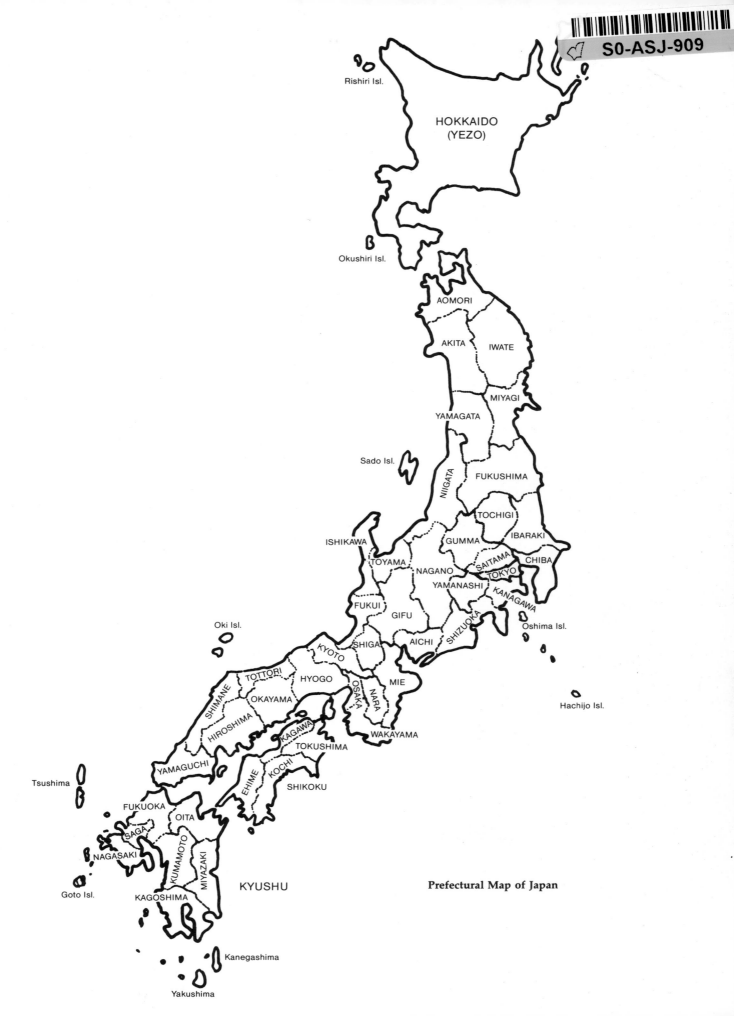

Rishiri Isl.

HOKKAIDO
(YEZO)

Okushiri Isl.

AOMORI

AKITA   IWATE

MIYAGI

YAMAGATA

Sado Isl.

NIIGATA   FUKUSHIMA

TOCHIGI

ISHIKAWA   GUMMA   IBARAKI

TOYAMA   SAITAMA   CHIBA

NAGANO   TOKYO

YAMANASHI   KANAGAWA

FUKUI   GIFU

Oki Isl.   SHIZUOKA   Oshima Isl.

SHIGA   AICHI

KYOTO   MIE

TOTTORI   HYOGO   Hachijo Isl.

SHIMANE   OKAYAMA   OSAKA   NARA

HIROSHIMA   KAGAWA   WAKAYAMA

Tsushima   YAMAGUCHI   TOKUSHIMA

EHIME   KOCHI   SHIKOKU

FUKUOKA   OITA

SAGA

NAGASAKI   KUMAMOTO

Goto Isl.   MIYAZAKI   KYUSHU   **Prefectural Map of Japan**

KAGOSHIMA

Kanegashima

Yakushima

THE GENUS *HOSTA*
GIBOSHI ZOKU

THE GENUS *HOSTA*
GIBOSHI ZOKU

Wolfram George Schmid

Technical Editor: Dr. Gilbert S. Daniels

TIMBER PRESS
Portland, Oregon

The author and publisher make no warranties, expressed or implied, as to the accuracy or adequacy of any information presented in this book. In no event will the author or publisher be liable for any damages arising from the use of any products or procedures mentioned in this book.

Also, by the omission of certain trade names and some of the formulated products available to the public, the author is not endorsing or recommending those companies whose brand names or products are listed to the exclusion of other products or vendors that may be suitable. For all products mentioned herein, the manufacturer's label recommendations and directions must be followed.

Japanese typesetting by
Johane Printing Company Ltd.,
Iwakuni City, Japan.

© 1991 by Timber Press, Inc.
Corrected reprint 1993
All rights reserved.

ISBN 0-88192-201-3
Printed in Hong Kong

TIMBER PRESS, INC.
9999 S.W. Wilshire, Suite 124
Portland, Oregon 97225

Library of Congress Cataloging-in-Publication Data

Schmid, Wolfram George.
    The genus Hosta = Giboshi zoku / Wolfram George Schmid : technical editor, Gilbert S. Daniels.
        p.   cm.
    Includes bibliographical references and index.
    ISBN 0-88192-201-3
    1. Hosta. I. Title. II. Title: Giboshi zoku.
SB413.H73S36 1991
635.9'34324--dc20   91-12491
                                                              CIP

Contents

To Hildegarde
for a lifetime of love, friendship, devotion, and support

Foreword

During the last 15 or so years we have seen a meteoric interest in hostas by horticulturists, landscape designers, nursery people, and keen gardeners. In addition, several important botanical studies on the genus *Hosta* were carried out.

In years before, this hardy herbaceous perennial, noted principally for its ornamental foliage and tolerance of shady growing sites, received almost scant attention. Today hostas rank among the most popular perennials in the United States, Britain, and other countries.

With this notable activity has come the need for a comprehensive reference source on the genus. This exhaustively researched, distinguished account amply fills this requirement, providing authoritative details for all.

In my view only W. George Schmid has the research steadfastness, technical acumen, and vast firsthand knowledge to overcome the numerous obstacles in producing the definitive botanical-horticultural-gardening book on the subject. His scientific and technological schooling provided the analytical and systematic approach for handling the many facets of this complex and often bewildering subject.

I first met George Schmid at the 1984 national convention of The American Hosta Society. Even before then he was concerned with the technical incompleteness and, in some cases, incorrectness of the plant's taxonomy. He had started to collect and study the botanical literature, planning to prepare a taxonomic treatise updating the 1940 monograph of Professor Fumio Maekawa and the works of other botanists, European as well as Japanese.

At the time I was editor of the society's journal, then named *The American Hosta Society Bulletin* and since 1986 *The Hosta Journal*. Recognizing that his studies would be of high interest to the members, I encouraged him to furnish a variety of articles for the publication, which he did articulately and abundantly.

That meeting led to a friendship between us with a very productive correspondence and interchange on many aspects involving *Hosta* but particularly on its taxonomy and cultivar nomenclature. George was a major contributor to the society's Nomenclature Committee when I was its chairman, and some of the information in this book stems from that association.

With zeal and scholarship not often found in this day and age, George Schmid has thoroughly examined the voluminous literature. His acknowledgment of the scores of people that have assisted him in this enterprise attests to the global comprehensiveness of his research. Also, he has visited Japan and European countries to obtain information directly.

Of significant help was his proficiency in Japanese, botanical Latin, and several European languages that enabled him to study texts in their original scripts. Further, he obtained and examined for himself herbarium specimens of *Hosta* leaves and flowers stored in botanical archives worldwide.

Many times over the years I would josh George that what he was producing would be a *handbuch*. This is a German term that I and my fellow graduate students used when we were writing our university dissertations to refer (with great reverence, I will add) to all-inclusive reference books of encyclopedic size and content on a specific subject. And indeed, this tome could correctly be titled *Handbook of the Genus* Hosta.

Long awaited by botanists and hosta specialists is this thorough, well-documented taxonomy monograph comprising an up-to-date classification of the genus. Included are new taxa, the latest scientific investigations, and Japanese names written in kana which will assist academics.

The technical arguments to support the multitude of changes in the taxonomy are clearly presented and can be followed by the nonbotanist with little trouble. Dr. Gilbert S. Daniels has provided a valuable taxonomic editorship; I consider it a scientific peer review. Without doubt this monumental effort, jammed with historical data, will be the authoritative source for a very long time.

To be commended is the handling of a vexing dilemma often mentioned by C. D. Brickell, director general of the Royal Horticultural Society and president of the British Hosta and Hemerocallis Society. Namely, it concerns the classification of plants that have been given species rank but undoubtedly are of garden origin.

George Schmid's treatment of this problem is straightforward and complies with the statutes of the latest editions of both the botanical and cultivated plant codes. First he determined which taxa are not "true species" and then transferred them to cultivar status. As examples, *H. lancifolia* is reduced to *H.* 'Lancifolia', *H. tardiflora* to *H.* 'Tardiflora', *H. fortunei albopicta* and *H. fortunei* 'Albopicta' to *H.* 'Fortunei Albopicta', and *H. tokudama aureonebulosa* and *H. tokudama* 'Aureonebulosa' to *H.* 'Tokudama Aureonebulosa'.

Those who do not like changes in plant names, and this usually applies to the nursery trade in particular, will find the new nomenclature a hard task to accept. But changes are mandatory to classify correctly this complex of plants.

The Chinese have a saying: the beginning of wisdom is getting things by their right names. This aptly applies to the genus *Hosta*. Many hostas have obsolete botanical synonyms, horticultural names which are often invalid, and Japanese and other foreign names. Welcomed by all who have to make sense out of this nomenclature quagmire is the listing of these names after the species and cultivar diagnoses.

Especially welcomed is the long-needed complete compilation of cultivars with technical descriptions, many with excellent photographs showing mature clumps. Importantly, the listing includes the nonregistered as well as registered varieties, a fair number of both never or no longer offered in the trade. This cultivar information alone will make this book a frequently used reference by hosta aficionados and others.

Lastly the nonspecialist will find considerable value in the extensive information on using hostas in the landscape which is copiously backed up with photographs taken in many prominent gardens, and in the hands-on cultural details, specially the instructions for control of viruses, slugs, and snails, and other problems from the author's experience in his own garden, Hosta Hill.

Rarely do we see a single volume meeting the total needs of the botanical, horticultural, nursery, specialist, and general gardening audience. I am sure everyone will find that *The Genus* Hosta does.

Dr. Warren I. Pollock

Wilmington, Delaware
1 January 1991

Preface and Acknowledgments

In 1959 I planted my first unnamed *Hosta* hybrids which I had received as gifts. They became star attractions in my first garden located near Nashville, Tennessee, as few Southerners had seen a hosta. Isolated from other lone enthusiasts I began to search for information on the genus in local libraries and nurseries, receiving a lot of courteous help but having very little success and gaining only very basic and mostly incorrect knowledge about these rather obscure plants. After moving to Atlanta in 1966 I purchased a suburban property near Tucker, Georgia. Interested in making another garden and keenly aware of the utility of hostas, I began a garden in 1969, calling it "Hosta Hill." Only species and named cultivars were planted, together with ferns and selected companion plants. Originally conceived as a private suburban garden for after-work pleasure and relaxation, it has become a garden for serious study and research, serving as a source for authenticated plant material used in biosystematic work at several universities. Although a private garden, it has also functioned as a show garden on special occasions, demonstrating to other gardeners how hostas can be used in formal, semiformal, and natural garden settings. In 1988 the garden was featured in *Southern Living*, a well-known monthly home and garden magazine circulated in the United States from Oklahoma to Delaware and south.

About 1980 my heretofore casual interest became preoccupation. Helped along by my botanical training I started a literature search and assembled a collection of scientific books and articles written on the genus *Hosta* from around the world, principally Japan, Great Britain, Sweden, Germany, and the Netherlands. My library now includes virtually all titles extant. Correspondence with botanists, horticulturists, gardeners, and students of the genus commenced at that time. Already proficient in translating botanical Latin, German, Dutch, and Swedish texts, I began studying the Japanese language for the purpose of accomplishing my own translations. These activities led to the establishment of many new contacts and the accession of authentic plant material from academic and private sources the world over.

In the early 1980s, with a comprehensive literature base at hand (see Bibliography), I started actual work on this definitive monographic revision of the genus *Hosta*. To support this endeavor I travelled to Japan, Germany, Austria, England, Sweden, Denmark, and the Netherlands, as well as all over the United States and Canada, to examine and photograph hostas in the wild and under cultivation. Wherever I went my contacts and hosts helped in every way possible and provided key information. I inspected, analyzed, and photographed several hundred Japanese herbarium specimens, including most Japanese holo-, lecto-, iso-, and syntypes. Also seen, studied, and photographed were most of the European herbarium specimens, which include all representative classic specimens prepared by Thunberg, von Siebold, Miquel, and contemporaries, as well as English and German specimens of great importance. All the herbaria in the world that maintain *Hosta* specimens are represented in the collections seen and studied, thanks to the courtesy of Dr. Samuel B. Jones, Jr., of the University of Georgia, Botany Department.

Under the leadership of Professor Jones, the University of Georgia has become the key institution in carrying out scientific investigations concerning the genus. More impor-

tant, this research has provided fresh, new data based on methodologies not employed thus far—like palynology as well as electrophoretic and other biosystematic procedures. The application of these data has provided significant support to determinations made in this work.

I began publishing articles on the genus in 1984, and this activity was encouraged by Dr. Warren I. Pollock, then editor of *The American Hosta Society Bulletin* (now *The Hosta Journal*). Warren's insistence to keep on writing finally culminated in the suggestion to put all my studies on paper and write a definitive book on the genus *Hosta*. I appreciate his professional advice, his continuing, staunch support, and the many hours he spent with me discussing difficult problems.

In the summer of 1987 I circularized the major hybridizers and other enthusiasts, gardeners, and growers, seeking information on new cultivar names and descriptions not yet publicized. I want to thank the following for contributing names, descriptions, catalogs, and, in some cases, photographs. Also included in this list are the gardeners who permitted me to take photographs in their gardens and to include them in this book: Kenneth A. Anderson, Farwell, MN; Pauline Banyai, Banyai's Hostas, Madison Heights, MI; Dr. R. H. Benedict, Hillsdale, MI; Dr. and Mrs. Paul F. Boon, Birmingham, AL; William Brincka, Michigan City, IN; J. R. Buckler and J. Renoud, Flower Farm, Kennett Square, PA; Ainie Busse, Busse Gardens, Cokato, MN; Peter Chappell, Spinners, Boldre, Lymington, Hampshire, UK; Roy and Mary Chastain, Ooltewah, TN; Gordon Collier, Titoki Point Garden, Taihape, New Zealand; George R. and Wilma Coney, Stone Mountain, GA; Jim Cooper, Raleigh, NC; Clyde Crockett, Indianapolis, IN; Dr. and Mrs. Gilbert S. Daniels, Indianapolis, IN; Allan M. Eddy, Jarrettsville, MD; Clarence H. Falstad III, Walters Gardens, Inc., Zeeland, MI; Hideko Gowen, Excelsior, MN; Robert A. Harris, Stone Mountain, GA; Handy Hatfield, Stoutsville. OH; Ursula Herz, Coastal Gardens and Nursery, Myrtle Beach, SC; Jere Housworth, Holiday Seeds, Stone Mountain, GA; Ann January, Indianapolis, IN; Betty Godwin Jernigan, Jernigan Gardens, Dunn, NC; Lloyd C. (Gil) Jones, Jackson, MI; Dr. Samuel B. and Carleen Jones, Piccadilly Farm, Bishop, GA; Roy Klehm, Chas. Klehm and Son Nursery, South Barrington, IL; Stauden-Gärtnermeister Heinz Klose, Lohfelden, Kassel, Germany; Robert Kuk, Kuk's Forest, Brecksville, OH; J. C. Kulpa, Warren, MI; William and Eleanor Lachman, Amherst, MA; Joe M. and Olive B. Langdon, Birmingham, AL; Lillian Maroushek, Maroushek Gardens, Hastings, MN; Eldren and Nancy Minks, Albert Lea, MN; Barbara Mitchell, Alpharetta, GA; W. D. Mitchell, Chadds Ford, PA; Dr. Robert. C. Olson, St. Louis Park, MN; Clarence Owens, Jackson, MI; Dr. Warren I. and Ali Pollock, Wilmington, DE; Nori and Sandra Pope, Hadspen House, Castle Cary, Somerset, UK; Pukeiti Trust, New Plymouth, New Zealand; Charles R. Seaver, Wilmington, DE; Mildred Seaver, Needham Heights, MA; Clarence and Marjorie C. Soules, Indianapolis, IN; Ray B. Stephens, Tucker, GA; Ann Stevens, Ivy Cottage, Ansty, Dorchester, Dorset, UK; Hajime Sugita, Okazaki, Aichi, Japan; Alex J. and Gene Summers, Honeysong Farm, Bridgeville, DE; Arie Van Vliet, De Heren C. Klijn en Co., Boskoop, Holland; F. J. Waitara, Taranaki, New Zealand; Mel Wallace, Birmingham, AL; John Walters, Walters Gardens, Inc., Zeeland, MI; and Frances Watkins, Birmingham, AL.

Extensive conversations and correspondence with several authorities contributed greatly to the accuracy and completeness of Chapters 3 and 4 and Appendix A. My thanks go to Dr. Myong Gi Chung, Department of Botany, University of Georgia, Athens, GA; Haynes Currie, ecologist-botanist, Law Environmental, Inc., Atlanta, GA; Mervin C. Eisel, registrar, International Registration Authority for *Hosta*, Chanhassen, MN; Dr. Ullrich Fischer, Braunschweig, Germany; Diana Grenfell, British Hosta and Hemerocallis Society (BHHS), Lymington, Hampshire, UK; Roger Grounds, BHHS, Lymington, Hampshire, UK; Yoshimichi Hirose, Iwakuni City, Japan; Carleen Jones, Piccadilly Farm, Bishop, GA; Dr. Samuel B. Jones, Jr., Department of Botany, University of Georgia, Athens, GA; Diplomgärtner Hermann Müssel, Staudensichtungsgarten Weihenstephan, University of Munich at Freising, Germany; Dr. Warren I. Pollock, formerly editor, *The Hosta Journal*, and past chairman, Nomenclature Committee, The American Hosta Society (AHS), Wilmington, DE; Robert M. Solberg, editor, *The Hosta Journal*, Green Hill Farms, Chapel Hill, NC; Alex Summers, past president and cofounder, AHS, Bridgeville, DE; Andre Viette, Andre Viette Farm and Nursery, Fishersville, VA; and Barry R. Yinger, Far Hills, NJ.

With the cooperation of Dr. S. B. Jones of the University of Georgia and his wife Carleen, I was able to study and photograph cultivated populations of the new Korean species and examine other hostas in their extensive reference collection at Piccadilly Farm, Bishop, GA, and at the greenhouses of the University of Georgia. Also of great assistance in describing the Korean species was Dr. Myong Gi Chung who provided original research material and commentary based on his palynological and biosystematic studies of populations of the genus in Korea and Tsushima Island, Japan. Likewise, conversations with Haynes Currie, who has compiled chemosystematic data on the Japanese species, proved to be of great value. I want to thank all these individuals for their assistance and cooperation.

In 1985 Diplomgärtner Hermann Müssel provided personal guidance through the vast grounds of Staudensichtungsgarten Weihenstephan, University of Munich at Freising, Germany; and with the expert direction of Diana Grenfell and Rogers Grounds my 1988 visit to England provided essential data for this book. Again I want to express my gratitude to all these individuals.

My deep appreciation goes also to Ursula Herz of Coastal Gardens and Nursery, Myrtle Beach, SC, who assisted me with Karl Foerster's books and articles; to Mary E. Pratt, Peoria, IL, who helped establish valuable connections in Japan and furnished slides and photographs taken in Japan; and to Clarence H. Falstad III of Walters Gardens, Inc., Zeeland, MI, who kept me informed about the latest developments in tissue culture. Rare plants were contributed by Kenneth Anderson, Dr. R. H. Benedict, Roy and Mary Chastain, Clarence H. Falstad III, Hideko Gowen, Robert A. Harris, Ursula Herz, Robert M. Solberg, Clarence and Marjorie C. Soules, and Arie Van Vliet, and these, as well as access to the living collections received from academic Japanese sources at the University of Georgia, were important in settling some of the problems encountered with little-known material.

Daniel S. Sweeney, my son-in-law, created some of the line drawings and map outlines which are key elements in the identification of technical terms and which provide a better idea of where in Japan the species can be found in the wild. His diligent and professional work provides an important dimension to this book and is much appreciated.

Van and Shirley Wade of Wade and Gatton Nurseries, Bellville, OH, allowed me to peruse a prepublication copy of their extensive catalog-handbook of cultivars (Wade and Wade, 1990), and their splendid cooperation has been very helpful and is appreciated.

William C. Burto of Cambridge, MA, provided a preliminary copy of his index to all the bulletins and journals published by The American Hosta Society, and his efforts facilitated the writing phase of this work. Suzy Wert, Indianapolis, IN, made several suggestions which make the book more useful to the average gardener, and I appreciate her input.

My thanks also to Norm Hatcher and other staff members of the public library system of DeKalb County, GA, the University of Georgia library, and the Atlanta Botanical Garden and Atlanta Historical Society Garden libraries, who expeditiously handled many of my many special requests for document search and interlibrary loans.

One of my most sincere wishes was to make this book useful in Japan from where most of the taxa of the genus came to the West in the first place. To accomplish this, in part at least, I have included all Japanese formal (academic) and horticultural names printed in kana. This required considerable assistance and cooperation from Japan to check and typeset my final list of Japanese kana names, a difficult process that was made possible by individuals to whom I owe a great debt of gratitude: Yoshimichi Hirose of Vari-Nine, Ltd., Iwakuni City, and Barry Yinger who checked my original listing; and Teruyuki Matsukawa, president of Yohane Printing Company, Ltd., Iwakuni City. Mr. Hirose, a member of The American Hosta Society, is an acknowledged expert and author on variegated plants. He is one of the coauthors of *The Hosta Book* (Aden, 1988). Mr. Hirose also arranged for the kana typesetting through Mr. Matsukawa. I want to express my deep appreciation to Messrs. Hirose, Matsukawa, and Yinger for their help in this important matter. Kudos also to the Timber Press production staff, under the able direction of Darcel Warren, who meticulously inserted the Japanese kana into the English text, no small feat.

Mr. Hirose also arranged for permission to include in this book photographs of a splendid Japanese garden, namely, that of Toshihiko Satake of Satake Engineering Co., Ltd., Higashi-Hiroshima, Hiroshima Prefecture. Mr. Satake is a life member of The American Hosta Society. My thanks to both these men for their assistance.

The editorial help and guidance provided by Dr. Gilbert S. Daniels and Richard Abel of Timber Press were of inestimable value to me as were their extensive and supportive knowledge of matters botanical and horticultural and their encouragement to press on with a difficult task. I consider myself very fortunate to have Dr. Daniels assist in this work as technical editor. This role is not new to him, as he has served as technical editor for two other encyclopedic works published by Timber Press, namely, Gerd Krüssmann's *Manual of Cultivated Broad-Leaved Trees and Shrubs* and *Manual of Cultivated Conifers*. Dr. Daniels is well known in the botanical community for his research on the taxonomy of the genus *Heliconia* and his directorship of the Hunt Botanical Library at Carnegie-Mellon University. He is also well recognized in horticultural circles as a member of the board of directors of the American Horticultural Society from 1969 until 1981, serving as president of the society from 1977 until 1981 and as acting executive director in 1983. His expert knowledge was instrumental in solving difficult taxonomic problems, and he helped greatly in resolving many nomenclatural difficulties presented by the genus. His collaboration and professional advice concerning the International Code of Botanical Nomenclature and other scientific and scholarly matters perfected the botanical sections of this book. Beyond matters botanical, Dr. Daniels' astute editorship provided many excellent suggestions which have fashioned this work into a reference book that can be useful to gardeners and horticulturists, as well as to botanists and other professionals. In all of this he was certainly helped by his own enthusiasm for hostas which he grows in his garden.

During the editing phase of this book Gil Daniels suggested that credit should also be given to a most important "assistant"—the computer. I must admit, without the aid of my computer and word-processing software, the writing phase of this book would probably never have been finished. I cannot imagine doing all this writing longhand. Beyond just writing, without a computer, conscientious editing could easily turn into a prolonged nightmare.

Last, but not least, I want to thank Linda Willms of Timber Press who served as principal editor. She patiently scrutinized every one of the six million keystrokes in this book to ascertain that each and every one produced the correct result. Her intuitive grasp of the many special requirements posed by the highly technical text helped fashion it into stylistically and grammatically correct passages, and I appreciate her professional help and advice on editorial matters.

My basic purpose in writing this book is to produce a definitive monographic reference work on the genus *Hosta* covering all important aspects—principally taxonomy, morphology, horticultural classification, and cultivation. A major part of the text is devoted to the descriptions of all known species and all registered cultivars, including information on many of the unregistered classic hostas as well. By necessity, some of the text is of a technical nature, and the parts of primary interest to professionals are concentrated in Appendixes A and B. All other chapters were written with the gardener in mind, and where technical terminology was unavoidable a glossary has been provided. I have also included basic information concerning cut-leaf show classification, macromorphological concepts, foreign names, biotic and abiotic factors in cultivation, propagation and hybridization, and a brief survey of economic and other uses of hostas.

To standardize horticultural classification I devised a system of uniform, summarized cultivar descriptions to aid in identification and sought to incorporate all historical and modern English and foreign names and synonyms used internationally, including Japanese names in kana. Since by necessity species and botanical varieties take up a large portion of this book, a basic revision of the taxonomy of the genus is included. All taxa known have been placed in accordance with this revised system to provide clarification of existing confusion in nomenclature.

To make sense out of all the names printed in this book—beyond their reference use—and to help average gardeners put them to practical use, I followed the sage advice of Richard Abel and provided specific horticultural recommendations for the use of hostas in landscaping. The chapter giving this information is comparatively short but profusely illustrated to show gardeners how to use hostas in the landscape, be it as a single specimen in a pot on the window sill, or interspersed with other perennials in a suburban backyard, or grown in large drifts in public gardens. To show good hosta gardening one picture is worth a thousand words.

I must end this preface with a caveat: *Hosta* is a complex genus. One has only to study its taxonomic treatment and nomenclatural history to learn very quickly that there are many differing opinions on this subject. For this reason I welcome discussion and will correspond with serious students of the genus. Likewise, readers are encouraged to comment on this work and transmit to me any emendations or additional information they can contribute. All this material will be incorporated in a future edition of this work.

W. George Schmid

5 August 1990

Botanical Summary

GENERAL NOTES

Following is a summary of the taxonomic revisions made to the genus *Hosta*:

A number of new infraspecific epithets were formulated to properly place taxa long known to science but not yet validly described or to allow revised placements which better reflect the character of particular natural populations.

The genus has been divided into three subgenera: *Hosta* (formerly *Niobe*), *Bryocles* and *Giboshi*. In subgenus *Bryocles*, a new section, *Arachnanthae*, has been established to place the spider-flowered Korean taxa.

A new species from Korea, viz., *H. laevigata*, has been named. It and the recently named *H. yingeri* S. B. Jones occur on remote islands off the southwestern coast of Korea (accessed by Yinger et al. and M. G. Chung) and have been placed in the new section *Arachnanthae*.

All taxa described under section *Foliosae* have been reduced to cultivar form, so the latter is eliminated from consideration in systematic keys.

The transfer of *Hosta lancifolia* var. *thunbergiana* f. *albomarginata* Maekawa 1940 to *H. albomarginata* (Hooker) Ohwi was accomplished by Ohwi (1942). The subsequent proposal forwarded by Ingram (1967) to follow the rules of priority and use the epithet *sieboldii* (based on *Hemerocallis sieboldii* Paxton) as *Hosta sieboldii* (Paxton) Ingram 1967 have been disputed by other authors who prefer to retain *H. albomarginata* on grounds of its persistent historical use. Notwithstanding, I have followed the rules of priority per Article 11 of the International Code of Botanical Nomenclature (ICBN) and the valid transfers made by Hara (1984), accepting *H. sieboldii* (Paxton) Ingram 1967 as the correct species name.

Following new requirements of the ICBN, Fujita (1976a) changed the name of the monotypic subgenus encompassing the generic type *H. plantaginea* from *Niobe* to *Hosta*. Hensen (1985) also adopted this name change. Unfortunately, neither Fujita nor Hensen explained the requirement for this change which perplexed many nonbotanists and horticulturists. Ordinarily, this revision should be a simple one because it is mandated by the ICBN, but the matter is more complicated: the subgeneric name *Giboshi*, which was validly published by Maekawa and used as a valid name for the subgenus which incorporates all the native Japanese hostas, in fact means *Hosta* when translated. *Giboshi* is merely the Japanese-language equivalent of *Hosta*. Neither Fujita nor Hensen used the trisubgeneric system, so subgenus *Giboshi* is not part of their classification and the problem of having two subgeneric names with the same meaning representing different subgenera within the same genus does not exist for them. In the present classification, however, Maekawa's name *Giboshi* is used, so I must deal with this problem. To avoid confusion I have decided to drop the name *Niobe*, which has been in use since 1812, but coincidental with each occurrence of that name, I am citing *Hosta* as a subgeneric name thus pointing out that use of the latter is correct and mandated by the ICBN, Article 22.

Finally, the problem of ranking validly published taxa of cultivated origin has been dealt with. These include the so-called European taxa described principally by Bailey, Hylander, and Stearn, which have been determined to be specioids (see Introduction) and, as a consequence, have been reduced to cultivar form. Additionally, many of the taxa described in Maekawa's 1940 monograph are cultigens and subsequently were eliminated by Maekawa himself in 1969. Fujita (1976a) carried out the de facto elimination of validly described species of cultivated origin, and I have followed his ecological studies and data on habitat, reducing to cultivar form a number of taxa originally described in Japan but not found in the wild as perpetuating natural populations.

SYSTEMATIC LISTING

HOSTACEAE.
GENUS *HOSTA*.
  H. plantaginea (type).

Subgenus *Hosta* (formerly subgenus *Niobe*).
  H. plantaginea (type).

Subgenus *Bryocles*.
Section *Eubryocles*.
  H. ventricosa (type).
Section *Lamellatae*.
  H. venusta (type).
  H. capitata.
  H. minor.
  H. nakaiana.
Section *Arachnanthae*.
  H. yingeri (type).
  H. laevigata.
Section *Stoloniferae*.
  H. clausa (type).

Subgenus *Giboshi*.
Section *Helipteroides*.
  H. montana (type).
  H. crassifolia.
  H. fluctuans.
  H. nigrescens.
  H. sieboldiana.
Section *Intermediae*.
  H. densa (type).
  H. kiyosumiensis.
  H. pachyscapa.
Section *Rynchophorae*.
  H. kikutii (type).
  H. shikokiana.
Section *Picnolepis*.
  H. longipes (type).
  H. aequinoctiiantha.
  H. hypoleuca.
  H. okamotoi.
  H. pulchella.
  H. pycnophylla.
  H. rupifraga.
  H. takiensis.

Section *Tardanthae*.
  H. tardiva (type).
  H. cathayana.
  H. gracillima.
  H. jonesii.
  H. takahashii.
  H. tibae.
  H. tsushimensis.
Section *Nipponosta*.
  H. sieboldii (type).
  H. alismifolia.
  H. atropurpurea.
  H. calliantha.
  H. clavata.
  H. ibukiensis.
  H. longissima.
  H. rectifolia.
  H. rohdeifolia.

NEW SUBGENERIC DIVISION (3 SUBGENERA)

Subgenus *Hosta*; autonym per ICBN.
Subgenus *Bryocles* (Salisbury) Maekawa.
Subgenus *Giboshi* Maekawa.

NEW SECTION

Subgenus *Bryocles*, section *Arachnanthae* W. G. Schmid.

NEW SPECIES, VARIETIES, AND FORMS

Hosta laevigata W. G. Schmid sp. nov.
H. kikutii var. *kikutii* f. *leuconota* W. G. Schmid f. nov.
H. longipes var. *vulgata* (Maekawa) W. G. Schmid and G. S. Daniels var. nov.
H. longissima var. *longifolia* (Honda) W. G. Schmid var. nov.
H. montana f. *macrophylla* W. G. Schmid f. nov.
H. rectifolia var. *australis* Maekawa ex W. G. Schmid var. nov.
H. sieboldii f. *angustifolia* (Regel) W. G. Schmid f. nov.

TRANSFERS IN RANK, NEW COMBINATIONS, EMENDATIONS

Hosta clausa var. *ensata* (Maekawa) W. G. Schmid stat. nov.
H. longipes f. *sparsa* (Nakai) W. G. Schmid stat. nov.
H. montana f. *ovatolancifolia* Araki ex W. G. Schmid comb. nov.
H. montana emend. taxonomic position.
H. rhodeifolia emend. epithet to *H. rohdeifolia* (Maekawa 1937).
H. sieboldii f. *bunchoko* (Maekawa) W. G. Schmid comb. nov.
H. sieboldii f. *campanulata* (Araki) W. G. Schmid comb. nov.
H. sieboldii f. *kifukurin* (Maekawa) W. G. Schmid comb. nov.
H. sieboldii f. *spathulata* (Miquel) W. G. Schmid comb. nov.

CULTIGENS WITH BOTANICAL RANK (SPECIOIDS) REDUCED TO CULTIVAR FORM

Hosta bella Wehrhahn 1936
  to   *H.* 'Bella'.
H. crispula Maekawa 1940
  to   *H.* 'Crispula'.
H. decorata Bailey 1930 f. *decorata*
  to   *H.* 'Decorata'.
H. decorata f. *normalis* Stearn 1931b
  to   *H.* 'Decorata Normalis'.
H. elata Hylander 1954
  to   *H.* 'Elata'.
H. fortunei (Baker) Bailey 1930
  to   *H.* 'Fortunei'.

H. fortunei var. *albopicta* Hylander 1954
  to   *H.* 'Fortunei Albopicta'.
H. fortunei var. *albopicta* f. *aurea* Hylander 1954
  to   *H.* 'Fortunei Aurea'.
H. fortunei var. *albopicta* f. *viridis* Hylander 1954
  to   *H.* 'Fortunei Viridis'.
H. fortunei var. *aureomarginata* Hylander 1969
  to   *H.* 'Fortunei Aureomarginata'.
H. fortunei var. *gigantea* Bailey 1915
  to   *H.* 'Fortunei Gigantea'.
H. fortunei var. *hyacinthina* Hylander 1954
  to   *H.* 'Fortunei Hyacinthina'.
H. fortunei var. *obscura* Hylander 1954
  to   *H.* 'Fortunei Obscura'.
H. fortunei var. *rugosa* Hylander 1954
  to   *H.* 'Fortunei Rugosa'.
H. fortunei var. *stenantha* Hylander 1954
  to   *H.* 'Fortunei Stenantha'.
H. helonioides Maekawa 1937
  to   *H.* 'Helonioides'.
H. helonioides var. *albopicta* Maekawa 1937
  to   *H.* 'Helonioides Albopicta'.
H. hippeastrum Maekawa 1940
  to   *H.* 'Hippeastrum'.
H. lancifolia Engler 1888
  to   *H.* 'Lancifolia'.
H. montana var. *aureomarginata* Maekawa 1940
  to   *H. montana* 'Aureomarginata'.
H. montana var. *liliiflora* Maekawa 1940
  to   *H. montana* 'Liliiflora'.
H. montana var. *praeflorens* Maekawa 1940
  to   *H. montana* 'Praeflorens'.
H. montana var. *transiens* Maekawa 1940
  to   *H. montana* 'Transiens'.
H. nigrescens f. *elatior* Maekawa 1940
  to   *H. nigrescens* 'Elatior'.
H. opipara Maekawa 1940
  to   *H.* 'Opipara'.
H. plantaginea f. *aphrodite* Maekawa 1940
  to   *H. plantaginea* 'Aphrodite'.
H. plantaginea f. *stenantha* Maekawa 1940
  to   *H. plantaginea* 'Stenantha'.
H. rectifolia var. *chionea* Maekawa 1940
  to   *H. rectifolia* 'Chionea'.
H. rectifolia var. *chionea* f. *albiflora* Maekawa 1940
  to   *H. rectifolia* 'Albiflora'.
H. rohdeifolia f. *rohdeifolia* Maekawa 1937
  to   *H.* 'Rohdeifolia'.
H. sacra Maekawa 1940
  to   *H.* 'Sacra'.
H. sieboldiana var. *amplissima* Maekawa 1940
  to   *H. sieboldiana* 'Amplissima'.
H. sieboldiana var. *fortunei* Maekawa 1940
  to   *H. sieboldiana* 'Fortunei'.
H. sieboldiana var. *hypophylla* Maekawa 1940
  to   *H. sieboldiana* 'Hypophylla'.
H. sieboldiana var. *mira* Maekawa 1940
  to   *H. sieboldiana* 'Mira'.
H. sieboldii f. *alba* (Irving) Hara 1984
  to   *H. sieboldii* 'Alba'.
H. sieboldii f. *bunchoko* (Maekawa) Schmid 1991
  to   *H. sieboldii* 'Bunchoko'.
H. sieboldii f. *kabitan* (Maekawa) Hara 1984
  to   *H. sieboldii* 'Kabitan'.
H. sieboldii f. *kifukurin* (Maekawa) Schmid 1991
  to   *H. sieboldii* 'Kifukurin'.
H. sieboldii f. *mediopicta* (Maekawa) Hara 1984
  to   *H. sieboldii* 'Mediopicta'.

H. sieboldii f. *subchrocea* (Maekawa) Hara 1984
   to   *H. sieboldii* 'Subcrocea'.
H. tardiflora (Irving) Stearn apud Grey 1938
   to   *H.* 'Tardiflora'.
H. tokudama Maekawa 1940
   to   *H.* 'Tokudama'.
H. tokudama f. *aureonebulosa* Maekawa 1940
   to   *H.* 'Tokudama Aureonebulosa'.
H. tokudama f. *flavocircinalis* Maekawa 1940
   to   *H.* 'Tokudama Flavocircinalis'.

H. tokudama f. *flavoplanata* Maekawa 1940
   to   *H.* 'Tokudama Flavoplanata'.
H. undulata Bailey 1930
   to   *H.* 'Undulata'.
H. undulata var. *albomarginata* Maekawa 1940
   to   *H.* 'Undulata Albomarginata'.
H. undulata var. *erromena* (Stearn) Maekawa 1936
   to   *H.* 'Undulata Erromena'.
H. undulata var. *univittata* (Miquel) Hylander 1954
   to   *H.* 'Undulata Univittata'.

Introduction

GIBOSHI ZOKU—THE GENUS HOSTA

Giboshi Zoku may read and sound very strange to most Western readers. It is the name used by the Japanese for the genus *Hosta*. I have chosen to use Japanese as well as English titles to emphasize the international scope of this book. In recent years it has become quite evident that serious study and cultivation of plant genera endemic to other parts of the world require the use of plant names coined in a plant's native habitat. Thus, it was no surprise when J. D. Vertrees' book on Japanese maples (Timber Press, Forest Grove, OR) appeared with the subtitle *"Momiji* and *Kaede"* and contained numerous Japanese names. Fred C. Galle's book on azaleas (Timber Press, Portland, OR) is also replete with Japanese names.

In this book the reader will again find numerous Japanese and other non-English names. These are necessary to establish species and cultivar relationships and to make this book useful the world over. The Japanese have published a number of botanical as well as horticultural articles and small books on their hostas. Unfortunately, most of them are printed in Japanese, which makes them inaccessible to the majority of Western gardeners, horticulturists, and botanists. Translated and excerpted, this material has been included in this book, with most Japanese names printed in kana (Japanese writing) and their transliteration, as well as Western meanings, also incorporated.

NOMENCLATURE PROBLEMS

The nomenclature of genus *Hosta* has been in a confused state for many years. This is partially due to a high number of botanical synonyms brought about by frequent name changing to which even the generic name was not immune. Kaempfer (1692) was the first botanist to draw a likeness of two hostas, which was followed in 1780 by Thunberg's formulation of *Aletris japonica*, the first species name to be used in the genus. It was not until 125 years later that the genus finally received a valid and accepted name. In the intervening period from 1780 until 1905 it had a number of generic names, each with its own set of specific epithets. In 1905 botanists attending the International Botanical Congress of Vienna agreed to conserve the name *Hosta* Trattinnick (1812) in spite of the fact that an earlier valid generic homonym existed against it and so, according to present rules, would be illegitimate. It is no surprise that, in addition to these botanical names, horticulturists came up with their own set of latinate horticultural names, and so confusion reigned supreme.

It became quite obvious to me this book could not be written unless a number of nomenclatural problems and other difficult taxonomic issues were resolved first. This undertaking became tantamount to a complete revision of the genus which has been accomplished in Chapter 3 and Appendix A.

SPECIOIDS—SPECIES KNOWN ONLY IN CULTIVATION

Fujita (1976a), in his treatise of the Japanese hostas, disregarded many of the validly published species and infraspecific taxa, principally because they could not be found in the wild in Japan. Thus, the very burdensome problem of what to do with these validly published names is an important matter which requires solution. Previously, they have been called *species of convenience* (Brickell, 1968, 1983) and *specioids* (Hensen, 1985). Hensen defines a specioid as a taxon that has been validly published but is only known in cultivation and is so different from all species described from natural habitats that it is considered a separate taxon of the same rank as a species. Unfortunately, the term specioid is currently not sanctioned by the International Code of Botanical Nomenclature (ICBN), although there is great need for a legitimate, separate category into which these cultigens could be placed. For the convenience of horticulturists I have, however, made occasional use of the term specioid where a concise label was required for validly published cultigens. Although the ICBN does not endorse the specioid concept, it nevertheless permits species to be reduced to cultivar rank without any intermediate steps, and I have elected this method to separate cultigens from taxa found in the wild. I have reduced all taxa falling within Hensen's specioid definition to cultivar form under the International Code of Nomenclature for Cultivated Plants (ICNCP) (1980, Article 10, note 5; 1990, Article 11, note 1). To indicate this in Chapter 3 headings, I have enclosed in double quotation marks all species and infraspecific taxa which have been reduced to cultivar form (see Chapter 3—Part 1). For example, *H. decorata* f. *decorata* becomes *"H. decorata"* (a specioid), which is subsequently reduced to *H.* 'Decorata', a cultivar. In this case use of a clonal cultivar name presents no problem because this particular taxon is clearly a single clone. Taxa consisting of groups of similar plants represented by several distinct clones have been reduced to cultivar status and designated as cultivar groups in accordance with Article 26 of the ICNCP. In less clearly defined cases a clonal cultivar name was established by redefinition of the taxon to permit that name to represent groups of very similar or virtually identical clones.

Other botanists, including Fujita (1976a), have dealt with this problem by simply eliminating all taxa not found as natural populations. I do not agree with this treatment because it ignores and eliminates the names of a large number of taxa which have seen extensive scientific treatment in the botanical literature and are well known in horticulture.

When reducing taxa to cultivar form it is highly desirable to assign the reduced taxon to a species, if this is possible. Unfortunately, it is now impossible to definitely connect some of the European species with a related botanical taxon. One example is *H.* 'Fortunei' which is represented by a fragmentary type specimen for which no living material is known (Hylander, 1954). All the taxa assembled under this epithet by Hylander and raised to botanical rank started out as horticultural material which has been so thoroughly hybridized that it is now impossible to ascribe parentage with any degree of certainty. To assign these taxa to a species would simply be conjecture, and rather than guessing, I have included the former species epithet within the cultivar name. An example is *H.* 'Fortunei Hyacinthina'. This method maintains all the old names familiar to gardeners and is least disturbing to horticultural nomenclature. Luckily, the ICNCP does not require that cultivars be assigned to a species, so this method is acceptable under its rules.

NOMENCLATURAL TRANSFERS

Adjustment of the nomenclature of the genus was required by several changes and additions made by botanists in recent years. Revising the genus also required several new transfers, and these have been accomplished by formulating new combinations and changes in rank. For example, in the West the required transfer of names proposed by Ingram (1967) from *H.* 'Lancifolia' and *H. albomarginata* to *H. sieboldii* had been carried out de facto in several horticultural works, including *The* Hosta *Book* (Aden, 1988), while in recent botanical papers (Chung, 1989; Jones, 1989) the name *H. albomarginata* continues to be used in spite of (1) Ingram's proposal, which must be accepted on grounds of priority, and (2) the transfer by Hara (1984)— who followed Fujita (1976a)—of a number of synonyms cited under *H. albomarginata* to the botanically correct *H. sieboldii*. In Japanese horticulture *H.* 'Lancifolia' and *H. albomarginata* continue to be considered the same taxon (as *Koba Giboshi*), and it may be some time before Hara's transfers are properly considered in Japanese horticulture. Other significant taxonomic disagreements within the genus required solutions and were also dealt with, including the *H.* 'Elata'/*H. montana* problem (see Appendix B).

NEW TAXA

A number of taxa new to science have been described in recent botanical literature. They have been included in this book along with a few others which are first named in this book. Inclusion of these names brings the nomenclature and taxonomy sections (Chapter 3 and Appendix A) in line with botanical developments as of July 1990, considering all the names published in *Index Kewensis* up to and including Supplement no. 18, 1981–1985 (1987). Chapter 4 includes all the taxa registered with the International Registration Authority for *Hosta* up to and including the 1989 and some 1990 registrations.

A botanical summary of all taxonomic changes is included in this book.

NEW RESEARCH

During the last several years, a start has been made in applying modern methods of investigation to the taxonomy and classification of the genus. This new work includes micromorphological as well as biosystematic methods. At the forefront of this research is the College of Arts and Sciences, Department of Botany, of the University of Georgia, USA. The work involves palynological and morphometric investigations as well as starch gel electrophoresis involving population studies, principal component analysis, cluster analysis, and isoenzyme analysis. It is conducted under the direction of Dr. Samuel B. Jones, Jr., by Dr. Myong Gi Chung, with the assistance of the staff of the university. Preliminary copies of research reports have been given to me by Dr. Chung through the courtesy of Dr. Jones. The conclusions reached by this valuable and important research have been considered throughout this book.

Professionals will notice, however, that I have not completely followed the recommendations of Chung (1990) because my approach to *Hosta* taxonomy is somewhat different in its philosophy than that of systematic researchers. This should in no way detract from the importance of the new, ongoing work. It is simply a difference in opinion.

Biosystematic research deals with the relationships and variations within populations and utilizes a number of analytical, statistical, and comparative methods, all of which are time-consuming, expensive, and therefore usually restricted in their application. Currently, these modern methods have been applied to limited populations only. Chung and Jones (1989) examined the pollen morphology of 22 Japanese, Chinese, and Korean taxa. The latest work of M. G. Chung (1990) involves 47 populations of Korean taxa as well as 2 from Tsushima Island, Japan, comprising a total of 6 species. Except for *H. tsushimensis*, all populations represent taxa indigenous to Korea so, unfortunately, his work has only very restricted application to the main populations of the genus in Japan. The slow and painstaking analytical work required in biosystematics will no doubt be eventually applied to the Japanese populations, but it may be a long time before definitive results are known. In the meantime the delimitation of the genus on the sectional as well as the species level is based principally on historical, macromorphological methodology and analysis, which in turn are based on very limited collections or even single specimens rather than on populations of plants. As these taxa come under increased scrutiny some changes may have to be made in the nomenclature. Plant taxonomy evolves with the knowledge we have about plants and as a consequence is constantly modified to reflect variability and biological relationships. Occasionally this flies in the face of horticulture which requires stability and simplicity in nomenclature.

M. G. Chung's latest study yields two examples of these changes and how they might affect horticultural nomenclature: Lee (1973) and Y. H. Chung and Y. C. Chung (1982) determined that *H. clausa* var. *clausa* and *H. clausa* var. *normalis* are the same and that varietal rank not be recognized. Maekawa (1969) also concluded that *H. clausa* var. *clausa* is a very rare form in the wild. Chung (1989: personal communication) states that he did not encounter the closed-flowered *H. clausa* var. *clausa* during his accessions of the wild populations. Likewise, the sword-leaved *H. clausa* var. *ensata* also occurs as part of the natural populations and appears to be a natural adaptation of the normal-flowered *H. clausa* var. *normalis* when growing on a rock base. There is a fourth form I have observed which never develops flower scapes but nevertheless propagates aggressively by a wide-ranging, stoloniferous root system. No botanical name has been assigned to this form, but one might call it *H. clausa* var. *stolonifera* (nom. nudum). This means that there are four forms occurring in the wild which are biologically one and the same species yet macromorphologically quite distinct having adapted to different environments. All these variants are vegetatively propagated, stable cultivars grown in gardens and so require names. This typical example shows the conflict between the taxonomist, who has in this case modified a currently accepted relationship, and the practical horticulturist, who looks to the botanist-scientist for help in naming the taxa. Unfortunately, this help is not always forthcoming or, as happens on occasion, researchers show little inclination to solve or even consider the horticulturist's nomenclatural problems, so the usual solution on the practical side of things is to give a particular taxon a name, any name, just to have a label or to retain an old, perhaps even invalid name. This is regrettable because the main economic importance of the genus is in its horticultural application: gardeners love the plants and cultivate them extensively the world over.

Most gardeners, horticulturists, and nursery operators find plant names indispensable and valuable. They depend on the botanical literature to supply the botanical names. As mentioned earlier, the horticultural nomenclature of *H. clausa* is not served by taxonomy if the forms in varietal ranks were eliminated—following Lee (1973), Y. H. Chung and Y. C. Chung (1982), and Maekawa (1969). All the variants of *H. clausa* (viz. *H. clausa* var. *clausa*, *H. clausa* var. *ensata*, *H. clausa* var. *normalis*, and the nonflowering *H. clausa* var. *stolonifera* nom. nudum) need names because they are stable forms in cultivation. It is possible to give them cultivar names, but they clearly occur in the wild. To indicate this they should be given botanical names or retain those given previously.

Similar problems are created by recent taxonomic findings concerning the taxa placed in section *Lamellatae* (Maekawa, 1940): *H. minor*, *H. venusta*, *H. nakaiana*, and *H. capitata*. Maekawa (1969) and others have determined that *H. nakaiana* and *H. capitata* are the same species, notwithstanding some distinct, major macromorphological differences in the cultivated and wild forms. In gardens the two are definitely distinct entities and labeled accordingly (per Maekawa, 1940), while most taxonomists no longer recognize *H. nakaiana* and consider it synonymous to *H. capitata*. In this case the equation *H. nakaiana* = *H. capitata* makes eminent sense to taxonomists who look at fundamental, biological relationships. On the other hand, horticulturists and gardeners, for obvious reasons, require and advocate a detailed as well as a stable nomenclature. This is the main reason why horticulturists embraced Maekawa's 1940 classification and virtually ignored Fujita's 1976 revision. Taxonomic research and horticultural nomenclature are constantly at odds because they have different objectives: Taxonomy, particularly biosystematics, looks at the biological relationships of populations and so takes a broad, population-based approach to delimiting a particular taxon. Horticulture seeks stability and rigidity in nomenclature. Gardeners despise name changes and are perplexed when taxonomists declare that *H. nakaiana* is the same species as *H. capitata* (Maekawa, 1969; Chung, 1990) when it is quite obvious that in gardens these taxa are quite different and easily recognizable. On the one hand, gardeners often do not realize they deal with clonal material, which is selected from natural populations and vegetatively propagated, so retaining its particular clonal characters. The taxonomist, on the other hand, makes a judgment by studying large collections or populations which have considerable variability and so blend into each other. I feel both positions have a legitimate purpose and must be considered. As a consequence I have retained *H. nakaiana* but pointed out its very close relationship to *H.*

capitata. A detailed discussion of this problem can be found in Appendix A—Part 1, under "The Korean Species."

An even more complicated case is presented by *H. minor* and *H. venusta*, with ridged scapes, which were linked by Chung (1990) to *H. tsushimensis* and *H. jonesii*, with terete scapes, not to mention major differences in flower and leaf morphology. This classification conflicts with Maekawa's and Fujita's sectional classifications. Although biosystematics definitively points to a (perhaps evolutional) link between these taxa, final conclusions are premature. Chung (1990) cautions that "without knowledge of the genetic basis of each isoenzyme band or morphological character . . . the phylogenetic relationships of these species cannot be determined" (for further discussion see Appendix A—Part 1). Clearly, it is too early to adjust the nomenclature.

Quite often minor changes are indicated which do not affect naming on the species level. Palynological studies of *H. clausa* show it to have a distinct pollen type (Chung and Jones, 1989), although it is macromorphologically similar to members of section *Tardanthae* and has been placed in this section by other authors. Chung (1990) supports a change from this earlier placement but does not make a specific recommendation. I have moved this taxon into subgenus *Bryocles* on ecological, palynological, evolutionary, and biosystematic grounds, but this transfer does not alter the species name, so has little effect on horticultural nomenclature.

In my opinion, it will be many years before the entire genus can be examined using the most up-to-date scientific tools and methods for analysis and before all its populations can be studied and their biological relationships determined. In the meantime professionals, horticulturists, and gardeners alike are looking for a system of classification which they can use and which will lend stability to nomenclature. In this book I have taken an intermediate position by retaining well-known names long in use in horticulture, but at the same time pointing to results obtained by the latest taxonomic and biosystematic research. This gives consideration to the important work done by scientific researchers while at the same time maintaining a stable nomenclature for gardeners who merit some regard. After all, it was hybridizers and gardeners who took plants once considered weeds in Asia and gave them economic importance the world over as valuable and cherished garden plants.

CHAPTER 1

How to Use This Book

GENERAL INSTRUCTIONS

To make use of this book as simple as possible, the descriptions of species and specioids in Chapter 3 and cultivated varieties in Chapter 4 are arranged in alphabetic order (rather than in systematic order) so most of the important names can be looked up directly in these chapters without consulting the indexes. There are, however, hundreds of incorrect, obscure, and obsolete synonyms and a host of other less significant names which are listed in Chapters 3 and 4 under a primary name entry. These must be looked up in the indexes, which contain all names included in the book and give page references that point to a primary entry under which these secondary names can be found. If a name cannot be found in the indexes, it is not included in the book.

Chapters 3 and 4 have separate introductions which contain important information and definitions relating to their respective chapters. I urge readers to study these introductions. For species, botanical varieties and forms, and specioids included in Chapter 3, a complete botanical diagnosis in English is given.

Cultivar descriptions in Chapter 4 follow, as much as possible, a uniform descriptive format based on the classification of cultivars in Chapter 2. It is very important to consider the preconditions and definitions in Chapter 2 before referring to Chapter 4.

A history of the genus follows in Chapter 5. It begins with Japanese records from the 11th century and covers historical aspects up to the 20th-century pioneers and hybridizers through whose efforts the genus gained renewed popularity. Nomenclature developed along historical lines, so emphasis is given to this subject from a historical point of view.

This book would not be complete without consideration of the primary use of the taxa in the genus as premier landscape plants, so Chapter 6 gives basic information relating to this subject together with key principles of gardening with hostas and lists of species and cultivars recommended for a number of gardening situations. Names and addresses of international societies concerned with the genus and nurseries selling hostas are also included.

Since the publication of Fumio Maekawa's monograph on the genus in 1940, no comprehensive treatment has been published, and in fact Maekawa's monograph did not contain the taxa named and described in Europe so was incomplete in that respect. For comprehensiveness this book encompasses all botanical taxa in the genus known today, and a complete botanical, taxonomic treatment has been included in Appendixes A and B. The determinations made in Appendix A are reflected in Chapter 3. They cover the taxonomical aspects in detail and validly correct many of the nomenclatural mistakes that have accumulated since Maekawa. Appendix B deals with the many problems in nomenclature from a historic standpoint and reviews analytically each important author since Kaempfer's contribution in 1712.

The American Hosta Society (AHS) has been conducting cut-leaf exhibitions since its inception in 1969. These shows go a long way in introducing the public to the pleasures of gardening with hostas, so Appendix C specifies the leaf-size classifications originated by the AHS for cut-leaf shows and also includes this society's national show schedule (as of 1990). To correlate these data to the descriptions given in Chapters 3 and 4, I have provided the AHS show classification number for each species, specioid, and registered cultivar, insofar as these numbers are available. Thus, readers can determine the AHS leaf type number by direct reference.

Appendix D is interrelated to Chapter 2. It gives definitions of sizes, color groupings, shapes, and other morphological plant features and discusses the basis of variegation in the genus and the finer points of flower macromorphology. It is intended primarily for the keen gardener and professionals in the field.

To make the book internationally useful, I have included non-English synonyms and common as well as academic local names, principally in Japanese, German, and Korean, and to make the names more useful and better understood, transliterations and/or translations for most of them have been included in the descriptions in Chapters 3 and 4. Appendix E introduces readers to a few important points about the Japanese language and gives translations for the most common Japanese and German names. It also contains a brief discourse on these languages as they relate to *Hosta*.

Abiotic and biotic factors influencing the cultivation of the genus are briefly discussed in Appendix F, and a condensed treatise on propagation and hybridizing is given in Appendix G. Appendix H gives information on economic and other uses of the genus beyond those covered in Chapter 6.

A number of abbreviations are used throughout this book, so I urge readers to familiarize themselves with the list of abbreviations which follows the appendixes. This list includes acronyms and many scholarly (Latin-based) abbreviations.

A collection of endnotes is provided to give additional information for those keenly interested in the more detailed and scientific aspects of this work.

A glossary to technical and botanical terminology is provided. Most gardeners only occasionally encounter botanical Latin, and when they do, then in the form of latinate plant names. No botanical Latin will be required to use the reference chapters of this book. It was inevitable, however, to make occasional use of specialized terms, most of which are based in either Latin or Greek, and to include brief Latin text to validate new taxa—as required by the International Code of Botanical Nomenclature (ICBN). These technical references are part of Appendix A. Use of this book for reference purposes does not require full understanding of the scientific language given in Appendix A, but because botanical Latin is the international language of botanists, it is indispensable to the very keen gardener who is bent on the study and cultivation of species and botanical varieties and forms. Quite regularly, even casual gardeners, who are primarily interested in cultivars, find themselves faced with latinate plant names, so they may want to learn some of the more frequently used descriptive latinate terms. The Glossary encompasses an adequate vocabulary of scientific terms rooted in Latin and Greek, but it is by necessity in abbreviated form. Readers wanting to consult a more comprehensive reference can obtain Stearn's (1986) *Botanical Latin*.

An extensive bibliography is provided with a separate listing of catalogs and price lists which served as reference material.

Finally, three indexes are provided: a general index covering general names and subjects; an index to plant names and synonyms associated with the genus *Hosta;* and an index to foreign *Hosta* names and synonyms. Page numbers for key references are in bold; plate and figure numbers are in italic type. The primary names and essential synonyms are arranged in alphabetic order in Chapters 3 and 4 so require no index search, but I want to emphasize that most of the more obscure and unimportant synonyms and historical names do not show up as primary entries in these chapters. However, they are included in the indexes, which must be used to locate them.

ILLUSTRATIONS

All black-and-white halftones and line drawings are arranged in numeric order, starting a new number sequence within each chapter or appendix. The illustration number is preceded by the chapter number or appendix letter—for example, 3-18 or D-5—to permit cross-referencing of illustrations. Thus Figure 3-18 is the 18th figure in Chapter 3, and Figure D-5 is the 5th figure in Appendix D. Color illustrations are numbered individually and consecutively without regard to chapter or appendix. They are referred to in the text by their unique number. Plate 27, for example, points to the 27th color illustration in the color section, which follows page 128.

Photographer's credit is provided for all photographs featured in this book. It is given at the end of each caption, printed in parenthesis. All photographs marked "(Hosta Hill)" were taken by the author at Hosta Hill. Along with the credit, and whenever possible, the gardens in which the photographs were taken are identified.

In some cases the photogenic quality of the illustrations is the highest that can be expected from slides taken for record purposes only. Occasionally, it was important to include historically or taxonomically important plants in spite of some obvious insect or hail damage to the plant.

METRIC CONVERSIONS

Both metric and U.S. mensurations are given in this book, principally for length and area measurements, so conversion is not required. For quick conversion calculations to the metric system, the following rounded-off equivalents can be used, and for readers who want to make precise calculations, exact equivalents are given in brackets.

Metric Units.
  Millimeter (mm): 1000 mm = 1 meter (m).
  Centimeter (cm): 100 cm = 1 m.
  Kilometer (km) = 1000 m.
  Are (a) = 100 square meters.
  Hectare (ha) = 10,000 square m.
  Square km = 1,000,000 square m.

Measures of Length (U.S. to Metric).
  1 inch = 25 mm or 2.5 cm [= 0.0254 m].
  1 foot = 300 mm or 30 cm [= 0.3048 m].
  1 yard = 900 mm or 90 cm [= 0.9144 m].
  1 mile (statute) = 1600 m [= 1609.344 m or 1.609344 km].
  1 mile (nautical) = 1850 m [= 1852 m or 1.852 km].

Measures of Length (Metric to U.S.).
  1 mm = 0.04 inch [= 0.03937 inch].
  1 cm = 0.4 inch [= 0.3937 inch].
  1 m = 40 inches [= 39.37 inches].
  1 m = 3.3 feet [= 3.2808 feet].
  1 km = 3300 feet [= 3280.8 feet].
  1 km = 0.6 mile (statute) [= 0.6214 mile].

Measures of Surface Area (U.S. to Metric).
  1 square inch = 640 square mm [= 645.2 square mm].
  1 square inch = 6.4 square cm [= 6.452 square cm].
  1 square foot = 930 square cm [= 929.03 square cm].
  1 square foot = 0.1 square m [= 0.0929 square m].
  1 square yard = 0.8 square m [= 0.8361 square m].
  1 acre = 43,560 square feet = 4000 square m [= 4046.7 square m].
  1 acre = 0.4 ha [= 0.40467 ha].
  1 square mile = 640 acres = 2.6 square km [= 2.5899 square km].
  1 square mile = 260 ha [= 258.99 ha].

Measures of Surface Area (Metric to U.S.).
  1 square millimeter = 0.0015 square inch [= 0.00155 square inch].
  1 square centimeter = 0.15 square inch [= 0.155 square inch].
  1 square meter = 10.8 square feet [= 10.764 square feet].
  1 square meter = 1.2 square yards [= 1.196 square yards].
  1 are = 120 square yards [= 119.6 square yards].
  1 hectare = 2.5 acres [= 2.471 acres].
  1 hectare = 0.004 square mile [= 0.003861 square mile].
  1 square kilometer = 0.4 square mile [= 0.3861 square mile].
  1 square kilometer = 250 acres [= 247.12 acres].

CHAPTER 2

A Classification System for *Hosta* Cultivars

GENERAL AND HISTORICAL NOTES

The genus *Hosta* is composed of 3 subgenera, 10 sections, and over 100 species, specioids, and subspecific botanical varieties and forms. There is also a profusion of cultivars, both registered and unregistered.

The botanical classification of species, varieties, and forms is a task carried out by plant taxonomists. There are considerable differences among them on how the genus should be divided and classified. Furthermore, classification is a continuing task because the conclusions reached in new investigations often require revisions. The system I have used is one that is a more or less accepted, considering the work of all major researchers. The resulting arrangement is reflected in the nomenclature of species, sub-species, and specioids included in Chapter 3 and the systematic keys to the genus presented in Appendix A.

Currently, no comprehensive, established system for classifying the hundreds of cultivars exists. It is clear, however, that there is a great need for such a system because hybridizers are constantly adding to the pool of existing named cultivars and in Japan new sports are being discovered in the wild, brought into cultivation, and named. To categorize these new taxa and to provide uniform descriptions for this book, I devised a horticultural classification system dealing with all important morphological features found in the genus. It is much more detailed than the current AHS cut-leaf show classification system which deals with leaf sizes and colors only.

The confused state of cultivar names in the genus has its roots, at least partially, in muddled botanical nomenclature. Due to the many synonyms used to designate the species in the genus, the association of cultivar names with particular species names has become equally difficult. The correct correlation of cultivars to their parental species is clearly important for both historic and horticultural reasons. Consequently, one or more synonyms are provided for a majority of the species and cultivar entries in Chapters 3 and 4.

Historically, only limited attempts have been made to provide comprehensive listings of registered and unregistered cultivars. The main publication[1] of The American Hosta Society (AHS) has provided an annual listing of all cultivars registered during the prior year. These lists are maintained by Mervin C. Eisel, registrar, International Registration Authority for *Hosta* (Eisel and Pollock, 1984). Before 1980 many of the entries, however, lacked descriptions. A few listings provided descriptions but they were often incomplete and did not follow a uniform pattern.

In 1969 the late Mrs. Glen (Eunice V.) Fisher published the first edition of a *Hosta* listing in booklet form which saw subsequent revisions in 1973 and 1979 (Fisher, 1969, 1973, 1979). Quite thorough, this work covered species and both registered and unregistered cultivars. It catalogued many of the classic cultivars for the first time within a single publication. A preliminary checklist for the genus was compiled by Ruh et al. (1980). This listing was prepared by a committee formed expressly for this purpose by the AHS. It was a preliminary undertaking, which lacked descriptions and was incomplete in other respects, but was, nevertheless, the most comprehensive list of names available at that time.

Since 1960 other authors attempted to catalogue the species and cultivars of the genus for horticultural purposes. These efforts included limited papers by Brickell (1968), Grenfell (1981), Hansen and Müssel (1964), Hansen et al. (1974), Hensen (1963a, 1963c, 1985), and Schmid (1986b). Additionally, *Hosta* listings were published in various horticultural encyclopedias in Japan, England, Germany, and the United States (Bailey and Bailey, 1976; Everett, 1984; Graf, 1978; Hansen, 1972; Hylander, 1969; Jellito-Schacht, 1963; Jellito et al., 1986; Maekawa, 1950, 1969; Thomas, 1985). Although some of these papers are quite complete in regard to species and botanical varieties, they contain a very limited number of cultivar entries and are therefore quite incomplete. I have used these publications as reference material and included them in the Bibliography.

In 1988 *The Hosta Book* was published. A cooperative effort of several authors, with Paul Aden acting as editor, this beautifully illustrated book was the first garden book exclusively devoted to the genus. An excellent source of standard information for aspiring gardeners, it serves its intended purpose well. General in scope, it is not a definitive reference work.

Lacking in all these endeavors were the key considerations enumerated earlier, but especially (1) a uniform classification method, (2) a simplified, descriptive format to represent *Hosta* cultivars, and (3) inclusion of all species, specioids, and practically all known cultivars, their names and synonyms.

BASIS FOR CLASSIFICATION

The following classification system is for cultivars only, because species display much greater variability than do cultivar clones. The latter, usually vegetatively propagated as the name *clone* implies, are quite uniform in growth and appearance. On the other hand, species and varieties growing in the wild differ considerably over their natural habitat. The simplified descriptions used for cultivars are not sufficiently accurate to characterize species growing in the wild. Consequently, all species, botanical varieties, and specioids have been provided with complete botanical descriptions in English and are gathered in Chapter 3. This will help the serious gardener identify them and permit clarification of many unsolved puzzles existing in today's gardens. Technicalities concerning color, variegation, and flower, as well as leaf morphology, have been included in Appendix D, while botanical terminology is interpreted in the Glossary. The cultivars which are classified by the following system are assembled in Chapter 4.

The basis used for the system of cultivar classification presented here is rooted in standard botanic taxonomic principles. The narrative that botanists use for species, called a *botanical diagnosis*, forms the basis for cultivar classification. It describes key morphological features in detail following a predetermined order from bottom to top—from root structure to flowers.

Obviously, a classification system must include all key features required for evaluating distinctiveness. It may appear complicated to some, but most gardeners, after carefully studying the following list of included characteristics, will recognize that it consists of the features they normally use for identification of hostas in their own gardens. Root structure is not included here because it is normally not seen. Except for the stoloniferous members of the genus, all others have a comparable root structure which is explained in the introductions to Chapters 3 and 4.

Plant shape.	Scape length.
Plant diameter.	Scape foliation.
Plant height.	Scape posture.
Leaf size.	Flower size.
Leaf venation.	Flower shape.
Leaf color.	Flower color.
Leaf shape.	Flower fragrance.
Leaf surface.	Blooming period.
	Fruiting.

Although the above list includes all key attributes, there are a few odd cultivars that defy the order in some respects. These are annotated in the descriptions to point out their unique features.

Most descriptions in Chapter 4 have a uniform arrangement following the above order. A sample description appears like this:

> Plant erect, 30 in. (76 cm) dia., 28 in. (71 cm) high. Leaf 9 by 6 in. (23 by 15 cm), veins 12, blue-green, not variegated, cordate, wavy-undulate. Scape 56 in. (142 cm), bare, straight. Flower medium, funnel-shaped, lavender, flowers during average period, sterile.

Each of the traits mentioned in this description is explained in detail on the following pages.

DEFINITIONS AND PRECONDITIONS

Before specifying the individual categories, some definitions and preconditions must be understood.

Plant Maturity. Classification must be made on mature plants. Due to the longevity of cultivars, the term *plant maturity* requires particularly careful definition. In this book plants are considered mature when they have completed their sixth growing season after being started from 1- or 2-year-old root divisions.

Some cultivars, especially when well established, will reach immense proportions as reflected in occasional descriptions published in rather florid language. But plants of such spectacular size are not normally encountered in average gardens. For this reason accounts of such sizes have been ignored in favor of average sizes attained under average growing conditions at the completion of six growing seasons.

Leaf Maturity. Many cultivars produce two distinct leaf forms, one being a juvenile, the other a mature form. Most, if not all, cultivars attain their mature leaf shapes and sizes after six growing seasons. Frequently, plants also produce a second crop of leaves, called *summer leaves*. These leaves are often different from those arising earlier. One cultivar which typically develops summer leaves is *H.* 'Undulata'. Its summer leaves are much narrower than its vernal leaves and usually green, not variegated.

Obviously, leaves are one of the most important characteristics, so care must be taken that only mature leaf forms are

used for categorization. As a consequence I exclude juvenile and summer leaf types. Leaf maturity also relates to the determination of other characteristics and vernal, juvenile, and summer leaf forms are discussed in detail later.

Plant Shapes and Outlines. Quite frequently the shape and outline of clumps change with the passage of time. Young plants may first possess an erect shape which later becomes dome-shaped after the plant has spread out, with a consequent lengthening of the petioles. This transformation should have taken place within the 6-year time limit adopted as a criterion. The descriptions in Chapter 4 assume a plant to be dome-shaped unless it is specifically characterized as being erect.

Cultural Conditions. These include the effect of climate, location, and soil (see Appendix F). Although most of the morphological cultivar characteristics, such as flowering and fruiting, are manifest within the period of maturity used here, some cultivars will not flower reliably nor bear fruit under certain conditions. Typically, this is due to improper location, climatic conditions, or cultivation. The climate might be too hot or too cold, or the plant may get too much shade. Clearly, the six growing seasons stipulated must pass under average climatic and growing conditions. Cultivation and conditioning of cultivars must include correct soil preparation and improvement, fertilizing and watering as and when required, and basic insect and disease control (see Appendix F). I assume most gardeners, having paid considerable sums of money for their acquisitions, are inclined to give their plants reasonable and adequate care.

Plant Mutability. Species growing in the wild show great diversity. They are also prone to produce mutations, many of which have been isolated and named. Species also hybridize freely in areas where the populations of two species overlap, so it is no surprise that cultivars follow this general pattern of variability. Even the so-called stable cultivars can and will vary with the passage of time. Some unstable center-variegated cultivars bought under one name may change in time and have to be renamed. The descriptions included in Chapter 4 represent the average plant as originally described and before any reversion may have taken place.

Nota Bene
In the following classification all key identifiers are marked with a bullet thus: ●.

PLANT SHAPE AND SIZE

Dome-shaped. Most cultivars develop into rounded dome-shaped mounds as exemplified by *H.* 'Blue Cadet' (Figure 2-1). These mounds may be quite flat and low in some cultivars, as in *H. longipes* 'Golden Dwarf' (Figure 2-2), or they can be as high as they are wide without actually being erect, in which case they are referred to as "cubed" mounds. An example of the latter is seen in young plants of *H.* 'Summer Fragrance' (Figure 2-3). A few cultivars that grow quite flat when young, with their leaves hugging the ground, are thought of as flat plants by many gardeners. But as these cultivars mature, they eventually fill out and become more dome-shaped. For this reason such flat plants are classified as dome-shaped types.

Stoloniferous plants, those with creeping roots, form colonies, resulting in mats of adjacent plants. These colonies considered as a whole may be quite flat, but the individual plants within the group are usually dome-shaped or erect. Consequently, this classification considers only a single plant among a stoloniferous group under cultivation.

Figure 2-1. *H.* 'Blue Cadet'; mounding habit: typical dome-shaped mound (Hosta Hill)

Figure 2-2. *H. longipes* 'Golden Dwarf'; mounding habit: flat mound (Hosta Hill)

Figure 2-3. *H.* 'Summer Fragrance' (young plant); mounding habit: "cubed" mound—as wide as high (Hosta Hill)

Figure 2-4. *H.* 'Krossa Regal'; mounding habit: erect mound, long petioles (Hosta Hill)

Erect. Some cultivars grow very erect, on upright petioles. Of these, most have vase-shaped, upright petiole bundles with the leaves either in line with the petioles or angled away from them. These plants which retain an erect, vase-shaped posture even as mature plants, after their petioles have elongated considerably, are classified as erect types, an example of which is seen in *H.* 'Krossa Regal' (Figure 2-4). This group also contains a number of plants bearing long, upright leaves with short petioles such as the members of the *H. sieboldii* group. It is important to understand that cultivars must be distinctly and permanently erect in habit to be considered erect plants. Several forms are erect when young, but become dome-shaped as they mature and leaves are added. Thus, they are classified as dome-shaped.

A true upright character can be seen in *H.* 'Krossa Regal' and *H. rectifolia*.

Thus, the descriptions for plant shape are

- Dome-shaped.
- Erect (upright, vase-shaped).

The description "dome-shaped" is, however, not included in the descriptions in Chapter 4, so when no descriptor is included, the plant described is assumed to be dome-shaped. Erect plants are described as "erect."

Plant Size. Terms such as large, medium, and small are frequently seen in nursery catalogs. These terms are too general and not useful for a true depiction of size. Plant size is therefore described using diameter and height given in inches and centimeters:

- Plant diameter.
- Plant height.

Plant Diameter. Average diameter is measured across the center of a plant from a leaf tip near the ground on one side to a comparable leaf tip on the other. Some gardeners refer to this measurement as width or breadth and, incorrectly, as girth.

Plant Height. This measurement is taken at the highest point above the ground surface reached by the leaves, usually near the center of the plant. Leaves on flower scapes, even very leafy scapes, are excluded from this measurement.

LEAF CHARACTERISTICS

Size Categories. In sanctioned cut-leaf shows, the AHS recognizes six general size categories. They are listed below and are further defined in terms of length-to-breadth ratios in Appendix C. A color code is also included in the AHS classification number, and the entire code number is included in Chapters 3 and 4 after the taxon's name, so allowing readers easy determination of the AHS cut-leaf show classification if they wish to enter one of these shows. The AHS size categories are

Class I: Giant = 144 square in. and larger.
Class II: Large = 81–144 square in.
Class III: Medium = 25–81 square in.
Class IV: Small = 6–25 square in.
Class V: Miniature = 2–6 square in.
Class VI: Dwarf = 2 square in. and smaller.

Leaf Size. The dimensions given in Chapter 4 have been obtained by averaging the measurements taken of vernal leaves (see below) on several mature clumps. In some instances actual plants were not available so photogrammetric methods, which have proven to be very reliable, were used to obtain calculated measurements from photographs. In the cases of some very new cultivars not available to the author or those not old enough to meet the 6-year maturity criterion, the introducer's data given in the registration form were utilized.

Determining leaf size requires an understanding of the factors which affect classification. Mature leaves must be used and certain leaf types must be excluded. Leaf size is given in length and breadth. While the breadth is easy to determine, the length is very difficult to obtain in taxa with margins continuously decurrent to the petiole as they give no clear indication where the leaf ends and the pseudo-petiole begins. An example is the new cultivar *H.* 'Gosan Lettuce' (Figure 2-5). In some taxa, for example, *H. laevigata* or *H. longissima* f. *longifolia*, the leaf emerges directly from the rhizome without a discernable petiole transition, so the leaf length is measured from ground level to leaf tip. This is also the case for some cultivars, for example, *H.* 'Gosan Gold Sword' (Figure 2-6). Even in cases where there is some visible petiole transition, some judgment is required to arrive at the point from which leaf length should be measured.

Leaf size is indicated by

- Leaf Length.
- Leaf Width.

Figure 2-6. *H.* 'Gosan Gold Sword'; leaf without petiole transition (Hosta Hill)

Vernal Leaves. The leaves which first unfurl in spring, called *vernal leaves,* are the first to attain a characteristic, mature leaf shape. They are customarily larger, broader, and more rugose than the inside leaves which emerge later in spring or as a second flush in early summer. This is especially true of younger plants, which produce few mature leaves. For this reason, the leaf sizes used in the descriptions are those of mature vernal leaves, growing at the periphery of the plant.

Juvenile Leaves. Many cultivars produce a variable type of leaf growth called *juvenile leaves* which do not result in mature shapes but which cannot be mistaken for summer leaves as they are formed with the vernal leaves. They are the innermost leaves in the crown, especially in young plants. In very young plants all leaves may be of juvenile form, none of which are characteristic of the mature leaf shape. A typical example is *H.* 'Ginko Craig' which has very desirable, small juvenile leaves, but sprouts mature leaves of rather overgrown proportions after the plant is in place 5–7 years (Figure 2-7). The transition is slow and at first only the margins increase in width and the leaves get moderately larger. Eventually, the mature plant grows much larger. Only continuous lifting and dividing will preserve the juvenile leaf form.

Figure 2-7. *H.* 'Ginko Craig'; juvenile leaves (right front), mature leaves beginning to show (left rear) (Hosta Hill)

Figure 2-5. *H.* 'Gosan Lettuce'; leaf lacking obvious petiole (Hosta Hill)

Summer Leaves. Occasionally a mature cultivar sprouts summer leaves which are atypical of the plant. These leaves should be ignored for classification. A typical example of nonvariegated summer leaf development can be observed in members of the variegated *H.* 'Undulata' group (Figure 2-8).

Figure 2-8. *H.* 'Undulata'; nonvariegated, green summer leaves (Hosta Hill)

Abnormal Development. In most gardens "melting out" (Schmid, 1987d; Pollock, 1988) prevents the leaves of certain variegated cultivars (featuring large central areas of white) from ever reaching registered leaf sizes. Reports indicate these taxa not only do not reach the sizes described but diminish in size year after year and finally succumb, never developing mature leaves. A lack of chlorophyll in center-variegated varieties that have large areas of albescent white causes this problem. In some locations the plants carry on but with much diminished vigor and size, so the ultimate mature sizes described for them may be much larger than they actually get. Some reports promote placing these taxa in full sunlight to reach the mature sizes portrayed in the registrations but this has not worked for many gardeners.

VENATION (VEINING)

Campylodrome Veining. The circulatory system of leaves exhibits a typical pattern of veining (see Figure 2-9) called *campylodrome.* Some taxa, for example, *H. jonesii,* appear to be camptodrome—where the primary nerves truly join a principal nerve along the midrib—when in actuality the primary nerves form nerve bundles along the midrib without ever joining. The arrangement and number of principal veins in leaves is an important diagnostic tool for botanists and gardeners alike. The veins are very conspicuous, and their analysis is uncomplicated and easily undertaken by any

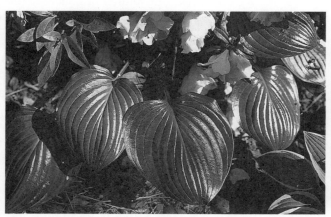

Figure 2-9. *H. ventricosa;* typical campylodrome veining pattern (Hosta Hill)

gardener as it simply involves counting the total number of principal vein pairs in a mature vernal leaf. Depending on the taxon observed, the number of veins observed varies from 2 to 20 pairs.

The number of principal veins is indicated by

• Veins.

Variability in Veining Count. As with other diagnostic features, a given cultivar displays some variability in the number of veins, and so the count given in the descriptions is the average maximum number of principal veins normally seen in that cultivar. Occasionally, this number may be exceeded by one or two, while the younger summer leaves may produce fewer veins. It is best to make a count on several mature vernal leaves and then take the average.

Abbreviated Veins. One significant point must be made: The outermost vein or veins are often abbreviated and do not extend to the leaf tip but usually terminate at the leaf margin between a third- and halfway up from the petiole intersection (see Figure 2-10). Although these veins end at the margin and are thus incomplete, they must be counted. In some cases they are hard to detect on the upper side of the leaf so it is helpful to search for them on the underside, where they are typically more prominent. In the taxa belonging to section *Helipteroides* these outer veins are submarginally connected and appear to merge with the next vein, but close examination shows they actually terminate (Figure 2-11) and are merely cross-connected.

There are other more complicated veining patterns than the ones described here. These are not dealt with to keep the system simple. *Hosta sieboldiana* and *H.* 'Tokudama' show submarginal connection patterns which may be useful in classification and diagnosis. More analytical work is needed on this attribute to make it useful.

Figure 2-10. *H.* 'Sum and Substance'; abbreviated outer veins (Hosta Hill)

Figure 2-11. *H.* 'Sum and Substance'; marginally connected outer veins (Hosta Hill)

PRIMARY AND SECONDARY COLORS

Variegation. Refer to Appendix D for a brief technical discussion of variegation.

Color Descriptions. A meaningful depiction of leaf colors is probably the most difficult cultivar classification characteristic to put into writing because color is based on very personal perceptions. The frequent references to "blue" and "gold" seen in cultivar names are typical of this difficulty. Obviously, there are no true blue or gold colors in leaves. The blue and gold are strictly in the eyes of the beholder. The quality of color is frequently influenced by emotion; many avid gardeners believe they see "true blue" or "pure gold," while more-detached and less-biased casual visitors to their gardens perceive these colors as just grey-green or plain yellow. This problem is compounded in color illustrations which are often exaggerated by using special color filters to emphasize blue coloration, making cultivars look a true blue color that is not perceptible by the human eye when it looks at the actual plants.

Another difficulty in classifying color arises from streaked and mottled leaf color patterns. These color patterns frequently differ from leaf to leaf on the same plant or from one season to the next and disappear altogether in certain unstable cultivars. Others start out with a nice yellow leaf color only to turn into a homely chartreuse or green. It is well known that leaf colors in most cultivars, whether all-green or highly variegated, do change perceptively with the passing seasons. This change is almost universally observed within the genus, so color must be assessed during its peak period, early May to mid-July, depending on geographic location.

Because of these complexities, a detailed definition of color is necessary to any classification scheme. The color descriptions used in horticulture are based on standardized color groups used by botanists. In the following, only broad color definitions are given, so for botanical technicalities and exact color groupings refer to Appendix D.

The AHS has included color codes in its cut-leaf show classification number (see Appendix C) and these are very broad in scope and useful for show purposes only. Whenever the AHS classification code was available it has been included in Chapters 3 and 4 for species and all registered cultivars after the taxon's name (see introductions to Chapters 3 and 4).

Color Dominance. One leaf color usually dominates in variegated hostas. This color is called the base color or *primary* leaf color, while the additional color or colors are called *secondary* colors and are those forming the variegation pattern.

Primary Leaf Color. Primary leaf color can be green, blue-green, yellow, or white and is defined here as occupying a minimum of 60% or more of the leaf surface. As discussed later, a primary color may be a blend of colors and not technically a true monochrome, although it may appear to be such.

Secondary Leaf Colors. Secondary leaf colors cover 40% or less of the leaf surface. They are also used to indicate the type of variegation, whether margin colors of green, blue-green, yellow, or white, or central variegation, such as central fields or stripes, streaking, or mottling of green, blue-green, yellow, or white. A detailed listing of the combinations utilized in the descriptions is discussed below (see "Variegation").

As pointed out previously, some secondary leaf color combinations in highly variegated cultivars almost defy description. They vary considerably from leaf to leaf within the same clump. The International Registration Authority for *Hosta* has discouraged the registration of such highly variable cultivars because they do not exhibit good color stability; many such cultivars are, in fact, unstable and revert to stable forms, usually producing a differently colored leaf margin or all-green or all-yellow leaf coloration. Fortunately, many variegated hostas have more or less stable configurations and can be described in relatively simple terms.

Not Variegated. Many cultivars are not variegated. They have a uniform coloration of blue-green, green, or yellow, or a blend of slight variations of one of these colors which gives the appearance of uniform coloration at a distance. Upon closer examination this blend of several hues is evident, but when viewed from a distance of 6 feet (1.8 m) or more it appears as uniform coloration and is considered here as a uniform color for classification purposes. For these monochrome leaves the secondary leaf color given in the descriptions is "not variegated."

COLOR STABILITY AND EFFECTS

Several phenomena relate to leaf color and must be noted: instability, viridescence, lutescence, albescence, and changing surface effects. In Chapters 3 and 4 color changes have been categorized into these major types and additional comment is given about the timing factors involved in these phenomena.

Unstable Colors. In most cultivars color and color effects (such as blue) are temporal conditions and change with the passing seasons. A high number of variegated hostas have unstable leaf colors and virtually every gardener has, always with some degree of sadness, seen blue hostas turn to plain green, a golden margin inevitably turn to a more-or-less nondescript white or plain light green, and glowing golden mounds change to chartreuse.

Viridescence. Many cultivars are viridescent, which means they emerge with white or yellow leaf colors that ultimately become increasingly green. There are differing degrees of viridescence. Certain cultivars produce beautiful yellow or white colors in spring, only to turn all-green by the onset of summer. In these cultivars, of which *H.* 'Fortunei Albopicta' is an example, viridescence is complete. Partial viridescence, a partial greening, is common. Examples are *H. sieboldii* 'Silver Kabitan' and *H.* 'Chinese Sunrise' in which the leaves emerge with white or yellow centers that later turn greenish by forming green streaks (the former) or uniformly (the latter).

Lutescence. Lutescent taxa emerge green or chartreuse (yellowish green) and turn to yellow or whitish yellow. This process is usually much more subtle and often less discernable than viridescence as frequently it involves only a very slight change from a greenish cast to a yellowish hue. The yellowing process appears to be influenced by environmental factors. During very dry and very hot weather the color change from greenish to yellowish may be delayed or not occur in certain cultivars, adding to the difficulty of classification.

Albescence. Albescent taxa have yellow, yellowish green, or green areas that turn to near white, as in *H.* 'Janet'. Frequently, yellow-margined taxa turn into white-margined ones, for example, *H. ventricosa* 'Aureomarginata'. Whitening due to bleaching by overexposure to strong sunlight destroys color-forming plastids, so is not true albescence.

Blue to Green. The loss of blue is caused by the loss of pruinose epidermal wax, which produces a blue, glaucous sheen over a green background color. When the wax is lost due to rain, overhead watering, and/or increasing day- and nighttime air temperature differentials, the plain green color becomes visible. Warming of the topsoil is also suspect as a contributing factor. Although technically a color change, the change from blue to green is not used for classification because it occurs after the prime period for judging colors (usually May to June). Gardeners can assume that the blue lasts longer in cooler locations but will sooner or later in the season turn to green.

White Surface Effects. The leaf underside of some species, including *H. hypoleuca, H. pycnophylla,* and *H. longipes* 'Urajiro', has a near white color which is actually a coating of a very opaque fine white powder. Some hybrids have inherited this trait, for instance, *H.* 'Sum and Substance'. For the purpose of simplification, it is considered a color and included in the descriptions as such.

Timing for Classification. Viridescence (greening with age), lutescence (yellowing with age), and albescence (whitening with age) create a considerable problem in arriving at descriptions, as the colors could obviously be described either before or after the color change. To standardize timing for the purpose of classification, cultivars have been described as they appear during their prime season as specified earlier. This is the stage at which most are pictured in print and seen on carefully timed garden tours. For example, *H. ventricosa* 'Aureomarginata' is classified with yellow margins, although they turn whitish soon after the high season. Another difficulty is caused by the AHS classification system which separates light and dark yellows, for example. Since light and dark may be caused by viridescence or lutescence and so are interrelated to a time factor, the classification number given by the AHS (see Appendix C) and included in Chapters 3 and 4 may not represent the actual color observed at a given time.

COLOR DESCRIPTIONS FOR CULTIVARS

The following cultivar color descriptions comprise a simplified version of the system used by botanists. It assigns only major color categories, and each category covers a range of colors (refer to Appendix D for color groupings).

- Blue-green (enhanced by temporary surface effects).
  A dull green passing into greyish blue, usually associated with a glaucous, caesious, pruinose, or glaucescent surface.
- Medium green.
  Grass-green, clear green, and olive-green.
- Dark green.
  Deep green verging on black, and deep green with a mixture of blue.
- Chartreuse.
  Distinctly more green than yellow, yellowish green.
- Yellow (viridescent) (begins as one of the yellows listed below and turns chartreuse or green—is yellow during prime observation time).
  Lemon-yellow, golden yellow, plain yellow, pale yellow, sulphur-yellow, straw-colored, waxy yellow, egg yolk, greyish yellow, yellow clouded with greyish or bluish.
- Yellow (lutescent) (begins as light green or chartreuse and becomes one of the yellows listed below—is yellow during prime observation time).
  Lemon-yellow, golden yellow, plain yellow, pale yellow, sulphur-yellow, straw-colored, waxy yellow, egg yolk, greyish yellow, yellow clouded with greyish or bluish.
- White (albescent) (begins as a yellow or greenish color becoming one of the listed whites).
  Pure white, ivory-white (with yellow), milk-white (with blue), chalk-white, silvery (white with bluish grey luster), whitish, white, whitened (covered with white).
- White (viridescent) (begins as one of the listed whites but turns chartreuse, whitish green, or green later; greens up).
  Pure white, ivory-white (with yellow), milk-white (with blue), chalk-white, silvery (white with bluish grey luster), whitish, white, whitened (covered with white).

Monochrome Colors. Most of the above colors can occur as solid, monochromatic coloration; all-white hostas have been found. Solid colors extend over the entire leaf surface. Monochromes are also formed by hues of two or more different greens that blend into one color when seen from a distance and thus are considered solid-colored. A distinct secondary color is absent so they are classified as "not variegated."

- Not Variegated. Absence of a distinct secondary color.

VARIEGATION

Margin Colors. The descriptions use three major margin types, defined by the margin color over a solid primary color. Margin colors must be judged at the prime observation time in May/June.

- White Margin on solid blue-green, green, chartreuse, or yellow.
- Yellow Margin on solid chartreuse, blue-green, green, or white.
- Green or Blue-Green Margin on solid chartreuse, yellow, or white.

Streaky Patterns. Many variegated cultivars have highly streaked, splashed, mottled, or otherwise irregular variegation (i.e., the center of the Benedict Cross, as discussed in Appendix D). Most, if not all, streaky color patterns are unstable as discussed earlier and in Appendix D. In Chapter 4 the streaky variegation pattern is described in simplified terms.

- Streaky White on green, chartreuse, or yellow.
- Streaky Yellow on green, chartreuse, or white.
- Streaky Green or Blue-green on chartreuse, yellow, or white.
- Streaky Multicolor. Several light colors on a darker color, several dark colors on a lighter color.

Multicolor variegation category may be streaky, splashed, mottled, or a combination of these. This description also includes light or dark margins as well as irregular variegation in combination with a streaky pattern. Although there is a margin of sorts this does not make it a marginate type.

LEAF SHAPE AND SURFACE

Classification of cultivar leaf shapes is relatively simple. When looking at a leaf, three main components stand out as the parts making up the outline shape of the leaf:

1. The basic shape.
2. The shape of the leaf tip.
3. The shape of the leaf base.

Definitions of Leaf Shapes. The combination of these three attributes makes up the actual leaf shape. Leaf shapes, tip shapes, and base shapes recognized by botanists, and their respective category numbers are discussed in detail in Appendix D, and definitions are included in the Glossary. For the purposes of this classification system, the three main leaf shape components listed above have been combined into five basic types which are used in the descriptions.

- Strap leaf (Figure 2-12).
    Strap-shaped, ratio 12 or more to 1;
basic leaf shape no. 12, band-shaped;
tip shapes no. 141, cuspidate, tapering gradually to a sharp point, or no. 149, acute, coming straight to a point;
base shape no. 175, wedge-shaped with straight sides converging and terminating at the crown without a distinct petiole.

Figure 2-12. *H. longissima* var. *longifolia*; leaf forms: strap leaf (Pratt)

- Lanceolate (Figure 2-13).
    Lance-shaped, ratio 6:1 to 3:1;
basic leaf shapes nos. 1 and 2, lanceolate, nos. 36 and 37, narrowly ovate, and nos. 45 and 46, narrowly obovate;
tip shapes no. 141, cuspidate, tapering gradually to a sharp point, or no. 149, acute, straight to a point;
base shapes no. 175, wedge-shaped, straight sides converging, or no. 176, attenuate, curved sides converging with distinct petiole.

Figure 2-13. *H. sieboldii* f. *spathulata* (right); *H. sieboldii* form (left); leaf form: lanceolate (Hosta Hill)

- Ovate (Figure 2-14) (includes oval to obovate).
    Egg-shaped, ratio 2:1 to 3:2;
basic leaf shapes nos. 3 and 4, oval (elliptical), nos. 38 and 39, ovate, and nos. 47 and 48, obovate;
tip shapes no. 141, cuspidate, tapering gradually to a sharp point, or no. 149, acute, straight to a point, and no. 153, blunt-pointed, terminated by a rounded end;
base shapes no. 171, truncate, as if cut straight across, no. 175, wedge-shaped, straight sides converging, or no. 176, attenuate, curved sides converging with distinct petiole.

Figure 2-14. *H.* 'Opipara'; leaf form: oval (Hosta Hill)

- Cordate (Figure 2-15).
    Broadly heart-shaped, ratio 6:5;
basic leaf shapes no. 5, roundish, and no. 40, broadly ovate;
tip shapes no. 140, mucronate, terminated by a sharp point, and no. 153, blunt-pointed, terminated by a rounded end;
base shapes no. 166, heart-shaped, having two equal, rounded lobes, or no. 171, truncate, as if cut straight across.

Figure 2-15. *H.* 'Blue Cadet'; leaf form: cordate (Hosta Hill)

- Round (Figure 2-16).
    Circular, ratio 1:1;
basic leaf shapes no. 6, orbicular, and no. 41, very broadly ovate;
tip shapes no. 140, mucronate, terminated by a sharp point, and no. 153, blunt-pointed, terminated by a rounded end;
base shape no. 166, heart-shaped, having two equal, rounded lobes.

Figure 2-16. *H.* 'Love Pat'; leaf form: rounded (Hosta Hill)

Leaf Topography (Surface). The leaf surface characteristics of cultivar leaves are determined by a combination of several factors: (1) markings or evenness, (2) superficial processes, and (3) polish or texture. The botanical definitions of these features are discussed in Appendix D and included in the Glossary. For cultivar classification this category has been simplified to the following major surface and margin types which have been isolated and included in the descriptions.

- Flat (even, smooth, without much rugosity) (Figure 2-17).
  Many cultivar leaves are "flat," but this should not be taken to mean flat as a board. Flat is defined as the absence of rugosity. The leaf area is depressed along the principal veins. But the tissue between the veins is smooth, albeit frequently arched, or level, with no intermittent concavity or convexity. Some cultivars show an occasional depressed or raised area between veins but are still considered flat. In fact, all leaf types which are not conspicuously rugose, cupped, contorted, or very undulate along the margins are placed in this category.

Figure 2-17. *H. cathayana* 'Chinese Sunrise'; leaf topography: "flat," indicating the absence of rugosity, not "flat as a board" (Hosta Hill)

- Rugose (Figure 2-18).
  Leaves in this class are distinctly and predominantly rugose; that is, leaf surface has uneven features. This includes dimpled, puckered, pursed, embossed, ruffled, pleated, wrinkled, and crinkled leaf surfaces. Examples

are *H. sieboldiana* and its hybrids. Although some juvenile leaves may lack rugosity, vernal leaves on mature plants are almost completely rugose.

Figure 2-18. *H.* 'Gosan Sigi Grey'; leaf topography: rugose (Hosta Hill)

- Cupped-rugose (Figure 2-19).
  In this group rugosity is accompanied by cupped leaves. Cultivars whose leaves have slight cupping or raised margins are not included here. Only those with distinct cupping and dominant rugosity are classified in this group.

Figure 2-19. *H.* 'Big Daddy'; leaf topography: cupped-rugose (Hosta Hill)

- Wavy-undulate (Figure 2-20).
  Hostas classified in this category lack rugosity. The leaves have a relatively smooth surface but are very wavy and undulate. Typically, there are several broad waves on the leaf, with smaller, irregular undulations interspersed which are sometimes confined to the margins only. Additionally, the leaf tip is slightly twisted on some leaves.

- Contorted (Figure 2-21).
  A few cultivars have contorted, warped, or distorted leaves and are gathered under this classification. Due to their unique leaf shapes which defy description, illustrations are provided to typify the several forms included under this class.

Figure 2-20. *H.* 'Undulata'; leaf topography: wavy-undulate (Hosta Hill)

Figure 2-21. *H.* 'Tortifrons'; leaf topography: contorted (Pratt)

• Piecrust (Figures 2-22, 4-15, 4-23).

The leaves of this group are essentially flat but have closely spaced marginal undulations which are commonly referred to as *piecrust* margins, a term I have retained because it is very descriptive. Leaves of a great many cultivars have sporadic and uneven undulations but they are included under wavy-undulate. Cultivars classified as having piecrust margins have distinct, regular, almost uniformly spaced, and plainly recognizable undulations on all mature leaves.

Figure 2-22. *H. montana*; leaf topography: piecrust (piecrust form ex Asuke-cho, Aichi Prefecture; cultivated at Hosta Hill)

• Furrowed (Figure 2-23).

The principal veins in most cultivar leaves are slightly sunken, creating a ribbed effect. Many leaf types classified as flat have these slightly depressed veins. In con-

trast, the furrowed group has very deeply sunken veins with the intervening leaf surface arching high to form rather deep V-shaped channels or furrows. The depth of these furrows can reach 0.16 in. (4 mm) or more. In these cases the leaf surface is called furrowed. An example is *H. montana* f. *macrophylla*.

Figure 2-23. *H. montana* f. *macrophylla*; leaf topography: furrowed (Hosta Hill)

SCAPE LENGTH

Scape Length. Due to variability in the orientation of the scape, scape height is obviously not the same as scape length. In this classification scape height is disregarded in favor of the actual length of the scape, measured along the scape from the crown at ground level to the tip of the raceme. Scape length including the raceme varies from 2–3 inches to 8 feet (5–7 cm to 2.4 m).

• Scape length.

SCAPE FOLIATION AND POSTURE

Scape and Raceme. All members of the genus carry flowers on a more-or-less elongated flower scape terminating in a more-or-less populated raceme (Figure 2-24). Some species—for example, *H. tibae* and *H. jonesii*—and some cultivars produce branched scapes (Figure 2-25).

Scape Foliation. The racemes bear fertile bracts from which single flowers emerge (Figure 2-26) below which, along the scape, a varying number of sterile (flowerless), subtending bracts develop (Figure 2-27). The latter can scarcely be seen in some cultivars, as they are tightly wrapped around the scape and do not open. This is typical of many cultivars in the *H. sieboldii* group (Figure 2-28). In other groups the bracts open and extend away from the stem, presenting a leafy appearance. Examples of foliated bracts are seen in many hybrids of *H. sieboldiana*, *H. montana*, *H. fluctuans*, and *H. kikutii* (Figure 2-29). In some taxa, fertile and sterile bracts develop to give the appearance of actual leaves of varying sizes along the scape. They are usually larger close to the ground and diminish in size towards the top of the raceme (Figure 2-30), and the upper bracts may be fertile (i.e., subtend a flower). Conversely, and occasionally, the bracts at the top of the raceme develop into large leafy shapes which initially envelope the bud. The taxa belonging to the *H. kikutii* complex and its hybrids illustrate this type of bract (Figure 2-31).

For the purpose of horticultural classification all scapes with tightly wrapped bracts are described as nonfoliated, bare (*nudus*) scapes. All others, with more-or-less developed, leafy, sterile bracts, are considered as leafy (foliaceous).

- Bare.
- Foliated.

Figure 2-28. *H. rohdeifolia* f. *viridis*; sterile bracts, amplexicaul (stem-clasping) (Hosta Hill)

Figure 2-24. *H. montana*; raceme (Hosta Hill)

Figure 2-29. *H. kikutii* × *H. pycnophylla* hybrid; sterile bracts, approaching foliaceous (leafy) (Hosta Hill)

Figure 2-25. *H. tibae*; branched scape (Hosta Hill)

Figure 2-26. *H. hypoleuca*; fertile bracts, seed pods forming (Hosta Hill)

Figure 2-30. *H.* 'Undulata'; sterile bracts, foliaceous, numerous large scape leaves (Hosta Hill)

Figure 2-27. *H. longipes* form; sterile bracts, subtending (Hosta Hill)

Figure 2-31. *H. kikutii* × *H. pycnophylla* hybrid; fertile, foliaceous bracts (large bud leaves) (Hosta Hill)

Scape Posture. Scapes grow from the rootstock in all directions, from vertical or near vertical (*H. nigrescens*, Figure 2-32), to obliquely bent (*H. ventricosa*), and in some cases, arching and becoming partially subhorizontal (*H.* 'Nakaimo', Figure 2-33), or flat along the ground, as in the *H.* 'Unazuki Soules' form of *H. kikutii* var. *caput-avis* (Figure 2-34). Cultivars originating with these and other species frequently inherit these traits.

The following types of scape posture have been used in this classification. Measurements are based on the angle of degrees from a horizontal position.

- Straight = 80–90°, erect.
- Oblique = 20–80°, inclined, bending.
- Prostrate = 0–20°, near horizontal.

It is important to note that these scape postures are to be judged shortly before full bloom (anthesis) on a dry scape. After seed development the weight of seed or rain or irrigation water adhering to flowers distorts the scape angle abnormally.

Figure 2-33. *H.* 'Nakaimo'; scape posture: oblique (inclined, bending, arching) (Hosta Hill)

Figure 2-34. *H.* 'Unazuki Soules' (a form of *H. kikutii* var. *caput-avis*); scape posture: prostrate (supine, flat on the ground) (Hosta Hill)

FLOWER MORPHOLOGY

Maekawa (1940) described scientifically the flower and its major parts (see Figure 2-35). Reference to and review of his detailed analysis, while informative, may prove too complicated for the casual reader interested in a gardener's cultivar classification system. Detailed botanical information concerning flower morphology and color determination is given in Appendix D, where I have also categorized the various color patterns found in the lobes and applied them in the morphological keys given in Appendix A. Fortunately, the flower has a relatively simple morphology. Consequently, only the key elements for recognition have been utilized in the descriptions in Chapter 4. These are

Figure 2-32. *H. nigrescens*; scape posture: straight

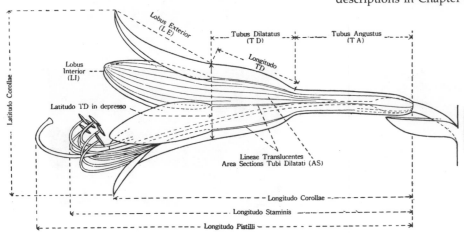

Figure 2-35. Flower morphology: diagram by Maekawa (1940:326)

1. Size of flower.
2. Shape of the expanded section of the perianth.
3. Color of the flower.
4. Fragrance.

There are some additional morphological complexities which should be mentioned. Subgenus *Hosta* (formerly *Niobe*), as represented by a single species, namely, *H. plantaginea*, has flowers carried on a degenerated compound raceme with one-flowered, sessile branches. It is also the only species that flowers nocturnally. There are also some species in other subgenera—for instance, *H. tibae*, *H. tsushimensis*, and *H. jonesii*—which carry branched racemes. Additionally, double-flowering forms have been reported, of which *H. plantaginea* 'Aphrodite' and some forms of *H. montana* are examples. Both *H. yingeri* and *H. laevigata* have a distinct spider-flowered perianth. Recently Japanese collectors have discovered several mutations with abnormally formed flowers, which are very much sought after in Japan. Some of these atypical forms have been excluded from the classification system to simplify it.

Flower Size. This measure is the total length of the perianth from its root at the pedicel to the furthest extension of the tips of the lobes (Maekawa's *longitudo corollae*). The stamens and pistils usually project beyond these tips but are not considered part of the perianth length. This easily measured characteristic has been divided into three categories:

- Large = 3 in. (7.5 cm) or more.
- Medium = 1–3 in. (2.5–7.5 cm).
- Small = Less than 1 in. (2.5 cm).

Most cultivars have medium-size flowers, save for some cultivars of *H. plantaginea*, which have large flowers, as does the species. Small flowers do occur, but rarely.

Flower Shape. Flowers are composed of a narrow tubular section followed by an expanding section formed by 6 lobes: 3 interior and 3 exterior. The center section of the perianth beginning at the point of expansion to the onset of the lobes is either funnel-shaped or bell-shaped. This central shape gives the flower either a funnel-shaped form (Figure 2-36) as in *H. montana* or a bell-shaped character (Figure 2-37) as in *H. ventricosa*. Most cultivars have a more-or-less bell-shaped flower, while a few have a truly funnel-shaped inflorescence. *Hosta yingeri* and *H. laevigata*, new species discovered in Korea recently, have very narrow lobes which open to what horticulturists consider a spider flower (Figure 2-38), but this characteristic, rare even in species, has so far not been observed in cultivars and so is not included for cultivar classification.

One exception to these two major types includes flowers that do not open. These closed-perianth types expand to the point in time when the flower would normally open its lobes, but it does not do so, and thus the flower remains closed until it dries and separates from the pedicel. An example is *H. clausa*.

The three classifiers used in the description for flower shape are

- Funnel-shaped.
- Bell-shaped.
- Closed perianth.

Perianth Colors. Detailed analysis of flower coloration is important to species identification and is presented in Appendix D. For cultivar identification it plays a secondary role and for this reason a simplified system of classifying cultivar flowers is included in the following.

The background color in cultivar flowers is usually white but some have suffused lavender or purple coloration. Background color either alone or combined with blue-lavender-

Figure 2-36. *H. montana* hybrid; flower morphology: funnel-shaped flower (Hosta Hill)

Figure 2-37. *H. ventricosa*; flower morphology: bell-shaped flower (Hosta Hill)

Figure 2-38. *H. laevigata*; flower morphology: spider-shaped flower (Hosta Hill)

purple striping or suffused effects results in the following categories, which are used in the descriptions.

Timing of Observation. For the purpose of arriving at a standard, color should be observed at the time the flower opens. This occurs just before or just after sunrise in day-blooming species and cultivars. Further detailed discussion on the coloration of flowers can be found in Appendix D.

- Whitish, white (corresponds to type A in Appendix D) (Plates 1, 193, 194, 195, 196).

  Flowers appear white, but are not actually a pure white. *Hosta plantaginea* has flowers that approach a pure white. This white is combined with a waxy-sheen surface effect. It has been called a waxy white. Representatives in section *Helipteroides*, such as *H. montana* and *H. nigrescens*, appear whitish. The veins are barely visible, but there may be a noticeable lavender tint in the lobes, and this coloration varies with abiotic factors which are detailed in Appendix D. Type A color is meant to be mostly white, or with a white appearance. A good example is *H. kikutii* which has wild populations with whitish flowers and was so diagnosed by Maekawa (1940). In cultivation it often takes on a distinct lavender color not normally seen in the wild, although Fujita (1976a) included some atypical populations with colored lobes.

- Purple (corresponds to type B in Appendix D) (Plates 2, 197, 198, 199, 200).

  Intensely purple-colored veins on each interior lobe are surrounded by more-or-less tinted (purple and dark mauve, lilac, or lavender) areas which are bordered by a thin white margin. Most of the inside of the perianth is colored. The narrow tube may be tinted or near white. On the outside this coloration appears as a uniform purple coloration, as seen in the species *H. ventricosa, H. capitata, H. nakaiana*, and many of their hybrids. The purple stripes (veins) are barely visible and a more-or-less uniform purple field surrounded by narrow white margins takes their place.

- Purple striped (corresponds to type C in Appendix D) (Plates 3, 201, 202, 203, 204).

  The veins in each inner lobe are intensely colored, usually a dark purple, with the adjacent areas a very pale and suffused lilac or near white, giving the flower a striped effect. On the outside these flowers are near white, with some tint showing through. This type of coloration is common in the *H. sieboldii* group and its variants and hybrids. Exceptions are the white-flowered variants of this group, such as *H. sieboldii* 'Alba' and *H. sieboldii* 'Louisa'. In these exceptions the flowers present albino forms which are predominantly whitish.

- Lavender (corresponds to type D in Appendix D) (Plates 4, 205, 206, 207, 208).

  A large group of cultivars has veins in the inner lobes which are very pale and barely visible because they are almost the same color as the background. In certain species this color field is surrounded by wide margins that are white or a very pale lavender. *Hosta longipes* and many of its hybrids demonstrate this feature which is useful for sectional classification. In many cultivars characterized as having lavender-colored flowers, the white margins overlap where the lobes join, so are hidden, and the overall effect is lavender or light purple. The entire perianth takes on a suffused-lavender or light purple color, which is also observable on the outside. This type of tinting is most often described in the horticultural literature as lavender, mauve, or lilac—reflecting the slight differences in shading and hue. *Hosta* 'Inaho' and *H.* 'Fortunei' are examples of this type of tinting. Because many other hybrids have this flower color, it is of little use for identification of hybrids.

Flower Fragrance. It was once thought that only the Chinese species, *H. plantaginea* in subgenus *Hosta*, its varieties, and some of its hybrid offspring were fragrant. However, several unrelated fragrant cultivars are grown in Japan with apparently no connection to *H. plantaginea*. One of these, *H.* 'Asuka', is dwarf with white fragrant flowers. Another, *H.* 'Otome No Ka', is dwarf and fragrant, with light purple flowers.

Most hostas are not fragrant. However, because fragrance is an important horticultural trait, when it occurs it has been included in the descriptions as

- Fragrant.

Season of Bloom. Depending on the species, blooming takes place between June and October. Most of them flower during the period June 1–July 15. Geographic location influences onset of blooming as do climatic conditions.

All dates of flowering have been recorded at Hosta Hill garden, Tucker, Georgia, located at 34° north latitude, with a mean January isotherm temperature of 43° F (6° C). This location approximates conditions in southwestern England and Ireland, the south-central and southern part of the Japanese archipelago—including Shikoku and Kyushu—southeastern Australia, and much of western New Zealand. For every 2 degrees of latitude north (or southward in the Southern Hemisphere), the onset of blooming occurs about one week later.[2] Thus the blooming period indicated in the listing must be adjusted for latitude. The following arrangement has been used to indicate the beginning period of flowering:

- Very early period = before June 1.
- Average period = June 1 to July 15.
- Summer period = July 15 to August 15.
- Late period = August 15 to October 1.
- Very late period = after October 1.

Blooming Time. The classification system developed for these descriptions pays no heed whether the cultivars are night- or day-blooming varieties. The species *H. plantaginea* and its varieties are the only night-blooming taxa of record, its flowers opening in late afternoon. All others are day-bloomers, the flowers opening in the morning hours.

Fruiting (Seed Set). The matter of fertility versus sterility in cultivars is complicated. Some cultivars are very fertile, while others produce viable seed only when carefully hand-pollinated. Still others produce seed capsules in abundance, giving the appearance of being fertile, but their capsules are filled with aborted or undeveloped ovules and no viable seed is found. Viable seeds are ovoid and black with winged appendages.

Some cultivars that bloom very late in the season are fertile, but fail to set seed in northern latitudes, due to the shortness of the growing season. A few, such as the night-blooming *H. plantaginea*, require narrowly defined climatic and environmental prerequisites to produce seed. Many cultivars are for all practical purposes sterile, but they will on rare occasions produce a few viable seeds. All of this makes it difficult to classify borderline cases.

I have assumed that under cultivation, opportunities for pollination are abundant and will additionally be helped along by careful human hands. Under these circumstances I have found that many cultivars once considered sterile produce viable seed, although rarely and in a rather sporadic fashion. For the purpose of the descriptions I have classified all cultivars which produce any kind of viable seed as fertile. Some never set seed and have been classified infertile. In a few instances I was not able to obtain reliable information and in these cases the taxon has been noted as "fertility(?)":

- Fertile.
- Sterile.
- Fertility(?).

CHAPTER 3—PART 1

Introduction to Plant Descriptions—Species

METHODS

The information presented in this chapter was obtained in several ways: (1) from the botanic literature as referenced in the Bibliography; (2) collecting authentic specimens in the wild or obtaining them from academic and private sources and observing them in cultivation; (3) studying the species and specioids in the wild or in botanic and private gardens the world over; (4) examining and analyzing most of the *Hosta* specimens in herbaria in Japan, Europe, and the United States, including a majority of the type specimens extant (in BH, BM, E, GA, K, KYO, L, M, MAK, NA, P, PE, SAP, SHIN, SNU, TI, TNS, TUS, U, UPS, WAG); (5) subjecting authenticated, live and dried specimens to a comparative, macromorphological analysis using 60 morphological characters—33 quantitative and 27 qualitative with 75 variables (see Appendix A—Part 1)—and delimiting the taxa on the basis of this analysis; (6) obtaining photographic material substantiating determinations made with a number of *Hosta* researchers and authorities; and (7) incorporating the results of the latest scientific macromorphlogical, palynological, and biosystematic investigation conducted in Japan (Hara, 1984; Maekawa 1984) and North America (Chung and Jones, 1989; Chung, 1990).

TYPOGRAPHIC PROTOCOL

The following typographic protocol has been followed for the main name headings to indicate their standing.

1. Names of recognized species are printed in **bold italic** type, as in **H. ventricosa**.
2. Names of specioids (see Introduction) reduced to cultivar form are preceded by the symbol ✠, printed in *"regular italic"* type, and enclosed in double quotation marks, as in ✠ *"H. sieboldii f. kabitan"*.
3. Essential botanical synonyms, including all those listed in *Index Kewensis* through Supplement 18, have been included as primary entries and are printed in *regular italic* type, as in *H. apoiensis*. A number of important horticultural synonyms are also included as primary entries. Usually, these are combinations of a species name with a Latinized or Japanese descriptive cultivar epithet, in which case the species name is printed in *regular italic* type, and the cultivar epithet is printed in 'Regular Roman' type and enclosed in single quotation marks; the combination appears thus: *H. sieboldii* 'Oze Mizu'.
4. Combinations of a recognized species name with a Latinized or Japanese descriptive cultivar epithet are printed in **bold italic** type for the species name, and the cultivar epithet is printed in **'Bold Roman'** type and enclosed in single quotation marks; the combination appears thus: **H. ventricosa 'Aureomarginata'**.
5. When a species has been reduced to cultivar form, it is written in cultivar form, with the epithet enclosed in single quotation marks and printed in **'Bold Roman'** type, as in *H.* **'Fortunei'**. Any descriptive cultivar epithet associated with the reduced species name is combined with it and the combination written as a cultivar name, as in *H.* **'Fortunei Albomarginata'**.

DEFINITION OF A SPECIES

Species, as currently delimited within the genus, do interbreed in the wild and so the classic definition of a species as "a population of similar individuals, alike in structural and functional characteristics, *which in nature breed only with each other*, and which have a common heritage" is of only limited use. I have therefore discussed this subject in more detail in Appendix A and defined *Hosta* species in this book as (1) natural (evolved or hybridized) populations which maintain themselves in the wild, and (2) which are recognized by botanists as distinct assemblages and upon which specific rank has been conferred, and (3) which conform to a given systematic type and the morphological limits of a valid diagnosis given for this type. This very simplified definition eliminates the very complex problem of interspecific hybrids treated as species by botanists. It also should clear up the mistaken belief often held by gardeners that any plant found in the wild is a species when in fact it must first be collected and thoroughly researched, a holotype designated, and a valid diagnosis published in Latin. Only after all these steps have been completed does a plant become a recognized species. Quite a number of Japanese plants brought to Western gardens under Japanese names are often incorrectly considered species. Equally incorrect is the view that a popular cultivar is a species because it breeds true from seed (Summers, 1990). Further comment on this matter is found later in this chapter under "Botanical Synonyms."

EXPLANATION OF DESCRIPTIONS

Hosta species, infraspecific taxa, and specioids have a number of characteristics in common which are listed below. Because they apply to all or most of the taxa described, they are not repeated in the individual descriptions.

1. Chromosome number: Unless noted otherwise, all are diploid with a chromosome number of $2n = 60$ (see also Appendix A—Part 3).
2. Root stock: Unless noted otherwise, all have a tuberlike, subterranean, rhizomatous rootstock with abbreviated internodes. The leaf bundles are produced at the apex of the rhizome and frequently the remnants of vascular bundles can be seen there in spring. The size and thickness of the rhizome depends on the kind of species, age, nutrition, environmental factors, and water economy.
3. Roots: Unless noted otherwise, all have roots emanating from the rhizome which are long, white, round in cross section, hairy, and from 1–4 mm (0.04–0.15 in.) in diameter.
4. Veins: The words "smooth" and "papillose" are used to characterize the texture of the projected veins on the leaf underside. The principal veins are almost always sunken on the leaf surface and more or less raised on the underside. In some species—*H. kikutii*, for example—this raised part feels smooth, but in others, like *H. montana*, it is covered with numerous excrescences (papillae) along its length and feels rough (papillose) to the touch, so the descriptors "smooth" or "papillose" are

used under the heading "Veins" to characterize the surface texture of the projected veins on the back of leaves.

5. Anthers: My study of anther coloration (Schmid, 1986–1989; unpublished) confirms that it is an important characteristic for classification. Judging color must be done before the anthers dehisce and release their yellow pollen, thereby masking the true anther color. Examination is best accomplished with a 30-power microscope on anthers removed from an unopened flower. *Hosta* anthers have two oblong, parallel pollen sacks which open at the dividing line and dehisce introversely, thus obscuring the exterior coloration. Preliminary results indicate that true species have either pure yellow or uniformly purple-dotted anthers, while interspecific hybrids have nonuniform purple dotting with several dot sizes, or irregular dot patterns, or they have one yellow-colored locule and the other purple-dotted to varying degrees, a condition called "bicolor anthers" in the descriptions.

6. Pollen: The pollen grains of all species are yellow, and they are basically egg-shaped—oblate-spheroidal, suboblate (Erdtman, 1966). Occasional references to pollen grain types are based on the 1989 palynological study by Chung and Jones and listed in Appendix A—Part 4, under "Morphology and Palynology."

To help the gardener identify *Hosta* species, varieties, and forms, as well as specioids, complete and detailed descriptions are provided. The characterization of species and specioids follows the general format used by botanists in plant diagnosis.

The main reason for the more detailed portrayal is the variability of natural populations. While cultivars are largely vegetatively (asexually) propagated clones with a very constant morphology, species vary considerably in the wild. To deal with this variation, species descriptions are traditionally of a wider latitude but must include sufficient data on often rather-minute details for petioles, leaves, veining, scape, bracts, raceme, flowers, anthers, and other pertinent features as necessary to accurately portray the entire morphological range of the species. These details must be carefully compared with an actual specimen to confirm they match a particular collected phenotype. This type is usually represented by a herbarium specimen called a *holotype*, or another accepted botanical type specimen, or, in the absence of such a specimen, concordance with the valid type diagnosis must be ascertained by careful observation. Under the ICBN rules the description of any taxon published after 1 January 1958 requires the indication of a nomenclatural type and the herbarium in which such a type specimen is located. Fortunately, type specimens exist for many *Hosta* species published before this date and appropriate reference to a nomenclatural type has been made in the classification of the genus in Appendix A.

As a consequence of this natural variability, the specific descriptions provided in this chapter are more detailed than those provided for cultivars in Chapter 4 which follow the uniform but summarized classification system detailed in Chapter 2. Both systems of description follow botanical convention which stipulates a uniform order commencing with the underground portions of the plants—rhizomes and roots—proceeding upwards to petioles and leaves, then to flower scape and flowers, and ending with parts of the flowers and seeds. Because botanists use metric measurements, the descriptions have been given metric measurements first, with English measurements following in parenthesis. All these characters taken together usually permit clear identification of a species. To further enhance a particular diagnosis,

photographs have been provided for most of the taxa listed. Some species—for example, Araki's—are very narrowly delimited and represented in the wild by very small populations, so it was not possible to obtain living plants for all his species. In these cases the holotype and other herbarium specimens were examined, and a specimen photograph serves to illustrate a particular species.

In addition to providing descriptive information for species and botanical varieties and forms, historical, ecological and nomenclatural information has also been included. This added information relates to discovery, habitat, history, unique features and the meaning of both Japanese formal and common names as well as the latinate botanical names.

BOTANICAL SYNONYMS

The meaning of *synonym* in botany is quite different from its horticultural application which is explained in Chapter 4. Botanically, each species has one correct scientific name by which it is known and which is composed of the generic name *Hosta* (abbreviated as *H.*) and a specific epithet, as in *H. plantaginea*. A species may also have one or more botanical synonyms which are validly published names that have been replaced when the taxonomic status of a particular taxon was changed due to modification, division, union, or change in rank, or any other legitimate procedure permitted under the rules of the ICBN. Such changes result in previously valid botanical names becoming superfluous, illegitimate, or otherwise invalid. In such cases these names are given the status of "valid botanical synonyms." Occasionally in this book, nomina nuda are included with the listing of botanical synonyms because they may have served as basionyms, provided essential facts in the identification of taxa, or been essential synonyms in prior botanical publications. Among these, I consider all the names published by von Siebold as essential synonyms realizing, of course, that they are nomina nuda. Most, but not all the essential synonyms appear in *Index Kewensis*, and all names incorporated in this index up to and including supplement 18, have been considered.

The synonyms are listed at the end of each species entry segregated into four categories: (1) **SY** = Botanical synonyms; (2) **HN** = Horticultural names; (3) **JN** = Japanese names; and (4) **ON** = Other-language common names synonymous to the main entry. Within each group the names are arranged in alphabetical order. The entire botanical synonymy of the genus *Hosta*, including bibliographic references, is given in Appendix A to positively identify and delimit each species on the basis of its nomenclatural history and available types.

The nomenclatural rules of the ICBN allow only one valid name for a particular taxon, and in the botanical literature this rule is strictly observed. Unfortunately, the rules are not always followed by horticulturists. Regrettably in the past, when new species were introduced into the trade, cultivar names were often given to an imported plant before it was identified as a species and its correct botanical name known. An example is the case of *H. nakaiana* which is also called *H.* 'Birchwood Gem'. There is nothing wrong with this naming process in principle because selected, cultivated clones of a species may be given cultivar names under the ICNCP. A problem arises, though, when the named clones are practically identical morphologically to the particular phase of a taxon that is propagated and sold as the species. Ordering under any of these names will yield plants that are virtually identical. This concerns gardeners who want to avoid duplication and unnecessary expense. To prevent such duplication all horticultural synonyms listed under a species entry are names representing the same or virtually the same clone or phase as the species. These synonyms are included in Chapter 4 as well, with the appropriate cross-references given.

Unfortunately, many taxa in the genus are either cultigens (specioids) or interspecific hybrids that, as a consequence, do not come true from seed. In these cases the makeup of the offspring is unpredictable because one or both parents lack complete dominance of inherited genes which results in multiple-factor inheritance. By way of an example, most gardeners know that *H. sieboldiana*, when carefully selfed, yields a multitude of different seedlings, large and small, green or glaucous, and tall-scaped as well as short-scaped. This is because what gardeners grow as the species *H. sieboldiana* is in fact a taxon that has been extensively hybridized during its 150 years of cultivation in the West and so is no longer representative of the wild population. Even in Japan the type used for this taxon by Maekawa was also probably hybridized, as much of his type material was of cultivated origin. Both Fujita (1976a) and Maekawa (1940) give this species extremely wide morphological latitude by including forms which Western horticulturists and gardeners do not normally consider *H. sieboldiana* even though botanically they are.

The detection of hybrids among the taxa named and described in the botanical literature is very important not only to the delimitation of the species but also to their placement and interpretation as true species. Gardeners who have carefully selfed *H. sieboldiana* have, in fact, carried out one of the tests which botanists use to detect hybrids within a specific population, namely, a progeny test. The morphological mixture of seedlings which results from mating *H. sieboldiana* × *H. sieboldiana* establishes that the *H. sieboldiana* cultivated in Western gardens is not a "pure" species but a heterozygous taxon which exhibits considerable genetic instability. Fujita (1976a) recognized this and defined his *H. sieboldiana* var. *sieboldiana* species in the broadest sense possible by including as synonyms the following species and specioids: *H.* 'Fortunei Gigantea', *H. sieboldiana* var. *gigantea*, *H. sieboldiana* var. *yakusimensis*, *H. montana*, *H.* 'Elata', *H. montana* 'Praeflorens', *H. montana* 'Liliiflora', *H. crassifolia*, and, had he not considered *H.* 'Tokudama' and its forms to be cultivars, he might have included them, too, as they clearly belong to this assembly. Maekawa (1940) considered many of the above taxa to be separate species, based on morphology alone, without reporting on seed viability, progeny testing, and controlled breeding.

Aside from rather involved cytotaxonomic and biosystematic methods, only controlled breeding and outcrossing can determine the basic nature of this and other "hybrid species," but no such work has been reported in the literature although some efforts in this direction are underway. Therefore, to resolve this problem for the purpose of this book, I have performed a limited number of progeny tests and controlled breeding experiments (author's data, 1985–1989) which indicate that two distinct lines exist in Fujita's synonymy of *H. sieboldiana*, namely, (1) the *H. montana* line with some purple coloration on the anthers, and (2) the *H. sieboldiana* line with yellow anthers. I believe the coloration of the anthers, judged in combination with other macromorphological features, is important enough diagnostically to separate the two lines taxonomically, following Maekawa (1940, 1969). The synonymy presented in this chapter and in Appendix A follows this arrangement.

While seeming the essence of nit-picking, these observations are very important to the correct naming of botanical taxa and the establishment of synonymy in species, because names which might be considered synonyms under Fujita's very broad species definition would certainly not qualify as such under Maekawa's narrower classification. Superficially, determination of botanical synonymy seems to be irrelevant to gardeners and of no practical use. But it should be pointed out

that acceptance of Fujita's synonymy in a strict sense would mean wholesale changing of species names well established in horticulture: *H. nigrescens* and *H. fluctuans* would become *H. sieboldiana* var. *glabra*, and *H. montana* and *H.* 'Elata' would have to be changed to *H. sieboldiana* var. *sieboldiana*, to name a few examples. Luckily in this case, Maekawa's arrangement, although challenged, has been better sanctioned in the literature, so gardeners, who have already struggled through a number of confusing name changes within the genus, can relax because Fujita's proposed changes have only limited acceptance.

Uninformed gardeners expect uniformity in plant material, so it is no surprise that they often make the mistake of considering botanical taxa, such as a species, to be morphologically invariable and to behave like clones. This false impression has been fostered by commercial nurseries who often use vegetative (asexual) mass propagation methods, such as tissue culture, to market a particular clone of a species selected in the wild (Appendix G). Obviously, all the plantlets resulting from such increase are clones of the original plant and do not display the full range of variation seen in natural populations which propagate sexually. So gardeners not infrequently reject other forms of the species differing from the marketed cloned form as not being the same species because they do not conform to their preconceived idea of what the species should look like.

To accommodate variegated taxa, "cultivar synonyms" have been included under group names, as explained in the Introduction to Chapter 4. For example, all yellow-marginate cultivar forms of *H. sieboldiana* have been gathered into a single group, a collection of similar plants, called the *H. sieboldiana* Aureomarginata group. Thus, *H. sieboldiana* 'Frances Williams', 'Aurora Borealis', 'Chicago Frances Williams', 'Gilt Edge', 'Golden Circles', 'Maple Leaf', 'Nifty Fifty', and 'Samurai' all belong to the yellow-marginate group of *H. sieboldiana* and are synonymous when considered as a group. Nevertheless, individually, these plants are held by many to be sufficiently different to justify their clonal names and so are described in Chapter 4 with cross-reference made to an associated group in Chapter 3. To illustrate, *H. sieboldiana* 'Frances Williams' is a separate entry in Chapter 4 with its narrow synonyms listed under its primary name, but it is included in Chapter 3 under the *H. sieboldiana* Aureomarginata group which includes all the yellow-marginate forms of *H. sieboldiana* as broad synonyms. They are certainly close enough in appearance for their names to be considered broadly synonymous, but in a narrow sense there are differences and purists may not consider them morphologically alike. In these cases I have attached the abbreviation "sim" (= similar) or "pp sim" (= similar in part) to the cross-referenced names. This approach should satisfy the knowledgeable hosta collector, who considers these cultivars as being distinctly different, as well as the average gardener, for whom they are practically identical and so perform interchangeable functions in the garden.

All this may seem daunting and unnecessary, but the confusion arising out of the marketing of the same species or botanical variety under several different names, including some cultivar names, has serious implications for the gardener. The botanist can readily ignore such horticultural mischief, but gardeners cannot. They face this problem every time they acquire a plant—whether a species or a species hiding under a cultivar name. Thus, whenever horticultural names are listed as synonyms under a species name, caution should be exercised to not duplicate plant material when ordering under one or more of these names.

HORTICULTURAL SYNONYMS AND "INCORRECT"

Many old botanical and horticultural synonyms exist which may not be incorrect technically but which are obsolete or nomina nuda—for example *Funkia viridimarginata* Siebold (1863) for *Hosta* 'Fortunei Albopicta'. These names are marked "incorrect" and should not be used. Modern latinate horticultural synonyms formulated in contravention of the rules of the ICNCP are always marked incorrect—for example, *H. aureomaculata* Foerster (1965b)—so should not be used. Validly published botanical synonyms are noted as incorrect only if they contain orthographic errors or if they are taxonomically incorrect. An example is *H. lancifolia* var. *thunbergii* f. *albomarginata* (= *H. sieboldii*). Obviously, these incorrect names should not be used. Finally, many cultivar synonyms exist for certain taxa. For example, *H. fortunei* var. *aureomarginata* Hylander (1969) includes these synonyms: *H.* 'Craig No. H-7', *H.* 'Ellerbroek', *H.* 'Ellerbroek L-7', *H.* 'Hirao No. 7', *H.* 'Gold Crown', *H.* 'Golden Crown', *H.* 'Sprengeri', and *H.* 'Yellow Band'. None of these cultivar names has been noted incorrect, because each represents a clonal name within the *H.* 'Fortunei Aureomarginata' group. But gardeners should be aware that some of these clones are virtually or absolutely identical and that they may receive duplicate plant material if they order under several of these names, so their use is discouraged.

FORMAL JAPANESE NAMES OF SPECIES

To the names of species and botanical varieties I have attached Japanese formal, "academic" names, so-called because they were cited along with the valid species name in Japanese botanical publications and thus linked taxonomically and scientifically. It is very important to note that these Japanese academic names are vernacular names that have no standing in botany. They are written solely with Japanese katakana phonetic symbols and are, at best, Japanese-language synonyms for species names. Because of the vast difference between botanical Latin and Japanese, use of the former by nonbotanists in Japan is difficult, and formal Japanese names have been included to allow correlation between them and Western names. I have used the word "formal" to distinguish these names from Japanese horticultural names which are written in katakana, hiragana, and kanji (ideographs derived from Chinese character symbols), as well as jukugo compound words made up of two or more kanji (see Appendix E). To indicate this distinction, all Japanese horticultural names have "hort." added at the end of the names, while formal, academic names are without this qualifier but include an author's name and date of formulation in most cases. Aside from assisting Japanese nonbotanists, these Japanese formal names are also important because of their use in the investigation of early collections appearing in the Japanese floristic literature of the 18th and 19th centuries. They are an essential element in the nomenclatural identification of species or subspecies and play an important role in the synonymy of most of the taxa because they represent a bridge between the Western botanical name and its equivalent Japanese name(s) as cited by early Japanese botanists. Notes on the Japanese language as it relates to the genus, an explanation of Japanese pronunciation, and the meaning of commonly used Japanese names are given in Appendix E.

DISTRIBUTION

Distribution maps and diagrams showing the natural habitat for the species are located in Appendix A—Part 4. Maps showing provincial, prefectural, or regional names can be found in the end papers.

In cases where populations overlap and the possibility for the generation of interspecific hybrid swarms exists, the distribution maps are annotated to point out these overlapping areas. These maps are based on (1) observations in the wild that I made as well as those made by Japanese, Korean, and U.S. botanists and collectors; (2) data published by Maekawa (1960, 1972), Fujita (1976a—modified to reflect the delimitation of species used in this book), M. G. Chung (1989; and personal communication), and S. B. Jones (1989); (3) collectors' data affixed to the herbarium sheets, of which virtually all in existence have been examined; (4) distribution and collection data given in the various original diagnoses; (5) numeric and graphic analysis of the association of characters in known intergrading phenotypes and their recorded locations; and (6) the interpretation of data derived from concordant and discordant variation patterns of the taxa examined. The character of the "standard" populations of species vary within a concordant (i.e., consistent) pattern, while interspecific hybrid swarms show discordant (i.e., abrupt and unforeseen) character combinations and a breakdown of specific lines (Anderson, 1951, 1957).

The genus is still evolving but the rate is very slow, so habitat and ecological influences apparently play a role secondary to intergradation of species. Due to the ability of most species within the genus to interbreed, the specific populations of Japan are in reality networks of interbreeding true species and interspecific hybrids. Individual local hybrid groups within these networks have an uncommonly high survival rate and will eventually segregate through backcrossing. But it appears that a high percentage of genes are eliminated in the formation of local varieties, which possess such a high survival rate. The human race has also contributed to this problem by displacing natural populations and thereby complicating the hybridization patterns even more due to escape of locally foreign species into the wild. This trend can clearly be seen in the herbarium samples studied. Interspecific hybridization and resulting intergradation take place at a relatively fast pace and local factors—such as water, soil, temperature, and geographic features—together with new gene combinations often result in the rather rapid production of local populations of incipient species or varieties. For this reason the distribution maps provided should be regarded as approximate. Further investigations are needed to furnish additional data on the very complex specific interrelationships which exist in the genus, particularly in Japan.

Note bene
Due to the continuing and contemporaneous shift in nomenclature for the genus *Hosta*, some references in the text do not point clearly to the current most-valid form. In an effort to provide the most current reference, the reader should look in the "Index of Names Asssociated With Genus *Hosta*" for the best contemporaneous reference.

CHAPTER 3—PART 2

Alphabetic Listing of Species

A

H. adunca nom. nudum.

ニシノイワギボウシ

Appeared in a list furnished by Dr. Yuasa, University of Tokyo. A selected form of *H. longipes*.

JN: *Nishino Iwa Giboshi* hort.

H. aequinoctiiantha Koidzumi ex Araki 1942.

AHS-IV/19A. (Figure 3-1; Plates 191, 207).

オヒガンギボウシ

Ohigan Giboshi, the "hosta of the equinox," was collected by Kitamura at Yoro-mura in Gifu Prefecture of Central Honshu in 1941. It grows on rocky ledges and outcrops and blooms two to three weeks later than *H. longipes*, around the time of the autumnal equinox, 22 September, hence the name. Similar to *H. longipes* but smaller, it has thin, papery leaves, fewer principal veins, and a more-undulate leaf surface and margin. Fujita considered it a variety of *H. longipes* as *H. longipes* var. *aequinoctiiantha*. *Hosta* 'Iwa Soules' Horinaka cultivated in North America has thicker leaves and blooms a little earlier, but is otherwise very similar to the species and may represent one of the many clones existing among the wild, polymorphic population. Available, but rarely seen, it is a collectors item.

Plant size 35–40 cm (14–16 in.) dia., 30 cm (12 in.) high. Petiole 12.5–17.5 by 0.3 cm (5–7 by 0.125 in.), erect, green, purple-dotted, starting at leaf base, becoming progressively darker towards ground. Leaf 7.5–12.5 by 5 cm (3–5 by 2 in.), erect and in line with petiole, entire, oval-ovate, petiole transition rounded, truncate, smooth, wavy, membranous, thin; tip acuminate, cuspidate; green to dark green above,

Figure 3-1. *H. aequinoctiiantha* (Hosta Hill)

lighter opaque green below. Venation 4–5, sunken above, very projected, smooth below. Scape 25–45 cm (10–18 in.), straight, but bending obliquely, purple-dotted entire length, smooth round. Fertile bracts 1 cm (0.3 in.) long, navicular, thin, membranous, white or whitish green, purple-tinted, imbricated, not withering. Raceme 15–20 cm (6–8 in.), 10–20 flowers. Flowers pale purple, held erect in horizontal position on long, strong horizontal or slightly ascending purple pedicels; perianth 5 cm (2 in.) long, funnel-shaped, expanding, in the central part dilated bell-shaped, lobes spreading straightly to ±angled to the axis of perianth, thin narrow hexagonal tube. Anthers purple, uniformly dotted. September/October. Fertile.

SY: *H. longipes* var. *aequinoctiiantha* Fujita 1976a na.

H. okamotoi Fujita 1976a sl na.

HN: *H.* 'Iwa Soules' hort. pp sim.

JN: *Ohigan Giboshi* Koidzumi 1942.

H. albomarginata Hooker 1838.

(see *H. sieboldii*).

H. alismifolia Maekawa 1984.

AHS-II/7B. (Figure 3-2; Plate 5).

バランギボウシ

Baran Giboshi, the "Baran hosta," for *Baran* which is the common Japanese name for *Aspidistra elatior*, the Cast Iron Plant. Large colonies of this species grow in wet sphagnum bogs and marshes in Gifu and Aichi prefectures along with *H. longissima*. Fujita (1976a) reported a similar sterile taxon in Kochi Prefecture. A natural triploid (2n = 90), it is sterile and propagates by creeping root stocks. The species epithet is derived from *Alisma*, aquatic or marsh herbs in the Alismataceae, to which Water Plantain belongs. Maekawa's holotype (in TI) and his diagnosis portray a very large taxon with leaves to 65 cm (26 in.) long (Figure 3-2). Imported plants and photographs taken in the wild purported to be this species (Plate 5) show a much smaller taxon, about the size of *H. sieboldii*. While variability is accepted in species, the size differences are consistently on the order of 10:1, and these recently imported plants are probably another taxon. The true *H. alismifolia*, as typified by Maekawa, has not been identified in Western gardens. One identifying characteristic of this species is the homogeneous light purple coloration of the perianth, with no stripes and purple anthers. Some of the plants imported from Japan purported to be this species are fertile, so are not this taxon but related to *H. sieboldii*, having stripes in the perianth and yellow anthers. Authentic plants conforming to Maekawa's (1940) diagnosis are in scientific collections but seldom seen in gardens.

Plant size 41 cm (16 in.) dia., 46 cm (18 in.) high. Petiole 20–30 by 0.6 cm (8–12 by 0.25 in.), erect, winged in the upper part, forming a vase-shaped plant, green. Leaf 50–65 by 4.5–6.5 cm (20–26 by 2–3 in.), erect and in line with petiole, obovate-lanceolate, petiole transition decurrent, gradual, dull dark green above, glossy lighter green below. Venation 5–7. Scape 70–80 cm (28–32 in.), straight and erect, bending slightly in the upper part, light green. Sterile bracts 2–3, foliaceous, navicular, pointed; fertile bracts similar, smaller, 10–40 mm (1–1.8 in.) long, 4–9 mm (0.1–0.3 in.) wide. Raceme long, secund, 16–20 flowers, widely spaced. Flowers 5 cm (2 in.) long, 3.5 cm (1.5 in.) broad, pale purple uniformly suffused, no stripes, thin narrow tube, perianth expanding, lily-shaped, lobes spreading rapidly, wide open, at first held horizontal, then nodding on short, purple-dotted pedicels 4–7 mm (0.5 in.) long; stamens equal or slightly longer than perianth. Anthers purple. July. Sterile.

JN: *Baran Giboshi* Maekawa 1972.

Figure 3-2. *H. alismifolia*; holotype in TI (Maekawa, 1984)

H. apoiensis Nakai ex Miyabe and Kudo 1932.
(see *H. rectifolia*).

H. atropurpurea Nakai 1930.
    AHS-IV/19B.　　　　　　　　　　(Figure 3-3; Plate 6).
クロバナギボウシ

    Kurobana Giboshi, the "dark-flowered hosta," is endemic to northern Honshu and Hokkaido, where it occurs in moist woodlands and forest margins. It shares its habitat with *Ezo Giboshi, H. rectifolia* var. *sachalinensis,* which see. Similar in habit to *H. rectifolia,* it is moderately smaller and initially slightly pruinose on leaves and bracts in spring. Hara (1984) considered it *H. sieboldii* var. *rectifolia* f. *atropurpurea,* but the connection to *H. rectifolia* is not accepted here because the anthers of the latter are purple, not yellow (see *H. rectifolia*). The flowers of this taxon have the darkest coloration in the genus with very dark purple lobes with even darker stripes. Climatic conditions similar to the native habitat are required to bring out the deep color. Related to *H. rectifolia,* this selected form has the same stately habit and can be used for mass plantings or specimen clumps, where massed tall, straight scapes are desired. Available, but rarely seen, it is often mislabeled, as is the fine specimen planted in the rock garden at RHS Wisley Garden, UK.

    Plant size 25 cm (10 in.) dia., 30 cm (12 in.) high.

Petiole 12.5–27.5 by 0.8 cm (5–7 by 0.33 in.), erect, winged in the upper part, forming a vase-shaped plant, lightly pruinose fading to dull green with no purple dots at the base. Leaf 15–17.5 by 5–7.5 cm (6–7 by 2–3 in.), erect and in line with petiole, ovate-lanceolate, petiole transition discernable, acuminate tip, flat, smooth, first moderately pruinose fading to dull, dark green above, glossy lighter green below. Venation 5–6, lightly impressed above, smooth below. Scape 60–90 cm (24–36 in.), straight and erect, bending slightly in the upper part, light green, no purple marks. Fertile bracts navicular, pointed, moderately pruinose, purple-tipped, withering at anthesis, but not falling away. Raceme long, 16–20 flowers, widely spaced. Flowers 5 cm (2 in.) long, 3 cm (1.5 in.) broad, dark purple-suffused, darker purple stripes, thin narrow tube, perianth expanding, lily-shaped, lobes spreading rapidly, wide-open, nodding on short, pruinose pedicels, stamens equal or slightly shorter than perianth. Anthers yellow. July. Fertile.

SY: *H. albomarginata* Fujita 1976a sl na.
      H. rectifolia f. *atropurpurea* (Nakai) Nakai ex Maekawa 1950.
      H. rectifolia subsp. *atropurpurea* (Nakai) Inagaki and Toyokuni 1963.
      H. rectifolia var. *atropurpurea* (Nakai) Tatewaki and Kawano ex Ito 1969.
      H. sieboldii var. *rectifolia* f. *atropurpurea* (Nakai) Hara 1984 na.

HN: *H. rectifolia* 'Atropurpurea' hort. incorrect.
JN: *Kurobana Giboshi* Nakai 1930.

Figure 3-3. *H. atropurpurea;* general habit (RHS Wisley/Schmid)

B

✤ *"H. bella"* Wehrhahn 1936.
    AHS-III/13B.　　　　　　　　　　(Figure 3-4).
Here reduced to cultivar form as *H.* 'Bella'.

    This taxon is equivalent to Hylander's (1954) *H. fortunei* var. *obscura,* and because it was validly published in Germany by Wehrhahn (1936) as *H. bella,* the latter name has priority over Hylander's and should be used instead. Inasmuch as both

C

taxa have been reduced to cultivar form and *H.* 'Bella' may represent a different clone in this group, the names are written *H.* 'Bella' and *H.* 'Fortunei Obscura' and can co-exist. Hylander (1953) had called this taxon *H. fortunei* var. *nova*, the "new" *H.* 'Fortunei', indicating he considered this to be the lost *H. fortunei* Baker, which see. *Hosta* 'Bella' is by description considered closest in morphology to Baker's lost taxon and is deemed by some to be the true *H. fortunei* Baker, although no proof exists because no authentic, living specimens of either one of these taxa have been found. The following description is based on Wehrhahn's Latin diagnosis and photograph.

Plant size 40–60 cm (16–24 in.) dia., 35–45 cm (14–18 in.) high. Sprouts grey-green. Petiole 20 by 0.8 cm (8 by 0.35 in.), ascending in an arch, forming a very large dome-shaped plant, winged, grooved, dull green. Leaf 20–30 by 15–20 cm (8–12 by 6–8 in.), leaf attitude at petiole arcuate spreading, entire-elliptical, ovate to cordate-ovate, petiole-leaf transition broadly open, round to cordate, transition broadly open, flat, truncate, acuminate tip, some rugose, flat surface with 1–2 waves, matte to shiny above, pruinose below. Venation 9–10, sunken above, very projected below. Scape 80–100 cm (32–38 in.), isolated fertile bracts and usually bending, solid, terete, green. Fertile bracts large, flat and broad, imbricate to obliquely patent, concave, green with purple. Raceme 25 cm (10 in.), 25–35 flowers, clustered. Flowers 5 cm (2 in.) long, 3.5 cm (1.5 in.) broad, white, suffused pale violet to purple, expanding, funnel-shaped, in the central part slightly dilated bell-shaped, lobes spreading straightly to ±angled to the axis of perianth, stamens superior. Anthers yellowish, with some purple spots. June. Some fertile seeds.

SY: *H. fortunei* var. *nova* Hylander 1952.
     H. fortunei var. *obscura* Hylander 1954.
HN: *H. fortunei* hort. incorrect.
     H. fortunei 'Obscura' hort.
     H. 'Ribbed Beauty' hort.
     USDA ARS No. 263131 Meyer 1963.
ON: Dunkelgrüne Schattenfunkie (German).
     Schattenfunkie (German).

H. calliantha Araki 1942.
AHS-III/13B.   (Figure 3-5).
フジギボウシ

Fuji Giboshi, the "Fuji hosta," was found in Kyoto and Hyogo prefectures of south-central Honshu, where it inhabits wet bottom lands in mountain valleys. Morphologically midway between *H. sieboldii* and *H. rectifolia*, it has very long, winged petioles and beautiful, purple-striped, bell-shaped flowers. The species epithet comes from *callianthus* = with beautiful flowers. Available in Japan it is rarely seen in the West.

Plant size 40 cm (16 in.) dia., 40 cm (16 in.) high. Petiole 15–30 by 0.8 cm (6–12 by 0.33 in.), erect, green with no purple dots at the base, broadly winged, with wings starting at base, becoming wider and merging into leaf base. Leaf 7.5–12 by 2.5–5.5 cm (3–4 by 1–2 in.), oblong-elliptical, erect, decurrent to petiole with very gradual transition, flat, smooth, shiny dark green above, tip obtuse. Venation 3–4, lightly impressed above, smooth below. Scape 50–80 cm (20–32 in.), straight and erect, perpendicular to ground, not bending, light green, no purple marks. Sterile bracts 3–4, small, tightly clasping stem; fertile bracts short, blunt, navicular, thin, membranous, green, not withering at anthesis. Raceme long, 7–19 flowers, widely spaced. Flowers 5 cm (2 in.) long, 3.5 cm (1.5 in.) broad, purple-striped, purple, thin narrow tube, perianth dilated bell-shaped, lobes half open, pedicels 0.5 cm (0.2 in.), slightly projecting stamen. Anthers yellowish, with some purple spots. August/September. Fertile.

SY: *H. albomarginata* Fujita 1976a sl na.
JN: *Fuji Giboshi* Araki 1942.

Figure 3-5. *H. calliantha*; general habit, young plant (Hosta Hill)

H. campanulata Araki 1942.
(see *H. sieboldii* f. *campanulata*).

H. campanulata var. *parviflora* Araki 1942.
(see *H. sieboldii* f. *campanulata*).

Figure 3-4. *H.* 'Bella'; type sketch (Wehrhahn, 1936)

H. capitata Nakai 1930.

AHS-IV/19A.   (Figure 3-6; Plate 7).

イヤギボウシ
カンザシギボウシ

Iya Giboshi, the "hosta from Iya," is the most distinct and largest species in section *Lamellatae*. It was collected by Koidzumi on Shikoku, Iya District, Tokushima Prefecture in 1916. Its Korean common name, when considered a synonym of *H. nakaiana* is *Ilwol-bibich'u* or *Banwool-bibich'u* (meaning "small ball" or "ball-shaped"). Specimens obtained in Japan have bicolor anthers pointing to the possibility of interspecific hybrid origin when, after migrating to western Japan, a Korean taxon belonging to section *Lamellatae* hybridized with a native Japanese species. The Korean populations as analyzed by M. G. Chung (1990) are very small and show little morphological diversity; they may be another taxon (see "The Korean Species" in Appendix A—Part 1). According to M. G. Chung (1989: personal communication) some natural groups near the rocky east coast of the southern part of Korea are in a state of retrogression showing declining membership. This may indicate failure to adapt to new environments and signals eventual disappearance in particular habitats. In cultivation the species flourishes but does not come true from seed, also pointing to interspecific origin. Many different forms exist in the wild, which may be hybrid swarms at various points of intergrading. The smaller forms resemble *H. nakaiana*, so Fujita (1976a) combined this taxon with *H. nakaiana* in synonymy, which is correct in a broad sense, but Fujita considered *H. capitata* a Japanese species, while Chung considers it a Korean endemic, at least from an evolutionary standpoint. There are, however, considerable macromorphological differences, including a disparity in the color of the anthers, as well as others which are further discussed under *H. nakaiana* and in Appendix A—Part 1, and so the question as to whether *H. nakaiana* and *H. capitata* are synonymous must await further study. Nevertheless, in Japan both *H. nakaiana* and *H. capitata* are by some authors called by the same name, *Kanzashi Giboshi*, the "ornamental hair pin hosta," because the closed, purple flower bud looks like a Japanese hairpin ornament. Its large globular flower bud is dark violet just before opening, leading to its epithet, which is derived from *capitatus* = with a knoblike head or tip. Its tightly bunched purple flowers are quite attractive. Scapes have ridges. Several distinct clones as well as lookalike F_1 hybrids have been seen in Western gardens under the species name.

Plant size to 35–40 cm (14–18 in.) dia., 25 cm (10 in.) high. Petiole 20 by 0.8 cm (8 by 0.35 in.), ascending in an arch, slender, narrowly open, purple-dotted, dark basal section, lighter to above middle. Leaf 10–12 by 5.5–8.5 cm (4–5 by 2–3.5 in.), ovate-cordate, with ruffled, piecrust, undulate, upturned margin, elsewhere surface "flat", membranous, not pruinose, but dull, dark yellowish green, some forms darker green, lighter below, opaque. Venation 7–9, sunken above, papillose below. Scape 60–70 cm (24–28 in.), distinct lamellar ridges parallel or slightly spiral to scape axis, straight, erect, mostly perpendicular to the ground, sometimes bending slightly after the weighty seed pods are formed. Fertile bracts navicular, grooved, thick, green or whitish green, tinted purple before anthesis, imbricated even during flowering and nearly equal in size, persisting at but withering after anthesis, developed unopened flower head very globular, capitate, 2–4 sterile bracts. Raceme short, compactly clustered, 15 cm (6 in.), 8–14 flowers. Flowers 4.5–5 cm (2 in.) long, 2.5 cm (1 in.) broad, very closely spaced on raceme, held erect in ±horizontal position on strong pedicels, dark purple veins

on a lighter colored background; perianth pale purple-violet, expanding, in the central part dilated bell-shaped, lobes ±angled to the axis; stamens exerted. Anthers bicolor, yellowish. July. Fertile. Capsules blunt tipped.

SY: *H. cœrulea* var. *capitata* Koidzumi 1916.
    H. nakaiana Maekawa 1969 sl na.
    H. nakaiana Fujita 1976a sl na.
    H. nakaiana Chung 1990 sl na.

HN: Capitate Plantain Lily.
    H. 'Krossa No. K-3' PI 319294.
    H. 'Nakaimo minor' Zager 1967.
    Summers No. 247 1967.

JN: *Iya Giboshi* Koidzumi 1916 pp sim.
    Kanzashi Giboshi Maekawa 1969 pp sl.

ON: *Banwool-bibich'u* (Korean).
    Ilwol-bibich'u (Korean).

Figure 3-6. *H. capitata*; flower bud opening (Hosta Hill)

H. capitata 'O Kanzashi' hort.

大カンザシギボウシ

O Kanzashi Giboshi is a selected, large-leaved form of the species found in the wild in Japan but not sufficiently different to be separated taxonomically and here considered a cultivated clone.

JN: *Oba Kanzashi Giboshi* hort.
    O Kanzashi Giboshi hort.

H. capitata 'Oba Kanzashi' hort.

オオバカンザシギボウシ

Oba Kanzashi Giboshi is a synonym for *O Kanzashi Giboshi*, *H. capitata* 'O Kanzashi'.

JN: *O Kanzashi Giboshi* hort.
    Oba Kanzashi Giboshi hort.

H. capitata 'Ogon' hort.

黄金カンザシ

Ogon Kanzashi Giboshi is a yellow mutation of the species found in cultivation.

JN: *Ogon Kanzashi Giboshi* hort.

H. caput-avis Maekawa 1952.

(see *H. kikutii* var. *caput-avis* Maekawa).

H. cathayana Maekawa 1940.

AHS-IV/19B.   (Plate 8).

アキカゼギボウシ

Akikaze Giboshi, the "autumn wind hosta," is often mistaken for the cultigen *H.* 'Lancifolia', because the only visible differences are the former's smaller, glossy leaves and shorter scapes, persistent bracts, and later flowering time ("blooms in autumn wind"). Most importantly, *H.* 'Lancifolia' is sterile, while *H. cathayana* is a fertile species not indigenous to Japan, but originally from China, as its species epithet indicates (*cathaiana* = from China). It is often cultivated under the incorrect name *H.* 'Lancifolia'.

Plant size 30–45 cm (12–18 in.) dia., 25 cm (10 in.) high. Petiole 15–20 by 0.5 cm (6–8 by 0.2 in.), erect, forming a vase-shaped plant, green, purple-spotted at the base. Leaf 10–12.5 by 5–6.5 cm (4–5 by 2–2.5 in.), erect, decurrent to the petiole, ovate-lanceolate, acuminate tip, slightly undulate, wavy in the margin, erect, rigid, smooth, glossy green above, glossy lighter green below. Venation 5–6, sunken above, very projected, smooth, below. Scape 35–60 cm (14–24 in.), straight and erect, ±perpendicular to the ground, green, purplish red dotted lower third. Fertile bracts short, navicular, grooved, thin, membranous, green, persisting after anthesis. Raceme long, 20–25 cm (8–10 in.), 10–20 flowers. Flowers 4–4.5 cm (1.5–2 in.) long, 4 cm (1.5 in.) broad, purple-violet; perianth expanding, funnel-shaped, in the central part slightly dilated bell-shaped, lobes spreading rapidly, recurving, widely open, blunt, short pedicels, projecting stamen. Anthers purple. August/September. Fertile.

SY: *H. japonica* var. *fortis* Maekawa incorrect.
      H. tardiva Fujita 1976a sl na.
HN: *H. lancifolia* hort. incorrect.
JN: *Akikaze Giboshi* Maekawa 1940.

H. cathayana 'Nakafu' hort.

AHS-IV/20A.   (Figure 2-17; Plate 9).
中斑アキカゼギボウシ
Nakafu Akikaze Giboshi is a fertile, viridescent, medio-variegated form of *H. cathayana*, also called *H.* 'Chinese Sunrise.' Many consider it a variegated form of *H.* 'Lancifolia', which it cannot be because the latter is sterile. Although the yellow center turns to light green by summer, a distinct two-color pattern can be discerned all season.
HN: *H. cathayana* 'Variegated' hort.
JN: *Nakafu Akikaze Giboshi* hort.
(see also *H.* 'Chinese Sunrise').

H. cathayana 'Ogon' hort.

黄金アキカゼギボウシ   (Plate 167).
Ogon Akikaze Giboshi is produced when *H. cathayana* 'Nakafu' (*H.* 'Chinese Sunrise') is carefully selfed. Most of these all-yellow, fertile seedlings are viridescent, but some remain yellow until anthesis and are sometimes mistaken for the stable, yellow forms of *H. sieboldii* and *H.* 'Lancifolia'.
JN: *Ogon Akikaze Giboshi* hort.

H. cathayana 'Shirofukurin' hort.

白覆輪アキカゼギボウシ
Shirofukurin Akikaze Giboshi is a horticultural name used in Japan for *H.* 'Vera Verde' (Figure 3-68; Plate 190) which formerly was called incorrectly *H. gracillima* 'Variegated'. *Hosta* 'Cheesecake' is a sport of it (Figure 4-12).
HN: *H.* 'Gracillima Variegata' hort. incorrect.
      H. gracillima variegata hort. incorrect.
      H. gracillima 'Variegata' hort. incorrect.
      H. gracillima 'Variegated' hort. incorrect.
      H. 'Gracillima Variegated' hort. incorrect.
      H. 'Vera Verde' Klehm 1986 (cat.).
JN: *Shirofukurin Akikaze Giboshi* hort.
(see also *H.* 'Cheesecake' stable form).
(see *H.* 'Vera Verde').

H. chibai nom. nudum Kaneko 1968a.

Although used in horticulture this name is a nom. nudum and botanically incorrect. This species was validly published as *H. tibai* by Maekawa in 1984, now *H. tibae* per ICBN. (see *H. tibae*).

H. clausa 'Stolon' hort.

A selected, cultivated clone of the species which may be identical to *H. clausa* var. *stolonifera*.

H. clausa var. *clausa* (Koidzumi) Nakai 1930.

AHS-IV/19B.   (Figures 3-7, A-9).
ツボミギボウシ
In Korea this species is called *Jookug-bibich'u* or *Ch'am-bibich'u* (both meaning "lanceolate hosta"), while its Japanese formal name, *Tsubomi Giboshi*, translates to "closed flower ball (= bud) hosta." It was discovered by Nakai on the Korean peninsula in Province Kyonggi-do (Keiki) in 1930. The largest concentration of natural populations occurs in central and northern Korea (M. G. Chung, 1989: personal communication; and 1990), and the northern components appear to be sympatric with populations of *H. sieboldii* and possibly also *H. cathayana* along and north of the Yalu River in Liaoning and Jilin provinces. Lee (1973) and Y. H. Chung and Y. C. Chung (1982) determined that *H. clausa* var. *clausa* (closed flowers) and *H. clausa* var. *normalis* (open flowers) are the same taxon and that varietal rank not be recognized. Maekawa (1969) reported that *H. clausa* var. *clausa* is a form very rare in the wild, and according to Chung (1990) it and *H. clausa* var. *normalis* are biologically one and the same species, although the former is a sterile triploid and the later a fertile diploid (Kaneko 1968a). The form with closed flowers has been cultivated for many years in Western gardens and has proven to be stable, and so the varietal name has been maintained. Growing along river banks it is exposed to periodic flooding, brought about by typhoons during the time of flowering and seed maturation, which severely disturbs normal sexual propagation resulting in evolutionary changes to a more efficient vegetative method by way of extensively creeping rhizomes. Among the natural populations a special form occurs under the dense cover of native willows (*Salix*). This form never develops flower stalks, which are useless in the dense cover, and its method of propagation is solely vegetative by way of creeping rhizomes. This form is also grown in Western gardens and has been called provisionally *H. clausa* var. *stolonifera* (nom. nudum). According to Chung (1990) and other authors, all these forms are biologically one and the same species, but because they have been cultivated extensively in Western gardens for many years and have proven stable I have retained their individual, varietal names. Further, recent accessions by M. G. Chung (1989, 1990, and personal communication) in the area of Nakai's original collections (Kangwon-do, Hongch'on-gun) indicate populations with scapes on which some flowers never open, while others on the same plant do open, pointing to the existence of transitional forms. In Korea it is used in gardens in much the same way as *H.* 'Lancifolia' is in North America and Europe. The leaves are rather plain, very similar to *H.* 'Lancifolia', but moderately larger and with more substance. The plant is outstanding when the rigidly held, purple, closed flower buds develop. The taxon with closed flowers is a sterile triploid (2n = 90; Kaneko, 1968a) which propagates by way of subterranean creeping roots. It has a unique rugulate-baculate pollen type (Type RB) (see Figure A-9). The species epithet is derived from *clausus* = closed (bud). It is available and cultivated worldwide and is excellent for ground cover.

Plant size 25–30 cm (10–12 in.) dia., 25–30 cm (10–12 in.) high. Rootstock stoloniferous, wide-ranging, arising sympodially to form new shoot. Petiole 5–10 by 0.5 cm (2–4 by 0.2 in.), erect, ribbed on back, green, forming a vase-shaped plant. Leaf 7.5–15 by 2.5–5 cm (3–6 by 1–2 in.), erect and in line with petiole, lanceolate, petiole transition very gradual, nonangular, acuminate tip, generally "flat" surface, no waves in margin, erect, rigid, very leathery, shiny, dark green above, glossy lighter green below. Venation 4–5, sunken above, very projected, smooth, below. Scape 35–40 cm (14–16 in.), straight and erect, ±perpendicular to the ground, green, slightly purplish red tinted at the base. Fertile bracts short, navicular, grooved, green or whitish green, imbricated, withering at anthesis, but not falling away. Raceme long, 20–25 cm (8–10 in.), densely imbricated at first, then evenly spaced, 15–25 flowers; perianth distended but remaining closed, very pointed bud, grooved, deep bluish violet, carried horizontally on strong, very short, incurved pedicels. Anthers purple. August. Closed flowers, which drop off unopened before producing fruit; sterile triploid (2n = 90) (Kaneko, 1968a).

SY: *H. clausa* Lee 1973.
    H. clausa Chung and Chung 1982.
    H. clausa M. G. Chung 1990.
HN: *H. 'Krossa No. B-7'* Summers No. 46 1966.
    H. 'Krossa No. K-4' PI 318545.
    Summers No. 149 1967.
    Sword-leaved Plantain Lily Maekawa 1969.
JN: *Tsubomi Giboshi* Nakai 1930.
ON: *Jookug-bibich'u* (Korean).
    Ch'am-bibich'u (Korean).

Figure 3-7. *H. clausa* f. *stolonifera* (nom. nudum); general habit, showing several plants arising from underground stolons (Hosta Hill)

H. clausa var. *ensata* (Maekawa) W. G. Schmid stat. nov.
ツルギギボウシ   (Plate 10).

Tsurugi Giboshi, the "sword-shaped hosta," is native to the Korean Peninsula and to northeastern China in Liaoning and Jilin provinces along the Yalu River. This variety occurs as a variant among natural, allopatric populations (M. G. Chung, 1989: personal communication). Although Maekawa (1940) validly published this taxon as a species, on his own herbarium sheets (in TI) he considered it a variety of *H. clausa*. The latter placement better reflects the distribution observed by Chung, so I have reduced this taxon to varietal rank. Its root system is not as wide-ranging as *H. clausa*. It is smaller and has very narrow, sword-shaped leaves (*ensata* = swordlike) on shorter petioles which are purple-dotted. Due to its similarity to small forms of the all-green *H. sieboldii*, other authors have misidentified it (Komarov, 1901; Mori, 1922). This sword-

leaved variant migrated from the river banks to rock outcrops and was modified by different growing conditions. Plants cultivated under this name in the United States with yellow anthers are not this species but belong to *H. sieboldii*. Plants conforming to the correct morphology are rarely seen.

Plant size 25–30 cm (10–12 in.) dia., 25 cm (10 in.) high. Rootstock stoloniferous, wide-ranging. Petiole 2.5–5 by 0.4 cm (1–2 by 0.2 in.), at leaf broadly winged, purple-spotted on back, green. Leaf 7.5–12.5 by 2.5–4 cm (3–5 by 1–1.5 in.), erect and in line with petiole, oblong-lanceolate, petiole transition very gradual, nonangular, acuminate tip, generally "flat" surface, no waves in margin, erect, rigid, leathery, shiny dark green above, glossy lighter green below. Venation 4–5, sunken above, very projected, smooth, below. Scape 30–55 cm (12–22 in.), straight and erect, ±perpendicular, green, slightly purplish red tinted at the base. Fertile bracts short, navicular, grooved, green or whitish green, imbricated, not persistent at anthesis. Raceme long, 25 cm (10 in.), 15–25 flowers. Flowers purple, held erect in horizontal position on strong pedicels, 5 by 2 cm (2 by 1 in.), funnel-shaped, rapidly expanding, at tips ±perpendicular to axis of perianth; stamens even with lobes. Anthers purple. August/September. Fertile.

SY: *H. clausa* Lee 1973.
    H. clausa Chung and Chung 1982.
    H. clausa M. G. Chung 1990.
    H. ensata Maekawa 1937.
    H. lancifolia Engler in Nakai 1911 incorrect.
    H. lancifolia Sprengel in Komarov 1901 incorrect.
    H. japonica var. *lancifolia* Nakai apud Mori 1922 incorrect.
JN: *Tsurugi Giboshi* Maekawa 1937.

H. clausa var. *normalis* Maekawa 1937.
AHS-IV/19B.
サクハナギボウシ

In Korea the common names *Jookug-bibich'u* or *Ch'am-bibich'u* which are used for the species (see *H. clausa*) are also used for this variety. In Japan it is known under the formal name *Sakuhana Giboshi*, the "open-flower hosta." Its features are identical to *H. clausa*, except the flowers open so it looks a little like *H. 'Lancifolia'* and is often mistaken for it. It propagates by seed as well as by creeping root stocks (Chung, 1990). This is the common form of the species in Korea (see *H. clausa* var. *clausa*) but is rare in cultivation. According to Chung (1990) this taxon is a diploid (2n = 60).

SY: *Funkia lancifolia* Sprengel; Czerniakovska in Komarov 1935 incorrect.
    Hosta cærulea Trattinnick in Nakai 1911 incorrect.
    H. clausa Lee 1973.
    H. clausa Chung and Chung 1982.
    H. clausa M. G. Chung 1990.
    H. japonica var. *lancifolia* Nakai 1918 incorrect.
HN: *H. 'Krossa No. B-6'* Summers No. 51 1967.
JN: *Sakuhana Giboshi* Maekawa 1937.

H. clausa var. *stolonifera* nom. nudum.

This variety occurs as a variant among natural populations, growing in dense willow growth along river banks. It does not develop flower scapes, but propagates asexually by extensively creeping rhizomes. It is described under *H. clausa* var. *clausa*, which see. This taxon is available and cultivated in Western gardens.

SY: *H. clausa* Lee 1973.
    H. clausa Chung and Chung 1982.
    H. clausa M. G. Chung 1990.

H. clavata Maekawa 1938b.
AHS-IV/19B. (Figure 3-8).
コギボウシ
ムサシノギボウシ

Ko Giboshi (by Makino), the "small hosta," occurs naturally in central Honshu, including Tsukude and Shimoyama districts. Also called *Musashino Giboshi* (by Maekawa), the "Musashi hosta," it is found in the old province of Musashi, now Tokyo Prefecture. In North America the species name was once incorrectly used for *H. sieboldii* 'Kabitan'. It looks like *H. sieboldii* f. *spathulata*, the all-green form of *H. sieboldii*, except for the club-shaped (clavate) flower bud and the bracts, and was placed in synonymy with the latter by Fujita (1976a) in a broad sense. The epithet *intermedia* used in the synonyms for this taxon indicates its taxonomic position between *H. sieboldii* and *H. rectifolia*, although it is much closer to the former. It is seldom seen in gardens.

Plant size 25 cm (9 in.) dia., 20 cm (8 in.) high. Petiole 10 by 0.5 cm (4 by 0.2 in.), green with no purple dots at the base. Leaf 7.5–12.5 by 2.5–4 cm (4–6 by 1–1.5 in.), erect and in line with petiole, spreading, lanceolate to oblong-lanceolate, petiole transition gradual, narrowing, decurrent, acuminate tip, slightly undulate, wavy in the margin, smooth, shiny light, dull dark green above, glossy lighter green below. Venation 3–4, lightly impressed above, smooth below. Scape 40–45 cm (16–18 in.), straight and erect, not bending, light green, no purple marks. Sterile bracts 2–3, clasping stem, persistent; fertile bracts short, navicular, thin, membranous, green, withering at anthesis, but not falling away. Raceme long, 10–24 flowers, spaced evenly on long raceme. Flowers in bud very clavate, blunt, 4 cm (1.5 in.) long, 3 cm (1.25 in.) broad, white, shiny, very lightly purple-suffused in the middle of the lobe, or white entirely, gradually expanding, lily-shaped, lobes rapidly expanding, at tips ±perpendicular to axis of perianth or recurving. Anthers yellowish. July to August. Fertile.

SY: *H. albomarginata* Fujita 1976a sl na.
H. intermedia (Makino) Maekawa 1938b.
H. japonica var. *intermedia* Makino 1910.
H. lancifolia var. *intermedia* (Makino) Maekawa 1950.
H. sieboldii var. *intermedia* (Makino) Hara 1984.
JN: *Ko Giboshi* Makino 1910.
Musashino Giboshi Maekawa 1938b.

Figure 3-8. *H. clavata*; bud detail, opening (Hosta Hill)

H. clavata 'Nagaba' hort.
ナガバムサシノギボウシ

Nagaba Musashino Giboshi, the "narrow leaf Musashi hosta." A narrow-leaf form of the species found in the wild but not sufficiently different for taxonomic separation. Maintained as a selected cultivar/clone.
JN: *Nagaba Musashino Giboshi* hort.

H. clavata 'Urajiro' hort.
裏白ムサシノギボウシ

Urajiro Musashino Giboshi, the "white-backed Musashi hosta," is rock-dwelling form with intense white coating on back of leaf. It may be an interspecific hybrid with *H. longipes* with which it occurs in central Honshu. Maintained as a cultivar form.
JN: *Urajiro Musashino Giboshi* hort.

H. cærulea Trattinnick 1812.
(see *H. ventricosa*).

H. crassifolia Araki 1943.
アツバギボウシ (Plate 11).

Atsuba Giboshi, the "thick-leaved hosta," was collected by Araki on Mount Ibukiyama in Shiga Prefecture. Very little information exists in written form but a holotype is in KYO. Araki considered it remotely related to *H. montana* and it was included by Fujita (1976a) in a very broad sense under *Oba Giboshi*, *H. sieboldiana* var. *sieboldiana*. Its thick-textured leaves are elongated, ovate-oblong, and decurrent to the petiole, a bright medium green above, moderately pruinose below, and smaller than the leaves of *H. montana*. Its flowers are white and similar to *H. montana* but more bell-shaped, and it has purple anthers. Morphology points to interspecific hybrid origin. It is rarely available and only a few specimens exist in scientific collections and herbaria.
JN: *Atsuba Giboshi* Araki 1943.
Atsuba (Oba) Giboshi Fujita 1976a.

✠ "H. crispula" Maekawa 1940.
AHS-III/16A. (Figures 3-9, 4-14, F-10; Plate 12).
Here reduced to cultivar form as *H.* 'Crispula'.
サザナミギボウシ
ヤキバギボウシ

Sazanami Giboshi, the "ripple-margin hosta," is described from cultivated specimens only, but according to annotations I found on two of von Siebold's herbarium specimens (0147/14 and 0147/15 in L), it was originally found growing in two separate locations in mountain valleys of Nagasaki Prefecture on the island of Kyushu in 1827. This taxon was specifically selected for its white margins, being a rare, variegated mutant. One of the original herbarium specimens (0147/9 in L) is marked *Yakiba Giboshi* (in kanji), which must be an old local name. Maekawa reported seeing specimens in Hokkaido, Ishikari, near Sapporo in 1937, but these do not represent natural accessions as they were grown in gardens like those in Tokyo. Now no longer found in the wild, it is considered a cultigen and has been reduced to cultivar form as it requires vegetative propagation to retain its variegation. It is often mistaken for *H.* 'Undulata Albomarginata', but the latter has widely winged petioles and is sterile. Sometimes it mutates to the all-green *H.* 'Crispula Viridis'. The species epithet comes from *crispus* = crispate, very undulate (as for margin). Used in gardens since the 1830s, this cultigen is one of the best white-margined hostas available. In Europe a very large, white-margined taxon has been seen and is called *H.* 'Crispula' but may in fact be *H. montana* 'Shirofukurin', which see. A white-margined sport of *H. montana* 'Aureomarginata' has been found in tissue culture. It is called *H.* 'Mountain Snow', which

Figure 3-9. *H.* 'Crispula Viridis'; leaf detail (Hosta Hill)

H. 'Lighthouse' incorrect (= *H.* 'Undulata Albomarginata').
H. longipes viridipes hort. incorrect.
H. 'Mack No. 5'.
H. 'Thomas Hogg' hort. incorrect.
H. 'Undulata Albomarginata' hort. incorrect.
Ripple-margined Plantain Lily Maekawa 1969.
USDA ARS No. 263123 Meyer 1963.
JN: *Sazanami Giboshi* Maekawa 1938b.
      Yakiba Giboshi Siebold 1827 herbarium annotation in L
         0147/9L.

H. cucullata (Siebold ex Miquel) Koidzumi 1936.
(see *H. montana*).
(see also *H. sieboldiana*).

D

see, and may also be closely related to the European taxon incorrectly called *H.* 'Crispula'.

Plant size 60–90 cm (24–36 in.) dia., 40–50 cm (16–20 in.) high. Petiole 20–40 by 0.8 cm (8–16 by 0.35 in.), ascending in an arch, forming a very large, dome-shaped plant, not winged, deeply grooved, dull green, with white margins. Leaf 20–30 by 12.5–15 cm (8–12 by 5–6 in.), leaf attitude at petiole arcuate spreading, wavy surface, waves irregular over entire surface, margin undulate, crispate, elongated, acuminate tip twisted and turned under, matte sheen, deep green with irregular fields of grey-green, margin irregular, silvery white to chalk-white. Venation 7–10, sunken above, very projected below. Scape 60–90 cm (24–36 in.), isolated fertile bracts and flowers widely spaced along scape away from raceme, straight, but occasionally bending, solid, terete, green. Fertile bracts large, flat and broad, thick and fleshy, green or whitish green, developing and opening in a stellar form when looked at from top, persisting. Raceme 25 cm (10 in.), 20–30 flowers, clustered. Flowers 4 cm (1.65 in.) long, 3.5 cm (1.5 in.) broad, mostly white; perianth expanding, funnel-shaped, lobes ±acutely angled to the axis of perianth; stamens very superior. Anthers light purple. June to July. Fertile.

SY: *Funkia albomarginata* nom. nudum Siebold 1882.
      Funkia marginata nom. nudum Siebold 1844.
      Funkia ovata δ *albomarginata* Regel 1876.
      Funkia ovata marginata Regel 1881.
      Funkia ovata var. β *intermedia* f. *marginata* Baker 1876.
      Funkia sieboldiana f. α *marginata* Miquel 1867.
      Funkia sieboldiana lusus β *marginata* Miquel 1869.
      Hosta fortunei var. *marginato alba* Bailey 1930 pp.
      H. latifolia var. *albimarginata* Wehrhahn 1936.
      Hostia cærulea f. *albomarginata* Voss 1896.
HN: *Funkia* 'Thomas Hogg' hort. incorrect.
      Hosta crispula Europe incorrect pp (see *H. montana* 'Shirofukurin').
      H. 'Crispula' Longstock form UK.
      H. 'Fortunei Albomarginata' hort. incorrect.
      H. japonica lanceolata albomarginata hort. Foerster 1956 incorrect.
      H. 'Krossa No. J-5' pp.

H. decorata f. *albiflora* hort. nom. nudum.
HN: *Shirobana Otafuku Giboshi*
(see *H. decorata* f. *decorata*).

✠ "*H. decorata* f. *decorata*" Bailey 1930.
   AHS-IV/22B.   (Plate 13).
Here reduced to cultivar form as *H.* 'Decorata'.
オタフクギボウシ

Otafuku Giboshi, the "moon-faced (rounded) hosta," for its distinctly rounded, blunt-tipped leaves and white margins, was reportedly (Maekawa, 1969, 1971) found in Chubu District, Nagano Prefecture, of central Honshu, where it purportedly evolved in the wild by mutation from the all-green form, *H.* 'Decorata Normalis'. Its yellow anthers point to an origin in the *H. sieboldii* branch of section *Nipponosta*. Field investigations by Fujita (1976a), however, did not verify the existence of natural populations and he considered it a cultigen, eliminating it. Following Fujita, and considering that it does not come true from seed, I have reduced it to cultivar form. In 1875 it was imported into North America by Thomas Hogg who obtained it from street vendors in Yokohama, and by virtue of this connection it was formerly called *H.* 'Thomas Hogg', but this name is now incorrect. It is probably the first hosta to come directly from Japan into the United States, where it is still found in old estate gardens, some dating back to before 1900. Moderately stoloniferous, a single plant will in time spread into large colonies. Its species epithet was derived from *decorus* = nice, ornate. A mutant with white flowers has been reported from Japan as *Shirobana Otafuku Giboshi*, but I have not been able to verify its existence. Apparently, this form also occurs in Europe and has been given a latinized name as *H. decorata* f. *albiflora* (Grenfell, 1990), which is a nomen nudum. The European mutant is just as elusive; I have not seen it nor have I found anyone who has. An excellent ground-cover and specimen plant, *H.* 'Decorata' is extensively cultivated in North America.

Plant size 45 cm (18 in.) dia., 30 cm (12 in.) high. Rootstock moderately stoloniferous, the shoots spread horizontally before breaking ground. Petiole 10–17.5 by 0.8–1.1 cm (4–7 by 0.33–0.5 in.), spreading horizontally, broadly winged, wider in the upper part, dark green with narrow, white margin continuing into leaf margin. Leaf 10–15 by 5–7.5 cm (4–6 by 2–3 in.), continuing and in line with petiole, entire, broadly elliptical to rounded, blunt, flat surface, ±keeled, 3–4 very slight waves in margin, contracted at the base, surface dull dark green with narrow, irregular white margin, and occasional white streaks extending into leaf center, paler green below. Venation 5–6, lightly impressed above, smooth below. Scape 50 cm (20 in.), straight and erect, perpendicular, dull light green, no purple marks. Sterile bracts 3–4, light green outside with whitish margins, clasping stem; fertile bracts, broadly ovate-elliptical, navicular, margined, not withering at anthesis, not falling away. Raceme compact, 10–18 flowers, closely spaced. Flowers 5 cm (2 in.) long, 3.5 cm (1.5 in.) broad, held erect on strong pedicels, whitish narrow tube, pale purple, striped dark purple inside, expanding, funnel-shaped, in the central part dilated bell-shaped, lobes spreading straightly to ±angled to the axis of perianth; stamens equal or shorter than perianth. Anthers yellow. July. Fertile.

SY: *H. decorata* f. *decorata* Brickell 1968.
      H. decorata f. *marginata* Stearn 1931b.
      H. decorata var. *marginata* Stearn 1931b.
HN: *Funkia* hybr. 'Thomas Hogg' hort.
      Funkia 'Thomas Hogg' hort. Hogg.
      Hosta decorata minor hort. incorrect.
      H. lancifolia var. *albomarginata* hort. (Netherlands) in syn.
        pp Hensen 1963a (not Stearn).
      H. 'Mack No. 12'.
      H. 'Thomas Hogg' hort. United States.
      H. 'Undulata Albomarginata' hort. incorrectly applied.
      Blunt Plantain Lily Gray & Cole 1941 (cat.).
      USDA ARS No. 263124 Meyer 1963.
      Whiterim Blunt Plantain Lily Mack 1960 (cat.).
JN: *Otafuku Giboshi* Maekawa 1938b.
ON: Zierliche Weissrandfunkie (German) Hansen et al., 1964.
[*H. sieboldii* derivative]

✤ "*H. decorata* f. *normalis*" Stearn 1931b.
    AHS-IV/19B.   (Plate 14).
Here reduced to cultivar form as *H.* **'Decorata Normalis'**.
ミドリオタフクギボウシ
アオバオタフクギボウシ

   Midori Otafuku Giboshi, the "green moon-faced hosta" (*midori* = green), is also called *Aoba Otafuku Giboshi* (*aoba* = green leaved). This form has all-green leaves but is otherwise identical to the white-margined species. It arose in cultivation at Koishikawa Botanic Garden, Tokyo, and occasionally this green form is found as a back-mutant or selfed seedling among populations of the white-margined cultigen. According to Fujita (1976a) it is not found in the wild, and so is here reduced to cultivar form. Available, but scarcely seen.
SY: *H. decorata* f. *normalis* Stearn 1931b.
      H. decorata var. *normalis* Stearn 1931b.
HN: Greenleaf Blunt Plantain Lily Mack 1960 (cat.).
      H. decorata 'Normalis' hort.
      H. 'Mack No. 13'.
JN: *Midori Otafuku Giboshi* Maekawa 1940.
      Aoba Otafuku Giboshi hort.

H. densa Maekawa 1940.
    AHS-III/13A.   (Figures 3-10, 3-11; Plate 15).
ケヤリギボウシ
   Keyari Giboshi, the "Keyari hosta," is native in south-central Honshu, primarily in the Kinki District. This species was found on Mount Odaigahara located in Yoshino-Kumano National Park on the Kii Peninsula (type in TI). A different form was collected not far from the original find in Mie Prefec-

Figure 3-10. *H. densa*; densely arranged, expanding raceme (Hosta Hill)

ture on Mount Nonobori. Plants growing south of the Suzuka mountain range in Mie and Nara prefectures have shorter and more oblique scapes and belong to *H. kikutii* so are not included here. This is the type species for section *Intermediae* which is a group with an intermediate morphological position between section *Helipteroides* (*H. sieboldiana* and *H. montana*) and section *Rynchophorae* (*H. kikutii*). Some of the members of this section originally published with specific rank are now considered cultigens and have been reduced to cultivar form. Specific rank has been retained for this taxon disregarding strong evidence (bicolor anthers) that it may represent an interspecific, intergrading hybrid swarm. It is highly variable and, depending on the particular population studied, other authors have placed it in diverse positions: Maekawa (1969) included it with *H. kikutii* as var. *densa* after having linked it to *H. kiyosumiensis* in 1940. Fujita (1976a) considered it synonymous to the latter. Authentic specimens cultivated in North America, originating from populations growing in Kii Peninsula, conform to Maekawa's 1940 diagnosis and are morphologically quite distinct, characterized by spreading leaves (like *H. montana*) and a densely arranged raceme with many, late flowers (like *H. kikutii*) with the narrow part of the perianth never grooved. The species epithet comes from *densus* = dense, alluding to the densely arranged flowers on the raceme. A collector's item, it is rarely cultivated. A very pruinose, blue-grey plant cultivated in North America under the species name *H. densa* is not this species, which has medium green leaves without pruinosity.

Figure 3-11. *H. densa*; general habit, bearing seeds (Hosta Hill)

Plant size 45–55 cm (18–22 in.) dia., 35–40 cm (14–16 in.) high. Petiole 22.5–30 by 0.9 cm wide (9–12 by 0.6 in.), erect, green, purple-dotted at the base, deeply grooved. Leaf 17.5–22.5 by 10–12.5 cm (7–9 by 4–5 in.), erect and in line with petiole, entire, ovate-elliptical to ovate-cordate, cuspidate, petiole-leaf transition cordate, truncate, acuminate tip, flat surface, but undulate-wavy along the margin, opaque dark green above, lighter green below. Venation 8–10, closely spaced, sunken above, very projected, smooth, below. Scape 60 cm (24 in.), 0.5 cm (0.2 in.) thick, inclining, green, purple-spotted at base, upper raceme partly bent back. Sterile bracts large, navicular, thin, membranous, soft, green, very pointed; fertile bracts whitish green. Raceme short, many flowers densely arranged, to 40. Flowers 5 cm (2 in.) long, 2.5 cm (1 in.) broad, medium size, white, but very slightly purple-suffused inside, expanding, funnel-shaped, in the central part dilated bell-shaped, lobes spreading straight to the axis of perianth; stamens not very superior, equal, or slightly shorter than perianth. Anthers bicolor purple-yellow. September. Fertile.

SY: *H. kikutii* var. *densa* Maekawa 1969 pp sl.
     H. kiyosumiensis Fujita 1976a sl na.
JN: *Keyari Giboshi* Maekawa 1938b.
(see also *H. kikutii*).

E

✠ "*H. elata*" Hylander 1954.
    AHS-I/1B.   (Figure F-8, Plates 16, 144).
Here reduced to cultivar form as *H.* 'Elata'.

    This taxon is not found in the wild and so no Japanese name exists. It has yellow anthers and is not conspecific with the Japanese *H. montana, Oba Giboshi*, which has yellowish purple anthers (actually uniform purple dotting on a yellow background). *Hosta* 'Elata' is a hybrid cultigen which originated in Europe from extremely polymorphic, cultivated hybrid stock and has a mixed background partially going back to Lindley's green-leaved *Funkia sieboldi* (1839). Taxa similar to this were known to von Siebold as *Funkia sinensis*. The name *Hosta elata* was used by Vilmorin in the 1860s and by Bailey in 1915. It is grown under this name in many gardens, but most plants so cultivated do not conform to Hylander's diagnosis. *Hosta* 'Elata', as described by Hylander, has 9–11 pairs of veins, and a specimen no. 039020 in L has 9–10 veins. But many other herbarium specimens (several in BH, s.n., no. 322 in BH, and in BH ex U, July 1950) are morphologically quite different from this specimen but were nevertheless determined to be *H.* 'Elata' by Hylander, and so the specimens provide no answer as to which is the true form. Due to the absence of a designated type, his 1954 English diagnosis is the only scientific basis for identification which confirms that most of the taxa cultivated in gardens nowadays under *H.* 'Elata' are not this taxon. *Hosta fortunei* var. *gigantea* Bailey (1915, 1930), placed by Hylander (1954) in synonymy, applies only in part, because many of the hybrid taxa cultivated under Bailey's varietal name are green-leaved hybrids of *H. sieboldiana* known in horticulture as *H. sieboldiana* var. *gigantea*. Summers (1984) and other authorities have confirmed that many of the plants in cultivation under the name *H.* 'Elata' are a mixture of hybrids of uncertain origin lacking morphological uniformity. For this reason Hylander's 1954 clone has been reduced to cultivar form and

the following description is based on his description. Plants which do not conform to this description should not be labeled *H.* 'Elata'. The epithet denotes its tall bloom scapes (*elatus* = tall). Many commercial sources offer *H.* 'Elata', but usually the plants do not conform to Hylander's description.

    Plant size 65–100 cm (26–40 in.) dia., 45–65 cm (18–26 in.) high. Petiole 30–50 by 1.5 cm (12–20 by 0.65 in.), ascending in an arch, forming a very large dome-shaped plant, slightly winged, deeply grooved, slightly pruinose, fading, dull green. Leaf 25–35 by 15–25 cm (10–14 by 6–10 in.), leaf attitude at petiole arcuate spreading, wavy surface, waves irregular over entire surface, margin undulate, slightly rugose, acuminate twisted tip, pruinose above fading later to a matte sheen, ±permanently pruinose below, green to sea green. Venation 9–11, sunken above, very projected, strigose below. Scape greatly exceeds height of plant, 90–120 cm (36–48 in.), some with bracteole sterile leaves in lower part, isolated fertile bracts and flowers widely spaced along scape away from raceme, usually bending, solid, terete, slightly pruinose, glaucous sea-green, fading to matte green. Fertile bracts large, flat and broad, thick and fleshy, green or whitish green, tinged purple, developing and opening in a stellar form as seen from above, persisting long after anthesis until dehiscence. Raceme 25–35 cm (10–14 in.), 15–30 flowers, clustered. Flowers 5.5 cm (2.25 in.) long, 3 cm (1.25 in.) broad, whitish; perianth expanding, funnel-shaped, in the central part dilated bell-shaped, lobes spreading straightly to ±angled to the axis of perianth; stamens not very superior, equal or slightly shorter than perianth. Anthers yellow in Hylander's form. Taxa with purple or bicolor anthers are not this taxon. June/July. Fertile.

SY: *Funkia latifolia* β *sinensis* Miquel 1869.
     Funkia ovata f. β *latifolia* Regel 1876.
     Funkia sinensis nom. nudum Siebold 1856 pp.
     Hosta fortunei var. *gigantea* Bailey 1930 pp sim sl.
     H. gigantea Koidzumi 1936 pp sim sl.
     H. latifolia Wehrhahn 1936.
     H. sieboldiana var. *sieboldiana* Fujita 1976a sl na.
     H. sinensis nom. nudum Siebold 1856 pp.
     Hostia cærulea f. *latifolia* Voss 1896.
HN: European Montana incorrect.
     Giant Fortune Plantain Lily.
     Hosta 'Elata' hort.
     H. fortunei 'Elata' hort. incorrect.
     H. fortunei 'Gigantea' hort. pp sim sl.
     H. 'FRW No. 128'.
     H. 'FRW No. 556' hybrid pp sim.
     H. 'Mack No. 10'.
     H. montana 'Elata' hort. incorrect.
     H. montana incorrect.
     H. sieboldi gigantea hort. Foerster 1952 incorrect.
     H. sieboldi 'Gigantea' hort. incorrect.
     H. sieboldiana gigantea hort. Foerster 1956 incorrect.
     H. sieboldiana 'Gigantea' hort. incorrect.
     H. sieboldiana hort. incorrect.
     USDA ARS No. 263125 Meyer 1963.
     H. 'Wavy Elata' hort.
ON: Grüne Riesenfunkie (German) Foerster 1952 pp.

H. ensata Maekawa 1937.
(see *H. clausa* var. *ensata*).

H. erromena Stearn apud Bailey 1932.
(see *H. undulata* var. *erromena*).

F

H. fluctuans Maekawa 1940.
AHS-II/7B.   (Plate 17).
クロナミギボウシ

Kuronami Giboshi, the "dark (-leaved and) wavy hosta," was originally found in northern Honshu, Aomori Prefecture. Its large, wavy (fluctuating) leaves are used in Japanese *ikebana* (flower arranging), and it is cultivated for this purpose in northern Honshu in addition to being raised as a food crop (see Appendix H). Apparently all Maekawa's specimens were of cultivated origin, but according to Fujita (1976a) natural populations exist in northern Nagano Prefecture. Also seen in Iwate Prefecture (Plate 17) it ranges north to Aomori. It differs from *H. nigrescens* by its wavy leaves that are farinose only on the underside, shiny above, and have a less-erect and more-spreading habit. The species epithet comes from *fluctus* = wave (wavy). Available but rarely seen.

Plant size 60–70 cm (24–28 in.) dia., 65 cm (26 in.) high. Petiole 25–50 by 1.5 cm (1–20 by 0.65 in.), horizontally spreading, forming a dome-shaped plant, pruinose, glaucous sea-green, purple-dotted, dark basal section, lighter above. Leaf 20–30 by 12.5–17.5 cm (8–12 by 5–7 in.), ovate-cordate, transition usually tight and contracted, truncate base, tip suddenly cuspidate, wavy, fluctuating, waves irregular, over entire surface, first pruinose then shiny light green above, glaucous green below, smooth. Venation 9–10, sunken above, projected, smooth below. Scape length to 130 cm (52 in.), farinose, glaucous sea-green, often bending, leaning horizontally to subhorizontally during anthesis, solid, terete, with several large sterile bracts, withering, but persisting after anthesis. Fertile bracts flat and broad, thick and fleshy, green or whitish green, developing and opening in a stellar form as seen from above. Raceme 25 cm (10 in.), 25–35 flowers, densely clustered. Flowers 5–6 (2–2.5 in.) cm long, 3.5 cm (1.5 in.) broad, whitish, suffused violet to pale purple; perianth expanding, funnel-shaped, in the central part dilated bell-shaped, lobes ±angled to the axis of perianth; stamens not superior, equal or slightly shorter than perianth. Anthers purple. July/August. Fertile.

SY: *H. fluctuans* f. *parvifolia* Maekawa 1940.
     H. sieboldiana var. *glabra* Fujita 1976a sl na.
HN: *H. sieboldiana* var. *fluctuans* hort.
JN: *Kuronami Giboshi* Maekawa 1940.
     Kobano Kuronami Giboshi Maekawa 1940.
     Nameru Giboshi Fujita 1976a sl na.

H. fluctuans 'Blue Sagae' hort.
Blue Sagae Giboshi, the "blue Sagae," is a blue backcross of *H. fluctuans* 'Variegated' and is cultivated under the name *H.* 'Blue Sagae', which see. The connection of this cultivar to *H. fluctuans* has not been scientifically established.

H. fluctuans f. parvifolia Maeka 1940.
コバノクロナミギボウシ

Kobano Kuronami Giboshi, the "small-leaved, wavy, dark hosta," was originally found by Kikuchi in northern Honshu, Aomori Prefecture, Hirosaki city area. It is a small-leaved form of the species which is rarely seen and may only represent a locally differentiated race. The varietal epithet is derived from *parvus* = small and *folius* = leaved, and is often seen incor-

rectly printed as *parviflora* (= small-flowered), as for example, in Zilis (1989), but this spelling is an orthographic error. This taxon is here considered synonymous to *H. fluctuans*.
HN: *H. fluctuans* 'Parvifolia' hort.
     H. fluctuans 'Parviflora' Zilis 1989 hort. incorrect.
JN: *Kobano Kuronami Giboshi* Maekawa 1940.
(see *H. fluctuans*).

H. fluctuans 'Gold Sagae' hort.
黄金サガエ

Ogon Sagae Giboshi, the "golden Sagae," is a yellow mutation of *H. fluctuans* 'Variegated' and is cultivated under the name *H.* 'Ogon Sagae', which see. The connection of this cultivar to *H. fluctuans* has not been scientifically established.

H. fluctuans 'Variegated' AHS-NC IRA/187.
AHS-II/10B.   (Plates 18, 146, 151, 153).
Here the registered Western cultivar name is maintained although *H.* 'Sagae' (used in Japan) is the correct, original name.
寒河江ギボウシ

The cultivar name registered for show purposes for *Sagae Giboshi* (hort.) or *H.* 'Sagae' (Watanabe, 1985), the "hosta from Sagae," is applied to a single clone discovered among cultivated taxa in northern Honshu, Yamagata Prefecture, near the town of Sagae, and now vegetatively propagated and cultivated the world over. One of the most cherished cultivars available, it has been extensively cultivated in Japanese gardens under the name *Sagae Giboshi*. Its Western name is technically incorrect because its connection to *H. fluctuans* has not been definitely established. Per the ICNCP, the original Japanese name should have been used without being translated. Also in doubt is its association in Japan with *H. montana*, as *H. montana* 'Sagae', because *Sagae Giboshi* has yellow anthers with very pale purple dots of two different patterns while *H. montana* has much darker purple ones indicating it is only remotely related; this holds true for *H. fluctuans* also. Although technically incorrect, its Western name has been retained because the AHS-NC has registered it with the IRA, and the registrar has accepted the name which is well established in North America and Europe. Under its Western name this taxon has won the AHS President's Exhibitor Trophy, 1982, exhibited by Kenneth Anderson; and the AHS Benedict Award, 1987, exhibited by Richard Ward. In Japan the correct name *H.* 'Sagae' (*Sagae Giboshi*), which also see, is preferred.

Plant size 55–65 cm (22–26 in.) dia., 50 cm (by 20 in.) high. Leaf 20–30 by 12.5–20 cm (8–12 by 5–8 in.), ovate-cordate, transition usually tight and contracted, truncate base, tip suddenly cuspidate, wavy, fluctuating, waves irregular, over entire surface, first pruinose then dull yellow green above, glaucous green below, bright pale yellow margin. Venation 9–10, sunken above, projected, smooth below. Scape length to 110 cm (44 in.), farinose, glaucous sea-green, often bending, leaning horizontally to subhorizontally during anthesis (due to weight of flowers), solid, terete, with several large sterile bracts, withering, but persisting after anthesis, one or more bracteolate leaves with yellow margins on the lower scape. Fertile bracts flat and broad, thick and fleshy, pruinose, green or whitish green, developing and opening in a stellar form as seen from above. Raceme 25 cm (10 in.), 25–35 flowers, densely clustered. Flowers 5–6 cm (2–2.5 in.) long, 3.5 cm (1.5 in.) broad, whitish, suffused violet to pale purple; perianth expanding, funnel-shaped, in the central part dilated bell-shaped, lobes ±angled to the axis of perianth; stamens not superior, equal or slightly

shorter than perianth. Anthers yellowish. July to
August. Fertile.
HN: *H. fluctuans* 'Variegata' hort. incorrect.
　　H. fluctuans 'Sagae' hort.
　　H. 'Sagae' hort. Japan.
(see also *H. montana* 'Sagae').
(see also *H.* 'Sagae').

✠ *"H. fortunei"* (Baker) Bailey 1930.
Here reduced to cultivar form as *H.* **'Fortunei'**.
レンゲギボウシ　　　　　　　　　　　(Plates 19, 170).

In 1930 Bailey briefly mentioned *H. fortunei* based on a
taxon named by Baker in 1876. Baker registered a herbarium
sheet of this taxon in K. No authentic, living specimens of this
plant have survived but the possibility of it still existing in
gardens cannot be ruled out. Hylander (1954) described a
novotype under the name *H. fortunei* var. *nova*, and Wehrhahn
(1936) described a taxon of identical morphology (as far as this
can still be determined) under the name *H.* 'Bella'. Maekawa
(1940) called it *Renge Giboshi*, but his description does not
match Hylander's. *Hosta* 'Fortunei' does not occur in the wild,
so has been reduced to cultivar form. In 1954 Hylander raised
to the rank of variety (under the species name *H. fortunei*) a
number hostas long known in Western cultivation. These are
either hybrids, or they originated as bud mutations from cultivated plants in Europe. Most had been grown under different names given by von Siebold and others from 1844 to
1879. All named *H.* 'Fortunei' varieties are morphologically
similar to this taxon with the differences being leaf color, texture, surface finish and variegation pattern. The many forms
purported to be and cultivated as the missing *H.* 'Fortunei'
are mostly all-green sports of the variegated forms. Totally
unrelated taxa, such as *H.* 'Undulata Erromena', are frequently
cultivated under the label *H.* 'Fortunei'. The following description is not intended to be for the specioid alone but for all taxa
in the *H.* 'Fortunei' group collectively, and it includes all the
common morphological characteristics. Specific differences
are given for each *H.* 'Fortunei' form under its respective
description.

Plant size 40–60 cm (16–24 in.) dia., 35–45 cm (14–18
in.) high. Sprouts green. Petiole 20 by 0.8 cm (8 by
0.35 in.), ascending in an arch, forming a very large,
dome-shaped plant, winged, grooved, dull green.
Leaf 20–30 by 15–20 cm (8–12 by 6–8 in.), leaf attitude at petiole arcuate spreading, entire-elliptical,
ovate to cordate-ovate, petiole-leaf transition broadly
open, round to cordate, transition broadly open, flat,
truncate, acuminate tip, some rugose, flat surface
with 1–2 waves, matte colored to shiny above,
pruinose below. Venation 7–10, sunken above, very
projected below. Scape 80–100 cm (32–38 in.), isolated fertile bracts and, straight, but usually bending,
solid, terete, green. Fertile bracts large, flat and broad,
imbricate to obliquely patent, concave, green with
purple. Raceme 25 cm (10 in.), 25–35 flowers,
clustered. Flowers 5 cm (2 in.) long, 3.5 cm broad (1.5
in.) broad, white, suffused pale purple to violet,
expanding, funnel-shaped, in the central part slightly
dilated bell-shaped, lobes spreading straightly to
±angled to the axis of perianth, stamens superior.
June. Most clones infertile but produce many seed
capsules with aborted seed. Occasionally, viable seed
can be produced by careful and timely hand-
pollination.
SY: *Funkia fortunei* Baker 1876.
　　Hosta fortunei Bailey 1915.
　　H. bella Wehrhahn 1936 pp sim.
　　H. fortunei Stearn 1931b.

H. fortunei var. *nova* Hylander pp.
H. sieboldiana var. *fortunei* Ascherson and Gräbner 1905
　　pp.
Niobe fortunei Nash 1911.
HN: *Hosta fortunei* 'Obscura' hort.
　　H. 'Fortunei Obscura'.
　　H. fortunei 'Viridis' hort.
　　H. 'Fortunei Viridis'.
　　H. 'FRW No. 152'.
　　H. 'Mack No. 11' pp sim.
JN: *Renge Giboshi* Maekawa 1940 pp.

H. 'Fortunei' cultivated varieties.

All forms broadly belonging to *H.* 'Fortunei' which have
received botanical treatment are described in this chapter. All
other named cultivars related to *H.* 'Fortunei'—for example, *H.*
'Fortunei Albomarginata'—are listed and described in
Chapter 4, which see.

✠ *"H. fortunei* var. *albopicta"* Hylander 1954.
AHS-III/14B.　　　　　　　　　　　(Plate 20).
Here reduced to cultivar form as *H.* **'Fortunei Albopicta'**.
黄中斑レンゲギボウシ

This cultivar evolved in von Siebold's garden at Leiden in
the 1860s and was first listed in 1874. Hylander (1954) selected
and named a plant identical to this clear yellow-centered
European taxon, stating that his several plants probably are
from the same clone so representation of this taxon by a clonal
cultivar name, viz., *H.* 'Fortunei Albopicta', presents no
problems. Hylander incorrectly assumed the plant was
imported by von Siebold from Japan, when in fact it arose as a
mutation in Siebold's garden. The plants in the trade as *H.*
'Fortunei Albopicta' are identical to Hylander's taxon and also
very uniform. Some time ago some were exported to Japan
where they are cultivated as *Kinakafu Renge Giboshi*. In addition
to this well-known clone, a number of different mutants
broadly related to this variety exist, some having the leaf center
substantially marbled or spotted with yellow which may
account for the historical epithets *aureomarmorata* (= marbled
with gold) and *aureomaculata* (= spotted with gold) sometimes seen in Germany and England. These atypical forms are
included in synonymy here in a broad sense only because they
were not involved originally in Hylander's clonal selection
and the entire complex is here considered the *H.* 'Fortunei
Mediovariegata' group. The clear yellow-centered clone is
widely distributed and one of the variegated, viridescent
classics which unfortunately loses its bright variegation by late
spring. The cultivar name *H. fortunei* 'Albo-picta' is registered
with the IRA and ostensibly applies to the specific clone isolated and named by Hylander (1954), but no description was
given with the registration. The cultivar name is in wide horticultural use. In the United Kingdom this taxon is cultivated
under the name *H.* 'Chelsea' because for many years it has
been prominently shown at the RHS (London) Chelsea
Flower Show.

Plant conforms to the basic morphology given under
H. 'Fortunei' except as follows: Leaf clear, golden-
yellow center, with narrow, dark green margin and
some green streaks submarginally into the yellow
center, viridescent, turning green before flowering.
SY: *Funkia aurea maculata* nom. nudum Siebold ex Miquel
　　1869 pp.
　　Funkia ovata (var.) c. *albopicta* Miquel 1869.
　　Funkia viridimarginata nom. nudum Siebold 1863.
　　Hosta fortunei var. *viridis marginata* Bailey 1915.
　　H. lancifolia var. *aureomaculata* Wehrhahn 1934 pp.
　　H. viridis marginata Bailey 1915.
HN: Fortune Greenrim Green Plantain Lily.

Greenrim Plantain Lily.
H. 'Albopicta' hort. incorrect.
H. 'Aureomaculata' hort. incorrect.
H. aureomaculata hort. Foerster 1965b incorrect.
H. aureomarmorata hort. Foerster 1952 incorrect.
H. 'Chelsea' UK.
H. 'Chelsea Babe' Smith/Grounds UK pp sim dwarf form.
H. fortunei albopicta hort.
H. fortunei 'Albo-picta' hort.
H. 'Fortunei Albopicta' hort.
H. fortunei aureomaculata hort. incorrect.
H. fortunei 'Aureo-maculata' Hensen 1963a.
H. fortunei aureo picta hort. UK incorrect.
H. fortunei aureo variegata hort. UK incorrect.
H. fortunei 'Elizabeth Campbell' UK pp sim.
H. 'Fortunei Mediovariegata' group.
H. fortunei picta hort. incorrect.
H. fortunei 'Picta' hort. incorrect.
H. fortunei 'Viridimarginata' hort.
H. fortunei viridis marginata hort.
H. fortunei 'Viridis Marginata' hort.
H. fortunei 'Zager Green Rim' hort.
H. 'Golden Forest' hort.
H. 'Golden Spring' hort.
H. 'Golden Variegated' hort.
H. japonica aureomarmorata Foerster 1956 incorrect.
H. lancifolia aurea margista Zager 1941 (cat.) incorrect.
H. lancifolia var. *aureomaculata* hort. incorrect pp.
H. 'Mack No. 9'.
H. 'Maya'.
H. 'Panaché Jaune' UK pp sim.
H. 'Spring Gold' pp sim hort. (viridescent).
USDA ARS No. 263123 Meyer 1963.
JN: *Kinakafu Renge Giboshi* hort.
ON: Gelbe Grünrandfunkie (German).
Gelbmarmorierte Funkie (German) Foerster 1952 pp sim.
Maiprachtfunkie (German) Foerster 1965b.

✠ "*H. fortunei* var. *albopicta* f. *aurea*" Hylander 1954.
AHS-III/17A. (Plate 21).
Here reduced to cultivar form as *H.* **'Fortunei Aurea'**.
黄金レンゲ
A form of *H.* 'Fortunei' with clear yellow leaves in spring evolved in von Siebold's garden at Leiden in the 1860s. The clonal name, *H.* 'Fortunei Aurea', applies to a specific chlorophyll variant with clear yellow leaves in spring isolated and named by Hylander (1954). This form originated in Western gardens by mutation from the yellow-centered form and is also of clonal origin, reflected by its clonal name *H.* 'Fortunei Aurea'. The cultivar name *H. fortunei* 'Aurea' is registered with the IRA. It has also been exported to Japan and is occasionally seen cultivated in Japanese gardens as *Ogon Renge Giboshi*. It is sometimes mistaken for the yellow form of the cultigen *H.* 'Lancifolia', but the latter has more lanceolate leaves of thinner texture.
Plant conforms to the basic description given under *H.* 'Fortunei' except as follows: Leaf slightly smaller, leaf viridescent, clear golden yellow turning to a dark green by anthesis.
SY: *Funkia aurea* nom. nudum Siebold 1874.
Hosta aurea Bailey 1915.
H. fortunei var. *albopicta* f. *lutescens* Hylander 1953 pp.
H. japonica aurea Nobis 1951 incorrect.
H. japonica f. *lutescens* Voss 1896 pp incorrect.
H. lancifolia var. *aurea* Wehrhahn 1934 incorrect.
HN: Fortune Yellowleaf Plantain Lily.

H. aurea hort. pp.
H. aurea praecox Foerster 1956 incorrect.
H. cærulea aurea hort. incorrect.
H. fortunei aurea hort.
H. 'Fortunei Aurea' hort.
H. 'Fortunei Aurea' group.
H. lancifolia aurea hort. incorrect.
H. 'Mack No. 33'.
USDA ARS No. 263128 Meyer 1963.
Wisley No. 821394 through 821397.
JN: *Ogon Renge Giboshi* hort.
ON: Frühlingsgoldfunkie (German) Foerster 1956.

✠ "*H. fortunei* var. *albopicta* f. *viridis*" Hylander 1954.
AHS-III/13B. (Figure 4-38; Plates 19, 170).
Here reduced to cultivar form as *H.* **'Fortunei Viridis'**.
The all-green form of *H.* 'Fortunei Albopicta' is a mutation and is considered by some the "true" *H. fortunei* (Baker) Bailey because its mature leaf resembles the one shown on Baker's herbarium specimen in K. It occurs as a reversion from the yellow-centered, viridescent *H.* 'Fortunei Albopicta', so is of clonal origin, and reduction of the botanical name to cultivar form presents no problems. The cultivar name *H. fortunei* 'Viridis' has been registered with the IRA. It is in horticultural use worldwide.
Plant conforms to the basic morphology given under *H.* 'Fortunei' except as follows: Leaf deep green, on rather short petioles, with a matte sheen above, ±permanently glaucous below. Fertile bracts large, stiff, patent, very persistent.
SY: *Funkia viridis* nom. nudum Siebold 1867 pp.
HN: Fortune Greenleaf Plantain Lily.
Hosta cærulea viridis Foerster 1957 incorrect.
H. fortunei albo-picta f. *viridis* hort.
H. fortunei albo-picta viridis hort.
H. fortunei viridis hort.
H. 'Fortunei Viridis' hort.
H. japonica cærulea viridis hort. Foerster 1956 incorrect.
H. viridis hort. Foerster 1952 incorrect.
H. viridis hort.
H. 'Mack No. 20'.
USDA ARS No. 263127 Meyer 1963.
ON: Frühgrüne Schmalblattfunkie (German) Hansen et al., 1964 pp.

✠ "*H. fortunei* var. *aoki*" Siebold ex Bailey 1915.
AHS-III/13B.
Here reduced to cultivar form as *H.* **'Fortunei Aoki'**.
Now considered a selected clone of the *H.* 'Fortunei Hyacinthina' group. Named by von Siebold before his death for Aoki Kon'yo, who produced the first Japanese-Dutch dictionary. Introduced by the von Siebold nursery in 1879 two years after *H.* 'Fortunei Hyacinthina', it is similar except that its leaf surface is entirely wrinkled, so much so that some authors believe it to be *H.* 'Fortunei Rugosa', which see. The cultivar name *H.* 'Fortunei Aoki' has been registered with the IRA.
SY: *Funkia aokii* nom. nudum Siebold 1879.
Hosta aoki Bailey 1915.
HN: *H. aoki* hort. incorrect.
H. 'Aoki' hort.
H. aokii hort. incorrect.
H. fortunei 'Aoki' hort.
H. 'Fortunei Aoki' hort.
H. fortunei var. *aokii* hort. incorrect.
H. fortunei var. *stenantha* hort. incorrect.
H. 'Krossa No. C-4'.
H. 'Mack No. 8'.
ON: Runzelblattfunkie (German) pp.

✠ "*H. fortunei* var. *aureomarginata*" Hylander 1969.
AHS-III/16B.   (Plates 22, 152).
Here reduced to cultivar form as *H.* **'Fortunei Aureo-marginata'**.
黄覆輪レンゲギボウシ

The clone used by Hylander (1954) as a basis for his diagnosis originally came from Germany, and he named it *H. fortunei* var. *obscura* f. *marginata*. It is identical to *H. lancifolia* f. *aureimarginata* Wehrhahn (1931), which has priority, so to adhere to the rules of priority, Hylander (1969) changed his species name to *H. fortunei* var. *aureomarginata*. This taxon is of clonal origin described from a single clone, so there are no impediments to reduce it to cultivar form. The cultivar name *H.* 'Fortunei Aureomarginata' has been selected to represent the specific clone isolated and named by Hylander (1954) and is registered (in slightly modified form) with the IRA. In addition to this well-known clone, a number of mutants exist which are of different clonal origin but broadly related to it. Because they are similar, they are grouped under the *H.* 'Fortunei Aureomarginata' group from which distinct clones can be selected and named. The latter group includes variants which bloom earlier and some with a whitish yellow margin. A few have already been given clonal names. Although Hylander's clone and most other members of this group produce capsules abundantly, the seed contained in them is usually abortive. Some years ago this taxon was exported to Japan where it is grown as *Kifukurin Renge Giboshi*. Cultivated the world over, it is well known to gardeners and commercially available, unfortunately, under a number of different synonyms.

Plant conforms to the basic morphology given under *H.* 'Fortunei' except as follows: Leaf deep green, with a matte sheen above, permanently glaucous below, with a yellow to golden-yellow margin that holds its color until flowering. In cultivars exposed to strong light the margin bleaches to a pale yellow-white or white. Some forms in this group have a leaf center which is olive green to green, also with a golden-yellow margin as above.

SY: *H. fortunei* var. *obscura* f. *marginata* Hylander 1954 nom. superfluum.
      H. japonica var. *aureamarginata* Nobis 1951 incorrect.
      H. lancifolia f. *aureimarginata* Wehrhahn 1931.
HN: *H.* 'Craig No. H-7' Summers No. 335.
      H. 'Ellerbroek' hort.
      H. 'Ellerbroek L-7' hort.
      H. 'Ellerbrook' hort. incorrect.
      H. fortunei 'Aurea Marginata' hort.
      H. fortunei aureamarginata hort. incorrect.
      H. fortunei aureomarginata hort. incorrect.
      H. fortunei 'Aureo-marginata' hort.
      H. 'Fortunei Aureomarginata' group.
      H. fortunei 'Gold Crown' hort.
      H. fortunei 'Golden Crown' hort.
      H. fortunei obscura aureomarginata hort. incorrect.
      H. fortunei 'Obscura Aureo-marginata' hort. incorrect.
      H. fortunei 'Obscura Marginata' hort. incorrect.
      H. fortunei 'Sprengeri' hort. incorrect.
      H. fortunei 'Sprengerii' hort. incorrect.
      H. fortunei 'Yellow Edge' pp.
      H. 'Gold Crown' hort.
      H. 'Golden Crown' hort.
      H. 'Golden Ruffles' Blackthorne.
      H. 'Hirao No. 7' pp sim.
      H. japonica aureomarginata Foerster 1956 incorrect.
      H. 'Krossa L-7' pp.
      H. 'Krossa Wide Band' pp.
      H. lancifolia aureomarginata hort. incorrect.
      H. 'Sprengeri' hort.

      H. 'Yellow Band' hort.
      H. 'Yellow Edge' hort. incorrect.
      Wisley No. 821364.
      Yellow Band Hosta.
JN: *Kifukurin Renge Giboshi*.
ON: Grüne Goldrandfunkie (German) Foerster 1952.
      Riesengoldrandfunkie (German) Foerster 1965b pp.

✠ "*H. fortunei* var. *gigantea*" Bailey 1915.
AHS-II/7B.   (Plate 23).
Here reduced to cultivar form as *H.* **'Fortunei Gigantea'**.

Hylander (1954) considered this taxon to be synonymous with *H.* 'Elata' but plants cultivated under this name are a group of hybrids of long standing, most having a venation count of 14–16, very large leaves, and large white flowers, and therefore they cannot be *H.* 'Elata'. In horticulture the varietal epithet has also been involved in the naming of the green form of *H. sieboldiana* as *H. sieboldiana* var. *gigantea*. Plants in the trade under this name are a mixture of different hybrids, most of them green forms of *H. sieboldiana* or hybridized forms of *H. montana* with nearly yellow anthers, but their authenticity and conformity to Bailey's taxon cannot be confirmed because Bailey's 1915 description is too short, contemporary illustrations are imprecise, and type specimens have not been found.
SY: *H. gigantea* Koidzumi 1936 pp.
      H. sieboldiana var. *gigantea* (Bailey) Kitamura 1966 pp.
HN: *H.* 'Fortunei Robusta' hort.
      H. fortunei var. *robusta* hort.
(see also *H. elata*).
(see also *H. fortunei* var. *robusta*).

✠ "*H. fortunei* var. *hyacinthina*" Hylander 1954.
AHS-III/13B.   (Figure 3-12; Plate 24).
Here reduced to cultivar form as *H.* **'Fortunei Hyacinthina'**.

Although this variety was first described and named by Hylander (1954) from Swedish material, it did not originate in Sweden nor was it imported from Japan. It evolved in von Siebold's garden before his death and was listed by Witte in 1877 as *H. glaucescens*, a name still used for this taxon in Germany in the 1950s. Glaucescens means "somewhat glaucous" in contrast to the very glaucous *H. sieboldiana* and *H.* 'Tokudama', which were also known then. Hylander considered this variety as a group, here called *H.* 'Fortunei Hyacinthina' group, represented by very similar clones. Because of this, reduction of the taxon to cultivar form under the clonal name *H.* 'Fortunei Hyacinthina' may be theoretically incorrect, but the material in commerce and now cultivated under this cultivar name is very uniform, virtually identical, and probably originated with the same clone originally propagated in Holland, and so the use of a clonal name can be accepted. The AHS-NC has in fact registered the cultivar name *H. fortunei* 'Hyacinthina' with the IRA. The taxon so selected and representing this group is more glaucous and pruinose than other *H.* 'Fortunei' forms, reflecting traits of one of the probable parents, *H. nigrescens*. The varietal epithet comes from *hyacinthinus* = violet, for the flower color and the violet cast observed in spring on the leaves. It is judged the best flowering form of the *H.* 'Fortunei' cultivars, is mainly sterile, but occasionally produces some fertile seeds. It is also very prone to bud mutation, so several variegated forms have been found and named. This taxon is extensively cultivated worldwide.

Plant conforms to the basic description given under *H.* 'Fortunei' except as follows: Leaf 20–30 by 15–20 cm (8–12 by 6–8 in.), leaf attitude at petiole spreading, patent, entire-elliptical, ovate to cordate-ovate, petiole-leaf transition involute, round to cordate, flat, truncate, acuminate tip, some rugose, flat surface with 1–2 waves, in spring distinctly pruinose, glaucous blue-green to dull greyish green above, very pruinose whitish grey below, with a very marked whitish marginal line, rugose in part, especially in the radical leaves. Venation 8–10, 'sunken above, very projected below. Scape 100 cm (38 in.), slightly bending, solid, terete, intense pruinose glaucous grey-green with purplish cast, suffused glaucous purple towards the top. Fertile bracts, large, flat and broad, imbricate, patent, concave, pruinose grey green, suffused purple before opening; sterile, several, below raceme, leaflike, persistent, not withering. Capsules pruinose grey.

SY: *Funkia glaucescens* nom. nudum Siebold 1877.
Funkia glaucescens nom. nudum Anonymous 1891a.
Hosta glauca Hensen 1963a pp.
H. glaucescens nom. nudum Siebold 1877 pp.

HN: *H. fortunei* 'Hyacinth' hort. incorrect.
H. fortunei 'Hyacintha' hort. incorrect.
H. 'Fortunei Hyacinthina' group.
H. fortunei 'Hyacinthina' hort.
H. 'Hyacinth' hort. incorrect.
H. 'Hyacintha' hort. incorrect.
H. 'Hyacinthia' hort. incorrect.
H. 'Hyacinthina' hort.
H. 'Hyacinths' hort. incorrect.
H. sieboldi glauca hort. incorrect.
H. sieboldiana glaucescens Foerster 1956 incorrect.
Hyacinths Hosta.
USDA ARS No. 263129 Meyer 1963.

ON: Blaue Siebold Funkie (German) Foerster 1956 pp.
Graublattfunkie (German).
Hyazinthenfunkie (German).

Figure 3-12. *H.* 'Fortunei Hyacinthina'; general habit (Wisley/Schmid)

✠ *"H. fortunei var. obscura"* Hylander 1954.
Here reduced to cultivar form as *H.* **'Fortunei Obscura'**.

The taxon described under this name by Hylander is by description identical to *H. bella* Wehrhahn (1934), and since that name has priority it should be used. Theoretically, in botanical rank, Wehrhahn's name should replace the name *H.* 'Fortunei' on grounds of priority, but I have not undertaken this transfer because the latter is a lost taxon, *H.* 'Fortunei Obscura' is established and widely used in horticulture, and both taxa have been reduced to cultivar form. For description refer to *H. bella*.
(see *H. bella*).

H. fortunei var. robusta Bailey 1915.
A synonym for *H. sieboldiana* 'Elegans' which is now considered a cultivar form. This name is also used in horticulture

for large, green hybrid forms of *H. sieboldiana*.
SY: *H. fortunei* var. *robusta* Silva-Tarouca 1910.
HN: *H. fortunei robusta* hort. Arends 1905.
(see *H. sieboldiana* 'Elegans').
(see also *H.* 'Fortunei Gigantea').

✠ *"H. fortunei var. rugosa"* Hylander 1954.
AHS-III/13B. (Figure 3-13).
Here reduced to cultivar form as *H.* **'Fortunei Rugosa'**.

Hylander's specimens came from Germany and probably originated with von Siebold. I believe this taxon is basically the same as *H.* 'Fortunei Aoki' which originated with von Siebold. The leaves are very wrinkled, pruinose, and glaucous, and the taxon is similar and very closely related to *H.* 'Fortunei Hyacinthina'. The cultivar name has been registered by the AHS-NC with the IRA as *H. fortunei* 'Rugosa' and is applied to the very uniform cultivated stock that is widely cultivated.

Plant conforms to the description given under *H.* 'Fortunei' except as follows: Leaf in spring very pruinose, sea-green above, turning glabrous green later, with slight sheen, permanently glaucous grey-green below, in the leaf tissue between the principal veins very rugose. Scape pruinose, with leafy sterile bracts, shorter than other varieties. Raceme also shorter, more compact. Fertile bracts large, stiff, patent, very persistent.

HN: *H. fortunei rugosa* hort. incorrect.
H. fortunei 'Rugosa' hort.
H. 'Rugosa' hort.

ON: Runzelblattfunkie (German).

Figure 3-13. *H.* 'Fortunei Rugosa'; landscape use, mass planting (Wisley/Schmid)

✠ *"H. fortunei var. stenantha"* Hylander 1954.
AHS-III/13A. (Plates 25, 26).
Here reduced to cultivar form as *H.* **'Fortunei Stenantha'**.

Hylander (1954) selected and named this taxon based on a collection of specimens from 8 Swedish gardens. It is theoretically a group of very similar clones but the cultivated material is very uniform nowadays and probably originated with one clone selected from this group in Holland, where it was first propagated after having been received from Hylander. Because of this uniformity I have reduced this variety to cultivar form as *H.* 'Fortunei Stenantha', conforming to Hylander's description. The cultivar name has been registered by the AHS-NC with the IRA as *H. fortunei* 'Stenantha'. Quite distinct from *H.* 'Fortunei Hyacinthina' and *H.* 'Fortunei Rugosa', the leaf color of this taxon is much lighter and little rugosity exists. The bracts are much smaller and wither soon after flowering. The scapes are short, with the raceme only slightly above the leaf mound. Flowers are very narrow, with lobes not spreading, hence the epithet *stenantha* (from *stenos anthos* = narrow flower). Variegated mutations occur often (Plate 26) and the cultivar is widely cultivated.

Plant conforms to the basic morphology given under *H.* 'Fortunei' except as follows: Leaf in spring distinctly pruinose, opaque greyish green above, in summer a much lighter green (virens to flavovirens), pruinose, glaucous green below, the leaf tissue between the principal veins flat or only moderately rugose, especially in the radical leaves. Scape slightly pruinose, considerably shorter than in other variants of the *H.* 'Fortunei' group. Fertile bracts withering soon after anthesis. Perianth gradually expanding, more narrowly funnel-shaped, lobes not fully opening, parallel to axis of corolla.

HN: *H. fortunei stenantha* hort. incorrect.
  H. fortunei 'Stenantha' hort.
  H. 'Mack No. 8'.
  H. stenantha hort. pp.
  H. 'Stenantha' hort. incorrect.
  H. 'Violet Bells'.

G

H. gigantea Koidzumi 1936.

Applied by Hylander (1954) to *H.* 'Elata' with respect to Bailey's synonym cited *H. fortunei* var. *gigantea*, but hardly in regard to the basionym which is rooted in *H. sieboldiana*. This species name has been used for different taxa and is considered a nom. confusum.
(see also *H.* 'Elata').

H. glauca (Siebold ex Miquel) Stearn 1931b.

Applied to *H. sieboldiana* by Stearn but this species name has many different botanical and horticultural applications so is no longer used and considered a nom. confusum.
(see also *H. sieboldiana*).

H. gracillima Maekawa 1936b.
  AHS-V/25B.   (Figure 3-14).
ヒメイワギボウシ

Hime Iwa Giboshi, the "small rock hosta," is one of the smallest species extant, and allopatric populations exist in the mountain valleys of Kochi Prefecture, Shikoku. Fujita (1976a) connects this taxon with Iwa Giboshi, *H. longipes*, on grounds of minor, macromorphological flower details, but the typifying coloration of the lobes is purple striped, not homogeneous. The type (in TI) was collected by Okamoto near Tosa and has late-blooming flowers with long, narrow tubes and a flaring perianth, so is maintained as a member of the late-blooming section *Tardanthae* following Maekawa (1940). The epithet comes from *gracilis* = gracefully slender, alluding to the very long and slender flowers with gracefully recurving lobes. This taxon was obtained by Craig in Japan and sent to Davidson in 1964, who grew it as No. 64 (Davidson, 1990). It was then called *H.* 'Rock Princess', an incorrect translation of *Hime Iwa Giboshi* which actually means "small rock hosta." *Hime* as a noun means princess and the Japanese formulation would be *Hime no Iwa Giboshi*. Unfortunately, several other taxa were called *H.* 'Rock Princess', among them *H. venusta* and possibly also *H. nakaiana*, so this name should not be used as it is confusing. Several forms are in the trade of which some may be interspecific hybrids with leaf length/width ratios from 2:1 to 3:1. In Japan this taxon is frequently and incorrectly called *H.*

venusta because some of its forms have leaves similar to the latter but the flowering scape of *H. gracillima* is smooth while that of *H. venusta* has ridges, and this difference can serve as a positive identifier. A variegated form closely resembling the species is in North America under the name *Shirofukurin Ko Mame Giboshi*, *H.* 'Shirofukurin Ko Mame', which see, and this form may be identical to *H. gracillima* 'Shirofukurin'. This taxon is excellent in the rock or miniature garden and is used in Japan for pot culture.

Plant size 20–24 cm (5–7 in.) dia., 7.5–10 cm (0.75 in.) high. Petiole 3–5 by 0.2 cm (1.2–2 by 0.1 in.), semierect, green. Leaf 2.5–6 by 1.1–2 cm (1–2.5 by 0.5–0.75 in.), semierect, ovate-lanceolate, acuminate tip, undulate, wavy in the margin, rigid, smooth, glossy green above, glossy lighter green below, contracted at the base. Venation 2–3, sunken above, smooth, below. Scape 20–25 cm (8–10 in.), erect, but leaning, green, purplish red dotted at base. Fertile bracts short, navicular, awl-shaped, spreading, green, rigid, persisting after anthesis. Raceme short, few flowers. Flowers 2.5–3.5 cm (1–1.5 in.) long, 2.5 cm (1 in.) broad, long narrow tube, perianth suddenly broadly funnel-shaped, in the central part very slightly dilated bell-shaped, lobes spreading rapidly, recurving, wide open, blunt, lavender outside, purple-striped inside, short pedicels, slightly projecting stamen. Anthers purple. September. Fertile.

SY: *H. longipes* var. *gracillima* Fujita 1976a sl na.
HN: *H. gracilliana* hort. incorrect.
  Rock Princess.
  Small Rock Hosta.
JN: *Hime Iwa Giboshi* Okamoto in Kikuchi 1934.

Figure 3-14. *H. gracillima*; general habit (Hosta Hill)

H. gracillima 'Saizaki' hort.
采咲ヒメイワギボウシ

Saizaki Hime Iwa Giboshi is a mutant form with deformed lobes and petaloid stamens treasured by the Japanese. Although found in the wild it is nonperpetuating so treated as a cultivar.
JN: *Saizaki Hime Iwa Giboshi* hort.

H. gracillima 'Shirofukurin' hort.
白覆輪ヒメイワギボウシ

Shirofukurin Hime Iwa Giboshi is a white-margined mutant form. Although found in the wild it is nonperpetuating so treated as a cultivar. *Shirofukurin Ko Mame Giboshi*, *H.* 'Ko Mame Shirofukurin', is very close to this taxon or may be the same.
JN: *Shirofukurin Hime Iwa Giboshi* hort.
  Shirofukurin Ko Mame Giboshi hort. sim.

H. gracillima 'Variegated' hort. incorrect.
   An incorrectly associated, horticultural name which has been replaced by the cultivar name *H.* 'Vera Verde'.
HN: *H. gracillima variegata* hort. incorrect.
        H. gracillima 'Variegata' hort. incorrect.
(see *H.* 'Vera Verde').
(see also *H. cathayana* 'Shirofukurin').

H

H. harunaensis Honda 1935b.
ハルナギボウシ
   Haruna Giboshi the "Mount Haruna hosta," is morphologically like *H. rectifolia* and is listed under its synonymy. Fujita (1976a) considered it synonymous to *H. sieboldii* in a broad sense but this placement is not accepted here in a narrow sense (see *H. rectifolia*).
SY: *H. albomarginata* Fujita 1976a sl na.
JN: *Haruna Giboshi.*
(see *H. rectifolia*).

✠ *"H. helonioides"* Maekawa 1937.
   AHS-IV/19A.   (Figure 3-15).
Here reduced to cultivar form as *H.* '**Helonioides**'.
ハカマギボウシ
   Hakama Giboshi, the "pleated (divided) skirt hosta," is still in cultivation near the site of its original discovery in Yamagata Prefecture of northern Honshu. Described on the basis of cultivated material, it is considered a cultivar by Fujita (1976a), and this placement has been maintained for both the all-green cultigen and the white-margined mutant form. In bud it looks similar to and has been named for *Helonias bulata,* the Swamp Pink, with tall, straight scapes on a basal leaf crown and there is a resemblance in the general leaf shape. The green form is identical in general habit and flowering to the margined form (Figures 3-15, 3-16). Compared to the latter, this green-leaved cultigen is of minor horticultural importance and seldom seen.
   Plant size 30 cm (12 in.) dia., 17.5 cm (7 in.) high. Sprouts green. Petiole 7.5–12.5 cm (3–5 in.) long, continuously tapering from leaf base towards rhizome where it is 0.6 cm (0.2 in.), broadly winged, unmarked green. Leaf 12.5–15 by 2.5 cm (5–6 by 1 in.), erect and in line with petiole, linear to oblanceolate, narrowing into petiole with no discernable transition between petiole and leaf, with flat surface, but undulate, wavy margin, acuminate tip, surface dull dark green, underside shiny, green. Venation 3–4, impressed above, projected, smooth below. Scape 45–55 cm (18–22 in.), straight and erect, perpendicular, not bending, light green, purple-dotted at base. Sterile bracts 3–6, clasping stem, navicular, incurved, persistent; fertile bracts short, navicular, thin, membranous, green, shiny, persisting at anthesis. Raceme long, 6–10 flowers, widely spaced. Flowers 5 cm (2 in.) long, 3.5 cm (1.5 in.) broad, purple-striped inside, thin narrow tube, perianth expanding, lily-shaped, lobes spreading, recurving, short pedicels; stamens shorter than the perianth. Anthers purple. August. Fertile.
HN: *H. helenioides* incorrect.
        H. helenoides incorrect.
JN: *Hakama Giboshi* Maekawa 1937.

Figure 3-15. *H.* 'Helonioides Albopicta'; flower detail (Hosta Hill)

✠ *"H. helonioides f. albopicta"* Maekawa 1937.
   AHS-IV/22A.   (Figures 3-15, 3-16).
Here reduced to cultivar form as *H.* '**Helonioides Albopicta**'.
斑入カラフトギボウシ
覆輪ハカマギボウシ
大型文鳥香ギボウシ
   Fukurin Hakama Giboshi, the "margined, pleated-(divided) skirt hosta," is widely known in Japan as *Hakama Giboshi.* Originally found and reported by Kikuchi in a cultivated colony in northern Honshu, Yamagata Prefecture, it has leaves with yellowish white margins and very characteristically shaped obtuse tips like those of the Swamp Pink. Ruh and Zilis (1989) reported that the particular taxon which has for many years been cultivated in North America under this botanical name is actually *H.* 'Rohdeifolia'. This information needs further confirmation because herbarium specimens I have examined of the all-green *H. rohdeifolia* f. *viridis* in KYO (Figure 3-60) portray a different taxon so do not confirm their placement. A further, more serious impediment to accepting their proposal is the coloration of the anthers. Maekawa's 1937 diagnosis for *H. rohdeifolia* calls for whitish anthers, which I conclude to be yellow (or more yellow than white—there are no white anthers in the genus). Fujita (1976a) in fact includes *H. rohdeifolia* as a synonym under *H. sieboldii,* which also has yellow anthers. The taxon now cultivated in North America as *H.* 'Helonioides Albopicta' and which, according to Ruh and Zilis, is *H.* 'Rohdeifolia', has purple anthers, so it is very unlikely that it is *H.* 'Rohdeifolia' which has yellow anthers. Their determination, which is based on Japanese horticultural information, appears to be incorrect and requires further study. *Hosta* 'Helonioides Albopicta' with purple anthers is much closer morphologically to *H. rectifolia* and, incidentally, was originally found in northern Honshu where the latter occurs. Illustrations in *The Hosta Journal* of young plant specimens purported to be *Hakama Giboshi, H.* 'Helonioides Albopicta', a species received from horticultural sources in Japan, look similar to *H.* 'Ginko Craig', which see, and show an apparent juvenile leaf form which may later change. A cultivar named *H.* 'White Border', imported from Japan by Soules Nursery, is identical to what is cultivated as *H.* 'Helonioides Albopicta'. Judging by the many Japanese cultivar names applied to this taxon in Japan, there is also considerable confusion as to its identity in that country, and determinations based on Japanese horticultural information have proven to be

inconclusive and in some cases incorrect. The plants received from Japan and purported to be H. 'Rohdeifolia' do not fundamentally match available herbarium material for H. rohdeifolia f. viridis nor do they match Maekawa's diagnosis. Until this problem can be settled, Maekawa's respective 1937 diagnoses may provide some help in identifying these taxa: H. 'Rohdeifolia' is a much larger taxon having 5–6 pairs of veins with yellow margins ("Lamina flavido-marginata") and yellowish white anthers (like H. sieboldii), while H. 'Helonioides Albopicta' has 3–4 pairs of veins on smaller leaves with white margins ("Folia albomarginata") and purple anthers (like H. rectifolia). The scapes are to 120 cm (48 in.) in the former and 65 cm (28 in.) in the latter (Schmid, 1987b). According to Maekawa (1940; cfr. ic. 84, 85, 86, pp. 402, 406), the white margins of H. 'Helonioides Albopicta' are much wider (4–8 mm/0.2–0.35 in.) and more irregular with streaking towards the leaf center, but H. 'Rohdeifolia' has a very narrow, well-defined margin of uniform width (2–4 mm/0.1–0.2 in.). Otherwise these taxa are very closely related and have similar-looking flowers.

Plant description is identical to that of the green form and as follows: Petiole 7.5–12.5 cm (3–5 in.) long, continuously tapering towards from leaf base towards rhizome where it is 0.6 cm (0.2 in.), broadly winged, white leaf margin extending from leaf uninterrupted in petiole, narrowing, otherwise green. Leaf 12.5–15 by 2.5 cm (5–6 by 1 in.), erect and in line with petiole, linear to oblanceolate, narrowing into petiole with no discernable transition between petiole and leaf, with flat surface, sub-obtuse tip, surface dull dark green with regular whitish margin, underside shiny, green. Venation 3–4, impressed above, projected, smooth below. Scape 65 cm (28 in.), with 3–4 amplexicaul, margined sterile bracts. Flower bud clavate. Flowers 5 cm (2 in.) long, 3.5 cm (1.5 in.) broad, purple-striped inside, thin narrow tube, perianth expanding, lily-shaped, lobes spreading, recurving, short pedicels; stamens shorter than the perianth. Anthers purple. August. Fertile.

HN: H. 'Craig No. 43' Summers No. 322 1969.
     H. helenioides 'Albo-picta' hort. incorrect.
     H. helenoides 'Albo-picta' hort. incorrect.
     H. helonioides 'Albo-picta' hort.
     H. helonioides var. albopicta hort. incorrect.
     H. 'Krossa No. H-7'.
     H. 'White Border' hort.

JN: Fuiri Karafuto Giboshi hort. incorrect.
     Fukurin Hakama Giboshi Maekawa 1937.
     Hakama Giboshi hort.
     Hime Karafuto Giboshi hort. pp sim.
     Ogata Bunchoko Giboshi hort.

Figure 3-16. H. 'Helonioides Albopicta'; general habit (Hosta Hill)

✠ "H. hippeastrum" Maekawa 1940.
     AHS-III/13A.   (Figure 3-17).
Here reduced to cultivar form as H. 'Hippeastrum'.
ラッパギボウシ

Rappa Giboshi, the "bugle horn hosta," was described by Maekawa (1940) as a new species, based on a cultivated form grown by Tutui in the city of Ueno, Mie Prefecture. It was named for its atypical, broad-lobed, light lavender flowers which bear a slight resemblance to the flowers of the genus *Hippeastrum* (*Amaryllis*). Fujita (1976a) ignored it, and Maekawa (1969) reduced it to cultivar status because of its genetic instability, made obvious by irregularities in stamen development, abortive pollen, and bicolor anthers. Japanese horticulturists consider it a cultivar broadly related to H. kiyosumiensis. It is seldom seen.

Plant size 40–50 cm (16–20 in.) dia., 35 cm (14 in.) high. Petiole 30–32.5 by 0.6 cm (12–13 by 0.2 in.), erect, green, purple-dotted below the middle. Leaf 13–20 by 8–12 cm (5–8 by 3–5 in.), spreading horizontally, entire, ovate-elliptical to ovate, openly cordate-truncate at base, very pointed, acuminate tip, generally flat surface, but undulate in the margin, thin papery texture, dark green, opaque, lighter green below. Venation 8–9, never sunken above, smooth below. Scape 50 cm (20 in.), straight, erect, perpendicular, purple-dotted lower half. Fertile bracts large, 2–2.5 cm (to 1 in.), navicular, green with greenish white margins, persistent, not withering at anthesis. Raceme short, 15 flowers, densely arranged. Flowers 3.5–4.5 cm (1.5–2 in.) long, 4.5 cm (1.5 in.) broad, pale purple-violet, narrow part expanding gradually, broad lobes expanding rapidly, recurving, perpendicular to axis of perianth, stamens exceeding length of perianth, in some flowers 1–2 petaloid or all missing. Anthers bicolor. June/July. Barely fertile.

SY: H. kiyosumiensis Fujita 1976a sl na.
HN: H. 'Hippeastrum' hort.
     H. kiyosumiensis 'Hippeastrum' hort.
JN: Rappa Giboshi Maekawa 1940.

Figure 3-17. H. 'Hippeastrum'; flower detail (Hosta Hill)

H. hypoleuca Murata 1962.
     AHS-I/1A.   (Figure 2-26, 3-18, 3-19, 3-20; Plates 27, 157, 208).
ウラジロギボウシ
一ッ葉裏白ギボウシ

Urajiro Giboshi, the "white-backed hosta," is uncommon in the wild and was first found in Chubu District, in the mountains of southeastern Aichi Prefecture, Mikawa area. Two colonies have recently been located in Shizuoka Prefecture near Tenryu in the Tenryu River District. Growing on sunny, south-facing canyon walls, it clings tenaciously to rock ledges.

In the wild it forms only 1–3, very large leaves (Figure 3-20) but in cultivation it grows 5–7 leaves and develops into a standard leaf mound (Plate 27). The intensely white, pruinose coating on the underside of the leaves and petioles is an evolutionary adaptation to protect against the extreme summer heat absorbed by the rocks and reradiated against the leaf bottom, a development which is also seen in other rock-dwelling taxa. Leaf color above is yellowish green, but some forms with darker green leaves exist. The principal veins are spaced far apart and very smooth below with transverse veins between them clearly visible. Several forms occur in the wild, some with elongated leaves, others with cordate-round leaves. A rare form with principal veins closer spaced and submarginally connected has also been found and is under observation in the United States. The species epithet is derived from the Greek *hypo* = back, beneath and *leucon* = white color. Commercially available, it is frequently seen in cultivation and has become one of the parents of several important breeding lines. In 1985 Aden named a form belonging to this taxon *H.* 'Maekawa'. It is, according to Aden (1988), the hosta most admired by the late botanist and researcher and a very large-leafed clone of *H. hypoleuca*, with a bluish green leaf color, heavy substance, and undulating margins. In Japan it is often used in elevated pots to show the very white coating of the leaf underside or to provide an accent at the entrance to a garden (Figure 3-18). The following description is for cultivated specimens, but annotated for natural plants.

Plant size 45–65 cm (18–26 in.) dia., 25–35 cm (10–14 in.) high. Sprouts pruinose, very black-green with a purple cast, green leaves unfurling in a twisted and contorted fashion. Petiole 15–25 by 0.8 cm (6–10 by 0.3 in.) spreading horizontally, light yellowish green, pruinose below. Leaf 25–45 by 20–30 cm (10–18 by 8–12 in.), entire, cordate to ovate-cordate, flat surface, undulate margin, not rugose, initially pruinose yellowish green or green later with a slight sheen above, permanently intensely white-coated below. The extremes given for leaf size occur in the wild, where the taxon grows only 1–3 very large leaves (Figure 3-20). Venation 9–11, widely spaced, projected below, transverse veins between principal veins very prominent. Scape 45–65 cm (18–26 in.), in the wild projecting obliquely to subhorizontally from the rock faces, in cultivation leaning with raceme occasionally becoming subhorizontal, smooth, round, light green, in the lower part intensely dark-purple spotted. Sterile bracts, 2–3, very large, persisting; upper fertile bracts large, clasping the flowers, thick, slightly pruinose, navicular, very light green, strongly persistent and still green after anthesis. Raceme short, 10–20 cm (4–8 in.), densely imbricated, 10–20 flowers. Flowers white, shiny, very lightly purple-suffused in the middle of the lobe, or white entirely, 4.5 by 3 cm (1.75 by 1.25 in.) across the lobes, carried horizontally on strong pedicels, 2.5 cm (1 in.) long, which are equal to the lower and extending beyond the upper fertile bracts; perianth expanding, funnel-shaped, in the central part dilated bell-shaped, lobes spreading ±angled to the axis of perianth; stamens equal to or slightly extended beyond the lobes. Anthers dark purple. Capsules round, light green. July. Fertile.

HN: *H. hypoleuca* 'Urajiro' hort. incorrect.
    H. 'Maekawa'.
    H. 'Mayan Seer' pp sim.
    H. 'Urajiro' hort. incorrect.
JN: *Hitotsuba Urajiro Giboshi* hort.
    Urajiro Giboshi Murata 1962.

Figure 3-18. *H. hypoleuca*; accent at entrance to Japanese garden (Sugita garden)

Figure 3-19. *H. hypoleuca*; showing white coating on leaf underside (Hosta Hill)

Figure 3-20. *H. hypoleuca*; native habitat, showing single large leaf (Mt. Chiiwa, Aichi Prefecture/Sugita)

H. hypoleuca 'Hitotsuba' hort.
一ッ葉裏白ギボウシ

Hitotsuba Giboshi is very similar to, and here considered synonymous to, *H. hypoleuca*, which see.

H. hypoleuca 'Ogon' hort.
黄金ウラジロギボウシ

Ogon Urajiro Giboshi is a yellow-leaved form of the species found as a nonperpetuating, natural variant. In the wild considerable color variations exist, with the main color light green with a tinge of yellow, but dark green as well as greenish yellow have been observed. These may be local adaptations so have not been separated taxonomically but are considered selected, horticultural forms.
JN: *Ogon Urajiro Giboshi* hort.

I

J

H. ibukiensis Araki 1942.
AHS-IV/19A.   (Figures 3-21, 3-22).
イブキギボウシ

Ibuki Giboshi, the "Mount Ibuki hosta," is named for the mountain where it was found. It is very closely related to *H. sieboldii*, has the same flowers with yellow anthers, and looks almost like the all-green *H. sieboldii* f. *spathulata*, except for the petioles which are wider and broadly winged. Fujita (1976a) declared it synonymous to *H. sieboldii* (as *H. albomarginata*) in a broad sense. The type colony was found on the slopes of Mount Ibukiyama in Shiga Prefecture, central Honshu, and small, allopatric populations exist in the wild, so this taxon is maintained as a species. It is not important horticulturally and of interest to serious collectors only.

SY: *H. albomarginata* Fujita 1976a sl na.
JN: *Ibuki Giboshi* Araki 1942.
       Ibukiyama Giboshi hort.
(see also *H. sieboldii* f. *spathulata*).

Figure 3-21. *H. ibukiensis*; general habit (Hosta Hill)

Figure 3-22. *H. ibukiensis*; holotype in KYO

H. intermedia (Makino) Maekawa 1938b.
(see *H. clavata*).

H. japonica Trattinnick 1812.
The epithet *japonica* has been used under the generic names *Aletris*, *Hemerocallis*, *Funkia*, *Niobe*, *Hostia*, and *Hosta*. As such it has been widely and persistently used for taxa not including its type and should be rejected as a nomen rejiciendum (ICBN, Article 69) or, at least, be considered a nomen confusum.
(see also *H. plantaginea*, *H. 'Lancifolia'*, and *H. 'Tokudama'* in this chapter and in Appendix A—Part 3).

H. japonica Ascherson 1888.
Refer to comment under the preceding entry.
(see also *H. plantaginea*).

H. jonesii M. G. Chung 1989.
AHS-IV/19B.   (Figures 3-23, 3-24; Plates 28, 200).
This Korean species is named in honor of Dr. Samuel B. Jones, botanist and taxonomist at the University of Georgia. Jones and his associates Carleen Jones and Myong Gi Chung are assembling a representative, living collection of the genus and the university staff is engaged in biosystematic and chemosystematic research involving the Korean populations. The Korean name *Tadohae-bibich'u* translates to "several islands," indicating habitat. This taxon is closely related to *H. tsushimensis* (*Tsushima Giboshi*), which see. The area of collection is Province Kyongsangnam-do, Namhae-gun, Sangju Myeon, and the holotype was collected on Mount Kumsan, Namhae Island (Namhae-do), where it grows in rocky humus in the shade of oak forests near the coast. Accessions in 1988 by M. G. Chung located additional colonies in Province Chollanam-do, Yoch'on-gun, Tolsan (or Dolsan) Island (Tolsan-do). *Hosta jonesii* differs from *H. tsushimensis* by its creeping rhizome, scapes with reddish purple dots at the base, and flowers that are larger, suffused purple, and bell-shaped. In cultivation *H. jonesii* is much more vigorous in growth than the former and is an attractive horticultural subject. Of high garden interest are the branched scapes which can be observed in some of the cultivated specimens. Branched scapes are also observed in *H. tibae* and *H. tsushimensis* which grow in Nagasaki Prefecture directly across the Korea Strait and on Tsushima Island located in the strait. I consider *H. jonesii* broadly related to these taxa, and this is substantiated by M. G. Chung (1989) who placed the latter in section *Tardanthae*, to which the former taxa also belong.

Plant size 45 cm (18 in.) dia., 20 cm (8 in.) high. Petiole 5–13 cm by 5–8 mm (2–5 by 0.2–0.35 in.), slightly winged, erect, green with purple dots. Leaf 10–20 by 5–10 cm (4–8 by 2–4 in.), elliptic-ovate to narrowly ovate, obtuse tip, flat, smooth, dull green above, glossy lighter green below, decurrent to petiole. Venation 5–7, not sunken above, slightly projected, smooth below. Scape 30–60 cm (12–24 in.), erect, straight to slightly obliquely ascending, green, reddish purplish dots at base. Sterile bracts, 2–3, clasping the stem; fertile bracts navicular, lanceolate, thick, green, persisting, not withering at anthesis. Raceme long, 25–30 cm (10–12 in.), loosely arranged, to 20 flowers, in some forms branched, 2–8 flowers per branch. Flowers 4–5 cm (1.5–2 in.) long and 2.5 cm (1 in.) broad, nearly purple, white nerves inside, whitish narrow tube, perianth expanding, in the central part dilated bell-shaped, lobes spreading but not recurving; pedicels obliquely ascending, 4–8 cm (0.15–0.35 in.), whitish green, purple-dotted, shorter than bracts; stamens equal or slightly longer than perianth; pistil projecting. Anthers purple. August. Fertile.

ON: *Tadohae-bibich'u* (Korean).

Figure 3-23. *H. jonesii*; general habit (Hosta Hill)

Figure 3-24. *H. jonesii*; type location; Namhae Island, Mt. Kumsan, near Yangha Ri (M. G. Chung)

K

H. kikutii Maekawa 1937.

AHS-III/13B.   (Figures 2-29, 2-31, 2-34, 3-25, 3-26, 3-27, 3-28, 3-30, 3-32; Plates 1, 29, 168, 195).

ヒュウガギボウシ

Hyuga Giboshi, the "hosta from Hyuga," is the type species for a section of hostas found primarily in the southern part of Japan. Widespread on Kyushu and adjacent small islands, the holotype was collected on Mount Boroishizan, Miyazaki Prefecture, in the old province of Hyuga, hence the Japanese name *Hyuga Giboshi.* The species epithet was given by Maekawa to honor Akio Kikuchi, a distinguished Japanese botanist under whose direction much research on the genus *Hosta* was done. In the wild this taxon is extremely variable and many distinct populations exist from which a number of botanical varieties have been isolated and named.

Distinct allopatric groups of *H. kikutii* exist on Shikoku, in Kochi Prefecture near the city of Tosa ranging east to Tokushima Prefecture, where they have been modified by their environment. Colonies growing south of the Suzuka mountain range in Mie and Nara prefectures differ slightly but belong to *H. kikutii* and are included (Fujita, 1976a). A majority

of these overlapping populations are partially differentiated from the type and may be interspecific hybrid swarms which are in the process of intergradation. *Hosta kikutii* offers a difficult classification problem because all the taxa belonging to this group have similar flower morphology but differ in other respects, including biosystematic evidence (Currie, 1988).

Maekawa (1969) and Fujita (1976a) approached the problem by classifying the differentiated forms as varieties of the species. Chemosystematic evidence (Currie, 1988: personal communication) points to greater separation of the taxa based on certain differences in flavonoid pigments so supports Maekawa's earlier classifications considering most of the taxa involved as being of specific rank. But these differences may be due to the extensive hybridization of this species in the habitat, and the differentiated taxa may represent intergrading hybrid swarms. This is corroborated by findings that *H. kikutii* is most differentiated at the northeastern limit of its habitat, where it is sympatric with populations of other species. This is exemplified by the polymorphic populations of *H. densa,* some of which approach *H. kikutii* morphology so much so that Maekawa (1969) classified selected groups in its population as a variety of *H. kikutii,* viz., *H. kikutii* var. *densa.*

Examination of the habitat shows some sympatric populations of *H. densa* on Honshu in Nara, Wakayama, and Mie prefectures are beginning to show some *H. kikutii* characteristics but are maintained as species in section *Intermediae* which is a group with an intermediate morphological position between section *Helipteroides* (*H. sieboldiana* and *H. montana*) and section *Rynchophorae* (*H. kikutii*).

Further southwest, on Shikoku, *H. kikutii* var. *tosana* and *H. kikutii* var. *caput-avis* have more-or-less acutely, characteristically bending scapes but otherwise show typical morphology.

Hosta kikutii var. *yakusimensis* is placed by Maekawa (1940) at the southwestern limit of the range in the Satsunan Islands. Located at the southern tip of the Japanese archipelago and lying between latitude 31° and 27°, the island group includes the large principal islands of Tanegashima (446 sq. km/172 sq. miles) and Yakushima (503 sq. km/194 sq. miles) on which the warm subtropical climate fosters rich vegetation. The type specimen of *H. kikutii* var. *yakusimensis* in TI, collected by Suzuki on Yakushima, shows a narrow-leaved taxon conforming to the illustration shown in Maekawa (1940: ic. 43, 44; 1969). In my classification only the populations found in the Satsunan Islands are included under this varietal name.

Also on Yakushima grows a pronounced pruinose form with a whitish coating on the leaf underside. This form has not been described before, but because it is represented in wild populations, comes reasonably true from seed, and is extensively cultivated, I have segregated it as *H. kikutii* f. *leuconota.*

Fujita (1976a) included *H. kikutii* var. *yakusimensis* as a synonym under *H. kikutii* var. *polyneuron,* which grows on Shikoku, as exemplified by the populations growing near Ikegawa-cho, Kochi Prefecture. While this placement is correct when considered under Fujita's very broad delimitation, I have not followed this synonymy but I have segregated the taxa as originally described and applied the species name *H. kikutii* var. *polyneuron* to the populations on Shikoku. *Hosta kikutii* var. *yakusimensis* has narrow, lanceolate leaves with 5–7 pairs of principal veins, while the former has 9–11 pairs and much wider, ovate leaves.

All this illustrates how involved the delimitation of this section is and that more field work is needed to arrive at a final disposition. Until this can be done the related taxa in section *Rhynchophorae* are kept in varietal rank, following Maekawa (1969) and Fujita (1976a). The atypical taxa included by the latter, however, some with strigose veins and others atypically blooming early in July, are not included here because of my narrower delimitation.

The specific forms have purple anthers, while some of the atypical taxa have distinct bicolor or yellow anthers with irregular purple-dot patterns, suggesting interspecific hybridization. In the species the leaves are elongated, lanceolate, with closely spaced veins and large, leaflike, sterile bracts. A key characteristic is the initially very pointed, green flower bud (Figure 3-30) which is in some forms strongly inclined (Figure 3-25). The overlapping bracts of the flower bud are green when closed and enveloped by the large, sterile, outer bract, but the bracts quickly change to white (Figure 3-26) as the elongation phase of the raceme begins (Figure 3-27). This characteristic change is common to all true forms of *H. kikutii* and so are the near-white flowers (Figure 3-27, 3-32) which are very closely spaced on the raceme. The very long pedicels remain horizontal and do not bend down even when heavy with seed pods (Figure 3-28).

Maekawa called it the Cranebeaked Plantain Lily, suggesting that the upper part of the scape with the closed bud looks like the long neck and head of a Japanese Crane, called *tsuru* (usually *Grus japonensis*, Gruidae) and *tancho*.

Available in most of its forms and horticulturally important as it has become both pod and pollen parent in a number of breeding lines and is extensively cultivated.

Plant size 45 cm (18 in.) dia., 25 cm (12 in.) high. Petiole 13 by 0.4 cm (5.2 by 0.15 in.), ascending in an arch, light green. Leaf 18–23 by 7.5–11 cm (7–9 by 3–4.5 in.), elliptical, ovate to lanceolate, petiole-leaf transition narrowly truncate, acuminate, very elongated, drooping tip, with flat surface, but convolute at the base, no waves or very slight waves in margin, not rugose, shiny dark green above, shiny light green below. Venation 8–10, closely spaced, projected below. Scape 50 cm (20 in.), erect, but leaning in the upper part, smooth round. Sterile lower bracts, leaflike, with exterior bracts enveloping the interior, occasionally ±2 large sterile leaflike bracts near bud forming beaklike configuration of the unopened flower bud; fertile bracts flat and broad, thick, first green, but opening white, withering, but persisting at anthesis, 2 by 1 cm (0.75 by 0.33 in.). Raceme short, densely imbricated, 10–20 flowers. Flowers white, shiny, sometimes very lightly suffused purple in the middle of the lobe, 4.5 by 3 cm (1.75 by 1.25 in.) across the lobes, carried horizontally on strong pedicels, 2.5 cm (1 in.) long which extend beyond the bracts; perianth expanding, funnel-shaped, in the central part dilated bell-shaped, lobes spreading ±angled to the axis of perianth; stamens as long as

perianth or extending beyond it. Anthers purple. August. Fertile.

SY: *H. kikutii* var. *densa* Maekawa 1969 pp.
      H. kikutii var. *kikutii* Maekawa 1950.
HN: Cranebeaked Plantain Lily.
      H. 'Huga Giboshi' United States incorrect.
      H. 'Kibutii' hort. United States incorrect.
      H. 'Kikuchiana Huga' hort. United States incorrect.
JN: *Hyuga Giboshi* Kikuchi and Maekawa 1937.

Figure 3-26. *H. kikutii*; bract, expansion phase, turning white (Hosta Hill)

Figure 3-27. *H. kikutii*; racemes, elongation phase (Hosta Hill)

Figure 3-28. *H. kikutii*; seed pods on long pedicels (Hosta Hill)

H. kikutii 'Harvest Delight' hort.
(see *H.* 'Harvest Delight').

H. kikutii 'Hosoba Urajiro' hort.
ホソバウラジロヒュウガギボウシ
    Hosoba Urajiro Hyuga Giboshi is a white-backed, strap-

Figure 3-25. *H. kikutii*; pointed flower bud, green, strongly inclined during initial phase of scape elongation (Hosta Hill)

leaved form of the species found in the wild which has been incorrectly associated with *H. longipes* and is here maintained under its Japanese cultivar name. It may be a specialized form of *H. kikutii* var. *kikutii* f. *leuconota*.

JN: *Hosoba Urajiro Hyuga Giboshi* hort.

H. kikutii 'Kifukurin' hort.
AHS-IV/22B.   (Plate 30).
A yellow-margined cultivar of cultivated origin. Morphologically similar to *H. kikutii* var. *tosana*, but the scape is not acutely bending. Although by name connected with *H. kikutii* it may be a hybridized taxon of mixed parentage.

H. kikutii 'Soules Pruinose' hort.
AHS-III/13B.   (Figure 3-29).
Several pruinose forms of *H. kikutii* exist from which a pronounced glaucous, permanently white-back form has been separated and named *H. kikutii* var. *leuconota*, which see. This form was imported by Soules Garden and is only slightly pruinose, but never shiny above, and lastingly dull glaucous below. It may be related to Maekawa's *H. kikutii* var. *polyneuron*, which see. The possibility that is an interspecific hybrid cannot be ruled out.

Plant has leaves with same shape as the species, but larger, to 25 by 10 cm (10 by 4 in.). Scapes moderately more erect. Similar to *kikutii* f. *leuconota* but with wider leaves, less permanently pruinose, and not as white on the leaf underside.

HN: *H. kikutii* 'Pruinosa' hort. United States incorrect.
     H. kikutii 'Soules Pruinose' hort.

Figure 3-29. *H. kikutii* 'Soules Pruinose'; general habit (Hosta Hill)

H. kikutii var. *caput-avis* Maekawa 1950.
III/1B.   (Figure 2-34; Plate 31).
ウナズキギボウシ
Unazuki Giboshi, the "bowing- (nodding-) head hosta," has the species epithet *caput-avis* which means "head of a bird." The Japanese name refers to the head (and long neck) of the Japanese crane, called *tsuru*. This hosta grows on rocky cliffs in Shikoku, where the type was collected by Yasui near Yanase in Kochi Prefecture. It shares habitat with *H. kikutii* var. *tosana*, to which it is closely related, and with which it ranges east into Wakayama and Tokushima prefectures. The scape of this taxon has a very characteristic posture, which bends acutely to a horizontal position at ground level. In the wild the flowers rest on adjacent rock surfaces or hang subhorizontally below the leaf mound and this posture is maintained in cultivation (Plate 31). Intermediate forms exist in the wild in which the bend in the scape occurs further up, similar to and approaching *H. kikutii* var. *tosana*. Many different forms exist, including dwarf forms (Figure 2-34) and may represent allopatric

populations in the process of speciation or, on the other hand, intergrading hybrid swarms. Leaf growth on some forms is sparse and its shape is similar to *H. kikutii* var. *polyneuron* or *H. kikutii* var. *yakusimensis*, while other forms have more leaves which are larger and approach in size those in the typical specific form. A yellow-streaked form has been found in the wild and is called *Fuiri Unazuki Giboshi*. The forms shown in Figure 2-34 and Plate 31 typify large and small taxa. In Japan this taxon is popular for pot culture and rock gardens, and its unique characteristics make it a collector's item.

Plant size 30 cm (12 in.) dia., 15 cm (6 in.) high. Petiole 7.5 by 0.4 cm (3 by 0.15 in.), spreading horizontally, light green. Leaf 15 by 5 cm (6 by 2 in.), elliptical to lanceolate, petiole-leaf transition decurrent, acuminate, very elongated, drooping tip, with flat surface, slight undulate in margin, not rugose, dark green with slight sheen above, shiny green below. Venation 7–9, closely spaced, projected below. Scape 15–30 cm (6–12 in.), smooth, round, bending acutely at ground level, growing horizontally (or subhorizontally on rocky cliffs), usually below the leaf mound. Sterile lower bracts, leaf-like, with exterior bracts enveloping the interior, in some specimens ±2 large sterile leaflike bracts near bud forming beaklike configuration of the unopened flower head; fertile bracts flat and broad, thick, first green, but turning mostly white, withering but persistent at anthesis, 2 by 1 cm (0.75 by 0.33 in.). Raceme short, densely imbricated, 6–20 flowers. Flowers white, shiny, rarely suffused very light purple in the middle of the lobe, 4.5 by 3 cm (1.75 by 1.25 in.) across the lobes, carried horizontally on strong pedicels, 2.5 cm (1 in.) long, which surpass the bracts; perianth expanding, funnel-shaped, in the central part dilated bell-shaped, lobes spreading ±angled to the axis of perianth; stamens as long as perianth or surpassing it. Anthers purple. July/August. Fertile.

SY: *H. caput-avis* Maekawa 1952.
     H. caput-avis f. *leucoclada* Maekawa 1948.
     H. kikutii var. *tosana* Fujita 1976a pp sl.
     H. tosana Maekawa 1940 pp sl.
     H. tosana var. *caput-avis* Maekawa 1948.
HN: *H. caput-avis* hort.
     H. 'Craig No. H-9' Summers No. 337 1969 ad int.
     Nodding Cranebeaked Plantain Lily.
JN: *Unazuki Giboshi* Maekawa 1952.

H. kikutii var. *kikutii* (see *H. kikutii*).

H. kikutii var. *kikutii* f. *leuconota* W. G. Schmid f. nov.
AHS-III/13B.   (Figures 3-30, 3-33; Plates 32, 196).
裏白ヒュウガギボウシ
Urajiro Hyuga Giboshi, the "white-backed Hyuga hosta," is a pruinose and distinctly white-backed form (Plate 32) occurring in the wild with the species and occasionally as small, separate populations. It is similar in size and leaf shape to *H. kikutii* var. *yakusimensis*, but the leaves are not as relaxed and are more stiffly erect. It is pruinose on both sides of the leaf and petiole, fading on the upper surface by flowering time but lasting on underside. It is well known in Japan and has been cultivated there for many years under its Japanese name. It is also widely cultivated in North America where it is labeled *H. kikutii* 'Pruinosa', but this name is invalid per the ICNCP. Not uncommon in the wild, it has never been validly described.

Plant size 45 cm (18 in.) dia., 25 cm (12 in.) high. Petiole 13–15 by 0.4 cm (5–6 by 0.15 in.), ascending in a low arch, light green. Leaf 18–23 by 5–7.5 cm (7–9 by 2–3 in.), elliptical, ovate to lanceolate, petiole-leaf transition decurrent to the petiole, acuminate, very elongated tip, with flat surface, not rugose, first lightly pruinose above, later shiny dark green above, greyish white pruinose below, lasting longer. Venation 6–9, closely spaced. Scape 40 cm (16 in.), leaning below 30°, smooth round, slightly pruinose green. Sterile lower bracts and fertile upper, bracts first navicular, then flattening, white, withering but persistent at anthesis, 2 by 0.6 cm (0.75 by 0.25 in.). Raceme short, densely imbricated, 10–20 flowers. Flowers white, shiny, 5 by 3 cm (2 by 1.25 in.) across the lobes, carried horizontally on strong pedicels, 1.5 cm (0.6 in.) long; perianth expanding, funnel-shaped, in the central part dilated bell-shaped, lobes spreading ±angled to the axis of perianth; stamens as long as perianth or longer. Anthers purple. August. Fertile.

HN: *H. kikutii* 'Pruinosa' hort. United States incorrect.
       H. kikutii 'Pruinose' hort.
       H. kikutii 'Urajiro' hort.
JN: *Urajiro Hyuga Giboshi* hort.

Figure 3-30. *H. kikutii* var. *kikutii* f. *leuconota*; pointed flower bud, green during initial phase of scape elongation (Hosta Hill)

H. kikutii var. *polyneuron* Fujita 1976a.

AHS-III/13B.   (Figure 3-31).
スダレギボウシ

Sudare Giboshi, the "bamboo blind hosta," has nerves closely spaced like the slats of a Japanese bamboo blind, hence the name. The Greek *polyneuron* means "many nerves" (principal veins). It is similar to *H. kikutii* var. *yakusimensis* but differs in the leaf being wider and having 9–11 closely spaced veins. It grows on Shikoku, Kochi Prefecture, near Ikegawa-cho. A number of seed-raised plants I obtained for testing and observed in cultivation in Europe were labeled *H. kikutii* var. *polyneuron* but are definitely not this taxon; they have bicolor anthers, fewer veins, lanceolate leaves, and are much smaller, they may represent intra- or interspecific hybrids. Authentic specimens of this taxon are in scientific collections but are rarely seen in Western gardens. Recently a white-margined form was discovered in the wild and is now grown in North America under the name *H. kikutii* var. *polyneuron* 'Shirofukurin'. The leaves of this taxon approach those of *H.*

densa which grows further east.

Plant is morphologically similar to the species but has leaves 20 by 8 cm (8 by 3 in.), ovate-elliptical to elliptical, petiole-leaf transition decurrent, acuminate, very elongated, slightly drooping tip, with flat surface, no waves or very slight waves in margin, not rugose, green with slight sheen above, shiny light green below. Venation 9–11, closely spaced, projected below.

SY: *H. kikutii* var. *yakusimensis* Fujita 1976a sl na.
       H. polyneuron Maekawa 1952.
HN: *H. polyneuron* hort.
JN: *Sudare Giboshi* Fujita 1976a.

Figure 3-31. *H. kikutii* var. *polyneuron*; bud detail (Hosta Hill)

H. kikutii var. *polyneuron* 'Ogon' hort.
黄金スダレ

Ogon Sudare Giboshi, the "yellow bamboo blind hosta," is a yellow form of the botanical variety and is otherwise identical to it.

H. kikutii var. *polyneuron* 'Shirofukurin' hort.
白覆輪スダレギボウシ   (Plate 33).
Shirofukurin Sudare Giboshi, the "white-margined bamboo blind hosta," is a white-margined form of the botanical variety and is otherwise identical to it. Recently brought to North America by Hideko Gowen it is now under cultivation in North America under the name *H. kikutii* var. *polyneuron* 'Albomarginata', which is invalid under the rules of the ICNCP because of its Latin formulation. The Japanese name *H. kikutii* var. *polyneuron* 'Shirofukurin' should be used.

H. kikutii var. *polyneuron* 'Shironakafu' hort.
白中斑スダレギボウシ
Shironakafu Sudare Giboshi, the "white-centered bamboo blind hosta," is an albopicta mediovariegated form of the botanical variety. It is smaller than the species but otherwise identical to it.

H. kikutii var. *tosana* (Maekawa) Maekawa 1950.
AHS-IV/19B.   (Figure 3-32).
トサノギボウシ

Tosa No Giboshi, the "hosta from (or of) Tosa," inhabits mountain valleys in the old province of Tosa, now Kochi Prefecture, where the type was found on Mount Kajigamine and at first described by Maekawa as a species, but later ranked as a variety. Its Latin varietal epithet also stands for Tosa Province. *Hosta kikutii* var. *tosana* is similar to *H. kikutii* var. *caput-avis*, and Fujita (1976a) considered the two synonymous. They are undoubtedly very closely related, and Fujita's placement is accepted in part, but they represent locally differentiated adaptations to particular habitats and show distinct macromorphological differences, including disparities in scape posture. As a consequence, Maekawa's (1940) delimitation has been followed, retaining this taxon on the varietal level following Maekawa (1950) and Kitamura (1964). It is rarely seen in the West, but some specimens are cultivated in North America.

Plant size 35 cm (14 in.) dia., 15 cm (6 in.) high. Petiole 10 by 0.4 cm (4 by 0.15 in.), spreading horizontally, light green. Leaf 10–15 by 7.5–10 cm (4–6 by 3–4 in.), elliptical to lanceolate, petiole-leaf transition decurrent, acuminate, very elongated, drooping tip, with flat surface, no waves or very slight waves in margin, not rugose, dark green with slight sheen above, shiny green below. Venation 6–9, closely spaced, projected below. Scape 35 cm (14 in.), acutely bending in the upper half and leaning considerably, sometimes becoming horizontal, smooth round. Sterile lower bracts, leaflike, with exterior bracts enveloping the interior, in some specimens ±2 large sterile leaflike bracts near bud forming beaklike configuration of the unopened flower head; fertile bracts flat and broad, thick, first green, but turning white, withering but persistent at anthesis, 2 by 1 cm (0.75 by 0.33 in.). Raceme short, densely imbricated, 10–20 flowers. Flowers white, shiny, very lightly purple-suffused in the middle of the lobe, or white entirely, 4.5 by 3 cm (1.75 by 1.25 in.) across the lobes, carried horizontally on strong pedicels, 2.5 cm (1 in.) long, which surpass the bracts; perianth expanding, funnel-shaped, in the central part dilated bell-shaped, lobes spreading ±angled to the axis of perianth; stamens as long as perianth or longer. Anthers purple. July/August. Fertile.

SY: *H. kikutii* var. *caput-avis* Fujita 1976a sl pp na.
    H. tosana Maekawa 1940.
JN: *Tosa No Giboshi* Maekawa 1950.

Figure 3-32. *H. kikutii* var. *tosana*; detail of scape bending acutely at beginning point of raceme (Hosta Hill)

H. kikutii var. *yakusimensis* Maekawa 1940.
    AHS-III/13B.   (Figure 3-33).
ヒメヒュウガギボウシ

Hime Hyuga Giboshi, the "small hosta from Yaku Island," grows in Kagoshima Prefecture, Kyushu. Smaller than the species but otherwise similar to it, it has a low-growing habit and spreads to form large colonies. The leaves are elongated and more lanceolate, the veins very closely spaced, the leaf tips drooping. It has large leaflike bracts, and closely imbricated, beaked buds. It should be noted that in the literature the species epithet *yakusimensis* is applied to two distinct and

segregated taxa, one of which is a larger form called *H. yakusimensis*. This larger form is considered part of section *Helipteroides* (*H. sieboldiana/H. montana* group) and so is excluded here. Flower color is white in the wild but when cultivated in more northern latitudes, where it also flowers later, lavendar color has been observed.

Plant size 45 cm (18 in.) dia., 13 cm (5 in.) high. Petiole 11 by 0.4 cm (4.5 by 0.15 in.), spreading horizontally, light green. Leaf 20 by 5–7 cm (8 by 2–3 in.), elliptical to lanceolate, petiole-leaf transition decurrent, acuminate, very elongated, drooping tip, with flat surface, no waves or slight waves in margin, not rugose, deep dark green, slight sheen above, shiny lighter green below. Venation 7–9, closely spaced, projected below. Scape 50 cm (20 in.), erect, but bending above the middle and leaning in the upper part, smooth round. Sterile lower bracts, leaflike, with exterior bracts enveloping the interior, in some specimens ±2 large sterile leaflike bracts near bud forming beaklike configuration of the unopened flower head; fertile bracts flat and broad, thick, first green, turning mostly white, withering but persistent at anthesis, 2 by 1 cm (0.75 by 0.33 in.). Raceme short, densely imbricated, 10–20 flowers. Flowers white, shiny, very lightly purple-suffused in the middle of the lobe, or white entirely, 4.5 by 3 cm (1.75 by 1.25 in.) across the lobes, carried horizontally on strong pedicels, 2.5 cm (1 in.) long, which surpass the bracts; perianth expanding, funnel-shaped, in the central part dilated bell-shaped, lobes spreading ±angled to the axis of perianth; stamens as long as perianth or longer. Anthers yellow background with uniform purple cast, looking "dirty" yellow. August. Fertile.

SY: *H. kikutii* var. *yakusimensis* Masamune 1932 pp.
    H. polyneuron Ohwi 1965 pp sl na.
    H. sieboldiana var. *yakusimensis* Masamune pp na.
    H. yakusimensis Maekawa pp na.
HN: *H.* 'Hirao No. 59' pp sim.
    H. 'Mack No. 18' pp ad int.
JN: *Hime Hyuga Giboshi* Maekawa 1940.

Figure 3-33. *H. kikutii* var. *yakusimensis*; general habit; *H. kikutii* var. *kikutii* f. *leuconota* (right) (Hosta Hill)

H. kiyosumiensis Maekawa 1935.
    AHS-III/13A.   (Figure 3-34; Plate 34).
キヨスミギボウシ

Kiyosumi Giboshi, the "Mount Kiyosumi hosta," was collected by Nakai on Mount Kiyosumi in the Kanto District of Honshu, Chiba Prefecture, and grows over a wide area in south-central Honshu along forest margins and river valleys. It

Figure 3-34. *H. kiyosumiensis*; leaf detail showing serrated margin (Hosta Hill)

modifies greatly over its range and several variants have been named. Its leaves are yellowish or very light green and thin, and they have microscopically toothed (serrated), slightly irregular margins (Figure 3-34), a trait rare in the genus. The latter are definite identifiers but some hybrids of this species also show this peculiarity. In spring the shoots arise with a yellowish green coloration. Maekawa's 1940 diagnosis is here emended in regard to scape height, flower count, and bract morphology, and this modification has been confirmed by observation of authentic specimens in Japan and cultivated material received from academic sources as well as recent accessions of natural populations by M. G. Chung (1989; personal communication). The populations observed and cultivated have higher scapes, more and larger flowers, and large subtending, foliaceous bracts which Maekawa (1940) compared to those of *H.* 'Lancifolia' and which make it appealing for garden use. Variegated forms have been found in the wild (Plate 34). A form of the species selected from cultivated material with well-defined bell-shaped flowers has been selected, but no Japanese name is known. This taxon has been compared with the green form of *H.* 'Crispula' (Maekawa, 1969) and also to *H.* 'Fortunei' (Maekawa, 1940). Both placements are incorrect because *H.* 'Crispula' has larger leaves, 8–10 pairs of veins, and flowers abundantly, while *H.* 'Fortunei' has 9–11 pairs of veins and also many more flowers. It is available but seldom seen.

Plant size 30–45 cm (12–18 in.) dia., 25 cm (10 in.) high. Petiole 7.5–10 by 0.7 cm (0.75 by 0.3 in.), erect, broadly grooved, keeled, triangular in cross section, green, at the base barely purple-dotted. Leaf 10–15 by 5–7.5 cm (4–6 by 2–3 in.), entire, ovate-elliptical to ovate, truncate at base, very pointed, acuminate, elongated tip, wavy surface, undulate-crispate in the margin, thin papery texture, light yellowish green, opaque, below, shiny light green. Microscopically serrated margin. Venation 5–6, sunken above, very projected, markedly strigose, below. Scape 30–90 cm (12–36 in.), straight, erect, perpendicular, barely purple-dotted at base. Sterile bracts, 1–3, large, leafy, sheathed at the base, green, similar to *H.* 'Lancifolia'; fertile bracts, 1–3 cm (0.5–1.25 in.) long, 0.5–1 cm (0.25–0.5 in.) broad, ovate-lanceolate, navicular, shiny light green, at first imbricate, fresh and persisting at anthesis, but later falling away. Raceme 35–75 cm (14–31 in.), 5–20 flowers. Flowers 5 by 2.5 cm (2 by 1 in.), medium size, whitish, very slightly purple-suffused inside, expanding, funnel-shaped, in the central part dilated bell-shaped, narrow tube long; stamens almost as long as the perianth, style longer projecting beyond perianth. Anthers purple. June/July. Fertile.

SY: *H. densa* Fujita 1976a sl na.
     H. kiyosumiensis var. *petrophila* Fujita 1976a.
     H. pachyscapa Fujita 1976a sl na.
HN: *H. praecox* hort.
JN: *Hayazaki Giboshi* Maekawa 1969 sl.
     Kiyosumi Giboshi Maekawa 1935.

H. kiyosumiensis 'Nakafu' hort.
中斑キヨスミギボウシ   (Plate 34).
    Nakafu Kiyosumi Giboshi, the "aureonebulosa Kiyosumi hosta," is yellow-centered form with thin green margin. It was found among the wild populations near Nukata-cho, Aichi Prefecture in 1984. Here it is considered a nonperpetuating mutant and maintained as a cultivar.
JN: *Nakafu Kiyosumi Giboshi* hort.

H. kiyosumiensis 'Shirobana' hort.
白花キヨスミギボウシ
    Shirobana Kiyosumi Giboshi, the "white-flowered Kiyosumi hosta," is a white-flowered form found in the wild and now cultivated. It may only represent a local adaptation, so it is not taxonomically separated but maintained as a cultivar. It should be noted that the standard form has flowers which are almost white in certain habitats and which are not true albino forms.
JN: *Shirobana Kiyosumi Giboshi*.

H. kiyosumiensis var. *petrophila* Maekawa 1940.
イワマギボウシ
    Iwama Giboshi, the "rock-dwelling hosta," was named by Maekawa in 1938 and made a variety in 1940. It inhabits the mountains of the Kinki District of Central Honshu, in Kyoto and Nara prefectures, with the range extending eastward to Aichi Prefecture, where colonies grow on rocks along the Oto River near Nukata-cho. The epithet *petrophila* (not *petrophylla*) comes from the Greek *petro* = rock and *philo* = loving, alluding to the plant's preferred rocky habitat. It is frequently smaller than the type and has shorter scapes and fewer flowers, but is otherwise identical and here considered synonymous to the species.

Plant similar to the species but smaller and has slightly darker flowers. Leaf shorter, 7.5–10 by 5–7.5 cm (3–4 by 2–3 in.), otherwise like the species.
SY: *H. kiyosumiensis* Fujita 1976a.
HN: *H. kiyosumiensis* var. *petrophylla* hort. incorrect.
JN: *Iwama Giboshi* Maekawa 1938b.

L

H. laevigata W. G. Schmid sp. nov.
    AHS-IV/19B. (Figures 2-38, 3-35, 3-36; Plates 35, 182).
    The species epithet is derived from *laevigatus* = polished, denoting the very smooth upper leaf surface and polished leaf underside, both characteristics this species has in common with *H. yingeri* to which it is closely related. Like the latter, the cultivated material was grown from seed originating with B. R. Yinger, then of the U.S. National Arboretum, from several accessions of *Hosta* collected from the islands of the Huksan group (Huksan-chedo) on Taehuksan (Tae-huksan-do) and Sohuksan (So-huksan-do) off the southwestern coast of Korea. Yinger (1991: personal communication) confirms the existence of highly variable populations on Taehuksan where *H. laevigata* originates. The area of collection is Province Chollanam-do, Shinan-gun, Huksan Myeon, where the

species inhabits remote, rocky islands near the coast in soil on talus slopes in some shade. It shares habitat with *H. yingeri* and like it has leaves that have very heavy substance and appear succulent, but that differ considerably from the latter's by being attractively lanceolate, and having a wavy, crispate margin and an elongated, twisted tip. The leaf color of *H. yingeri* is a dark green, while *H. laevigata* has light green leaves.

Populations of this new species have been observed by M. G. Chung who collected in the Huksan group in 1987 and 1988 (1989: personal communication). A form with very glossy, short leaves exists (Plate 35), but further study is needed before its status can be determined. The type and short-leaved form of *H. laevigata* have identical flower morphology which differs from *H. yingeri*. Of the 3 taxa shown in Plate 35 the short-leaved form has the glossiest leaves I have encountered in the genus. The very heavy substance of the type of *H. laevigata* is thought to be an adaptation to its coastal habitat. It has flowers larger than those of *H. yingeri* are purple-suffused with very narrow lobes looking spider-flowered. Both species have been placed in the new section *Arachnanthae* (see Appendix A). The 6 filaments carrying the anthers are of equal length (see Figure 2-38; Plate 182), unlike *H. yingeri* which has 2 sets of 3 filaments, one set shorter than the other (Figure 3-80). The pedicels of *H. laevigata* are very short (4–6 mm/0.16–0.24 in.) while *H. yingeri* has very long pedicels (to 20 mm). *Hosta laevigata* has very thick, slug-resistant leaves and unusual flowers, and it will in the future be of great horticultural merit as a parent and a substitute for the many lanceolate, thin-leaved cultivars in the *H. sieboldii* breeding line.

Plant size 25–35 cm (10–15 in.) dia., 10 cm (4 in.) high. Petiole 1.5–2.5 by 0.5 cm (0.75–1 by 0.2 in.), erect, spreading, tapering into and becoming part of

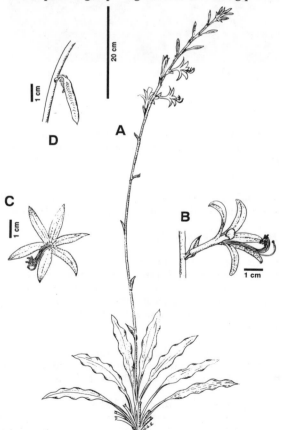

Figure 3-35. *H. laevigata*; (A) habit; (B) view; (D) seed pod (drawing by the author from holotype/Hosta Hill)

leaf without noticeable transition, forming a vase-shaped plant, medium green. Leaf 9–12 by 2–3 cm (3.5–5 by 0.75–1.25 in.), erect and in line with petiole, petiole transition gradual, narrowly lanceolate, undulate, wavy-crispate in the margin, keeled, long, acuminate, contorted tip, erect-spreading, very shiny, light green above, smooth, extremely glossy, polished, lighter green below. Venation 3, very smooth above, projected, smooth below. Scape 35–90 cm (14–36 in.), straight and erect, stiff, green. Sterile bracts, 3–5, lowest lanceolate, wavy, foliaceous 3–5 cm (1–2 in.); fertile bracts short, 5–10 mm (0.25–0.5 in.), navicular, green, remaining fresh at anthesis. Pedicels, short 4–6 mm (0.16–0.224 in.), shorter or equal to fertile bracts, bending down. Raceme long, 12–20 cm (5–8 in.), 5–20 flowers. Flowers large, 5 cm (2 in.) long, 4 cm (1.5 in.) broad, purple-suffused, lobes very narrow, spreading rapidly, recurving, wide open, spider-flowered. Stamens 6, on filaments of equal length, 30 mm (1.25 in.), not projecting, Anthers light uniform purple. August. Fertile.

Figure 3-36. *H. laevigata*; flower bud detail, type (Hosta Hill)

✠ *"H. lancifolia"* Engler 1888.
AHS-IV/19B. (Figure 3-37).
Here reduced to cultivar form as *H.* **'Lancifolia'**.
サジギボウシ

Saji Giboshi, the "little hosta," was the first representative of the genus to be introduced to Western botany as *Giboosi altera* based on a drawing made by Kaempfer in 1692. Almost 100 years later Thunberg collected herbarium specimens in Japan and there is no doubt that one of them, the lectotype of *Aletris japonica* in UPS, is identical to the cultigen *Hosta* 'Lancifolia'. It should be noted, though, that Thunberg's specimen could also have been *H. cathayana*, which is practically indistinguishable in a dried state and also occurs in Nagasaki Prefecture, where Thunberg collected. This taxon is a hybrid cultigen of ancient origin and is represented by a number of very similar-looking clones. It is known that one of Kaempfer's Japanese guards purchased plants for him in Osaka during his travel to Edo (see Chapter 5). He certainly did not find it in the wild. Some of the wild populations of the all-green form of *H. sieboldii* in Japan have representatives which are superficially comparable to *H.* 'Lancifolia', so they have frequently been mistaken for each other. In a number of publications the synonyms cited for one are in reality applicable to the other (see synonymy for this taxon and for *H. sieboldii* f. *spathulata* for correct relationships). The lectotype of *Aletris japonica*, for example, was cited as recently as 1984 by

Hara as the type for his *Hosta sieboldii* var. *sieboldii* f. *lancifolia*, so there can be no doubt that he meant to classify the sterile *H.* 'Lancifolia' as a forma under the fully fertile *H. sieboldii*. In doing this Hara reversed the usual arrangement of *H. sieboldii* as a variety under *H.* 'Lancifolia', so did not separate these as Hylander had done in 1954. Details of these placements are discussed in Appendixes A and B. In Japan *H.* 'Lancifolia' is sometimes called *Koba Giboshi*, the "small leaf hosta," a name which is also used for the all-green *H. sieboldii* f. *spathulata*. The name *Saji* (or *Sazi*) *Giboshi* appears on Kaempfer's drawing and has also been used for this taxon. According to Maekawa (1940) this name was applied as well to *H. longissima* var. *brevifolia* by Iinuma (1874), but the widely expanded, bell-shaped flowers and 4 pairs of veins shown on Iinuma's drawing point to a taxon other than our present-day *H.* 'Lancifolia'. All this establishes that *H.* 'Lancifolia' was mistaken for a number of unrelated taxa. The first live plants were sent to Holland by von Siebold in 1829. Today the species is cultivated around the world as an excellent ground cover and edger. It is often mistaken for *H. cathayana* which it resembles, but while the latter is fertile, the former rarely sets fruit and is considered pod-sterile. It is a popular garden plant, and if left undisturbed it spreads into very large colonies.

Plant size 35–50 cm (14–20 in.) dia., 30 cm (12 in.) high. Petiole 17.5–25 by 0.5 cm (7–18 by 0.2 in.), erect, forming a vase-shaped plant, green, with purple-dotted base. Leaf 10–15 by 5–7.5 cm (4–6 by 2–3 in.), erect and in line with petiole, ovate-lanceolate, petiole transition gradual, broadly narrowed, acuminate tip, slightly undulate, wavy in the margin, erect, smooth, shiny, medium green above, glossy lighter green below. Venation 5–6, sunken above, very projected, smooth below. Scape 40–50 cm (16–20 in.), straight and erect, but bending, lax, green, purplish red dots on lower third. Sterile bracts 3–5, leafy, large; fertile bracts short, navicular, grooved, thin, membranous, green, withering at anthesis, but not falling away. Raceme long, 17.5–20 cm (7–8 in.), 10–20 flowers. Flowers 4–4.5 cm (1.5–2 in.) long, 4 cm (1.5 in.) broad, purple-violet; perianth expanding, funnel-shaped, in the central part slightly dilated bell-shaped, lobes spreading rapidly, recurving, wide open, blunt, short pedicels, projecting stamen. Anthers purple. September. Sterile.

SY: *Aletris japonica* Thunberg ex Houttuyn 1780.
      Funkia japonica α *typica* Regel 1876.
      Funkia japonica Druce 1917.
      Funkia lanceaefolia Denst. ex Don. (in *Ind. Kew.* Ed. 1).
      Funkia lancifolia Sprengel 1825.
      Funkia ovata var. *lancifolia* Miquel 1869.
      Giboosi altera nom. nudum Kaempfer 1692.
      Hemerocallis japonica Thunberg 1784.
      Hemerocallis lancifolia Thunberg 1794.
      Hosta albomarginata f. *lancifolia* (Miquel) Ohwi 1942.
      H. cærulea f. *lancifolia* Matsumura 1905.
      H. japonica Koidzumi 1925.
      H. japonica Nash 1911.
      H. japonica var. *fortis* Bailey 1930 incorrect (*H.* 'Undulata Erromena').
      H. japonica var. *fortis* Bailey 1932.
      H. lancifolia var. *thunbergiana* Maekawa 1940.
      H. lancifolia var. *thunbergii* Stearn 1931a.
      H. sieboldii var. *sieboldii* f. *lancifolia* Hara 1984.
      Hostia japonica f. *typica* Voss 1896.
      Niobe japonica Thunberg Nash 1911.
      Saussurea japonica Kuntze 1891.
HN: *Hosta angustifolia* Foerster 1965b incorrect.

H. cathayana incorrect.
H. 'Craig No. C-5' Summers No. 340.
H. 'Craig No. C-6' Summers No. 339.
H. cærulea viridis Foerster 1956 incorrect.
H. 'Fortis' hort. incorrect.
H. 'Green Lance' hort.
H. japonica hort. incorrect.
H. 'Krossa No. 6' Summers No. 45 incorrect.
H. lancifolia 'Pleasant Hill' sim.
H. lancifolia var. *fortis* hort. incorrect.
H. laurifolia Buist 1854 ad int.
H. 'Mack No. 16'.
H. tardiva hort. incorrect.
H. viridis Foerster 1952 incorrect.
Lanceleaf Plantain Lily.
Narrow Leaved Plantain Lily.
Narrowleaf Plantain Lily.
JN: *Saji Giboshi* Kaempfer 1692.
      Sazi Giboshi hort.
ON: Frühgrüne Schmalblattfunkie (German) Foerster 1956.
      Lanzenfunkie (German) Hansen et al. 1964.
      Schmalblattfunkie (German) Foerster 1956 pp.

Figure 3-37. *H.* 'Lancifolia'; mass planting (Inniswood Botanic Garden/Schmid)

H. lancifolia var. *thunbergiana* f. *bunchoko* Maekawa 1969.
     Here transferred to a new combination as *H. sieboldii* f. *bunchoko*.
(see *H. sieboldii* f. *bunchoko*).

H. lancifolia var. *thunbergiana* f. *kifukurin* Maekawa 1969.
     Here transferred to a new combination as *H. sieboldii* f. *kifukurin*.
(see *H. sieboldii* f. *kifukurin*).

H. latifolia (Miquel) Matsumura 1905.
     Matsumura transferred this taxon to *Hosta* in name only and without description, so it is impossible to identify it. Hylander (1954) associated it with *H. ventricosa*. Wehrhahn amplified on this species name with a different opinion, which see in the following entry.

H. latifolia (Miquel) Wehrhahn 1936.
     Wehrhahn identified this taxon and described it as being illustrated in Bailey (1930: ic. 190), as *H.* 'Elata'.

H. laurifolia nom. nudum Buist 1854.
     A listing from the *American Gardening Dictionary* (Buist, 1854), which is a nom. nudum and may have stood for *H.* 'Lancifolia'.
(see *H. lancifolia*).

H. leptophylla nom. nudum Maekawa 1950.
ウスバイワギボウシ

A nom. nudum originally used for *H. longipes* var. *caduca*.
JN: *Usuba Iwa Giboshi* Maekawa 1950.
(see *H. longipes* var. *caduca*).

H. leucantha nom. nudum hort.

In specific rank this species name is a nom. nudum used incorrectly in horticulture for an unspecified form. It is derived from the Greek *leucanthes* = white flowering. As a forma name it was originally published by K. Ito (1969) as *H. rectifolia* var. *atropurpurea* f. *leucantha*, transferred to *H. sieboldii* as *H. sieboldii* var. *rectifolia* f. *leucantha* by Hara (1984), and is here considered synonymous to *H. rectifolia* var. *chionea* f. *albiflora*. (see *H. rectifolia* var. *chionea* f. *albiflora*).

H. leucoclada nom. nudum hort.

A nom. nudum as a species name used for an unspecified form. The epithet is derived from the Greek *leucon* = white and *clados* = branch, shoot. In 1948 Maekawa named *H. caput-avis* f. *leucoclada* nom. nudum but did not validate this name because white shoots are not uncommon in *H. kikutii*.

H. lilacina nom. nudum Bailey 1976.
An obsolete name printed in *Hortus Third*.

H. liliiflora nom. nudum Maekawa 1938a.
(see *H. montana* var. *liliiflora*).

H. liliiflora nom. nudum Maekawa ex Araki 1942.

This species name was first published by Maekawa (1938a) (in observation). As such it was a nom. nudum. Araki took up the name and republished it without description, so the species name ex Araki is still a nom. nudum. Although Maekawa validly published the combination *H. montana* var. *liliiflora*, the varietal name does not have priority outside its rank. Although Araki provided a valid diagnosis for his *H. liliiflora* var. *ovatolancifolia*, the latter must be considered a comb. nudum because the species name was never validated. (see *H. montana* var. *liliiflora*).

H. liliiflora var. *ovatolancifolia* nom. nudum Araki 1942.
ナガレギボウシ

Nagare Giboshi was collected in west-central Honshu, Kyoto, and Hyogo prefectures and is represented by several specimens and the type in KYO. The name is based on the invalid basionym *H. liliiflora* and is a comb. nudum. To give this taxon a valid name I have transferred it to *H. montana* as *H. montana* f. *ovatolancifolia*, which see.
JN: *Nagare Giboshi*.

H. longipes. (see *H. longipes* var. *longipes*).

H. longipes f. *hypoglauca* Maekawa 1940.
AHS-IV/19A.   (Plates 36, 206).
コフキイワギボウシ

Kofuki Iwa Giboshi, the "pruinose rock hosta," grows in central Honshu, Tochigi Prefecture, Nikko area. It differs from *Urajiro Iwa Giboshi* by being initially glaucous allover. The latter is white-backed only and is included under the species. Variability is common in the wild. Two variants were selected by Davidson (1970, 1990) in Japan and named *H. longipes* 'Tagi' and *H. longipes* 'Setsuko', which see. In 1969 Davidson sent many of these collected forms to Summers who cultivated them under nos. 347–354. A selected form of this variety, probably an F_1 hybrid, is in the North American trade under the name *H.* 'Fall Bouquet'. When carefully selfed, this botanical variety produces both glaucous and nonglaucous

forms which are macromorphologically very close to the holotype *Funkia longipes* Franchet et Savatier 1876.

Plant size 20–30 cm (8–12 in.) dia., 15–20 cm (6–8 in.) high. Petiole 10–30 by 0.4 cm (4–12 by 0.15 in.), erect, spreading, purple-dotted entire length, extending into leaf base, pruinose coating, with long and short petiole forms existing side by side in the wild. Leaf 7.5–12.5 by 5–7.5 cm (3–5 by 2–3 in.), erect and in line with petiole, cordate, transition tight and contracted, acuminate tip, with generally flat surface, ±keeled, no waves in margin, not rugose, bright glaucous green, bluish white, farinose, below. Venation 5–7, projected, smooth below. Scape 25–30 cm (10–12 in.), straight, but leaning, smooth, round, sea-green, slightly pruinose, permanently purple-dotted, more densely in lower half. Fertile bracts small, navicular, grooved, thin, membranous, white, tinted purple, withering, falling away during anthesis. Raceme 8–12 flowers, widely spaced. Flowers whitish purple, purple striped, 4.5 cm (1.75 in.) long, 3 cm (1.25 in.) across the lobes, carried horizontally on strong pedicels; perianth expanding, funnel-shaped, lobes spreading lily-shaped; stamens very superior, surpassing the lobes. Anthers purple. August/September. Fertile.
SY: *Funkia longipes* Franchet et Savatier 1876 pp sim.
HN: *Hosta* 'Fall Bouquet'.
      H. longipes f. *hypoglauca* 'Setsuko' sim.
      H. longipes f. *hypoglauca* 'Tagi' sim.
JN: *Kofuki Iwa Giboshi* Maekawa 1940.
      Setsuko Iwa Giboshi hort. pp.
      Tagi Iwa Giboshi hort. pp.
      Urajiro Iwa Giboshi hort. incorrect.

H. longipes f. *sparsa* (Nakai) W. G. Schmid stat. nov.
AHS-IV/19B.   (Plate 37).
アキギボウシ
ホソバイワギボウシ

Aki Giboshi, the "fall(-blooming) hosta," was originally named as the species *H. sparsa* by Nakai in 1930. The type was described from stock cultivated near Nagoya, Aichi Prefecture, Honshu. The cultivated *H. sparsa* is virtually identical to natural allopatric populations found in the wild in Tenryu District, near Nagoya, growing on wet rocks along river banks. These are locally called *Hosoba Iwa Giboshi*, the "narrow-leaved rock hosta," which is *H. longipes* var. *lancea*, and this named form is considered synonymous to *H. sparsa*, at least in part. Other authors have judged *H. sparsa* to be the same as *H.* 'Tardiflora', but this is incorrect as the latter produces yellow anthers and many flowers, while the former flowers sparsely (hence the epithet) and has purple anthers. I have formed a new combination *H. longipes* f. *sparsa*, preferring the older name *sparsa* (Nakai, 1930) over *lancea* (Honda, 1935a), to designate the distinct populations in the river valleys of Shizuoka and Aichi prefectures, and thus treating *Hosoba Iwa Giboshi* and other wild forms conforming to *Aki Giboshi* morphology (narrow leaves, sparse flowers, purple anthers) as a forma under *H. longipes*. A dwarf yellow form of *H. sparsa* has been reported, and this taxon may in fact be the same as *H. longipes* 'Golden Dwarf', which see. Beginning to be appreciated in Japan as a pot plant, it will play a future role in Western gardens and is of high interest to collectors.

Plant size 40 cm (16 in.) dia., 30 cm (12 in.) high. Petiole 12.5–17.5 cm by 0.3 cm (5–7 by 0.12 in.), erect, green, purple dotted, starting at leaf base, becoming progressively darker towards ground. Leaf 7.5–15 cm by 5–7.5 cm (3–6 by 2–3 in.), erect and in line with petiole, broadly lanceolate, petiole transition very gradual, not decurrent, acuminate tip, flat surface, erect, rigid, leathery, glossy light green to dark green above, lighter, opaque green below. Venation 4–5, sunken above, very projected, smooth below. Scape 25–30 cm (10–12 in.), straight, but bending obliquely, purple-dotted entire length, smooth round. Fertile bracts 1 cm (0.3 in.) long, navicular, grooved, thin, membranous, white or whitish green purple-tinted, imbricated, withering at anthesis. Raceme 12 cm (5 in.), 6–8 flowers. Flowers pale purple, held erect in horizontal position on long, strong horizontal or slightly ascending purple pedicels; perianth 5 cm (2 in.) long, funnel-shaped, expanding, in the central part dilated bell-shaped, lobes spreading straightly to ±angled to the axis of perianth, thin narrow hexagonal tube. Anthers purple. September. Fertile.

SY: *H. sparsa* Nakai 1930.
      H. longipes var. *lancea* Honda 1935a pp, with respect to the populations in Tenryu River Basin.
HN: *H. tardiflora* f. *sparsa* incorrect.
      H. tardiflora incorrect.
JN: *Aki Giboshi* Nakai 1930.
      Hosoba Iwa Giboshi hort. pp.

H. longipes f. *sparsa* 'Kinakafu' hort.
黄中斑アキギボウシ

Kinakafu Aki Giboshi is probably the mediovariegated form of *H.* 'Tardiflora'. Plants observed under this name have yellow anthers, not purple ones, so are not *Aki Giboshi*.
(see *H.* 'Tardiflora Kinakafu').

H. longipes f. *viridipes* Maekawa 1940.
AHS-IV/19A.
アオジクイワギボウシ

Aojiku Iwa Giboshi, the "green-petioled rock hosta," grows near Nikko in Tochigi Prefecture and is a form of *H. longipes* with pure green petioles. The typical purple dotting of petioles and scape observed in all other forms is absent. Except for this it is identical to *H. longipes* var. *vulgata*.
JN: *Aojiku Iwa Giboshi* Maekawa 1940.

H. longipes 'Golden Dwarf' hort.
AHS-VI/35A.   (Figure 2-2).
A miniature plant found among cultivated populations. Reportedly, it also exists in the wild, but lacking confirmation it is maintained as a cultivar.
    Plant size 10 cm (4 in.) dia., 7.5 cm (3 in.) high. Leaf 6 by 2 cm (2.5 by 0.75 in.), yellow, with a long, twisting tip, lasting color, and only slight viridescence. Petioles 5 cm (2 in.), purple-dotted.
HN: Dwarf Golden Rock Hosta.
      H. longipes Yellow group.
JN: *Ogon Hime Iwa Giboshi* hort.

H. longipes 'Harvest Dandy' hort.
(see *H.* 'Harvest Dandy').

H. longipes 'Ogon Amagi' hort.
AHS-III/17A.
黄金アマギギボウシ

Ogon Amagi Giboshi, the "golden Amagi rock hosta," is a yellow form of *H. longipes* var. *latifolia* (*Amagi Iwa Giboshi*). Many yellow forms exist in a variety of leaf shapes. Most are viridescent, turn to chartreuse or light green by anthesis, and are best considered a group. Some, including this taxon, have lasting yellow leaf color and have been isolated and named.

HN: Golden Rock Hosta.
JN: *Ogon Amagi Giboshi* hort.
      Ogon Iwa Giboshi hort.

H. longipes 'Setsuko' Davidson 1969.
AHS-IV/19A.
セツコイワギボウシ

Setsuko Iwa Giboshi, the "Setsuko's rock hosta," named for Dr. A. Moriya's wife, was collected near Tagi Shrine, Tochigi Prefecture. It is close to *H. longipes* f. *hypoglauca*, but larger and less pruinose allover with very dark and attractive purple-colored petioles, scapes, and bracts.
HN: *H. longipes* f. *hypoglauca* 'Setsuko'.
JN: *Setsuko Iwa Giboshi* hort.

H. longipes 'Shirobana' hort.
白花イワギボウシ

Shirobana Iwa Giboshi, the "white-flowered rock hosta," is a form of the species with pure white flowers.
JN: *Shirobana Iwa Giboshi* hort.
      Tama No Yuki Giboshi hort. sim white, bell-shaped flowers.

H. longipes 'Shirofukurin' hort.
白覆輪イワギボウシ

Shirofukurin Iwa Giboshi, the "white-margined rock hosta," is a white-margined form of the species occurring in the wild. Several clones exist, all mutations which are nonperpetuating so maintained as cultivar forms.
JN: *Shirofukurin Iwa Giboshi* hort.

H. longipes 'Tagi' hort.
AHS-V/25A.   (Figure 3-38; Plate 4).
タギイワギボウシ

Tagi Iwa Giboshi, the "Tagi rock hosta," discovered and named for the Tagi shrine by Davidson (1970, 1990) during an expedition into Tochigi Prefecture, including the Nikko area, where the shrine is located. It is very close to *H. longipes* f. *hypoglauca*, but has smaller, more lance-shaped leaves with light green, pruinose coloration and purple-dotted petioles and scapes.
HN: *H. longipes* f. *hypoglauca* 'Tagi'.
JN: *Tagi Iwa Giboshi* hort.

Figure 3-38. *H. longipes* 'Tagi'; a small narrow-leaved form of *H. longipes* var. *longipes* (Hosta Hill)

H. longipes 'Urajiro' hort.
裏白イワギボウシ   (Figure 3-39).

Urajiro Iwa Giboshi, the "white-backed rock hosta," represents forms with more or less dense, lasting whitish pruinose coatings on the leaf underside. They inhabit the river valleys of

Shizuoka and Aichi prefectures, and the type was found on Mount Tanayama. Some forms have narrow leaves while others are broad-leaved approaching var. *latifolia*. Several have been given Japanese cultivar names. The Japanese name is also used frequently as an incorrect synonym for *H. longipes* f. *hypoglauca* Maekawa 1940 (*Kofuki Iwa Giboshi*).
HN: White-backed Rock Hosta.
JN: *Urajiro Iwa Giboshi* hort.
(see also *H. longipes* f. *hypoglauca*).

Figure 3-39. *H. longipes* 'Urajiro'; leaf detail showing white underside (Hosta Hill)

H. longipes 'Usuba' Maekawa 1950.
ウスバイワギボウシ

Usuba Iwa Giboshi is a formal Japanese synonym for *H. longipes* var. *caduca*, which see.

H. longipes var. *aequinoctiiantha* Fujita 1976a.
(see *H. aequinoctiiantha*).

H. longipes var. *caduca* Fujita 1976a.
AHS-IV/19A.   (Figure 3-40).
サイコクイワギボウシ

Saikoku Iwa Giboshi, the "Shikoku rock hosta," inhabits several mountainous areas of Kyushu. The name is puzzling because the type was found on Kyushu in Shiiba-mura, Miyazaki Prefecture, and wild populations occur principally on this island, while it is only rarely found in Kochi Prefecture on Shikoku. This taxon differs from *H. longipes* var. *vulgata* only

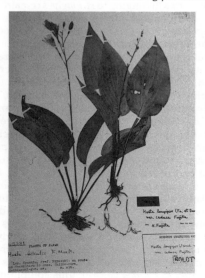

Figure 3-40. *H. longipes* var. *caduca*; holotype in KYO

in that the bracts, which are first densely imbricate, wither almost immediately, hence the epithet var. *caduca* (= wither). Except for this difference it is also very much like *H. longipes* but with leaves longer and narrower. Originally named *Usuba Iwa Giboshi*, the "slender-leaved rock hosta," by Maekawa, together with the invalid species name *H. leptophylla* nom. nudum—from *leptos* = slender and *phyllon* = leaf—but unexplained, the holotype does not show a distinctly slender leaf.
SY: *H. leptophylla* nom. nudum Maekawa 1950.
JN: *Saikoku Iwa Giboshi* Fujita 1976a sl.
Usuba Iwa Giboshi Maekawa 1950.

H. longipes var. *latifolia* Maekawa 1940.
AHS-III/13B.   (Plate 38).
アマギイワギボウシ
イズイワギボウシ

Amagi Iwa Giboshi, the "Amagi rock hosta," was named for its habitat on Mount Amagi on the Izu Peninsula. Similar to *H. rupifraga* it was first described by Maekawa in 1940. The species epithet means "broad-leaved." This taxon was combined by Fujita (1976a) with *H. rupifraga* under the new name *Izu Iwa Giboshi*, the "Izu rock hosta." But *H. rupifraga* is a species with a solitary allopatric colony on Hachijo Island and represents an evolved population which has adapted to a new environment. Several forms of *H. longipes* var. *latifolia* exist in the wild, some rather large, others variegated. *Maruba Iwa Giboshi*, the "round-leaved rock hosta," (a Japanese horticultural name), comes macromorphologically very close to *H. longipes* var. *latifolia*, has the characteristically wide, round leaf, but is smaller and lacks the purple dotting on the petioles and scapes. It may be an intergrading interspecific hybrid between *H. rupifraga* and *H. longipes* var. *latifolia*. A white-backed form is known as *Urajiro Hachijo Giboshi* and may be a form of *H. longipes* var. *latifolia* rather than *H. rupifraga*, as the Japanese name indicates.

Leaf 12.5–15 by 10–12.5 cm (5–6 by 4–5 in.), erect and in line with petiole, cordate, very round, orbicular, transition tight and contracting, very acuminate tip, undulate in the margin, smooth surface, dark green above, lighter green below. Venation 7–9, widely spaced, projected, smooth below. Scape 25–30 cm (10–12 in.), straight, but leaning, smooth, round, seagreen. Fertile bracts small, navicular, grooved, thin, membranous, white, tinted purple, withering, falling away during anthesis. Raceme 8–12 flowers, widely spaced. Flowers whitish, 4.5 by 3 cm (1.75 by 1.25 in.) across the lobes, carried horizontally on strong pedicels; perianth expanding, funnel-shaped, in the central part dilated bell-shaped, lobes spreading straightly to ±angled to the axis of perianth, stamens not superior. Anthers purple. August. Fertile.
SY: *H. longipes* var. *latifolia* Fujita 1976a pp.
HN: Round-leaved Rock Hosta.
JN: *Amagi Iwa Giboshi* Maekawa 1940.
Izu Iwa Giboshi Fujita 1976a.
Maruba Iwa Giboshi hort. pp sim.

H. longipes var. *latifolia* 'Amagi Nishiki' hort.
HN: *H. longipes* 'Amagi Nishiki' hort.
(see *H.* 'Amagi Nishiki').

H. longipes var. *latifolia* 'Izu' hort.
イズイワギボウシ

Izu Iwa Giboshi, the "Izu rock hosta," is a selected, named form of *H. longipes* var. *latifolia* found among the natural populations on Izu Hanto. This name was given by Fujita (1976a) as a Japanese formal name for *H. longipes* var. *latifolia*.

HN: *H. longipes* 'Izu' hort.
JN: *Izu Iwa Giboshi* Fujita 1976a.
(see also *H. longipes* var. *latifolia*).

H. longipes var. *latifolia* 'Maruba' hort.

マルバイワギボウシ   (Figure 3-41).
    Maruba Iwa Giboshi, the "round-leaved rock hosta," is a selected, rounded leaf form of *H. longipes* var. *latifolia* found among the natural populations.
HN: *H. longipes* 'Maruba' hort.
(see *H.* 'Maruba Iwa').
(see also *H. longipes* var. *latifolia*).

Figure 3-41. *H. longipes* var. *latifolia* 'Maruba'; general habit (Hosta Hill)

H. longipes var. *latifolia* 'Urajiro Hachijo' hort.
AHS-III/13B.

裏白八丈

    Urajiro Hachijo Giboshi, the "white-backed Hachijo hosta," is a horticultural name for a mutation found among the wild population. Its name notwithstanding, it is not a form of *H. rupifraga* but rather a white-backed form of *H. longipes* var. *latifolia*, which grows on the Izu Peninsula. Except for the "white back" this taxon is very similar to the latter.
    Plant size 50 cm (20 in.) dia., 23 cm (10 in.) high. Petioles 23 cm by 0.8 cm (9 by 0.3 in.), rigid, blunt on back, not keeled, purple-dotted full length. Leaf 12.5–15 by 10–12.5 cm (5–6 by 4–5 in.), erect and in line with petiole, leathery, cordate, transition open, undulate in the margin, smooth surface, light green above, lighter grey-green below, with a heavy coating of whitened bloom, tip acuminate. Venation 10–11, widely spaced, projected, glabrous below. Scape to 60 cm (24 in.) long, obliquely arching, smooth, round, sea-green, slightly pruinose, permanently purple-dotted full length. Sterile bracts 1–2; fertile bracts 2.5 cm by 0.8 cm (1 by 0.3 in.), navicular, thick in substance, whitish green, subtle darker stripes, remaining fresh until seeds are released. Raceme 20 cm (8 in.), evenly spaced flowers, 25–30 flowers. Flowers 4 cm (1.7 in.) long, 2 cm (0.8 in.) broad, purple inside, thin narrow tube, perianth expanding, lobes straightly spreading, bell-shaped, pedicels 1.2 cm (0.5 in.), abruptly nodding, stamens shorter than the perianth. Anthers evenly purple-spotted. August/September. Fertile.
JN: *Urajiro Hachijo Giboshi* hort.
     Urajiro Iwa Giboshi hort. pp.
(see also *H. longipes* var. *latifolia*).

H. longipes var. *longipes* Fujita 1976a.
    Fujita cited Maekawa's 1940 type (in TI) in synonymy with this taxon, which is represented by the holotype in P. According to the ICBN, the name *H. longipes* var. *longipes* must be assigned to and remain with the type of the name (in P). Under my classification Maekawa's type (in TI) represents a different phase of *H. longipes*, and I have described Maekawa's phenotype under the new varietal name *H. longipes* var. *vulgata*, which see. The description of the latter is based on Maekawa's 1940 diagnosis, while *H. longipes* var. *longipes* is described on the basis of the type in P.

H. longipes var. *longipes* (Franchet et Savatier) Matsumura 1894 (not Fujita).
    AHS-IV/19A.   (Figures 3-42, 3-43; Plates 39, 205).

イワギボウシ

    Iwa Giboshi, the "rock hosta," has large populations growing in central Honshu and ranging into Shikoku and Kyushu. Botanically known as *H. longipes* (var. *longipes*), it is a highly polymorphic species represented by many different forms, and it interbreeds with other species in the overlapping areas of habitat. This diversity clearly shows in the illustrations provided by Maekawa (cfr. 1940: photographs 60, 62, and 63, pp. 386 and 387), which show a form which approaches *H. longipes* var. *lancea* (Honda, 1935a), with narrower leaves which are decurrent to the petiole, and this diversity is reflected by Maekawa's type in TI and several other herbarium specimens. Populations of this distinct form are common. In a narrow sense, the holotype in P represents a relatively rare form of the species, as exemplified by Maekawa's photograph 61, (1940: 386), with slightly pruinose leaves, which are broadly cordate, fewer flowers, and shorter scapes approaching *H. longipes* f. *hypoglauca*.
    Discrete allopatric populations of each type exist, and to segregate them I have named a new variety to represent Maekawa's type (in TI), viz., *H. longipes* var. *vulgata* (*vulgata* = common, indicating its much more common and widespread occurrence). Thus, *H. longipes* var. *longipes*, according to ICBN rules, remains assigned to the type (in P; Figure 3-42), while *H. longipes* var. *vulgata* is attached to Maekawa's more common taxon as emended in Appendix A. The varietal epithet *longipes* had also seen use in *H. sieboldiana* var. *longipes* Matsumura, but not all taxa listed in its synonymy belong to *H. longipes* as exemplified by several specimens at K and TI.
    Fujita (1976a), under his very broad delimitation, combined many of the distinct taxa comprising the basic form, but this broad approach is not followed here. In the wild most of the different forms belonging to *H. longipes* remain small due to lithophytic and occasionally epiphytic habit but have been observed growing larger in deeper soil. Because of the many different forms belonging to this species, a detailed analysis of the distribution follows, and the main forms are illustrated under their individual descriptions to permit visual comparison.
    The primary habitats are Kanagawa, Saitama, Tochigi and Tokyo prefectures, the Kanto Plain, and Izu Hanto. In the mild climate of Izu Peninsula (Izu = Yu-Izu, "hot water spring") a broad-leaved form has evolved which is described as *H. longipes* var. *latifolia*, but even within this population differences exist. Around Mount Amagi (1407 m/4616 ft.) in the east central part of Izu Peninsula, Maekawa's *H. longipes* var. *latifolia* is found and referred to as *Amagi Iwa Giboshi*; another variant, locally called *Maruba Iwa Giboshi*, occurs further south and east on Izu and may represent intergrading hybrid swarms between the various forms of *H. longipes* var. *latifolia* and *H. rupifraga*, the *Hachijo Giboshi*. Apparently, the latter evolved in isolation on Hachijojima, the southernmost of the seven Izu islands. Fujita treated all the variants within this geographic area as *Izu Iwa Giboshi*, thus combining under his *H. longipes* var. *latifolia* all phases growing south of Fuji-san

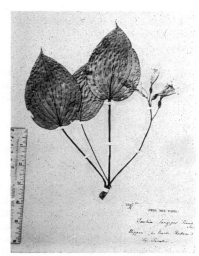

Figure 3-42. *H. longipes* var. *longipes*; holotype in P

(Mount Fuji) to the island of Hachijojima. I have combined only the taxa growing on Izu Peninsula proper into *H. longipes* var. *latifolia*, but treated *H. rupifraga* as a separate species following Maekawa (1940). The type upon which the name *H. longipes* is founded is in P, No. 1297. It was collected by Savatier on Mount Hakone and described by Franchet and Savatier in 1876. This mountain is located in the Hakone region, an area bounded on the north by Mount Fuji and on the south by Izu Peninsula. The entire area lies within the Fuji-Hakone-Izu National Park.

The Paris specimen, representing the populations of *H. longipes* var. *longipes* occurring in this general area, is a small pruinose form, with intense purple dotting on the petioles extending into the leaf base. The holotype approaches the morphology of Maekawa's *H. longipes* f. *hypoglauca* (*Kofuki Iwa Giboshi*) collected in the old province of Shimotsuke, now Tochigi Prefecture, at Fubasami, the eastern limit of distribution. From there *H. longipes* f. *hypoglauca* extends west and southwest to the Kanto and Fuji-Hakone areas, where the Paris specimen was collected, so this variety and the type are similar but differ moderately in flower morphology. Also in Tochigi, near Fubasami, the type for *H. longipes* f. *viridipes*, having green petioles without purple dotting, was found by Nakai and Maekawa.

West of Kanto *H. longipes* becomes more differentiated, and some of these local modifications are treated as species or varieties: *H. aequinoctiiantha* ranges from Gifu Prefecture in west-central Chubu District into the Kansai region, with the type collected by Kitamura at Yoro-mura in Gifu. Isolated allopatric populations occur outside this main habitat.

In the Tenryu River area of Aichi and Shizuoka prefectures, *H. longipes* has developed populations with lance-shaped leaves which typify *H. longipes* var. *lancea* (Honda, 1935a), *Hosoba Iwa Giboshi*. This form overlaps with the variant described by Maekawa (1940) as *H. longipes* (reclassified by me as *H. longipes* var. *vulgata*) into Kanagawa, Tokyo, and Saitama prefectures. Maekawa's 1940 type of *H. longipes* var. *vulgata* was collected at Tokura and occurs in parts of Kanto, Chubu, and Kansai districts. A very similar form has been observed growing in Shizuoka Prefecture, in the Tenryu River area. It is very sparsely flowered and indistinguishable from *H. sparsa*, so I have handled the latter as a forma under *H. longipes*, viz., *H. longipes* f. *sparsa*. The classification of *H. sparsa* in synonymy with *H.* 'Tardiflora' is incorrect, because the latter has yellow anthers, while *H. longipes* f. *sparsa* has purple anthers. Other

differentiating characteristics are given under the respective species names.

Further west Araki (1942) isolated distinct forms in northern Kansai district with specimens collected from populations in Hyogo and Kyoto prefectures. These are treated as the separate species *H. okamotoi* (*Okuyama Giboshi*) and *H. takiensis* (*Taki Giboshi*).

Fujita (1976a) described a new taxon as *H. longipes* var. *caduca*. It is representative of the form growing on Shikoku, known as *Saikoku Iwa Giboshi* and characterized by bracts which wither immediately after opening.

In Aichi and Shizuoka prefectures, along the open valleys of the Tenryu, Keta, and Osuzu rivers, allopatric populations growing on rocks and at waterfalls have evolved into white-backed forms *H. longipes* 'Urajiro', *Urajiro Iwa Giboshi*, or *Hachijo Urajiro Iwa Giboshi*, which grow near Mount Tamayama. In the same area the highly differentiated *H. hypoleuca*, *Urajiro Giboshi*, is handled as a species.

Other, even more-specialized forms grow beyond the normal habitat of central Honshu: *H. pycnophylla* grows on Oshima Island, Yamaguchi Prefecture; and *H. pulchella*, which grows on rock outcrops at elevation 1600 m (5250 ft.) in north-western Kyushu, Oita Prefecture, has previously been associated with section *Tardanthae*, although its early flowering casts doubt on this placement. It has more macro-morphological features in common with section *Picnolepis* so is included with the latter.

The epithet *longipes* means "long-stalked," but the exact morphological interpretation of this name in relation to this species is not known. The original *Funkia longipes* (Franchet et Savatier, 1876) had unusually long (±35 mm/1.5 in.) pedicels, so the epithet may have been chosen to indicate this. The name "stalk" is traditionally applied to the flower scape, but the type (in P) has short scapes, while most of the forms of this species have long scapes. Furthermore, stalk also sometimes implies "(leaf-)stalk," and since the species has very long petioles in most of its variants, this could also apply. The meaning "long-footed" has also been mentioned, implying long roots, but this connotation is in doubt because in the wild this taxon has a relatively compact root structure.

Although many plants are cultivated under the names *Hosta longipes* and *Iwa Giboshi* in Western gardens, they are frequently not this species and authentic forms are uncommon in cultivation.

Plant size 20–30 cm (8–12 in.) dia., 15–20 cm (6–8 in.) high. Petiole 10–30 by 0.4 cm (4–12 by 0.15 in.), erect, spreading, purple-dotted entire length, extending into leaf base. Leaf 10–13 by 5–7 cm (4–5 by 2–3 in.), erect and in line with petiole, cordate, transition tight and contracted, with generally flat surface, ±keeled, no waves in margin, not rugose, bright glaucous or

Figure 3-43. *H. longipes* var. *longipes*; detail of flower (Hosta Hill)

shiny green, acuminate tip. Venation 5–6, projected, smooth below. Scape 15–20 cm (6–8 in.), occasionally to 30 cm (12 in.) straight, but leaning, smooth, round, sea-green, slightly pruinose or shiny, permanently purple-dotted, very dark in lower half. Bracts small, navicular, grooved, thin, membranous, white, tinted purple, withering, falling away during anthesis. Raceme 8–12 flowers, widely spaced, sparse. Flowers whitish with purple field, 4.5 by 3 cm (1.75 by 1.25 in.) across the lobes, carried horizontally on strong pedicels; perianth expanding, funnel-shaped, lobes spreading lily-shaped; stamens very superior, surpassing the lobes. Anthers purple. August/September. Fertile.

SY: *Funkia longipes* Franchet et Savatier 1876.
     Hosta longipes Bailey 1930 pp(?).
     H. longipes var. *longipes* (not Fujita 1976a).
     H. sieboldiana var. *longipes* Matsumura 1905 pp.
HN: *H.* 'Tardiflora Minor' hort. incorrect pp sim.

H. longipes var. *vulgata* W. G. Schmid et G. S. Daniels var. nov. (in the sense of Maekawa 1940).

AHS-IV/19B.   (Figure 6-5; Plates 40, 170).

イワギボシ

Iwa Giboshi, the "rock hosta," has a common type which was described by Maekawa (1940) but is unfortunately very different from the holotype *Funkia longipes* (Franchet et Savatier, 1876; No. 1297 in P) which represents a specialized population. *Hosta longipes* var. *vulgata* is a new name for the common *H. longipes* described by Maekawa (1940) (type in TI), a highly polymorphic taxon represented by many different forms and interbreeding with other species in the fringe areas of its habitat. White-backed, yellow, yellow dwarf, and variegated forms exist. Gardeners should be aware that there are many forms of this species and not all have been described, so considerable variation should be expected in plants collected in the wild. The typical species has intensely purple-dotted petioles and scapes and is popular in Japan where it is widely cultivated. Even though plants are cultivated under the names *H. longipes* and *Iwa Giboshi* in Western gardens, they are frequently not this species so in its authentic form it is still uncommon.

Plant size 35–45 cm (14–18 in.) dia., 20 cm (8 in.) high. Rootstock normal rhizomatous, under lithophytic and epiphytic conditions shallow and clinging tenaciously to rock and bark. Petiole 14–15 by 0.5 cm (5–6 by 0.2 in.), spreading horizontally, light green, purple-dotted entire length. Leaf 12–14 by 8–9.5 cm (5–6 by 3–4 in.), elliptical, ovate-elliptical, sometimes approaching cordate to round, truncate at the base, with generally flat surface, but undulate, wavy at the margin, erect, almost straight ±arching midrib, shiny dark green above, glossy lighter green below, cuspidate, acuminate tip. Venation 7–8, projected, smooth below. Scape 20–30 cm (8–12 in.), mostly oblique, in some epiphytic specimens bending to horizontal or subhorizontal, smooth, round, green, permanently purple-dotted, more densely in lower half. Fertile bracts navicular, grooved, thin, membranous, white, tinted purple, withering, but not falling away during anthesis and nearly equal in size to the 1 cm long, erect, spreading pedicels. Raceme short 10–15 cm (4–6 in.), 20–40 flowers. Flowers whitish purple to purple, 4.5 by 2.5 cm (1.75 by 1.25 in.) across the lobes, carried horizontally on strong pedicels; perianth expanding, funnel-shaped, in the central part dilated bell-shaped, lobes spreading

straightly to ±angled to the axis of perianth; stamens superior, surpassing the lobes. September. Fertile.

SY: *H. longipes* Maekawa 1937.
     H. longipes Maekawa 1940.
     H. longipes var. *lancea* Honda 1935a pp.
     H. longipes var. *longipes* Fujita 1976a incorrect.
HN: *H.* 'Tardiflora Minor' hort. incorrect pp sim.
     Purplebracted Plantain Lily.
JN: *Hosoba Iwa Giboshi* hort. pp.
     Iwa Giboshi Iwasaki 1874.

H. longissima Honda 1935a var. *longissima*.

AHS-IV/19B.   (Plate 41).

ミズギボウシ

Mizu Giboshi, the "swamp hosta," grows in Aichi, Gifu, and Shizuoka prefectures of central Honshu. It is a polymorphic species which is represented by differentiated forms in central and western Honshu, Shikoku, and Kyushu with the area around Hamamatsu City in Shizuoka reportedly being the eastern limit of distribution. Like *H. sieboldii*, to which it is broadly related, it inhabits open, grassy swampland and wet places receiving considerable direct sun in spring before grasses, weeds, and subshrubs emerge and provide cover for the leaf mound. The type has a linear-lanceolate leaf form, gradually narrowed at the base of the petiole, but with the petiole distinguishable. The forms with true, linear strap-leaves and no discernable petiole transition are described under *H. longissima* var. *longifolia*, which see. Many variegated and unusual forms have been isolated and named. This taxon was not named until 1937, but the Japanese name dates to Iinuma (1856, 1874). Von Siebold brought live specimens from Japan in 1829 assigning the name *Funkia lanceolata* which is the classic *Hosta longissima* as represented by herbarium specimen No. 908/106 1023 in L. Maekawa's *H. longissima* var. *brevifolia* is included here because according to herbarium sheets (in BH, L, MAK and TI) and Maekawa's descriptions there is no macromorphological difference between it and the species. Thus it is treated as a synonym under *H. longissima*. Hylander (1954) pointed this out, and Fujita (1976a) supported this synonymy. The strap-leafed form is treated as a variety of the species, that is *H. longissima* var. *longifolia*, following Honda (1930, 1935a). It is important to note that some variants of *Koba Giboshi*, *H. sieboldii*, have very elongated leaves and are often mistaken for *H. longissima*, a mistake reflected in herbarium material (in BH, MAK), but their leaves have less substance and their flowers have yellow anthers, while *H. longissima* has purple anthers. These narrow-leaved forms are *H. sieboldii* f. *angustifolia*, which see. (See also "The Identities of *H. longissima*" under Maekawa in Appendix B.)

Plant size 25 cm (9 in.) dia., 15 cm (6 in.) high. Petiole in most representatives is not measurable because the leaf narrows steadily and a petiole transition is not discernable. Leaf 16–20 by 1.5–2.5 cm (6–8 by 0.5–1 in.), erect, vase-shaped arrangement, green with no purple dots at the base, and in line with petiole, linear to linear-lanceolate, very attenuate, gradually narrowing into petiole with no discernable transition between petiole and leaf, some forms very linear strap-leaf, very flat surface, not rugose, surface dull, underside shiny, dark green above, acuminate tip. Venation 3, lightly impressed above, projected, smooth below. Scape 35–55 cm (14–22 in.), straight and erect, not bending, light green, no purple marks. Sterile bracts 2–3, clasping stem, persistent; fertile bracts short, navicular, thin, membranous, green, withering at anthesis, but not falling away. Raceme long, 4–8 flowers, widely spaced. Flowers 4 cm (1.5 in.) long by 3 cm (1.25 in.) across the lobes, carried horizontally on strong pedicels, purple-striped, thin narrow tube, perianth expanding, lily-shaped, lobes spreading rapidly, recurving, wide open, short pedicels, long projecting stamens. Anthers purple. August. Fertile.

SY: *Funkia lanceolata* Siebold 1844 nom. nudum.
Funkia lancifolia ε angustifolia Regel 1876 pp.
Funkia ovata var. *lancifolia* Miquel 1869 pp as described only and without the synonyms.
Hosta japonica var. *angustifolia* Ascherson and Gräbner 1905 pp.
H. japonica var. *angustifolia* Makino in Iinuma.
Hosta lancifolia var. *angustifolia* Koidzumi 1936 pp.
H. longissima var. *brevifolia* Maekawa 1940.

HN: *Funkia lanceolata* Manning 1897 (cat.).
Hosta lanceolata hort. incorrect.
H. lancifolia var. *angustifolia* hort. incorrect.
Narrowleaf Plantain Lily.

JN: *Mizu Giboshi* Iinuma 1874.
Saji Giboshi Iinuma 1874 pp.

ON: Langblattfunkie (German) Hansen et al. 1964.
Schmalblattfunkie (German) Hansen et al. 1964 pp.

H. longissima 'Fukurin' hort.
覆輪ミズギボウシ
Fukurin Mizu Giboshi, the "margined swamp hosta," is generally applied to all margined forms of the species from which several have been selected and named.
JN: *Fukurin Mizu Giboshi* hort.

H. longissima 'Hanazawa' hort.
ハナザワミズギボウシ
Hanazawa Mizu Giboshi, the "Hanazawa swamp hosta," is a white-margined form of the species found in the wild in Shimoyama. It is also called *Hanazawa Fukurin Giboshi* hort.
JN: *Fukurin Mizu Giboshi* hort.
Hanazawa Fukurin Giboshi hort.
Hanazawa Mizu Giboshi hort.
(see also *H.* 'Hanazawa Fukurin').

H. longissima 'Hosoba' hort.
ホソバミズギボウシ
Hosoba Mizu Giboshi is a Japanese synonym for *H. longissima* var. *longifolia*, which see.
JN: *Hosoba Mizu Giboshi* hort.

H. longissima 'Isshiki Fukurin' hort.
イッシキミズギボウシ
Isshiki Mizu Giboshi, the "Isshiki swamp hosta," is a yellow-margined form of the species found in the wild in Nukata. It is also called *Isshiki Fukurin Giboshi* hort.
JN: *Isshiki Fukurin Giboshi* hort.
Isshiki Mizu Giboshi hort.
Kifukurin Mizu Giboshi hort. pp sim.
(see also *H. longissima* 'Kifukurin').

H. longissima 'Kifukurin' hort.
黄覆輪ミズギボウシ
Kifukurin Mizu Giboshi, the "yellow-margined swamp hosta," is a yellow-margined form of the species found in the wild in Nukata. It is also called *Isshiki Fukurin Giboshi*.
JN: *Isshiki Fukurin Giboshi* hort.
Isshiki Mizu Giboshi hort.
Kifukurin Mizu Giboshi hort. pp sim.
(see also *H.* 'Isshiki Fukurin').

H. longissima 'Kikeika' hort.
キケイカミズギボウシ
Kikeika Mizu Giboshi, the "deformed flower swamp hosta," is a form with deformed and joined lobes and, occasionally, petaloid stamens. It is found in Nukata District. A nonperpetuating mutant, so maintained as a cultivar form.
JN: *Kikeika Mizu Giboshi* hort.

H. longissima 'Nikazaki' hort.
ニカザキミズギボウシ
Nikazaki Giboshi, the "double-flowered (swamp) hosta," is a double-flowered form found in Tsukude. A nonperpetuating mutant, so maintained as a cultivar form.
JN: *Nikazaki Giboshi* hort. pp sim.

H. longissima 'Shirobana' hort.
白花ミズギボウシ
Shirobana Mizu Giboshi, the "white-flowered swamp hosta," is a white-flowered form found in Nukata. A nonperpetuating mutant, so maintained as a cultivar form.
JN: *Shirobana Mizu Giboshi* hort. pp sim.

H. longissima 'Sotoyama Fukurin' hort.
Sotoyama Fukurin Giboshi, the "variegated Sotoyama (swamp) hosta," is a selected and named form broadly belonging to the *Fukurin Mizu Giboshi* group of margined cultivars.
JN: *Sotoyama Fukurin Giboshi* hort.
Fukurin Mizu Giboshi hort. pp sim.
(see also *H.* 'Sotoyama Fukurin').

H. longissima var. *brevifolia* Maekawa 1940.
AHS-IV/19B.
ミズギボウシ
The varietal epithet means "short-leaved." This taxon is now held to be identical to Maekawa's type (Maekawa, 1940). Herbarium specimens (in BH, L, MAK, and TI) corroborate that this variety and the species conform to the "short-leaf" diagnosis, while the long-leaf, strap-leaf form, in Japan *Nagaba Mizu Giboshi*, is a special form I have segregated as *H. longissima* var. *longifolia*, which see. *Hosta longissima* var. *brevifolia* is here considered synonymous with the species.
(see *H. longissima*).

H. longissima var. *longifolia* (Honda) W. G. Schmid var. nov.
ナガバミズギボウシ   (Figure 2-12).
Hosoba Mizu Giboshi, "the strap-leaved swamp hosta," or *Nagaba Mizu Giboshi*, the "long-leaved swamp hosta," is endemic in Aichi and Gifu prefectures. Although the Japanese formal name was included by Maekawa (1940), his description does not match the morphology of this variant. To permit separate taxonomic treatment of this very distinct taxon it is included as a new variety, *H. longissima* var. *longifolia*, using *H. japonica* var. *longifolia* Honda (1930) as the type and basionym. This type has true strap leaves with no discernable petiole or petiole transition, and has small flowers and long, thin scapes. It is a very distinct taxon with little representation in herbaria, but some specimens attributable to this variety and the type are in TI.

Plant size 20 cm (8 in.) dia., 20 cm (8 in.) high. Petiole not measurable because leaves have linear, strap shape. Plant erect, vase-shaped, green with no purple dots at the base. Leaf 10–20 by 0.8–1.2 cm (4–8 by 0.3–0.5 in.), erect, flat surface, not rugose, surface dull, underside shiny, dark green above. Venation 2-3, lightly impressed above, projected, smooth below. Scape 35–65 cm (14–26 in.), straight and erect, not bending, light green, no purple marks, except at base. Sterile bracts 2–4, clasping stem, persistent; fertile bracts short, navicular, thin, membranous, green, withering at anthesis, but not falling away. Raceme long, 4–6 flowers, widely spaced, few. Flowers small, striped purple, thin narrow tube, perianth expanding, lily-shaped, lobes spreading rapidly, recurving, wide open, short pedicels, long projecting stamen. Anthers purple. August. Fertile.

SY: *H. japonica* var. *longifolia* Honda 1930.
       H. lancifolia var. *angustifolia* hort. incorrect.
       H. lancifolia var. *angustifolia* Koidzumi 1936 pp.
       H. lancifolia var. *longifolia* Honda 1935a pp.
JN: *Hosoba Mizu Giboshi* hort.
       Mizu Giboshi Iinuma 1874 pp.
       Nagaba Mizu Giboshi Honda 1935a pp.

H. longissima var. *longifolia* 'Kifukurin' hort.
黄覆輪ナガバミズギボウシ
アサヒ黄覆輪ギボウシ

Kifukurin Nagaba Mizu Giboshi, the "yellow-margined, narrow-leaved swamp hosta," is a yellow-margined form of the species with very narrow leaves found in the wild. It is named and registered as *H.* 'Asahi Sunray' Kato/Zumbar IRA/1984. It is also called *Fukurin Giboshi* hort.
JN: *Asahi Kifukurin Giboshi* hort.
       Kifukurin Mizu Giboshi hort. pp sim.
       Kifukurin Nagaba Mizu Giboshi hort.
(see *H.* 'Asahi Sunray' Kato/Zumbar IRA/1984).

H. longissima var. *longifolia* 'Kinakafu' hort.
Kinakafu Nagaba Mizu Giboshi, the "mediovariegated narrow-leaved swamp hosta," is a yellow mediovariegated form of the species with very narrow leaves found in the wild.
JN: *Kinakafu Nagaba Mizu Giboshi* hort.

H. longissima var. *longifolia* 'Shirofukurin' hort.
白覆輪ナガバミズギボウシ
アサヒ白覆輪ギボウシ

Shirofukurin Nagaba Mizu Giboshi, the "white-margined, narrow-leaved swamp hosta," is a white-margined form of the species with very narrow leaves found in the wild. It is named and registered as *H.* 'Asahi Comet' Kato/Zumbar IRA/1984. It is also sometimes called *Fukurin Giboshi* hort.
HN: *H. longissima aureomacrantha* hort. incorrect.
JN: *Asahi Shirofukurin Giboshi* hort.
       Shirofukurin Nagaba Mizu Giboshi hort.
(see *H.* 'Asahi Comet' Kato/Zumbar IRA/1984).

M

H. minor Nakai 1911.
AHS-V/25A.   (Figures 3-44, 3-45; Plate 42).
ケイリンギボウシ

Keirin Giboshi, the "Korean hosta," evolved along the southern and eastern coast of Korea in the provinces of Chollanam-do, Kyongsangnam-do, Kyongsangbuk-do, and extending through the T'aebaek-sanmaek region to Kangwon-do. It is also reported on Cheju Do (Quelpaert Island) and the type was collected in Kangwon-do (Kogen) on Mount Sorak. It is also found in the Lushan Mountains, Jiangxi Province, China, and in Japan, on Kyushu, Nagasaki Prefecture. These removed populations are undoubtedly escaped transplants from cultivation, an opinion which Fujita (1976a) confirmed (at least for Japan) when he did not include *H. minor* as a Japanese native species in spite of its occurrence there.

Figure 3-44. *H. minor*; scape detail showing pointed bud and ridges (Hosta Hill)

This species is highly variable in the wild and has white-flowered and white-margined forms. It is characterized by lamellar ridges on the scape, a definite identifier for section *Lamellatae*. Most of the taxa cultivated in North America and Europe under the specific name *H. minor* do have the ridges on the scape, but are much smaller and have 3–4 pairs of principal veins with a shiny, deep green leaf color. Thus, they are not the species but are either *H. nakaiana* forms or representatives of intergrading hybrid swarms formed by members of section *Lamellatae*, including the true *H. minor*, with other species.

There are also many plants in cultivation under the name *H. minor* which lack the ridges on the scape and as a consequence are not *H. minor*. Recent accessions of the natural populations of *H. minor* in Korea (Chung, 1988) are illustrated (Plate 42) to allow comparison with the true form conforming to Nakai's description and showing a larger leaf with 5–6 pairs of veins and a light green leaf color that has a metallic grey sheen. The true form is quite different from the garden forms in commerce which are purported to be this species although they are only hybridized forms. Authentic specimens of *H. minor* are in scientific collections but seldom seen in gardens. I obtained 17 specimens under the name *H. minor* from various private sources and specialty nurseries allover North America and found that none were representative of the natural populations as accessed by M. G. Chung in 1988.

The North American cultivated population did not originate in Korea but in Japan; Craig obtained a specimen from commercial Japanese sources and sent it under the name *H. numor* nom. nudum to Davidson in 1962 who in turn assigned it cultivar No. 70. According to Davidson it was also incorrectly named *H. nimor* (Davidson, 1990). These imported specimens might have been the true species, which has since been hybridized, or they could have been hybridized material to begin with. In any case, the material is of uncertain lineage which does not match field-collected Korean voucher specimens (M. G. Chung, 1988). In its authentic form it is a good species for the rock garden, and in Japan it is used for pot culture. In the warm climate of Georgia, USA, it appears early in the spring; it does not hold well into the fall period as the leaves disappear long before the first freeze. (For further comments on *H. minor* see *H. nakaiana* and, in Appendix A—Part 1, "The Korean Species.")

Plant size to 16–20 cm (6–8 in.) dia., 12 cm (5 in.) high. Rootstock obliquely creeping. Petiole 5–10 by 0.4 cm (2–4 by 0.135 in.), forming a dome-shaped plant, slender, narrowly open. Leaf 8–10 by 6–8 cm (3–4 by 2.5–3 in.), ovate-cordate, transition tight and contracting, acuminate tip, interior leaf flattish, barely wavy, not pruinose, surface yellowish green with metallic sheen, below, light green, shiny; texture papery. Venation 5–6, not much sunken above, projected, smooth below. Scape 35–45 cm (14–18 in.), distinct lamellar ridges parallel or slightly spiral to scape axis, straight, erect, perpendicular. Sterile bracts 2–3 below raceme, withering by anthesis; fertile bracts navicular, grooved, thick, green or whitish green, ascending, imbricated even during flowering and nearly equal in size, developed unopened flower head spicate. Raceme 15 cm (8 in.), 8–12 flowers. Flowers 4.5–5 cm (2 in.) long, 2.5 cm (1 in.) broad, held erect in ±horizontal position on strong pedicels, dark veins on a lighter colored background; perianth pale purple-violet, expanding, funnel-shaped, in the central part dilated bell-shaped, lobes ±angled to the axis, stamens exerted. Anthers evenly purple-dotted on yellow background. Looks purple. July, reblooms. Fertile.

SY: *Funkia ovata* var. *minor* Baker 1870.
HN: *Funkia ovata minor* hort. incorrect.
      Hosta 'Krossa No. K-1' PI 318546/Summers No. 151 pp.
      H. 'Nakaimo Minor' hort. incorrect.
      H. nakaimo minor hort. incorrect.
      H. nimor hort. incorrect.
      H. numor hort. (Davidson No. 70) incorrect.
      H. ventricosa 'Minor' hort. incorrect.
      H. ventricosa 'Nana' hort. incorrect.
      Korean Dwarf Hosta.
JN: *Keirin Giboshi* Maekawa 1937.
      Ko Giboshi Maekawa 1940 pp na.

Figure 3-45. *H. minor;* detail of seed pod (Hosta Hill)

H. minor Goldbrook form hort.

An interspecific hybrid of the species shown by Goldbrook Nursery (UK), having shiny, green, wavy leaves and scapes with ridges. Broadly related to *H. minor*, it is not that species but probably an interspecific hybrid with another member of section *Lamellatae*, most likely *H. nakaiana* or *H. capitata*.

✠ "*H. minor* f. *alba*" Maekawa 1940.
AHS-V/25A 1940.
Here reduced to cultivar form as *H. minor* 'Alba'.
白花ケイリンギボウシ
Shirobana Keirin Giboshi, the "white-flowered Korean hosta," is a mutant form of the species with white flowers. Two horticultural names written incorrectly in latinate form as "*H. minor* var. *alba*" (hort) or "*H. minor alba*" (hort) have been used for many years incorrectly for the white-flowered *H. sieboldii* 'Alba' which is a different taxon without ridges on the scape

and with yellow anthers and more lanceolate leaves. The white-flowered form of *H. minor* has purple anthers and ridges on the scape. In the wild it occurs as a seldom-seen, non-perpetuating mutation, so is treated as a cultivar. I have not seen it in cultivation.

SY: *H. longipes* var. *alba* Nakai 1918.
HN: *H. albomarginata alba* hort. incorrect.
      H. minor alba hort. (not *H. sieboldii* 'Alba').
      H. minor 'Alba' hort. (not *H. sieboldii* 'Alba').
      White-flowered Korean Dwarf Hosta.
JN: *Shirobana Keirin Giboshi* Maekawa 1940.

H. miquelii Moldenke 1936.
Published with respect to a new name for *H. latifolia* in the sense of Matsumura 1905.
(see *H. ventricosa*).

H. mira Maekawa 1934.
(see *H. sieboldiana* var. *mira*).

H. montana Maekawa 1940.
AHS-II/7A.   (Figures 2-22, 2-36, 3-46, F-3, F-6; Plates 43, 44, 194).
オオバギボウシ
Oba Giboshi, the "large-leaved hosta," grows in central and northern Honshu and southern Hokkaido in mountain valleys along forest margins. It is one of the most prevalent hostas in Japan with its type (in TI) based on a cultivated specimen from a population collected by Maekawa near Lake Yamanaka (Fuji-Goko) in Yamanashi Prefecture. The name *Oba Giboshi* originated with Iinuma in 1874, and horticulturally it embraces a number of broadly related, but different taxa in Japan. This classification originated with Fujita 1976a, who very broadly applied this name to all species falling within the *Oba Giboshi* (*H. montana*) and *H. sieboldiana* complexes in section *Helipteroides*. This arrangement brings together under one name all the taxa broadly related to *H. sieboldiana, H. montana,* and *H.* 'Elata', including *H. nigrescens, H. fluctuans,* and *H.* 'Tokudama', and, if accepted, would cause endless confusion, so is not adopted here.

Under my classification *H. montana* is treated in the narrower sense as proposed by Maekawa (1940) but with most of the listed varieties and forms reduced to cultivar forms. *Hosta montana* is a very variable species displaying many forms with distinctly different leaf shapes and variegations. Many of the wild populations have flat leaves, but forms in Asuke-cho, Aichi Prefecture, have "piecrust" margins (Figure 2-22), and others seen further north have wavy leaves and approach the morphology of *H. fluctuans*. Variegation color ranges from white to yellow, and there are viridescent and lutescent examples which include margined and medio variegated forms along with streaked, spotted, and clouded variants. Many of these mutations have been found among the wild populations of the species and have been isolated and named.

Forms with verticillately grouped flowers occur in the wild as well as forms with true hose-in-hose flowers (Plate 45; see *H. montana* 'Yae'). I have also observed true double flowers with double the number of tepals, pistils, and stamens (Figure 3-46). White-backed and branched-scape forms also occur, with the latter named informally *H. montana ramosa* Satomi (1957?) but I have not found validation of this name. Most of these mutants do not perpetuate in the wild so are considered cultivar forms.

The European hybrid *H.* 'Elata' (with yellow anthers) is frequently compared to *H. montana* (with purple anthers), but

Figure 3-46. *H. montana*; double flower, detail showing 12 tepals, 2 pistils, and 12 anthers (Hosta Hill)

the two are not synonymous. Because of the great variability of *H. montana* in the wild, selected clones brought into cultivation often look quite different, but they all fall within the general limits of the following diagnosis. Correct identification of cultivated material is sometimes difficult because, aside from natural variability, a number of putative hybrids are cultivated under the species name. Very large-leaved hostas have been identified with *H. montana*, but they are probably interspecific hybrids (with *H. sieboldiana*).

Plant size 40–100 cm (16–40 in.) dia., 35–55 cm (14–22 in.) high. Petiole 25–40 by 1.2 cm (10–16 by 0.5 in.), ascending in an arch, forming a large dome-shaped plant, slightly winged, deeply grooved, dull dark green. Leaf 20–25 by 12.5–17.5 cm (8–10 by 5–7 in.), leaf attitude at petiole arcuate spreading, very contracted, broadly ovate, oblong-ovate, or ovate-cordate, generally flat surface, open, margin with slight or no waves, surface neither undulate nor rugose, acuminate tip, sometimes twisted and turned under, surface with matte sheen or shiny deep green, dull green below. Venation 10–14, mostly 12, sunken above, very projected, strigose below. Scape exceeding height of plant, 90–110 cm (36–44 in.), 2–3 isolated fertile bracts widely spaced along scape away from raceme, straight, erect, solid, terete, matte green (virescent), lightly purple-spotted at base. Fertile bracts large, flat and broad, thick and fleshy, very whitish green, tinged purple, developing and opening in a stellar form as seen from above, withering, but persisting long after anthesis. Raceme 25–35 cm (10–14 in.), 15–30 flowers, compactly clustered. Flowers 5 cm (2 in.) long, 3 cm (1.25 in.) broad, mostly white to white very lightly purple-suffused; perianth expanding, funnel-shaped, in the central part dilated bell-shaped, lobes spreading straightly to ±angled to the axis of perianth; stamens superior, surpassing the perianth. Anthers purple dotted on yellow background, looks purple. June/July. Fertile.

SY: *Funkia sieboldi* Lindley 1839 pp.
      Funkia sinensis Miquel 1869 pp.
      Hosta cucullata Koidzumi 1936 pp.
      H. fortunei Maekawa 1938a incorrect.
      H. sieboldiana Makino 1910 pp.

H. sieboldiana var. *sieboldiana* Fujita 1976a sl na.
HN: *H. elata* hort. incorrect.
      H. 'Elata' hort. incorrect.
      H. fortunei 'Gigantea' hort. incorrect.
      H. 'Krossa No. B-1' pp sim hybr.
      H. 'Krossa No. B-2' pp sim.
      H. 'Krossa No. B-3' hort. (= *H. montana* f. *macrophylla*).
      H. 'Krossa No. X-3' pp.
      H. 'Krossa No. X-5' pp.
      H. montana 'Mount Tsukuba'.
      H. montana ramosa nom. nudum Satomi (1957) (?).
      H. sieboldiana gigantea hort. pp.
      H. sieboldiana hort. incorrect.
JN: *Oba Giboshi* Iinuma 1874.

H. montana 'Aureomarginata'.

The cultivar name registered for show purposes (in modified form) as *H. montana* 'Aureo-marginata' AHS-NC IRA/1987 for *H. montana* f. *aureomarginata*, which see.

H. montana 'Chirifu' hort.

散斑オオバギボウシ

Chirifu Oba Giboshi, also sometimes simply called *Chirifu*, an "overall variegated" hosta, is a natural mutation which occurs in Gumma, Tokyo, and Shizuoka prefectures. Recently a slightly different form from Tochigi Prefecture has been brought to the United States by Hideko Gowen. All are large *H. montana* forms with whitish or yellow variegation ranging from mottling to streaking. The form observed in North America will grow to the size of *H. montana* f. *macrophylla*, which see. These cultivars have good horticultural potential, and the large funnel-shaped flowers are excellent.
(see also *H.* 'Chirifu').

✠ "*H. montana* f. *aureomarginata*" Maekawa 1940.
      AHS-II/10A.   (Plate 45).
Here reduced to cultivar form as *H. montana* 'Aureo-marginata'.

キフクリンオオバギボウシ

Kifukurin Oba Giboshi, the "yellow-margined, large-leaved hosta," was first described by Makino as a variety of *H. sieboldiana* in 1928. Wild plants are found in central Honshu and probably occur occasionally within the entire range occupied by the standard form. The type was found as a non-perpetuating mutant in Tokyo Prefecture, at the foot of Mount Takao, near Hachioji city. This is the only variegated form of *H. montana* with a valid botanical description, although many other variegated sports have appeared naturally among the wild populations with a number of them collected and named.

All the aureomarginata forms of this species are here considered an assembly of similar plants informally called the *H. montana* Aureomarginata group. It has the typical cordate leaves of the species, with a few more undulations in the margin. It is ribbed with deeply sunken veins but otherwise not rugose. Young plants have a very elongated leaf, and it takes several years for the characteristic cordate leaf shape to develop. The irregular yellow margin has occasional streaks which extend towards the midrib. Margin turns whitish with approaching anthesis. This is a robust form growing nearly as large as the species. It is one of the first hostas to sprout in spring, so it is subject to damage by late frosts and the emerging sprouts need protection. During hot, dry summers the leaves have a tendency to burn out; this taxon goes heat-dormant before any other hosta, especially when grown in direct sun. Sometimes in early fall, second flushes of summer leaves emerge with an occasional reblooming scape. Occasionally, double-flowered forms occur, but these mutations require more study to test their stability. This large variegated hosta is very popular in the United States where it is widely cultivated. In 1985 it was selected as the AHS Alex J. Summers Distinguished Merit Hosta by Warren I. Pollock.

Plant size 40–90 cm (16–36 in.) dia., 35–50 cm (14–20 in.) high. Petiole 25–35 by 1.2 cm (10–14 by 0.5 in.), ascending in an arch, deeply grooved, slightly pruinose, fading, dull grass-green, with yellow, variegated, petiole marginal wings extending from leaf margin to crown. Leaf 20–25 by 12.5–17.5 cm (8–10 by 5–7 in.), leaf attitude at petiole arcuate spreading, very contracted, broadly ovate, oblong-ovate, ovate-cordate, ribbed, but generally flat surface, open, margin with slight waves but not undulate, not rugose but furrowed, acuminate twisted tip turned under, surface with matte sheen or shiny deep green, dull green below, broad, irregular golden yellow margin, with streaks running to the leaf midrib and extending into petiole. Anthers purple dotted on yellow background, looks purple. June/July. Fertile.

SY: *H. sieboldiana* var. *aureomarginata* Makino 1928.
HN: *H. elata aureomarginata* Kitchingman 1984 nom. nudum incorrect.
H. montana 'Aureo-marginata' AHS IRA/1987.
H. montana Aureomarginata group sl.
H. montana var. *aureomarginata* hort.
H. montana variegata hort. incorrect.
H. sieboldiana var. *glauca variegata* hort. incorrect.
JN: *Kifukurin Oba Giboshi* Maekawa 1940.
Kifukurin To Giboshi Makino 1928 pp.
Ogon Fukurin Oba Giboshi hort. pp sim.

H. montana f. *macrophylla* W. G. Schmid f. nov.

AHS-I/1B. (Figures 2-23, 3-47; Plate 46).

This taxon is grown under the cultivar name *H. montana* 'Praeflorens', which is technically incorrect (see *H. montana* var. *praeflorens*) but widely used in North America and Europe. To avoid confusion and the use of an incorrect name, a new forma has been named: *H. montana* f. *macrophylla*. One of the largest hostas cultivated in North America, it has a number of other cultivar names. It originated with the importations of Krossa coming from Osaka University in the early 1950s (see Chapter 5) and occurs in west-central Honshu, Kyoto, Hyogo, and Nara prefectures. It flowers earlier than *H. montana* and is unique not only for its unusual size, which can exceed 150 cm (60 in.) dia., and 90 cm (36 in.) high, but also for its lasting, fertile bracts, which roll under (Figure 3-47). It grows much faster than *H. sieboldiana* and can substitute for it where a large green specimen plant is required. This taxon breeds relatively true when carefully selfed. A number of cultivar names have been given to F$_1$ hybrids; they are listed later. There are some minor differences in these named hybrids, but all look very similar. Although this hosta is considered a true *H. montana*, its veining count and anther color indicates it may be an interspecific, intergrading hybrid between *H. montana* and a *H. sieboldiana* form. Some cultivars, such as *H.* 'Green Acres', look very similar and may be closely related to this taxon. Although given the horticultural cultivar name *H. montana* 'Praeflorens', this taxon has nothing to do with the botanical variety *H. montana* var. *praeflorens* described by Maekawa (1940).

Plant size 100–135 cm (40–54 in.) dia., 60–80 cm (24–32 in.) high. Petiole 50–60 by 1.2 cm (20–24 by 0.5 in.), stiffly erect, forming a large, dome-shaped plant, slightly winged, deeply grooved, dull dark green. Leaf 40–45 by 25–30 cm (16–18 by 10–12 in.), leaf attitude at petiole at right angles, spreading, very contracted at base, broadly ovate-cordate, deeply ribbed surface created by sunken veins, acuminate tip, surface deep matte green, duller green below. Venation 14–18, very sunken above, very projected, strigose below. Scape 90–110 cm (36–44 in.), 2–3 isolated fertile bracts widely spaced along scape away from raceme, straight, erect, solid, terete, matte green (virescent), lightly purple-spotted at base. Sterile bracts 2–3 below raceme, large, fleshy; fertile bracts flat and broad, thick and fleshy, very whitish green, tinged purple, developing and opening in a stellar form as seen from above, persisting long after anthesis, with the lower bracts in the raceme rolling under in circular fashion (Figure 3-47). Raceme 25–35 cm (10–14 in.), 15–30 flowers, spread evenly. Flowers 5 cm (2 in.) long, 3 cm (1.25 in.) broad, white; perianth expanding, funnel-shaped, in the central part dilated bell-shaped, lobes spreading straightly to ±angled to the axis of perianth; stamens superior, exceeding the perianth. Anthers yellow background with very pale purple dotting, appearing yellow. June. Fertile.

HN: *H.* 'Krossa No. B-3'.
H. montana 'Praeflorenz' Klose 1982 (cat.).
The following cultivar names have been given to horticultural forms very similar or identical to this taxon:
H. montana 'Praeflorens' hort.
H. 'Green Acres' pp.
H. 'King Michael' pp.
H. 'Mikado'.

Figure 3-47. *H. montana* f. *macrophylla*; revolute, rolled-under bracts with seed pods, type (Hosta Hill)

H. montana f. *ovatolancifolia* (Araki) W. G. Schmid comb. nov.

AHS-III/13B. (Figure 3-48).

ナガレギボウシ

Nagare Giboshi was collected in west-central Honshu, Kyoto, and Hyogo prefectures and is represented by several specimens in KYO. The holotype (In KYO, No. 15862; Y. Araki) was collected in Kitakuwada-gun, Kuroda-mura. Populations occur north into the old province of Tango (Kyoto Prefecture), at Amada-gun, Kamimutobe-mura, and Kasa-gun with accessions on the flanks of Mount Iwatoyama. The transferred name is based on the invalid basionym *H. liliiflora* var. *ovatolancifolia* nom. nudum. This taxon is a modified form of *H. montana* with ovate-lanceolate or lanceolate leaves. It may be an interspecific hybrid.

Petiole 10–20 by 0.5 cm (4–8 by 0.2 in.), erect, grooved, dark green. Leaf 10–30 by 5–10 cm (4–12 by 2–4 in.), spreading, rounded at base, ovate-lanceolate to lanceolate, deeply ribbed, acuminate tip, surface green, duller green below. Venation 6–8, sunken above, projected, strigose below. Scape 70 cm (28 in.), straight, erect, solid, terete, matte green (virescent), lightly purple-spotted at base. Sterile bracts 2–3 below raceme are large, 2–3 by 0.8 cm (1 by 0.3 in.); fertile bracts smaller, flat and broad, thick and fleshy, very whitish green, tinged purple, developing and opening in a stellar form as seen from above, withering, but persisting long after anthesis. Raceme has 30–40 flowers, spread evenly. Flowers 4.5 cm (2 in.) long, 3 cm (1.25 in.) broad, white; perianth expanding, funnel-shaped. Anthers yellow background with very pale purple dotting, appearing yellow. June. Fertile.

SY: _H. liliiflora_ var. _ovatolancifolia_ Araki 1942.
JN: _Nagare Giboshi._

Figure 3-48. _H. montana_ f. _ovatolancifolia_; general habit (Hosta Hill)

H. montana 'Gohonmatsu Fukurin' hort.
五本松覆輪
JN: _Gohonmatsu Fukurin Giboshi_ hort.
(see _H._ 'Gohonmatsu Fukurin').

H. montana 'Kurumazaki' hort.
車咲キオオバギボウシ
Kurumazaki Oba Giboshi, a rare mutant found in the wild with verticillate flowering habit (bracts and flowers arranged in whorls with several groups along the raceme). Reported stable. Only the horticultural name exists; it is maintained as a cultivar name because this form does not perpetuate in the wild.
JN: _Kurumazaki Oba Giboshi_ hort.

H. montana 'O Fuji Fukurin' hort.
大富士覆輪
JN: _O Fuji Fukurin Giboshi_ hort.
(see _H._ 'O Fuji Fukurin').

H. montana 'Ogon' hort.
黄金オオバギボウシ
Ogon Oba Giboshi, the "golden large-leaved hosta," occurs occasionally among the wild populations but has never been validly described. One form called _Ogon Oba Giboshi_ is viridescent and discolors to green with the advancing season. Mutation to all-gold forms has also occurred among the cultivated forms of _H. montana_ 'Aureomarginata' in the United States and a yellow mutation found recently has been selected

and named _H._ 'Emma Foster', which see. Other yellow forms exist and are here considered part of the _H. montana_ Yellow group. Most are not as large as the species and reportedly much weaker in growth. No botanical name has been given because the mutants do not perpetuate in the wild.
HN: Golden Montana.
      H. montana Yellow group.
JN: _Ogon Oba Giboshi_ hort.
(see also _H._ 'Emma Foster').

H. montana 'Ogon Fukurin' hort.
黄金覆輪オオバギボウシ
Ogon Fukurin Oba Giboshi, the "gold-margined large-leaved hosta," is a special cultivar selection of a yellow-margined _H. montana_. Reported to be more vigorous than the botanical form described by Maekawa 1940. It has a clear golden yellow margin.
JN: _Ogon Fukurin Oba Giboshi_ hort.
(see also _H. montana_ var. _aureomarginata_).

H. montana 'Praeflorens' hort./USA incorrect.
This cultivar name is widely and incorrectly used in North America. It is illegitimate because it uses the botanical varietal epithet _praeflorens_ given by Maekawa to a different taxon and because it is in latinate form. A description of the taxon to which it is incorrectly applied is given under its new botanical name _H. montana_ f. _macrophylla_, which see. The name _H. montana_ 'Praeflorens' (hort.) should not be used for the latter, but applies to Maekawa's taxon which is not in the trade.

H. montana 'Sagae' hort.
寒河江ギボウシ
An incorrect name for _H._ 'Sagae' hort, which see.
HN: _H. fluctuans variegata_ hort. incorrect.
      H. fluctuans 'Variegata' hort. incorrect.
      H. fluctuans 'Variegated' hort.
      _H._ 'Sagae' hort.
JN: _Sagae Giboshi_ hort.
(see _H. fluctuans_ 'Variegated').

H. montana 'Shirobana' hort.
白花オオバギボウシ
Shirobana Oba Giboshi, the "white-flowered large-leaved hosta," is a cultivated form with pure white flowers. In the wild _H. montana_ normally has white flowers, but they are not pure white due to extensive interspecific hybridization.
HN: _H. montana alba_ hort. incorrect.
JN: _Shirobana Oba Giboshi_ hort.

H. montana 'Shirofukurin' hort.
白覆輪オオバギボウシ
Shirofukurin Oba Giboshi, the "white-margined large-leaved hosta," is a collective name for any white-margined form, whether the margin is wide, narrow, splashed, streaked to the central vein, wider in the upper part of the leaf (_Tsume Fu_ = nail variegation), or with half the leaf along the central vein variegated (_Han Fu_ = half-variegated). All are found as mutants among the wild population and are collectively referred to as _Shirofukurin Oba Giboshi_, which should be considered a group name, here called _H. montana_ Albomarginata group of clones. These mutants do not propagate in the wild, so are considered cultivars. Selected clones have been named. A white-margined mutant of _H. montana_ 'Aureomarginata' discovered in tissue culture has recently been named _H._ 'Mountain Snow', which see. A very large _albomarginata_ form has been observed in Europe where it is cultivated under the incorrect name _H._ 'Crispula'. Its leaves are larger than those of the latter and have 11–15 principal veins instead of 9–10, but it

may be a mutant of *H. fortunei* var. *gigantea* and not directly related to *H. montana*.

HN: *H. montana* Albomarginata group.
JN: *Shirofukurin Oba Giboshi* hort.

H. montana 'Taika' hort.
帯化オオバギボウシ
JN: *Taika Oba Giboshi* hort.
(see *H.* 'Taika').

H. montana 'Tsunotori Fukurin' hort.
角取り覆輪
JN: *Tsunotori Giboshi* hort.
(see *H.* 'Tsunotori Fukurin').

H. montana 'Urajiro' hort.
裏白オオバギボウシ
Urajiro Oba Giboshi, the "white-backed large-leaved hosta," occurs among the wild population. It has a white, pruinose-farinose coating on the back of the leaves, but looks otherwise identical to the species so is not taxonomically separated.
JN: *Urajiro Oba Giboshi* hort.

✠ "*H. montana* var. *liliiflora*" Maekawa 1940.
AHS-II/7A.   (Figure D-4).
Here reduced to cultivar form as *H. montana* 'Liliiflora'.
ウノハナギボウシ
Unohana Giboshi, the "lily-flowered large-leaved hosta," was found on Mount Aoba, Kyoto Prefecture, and has representatives among the natural populations in the prefectures of Hyogo, Shizuoka and Tottori. Although Maekawa (1969) confirmed the name, it is today considered a cultivar in Japan, its only difference being the shape of the flower. The lobes are more open and the tips recurved. Maekawa linked this hosta with *H.* 'Crispula' and pointed out its peculiar existence in the marginal areas of distribution for the species *H. montana*, indicating with this the possibility of interspecific hybridization. This taxon may represent intergrading hybrid swarms existing among the overlapping specific populations of *H. montana* with *H. kiyosumiensis* and *H. longipes*. It looks very similar to the all-green mutant form of *H.* 'Crispula' and is morphologically very close to it. Its leaves are smaller, and it has fewer principal veins than the species (7–9 versus 10–13). It is not in the trade and of little horticultural importance.
Venation 7–9. Flowers 5 cm (2 in.) long, 3 cm (1.25 in.) broad, white very purple-suffused, lily-shaped, rapidly expanding, at tips ±perpendicular to axis of perianth, stamens superior, far surpassing the perianth. June. Fertile.
SY: *H. liliiflora* nom. nudum Maekawa 1938a.
H. liliiflora var. *ovatolancifolia* comb. nudum Araki 1942 pp sim.
HN: *H. montana* 'Liliiflora' hort.
JN: *Nagare Giboshi* Araki 1942 pp sim.
Unohana Giboshi Maekawa 1938a.

✠ "*H. montana* var. *praeflorens*" Maekawa 1940.
AHS-II/7A.
Here reduced to cultivar form as *H. montana* 'Praeflorens'.
ハヤザキギボウシ
ハヤザキオオバギボウシ
Hayazaki Giboshi or *Hayazaki Oba Giboshi*, the "early-flowering (large-leaved) hosta," is endemic in Shikoku outside the normal *H. montana* distribution and is here considered an interspecific hybrid with another species. Its early flowering character may also be partially due to its habitat which is further south than that of the group in general. In 1969

Maekawa no longer listed this hosta, and it is treated as a cultigen. It is important to note that plants cultivated in North America under the name *H. montana* 'Praeflorens' (hort./USA), now called *H. montana* f. *macrophylla*, have nothing to do with the taxon described here and do not conform to Maekawa's diagnosis for it (see *H. montana* f. *macrophylla*). Maekawa's true *H. montana* 'Praeflorens' is not cultivated in the West and is rarely seen in Japan.
Leaf 17.5–20 by 8–10 cm (7–8 by 3–4 in.), leaf attitude at petiole arcuate spreading, very contracted, broadly ovate, oblong-ovate, generally flat surface, open, acuminate tip, surface shiny deep green, dull green below. Flowers 5 cm (2 in.) long, 3 cm (1.25 in.) broad, white, suffused purple; perianth expanding, funnel-shaped, lobes spreading straightly to ±angled to the axis of perianth; stamens superior, surpassing the perianth. Anthers purple. May-June. Fertile.
JN: *Hayazaki Giboshi* Maekawa 1940.
Hayazaki Oba Giboshi hort.

✠ "*H. montana* var. *transiens*" Maekawa 1940.
AHS-III/15A.
Here reduced to cultivar form as *H. montana* 'Transiens'.
ウツリギボウシ
Utsuri Giboshi, the "Utsuri hosta," is reportedly growing in south-central Honshu, in Kyoto and Hyogo Prefectures. Maekawa (1969) no longer listed this variety nor did Fujita (1976a) support this name, so it has been reduced to cultivar form. The taxon was described with round leaves which are glaucous blue-green, like those of *H.* 'Tokudama', much taller scapes, and 14–16 pairs of veins. In 1940 Maekawa placed *H. bella* Wehrhahn 1934 in its synonymy (without having seen the latter) and this placement has been used by Hylander (1954) as sufficient reason for declaring the name *H. montana* superfluous and replacing it with *H.* 'Elata'. Detailed examination of this transfer is given in Appendixes A and B. *Hosta montana* 'Transiens' has been conclusively confirmed as an intraspecific hybrid with another member of section *Helipteroides*, probably a *H. sieboldiana* form, as the pod parent. The photograph shown by Maekawa (1940) agrees only partially with his description and leaf sizes and areas, when examined by photogrammetric methods, differ. *Hosta montana* 'Transiens' is not cultivated in the West.
Leaf 20–30 by 15–20 cm (8–12 by 6–8 in.), leaf attitude arcuate-spreading, very contracted, orbicular, ovate-orbicular, flat surface with slightly raised margins, not undulate, cuspidate tip, surface glaucous sea-green, dull green to greyish blue below. Venation 14–16, sunken above, very projected, strigose below. Scape 80–90 cm (32–36 in.), straight, erect, solid, terete, glaucous sea-green.
SY: *H. sieboldiana* var. *sieboldiana* Fujita 1976a sl.
HN: *H. montana* 'Transiens' hort.
JN: *Utsuri Giboshi* Maekawa 1940.
Utsuri Oba Giboshi hort.

H. montana 'Yae' Schmid.
ヤエノオオバギボウシ   (Figures 3-49, 3-50).
Yae No Oba Giboshi, the "double-flowered large-leaved hosta," is a mutation occasionally reported among the natural populations and has also occurred in cultivation in North America. It is probably unstable, but some reports characterize it as permanent. The flowers are true hose-in-hose double flowers with 12 full-size lobes and with occasional petaloid stamens in addition to the double number of lobes

(see also Figure 3-46). I am treating it as a cultivar because in the wild it is a nonperpetuating form.

HN: Double-Flowered Montana.

JN: *Yae No Oba Giboshi.*

Figure 3-49. *H. montana* 'Yae'; flower detail, "hose-in-hose" flower (Hosta Hill)

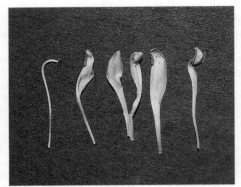

Figure 3-50. *H. montana* 'Yae'; petaloid stamens

N

H. nakaiana Maekawa 1935.

AHS-V/25B.   (Figure 3-51; Plates 47, 190, 198).

カンザシギボウシ

Kanzashi Giboshi, the "ornamental hairpin hosta," is called so because the scape with the capitate flower bud looks like the traditional ornamental hairpin worn by Japanese women. It is native to southern and central Korea, found in the provinces of Chollanam-do, Chollabuk-do, Kyongsangnam-do, and Kyongsangbuk-do. It also grows in Japan on Kyushu, in Saga and Nagasaki prefectures, and on Honshu, in Hyogo Prefecture. The non-Korean populations may have been carried to Japan by travellers and plant collectors. Several forms have evolved but they are very close macromorphologically and yellow as well as variegated mutants have also been found.

Hosta nakaiana is larger than *H. venusta,* the flower bud is globular-capitate not spicate (pointed), the scapes solid not hollow, and the raceme very abbreviated, densely arranged, not racemose—all are principal differences. It has the characteristic lamellar ridges of section *Lamellatae* on the scape. Maekawa (1969) and Fujita (1976a) considered it synony-

mous to *H. capitata,* which is closely related, and this relationship is not questioned. Herbarium specimens indicate that *H. capitata* and *H. nakaiana* as currently delimited are but two forms of many more which make up interspecific hybrid swarms formed by the union of cultivated specimens of the Korean *H. minor* and *H. venusta* with native Japanese or other Korean species. It is highly significant that the projecting underside leaf veins of *H. capitata* are papillose, while all other members of section *Lamellatae,* including *H. nakaiana,* have smooth veins. No other Korean species has papillose veins, but several Japanese species do and *H. capitata* is considered a Japanese species by Fujita (1976a), while Chung (1990) regards it a Korean species. Both are maintained as individual species because of considerable macromorphological differences (color of anthers, papillose and non-papillose veins) and the existence of natural allopatric populations. The leaves of *H. nakaiana* are smaller and flat, entire, while the leaves of *H. capitata* are larger, with undulate, crispate margins. (For further information on the relationship between these species, see "The Korean Species" in Appendix A—Part 1.) *Hosta nakaiana* first reached the United States in the 1950s from Osaka University (Krossa, 1966) but was not identified until much later. It was given several cultivar names in the interim which are treated as cultivar synonyms. It was subsequently imported by Craig who bought it at a market stall and sent it to Davidson in 1962 (Davidson, 1990) under its Japanese formal name *Kanzashi Giboshi.* The white-margined form, *Shirofukurin Kanzashi Giboshi,* is now cultivated under the cultivar name *H.* 'Allan P. McConnell', which see. *Hosta nakaiana* is the parent of many important garden hybrids, particularly the lines bred by Eunice Fisher and Savory, and is horticulturally useful where a small free-blooming hosta is required.

Plant size to 16–22 cm (6–9 in.) dia., 12 cm (5 in.) high. Petiole 9–10 by 0.4 cm (2–4 by 0.135 in.), ascending in an arch, forming a dome-shaped plant, slender, narrowly open. Leaf 6–9 by 3.5–6 cm (2.5–3.5 by 1.5–2.5 in.), ovate-cordate, very truncate at the base, transition usually very contracted, recurving, acuminate tip, interior leaf flattish, margin undulate, wavy, not pruinose, surface with metallic sheen, nearly shiny, dark green above, lighter green below, opaque. Venation 5–7, very thin, not very sunken above, smooth below. Scape 40–50 cm (16–20 in.), distinct lamellar ridges parallel or slightly spiral to scape axis, straight, erect, usually perpendicular, sometimes bending slightly. Fertile bracts navicular, grooved, thick, green or whitish green, ascending, imbricated even during flowering and nearly equal in size, persisting at anthesis but withering soon after, developed unopened flower head globular, capitate, usually one sterile bract. Raceme 12 cm (8 in.) 6–10

Figure 3-51. *H. nakaiana;* flower bud detail (Hosta Hill)

flowers. Flowers 4.5–5 cm (2 in.) long, 2.5 cm (1 in.) broad, closely spaced on raceme, held erect in ±horizontal position on strong pedicels, dark veins on a lighter colored background; perianth pale purple-violet, expanding, in the central part dilated bell-shaped, lobes ±angled to the axis, stamens exerted. Anthers purple. July. Fertile.

SY: *H. capitata* Fujita 1976a sl na.
HN: Capitate Plantain Lily pp.
    H. 'Birchwood Gem' hort.
    H. 'Burkes Dwarf' hort.
    H. 'Krossa No. E-6'.
    H. 'Mukayama' hort. UK incorrect.
    H. nakaimo minor hort. incorrect.
    H. nakiana hort. incorrect.
    H. 'Sweetheart' hort.
    H. 'Sybl' hort.
    H. venusta 'Carder' pp.
JN: *Kanzashi Giboshi* Maekawa 1935.

H. nakaiana 'Ogon' hort.
AHS-V/29A. (Plate 120).
黄金カンザシ

Ogon Kanzashi Giboshi, the "golden ornamental hairpin hosta," is composed of several yellow forms closely related to the species, including *Hosta* 'Hydon Sunset' (Plate 120), a hybridized form with traces of ridges on the lower scape. A cultivar called Golden Nakaiana in the United Kingdom has nothing to do with this taxon but is *H.* 'Birchwood Parkys Gold', which see. Because *H. nakaiana* and *H. capitata* are considered synonymous by some, the Japanese name is applied to the yellow form of either species.

HN: Golden Nakaiana incorrect UK.
    H. 'Golden Scepter' Savory pp sim.
    H. 'Hydon Sunset' pp sim hybridized.
JN: *Ogon Kanzashi Giboshi* hort.

H. nakaiana 'Shirofukurin' hort.
白覆輪カンザシギボウシ (Plate 85).

Shirofukurin Kanzashi Giboshi, the "white-margined ornamental hairpin hosta," has ridges on the scape like the species and is widely grown in North America under the name *H.* 'Allan P. McConnell' (Plate 85), which see.

JN: *Shirofukurin Kanzashi Giboshi* hort.

H. nigrescens Maekawa 1937.
AHS-II/9B. (Figure 2-32; Plates 48, 93).
クロギボウシ

Kuro Giboshi, the "black hosta," has been known in Japan for many years and is mentioned in a floristic work by Iinuma (1874). Not actually black, but very dark-green, and pruinose initially except for the sprouts which are dull black initially. The species epithet *nigrescens* means blackish, or very dark colored. This taxon evolved in northern Honshu, Aomori Prefecture, and natural populations are said to exist in Iwate and Akita prefectures. It is now rarely seen in the wild but is extensively cultivated. Many plants sold under this name are hybridized forms. Specimens conforming to the lectotype can be recognized by scape length, which was given by Maekawa (1969) as 150 cm (60 in.), but they will reach a height of ±180 cm (72 in.). The scape retains its glaucous grey coating until fall, and the seed pods are also a glaucous grey. Fujita (1976a) considered this taxon synonymous with *H. sieboldiana* var. *glabra*, which has a habitat in southern and south-central Honshu, including the prefectures of Shimane, Toyama, Nagano, Niigata and Oki Gunto (Gunto Island). Because Oki Gunto is geographically isolated from the area in northern Honshu where *H. nigrescens* was originally reported, *H. nigres-*

cens is treated as separate species following Maekawa (1940, 1969). *Hosta nigrescens* is an important species horticulturally and has been extensively hybridized.

Plant size 60–70 cm (24–28 in.) dia., 65 cm (26 in.) high. Sprouts lightly pruinose, blackish grey. Petiole 30–50 by 1.2 cm (12–20 by 0.5 in.), slightly arching but erect, forming a tall plant, dark pruinose glaucous green. Leaf 25–30 by 17.5–22.5 cm (10–12 by 7–9 in.), ultimate size can be 45 cm by 35 cm (18 by 14 in.), leaf attitude at petiole acutely angled at joint then ±arcuate spreading, ovate-cordate, transition usually tight and contracted, acuminate tip, rugose in part, ±keeled, no waves in margin, entire plant very pruinose initially, farinose, deep green initially, changing to shiny deep green. Venation 11–13, sunken above, very projected, strigose below. Scape far exceeding height of plant, to 140 cm (56 in.), measured to 180 cm (72 in.) on mature plants, with ±3 sterile bracts, very straight, erect, upper part rarely but occasionally bending, solid, terete, permanently pruinose, lasting until dehiscence. Bracts flat and broad, thick and fleshy, green or whitish green, developing and opening in a stellar form as seen from above. Raceme 30 cm (12 in.), 15–25 flowers, widely spaced. Flowers 5 cm (2 in.) long, 3 cm (1.25 in.) broad, mostly white to white suffused very lightly purple; perianth expanding, funnel-shaped, in the central part dilated bell-shaped, lobes spreading straightly to ±angled to the axis of perianth; stamens not very superior, equal or slightly shorter than perianth. Average anthesis July/August. Anthers have widely spaced purple dots outside and dense dotting inside, approaching bicolor, looks very light purple. June. Fertile.

SY: *H. sieboldiana* var. *glabra* Fujita 1976a sl pp na.
    H. sieboldiana var. *nigrescens* Makino 1902.
HN: Darkgreen Plantain Lily.
JN: *Kuro Giboshi* Iinuma 1874.
    Nameru Giboshi Fujita 1976a sl pp na.

✠ "*H. nigrescens* f. *elatior*" Maekawa 1940.
Here reduced to cultivar form as *H. nigrescens* 'Elatior'.
AHS-I/1A. (Figure 3-52).
セイタカクロギボウシ

Seitaka Kuro Giboshi, the "black hosta with tall stature," was found by Yamanaka in cultivation. Maekawa (1940) published the name based on a cultivated plant without number in Kikuchi's garden in Kyoto. The description reads: "A typo ex omnibus partibus robustioribus, scapo alteriori (170 cm longio), floribus majoribus (ca 65 mm longis) recedit." In this description, no reference is made to pruinosity, and it basically states the taxon differs from the type by being larger in all parts, and by having longer scapes (170 cm long) and larger flowers (ca. 65 mm long). This has puzzled horticulturists, who expect *H. nigrescens* f. *elatior* to be as pruinose as the type. This consistency is not required for delimiting a forma, and Maekawa may have used the absence of pruinosity as a reason to segregate this taxon from the type, without actually mentioning this character. Specimens in North America, originating with Kaneko and cultivated under the name *H. nigrescens* f. *elatior*, now *H. nigrescens* 'Elatior', are not farinose-glaucous dark green, but shiny, light green. Yet, they match in all respects photo 2, page 323, of Maekawa 1940, and are therefore considered representatives of this taxon. Maekawa (1969) eliminated this taxon as a cultigen for which no representative wild populations have been found. I am also treating it as a specioid and believe it to be an interspecific hybrid of uncertain origin.

There is also a *H.* 'Elatior' at Wisley, United Kingdom, No. 821363, but its connection, if any, has not been established. This taxon did not originate with the cultivated populations in North America, but came to England from an unknown source. In any case, the name *H.* 'Elatior', used in this manner, is incorrect.

A similar hosta with a foliage height of more than 100 cm (40 in.) and scapes of more than 200 cm (80 in.) is in cultivation in an area near the Tenryu River, Shizuoka Prefecture, under the horticultural name *Tenryu Giboshi, H.* 'Tenryu', which see. Its leaves are described as whitish farinose on both sides, similar to *H. nigrescens. Hosta* 'Tenryu' has been mentioned in connection with *H. nigrescens*; however, it is geographically far removed from the latter's natural habitat in northern Honshu. As a consequence, I believe this Japanese cultivar is only very distantly related.

Hosta 'Green Wedge' Aden is a selected clone of this taxon. It and *H. nigrescens* 'Elatior' are excellent accent plants which stay in prime condition from spring until late summer.

Plant size 80–100 cm (32–40 in.) dia., 75 cm (30 in.) high. Scape far exceeding height of plant, to 180 cm (72 in.), not as straight as the species but bending in the middle forming an arch. Anthers yellow, lightly purple-dotted. July. Fertile.

HN: *H.* 'Elatior' Wisley, UK incorrect.
     H. elatior hort. incorrect.
     H. 'Green Wedge' Aden.
     H. nigrescens 'Elatior' hort.
JN: *Seitaka Kuro Giboshi* Maekawa 1940.
     Tenryu Giboshi hort. Yoshie pp sim.

Figure 3-52. *H. nigrescens* 'Elatior'; general habit (Hosta Hill)

H. nigrescens 'Krossa Regal' hort. IRA/1980.
(see *H.* 'Krossa Regal').

H. nimor nom. nud. hort.
(see *H. numor*).

H. numor nom. nud. hort.
Hosta nimor and *H. numor* are names of uncertain origin. Davidson (1990), who imported and distributed many Japanese hostas when these names first appeared, considers them incorrect formulations for *H. minor*. Several taxa have been sold under these names, including *H. gracillima, H. minor, H. nakaiana, H. venusta*, and probably also others, all small to miniature size. Both names are invalid and should not be used.

O

H. okamii Maekawa 1938a.
(see *H. sieboldii* f. *okamii*).

H. okamotoi Araki 1942.
  AHS-IV/19B.   (Plate 49).
オクヤマギボウシ

Okuyama Giboshi, the "hosta from Okuyama," was collected by Shogo Okamoto who found it growing epiphytically on tree trunks in the shady valleys of Mount Okuyama near Chii-mura, Kyoto Prefecture, Honshu. The species epithet honors Mr. Okamoto. This taxon is similar to *H. longipes* and closely related, but has longer scapes and more widely spaced flowers. Fujita (1976a) placed it with *H. longipes* var. *aequinoctiiantha* because it blooms concurrently with it in some areas, but there are sufficient differences to maintain them as separate species. It is rarely available, but in time its attractive, purple petioles and scapes will make it important horticulturally.

Plant size 35–40 cm (14–16 in.) dia., 30 cm (12 in.) high. Petiole 12.5–15 by 0.4 cm (5–6 by 0.16 in.), erect, purple-dotted from base towards the center. Leaf 10–12.5 by 5–7.5 cm (4–5 by 2–3 in.), erect and in line with petiole, entire, subcordate, truncate, petiole transition rounded, cuspidate tip, flat or wavy surface, erect, fleshy-leathery, smooth, green above, lighter, opaque green below. Venation 5–7, sunken above, very projected, smooth below. Scape 25–45 cm (10–18 in.), straight, but growing obliquely, purple-dotted entire length, smooth round. Fertile bracts 1 cm (0.3 in.) long, navicular, thin, membranous, white or whitish green, purple-tinted, imbricated, not withering. Raceme 20–25 cm (8–10 in.), 10–20 flowers, spaced apart. Flowers white outside, pale purple-suffused inside, held erect in horizontal position on long, strong, horizontal or slightly ascending purple pedicels; perianth 5 cm (2 in.) long, funnel-shaped, expanding, in the central part dilated bell-shaped, lobes spreading straightly to ±angled to the axis of perianth, thin narrow hexagonal tube. Anthers yellow background, purple-dotted, looks purple. September. Fertile.

SY: *H. longipes* var. *aequinoctiiantha* Fujita 1976a sl pp na.
HN: *H. longipes* var. *okamotoi* hort.
JN: *Okuyama Giboshi* Araki 1942.

✠ "*H. opipara*" Maekawa 1937.
  AHS-II/10A.   (Figures 2-14, 3-53; Plate 50).
Here reduced to cultivar form as *H.* '**Opipara**'.
ニシキギボウシ

Nishiki Giboshi, the "sumptuous hosta," has a broad, golden yellow margin. The species epithet means "with cloth of gold (brocade)," but is translated as sumptuous. It was found among cultivated plants near the city of Hirosaki in Aomori Prefecture of northern Honshu and is now considered a cultivar. This taxon together with *Otafuku Giboshi, H.* 'Decorata', forms a distinct (cultivar) group with widely winged petioles and rounded ovate leaves. The two taxa also share a slightly "stoloniferous" root system (Figure 3-53), actually lateral shoots. *Hosta opipara* is one of the best of the yellow-margined hostas with both leaf and margin color enduring until fall especially if the plant is located in light shade. It does not thrive in deep shade and needs optimum amount of sun as all other members of section *Nipponosta*.

Some clones distributed in commerce have a viral disease (Pollock, 1989; Vaughn, 1989a; Vaughn 1989b) that is highly infectious. Such plants should be destroyed. Several virtually identical clones which vary slightly in size are in cultivation. A cultivar named *H.* 'Opipara Bill Brincka' has been registered in 1988, and an earlier name for this taxon, *H.* 'Opipara Noble One', is now considered a synonym. These are reportedly stronger, larger growing clones of *H.* 'Opipara', but given optimum growing conditions and time (without dividing), all will eventually develop into magnificent clumps.

Plant size 50 cm (20 in.) dia., 35 cm (14 in.) high. Petiole 15–20 by 0.8–1 cm (6–8 by 0.33–0.45 in.), spreading horizontally, broadly winged, considerably wider in the upper part, to 1.8 cm (0.75 in.), green with yellow margin continuing into leaf margin. Leaf 17.5–22.5 by 10–12.5 cm (7–9 by 4–5 in.), continuing and in line with petiole, entire, elliptical to broadly ovate-elliptical, acuminate tip, flat surface, ±keeled, 3–5 very slight waves in margin, slight rugosity in parts of vernal leaves, broadly contracted at the base, surface shiny dark green with broad golden yellow irregular margin, with occasional yellow streaks extending into leaf center, margin 1.2–2.5 cm (0.5–1 in.) wide, planted in intense light it bleaches to white by anthesis, in deep shade it remains golden yellow, glossy below. Venation 8–9, impressed above, smooth below. Scape 80 cm (32 in.), straight but obliquely bending during flowering and seed production, dull light green, no purple marks. Sterile bracts 3–4, green with yellowish green margins, tightly clasping stem; fertile bracts broadly ovate-elliptical, navicular, margined, not withering at anthesis, not falling away. Raceme compact, 10–15 flowers, closely spaced. Flowers 5 cm (2 in.) long, 3.5 cm (1.5 in.) broad, held erect on strong pedicels, whitish, pale purple, striped dark purple, expanding, funnel-shaped, in the central part dilated bell-shaped, lobes spreading straightly to ±angled to the axis of perianth. Anthers yellow, purple-dotted. July. Fertile.

HN: *H.* 'Bill Brincka' Brincka IRA/1988.
    H. 'Opipara Bill Brincka' Brincka IRA/1988.
    H. 'Opipara Noble One' Pollock.
    H. opipera Grey 1938 incorrect.
    H. opipera hort. incorrect.
    H. oporia hort. incorrect.
JN: *Nishiki Giboshi* Maekawa 1937.

P

H. pachyscapa Maekawa 1940.

    AHS-III/13B.   (Figures 3-54, 3-55; Plate 51).
ベンケイギボウシ

Benkei Giboshi, the "Benkei hosta," is based on a form collected by Toyama near Inae, Shiga Prefecture, and cultivated in Kikuchi's garden. The valid description is based on cultivated plants. Populations are reported in Honshu, including Shiga Prefecture in Kansai District and Shizuoka Prefecture in Chubu District, where they inhabit open valleys and forest margins in good soil. Related to and possibly a locally differentiated race of *H. kiyosumiensis*, it is a much larger species with tall and thick flower scapes, which Maekawa measured as 11 mm (0.5 in.) in diameter. This feature prompted the epithet which means "thick scape." In North America it has been cultivated under several incorrect names.

Figure 3-54. *H. pachyscapa*; expanding raceme (Hosta Hill)

Figure 3-53. *H.* 'Opipara'; lateral shoots (Hosta Hill)

Figure 3-55. *H. pachyscapa*; scape detail, 14 mm (over 0.5 in.) dia. (Hosta Hill)

It prefers heavy, moist clay soils in which it will grow to exceed some of Maekawa's size limits for the species. I have measured the scape diameter to 14 mm (over 0.5 in.) (Figure 3-55). This taxon is a good green specimen hosta with impressive tall scapes and many attractive flowers.

Plant size 65–90 cm (26–36 in.) dia., 50 cm (20 in.) high. Petiole 20–30 by 1.2 cm (8–12 by 0.5 in.), erect, green, lightly purple-dotted at base. Leaf 12.5–20 by 7.5–15 cm (5–8 by 3–6 in.), spreading horizontally, entire, ovate-elliptical to ovate, truncate and contracted at base, generally flat surface, but slightly undulate in the margin, shiny dark green, lighter green below, tip acuminate. Venation 7–8, slightly sunken above, smooth below. Scape 70–125 cm (28–50 in.), to 1.2 cm (0.5 in.) dia., rising upwards but leaning, purple-dotted at base and at tip, later bending under weight of flowers and seed. Sterile bracts, several large, leaflike; fertile bracts, navicular, imbricate, green with purple margins, persistent. Raceme 30–50 flowers, evenly spaced, but densely arranged. Flowers 4.5 cm (2 in.) long, 3.5 cm (1.5 in.) broad, pale purple-violet, gradually expanding, lobes expanding, angled to axis of perianth, stamens exceeding the perianth. Anthers purple-dotted. June/July. Fertile.

SY: *H. kiyosumiensis* Fujita 1976a sl pp.
HN: *H.* 'Craig No. C-1' ad int.

H. petrophila Maekawa 1938a.
(see *H. kiyosumiensis*).

H. plantaginea Ascherson 1838 var. *plantaginea*.
AHS-III/13A.   (Figures 3-56, A-5, A-6, D-4; Plate 52).
マルバタマノカンザシ
玉簪 Chinese name.

Maruba Tama No Kanzashi, the "round-leaved jewel of the hairpin (hosta)," has a Japanese formal name dating from 1937 which was given by Kikuchi and is a translation of its Chinese name *Yu-san*. The species is native to China where records show it is cultivated in Hebei (also Hopei or Hopeh) Province and other parts of China as well as the world over. Province Hebei surrounds Beijing and Tiantjin and is occasionally mentioned as the original, evolutionary habitat for the species, but plant physiological-ecological requirements for successful seed production point slightly further south. Unconfirmed reports place it in Zhejing Province, which would place its natural populations further south than any other taxon in the genus, and cultural requirements tend to confirm such warm habitat. In cultivation this species produces seed abundantly during prolonged hot summers in southeastern North America. This taxon was the first hosta on the continent of Europe grown from seeds, which were sent from Macao by the French consul Charles de Guignes before 1784. It was first described by Lamarck in 1789 based on mature specimens grown from this seed at the Jardin des Plantes in Paris and the type is in P. In 1790 the first live plants were imported into England by George Hibbert where they were at first grown under glass. Some specimens were part of an extensive collection of rare, ornamental plants that Josephine Bonaparte assembled at the gardens of Malmaison. Soon it became such a popular outdoor specimen plant that it was referred to as the "Parisian Funkia" and seen allover Paris where it was planted in public and private gardens. It spread to other areas of France, arrived in Germany before 1800, and was cultivated in the Copenhagen Botanic Garden in 1802.

This species has the best flowers in the genus; they are more than twice as large as those in other species, with a pure white color, heavy substance and a waxy surface. It is the only night-blooming species in the genus. The flowers open late in the afternoon and their fragrance is most noticeable during evening hours. The light green, shiny leaves provide a beautiful foil. Planting this hosta near garden seating or walks will take full advantage of its unique look and lovely fragrance. Considered by many a medium-sized hosta, it will grow into a large clump in time. *Hosta plantaginea* is pod parent to a number of fragrant hybrids which include variegated forms. This species requires extended, warm summers to properly set seed.

It is important to note that this taxon is not the same one brought by von Siebold from Japan in the early 1840s. Siebold's plant—*H. plantaginea* var. *japonica* (see jacket back)—had longer, narrower leaves, and was most likely an interspecific hybrid with a species that had been cultivated in Japan for a very long time. In 1940 Maekawa confirmed that the native Chinese species with rounded leaves, which is now the predominant form cultivated, was introduced into Japan from Europe relatively recently.

Plant size 60 cm (24 in.) dia. by 45 cm (18 in.) high. Petiole 24 cm by 0.9 cm (10 by 0.35 in.), erect and spreading, unmarked glossy light green. Leaf 16–25 cm by 15–21 cm (6.5–10 by 6–8 in.), erect and in line with petiole, becoming subpendulous, orbicular-cordate, nearly round, transition tight and contracted to slightly open, cuspidate, interior surface "flat", but undulate, wavy in the margin, not pruinose, surface dull, semiglossy, below very glossy, light yellow green, tip acuminate, projecting. Venation 8–9, sunken above, very projected, smooth below. Scape 60–80 cm (24–32 in.), straight, erect, yellow-green, smooth round. Fertile bracts, glossy green, ovate-lanceolate, grooved in the lower part, pointed; 2-bracted, bracteole within external bract, opposite to lower fertile bracts, flat, large to 8 cm (3 in.), fleshy and rigid, green or greenish white; lower, sterile bracts often foliaceous. Raceme 25 cm (10 in.), 10–15 flowers. Flowers degeneratively duplicate, with one-flowered, sessile branches, appearing racemose, held erect in ±horizontal position on strong pedicels, fragrant, very large, to 12.5 cm (5 in.) long and 7.5 cm (3 in.) broad, waxy, shiny, lily-shaped, sharply recurving lobes, shiny white entirely, occasionally shades of white and pale cream, stamens not superior, parallel, joined to perianth tube. Capsules very large, elongated, round, with a pointed tip. Anthers yellow. August, night-flowering. Fertile.

SY: *Funkia alba* Sweet 1827.
Funkia alba 'Thomas Hogg' de Noter 1905.
Funkia japonica Mottet 1897 incorrect.
Funkia sieboldiana bracteata Miquel 1867 nom. confusum incorrect.
Funkia subcordata Sprengel 1825 nom. illegitimum.
Funkia subcordata var. *grandiflora* Miquel 1869.
Hemerocallis alba Andrews 1801.
Hemerocallis cordata Cavanilles 1801.
Hemerocallis cordifolia Salisbury 1807.
Hemerocallis japonica Redouté 1802 incorrect.
Hemerocallis plantaginea Lamarck 1789.
Hosta Iaponica Trattinnick 1812 incorrect.
H. plantaginea f. *grandiflora* Ascherson and Gräbner 1905.
Niobe cordifolia Salisbury 1812 incorrect.
Niobe plantaginea Nash 1911.
Saussurea plantaginea Kuntze 1891.
HN: August Lily.
Corfu Lily Robinson 1883.
Fragrant Plantain Lily.
Funkia grandiflora hort.

Funkia liliiflora Foerster 1956 incorrect.
Funkia subcordata grandiflora hort.
Hosta 'Grandiflora' incorrect.
H. 'Krossa No. K-2' CL No. 318547.
H. plantaginea subcordata grandiflora hort. incorrect.
H. plantaginea 'Long Tom' hort. large flowers.
H. 'Mack No. 14'.
Large White Plantain Lily.
Paris Lily or Funkia.
White Plantain Lily.
JN: *Maruba Tama No Kanzashi* Kikuchi 1934.
ON: Lilienfunkie (German).
Wegerichblätterige Funkie (German).
Yu-san (Chinese).

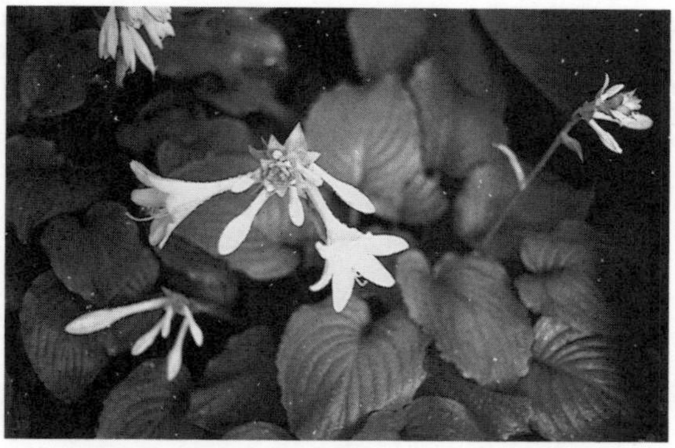

Figure 3-56. *H. plantaginea*; flower detail (Hosta Hill)

✠ "*H. plantaginea* f. *aphrodite*" Maekawa 1940.
AHS-III/13A. (Figure 3-57).
Here reduced to cultivar form as ***H. plantaginea* 'Aphrodite'**.
ヤエノマルバタマノカンザシ

Yae No Maruba Tama No Kanzashi, the "double-flowered, round-leaved leaf jewel of the ornamental hairpiece," is a double-flowered, fragrant hosta. It differs from the species by the outer stamens which are petaloid, spatulate, projected, 11 by 5 cm (4.5 by 2 in.), pointed, cuneate at the base, and the inner stamens which are shorter, 3.5 cm (1.5 in.) long, inserted. A naturally occurring mutation which is rare and seldom cultivated, it has reached Japan, the United States, and Germany, and is a collector's item. In North America it is called *H. plantaginea* 'Flora Plena' or *H. plantaginea* 'Plena', but these names are invalid per the ICNCP because of their latinized form. This taxon should be named 'Aphrodite' following Maekawa (1940). In China this taxon also has been named *H. plantaginea* var. *plena* by Yan Liang Fei (1983; cfr. Licht 1989), but for now Maekawa's name *H. plantaginea* var. *aphrodite* has priority, so the former name is a nomen superfluum. The Chinese name is *Chingban Yu-san*. Research in China is attempting to establish that an even earlier valid name exists, because this taxon has been cultivated in China for over 150 years (Licht, 1989). Not perpetuating in the wild, it has been reduced to cultivar form, adopting Maekawa's epithet as a cultivar name.

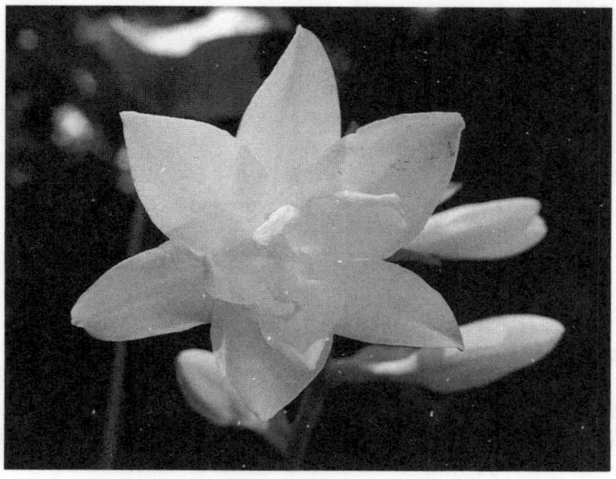

Figure 3-57. *H. plantaginea* 'Aphrodite'; flower detail

SY: *H. plantaginea* var. *plena* Fei 1983.
HN: Double-flowered White Plantain Lily.
H. plantaginea 'Aphrodite'.
H. plantaginea 'Flora Plena' incorrect.
H. plantaginea 'Plena' incorrect.
JN: *Yae No Maruba Tama No Kanzashi* Maekawa 1940.
ON: *Chingban Yu-san* (Chinese).

✠ "*H. plantaginea* f. *stenantha*" Maekawa 1940.
AHS-III/13A.
Here reduced to cultivar form as ***H. plantaginea* 'Stenantha'**.
クダザキマルバタマノカンザシ

Kudazaki Maruba Tama No Kanzashi is the "narrow-flowered, round-leaved leaf jewel of the ornamental hairpiece." The species epithet is derived from Greek *stenos* = narrow and *anthos* = flower. Reported by Kikuchi in Province Hebei, China, it differs from the species only in the shape of the perianth, which is more narrow in appearance, and the lobes which are slimmer. The stamens project slightly beyond the perianth. This hosta is a natural modification of the typical species form and occurs among the members of natural colonies. It is not sufficiently differentiated to be maintained as a separate taxon, so it is reduced to cultivar form. Now and then observed among cultivated specimens of *H. plantaginea*, it is strictly a collector's item and seldom seen.
HN: *H. plantaginea* 'Stenantha'.
Narrow-Flowered White Plantain Lily.
JN: *Kudazaki Maruba Tama No Kanzashi* Maekawa 1940.

H. plantaginea var. ***japonica*** Maekawa 1938a.
AHS-III/13A. (Figure B-1; jacket back).
タマノカンザシ

Tama No Kanzashi, the "jewel of the hairpiece (hosta)," was first named by Ranzan Ono in 1847 but reportedly cultivated in Japan for a long before this date. Maekawa stated it "was introduced from China," and it is widely cultivated in Japan and in Korea. In 1830, while returning to Holland, von Siebold brought this taxon to Batavia's Buitenzorg gardens where it was planted. According to Hensen (1963b), in 1841 J. Pierot of the Rijksherbarium Leiden (L) stopped over in Batavia, Java, retrieved *H. plantaginea* var. *japonica* and sent it to von Siebold in Leiden under the name *Funkia grandiflora*. This hosta is portrayed very precisely in a drawing made by van Houtte in 1846 working from plants provided by von Siebold to the Jardin de la Société Royale d'Horticulture des Pays-Bas (see jacket back). The illustration and description verify that this was *Hosta plantaginea* var. *japonica* from Japan, and this is further corroborated by herbarium specimens (in L). First listed by von Siebold (1844) as *Funkia grandiflora* and as *Funkia subcordata grandiflora* in 1856, it probably is an interspecific, natural hybrid with a native Japanese species. The "Japanese plantaginea" differs from the Chinese species by having longer and narrower leaf blades, by making a taller, less compact leaf mound, by the yellow anthers with slight purple dotting, and by the lobes which are more narrow and straight looking and less recurving. Even with careful hand-pollination, seed set is difficult to accomplish; for this reason some consider this taxon infertile even though it is not. Its use in the landscape is identical to that described for the species

Hosta plantaginea, but it is rarely offered and seldom seen. Plant size 65 cm (25 in.) dia., 45 cm (18 in.) high. Petiole 24 by 0.9 cm (10 by 0.35 in.), erect and spreading, unmarked glossy light green. Leaf 20–28 cm by 14–20 cm wide (8–11 by 5.5–8 in.), erect but more relaxed than the type and in line with petiole, becoming subpendulous, orbicular-cordate, nearly round, transition tight and contracted to slightly open, interior surface "flat", but undulate, wavy in the margin, not pruinose, surface dull, shiny above, below very glossy, light yellow green, cuspidate, tip acuminate. Venation 8–9, sunken above, very projected, smooth below. Scape 60–80 cm (24–32 in.), straight, erect, yellow-green, smooth round. Fertile bracts, 2-bracted, bracteole within external bract, opposite to lower fertile bracts, flat, large to 9 cm (3.5 in.), fleshy and rigid, green or greenish white, glossy or glossy green, ovate-lanceolate, grooved in the lower part, pointed; lower sterile bracts often foliaceous. Raceme 25 cm (10 in.), 10–15 flowers. Flowers degeneratively duplicate, with one-flowered, sessile branches, appearing racemose, held erect in ±horizontal position on strong pedicels, fragrant, very large, to 13.5 cm (5.5 in.) long and 7.5 cm (3 in.) broad, waxy, shiny, lily-shaped, recurving lobes (but not as much as the type), shiny white entirely, occasionally shades of white and pale cream, stamens not superior, parallel, joined to perianth tube. Anthers yellow, with light purple dotting. August, night-flowering. Rarely makes viable seeds when open-pollinated, but this can be occasionally accomplished with hand-pollination.

SY: *Funkia grandiflora* Siebold and Zuccarini in Lemaire 1846.
　　 Hosta plantaginea Matsumura 1905.
　　 H. plantaginea var. *grandiflora* Hylander 1954.
HN: *H. plantaginea* 'Japonica'.
　　 Japanese White Plantain Lily.
　　 Narrow-Leaf White Plantain Lily.
JN: *Tama No Kanzashi* Ono 1847.

H. polyneuron Maekawa 1952.
(see *H. kikutii* var. *polyneuron*).

H. praecox Maekawa 1938a.
(see *H. kiyosumiensis*).

H. pulchella Fujita 1976a.
　　 AHS-VI/31B.　　　　　　　 (Figures 3-58, 4-41; Plate 53).
ウバタケギボウシ
祖母ヒメイワギボウシ

Ubatake Giboshi, the "grandmother mountain hosta," was found by Fujita and Takahashi at elevation 1600 meters on Mount Sobo-san (Grandmother Mountain) in Kyushu, Oita Prefecture. It grows along the ridge lines on rock outcrops. Recently, it has also been reported in Miyazaki Prefecture. The species epithet, which is derived from *pulchellus*=beautiful and little, is fitting, and the small heart-shaped, glossy leaves topped by large purple flowers present a pretty picture. Most specimens received from academic sources in Japan are much smaller than Fujita's description. Examination of the herbarium specimens for this taxon indicate that the illustration depicted in Fujita (1976a) is not that of the holotype No. 1001 cited by him. Instead it is another isotype—No. 1001 (as No. 32413 in KYO), collected by Fujita and Takahashi, which has two very small hosta specimens mounted on the sheet. The description below has been adjusted to reflect the size of these specimens, and the isotype itself has been accepted as the

holotype because of its close morphological agreement with authentic plants received from Kyoto. This taxon has been placed in section *Picnolepis* on morphological and ecological grounds, and Fujita's placement in section *Tardanthae* is not maintained although there is some palynological congruence. Sectional placement of his taxon is very difficult because it has purple-striped flowers, like *H. tardiva* of section *Tardanthae*, but blooms very early, preceding even section *Helipteroides*—it has been observed at Hosta Hill to bloom as early as May 15 with seed capsules fully formed by June 1. All other characteristics are those of section *Picnolepis*, and it may represent an isolated, introgressive, allopatric hybrid population which has survived in its rather hostile habitat through amalgamation of modifying parental genes. Some Japanese horticulturists call it *Hime Iwa Giboshi*, the "little rock hosta." Several fragrant variants have been reported, but their relationship has not been confirmed. Specimens now cultivated in North America are all diminutive, as the epithet implies, and can be used in the garden like other small hostas, such as *H. venusta*, which see.

Plant size 15–20 cm (6½–8) dia., 10 cm (4 in.) high. Rootstock creeping, moderately stoloniferous. Petiole 2.5–4.5 cm by 0.4 cm (1–2 by 0.20, in.), purple-spotted on back, green. Leaf 2.5–4.5 cm by 1–2.5 cm (1–2 by 0.5–1 in.), erect and in line with petiole, ovate-cordate, moderately wavy margin, erect, rigid, leathery, polished dark green above, glossy lighter green below, tip tapering to mucronate. Venation 3–4, sunken above, very projected, smooth, below. Scape 12.5–30 cm (5–12 in.), straight, obliquely ascending, green, purplish red tinted for entire length. Sterile bracts 1–3, clasping stem, withering by anthesis; fertile bracts short, navicular, grooved, green, loosely imbricate, persisting and not opening at flowering. Raceme short, 3–10 flowers. Flowers purple lobes, narrow tube white, held erect on purple-tinted pedicels, 5 cm (2 in.) long, 2 cm (0.8 in.) broad, funnel-shaped, stamens conspicuously exserted. Average anthesis July. Anthers purple. Fertile.

HN: Pretty Plantain Lily.
　　 Rock Princess.
JN: *Hime Iwa Giboshi* hort. incorrect.
　　 Sobo Hime Iwa Giboshi hort. incorrect.
　　 Ubatake Giboshi Fujita 1976a.

Figure 3-58. *H. pulchella*; flower detail (Hosta Hill)

H. pulchella 'Kifukurin' hort.
黄覆輪ウバタケギボウシ

Kifukurin Ubatake Giboshi, the "yellow-margined grandmother mountain hosta," was found as a wildling in Miyazaki Prefecture, on the south side of Mount Sobo. A nonperpetuating mutant, it is maintained as a cultivar form.
JN: *Kifukurin Ubatake Giboshi*.

H. pulchella 'Sobo' hort.
祖母ヒメイワギボウシ

Sobo Hime Iwa Giboshi, the "Mount Sobo hosta," is considered an incorrect Japanese synonym for the species *H. pulchella* which was found on Mount Sobo (Ubatake).
JN: *Sobo Hime Iwa Giboshi.*

H. pulchella 'Urajiro' hort.
裏白ウバタケギボウシ

Urajiro Ubatake Giboshi, the "white-backed grandmother mountain hosta," was discovered growing on south-facing cliffs in Miyazaki Prefecture among the typical population. A nonperpetuating mutation, it is maintained as a cultivar form.
JN: *Urajiro Ubatake Giboshi* hort.

H. pycnophylla Maekawa 1976.
AHS-III/13A.   (Figures 2-29, 2-31, 3-59; Plate 54).
セトウチギボウシ

Setouchi Giboshi, the "Setouchi hosta,' grows in Eastern Honshu, Yamaguchi Prefecture. The type (No. 35673 in TI, coll. K. Oka) was discovered on the mountain ridges of Oshima Island (there are several islands which have this name) located in the Japanese Inland Sea opposite the town of Yanai. The species epithet means "densely arranged leaves." The taxon has a thick, white, pruinose coating on the underside of the leaves and the petioles and forms dense leaf mounds to provide shading for the shallow root system. The leaves have a piecrust margin, and the bracts are large and glaucous. The reddish-purple dotting (actually elongated streaks) on the petioles is very distinct. Multibranched scapes have been observed in the wild and in cultivation. In Japan it is cultivated in elevated pots to show the white-backed leaves. Aside from being a collector's item this hosta is used for breeding. A specimen conversation piece in the garden, it should be planted in front where its many outstanding features, such as the attractive red-purple-spotted petioles, can be closely examined.

Plant size 45 cm (18 in.) dia., 25 cm (10 in.) high. Petiole 25–30 by 0.8 cm (10–12 by 0.3 in.), spreading horizontally, light yellowish green, distinct red-purple spots (streaks) increasing in frequency towards the ground, pruinose below. Leaf 20–25 by 17.5 cm (8–10 by 7 in.), entire, ovate to ovate-cordate, with flat surface and piecrust margin, dull rust green to olive-green, later with a slight sheen above, permanently intensely pruinose, white below. Venation 8–9, projected below. Scape 35 cm (16 in.), projecting obliquely from crown, smooth, round, rust green.

Figure 3-59. *H. pycnophylla*; expanding raceme detail (Hosta Hill)

Sterile bracts, 2–3, navicular, large; fertile bracts, large, imbricated, thick, slightly pruinose, light green, persistent. Raceme short, densely imbricated, 10–20 flowers. Flowers purple to dark purple, 4.5 by 3 cm (1.75 by 1.25 in.) across the lobes, carried horizontally on strong pedicels, 2.5 cm (1 in.) long, extending beyond the bracts; perianth expanding, funnel-shaped, in the central part dilated bell-shaped, lobes spreading ±angled to the axis of perianth; stamens far exceeding the lobes. Anthers purple. August. Fertile.
HN: *H. pycnophylla* 'Setouchi' hort. incorrect.
        H. 'Setouchi' hort. incorrect.
JN: *Noshi Setouchi Giboshi* Grenfell 1990 (?).
        Setouchi Giboshi Fujita 1976a.
        Urajiro Setouchi Giboshi hort. incorrect.

H. pycnophylla 'Ogon' hort.
黄金セトウチギボウシ

Ogon Setouchi Giboshi, the "golden Setouchi hosta," is one of the naturally occurring chlorophyll variants of the species with yellowish leaves. It is represented by several very similar clones.
JN: *Ogon Setouchi Giboshi* hort.

H. pycnophylla 'Urajiro' hort.

Urajiro Setouchi Giboshi is a superfluous Japanese synonym for the species.

R

H. rectifolia Nakai 1930 var. *rectifolia*.
AHS-IV/19B.   (Plates 55, 153).
タチギボウシ

Tachi Giboshi, the "erect (upright, stately) hosta," ranges from northern Honshu, Tohoku District, to the north and west as far as the South Kurile Islands and the Ussuri region of the USSR. The type (in TI) was collected by Nakai in southern Hokkaido (Ezo, Yezo), Province Hidaka, on Mount Apoi near Urakawa. The leaves of this taxon have a very distinct, erect habit and form a vase-shaped clump. The species epithet means "erect leaves." The taxon is broadly related to *H. sieboldii*, and Fujita declared the two synonymous based on flower morphology. I do not accept this broad placement on grounds of micromorphological evidence presented by M. G. Chung and S. B. Jones (1989), which shows that *H. sieboldii* has a pollen type (RG-II-B) different from that of *H. rectifolia* (RG/IV). Macromorphologically, the latter typifies a group of hostas which are larger in all respects than *H. sieboldii*, with much darker flowers and with taller, very erect scapes, and purple instead of yellow anthers. The anthers have been characterized as being whitish or yellowish with purple margins, but this observation was made after dehiscence. In the unopened flower they are uniformly purple-dotted on a yellow background, looking light purple. Many different forms exist, some with narrow leaves and others with moderately wide leaves that approach *H. rectifolia* var. *australis* in form, and several have been given botanical rank. A number of yellow-leaved and variegated forms have been found as mutations in the wild as well as in cultivation, and a few have been given Japanese cultivar names, for example, *H.* 'Tsugaru Nishiki', which see. *Hosta rectifolia* is an extremely useful landscape hosta for mass plantings, large edgings, and as specimen clumps. The leaves are larger and more erect than *H. lancifolia*, and the very straight, tall scapes with many dark purple flowers present an imposing picture (Plate 55).

Plant size 30 cm (12 in.) dia., 35 cm (14 in.) high. Petiole 17.5–20 by 0.8 cm (7–8 by 0.33 in.), erect, forming a vase-shaped plant, green with no purple dots at the base. Leaf 17.5–20 by 7.5–10 cm (7–8 by 3–4 in.), erect and in line with petiole, lanceolate, petiole transition decurrent, flat, smooth, shiny light, dull, dark green above, glossy lighter green below, tip acuminate. Venation 6–7, lightly impressed above, smooth below. Scape 80–100 cm (32–40 in.), straight and erect, perpendicular, not bending, light green, no purple marks. Sterile bracts, 2–4, clasping stem; fertile bracts, short, blunt, navicular, thin, membranous, green purple-tipped, withering at anthesis, but not falling away. Raceme 16–25 flowers, widely spaced. Flowers 5 cm (2 in.) long, 3.5 cm (1.5 in.) broad, purple-striped; purple, thin narrow tube, perianth expanding, lily-shaped, lobes spreading rapidly, recurving, widely open, pedicels 9–12 mm (0.5 in.), very projecting stamen. Anthers purple. August. Fertile.

SY: *Funkia longipes* Irving 1903 incorrectly applied.
     Hosta albomarginata Fujita 1976a sl na.
     H. apoiensis Nakai ex Miyabe and Kudo 1932 in syn.
     H. atropurpurea Nakai 1930 pp sim.
     H. harunaensis Honda 1935b.
     H. rectifolia var. *sachalinensis* Maekawa 1940 pp sim.
     H. sieboldii var. *rectifolia* Hara 1984 na.
HN: Erect-leaved Plantain Lily.
     H. recta hort. incorrect.
     H. rectifolia '1666' hort. UK incorrect.
     H. sachalinensis Koidzumi 1936 pp sim.
JN: *Ezo Giboshi* Koidzumi 1936 pp sim.
     Oze Mizu Giboshi hort. incorrect.
     Rishiri Giboshi hort. incorrect.
     Tachi Giboshi Nakai 1930.

H. rectifolia 'Kinbuchi' hort.
キンブチタチギボウシ

Kinbuchi Tachi Giboshi, the "yellow-margined, erect-leaved hosta," was discovered by Hachiro Negishi. This mutation is like the white-margined form except the margins are yellow. Cultivated in Japan, it is a collector's item. A nonperpetuating mutation, it is maintained as a cultivar form.
JN: *Kinbuchi Tachi Giboshi* hort.

H. rectifolia 'Maruba' hort.
マルバタチギボウシ   (Plate 56).

Maruba Tachi Giboshi, the "round-leaved, erect hosta," looks like the species but has leaves that are ovate-rounded. This taxon is macromorphologically the same as *H. rectifolia* var. *australis* (Plate 56), which see.
SY: *H. rectifolia* var. *australis* pp.
JN: *Maruba Tachi Giboshi* hort.

H. rectifolia 'Ogon' hort.
AHS-IV/23A.
黄金タチ

Ogon Tachi Giboshi, the "golden erect-leaved hosta," represents a group of yellow sports occasionally found among the wild and cultivated populations. Several types are known, all smaller than the species, some remaining yellow, others turning chartreuse or light green by anthesis. Nonperpetuating mutations, they are maintained as cultivar forms.
HN: *H. rectifolia* 'Foliis Luteis' hort. incorrect.
JN: *Ogon Tachi Giboshi* hort.

H. rectifolia 'Oze' hort.
オゼギボウシ
オゼミズギボウシ

Oze Giboshi or *Oze Mizu Giboshi* are Japanese synonyms applied to *H. rectifolia*. They are generally considered incorrect and/or superfluous.
JN: *Oze Giboshi* hort.
     Oze Mizu Giboshi hort.
(see *H. rectifolia*).

H. rectifolia 'Rishiri' hort.
利尻ギボウシ

Rishiri Giboshi is a Japanese synonym applied to *H. rectifolia* and generally considered incorrect or superfluous.
JN: *Rishiri Giboshi* hort.
(see *H. rectifolia*).

H. rectifolia var. *australis* Maekawa ex W. G. Schmid var. nov.
AHS-IV/19B.   (Plate 56).
マルバタチギボウシ

Maruba Tachi Giboshi is the "round-leaved erect hosta." The varietal epithet appears on herbarium sheet 643 225/6560 in TI. No Japanese formal name was given, but I have assigned a descriptive Japanese name which is also used in Japanese horticulture. The botanical name means "the southern rectifolia." The type was collected in central Honshu, Gumma Prefecture, in the Ozegahara Plain near Tone-gun by M. Mizushima, 29 August 1954. The plain is a great moorland located near Lake Ozenuma at the western end of Nikko National Park bordering Gumma and Fukushima prefectures. The leaves differ considerably, being shorter and more rounded than those of the type, and the plant is smaller. There is some representation of this taxon in TI. According to collector's records on herbarium sheets, the northern limit of habitat is in the Hokkada mountains in Aomori Prefecture, south of Aomori City, where populations are found at 1400 m (4600 ft.) on Mount Odake (or Sukayu; 1585 m/5200 ft.). The area lies within the northern part of Towada-Hachimantai National Park, so is protected and has still largely untouched forests. The specimen representing the northern populations of this taxon has slightly shorter scapes and petioles and was collected by H. Koyama, 5 September 1952, in TI, No. 643 29052 (No. 1563). Cultivated at Fuchu, Tokyo, this hosta is not in Western gardens at this time but is represented in scientific collections. *Hosta rectifolia* 'Maruba', a cultivated variety, belongs to this taxon. Because of the existence of allopatric populations in the wild I have validated Maekawa's name in Appendix A electing Mizushima's specimen as a lectotype.

Plant similar to *H. rectifolia* but with ovate elliptical leaves, not as decurrent to the petiole as the type: Plant 25 cm (10 in.) dia., 25 cm (10 in.) high. Petiole 15–25 cm (6–10 in.), erect, winged only in the upper part, forming a vase-shaped plant, green. Leaf 13–15 by 8–10 cm (5–6 by 3–4 in.), erect and in line with petiole, ovate-elliptical, petiole transition not as decurrent as in the type, flat, smooth, shiny light, dull, dark green above, glossy lighter green below, tip obtuse. Venation 5–6, lightly impressed above, smooth below. Scape 45–90 cm (18–36 in.), straight and erect, perpendicular, not bending, light green, no purple marks. Sterile bracts, 1–3, clasping stem; fertile bracts, short, blunt, navicular, thin, membranous, green purple-tipped, withering at anthesis, but not falling away. Raceme 16–25 flowers, widely spaced. Flowers 5 cm (2 in.) long and 3.5 cm (1.5 in.) broad, purple-striped; purple, thin narrow tube, perianth expanding, lily-shaped, lobes spreading rapidly, recurving, widely open, pedicels 9–12 mm (0.5 in.), very projecting stamen. Anthers purple. August. Fertile.

HN: *H. rectifolia* 'Maruba' hort. sim.
JN: *Maruba Tachi Giboshi* Schmid.

✠ *"H. rectifolia* var. *chionea"* Maekawa 1938b.
AHS-IV/22A.
Here reduced to cultivar form as *H. rectifolia* 'Chionea'.
ギンブチタチギボウシ

Ginbuchi Tachi Giboshi, the "silver (white)-margined, erect(-leaved) hosta," was found among a cultivated group in northern Honshu, Aomori Prefecture, Hirosaki City. It is considered a cultivar. This clone has 5 pairs of veins versus the species, which has 7, and it is smaller and different in other respects and rarely seen cultivated. Associated with *H. sieboldii* by Hara (1984) as *H. sieboldii* var. *rectifolia* f. *chionea*, this relationship is not accepted in a narrow sense on palynological grounds.

Petiole 15–20 cm (6–8 in.) long, green, flattened. No purple dots on the petiole and scape. Leaf 10–15 by 5 cm (4–6 by 2 in.), erect and in line with petiole, lanceolate, petiole transition gradual, decurrent, flat, erect, smooth, thin textured, silvery white (argenteus) margin on dark green leaf, tip acuminate. Venation 5, impressed above, smooth below. August. Barely fertile.

SY: *H. rectifolia* var. *chionea* Maekawa 1938b.
H. rectifolia f. *chionea* Maekawa 1950.
H. sieboldii var. *rectifolia* f. *chionea* Hara 1984 na.
HN: *H. rectifolia* 'Chionea' hort.
H. rectifolia f. *chionea* hort.
JN: *Ginbuchi Tachi Giboshi* Maekawa 1938b.

✠ *"H. rectifolia* var. *chionea* f. *albiflora"* (Tatewaki) Maekawa 1940.
AHS-IV/22A.
Here reduced to cultivar form as *H. rectifolia* 'Albiflora'.
シロバナタチギボウシ

Shirobana Tachi Giboshi, the "white flowered, erect-leaved hosta," was found as a naturally occurring mutation among dark-flowered colonies in southern Hokkaido. First published by Tatewaki in 1934, it is nonperpetuating and here reduced to cultivar form. It is a white-flowered form of *H. rectifolia* var. *chinoea*, to which it is morphologically identical except for the flower color. It was associated with *H. sieboldii* by Hara (1984), based on Tatewaki (1934). Other white-flowered forms very closely related to *H. rectifolia*, including *H. atropurpurea* f. *albiflora* Tatewaki and *H. rectifolia* f. *leucantha* Ito (1934), have been combined into this taxon because very few macromorphological differences exist between them, and all of them have the key differentiating feature of white flowers. It is not often seen in cultivation and is a collector's item.

SY: *H. atropurpurea* f. *albiflora* Tatewaki 1934.
H. rectifolia f. *albiflora* Tatewaki 1934.
H. rectifolia var. *atropurpurea* f. *albiflora* Ito 1969.
H. sieboldii var. *rectifolia* f. *albiflora* Hara 1984 na.
H. sieboldii var. *rectifolia* f. *leucantha* Hara 1984 na.
HN: *H. rectifolia* 'Albiflora' hort.
H. rectifolia 'Chionea Alba' hort.
JN: *Shirobana Tachi Giboshi* Tatewaki 1934.

H. rectifolia var. *rectifolia* f. *pruinosa* Maekawa 1940.
AHS-IV/19A.
トノコタチギボウシ

Tonoko Tachi Giboshi, the "pruinose, erect-leaved hosta," is a natural modification of the species. The type (in TI) was collected in eastern Hokkaido, Province Kushiro, Higashi-

Kushiro. It is much like the species except that the leaves, scapes, and bracts are pruinose. The pruinosity fades by anthesis. This hosta is rarely cultivated in Western gardens but has been observed at the botanic garden, Uppsala, Sweden. It was associated with *H. sieboldii* by Hara (1984). It blooms in August and is fertile.

SY: *H. sieboldii* var. *rectifolia* f. *pruinosa* Hara 1984 na.
HN: *H. rectifolia* 'Pruinosa' hort.
JN: *Tonoko Tachi Giboshi* Maekawa 1940.

H. rectifolia var. *sachalinensis* (Koidzumi) Maekawa 1940.
AHS-IV/19B. (Plate 203).
エゾギボウシ

Ezo Giboshi, the "hosta from Ezo," was discovered by Koidzumi on Sakhalin, near Sakaehama, in 1930. The Japanese name is derived from Ezo (Yezo, Yeso), an old name for Hokkaido. Allopatric populations occur in the Chishima volcanic range, in Karafuto, and in the Ussuri River region, far eastern USSR. It is identical to *H. rectifolia*, except that it is moderately larger and the flowers are darker. Fujita's synonymy with *H. sieboldii* is not accepted by me on palynological grounds (see under *H. rectifolia*). The names *Tachi Giboshi* and *Ezo Giboshi*, are frequently used as synonyms. Maintained as a botanical variety on ecological and palynological grounds, this taxon is similar to *H. rectifolia* but has very dark purple-suffused flowers. It is available in the West but seldom seen.

SY: *H. albomarginata* Fujita 1976a sl na.
H. rectifolia var. *sachalinensis* Maekawa 1969.
H. sachalinensis Koidzumi 1936.
JN: *Ezo Giboshi* Maekawa 1940.

"H. rhodeifolia" Maekawa sphalm.
This orthographically incorrect spelling of the species epithet has been corrected.
(see *H. rohdeifolia*).

✠ *"H. rohdeifolia* f. *rohdeifolia"* Maekawa 1937.
AHS-IV/22A. (Figure 2-28).
Here reduced to cultivar form as *H. rohdeifolia* 'Rohdeifolia' or abbreviated as *H.* 'Rohdeifolia'.
オモトギボウシ
黄覆輪オモトギボウシ

Omoto Giboshi or *Kifukurin Omoto Giboshi*, the "yellow-margined Rohdea(-leaved) hosta," was described by Maekawa (1940) as a species. However, it has not been found in the wild but rather as a mutation among cultivated populations of the all-green species. The leaves are comparable to *Omoto*, the Japanese rohdea (*Rohdea japonica*); hence the name. In Japan horticulturists combine the margined and all-green forms under the name *Omoto Giboshi*. Taxa cultivated in North America under *H. rohdeifolia* 'Aureo-marginata' and *H. rhodeifolia* 'Albo-marginata' are named incorrectly; they do not relate to this hosta, but belong to the *H.* 'Fortunei' complex. As reported by Schmid (1987b), the spelling "rhodeifolia" (Gr. *rhodon* = rose, leaves like a rose) as used by Maekawa and repeated in most of the botanical and horticultural literature, is an orthographic error and should be "rohdeifolia." The latter means "with leaves like the *Rohdea*," which in Japan is known as *Omoto*. The name has been corrected here and in Appendix A. *Rohdea japonica* is named for Michael Rohde, a German physician and botanist. This taxon is similar to and closely related to *H. sieboldii*, but it is larger and has narrow yellow margins. Fujita considered it synonymous with *H. sieboldii*; both taxa have whitish yellow anthers. Ruh and Zilis (1989) reported that some of the plants in the United States under the name *H.* 'Helonioides Albopicta' are the yellow-margined *H.*

rohdeifolia. This can be verified by the latter's anther color, which is yellowish white, and by its venation count, which is 5–6 versus purple anthers and 3–4 pairs of veins for *H.* 'Helonioides Albopicta'. This report requires further verification because most of the plants cultivated in North America as *H.* 'Helonioides Albopicta' have purple anthers, so cannot be *H. rohdeifolia* as stated by Ruh and Zilis. Originally found with all-green leaves in Kansai region, this taxon is difficult to delimit because in some parts of its range it is a cultivar near housing (Fujita, 1976a). From there it has escaped back into the wild where it occurs sympatrically with *H. sieboldii*. It should be pointed out that all these taxa have all-green leaves. The yellow-margined form described here is a rare mutant which does not perpetuate in the wild and was brought into cultivation where it is maintained as a cultivar. This means that the species turns out to be a cultivar while its all-green form *H. rohdeifolia* f. *viridis* is in fact the naturally occurring taxon. The specific name *H. rohdeifolia* f. *rohdeifolia* has been reduced to cultivar form as *H. rohdeifolia* 'Rohdeifolia'. Horticulturists and gardeners may simply call it *H.* 'Rohdeifolia'.

Plant size 30–40 cm (12–16 in.) dia., 35–40 cm (14–16 in.) high. Petiole 12.5–25 by 0.5 cm (5–10 by 0.2 in.), erect, marginal yellowish striation bleaching to white by anthesis, otherwise green. Leaf 12.5–15 by 5 cm (5–6 by 2 in.), erect and in line with petiole, lanceolate to oblong-lanceolate, broadened in the upper part (like the leaf of *Rohdea japonica*), petiole transition discernable, angled, sub-obtuse tip, ±arching midrib, flat margins, slightly convolute, green with narrow yellow margins in spring, bleaching to white by anthesis, moderate sheen above, shiny below. Venation 5–6, impressed above, projected, smooth below. Scape 75–120 cm (30–48 in.), straight and erect, not bending, light green, no purple marks. Sterile bracts 3–6, convolutely clasping stem, green with whitish green margin, persistent; fertile bracts short, navicular, thin, membranous, green, withering at anthesis, but not falling away. Raceme has 6–10 flowers, widely spaced. Flowers 5 cm (2 in.) long and 3.5 cm (1.5 in.) broad, purple-striped inside, thin, narrow tube, perianth expanding, lily-shaped, lobes spreading, recurving, short pedicels, stamens shorter than the perianth, abruptly nodding. Anthers light yellow. August. Fertile.

SY: "*H. rhodeifolia*" Maekawa 1937 incorrect.
       "*H. rhodeifolia*" Maekawa 1940 incorrect.
HN: *H. rhodeifolia* hort. incorrect.
       H. rhodeifolia 'Albo-marginata' hort. incorrect (= *H.* 'Fortunei Gloriosa').
       H. rhodeifolia 'Aureo-marginata' hort. incorrect (= *H.* 'Fortunei Aureomarginata'.
       H. rhodiefolia aureo marginata hort. incorrect.
       H. rhodiefolia 'Aureus' hort. incorrect.
JN: *Kifukurin Omoto Giboshi* hort.
       Omoto Giboshi Maekawa 1937.
       Omotoba Giboshi hort.

H. rohdeifolia f. *viridis* Maekawa 1940.
   AHS-IV/19A.   (Figure 3-60).
アオバオモトギボウシ

Aoba Omoto Giboshi, the "green-leaved hosta with leaves like *Rohdea*," grows around Mount Hiei, in western Japan, principally in Chugoku District, Kyoto Prefecture, and it also occurs in marshy areas in Kansai District. Populations with slightly modified forms are reported in Nagano and Aichi prefectures, and west of this area this taxon forms sympatric populations with *H. sieboldii*. This is the naturally occurring taxon from which the yellow-margined mutation was selected.

One of the herbarium specimens (No. 643/39519 in MAK ex KYO) has the annotation "Koosodani in Mount Hieizan," Kyoto Prefecture, and since no type has been designated this specimen has been elected the lectotype. Mount Hiei (848 m/382 ft.) is a short distance northeast of Kyoto near the shores of Lake Biwa. Morphologically this taxon is similar to *H. sieboldii* but has much longer petioles, different leaf shape and bracts, and it may be an interspecific hybrid. Authentic, collected specimens of this taxon are rarely available and sparsely represented in herbaria. I have not seen authentic specimens of it in cultivation in the West.

SY: *H. rhodeifolia* f. *viridis* Maekawa 1940 (sphalm) incorrect.
HN: *H. rhodeifolia* 'Viridis' hort.
JN: *Aoba Omoto Giboshi* Maekawa 1940.

Figure 3-60. *H. rohdeifolia* f. *viridis*; specimen in KYO

H. rupifraga Nakai 1930.
   AHS-IV/19A.   (Figure 3-61; Plate 57).
ハチジョウギボウシ

Hachijo Giboshi, the "Hachijo hosta," is named for Hachijojima, the island upon which it evolved. The type was based on specimens collected by Matsuzaki and Ogata on this volcanic island located in the subtropical region of the Pacific Ocean 350 km (220 miles) south of Tokyo. The epithet was derived from *rupifragus* (= growing in the cleft of rocks) and is often incorrectly ascribed to *rupifractus* (from *frangere* = breaking rocks) (Smith, 1963). Reportedly, this species evolved in total isolation from other members of the genus, and although Maekawa (1940) reported purple anthers, specimens vegetatively propagated from plants collected at the site have distinctly bicolor anthers pointing to introgressive hybridization. Characters acquired from both parental species may have produced a new race capable of surviving in the hostile environment of the rocky rim of Mount Nishi (Hachijo-Fuji, 854m/2802 ft.). More detailed study is needed to solve this puzzle but it should be pointed out that Fujita (1976a) held this taxon to be synonymous with *H. longipes* var. *latifolia* which occurs as isolated colonies in the mountains of Izu Peninsula. Retaining many of the features of *H. longipes*, this taxon has more broadly ovate, leathery, almost succulent leaves. Many *Hosta* discoveries have been made in this volcanic chain beginning with Mount Fuji (Fuji-san) and Mount Hakone to the north and extending south where it formed the seven Izu Islands (Izu-Shichito), Hachijojima being the southernmost. Fujita (1976a) stated he had not seen the type

Figure 3-61. *H. rupifraga*; expanding raceme detail (Hosta Hill)

species of *H. rupifraga*, so Maekawa's 1940 classification has been maintained.

This hosta is relatively rare in its habitat and the natural allopatric population is limited to an area of less than one acre on the rim of Hachijo-Fuji at elevation 2500 feet (845 meters). In spring it arises together with *Astilbe hachijoensis* and other alpines in full sun and by early summer the leaf mounds are shaded by taller grasses and stay in this shade for the remainder of the season (Craig, 1971). In 1969 several authentic specimens were collected by Craig on the rim of the volcano and sent to Summers (Nos. 430–437) and Davidson. These have been extensively and vegetatively propagated, making the very scarce *H. rupifraga* available for cultivation in North America and elsewhere. This collection can be considered extremely fortuitous because a few years ago the volcano erupted (Davidson, 1990) and in all probability destroyed the entire population growing around its rim. I have not been able to confirm this, however.

Unfortunately, some plants in the trade under this name are not this species but hybridized taxa. *Hosta longipes* var. *latifolia* 'Maruba' (*H.* 'Maruba Iwa') is morphologically similar but its scapes are longer. Although native to a subtropical region, the adaptability of *H. rupifraga* to colder climates has been demonstrated and it is a highly desirable hosta for the rock garden as it will grow in a man-made scree. Its heavy leaf substance makes it virtually slugproof, and many hybridizers are using it to impart that trait to other hostas. Authentic specimens are scarce but occasionally available.

Plant size 25–30 cm (10–12 in.) dia., 15–20 cm (6–8 in.) high. Petiole 25–7.5 cm by 0.8 cm (1–3 by 0.30 in.), rigid, blunt on back, not keeled, green. Leaf 12.5–15 by 10–12.5 cm (5–6 by 4–5 in.), erect and in line with petiole, leathery, ovate to ovate-cordate, transition tight and contracted, very acuminate tip, undulate in the margin, smooth surface, dark green above, lighter green below. Venation 7–9, widely spaced, projected, glabrous below. Scape 25–30 (10–12 in.), obliquely arching, smooth, round, sea-green, slightly pruinose, permanently purple-dotted in lower half. Sterile bracts 4–5; fertile bracts 2 cm, navicular, thick, densely imbricated, whitish green, tinted purple, withering, falling away during anthesis. Raceme densely arranged, 8–12 flowers. Flowers 4 cm (1.7 in.) long and 2 cm (0.8 in.) broad, purple-striped inside, thin narrow tube, perianth expanding, lobes straightly spreading, bell-shaped, pedicels 1.2 cm (0.5 in.), abruptly nodding, stamens shorter than the perianth. Anthers bicolor purple-yellow. August. Fertile.

SY: *H. longipes* var. *latifolia* Fujita 1976a sl na.
HN: Hachijo Mountain Hosta.
Hachijo Plantain Lily.
Hosta rubrafraga incorrect.
JN: *Hachijo Giboshi* Nakai 1930.
Izu Iwa Giboshi Fujita 1976a sl na.

H. rupifraga 'Ki Hachijo' hort.
黄八丈
Ki Hachijo (Giboshi), the "(golden-) yellow Hachijo hosta," is a horticultural hybrid that has a golden yellow leaf resulting from cross-breeding the species.
JN: *Ki Hachijo (Giboshi)* hort.

H. rupifraga 'Kifukurin Ki Hachijo' hort.
黄覆輪黄八丈
Kifukurin Ki Hachijo (Giboshi), the "yellow-margined, yellow Hachijo hosta," is a horticultural hybrid having a golden yellow margin on a yellowish white leaf resulting from cross-breeding the species.
JN: *Kifukurin Ki Hachijo (Giboshi)*.

H. rupifraga 'Koriyama' hort.
This cultivar name is of unknown origin and apparently incorrect, because plants received from Japan and cultivated in North America under this name are identical to *Urajiro Hachijo Giboshi*, the white-backed form of *H. longipes* var. *latifolia*. Koriyama is a place name and there is no record of the cultivar growing there.

H. rupifraga 'Urajiro' hort.
This name is used as a synonym for the white-backed form of *H. longipes* var. *latifolia*. (see *H. longipes* var. *latifolia* 'Urajiro Hachijo').

S

✤ *"H. sacra"* Maekawa 1938b.
AHS-III/15A.   (Plates 58, 159).
Here reduced to cultivar form as *H.* 'Sacra'.
サクラギボウシ
Sakura Giboshi, the "sacred hosta" grows in northern Honshu. The Japanese name as well as the species epithet mean "sacred," intimating the use of this stately hosta around religious shrines and in temple gardens. Discovered by Kikuchi in cultivation near the town of Hirosaki, located in Aomori Prefecture in northern Honshu, it is close to *H. nigrescens* except for the fertile bracts which are very boat-shaped, not flat. It has large, flattened leaves and strong, deeply grooved, widely spreading petioles, resulting in a flat mound that is quite different from the erect mound seen in *H. nigrescens*. The narrow part of the perianth is never grooved. In 1969 Maekawa no longer listed this taxon as a species, and in 1976 Fujita also ignored it, so it is treated as a cultigen and reduced to cultivar form. Horticulturists in Japan occasionally place it with *H. kiyosumiensis* even though the two taxa are not related. Its place of discovery indicates it may be an interspecific hybrid of *H. nigrescens* with a *Helipteroides* species as the other parent. Being similar to many of the tall-scaped hybrids of the *H. sieboldiana/H. nigrescens* group it has not been widely distributed. It can be seen around religious shrines in central and northern Honshu. Plants cultivated in North America under the name *H. sacra* are green-leaved with no pruinosity and

differ considerably from Maekawa's diagnosis, so they are not this taxon.

Plant size 50–65 cm (20–26 in.) dia., 35 cm (14 in.) high. Petiole 22.5–30 by 2.5 cm (9–12 by 1 in.), spreading horizontally, deeply canaliculate, green, purple-dotted at base. Leaf 17.5–30 by 15–22.5 cm (7–12 by 6–9 in.), entire, ovate-elliptical to ovate-cordate, truncate at base, very pointed, generally "flat" surface, but slightly undulate in the margin, pruinose grey-green to green to dark green, opaque above, lighter green, pruinose below, tip acuminate. Venation 12–13, sunken above, very projected, smooth, below. Scape 75–100 cm (30–40 in.), straight, erect, glaucous, purple-dotted lower third. Sterile bracts, 1–2; fertile bracts, large, navicular, imbricate, membranous, green suffused with purple, remaining fresh at anthesis. Raceme short, up to 20 flowers, densely arranged. Flower 5 cm (2 in.) long and 2.5 cm (1 in.) broad, medium size, white, but suffused very slightly purple inside, expanding, funnel-shaped, in the central part dilated bell-shaped, lobes spreading straight to the axis of perianth, stamens not very superior, equal or slightly shorter than perianth. Anthers purple. June/July. Fertile.

HN: *H. kiyosumiensis* 'Sacra' hort. incorrect.
H. kiyosumiensis var. *sacra* hort. incorrect.
JN: *Sakura Giboshi* Maekawa 1938b.

H. shikokiana Fujita 1976a.
AHS-IV/19A.   (Figure 3-62; Plate 59).
シコクギボウシ

Shikoku Giboshi, the "hosta from Shikoku," is found in northern Shikoku, Kochi Prefecture south of the Ishizuki and Akaishi mountain ranges, and in Ehime Prefecture, where the type was collected by Yamanaka on Mount Higashiakaishi. It is a mountain-dwelling species, growing on wet rock outcrops and ridge lines above altitude ±3000 ft. (±1000 m). After examination of several herbarium specimens including the holotype, placement of this species in *Eubryocles* as proposed by Fujita is not accepted here on macromorphological and ecological grounds. A small hosta, it looks very much like *H. longipes* and occurs sympatrically with it in overlapping areas of habitat. It combines morphological characteristics of *H. longipes*, *H. kikutii*, and *H. montana* (papillose veins), and I have placed it in section *Rhynchophorae* on a provisional basis. Although available through academic sources, this hosta species is of minor horticultural value and is of interest to collectors only.

Plant size 25 cm (12 in.) dia., 15 cm (6 in.) high. Petiole 10 by 0.6 cm (4 by 0.25 in.), erect, green, purple-spotted lower half. Leaf 18–20 by 7.5–8 cm (7–8 by 3–4 in.), entire-elliptical, ovate to ovate-cordate, petiole-leaf transition shortly attenuate, no waves or very slight waves in margin, not rugose, shiny green above, shiny lighter green below, tip very pointed, acuminate. Venation 8–10, closely spaced, projected below and papillose. Scape 40 cm (16 in.), oblique, leaning in the upper part, smooth round, purple-dotted for the most part. Sterile bracts, 2–3 tightly clasping stem; fertile bracts, lanceolate, navicular, loosely imbricate, not open at flowering, purplish, withering but persistent at anthesis, ±2 by 0.5 cm (0.75 by 0.2 in.). Raceme short, densely imbricated, 5–8 flowers. Flowers purple to pale purple, 5 cm (2 in.) long, carried horizontally on strong pedicels, 1.2 cm (0.5 in.) long, purple; perianth expanding, funnel-shaped, in the central part dilated bell-shaped, lobes spreading ±angled to the axis of perianth; stamens exceeding the perianth. Anthers purple. July. Fertile.

JN: *Shikoku Giboshi* Fujita 1976a.

H. sieboldi nom. illeg. hort.   (Figure A-1).
This name based on *Funkia sieboldi* Lindley 1839 is an illegitimate name that was never validated under *Hosta*. *Funkia sieboldi* is listed as a synonym for *Hosta sieboldiana*, although Lindley's taxon may not have been *H. sieboldiana* at all; the original illustration looks more like a *H.* 'Fortunei' type. The names *H. sieboldi*, *H. sieboldii*, *Funkia sieboldi*, and *Funkia sieboldii* have been used frequently in the horticultural literature to label *Hosta sieboldiana* (Downing, 1841; Henderson, 1881; Jekyll, 1899, 1901). This horticultural use is incorrect and illegitimate because the earlier, valid homonym, *H. sieboldii* (based on *Hemerocallis sieboldii* Paxton 1838), exists against it, and the use of these names in this manner is against the rules. The name *Hosta sieboldii* is the correct name for a taxon formerly called *H. albomarginata*. Some gardeners have complained in print that the correct name is confusing, so to them I offer an easy way to remember the difference: *H. sieboldii* ends with an *i* as in little and applies to the smaller taxon, while *H. sieboldiana* ends with an *a* as in large and applies to the very large hosta cultivated under this name.

H. sieboldiana (Hooker) Engler 1888.
AHS-I/3B.   (Figures 3-63, 3-64, 3-71, 6-3, A-1, A-2; Plates 60, 164, 166, 172, 193).
トウギボウシ

Philipp Franz Balthasar von Siebold, who popularized *Hosta* in Europe, was recognized by four naturalists-botanists, who named hostas using his name: Loddiges in 1832 with *Hemerocallis sieboldtiana*; Paxton in 1838 with *Hemerocallis sieboldii*; Hooker in 1839 with *Funckia sieboldiana*; and Lindley, also in 1839 with *Funkia sieboldi* (not *sieboldii*). Except for Paxton's *Hemerocallis sieboldii*, the names are today applied to and considered synonyms of *Hosta sieboldiana*. But a study of contemporary illustrations show Loddiges' hosta to be a *H.* 'Fortunei' form with 10 pairs of veins (Figure A-2) and Lindley's hosta to be a *H. montana* form with 12–13 pairs of veins (Figure A-1). Only Hooker's plant appears to be a "typical" *H. sieboldiana* form with 14–16 pairs of veins. Paxton's is a different taxon, namely *H. sieboldii*, formerly called *H. albomarginata*.

A selected clonal form of *H. sieboldiana* has been made the quasi lectotype in Western gardens. It is large, stately, impres-

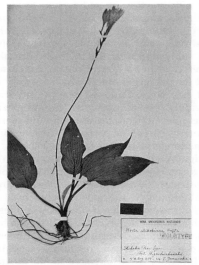

Figure 3-62. *H. shikokiana*; holotype in KYO

sive, and has been called the "Queen of Hosta." The selected clone named *H. sieboldiana* 'Gray Cole' (Kuk) exemplifies this Western form which can reach immense proportions of 1 m (3 ft.) high by 3 m (9 ft.) diameter (see Figure 3-63). The cultivated population includes many F_1 hybrid seedlings which have been selected for conformity to the accepted norm over the last century and a half. Subsequently propagated by vegetative methods to retain the desirable features, many of these cultivar/clones have been named and there is now a proliferation of well over 100 named cultivars which look very much like the idealized form of the species. In spite of its popularity and the accolades given to it, the form grown in Western gardens is by no means typical of the natural populations. Sugita (1988: personal communication) and several other Japanese naturalists have reported that they have never encountered wild colonies of *H. sieboldiana* which looked like the "European" form.

In Japan this taxon is called *To Giboshi* (Iwasaki and Iinuma, 1874), the "hosta of old," with natural populations in northern Ura-Nihon (Hokurikudo), the prefectures bordering the western side of central and northern Honshu, from Kyoto and Tottori prefectures, along the coast provinces, and beyond, north to Aomori Prefecture. The "type" was collected in Tottori Prefecture. Maekawa (1940) included in his description many features which do not conform to the Western concept of what *H. sieboldiana* should look like. For example, he referred to green leaves (a nonpruinose form included with the remark: "*planta glaucina vel viridis*" (= plant glaucous or green), tall scapes, and different leaf forms (Figure 3-64). Also recognizing the full extent of polymorphism in this species, Fujita (1976a) took an extreme position on synonymy by including the hybrid form *H.* 'Elata', *H. montana* and many of its varieties, and a number of other related hostas under the collective species name *H. sieboldiana* var. *sieboldiana*, thus widening its natural range to practically all Japan. He included, for example, *H. sieboldiana* var. *yakusimensis* Masamune 1932 and *H. yakusimensis* Maekawa 1950 growing at the extreme southern end of Japan on Yakushima.

This very broad view of the species has not been accepted here, and the evolutionary range of this taxon as delimited in this book is considered in a more narrow sense and within the area in Ura-Nihon specified by Maekawa. *Hosta sieboldiana* was first validly published by European botanists, and it is the "European type" grown in Western gardens that is considered here as the species in a more narrow sense and that is reflected in the description given by Hylander (1954). The European taxa are obviously described from cultivated and probably also hybridized material and do not represent Maekawa's natural populations. The taxon most often considered the archetypal, standard form in Western gardens is, in fact, a hybrid, namely, *H. sieboldiana* 'Elegans' (Arends, 1905; Hylander, 1954). But in Japan these hostas have also been extensively and selectively cultivated for centuries and include many "improved" clones. Some authors, including Hylander, have suggested that this "species" be used as a type species for subgenus *Giboshi*. Obviously, this can be done only if *H. sieboldiana* is regarded in a much broader sense, such as that proposed by Fujita.

Several plants of *H. sieboldiana*, apparently representing different clones, were introduced from Japan by von Siebold in 1829/1830. All these plants were obtained by von Siebold as cultivated specimens; they were not collected in the wild. They were sufficiently different to be given unique names, such as *Funkia cucullata*, *Funkia glauca*, and *Funkia sieboldiana*. One of these plants was first introduced into the botanic garden at Leiden with von Siebold's first shipment in 1829. He sent it to George Loddiges, England, who coined the basionym *Hemerocallis Sieboldtiana* in 1832. Another, somewhat different plant was sent to Hooker in Glasgow, from the nursery of L. J.

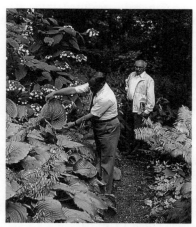

Figure 3-63. *H. sieboldiana*; general habit, seed-bearing; author holding huge leaf of immense clumps with Herr Becherer looking on; *Hydrangea aspera* ssp. *sargentiana* (left background) (Munich Botanic Garden/Dr. U. Fischer)

Makoy at Liège, Belgium. Originating with the hostas von Siebold had to leave behind in Ghent due to war action, it was described as *Funckia sieboldiana* in 1838. It has now been identified as the same one that was originally named *Funkia cucullata* (Hensen, 1963b). Thus, from the very beginning, very different plants were cultivated as *Hosta sieboldiana* and these differences can still be seen among the present garden cultivars. In its selected "best" form *H. sieboldiana* is a magnificent, very large specimen plant. Many of today's small gardens may have difficulty placing it, although it has been seen in small courtyards and garden borders as a specimen or accent plant. Public parks and gardens in Europe and North America include breathtaking mass plantings. It grows slowly and if undisturbed will reach its truly mature form in 15 years.

Plant size 70–90 cm (28–36 in.) wide, 35–45 cm (16–20 in.) high, ultimate size of plants in one place for 15 years was measured 140–160 by 80 cm (56–64 by 32 in.). Petiole 30–50 by 1.5 cm (12–20 by 0.75 in.), not or slightly winged, deeply grooved, slightly pruinose, fading, grey-green. Leaf 25–35 by 20–25 cm (10–14 by 8–10 in.), ultimate size can be 45 by 35 cm (18 by 14 in.), attitude at petiole spreading in a ±continuing flat arch, cordate, broadly ovate to orbicular-cordate in the radical leaves to ovate-cordate, longer pointed in the inner leaves, transition truncately, flattened, surface generally rugose, glaucous, pruinose, with some pruinosity remaining at sunken veins after anthesis, more glaucous on back ±permanent, grey-green. Venation 14–20, sunken above, very projected, strigose below, convergent and submarginally connected at tip area. Scape height identical to plant height or slightly above, 45–60 cm (20–24 in.), in long-established plants to 80 cm (32 in.), permanently pruinose, lasting at least until anthesis, erect, but bending back in upper part, yellow-green, smooth round. Sterile bracts, 1–3, large, sometimes foliaceous; fertile bracts, flat and broad, thick and fleshy, green or whitish green, developing and opening in a stellar form as seen from above. Raceme 25 cm (10 in.), 15–25 flowers. Flowers 5.5 cm (2.25 in.) long, 3 cm (1.25 in.) broad, mostly white, shiny, suffused very light purple in the middle of the lobe, densely arranged, expanding, funnel-shaped, in the central part dilated bell-shaped, lobes spreading straightly to ±angled to the axis of perianth, heavy textured, thick; stamens not superior, equal or slightly shorter than perianth. Anthers yellow. June. Fertile.

SY: *Funckia sieboldiana* Hooker 1838.
Funkia glauca Miquel 1869 pp.
Funkia sieboldi Lindley 1839 pp sl.
Funkia sieboldiana Baker 1870.
Funkia sieboldiana var. *glauca* Witte 1868.
Hemerocallis sieboldtiana Loddiges 1832 pp sl.
Hosta crassifolia Fujita 1976a sl na.
H. elata Fujita 1976a sl na.
H. fortunei var. *gigantea* Fujita 1976a sl na.
H. glauca Stearn 1931b.
H. kikutii var. *yakusimensis* (Masamune) Maekawa in Fujita 1976a na.
H. liliiflora Fujita 1976a sl na.
H. liliiflora var. *ovatolancifolia* Fujita 1976a sl na.
H. montana Fujita 1976a na.
H. montana var. *liliiflora* Fujita 1976a sl na.
H. montana var. *praeflorens* Fujita 1976a na.
H. sieboldiana var. *glauca* Makino 1902.
H. sieboldiana var. *sieboldiana* Hensen 1963a.
H. sieboldiana var. *sieboldiana* Fujita 1976a sl na.
H. sieboldiana var. *yakusimensis* Masamune in Fujita 1976a sl na.
H. yakusimensis (Masamune) Maekawa 1950 in Fujita 1976a sl pp na.
Hostia sieboldiana Voss 1896.
Niobe sieboldiana Nash 1911.
Saussurea sieboldiana Kuntze 1891.

HN: Cushion Plantain Lily.
Funkia glauca hort.
Funkia glaucescens hort. incorrect.
Hosta 'Brigham Blue' hort.
H. glauca hort. incorrect.
H. 'Mack No. 1'.
H. sieboldi hort. incorrect.
H. sieboldii hort. incorrect.
Seersucker Plantain Lily.
Short-Cluster Plantain Lily.
Siebold Funkia.
Siebold Plantain Lily.
Siebold's Funkia.
Siebold's Plantain Lily.

JN: *Oba Giboshi* Fujita 1976a sl na (incorrect in a strict sense).
To Giboshi Iwasaki and Iinuma 1874.

ON: Blaublattfunkie (German) pp.
Grosse Blaublatt Funkie (German) pp.
Siebold Funkie (German).
Siebold's Funkie (German).

Figure 3-64. *H. sieboldiana*; general habit, green, taller-scaped form (Hosta Hill ex Ura-Nihon, Yamagata Prefecture)

H. sieboldiana 'Aurea' hort.

An imprecise cultivar name applied to a variety of yellow forms of the species. I recommend the use of unique cultivar names for distinct, yellow forms.

H. sieboldiana Aureomarginata group.
黄覆輪トウギボウシ

Kifukurin To Giboshi is a group of yellow-margined sports of *H. sieboldiana* which have been found as mutations in the wild as well as in cultivation in Japan and in Western gardens. These mutations occur in several sizes and vary from the species only by the leaves which have very irregular, yellow margins. The best known of these sports is *H. sieboldiana* 'Frances Williams', which see. Botanically, these taxa should be considered a group of related plants of different origins, forms, and sizes, which also includes yellow-margined intermediate types belonging to *H. sieboldiana* related specioids, such as *H.* 'Tokudama'. Primary leaf color varies from intense blue-green to lighter greenish grey to medium green. Margin color can be chartreuse to yellowish white. Many different named forms are in the trade (see list of cultivar names). The variegation of some of these forms is unstable in the long run. In mature plants reversions to all-green and all-yellow leaves are common, as are very wide margins and half-green/half-yellow leaves. This instability is most common in older, mature plants and has been typified for the *H.* 'Frances Williams' clone by Zilis (1987). In Japan *marginata* forms of *To Giboshi* have been observed and collected in the wild as mutations and are now cultivated as *Kifukurin To Giboshi* or under one of the Western names. Some plants are necrotic (see under *H. sieboldiana* 'Frances Williams'), but on the other hand, according to their descriptions, a number of cultivars belonging to this group do not show marginal necrosis. Many horticultural articles have reported that all yellow margined forms of *H. sieboldiana* have a common, clonal origin, but this is clearly incorrect, and for this reason I have established this group under which the many different forms can be assembled.

Plant size 70–90 cm (28–36 in.) dia., 35–45 cm (16–20 in.) high, but it can be larger. Petiole 30–50 by 1.5 cm (12–20 by 0.75 in.), not or slightly winged, deeply grooved, slightly pruinose, fading, grey-green. Leaf 25–35 by 20–25 cm (10–14 by 8–10 in.), ultimate size can be larger, attitude at petiole spreading in a ±continuing flat arch, cordate, broadly ovate to orbicular-cordate in the radical leaves to ovate-cordate, longer pointed in the inner leaves, transition truncately flattened, surface rugose, irregularly undulate in the margin, glaucous, pruinose with some pruinosity remaining at sunken veins after anthesis, more glaucous on back ±permanent, bluish grey-green to greyish green to bright medium green leaf center with chartreuse to yellow margin, which is wide, irregular, and differing from leaf to leaf, with some much more yellow than others, occasionally showing all-yellow and all-green mutations in some leaves. Venation 13–19, sunken above, very projected below, convergent and submarginally connected at tip area. Scape height identical to plant height or slightly above, 45–60 cm (20–24 in.), in long-established plants to 80 cm (32 in.), permanently pruinose, lasting until at least anthesis, erect, but bending back in upper part, yellow-green, smooth round. Sterile bracts, 1–3, large, sometimes foliaceous; fertile bracts, flat and broad, thick and fleshy, green or whitish green, developing and opening in a stellar form as seen from above. Raceme 25 cm (10 in.). Flowers 5.5 cm (2.25 in.) long, 3 cm (1.35 in.) broad, mostly white, shiny, suffused very lightly purple in the middle of the lobe, densely arranged, expanding, funnel-shaped, in the central part dilated bell-shaped, lobes spreading straightly to ±angled to the axis of perianth, heavy textured, thick; stamens not superior, equal or slightly shorter than perianth. Anthers yellow. June. Fertile.

HN: *H.* 'Aurora Borealis' Wayside IRA/1986 pp sim.
H. 'Chicago Frances Williams' Rudolph/Hatfield.
H. 'Frances Williams Sport' Rudolph.
H. 'Frances Williams' Robinson/Williams IRA/1986.
H. 'FRW No. 1141' pp sim.
H. 'FRW No. 383'.
H. 'Glauca Gold' hort.
H. glauca var. *aureovariegata* hort. pp incorrect.
H. 'Golden Circles' (FRW No. 1141) pp sim.
H. 'Mack No. 19'.
H. sieboldiana aureovariegata hort.
H. sieboldiana aureus marginata hort. Zager 1960 (cat.).
H. sieboldiana 'Elegans Aureomarginata'.
H. sieboldiana fortunei aureomarginata Foerster 1952 pp sim incorrect.
H. sieboldiana 'Frances Williams' Robinson.
H. sieboldiana glauca(ns) 'Golden Edged' Thompkins pp sim.
H. sieboldiana 'Golden Circles' (FRW No. 1141) pp sim.
H. sieboldiana var. *marginata* hort. incorrect.
H. sieboldiana 'Yellow Edge' (FRW No. 383).
H. 'Squash Edge' Donahue.
H. 'Yellow Edge' (FRW No. 383).
Yellowedge Shortcluster Plantain Lily.
Yellowedge Siebold Plantain Lily.
JN: *Kifukurin Oba Giboshi* hort. incorrect.
Kifukurin To Giboshi hort.
ON: Blaue Gelbrandfunkie Foerster 1952 (German).

Following are the full cultivar names of some cultivars belonging to the *H. sieboldiana* Aureomarginata group (collectively). All are described in Chapter 4. Use of the group name is optional per the ICNCP, and the names may be written *H. sieboldiana* 'Aurora Borealis' or simply *H.* 'Aurora Borealis':

H. sieboldiana (Aureomarginata group) 'Aurora Borealis'.
H. sieboldiana (Aureomarginata group) 'Chicago Frances Williams'.
H. sieboldiana (Aureomarginata group) 'Frances Williams'.
H. sieboldiana (Aureomarginata group) 'Maple Leaf'.
H. sieboldiana (Aureomarginata group) 'Nifty Fifty'.
H. sieboldiana (Aureomarginata group) 'Olive Bailey Langdon'.
H. sieboldiana (Aureomarginata group) 'Samurai'.
H. sieboldiana (Aureomarginata group) 'Squash Edge'.
H. sieboldiana (Aureomarginata group) 'Wagon Wheels'.
H. sieboldiana (Aureomarginata group) 'Zager Pride'.

H. sieboldiana 'Elegans Alba' hort.

A selected, cultivated German form by Klose with white flowers. The latinized cultivar name is incorrect per the ICNCP. It is also called *H. sieboldiana* 'Alba'. It should be pointed out that the flowers of the species are almost a pure white. Many hybridized *H. sieboldiana* forms have tinted flowers.

H. sieboldiana 'Frances Williams' Robinson IRA/1986.

AHS-II/10B.   (Plates 141, 160, 175, 176).
AHS Alex J. Summers Distinguished Merit Hosta, 1984, selected by Constance Williams. One of the most popular hostas in North America and a perennial favorite in the AHS popularity poll, it belongs to a group of related plants com-

prising the Aureomarginata group of *H. sieboldiana*. Due to instability and variability of margins in older plants (Zilis types A to F, cfr. Zilis, 1987) many different transitional forms exist and have been named, but all these forms are unstable in the long term (see other clonal cultivar names and synonyms under *H. sieboldiana* Aureomarginata group). Summers (1989b) reported that the taxon *H. sieboldiana* 'Frances Williams' is a quasi-juvenile form which turns into *H. sieboldiana* 'Aurora Borealis', but not all yellow-margined forms of *H. sieboldiana* originated with *H. sieboldiana* 'Frances Williams' so this opinion is only partially correct. The origin of this yellow-margined form is in dispute, and some authors maintain that all these *H. sieboldiana* mutants are a single taxon (i.e., *Hosta sieboldiana* 'Frances Williams'), but this opinion is also incorrect. There are many variegated forms of *H. sieboldiana* which have different points of origin (see *H. sieboldiana* Aureomarginata and *H. sieboldiana* Mediovariegata groups). Some clones suffer from marginal necrosis, probably a genetic disorder, which causes the yellow marginal tissue to "burn" and eventually turn brown, develop holes, and disintegrate. Exposure to strong sunlight in early spring and frequent rain seems to exacerbate the malady.

Plant is similar to *H. sieboldiana* 'Elegans', growing to 122 cm (48 in.) dia., 53 cm (22 in.) high. Leaf 33 by 28 cm (13 by 11 in.), blue-green, yellow margin, cordate, rugose. Venation 16. Scape 66 cm (26 in.), foliated, straight. Flower medium, bell-shaped, white. Anthers yellow. June/July. Fertile.

HN: *H.* 'Eldorado' UK.
H. 'Frances Williams'.
H. 'FRW No. 383'.
H. sieboldiana 'Frances Williams' hort.
(see also *H. sieboldiana* Aureomarginata group).

H. sieboldiana Mediovariegata group.

Several *mediovariegata* sports of *H. sieboldiana* have been found as mutations in the wild as well as in cultivation in Japan and in Western gardens. They occur in several sizes and vary from the species only by the leaves which have irregular green margins with the leaf center being chartreuse, yellow, yellowish white, or white. Also included in this group are the center-variegated, streaked, and splashed cultivars of which *H. sieboldiana* 'Northern Mist'™ Walters IRA/1988 is an outstanding example. Additionally, the center variegation can be albescent or viridescent, and the latter case is exemplified by *H. sieboldiana* 'Northern Sunray'™ Walters IRA/1987. These Walters cultivars look quite different from some others in this group, but belong here. Some of the smaller forms in this group approach *H.* 'Tokudama' in size. All these mutants are included here in a broad sense because botanically, they are considered a group of related plants of different forms and sizes. The variegation of some of these forms is unstable in the long run. In mature plants reversions to all-green and all-yellow leaves can occur. In Japan *mediovariegata* forms of *To Giboshi* have been observed and collected in the wild; they are broadly considered *Kinakafu To Giboshi* but mostly cultivated under a Japanese cultivar name.

A few names of cultivars which broadly belong to this group have been given below to typify it. All are individually described in Chapter 4. Use of the group name is optional per the ICNCP and the names may be written *H. sieboldiana* 'Borwick Beauty' or simply *H.* 'Borwick Beauty'. Some of the names may apply to the same plant; for example, *H. sieboldiana* 'Heslington' is a name once used for *H. sieboldiana* 'George Smith' (Pollock, 1990). Many different named forms are in the trade and all are more-or-less distinct and described under their respective names. There may be a problem with some of the names, as an example, *H. sieboldiana* 'George Smith' and *H. sieboldiana* 'Borwick Beauty' which, according to some reports, are morphologically identical. If they are, one of the registered names will become invalid because per the ICNCP identical taxa cannot have different names regardless of mode of origin.

> *H. sieboldiana* (Mediovariegata group) 'Borwick Beauty' (McBurnie IRA/1988).
>
> *H. sieboldiana* (Mediovariegata group) 'Chippewa' (Arett IRA/1986).
>
> *H. sieboldiana* (Mediovariegata group) 'Color Glory' (Aden/Klehm 1988 [cat.] not Aden IRA/1980).
>
> *H. sieboldiana* (Mediovariegata group) 'George Smith' (George Smith IRA/1983).
>
> *H. sieboldiana* (Mediovariegata group) 'Great Expectations' (Bond/Aden IRA/1988).
>
> *H. sieboldiana* (Mediovariegata group) 'Heslington' (George Smith).
>
> *H. sieboldiana* (Mediovariegata group) 'Northern Lights'™.
>
> *H. sieboldiana* (Mediovariegata group) 'Northern Mist'™.
>
> *H. sieboldiana* (Mediovariegata group) 'Northern Sunray'™.

H. sieboldiana 'Semperaurea' Foerster 1952.
AHS-I/5A.   (Plate 61).

黄金ダイオウギボウシ

Ogon Daio Giboshi, the "golden rhubarb hosta," is also referred to as *Ogon To Giboshi*, but the latter has a more rounded leaf, like *H. sieboldiana* 'Golden Sunburst'. In a broad sense this taxon belongs to the *H. sieboldiana* Yellow group. It will get larger than other yellow forms of *H. sieboldiana* and was reportedly brought from Japan by Foerster of Germany in the 1930s. A plant originating with Foerster is at Staudensichtungsgarten Weihenstephan, University of Munich at Freising, Germany. When selfed, this clone produces a high percentage of yellow seedlings and a few, mostly unstable, yellow-margined and yellow-centered forms. Selected golden seedlings have been named, one of them being *H.* 'Kasseler Gold' (Klose). Neither this taxon nor its selfed offspring have the necrotic traits seen in *H. sieboldiana* 'Golden Sunburst' (which see), and they are also less sensitive to direct sunlight. Becoming very large in time, it should be a carefully placed accent specimen in the garden.

Plant size 80–125 cm (32–48 in.) dia., 60 cm (24 in.) high. Sprouts lightly pruinose, grey. Petiole 40–50 by 1.8 cm (16–20 by 0.75 in.), not or slightly winged, deeply grooved, slightly pruinose, fading, yellow green. Leaf 35–40 by 20–25 cm (14–16 by 8–10 in.), attitude at petiole spreading in a ±continuing flat arch, cordate, broadly ovate-cordate, lower lobes clasping the petiole (cordatis lobis basalibus semiamplexicaulis), irregularly and broadly undulate in the margin, rugose, cuspidate, glaucous, pruinose, with some pruinosity remaining after anthesis, more glaucous on back ±permanent, lutescent, first green, then chartreuse to yellowish green in spring, golden yellow by anthesis or before. Venation 11–17, sunken above, very projected below, convergent and submarginally connected at tip area. Scape height to slightly above leaf mound, 65–75 cm (28–32 in.), but some scapes terminate below leaf canopy, pruinose, erect, but bending in upper part, light yellow-green, smooth round. Sterile bracts, 1–3, large, sometimes foliaceous; fertile bracts, flat and broad, thick and fleshy, green or whitish green, developing and opening in a stellar form as seen from above. Raceme 25 cm (10 in.), 15–30 flowers. Flowers 5.5 cm (2.25 in.) long, 3 cm (1.25 in.) broad, mostly white, shiny, suffused very lightly purple in the middle of the lobe, densely arranged, expanding, funnel-shaped, in the central part dilated bell-shaped, lobes spreading straightly to ±angled to the axis of perianth, heavy textured, thick; stamens not superior, equal or slightly shorter than perianth. Anthers yellow. June. Fertile, produces seed-containing capsules from each fertilized flower, seed comes true to a high percentage. Seed capsules triangular, hanging down, to 4.5 cm (1.75 in.) long, pruinose.

HN: *H. grandifolia semperaurea* Foerster 1952 hort. incorrect.
    H. japonica semperaurea Foerster 1956 incorrect.
    H. semperaurea Foerster 1965a/1965b incorrect.
    H. 'Semperaurea' hort.
    H. sieboldiana 'Semperaurea'.
    H. sieboldiana var. *mira* 'Semperaurea' hort.
    H. sieboldiana Yellow group pp sim.

JN: *Ogon Daio Giboshi*.
    Ogon Oba Giboshi hort. incorrect.
    Ogon To Giboshi pp sim.

ON: Dauergoldfunkie (German).
    Goldblattfunkie (German).
    Grosse Goldblattfunkie (German).
    Riesengoldblattfunkie (German).

✣ "*H. sieboldiana* var. *amplissima*" Maekawa 1940.
AHS-I/1A.

Here reduced to cultivar form as *H. sieboldiana* 'Amplissima'.

ウチワギボウシ

Uchiwa Giboshi, the "Uchiwa hosta," was found among cultivated plants in northern Honshu. Although included by Maekawa in 1969, it is now considered a cultivar. In the district of Hirosaki (now Aomori Prefecture), it is cultivated for its leaves which are used to wrap rice balls (see Appendix H). The varietal epithet translates to "the largest." This hosta is larger than the species and differs only in the scapes which are longer and the leaves which are concave and marginally incurved.

Plant size 80–95 cm (32–38 in.) dia., 60 cm (24 in.) high, compactly clustered, ultimate size much larger. Leaf 25–30 by 18–25 cm (10–12 by 7–10 in.), very cordate, ovate to elliptic, broad, surface cupped, ribbed and rugose, margins up-turned, incurved, color green. Venation 12–18, very sunken above. Scape higher than leaf mound, 70–80 cm (28–32 in.). Sterile bracts, 1–3, large, sometimes foliaceous; fertile bracts, flat and broad, thick and fleshy, green or whitish green, developing and opening in a stellar form as seen from above. Anthers yellow. June. Fertile.

HN: *H. sieboldiana* 'Amplissima' hort.
JN: *Uchiwa Giboshi* Maekawa 1940.

✣ "*H. sieboldiana* var. *elegans*" Hylander 1954 AHS-NC IRA/1987.
AHS-I/3B.   (Figure 3-65; Plates 60, 172).

Here reduced to cultivar form as *H. sieboldiana* 'Elegans'.

The cultivar name was registered for show purposes for *H. sieboldiana* var. *elegans* Hylander. This hosta was originally described as a botanical variety but is now known to be a hybrid made by Arends (1905) and named *H.* 'Robusta'. Apparently further developed and hybridized, many different forms are now labeled *H. sieboldiana* 'Elegans', and according to Hansen and Müssel (1964), five different forms are cultivated at the trial gardens of Weihenstephan, Freising, Germany, and many other, similar looking clones and hybrids are offered under this cultivar name. Unfortunately, which of these is Arend's clone can no longer be established with any

Figure 3-65. *H. sieboldiana* 'Elegans'; general habit with taller scapes (ex Hylander, Type I; Weihenstephan/Schmid)

degree of certainty. It should be considered a group of similar garden plants, but the form usually cultivated under this name looks like the archetypal *H. sieboldiana*. In Europe this plant has been grown for many years as *H.* 'Blue Angel' or *H.* 'Blauer Engel', which should not be mistaken for *H.* 'Blue Angel' (Aden), a different, but closely related, cultivar. This hybrid has moderately taller scapes and is more robust than the species *H. sieboldiana* and has slight lavender coloration inside the perianth. It is used horticulturally just like the species. There are more than 100 named cultivars which look more or less like *H. sieboldiana* or *H. sieboldiana* 'Elegans' when taken in the broader botanical sense. Most of these show some emphasized macromorphological characteristics, like rugosity, or pruinosity, but all are technically none other than the species, because they are either reversions from variegated types of the *H. sieboldiana* line or hybrids where both parents are of the *H. sieboldiana* line. When breeding within this line even in the broader sense—for example, the cross *H. sieboldiana* 'Frances Williams' × *H.* 'Sieboldiana Elegans'—the resulting hybrids will be morphologically close to the species.

Plant size 80–100 cm (32–40 in.) dia., 65–75 cm (26–30 in.) high, ultimate size of plants can be much larger. Petiole 30–60 by 1.5 cm (12–24 by 0.75 in.), not or slightly winged, deeply grooved, slightly pruinose, fading, grey-green. Leaf 25–40 by 20–30 cm (10–16 by 8–12 in.), attitude at petiole spreading in a ±continuing flat arch, cordate, broadly ovate to orbicular-cordate in the radical leaves to ovate-cordate, longer pointed in the inner leaves, transition truncately, flattened, surface cupped, very rugose between veins, irregularly undulate in the margin, glaucous, very pruinose, with some pruinosity remaining after anthesis, more glaucous on back ±permanent, bluish grey-green. Venation 14–20, sunken above, very projected, strigose below, convergent and submarginally connected at tip area. Scape overtopping leaf mound, 60–100 cm (24–40 in.), permanently pruinose, lasting until at least anthesis, erect, but bending back in upper part, grey-green, smooth round. Sterile bracts, 1–3, large, sometimes foliaceous; fertile bracts, flat and broad, thick and fleshy, green or whitish green, developing and opening in a stellar form as seen from above. Raceme 35 cm (14 in.), 15–30 flowers. Flowers 5.5 cm (2.25 in.) long, 3 cm (1.25 in.) broad, mostly white, shiny, suffused very light purple in the middle of the lobe, densely arranged, expanding, funnel-shaped, in the central part dilated bell-shaped, lobes spreading straightly to ±angled to the axis of perianth, heavy textured, thick, stamens not superior, equal or slightly shorter than perianth. Anthers yellow. June. Fertile.

SY: *H. fortunei robusta* Bailey 1915 pp.
     H. fortunei var. *robusta* Silva-Tarouca 1910.
     H. sieboldiana var. *elegans* Hylander 1954.
HN: *H.* 'Blue Angel' (Aden) incorrect.
     H. 'Blue Giant' hort.
     H. 'Blue Heart' hort.
     H. 'Elegans' hort. incorrect.
     H. fortunei robusta hort. Arends 1905.
     H. fortunei 'Robusta' hort. Arends 1905.
     H. glauca robusta hort. USA pp incorrect.
     H. glauca 'Robusta' pp incorrect.
     H. 'Mack No. 2'.
     H. 'Robusta' hort. incorrect.
     H. sieboldi elegans hort. incorrect.
     H. sieboldiana 'Blue Angel' hort.
     H. sieboldiana 'Coerulea' hort. UK incorrect.
     H. sieboldiana elegans 'Blue Angel' hort. incorrect.
     H. sieboldiana fortunei robusta Foerster 1955 incorrect.
     H. sieboldiana 'Robusta' Hensen 1985.
     USDA ARS No. 263132 Meyer 1963.
ON: Grosse Blaublattfunkie Hansen and Müssel 1964 (German).
     H. 'Blauer Engel' hort. Europe pp sim (German).
     Riesenblaublattfunkie Foerster 1955 incorrect (German).

✠ "*H. sieboldiana* var. *fortunei*" (Regel) Maekawa.
     This name is a synonym of *H.* 'Tokudama', which has been reduced to cultivar form.
     (see *H. tokudama*).

H. sieboldiana var. *glabra* Fujita 1976a.

AHS-III/13A.   (Figure 3-66).

ナメルギボウシ

Nameru Giboshi, the "Nameru hosta," represents yet another form of *H. sieboldiana* on the varietal level. The type (in KYO) was collected by Ibuka on the Japan Sea coast of Honshu in Shimane Prefecture on Oki Island. Other specimens have been found growing further north in Toyama and Nagano prefectures, and in the mountains along the Japan Sea coast, with the most northern occurrence reported in Niigata Prefecture. A good representation of specimens is in KYO, SHIN, TI, TNS, and TUS. Other representatives of *H. sieboldiana* are also found in this general area but range further north. This taxon has the well-rounded leaves of *H. sieboldiana*, except they have a smoother surface and are green with no pruinosity. The veins are smooth on the back, in contrast to *H. sieboldiana*, and this gave rise to the varietal epithet *glabra* = smooth. The scapes are tall, to 120 cm (48 in.), and they have 30–35 white flowers. By publishing this taxon Fujita extended the normal range of *H. sieboldiana* further south to the Oki Archipelago, and perhaps these are the types Maekawa included as "green" variants without actually specifying this habitat, which occurs in an area where *H. longipes* and *H. sieboldiana* overlap. *Hosta sieboldiana* var. *glabra* may have originated with one of the intergrading hybrid swarms existing in this area and this is positively indicated by this taxon having characteristics of both these species. Taxa now considered var. *glabra* were previously identified as *H. sieboldiana* var. *longipes*, according to notes on specimens in KYO. This indicates the perceived connection of this taxon between *H. sieboldiana* and *H. longipes*. Although available, this hosta is rarely seen outside scientific collections.

Plant size 70–90 cm (28–36 in.) dia., 35–45 cm (16–20) high. Petiole 30–40 by 1.2 cm (12–16 by 0.5 in.), winged, whitish green, purple-spotted at base. Leaf 25 by 18–22 cm (10 by 7–9 in.), attitude at petiole erect-spreading, cordate, broadly ovate to orbicular-cordate, transition truncately flattened, surface generally flat, green, glabrous on the nerves below. Venation 14–16, sunken above, projected smooth below. Scape to 120 cm (48 in.), obliquely ascending, whitish green, sparsely dotted with purple, smooth, round. Sterile bracts 1–4; fertile bracts flat and broad, thick and fleshy, ovate-lanceolate, 2–4 by 1.2 cm (1–1.5 by 0.5 in.), whitish green, developing and opening in a stellar form as seen from above. Raceme 50 cm (20 in.), 15–35 flowers. Flowers 5.5 cm (2.25 in.) long and 3 cm (1.25 in.) broad, mostly white, shiny, densely arranged, expanding, funnel-shaped, in the central part dilated bell-shaped, lobes spreading straightly to ±angled to the axis of perianth, heavy textured, thick; stamens equal or slightly protruding. Anthers yellow. June. Fertile.

SY: *H. sieboldiana* var. *longipes* herbarium annotation KYO, Murata, s. n. dated August 1903.

JN: *Nameru Giboshi* Fujita 1976a.

Figure 3-66. *H. sieboldiana* var. *glabra*; holotype in KYO

✠ *"H. sieboldiana* var. *hypophylla"* Maekawa.
AHS-I/B.   (Plate 138).
Here reduced to cultivar form as *H. sieboldiana* 'Hypophylla'.
ハガクレギボウシ

Hagakure Giboshi, the "hosta (with scape and flowers) hidden under leaves," also has a varietal epithet which means "below (beneath) leaves." A selected clone of the species, this is the most pruinose variety described by Maekawa. It comes very close to the "European prototype" for *H. sieboldiana*. It can be identified quickly by its very short scapes with flowers hidden or almost hidden under the leaves. It was introduced by von Siebold in 1830 and called *Funkia cucullata* (= hoodlike). This taxon is probably the genetic ancestor of today's very glaucous, pruinose types. Its pruinosity lasts longer, and its mound is broader and not as high as the standard species. It is not cultivated under its name in today's gardens, yet occasionally named cultivars can be seen which have all the characteristics of *Hosta sieboldiana* 'Hypophylla'; an example is *H.* 'Ryans Big One' (Plate 138). It also occurs in the seedling progeny when interbreeding *H. sieboldiana* forms.

Plant size 80–95 cm (32–38 in.) dia., 40 cm (16 in.) high, ultimate size larger. Leaf 25–33 by 22–27 cm (10–13 by 9–11 in.), attitude at petiole spreading in a ±continuing flat arch, cordate, broadly ovate, surface wavy, twisted, very rugose, truncate, short acumi-

nate tip, very glaucous, farinose, with some pruinosity remaining longer than in the other varieties, bluish grey-green. Venation 14–20, sunken above, convergent and submarginally connected at tip area. Scape shorter than leaf mound, 38 cm (16 in.), pruinose, round. Sterile bracts, 1–3, large, sometimes foliaceous; fertile bracts, flat and broad, thick and fleshy, green or whitish green, developing and opening in a stellar form as seen from above. Anthers yellow. June. Fertile.

SY: *Funkia cucullata* hort. Bailey 1915.
   Funkia cucullata nom. nudum Siebold 1844.
   Funkia glauca cucullata Miquel 1869.

HN: *Funkia glauca* hort. pp.
   Funkia glaucescens hort. pp.
   Hosta glauca hort. pp.
   H. sieboldiana hort. pp.
   H. sieboldiana 'Hypophylla' hort.
   H. sieboldi hort. incorrect.
   H. sieboldii hort. incorrect.
   H. 'True Glauca' Krossa pp.

JN: *Hagakure Giboshi* Maekawa 1940.

ON: Siebold Funkia pp (German).
   Siebold Funkie pp (German).

✠ *"H. sieboldiana* var. *mira"* Maekawa 1940.
AHS-I/A.   (Figure 3-67).
Here reduced to cultivar form as *H. sieboldiana* 'Mira'.
ダイオウギボウシ

Daio Giboshi, the "rhubarb hosta," is so called because of its large size, but "daio" also means "great monarch" which is fitting as well. The varietal epithet is derived from *mirus* = extraordinary, exceptional. It was found in cultivation in Hisai City, Mie Prefecture. Although retained by Maekawa in 1969, it is now considered a cultivar because it is morphologically just like the species, differing only by its larger leaves that are less round and more pointed. As with other clonal types, it also occurs in the seedling progeny when interbreeding *H. sieboldiana*. This accounts for forms of *H. sieboldiana* 'Mira' having been in the United States since the early 1900s, according to Summers, who found specimens of it in the Meissner garden in Garden City, Long Island, New York. This particular variety has been used in estate gardens in Europe and North America for some time, and some of these plantings survive today. It can be used in a garden in the same way as the species. A golden-yellow form exists which is identical to *H. sieboldiana* 'Semperaurea', which see.

Plant size 80–95 cm (32–38 in.) dia., 50 cm (20 in.) high, ultimate size of plants in situ 15 years larger. Leaf 33–39 by 18–27 cm (13–15.5 by 7.25–11 in.), attitude at petiole spreading in a ±continuing flat arch,

Figure 3-67. *H. sieboldiana* 'Mira'; general habit (Hosta Hill)

cordate, broadly ovate but more elongated than the type, long-pointed, transition truncate, funnel-shaped, cuspidate tip, glaucous, with some pruinosity remaining at sunken veins after anthesis, more glaucous on back ±permanent, not as rugose as the typical form, grey-green. Venation 12–17, sunken above, very projected, convergent and sub-marginally connected at tip area. Scape higher than leaf mound, 60–70 cm (24–28 in.), pruinose, lasting until at least anthesis, erect, yellow-green, smooth round. Sterile bracts, 1–3, large, sometimes foliaceous; fertile bracts, flat and broad, thick and fleshy, green or whitish green, developing and opening in a stellar form as seen from above. Anthers yellow. June. Fertile.

HN: *H. sieboldiana* 'Mira'.
JN: *Daio Giboshi* Maekawa 1938b.

H. sieboldiana Yellow group.

黄金トウギボウシ (Plates 61, 161, 176.)

Ogon To Giboshi, the "golden hosta of old," broadly represents a group of yellow cultivars with *H. sieboldiana* parentage, originating either as hybrids of the *H. sieboldiana* Aureomarginata group or as sports in cultivation or tissue culture. They also result from natural mutations of the long-term unstable aureomarginata forms (Zilis type F, cfr. Zilis, 1987). All of them look much like *H. sieboldiana*, and their descriptions are identical to that of the species in every respect, except that this group has yellow (lutescent) leaves and is slightly smaller. The all-yellow forms which originate or mutate from ancestors with necrotic margins are also severely necrotic. Entire leaves may disintegrate in late spring, but it should be pointed out that many of the named cultivars/clones appear to be free of this malady. Many distinct forms exist, have been named, and are described under their respective cultivar names in Chapter 4 with cross-reference to this group given. Most of the yellow forms of *H. sieboldiana* make large, prominent accents and require careful placement. Singly, backed by an all-green foil, any of these cultivars makes an outstanding display and accent (Plate 176).

HN: Golden Sieboldiana incorrect.
   H. 'FRW No. 1142'.
   H. 'Golden Sunburst' AHS-NC IRA/1984.
   H. 'Golden Mammoth' Blackthorne.
   H. sieboldiana aurea hort. incorrect.
   H. sieboldiana Golden group.
   H. sieboldiana 'Golden' incorrect.
   H. sieboldiana 'Golden Sunburst' AHS-NC IRA/1984.
   H. sieboldiana 'Semperaurea' Foerster 1952 pp sim sl.

H. sieboldii (Paxton) Ingram.

AHS-IV/22A. (Figure 6-6; Plates 3, 62, 201; see jacket front).

フクリンギボウシ
ヘリトリギボウシ

Fukurin Giboshi, the "hosta with ornamental margin," also *Heritori Giboshi*, and its many differentiated forms are endemic in the Japanese archipelago. Generally, central Honshu is the primary habitat of the type, while the forms to the north, in northern Honshu and Hokkaido, as well as variants to the west and south in western Honshu, Shikoku, and Kyushu have been classified as separate taxa. Virtually all the wild population is all-green and known as *Koba Giboshi*, but the white-margined form, which was uncommon in the wild, was the first representative of this species to be validly published by Paxton (1838) and has served as the type for the entire group for many years. The white-margined type does not come true from seed and is nonperpetuating in the wild, so it is technically a mutant

form which should be reduced to cultivar form. But as the type for a large group, its name is inseparably linked with its type taxonomically, and to change this taxon's status would be tantamount to reclassifying the entire section. For this reason all previous authors have accepted and maintained the historic arrangement, and I am also endorsing it. I have, however, only partially followed Hara's recent reclassification of the *H. sieboldii* complex (Hara, 1984), which includes *H.* 'Lancifolia' as a forma. The latter is not part of this group and has been moved to section *Tardanthae* following Hylander (1954). As a consequence, many of the synonyms formerly used under *H. sieboldii* have also been removed. In 1940 Maekawa gave the margined form the Japanese formal (academic) name *Fukurin Giboshi*, but a much earlier, formal Japanese name exists in *Heritori Giboshi* formulated by Makino and Tanaka in 1928.

Most of this taxon's populations exist as lowland plants, where they grow in moors and damp areas, including open, weedy meadows, but evolved variants occasionally grow in elevated grasslands. *Hosta sieboldii* is the sectional type for one of the largest and most diversified groups of hostas existing in the wild in Japan, and so Maekawa named this group section *Nipponosta* (= of Japan). *Hosta sieboldii* was one of the first variegated hostas removed from Japan by von Siebold who brought it with him when he returned in 1830. He planted it at Makoy's garden in the city of Ghent, Belgium, naming it *Funkia spatulata* Siebold *foliis albomarginatis*. Shortly after von Siebold's return, war broke out between Belgium and Holland, and von Siebold had to retreat to Leiden, Holland, but in haste left some of his hostas behind. It was J. L. Makoy, nurseryman of Liège, who sent this species to the Glasgow Botanic Garden, labeled *Funkia* spec. *foliis marginatis*. At Glasgow Hooker published an illustrated description of it and named it *Funckia albomarginata* (see jacket front). Von Siebold, who had taken some of his plants with him when retreating to Leiden, sent a specimen of *Hosta sieboldii* to the English botanist Paxton, who published a short specific diagnosis under the name *Hemerocallis sieboldii* in honor of the collector. Stearn (1931b) correctly pointed out the priority of the name *Hosta sieboldii* over *H. albomarginata*, but it was not until 1967 that a change was formally proposed by Ingram and 1984 when the valid transfers were actually made by Hara. Because Hara's classification includes other varieties under *H. sieboldii*, he wrote the name as *H. sieboldii* var. *sieboldii* f. *sieboldii* (see *H. sieboldii* var. *sieboldii* Hara 1984). Some botanists, including Hylander (1954) and Hensen (1963a, 1985), have argued against acceptance of the name *H. sieboldii*, but the latter must be used in accordance with the rules of the ICBN. Unfortunately, starting with Miquel (1869), many authors have incorrectly included this species under *H. lancifolia* Engler (now *H.* 'Lancifolia'). Maekawa's *H. lancifolia* var. *thunbergiana* f. *albomarginata* is an example. This has contributed considerably to the earlier nomenclatural confusion which is fully discussed in Appendix B. Some of the many variants existing in the wild have been selected and validly published in the botanical literature. As demonstrated by Yasui (1929), *H. sieboldii* progeny is rather prone to mutate and so quite a number of variegated forms, unusual flower formations, and white-flowered forms have been observed in this group. Dwarf forms exist under several Japanese horticultural names—*Yakushima Giboshi, Hime Yakushima Giboshi, Yakushima Mizu Giboshi*, and *Hime Koba Giboshi*—although some of these names also relate to other species. Yellow-margined cultivars with either purple-striped or white flowers exist. In Japan they are called *Kifukurin Koba Giboshi*. In Western gardens similar cultivars are grown as *H. (sieboldii)* 'Butter Rim' (IRA/1986) or *H. (sieboldii)* 'Marble Rim' (IRA/1986). A viridescent form is called *H. (sieboldii)* 'Mentor Gold' (IRA/1978). Yellow leaf clones with white margins exist in the United States under the

name *H. (sieboldii)* 'Anne Arett' (IRA/1975), and another clone
is called *H. (sieboldii)* 'Little Ann'. *Hosta sieboldii* is in a broad
sense the parent of the taxa just mentioned and many other
sports. This does not necessarily mean that *H. sieboldii* is
directly involved as a parent, but all the cultivars listed are
derivatives of *H. sieboldii*. Most of these sports and hybrids are
much in demand and widely cultivated. Quite to the contrary,
the species itself is of minor horticultural importance, because
its margin is viridescent and almost completely disappears by
summer. Many other, more-stable, better-looking, white-
margined cultivars of this size are available—some closely
related to *H. sieboldii*—and are replacing the species in
gardens. For the collector this cultivar is a must as it represents one of the classic hostas which has been cultivated in
Western gardens for over 150 years.

Plant size 25 cm (10 in.) dia., by 20 cm (8 in.) high.
Petiole 10–15 by 0.5 cm (4–6 by 0.2 in.), erect,
forming a vase-shaped plant, green with no purple
dots at the base. Leaf 10–15 cm by 5 cm wide (4–6 by 2
in.), erect and in line with petiole, lanceolate, petiole
transition gradual, decurrent, slightly undulate, wavy
in the margin, erect, smooth, shiny light, dull, dark
green above, with a narrow, yellowish white margin,
glossy lighter green below, tip acuminate. In exposed
areas the margin color is moderately viridescent and
turns to whitish green or green after anthesis. Venation 3–4, very lightly impressed above, smooth
below. Scape 25–50 cm (10–20 in.), straight and erect,
not bending, light green, no purple marks. Sterile
bracts 2–3, tightly clasping stem, persistent; fertile
bracts, short, navicular, thin, membranous, green,
withering at anthesis, but not falling away. Raceme 6–
12 flowers, widely spaced. Flowers 5 cm (2 in.) long
and 3.5 cm (1.5 in.) broad, purple-striped, purple,
thin narrow tube, perianth expanding, lily-shaped,
lobes spreading rapidly, recurving, widely open,
short pedicels, very projecting stamen. Anthers
yellow. July. Fertile.

SY: *Funckia albomarginata* Hooker (May) 1838.
Funkia lancifolia f. *albomarginata* Baker 1870 incorrect.
Funkia lancifolia f. *albomarginata* Regel 1876 incorrect.
Funkia ovata f. *spathulata* lusus α Miquel 1869.
Funkia ovata var. β *albomarginata* Miquel 1869.
Funkia spatulata foliis albomarginatis nom. nudum Siebold
1844.
Hemerocallis sieboldii Paxton (March) 1838 (basionym).
Hosta albomarginata Ohwi 1942.
H. albomarginata f. *albomarginata* Hensen 1963a.
H. cærulea f. *albomarginata* Matsumura 1905.
H. japonica f. *albomarginata* Makino 1925.
H. japonica var. *albimarginata* Ascherson and Gräbner
1905.
H. lancifolia var. *albomarginata* Stearn 1931b.
H. lancifolia var. *thunbergiana* f. *albomarginata* Maekawa
1940.
H. lancifolia var. *thunbergiana* f. *sieboldii* Maekawa 1950.
H. sieboldii var. *sieboldii* f. *sieboldii* Hara 1984.
Hostia japonica f. *albomarginata* Voss 1896.
Niobe japonica var. *albomarginata* Nash 1911.
HN: *Hosta albomarginata* 'Albo-marginata' Hensen 1963a.
H. albomarginata hort. Japan 1985.
H. 'FRW No. 1246'.
H. lancifolia 'Albomarginata' hort. incorrect.
H. lancifolia var. *albomarginata* hort. incorrect.
H. sieboldii 'Albomarginata' hort. incorrect.
H. sieboldii f. *albomarginata* hort. incorrect.
H. sieboldii (syn. *albomarginata*) hort.

Whiterim Plantain Lily.
Whiterim Purple Plantain Lily.
JN: *Fukurin Giboshi* Maekawa 1940.
Heritori Giboshi Makino and Tanaka 1928.
Oze Mizu Giboshi hort. incorrect.
ON: Schmale Weissrandfunkie Hansen and Müssel 1964
(German).
Weissrandfunkie Foerster 1957 (German).

✠ *"H. sieboldii* f. *alba"* (Irving) Hara 1984.
AHS-IV/19B.
シロバナコバギボウシ
Here reduced to cultivar form as *H. sieboldii* 'Alba'.

Shirobana Koba Giboshi, the "white-flowered, small-leaf
hosta," is now and then found as a wildling, and it also occurs
as a mutation in cultivation. Several distinct forms are in cultivation which can be considered a group of white-flowered
forms, but I have established no formal group name because
well-established registered cultivar names exist. The existence of several legitimate Japanese names also points to polymorphism: *Shirobana Koba Giboshi* Maekawa (1969), *Shirobana
Ko Giboshi* Maekawa (1950), and *Shirobana Mizu Giboshi*
Makino (1910). As a consequence, classification of the white-
flowered taxa in this group is difficult because several phases
do exist. The synonyms listed are based upon material which,
applies in part to white-flowered forms of *H. sieboldii* f. *angustifolia* and may even include the white-flowered *H. longissima*
form, as alluded to by Makino's Japanese name listed earlier.
Because these taxa are nonperpetuating, occasional mutants
which have been reduced to cultivar form, they do not play an
important role in the classification of section *Nipponosta*, and I
have not attempted further separation of these taxa. The
original sport was discovered in von Siebold's garden in 1868
and given the name *Funkia japonica flore albo*. Often referred to
as *Hosta albomarginata* 'Alba', it is now correctly *H. sieboldii* f. *alba*
(Irving) Hara 1984, and this taxon has been reduced to cultivar form. This special form of *H. sieboldii* has long been cultivated under the incorrect name of "*H. minor alba*". The true *H.
minor* f. *alba*, which see, has longitudinal ridges on the scape,
whereas *H. sieboldii* 'Alba' has a smooth scape and a different
leaf form. In Japan the white-flowered form known as
Shirobana Kika Koba Giboshi, is occasionally found as a rare
mutation with an unstable number of petals, between four and
six, and with the anthers projecting from the unopened flower.
The standard form is very much like the species and is cultivated under many different names. One of the best, named
European clones of this form is *H. sieboldii* 'Weihenstephan'
(Plate 143), and a North American form is *H. sieboldii* 'Mount
Royal', although neither of these may have originated from the
species but from related, heterozygous material as evidenced
by the higher count of principal veins and other features
atypical of the species.

Plant size 25 cm (10 in.) dia. by 20 cm (8 in.) high.
Petiole 10–15 by 0.5 cm (4–6 by 0.2 in.), erect,
forming a vase-shaped plant, green with no purple
dots at the base. Leaf 10–15 by 4–5 cm (4–6 by 1.5–2
in.), erect and in line with petiole, lanceolate, petiole
transition gradual, decurrent, slightly undulate, wavy
in the margin, erect, smooth, shiny light, dull, dark
green above, glossy lighter green below, tip acuminate. Venation 3–4, very lightly impressed above,
smooth below. Flowers 5 cm (2 in.) long and 3.5 cm
(1.5 in.) broad, pure white, thin narrow tube,
perianth expanding, lily-shaped, lobes spreading
rapidly, recurving, widely open, short pedicels, very
projecting stamen. Anthers yellow. August. Fertile.
SY: *Funkia japonica flore albo* nom. nudum Siebold 1868.
Funkia ovata f. lusus *spathulata* Miquel 1869.

Funkia ovata spathulata β floribus subalbidis Miquel 1869 pp.
Hosta albomarginata var. *alba* Hylander 1954.
Hosta cærulea var. *minor albiflora* Nobis 1951.
H. japonica var. *angustifolia* f. *albiflora* Makino 1910.
H. lancifolia [var.] *alba* Irving 1903.
H. lancifolia var. *thunbergiana* f. *alba* Maekawa 1940.
H. lancifolia var. *thunbergiana* f. *albiflora* Ikegami 1967.
H. lancifolia var. *thunbergiana* f. *albiflora* Maekawa 1950.
HN: Dwarf White Plantain Lily Mack
    Funkia lancifolia var. *alba* hort. incorrect.
    Hosta albiflora Mack.
    H. albomarginata alba hort. Grenfell 1981.
    H. albomarginata 'Alba' Hensen 1963a.
    H. albomarginata 'Alba' hort.
    H. albomarginata f. *alba* hort.
    H. albomarginata var. *alba* hort. incorrect.
    H. 'FRW No. 537'.
    H. lancifolia 'Alba' incorrect.
    H. lancifolia albomarginata alba hort. incorrect.
    H. lancifolia f. *alba* incorrect.
    H. 'Mack No. 15'.
    H. minor alba grandiflora Foerster 1956 incorrect.
    H. minor alba hort. incorrect.
    H. minor hort. incorrect.
    H. sieboldii alba hort. incorrect.
    H. sieboldii 'Alba' hort.
    H. sieboldii var. *alba* incorrect.
JN: *Shirobana Kika Koba Giboshi* hort. unstable number of petals.
    Shirobana Ko Giboshi Maekawa 1950.
    Shirobana Koba Giboshi Maekawa 1969.
    Shirobana Mizu Giboshi Makino 1910 pp.
ON: Weissblühende Zwergfunkie Foerster 1956 (German).

H. sieboldii f. *angustifolia* (Regel) W. G. Schmid comb. nov.

(Figure 3-68; Plate 190).

Although no Japanese formal name is known for this taxon, the horticultural name *Nagaba Mizu Giboshi* is sometimes incorrectly applied because it looks very similar to *H. longissima*. Both taxa have all-green, narrow leaves, and their diagnoses are virtually identical. However, *H. sieboldii* blooms in July-August and has yellow anthers, while *H. longissima* has purple anthers and blooms 3–4 weeks later. Narrow-leaved, all-green forms of *H. sieboldii* are known to occur among the allopatric and sympatric populations of the latter and have also been found among selfed *H. sieboldii* seedlings. This hosta is often mistaken for and labeled *H. longissima*. Long known in horticulture and botanically described under many illegitimate names, Regel's varietal epithet has been used as the

basionym for a new combination. Frequently, the difference between *H. sieboldii* f. *angustifolia* and *H. longissima* var. *brevifolia* can be detected only during flowering by examining the anthers and perianth lobes, because in general aspect and in leaf form these two hostas are very much alike. A collector's hosta, it is frequently seen among cultivated populations, but hardly ever identified and labeled correctly.
SY: *Funkia lancifolia* ε *angustifolia* Regel 1876 pp.
    Funkia ovata var. *lancifolia* Miquel 1869 pp.
    Hosta japonica var. *angustifolia* Ascherson and Gräbner 1905 pp.
    H. japonica var. *angustifolia* Makino in Iinuma 1910 pp.
    H. lancifolia var. *angustifolia* Koidzumi 1936 pp.
HN: *H. lancifolia* var. *angustifolia* hort. incorrect pp.
    Narrowleaf Plantain Lily pp.
JN: *Nagaba Mizu Giboshi* incorrect.
ON: Schmalblattfunkie Hansen et al., 1964 pp sim (German).

✠ *"H. sieboldii* f. *bunchoko"* (Maekawa) W. G. Schmid comb. nov.

文鳥香
斑入チシマギボウシ

Here transferred from *H. lancifolia* var. *thunbergiana* f. *bunchoko* Maekawa 1969 and reduced to cultivar form as *H. sieboldii* **'Bunchoko'**.

Bunchoko Giboshi, the "small morning sunray hosta," is a dwarf form of the species with a narrow white margin that stays white. It evolved in cultivation and several similar hostas have arisen from *H. sieboldii* as mutants or mutant seedlings. Described as a white-flowered taxon, forms with purple-striped flowers have also been seen under this name, so there is some confusion, but reversions from white to purple-striped flowers are not unusual in the *H. sieboldii* line. The white-flowered taxon is similar to *H. sieboldii* 'Louisa', but specimens received from Japanese nurseries look like *H.* 'Ginko Craig' in its juvenile form. The flowers are also comparable, and more study is needed to determine the exact interrelationship of the imported plants with taxa already in North America, particularly because some of the latter have purple-striped flowers. How this will affect the naming is not known. Inasmuch as *H.* 'Ginko Craig' develops into a coarser, less-desirable mature form it remains to be seen if *H. sieboldii* 'Bunchoko' also follows this trait. *Hosta* 'Emerald Isle', a cultivar grown in the United Kingdom and reportedly less vigorous, has similar leaves except they look more like those of *H. sieboldii* 'Louisa'. In Japan *H. sieboldii* 'Bunchoko' is used in pot culture. It will be an attractive subject if its graceful leaf form turns out to be permanent.

Plant size 20 cm (8 in.) dia., 18 cm (7 in.) high. Petiole 10–15 by 0.5 cm (4–6 by 0.2 in.), erect, forming a vase-shaped plant, green with no purple dots at the base. Leaf 8–12 by 4–5 cm (3–5 by 1.5–2 in.), erect and in line with petiole, lanceolate, petiole transition gradual, decurrent, moderately undulate, wavy in the margin, erect, smooth, shiny light, dull, dark green above, with a narrow white margin, glossy lighter green below, tip acuminate. Venation 3–4, very lightly impressed above, smooth below. Flowers 5 cm (2 in.) long and 3.5 cm (1.5 in.) broad, pure white (purple-striped forms exist), thin narrow tube, perianth expanding, lily-shaped, lobes spreading rapidly, recurving, widely open, short pedicels, very projecting stamen. July. Anthers yellow. Barely fertile.
SY: *H. lancifolia* var. *thunbergiana* f. *bunchoko* Maekawa 1969.
HN: *H.* 'Bunchoko' hort.
    H. 'Emerald Isle' Smith pp sim.
    H. 'Krossa No. H-8' pp sim.
    H. lancifolia 'Bunchoko' hort. incorrect.

Figure 3-68. *H. sieboldii* f. *angustifolia*; general habit, young plant; *H.* 'Vera Verde' (right) (Hosta Hill)

H. 'Louisa' Williams IRA/1986 pp sim.
H. sieboldii 'Bunchoko' hort.
H. sieboldii f. alba 'Variegated' hort. pp sim.
H. sieboldii 'Louisa' Williams IRA/1986 pp sim.
Whiterim White Plantain Lily Mack.

JN: Bunchoko Giboshi Maekawa 1969.
     Bunchoko Koba Giboshi hort.
     Fuiri Chishima Giboshi hort. incorrect.

H. sieboldii f. *campanulata* (Araki) W. G. Schmid comb. nov.

AHS-IV/19B.

ツリガネギボウシ
コバナツリガネギボウシ

Tsurigane Giboshi, the "temple bell hosta," is named for its bell-shaped flowers. The Latin epithet also means "bell-shaped (flowers)." This taxon has natural populations in south-central Honshu, in Kyoto and Hyogo prefectures. The type was collected by Araki in Taki-gun, Kumobe-mura. It colonizes wetlands and meadows in open mountain valleys and is very similar in habit to *H. sieboldii*, the only difference being in the flowers. The latter has a funnel-shaped, wide-open perianth with recurving lobes, while *H. sieboldii* f. *campanulata* has a bell-shaped perianth which opens partially. Fujita (1976a) included it in the synonymy of *H. sieboldii* in a broad sense, but here it is treated as a forma of this species, due to its quite different flower form and other significant macromorphological differences evident in holotype No. 14562b in KYO. The type specimen shows a branched scape with long, winged petioles and purple-striped, bell-shaped flowers. It is recorded to bloom very late in September/October. A variant of this taxon occurs among natural colonies, named *Kobana Tsurigane Giboshi*, the "small-flowered temple bell hosta," (holotype No. 14562a, KYO). It has flowers barely smaller than the specific type—4.5 cm (1.75 in.) versus 5 cm (2 in.). Araki (1942) named it *H. campanulata* var. *parviflora*, the latter meaning "small-flowered," but following Fujita (1976a), I consider it synonymous with the species and have placed it thus. Both are collector's hostas which are rarely seen.

Plant size 40 cm (16 in.) dia., 40 cm (16 in.) high. Petiole 10–20 by 0.8 cm (4–8 by 0.33 in.), erect, green with purple dots at the base. Winged, with wings starting at base and extending to leaf base. Leaf 7.5–15 by 2.5–5 cm (3–5 by 1–2 in.), oblanceolate-oblong, erect, decurrent to petiole, obtuse tip, flat, smooth, shiny green above. Venation 3–4, impressed above, smooth below. Scape 65–80 cm (26–32 in.), straight and erect, perpendicular, not bending, light green, purple-dotted near base. Sterile bracts 3–4, small, clasping stem, some slightly opening; fertile bracts, short, blunt, navicular, thick, green, not withering at anthesis. Raceme 10–24 flowers, widely spaced. Flowers 4.5–5 cm (2 in.) long and 3.5 cm (1.5 in.) broad, purple-striped, thin narrow tube, perianth dilated bell-shaped, lobes half-open, short pedicels, stamens equal with perianth. Anthers yellow. September/October. Fertile.

SY: H. campanulata Araki 1942.
     H. campanulata var. parviflora Araki 1942.
JN: Kobana Tsurigane Giboshi Araki 1942.
     Tsurigane Giboshi Araki 1942.

✠ "*H. sieboldii* f. *kabitan*" (Maekawa) Hara 1984.

AHS-IV/20B.   (Plates 63, 64).

カビタン

Here reduced to cultivar form as *H. sieboldii* 'Kabitan'.

Kabitan Giboshi, the "captain hosta," was named by Iwasaki in the late 1800s. It was first described by Iwasaki (1916–1918),

confirming this taxon has been in cultivation for a long time. The original plant may have been found in the wild as a mutation. In Europe similar variegated forms appeared in von Siebold's garden, purportedly also as mutations or mutated seedlings, which he called *Funkia spathulata albomarginata* var. *lutescens*. In the scientific literature the occurrence of yellow variegated sports among *Hosta sieboldii* seedlings is documented by Yasui (1929), and these mutant forms also develop occasionally in the wild.

The origin of Maekawa's epithet "kabitan" is subject to conjecture. Some authors think it is derived from the Dutch or German "Kapitän," which means "captain." The governor of the Dutch settlement on Dejima Island in Nagasaki harbor was called kapitain (or kapitän, kabitan). Others link it with a beautiful, striped piece of cloth brought as a gift to the shogun in Edo (Tokyo) on the occasion of obligatory visits by the captain of the Dutch settlement on Dejima. This cloth would subsequently be called by the same name: kaptain. I happen to think it is simply a fancy name much like those Westerners give their hostas: *kabi* means "beautiful," and *tan* stands for "cloth," hence kabitan = beautiful cloth.

The name *H.* 'Kabitan' has been registered for this cultivar by The American Hosta Society in 1978, but many horticulturists prefer *H. sieboldii* 'Kabitan' to indicate the parental line. A cultivar imported by Soules Nursery from Japan to the United States, named *Ogon Waisei Giboshi* (Ogon Waisei = the golden one of small stature), is virtually identical. Being a mutation, this variant of *H. sieboldii* is now considered a cultivar. Problems in growing this hosta have been reported by gardeners. These problems may stem from a misunderstanding of its cultural requirements which call for moist soil conditions combined with fairly strong sunlight and high temperatures, with direct sun in early spring and some shade as late spring approaches. These are the same conditions under which *H. sieboldii* grows in the wild. Sunlight must be carefully balanced, because too much will bleach the colors and not enough will cause the plant to languish or dwindle. *Hosta* 'Sea Sprite' is similar but sufficiently distinct to have its own name. Planted in a place to its liking this cultivar grows into a colorful, yellow-green mound which increases rapidly in size due to the ranging habit of root systems. Reversions to green have been reported but seem to be uncommon (Plate 64). It is widely available, inexpensive, and a must for every garden.

Plant size 25 cm (10 in.) dia., 20 cm (8 in.) high. Petiole 10–15 by 0.5 cm (4–6 by 0.2 in.), erect, forming a vase-shaped plant, green with no purple dots at the base. Leaf 10–12.5 by 2.5–4 cm (4–5 by 1–1.5 in.), erect and in line with petiole, lanceolate, petiole transition gradual, decurrent, undulate in the margin, erect, smooth, egg-yolk yellow (vitellinus) with a narrow, well-defined dark green margin; strong light levels cause moderate bleaching to whitish yellow, tip acuminate. Venation 3–4, very lightly impressed above, smooth below. Scape and flowers same as the species. Anthers yellow. August. Fertile.

SY: Funkia spathulata albomarginata var. lutescens nom. nudum
     Siebold 1877.
     Hosta albomarginata f. kabitan Ohwi 1942.
     H. albomarginata f. variegata Ohwi 1965.
     H. japonica var. angustifolia f. variegata Oonuma in Iwasaki
     1916 pp.
     H. lancifolia var. thunbergiana f. kabitan Maekawa 1940.
HN: H. albomarginata f. kabitan hort.
     H. albomarginata 'Kabitan' Hensen 1985.
     H. albomarginata 'Kabitan' hort.
     H. clavata hort. incorrect.
     H. 'Kabitan' AHS-NC IRA/1987

H. lancifolia f. *kapitan* Jellito/Schacht/Fessler 1986
incorrect.
H. lancifolia 'Kabitan' Grenfell 1981 incorrect.
H. lancifolia 'Kabitan' hort. incorrect.
H. lancifolia var. *kabitan* hort. incorrect.
H. lancifolia 'Viridis-marginata' incorrect.
H. 'Ogon Waisei' hort.
H. 'Sea Sprite' pp sim.
H. sieboldii 'Kabitan' hort.
H. 'Wogon Waisei' hort.

JN: *Aofukurin Giboshi* hort. incorrect.
Hime Giboshi 'Kin Cho' hort. incorrect.
Kabitan Giboshi Maekawa 1940.
Konfukurin Giboshi hort. pp.
Ogon Hime Giboshi hort. incorrect.
Ogon Waisei Giboshi hort.

✠ "*H. sieboldii* f. *kifukurin*" (Maekawa) W. G. Schmid comb. nov.
AHS-IV/22A.   (Plate 65).
キフクリンギボウシ
Here transferred from *H. lancifolia* var. *thunbergiana* f. *kifukurin* Maekawa 1969 and reduced to cultivar form as *H. sieboldii* 'Kifukurin'.

Kifukurin Giboshi, the "yellow-margined hosta," is a small form similar to the species but with narrow yellow or whitish yellow margins. In most clones the margins stay yellow, but a few are viridescent and loose their margin color, such as in *H.* 'Krossa Cream Edge', which can be included in this group. Evolving in cultivation, several similar-looking hostas have arisen as mutants or mutant seedlings, broadly related to *H. sieboldii*. These include *H. sieboldii* 'Butter Rim' and *H. sieboldii* 'Marble Rim' in North America and the Japanese *Kifukurin Ko Mame Giboshi* hort., a dwarf, yellow-margined form, and *H.* 'Koriyama', which see. Being similar in size to the species, most are available and make good garden subjects.
SY: *H. lancifolia* var. *thunbergiana* f. *kifukurin* Maekawa 1969.
HN: *H.* 'Butter Rim'.
H. 'Krossa Cream Edge' pp sim.
H. 'Marble Rim'.
JN: *Kifukurin Giboshi*.

✠ "*H. sieboldii* f. *mediopicta*" (Maekawa) Hara 1984.
AHS-IV/20A.   (Plate 66).
キスジギボウシ
Here reduced to cultivar form as *H. sieboldii* 'Mediopicta'.

Kisuji Giboshi, the "yellow-striped hosta," is found in the wild as a mutant. It does not come true from seed, so is here considered a cultivar form. Its variegation is moderately viridescent, and its bright yellow streaking turns to chartreuse or light green by summer. This hosta has a more lanceolate leaf than another, quite similar form called *H.* 'Inaho', *Inaho Giboshi*, which see. The latter is reported practically sterile and a mutation of *H.* 'Lancifolia', while *H. sieboldii* f. *mediopicta* is fertile. More study is required to determine exact relationships. *Hosta sieboldii* 'Mediopicta' is not generally available for cultivation and is a collector's item.
Plant size 20 cm (8 in.) dia., 18 cm (7 in.) high. Petiole 10 by 0.4 cm (4 by 0.15 in.), erect, forming a vase-shaped plant, green with no purple dots at the base. Leaf 10 by 4–5 cm (4 by 1.5–2 in.), erect and in line with petiole, lanceolate, petiole transition gradual, decurrent, undulate, erect, smooth, green leaf, bright yellow (flavus) striped; moderately viridescent, the yellow color slowly darkens to a light green and the leaf becomes green with lighter green stripes, or all-green by anthesis, tip acuminate. Venation 3–4, very

lightly impressed above, smooth below. Anthers yellow. August. Fertile.
SY: *H. albomarginata* f. *mediopicta* Ohwi 1942.
H. lancifolia var. *thunbergiana* f. *mediopicta* Maekawa 1940.
HN: *H.* 'Inaho' incorrect.
H. lancifolia 'Aureostriata' hort. incorrect.
H. sieboldii 'Mediopicta' hort.
H. tardiva 'Aureostriata' hort. incorrect.
JN: *Inaho Giboshi* hort. incorrect.
Kisuji Giboshi Maekawa 1940.
Kisuji (Koba) Giboshi hort.

H. sieboldii f. *okamii* (Maekawa) Hara 1984.
AHS-IV/19B.
ムラサメギボウシ
Murasame Giboshi, "the purple shower hosta," occurs naturally in central Honshu, in the mountain valleys of Mie and Kyoto prefectures and on Shikoku, Kochi Prefecture. The varietal epithet honors Okami who collected the type. It is similar to *H. sieboldii* but smaller and blooms considerably later. As in the type, the flowers are purple-striped but almost bell-shaped. The anthers point to an interspecific hybrid origin, and it is rarely seen in cultivation.
Plant size 20 cm (8 in.) dia., 15 cm (6 in.) high. Petiole 5–7.5 by 6–1 cm (2–3 by 0.25–0.4 in.), broadly winged, erect, green with no purple dots at the base. Leaf 7.5–10 by 2.5–3 cm (3–4 by 2 in.), erect and in line with petiole, moderately thick, lanceolate to oblong-lanceolate, petiole transition cuneately decurrent, acute tip, flat but wavy in the margin, surface shiny green, scarcely apparent variegation, striped, greenish white, underside shiny. Venation 3–4, very lightly impressed above, smooth below. Scape 50 cm (20 in.), straight and erect, not bending, light green, no purple marks. Sterile bracts 2–3, clasping stem, persistent; fertile bracts, short, navicular, thin, membranous, green, translucent at anthesis. Raceme 10–12 flowers, widely spaced. Flowers 4 cm (2 in.) long and 3.5 cm (1.5 in.) broad, purple-striped, purple, thin narrow tube, perianth expanding, broadly funnel-shaped, lobes spreading straightly, short pedicels, very projecting stamen. Yellow anthers with irregular purple-dot pattern. September. Fertile.
SY: *H. lancifolia* var. *thunbergiana* f. *okamii* Maekawa 1950.
H. okamii Maekawa 1940
HN: *H.* 'Davidson No. 75'.
H. 'Davidson No. 90'.
JN: *Murasame Giboshi* Maekawa 1940.

H. sieboldii f. *polycarpellata* (Maekawa) Hara 1984.
AHS-IV/19B.   (Figure 3-69).
ヤツブサギボウシ
Yatsubusa Giboshi was illustrated and validly published by Maekawa (1944). The type is in TI. The epithet is derived from *poly* = many and *carpellum* = fruit. At first examination the name seems strange because all taxa in the genus are normally polycarpellate. Fruit in *Hosta* is a dry, dehiscent, poly-carpellary round or triangular siliqua, meaning a fruit capsule which, in this case, contains three double rows of seeds which are released by the capsule splitting loculicidally into three, recurving shells. Maekawa (1944), however, as part of his carpel studies of the genus discovered carpel connation (Figure 3-69A), carpellar stamina (Figure 3-69B), and pistils (Figure 3-69C). These formations should be considered monstrous, which Maekawa in fact indicated by the name *H. lancifolia* var. *thunbergiana* f. monstr. *polycarpellata*. He also indicated the occurrence of deviation of floral symmetry in these

monstrosities (Figure 3-69D). Maekawa used several synonyms in his article, which are listed later. Hara (1984) validly transferred this forma to *H. sieboldii* as *H. sieboldii* var. *sieboldii* f. *polycarpellata*. This taxon is here considered a monstrosity of scientific interest but of very minor horticultural importance. As such, I have included it in the synonymy of *H. sieboldii* f. *spathulata*, which see.

SY: *H. lancifolia* f. *carpellata* Maekawa 1944.
  H. lancifolia f. *polycarpellata* Maekawa 1944.
  H. lancifolia var. *thunbergiana* f. *polycarpellata* Maekawa 1944.
  H. lancifolia var. *thunbergiana* f. monstr. *polycarpellata* Maekawa 1944.
JN: *Yatsubusa Giboshi* Maekawa 1944.

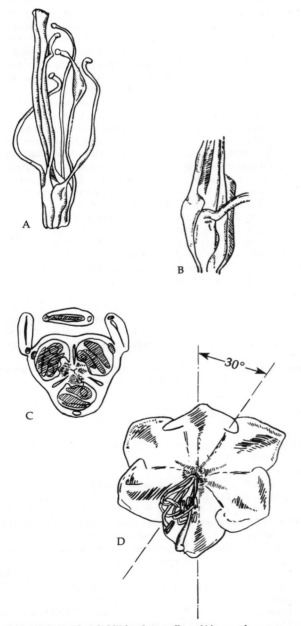

Figure 3-69. *H. sieboldii* f. *polycarpellata*; (A) carpel connation; (B) carpellar stamina and pistils; (C) detail of carpellar stamina; (D) floral asymmetry (drawing by author from Maekawa's [1944] original)

H. sieboldii f. *spathulata* (Miquel) W. G. Schmid comb. nov.

AHS-IV/19B.   (Figures 2-13, 3-70; Plates 190, 202).
コバギボウシ

Koba Giboshi, the "small-leaved hosta," has a name which in Japan applies horticulturally to the all-green as well as the white-margined forms. Because the white-margined form was first validly published as the species *H. sieboldii*, the all-green form has been placed in the rank of forma. Nevertheless, this all-green form is the form found principally in the wild, and a preponderance of Japanese herbarium specimens exemplify this taxon under the name *Koba Giboshi*, although some of them incorrectly classify it as *H.* 'Lancifolia'. The name *Koba Giboshi* is also applied occasionally by Japanese horticulturists to the white-margined form, namely *H. sieboldii*. The all-green *H. sieboldii* f. *spathulata* is endemic to the Japanese archipelago, being abundant in central and western Honshu, Shikoku, and Kyushu. It is most often found as a lowland plant that occurs in moors and damp areas, with some forms ranging into elevated grasslands. In wild populations an incredible number of differentiated leaf forms and sizes exists, which includes leaves with a distinct petiole transition as well as those with margins decurrent to the petiole (Figure 2-13). Some are short, as in the typical form; others are elongated, approaching the morphology of *H. sieboldii* f. *angustifolia*. This well-established and prevalent species varies from place to place, having adapted to local conditions, and these adaptations have in overlapping habitats formed populations of hybrid swarms that are in the process of developing further into new forms by interbreeding and consequent intergrading with other races and species. Evidence of this process can be seen in herbaria, where many different forms of *Koba Giboshi* exist, and some of the more divergent and distinct morphological varieties have been given botanical rank. In all these variations the flower morphology remains relatively constant. This was recognized by Fujita (1976a) who combined many of these forms in synonymy. Selfed crosses made of *H. sieboldii* in cultivation will yield the same conglomeration of all-green forms, and a number of hybrids have been selected and given cultivar names. In the recent past this taxon has been incorrectly associated with *H.* 'Lancifolia'. In its typical form this hosta does not have great importance for gardening purposes. It is occasionally seen in edgings and specimen plantings (Figure 3-70) and many gardeners use plants obtained by sowing seed. Hardly ever does it have correct labeling, and cultivar names are frequently used to identify it, as for example, *H. sieboldii* 'Royal Lady'.

Plant size 25 cm (9 in.) dia., 20 cm (8 in.) high. Petiole 10–15 by 0.5 cm (4–6 by 0.2 in.) wide, erect, forming a vase-shaped plant, green with no purple dots at the base. Leaf 10–15 by 5 cm (4–6 by 2 in.), erect and in line with petiole, lanceolate, petiole transition gradual, decurrent, a little undulate, marginally wavy, erect, smooth, shiny, dull, dark green above, glossy lighter green below. The character of the leaves can vary considerably between local races, and statistically infrequent dwarf and giant forms are excluded from this diagnosis, tip acuminate. Venation 3–4, very lightly impressed above, smooth below. Scape 25–30 cm (10–12 in.), straight and erect, not bending, light green, no purple marks. Sterile bracts, 2–3, clasping stem, persistent; fertile bracts, short, navicular, thin, membranous, green, withering at anthesis, but not falling away. Raceme 6–12 flowers, widely spaced. Flowers 5 cm (2 in.) long and 3.5 cm (1.5 in.) broad, purple-striped, thin narrow tube, perianth expanding, lily-shaped, lobes spreading rapidly, recurving, widely open, short pedicels, very projecting stamens. August. Anthers yellow. Fertile.

SY: *Funkia japonica foliis viridimarginatis* Rodigas 1864.
Funkia ovata var. (f). *spathulata* Miquel 1869.
Funkia spatulata nom. nudum Siebold 1860.
Hosta albomarginata f. *spathulata* Hensen 1963b.
H. albomarginata f. *spathulata* Hansen and Müssel 1964.
H. albomarginata f. *viridis* Hylander 1954.
H. harunaensis Honda 1935b pp.
H. ibukiensis Fujita 1976a pp sl na.
H. lancifolia f. *carpellata* Maekawa 1944.
H. lancifolia f. *polycarpellata* Maekawa 1944.
H. lancifolia var. *thunbergiana* Maekawa 1940.
H. lancifolia var. *thunbergiana* f. *polycarpellata* Maekawa 1944.
H. lancifolia var. *thunbergiana* f. monstr. *polycarpellata* Maekawa 1944.
H. sieboldii var. *sieboldii* f. *polycarpellata* Hara 1984.

HN: *H. albomarginata spathulata* hort. incorrect.
H. albomarginata 'Spathulata' Hansen and Müssel 1964.
H. albomarginata 'Thunbergiana' incorrect.
H. 'Beatrice Green Form' hort. incorrect.
H. 'Craig No. C-2'.
H. 'Green Beatrice' Williams/Ruh IRA/1987.
H. lancifolia 'Hausers Narrow Leaf' pp incorrect.
H. lancifolia thunbergiana hort. incorrect.
H. sieboldii 'Spathulata' hort.
H. sieboldii thunbergiana hort. incorrect.
H. sieboldii 'Viridis' hort. incorrect.
H. sieboldii viridis hort. incorrect.
H. thunbergiana hort. incorrect.
H. 'Thunbergiana' hort. incorrect.
H. 'Thunbergii' hort. incorrect.
H. thunbergii hort. incorrect.

JN: *Koba Giboshi* Makino 1940.
Oze Giboshi hort.
Oze Mizu Giboshi hort. incorrect.

Figure 3-70. *H. sieboldii* f. *spathulata*; general habit, landscape use (Hosta Hill)

H. sieboldii f. *spathulata* Dwarf group hort.

ヒメコバギボウシ
姫ヤクシマギボウシ
コマメギボウシ
サイシュウジマギボウシ
ヤクシマギボウシ
ヤクシマミズギボウシ

(Figure 6-6).

Hime Koba Giboshi, Hime Yakushima Giboshi, Ko Mame Giboshi, Saishu Jima Giboshi, Yakushima Giboshi, and *Yakushima Mizu Giboshi* are all small cultivars which make up a group of dwarf forms of the green form of the species. Many different variants exist. Here they are recognized as a group from which individuals can be selected and named. The named varieties are listed under their respective cultivar names. Not all the plants named in horticulture belong to the *H. sieboldii* complex; some are related to *H. longissima* and *H. gracillima*. An example is *H.* 'Yakushima Mizu', a form of *H. gracillima*, but I have also seen *H. sieboldii* related material under this name. There is considerable confusion in Japan as well as in North America because many small seedlings from a variety of species are in commerce under these names.

HN: *H. albomarginata* dwarf form, hort. incorrect.
H. 'Hakujima' hort.
H. 'Hime Yakushima' hort.
H. 'Ko Mame' hort.
H. 'Saishu Jima' pp sim.
H. 'Yakushima Mizu' hort. pp sl.

JN: *Hime Koba Giboshi* hort.
Hime Yakushima Giboshi hort.
Ko Mame Giboshi hort.
Saishu Jima Giboshi hort.
Yakushima Giboshi hort. pp.
Yakushima Mizu Giboshi hort. pp sl.

✠ *"H. sieboldii* f. *subchrocea"* (Maekawa) Hara 1984.

AHS-IV/23B. (Plates 67, 97, 159, 160).

シロカビタン
黄金カビタン

Here orthographically corrected to f. *subcrocea* and reduced to cultivar form as *H. sieboldii* 'Subcrocea'.

Shiro Kabitan Giboshi is no longer listed by Maekawa (1969) as a botanical form. It was described by him in 1940 under the Latin epithet *subchrocea,* which is here considered an orthographic error and has been corrected to "subcrocea," meaning "light cadmium yellow," which is correct in a Western sense. The latter name is used in the registration of this taxon. Maekawa's very brief description reads, "Folia aureovariegata margine valde undulata [leaves gold-variegated with strongly undulate margin]," so he undoubtedly described the typical yellow form of *H. sieboldii* now known in the West as *H. sieboldii* 'Subcrocea'. Why he applied the Japanese name *Shirokabitan Giboshi*, "the white kabitan," to a yellow taxon is not known. Unfortunately, and to complicate matters, Japanese horticulturists use the name *Shirokabitan Giboshi* with a plant similar to the green-margined, white taxon known in the West as *H.* 'Haku Chu Han', not a yellow one, so there is some confusion. In the West the Nomenclature Committee of The American Hosta Society has registered the names *H.* 'Haku Chu Han' (1986) and *H.* 'Subcrocea' (1987) without descriptions, with the latter ostensibly applying to the all-yellow taxon. *Hosta* 'Shirokabitan', on the other hand, has not been registered and should not be used. It is a confusing name used in horticulture for a white-centered, green-margined taxon, while at the same time being formally and taxonomically applied to the taxon gardeners know as *H.* 'Subcrocea'. The latter, in its most frequently cultivated form, is very similar *H. sieboldii* f. *kabitan,* except that it lacks the green margin and has a more undulate leaf. The description is based on this form. In Japan these yellow forms are not gathered under *Shirokabitan Giboshi* (the academic Japanese name) but under *Ogon Koba Giboshi*, and *H.* 'Ogon Koba'. Occasionally the name *Ogon Kabitan*, *H.* 'Ogon Kabitan', the "golden Kabitan," is used. What the Japanese call *Shirokabitan Giboshi*, I have renamed *H. sieboldii* 'Silver Kabitan', which see, because, in this case, use of the Japanese name is contrary to the rules and confusing. As with the other variegated forms of *H. sieboldii*, it originated with the species either by way of self-pollination (Yasui, 1929) or mutation. It has been found as rare mutations in the wild but the latter do not perpetuate in the wild so are considered cultivars. Cultural requirements are the same as listed under *H. sieboldii* f. *kabitan*. The obvious heterozygous background of the parent plant *H. sieboldii* is revealed in the many leaf shapes which occur in the yellow forms derived from selfing the species.

Plant size 20 cm (8 in.) dia., 18 cm (7 in.) high. Petiole 10 by 0.4 cm (4 by 0.15 in.), erect, forming a vase-shaped plant, green with no purple dots at the base. Leaf 10–12.5 by 2.5–4 cm (4–5 by 1–1.5 in.), erect and in line with petiole, lanceolate, petiole transition gradual, decurrent, very undulate, crispate in the margin, erect, smooth, bright yellow (flavus). All existing forms are viridescent in varying degrees. Strong light causes moderate bleaching to whitish yellow in some clones, tip acuminate. Venation 3–4, very lightly impressed above, smooth below. Anthers yellow. August. Fertile.

SY: *H. albomarginata* f. *subchrocea* Ohwi 1942.
     H. albomarginata f. *variegata* Ohwi 1965.
     H. lancifolia var. *thunbergiana* f. *subchrocea* Maekawa 1940.

HN: *H. albomarginata* 'Subcrocea' hort.
     H. clavata hort. Krossa incorrect.
     H. 'Golden Dewdrop' hort.
     H. 'Krossa Clavata' Summers No. 49.
     H. lancifolia 'Subcrocea' incorrect.
     H. lancifolia var. *subchrocea* hort. incorrect.
     H. lancifolia var. *thunbergiana* 'Aurea' hort. UK incorrect.
     H. lancifolia var. *thunbergiana* f. *subchrocea* hort. incorrect.
     H. 'Ogon' incorrect.
     H. sieboldii f. *subchrocea*.
     H. sieboldii 'Subcrocea' hort.
     H. 'Subcrocea' AHS-NC IRA/1987.
     H. 'Wogon' incorrect.

JN: *Ogon Kabitan Giboshi* hort.
     Ogon Koba Giboshi hort. pp.
     Shiro Kabitan Giboshi Maekawa 1940.

H. sieboldii 'Fuiri Chishima' hort.
斑入チシマギボウシ

Fuiri Chishima Giboshi is a name occasionally and incorrectly used as a Japanese synonym for *H. sieboldii* 'Bunchoko' (*Bunchoko Giboshi*), which see.

H. sieboldii 'Hime Kin Cho' hort.
姫ギボウシ金鳥

Hime Giboshi Kin Cho is a name occasionally and incorrectly used as a Japanese synonym for *H. sieboldii* 'Kabitan' (*Kabitan Giboshi*), which see.

H. sieboldii 'Ogon Hime' hort.
黄金姫ギボウシ

Ogon Hime Giboshi is a name occasionally and incorrectly used as a Japanese synonym for *H. sieboldii* 'Kabitan' (*Kabitan Giboshi*), which see, and also for *H. sieboldii* 'Subcrocea'.

H. sieboldii 'Ogon Kobano' hort.
黄金コバノ ギボウシ

Ogon Kobano Giboshi is a name occasionally and incor-

rectly used as a Japanese synonym for *H. sieboldii* 'Subcrocea' (*Ogon Giboshi*), which see.

H. sieboldii 'Oze' hort.
オゼギボウシ

Oze Giboshi is a name occasionally and incorrectly used as a Japanese synonym for *H. sieboldii* f. *spathulata* (*Koba Giboshi*), which see.

H. sieboldii 'Oze Mizu' hort.
オゼミズギボウシ

Oze Mizu Giboshi is a name occasionally and incorrectly used as a Japanese synonym for *H. sieboldii* f. *spathulata* (*Koba Giboshi*), which see.

H. sieboldii 'Silver Kabitan'.
(Plates 30, 68).

Shirokabitan Giboshi, the "white captain hosta," is a name which is taxonomically linked with *H. sieboldii* 'Subcrocea', an all-yellow plant. The name is applied by Maekawa (1940, 1969), Ohwi (1942), and Hara (1984) as the formal Japanese name for *H. sieboldii* "Subcrocea", which see. Unfortunately, in Japanese horticulture a white-centered taxon, not a yellow one, is cultivated under the name *Shirokabitan Giboshi* and so, from a taxonomic standpoint, incorrectly associated and applied. Since the latter name is confusing and should not be used, I have assigned a Western cultivar name to represent what Japanese horticulturists incorrectly call *Shirokabitan Giboshi*, namely, *H. sieboldii* 'Silver Kabitan', for its silvery white leaf center in spring. The name *H. sieboldii* 'White Kabitan' would be more fitting but cannot be used per Article 32 of the ICNCP because it is merely a translation of *Shirokabitan*. Several forms of this taxon exist, and one of them has been registered as *H. (sieboldii)* 'Haku Chu Han', which see. In Japan this name is not used; instead Maekawa's 1969 name, *Shirokabitan Giboshi*, is incorrectly applied in a broad sense. Originating from the species by hybridization or mutation in the wild, the several different clones of this form are smaller than the species *H. sieboldii* (compare leaves in Plate 68), and some have different leaf forms because the species itself is a heterozygous taxon (see *H. sieboldii*). Varying chlorophyll deficiencies cause these variants to exhibit different degrees of viridescence. *Shirokabitan Giboshi*, now called *H. sieboldii* 'Silver Kabitan', received from Japan, for example, turns more green and is slightly more vigorous than *H.* 'Haku Chu Han'. Some variants (either mutants or hybrids) are very small, for example, *H.* 'Bobbin' which is related. Most of these have purple-striped flowers. *Hosta* 'Silver Spoon' has white flowers and represents an albino form. Due to their viridescence, the white leaf areas of these white-centered forms of *H. sieboldii* do not melt out as severely as is the case with many other white-centered cultivars which are albescent. Being small and mostly white-leaved, all must be given the correct cultural conditions as outlined under *H. sieboldii* f. *kabitan* and they must be carefully placed in the garden.

Plant size 15 cm (6 in.) dia., 10 cm (4 in.) high. Petiole 5 by 0.4 cm (2 by 0.15 in.), erect, forming a vase-shaped plant, white, green striped at margin, with no purple dots at the base. Leaf 7.5 by 1.8 cm (3 by 0.6 in.), erect and in line with petiole, lanceolate, petiole transition gradual, decurrent, very undulate in the margin, erect, smooth, white, slightly viridescent, with a narrow, well-defined dark green margin, in summer turning whitish green, sometimes with green streaks, tip acuminate. Venation 3–4, very lightly impressed above, smooth below. Anthers yellow. August. Fertile.

HN: *H.* 'Bobbin' pp sim dwarf form.

H. 'Haku Chu Han' Japan IRA/1986.
H. 'Shirokabitan' hort. incorrect.
H. sieboldii 'Shirokabitan' hort. incorrect.
H. 'Silver Spoon' pp sim white flowers.
H. thunbergii 'Argenteomaculata' hort. incorrect.
H. 'Tiny Tim' Summers (No. 171) pp mutation sim.
JN: *Hime Shirokabitan Giboshi* hort.
      Shironakafu Koba Giboshi hort.
      Tsugaru Komachi Giboshi hort. pp sim.

H. sieboldii var. *intermedia* (Maekawa) Hara 1984.
(see *H. clavata*).

H. sieboldii var. *rectifolia* (Maekawa) Hara 1984.
(see *H. rectifolia*).

H. sieboldii var. *rectifolia* f. *albiflora* (Tatewaki) Hara 1984.
(see *H. rectifolia* var. *chionea* f. *albiflora*).

H. sieboldii var. *rectifolia* f. *atropurpurea* (Nakai) Hara 1984.
(see *H. atropurpurea*).

H. sieboldii var. *rectifolia* f. *chionea* (Maekawa) Hara 1984.
(see *H. rectifolia* var. *chionea*).

H. sieboldii var. *rectifolia* f. *leucantha* (K. Ito) Hara 1984.
(see *H. rectifolia* var. *chionea* f. *albiflora*).

H. sieboldii var. *rectifolia* f. *pruinosa* (Maekawa) Hara 1984.
(see *H. rectifolia* var. *pruinosa*).

H. sieboldii var. *sieboldii* Hara 1984.
     Under the classification of the *H. sieboldii* complex presented in this volume, I have not accepted Hara's placement of *H. rectifolia* and *H. intermedia* as varieties under *H. sieboldii*. As a consequence, there exist no other valid varieties to justify the citation of var. *sieboldii* under the species name, and thus it has not been used.
(see *H. sieboldii* [Paxton] Ingram).

H. sieboldii var. *sieboldii* f. *sieboldii* Hara 1984.
     See comments under *H. sieboldii* var. *sieboldii* Hara 1984.
(see *H. sieboldii* [Paxton] Ingram).

H. sparsa Nakai 1930.
(see *H. longipes* f. *sparsa*).

H. stenantha nom. nudum hort. incorrect.
(see *H. fortunei* var. *stenantha*).

T

H. takahashii Araki 1942.
シヒゾギボウシ   (Figure 3-71; Plates 69, 199).
     Shihizo Giboshi, the "hosta of Shihizo," was named for the collector Shihizo Takahashi, who found it on Mount Ibukiyama, Shiga Prefecture, central Honshu. The epithet also honors the collector. In Japan it is sometimes included as a variety of *H. tardiva* or *H. kiyosumiensis*. It is like the former, but handled as a species due to its larger, widely ovate leaves with cordate-truncate base, much longer scapes, and purple-striped, bell-shaped flowers. It blooms quite late, so this taxon has been placed in section *Tardanthae*. Growing into a large

clump with bright green leaves and many flowers on straight scapes, it is a good background plant where a green, late-blooming hosta is required.
     Plant size 50–65 cm (20–26 in.) dia., 30 cm (12 in.) high. Petiole 17.5–25 by 4–1 cm (7–18 by 0.16–0.45 in.), slightly winged, erect, green with purple dotted at the base, lighter above. Leaf 12.5–17.5 by 10–15 cm (5–7 by 4–6 in.), erect, broadly ovate, petiole transition truncate, cordate, slightly undulate, wavy in the margin, smooth, shiny light, elm green above, glossy lighter green below, tip acuminate. Venation 5–6, sunken above, very projected, smooth below. Scape 65–80 cm (26–32 in.), erect, green, purplish red dotted at the base. Sterile bracts 3, clasping the stem; fertile bracts, navicular, long, thick, grooved, green, persisting, not withering at anthesis. Raceme 30 cm (12 in.), 15–30 flowers. Flowers 3.5–4.5 cm (1.5–2 in.) long and 3–4 cm (1.25–1.5 in.) broad, purple-violet; perianth expanding, in the central part slightly dilated bell-shaped, lobes spreading but not recurving, half open, short pedicels; projecting stamens. Seed pods light green, purple-dotted. Anthers densely purple-dotted. September. Fertile.
SY: *H. kiyosumiensis* hort. incorrect.
      H. tardiva Fujita 1976a sl na.
JN: *Shihizo Giboshi* Araki 1942.

Figure 3-71. *H. takahashii*; general habit; *H. sieboldiana* green form (behind) (Hosta Hill)

H. takiensis Araki 1942.
タキギボウシ   (Plate 70).
     Taki Giboshi, the "hosta from Taki," was found growing on rocks in mountain valleys near Taki-gun, Murakumo-mura, Kyoto Prefecture, Honshu. Formerly compared to *H. cathayana*, it is not related to it. Morphologically and ecologically it is connected to *H. aequinoctiiantha*, so Fujita (1976a) included it as a synonym under this species. It belongs in section *Picnolepis*. It is treated as a species due to its geographic isolation and macromorphological distinctiveness. Observed only at scientific institutions, it is not generally available and is of interest to collectors only.
     Plant size 35–45 cm (14–18 in.) dia., 30 cm (12 in.) high. Petiole 7.5–12.5 by 0.6 cm (3–5 by 0.25 in.), erect, green, purple-dotted only lightly at the base. Leaf 7.5–12.5 by 3.5–7.5 cm (3–5 by 1.5–3 in.), erect and in line with petiole, entire, broadly ovate to ovate, petiole transition rounded, erect, moderately textured, smooth, shiny green above, lighter, opaque green below, tip acute. Venation 6–9, smooth above. Scape 25–32.5 cm (10–13 in.), straight, erect, slightly purple-dotted at base only, smooth round. Sterile bracts 2–4, sessile; fertile bracts, navicular, thin,

membranous, white or whitish green, purple-tinted, imbricated, persistent, not withering. Raceme 10–12.5 cm (4–5 in.), 20–30 flowers, densely arranged. Flowers white outside, suffused pale purple inside, held erect in horizontal position on long, strong horizontal or slightly ascending purple pedicels, perianth 5 cm (2 in.) long, funnel-shaped, expanding, in the central part dilated bell-shaped, lobes spreading straightly to ±angled to the axis of perianth. Anthers yellow background uniformly purple-dotted. September. Fertile.

SY: *H. longipes* var. *aequinoctiiantha* Fujita 1976a sl pp na.
JN: *Taki Giboshi* Araki 1942.
(see also *H. aequinoctiiantha*).

✠ "*H. tardiflora*" (Irving) Stearn apud Grey 1938.
AHS-IV/19B.   (Figure 3-72; Plates 39, 71).
Here reduced to cultivar form as *H*. '**Tardiflora**'.

This taxon is considered by many authorities to be a Japanese species, but it has not been matched with any of the taxa growing in the wild. Its morphological character connects it with section *Picnolepis*, but it has yellow anthers and so differs in this key attribute. It was brought from Japan to Germany by Leichtlin in 1894, who sent a specimen to the Royal Botanic Garden, Kew, in 1895. Leichtlin named this hosta but did not record its origin. Maekawa (1940) included *H. tardiflora* as a synonym for *H. sparsa* Nakai, *Aki Giboshi*, but this synonymy is doubtful because the latter has purple anthers. There are other key morphological differences, including 5–8 flowers per raceme for *H. sparsa* and 14–20 per raceme for *H*. 'Tardiflora'. For this reason I have included *H. sparsa* as a forma under *H. longipes*, the *Iwa Giboshi*. A variant of *H. longipes*, namely, *H. longipes* var. *lancea*, grows in Shizuoka Prefecture in the Tenryu River area and has been reported to be identical to *H*. 'Tardiflora' by Junichi Sugimoto (H. Sugita, 1988: personal communication), but the former also has purple anthers. If *H. sparsa* is considered a synonym of *H. tardiflora*, then the latter name has priority. Maekawa (1969), recognizing this, reversed the synonymy and used the Japanese katakana equivalent, that is, *Tarudeifuro-ra Giboshi*, and put *H. sparsa* as a synonym under *H. tardiflora*. This reverse placement is just as questionable as the earlier one. There are no natural populations of this taxon in Japan, and a collected type has never been designated. As a consequence Fujita (1976a) disregarded this taxon, considering it a cultigen; I have reduced it to cultivar form. This should in no way detract from its horticultural status as the premier late-blooming, fertile cultivar. It is cultivated the world over. Occasionally, late-blooming forms of *H*. 'Lancifolia' and *H. sieboldii* (see *H*. 'Lancifolia Cathy Late') masquerade as this specioid and are often found in gardens labeled *H*. 'Tardiflora', which they are not. They bloom earlier and have leaves of comparatively thin substance, while *H*. 'Tardiflora' is a later blooming hosta with frost-resistant foliage of considerable substance. *Hosta* 'Tardiflora' is an excellent plant for borders, lasting well into fall and providing a late flower showing. It is the best substitute for *H*. 'Lancifolia'. The heavy leaf substance provides good resistance against slug and snail damage and survives light frosts. In colder climates this taxon will flower, but its flowers are occasionally spoiled by early freezes, and the plant fails to develop seeds due to the onset of winter. It has been widely used by hybridizers (see *H*. Tardiana grex).

Plant size 40 cm (16 in.) dia., 25 cm (10 in.) high. Petiole 11–13 by 0.3–0.6 cm (4.5–5 by 0.12–0.25 in.), erect, green covered with vertical dull purple dots (actually elongated streaks 0.1 by 1mcm/0.004 by 0.04 in.), starting at leaf base, becoming progres-sively darker towards ground. Leaf 7–14 by 5–6 cm (3–6 by 2–2.5 in.), erect and in line with petiole, broadly lanceolate, petiole transition very gradual, decurrent, flat surface, slight waves in margin, erect, rigid, leathery, glossy dark green above, lighter shiny green below, tip acuminate. Venation 6–8, sunken above, very projected, smooth below. Scape 25–30 cm (10–12 in.), straight, erect, tinted purplish red at the base, smooth round. Fertile bracts 1 cm (0.3 in.), navicular, grooved, white or whitish green, purple tinged, imbricated, withering at anthesis. Raceme 12 cm, 15–20 flowers. Flowers pale purple, held erect in horizontal position on strong horizontal or slightly ascending purple pedicels, evenly spaced on raceme, perianth 4 cm (1.5 in.) long, funnel-shaped, thin narrow hexagonal tube. Anthers yellow. October. Fertile.

SY: *Funkia tardiflora* Irving 1903.
        Funkia tardiflora Leichtlin.
        Hosta japonica var. *tardiflora* Bailey 1915 pp.
        H. lancifolia var. *tardiflora* Bailey 1930 incorrect.
        H. longipes var. *lancea* Honda incorrectly attributed.
        Niobe japonica var. *tardiflora* Nash.
HN: *Funkia lancifolia* var. *tardiflora* hort. incorrect.
        Hosta 'Krossa No. F-1' pp sim.
        H. lancifolia var. *tardiflora* hort. incorrect.
        H. 'Mack No. 17'.
        H. sparsa incorrect.
        H. tardiflora 'Hybrida' Arends pp.
JN: *Aki Giboshi* incorrect.

Figure 3-72. *H*. 'Tardiflora; flowering plant (Hosta Hill)

H. **tardiva** Nakai 1930.
AHS-IV/19B.   (Figure 3-73).
ナンカイギボウシ

Nankai Giboshi, the "hosta of the southern ocean," alludes to its habitat in southern Japan. *Hosta tardiva*, from *tardus* = late, as well as the common name, Serotinous Plantain Lily, from *sero* = late, allude to its late flowering. The type was collected by Nakai in Shikoku, Tokushima Prefecture, and it ranges into Kyushu and Kii Peninsula. Although found in the wild it is sterile. According to Kaneko (1968a), it is a diploid 2n = 60. Fujita (1976a) reported dispersal through human cultivation on Shikoku, where it is found near human habitation, but outside Shikoku he considered it a cultivar. Its leaves are very shiny, which may have given rise to the name *H. tardiva* var. *lucida*, but it is difficult to identify this taxon by the leaves alone because they are very much like those of *H*. 'Lancifolia' or *H. cathayana*. Its bracts always wither at flowering time, so this trait can be used to separate it from the latter, and the flowers have a larger, expanding perianth. By some Japanese horticulturists it is regarded as an interspecific hybrid, *H. rohdeifolia* f. *viridis* × *H. longipes*. Interplanting with the very similar *H.* 'Lancifolia' or *H. cathayana* extends the blooming period because it blooms later, but otherwise it is of interest primarily to the collector only. A large cultivar grown in North America under this name (cfr. Aden, 1988:32) with large leaves, 6–9 pairs of veins, and tall scapes with many flowers does not conform to Maekawa's description so is not this taxon.

Plant size 45–55 cm (18–22 in.) dia., 30 cm (12 in.) high. Petiole 17.5–25 by 0.5 cm (7–18 by 0.2 in.), erect, forming a vase-shaped plant, green, purple-spotted at the base. Leaf 10–17.5 by 5–7.5 cm (4–7 by 2–3 in.), erect and in line with petiole, ovate-lanceolate, petiole transition broadly narrowed, sometimes blunt, tip acuminate, slightly undulate, wavy in the margin, erect, rigid, smooth, shiny light, elm green above, glossy lighter green below. Venation 4–6, sunken above, very projected, smooth, below. Scape 50–60 cm (20–24 in.), straight and erect, ±perpendicular to the ground, green, lower third dotted purplish red. Fertile bracts short, navicular, grooved, thin, membranous, green, withering at anthesis, but not falling away. Raceme 20–25 cm (8–10 in.), 10–20 flowers. Flowers 4–4.5 cm (1.5–2 in.) long and 4 cm (1.5 in.) broad, purple-violet; perianth expanding, funnel-shaped, in the central part slightly dilated bell-shaped, lobes spreading rapidly, recurving, widely open, blunt, short pedicels, projecting stamen. Anthers purple. September. Sterile.

SY: *H. cathayana* Fujita 1976a sl na.
      H. takahashii Fujita 1976a sl na.
      H. tardiva var. *lucida* nom. nudum Maekawa 1940.
      H. tardiva var. *takina* nom. nudum Kaneko 1968a.
HN: *H.* 'Craig No. H-1' sim.
      H. 'Craig No. H-2' sim.
      H. 'Craig No. H-8' sim.
      Serotinous Plantain Lily Maekawa 1969.
JN: *Nankai Giboshi* Nakai 1930.

Figure 3-73. *H. tardiva*; general habit (Hosta Hill)

H. tardiva 'Aureostriata' hort.

This name is a nomen confusum because it is applied to different taxa. It is invalid per the ICNCP because of its Latin formulation.
(see *H.* 'Inaho').

H. tardiva var. *lucida* nom. nudum Maekawa 1940.

The name *H. tardiva* var. *lucida* was mentioned by Maekawa (1940), but he did not elaborate on it. The varietal epithet may have been used to indicate the glossy leaf surface of this taxon (*lucida* = shining). It is here considered a nomen nudum.

H. tardiva var. *takina* nom. nudum Kaneko 1968a.

This taxon is mentioned in a cytological study by Kaneko (1968a), and was grown in Maekawa's garden as No. 180. Collected by Yoshinaga in Kochi Prefecture, Shikoku, it is very close to the species and here considered synonymous to it. (see *H. tardiva*).

H. tibae Maekawa 1984 (as *H. tibai*).

AHS-III/13A. (Figures 2-25, 3-74, D-4; Plates 72, 204). ナガサキギボウシ

Nagasaki Giboshi, the "Nagasaki hosta," was rediscovered by Tsunesaburo Chiba (latinized = Tiba) on the flanks Mount Inasa-dake (333 m/1000 ft.), which is located on Nagasaki Harbor across from the city proper and east of the suburb Inasa-machi. In 1827 von Siebold also collected this hosta on the same mountain which can be seen from the historical site of his house in Katafuchi-machi, Nagasaki. Two herbarium specimens of von Siebold's *H. tibae* exist in L (Nos. 8147/36 and 8147/37), both marked syntypes of *Funkia ovata* var. *ramosa* Miquel (*ramosus* = bearing branches, multi-branched) (Plate 72). In 1957 Hylander believed these were varieties of *Hosta* 'Lancifolia' and affixed his incorrect determination to these specimens under his signature. Although imported by and known to von Siebold and identified by Miquel as a distinct botanical variety, this species remained unrecognized in Western gardens and disappeared. It was sent to the United States by Kaneko in the late 1960s as *H. chibai* (Kaneko, 1968a) which is a nom. nudum, is invalid and should not be used. This hosta was validly published by Maekawa in 1984 under the name *H. tibai*, which becomes *H. tibae* following Article 73C.1.(a) of the ICBN. A broad relationship exists with the recently discovered species *H. jonesii*, which see. It occurs in a relatively small mountainous area around the city of Nagasaki, Nagasaki Prefecture, and can be found in rocky areas as well as on forest soil. With its many-branched racemes (Plate 72) carrying many light-purple-striped flowers, it is of considerable horticultural interest. As many as 120 flowers have been counted on one scape and its multiple branches. A good conversation piece for specimen planting, it blooms in September and provides a late show of color.

Plant size 45–55 cm (18–22 in.) dia., 30 cm (12 in.) high. Petiole 17.5–25 by 0.5 cm (7–10 by 0.2 in.), erect, green, purple-spotted at the base. Leaf 17.5–22.5 by 10–12.5 cm (7–9 by 4–5 in.), erect and in line with petiole, ovate to ovate-cordate, petiole transition broadly narrowed, tapering, tip acuminate, slightly undulate, wavy in the margin, erect, rigid, smooth, shiny light green above, glossy lighter green, glabrous below. Venation 6–8, sunken above, very projected, smooth, below. Scape 50–60 cm (20–24 in.), straight, erect, perpendicular to the ground, 3–6 branches per main scape with 5–12 flowers per branch, purple-dotted lower third. Fertile bracts short, navicular, grooved, thin, membranous, green, withering at anthesis, but not falling away. Raceme on each of several side branches, central raceme long, lateral ones short, average to 80 flowers per scape, 25–30 on main raceme, the remainder on lateral racemes. Flowers 5 cm (2 in.) long and 3.5 cm (1.25 in.) broad, purple-violet; perianth expanding, funnel-shaped, in the central part slightly dilated bell-shaped, lobes barely spreading, short pedicels, projecting stamen. Anthers yellow. September. Fertile.

SY: *Funkia ovata* Sprengel var. *ramosa* Miquel; herbarium annotation (Nos. 8147/36 and 8147/37) in L.
Hemerocallis japonica var. *mihi* nom. nudum Siebold 1830; herbarium annotation (Nos. 8147/36 and 8147/37) in L.
Hosta chibai Kaneko 1968a nom. nudum incorrect.
H. tibai Maekawa 1940.
JN: *Nagasaki Giboshi* Maekawa ex Toyama 1940.

Figure 3-74. *H. tibae*; specimen collected by von Siebold near Nagasaki, now in L; named *Funkia ovata* var. *ramosa* Miquel; note the branching scapes (UGA/Schmid)

✣ *"H. tokudama"* Maekawa 1940.
AHS-III/15B. (Figure 3-75; Plates 73, 173, 186).
トクダマ
Here reduced to cultivar form as *H.* **'Tokudama'**.

Tokudama, the "well-rounded hosta," is named for its rounded leaves. Although Maekawa stated, "Seems to be spontaneous in Inaba Province (Tottori Prefecture)," all the specimens he lists are numbered cultivars in Kikuchi's garden. This taxon is considered a cultivar by most authorities, and following Fujita (1976a), who did not list it, I am treating it as a cultigen, reducing it to cultivar form. It is possible that *H.* 'Tokudama' forms occur in the wild among allopatric populations of *H. sieboldiana*, but these are considered differentiated forms of the latter, nothing more. European botanists have considered it a variety of *H. sieboldiana*, as *H. sieboldiana* var. *fortunei*, since the 1870s. The latter name is synonymous to *H.* 'Tokudama'. This taxon was brought to Europe by both Fortune and von Siebold, Fortune obtaining it from von Siebold during a visit to his Nagasaki home in Japan in the fall of 1860. In early 1862 both naturalists returned to Europe with live specimens of this cultigen. It was shown in England in 1863 as a single specimen; von Siebold, on the other hand, did not publicize it but simply planted it in his garden. Due to its slow growth, propagation was delayed in England and Holland, and it was not introduced into commerce until after von Siebold's death (1866) by Witte in Holland in 1870, who also stated that it was an extremely slow grower. This variable taxon has been extensively hybridized in cultivation and should be considered as a group of very similar clones although no group name has been established due to the very minor macromorphological differences in the cultivated population. Many of the clones which have been selected and given cultivar names are described in Chapter 4, such as *H.* 'Love Pat'. This taxon is prone to mutation resulting in various variegated forms. When it was first cultivated in the United States, cultivar names were attached to it or its selfed hybrids—for example, 'Rabinau' or 'Carder'. Some of these clones were considered the "true form." Most propagated clones have round leaves with upturned margins and white flowers that never fully open. They are slow growing and take years to grow into specimen clumps. They are, nevertheless, extensively cultivated, by virtue of their very pruinose blue spring color and cupped, highly rugose leaves. Other forms are known which do not have cupped leaves, but otherwise are within the morphological limits of *H.* 'Tokudama' as described by Maekawa (1940) (Figure 3-75).

Plant size 40–70 cm (16–28 in.) dia., to 30–40 cm (12–16 in.) high. Petiole 15–30 by 1.2 cm (6–12 by 0.5 in.), not or slightly winged, deeply grooved, very pruinose, lasting, verdigris-green. Leaf 20–30 by 15–20 cm (8–12 by 6–8 in.), attitude at petiole spreading in a ±continuing flat arch, cordate, broadly ovate-cordate, some leaves orbicular, undulate, many, but not all leaves with upturned margins, concave, very rugose, puckered, coriaceous, very pruinose, with some pruinosity remaining after anthesis, pruinose on back ±permanent, cuspidate tip, glaucous sea-green. Venation 10–13, sunken above, very projected, strigose below, convergent and sub-marginally connected at tip area. Scape height to slightly above leaf mound, 45 cm (18 in.), pruinose, erect, round, glaucous green. Fertile bracts flat and broad, thick and fleshy, green or whitish green, tinged with purple, developing and opening in a stellar form as seen from above, horizontally spreading during anthesis, triangular, very persisting. Raceme 15 cm (6 in.), 10–15 flowers. Flowers 4–4.5 cm (1.5 in.) long and 2.5 cm (1 in.) broad, white, suffused very pale violet to violet, distinctly globular in the expanded tube, during anthesis lobes gradually expanding, never fully open, ±parallel to axis of perianth, heavy textured, thick; stamens not superior, equal or slightly shorter than perianth. Anthers pale yellow to whitish yellow, top and margins. July. Fertile.

SY: *Funkia fortunei* nom. nudum Siebold 1870.
Funkia sieboldiana f. *fortunei* Regel 1876.

Figure 3-75. *H. tokudama*; mature specimen, showing ultimate size, and also the devastating effect fully grown mollusks (slugs and snails) can have on leaves in spite of heavy substance (Spinners/Schmid)

Funkia sieboldiana var. *condensata* Miquel 1867.
Funkia sieboldiana var. *fortunei* Witte 1877.
Hemerocallis tokudama Trattinnick in Maekawa 1940
Hosta sieboldiana var. *glauca* Makino 1902.
Hostia sieboldiana f. *fortunei* Voss 1896.

HN: *Hosta* 'Blue Pearl' hort.
　　H. fortunei hort. Europe pp.
　　H. glauca hort. pp.
　　H. glauca minor Foerster 1957 incorrect.
　　H. 'Krossa No. K-6' pp sim.
　　H. 'Moscow Blue' hort. pp sim.
　　H. odudama Foerster 1965b incorrect.
　　H. okudama Foerster 1965a incorrect.
　　H. sieboldiana fortunei minor Foerster 1956 incorrect.
　　H. sieboldiana var. *fortunei* hort.
　　H. tokudama 'Carder' Carder.
　　H. tokudama 'Rabinau' Summers No. 15 hort.
　　H. tokudama 'True' hort. incorrect.
　　Tokudama Plantain Lily.

JN: *Tokudama* Iinuma 1874.
　　Tokudama Giboshi hort.

ON: Blaue Löffelblattfunkie (German).
　　Kleine Löffelblattfunkie Foerster 1956 (German).
　　Löffelblattfunkie Foerster 1957 (German).

✠ *"H. tokudama* f. *aureonebulosa"* Maekawa 1940.
アケボノトクダマ　　　　　　　　　　　(Plate 74).
青覆輪トクダマ
逆斑ギボウシ

Here reduced to cultivar form as *H.* **'Tokudama Aureonebulosa'**.

Akebono Tokudama, the "dawn of day hosta," is based on a cultivated type grown in Kikuchi's garden as No. 213 and was reportedly found by T. Susa in Aomori Prefecture. Although Maekawa (1969) maintained the name, this taxon is now considered a cultivar form. However, aureonebulosa (Japanese = *kinakafu*) forms of the *To Giboshi/H. sieboldiana* group (to which *H.* 'Tokudama' belongs) are still being found in the wild as mutations, and some of these have the general features of *H.* 'Tokudama'. Many sizes and variegation patterns exist and have been named, including the reverse form, an *aureomarginata* form, known as *H. tokudama* 'Sun Splash' (Soules). All these clones belong to the Aureonebulosa group of *H.* 'Tokudama'. In the United Kingdom it is occasionally called *H. tokudama variegata* hort., nom. nudum, but this epithet is ambiguous and illegitimate under the ICNCP as well. It causes errors by being incorrectly applied to any of the variegated forms of *H.* 'Tokudama'. Some of the many distinct clones have been named; *H.* 'Blue Shadows', which see, is one of them (Plate 95). This cultivar shows one extreme of variegation: it is more blue-green than yellow, while the typical form contains much more yellow in the variegation than blue-green. Occasionally, this taxon can revert to all blue-green or yellow. A form with almost clear yellow leaves and a thin blue-green margin has been named by Maekawa *H. tokudama* f. *flavoplanata* Maekawa (1940), which see. Another form observed at the Munich Botanic Garden, labeled *H. sieboldiana fortunei* f. *variegata*, has a principally blue-green leaf, with yellow mottling rather than streaking. This taxon is identical to *Funkia fortunei variegata* Siebold 1870. Although slow in growth *Hosta* 'Tokudama Aureonebulosa' is highly desirable and widely grown. In time it forms a splendid specimen clump. It has been selected the AHS Alex J. Summers Distinguished Merit Hosta by Mildred Seaver in 1988 and garnered the 1985 AHS Alabama Hosta Society Award exhibited by Henry Ross in Gardenview Horticultural Park.

Plant size 30–60 cm (12–24 in.) dia., 25–35 cm (10–14 in.) high. Petiole 15–20 by 0.8 cm (6–8 by 0.3 in.), not or slightly winged, deeply grooved, very pruinose, lasting, verdigris-green. Leaf 20–25 by 12.5–17.5 cm (8–10 by 5–7 in.), attitude at petiole spreading in a ±continuing flat arch, cordate, ovate-cordate, some leaves orbicular, undulate, many, but not all leaves with upturned margins, concave, very rugose, puckered, coriaceous, very pruinose, with some pruinosity remaining after anthesis, pruinose on back ±permanent, cuspidate tip, glaucous sea-green margin, with leaf center pale yellow to livid (lividus) clouded bluish, mottled, clouded, extremely variable, covering 15–70% of the leaf area, in some leaves with streaks, some forms initially very livid, turning to mottled pale yellow after anthesis. Venation 10–13, sunken above, very projected, strigose below, convergent and submarginally connected at tip area. Scape height to slightly above leaf mound, 40–45 cm (16–18 in.), pruinose, erect, round, glaucous green. Fertile bracts flat and broad, thick and fleshy, green or whitish green, tinged with purple, developing and opening in a stellar form as seen from above, horizontally spreading during anthesis, triangular, very persisting. Raceme 15 cm (6 in.), 15–20 flowers, tightly packed. Flowers 4–4.5 cm (1.5 in.) long and 2.5 cm (1 in.) broad, white, with traces of pale violet, distinctly globular in the expanded tube, during anthesis lobes gradually expanding, never fully open, ±parallel to axis of perianth, heavy textured, thick, stamens not superior, equal or slightly shorter than perianth. Anthers pale yellow. July. Fertile.

SY: *Funkia fortunei variegata* nom. nudum Siebold 1870.
　　Hosta glauca var. *variegata* nom. nudum Siebold 1861 pp.
　　H. tokudama f. *mediopicta* Kaneko 1968a.

HN: *H.* 'Aureo-nebulosa' incorrect.
　　H. 'Blue Shadows' Anderson pp sim.
　　H. 'Bright Lights' Aden/Klehm.
　　H. 'Golden Bowls' hort.
　　H. sieboldiana 'Aureonebulosa' Hensen 1985.
　　H. sieboldiana fortunei f. *variegata* hort. incorrect.
　　H. tokudama aureonebulosa hort. incorrect.
　　H. tokudama 'Aureonebulosa' hort.
　　H. tokudama Aureonebulosa group.
　　H. tokudama f. *variegata* hort. UK incorrect.
　　H. tokudama variegata hort. UK incorrect.
　　H. tokudama 'Variegata' Hensen 1963a incorrect.
　　H. tokudama 'Variegata' hort. UK incorrect.

JN: *Akebono Tokudama* Kikuchi 1934.
　　Aofukurin Tokudama hort. incorrect.
　　Gyakufu Giboshi hort. incorrect.
　　Kinakafu Tokudama hort. pp.

ON: Gefleckte Löffelblattfunkie (German).

✠ *"H. tokudama* f. *flavocircinalis"* Maekawa 1940.
キフクリントクダマ
　　　　　　　　　　　　　　　　　(Plate 75).
Here reduced to cultivar form as *H.* **'Tokudama Flavocircinalis'**.

Kifukurin Tokudama, the "yellow-margined, well-rounded hosta," is now considered a cultivar and treated as a specioid. The original description and type were based on a cultivated plant of unknown origin growing in Maekawa's garden as no. 65. Different forms and sizes exist, and horticulturally the most fitting name is the group name listed in the synonymy. This taxon has been known in Europe for many years. In the United Kingdom it is customarily cultivated as *H. tokudama* 'Variegata', but this name is ambiguous and has been incorrectly applied to all the variegated forms of *H.* 'Tokudama'. To illustrate, in

Holland and Germany *H. tokudama* 'Variegata' is not a *marginata* form, but more of a *nebulosa* form with clouded and spotted center variegation and much more blue-green in the leaf, similar to *H. tokudama* 'Blue Shadows', but not streaked. In North America a clonal form has been selected and registered without description under the cultivar name *H. tokudama* 'Flavo-circinalis'. This clonal form is propagated by vegetative means, so the population is relatively uniform in appearance. Other forms have been selected and named, and all of them belong to the group in a broad sense. The most appropriate classification for these mutants is with the *H.* 'Tokudama Flavocircinalis' group. The taxon bearing the clonal/cultivar name *H.* 'Tokudama Flavocircinalis' in North America differs from the species by its yellow (viridescent) irregular margin and more elongated leaves, which are more pointed and heart-shaped and do not represent a typical *H.* 'Tokudama' leaf form. This taxon may not be a *H.* 'Tokudama' form at all but belong to the *H. sieboldiana* Aureomarginata group, which see. Both groups are very closely related. Some mature clumps of *H.* 'Tokudama Flavocircinalis' become very large and take on the appearance of a yellow-margined *H. sieboldiana*. In Japan *Kara Giboshi*, *H.* 'Kara', is much like this taxon but differs in having petioles that are broadly winged and leaves that have less puckering between the principal veins but are more rounded and thus similar to the specioid. The flowers have some lavender in the lobes, while those of *H.* 'Tokudama' are pure white. All the yellow margined forms of this group are slow growers but, left undisturbed, will grow into large clumps.

Plant size 40–70 cm (16–28 in.) dia., to 30–40 cm (12–16 in.) high. Petiole 15–30 by 1.2 cm (6–12 by 0.5 in.), not or slightly winged, deeply grooved, very pruinose, lasting, verdigris-green. Leaf generally more cordate, elongated, and pointed than *H.* 'Tokudama Aureonebulosa', 20–30 by 15–20 cm (8–12 by 6–8 in.), attitude at petiole spreading in a ±continuing flat arch, cordate, ovate-cordate, undulate, rugose, very pruinose, with some pruinosity remaining after anthesis, pruinose on back ±permanent, cuspidate tip, glaucous sea-green, margin golden yellow, very irregular, covering 20–50% of the leaf area, in some leaves extending in streaks to midrib, turning to pale yellow after anthesis. Venation 11–13, sunken above, very projected, strigose below, convergent and submarginally connected at tip area. Scape height to slightly above leaf mound, 45 cm (18 in.), pruinose, erect, round, glaucous green. Fertile bracts flat and broad, thick and fleshy, green or whitish green, tinged with purple, developing and opening in a stellar form as seen from above, horizontally spreading during anthesis, triangular, very persisting. Raceme 15 cm (6 in.), 15–20 flowers, tightly packed. Flowers 4–4.5 cm (1.5 in.) long and 2.5 cm (1 in.) broad, white, with traces of pale lavender, distinctly globular in the expanded tube, during anthesis lobes gradually expanding, never fully open, ±parallel to axis of perianth, heavy textured, thick, stamens not superior, equal or slightly shorter than perianth. July. Anthers pale yellow. Fertile.

SY: *H. glauca* var. *variegata* nom. nudum Siebold 1861 pp.
HN: *H.* 'Flavo-circinalis' incorrect.
    H. 'Abiqua Hallucination' Walden-West sim.
    H. fortunei aureomarginata hort. pp.
    H. 'Kara' hort. pp sim.
    H. sieboldiana fortunei aureomarginata pp.
    H. tokudama aureomarginata hort. incorrect.
    H. tokudama Flavocircinalis group.
    H. tokudama flavocircinalis hort. incorrect.

    H. tokudama 'Flavocircinalis' hort.
    H. tokudama f. *variegata* hort. UK incorrect.
    H. tokudama variegata hort. UK incorrect.
    H. tokudama 'Variegata' hort. UK incorrect.
JN: *Kara Giboshi* hort. pp sim.
    Kifukurin Tokudama Maekawa 1940.
ON: Blaue Gelbrandfunkie pp (German).

✣ "*H. tokudama* f. *flavoplanata*" Maekawa 1940.
コアケボノトクダマ (Plate 76).
Here reduced to cultivar form as *H.* 'Tokudama Flavoplanata'.

Ko Akebono Tokudama, the "shining (or small) dawn-of-day, well-rounded hosta," is now considered a cultigen and reduced to cultivar form. Broadly, it belongs to the *H. tokudama* Aureonebulosa group. Described by Maekawa from a plant of cultivated origin in Kikuchi's garden, Kyoto, it does not attain the size of *H.* 'Tokudama Aureonebulosa' and may be a more advanced mutation of the latter with more yellow in the leaf. In the United States, the leaf of *H.* 'Tokudama Aureonebulosa' has been observed to turn more yellow in time, with a concurrent reduction in size. It is rarely available under its name, but occasionally *aureonebulosa* forms sport to an analogous form.

Plant size 30–50 cm (12–20 in.) dia., 20–30 cm (8–12 in.) high. Leaf 12.5–17.5 by 10–15 cm (5–7 by 4–6 in.), attitude at petiole spreading in a ±continuing flat arch, cordate, orbicular-cordate, slightly undulate, concave, very rugose, puckered, coriaceous, very pruinose, with some pruinosity remaining after anthesis, pruinose on back ±permanent, cuspidate, glaucous sea-green thin margin, with leaf center pale yellow to sulphur-yellow variable, to 90% of the leaf area. Venation 10–13, sunken above, very projected, strigose below, convergent and submarginally connected at tip area.

HN: *H. tokudama* Aureonebulosa group.
    H. 'Flavo-circinalis' incorrect.
    H. tokudama 'Flavoplanata' hort.
    H. tokudama flavoplanata hort. incorrect.
JN: *Ko Akebono Tokudama* Kikuchi 1934.

✣ "*H. tortifrons*" Maekawa 1940.
AHS-V/25B. (Figure 2-21).
コガラシギボウシ
アレチギボウシ
姫アレチノコガラシギボウシ
Here reduced to cultivar form as *H.* 'Tortifrons'.

Kogarashi Giboshi, the "autumn wind hosta," is a clonal selection which probably originated with a natural mutation. Its type was described by Maekawa based on a specimen found among cultivated material in Honshu, near Tokyo, by Okami. It is considered a cultivar and reduced to cultivar form because there are no wild populations. It does not come true from seed, and the cultivated stock must be vegetatively propagated to retain its very narrow, twisted leaves that give it a unique look. The Japanese name stems from its late blooming (in the autumn wind), and the specific epithet means "twisted (contorted) leaves." This taxon conforms in all respects to the diagnosis of *H.* 'Tardiflora', including the yellow anthers, except that it is smaller and has very twisted, contorted leaves. In Japan discerning horticulturists call it *H. tardiflora* var. *tortifrons*, although this is a nom. nudum. In Japan the incorrect horticultural synonyms *Arechi Giboshi* and *Hime Arechino Kogarashi Giboshi* are occasionally used. It is an interesting rock garden or foreground subject which is certain to attract attention. Unfortunately, it grows extremely slowly and is therefore difficult to obtain.

Plant size 20 cm (8 in.) dia., 15 cm (6 in.) high. Petiole is part of leaf. Leaf 15–17.5 by 1.2 cm (6–7 by 0.5 in.), erect, rigid, leathery, shiny dark green, contorted, very twisted and undulate, each leaf different. Venation 2–3. Scape 25–30 cm (10–12 in.), purple-dotted, straight, smooth round. Fertile bracts 1 cm (0.3 in.) long, navicular, grooved, thin, membranous, white or whitish green purple-tinted, imbricated, withering at anthesis. Raceme 7.5 cm (3 in.), 6–10 flowers. Flowers whitish to pale purple, held erect in horizontal position on long, strong horizontal or slightly ascending purple pedicels, perianth 5 cm (2 in.) long, funnel-shaped, expanding, in the central part dilated bell-shaped, lobes spreading straightly to ±angled to the axis of perianth, thin narrow hexagonal tube. Anthers yellow. September. Fertile.

HN: *H.* 'Craig No. 13'.
     H. tardiflora 'Twisted' pp sim.
     H. tardiflora var. *tortifrons* nom. nudum hort.
     H. 'Twisted Leaf' hort. pp sim.
JN: *Arechi Giboshi* hort. incorrect.
     Hime Arechino Kogarashi Giboshi hort. incorrect.
     Kogarashi Giboshi Maekawa 1940.

H. tosana Maekawa 1940.
(see *H. kikutii* var. *tosana*).

H. tsushimensis Fujita 1976a.
AHS-IV/19A.   (Figures 3-76, A-10; Plate 77).
ツシマギボウシ

Tsushima Giboshi, the "hosta from Tsushima," was described from a population found on Mount Ariake, Tsushima Islands, located in the Korea Strait (Korea Kaikyo), between Kyushu and South Korea, hence the name. It is also found in Nagasaki Prefecture of southern Honshu, but these populations may actually be intermediates of *H. tsushimensis* and *H. tibae*. Accessions of *H. tsushimensis* by M. G. Chung in 1988 located colonies on Mount Izuhara where the plant grows in relatively dry, open areas. Chung considered only material collected on Tsushima Island in his 1990 study, so it is difficult to correlate the taxon to *H. jonesii* and *H. tibae* which are closely related (see "The Korean Species" in Appendix A—Part 1). All three taxa produce branched scapes (Figure 3-76), but the flowers of *H. tsushimensis* are much lighter in color. The taxon is similar to *H. tardiva* and frequently mistaken for it, as the only differences are its somewhat later flowering time, its wider, more glossy, cordate leaves with smooth veins underneath, and its fertility. The natural populations are very polymorphic and many leaf shapes can be found from narrow lanceolate to widely ovate. A number of variegated mutants found in the wild have been selected and named. This species can substitute for *H.* 'Lancifolia', especially when a slightly later flowering period is required. Available, but still scarce, this taxon has reddish purple coloration on the petioles extending in some clones for the entire length and contrasting nicely with the light green leaves. It deserves to be more widely grown.

Plant size 45 cm (18 in.) dia., 20 cm (8 in.) high. Petiole 17.5–25 by 6–8 cm (7–18 by 0.25–0.35 in.), slightly or broadly winged, erect, green, with purple dots. Leaf 15–22.5 by 7.5–12.5 cm (6–9 by 3–5 in.), erect, ovate to ovate-cordate, tip acuminate, slightly undulate, wavy in the margin, smooth, light green above, glossy lighter green below. Venation 5–9, sunken above, projected, smooth below. Scape 65–75 cm (26–30 in.), erect, obliquely ascending, lax, green, purplish red dotted. Sterile bracts 2–3, clasping the stem; fertile bracts navicular, long, thick, grooved, whitish green, persisting, not withering at anthesis. Raceme 25–30 cm (10–12 in.), loosely arranged, to 30 flowers, frequently branching. Flowers 4–5 cm (1.5–2

in.) long and 4 cm (1.5 in.) broad, nearly white, purple nerves inside, whitish narrow tube, perianth expanding, funnel-shaped, in the central part slightly dilated bell-shaped, lobes spreading but not recurving, half-open, pedicels to 1.5 cm (0.5 in.), white, purple-dotted, very projecting stamen. Anthers purple. September. Fertile.

HN: *H. lancifolia* var. *thunbergiana* hort. incorrect.
     H. minor hort. incorrect.
JN: *Tsushima Giboshi* Fujita 1976a.

Figure 3-76. *H. tsushimensis*; branching scape detail (Hosta Hill)

H. tsushimensis 'Ogon' hort.
黄金ツシマ

Ogon Tsushima Giboshi, the "golden Tsushima," is a yellow form found in cultivation which retains its color. It is slightly smaller than the type. It is also called *H. tsushimensis* 'Golden', but this name goes against the recommendations of the ICNCP. Use of the Japanese name is preferred.
HN: *H. tsushimensis* 'Golden' incorrect.
JN: *Ogon Tsushima Giboshi* hort.

H. tsushimensis 'Sanshoku' hort.
三色ツシマギボウシ

Sanshoku Tsushima Giboshi is a mutation found in the wild with tri-colored flowers that are dark crimson at the base of the narrow tube, purple on the petals, and have white transparent lines. The plant does not come true from seed so is considered a cultivar. The flowers are not at all like those of the species, but more like those of *H. jonesii*. This taxon may be related to the latter; only the very perceptive connoisseur will appreciate the difference.
JN: *Sanshoku Tsushima Giboshi* hort.

H. tsushimensis 'Shirobana' hort.
白花ツシマギボウシ

Shirobana Tsushima Giboshi, the "white-flowered Tsushima," is a form with near white flowers found in the wild as a mutation.
HN: *H. tsushimensis alboflora* hort. incorrect.
JN: *Shirobana Tsushima Giboshi* hort.

U

✤ *"H. undulata"* Bailey 1930.
  AHS-IV/20A.   (Figures 2-8, 2-20, 2-30, A-11; Plates 78, 79, 155, 183).
スジギボウシ
Here reduced to cultivar form as *H.* 'Undulata'.

Suji Giboshi, the "striped hosta," is named so for its multi-colored, striped appearance which in its best form contains light and dark green, chartreuse, and white. Its specific epithet comes from *undulatus* = wavy, alluding to its undulating, wavy, even twisted leaves. This is the type species of section *Foliosae* and one of the first variegated hostas to be validly published as a species in Europe in 1833. It is not a true species, but is a pod-sterile hybrid of long standing. Persistent reports that *H.* 'Undulata' grows on Mount Kurokami, in the old province of Hizen (Saga Prefecture), have definitely not been verified (Maekawa, 1940). Von Siebold received it as a cultivated plant in the late 1820s, and even then, it was quite common in Japan. As early as 1776 Thunberg learned about it and returned with a herbarium specimen. It is considered a cultivar of hybrid origin and here reduced to cultivar form. Living plants were imported by von Siebold in 1829 and it was the first mediovariegated hosta to be cultivated in Western gardens. A number of different clones have been reported in the literature and there are countless intermediate forms, some looking quite distinct. These are, nevertheless, not true, stable clones but represent *H.* 'Undulata' in its various transitional stages from a mostly white plant to the all-green form *H.* 'Undulata Erromena'. They should be considered unstable forms which will eventually change their variegation. The variations not only include leaf variegation, form, and size, but may involve the flower scape, with some being extremely leafy, carrying large, variegated bracteoles, enveloping the flower bud. This can be seen more frequently on recently disturbed clumps. This taxon is one of the best-known classic, cultivated hostas and is used extensively in mass plantings, edgings, and as an accent plant the world over. It sprouts all-green summer leaves occasionally with white striate variegation. The latter gave rise to the names *Funkia argenteostriata* Siebold (1861), and *Funkia undulata argentea variegata* Siebold (1862) which were then considered distinct forms of *Hosta* 'Undulata'. Von Siebold, realizing the temporary nature of these aberrant forms, listed these names only once in his catalog and then dropped them. These summer leaves spoil the colorful spring picture, and for this reason *H.* 'Undulata' is often replaced by other, more stable mediovariegated cultivars. Due to its wide availability and low cost, however, it will remain an important landscape plant. When planting this hybrid its instability in the long term must be realized; it will eventually turn into the *H.* 'Undulata Univittata' form, finally mutating to the all-green *H.* 'Undulata Erromena', but this change may take years (Plate 78). By many considered absolutely sterile, it has nevertheless yielded very rare hybrids to persistent hybridizers. An example is *H.* 'Unducosa', which see.

Plant size 40–45 cm (16–18 in.) dia., 35 cm (14 in.) high. Petiole 10–12.5 by 1.2 cm (4–5 by 0.5 in.), broadly winged, erect, then horizontally spreading, forming a dome-shaped plant, green with yellowish green and white central stripes, no purple dots at the base. Vernal leaf 10–15 by 7.5–10 cm (4–6 by 3–4 in.), erect and in line with petiole, ovate-cordate to ovate, tip acuminate, torsionally twisted with spiral curl in tip, usually turned under, largely creamy white in center with a margin of dark green interspersed with light yellow-green streaks, shiny below; summer leaves all-green or green with white striations or white margins, shiny below. Venation 7–8, lightly impressed above, smooth below. Scape 80–100 cm (32–40 in.), erect but leaning and bending in upper part, purple-dotted at base and in the lower third and in the upper part. Bracts, stem nodes with large foliaceous bracts, remaining fresh, variegated; fertile bracts navicular, small, thin, soft, green and greenish white, withering soon after anthesis, but not falling away. Raceme 16–25 flowers, widely spaced. Flowers 5.5 cm (2 in.) long and 3.5 cm (1.5 in.) broad, suffused pale purple, violet, gradually expanding, funnel-shaped, ±parallel or angled to axis of perianth; stamens not very superior, equal or slightly shorter than perianth. Anthers purple. June. Sterile.

SY: *Funkia argenteostriata* nom. nudum Siebold 1861 pp.
  Funkia lancifolia δ *undulata* Regel 1876.
  Funkia ovata var. *undulata* Miquel 1867.
  Funkia undulata argentea variegata nom. nudum Siebold 1862 hort.
  Funkia undulata argenteo vittata nom. nudum Siebold 1863.
  Funkia undulata foliis variegatis nom. nudum Siebold 1844.
  Funkia undulata mediovariegata nom. nudum Siebold 1867.
  Funkia undulata Otto and Dietrich 1833.
  Hemerocallis undulata Thunberg 1797.
  Hosta cærulea f. *undulata* Matsumura 1905.
  H. japonica var. *angustifolia* f. *undulata* Ascherson and Gräbner 1905.
  H. japonica var. *undulata* f. *albovariegata* Makino 1935.
  H. lancifolia var. *undulata* Bailey 1903.
  H. pachycarpa Maekawa 1940 pp.
  Hostia japonica f. *undulata* Voss 1896.
  Niobe undulata var. *variegata* hort. Nash 1911.
HN: *Funkia lancifolia undulata variegata* hort.
  Funkia ovata undulata argentea hort.
  Funkia robusta elegans foliis variegatis hort.
  Funkia sieboldiana variegata hort. Lowe and Howard.
  Hosta 'Craig No. 38' Summers No. 321.
  H. 'Cream Delight' hort. UK.
  H. 'Curly Hosta' hort.
  H. japonica albo undulata Foerster 1957 incorrect.
  H. japonica undulata hort. Rockmont 1944 (cat.).
  H. 'Krossa No. B-6' Summers No. 51.
  H. 'Mack No. 39' 1960.
  H. 'Silver Splash' hort.
  H. 'Swirling Seas' hort.
  H. undulata 'Argentea variegata' hort. UK incorrect.
  H. undulata medio picta hort. incorrect.
  H. undulata medio variegata hort. incorrect.
  H. undulata variegata hort. Zager 1960 (cat.).
  H. 'Unitalis' hort. pp sim.
  H. variegata hort. incorrect.
  Wavyleaf Plantain Lily.
JN: *Suji Giboshi* Maekawa 1940.
ON: Weissgrüne Wellblattfunkie Foerster 1956 (German).
  Zierliche Schneefederfunkie Hansen and Müssel, 1964 pp (German).

✤ *"H. undulata* var. *albomarginata"* Maekawa 1936a.
覆輪オハツキギボウシ   (Figures 6-2, 6-4, 6-5; Plates 79, 165, 170, 184, 189).
Here reduced to cultivar form as *H.* 'Undulata Albomarginata'.

Fukurin Ohatsuki Giboshi, the "leafy-scaped hosta with ornamental margin," is a classic Japanese cultivar which came into Western cultivation by way of the United States, having been brought by Thomas Hogg from Japan in 1875 and initially, for lack of another name, cultivated under the name *Funkia* 'Thomas Hogg' (see Chapter 5). It is still found along with other classic hostas in old U.S. estate gardens. Frequently it is confused with *Hosta* 'Crispula', but the latter is fertile and has narrow petioles (0.4 to 0.6 cm) that are not winged. When young it is similar to *H.* 'Decorata' and so the name *Funkia* 'Thomas Hogg' was used for both cultivars. It also sprouts green summer leaves, but not as profusely as *Hosta* 'Undulata'. This white-margined form is stable and mutations to all-green or all-white forms are rare but have been observed. This is one of the most widely available and inexpensive hostas for variegated mass plantings and wide edgings. It will eventually be 80–100 cm (32–40 in.) across. It multiplies rapidly, grows in any soil, is widely cultivated, and is an excellent beginner's hosta.

Plant size 50–90 cm (20–36 in.) dia., 45 cm (18 in.) high. Vernal leaf 15–20 by 7.5–12.5 cm (5–8 by 3–5 in.), erect and in line with petiole, ovate-cordate to ovate, with flat surface, but slightly undulate, crispate in the margin, center is dark green with irregular streaks of a grey-green and a lighter greenish grey; creamy white margin, very irregular, interspersed with light green streaks at the green to white junction, principal veins green in white margin; summer leaves may be all-green or green with a thin creamy white margin. Leaf occasionally linear-lanceolate with no discernable transition between petiole and leaf, tip acuminate, glossy below. Venation 8–9, lightly impressed above, smooth below. Anthers purple. June. Sterile.

SY: *H. undulata* var. *decolorans* Maekawa 1936a.
HN: *Funkia* 'Thomas Hogg' hort. pp in UK incorrect.
    Hosta alba marginata hort. Zager 1958 (cat.) incorrect.
    H. 'Craig No. H-4' Summers No. 333.
    H. fortunei albo marginata hort. Zager 1941 (cat.) incorrect.
    H. 'Frank Sedgwick' hort.
    H. 'Krossa No. G-5'.
    H. 'Mack No. 5'.
    H. 'Silver Rim' hort.
    H. 'Thomas Hogg' hort. pp in UK incorrect.
    H. undulata 'Albomarginata' hort.
    H. undulata var. *albomarginata* hort. Mack 1960 (cat.).
    Wavyleaf Whiterim Plantain Lily Mack 1960 (cat.).
JN: *Fukurin Ohatsuki Giboshi* Maekawa 1936a.
ON: Weissgrüne Wellblattfunkie Hansen and Müssel 1964 incorrect (German).
    Weissrandige Wellblattfunkie Hansen and Müssel 1964 (German).

✠ *"H. undulata* var. *erromena"* (Stearn) Maekawa 1936a.
    AHS-III/13A.   (Plates 78, 150).
オハツキギボウシ
Here reduced to cultivar form as *H.* **'Undulata Erromena'**.

Ohatsuki Giboshi, the "leafy-scaped hosta," does not grow in the wild in Japan but evolved in cultivation from the variegated *H.* 'Undulata' in a number of different locations as the final, stable form of the specioid. Both the mediovariegated and margined forms will sport to this all-green cultivar. The leaves are entirely different from those of *H.* 'Undulata'—much larger, almost flat, light green—and the plant is twice as large in a clump. Von Siebold's firm first listed it as *Funkia viridis* in 1867. It is an inexpensive garden plant which is available and cultivated worldwide in mass plantings, edgings, and foundation plantings.

Plant size 50–90 cm (20–36 in.) dia., 45 cm (18 in.) high. Vernal leaf 15–20 by 7.5–12.5 cm (5–8 by 3–5 in.), erect and in line with petiole, ovate-cordate to ovate, with flat surface, but slightly undulate, wavy in the margin, bright shiny green above, lighter green below and very glossy. Venation 7–8, lightly impressed above, smooth below. Anthers purple-dotted, appearing uniformly purple. Sterile.

SY: *Funkia sieboldiana* Miquel 1869 incorrect.
    Funkia viridis nom. nudum Siebold 1867.
    Hosta erromena Stearn 1931b.
    H. japonica var. *fortis* Bailey 1932.
    H. lancifolia var. *fortis* Stearn 1931b.
    H. viridis Koidzumi 1936.
    Niobe undulata Nash 1911 obs pp.
HN: *Funkia viridis* hort.
    Hosta 'Green Ruffles' hort.
    H. 'Mack No. 3'.
    H. undulata 'Erromena' hort.
    H. undulata viridis hort. incorrect.
    H. viridis hort. incorrect.
    Leafy-scaped Plantain Lily Maekawa 1969.
    Midsummer Plantain Lily Mack 1960 (cat.).
JN: *Ohatsuki Giboshi* Maekawa 1940.
ON: Grüne Wellblattfunkie Hansen and Müssel 1964 (German).

✠ *"H. undulata* var. *univittata"* (Miquel) Hylander 1954.
    AHS-III/16A.   (Figure 3-77; Plates 78, 79).
Here reduced to cultivar form as *H.* **'Undulata Univittata'**.

This hosta has not been given a Japanese formal name as it represents a transitional stage of *H.* 'Undulata' reverting to *H.* 'Undulata Erromena'. It was first listed by von Siebold in 1863, crediting the varietal epithet *univittata* (= with one stripe) to van Houtte. It evolved in cultivation in Holland as a mutation of *H.* 'Undulata', sprouting all-green summer leaves, although to a lesser extent. It is one of the transitory forms of *H.* 'Undulata' and differs by the much narrower creamy white center variegation which can be characterized as a white stripe on a green leaf. It is more robust and grows larger. Its garden use is comparable to *H.* 'Undulata' and is indicated where a more subdued variegation pattern is desired. Named clones, such as *H.* 'Middle Ridge', which have wider or narrower leaves or center stripe, represent nothing more than the normal variation pattern of this taxon and will sooner or later also change to the next stage of back-mutation. All will eventually turn all-green, but this may take years and can be delayed by lifting and replanting, cutting out all-green sprouts in the process.

Plant size 50–90 cm (20–36 in.) dia., 40 cm (16 in.) high. Vernal leaf 12.5–17.5 by 7.5–12.5 cm (5–7 by 3–5 in.), erect and in line with petiole, ovate-cordate to ovate, tip acuminate, twisted or wavy surface, but less than the type, tip acuminate, usually turned under, creamy white (eborinus), narrow stripe in center of dark green leaf interspersed with light green streaks at the green to white junction; summer leaf may be all-green or green with greenish white stripe, shiny below. Venation 7–8, lightly impressed above, smooth below. Flowers 5.5 cm (2 in.) long and 3.5 cm (1.5 in.) broad, suffused pale purple, violet, gradually expanding, funnel-shaped, ±parallel or angled to axis of perianth; stamens not very superior, equal or slightly shorter than perianth. Anthers purple. June/July. Sterile.

SY: *Funkia lancifolia* var. *univittata* hort. Bailey 1915.
    Funkia sieboldiana lusus α *univittata* Miquel 1869.
    Funkia univittata nom. nudum van Houtte in Siebold 1863.

Hosta univittata Grey 1938.
HN: *H. japonica univittata* Foerster 1956 incorrect.
      H. 'Mack No. 6'.
      H. 'Silver Splash' hort.
      H. undulata 'Unitalis' hort.
      H. undulata 'Univittata' hort.
      H. undulata 'White Ray' hort.
      H. unitalis hort. pp incorrect.
ON: Schneefederfunkie Foerster 1956 (German).

Figure 3-77. *H. ventricosa*; landscape use; *H.* 'Undulata' and *H.* 'Undulata Univittata' (left) (Flower Farm/ Schmid)

V

H. variegata hort.

Although this name has been persistently used for many variegated taxa, its use should be discontinued because is a nom. nudum, a nom. confusum and a nom. ambiguum as well. As a cultivar name 'Variegata' is also confusing because it gives no precise indication as to the type of variegation. It is also used for several taxa, so should be eliminated.

H. ventricosa Stearn 1931b.

AHS-III/13B.   (Figures 2-9, 2-37, 3-77, 6-1, A-7, A-8, F-5,
ムラサキギボウシ   F-6; Plates 2, 197).
Murasaki Giboshi, the "dark purple(-flowered) hosta," was not named in Japan until 1937 by Kikuchi. It became known to European naturalists travelling in China during the latter part of the 18th century, and it is native to China, ranging into northern Korea. It was one of the first hostas to be grown on the continent of Europe and probably described there before it was generally known in Japan. In 1790 live specimens were imported into England by George Hibbert, a wealthy Englishman and collector of unique plants. He considered it rare and grew it under glass at first. Its hardiness was quickly discovered, and it was then transferred to open gardens. Distributed from England it reached France before 1800 and was part of the collection Josephine Bonaparte assembled at the gardens of Malmaison. There it served as a model for one of the two watercolors Redouté made of hostas while employed at the gardens. It appeared in Germany around 1805 and was included by Trattinnick as *H. cærulea* in 1814. The old epithet *cærulea* was used for over 160 years, and this taxon possessed no correct, valid name under *Hosta* until Stearn resurrected the basionym *Bryocles ventricosa* and transferred the epithet to *Hosta* as *H. ventricosa* Stearn (1931b). *Hosta ven-*

tricosa is the only natural tetraploid species in the genus with a chromosome number of 120 (2n). It will not produce hybrids as a pod parent because it produces seed without actual fertilization, through a process called pseudogamous apomixis, which is a specialized form of vegetative reproduction referred to as agamospermy. This process, often mistaken for self-pollination, initiates seed production by diffusing growth substances from the pollen and proceeds without the usual chromosome cycle of reduction divisions and fertilization. The resulting seedlings are true (vegetative) clones of the mother plant. On the other hand, *H. ventricosa* makes an excellent pollen parent. With its widely bell-shaped purple (actually purple-striped) flowers and dark green, shiny leaves *H. ventricosa* is an excellent landscape hosta which can be used for mass plantings, in the border, as edgings, and as a specimen plant. It is cultivated worldwide and can be found in many old gardens. Several variegated and yellow forms exist.

Plant size 80 cm (32 in.) dia., 50 cm (20 in.) high. Petiole 18–22 by 1 cm (7–9 by 0.35 in.), spreading horizontally (patens), forming a rosette-shaped plant, unmarked except for light purple spotting at base, glossy light green, deeply grooved. Leaf 20–30 by 15–20 cm (8–12 by 6–8 in.), cordate, broadly ovate, transition truncate, open, flattened, cuspidate, torsionally twisted with spiral curl in tip, usually turned under, central leaf surface generally "flat," not arched but flat between veins, irregularly undulate in the margin, not pruinose, semiglossy, below very glossy, dark emerald green. Venation 8–9, sunken above, projected, papillose-strigose below. Scape 80–95 cm (32–38 in.), straight, later bending under weight of heavy seed set often subhorizontally, terete, mostly uniformly semigloss light green, lightly reddish, purple-dotted at base. Fertile bracts navicular, grooved, thin, membranaceous, green at first, then white, withering, imbricated, nearly equal in size. Raceme 25 cm (10 in.) 20–30 flowers. Flowers 5.5 cm (2.2 in.) long and 3 cm (1.2 in.) broad, dark veins on a lighter colored background, general color very dark, bluish violet, purple-violet, perianth acutely expanding, bell-shaped, lobes at tips ±parallel to axis of perianth, average anthesis. Anthers purple. July. Fertile, propagates by pseudogamous apomixis without the aid of pollen, capsule triangular, short, stubby, blunt tip. Chromosome count 2n = 120, a natural tetraploid.

SY: *Bryocles ventricosa* Salisbury 1812.
      Funkia coerulea hort. incorrect.
      Funkia cærulea Sweet 1827.
      Funkia latifolia Miquel 1869.
      Funkia ovata Sprengel 1817.
      Funkia ovata var. *α typica* Regel 1876.
      Funkia ovata var. *cærulea* Miquel 1869.
      Hemerocallis cærulea Andrews 1797.
      Hemerocallis cærulea flore violaceo Ker-Gawler 1812.
      Hosta cærulea Trattinnick 1814.
      H. japonica var. *cærulea* Ascherson 1863.
      H. miquelii Moldenke 1936.
      H. ventricosa f. *ventricosa* Hensen 1963a.
      Niobe cærulea Nash 1911.
      Saussurea cærulea Kuntze 1891.
HN: *Hosta* 'Barlow Hall Castle' hort.
      H. 'Blue Bugles' hort.
      H. 'Borsch No. 3' hort.
      H. 'Chartreuse Ruffles' hort.
      H. coerulea hort. incorrect.
      H. 'Green Satin' hort.
      H. 'Krossa No. E-4' Krossa.

H. 'Mack No. 7'.

H. ventricosa 'Russels Form' hort. UK.

JN: *Murasaki Giboshi* Kikuchi and Maekawa 1937.

ON: Blaue Glockenfunkie (German).

Glockenfunkie (German).

H. ventricosa 'Aureo-maculata' AHS-NC IRA/1987.

AHS-III/18B.

This cultivar name is registered for show purposes (in modified form) as *H. ventricosa* 'Aureo-maculata' AHS-NC IRA/1987, which see.

H. ventricosa 'Aureomaculata' Hensen 1963b.

AHS-III/18B.   (Plate 80).

斑入ムラサキギボウシ

Fuiri Murasaki Giboshi, the "variegated purple-flowered hosta," is not mentioned in the academic Japanese literature but is cultivated in Japan. It arose as a mutation or from a mutated apomictic seedling in the garden of von Siebold at Leiden before 1856 and was first mentioned that year. A number of valid synonyms exist under *Funkia*, but none of them were ever transferred to *Hosta*, and several horticultural nomina nuda are on record. All these listed later have been connected to this taxon. Hensen (1963b, 1985) treated it as a cultivar form, and I have followed this placement. Several forms exist and in most the variegation is viridescent, but in England a form that holds its variegation longer has been reported. It differs from the species by having slightly smaller leaves with distinct yellow center variegation in spring.

Plant size 70 cm (28 in.) dia., 45 cm (18 in.) high. Leaf 20–30 by 15–20 cm (8–12 by 6–8 in.), cordate, broadly ovate, transition truncate, open, flattened, cuspidate, torsionally twisted with spiral curl in tip, usually turned under, central leaf surface generally "flat," not arched but flat between veins, irregularly undulate in the margin, not pruinose, semiglossy, below very glossy, dark emerald green margins with irregular, streaky, yellow-green leaf center, which darkens by anthesis to almost the margin color. June. Fertility: See species.

SY: *Funkia latifolia* lusus γ *aureomaculata* Miquel 1869.

Funkia ovata (f.) γ *aureovariegata* Regel 1876.

Funkia ovata foliis *aureomaculatis* nom. nudum Siebold 1856.

Funkia ovata foliis *aureomaculatis* nom. nudum Anonymous 1891a.

Hostia cærulea f. *aureovariegata* Voss 1896.

HN: *Funkia cærulea variegata* hort. pp.

Hosta cærulea gold-variegated form Bailey 1915.

H. cærulea var. *viridimarginata* hort.

H. ventricosa 'Aurea Maculata' Hansen and Müssel 1964.

H. ventricosa 'Maculata' hort. incorrect.

JN: *Fuiri Murasaki Giboshi* hort.

ON: Panaschierte Glockenfunkie (German).

H. ventricosa 'Aureo-marginata'.

AHS-III/16B.

This cultivar name is registered for show purposes (in modified form) as *H. ventricosa* 'Aureo-marginata' AHS-NC IRA/1987, which see.

H. ventricosa 'Aureomarginata' Hensen 1985.

AHS-III/16B.   (Plates 81, 122, 152).

黄覆輪ムラサキギボウシ

Kifukurin Murasaki Giboshi, the "yellow-margined purple(-flowered) hosta," is not mentioned in the Japanese academic literature. The Japanese name is of horticultural origin. The taxon arose in Europe as a mutation or a mutated apomictic seedling. It was discovered in Holland and introduced by Alan Bloom's nursery at Bressingham, near Diss, Norfolk, England. He called it *H. ventricosa* 'Aureo-Variegata' or 'Variegata', but these names should not be used because they are not specific as to the form of variegation. Hensen (1985) treated it as a cultivar form, assigning it a correct cultivar name, and I have followed this placement. In 1986 The American Hosta Society registered this taxon as *H. ventricosa* 'Aureo-marginata'. It received the 1987 AHS Alabama Hosta Society Award exhibited by Warren and Ali Pollock, the 1987 AHS Eunice Fisher Award, and the 1984 President's Exhibitor Trophy exhibited by Warren Pollock. The existence of several variegated forms of *H. ventricosa* has been known since the 1850s and a number of synonyms describing a *marginata* form are included in the synonymy to validate the cultivar name. This variegated clone is vegetatively propagated and differs from the species only by its distinct, very irregular margin that is golden yellow in spring (Plate 122) and fades to a yellowish white later in the season (Plate 81). In sunny positions the variegation may bleach to almost white. Some plants develop much wider margins and exhibit more yellow-white than green in the leaf, modifications that appear to be permanent. Held in high esteem by many gardeners, it is cultivated worldwide and one of the best yellowish white-margined hostas for specimen planting.

Plant size 70 cm (28 in.) dia., 45 cm (18 in.) high. Leaf 20–30 by 15–20 cm (8–12 by 6–8 in.), cordate, broadly ovate, transition truncate, open, flattened, cuspidate, torsionally twisted with spiral curl in tip, usually turned under, central leaf surface generally "flat," not arched but flat between veins, irregularly undulate in the margin, not pruinose, semiglossy, below very glossy, dark emerald green color in leaf center with irregular yellow margins, wide, in some leaves occupying more than 50% of leaf surface, occasionally extending into leaf center, margin color ±permanent, but turning to creamy white by anthesis. Anthers purple. July. Fertility: See species.

SY: *Funkia cærulea variegata* nom. nudum Siebold 1867 (?).

Funkia ovata (f.) β *late-(aureo)marginata* Regel 1876.

Hostia cærulea f. *latemarginata* Voss 1896.

HN: *Funkia cærulea variegata* hort.

Hosta cærulea variegata hort. incorrect.

H. ventricosa 'Albo-marginata' Germany/Klose incorrect.

H. ventricosa 'Aureomarginata' Summers AHS-NC IRA/1986.

H. ventricosa 'Aureo-variegata' UK incorrect.

H. ventricosa 'Luteo-variegata' UK incorrect.

H. ventricosa 'Variegata' UK incorrect.

Variegated Blue Plantain Lily pp.

JN: *Kifukurin Murasaki Giboshi* hort.

H. ventricosa Dwarf group hort.

AHS-IV/19B.   (Figure 4-34).

姫紫

Hime Murasaki Giboshi, the "dwarf purple-flowered hosta," is a form identical to the species, except smaller. Several sizes exist, all evolving from seedling populations; one of the most representative is *H. ventricosa* 'Peedee Elfinbells' Syre-Herz. Due to the difference in the existing clones these taxa are best considered a group.

HN: *H. ventricosa* 'Little Blue' Englerth IRA/1976 pp sim.

H. ventricosa 'Minima' hort. incorrect.

H. ventricosa 'Minor' hort. incorrect.

H. ventricosa 'Nana' hort. incorrect.

H. ventricosa 'Peedee Elfinbells' Syre-Herz IRA/1987.

JN: *Hime Murasaki Giboshi* hort.

H. ventricosa **Yellow group** hort.

AHS-III/17B.   (Plate 82).

Yellow and yellow-streaked forms of *H. ventricosa* are well known. All are viridescent and turn green in early summer. A number of hybrids emanating from *H. ventricosa* 'Aureomaculata' have been named by Wallace in 1986. These are yellow in spring but, being viridescent, turn to green in summer, also sprouting summer leaves in the center of the plant which are yellowish white streaked with green. Variegation of these summer leaves is stable. Yellow forms which are stable also have been reported.

HN: *H. ventricosa* 'Early Dawn' Wallace pure yellow viridescent.

  H. ventricosa 'Fury of Flame' Zilis IRA/1985.

  H. ventricosa 'Gold Flush' Bloom.

H. venusta Maekawa 1935.

AHS-VI/31B.   (Figure 3-78; Plate 83).
オトメギボウシ

Otome Giboshi, the "(beautiful) maiden hosta," evolved on Cheju Island (Cheju Do). Accessions by M. G. Chung in 1988 located allopatric populations on Cheju Do, Cheju City, near Ch'onwangsa, at altitude 600 m (Plate 83). The Korean common name is *Hanra-bibich'u* (M. G. Chung), indicating its habitat on Mount Halla. Fujita (1976a) did not consider *H. venusta* an indigenous Japanese hosta. It is treated as a Korean species, which is confirmed by Chung whose latest research indicates that *H. venusta* probably developed from remnants of *H. minor* after the last glacial epoch (see "The Korea Species" in Appendix A—Part 1). *Hosta venusta* var. *decurrens* (Maekawa, 1937) is regarded as being a minor modification of the species and so is treated here as a synonym. As the type species of section *Lamellatae*, *H. venusta* has characteristic lamellar ridges on the scape. Several variegated and yellow forms are known. Davidson (1990) reports that he received this taxon from Craig under the name *H.* 'Suzuki Thumbnail' in 1964, and he assigned it No. 86. Davidson acquired this taxon directly from Suzuki's nursery under the name *H.* 'Suzuki Thumbnail' when he visited central Honshu in 1969. He subsequently sent it to many North American locations and also to Beth Chatto and Kew Garden in England.

Hosta venusta is one of the smallest species extant and has been widely used in hybridizing. Because a high proportion come true from seed when carefully selfed, many of the resulting seedlings are none other than forms of the species. Yet they have been given cultivar names, which are listed as cultivar synonyms. These F$_1$ hybrids are in most cases virtually identical to the species. One popular form of this species is *H.* 'Minuta', a name invalid per the ICNCP because of its Latin formulation. The invalid names *H. nimor* and *H. numor* also have been incorrectly applied to this species. *Hosta venusta* should be planted up close in the rock garden or border and isolated, where it can be noticed. Mass plantings and drifts of large groups in prominent areas are very impressive.

Plant size 10 cm (4 in.) dia., 8 cm (3 in.) high. Petiole 3.5–6 by 0.3 cm (1.5–2.25 by 0.125 in.), forming a dome-shaped plant, slender, narrowly open. Leaf 3–4.5 by 2–3 cm (1.25–2 by 1 in.), ovate-cordate, transition usually tight and suddenly contracted, decurrent, tip acuminate, interior leaf flattish, margin undulate, wavy, not pruinose, surface with metallic sheen, shiny below, dark green, opaque. Venation 3–4, very thin, not much sunken above. Scape 18–24 cm (7–10 in.), distinct lamellar ridges parallel or slightly spiral to scape axis, straight, erect, mostly perpendicular to the ground, sometimes bending. Fertile bracts navicular, grooved, thick, green or whitish green, ascending, imbricated even during

flowering and nearly equal in size, developed unopened flower head globular with spicate top. Raceme 8 cm (3 in.), 4–8 flowers. Flowers 2.5–3.5 cm (1–1.5 in.) long and 2 cm (by 1 in.) broad, held erect in ±horizontal position on strong pedicels, dark veins on a lighter colored background, perianth pale purple-violet, expanding, funnel-shaped, in the central part dilated bell-shaped, lobes ±angled to the axis, stamens exserted. Anthers uniformly purple dotted, but look yellow. July. Fertile.

SY: *Funkia subcordata* var. *taquetii* Léveillé 1911 pp.

  Hosta venusta var. *decurrens* Maekawa 1937.

HN: *H.* 'Akarana' pp.

  H. 'Carder Venusta' incorrect.

  H. 'Craig No. C-7' incorrect.

  H. 'Davidson No. 87'.

  H. 'Minuta' hort.

  H. nimor incorrect.

  H. numor incorrect.

  H. 'Suzuki Thumbnail' Davidson No. 86.

  H. 'Thumbnail' pp.

  H. 'Tiny Tears' pp.

  H. venusta 'Shikoku' pp sim.

  H. venusta 'Shikou' hort. incorrect.

  H. 'Venustula' incorrect.

  H. venuta incorrect.

JN: *Bunchoko Giboshi* hort. incorrect.

  Otome Giboshi Maekawa 1935.

  Yakushima Mizu Giboshi hort. incorrect.

ON: Anmutige Funkie (German).

  Hanra-bibich'u (Korean).

  Zwergfunkie (German).

Figure 3-78. *H. venusta*; landscape use, mass planting (Hosta Hill)

H. venusta **'Kifukurin'** hort.
黄覆輪オトメギボウシ

Kifukurin Otome Giboshi, the "yellow-margined (beautiful) maiden hosta," is a variegated form of the species reported in Japan.

HN: *H. venusta* 'Aureomarginata' hort.

JN: *Kifukurin Otome Giboshi* hort.

H. venusta **'Kinakafu'** hort.
黄中斑オトメギボウシ

(Ki) Nakafu Otome Giboshi, the "aureonebulosa (beautiful) maiden hosta," is a mediovariegated form of the species reported in Japan.

HN: *H. venusta* 'Aureonebulosa' hort.

JN: *Kinakafu Otome Giboshi* hort.

H. venusta 'Ogon' hort.

Ogon Otome Giboshi, the "yellow (beautiful) maiden hosta," is a yellow form of the species. One of the named hybrid forms is *H.* 'Gosan Gold Midget' (Plate 153).
JN: *Ogon Otome Giboshi* hort.

H. venusta 'Shironakafu' hort.

Shironakafu Otome Giboshi is a Japanese synonym of *H. venusta* 'Variegated', which see.
JN: *Shironakafu Otome Giboshi* hort.

H. venusta var. *decurrens* Maekawa 1937.
(see *H. venusta*).

H. venusta 'Variegated' hort.

白中斑オトメギボウシ   (Figure 3-79).

Shironakafu Otome Giboshi, the "white-in-center (beautiful) maiden hosta," is a viridescent taxon that turns greenish white in summer. A cultivated plant which reverted to an all-green form at Hosta Hill turned out to be identical morphologically to *H. sieboldii* f. *spathulata* (Figure 3-79), although barely discernable traces of lamellar ridges on the scape close to the ground point to some conceivable involvement of *H. venusta* in its hybrid background. Preliminary micromorphological studies and anther coloration indicate it is a hybridized, medio-variegated form of *H. sieboldii* × *H. venusta*. For this reason I have retained the name, but its nomenclatural positioning under *H. venusta* is probably incorrect and may have to be changed. Early disintegration of white leaf tissue, as reported in other primarily white cultivars, has not been reported to date.

Plant erect, 15 cm (6 in.) dia., 10 cm (4 in.) high. Leaf 5 by 2.5 cm (2 by 1 in.), white (viridescent), margin green, lanceolate, flat. Venation 3. Scape 10 in. (25.5 cm), foliated, straight. Flower medium, funnel-shaped, purple-striped. Anthers purple. August. Fertile.
HN: *H. venusta* 'Variegata' hort. incorrect.
JN: *Shironakafu Otome Giboshi* hort.

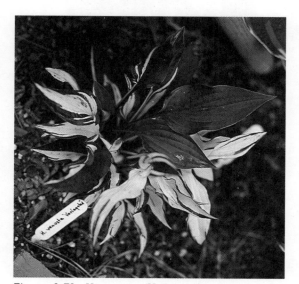

Figure 3-79. *H. venusta* 'Variegated'; general habit, partially reverting to all-green form (Hosta Hill)

Y

H. yakusimensis (Masamune) Maekawa 1950.
HN: *H. yakusimana* hort. incorrect.
(see *H. sieboldiana*).

H. yingeri S. B. Jones 1989.

AHS-IV/19B.   (Figures 3-80, 3-81, 3-82; Plate 35).

This is a new species published in 1989 by S. B. Jones and named for the horticulturist Barry R. Yinger, who, while at the National Arboretum, supplied collected seeds to Jones. This is a Korean species with the holotype (in NA) from Chollanam-do, Shin An Gun, Huksan Myeon, Taehuksan Island (Taehuksan-do), east side of Yeri village. The island is remotely located off the southwestern coast of Korea. Its Korean common name *Huksando-bibich'u* (M. G. Chung) denotes its habitat. Accessions by M. G. Chung in 1988 located populations on Taehuksan Island at Ye Ri, altitude 15 m, and on Sohuksan Island at Gakodo-l-Gu, altitude 150 m, near the coast. Although described only recently, according to M. G. Chung (1989: personal communication) a herbarium specimen from an earlier 1919 collection by T. Ishidoya and T. H. Chung on Hong Island (Hong-do) exists in SNU (No. 3374) labeled *Hosta japonica* Ascherson.

After 1945 Japanese botanists accessed the Korean populations on several remote islands and the possibility exists that they also located populations of the Korean taxa described recently. Japanese horticulturists connect the name *Fugire Giboshi* (フギレギボウシ) with *H. yingeri* but no botanical validation of this has been found.

This taxon is common, rock-dwelling on shady, northwest-facing talus slopes and cut-over hillsides at elevation 2–60 m (7–200 feet) above sea level. It also occurs on adjacent islands in the Huksan group, including Sohuksan Island. Its habitat includes pine forests where it shares the habitat primarily with grasses and ferns. It is distinct from other species in its thick, succulent leaves, which have a very shiny, flat, upper surface with inconspicuous veins and a "polished" surface on the back (Figure 3-82). Some variation exists in leaf color from dark green to light green and in surface polish which is very glossy in some forms and barely glossy in others. It has a delicate raceme with the flowers evenly spaced around the central shaft, unlike most other species which have the flowers pointed in one direction. The stamens are exserted considerably past the perianth and divided into 2 sets of 3 each, one set being longer than the other. The flowers are atypical of others in the genus: their lobes spread in "spider-flower" fashion, a characteristic shared with *H. laevigata*. Due to its significantly different morphology and ecological isolation, the proposed placement with subgenus *Bryocles*, section *Tardanthae*, is not accepted here. Due to its earlier flowering habit and distinct morphology of the perianth, it has been placed in a new section *Arachnanthae* (see Appendix A). This taxon has considerable horticultural merit and its use as a pod or pollen parent to transmit its very heavy leaf substance and attractive flowers to other species. Hybridization will undoubtedly create exciting new cultivars. It is still scarce but becoming available and a must for the collector.

Plant size 40 cm (16 in.) dia., 15 cm (6 in.) high. Petiole 3–7 by 0.5 cm (1.5–3 by 0.25 in.), semierect, V-shaped, green, some purple spots. Leaf 10–15 by 5–7 cm (6 by 2.75 in.), elliptic, rigid, thick and with very heavy substance, very shiny above, medium to dark green, polished light grey-green below, decurrent to the petiole and becoming V-shaped, elongated, tip acuminate. Venation 3–4, not sunken above, projected, smooth below. Scape to 65 cm (25 in.), straight, smooth, round, erect, mostly perpendicular to the ground, sometimes bending slightly, green. Sterile bracts, 1–4, linear-lanceolate, 1–2 by 0.25 cm (0.5–1 by 0.1 in.), navicular, green; fertile bracts flat, green with papillose apex, to 1.2 by 0.3 cm (0.5 by 0.1 in.); bracts not withering. Pedicels very long, green, purple spotted, slender, horizontal, to 2 cm (1 in.). Raceme 25–30 cm (10–12 in.), 15–25 flowers. Flowers 4 cm (1.5 in.) long and 4 cm (1.5 in.) broad, equally arranged around the stem, held erect in ±horizontal position on strong pedicels, lobes pale purple-suffused with slightly darker veins, white throat, expanding, funnel-shaped, spider-flowered. Stamens conspicuously exserted, 3 short and 3 long with filaments attached to narrow tube. July/August. Anthers purple. Fertile.

SY: *Hosta japonica* Ascherson herbarium annotation, T. Ishidoya and T. H. Chung, No. 3374 in SNU on the faith of M. G. Chung.

JN: *Fugire Giboshi* Maekawa (from horticultural sources; not validated botanically).

ON: *Huksando-bibich'u* (Korean).

Figure 3-81. *H. yingeri*; natural habitat; growing near rocks in Korea, Chollanam-do, Shin An Gun, Huksan Myeon, Sohuksan Island (Sohuksan-do), Yeri village (M. G. Chung)

Figure 3-80. *H. yingeri*; flower detail, showing two sets of stamens unequal in length (Hosta Hill)

Figure 3-82. *H. yingeri*; leaf detail, showing very glossy underside (Hosta Hill)

CHAPTER 4—PART 1

Introduction to Plant Descriptions—Cultivated Varieties

METHODS

The information presented in this chapter was derived from thousands of sources the world over. Those in printed form are included in the Bibliography. Much additional information was obtained from hybridizers, gardeners, and others interested in the genus. Still more was gleaned from hundreds of catalogs, magazines, and newspapers, both old and new. A lively correspondence with a number of *Hosta* experts contributed additional data. Photographs were made in gardens in Austria, Canada, Denmark, England, Germany, Japan, the Netherlands, New Zealand, Sweden, and the United States of America.

The descriptions in this chapter utilize the uniform descriptive format detailed in Chapter 2 whenever complete morphological information is available for a cultivar. Unfortunately, in several cases, such as some recent Japanese introductions, only partial information could be obtained, and for these all that is known has been included in abbreviated form. I consider partial information better than none.

The breeding line or exact parental cross is given for most cultivars, but for some hybrids it was impossible to include this information because a few hybridizers keep it secret. If a plant's morphology allows a well-founded guess about its parentage, I have indicated the possible derivation. In cases, where no definite link could be established through macromorphological features, I left the origin out, to be added in future editions, perhaps, when such data are released.

Insofar as possible, the morphology of cultivars still in cultivation has been verified by growing them in my garden or by observing them in other locations the world over. However, for named cultivars that have disappeared, the task was virtually impossible, so some entries contain only a name. These historical entries are included in the interest of comprehensiveness.

There are also a number of names which have been registered by the IRA without descriptions, ostensibly to reserve the name—for example, a number of names in the *H. Tardiana* grex—so these are listed by name only. The validity of these names is questionable, however, because according to Article 39 of the ICNCP (1980), any cultivar name published on or after 1 January 1959 must be accompanied by a description or refer to a previously published description. Although provisional registration of these *H. Tardiana* grex names without description is invalid according to the rules, it can probably be tolerated because a committee of the BHHS is actively working on the development of descriptions derived from "standard specimens." Thus the registered names can be emended with these descriptions in the near future and brought in line with ICNCP rules.

On the other hand, many new cultivars have not been in the trade long enough to conform to the 6-year maturity requirement stipulated in Chapter 2. In these cases, the registration information given by the hybridizer was utilized or only the name is given. Unfortunately, the information provided by hybridizers to the registrar is not always accurate because some cultivars are registered when still very young. What they will look like as mature plants is speculation.

These limited entries and other morphological data

coming from third parties for which no verification could be obtained may have to be revised or completed in the future. Readers are requested to contribute any information missing and to provide revised data where this is necessary. I hope in a subsequent edition to incorporate this information in sufficient detail to complete the entries.

It was not possible to include all the cultivar names known because (1) new names are constantly being formulated, and some were published after the deadline for this book; (2) some hybridizers who reported that they have named every seedling in their garden (in one case exceeding 600 in number), were not able or willing to supply the names or descriptions nor was it possible for me to visit every such garden to compile the information; and (3) many of these names are horticulturally insignificant and may never see widespread horticultural use. These obscure names have been excluded, but if they become important in time for future editions, some of them will have to be included then.

Inclusion of many of these unregistered new names appears worthwhile for the sake of comprehensiveness, although such action could be justified only if the named cultivars satisfy three conditions: (1) that their registration with the IRA is intended; (2) that propagation is anticipated; and (3) that gardeners will eventually be able to purchase the cultivars. To solve this dilemma I have compromised and selected a few of the more promising new cultivars and included them in this chapter. Obviously, any of the unregistered names I have included are not "reserved" (i.e., they can be used by anyone else to register any other taxon belonging to the genus) and this could cause nomenclature problems in the future. For this reason I urge all hybridizers to register their cultivars with the International Registration Authority for *Hosta*, Mervin C. Eisel, Registrar, University of Minnesota Landscape Arboretum, 3675 Arboretum Drive, P.O. Box 39, Chanhassen, MN 55317, USA. This is the only way names can become valid and recognized cultivar names and thus permanently attached to a given taxon.

TYPOGRAPHIC PROTOCOL

The following typographic protocol has been followed for the main name headings to indicate their standing:

1. For all cultivar names, the generic name is printed in **bold italic** type abbreviated *H.*, and the cultivar epithet is printed in **'Bold Roman'** type and enclosed in single quotation marks; the combination appears thus: *H.* **'August Moon'**.

2. Combinations of a species name with a Latinized or Japanese descriptive cultivar epithet are printed in **bold italic** type for the species name, and the cultivar epithet is printed in **'Bold Roman'** type and enclosed in single quotation marks; the combination appears thus: *H. ventricosa* **'Aureomarginata'**. These names are described in Chapter 3, but included as main headings in this chapter to provide a cross-reference.

3. When a species has been reduced to cultivar form in Chapter

3, it is written in cultivar form, with the epithet enclosed in single quotation marks and printed in **'Bold Roman'** type, as in *H*. **'Fortunei'**. Any descriptive cultivar epithet associated with the reduced species name is combined with it and the combination written as a cultivar name, as in *H*. **'Fortunei Albomarginata'**. All validly published taxa that have been reduced to cultivar form are described in Chapter 3, and their names are included as main entries in Chapter 4 to provide a cross-reference. All cultivar names associated with these taxa—as for example, *H*. 'Fortunei Albomarginata' or *H*. 'Lancifolia Aurea'—are described in this chapter.

4. Superseded or incorrect horticultural synonyms in main headings are printed in *regular italic* for the species name, if used, and the epithet is printed in regular Roman and enclosed in single quotation marks, as in *H*. 'Japonica'.

DEFINITION OF A CULTIVAR

Use of the word *variety* is confusing because in English it can refer to a botanical variety (*varietas*) or a cultivated variety (*cultivarietas*). Plants described in this chapter are cultivated varieties while botanical varieties are described in Chapter 3. The concept of cultivated variety as opposed to botanical variety allows clear and definite recognition of the status of a taxon, the former being a garden variety and the latter a botanical category below that of species. The term *cultivar* is derived from **CULTI**vated **VAR**iety, and per the ICNCP (1980: Article 10; 1990: Article 3), a cultivar is defined as an assemblage of cultivated plants which is clearly distinguished by one or more characters (morphological, physiological, cytological, chemical, or others), and which, when reproduced (sexually or asexually), retains its distinguishing characters. In the genus *Hosta* the distinguishing characters are principally macromorphological (i.e., the shape and size of leaves, plant size, and variegation, among others), but can include attributes less obvious to gardeners, such as cytological and chemical characters. Cultivars may originate in gardens or they may be plants selected from wild populations which are brought into cultivation and named.

The propagation method of choice employed by commercial growers and gardeners is asexual and involves division of the rhizome. Large propagators use tissue culture almost exclusively. It is only through these methods that a cultivar retains its distinguishing characters because *Hosta* cultivars and most cultivated species do not come true from seed. They must always be vegetatively (asexually) propagated, and so without human intervention they cannot perpetuate themselves and would eventually revert to another form or disappear.

In some foreign languages the distinction between botanical and cultivated varieties is much more precise because special terms are used for each. For example, in German "Art" means botanical variety and "Sorte" means cultivar. The 1980 ICNCP lists the terms meaning cultivar as follows: *Pinzhong* (*p'inchung*) in Chinese, *varieteit* or *ras* in Dutch, *variété* in French, *Sorte* in German, *varietà* or *razza* in Italian, *hinshu* in Japanese, *variedade* in Portuguese, *sort* in Russian and the Scandinavian languages, and *variedad* in Spanish.

The new ICNCP (1990: Article 4) stipulates that a cultivar name must be freely available in all countries for use by any person. Trademarks attached to cultivar names are discouraged because they are not freely available for use by any person and so are contrary to the new ICNCP.

The ICNCP (1990: Article 12) recognizes several different types of cultivars, but for the genus *Hosta* the only important one is the clone, which is defined as an individual or a group of individuals which may not necessarily be genetically uniform and which can be consistently distinguished by one or more characters. Virtually all cultivars in the genus either produced or selected as hybrids or mutations (sports) must be propagated vegetatively to retain their distinctive characters because they do not come true from seed. So all cultivar names can also be defined as clonal names and apply to what is called a specific cultivar/clone. Clones that have different origins, but are in all other characters alike and cannot be distinguished from each other, are given the same cultivar name.

EXPLANATION OF DESCRIPTIONS

This chapter contains a brief description for most cultivars; all their known synonyms, obsolete and incorrect names; their parentage or other origin, if known; cross-references, where appropriate; and additional comments, as required.

The following example illustrates the basic format used and the information given for each cultivar entry:

1. *H*. **'Blue Moon'** Smith/Aden IRA/1976.
   AHS-IV/21A.   Fig. 0-00; Plates 000, 000.
2. AHS Midwest Blue Award, 1982, exhibited by Kenneth Anderson. Plant 10 in. (25.5 cm) dia., 8 in. (20 cm) high. Leaf 3 by 2 in. (7.5 by 5 cm), veins 9, blue-green, not variegated, cordate, flat. Scape 12 in. (31 cm), bare, straight; flower small, bell-shaped, white, flowers during average period, fertile.
3. HN: *H*. 'Halo'.
   H. Tardiana grex TF 2 × 2.
4. [*H*. 'Tardiflora' × *H*. *sieboldiana* 'Elegans'].
5. (see also *H*. Tardiana grex).
6. (see . . .).

Detailed explanations for each entry as identified by numbers in the example above are as follows:

1. *Name, Originators, Dates, AHS Classification Number, Year, and Illustration Numbers* (when available). The primary horticultural name is followed by the name of the originator and the year of first use of the name, if other than the introduction year. When a long-established or important primary name has become invalid, incorrect, superseded, or is no longer used or recommended for other reasons, no further information is included and a cross-reference to the correct name is always given (as "see . . ."). When the names of several individuals follow the primary horticultural name, the first name is that of the plant originator or discoverer, the second is that of the namer, and the third is that of the introducer. If known, the year of first use of the name, or its publication date is also given, if other than the year of registration. Occasionally only a country of origin is known and given. Cultivars registered with the International Registration Authority for *Hosta* give the year of registration after "IRA."

If a classification number for a particular taxon was officially issued and available from the AHS, it has been included following the primary name. These classification numbers are explained in Appendix C.

Also following the primary entry are references to illustrations. Black-and-white illustrations, called figures, are double-numbered thus: 3-123 or A-7. The first number indicates the chapter or appendix in which the illustration occurs; the number following is the illustration number, which starts with "1" for each chapter or appendix. Each color illustration has a unique, consecutive number—for example, Plate 123.

For cultivars of Japanese origin, following the transliterated roman name I have included the Japanese name written in Japanese writing. These names are further explained below under "Names of Japanese Cultivars." Additional notes on the Japanese language in relation to the genus, an explanation of Japanese pronunciation, and the meaning of commonly used Japanese names are given in Appendix E.

2. *Description.* A uniformly formatted short description is provided for each cultivar. The format for cultivar descriptions is explained in Chapter 2. Uniformity of description allows easy comparison of one cultivar to another. For some important cultivars additional information is included on nomenclature, synonymy, stability of variegation, and awards given; for other taxa only partial information could be obtained. The author welcomes contributions from readers to complete such partial information.

3. *Synonyms, Associated Names, and Historical Names.* The third element in the description lists synonyms, associated names, historical names, and common names in other languages. These are arranged in alphabetic order. The following abbreviations are used for synonyms and other names:

SY: = Botanical synonyms.
HN: = Horticultural names.
JN: = Japanese names.
ON: = Other-language common names.

It is important to note that year dates cited along with an author's name for horticultural synonyms (HN), Japanese synonyms (JN), and other non-English synonyms (ON) do not refer to bibliographic entries, but are derived from many different sources, including catalogs, magazine articles, and correspondence, and so are not individually listed in the Bibliography. On the other hand, year dates cited along with an author's name for botanical synonyms (SY) always refer to a matching bibliographic entry.

A detailed definition of the term synonym is given later in this introduction.

Associated names are names that have been given to cultivars which are very similar macromorphologically to the listed taxon or represent groups of closely related clones.

Historical botanical names that were once applied to taxa, which now have been reduced to cultivar form, retain their status as synonyms even though they are obsolete. Other historical names included are those which were formerly used in horticultural publications, but have been superseded by contemporary cultivar names. In most cases these old names are obsolete and should not be used, but they are listed because they are synonyms and their inclusion contributes to historical completeness.

In some cases additional historical names or stock numbers are provided: Between 1930 and 1970 several early *Hosta* enthusiasts created gardens which included large hosta collections: Krossa, Summers, Williams, and others. Their plant lists (Krossa, 1966–1970; Summers, 1972; Williams, 1966–1968) are very important historically because they trace the historical development of modern *Hosta* cultivation in North America. I have included the stock numbers which appeared on the inventory lists of several of these gardens and their equivalent, current names insofar as these can still be determined.

4. *Parentage or Origin.* Knowing the parentage of a cultivar, whether a hybrid or a sport, gives important clues to overall cultural requirements. The breeding line of many hybrids, as well as the parental derivation of many mutations, when known, are shown in square brackets thus [...]. For hybrids, the pod parent is listed first and the pollen parent second. In a few instances conflicting reports of parentage have been uncovered in which case both versions are listed. The horticul-

turally less defensible of the two, in my opinion, has been marked "al," which stands for *aliorum*, meaning "of others (and less acceptable in this case)." Regrettably, some hybridizers do not release information concerning the parentage of their hybrids so it could not be included. Specifically, parental information is shown as follows:

[*H.* **A** × *H.* **B**] means a hybrid between **A** (female parent) and **B** (male parent).
[*H.* **C** hybrid] means a hybrid with **C** as pod parent but for which the male parent is unknown or uncertain.

Somatic mutations, called *sports* by gardeners, are more difficult to trace, because they can be bud mutations on the plant of origin or they can start as mutated seedlings several generations removed from the original parent (Yasui, 1929). Some bud mutations are well known—for example, *H. sieboldiana* 'Frances Williams', whose discovery is documented in great detail. In some cases the origin of a particular cultivar can be established in a broad sense only by way of macromorphological features. In these cases I have indicated a derivative origin:

[*H.* **D** mutation] means a sport (somatic mutation) of **D**.
[*H.* **E** form] or [*H.* **E** derivative] means a derivative of **E** which may be a hybrid or a mutation one to several generations removed but sharing key morphological characters with it.

5. *Cross-References.* The final element in the entry may be a cross-reference: It is always used here when the main entry is a superseded synonym, and it points to the correct name indicated by "(see ...)." References are also employed to indicate broad relationships. For example, *H. sieboldiana* 'Frances Williams' is cross-referenced to the *H. sieboldiana* Aureomarginata group, of which it is a member. Because of the broader relationship, this reference is indicated by "(see also ...)." In this case additional information relating to the named taxon can be found under the referenced name.

All recognized and valid botanical names, as well as all former botanical names which have been reduced to cultivar form, are gathered in Chapter 3, and whenever a cross-reference to a botanical name or a latinate cultivar name is given, that name can be found in Chapter 3. Chapter 4 also lists all botanical names that have been reduced to cultivar form and gives appropriate cross-references to Chapter 3 which encompasses details for such taxa. For example:

H. **'Undulata Univittata'.**
H. undulata var. *univittata*.

In this typical arrangement, the first line is the heading in Chapter 4, and the second line is the botanical name under which this taxon is described in Chapter 3.

UNSTABLE VARIEGATION = NOMENCLATURE PROBLEMS

Variegation in the genus is not absolutely permanent. Most seasoned gardeners have observed the slow change of the highly variegated *H.* 'Undulata' to the all-green *H.* 'Undulata Erromena'. Zilis (1987) reported that *H. sieboldiana* 'Frances Williams', hitherto by many thought to be a stable form, will eventually revert to all-green and all-yellow forms. This metamorphosis may take many years, so these taxa appear to have stable variegation. Some cultivars, however, have unstable variegation in the short term and undergo morphological modification by way of chimeral rearrangement. Most cultivars with unstable variegation in the short term belong to the mediovariegated group which is characterized by streaky or mottled multicolor variegation usually concentrated in the leaf center but occasionally also involving the leaf margins. They will sooner or later change to a more stable periclinal chimera form (see Glossary), either margined or solid-colored as explained by the Benedict Cross in Appendix D. The change may take place very rapidly, within 2 or 3 growing seasons, or it may take several years.

The unstable, streaky medio variegation can be maintained by constantly cutting away shoots with stable variegation—a method used in Japan. If left alone, the cultivar's more robust, stable shoots will eventually overwhelm the usually weaker, variegated parts of the plant which will succumb in time or many of the leaves will simply change to all-yellow, all-green, or a nonstreaky form of variegation, such as variegated margins (Plate 103).

Variegated taxa occur in the wild, usually originating with bud mutations, but these forms will inevitably backcross to a nonvariegated parental form or undergo periclinal rearrangement to a more stable, usually all-green form. This seems to apply to all variegated mutants in the wild, and the occurrence of variegated forms is an abnormal and nonperpetuating event. The manifestation of temporal variegation in the wild is higher in some taxa than in others, and abiotic conditions seem to influence it. Some of the variegated forms found in the wild are stable in the long term and have been brought into cultivation where they persist by human intervention. A documented case is *H.* 'Crispula' (which see), found by von Siebold around 1827/1828 at two locations near the city of Nagasaki, Nagasaki Prefecture, but variegated forms of this taxon have not been found since that time in spite of some diligent searches. The possibility exists that they may occur undetected from time to time and disappear within a relatively short time. Plant hunters in Japan still find variegated forms among wild populations, but such occasions are infrequent. *Hosta* 'Decorata', on the other hand, was bought by Hogg (see Chapter 5) in Yokohama, and no one knows where it came from. Presumably, it was a "find" in the wild—one that has not been repeated. Both these taxa are asexually propagated and thus perpetuated under cultivation, but without this human intervention they also would disappear completely sooner or later. In fact, they have been observed to produce all-green forms, but I have found no records concerning the time required for this change nor the frequency of its occurrence and, in any case, these situations present absolutely no nomenclature problems to horticulture because the all-green forms already have valid names.

On the other hand, rapid changes in variegation patterns by way of chimeral rearrangement pose significant nomenclature difficulties. Many hosta gardeners are familiar with the problems by *H.* 'Flamboyant' changing into *H.* 'Shade Fanfare' or *H.* 'Yellow Splash' changing into *H.* 'Yellow Splash Rim'. In each case the first name represents a streaky, splashed cultivar, while the second name is a long-term stable-margined form. While tissue culturing an unstable cultivar, both the unstable as well as the stable forms are produced, with the latter representing a high percentage of the yield. When this problem first appeared, both the unstable, streaked and the stable-margined form were sold under the name *H.* 'Flamboyant'. This obviously untenable situation caused considerable confusion among gardeners and was contrary to the rules of the ICNCP. As a consequence, in 1987 the Nomenclature Committee of The American Hosta Society, under the chairmanship of Dr. Pollock, approached the International Commission on Nomenclature of Cultivated Plants with a request to review this matter and, if possible, to arrive at a ruling which would govern these cases (Pollock, 1987). The

commission met on 17 August 1985 in Wageningen, Netherlands, in conjunction with the International Symposium on the Taxonomy of Cultivated Plants sponsored by the International Society for Horticultural Science (ISHS). It should be noted that the ISHS appoints the registrars for the various plant genera and families. The commission's chairman, C. D. Brickell, responded personally and conveyed the following ruling:

1. *"The stable periclinal chimeral form must be given a different cultivar name than that applied to the unstable form."* Interpretation: When the unstable cultivar *H.* 'Flamboyant', which is registered as having streaky variegation, changes to a distinct stable-margined form, it must be given a new name. The new name selected for it and registered with the IRA is *H.* 'Shade Fanfare'. In this case the relationship of the two cultivars is not obvious from the formulation of the names.

2. *"It is not essential for the two forms to have names indicating a relationship but it is very desirable that this should be done wherever it is appropriate and does not conflict with the ICNCP."* Interpretation: When the unstable *H.* 'Neat Splash' transforms to a distinct stable-margined form, its name changes to *H.* 'Neat Splash Rim'. In this case the relationship of the two cultivars is clearly established.

Brickell (in Pollock, 1987) further explains that "the stable form (name Y) must not be labeled or sold under the name of the unstable form (name X)." This determination has its roots in article 39 of the ICNCP (1980) which stipulates that to be valid a description must accompany the registration of a name. The description and name combination are inseparable, and there is no mechanism provided by the ICNCP for changing a description at a later date to make it fit a particular cultivar's morphology after it has undergone chimeral rearrangement (i.e., changed from an unstable to a stable form). To permit major emendations of cultivar descriptions after registration would, in my opinion, contravene the spirit and letter of the ICNCP as it would seriously destabilize cultivar nomenclature.

Premature registration of cultivars is the primary reason for these difficulties. Frequently, hybridizers name, describe, and register a cultivar before that particular plant has had a chance to grow to a mature form and remained stable for several years. The registration lists of the IRA for *Hosta* are replete with descriptions which were obviously written on the basis of an immature or juvenile plant, and in most circumstances the ICNCP will require that a new name be selected and the changed taxon reregistered with a new description. In a large number of cases the original names chosen are neutral, contrived, or of a general nature, so no real diplomatic problems ensue. On the other hand, changes mandated by the ICNCP in certain cases are difficult when names of people are involved. To mention an example, the popular and attractive cultivar, *H.* 'Mildred Seaver' (Vaughn), named to honor one of North America's leading hybridizers, was originally registered as a cultivar with streaky variegation, but this taxon has since changed into a more stable margined form which is in the trade under the original name. This is contrary to the rules of the 1980 and proposed 1990 ICNCP, and the more-stable form must be given a new name and reregistered. Obviously, a total name change in this case is difficult because of the honorific intentions of the name and also because the original name, once used, is no longer available for registration. However, following the second recommendation of the ISHS committee (listed above), Mrs. Seaver's name can be retained with the addition of a third name, "Y"; thus *H.* 'Mildred Seaver Y'.

This preserves the honorable meaning and satisfies the ICNCP.

Still, the very serious problem of incorrect descriptions filed with the IRA remains. These incorrect descriptions not only involve variegation, but also plant and leaf size and shape and other morphological features. I discussed this problem with the registrar for *Hosta* (in 1990) and he agrees with the rules promulgated but cautions that it may take considerable time to overcome this dilemma because of resistance in the horticultural community. Gardeners tend to make their own rules, as can be seen in the many latinate cultivar names still used contrary to ICNCP rules. One such example is *H. kikutii* var. *polyneuron* 'Albomarginata' which was seen recently although it is invalid per the rules. In this case it is better to use the Japanese version of the name, *H. kikutii* var. *polyneuron* 'Shirofukurin', which is legal.

MELTING OUT

Melting out is the disintegration of large white leaf areas due to a lack of chlorophyll. The severity of melting out appears to be influenced by microclimate and other abiotic conditions. In some gardens it is a minor problem, while in others it is so severe as to cause the rapid demise of the affected cultivars. Whenever instability or melting out has been reported in the literature I have indicated this information in the descriptions. This should not be construed as a judgment of inferiority, but simply as additional information provided to readers for their consideration.

DEFINITION OF A SYNONYM

Unfortunately, there is considerable confusion about the true meaning of the word *synonym*. For this reason I feel it is necessary to provide a detailed explanation of the origin, application, and various connotations of the word as it relates to matters botanic and horticultural. The meaning of synonym in botany is quite different from its horticultural application, and its specific botanic usage is dealt with in Chapter 3. The following is an interpretation of its horticultural application.

The word is derived from the Greek and is a combination of *syn*, meaning "together," and *onyma*, meaning "name." Most dictionaries define it as "a word having the same or nearly the same meaning in one or more senses as another word." For example, the words "house" and "home" are certainly synonymous, but it is immediately apparent that their associations differ. To most readers "house" is a dwelling, a place of residence, while "home" has a more emotional connotation, suggesting family ties and domestic comfort. To paraphrase Edgar A. Guest: "It takes a heap o' living and some love to make a house a home."

The ICNCP (1980) deals with the use of cultivar synonyms under Article 35:

> Each cultivar has one correct cultivar name, the single name by which it is internationally known. It may also have one or more legitimate synonyms. A commercial synonym is an alternative name of a cultivar which may be used instead of its correct name under restricted particular circumstances, for instance when a name is commercially unacceptable in a particular country.

"Restricted particular circumstances" cited by the ICNCP include difficult pronunciation or when the original name, or a translation, would have an undesirable connotation or implication. The Code (ICNCP, 1980) makes recommendation 35A as follows: "It is highly desirable that only one cultivar name for a single cultivar should be current under any particular circumstances."

The ICNCP makes it quite clear that only one name should be used. This is not always the case. For example, the commercial names *H.* 'Gold Crown' or 'Golden Crown' are used for the yellow-margined cultivar *H.* 'Fortunei Aureomarginata'. These names are synonyms in the truest sense because they are different names given to the same identical clone. The gardener buying these plants under their respective different names will receive identical plants.

Regrettably, synonymy in horticulture is not quite this simple. In the past, cultivar names were given to a species before it was identified and the specific name known. An example is the case of *H. nakaiana* which is also called *H.* 'Birchwood Gem'. Cultivar synonyms given to a species are included in Chapter 3 as well as in Chapter 4 to permit cross-referencing of species names to cultivar names. In this case the names usually apply to different clones because species show natural variability and are represented by several clones.

Probably the greatest difficulty arises when cultivar names are given to very similar looking clones. For example, *H. fortunei* 'Ellerbroek', 'L-7', and 'Krossa L-7' are names in the trade given to cultivars which look very much like *H.* 'Gold Crown', 'Golden Crown', or *H.* 'Fortunei Aureomarginata'.

Theoretically, in accordance with the ICNCP, slightly different clones can be called by different names, but from a practical standpoint this causes many problems. Gardeners who order these look-alike cultivars under different names are angered when they receive nearly identical hostas. Falling into this category is the proliferation of cultivars with *H. sieboldiana* parentage which look virtually like the species. Slight differences may be noted by the cognoscenti but to the average gardener these do not matter. To satisfy the requirements of both groups of people, I have adopted the stance that horticultural synonyms are plant names that are applied to cultivar-clones having the same or nearly the same morphology. I fully realize that applying synonyms to clones is fundamentally incorrect, because hypothetically, in accordance with the ICNCP, a distinct clone should have one name only. But in horticultural practice this distinctness is often lacking, and plants originally named differently but later identified as having the same or nearly the same morphology become horticulturally synonymous and should, according to the ICNCP, have only one name.

Plant names can be synonymous in a broad sense, as well as in a very restricted sense. For instance, all yellow-marginate cultivar forms of *H. sieboldiana* can be gathered into a single group of similar plants called the *H. sieboldiana* Aureomarginata group. Thus, *H. sieboldiana* 'Frances Williams', 'Aurora Borealis', 'Chicago Frances Williams', 'Gilt Edge', 'Golden Circles', 'Maple Leaf', 'Nifty Fifty', and 'Samurai' all belong to the yellow-margined group of *H. sieboldiana* and are broadly synonymous when regarded as a group. Nevertheless, individually these plants are considered by some to be sufficiently different to justify their clonal names although this is disputed by others. In any case, the primary entry for each cultivar is under its correct cultivar name, with reference made to an associated group in Chapter 3, where necessary. To illustrate, *H.* 'Frances Williams' is a separate entry in Chapter 4 with its narrow synonyms listed under this primary name, but it is also referenced to either the cultivar name *H. sieboldiana* 'Frances Williams' or the group name *H. sieboldiana* Aureomarginata group, in Chapter 3. In fact, all the yellow-marginate forms of *H. sieboldiana* are included in this group as broad synonyms, because all of them are yellow-margined forms of the species.

Conversely, synonyms can be applied in a very strict sense, as has been seen in the above examples and as is the case with *H.* 'Frances Williams' and *H.* 'Yellow Edge'. The latter name was used for some time for the same clone until the name now used was registered. While the older name is a valid synonym, it should no longer be used.

Occasionally, synonyms are merely different formulations of the same name applied to the same clone. For example, many gardeners prefer the cultivar name in its simplest form: *H.* 'Frances Williams'. The Perennial Plant Association (PPA) and many of its plant nursery members follow the recommendation of the ISHS and the International Stauden Union (ISU) to include the species name to indicate the parental line: *H. sieboldiana* 'Frances Williams'. I, too, have adopted this practice and thus most cultivar names associated with a valid species name are dealt with in Chapter 3 with a cross-reference to this name in Chapter 4. On the other hand, cultivars of species that have been reduced to cultivar form are dealt with in Chapter 4. More detailed still, Article 18 of the ICNCP (1980) allows the formulation of a cultivar name containing the collective group name when the latter is enclosed in parenthesis, thus: *H. sieboldiana* (Aureomarginata group) 'Frances Williams'. While more precise, the latter name is considered too long for commercial purposes, so the short form is commonly used. All these names apply to the same cultivar, and so are synonyms of different formulations permitted by the ICNCP. Where a species itself has been reduced to cultivar form, the species name is either written as a cultivar name or included with a descriptive name—for example, *H.* 'Decorata' or *H.* 'Fortunei Aureomarginata'.

The morphologies of *H.* 'Royal Standard' and *H.* 'White Knight' represent an in-between case. They are certainly close enough in appearance to be considered broadly synonymous, but in a narrow sense there are slight differences and the purist may argue they are not synonyms. In these cases I have cross-referenced the names and attached the abbreviation "sim" (= similar) or "pp sim" (= similar in part). This approach should satisfy both the knowledgeable hosta collector who considers these cultivars as different and the average gardener to whom they are practically identical and for whom they perform identical functions in the garden.

"INCORRECT" NAMES

The term "incorrect" is used frequently in the descriptions with several connotations. When a name is noted as incorrect, usually in the synonymy, it should not be used. Names are incorrect for the following reasons:

1. Orthographically incorrect, containing errors in spelling. Example: *H.* 'Nakiomi' (should be 'Nakaimo').
2. Horticulturally incorrect, that is, invalid latinate names. Example: *H. fluctuans* 'Variegata'. The ICNCP (1980: Article 27a), stipulates that a *Hosta* cultivar name published after 1 January 1959 must be a fancy name, not a botanical name in Latin form. In this example, 'Variegata' is invalid and should be 'Variegated'. Combinations like *H. kikutii* var. *polyneuron* 'Albomarginata' are invalid because of the latinate formulation. It is preferable to use the Japanese version of the name—*H. kikutii* var. *polyneuron* 'Shirofukurin'. Shirofukurin means "white-margined (*albomarginata*)" and its use is not restricted.
3. Formulation incorrect. Example: *H.* 'Karafuto G'. The letter "G" in the name stands for *Giboshi* and is superfluous (should be *H.* 'Karafuto').
4. Combination invalid and incorrect. Examples: *H.* 'Obscura Albomarginata' and *H.* 'Fortunei Obscura Albomarginata', which are combinations never validly pub-

lished but only trade inventions. The only valid botanical names containing the epithet *obscura* are *H. fortunei* var. *obscura* and *H. fortunei* var. *obscura* f. *marginata*. These have been reduced to cultivar forms as *H.* 'Fortunei Obscura' and *H.* 'Fortunei Aureomarginata'.
5. Use of obsolete botanical names as incorrect horticultural names. Example: *H. japonica cærulea viridis* Foerster 1956. Although published before 1 January 1959, the name *japonica* was set aside along with *Funkia* in 1905 and the combination is obsolete, invalid, and incorrect.

DEFINITION OF A GROUP—A GREX

The ICNCP (1980: Article 26) includes provisions for group designation of cultivars. "When a species, interspecific hybrid or intergeneric hybrid includes many cultivars, an assemblage of similar cultivars may be designated as a group." As mentioned earlier, I have adopted the technical term "group" to indicate the collective nature of a given cultivar assemblage which share common morphology and lineage. For instance, there are a number of yellow-marginate forms of *H.* 'Fortunei'. The botanical name is *H. fortunei* var. *aureomarginata* (now reduced to cultivar form as *H.* 'Fortunei Aureomarginata'). However, there are many other named yellow-margined clones of *H. fortunei* which are not exactly alike but undoubtedly belong to the specioid and so are members of the *H.* 'Fortunei Aureomarginata' group. In accordance with the ICNCP (1980), the group name, when used in combination with the species name alone, is placed next to it without parenthesis: *H.* 'Fortunei Aureomarginata' group. From this assembly many distinct cultivars have been selected and named. The ICNCP requires that the group name be enclosed in parenthesis and placed between the specific and cultivar names: *H.* ('Fortunei Albomarginata' group) 'Carol'. Once a cultivar belonging to a group is registered with the IRA for *Hosta*, the species or specioid name may be, and is usually, dropped and the cultivar listed under its simplified registered name, *H.* 'Carol'. *Hosta* 'Fortunei Carol' is also correct to indicate the cultivar's original breeding line and can be done in full accord with Article 26 of the ICNCP, but most commercial establishments have adopted the simplified form.

The term "grex," while similar to group, is used for assemblage of hybrids from the same mating when both parents are known. When only one parent is known, the 1990 ICNCP disallows the use of grex. An example of a grex is the *H.* Tardiana grex. Members of this grex have names like *H.* (Tardiana grex) 'Blue Moon' or *H.* (Tardiana grex) 'Dorset Blue', and these names are usually shortened to *H.* 'Blue Moon' and *H.* 'Dorset Blue'.

In the descriptions, cross-reference to a group is made, when appropriate, and group names are also listed in the indexes with a page reference. This permits the reader to determine which cultivars are closely related and considered part of a group and which hybrids are members of a grex. As already stated, some members of a group may be so much alike as to be virtually identical, so the reader should exercise caution to avoid duplication when ordering cultivars belonging to the same group. Unfortunately, this duplication may occur even when ordering registered hostas belonging to the same group because the criterion of distinctness has not always been fully adhered to in the registration process, to no fault of the registrar who has adopted a policy which leaves the determination of distinctness to the hybridizer's judgment. Generally, whenever a group name is referenced, the cultivars involved are similar if not alike and so are suffixed with "pp" and/or "sim," as explained earlier.

CONVENTIONS

The following practices have been used as guidelines for the formation and spelling of *Hosta* cultivar names. The principal references for these conventions are the 1980 *International Code of Nomenclature for Cultivated Plants* (ICNCP), with the 1990 proposal occasionally referred to, issued by the International Bureau for Plant Taxonomy and Nomenclature, Tweede Transitorium, Uithof, Utrecht, Netherlands (copies obtainable from the American Horticultural Society, Mount Vernon, VA 22121, USA, or the Royal Horticultural Society, Vincent Square, London, SW1P2PE, Great Britain) and the 1988 *International Code of Botanical Nomenclature* (ICBN), with the 1983 ICBN and earlier issues occasionally referred to, issued by the International Association for Plant Taxonomy (copies obtainable from Koeltz Scientific Books, R.R. 7, Box 39, Champaign, IL 61821, USA, direct or special order through bookstores):

1. Formation of *Hosta* cultivar names follows Articles 27 to 31B of the ICNCP. Accordingly, Latin names were considered valid only if they were published before 1 January 1959. When specioids have been reduced to cultivar form, the botanical names published in conformity with the ICBN have been retained, following Article 27b of the ICNCP, and are written as cultivar names enclosed in single quotation marks. Latinate descriptive epithets which were part of the botanical specioid name—for example, *H. fortunei* var. *aureomarginata*—are included as *H.* 'Fortunei Aureomarginata'.

2. Article 31A of the ICNCP rejects the use of abbreviations in horticultural names. Accordingly, the name *H.* 'Mt. Kirishima' is an improper formulation and should be *H.* 'Mount Kirishima'.

3. After consultation with Mervin C. Eisel, registrar, International Registration Authority for *Hosta*, and in accordance with his practice, apostrophes within cultivar names have been eliminated. Thus, *H.* 'Arett's Wonder' becomes *H.* 'Aretts Wonder'. It should be noted that the ICNCP does not impede the use of apostrophes, and their use would improve orthographic precision in some cases, but I am following, albeit reluctantly, the registrar's convention.

4. In accordance with Article 32 of the ICNCP, *Hosta* cultivar names rendered in a language other than English have been retained in their original language. In most cases translations and/or transliterations have been included, but the ICNCP preferred usage is the name in its original, non-English form. For example, *H.* 'Koryu' is transliterated from the Japanese kanji using the Hepburn method, but it is not a translated form even though an explanation of its meaning is given. Some non-English descriptive names must be used in conjunction with a species name because they are applicable to many different species. *Hosta kiyosumiensis* 'Nakafu' or *H. kiyosumiensis* 'Shirobana' are examples. *Nakafu* means "aureonebulosa" (yellow-centered variegation), and *shirobana* means "white-flowered," but neither of these characterizations are unique. Because they can be applied to many different species, they must be used in conjunction with a species name (see "Names of Japanese Cultivars" following). The same applies to similar names in English, such as "Albomarginata" or "Aureomarginata," which also must be used in combination with a species or specioid name, as in *H.* 'Fortunei Aureomarginata'.

5. The word specifying grey color is spelled both "gray" and "grey." Although "gray" is the common spelling in the United States, the word "grey" is preferred in international and botanical use and is used in this book. Proper names, however, which are spelled "gray," retain their original spelling.

6. Without listing all of them specifically I have followed all points of ICNCP recommendation 31A for correct formulation of cultivar names.

7. Hyphens have been eliminated (per Article 26 of the proposed 1990 ICNCP) from Japanese names. For consistency I have also removed them from Latinized names as they have no basis in Latin.

NAMES OF JAPANESE CULTIVARS

The genus *Hosta* is largely native to Japan. As a consequence the Japanese have over the years bred, selected, and named many cultivars. For this reason it is necessary to explain and define the usage of Japanese names which have been applied to the genus.

It must be noted that the current rules of the ICNCP (1980) discourage translation of cultivar names, although transliteration is permitted. The proposed rules of the 1990 ICNCP will be far more restrictive. Article 29a states: "Cultivar names must not be translated." If a name has been translated, the translated form becomes a synonym, and the correct cultivar name is the one formulated in its original language. Article 29b permits transliteration of Japanese names following the rules of Hepburn (see Appendix E). Article 27a of the 1990 ICNCP proposes that cultivar names originally in Japanese kanji must not consist of more than four characters. This restriction seems too severe, and in this book several Japanese names originally written with more than four kanji have been transliterated. I have contacted the secretary of the Horticultural Taxonomy Group with the recommendation that the permissible number of kanji be expanded to six in the final version of the 1990 ICNCP.

Japanese names fall into two main categories: (1) academic names given in conjunction with Latin binomials and valid descriptions in the Japanese botanical literature, and (2) all other Japanese names. The former are formal names which are part of the botanical identification of species and subspecific taxa; these are covered in detail in Chapter 3. The remaining Japanese names are principally cultivar names and have several origins:

1. Metaphorical names—usually written with kanji ideographs (derived from Chinese character symbols)—as well as jukugo compound words—made up of two or more kanji—are invented names and roughly equivalent to Western fancy cultivar names. For example, 'Haru no Yume' means 'Spring Dream'. I believe the Japanese names, some of which have been used for many years, should be preserved and that the transliterated Japanese word should be used, as is already the case in other genera such as Japanese maples, Japanese pines, and Japanese flowering cherries. This is the practice I have followed. Obviously, most Western gardeners cannot translate kanji, so a translation is given to let those interested know what the Japanese name means, but this should in no way be taken as encouragement on my part to use the translated English names in lieu of the transliterated Japanese names. In this book I have provided these names in kana as well as in the transliterated form to assist Japanese and Western readers in the correlation and identification of these cultivars.

2. Descriptive (literal) names correspond to English descriptive names. For example, 'Kifukurin' equates to 'Aureo-

marginata'. These descriptive names must be used in combination with a species names, because there are yellow-marginate forms in several different species (see paragraph 4 under "Conventions"). In some cases these descriptive names are written in kanji, but they are also frequently written with Japanese phonetic symbols, comprising the katakana and hiragana syllabaries. Most Japanese academic and descriptive cultivar names use the katakana syllabary, so I have written descriptive Japanese names with these phonetic characters. It should be pointed out that the Japanese have transliterated many Western fancy cultivar names into katakana, sounding them out with these phonetic language symbols. For example, *H.* 'Neat Splash' is phonetically spelled 'ni-to su-pu-ra-tsu-sho'.

3. Combination metaphorical and descriptive names are often used which call for inclusion of kanji or jukugo compound words (made up of two or more kanji), following Japanese horticultural convention. I have written these Japanese names with a combination of kanji, jukugo, katakana, and hiragana.

4. Different metaphorical names applying to the same taxon are relatively rare in Japanese horticulture, but there are a few duplicate, descriptive, literal names. In these cases I have provided the Japanese writing in katakana and stated which of the names is preferred in Japan.

Notes and explanations of Japanese pronunciation and the meaning of commonly used Japanese names are given in Appendix E.

Note bene
Due to the continuing and contemporaneous shift in nomenclature for the genus *Hosta,* some references in the text do not point clearly to the current most-valid form. In an effort to provide the most current reference, the reader should look in the "Index of Names Assocciated With Genus *Hosta*" for the best contemporaneous reference.

Plate 1. *H. kikutii*; whitish or white petals, veins barely visible (Hosta Hill)

Plate 2. *H. ventricosa*; purple; the darker veins are contrasted against a dark background with a white margin (Hosta Hill)

Plate 3. *H. sieboldii*; purple striped; purple veins on a white, lavender, or light purple background (Hosta Hill)

Plate 4. *H. longipes* 'Tagi'; lavender; more or less uniform lavender or light purple color field with veins blending into background, margins white, varying from very wide to very narrow (Hosta Hill)

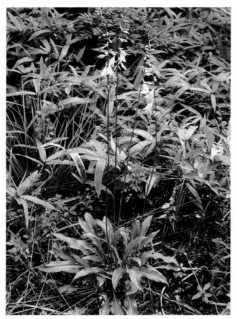

Plate 5. *H. alismifolia*; natural habitat of plant considered to be this taxon (Tsukude, Aichi/Sugita)

Plate 6. *H. atropurpurea*; flower bud detail (Hosta Hill)

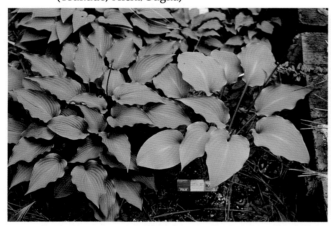

Plate 7. *H. capitata*; general habit; 2 different forms (Hosta Hill)

Plate 8. *H. cathayana*; general habit (Stanley Park, Vancouver, BC/Schmid)

Plate 9. *H. cathayana* 'Nakafu' (*H.* 'Chinese Sunrise)'; general habit (Hosta Hill)

Plate 10. *H. clausa* var. *ensata*; general habit (Hosta Hill)

Plate 11. *H. crassifolia*; general habit, young plant (Hosta Hill)

Plate 12. *H.* 'Crispula'; general habit (Hosta Hill)

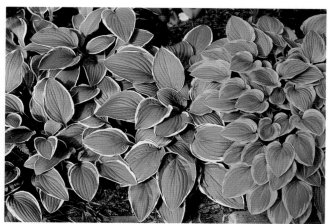

Plate 13. *H.* 'Decorata' (left); *H.* 'Golden Tiara' (right) (Hosta Hill)

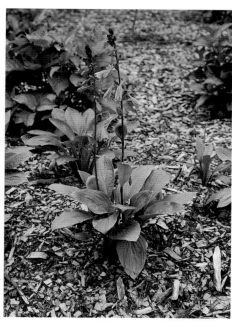

Plate 14. *H.* 'Decorata Normalis' (Savill/Schmid)

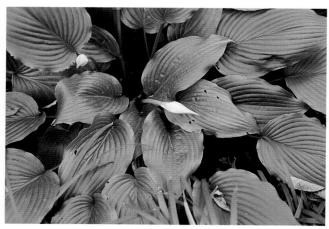

Plate 15. *H. densa*; general habit, showing *kikutii*-shaped bud (Hosta Hill)

Plate 16. *H.* 'Elata'; general habit (hail damaged), showing original form received from Hylander (Weihenstephan/Schmid)

Plate 17. *H. fluctuans*; natural habitat (Iwate Prefecture).

Plate 18. *H. fluctuans* 'Variegated' (*Sagae*); general habit (Gotemba/Pratt)

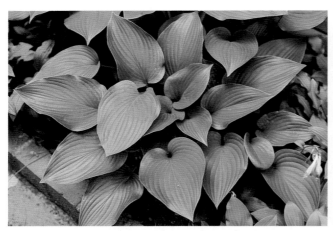

Plate 19. *H.* 'Fortunei Viridis'; general habit (Hosta Hill)

Plate 20. *H.* 'Fortunei Albopicta'; general habit (Klose)

Plate 21. *H.* 'Fortunei Aurea'; general habit (Klose)

Plate 22. *H.* 'Fortunei Aureomarginata'; general habit (Blowing Rock/Schmid)

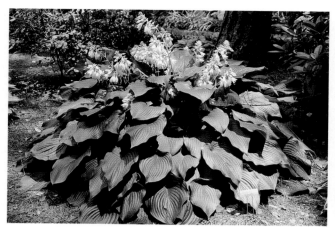

Plate 23. *H.* 'Fortunei Gigantea'; general habit (Coney garden/Schmid)

Plate 24. *H.* 'Fortunei Hyacinthina'; landscape use; *Primula helodoxa* and *Mimulus luteus,* (right) (Pukeiti Trust garden, New Plymouth, New Zealand/J. Mathews)

Plate 25. *H.* 'Fortunei Stenantha'; landscape use (Dr. Sun Yat-Sen Chinese Garden, Vancouver, BC/Schmid)

Plate 26. *H.* 'Fortunei Stenantha Variegated'; general habit (Hosta Hill)

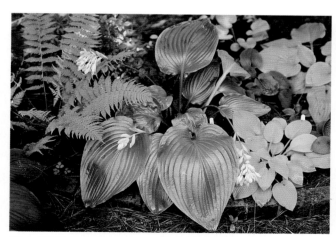

Plate 27. *H. hypoleuca*; general habit of cultivated specimen; *H.* 'Bright Glow' (right front) (Hosta Hill)

Plate 28. *H. jonesii*; detail of flowers and buds (Hosta Hill)

Plate 29. *H. kikutii*; general habit in full flower, average form; leaves showing damage caused by night-feeding moth larvae (Hosta Hill)

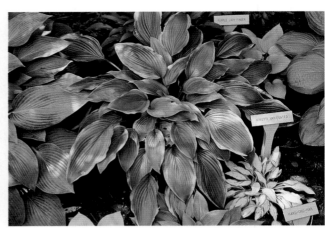

Plate 30. *H. kikutii* 'Kifukurin'; general habit; *H.* 'Haku Chu Han' (bottom right) (Olson garden/Schmid)

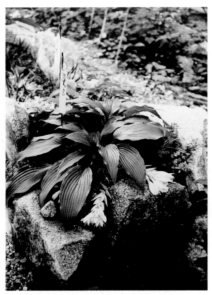

Plate 31. *H. kikutii* var. *caput-avis*; large form (Sugita)

Plate 32. *H. kikutii* var. *kikutii* f. *leuconota*; leaf details, showing pruinose-white underside, type (Hosta Hill)

Plate 33. *H. kikutii* var. *polyneuron* 'Shirofukurin'; general habitat (Hideko Gowen garden/Schmid)

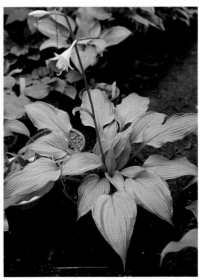

Plate 34. *H. kiyosumiensis* 'Nakafu'; discovered in Nukata-cho by H. Sugita (Sugita)

Plate 35. *H. laevigata*; the type and short-leaved form of *H. laevigata* (left and top) compared to *H. yingeri* (right) (Hosta Hill)

Plate 36. *H. longipes* f. *hypoglauca*; leaf details (Hosta Hill)

Plate 37. *H. longipes* f. *sparsa*; natural habitat; Tenryu River, Shizuoka Prefecture (Sugita)

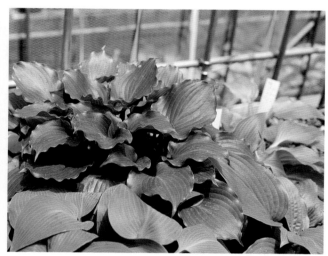

Plate 38. *H. longipes* var. *latifolia*; general habit (Gotemba/Pratt)

Plate 39. *H. longipes* var. *longipes*; general habit; *H. 'Tardiflora'* (bottom right) (Hosta Hill)

Plate 40. *H. longipes* var. *vulgata*   (Hosta Hill)

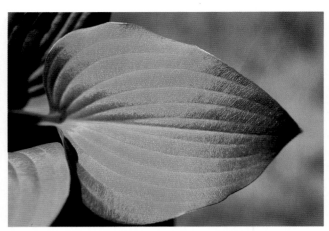

Plate 42. *H. minor*; leaf detail showing characteristic 'metallic' indumentum (cultivated at Hosta Hill, collected Kyongsang-nam-do, Korea)

Plate 41. *H. longissima*; general habit (incorrectly labeled var. *brevifolia*) (Klose)

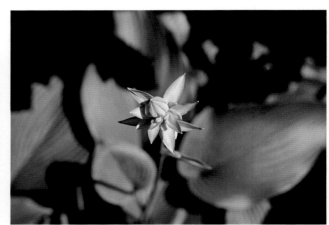

Plate 44. *H. montana*; flower bud detail, typical *Helipteroides* form (Hosta Hill)

Plate 43. *H. montana*; typical fall coloration of hosta leaves evident after first light frosts (Hosta Hill)

Plate 45. *H. montana* 'Aureomarginata'; general habit; *H.* 'Shade Fanfare' (bottom right) (January garden/Schmid)

Plate 46. *H. montana* f. *macrophylla*; general habit, type (Hosta Hill)

Plate 47. *H. nakaiana*; mass planting (Flower Farm/Schmid)

Plate 48. *H. nigrescens*; general habit (Hosta Hill)

Plate 50. *H.* 'Opipara' (Brincka form); general habit (Brincka garden/C. Seaver 1988)

Plate 49. *H. okamotoi*; general habit (Hosta Hill)

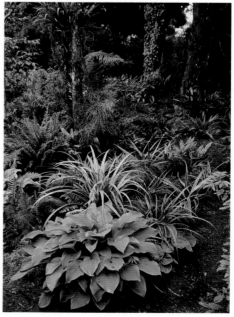

Plate 52. *H. plantaginea*; general habit, growing in shade of 100-year-old Rimu (*Dacrydium cupressinum*) with astelias, bromeliads and ferns (F. J. Waitara garden, Taranaki, New Zealand/J. Matthews)

Plate 51. *H. pachyscapa*; general habit (Hosta Hill)

Plate 53. *H. pulchella*; general habit (Hosta Hill)

Plate 54. *H. pycnophylla*; general habit, showing white coating on leaf underside, with Strawberry Geranium (*Saxifraga stolonifera*) (Hosta Hill)

Plate 55. *H. rectifolia*; landscape use, mass planting (RHS Wisley Garden/Schmid)

Plate 56. *H. rectifolia* var. *australis*; natural habitat (Mount Odake, Aomori Prefecture)

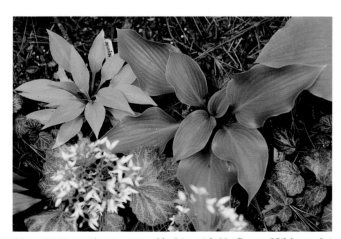

Plate 57. *H. rupifraga*; general habit, with *H.* 'Gosan Hildegarde' (Hosta Hill)

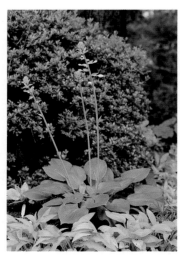

Plate 58. *H.* 'Sacra'; general habit (Hosta Hill)

Plate 59. *H. shikokiana*; general habit (Hosta Hill)

Plate 60. *H. sieboldiana* 'Gray Cole' (Kuk); general habit, a clone exemplifying the best Western garden form (Kuk's Forest garden/Schmid)

Plate 61. *H. sieboldiana* 'Semperaurea' (Foerster); general habit (ex Foerster; Weihenstephan/Schmid)

Plate 62. *H. sieboldii*; general habit (Hosta Hill)

Plate 63. *H. sieboldii* 'Kabitan'; mass planting (J. C. Taylor garden/Schmid)

Plate 64. *H. sieboldii* 'Kabitan'; plant reverting to green (Hosta Hill)

Plate 66. *H. sieboldii* 'Mediopicta'; general habit (right) compared with *H.* 'Lancifolia Inaho' (left) (Hosta Hill)

Plate 65. *H. sieboldii* 'Kifukurin'; general habit (Hosta Hill)

Plate 68. *H. sieboldii* 'Silver Kabitan'; general habit, showing the maximum degree of viridescence of leaves (*H.* 'Haku Chu Han' is very similar); for comparison, *H. sieboldii* leaves (top right) (Hosta Hill)

Plate 67. *H. sieboldii* 'Subcrocea'; landscape use, flanking steps (Watkins garden/Schmid)

Plate 69. *H. takahashii*; flower detail (Hosta Hill)

Plate 70. *H. takiensis*; general habit,, with Japanese Painted Fern (*Athyrium niponicum* var. *pictum*) (Hosta Hill)

Plate 71. *H.* 'Tardiflora; general habit (Hosta Hill)

Plate 72. *H. tibae;* general habit, full bloom (Hosta Hill)

Plate 73. *H.* 'Tokudama'; general habit, with *H.* 'Gold Edger' and *H.* 'Wide Brim' right (Hosta Hill)

Plate 74. *H.* 'Tokudama Aureonebulosa'; general habit (Pollock garden/Schmid)

Plate 75. *H.* 'Tokudama Flavocircinalis'; general habit (Coney garden/Schmid)

Plate 76. *H.* 'Tokudama Flavoplanata'; general habit (Hosta Hill)

Plate 77. *H. tsushimensis*; general habit (Hosta Hill)

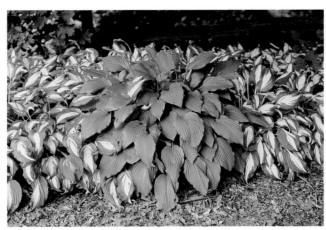

Plate 78. *H.* 'Undulata'; landscape use, center plant sporting to the all-green *H.* 'Undulata Erromena'; *H.* 'Undulata Univittata' form (left and right) (Flower Farm/Schmid)

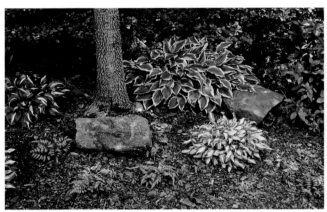

Plate 79. *H.* 'Undulata' forms; landscape use, *H.* 'Undulata Univittata' (left), *H.* 'Undulata Albomarginata' (center), and *H.* 'Undulata' standard form (right front) (Mitchell garden/ Schmid)

Plate 80. *H. ventricosa* 'Aureomaculata'; landscape use, with *H.* 'Middle Ridge' (Hosta Hill)

Plate 81. *H. ventricosa* 'Aureomarginata'; general habit, with *H.* 'Little Aurora' (bottom) (Hosta Hill)

Plate 82. *H. ventricosa* Yellow group; general habit (Hosta Hill)

Plate 83. *H. venusta*; natural habitat; Island Cheju Do, near Cheju City, Ch'onwangsa, alt. 600 m (1968 ft.) (M. G. Chung)

Plate 84. *H.* 'Abiqua Moonbeam'; general habit (top left), with other sports of *H.* 'August Moon': (top center) white margined, like *H.* 'Lunar Eclipse', but not cupped; (top right) *H.* 'Gosan August Clouds'; (bottom row) two *H.* 'September Sun' (originator's stock); all young plants (Hosta Hill)

Plate 85. *H.* 'Allan P. McConnell'; general habit (Hosta Hill)

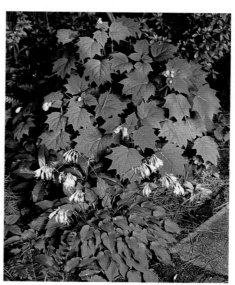

Plate 86. *H.* 'Amanuma'; general habit, landscape use, with *Kirengeshoma palmata* (Hosta Hill)

Plate 87. *H.* 'Anne Arett'; general habit (Hosta Hill)

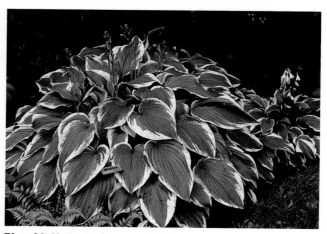

Plate 88. *H.* 'Antioch'; general habit (Hatfield garden/Schmid)

Plate 89. *H.* 'August Moon'; general habit (Hosta Hill)

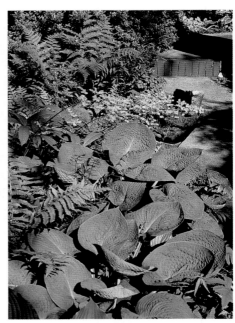

Plate 90. *H.* 'Big Daddy'; general habit, with ferns and blooming *Rodgersia sambucifolia* (Hosta Hill)

Plate 91. *H.* 'Birchwood Parkys Gold'; general habit, with *H.* 'Pearl Lake' (right) (Hosta Hill)

Plate 92. *H.* 'Blue Angel'; landscape use (Santa Lucia garden/Schmid)

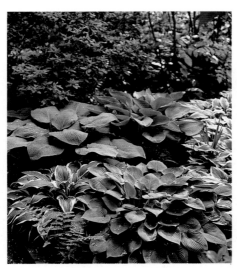

Plate 93. *H.* 'Blue Cadet'; general habit, with *H.* 'Neat Splash Rim' (left), *H.* 'Housatonic' (left rear), and *H. nigrescens* (right rear) (Hosta Hill)

Plate 94. *H.* 'Blue Rock'; general habit (Langdon garden/Schmid)

Plate 95. *H.* 'Blue Shadows'; general habit (Soules garden/Schmid)

Plate 96. *H.* 'Blue Wedgwood'; general habit (Pollock garden/Schmid)

Plate 97. *H.* 'Brim Cup'; landscape use (right), with *H.* 'So Sweet' (center) and *H.* 'Fragrant Gold' (left); *H. sieboldii* 'Subcrocea' (bottom) (Hosta Hill)

Plate 98. *H.* 'Carrie'; general habit (Hosta Hill)

Plate 99. *H.* 'Christmas Tree'; general habit (Soules garden/Schmid)

Plate 100. *H.* 'Color Glory' (right) showing different leaf form and color than *H.* 'Great Expectations' (left) (Hosta Hill)

Plate 101. *H.* 'Exotic Frances Williams'; general habit (Hosta Hill)

Plate 102. *H.* 'Fascination'; general habit (left), with *H.* 'Center Stage' (right) (Langdon garden/Schmid)

Plate 103. *H.* 'Flamboyant'; general habit, several clumps in various states of reversion to all-gold, white-centered, or white-margined forms (Wallace garden/Schmid)

Plate 104. *H.* 'Fortunei Albomarginata'; general habit, typical mature form (Blowing Rock/Schmid)

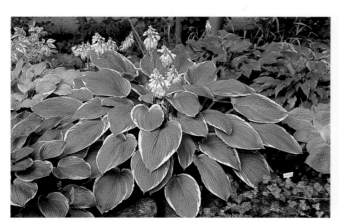

Plate 105. *H.* 'Frosted Jade'; general habit, typical mature form, in the border (Crockett garden/Schmid)

Plate 106. *H.* 'Gaiety'; general habit (Soules garden/Schmid)

Plate 107. *H.* 'Galaxy'; general habit (Soules garden/Schmid)

Plate 108. *H.* 'Gay Feather'; general habit (front), with *H.* 'Celebration' (rear) (Olson garden/Schmid)

Plate 109. *H.* 'Geisha'; general habit (Hosta Hill)

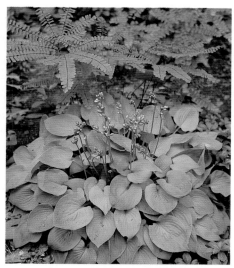

Plate 110. *H.* 'Gold Drop'; general habit, with Northern Maidenhair fern, *Adiantum pedatum* (Boon garden/Schmid)

Plate 111. *H.* 'Gold Regal'; general habit (Honeysong Farm/Schmid)

Plate 112. *H.* 'Gold Standard'; general habit (Coney garden/Schmid)

Plate 113. *H.* 'Golden Prayers'; general habit (Coney garden/Schmid)

Plate 114. *H.* 'Gosan Gold Sword'; general habit (Hosta Hill)

Plate 115. *H.* 'Gosan Mina'; general habit (Hosta Hill)

Plate 116. *H.* 'Green Marmalade'; general habit (Owens garden/Schmid)

Plate 117. *H.* 'Hadspen Hawk'; general habit (Pollock garden/Schmid)

Plate 118. *H.* 'Heaven Scent'[PPAF]; general habit; (Walters Gardens, Inc./Falstad)

Plate 119. *H.* 'Herifu'; general habit, with Japanese Painted Fern (*Athyrium niponicum* var. *pictum*) (Hosta Hill)

Plate 120. *H.* 'Hydon Sunset'; general habit (Hosta Hill)

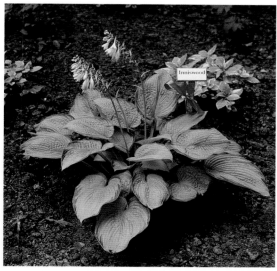

Plate 121. *H.* 'Inniswood'; general habit (Inniswood Botanic Garden/Schmid)

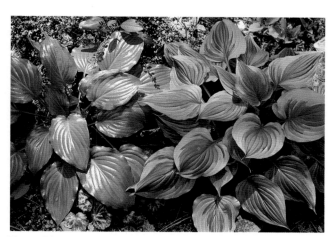

Plate 122. *H.* 'Invincible'; general habit (left), with *H. ventricosa* 'Aureomarginata' (right) (Hosta Hill)

Plate 123. *H.* 'Koriyama'; general habit (Hosta Hill)

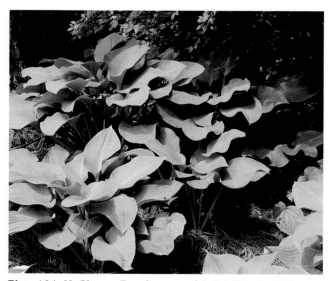

Plate 124. *H.* 'Krossa Regal'; general habit (Hosta Hill)

Plate 125. *H.* 'Leola Fraim'; general habit; (Hatfield garden/Schmid)

Plate 126. *H.* 'Lime Krinkles'; general habit (Soules garden/Schmid)

Plate 127. *H.* 'Little Jim'; general habit (Hosta Hill)

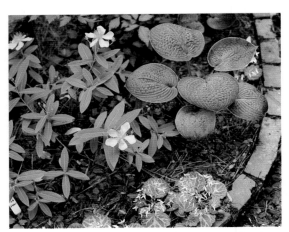

Plate 128. *H.* 'Love Pat'; general habit; young planting with yellow St. John's Wort (*Hypericum calycinum*) and Strawberry Geranium (*Saxifraga stolonifera*) (Hosta Hill)

Plate 129. *H.* 'Lunar Eclipse'; general habit; showing greenish vernal leaves and yellow summer leaves (Hosta Hill)

Plate 130. *H.* 'Mary Marie Ann'; general habit (Hosta Hill)

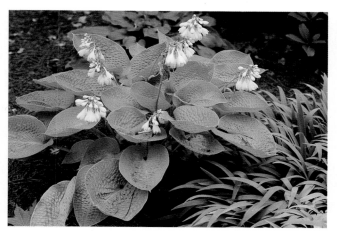

Plate 131. *H.* 'Midas Touch'; general habit (Coney garden/Schmid)

Plate 132. *H.* 'Moon Glow'; general habit; *H.* 'Hadspen Blue' on both sides (Coney garden/Schmid)

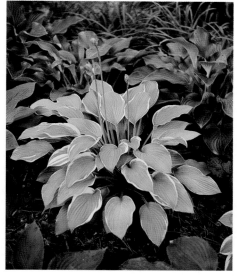

Plate 133. *H.* 'Moonlight'; general habit (Hosta Hill)

Plate 134. *H.* 'Northern Halo'; general habit; (Jones garden/Falstad)

Plate 135. *H.* 'Northern Lights'; general habit; (Jones garden/Falstad)

Plate 136. *H.* 'Piedmont Gold'; general habit (Hosta Hill)

Plate 138. *H.* 'Ryans Big One'; general habit, a cultivar form very close to *H. sieboldiana* 'Hypophylla' (Walters Gardens, Inc./Falstad)

Plate 137. *H.* 'Reginald Kaye'; general habit (front), with *H.* 'Shade Fanfare' (center), and *H.* 'Krossa Regal' (Hosta Hill)

Plate 139. *H.* 'Sea Thunder'; general habit (Hosta Hill)

Plate 140. *H.* 'September Sun'; general habit (Cooper garden/Solberg)

Plate 141. *H.* 'Snowden'; (center) in the border with yellow-margined *H. sieboldiana* 'Frances Williams' (foreground), and yellow-flowered potentilla (*Potentilla fructicosa*) (behind) (Hadspen House, UK/Schmid)

Plate 142. *H.* 'Sundance'; general habit; (Walters Gardens, Inc./Falstad)

Plate 143. *H.* 'Weihenstephan'; mass planting (RHS Wisley Garden/Schmid)

Plate 144. *H.* 'White Trouble'; general habit; *H.* 'Elata' (foreground) (Hosta Hill)

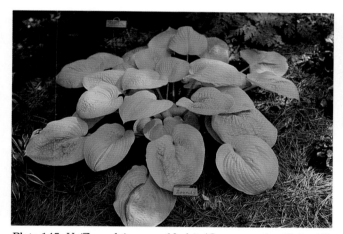

Plate 145. *H.* 'Zounds'; general habit (Coney garden/Schmid)

Plate 146. *H. fluctuans* 'Variegated' (*Sagae Giboshi*) (rear) dominates a splendid hosta garden (Satake garden, Higashi-Hiroshima)

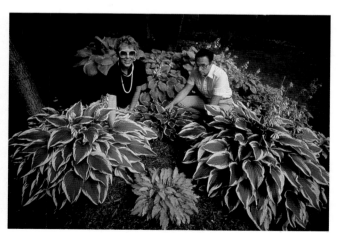

Plate 147. *H.* 'Antioch' (right and left), with *H.* 'Rosanne' (center), *H.* 'Sum and Substance' (left rear) (Pollock garden/Ali Pollock)

Plate 148. *Hosta* lining side entrance to Hosta Hill accentuates perspective and leads to a surprise (Hosta Hill)

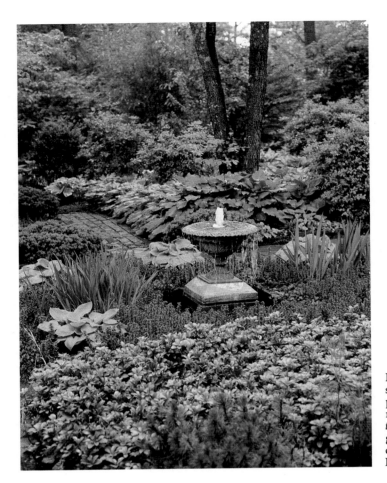

Plate 149. *H.* 'August Moon' clumps in a sea of blooming *Ajuga reptans* 'Atropurpurea' with *Crocosmia* 'Lucifer' surrounding a fountain; green *Pachysandra terminalis* (front), *H.* 'Honeybells' (background); this is seen after turning the corner on the walk in Plate 148 (Hosta Hill)

Plate 150. *H.* 'Undulata Erromena'; landscape use (private garden/Schmid)

Plate 151. *H.* 'Sum and Substance'; used as accent plant, with *H.* 'Blue Wedgwood' (bottom), *H.* 'Gold Standard' and *H. fluctuans* 'Variegated' (*Sagae*) (bottom right); *Azalea* 'Silver Sword' (above right) (Hosta Hill)

Plate 152. *H.* 'Gold Standard' (center) brightens area; *H. ventricosa* 'Aureomarginata' (left), with *H.* 'Fortunei Aureomarginata' (right) (Pollock garden/Ali Pollock)

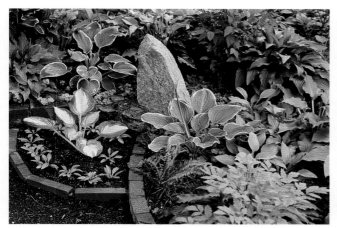

Plate 153. *H.* 'Great Expectations'; young plant used as accent, underplanted with *H.* 'Gosan Gold Midget'; *H.* 'Frosted Jade' (behind) and *H. fluctuans* 'Variegated' (*Sagae*) (right); *H. rectifolia* (top right background) (Hosta Hill)

Plate 154. *H.* 'Island Forest Gem'; used as focal point; *H.* 'Golden Tiara' (front) and *H.* 'Yellow Splash Rim' (behind) (Mitchell garden/Schmid)

Plate 155. *H.* 'Undulata'; used as edging (Flower Farm/Schmid)

Plate 156. *H.* 'Golden Tiara' (right) with *H.* 'Golden Scepter' blending into *Lamium maculatum* 'Beacon Silver', and *Ajuga reptans* 'Atropurpurea' framed by azaleas and *H.* 'Blue Ripples' (rear) (Hosta Hill)

Plate 157. *H.* 'Bright Glow' (focal point) with *H. hypoleuca* (left); the radiating leaf crown of *Amorphophallus rivieri* (above) with dark green Cast Iron Plant (*Aspidistra elatior*); blooming *H.* 'Nakaimo' (left) framed by *Acer japonicum* f. *aconitifolium* 'Maiku Jaku', and *Acer palmatum dissectum* 'Flavescens' (right) (Hosta Hill)

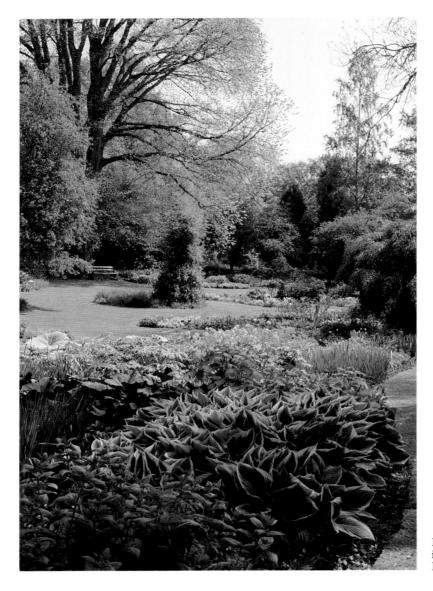

Plate 158. *H.* 'Fortunei Albomarginata' in island bed (Bressingham Gardens/Dr. Fischer)

Plate 159. *H.* 'Sacra' (right) anchoring the patio garden, framed by azaleas and *Acer palmatum dissectum*, with *H.* 'Fragrant Gold' and *H.* 'So Sweet' providing summer fragrance; *H. sieboldii* 'Subcrocea' used as edger (Hosta Hill)

Plate 160. *H. sieboldiana* 'Frances Williams' (rear) and *H.* 'Blue Cadet' forming a geometric pattern of threes; single clumps of yellow *H.* 'Zounds' (left) and *H.* 'Gold Edger' share the formal arrangement with ferns and azaleas; several more clumps of *H. sieboldii* 'Subcrocea' hide behind the front edging of *Liriope* (Mitchell garden/Schmid)

Plate 161. *H. sieboldiana* 'Golden Sunburst' used as accent (Pollock garden/Ali Pollock)

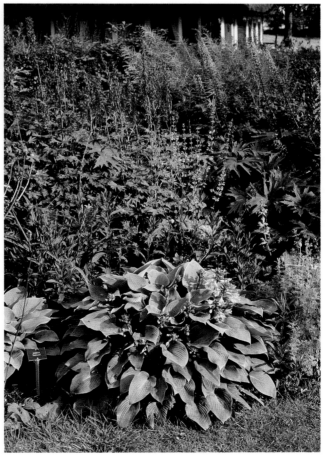

Plate 162. *H.* 'Halcyon' in a traditional English border (Stevens garden, UK/Schmid)

Plate 163. *H.* 'Snowden' with *Rodgersia* and *Miscanthus* at the lily pond (Hadspen House, UK/Schmid)

Plate 164. *H. sieboldiana* in the border with *Ligularia przewalskii* 'The Rocket' (Savill garden/Schmid)

Plate 165. *H.* 'Undulata Albomarginata' and *H.* 'Honeybells' used as foundation planting (Hosta Hill)

Plate 166. *H.* 'Golden Tiara' surrounding *Iris pallida* 'Argenteovariegata' at corner of raised island bed; *H.* 'Gosan Sigi Grey' (behind), followed by *H. sieboldiana* green form (right and left rear) (Hosta Hill)

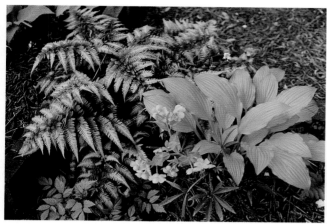

Plate 167. *H. cathayana* 'Ogon' with blooming *Helleborus foetidus* and Japanese Painted Fern (*Athyrium niponicum* var. *pictum*) (Hosta Hill)

Plate 168. *H. kikutii* with *Lamium maculatum* 'Beacon Silver' and Strawberry Geranium (*Saxifraga sarmentosa* or *stolonifera*) (Hosta Hill)

Plate 169. *H.* 'Shade Fanfare' planted in a group brightens up a dark area in Ursula Syre–Herz garden; underplanted with *Lamium maculatum* 'Beacon Silver' (Coastal Gardens/Schmid)

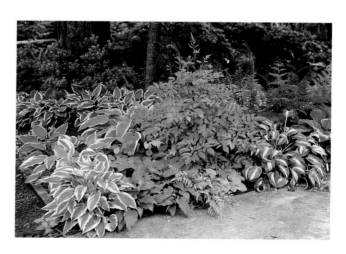

Plate 170. *H.* 'Little Aurora', next to Japanese Painted Fern (*Athyrium niponicum* var. *pictum*) dominated by *Astilbe*; *H.* 'Undulata Albomarginata' (left) followed by *H. longipes* var. *vulgata* and *H.* 'Fortunei Viridis'; *H.* 'Middle Ridge' (right) and *H.* 'Big Mama' (far right) (Patio garden, Hosta Hill)

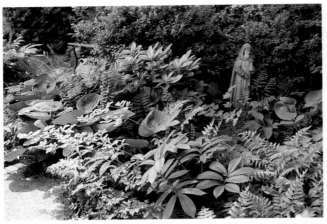

Plate 171. *H.* 'Big Daddy' and blooming *Rodgersia sambucifolia* (front), with rhododendron, azaleas, and ferns (Saint Fiacre Garden, Hosta Hill)

Plate 172. *H. sieboldiana* 'Elegans' with *Zantedeschia aethiopica* 'Crowborough' in Gordon Collier's bog garden, Taihape, New Zealand (Titoki Point garden/Collier)

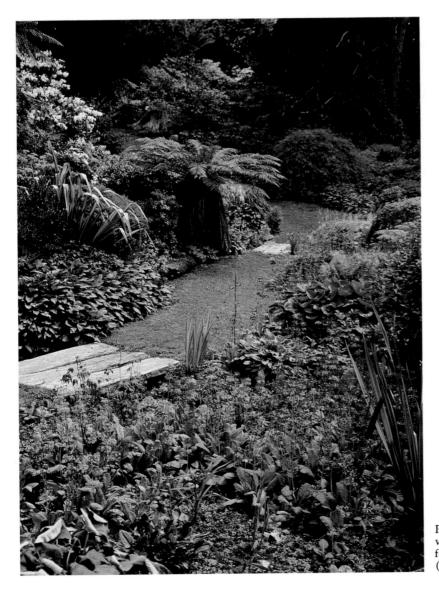

Plate 173. *H.* 'Tokudama' (right center), with other hostas, primulas, and tree fern, *Dicksonia fibrosa*, in the border (Titoki Point garden/Matthews)

Plate 174. *Hosta* border fronting the Director's House, RHS Wisley Garden (Wisley/Schmid)

Plate 175. *H. sieboldiana* 'Frances Williams' (right front) in the 'Great Hosta Border' at Hadspen House, UK (Schmid)

Plate 176. *H. sieboldiana* 'Golden Sunburst' backed by five *H. sieboldiana* 'Frances Williams' that form an accent group; *H.* 'Krossa Regal' (right and left in the rear) (Pollock garden/Schmid)

Plate 177. *Hosta* mass plantings alongside walks at RHS Wisley Garden (Schmid)

Plate 178. *H.* 'Fortunei Albomarginata'; mass planting (Satake garden, Higashi-Hiroshima)

Plate 179. *H.* 'Tall Boy' in the border with *Rheum palmatum* 'Atrosanguineum' at RHS Wisley Garden (Schmid)

Plate 180. *H.* 'Bold Edger' used as accent; *H.* 'Perrys True Blue' in background (J. C. Taylor garden/Schmid)

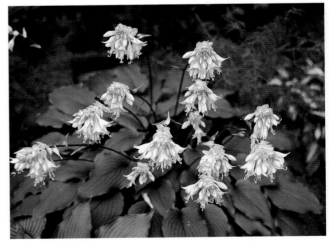

Plate 181. *H.* 'Nakaimo' flowers (Hosta Hill)

Plate 182. *H. laevigata* flower (Hosta Hill)

Plate 183. *H.* 'Undulata'; foliaceous bracts looking like a flower (Hosta Hill)

Plate 185. *Hosta* collection in border garden (Watkins garden/Schmid)

Plate 184. *H.* 'Fortunei' form with *H.* 'Undulata Albomarginata' fronted by yellow pansies (*Viola wittrockiana*) (Villa de Bella Fiore, Dorough design/Schmid)

Plate 186. *H.* 'Tokudama' used as focal point in very small garden corner framed by *Aucuba japonica* 'Gold Dust' and azaleas; rock, ferns, and contrasting hosta complete the design (Mitchell garden/Schmid)

Plate 187. *H.* hybrid used as accent plant on small rock promontory (UBC Botanic Garden, BC/Schmid)

Plate 188. *Hosta* collection in pots decorating front entrance (Coney garden/Schmid)

Plate 189. *H.* 'Undulata Albomarginata' in elevated terra cotta pot (Jasmine Hill garden/Schmid)

Plate 190. *H. sieboldii* f. *spathulata* (center), sharing small garden bed with *H. nakaiana* (left), *H. sieboldii* f. *angustifolia* (right), and *H.* 'Vera Verde' (extreme right) (Hosta Hill)

Plate 191. *H.* 'Saishu Jima' in a natural setting, growing on a rock ledge above stream; *H. aequinoctiiantha* (top left) (Hosta Hill)

Plate 192. *H.* 'Spinners' in the border (left center); *H.* 'Snowden' in full bloom behind it (left) (Spinners/Schmid))

Plate 193. *H. sieboldiana;* type A color lobes (Hosta Hill)

Plate 194. *H. montana;* type A color lobes (Hosta Hill)

Plate 195. *H. kikutii;* type A color lobes (Hosta Hill)

Plate 196. *H. kikutii* f. *leuconota* type A color lobes (Hosta Hill)

Plate 197. *H. ventricosa*; type B color lobes (Hosta Hill)

Plate 198. *H. nakaiana*; type B color lobes (Hosta Hill)

Plate 199. *H. takahashii*; type B color lobes (Hosta Hill)

Plate 200. *H. jonesii*; type B color lobes (Hosta Hill)

Plate 201. *H. sieboldii*; type C color lobes (Hosta Hill)

Plate 202. *H. sieboldii* f. *spathulata*; type C color lobes (Hosta Hill)

Plate 203. *H. rectifolia* var. *sachalinensis*; type C color lobes (Hosta Hill)

Plate 204. *H. tibae*; type C color lobes (Hosta Hill)

Plate 205. *H. longipes*; type D color lobes (Hosta Hill)

Plate 206. *H. longipes* f. *hypoglauca*; type D color lobes (Hosta Hill)

Plate 207. *H. aequinoctiiantha*; type D color lobes (Hosta Hill)

Plate 208. *H. hypoleuca*; type D color lobes (Hosta Hill)

Alphabetic Listing of Cultivated Varieties

A

H. **'Abiqua Ambrosia'** Walden-West IRA/1987.
AHS-III/13B.
Plant erect, 32 in. (81.5 cm) dia., 16 in. (40.5 cm) high. Leaf 6 by 5 in. (15 by 13 cm), veins 10, dark green, not variegated, round-cordate, cupped-rugose. Scape 18 in. (46 cm), foliated, straight. Flower medium, funnel-shaped, lavender, fragrant, flowers during average period, fertile.

H. **'Abiqua Blue Edger'** Walden-West IRA/1987.
AHS-IV/21B.
Plant 16 in. (40.5 cm) dia., 8 in. (20 cm) high. Leaf 4 by 4 in. (10 by 10 cm), veins 9, blue-green, not variegated, round-cordate, flat. Scape 16 in. (40.5 cm), foliated, straight. Flower medium, funnel-shaped, lavender, flowers during average period, fertile.

H. **'Abiqua Blue Jay'** Walden-West IRA/1988.
AHS-III/15B.
Plant, when young, is similar to the much smaller *H.* 'Blue Jay' (Benedict), which see. Plant 40 in. (101.5 cm) dia., 15 in. (38 cm) high. Leaf 7 by 4 in. (18 by 10 cm), veins 12, blue-green, not variegated, round-cordate, cupped-rugose. Scape 36 in. (91.5 cm), foliated, straight. Flower medium, white, flowers during summer period, fertile.
(see also *H.* 'Blue Jay').

H. **'Abiqua Blue Madonna'** Walden-West IRA/1988.
AHS-II-15A.
Plant 30 in. (76 cm) dia., 11 in. (28 cm) high. Leaf 7 by 6 in. (18 by 15 cm), veins 11, green, not variegated, cordate, flat. Scape 24 in. (61 cm), foliated, oblique. Flower medium, flowers during average period, fertile.

H. **'Abiqua Blue Shield'** Walden-West IRA/1988.
AHS-II/9B.
Plant 50 in. (127 cm) dia., 22 in. (56 cm) high. Leaf 7 by 6 in. (18 by 15 cm), veins 11, green, not variegated, cordate, flat. Scape 22 in. (56 cm), foliated, straight. Flower medium, bell-shaped, white, flowers during average period, fertile.
[*H. sieboldiana* hybrid].

H. **'Abiqua Drinking Gourd'** Walden-West IRA/1989.
Plant 14 in. (35.5 cm) dia., 16 in. (40.5 cm) high. Leaf 8 by 8 in. (20 by 20 cm), veins 15, blue-green, not variegated, round-cordate, cupped-rugose. Scape 22 in. (56 cm), foliated, straight. Flower medium, bell-shaped, white, flowers during average period, fertile.
[*H.* 'Tokudama' × *H. sieboldiana*].

H. **'Abiqua Gold Shield'** Walden-West IRA/1987.
AHS-II/11B.
Plant 32 in. (81.5 cm) dia., 20 in. (51 cm) high. Leaf 11 by 8 in. (28 by 20 cm), veins 15, chartreuse, not variegated, round-cordate, rugose. Scape 24 in. (61 cm), foliated, straight. Flower medium, bell-shaped, whitish, flowers during average period, fertility(?).
[*H.* 'White Vision' hybrid].

H. **'Abiqua Ground Cover'** Walden-West IRA/1988.
AHS-V/25B.
Plant is stoloniferous, 12 in. (31 cm) dia., 9 in. (23 cm) high. Leaf 2.5 by 2 in. (6 by 5 cm), veins 6, green, not variegated, cordate, flat. Scape 15 in. (38 cm), foliated, straight. Flower medium, bell-shaped, lavender, flowers during average period, fertile.

H. **'Abiqua Hallucination'** Walden-West.
Plant has been reported as a reverse mutation of *H. tokudama* 'Flavocircinalis', with yellow leaf center and sea-green margin. Summers (1989b) remarked it may be *H.* 'Tokudama Flavoplanata'.

H. **'Abiqua Miniature'** Walden-West IRA/1988.
AHS-VI/31A.
Plant 7 in. (18 cm) dia., 3 in. (7.5 cm) high. Leaf 1.5 by 0.5 in. (4 by 1 cm), veins 3, green, not variegated, cordate, flat. Scape 8 in. (20 cm), foliated, straight. Flower medium, bell-shaped, lavender, flowers during average period, fertility(?).

H. **'Abiqua Moonbeam'** Walden-West IRA/1987.
AHS-III/16B. (Plate 84).
Plant is reported by Solberg (1988a) and Summers (1989a) to be equal to *H.* 'Mayan Moon' (never registered). This has been confirmed, so the correct name for the latter will be *H.* 'Abiqua Moonbeam'. Plant 30 in. (76 cm) dia., 26 in. (66 cm) high. Leaf 7 by 6 in. (18 by 15 cm), veins 9, blue-green, chartreuse margins, round-cordate, rugose. Scape 24 in. (61 cm), bare, straight. Flower medium, bell-shaped, whitish, flowers during average period, fertile.
[*H.* 'August Moon' mutation].
(see also *H.* 'Mayan Moon').

H. **'Abiqua Pagoda'** Walden-West IRA/1989.
Plant 38 in. (96.5 cm) dia., 28 in. (71 cm) high. Leaf 13 by 12 in. (33 by 30 cm), veins 13, blue-green, not variegated, round-cordate, rugose, margins down-turned at tip. Scape 32 in. (81.5 cm), bare, straight. Flower medium, bell-shaped, whitish, flowers during average period, fertile.
[*H. sieboldiana* hybrid].

H. **'Abiqua Parasol'** Walden-West IRA/1987.
AHS-I/3B.
Plant 48 in. (122 cm) dia., 26 in. (66 cm) high. Leaf 14 by 10 in. (36 by 25.5 cm), veins 14–16, blue-green, not variegated, round-cordate, rugose, margins ruffled and down-turned. Scape 32 in. (81.5 cm), bare, straight. Flower medium, bell-shaped, whitish, flowers during average period, fertile.
[*H. sieboldiana* 'Elegans' hybrid].

H. **'Abiqua Recluse'** Walden-West IRA/1989.
  Plant 30 in. (76 cm) dia., 18 in. (46 cm) high. Leaf 13 by 8 in. (33 by 20 cm), veins 15, yellow, not variegated, cordate, rugose. Scape 32 in. (81.5 cm), bare, straight. Flower medium, funnel-shaped, whitish lavender, flowers during average period, fertile.
  [*H.* 'White Vision' × *H.* 'Sum and Substance'].

H. **'Abiqua Trumpet'** Walden-West IRA/1987.
  AHS-IV/21B.
  Plant 21 in. (53.5 cm) dia., 10 in. (25.5 cm) high. Leaf 4 by 4 in. (10 by 10 cm), veins 7, blue-green, not variegated, round-cordate, cupped-rugose. Scape 18 in. (46 cm), foliated, straight. Flower medium, bell-shaped, lavender, flowers during summer period, fertile.
  [*H.* 'Tokudama' form]

H. **'Ada Reed'** Suggs IRA/1988.
  AHS-III/17B.
  Plant erect, 24 in. (61 cm) dia., 18 in. (46 cm) high. Leaf 4 by 3 in. (10 by 7.5 cm), veins 6, chartreuse, not variegated, cordate, wavy. Scape 18 in. (46 cm), foliated, straight. Flower medium, lavender, flowers during average period, fertile.
  [*H.* 'August Moon' × *H.* 'Sunglow'].

H. **'Aden No. 000'** Aden.
  Plants numbered by Paul Aden, well-known hybridizer, to record the parents of his crosses; for example, *H.* 'Aden No. 365' × *H.* 'Aden No. 361' (=*H.* 'Blue Angel'). Reference to these numbers is made frequently in this chapter. While Aden has published the numbers he has not identified or described most of them. They have been included here for comprehensiveness and may be identified in a future edition of this book.

H. **'Ahamo Gold'** Geissler IRA/1969.
  AHS-III/17B.
  Plant's name is derived from the city of Omaha, spelled backwards. Holds color. Plant 24 in. (61 cm) dia., 11 in. (28 cm) high. Leaf 9 by 8 in. (23 by 20 cm), veins 14, chartreuse, not variegated, cordate, rugose. Scape, 20 in. (51 cm), bare, straight. Flower medium, bell-shaped, white, flowers during average period, fertile.
  HN: *H.* 'Ahoma Gold' incorrect.
  [*H. sieboldiana* hybrid].

H. **'Akarana'** Applegate 1985.
  Plant is one received by Wade and Gatton Nurseries from C. Applegate. Similar to *H. venusta* and probably an F$_1$ hybrid form of the species.
  (see *H. venusta*).

H. 'Akebono' Krossa incorrect.
  Plant is one received by Krossa from Japan and sent to Hensen, Wageningen Botanic Garden, Netherlands, in 1967. A herbarium specimen in WAG, no. DE-41/525-46, is identified incorrectly by Hensen as *H. tsushimensis*. Identification from a dried specimen is difficult but this taxon is similar to a glaucous, blue-green cultivar which has been found in North American gardens where it is mistakenly labeled *H. densa*. This is not the same as *Akebono Tokudama Giboshi* Kikuchi 1934 = *H.* 'Tokudama Aureonebulosa'. The name *H.* 'Akebono' is invalid when applied to Krossa's plant.
  HN: *H. densa* incorrect.

H. **'Aksarben'** Geissler/Ruh IRA/1988.
  AHS-I/3B.
  Plant's name is Nebraska spelled backwards. Plant 36 in. (76 cm) dia., 21 in. (53.5 cm) high. Leaf 12 by 9 in. (31 by 23 cm), veins 10–13, blue-green, not variegated, round-cordate, rugose. Scape 28 in. (71 cm), foliated, straight. Flower medium, bell-shaped, white, flowers during average period, fertile.
  HN: *H.* 'Omaha Gold' Geissler.
  [*H. sieboldiana* × *H.* 'Tokudama'].

H. **'Alabama Bowl'** Suggs IRA/1986.
  AHS-II/9B.
  Plant 36 in. (91.5 cm) dia., 24 in. (61 cm) high. Leaf 11 by 9 in. (28 by 23 cm), veins 15, blue-green, not variegated, round-cordate, cupped-rugose. Scape 28 in. (71 cm), bare, straight. Flower medium, bell-shaped, white, flowers during average period, fertile.
  [*H. sieboldiana* 'Elegans' × *H.* 'Big Mama'].

H. **'Alabama Gold'** Suggs IRA/1986.
  AHS-II/11A.
  Plant 33 in. (84 cm) dia., 25 in. (63.5 cm) high. Leaf 11 by 9 in. (28 by 23 cm), veins 15, yellow (lutescent), not variegated, cordate, rugose. Scape 28 in. (71 cm), bare, straight. Flower medium, bell-shaped, white, flowers during average period, fertile.
  HN: *H. sieboldiana* Yellow group.
  [*H.* 'Golden Waffles' hybrid].

H. 'Albo-Aurea' hort. UK.
  Plant name is an incorrect synonym.
  (see *H.* 'Antioch').

H. 'Albomarginata' hort.
  Plant name is an incorrect synonym.
  (see *H. sieboldii*).

H. 'Albomarginata Thunbergiana' hort.
  Plant name is an incorrect synonym.
  (see *H. sieboldii* f. *spathulata*).

H. **'Alex Summers'** Santa Lucia IRA/1989.
  Plant is a mutation of *H.* 'Gold Regal' with a wide, irregular, chartreuse margin. All other characteristics similar to *H.* 'Gold Regal'. Plant erect, 24 in. (61 cm) dia., 20 in. (51 cm) high. Leaf 7 by 5 in. (18 by 13 cm), veins 13, yellowish chartreuse, darker chartreuse margin, ovate, flat. Scape 28 in. (71 cm), bare, straight. Flower medium, bell-shaped, purple, flowers during average period, fertile.
  [*H.* 'Gold Regal' mutation].

H. **'Allan P. McConnell'** McConnell/Seaver IRA/1980.
  AHS-IV/22A.   (Plate 85).
  Plant is a white-margined hybrid of *H. nakaiana* and has ridges on scape which are identical to those of the species *H. nakaiana*. As a cultivar it is widely planted; it is an excellent small white-margined hosta. Plant 18 in. (46 cm) dia., 8 in. (20 cm) high. Leaf 3 by 2 in. (7.5 by 5 cm), veins 4, dark green, white margin, ovate, flat. Scape 15 in. (38 cm), bare, straight. Flower medium, bell-shaped, purple, flowers during average period, fertile.
  (see also *H. nakaiana* 'Shirofukurin').

H. **'Alpha Beta'** Calderara.
  Plant 6 in. (15 cm) dia., 6 in. (15 cm) high. Leaf 2 by 2 in. (5 by 5 cm), veins 8, blue-green, not variegated, cordate, flat.
  HN: *H.* 'Carl Calderaras Hybrid'.

H. **'Alpine Aire'** Minks 1973 IRA/1980.
  AHS-III/17B.
  Plant 20 in. (51 cm) dia., 14 in. (35.5 cm) high. Leaf 5 by 4

in. (13 by 10 cm), veins 10, yellow (lutescent), not variegated, cordate, rugose. Scape 20 in. (51 cm), bare, straight. Flower medium, bell-shaped, white, flowers during summer period, fertile.
[*H.* 'August Moon' × *H.* 'Wagon Wheels'].

H. 'Alpine Dream' Savory IRA/1982.
AHS-IV/19A.
Plant 20 in. (51 cm) dia., 9 in. (23 cm) high. Leaf medium green, not variegated, cordate, rugose. Scape 18 in. (46 cm), bare, straight. Flower medium, bell-shaped, purple, flowers during average period, fertile.
[*H. venusta* × *H. venusta*].

H. 'Alvantine Taylor' Minks.
Plant of excellent morphology. Medium-to-large-size leaves of dark greyish green with even yellowish white margins and a surface sheen later in the season, veins 11.

H. 'Amagi Nishiki' Japan.
天城錦
Plant is a large-leaved sport of *H. longipes* var. *latifolia* with yellow center and narrow green margin; found on Izu Peninsula.
HN: *H. longipes* var. *latifolia* 'Amagi Nishiki'.
JN: *Amagi Nishiki Giboshi* hort.
(see also *H. longipes* var. *latifolia* 'Amagi Nishiki').

H. 'Amanogawa' Japan.
天の川
Plant is a *H. montana* with light green leaves and yellow suffused, center with yellow stripes and streaks.
HN: *H.* 'Ama no gawa'.
H. montana 'Ama no gawa'.
H. montana 'Amanogawa'.
JN: *Amanogawa Giboshi* hort.

H. 'Amanuma' Maekawa 1960.
アマヌマギボウシ (Figure 4-1; Plate 86).
Plant is a hybrid made by Maekawa and named for the address of his garden in Tokyo. Maekawa (1960) published a diagram of his experimental cross, showing it to be *H. venusta* × *H. capitata*. It is similar to *H. nakaiana*, but has slightly larger leaves; the ridges on the scape are identical to those on the species. Plant 14 in. (35.5 cm) dia., 8 in. (20 cm) high. Leaf 3 by 2 in. (7.5 by 5 cm), veins 5, medium green, not variegated, ovate, flat. Scape 16 in. (40.5 cm), bare, straight. Flower small, bell-shaped, purple, flowers during early period, fertile.
JN: *Amanuma Giboshi* (*H. amanuma*) hort.
[*H. venusta* × *H. capitata*].

Figure 4-1. *H.* 'Amanuma'; general habit, detail (Hosta Hill)

H. 'Amber Maiden' Walters Gardens IRA/1988.
AHS-IV/22B.
Plant has deep green center with chartreuse margin which becomes yellow. Plant 16 in. (40.5 cm) dia., 14 in. (35.5 cm) high. Leaf 5 by 4 in. (13 by 10 cm), veins 10, green (lutescent), chartreuse margin, cordate, cupped. Scape 22 in. (56 cm), bare, straight. Flower medium, bell-shaped, lavender, flowers during average period, sterile.
[*H.* 'Candy Hearts' mutation].

H. 'Amy Aden' Aden IRA/1980.
AHS-IV/22A.
Plant 22 in. (56 cm) dia., 14 in. (35.5 cm) high. Leaf 3 by 2 in. (7.5 by 5 cm), veins 6, chartreuse, white-and-green streaked, ovate, flat. Scape 18 in. (46 cm), foliated, straight. Flower medium, bell-shaped, lavender, flowers during average period, fertility(?).
[*H.* 'Fascination' × *H.* 'High Fat Cream'].

H. 'Amy Aden Rim' Aden.
Plant 22 in. (56 cm) dia., 14 in. (35.5 cm) high. Leaf 3 by 2 in. (7.5 by 5 cm), veins 7, chartreuse, white margin, ovate, flat. Scape 18 in. (46 cm), foliated, straight. Flower medium, bell-shaped, lavender, flowers during average period, fertility(?).
[*H.* 'Fascination' × *H.* 'High Fat Cream' mutation].

H. 'Anderson No. 120' Anderson.
[*H.* 'Gold Drop' hybrid].

H. 'Ani Machi' Japan.
阿仁ギボウシ
Ani Giboshi, the "hosta (from) Ani Machi," is named for the town of Ani, Akita Prefecture, northeastern Honshu. A *H. sieboldii* × *H. rectifolia* intermediate form with yellow center and green margin. Reported to be similar or equal to *H.* 'Geisha' (Plate 109) or a selected form of it. This has not been confirmed and different plants have been observed under this name.
HN: *H. animachi* hort. incorrect.
H. 'Geisha' sel pp.
JN: *Ani Giboshi.*
Michinoku Nishiki Giboshi pp sim.
[*H. rectifolia* mutation] (?).
(see also *H.* 'Geisha').

H. 'Anne Arett' Arett IRA/1975.
AHS-IV/20B. (Plate 87).
Plant erect, 8 in. (20 cm) dia., 10 in. (25.5 cm) high. Leaf 5 by 1 in. (13 by 2.5 cm), veins 3, yellow (viridescent), white margin, flat. Scape 14 in. (35.5 cm), bare, straight. Flower medium, funnel-shaped, purple striped, flowers during summer period, fertile.
HN: *H. sieboldii* 'Anne Arett'.
[*H. sieboldii* 'Subcrocea' mutation].
[*H. sieboldii* derivation].

H. 'Anteach'.

H. 'Anticipation' Savill Gardens UK.
Plant looks like *H. sieboldiana* but has pruinose medium-green leaves.
[*H. sieboldiana* × *H.* 'Fortunei' form].

H. 'Antioch' Tompkins/Ruh/Hofer IRA/1979.
AHS-III/16A. (Figure 6-5; Plates 88, 147).
AHS multiple award winner: Eunice Fisher Award, 1986, exhibited by Richard Ward; ALAHOSO Bowl, exhibited by Richard Ward; AHS Alex J. Summers Distinguished Merit

Hosta, 1984, selected by Peter Ruh. It is inexpensive and one of the best white-margined hostas. Plants sold in the United Kingdom under the names *H.* 'Goldbrook' and *H.* 'Spinners' are very similar but have narrower leaves which may become wider and equal to *H.* 'Antioch' when plants are allowed to mature. *Hosta* 'Moerheim' is a name used in the Netherlands for a taxon which also looks like *H.* 'Antioch', as verified by a plant sent to Hosta Hill by C. Klyne and Co., Netherlands. According to Tompkins (1985), a similar taxon was given the seedling number 1928-7 W E in the 1920s and has subsequently been identified as *H.* 'Antioch'. Side-by-side comparisons of *H.* 'Shogun' and *H.* 'Antioch' show both taxa to be very much alike. In all these plants the margin color starts out yellow and turns white. *Hosta* 'Antioch' is frequently and incorrectly sold as *H.* 'Fortunei Albomarginata' but the latter is a distinct taxon when mature (compare Plate 88 with Plate 104), and has margins that start out almost white and remain that color.

    Plant 36 in. (91.5 cm) dia., 20 in. (51 cm) high. Leaf 10 by 8 in. (25.5 by 20 cm), veins 7, medium green, white margin, ovate, flat. Scape 32 in. (81.5 cm), foliated, oblique. Flower medium, funnel-shaped, lavender, flowers during average period, sterile.

HN: *H.* 'Albo-Aurea' hort. UK incorrect.
      H. fortunei albo aurea hort. sim UK incorrect.
      H. fortunei aureo alba hort. sim incorrect.
      H. fortunei aureomarmorata hort. incorrect.
      H. 'Fortunei Goldbrook'.
      H. 'Fortunei Moerheim' sim.
      H. 'Fortunei Moerheimii' sim incorrect.
      H. fortunei moerheimii hort. sim incorrect.
      H. 'Goldbrook' sim Goldbrook UK.
      H. 'Moerheim' sim Holland.
      H. 'No. 1928-7 W E' Tompkins 1984.
      H. 'Shogun' pp sim.
      H. 'Spinners' sim Smith/Chappell UK.
      H. 'Yellow Boy'.
[*H.* 'Fortunei' hybrid].

H. 'Aochidori' Japan.
アオチドリギボウシ
JN: *Aochidori Giboshi.*

H. 'Aoki' Siebold 1879.
(see *H. fortunei aoki*).

H. 'Aoki Variegated' hort.
(see *H.* 'Fortunei Aoki Variegated').

H. 'Apple Court Gold' Grenfell and Grounds 1988.
    Plant is named for Apple Court, the garden of Grenfell and Grounds, Lymington, Hampshire, UK. Leaf 7 by 5 in. (18 by 13 cm), veins 13, yellow (lutescent), not variegated, round-cordate, rugose. Scape 25 in. (63.5 cm), foliated, straight. Flower medium, funnel-shaped, lavender, flowers during average period, fertile.
[*H. sieboldiana* 'Semperaurea' × *H.* 'Tokudama Flavocircinalis'].

H. 'Apple Green' Anderson IRA/1982.
    AHS-IV/19B.
    Plant 16 in. (40.5 cm) dia., 10 in. (25.5 cm) high. Leaf 4 by 3 in. (10 by 7.5 cm), veins 6, chartreuse to light green, not variegated, cordate, flat. Scape 18 in. (46 cm), bare, straight. Flower medium, bell-shaped, white, flowers during average period, fertile.
[*H. nakaiana* hybrid].

H. 'Aqua Velva' Vaughn IRA/1983.
    AHS-II/9B.
    Plant 36 in. (91.5 cm) dia., 28 in. (71 cm) high. Leaf 9.5 by 4 in. (24 by 20 cm), veins 12, blue-green, not variegated, ovate, rugose. Scape 33 in. (84 cm), foliated, oblique. Flower medium, bell-shaped, lavender, flowers during average period, fertile.
[*H.* 'Polly Bishop' × *H.* 'Blue Lace'].

H. 'Arctic Circle' Tompkins 1985.
    Plant is a white-margined form with rather elongated, cordate leaves. Pruinose in spring.

H. 'Arechi' Japan.
アレチギボウシ
    Plant name is an incorrect Japanese synonym for *H.* 'Tortifrons'.
JN: *Arechi Giboshi.*
(see *H.* 'Tortifrons').

H. 'Aretts Wonder' Arett IRA/1986.
    AHS-I/3B.
    Plant looks like the parent and is very large.
[*H. sieboldiana* hybrid].

H. 'Art Shane' Aden.

H. 'Artists Palette' Kuk's Forest IRA/1986.
    AHS-V/28B.
    Plant erect, 6 in. (15 cm) dia., 6 in. (15 cm) high. Leaf 3 by 1 in. (7.5 by 2.5 cm), veins 3, medium green, streaked white, lanceolate, flat. Scape 14 in. (35.5 cm), bare, straight. Flower medium, bell-shaped, purple striped, flowers during summer period, fertile.
[*H.* 'Neat Splash' hybrid].

H. 'Asahi Comet' Kato/Zumbar IRA/1984.
    AHS-V/4A.
アサヒ白覆輪ギボウシ
    Plant erect, 8 in. (20 cm) dia., 6 in. (15 cm) high. Leaf 5 by 0.5 in. (13 by 1 cm), veins 3, medium green, white margin, strap-leaf, flat. Scape 16 in. (40.5 cm), bare, straight. Flower medium, bell-shaped, purple striped, flowers during summer period, fertile.
HN: *H. longissima* 'Asahi Comet'.
JN: *Asahi Shirofukurin Giboshi* hort.
      Shirofukurin Nagaba Mizu Giboshi hort.
(see also *H. longissima* var. *longifolia* 'Shirofukurin').

H. 'Asahi Sunray' Kato/Zumbar IRA/1984.
    AHS-V/4A.
アサヒ黄覆輪ギボウシ
    Plant erect, 12 in. (31 cm) dia., 8 in. (20 cm) high. Leaf 6 by 0.75 in. (15 by 2 cm), veins 3, medium green, yellow margin, strap-leaf, flat. Scape 18 in. (46 cm), bare, straight. Flower medium, bell-shaped, purple striped, flowers during summer period, fertile.
HN: *H. longissima* 'Asahi Sunray'.
JN: *Asahi Kifukurin Giboshi* hort.
      Kifukurin Nagaba Mizu Giboshi hort.
(see also *H. longissima* var. *longifolia* 'Kifukurin').

H. 'Aspen Gold' Grapes 1970 IRA/1986.
    AHS-III/17A.
    Plant attributed to *H.* 'Tokudama' line, but vein count of mature plants indicates *H. sieboldiana* is also involved. Plant erect, 36 in. (91.5 cm) dia., 20 in. (51 cm) high. Leaf 8 by 7 in. (20 by 17 cm), veins 14–18, chartreuse to yellow, not

variegated, round-cordate, cupped-rugose. Scape 25 in. (63.5 cm), foliated, straight. Flower medium, funnel-shaped, white, flowers during average period, fertile.
[*H. sieboldiana* Yellow group form].
[*H.* 'Tokudama Aureonebulosa Yellow' group form].

H. 'Assuage' Aden 1975.

H. 'Asuka' Japan.
明日香
Plant is a dwarf with fragrant white flowers. Named for Asuka, an old district name in Nara Prefecture.
JN: *Asuka Giboshi* hort.

H. 'August Moon' Langfelder/Summers IRA/1968.
AHS-III/17B.   (Figures 6-8; Plates 84, 89, 149).
AHS President's Exhibitor Trophy, 1978, exhibited by Loleta Powell. Often called a "Golden Sieboldiana," which is not. Mature leaves have only 9 principal veins. The flowers are similar to those of *H. sieboldiana*, so it is probably a hybrid between *H.* 'Fortunei' and *H. sieboldiana*. The leaves appearing in spring are rugose and greenish yellow after which a flush of summer leaves appear that are yellow and flat. Of unknown origin, it was found in Langfelder's garden, Chappaqua, NY, in 1964. Summers named and registered it in 1969. It has been extensively used for breeding and is predisposed to mutate to various variegated forms: dark green center/chartreuse margin = *H.* 'Abiqua Moonbeam' and *H.* 'Mayan Moon'; chartreuse to pale green center/pale green margin unnamed (referred to as the "False September Sun"); yellow center/dark green margin = *H.* 'September Sun'; yellow center/white margin = *H.* 'Lunar Eclipse'; yellow leaf/white splashes and streaks = *H.* 'Gosan August Clouds'; and others (Plate 84).
Plant 30 in. (76 cm) dia., 20 in. (51 cm) high. Leaf 6 by 5 in. (15 by 13 cm), veins 9, yellow (lutescent), not variegated, round-cordate, cupped-rugose. Scape 28 in. (71 cm), bare, straight. Flower medium, bell-shaped, white, flowers during average period, fertile.
HN: *H.* 'Golden Sieboldiana' incorrect.
H. 'Late Gold' Summers no. 30 1966.
H. 'Krossa F-7' Summers no. 30 1966.
[*H.* 'Fortunei' form × *H. sieboldiana* form ad int].

H. 'Aurea Folia' Starker incorrect.
Plant name is an incorrect synonym.
(see *H.* 'Starker Aureafolia').

H. 'Aurora Borealis' Wayside IRA/1986.
AHS-II/10B.
Plant is a robust yellow marginate form of *H. sieboldiana*. Grows larger than and is reportedly not as prone to necrosis as *H. sieboldiana* 'Frances Williams'. Other authors consider it merely the mature form of the latter. Plant 44 in. (112 cm) dia., 24 in. (61 cm) high. Leaf 13 by 11 in. (33 by 28 cm), veins 16, blue-green, yellow margin, cordate, rugose. Scape 30 in. (76 cm), bare, straight. Flower medium, bell-shaped, white, flowers during average period, fertile.
HN: *H.* 'Chicago Frances Williams'.
H. sieboldiana Aureomarginata group.
[*H. sieboldiana* 'Frances Williams' mutation].

H. 'Aztec Treasure' Vaughn IRA/1987.
AHS-III/17A.
Plant 26 in. (66 cm) dia., 12 in. (31 cm) high. Leaf, veins 13, chartreuse, not variegated, cordate, rugose. Scape 28 in. (71 cm), bare, straight. Flower medium, bell-shaped, purple, flowers during average period, fertile.
[*H.* 'Golden Waffles' × *H.* 'Rough Waters' hybrid].

B

H. 'Baby Bunting' Savory IRA/1982.
AHS-IV/21A.
AHS Savory Shield Award, 1980, exhibited by Robert Savory. Round leaf, blue-green, small. Plant 12 in. (31 cm) dia., 6 in. (18 cm) high. Leaf 1.5 by 1.5 in. (4 by 4 cm), veins 4, blue-green, not variegated, cordate-round, flat. Scape 20 in. (51 cm), bare, oblique. Flower medium, bell-shaped, white, flowers during average period, sterile.
Savory no. 279.
HN: *H.* 'Betsy Bunting' incorrect.
[*H.* 'Rough Waters' hybrid × hybrid] (?).

H. 'Baby Moon'.

H. 'Ballerina' Savory IRA/1982.
AHS-IV/19A.
Plant 24 in. (61 cm) dia., 12 in. (31 cm) high. Leaf 4 by 3 in. (10 by 7.5 cm), medium green, not variegated, cordate, flat. Scape 20 in. (51 cm), bare, straight. Flower medium, bell-shaped, white, flowers during average period, fertile.
[*H. venusta* hybrid].

H. 'Balsam' Houseworth 1986.
Plant 24 in. (61 cm) dia., 14 in. (35.5 cm) high. Leaf 7 by 6 in. (18 by 15 cm), veins 8, dark green, not variegated, cordate, rugose. Scape 24 in. (61 cm), bare, oblique. Flower medium, bell-shaped, white, flowers during average period, fertile.
[*H.* 'August Moon' hybrid].

H. 'Banana Sundae' Minks 1973 IRA/1980.
AHS-III/14A.   (Figure 4-2).
Plant's variegation is reported unstable and different from leaf to leaf. Parts of plant revert to all green. Plant 26 in. (66 cm) dia., 20 in. (51 cm) high. Leaf 8 by 6 in. (20 by 15 cm), veins 9, chartreuse, streaked white, ovate, flat. Scape 32 in. (81.5 cm), bare, oblique. Flower medium, funnel-shaped, lavender, flowers during average period, sterile.
[*H.* 'Fortunei' hybrid mutation].

Figure 4-2. *H.* 'Banana Sundae'; general habit (Hosta Hill)

H. 'Banyais Dancing Girl' Banyai IRA/1987.
AHS-IV/21A.
Plant 18 in. (46 cm) dia., 12 in. (31 cm) high. Leaf 4 by 3 in. (10 by 7.5 cm), veins 7, pruinose blue-green, flat. Scape 18 in. (46 cm), bare, straight. Flower medium, bell-shaped, lavender, flowers during average period, fertile.
[*H.* 'Blue Boy' hybrid].

H. **'Barbara'** Stone/Ruh IRA/1987.
AHS-IV/21A.
Plant 12 in. (31 cm) dia., 10 in. (25.5 cm) high. Leaf 4 by 2.5 in. (10 by 6 cm), veins 6, blue-green, not variegated, cordate, flat. Scape 20 in. (51 cm), bare, oblique. Flower medium, bell-shaped, lavender, flowers during average period, sterile.
HN: *H.* 'Barbra' incorrect.
       H. 'DSM No. 10' Stone.
[*H. nakaiana* hybrid ad int].

H. **'Barbara White'** Goldbrook.
Plant has round, lutescent chartreuse leaves and white flowers. The name honors the late Miss Barbara White of Reading, Berkshire, England, who served as secretary of The Hardy Plant Society for 23 years until her death in 1987.

H. **'Beatrice Green'** hort.
Plant is an all-green stable reversion from the unstable variegated form. The reverted plant is the green form of *H. sieboldii*, botanically known as *H. sieboldii* f. *spathulata*, of which many different forms exist.
HN: *H.* 'Beatrice Green Form' hort. incorrect.
[*H. sieboldii* hybrid].
[*H. sieboldii* mutation al].
[*H. sieboldii* 'Subcrocea' mutation].
[*H. sieboldii* derivative].
(see *H. sieboldii* f. *spathulata*).
(see also *H.* 'Green Beatrice').

H. **'Beatrice'** Williams (No. 1399A) 1962.
Plant is similar in habit to hybrids of *H. sieboldii*, but is an unstable, variegated form, streaked yellow, with some leaves margined yellow. No two leaves alike and a number of different plants bear this name.
HN: *H.* 'Beatrice Variegated' incorrect.
       H. 'FRW No. 1399A'.
[*H.* 'FRW No. 1246' hybrid].
[*H. sieboldii* hybrid].

H. **'Beaulah'** Stone/Ruh IRA/1988.
AHS-IV/22A.
Plant 16 in. (40.5 cm) dia., 8 in. (20 cm) high. Leaf 5 by 4 in. (13 by 10 cm), veins 4–5, green, yellowish white margin, broadly lanceolate, wavy, flat. Scape 22 in. (56 cm), foliated, straight. Flower medium, purple striped, flowers during summer period, fertility(?).
HN: *H.* 'DSM No. 7' Stone.

H. **'Behemoth'** Savory IRA/1988.
AHS-I/1A.
Plant 48 in. (122 cm) dia., 36 in. (91.5 cm) high. Leaf 15 by 10 in. (38 by 25.5 cm), veins 14, medium green, not variegated, cordate, rugose. Scape 42 in. (106.5 cm), bare, straight. Flower medium, lavender, flowers during average period, fertile.
[*H. montana* hybrid].

H. **'Bella'.**
H. bella.

H. **'Belle Robinson'** Stillwell.
HN: Summers No. 317 1969.

H. **'Belles Baby'.**
HN: *H.* 'Krossa No. Z-4'.

H. **'Bengee'** Harrison/Bemis/Palmer 1970.
Plant is a chartreuse-to-yellow *H.* 'Tokudama'. Color holds but can be more greenish or yellowish depending on

culture and location. An all-green taxon is cultivated incorrectly under this name.
HN: *H.* 'Tokudama Aureonebulosa Yellow' group.

H. **'Bennie McRae'** Suggs IRA/1989.
Plant 30 in. (76 cm) dia., 24 in. (61 cm) high. Leaf 11 by 5 in. (28 by 7.5 cm), veins 6, medium green, glossy, not variegated, ovate-lanceolate, wavy margin, flat. Scape 60 in. (152 cm), foliated, oblique. Flower medium, funnel-shaped, lavender, fragrant, flowers during summer period, fertility(?).
[*H. plantaginea* hybrid].

H. **'Bensheim'** Zieke/Klose 1982.
Plant is a *H.* 'Fortunei' form with irregular yellow stripes.
HN: *H.* 'Fortunei Bensheim' Klose 1982.
[*H.* 'Fortunei Aoki' mutation].
(see *H.* 'Fortunei Aoki Variegated').

H. **'Betchers Blue'** Betcher IRA/1986.
AHS-III/15B.
Plant is a blue-green *H.* 'Tokudama' form.
[*H.* 'Tokudama' hybrid].

H. **'Bethel Big Leaf'** Lantis IRA/1979.
AHS-I/1B.
Plant 56 in. (142 cm) dia., 36 in. (91.5 cm) high. Leaf 13 by 11 in. (33 by 28 cm), veins 14, medium green, not variegated, cordate, rugose. Scape 42 in. (106.5 cm), bare, straight. Flower medium, bell-shaped, white, flowers during average period, fertile.
HN: *H.* 'Lantis Montana Seedling' incorrect.
[*H. montana* hybrid].

H. 'Betsy Bunting' Savory.
Plant's name is incorrect, but as it appeared on the 1982 registration list for *H.* 'Baby Bunting' Savory, which see.

H. **'Betsy King'** Williams 1943 IRA/1968.
AHS-IV/19B.   (Figure 4-3)
Plant 20 in. (51 cm) dia., 14 in. (35.5 cm) high. Leaf 4 by 3 in. (10 by 7.5 cm), veins 5, medium green, not variegated, ovate, flat. Scape 24 in. (61 cm), bare, straight. Flower medium, funnel-shaped, purple striped, flowers during early period, fertile.
HN: *H.* 'FRW No. 502'.
[*H. decorata* × *H. sieboldii* form].

Figure 4-3. *H.* 'Betsy King'; general habit (Hosta Hill)

H. **'Bette Davis Eyes'** Vaughn IRA/1987.
AHS-III/13B.
Plant 18 in. (46 cm) dia., 10 in. (25.5 cm) high. Leaf 8 by 3 in. (20 by 7.5 cm), veins 7, dark green, not variegated, cordate,

flat. Scape 24 in. (61 cm), foliated, oblique. Flower medium, funnel-shaped, purple, tipped white, fragrant, flowers during summer period, fertile.
[*H.* 'Summer Fragrance' × *H.* 'Christmas Tree'].

H. **'Betty'** Benedict IRA/1983.
AHS-III/13B.
Plant 12 in. (31 cm) dia., 6 in. (15 cm) high. Leaf 4 by 3 in. (10 by 7.5 cm), veins 7, dark green, not variegated, cordate, undulate-crispate margin. Scape 18 in. (46 cm), foliated, straight. Flower medium, funnel-shaped, purple, flowers during early period, fertile.
[*H. nakaiana* × *H. ventricosa* hybrid].

H. **'Betty Darling'** Owens IRA/1989.
Plant 10 in. (25 cm) dia., 4 in. (10 cm) high. Leaf 3 by 2 in. (7.5 by 5 cm), veins 4, dark green, irregular white margin, ovate, flat. Scape 10 in. (25 cm), bare, straight. Flower medium, bell-shaped, purple, flowers during average period, fertile.

H. **'Big Boy'** Simpers IRA/1986.
AHS-I/1B
Plant, as compared by Herz (cfr. Crockett, 1989), shows this taxon similar to *H. montana* f. *macrophylla* (formerly *H. montana* 'Praeflorens' or *H.* 'Krossa B-3') but slightly larger. It may be a hybrid of one of these. Plant 48 in. (122 cm) dia., 36 in. (91.5 cm) high. Leaf 16 by 11 in. (40.5 by 28 cm), veins 18, medium green, not variegated, cordate, furrowed-rugose. Scape 42 in. (106.5 cm), bare, straight. Flower medium, bell-shaped, white, flowers during early period, fertile.
[*H. montana* derivative].

H. **'Big Daddy'** Aden 1976 IRA/1978.
AHS-II/9B.   (Figures 2-19, 4-14; Plates 90, 171).
AHS President's Exhibitor Trophy Award, 1989, and Midwest Blue Award, 1989, exhibited by Richard Ward. Mature leaves have 16 veins indicating *H. sieboldiana* relationship. Otherwise leaves look like a large *H.* 'Tokudama'. Plant erect, 36 in. (91.5 cm) dia., 24 in. (61 cm) high. Leaf 11 by 9 in. (28 by 23 cm), veins 16, blue-green, not variegated, round-cordate, cupped-rugose. Scape 36 in. (91.5 cm), bare, straight. Flower medium, bell-shaped, white, flowers during average period, fertile.
[*H. sieboldiana* derivative].

H. **'Big Hearted'** Benedict IRA/1983.
AHS-III/13B.
Plant 36 in. (91.5 cm) dia., 18 in. (46 cm) high. Leaf 8 by 7 in. (20 by 18 cm), veins 10, medium green, not variegated, cordate, piecrust margin. Scape 32 in. (81.5 cm), bare, straight. Flower medium, bell-shaped, purple, flowers during average period, fertile.
[*H. nakaiana* × *H. sieboldiana* 'Zagers Giant'].

H. **'Big John'** IRA/1986.
AHS-I/3B.
AHS Eunice Fisher Award, 1988, exhibited by Clarence Owens. A very large *H. sieboldiana* form. Plant 48 in. (122 cm) dia., 30 in. (76 cm) high. Leaf 18 by 15 in. (46 by 37.5 cm), veins 16, medium green, not variegated, cordate, rugose. Scape 32 in. (81.5 cm), bare, straight. Flower medium, bell-shaped, white, flowers during average period, fertile.
[*H. sieboldiana* 'Mira' hybrid].

H. **'Big Mama'** Aden 1976 IRA/1978.
AHS-I/3B.   (Plate 170).
Plant 48 in. (122 cm) dia., 36 in. (91.5 cm) high. Leaf 13 by 12 in. (33 by 31 cm), veins 16, blue-green, not variegated, cor-

date, rugose. Scape 48 in. (122 cm), bare, straight. Flower medium, bell-shaped, white, flowers during average period, fertile.
[*H.* 'Blue Tiers' × *H. sieboldiana* 'Blue Angel'].

H. **'Big Sam'** Klopping 1963 IRA/1986.
AHS-I/1B.   (Figure 4-4).
Plant has a typical *H. montana* leaves with crispate margins. Plant 48 in. (122 cm) dia., 36 in. (91.5 cm) high. Leaf 16 by 14 in. (40.5 by 36 cm), veins 13, medium green, not variegated, cordate, rugose. Scape 42 in. (106.5 cm), bare, straight. Flower medium, bell-shaped, white, flowers during average period, fertile.
[*H. montana* × *H. sieboldiana*].

Figure 4-4. *H.* 'Big Sam'; general habit (Honeysong Farm/Schmid)

H. **'Bill Brincka'** Brincka IRA/1988.
AHS-II/10A.   (Figure 3-53; Plate 50).
AHS Benedict Award, 1988, exhibited by William Brincka. Plant is a clonal selection of *H.* 'Opipara'. Plant 48 in. (122 cm) dia., 24 in. (61 cm) high. Leaf 11 by 8 in. (28 by 20 cm), veins 10, medium green, yellow margin, oval, flat. Scape 30 in. (76 cm), bare, straight. Flower medium, purple-striped, flowers during summer period, fertile.
(see *H.* 'Opipara').

H. **'Birchwood Blue'** Shaw 1966 IRA/1986.
AHS-III/15B.
Plant erect, 36 in. (91.5 cm) dia., 24 in. (61 cm) high. Leaf 10 by 8 in. (25.5 by 20 cm), veins 16, blue-green, not variegated, round-cordate, cupped-rugose. Scape 36 in. (91.5 cm), bare, straight. Flower medium, bell-shaped, white, flowers during average period, fertile.
HN: *H.* 'Birchwood Parkys Blue' Shaw pp sim.
[*H. sieboldiana* × *H.* 'FRW No. 382'].

H. **'Birchwood Elegance'** Shaw IRA/1986.
AHS-I/1B.
Plant 48 in. (122 cm) dia., 36 in. (91.5 cm) high. Leaf 16 by 11 in. (40.5 by 28 cm), veins 16, medium green, not variegated, cordate, rugose. Scape 42 in. (106.5 cm), bare, straight. Flower medium, funnel-shaped, white, flowers during average period, fertile.
[*H. sieboldiana* × *H.* 'FRW No. 382'].

H. **'Birchwood Florence Shaw'** Shaw 1966.

H. **'Birchwood Gem'** Shaw/Ruh IRA/1989.
　　Plant is a selected, small clone of *H. nakaiana* or may be an F₁ selfed seedling. It has ridged scapes and is very similar to the species.
(see *H. nakaiana*).

H. **'Birchwood Gold'** Shaw 1966 IRA/1986.
　　AHS-III/17B.　　　　　　　　　　　　　　　　(Plate 91).
　　Plant is similar to *H.* 'Birchwood Parkys Gold' and from the same mating. Plant erect, 30 in. (76 cm) dia., 18 in. (46 cm) high. Leaf 5 by 4 in. (13 by 10 cm), veins 8, yellow (lutescent), not variegated, cordate, flat. Scape 38 in. (96.5 cm), bare, straight. Flower medium, bell-shaped, lavender, flowers during average period, fertile.
HN:　*H.* 'Birchwood Gold No. 391'.
　　　H. 'Parkman Shaw No. 391'.
[*H.* 'Sunlight' hybrid].
(see also *H.* 'Birchwood Parkys Gold').

H. **'Birchwood Green'** Shaw 1966 IRA/1986.
　　AHS-II/7B.
　　Plant is a very large *H. sieboldiana* form with rugose green leaves.
[*H. sieboldiana* × *H.* 'FRW No. 382'].

H. **'Birchwood Parkys Blue'** Shaw IRA/1986.
　　AHS-III/15B.
　　Plant is similar to *H.* 'Birchwood Blue'. Plant 36 in. (91.5 cm) dia., 24 in. (61 cm) high. Leaf 10 by 8 in. (25.5 by 20 cm), veins 16, blue-green, not variegated, round-cordate, cupped-rugose. Scape 36 in. (91.5 cm), bare, straight. Flower medium, bell-shaped, white, flowers during average period, fertile.

H. **'Birchwood Parkys Gold'** Shaw IRA/1986.
　　AHS-III/17B.　　　　　　　　　　　　　　　　(Plate 91).
　　Plant is similar to *H.* 'Birchwood Gold'. Plant erect, 30 in. (76 cm) dia., 18 in. (46 cm) high. Leaf 5 by 4 in. (13 by 10 cm), veins 8, yellow (lutescent), not variegated, cordate, flat. Scape 38 in. (96.5 cm), bare, straight. Flower medium, bell-shaped, lavender, flowers during average period, fertile.
HN:　Golden Nakaiana UK incorrect.
　　　H. 'Birchwood Gold'.
　　　H. nakaiana 'Golden form' incorrect.
　　　H. 'Parky'.
　　　Wisley No. 821377.
[*H.* 'Sunlight' × *H. nakaiana* ad int].
[*H.* 'Sunlight' × *H.* 'Sunlight' al].
(see also *H.* 'Birchwood Gold').

H. **'Birchwood Ruffled Queen'** IRA/1986.
　　AHS-II/7B.
　　Plant 28 in. (71 cm) dia., 18 in. (46 cm) high. Leaf 12 by 9 in. (31 by 23 cm), veins 9, yellow (viridescent), not variegated, cordate, piecrust margin. Scape 36 in. (91.5 cm), bare, straight. Flower medium, funnel-shaped, lavender, flowers during average period, fertile.
[*H.* 'Green Piecrust' hybrid].

H. **'Birgladj Berbon'** (incorrect).

H. **'Bitsy Gold'** Savory IRA/1985.
　　AHS-V/29A.
　　Plant 12 in. (31 cm) dia., 4 in. (10 cm) high. Leaf 5 by 1 in. (13 by 2.5 cm), veins 3, yellow (lutescent), not variegated, lanceolate, flat. Scape 6 in. (15 cm), bare, straight. Flower

medium, bell-shaped, lavender, flowers during summer period, fertile.
[*H. longissima* × hybrid yellow form].

H. **'Bitsy Green'** Savory IRA/1985.
　　AHS-V/25B.
　　Plant 12 in. (31 cm) dia., 4 in. (10 cm) high. Leaf 5 by 1 in. (13 by 2.5 cm), veins 3, green, not variegated, lanceolate, flat. Scape 6 in. (15 cm), bare, straight. Flower medium, bell-shaped, lavender, flowers during summer period, fertile.
[*H. longissima* × hybrid green form].

H. **'Bizarre'** Kuk Forest IRA/1986.
　　AHS-IV/20A.
　　Plant erect, 8 in. (20 cm) dia., 8 in. (20 cm) high. Leaf 6 by 2 in. (15 by 5 cm), veins 4, chartreuse, white margin, ovate-lanceolate, flat. Scape 24 in. (61 cm), bare, straight. Flower medium, funnel-shaped, purple striped, flowers during average period, fertile.
[*H. sieboldii* 'Kabitan' hybrid].

H. **'Black Beauty'** Carpenter IRA/1984.
　　AHS-II/7B.
　　Plant 48 in. (122 cm) dia., 30 in. (76 cm) high. Leaf 14 by 11 in. (35.5 by 28 cm), veins 13, very dark green, not variegated, cordate, rugose. Scape 32 in. (81.5 cm), foliated, straight. Flower medium, funnel-shaped, lavender, flowers during average period, fertile.
[*H.* 'Green Piecrust' hybrid].

H. **'Black Forest'** Bemis.

H. **'Black Hills'** Savory IRA/1983.
　　AHS-III/13B.　　　　　　　　　　　　　　　　(Figure 4-5).
　　Plant 36 in. (91.5 cm) dia., 24 in. (61 cm) high. Leaf 8 by 7 in. (20 by 18 cm), class, veins 13, dark green, not variegated, cordate, cupped-rugose. Scape 32 in. (81.5 cm), foliated, straight. Flower medium, funnel-shaped, lavender, flowers during average period, fertile.
[*H.* 'Green Gold' hybrid].

Figure 4-5. *H.* 'Black Hills'; general habit (Savory garden/Schmid)

H. **'Black Pod'** Fisher 1963.
　　Plant's seed pods are dotted with dark purple, appearing black. Otherwise like *H. sieboldii* f. *spathulata*.
Summers' No. 101 1963.
[*H. sieboldii* hybrid].

H. **'Blade Runner'** Taylor.
　　Plant has long linear green leaves with even, whitish yellow margins. The arching leaves form a regular mound.

H. **'Blaue Venus'** Klose.

Plant is a *H.* Tardiana grex hybrid with blue cordate leaves and lavender flowers. Reported by Klose to be the bluest of the German tardianas. The name means "Blue Venus."
HN: *H.* Tardiana grex.
[*H.* 'Tardiflora' × *H. sieboldiana* 'Elegans'].
(see also *H.* Tardiana grex).

H. **'Blaue Wolke'** Klose.

Plant has round, cupped blue-green leaves and lavender flowers. The name means "Blue Cloud."
[*H. sieboldiana* hybrid].

H. **'Blauglut'** Klose.

Plant is medium size, cupped, with blue-green leaves and lavender flowers. The name means "Blue Glow."
[*H. sieboldiana* hybrid].

H. **'Blaumeise'** Klose.

Plant is a medium-size *H.* Tardiana grex hybrid with blue round leaves and lavender flowers. The name means "Blue Titmouse."
HN: *H.* Tardiana grex.
[*H.* 'Tardiflora' × *H. sieboldiana* 'Elegans'].
(see also *H.* Tardiana grex).

H. **'Blauspecht'** Klose.

Plant is a small *H.* Tardiana grex hybrid with blue round leaves and lavender flowers. The name means "Blue Woodpecker."
HN: *H.* Tardiana grex.
[*H.* 'Tardiflora' × *H. sieboldiana* 'Elegans'].
(see also *H.* Tardiana grex).

H. **'Blessings'** Aden IRA/1983.
AHS-III/14A.

Plant erect, 12 in. (30 cm) dia., 6 in. (15 cm) high. Leaf 4 by 1.5–2.5 in. (10 by 4–6 cm), veins 5, yellow (lutescent), thin white margin, lanceolate, flat. Scape 12 in. (31 cm), foliated, straight. Flower medium, funnel-shaped, lavender, flowers during average period, fertile.
HN: *H.* 'Aden No. 425'.
[*H.* Tardiana Yellow group hybrid].

H. **'Blonde Elf'** Aden.

Plant 24 in. (61 cm) dia., 8 in. (20 cm) high. Leaf yellow, not variegated, lanceolate, undulate margin. Flower medium, lavender, flowers during summer period, fertility(?).

H. **'Blondie'** Harshbarger 1973 IRA/1982.
AHS-III/17B.

Plant 14 in. (35.5 cm) dia., 10 in. (25.5 cm) high. Leaf 5 by 4 in. (13 by 10 cm), veins 12, yellow (lutescent), not variegated, round-cordate, cupped-rugose. Scape 18 in. (46 cm), bare, straight. Flower medium, bell-shaped, white, flowers during average period, fertile.
HN: Harshbarger GH-4.
[*H.* 'Tokudama Aureonebulosa' hybrid].

H. **'Blue Angel'** Aden IRA/1986.
AHS-I/3B.   (Plate 92).

Plant is not the European *H.* 'Blue Angel' which is *H. sieboldiana* 'Elegans'. Plant 48 in. (122 cm) dia., 36 in. (91.5 cm) high. Leaf 16 by 13 in. (40.5 by 33 cm), veins 13, blue-green, not variegated, cordate, rugose. Scape 48 in. (122 cm), bare, straight. Flower medium, bell-shaped, white, flowers during average period, fertile.
[*H.* 'Aden No. 365' × *H.* 'Aden No. 361'].
(see also *H. sieboldiana* 'Elegans').

H. **'Blue Arrow'** Anderson IRA/1982.
AHS-III/15B.

Plant erect, 18 in. (46 cm) dia., 10 in. (25.5 cm) high. Leaf 5 by 1.5 in. (13 by 4 cm), veins 10, blue-green, not variegated, lanceolate, flat. Scape 18 in. (46 cm), bare, straight. Flower medium, bell-shaped, white, flowers during average period, fertile.

H. **'Blue Bayou'** Vaughn IRA/1987.
AHS-II/9B.

Plant 40 in. (101.5 cm) dia., 32 in. (81.5 cm) high. Leaf 10 by 8.5 in. (25.5 by 21 cm), veins 12, blue-green, not variegated, round-cordate, rugose. Scape 44 in. (112 cm), bare, oblique. Flower medium, bell-shaped, lavender, flowers during average period, fertile.
[*H. sieboldiana* 'Frances Williams' hybrid].

H. **'Blue Beau'** Aden 1975.

H. **'Blue Beauty'** Summers/Shaw IRA/1986.
AHS-II/9B.   (Figure 4-6).

Plant 40 in. (101.5 cm) dia., 32 in. (81.5 cm) high. Leaf 10 by 8.5 in. (25.5 by 21 cm), veins 12, blue-green, not variegated, round-cordate, rugose. Scape 44 in. (112 cm), bare, oblique. Flower medium, bell-shaped, white, flowers during average period, fertile.
[*H. sieboldiana* hybrid].

Figure 4-6. *H.* 'Blue Beauty'; mass planting (Honeysong Farm/Schmid)

H. **'Blue Belle'** Smith/BHHS IRA/1988.
AHS-IV/21B.

Plant 22 in. (56 cm) dia., 16 in. (40.5 cm) high. Leaf 5 by 4 in. (13 by 10 cm), veins 8, blue-green, not variegated, round-cordate, cupped. Scape 11 in. (28 cm). Flower medium, bell-shaped, lavender, flowers during average period, fertile.
HN: Wisley No. 821424.
    H. Tardiana grex TF 2 × 22.
[*H.* 'Tardiflora' × *H. sieboldiana* 'Elegans'].
(see also *H.* Tardiana grex).

H. **'Blue Betty Lou'** Owens IRA/1987.
AHS-II/9B.

Plant 32 in. (81.5 cm) dia., 24 in. (61 cm) high. Leaf 10 by 9 in. (25.5 by 23 cm), veins 16, blue-green, not variegated, round-cordate, cupped. Scape 32 in. (81.5 cm), bare, straight. Flower medium, bell-shaped, lavender, flowers during average period, fertile.
HN: *H.* 'Blue Betty Blue' incorrect.
[*H.* 'True Blue' × *H.* 'Gold Regal'].

H. **'Blue Blazes'** Vaughn IRA/1988.
  AHS-II/9A.
    Plant 35 in. (89 cm) dia., 30 in. (76 cm) high. Leaf 13 by 11 in. (33 by 28 cm), veins 12, blue-green, not variegated, round-cordate, cupped-rugose. Scape 38 in. (96.5 cm), bare, straight. Flower medium, bell-shaped, lavender, flowers during average period, fertility(?).
  [*H.* 'Polly Bishop' × *H.* 'Blue Boy'].

H. **'Blue Blush'** Smith/BHHS IRA/1988.
  AHS-IV/21B.
    Plant is small, similar to *H.* 'Blue Heron' but darker bluish-green color. Plant 12 in. (31 cm) dia., 6 in. (15 cm) high. Leaf 4 by 1.5 in. (10 by 4 cm), veins 6, blue-green, not variegated, lanceolate, flat. Scape 11 in. (28 cm), bare, straight. Flower medium, bell-shaped, lavender, flowers during average period, fertile.
  HN: *H.* Tardiana grex TF 3 × 1.
  [*H.* 'Tardiflora' × *H. sieboldiana* 'Elegans'].
  (see also *H.* Tardiana grex).

H. **'Blue Boy'** Stone IRA/1986.
  AHS-III/15B.
    Plant 20 in. (51 cm) dia., 14 in. (35.5 cm) high. Leaf 5 by 4 in. (13 by 10 cm), veins 10, blue-green, not variegated, cordate, flat. Scape 22 in. (56 cm), bare, straight. Flower medium, bell-shaped, white, flowers during average period, fertile.
  [*H. nakaiana* × *H. sieboldiana*].

H. **'Blue Cadet'** Aden (No. 359) IRA/1974.
  AHS-IV/21B.   (Figures 2-1, 2-15, F-7; Plates 93, 160).
  AHS Nancy Minks Award, 1986, exhibited by Paul Aden. Plant 28 in. (71 cm) dia., 16 in. (40.5 cm) high. Leaf 5 by 4 in. (13 by 10 cm), veins 10, blue-green, not variegated, cordate, flat. Scape 26 in. (66 cm), bare, straight. Flower medium, bell-shaped, lavender, flowers during average period, fertile.
  HN: Wisley No. 821432, 821434.
  [*H.* 'Tokudama' hybrid].

H. **'Blue Danube'** Smith/BHHS IRA/1988.
  AHS-IV/21B.
    Plant 14 in. (35.5 cm) dia., 8 in. (20 cm) high. Leaf 4 by 4 in. (10 by 10 cm), veins 10, blue-green, not variegated, cordate, flat. Scape 24 in. (61 cm), bare, straight. Flower medium, bell-shaped, lavender, flowers during average period, fertile.
  HN: *H.* Tardiana grex TF 2 × 24.
      Wisley No. 821422.
  [*H.* 'Tardiflora' × *H. sieboldiana* 'Elegans'].
  (see also *H.* Tardiana grex).

H. **'Blue Diamond'** Smith/BHHS IRA/1988.
  AHS-III/15B.
    Plant 17 in. (43 cm) dia., 12 in. (31 cm) high. Leaf 7 by 5 in. (18 by 13 cm), veins 10, blue-green, not variegated, cordate, flat. Scape 18 in. (46 cm), bare, straight. Flower medium, bell-shaped, lavender, flowers during average period, fertile.
  HN: *H.* 'Blauer Diamant' Klose.
      H. Tardiana grex TF 2 × 23.
      Wisley No. 821436.
  [*H.* 'Tardiflora' × *H. sieboldiana* 'Elegans'].
  (see also *H.* Tardiana grex).

H. **'Blue Dimples'** Smith/BHHS IRA/1988.
  AHS-III/15B.
    Plant is often incorrectly sold as *H.* 'Blue Wedgwood'. Plant 20 in. (51 cm) dia., 14 in. (35.5 cm) high. Leaf 7 by 5 in. (18 by 13 cm), veins 10, blue-green, not variegated, cordate, rugose. Scape 20 in. (51 cm), bare, straight. Flower medium,

bell-shaped, lavender, flowers during average period, fertile.
  HN: *H.* Tardiana grex TF 2 × 8.
  [*H.* 'Tardiflora' × *H. sieboldiana* 'Elegans'].
  (see also *H.* Tardiana grex).

H. **'Blue Dome'** Minks IRA/1980.
  AHS-III/15B.
    Plant 28 in. (71 cm) dia., 18 in. (46 cm) high. Leaf 4 by 3 in. (10 by 7.5 cm), veins 12, blue-green, not variegated, round-cordate, cupped-rugose. Scape 24 in. (61 cm), bare, straight. Flower medium, bell-shaped, white, flowers during average period, fertile.
  [*H.* 'Tokudama' × *H.* 'Tokudama'].

H. **'Blue Fan Dancer'** Aden IRA/1976.
  AHS-III/15B.
    Plant 26 in. (66 cm) dia., 16 in. (40.5 cm) high. Leaf 5 by 4 in. (13 by 10 cm), veins 14, blue-green, not variegated, round-cordate, cupped-rugose. Scape 22 in. (56 cm), foliated, straight. Flower medium, bell-shaped, white, flowers during average period, fertile.
  [*H.* 'Blue Cadet' × *H.* 'Aden No. 355'].

H. **'Blue Frost'** Nesmith 1965 IRA/1986.
  AHS-I/3B.
    Plant is a large blue-grey *H. sieboldiana* form.
  [*H. sieboldiana* hybrid].

H. **'Blue Giant'** Piedmont Gardens.
    Plant is a selected form of the species *H. sieboldiana*.
  (see *H. sieboldiana* 'Elegans').

H. **'Blue Giant'** hort.
    A horticultural name for a selected form of the species *H. sieboldiana*.
  (see *H. sieboldiana* 'Elegans').

H. **'Bluegee'**.

H. **'Blue Happiness'** Aden 1974.
    Plant 20 in. (51 cm) dia., 14 in. (35.5 cm) high. Leaf 4 by 2.5 in. (10 by 6 cm), veins 10, blue-green, not variegated, cordate, flat. Scape 22 in. (56 cm), bare, straight. Flower medium, bell-shaped, white, flowers during average period, fertile.

H. **'Blue Heaven'** Aden IRA/1976.
  AHS-III/15B.
    Plant is a very silvery-blue cultivar. Plant 22 in. (56 cm) dia., 12 in. (31 cm) high. Leaf 6 by 5 in. (15 by 13 cm), veins 10, blue-green, not variegated, cordate, flat. Scape 22 in. (56 cm), bare, straight. Flower medium, bell-shaped, white, flowers during average period, fertile.
  [*H.* 'Blue Cadet' × *H.* 'Aden No. 355'].

H. 'Blue Heron' Smith.
    Plant name is an incorrect synonym.
  (see *H.* 'Hadspen Heron').

H. **'Blue Horizon'** Englerth IRA/1985.
  AHS-III/15B.
    Plant 32 in. (81.5 cm) dia., 14 in. (35.5 cm) high. Leaf 8 by 6 in. (20 by 15 cm), veins 14, blue-green, not variegated, round-cordate, cupped-rugose. Scape 18 in. (46 cm), bare, straight. Flower medium, bell-shaped, white, flowers during average period, fertile.
  [*H.* 'Tokudama' hybrid].

H. **'Blue Ice'** Benedict IRA/1987.
AHS-VI/33B.
Plant 8 in. (20 cm) dia., 4 in. (10 cm) high. Leaf 4 by 4 in. (10 by 10 cm), veins 8, blue-green, not variegated, round-cordate, cupped-rugose. Scape 10 in. (25.5 cm), bare, straight. Flower medium, bell-shaped, lavender, flowers during average period, fertile.
[*H.* (Tardiana grex) 'Dorset Blue' × *H.* 'Blue Moon'].

H. **'Blue Jay'** Benedict IRA/1987.
AHS-III/15B.
Plant is similar to the much larger *H.* 'Abiqua Blue Jay' (Walden-West), which see. Plant 12 in. (31 cm) dia., 8 in. (20 cm) high. Leaf 7 by 5 in. (18 by 13 cm), veins 8, blue-green, not variegated, round-cordate, cupped. Scape 12 in. (31 cm), bare, straight. Flower medium, bell-shaped, lavender, flowers during average period, fertile.
[*H.* (Tardiana grex) 'Dorset Blue' × *H.* 'Dorset Blue' hybrid].
(see also *H.* 'Abiqua Blue Jay').

H. **'Blue June'** Benedict IRA/1987.
AHS-III/15B.
Plant 16 in. (40.5 cm) dia., 12 in. (31 cm) high. Leaf 10 by 5 in. (25.5 by 13 cm), veins 10, blue-green, not variegated, cordate, cupped-rugose. Scape 14 in. (35.5 cm), bare, straight. Flower medium, bell-shaped, lavender, flowers during average period, fertile.
[*H.* (Tardiana grex) 'Blue Diamond' × *H.* Tardiana grex hybrid].

H. **'Blue Lace'** Vaughn IRA/1977.
AHS-II/9B.
Plant erect, 6 in. (15 cm) dia., 24 in. (61 cm) high. Leaf 13 by 11 in. (33 by 28 cm), veins 9, blue-green, not variegated, cordate, rugose. Scape 30 in. (76 cm), bare, straight. Flower medium, bell-shaped, white, flowers during average period, fertile.
[*H.* 'Frances Williams' hybrid].

H. **'Blue Lady'** Fisher 1978.
Plant erect, 10 in. (25.5 cm) dia., 8 in. (20 cm) high. Leaf 5 by 1 in. (13 by 2.5 cm), veins 3, medium green, not variegated, lanceolate, flat. Scape 20 in. (51 cm), bare, straight. Flower medium, funnel-shaped, purple striped, flowers during summer period, fertile.
[*H.* sieboldii hybrid].

H. **'Blue Lagoon'** Woodruff IRA/1972.
AHS-III/15B.
Plant 24 in. (61 cm) dia., 12 in. (31 cm) high. Leaf 6 by 5 in. (15 by 13 cm), veins 9, blue-green, not variegated, cordate, rugose. Scape 20 in. (51 cm), bare, straight. Flower small, bell-shaped, white, flowers during average period, fertile.
[*H.* 'Tokudama' hybrid].

H. **'Blue Line'** Aden IRA/1987.
AHS-V/27B.
Plant 8 in. (20 cm) dia., 4 in. (10 cm) high. Leaf 6 by 1 in. (15 by 2.5 cm), veins 4, blue-green, not variegated, lanceolate, flat. Scape 12 in. (31 cm), bare, straight. Flower medium, bell-shaped, lavender, flowers during summer period, fertile.
[*H.* 'Aden No. 412' × *H.* pulchella mutation].

H. **'Blue Mammoth'** Aden.
Plant 36 in. (91.5 cm) dia., 24 in. (61 cm) high. Leaf 13 by 11 in. (33 by 28 cm), veins 16, blue-green, not variegated, cordate, rugose. Scape 30 in. (76 cm), bare, straight. Flower medium, bell-shaped, white, flowers during average period, fertile.
[*H.* sieboldiana hybrid].

H. **'Blue Max'**.
(see *H.* 'Helen Doriot').

H. **'Blue Moon'** Smith/Aden IRA/1976.
AHS-IV/21A.
AHS Midwest Blue Award, 1982, exhibited by Kenneth Anderson. Plant 10 in. (25.5 cm) dia., 8 in. (20 cm) high. Leaf 3 by 2 in. (7.5 by 5 cm), veins 9, blue-green, not variegated, cordate, flat. Scape 12 in. (31 cm), bare, straight. Flower small, bell-shaped, white, flowers during average period, fertile.
HN: *H.* 'Halo'.
    H. Tardiana grex TF 2 × 2.
[*H.* 'Tardiflora' × *H.* sieboldiana 'Elegans'].
(see also *H.* Tardiana grex).

H. **'Blue Ox'**.
Plant is a selected *H.* sieboldiana form. Leaf has 14–16 veins.
[*H.* sieboldiana hybridized form].

H. **'Blue Pearl'** Holland/Krossa/Ruh.
Plant 24 in. (61 cm) dia., 16 in. (40.5 cm) high. Leaf 6 by 5 in. (15 by 13 cm), veins 12, blue-green, not variegated, round-cordate, cupped-rugose. Scape 22 in. (56 cm), bare, straight. Flower medium, bell-shaped, white, flowers during average period, fertile.
[*H.* 'Tokudama' form].

H. **'Blue Piecrust'** Summers IRA/1986.
AHS-II/9A.
Plant 44 in. (112 cm) dia., 32 in. (81.5 cm) high. Leaf 13 by 11 in. (33 by 28 cm), veins 13, blue-green, not variegated, cordate, piecrust margin. Scape 42 in. (106.5 cm), bare, straight. Flower medium, funnel-shaped, white, flowers during average period, fertile.

H. **'Blue Plisset'** Soules.
Plant is a *H.* sieboldiana derivative. Plant 64 in. (162 cm) dia., 30 in. (76 cm) high. Leaf 10 by 8 in. (25 by 20 cm), veins 14–16, blue-green, not variegated, cordate, very rugose. Scape 30 in. (76 cm), bare, straight. Flower medium, bell-shaped, white, flowers during average period, fertile.
[*H.* sieboldiana × *H.* 'Tokudama'].

H. **'Blue Prince'** Benedict.

H. **'Blue Reflection'** Tompkins.

H. **'Blue Ripples'** Stark.   (Plate 156).
Plant 40 in. (101.5 cm) dia., 26 in. (66 cm) high. Leaf 12 by 10 in. (31 by 25.5 cm), veins 13, medium green, not variegated, cordate, piecrust margin. Scape 42 in. (106.5 cm), bare, straight. Flower medium, bell-shaped, white, flowers during average period, fertile.
[*H.* sieboldiana hybrid].

H. **'Blue Rock'** Stone/Fisher IRA/1986.
AHS-II/9B.   (Plate 94).
Plant 36 in. (91.5 cm) dia., 20 in. (51 cm) high. Leaf 8 by 6 in. (20 by 15 cm), veins 16, blue-green, not variegated, cordate, rugose. Scape 26 in. (66 cm), bare, straight. Flower medium, bell-shaped, white, flowers during average period, fertile.
[*H.* sieboldiana hybrid].

H. **'Blue Rogue'** Walters.

H. **'Blue Sagae'** Japan.
Plant is a Japanese cultivar similar to *H.* 'Sagae' (*H. fluctuans* 'Variegated') with blue-grey, not variegated leaves, and probably a seedling or sport of the latter.
[*H.* 'Sagae' hybrid or mutation].

H. **'Blue Saucers'** Powell IRA/1977.
    AHS-II/9B.
Plant 36 in. (91.5 cm) dia., 24 in. (61 cm) high. Leaf 13 by 11 in. (33 by 28 cm), veins 13, blue-green, not variegated, cordate, rugose. Scape 20 in. (51 cm), bare, straight. Flower medium, bell-shaped, white, flowers during average period, fertile.
[*H. sieboldiana* 'Elegans' × *H. sieboldiana* 'Frances Williams'].

H. **'Blue Seer'** Aden.
Plant is a *H. sieboldiana* form selection.

H. **'Blue Shadows'** Anderson IRA/1980.
    AHS-III/14B.   (Plate 95).
AHS President's Exhibitor Trophy, 1980, exhibited by Kenneth Anderson. A special selection of *H.* 'Tokudama Aureonebulosa'. It has more dark green variegation. Reversion to the standard form has been reported from some areas. Plant 24 in. (61 cm) dia., 14 in. (35.5 cm) high. Leaf 7 by 6 in. (18 by 15 cm), veins 13, blue-green, streaked yellow, cordate, rugose. Scape 18 in. (46 cm), bare, straight. Flower medium, bell-shaped, white, flowers during average period, fertile.
HN: *H.* 'Tokudama Blue Shadows'.
(see also *H.* 'Tokudama Aureonebulosa').

H. **'Blue Skies'** Smith/BHHS IRA/1988.
    AHS-IV/21A.
Plant 12 in. (31 cm) dia., 9 in. (23 cm) high. Leaf 5 by 4 in. (13 by 10 cm), veins 9, blue-green, not variegated, cordate, flat. Scape 16 in. (40.5 cm), bare, straight. Flower medium, bell-shaped, lavender, flowers during average period, fertile.
HN: *H.* Tardiana grex TF 2 × 6.
         Wisley No. 821406.
[*H.* 'Tardiflora' × *H. sieboldiana* 'Elegans'].
(see also *H.* Tardiana grex).

H. **'Blue Skirt'** Geissler 1970 IRA/1970.
    AHS-II/9B.
Plant 36 in. (91.5 cm) dia., 20 in. (51 cm) high. Leaf 14 by 9 in. (35.5 by 23 cm), veins 13, blue-green, not variegated, cordate, rugose. Scape 26 in. (66 cm), bare, straight. Flower medium, bell-shaped, white, flowers during average period, fertile.
[*H. sieboldiana* hybrid].

H. **'Blue Steel'** Benedict.

H. **'Blue Swarm'** Aden.
(see *H.* 'Serendipity').

H. **'Blue Tiara'** Savory.

H. **'Blue Tiers'** Aden IRA/1976.
    AHS-III/15B.
Plant 36 in. (91.5 cm) dia., 20 in. (51 cm) high. Leaf 9 by 6 in. (23 by 15 cm), veins 13, blue-green, not variegated, cordate, rugose. Scape 30 in. (76 cm), bare, straight. Flower medium, bell-shaped, white, flowers during average period, fertile.
[*H.* 'Tokudama' hybrid × *H.* 'Tokudama' hybrid].

H. **'Blue Troll'** Savory IRA/1973.
    AHS-III/15B.
Plant 24 in. (61 cm) dia., 12 in. (31 cm) high. Leaf 7 by 5 in. (18 by 13 cm), veins 13, blue-green, not variegated, cordate, flat. Scape 18 in. (46 cm), bare, straight. Flower medium, bell-shaped, white, flowers during average period, fertile.
[*H. sieboldiana* hybrid].

H. **'Blue Umbrellas'** Aden 1976 IRA/1978.
    AHS-I/3A.   (Figure 4-7).
AHS Midwest Blue Award, 1987, exhibited by Richard Ward. Plant 48 in. (122 cm) dia., 36 in. (91.5 cm) high. Leaf 13 by 10 in. (33 by 23 cm), veins 13, blue-green, not variegated, cordate, rugose. Scape 42 in. (106.5 cm), bare, straight. Flower medium, bell-shaped, white, flowers during average period, fertile.
[*H.* 'Tokudama' × *H. sieboldiana* 'Elegans'].

Figure 4-7. *H.* 'Blue Umbrellas'; general habit (Langdon garden/Schmid)

H. **'Blue Veil'** Aden.
The stable form of *H.* 'Vickie Aden'. Leaf 9 by 6 in. (23 by 15 cm), blue-green, not variegated. Flower medium, lavender, flowers during summer period, fertility(?).
[(*H.* 'Flamboyant' hybrid) mutation].

H. **'Blue Velvet'** Aden IRA/1976.
    AHS-III/15B.
Plant erect, 24 in. (61 cm) dia., 20 in. (51 cm) high. Leaf 8 by 7 in. (20 by 17 cm), veins 13, blue-green, not variegated, round-cordate, cupped-rugose. Scape 28 in. (71 cm), bare, straight. Flower medium, bell-shaped, white, flowers during average period, fertile.
[*H.* 'Tokudama' hybrid × *H.* 'Tokudama' hybrid].

H. **'Blue Vision'** Aden IRA/1976.
    AHS-II/9B.
Plant erect, 36 in. (91.5 cm) dia., 32 in. (81.5 cm) high. Leaf 12 by 9 in. (31 by 23 cm), veins 16, blue-green, not variegated, round-cordate, cupped-rugose. Scape 36 in. (91.5 cm), bare, straight. Flower medium, bell-shaped, white, flowers during average period, fertile.
[*H.* 'Aden No. 355' × *H.* 'Aden No. 353'].

H. 'Blue Wedgewood' Smith/Summers.
Plant name is an earlier name for *H.* 'Blue Wedgwood' and is now considered incorrect because the latter name has been registered.
(see *H.* 'Blue Wedgwood').

H. **'Blue Wedgwood'** Smith/Summers/BHHS IRA/1988.
    AHS-III/15B.   (Plates 96, 151).
Plant named *H.* 'Blue Wedgewood' by Summers, alluding to wedge-shaped leaves, but registered as *H.* 'Blue Wedg-

wood', which is correct, referring to the light blue color of Jasperware made by Wedgwood & Sons. Both names are in use. Due to distribution errors some of the plants cultivated under this name are actually *H.* 'Blue Dimples', which does not have wedge-shaped leaves. Plant 24 in. (61 cm) dia., 14 in. (35.5 cm) high. Leaf 6 by 5 in. (15 by 13 cm), veins 12, blue-green, not variegated, round-cordate, cupped-rugose. Scape 16 in. (40.5 cm), bare, straight. Flower medium, bell-shaped, lavender, flowers during average period, fertile.
HN: *H.* 'Blue Wave'.
　　H. 'Blue Wedgewood' Summers incorrect.
　　H. 'Wedgewood Blue' incorrect.
　　H. 'Wedgewood' incorrect.
　　H. 'Wedgwood' incorrect.
　　H. Tardiana grex TF 2 × 9.
[*H.* 'Tardiflora' × *H. sieboldiana* 'Elegans'].
(see also *H.* Tardiana grex).

H. 'Blue Whirls' Aden IRA/1978.
　　AHS-III/15B.
　　Plant 30 in. (76 cm) dia., 20 in. (51 cm) high. Leaf 9 by 7 in. (23 by 18 cm), veins 13, blue-green, not variegated, ovate, cupped-rugose. Scape 28 in. (71 cm), bare, straight. Flower medium, bell-shaped, white, flowers during average period, fertile.
[*H.* hybrid × *H.* 'Blue Vision'].

H. 'Bluebells' Lewis 1963.

H. 'Bluebird' Savory/Summers IRA/1985.
　　AHS-III/15B.
　　Plant 24 in. (61 cm) dia., 18 in. (46 cm) high. Leaf 6 by 4 in. (15 by 10 cm), veins 10, blue-green, not variegated, round-cordate, cupped-rugose. Scape 22 in. (56 cm), bare, straight. Flower medium, bell-shaped, white, flowers during average period, fertile.

H. 'Blütenspiel' Klose.
　　Plant has small round green leaves and many lavender flowers. The name means "Blossom Play."

H. 'Bobbin' O'Harra.
　　AHS Savory Shield Award, 1987, exhibited by Russell O'Harra. A dwarf form of *H. sieboldii* 'Silver Kabitan' arising as a sport. Plant erect, 4 in. (10 cm) dia., 2 in. (5 cm) high. Leaf 1.25 by 0.5 in. (3 by 1 cm), veins 3, white, green margin, cordate, flat. Scape 5 in. (13 cm), bare, straight. Flower small, funnel-shaped, lavender, flowers during summer period, sterile.
[*H. sieboldii* derivative].
(see also *H. sieboldii* 'Silver Kabitan).

H. 'Bold and Brassy' Seaver.
　　Plant is a large *H. sieboldiana* form, crinkled leaves 11 by 9 in. (28 by 23 cm), veins 14–16, chartreuse (lutescent).
[*H. sieboldiana* Yellow group].

H. 'Bold Eagle' Vaughn.

H. 'Bold Edger' Vaughn IRA/1983.
　　AHS-III/16B.　　　　　　　　　　　　　(Plate 180).
　　Plant erect, 20 in. (51 cm) dia., 20 in. (51 cm) high. Leaf 6 by 4 in. (15 by 10 cm), veins 8, medium green, white margin, cordate, wavy-undulate. Scape 30 in. (76 cm), foliated, straight. Flower medium, funnel-shaped, lavender, flowers during summer period, fertile.
[*H.* 'Beatrice' × *H. sieboldiana* 'Frances Williams'].

H. 'Bold One' Aden IRA/1978.
　　AHS-III/16A.
　　Plant is a *H.* 'Fortunei' form. Leaf 7 by 5 in. (18 by 13 cm), splashed gold, chartreuse, and white. Unstable.
[*H.* 'Fortunei' derivative].

H. 'Bold Ribbons' Aden IRA/1976.
　　AHS-III/16B.
　　Plant 18 in. (46 cm) dia., 16 in. (40.5 cm) high. Leaf 6 by 4 in. (15 by 10 cm), veins 5, medium green, white margin, lanceolate, flat. Scape 28 in. (71 cm), bare, straight. Flower medium, funnel-shaped, lavender, flowers during average period, fertile.

H. 'Bold Ruffles' Arett IRA/1975.
　　AHS-I/3B.
　　Plant is similar to the parent but has distinctly ruffled edges on 12 by 9 in. (31 by 23 cm) leaves.
HN: *H. sieboldiana* 'Ruffled'.
　　Ruffled Sieboldiana.
[*H. sieboldiana* 'Elegans' derivative].

H. 'Bon Voyage' Minks IRA/1980.
　　AHS-III/15B.
　　Plant 24 in. (61 cm) dia., 16 in. (40.5 cm) high. Leaf 5 by 4 in. (13 by 10 cm), veins 6, medium green, not variegated, cordate, piecrust margin. Scape 32 in. (81.5 cm), bare, straight. Flower medium, bell-shaped, lavender, flowers during average period, fertile.
[*H.* 'Tokudama' × *H.* 'Dear Heart'].

H. 'Bonanza' Nesmith.
　　Plant is plain green, similar to *H.* 'Fortunei'. Leaf 7 by 5 in. (18 by 13 cm).
[*H.* 'Fortunei' hybrid].

H. 'Bonnie' Stone/Ruh IRA/1987.
　　AHS-III/15B.
　　Plant 22 in. (56 cm) dia., 14 in. (35.5 cm) high. Leaf 8 by 6 in. (20 by 15 cm), veins 14, blue-green, not variegated, cordate, rugose-furrowed. Scape 14 in. (35.5 cm), bare, straight. Flower medium, bell-shaped, whitish, flowers during average period, sterile.
HN: *H.* 'DSM No. 3' Stone.
[*H. sieboldiana* hybrid ad int].

H. 'Booka' Weissenberger IRA/1986.
　　AHS-IV/21B.
　　Plant 16 in. (40.5 cm) dia., 6 in. (15 cm) high. Leaf 2.5 by 2 in. (6 by 5 cm), veins 6, medium green, not variegated, cordate, flat. Scape 13 in. (33 cm), bare, straight. Flower medium, bell-shaped, lavender, flowers during average period, fertile.
[*H.* 'Blue Cadet' hybrid].

H. 'Boots and Saddles' Minks IRA/1983.
　　AHS-III/14B.
　　Plant 24 in. (61 cm) dia., 14 in. (35.5 cm) high. Leaf 5 by 4 in. (13 by 10 cm), veins 13, blue-green, yellow stripe in center, occasional yellow streaks, round-cordate, cupped-rugose. Scape 18 in. (46 cm), bare, straight. Flower medium, bell-shaped, white, flowers during average period, fertile.
[*H.* 'Tokudama Aureonebulosa' form].

H. 'Borsch 1' Borsch Nursery 1930.
　　Plant is identical to *H.* 'King James', a name given by Summers to a *H. montana* form plant received under number (probably B-1) from Krossa.
HN: *H.* 'King James' Summers.
[*H. montana* form].

H. **'Borsch 2'** Borsch Nursery 1930.
[*H. montana* form].

H. **'Borsch 3'** Borsch Nursery 1930.
(see *H. ventricosa*).

H. **'Borsch 4'** Borsch Nursery 1930.
[*H. montana* form].

H. **'Borwick Beauty'** McBurnie/BHHS IRA/1988.
    AHS-II/8B.
    Plant is one of the several mediovariegated mutants of *H. sieboldiana*. Other similar forms exist and have been named. Plant 26 in. (66 cm) dia., 14 in. (35.5 cm) high. Leaf 9 by 9 in. (23 by 23 cm), veins 13, yellowish white (albescent), blue-green margin, round-cordate, cupped-rugose. Scape 18 in. (46 cm), foliated, straight. Flower medium, funnel-shaped, white, flowers during average period, fertile.
HN: *H. sieboldiana* Mediovariegata group.
[*H. sieboldiana* hybrid mutation].
(see also *H. sieboldiana* Mediovariegata group).

H. **'Bountiful'** Fisher IRA/1971.
    AHS-IV/19A.
    Plant 18 in. (46 cm) dia., 14 in. (35.5 cm) high. Leaf 7 by 3 in. (18 by 7.5 cm), veins 7, medium green, not variegated, ovate, flat. Scape 22 in. (56 cm), foliated, straight. Flower medium, bell-shaped, lavender, flowers during summer period, fertile.
[*H. nakaiana* hybrid].

H. **'Bouquet'** Moldovan.

H. **'Bravo'** Aden IRA/1980.
    AHS-III/16A.   (Figure 4-8).
    Plant 20 in. (51 cm) dia., 14 in. (35.5 cm) high. Leaf 7 by 5 in. (18 by 13 cm), veins 6, green, streaked yellow, ovate, flat. Scape 22 in. (56 cm), foliated, straight. Flower medium, bell-shaped, white, flowers during summer period, fertile.
[*H.* 'Reversed' × *H.* 'Fascination'].

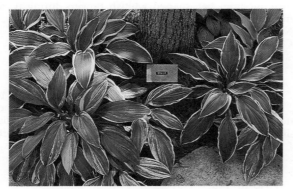

Figure 4-8. *H.* 'Bravo'; general habit; population reverting to marginata form (Soules garden/Schmid)

H. **'Breeders Choice'** Vaughn/Seaver IRA/1987.
    AHS-III/16A.
    Plant 16 in. (40.5 cm) dia., 10 in. (25.5 cm) high. Leaf 6 by 5 in. (15 by 13 cm), veins 11, medium green, multicolored streaked and/or margined, extremely variable, cordate, flat. Scape 30 in. (76 cm), bare, oblique. Flower medium, bell-shaped, lavender, flowers during average period, fertile.
[*H.* 'Beatrice' hybrid (V73-2) × *H. sieboldiana* 'Frances Williams'].

H. **'Brenner Pass'** Woodroffe IRA/1972.
    AHS-III/16B.
    Plant 24 in. (61 cm) dia., 14 in. (35.5 cm) high. Leaf 6 by 4 in. (15 by 10 cm), veins 13, blue-green, streaked yellow, round-cordate, cupped-rugose. Scape 18 in. (46 cm), bare, straight. Flower medium, bell-shaped, white, flowers during average period, fertile.
[*H.* 'Tokudama Aureonebulosa' hybrid].

H. **'Bressingham Blue'** Bloom.
    Plant 24 in. (61 cm) dia., 20 in. (51 cm) high. Leaf 6 by 4 in. (15 by 10 cm), veins 13, blue-green, not variegated, cordate, flat. Scape 28 in. (71 cm), bare, straight. Flower medium, bell-shaped, white, flowers during average period, fertile.
[*H. sieboldiana* × *H.* 'Tokudama'].

H. **'Bridegroom'** Benedict 1990.
    Plant 12 in. (30 cm) dia., 10 in. (25.5 cm) high. Leaf 5 by 3 in. (13 by 8 cm), veins 8, medium green, not variegated, ovate, wavy/contorted, unique shape. Fertile.

H. **'Bridgeville'** Summers 1986.
    Plant 16 in. (40.5 cm) dia., 10 in. (25.5 cm) high. Leaf 5 by 2 in. (13 by 5 cm), veins 9, medium green, white margin, ovate, wavy. Scape 22 in. (56 cm), bare, straight. Flower medium, funnel-shaped, lavender, flowers during average period, fertile.

H. **'Brigham Blue'** Van Bourgondien.
(see *H. sieboldiana*).

H. **'Bright Edge'**.

H. **'Bright Glow'** Aden IRA/1986.
    AHS-III/17A.   (Figure F-9; Plates 27, 157).
    Plant 16 in. (40.5 cm) dia., 12 in. (31 cm) high. Leaf 6 by 4 in. (15 by 10 cm), veins 10, yellow (lutescent), not variegated, cordate, flat. Scape 18 in. (46 cm), bare, straight. Flower medium, bell-shaped, white, flowers during average period, fertile.
HN: *H.* 'Golden Tardiana' incorrect.
       H. Tardiana Yellow group.
[*H.* 'Aden No. 380' × *H.* 'Aden No. 382'].

H. **'Bright Lights'** Aden/Klehm.
    Plant is a named clone of *H.* 'Tokudama Aureonebulosa', which see, and reported to be more vigorous.
(see *H.* 'Tokudama Aureonebulosa').

H. **'Brim Cup'** Aden IRA/1986.
    AHS-III/16B.   (Plate 97).
    Plant 16 in. (40.5 cm) dia., 12 in. (31 cm) high. Leaf 6 by 5 in. (15 by 13 cm), veins 10, medium green, white margin, round-cordate, cupped-rugose. Scape 18 in. (46 cm), bare, straight. Flower medium, bell-shaped, white, flowers during average period, fertile.
(*H.* 'Aden No. 392' × *H.* 'Wide Brim').

H. **'Broad Band 1'** Krossa.
HN: *H.* 'Broad Band A'.

H. **'Broad Band 2'** Krossa.
HN: *H.* 'Broad Band B'.
       H. 'Krossa No. H-3'.
(see *H.* 'Viettes Yellow Edge').

H. **'Brooke'** Stone/Ruh IRA/1987.
AHS-III/13A.
Plant 12 in. (31 cm) dia., 10 in. (25.5 cm) high. Leaf 8 by 7 in. (20 by 18 cm), veins 10, blue-green, not variegated, cordate, flat. Scape 20 in. (51 cm), bare, oblique. Flower medium, bell-shaped, white, flowers during average period, sterile.
HN: *H.* 'DSM No. 12' Stone.

H. **'Brookwood Blue'** Fraim.
Plant 48 in. (122 cm) dia., 32 in. (81.5 cm) high. Leaf 14 by 11 in. (35.5 by 28 cm), veins 16, blue-green, not variegated, cordate, rugose. Scape 34 in. (86.5 cm), bare, straight. Flower medium, bell-shaped, white, flowers during average period, fertile.
[*H. sieboldiana* hybrid].

H. **'Brother Ronald'** Smith/BHHS IRA/1988.
AHS-III/15B.
Plant 20 in. (51 cm) dia., 15 in. (38 cm) high; 6 by 4 in. (15 by 10 cm), veins 11, blue-green, not variegated, cordate, flat. Scape 16 in. (40.5 cm), bare, straight. Flower medium, bell-shaped, lavender, flowers during average period, fertile.
HN: *H.* Tardiana grex TF 2 × 30.
[*H.* 'Tardiflora' × *H. sieboldiana* 'Elegans'].
(see also *H.* Tardiana grex).

H. **'Bryce'**.

H. **'Buckanon'** Moldovan IRA/1983.
AHS-I/3B.
Plant 48 in. (122 cm) dia., 32 in. (81.5 cm) high. Leaf 14 by 12 in. (35.5 by 31 cm), veins 16, blue-green, not variegated, cordate, rugose. Scape 36 in. (91.5 cm), bare, straight. Flower medium, bell-shaped, white, flowers during average period, fertile.
[*H. sieboldiana* hybrid].

H. **'Buckeye Blue'** Hatfield.   (Figure 4-9).
Plant 48 in. (122 cm) dia., 32 in. (81.5 cm) high. Leaf 14 by 12 in. (35.5 by 31 cm), veins 16, blue-green, not variegated, cordate, rugose. Scape 36 in. (91.5 cm), bare, straight. Flower medium, bell-shaped, white, flowers during average period, fertile.
[*H. sieboldiana* hybrid].

Figure 4-9. *H.* 'Buckeye Blue'; general habit (Soules garden/Schmid)

H. **'Buckshaw Blue'** Smith IRA/1986.
AHS-III/15B.   (Figure 4-10).
AHS multiple award winner: Midwest Blue Award, 1980, exhibited by Mervin Eisel; AHS Nancy Minks Award, 1976, exhibited by Alex Summers. Award of Merit, Wisley Trials,

UK. Raised by Smith at Hilliers Nursery of Winchester and named for Buckshaw Gardens, Sherborne, Dorset, UK. Plant erect, 18 in. (46 cm) dia., 12 in. (31 cm) high. Leaf 6 by 4 in. (15 by 10 cm), veins 13, blue-green, not variegated, cordate, flat. Scape 14 in. (35.5 cm), bare, straight. Flower medium, bell-shaped, white, flowers during average period, fertile.
HN: Wisley No. 821437.
[*H. sieboldiana* × *H.* 'Tokudama'].

Figure 4-10. *H.* 'Buckshaw Blue'; general habit (Honeysong Farm/Schmid)

H. **'Buckwheat Honey'** Benedict IRA/1984.
AHS-III/13A.
Plant 12 in. (31 cm) dia., 10 in. (25.5 cm) high. Leaf 6 by 3 in. (15 by 7.5 cm), veins 6, light green, not variegated, ovate, flat. Scape 36 in. (91.5 cm), foliated, straight. Flower medium, bell-shaped, lavender, summer period, fertile.
[*H.* 'Ginko Craig' × *H. plantaginea*].

H. **'Buffy'** Weissenberger IRA/1986.
AHS-III/15B.
Plant 16 in. (40.5 cm) dia., 6 in. (15 cm) high. Leaf 4 by 2 in. (10 by 5 cm), veins 8, blue-green, not variegated, ovate, flat. Scape 14 in. (35.5 cm), bare, straight. Flower medium, bell-shaped, white, flowers during average period, fertile.
[*H.* 'Hadspen Blue' hybrid].

H. **'Bunchoko'** hort. Japan.
文鳥香
(see *H. sieboldii* 'Bunchoko).
(see also *H.* 'Ginko Craig').

H. **'Butter Rim'** Summers 1969 IRA/1986.
AHS-IV/22A.   (Plate 65)
Plant is similar to *H. sieboldii* 'Kifukurin', which see. Considered a *H.* 'Decorata' hybrid or mutation by some. Broadly, it is a *H. sieboldii* derivative, as is *H.* 'Decorata'. Plant 18 in. (46 cm) dia., 10 in. (25.5 cm) high. Leaf 4 by 2 in. (10 by 5 cm), veins 5, medium green, yellow margin, ovate, flat. Scape 20 in. (51 cm), bare, straight. Flower medium, funnel-shaped, white, flowers during average period, fertile.
[*H.* 'Decorata' hybrid or mutation].
[*H. sieboldii* derivative al].
(see also *H. sieboldii* 'Kifukurin').

H. **'Butter White Rim'** Summers 1987.
Plant 18 in. (46 cm) dia., 10 in. (25.5 cm) high. Leaf 4 by 2 in. (10 by 5 cm), veins 5, green, white margin, ovate, flat. Scape 20 in. (51 cm), bare, straight. Flower medium, funnel-shaped, white, not fragrant, flowers during average period, fertile.
[*H.* 'Butter Rim' mutation].

H. **'Butter Yellow'** Vaughn IRA/1982.
AHS-II/11A.
Plant is low growing, 24 in. (61 cm) dia., 8 in. (20 cm) high. Leaf yellow. Scape 26 in. (66 cm). Flower lavender.

C

H. **'Calypso'** Lachman IRA/1987.
AHS-IV/22A.
Plant erect, 14 in. (35.5 cm) dia., 7 in. (18 cm) high. Leaf 9 by 1.5 in. (23 by 4 cm), veins 4, yellow-white, dark green margin, lanceolate, flat. Scape 18 in. (46 cm), bare, straight. Flower medium, funnel-shaped, lavender, flowers during average period, fertile.
[*H.* (unnamed hybrid) × *H.* 'White Christmas'].

H. **'Camelot'** Smith/BHHS IRA/1988.
AHS-III/15B.
Plant 22 in. (56 cm) dia., 15 in. (38 cm) high. Leaf 7 by 5 in. (18 by 13 cm), veins 12, blue-green, not variegated, cordate, flat. Scape 15 in. (38 cm), bare, straight. Flower medium, bell-shaped, lavender, flowers during average period, fertile.
HN: *H.* Tardiana grex TF 2 × 27.
[*H.* 'Tardiflora' × *H. sieboldiana* 'Elegans'].
(see also *H.* Tardiana grex).

H. **'Candle Glow'** Arett/Minks.
Plant small with mound low. Leaf 5 by 3 in. (13 by 7.5 cm), veins 7, clear to streaky white center with chartreuse margins and yellow streakings along the edge.

H. **'Candle Wax'** Minks IRA/1974.
AHS-III/13A.
Smooth, waxy-looking leaf surface. Plant 12 in. (31 cm) dia., 12 in. (31 cm) high. Leaf 5 by 3 in. (13 by 7.5 cm), veins 8, medium green, not variegated, ovate, wavy. Scape 18 in. (46 cm), foliated, straight. Flower medium, funnel-shaped, white, flowers during average period, fertile.

H. **'Candy Dish'** Houseworth 1986.

H. **'Candy Hearts'** Fisher IRA/1971.
AHS-III/13A.
Plant 28 in. (71 cm) dia., 16 in. (40.5 cm) high. Leaf 6 by 5 in. (15 by 13 cm), veins 12, blue-green, not variegated, cordate, flat. Scape 26 in. (66 cm), bare, straight. Flower medium, bell-shaped, white, flowers during average period, fertile.
[*H. nakaiana* hybrid].

H. capitata **'O Kanzashi'**.

H. capitata **'Oba Kanzashi'**.

H. capitata **'Ogon'**.

H. **'Capitol Dome'** Minks IRA/1980.
AHS-II/7A.
Plant 20 in. (51 cm) dia., 12 in. (31 cm) high. Leaf has pie-crust edge.
[*H.* 'Crested Reef' × *H.* 'Crinkle Cup'].

H. **'Carder Blue'** Summers IRA/1986.
AHS-III/15B.
Plant is a small hybrid (selfed) form of the specioid. One of the many forms extant.
HN: *H.* 'Tokudama Carder Blue'.
H. 'Tokudama Carder Seedling' incorrect.
H. tokudama, Carder seedling.
H. 'Tokudama Mrs Carder'.
[*H.* 'Tokudama' hybrid].

H. **'Carder Venusta'**.
Plant name is an incorrect and obsolete synonym.
(see *H. venusta*).

H. **'Cardwell Yellow'** Ruh/Krossa IRA/1981.
AHS-III/17B.
Plant erect, 24 in. (61 cm) dia., 20 in. (51 cm) high. Leaf 6 by 3 in. (15 by 7.5 cm), veins 13, yellow (lutescent), not variegated, ovate, flat. Scape 32 in. (81.5 cm), bare, straight. Flower medium, bell-shaped, lavender, flowers during average period, fertile.
HN: *H.* 'Krossa No. F-9'.

H. **'Carefree'** Fisher IRA/1971.
AHS-II/7B.
Plant 26 in. (66 cm) dia., 16 in. (40.5 cm) high. Leaf 9 by 6 in. (23 by 15 cm), veins 11, yellow (viridescent), not variegated, ovate, flat. Scape 24 in. (61 cm), bare, straight. Flower medium, bell-shaped, white, flowers during average period, fertile.
[*H.* 'Golden Anniversary' hybrid].

H. **'Carnival'** Lachman No. L81-9-6 IRA/1986.
AHS-II/10B.
Plant 34 in. (86.5 cm) dia., 16 in. (40.5 cm) high. Leaf 17 by 9 in. (43 by 23 cm), veins 10, medium green, bright yellow margin, oval, flat. Scape 34 in. (86.5 cm), foliated, straight. Flower medium, funnel-shaped, lavender, flowers during summer period, fertile.
[*H.* 'Beatrice' hybrid × *H. sieboldiana* 'Frances Williams' hybrid].

H. **'Carol'** Williams (No. 1429) 1963 IRA/1986.
AHS-III/16B.   (Figure 4-11).
Plant 36 in. (91.5 cm) dia., 20 in. (51 cm) high. Leaf 9 by 7 in. (23 by 18 cm), veins 8, dark green, white margin, cordate, flat. Scape 40 in. (101.5 cm), foliated, oblique. Flower medium, funnel-shaped, lavender, flowers during average period, sterile.
HN: *H.* 'Fortunei Albomarginata' group.
H. 'Fortunei Carol'.
H. 'FRW No. 1429'.
[*H.* 'FRW No. 152' mutation].
(see also *H.* 'Fortunei Albomarginata' group).

Figure 4-11. *H.* 'Carol'; general habit (Kuk's Forest garden/Schmid)

H. **'Carols Sister'** Williams.

H. **'Carousel'** Lachman IRA/1989.
Plant erect, 13 in. (30 in.) dia., 9 in. (23 cm) high. Leaf 5 by 3 in. (13 by 7.5 cm), veins 6, dark green, yellow margin, cordate, flat. Scape 15 in. (38 cm), bare, straight. Flower medium, funnel-shaped, lavender, flowers during summer period, fertile.
HN: Lachman No. L83-9-1.
[Hybrid × *H.* 'Reversed'].

H. **'Carrie'** Stone/Ruh IRA/1988.
AHS-IV/22A. (Plate 98).
Listed as *H.* 'Carrie' in the registration list (*The Hosta Journal* 20, no. 1, 1989) but listed as *H.* 'Carrie Ann' in the official judge's handbook (Minks, 1990). Plant 10 in. (25 cm) dia., 4 in. (10 cm) high. Leaf 3.5 by 1.25 in. (9 by 3 cm), green, yellowish to whitish margin, lanceolate, slightly wavy. Scape 22 in. (56 cm), foliated, straight. Flower medium, funnel-shaped, white, flowers during summer period, fertile.
HN: *H.* 'Carrie Ann' Piedmont.
   H. 'DSM No. 6' Stone.
[*H. sieboldii* mutant].

H. **'Carrie Ann'** Piedmont.
(see *H.* 'Carrie').

H. **'Cartwheels'** Summers.
Plant 40 in. (101.5 cm) dia., 28 in. (71 cm) high. Leaf 6 by 5 in. (15 by 13 cm), veins 13, blue-green, yellow margin, cordate, rugose. Scape 32 in. (81.5 cm), bare, straight. Flower medium, bell-shaped, white, flowers during average period, fertile.
HN: *H.* 'Wagon Wheel Sport'.
[(*H. sieboldiana* hybrid) mutation].

H. **'Cassandra'** Wagner IRA/1985.
AHS-V/29B.
Plant 12 in. (31 cm) dia., 6 in. (15 cm) high. Leaf 3 by 1 in. (7.5 by 2.5 cm), veins 3, chartreuse, not variegated, lanceolate, flat. Scape 16 in. (40.5 cm), foliated, straight. Flower medium, funnel-shaped, lavender, flowers during summer period, fertile.
[*H.* 'Petite Gold' × *H.* 'Piedmont Gold'].

H. cathayana **'Nakafu'**.

H. cathayana **'Ogon'**.

H. cathayana **'Shirofukurin'**.

H. **'Cathy Late'** Ruh 1985.
Plant is a later (1–3 weeks) blooming clone of *H.* 'Lancifolia' Engler. Not *H.* 'Tardiflora'. Plant erect, 14 in. (35.5 cm) dia., 10 in. (25.5 cm) high. Leaf 5 by 2 in. (13 by 5 cm), veins 5, green, not variegated, lanceolate, flat. Scape 22 in. (56 cm), bare, straight. Flower medium, funnel-shaped, purple striped, flowers during late period, sterile.
HN: *H.* 'Lancifolia Cathy Late'.
   H. lancifolia tardiflora hort. incorrect.
   H. 'Mack No. 17'.
(see also *H.* 'Lancifolia Cathy Late').

H. **'Celebration'** Aden IRA/1978.
AHS-IV/20A. (Plate 108).
Plant is reported to be the same or nearly the same as *H.* 'Gay Feather', but the latter is a larger cultivar (see Plate 108). Melting out has been reported and can be delayed by planting in optimum sun. Plant erect, 14 in. (35.5 cm) dia., 10 in. (25.5 cm) high. Leaf 5 by 1.5 in. (13 by 4 cm), veins 4, white (albescent), green margin, lanceolate, flat. Scape 18 in. (46 cm), bare, straight. Flower medium, funnel-shaped, purple striped, flowers during average period, sterile.
HN: *H.* 'Gay Feather' sim.
[*H.* 'Aden No. 378' × *H.* 'Aden No. 322'].
(see also *H.* 'Gay Feather').

H. **'Center Stage'** Vaughn IRA/1982.
AHS-IV/20A. (Plate 102).
AHS Nancy Minks Award, 1984, exhibited by Kevin Vaughn. Plant 20 in. (51 cm) dia., 14 in. (35.5 cm) high. Leaf 5 by 1.5 in. (13 by 4 cm), veins 5, white (albescent), green margin, lanceolate, flat. Scape 18 in. (46 cm), bare, straight. Flower medium, funnel-shaped, purple striped, flowers during average period, sterile.

H. **'Century One'** Moldovan IRA/1983.
AHS-I/1A.
Plant 42 in. (106.5 cm) dia., 30 in. (76 cm) high. Leaf 14 by 11 in. (35.5 by 28 cm), veins 16, medium green, not variegated, cordate, rugose. Scape 38 in. (96.5 cm), bare, straight. Flower medium, bell-shaped, white, flowers during average period, fertile.
[*H. sieboldiana* hybrid].

H. **'Challenger'** Fisher IRA/1971.
AHS-II/7A.
Plant 36 in. (91.5 cm) dia., 26 in. (66 cm) high. Leaf 11 by 8 in. (28 by 20 cm), veins 13, medium green, not variegated, cordate, wavy. Scape 36 in. (91.5 cm), foliated, straight. Flower medium, funnel-shaped, white, flowers during average period, fertile.
[*H.* 'Elata' hybrid].

H. **'Chameleon'** Marx/Rodgers IRA/1986.
AHS-III/16B.
Plant 48 in. (122 cm) dia., 34 in. (86.5 cm) high. Leaf 12 by 7 in. (31 by 18 cm), veins 10, medium green, white margin, cordate, rugose. Scape 42 in. (106.5 cm), bare, straight. Flower medium, bell-shaped, white, flowers during average period, fertile.

H. **'Chameleon'** Smith.
HN: *H.* 'Chamaeleon'.
   Wisley No. 821374.
[*H.* 'Fortunei' × *H. sieboldii*].

H. **'Champion'** Simpers/Soules IRA/1985.
AHS-I/3B.
Plant 48 in. (122 cm) dia., 20 in. (51 cm) high. Leaf 13 by 11 in. (33 by 28 cm), veins 16, medium green, not variegated, round-cordate, cupped-rugose. Scape 24 in. (61 cm), bare, straight. Flower medium, bell-shaped, white, flowers during average period, fertile.
[*H. sieboldiana* × *H.* 'Tokudama'].

H. **'Change of Tradition'** Zilis IRA/1988.
AHS-IV/22B.
Plant 40 in. (101.5 cm) dia., 20 in. (51 cm) high. Leaf 6 by 2 in. (15 by 5 cm), veins 8, green, white margin, lanceolate, flat. Scape 24 in. (61 cm), bare, straight. Flower medium, funnel-shaped, lavender, flowers during late period, fertility(?).
[*H.* 'Lancifolia' mutation] (?).

H. 'Changing Moods' Vaughn IRA/1983.
    AHS-V/29A.
    Plant 8 in. (20 cm) dia., 4 in. (10 cm) high. Leaf 4 by 2 in. (10 by 5 cm), veins 7, yellow (albescent), not variegated, lanceolate, flat. Scape 12 in. (31 cm), bare, straight. Flower medium, funnel-shaped, lavender, flowers during average period, fertile.
[H. 'Janet' hybrid × H. 'William Lachman' hybrid].

H. 'Chantilly Lace' Lachman IRA/1988.
    AHS-IV/22B.
    Plant 14 in. (35.5 cm) dia., 9 in. (23 cm) high. Leaf 6 by 2 in. (15 by 5 cm), veins 5, medium green, whitish margin, lanceolate, wavy. Scape 12 in. (31 cm), foliated, straight. Flower medium, white, flowers during summer period, fertility(?).
[H. 'Calypso' × H. 'Halcyon'].

H. 'Chariot Wheels'.
    Plant 24 in. (61 cm) dia., 16 in. (40.5 cm) high. Leaf 6 by 5 in. (15 by 13 cm), veins 13, medium green, yellow margin, cordate, rugose. Scape 22 in. (56 cm), bare, straight. Flower medium, bell-shaped, white, flowers during average period, fertile.

H. 'Charldon' Williams No. 1380.
Summers No. 143.

H. 'Charlie John' Hatfield.

H. 'Charlotte Holman' Solberg.
    Plant has variegated leaves, with some leaves all green. Plant 8 in. (20 cm) dia., 5 in. (13 cm) high. Leaf 3 by 1 in. (7.5 by 2.5 cm), veins 4, green, variegated, lanceolate, flat. Scape 12 in. (31 cm), bare, straight. Flower medium, funnel-shaped, purple-striped, flowers during summer period, fertile.
[H. sieboldii derivative].

H. 'Charon' Klose 1982.
HN: H. 'Fortunei Charon' Klose 1982.
[H. 'Fortunei' hybrid].

H. 'Chartreuse' Holly 1955 IRA/1968.
    AHS-III/18B.
    Plant has long narrow leaves, chartreuse in spring, turn green.
HN: H. 'Krossa No. C-2'.

H. 'Chartreuse Edger' Aden 1975.

H. 'Chartreuse Piecrust' Owens IRA/1985.
    AHS-III/17B.
    Plant 24 in. (61 cm) dia., 10 in. (25.5 cm) high. Leaf 6 by 5 in. (15 by 13 cm), veins 13, chartreuse, not variegated, cordate, piecrust margin. Scape 26 in. (66 cm), foliated, straight. Flower medium, bell-shaped, white, flowers during average period, fertile.
[H. 'Bengee' hybrid].

H. 'Chartreuse Waves' Aden 1974.

H. 'Chartreuse Wedge' Aden IRA/1976.
    AHS-I/5B.
    Plant 48 in. (122 cm) dia., 20 in. (51 cm) high. Leaf 14 by 10 in. (35.5 by 25.5 cm), veins 12, chartreuse, not variegated, ovate, flat. Scape 56 in. (142 cm), bare, straight. Flower medium, bell-shaped, white, flowers during average period, fertile.
[H. 'Green Wedge' × H. 'Green Wedge'].

H. 'Chartreuse Wiggles' Aden IRA/1976.
    AHS-V/29B.
    AHS Nancy Minks Award, 1967, exhibited by Paul Aden. Plant erect, 10 in. (25.5 cm) dia., 8 in. (20 cm) high. Leaf 5 by 1 in. (13 by 2.5 cm), veins 3, chartreuse, not variegated, lanceolate, wavy-undulate. Scape 18 in. (46 cm), bare, straight. Flower medium, funnel-shaped, purple striped, flowers during average period, fertile.
[H. 'Wogon' hybrid].
[H. sieboldii form].

H. 'Checkerboard' Tompkins.
    Plant is a H. montana form with uneven, sometimes checkerboard-patterned, greyish green variegation over a dark green leaf, 10 in. (25.5 cm) long by 8 in. (20 cm) wide.

H. 'Cheesecake' Klehm 1983.   (Figure 4-12).
    Plant is a sport found in H. 'Vera Verde' clumps. Many different leaf variegations found but principally white leaf centers with green margins. Unstable and will revert to H. 'Vera Verde'. Plant erect, 9 in. (23 cm) dia., 6 in. (15 cm) high. Leaf 3 by 0.5 in. (7.5 by 1 cm), veins 3, white (viridescent), green margin, lanceolate, flat. Scape 14 in. (35.5 cm), bare, straight. Flower medium, funnel-shaped, purple striped, flowers during average period, fertile.
[H. 'Vera Verde' mutation].
(see also H. 'Vera Verde').

Figure 4-12. H. 'Cheesecake'; general habit, reverting to H. 'Vera Verde' (Hosta Hill)

H. 'Chelsea' UK.
    Plant is same as H. 'Fortunei Albopicta'.
HN: Chelsea Hosta.
(see H. 'Fortunei Albopicta').

H. 'Chelsea Babe' BHHS IRA/1988.
    AHS-IV/20A.
    Plant is a purported dwarf form of H. 'Fortunei Albopicta'. Named by Smith/Grounds. Has only 5 to 6 pairs of veins and may not be related to H. 'Fortunei' but may be a viridescent mediovariegated form of another taxon. By some authorities connected with H. 'Maya'.
(see also H. 'Fortunei Albopicta').
(see also H. 'Maya').

H. 'Chelsea Ore' Compton/Chelsea Physic Garden IRA/1989.
    Plant has a dark green, irregular margin on yellow green leaf. The leaf is albescent becoming almost white. Root system moderately stoloniferous. Leaf 6 by 2 in. (15 by 5 cm), veins 6. Flower white, fragrant as the parent plant.
[H. plantaginea derivative].

H. 'Cherub' Lachman IRA/1989.
Plant 9 in. (23 cm) dia., 6 in. (15 cm) high. Leaf 3 by 2.5 in. (7.5 by 6 cm), veins 6, medium green, white margin, cordate, slightly rugose. Scape 8 in. (20 cm), bare, straight. Flower funnel-shaped, medium, lavender, flowers during average period, fertility(?).
[H. 'Crepe Suzette' × H. 'Blue Moon'].

H. 'Chicago Frances Williams'.
HN: H. 'Squash Adler Variegated'.
[H. sieboldiana Aureomarginata group].
(see H. 'Aurora Borealis').

H. 'Chiffon' O'Harra.
Plant 22 in. (56 cm) dia., 16 in. (40.5 cm) high. Leaf 3 by 2 in. (7.5 by 5 cm), veins 8, yellow (viridescent), not variegated, ovate, flat. Scape 24 in. (61 cm), bare, straight. Flower medium, funnel-shaped, lavender, flowers during average period, fertile.

H. 'China Doll' Savory IRA/1988.
AHS-IV/23B.
Plant erect, 15 in. (38 cm) dia., 8 in. (20 cm) high. Leaf 4 by 1.5 in. (10 by 4 cm), veins 6, chartreuse, not variegated, lanceolate, flat. Scape 14 in. (35.5 cm), foliated, straight. Flower medium, funnel-shaped, lavender striped, flowers during summer period, fertility(?).
[H. 'August Moon' × hybrid].

H. 'Chinese Sunrise' Summers.
(Figure 2-17; Plate 9).
Plant 28 in. (71 cm) dia., 14 in. (35.5 cm) high. Leaf 6 by 3 in. (15 by 7.5 cm), veins 5, yellow (viridescent), green margin, lanceolate, flat. Scape 28 in. (71 cm), foliated, oblique. Flower medium, bell-shaped, lavender, flowers during late period, fertile.
HN: H. cathayana variegata hort. incorrect.
     H. cathayana 'Variegata' incorrect.
     H. cathayana 'Variegated'.
(see also H. cathayana 'Nakafu').

H. 'Chippewa' Arett IRA/1986.
AHS-II/8B.
Plant is similar to the parent plant but smaller. Variegation is reversed: center yellow, margin green.
HN: H. sieboldiana Mediovariegata group.
[H. sieboldiana Aureomarginata group derivative].

H. 'Chiquita' Eisel IRA/1979.
AHS-III/17A.
Plant 48 in. (122 cm) dia., 24 in. (61 cm) high. Leaf 9 by 7 in. (23 by 17 cm), veins 13, yellow (viridescent), not variegated, ovate, flat. Scape 32 in. (81.5 cm), foliated, oblique. Flower medium, funnel-shaped, lavender, flowers during average period, fertile.

H. 'Chirifu' Japan incorrect.
散斑オオバギボウシ
Plant is a mutation of H. montana and there are 2 forms, either white- or yellow-spotted/variegated. In the wild from Gumma and Tokyo prefectures. Correct name is H. montana 'Chirifu'.
JN: Chirifu Oba Giboshi hort.
[H. montana mutation].
(see H. montana 'Chirifu').

H. 'Choko Nishiki' Japan.
朝光錦
Choko Nishiki Giboshi, "colorful morning sunray hosta." A H. montana sport discovered in the wild by Asami. Name derived from combining the Japanese characters for Mr. Asami and "ray (light)." Clear yellow center and green margin. Stable variegation. Highly valued in Japan. Similar variegated forms are still being found. When mature it is similar to H. 'On Stage', which see.
HN: H. 'Choukou Nishiki'.
     H. 'Morning Sunray'.
JN: Choko Nishiki Giboshi hort.
     Choukou Nishiki Giboshi hort.
[H. montana derivative].

H. 'Christmas Gold' Seaver.
Plant has medium-sized, rugose, cupped leaves that spread. Retains its lemon-yellow color which contrasts with the purple seed capsules in fall.

H. 'Christmas Tree' Vaughn IRA/1982.
AHS-II/10B.   (Plate 99).
Plant 36 in. (91.5 cm) dia., 20 in. (51 cm) high. Leaf 8 by 5 in. (20 by 13 cm), veins 8, medium green, white margin, cordate, rugose. Scape 32 in. (81.5 cm), foliated, oblique. Flower medium, funnel-shaped, white, flowers during average period, fertile.
[H. 'Vaughn V 73-2' × H. sieboldiana 'Frances Williams'].

H. 'Circus Clown' Minks IRA/1983.
AHS-II/7A.
Plant 36 in. (91.5 cm) dia., 20 in. (51 cm) high. Leaf 10 by 8 in. (25.5 by 20 cm), veins 13, medium green, not variegated, cordate, ruffled piecrust margin. Scape 32 in. (81.5 cm), bare, straight. Flower medium, bell-shaped, lavender, flowers during average period, fertile.
[H. 'Ruffles' × H. 'Green Piecrust'].

H. 'Citation' Aden IRA/1980.
AHS-III/14B.
Plant 14 in. (35.5 cm) dia., 8 in. (20 cm) high. Leaf 4 by 2 in. (10 by 5 cm), veins 7, medium green, white margin, ovate, wavy-undulate. Scape 1 in. (2.5 cm), foliated, oblique. Flower medium, funnel-shaped, white, flowers during average period, fertile.
[H. 'Vicki Aden' hybrid].

H. 'City Lights' Aden IRA/1978.
AHS-II/11A.
Plant 36 in. (91.5 cm) dia., 24 in. (61 cm) high. Leaf 11 by 8 in. (28 by 20 cm), veins 13, yellow (lutescent), not variegated, cordate, flat. Scape 38 in. (96.5 cm), bare, straight. Flower medium, bell-shaped, white, flowers during average period, fertile.
[H. 'White Vision' × H. 'Golden Prayers'].

H. 'Classic Delight' Fisher IRA/1973.
AHS-II/7B.
Plant 32 in. (81.5 cm) dia., 18 in. (46 cm) high. Leaf 10 by 8 in. (25 by 20 cm), veins 11, medium green, not variegated, cordate, piecrust margin. Scape 34 in. (86.5 cm), bare, oblique. Flower medium, funnel-shaped, white, flowers during average period, fertile.
[H. 'Green Piecrust' hybrid].

H. 'Claudia' Grenfell 1990.
Plant is named for Diana Grenfell's daughter and has lanceolate leaves of medium green color. The flowers are

purple and appear in late summer. Leaf 6 by 1 in. (15 by 2 cm). [*H. sieboldii* × *H. clausa* var. *normalis* hybrid].

H. clausa 'Stolon'.

H. clavata 'Nagaba'.

H. clavata 'Urajiro'.

H. 'Clokei' Viette.

H. 'Color Accord' Aden IRA/1982.
    AHS-III/16A.
    Plant 26 in. (66 cm) dia., 18 in. (46 cm) high. Leaf 5 by 4 in. (13 by 10 cm), veins 12, medium green, streaked yellow, cordate, flat. Scape 22 in. (56 cm), bare, oblique. Flower medium, funnel-shaped, lavender, flowers during summer period, sterile.
[*H.* 'Fascination' hybrid].

H. 'Color Fantasy' Aden IRA/1980.
    AHS-III/16A.
    Plant 18 in. (46 cm) dia., 10 in. (25.5 cm) high. Leaf 6 by 4 in. (15 by 10 cm), veins 6, green, streaked chartreuse and near white, cordate, flat. Scape 16 in. (40.5 cm), foliated, straight. Flower medium, funnel-shaped, lavender, flowers during late period, sterile.
[*H.* 'Gala' hybrid].

H. 'Color Glory' Aden IRA/1980.
    AHS-III/14B.
    The following description is the original one provided to the IRA and is for a plant which is not in commerce. The plant marketed by Klehm Nursery (cfr. Aden, 1988: ic. p. 121) under the same name, *H.* 'Color Glory', is a different taxon, being a mutation of *H. sieboldiana* 'Elegans' and similar to *H.* 'George Smith', which see. Plant 34 in. (86.5 cm) dia., 26 in. (66 cm) high. Leaf 5 by 4 in. (13 by 10 cm), veins 8, green, streaked multicolor, cordate, flat. Scape 34 in. (86.5 cm), foliated, straight. Flower medium, funnel-shaped, lavender, flowers during average period, sterile.
[*H.* 'Fascination' × *H.* 'Intrigue'].

H. 'Color Glory'[PPAF] Aden/Klehm 1988.
    AHS-III/14B.   (Plate 100).
    The following description is for the plant marketed by Klehm Nursery (cfr. Aden, 1988: ic. p. 121). This taxon is different from *H.* 'Great Expectations', which see (Pollock, 1990). Compare leaf colors and shapes in Plate 100. Plant 40 in. (101.5 cm) dia., 30 in. (76 cm) high. Leaf 9 by 8 in. (23 by 20 cm), veins yellow (albescent), blue-green margin, round-cordate, cupped-rugose. Scape 32 in. (81 cm), foliated, straight. Flower medium, bell-shaped, white, flowers during average period, fertile.
HN: *H. sieboldiana* Mediovariegata group.
[*H. sieboldiana* 'Elegans' mutation].
(see also *H. sieboldiana* Mediovariegata group).

H. 'Color Riot'.

H. 'Color Splash'.

H. 'Colossal' Savory IRA/1977.
    AHS-I/1B.
    Plant 48 in. (122 cm) dia., 28 in. (71 cm) high. Leaf 14 by 10 in. (35.5 by 25.5 cm), veins 12, medium green, not variegated, cordate, furrowed. Scape 35 in. (89 cm), foliated, straight. Flower medium, funnel-shaped, lavender, flowers during average period, fertile.
[*H. montana* hybrid] .

H. 'Columbus Circle' Santa Lucia.
    Plant 26 in. (66 cm) high. Leaf 6 by 6 in. (15 by 15 cm), medium green, wide yellow margin, cordate. Flower medium, lavender, fertile.
[(*H.* 'Iron Gate Supreme' × *H. sieboldiana* 'Frances Williams' hybrid) mutation].

H. 'Comeuppance' Aden IRA/1982.
    AHS-III/14A.
    Plant erect, 20 in. (51 cm) dia., 16 in. (40.5 cm) high. Leaf 6 by 4 in. (15 by 10 cm), veins 12, yellow (lutescent), streaked yellow, cordate, flat. Scape 20 in. (51 cm), bare, straight. Flower medium, funnel-shaped, white, flowers during average period, sterile.
[*H.* 'Vicki Aden' × *H.* 'Fascination'].

H. 'Connie' Benedict IRA/1987.
    AHS-II/8A.
    Plant 30 in. (76 cm) dia., 20 in. (51 cm) high. Leaf 12 by 8 in. (31 by 20 cm), veins 12, medium green, yellow margin, cordate, rugose. Scape 24 in. (61 cm), bare, straight. Flower medium, funnel-shaped, lavender, flowers during average period, fertile.
[*H.* 'Sunlight' × *H. sieboldiana* 'Frances Williams' mutation].

H. 'Copenhagen Blue' Houseworth 1986.
[*H.* 'August Moon' hybrid].

H. 'Coquette' Benedict IRA/1987.
    AHS-IV/22B.
    Plant has irregular margins streaky to center. Plant erect, 14 in. (35.5 cm) dia., 12 in. (31 cm) high. Leaf 5 by 4 in. (13 by 10 cm), veins 7, medium green, chartreuse to whitish margin, ovate, flat. Scape 18 in. (46 cm), bare, oblique. Flower medium, funnel-shaped, lavender, flowers during average period, fertile.
[*H.* 'Neat Splash' × *H.* 'Neat Splash' hybrid].

H. 'Corduroy' Moldovan IRA/1983.
    AHS-I/1B.
    Plant 60 in. (152.5 cm) dia., 36 in. (91.5 cm) high. Leaf 15 by 11 in. (38 by 28 cm), veins 13, medium green, not variegated, cordate, flat. Scape 42 in. (106.5 cm), bare, straight. Flower medium, funnel-shaped, lavender, flowers during average period, fertile.
[*H.* 'Green Acres' hybrid].

H. 'Counter Point' Aden IRA/1982.
    AHS-III/16B.
    Plant 24 in. (61 cm) dia., 18 in. (46 cm) high. Leaf 7 by 5 in. (18 by 13 cm), veins 9, chartreuse, streaked blue-green and yellow, white margin, cordate, flat. Scape 24 in. (61 cm), bare, straight. Flower medium, funnel-shaped, lavender, flowers during average period, sterile.
[*H.* 'Fortunei Francee' derivative].

H. 'County Park' Grounds/Hutchins IRA/1983.
    AHS-III/13A.
    Plant has very short petioles, making a dense clump, and is 16 in. (40.5 cm) dia., 8 in. (20 cm) high. Leaf 5 by 4 in. (13 by 10 cm), veins 10, medium green, not variegated, cordate, flat. Scape 18 in. (45 cm), bare, straight. Flower medium, bell-shaped, white, flowers during average period, sterile.
HN: *H.* 'Country Park' Grenfell (1990) incorrect.
[*H.* 'Elata' hybrid].
[*H.* 'Fortunei' × *H.* 'Tokudama' al].

H. 'Cover Girl'.
(see *H.* 'Olive Bailey Langdon').

H. 'Craig No. 00' Craig.

Plants numbered by Jack E. Craig, who resided in Japan for a period of time and reported on a number of field trips where he examined wild populations and collected some specimens (Craig, 1970, 1971, 1972). Having no identification for most of his plant, he numbered collected specimens as well as some specimens which he received from other collectors. He sent several specimens to Summers whose numbers are included with Craig's for cross-checking, and also their current identification, where known:

H. 'Craig No. 13' Craig/Summers No. 183 1969
= *H.* 'Tortifrons'.
H. 'Craig No. 19' Craig/Summers No. 185 1969
= *H. longipes* dwarf form ad int.
H. 'Craig No. C-1' Craig/Summers No. 184 1969
= *H. pachyscapa* ad int.
H. 'Craig No. C-2' Craig/Summers No. 324 1969
= *Oze Giboshi* hort
= *H. sieboldii* 'Spathulata'.
H. 'Craig No. C-3' Craig/Summers No. 181 1969
= [*H. longipes* × *H. montana*].
H. 'Craig No. C-4' Craig/Summers No. 182 1969
= [*H. montana* × *H. sieboldii*].
H. 'Craig No. H-1' Craig/Summers No. 331 1969
= *H. tardiva* ad int.
H. 'Craig No. H-2' Craig/Summers No. 332 1969
= *H. tardiva* ad int.
H. 'Craig No. H-6' Craig/Summers No. 334 1969
= *H.* 'Purple Bloom Stock'.
H. 'Craig No. H-7' Craig/Summers No. 335 1969
= *H.* 'Hirao No. 7'
= *Kifukurin Renge Giboshi* (see *H.* 'Fortunei Aureomarginata').

H. 'Craigs Temptation' Craig/Schenk 1970.

Plant was collected in Aichi Prefecture near ancient temple grounds by J. E. Craig (1970; see also Chapter 5 of the present volume) and named by George Schenk. A plant seen under this name in exhibitions looks like *H. nakaiana* or a hybridized form of it, but is probably not *H.* 'Craigs Temptation' because according to his own report (Craig, 1990), Craig did not collect *H. nakaiana*; he bought it in a flower market.

In 1969 Craig and his friend Atsuya Hamada, guided by Hirano, made an extensive study of *H. hypoleuca* growing in the wild in the southern Kiso range of the Central Alps, near the village of Horaiji, in Aichi Prefecture. He observed many different forms of this species, which he later wrote about in detail (Craig, 1970), but he was not able to collect any specimens. This species is, according to Craig, his favorite one and one that is difficult to collect because it is scarce. Although not protected, it grows on inaccessible, vertical rock cliffs, usually out of reach of collectors. Tempted, he later returned and collected a few wild plants, sending them on to Roy Davidson. Craig (1990) surmises that it was one of the many types of *H. hypoleuca* which he sent to Davidson that was named *H.* 'Craigs Temptation' by Schenk.

H. 'Cream Edge' Fisher 1960.
(see *H.* 'Fisher Cream Edge').

H. 'Cream Edge Seer' Tompkins.

H. 'Cream Flash' Wallace No. 86-111.

Plant is a center-variegated sport with the outer leaves becoming green and inner leaves yellow streaked. All yellow in spring, viridescent. Several clones exist. Plant 32 in. (81.5 cm) dia., 16 in. (40.5 cm) high. Leaf 9 by 7 in. (23 by 18 cm), veins 8, medium green, streaked yellow, cordate, flat. Scape 34 in. (86.5 cm), bare, straight. Flower medium, bell-shaped, purple, flowers during average period, fertile.
HN: *H. ventricosa* 'Cream Flash'.
[*H. ventricosa* 'Aureomaculata' hybrid].

H. 'Cream Puff'.

H. 'Crepe Suzette' Lachman IRA/1986.
AHS-IV/22B.

AHS Nancy Minks Award, 1986, exhibited by Eleanor and William Lachman. Plant 12 in. (31 cm) dia., 6 in. (15 cm) high. Leaf 5 by 2 in. (13 by 5 cm), veins 4, medium green, white margin, ovate, flat. Scape 12 in. (31 cm), foliated, straight. Flower medium, funnel-shaped, lavender, flowers during average period, fertile.
HN: Lachman L80-2-1.
[*H.* 'Flamboyant' hybrid].

H. 'Crescent Moon' Walters Gardens IRA/1988.
AHS-III/16A.

Plant has a pure white margin wider at the tip and extending toward midrib. Plant 28 in. (71 cm) dia., 20 in. (51 cm) high. Leaf 6 by 5 in. (15 by 13 cm), veins 12, medium green, white margin, cordate, flat-wavy. Scape 30 in. (76 cm), bare, straight. Flower medium, lavender, flowers during average period, fertile.
[*H.* 'Lunar Eclipse' mutation].

H. 'Crested Reef' Minks IRA/1975.
AHS-II/7A.   (Figure 4-13).

Plant 32 in. (81.5 cm) dia., 20 in. (51 cm) high. Leaf 9 by 8 in. (23 by 20 cm), veins 12, medium green, not variegated, cordate, flat, ruffled margin. Scape 30 in. (76 cm), bare, oblique. Flower medium, funnel-shaped, lavender, flowers during average period, fertile.
[*H.* 'August Moon' × *H.* 'Ruffles'].

Figure 4-13. *H.* 'Crested Reef'; general habit (Hosta Hill)

H. 'Crested Surf' Wade.

Plant small. Leaf 5 by 2 in. (13 by 5 cm), veins 5, medium green, white margin, lanceolate, ruffled.

H. 'Crinkle Cup' Fisher IRA/1971.
AHS-III/13A.

Plant 24 in. (61 cm) dia., 14 in. (35.5 cm) high. Leaf 8 by 6 in. (20 by 15 cm), veins 8, medium green, yellow (viridescent), cordate, cupped-rugose. Scape 20 in. (51 cm), bare, straight. Flower medium, funnel-shaped, lavender, flowers during average period, fertile. In 1979 Fisher used the spelling "crinkled."
HN: *H.* 'Crinkled Cup' Fisher 1979.
[*H.* 'Golden Anniversary' hybrid].

H. 'Crinkled Joy'.

Plant 32 in. (81.5 cm) dia., 22 in. (56 cm) high. Leaf 7 by 5 in. (18 by 13 cm), veins 13, blue-green, not variegated, cordate, rugose. Scape 32 in. (81.5 cm), foliated, straight. Flower medium, bell-shaped, white, flowers during average period, fertile.

H. 'Crinoline Petticoats' Soules.

Plant is a huge, very rugose *H. sieboldiana* form plant with scapes slightly taller than the form.

H. 'Crispula'.

H. crispula.

H. 'Crispula Lutescens' nom. nudum Hylander 1954.

An unstable, European, mosaic, mutant form of *H.* 'Crispula Viridis'. Emerges green, becomes yellow spotted, but eventually reverts to all-green. Several clones exist, all being more-or-less unstable. In North America a cultivar infected with a virus looks much the same but is infectious and should be destroyed (see Appendix F).

HN: *Funkia marginata lutescens* Anonymous, in Siebold, 1876.

H. 'Crispula Viridis' hort.

AHS-III/133A   (Figures 3-9, 4-14).
アオバサザナミギボウシ

An all-green form of the species, but the leaf margin is not as undulate. *Aoba* in *Aoba Sazanami Giboshi* means green leaf, and the name indicates that a green-leaved form also exists in Japan. Maekawa considered *H. kiyosumiensis* to be very closely related to *H.* 'Crispula' but the latter has a taller scape and a much higher flower count.

HN: *H. crispula* f. *viridis* hort. nom. nudum
  H. 'Crispula Viridis' hort.
  H. 'Krossa No. K-7'.
  H. 'Krossa No. G-1'.
  H. 'Viridis' hort. pp incorrect.
  H. viridis incorrect.
JN: *Aoba Sazanami Giboshi.*

Figure 4-14. *H.* 'Crispula Viridis'; general habit (right center); *H.* 'Big Daddy' (top right and behind); white-margined *H.* 'Herifu' (left front) used as edger with Japanese Painted Fern (*Athyrium niponicum* var. *pictum*); *H. sieboldiana* green form (left center) (Hosta Hill)

H. 'Crown Jewel' Walters Gardens IRA/1984.

AHS-IV/20B.   (Figure 4-41).

Plant 8 in. (20 cm) dia., 4 in. (10 cm) high. Leaf 4 by 2 in. (10 by 5 cm), veins 7, chartreuse, white margin, cordate, cupped. Scape 10 in. (25.5 cm), bare, straight. Flower medium, funnel-shaped, lavender, flowers during average period, sterile.

[*H.* 'Gold Drop' mutation].

H. 'Crown Prince' Ross/Ruh 1977 IRA/1978.

AHS-IV/20A.

Plant erect, 18 in. (46 cm) dia., 10 in. (25.5 cm) high. Leaf 5 by 3 in. (13 by 7.5 cm), veins 7, chartreuse, pale green margins and splashes, ovate, wavy-undulate. Scape 18 in. (46 cm), bare, straight. Flower medium, funnel-shaped, purple, flowers during average period, sterile.

H. 'Crowned Imperial' Walters Gardens IRA/1988.

AHS-III/16B.

Plant 32 in. (81.5 cm) dia., 26 in. (66 cm) high. Leaf 9 by 6 in. (23 by 15 cm), veins 9, dark green, white margin, cordate, flat. Scape 48 in. (122 cm), foliated, straight. Flower medium, funnel-shaped, lavender, flowers during average period, sterile.

HN: *H.* 'Crown Imperial' incorrect.
  H. 'Fortunei Crowned Imperial'.
  [*H.* 'Fortunei Hyacinthina' mutation].

H. 'Crusader' Lachman IRA/1989.

Plant 30 in. (76 cm) dia., 16 in. (40 cm) high. Leaf 7 by 5 in. (18 by 13 cm), veins 9–10, dark green, irregular white margin, cordate, some rugosity. Scape 26 in. (65 cm), bare, straight. Flower medium, funnel-shaped, lavender, flowers during summer period, sterility(?).

HN: Lachman No. L83-89-3.
  [(*H.* 'Resonance' × *H.* 'P14-3)' × *H.* 'Halcyon']

H. 'Cup of Cheer' Houseworth 1986.

H. 'Cupids Arrow' Walters Gardens IRA/1988.

AHS-IV/20A.

Plant 18 in. (46 cm) dia., 10 in. (25.5 cm) high. Leaf 5 by 3 in. (13 by 7.5 cm), veins 8, white (albescent), green margin, lanceolate, flat. Scape 20 in. (51 cm), bare, straight. Flower medium, lavender, flowers during average period, sterile.

[*H.* 'Candy Hearts' mutation].

H. 'Curlew' Smith/BHHS IRA/1988.

AHS-III/15B.

Plant 21 in. (53.5 cm) dia., 10 in. (25.5 cm) high. Leaf 5 by 4 in. (13 by 10 cm), veins 9, blue-green, not variegated, cordate, flat. Scape 22 in. (56 cm), bare, straight. Flower medium, lavender, flowers during average period, fertility(?).

HN: *H.* Tardiana grex TF 2 × 5.
  [*H.* 'Tardiflora' × *H. sieboldiana* 'Elegans'].
  (see also *H.* Tardiana grex).

H. 'Curley Top' Benedict IRA/1985.

AHS-IV/19A.

Plant 14 in. (35.5 cm) dia., 10 in. (25.5 cm) high. Leaf 4 by 1 in. (10 by 2.5 cm), veins 4, medium green, not variegated, lanceolate, wavy-undulate. Scape 18 in. (46 cm), foliated, straight. Flower medium, funnel-shaped, lavender, flowers during summer period, sterile.

[*H.* 'Ginko Craig' × *H. plantaginea*].

H. 'Curls' Minks.

Plant is similar to *H.* 'Tall Twister' but larger and more erect. Plant 18 in. (36 cm) dia., 18 in. (36 cm) high. Leaf 7 by 2 in. (13 by 5 cm), veins 6, green, not variegated lanceolate, wavy-undulate. Scape 28 in. (70 cm), bare, straight. Flower medium, funnel-shaped, purple striped, flowers during summer period, fertile.

[*H. rectifolia* form hybrid].

H. **'Curly Locks'** Lachman IRA/1989.
Plant 14 in. (35.5 cm) dia., 5 in. (13 cm) high. Leaf 5 by 2 in. (13 by 5 cm), veins 3–4, dark green, yellowish green (albescent) margin, lanceolate, wavy-undulate. Scape 14 in. (35 cm), bare, straight. Flower medium, funnel-shaped, purple striped, flowers during summer period, fertile.
HN: Lachman No. L84-83-1.
[Hybrid (L82-18) × Hybrid]

H. **'Cyclops'** Tompkins.
Plant large, leaf 13 by 10 in. (33 by 25.5 cm), veins 16.
[*H. sieboldiana* hybrid].

H. **'Cynthia'** Tompkins IRA/1984.
AHS-II/12A.
Plant has unstable variegation and all-green leaves often appear. No two leaves alike, variegation whitish green on bluish green, blotches, patches, streaks, very irregular. Plant 36 in. (91.5 cm) dia., 16 in. (40.5 cm) high. Leaf 13 by 10 in. (33 by 25.5 cm), veins 12, yellow (viridescent), green margin, cordate, piecrust margin. Scape 34 in. (86.5 cm), bare, straight. Flower medium, funnel-shaped, lavender, flowers during average period, sterile.
[*H. montana* hybrid].

D

H. **'Daily Joy'** Fisher IRA/1973.
AHS-III/13B.
Plant 27 in. (68.5 cm) dia., 20 in. (51 cm) high. Leaf 11 by 9 in. (28 by 23 cm), veins 12, medium green, not variegated, cordate, piecrust margin. Scape 30 in. (76 cm), foliated, straight. Flower medium, funnel-shaped, white, flowers during average period, sterile.
[*H.* 'Crispula' hybrid].

H. **'Dancing Eddie'** Japan.
(see *H.* 'Uzu No Mai').

H. **'Daniel'** Weissenberger IRA/1986.
AHS-IV/21B.
Plant 12 in. (31 cm) dia., 6 in. (15 cm) high. Leaf 2 by 1.5 in. (5 by 4 cm), veins 5, blue-green, not variegated, round-cordate, cupped-rugose. Scape 14 in. (35.5 cm), bare, straight. Flower medium, funnel-shaped, lavender, flowers during average period, sterile.
[*H.* 'Blue Cadet' hybrid].

H. **'Dark Victory'** Savory IRA/1977.
AHS-IV/19B.
Plant 22 in. (56 cm) dia., 14 in. (35.5 cm) high. Leaf 5 by 2 in. (13 by 5 cm), veins 5, dark green, not variegated, ovate, rugose. Scape 30 in. (76 cm), bare, straight. Flower medium, funnel-shaped, purple, flowers during average period, sterile.
[*H. sieboldii* f. *spathulata* hybrid ad int].

H. **'Davidson Green'**.
Plant 30 in. (76 cm) dia., 18 in. (46 cm) high. Leaf 9 by 7 in. (23 by 18 cm), veins 12, medium green, not variegated, cordate, rugose. Scape 24 in. (61 cm), foliated, straight. Flower medium, bell-shaped, white, flowers during average period, fertile.

H. **'Daybreak'** Aden IRA/1986.
AHS-II/11A.
Plant 36 in. (91.5 cm) dia., 22 in. (56 cm) high. Leaf 12 by 8 in. (31 by 20 cm), veins 12, chartreuse, not variegated, cordate, flat. Scape 28 in. (71 cm), bare, straight. Flower medium, funnel-shaped, lavender, flowers during summer period, sterile.

H. **'Dear Heart'** Minks IRA/1975.
AHS-IV/19A.
Plant 14 in. (35.5 cm) dia., 10 in. (25.5 cm) high. Leaf 4 by 3 in. (10 by 7.5 cm), veins 8–10, blue-green, not variegated, cordate, cupped. Scape 18 in. (46 cm), foliated, straight. Flower medium, funnel-shaped, lavender, flowers during average period, sterile.
[*H. nakaiana* × *H.* 'Blue Boy'].

H. **'Debutante'** Aden IRA/1978.
AHS-III/16B.
Plant erect, 16 in. (40.5 cm) dia., 12 in. (31 cm) high. Leaf 4 by 3 in. (10 by 7.5 cm), veins 9, blue-green, streaked yellow, cordate, flat. Scape 18 in. (46 cm), bare, straight. Flower medium, funnel-shaped, lavender, flowers during summer period, sterile.
[*H.* 'Wahoo' × *H.* 'Flamboyant'].

H. **'Decorata'**.
H. decorata.

H. **'Decorata Minor'** hort. incorrect.
Plant name is an incorrect synonym.
HN: *H. decorata minor* hort. incorrect.
(see *H.* 'Decorata').

H. **'Decorata Normalis'**.
H. decorata f. *normalis*.

H. **'Delta Dawn'** Vaughn 1990.
Plant is a large bright yellow cultivar with leaves that have an irregular white margin. The scape is foliated and the flowers are white.
[*H.* 'Aztec Treasure' hybrid × *H.* 'William Lachman' hybrid].

H. **'Density'** Minks.

H. **'Devon Blue'** Smith/Archibald/Bowden BHHS IRA/1988.
AHS-III/15B.
Plant named by Ann and Roger Bowden at Cleave House Garden, Okehampton, Devon, UK. Plant 40 in. (101.5 cm) dia., 20 in. (51 cm) high. Leaf 7 by 4 in. (18 by 10 cm), veins 10, blue-green, not variegated, ovate-cordate, flat. Scape 28 in. (71 cm), bare, straight. Flower medium, bell-shaped, lavender, flowers during average period, sterile.
HN: *H.* Tardiana grex hybrid F_1.
[*H.* 'Tardiflora' × *H. sieboldiana* 'Elegans'].
(see also *H.* Tardiana grex).

H. **'Dew Drop'** Walters Gardens IRA/1988.
AHS-IV/22B.
Plant 8 in. (20 cm) dia., 6 in. (15 cm) high. Leaf 3.5 by 2.5 in. (9 by 6 cm), veins 8, dark green, whitish margin, cordate, flat. Scape 14 in. (35.5 cm), foliated, straight. Flower medium, bell-shaped, white, flowers during average period, reblooms.
[*H.* 'Gold Drop' mutation].

H. **'Dewline'**.

H. 'Diamond Tiara' Zilis IRA/1985.
    AHS-IV/22B.
    Plant 26 in. (66 cm) dia., 14 in. (35.5 cm) high. Leaf 4 by 3 in. (10 by 7.5 cm), veins 6, medium green, white margin, cordate, wavy-undulate. Scape 28 in. (71 cm), bare, straight. Flower medium, bell-shaped, purple, flowers during average period, sterile.
[*H.* 'Golden Tiara' mutation].

H. 'Dianas Hyacinth' Alburg.
    Plant is a hybrid related to *H. longipes*.
[*H. longipes* form].

H. 'Dianne' Owens IRA/1985.
    AHS-III/14B.
    Plant 30 in. (76 cm) dia., 20 in. (51 cm) high. Leaf 4 by 3 in. (10 by 7.5 cm), veins 9, chartreuse, streaked yellow, cordate, rugose. Scape 28 in. (71 cm), bare, straight. Flower medium, bell-shaped, lavender, flowers during average period, fertile.
[*H.* 'August Moon' mutation].

H. 'Distinction' Fisher 1965.
    Plant is a Zager *H. montana* hybrid incorrectly attributed to *H. sieboldiana* var. *gigantea*. Large montana form with white flowers.
[*H. montana* hybrid].

H. 'Dixie Joy' Aden IRA/1983.
    AHS-IV/22B.
    Plant 10 in. (25.5 cm) dia., 6 in. (15 cm) high. Leaf 10 by 1.5 in. (25.5 by 4 cm), veins 3, chartreuse, streaked multicolor, lanceolate, flat. Scape 11 in. (28 cm), bare, straight. Flower medium, funnel-shaped, lavender, flowers during average period, fertile.
[*H.* 'Gala' × *H.* 'Halo'].

H. 'Dixie Queen' Savory IRA/1982.
    AHS-IV/19A.
    Plant 18 in. (46 cm) dia., 8 in. (20 cm) high. Leaf 3 by 2.5 in. (7.5 by 6 cm), veins 6, medium green, not variegated, cordate, flat. Scape 16 in. (40.5 cm), bare, straight. Flower medium, bell-shaped, lavender, flowers during average period, fertile.
[*H. nakaiana* hybrid].

H. 'Don Stevens' Stevens/Seaver.
    Plant is small with medium-sized glossy, green leaves that have a yellowish white margin. Scapes are purple spotted and flowers are purple. A form that has streaked variegation is known under the name *H.* 'Don Stevens Streaked'.

H. 'Donahue Piecrust' Donahue.   (Figure 4-15).
    Plant is one of the best with piecrust margins and has become the parent of many piecrust-margined hybrids. Similar in part to *H.* 'Ruffles'. Plant 30 in. (76 cm) dia., 22 in. (56 cm) high. Leaf 10 by 7 in. (25 by 17 cm), veins 12, medium green, not variegated, round-cupped. Scape 34 in. (86.5 cm), foliated, oblique. Flower medium, bell-shaped, white, flowers during average period, fertile.
HN: *H.* 'Ruffles' pp sim.
[*H. montana* hybrid].
(see *H.* 'Ruffles').

Figure 4-15. *H.* 'Donahue Piecrust'; general habit (Honeysong Farm/Schmid)

H. 'Dorothy' Williams (FRW No. 511) 1943 IRA/1986.
    AHS-III/13B.
    Plant is a hybrid with leaves like *H. decorata* and funnel-shaped lavender flowers like *H.* 'Fortunei'. Leaf grey on back. Flowers in July.
HN: *H.* 'FRW No. 511'.
[*H.* 'Decorata' × *H.* 'Fortunei'].

H. 'Dorothy Benedict' Benedict IRA/1983.
    AHS-II/7OB.
    Plant 20 in. (51 cm) dia., 10 in. (25.5 cm) high. Leaf, veins 10, blue-green, streaked yellow, cordate, rugose. Scape 12 in. (31 cm), foliated, straight. Flower medium, bell-shaped, white, flowers during average period, fertile.
[*H. sieboldiana* 'Frances Williams' × *H. sieboldiana* 'Frances Williams'].

H. 'Dorset Blue' Smith/Aden IRA/1977.
    AHS-IV/21B.   (Figure 4-16).
    Plant 12 in. (31 cm) dia., 8 in. (20 cm) high. Leaf 3 by 2.5 in. (7.5 by 6 cm), veins 9, blue-green, not variegated, round-cordate, cupped-rugose. Scape 12 in. (31 cm), foliated, straight. Flower medium, bell-shaped, white, flowers during average period, fertile.
HN: *H.* 'Blue Lagoon' pp.
     H. 'Two by Four' Smith pp.
     H. Tardiana grex TF 2 × 14.
[*H.* 'Tardiflora' × *H. sieboldiana* 'Elegans'].
(see also *H.* Tardiana grex).

Figure 4-16. *H.* 'Dorset Blue'; general habit (Honeysong Farm/Schmid)

H. 'Dorset Charm' Smith 1961.

Plant 22 in. (56 cm) dia., 12 in. (31 cm) high. Leaf 5 by 3 in. (13 by 7.5 cm), veins 9, blue-green, not variegated, round-cordate, cupped-rugose. Scape 18 in. (46 cm), foliated, straight. Flower medium, bell-shaped, white, flowers during average period, fertile.

HN: H. Tardiana grex TF 1 × 1.
[H. 'Tardiflora' × H. sieboldiana 'Elegans'].
(see also H. Tardiana grex).

H. 'Dorset Cream' Smith.

Plant is a yellow-leaved cultivar of Smith's GL series which is no longer in the UK National Reference Collection but may exist in some gardens.
[H. 'Fortunei Aurea' × H. sieboldiana 'Elegans'].

H. 'Dorset Flair' Smith 1961.

Plant 26 in. (66 cm) dia., 14 in. (35.5 cm) high. Leaf 7 by 5 in. (18 by 13 cm), veins 10, blue-green, not variegated, round-cordate, cupped-rugose. Scape 18 in. (46 cm), foliated, straight. Flower medium, bell-shaped, white, flowers during average period, fertile.

HN: H. Tardiana grex TF 1 × 4.
[H. 'Tardiflora' × H. sieboldiana 'Elegans'].
(see also H. Tardiana grex).

H. 'Double Edge' Aden IRA/1982.

AHS-III/16B.

Plant 26 in. (66 cm) dia., 18 in. (46 cm) high. Leaf 4 by 2 in. (10 by 5 cm), veins 9, medium green, yellow margin, cordate, rugose. Scape 24 in. (61 cm), bare, straight. Flower medium, funnel-shaped, white, flowers during average period, fertile.
[H. 'Flamboyant' × H. 'Fascination'].

H. 'Drip Drop' Walters Gardens IRA/1988.

AHS-IV/20B.

Plant 20 in. (51 cm) dia., 16 in. (41 cm) high. Leaf 5.5 by 3.5 in. (14 by 9), veins 8, yellow green, whitish margin, cordate, flat. Scape 26 in. (66 cm), foliated, straight. Flower medium, bell-shaped, white, flowers during average period, fertile.
[H. 'Gold Drop' mutation].

H. 'Drummer Boy' Moldovan IRA/1983.

AHS-IV/19B.

Plant 36 in. (91.5 cm) dia., 16 in. (40.5 cm) high. Leaf 5 by 4 in. (13 by 10 cm), veins 6, medium green, not variegated, round-cordate, cupped-rugose. Scape 30 in. (76 cm), bare, oblique. Flower medium, bell-shaped, lavender, flowers during average period, fertile.
[H. nakaiana × H. 'Birchwood Ruffled Queen'].

H. 'DSM 1' Stone 1969.

Plant is a small-leaved cultivar with leaves like H. 'Fortunei'. Yellow in spring, turns green later. This may be the same as H. 'Hazel'.

HN: H. 'Hazel'(?).
  H. 'Spring Gold'.
  H. 'S F No. 1'.

H. 'DSM No. 00' Stone/Ruh.

Plants numbered by David M. Stone (1919–1978) of Wolcott, Connecticut, internationally famous for his well-known work with the Lilium Connecticut hybrids. He made a number of Hosta hybrids of which the smaller were grouped under the acronym DSM (David Stone Miniatures). Peter Ruh has posthumously named and registered a number of these and descriptions can be found under their respective cultivar names:

H. 'DSM No. 1' Stone
= H. 'Hazel' Stone/Ruh IRA/1987.
H. 'DSM No. 2' Stone
= H. 'Dustin' Stone/Ruh IRA/1988.
H. 'DSM No. 3' Stone
= H. 'Bonnie' Stone/Ruh IRA/1987.
H. 'DSM No. 5' Stone
= H. 'Sunnybrook' Stone/Ruh IRA/1987.
H. 'DSM No. 6' Stone
= H. 'Carrie Ann' Stone/Ruh IRA/1988.
H. 'DSM No. 7' Stone
= H. 'Beaulah' Stone/Ruh IRA/1988.
H. 'DSM No. 9' Stone
= H. 'Ellen' Stone/Ruh IRA/1987.
H. 'DSM No. 10' Stone
= H. 'Barbara' Stone/Ruh IRA/1987.
H. 'DSM No. 11' Stone
= H. 'Mary Jo' Stone/Ruh IRA/1987.
H. 'DSM No. 12' Stone
= H. 'Brooke' Stone/Ruh IRA/1987.
H. 'DSM No. 13' Stone
= H. 'Pauline' Stone/Ruh IRA/1987.
H. 'DSM No. 16' Stone
= H. 'Oakview' Stone/Ruh IRA/1987.
H. 'DSM No. 17' Stone
= H. 'Jo Jo' Stone/Ruh IRA/1987.
H. 'DSM No. 19' Stone
= H. 'Margaret' Stone/Ruh IRA/1987.

H. 'Duchess' Savory IRA/1982.

AHS-IV/22B.

Plant 12 in. (31 cm) dia., 6 in. (15 cm) high. Leaf 3 by 1.5 in. (7.5 by 3 cm), veins 5, medium green, whitish yellow margin, cordate, wavy. Scape 18 in. (46 cm), foliated, straight. Flower medium, bell-shaped, purple, flowers during average period, fertile.
[(H. nakaiana hybrid) mutation].

H. 'Duke' Savory IRA/1988.

AHS-II/7B.

Plant 48 in. (122 cm) dia., 30 in. (76 cm) high. Leaf 12 by 9 in. (31 by 23 cm), veins 13, dark green, not variegated, cordate, rugose. Scape 48 in. (122 cm), foliated, straight. Flower medium, bell-shaped, lavender, flowers during average period, fertile.

H. 'Dustin' Stone/Ruh IRA/1988.

AHS-IV/22B.

Plant 12 in. (31 cm) dia., 12 in. (31 cm) high. Leaf 5 by 1.5 in. (13 by 4 cm), veins 6, dark green, whitish margin, lanceolate, flat. Scape 23 in. (58.5 cm), foliated, straight. Flower medium, lavender, flowers during average period, fertility(?).
HN: H. 'DSM No. 2' Stone.

H. 'Dwarf Gray Leaf' Fischer.

Plant name is an incorrect synonym.
(see H. 'Helen Field Fischer').

E

H. **'Eagle Wings'** Houseworth 1986.

H. **'Early Dawn'** Wallace 1986.
Plant's leaves are all gold in spring, greening later. Inner leaves (second flush) are permanently yellow streaked. Plant 32 in. (81.5 cm) dia., 16 in. (40.5 cm) high. Leaf 9 by 7 in. (23 by 18 cm), veins 8, medium green, streaked yellow (viridescent), cordate, flat. Scape 34 in. (86.5 cm), bare, straight. Flower medium, bell-shaped, purple, flowers during average period, fertile.
HN: *H. ventricosa* 'Early Dawn' Wallace 1986.
[*H. ventricosa* 'Aureomaculata' hybrid].

H. **'Early Gold'** Viette/Summers No. 40 1964.
Plant is a viridescent yellow form of the parent.
(*H. sieboldiana* form).

H. **'Edge of Night'** Savory IRA/1988.
AHS-III/13B.
Plant 40 in. (101.5 cm) dia., 24 in. (61 cm) high. Leaf 10.5 by 8 in. (27 by 20 cm), veins 10, blue-green, not variegated, round-cordate, rugose. Scape 30 in. (76 cm), bare, straight. Flower medium, funnel-shaped, lavender, flowers during average period, fertility(?).
[*H.* 'Green Gold' × *H.* 'Halcyon'].

H. **'Edina Heritage'** Savory IRA/1987.
AHS-II/9B.
Plant 40 in. (101.5 cm) dia., 30 in. (76 cm) high. Leaf 12 by 10 in. (31 by 25.5 cm), veins 16, blue-green, not variegated, round-cordate, rugose. Scape 40 in. (101.5 cm), foliated, straight. Flower medium, bell-shaped, lavender, flowers during average period, fertile.
[*H. sieboldiana* hybrid].

H. **'Edward Wargo'** Weissenberger IRA/1986.
AHS-III/15B.
Plant 26 in. (66 cm) dia., 10 in. (25.5 cm) high. Leaf 5 by 4 in. (13 by 10 cm), veins 7, blue-green, not variegated, round-cordate, cupped-rugose. Scape 16 in. (40.5 cm), bare, straight. Flower medium, bell-shaped, white, flowers during average period, fertile.
[*H.* 'Hadspen Blue' hybrid].

H. **'Egret'** Savory IRA/1984.
AHS-IV/19A.
Plant 12 in. (31 cm) dia., 6 in. (15 cm) high. Leaf 3 by 2 in. (7.5 by 5 cm), veins 6, medium green, not variegated, cordate, flat. Scape 14 in. (35.5 cm), bare, straight. Flower medium, funnel-shaped, white, flowers during average period, fertile.
[*H. nakaiana* hybrid].

H. **'El Capitan'** Lachman IRA/1987.
AHS-II/10B.
Plant 40 in. (101.5 cm) dia., 24 in. (61 cm) high. Leaf 10 by 9 in. (25.5 by 23 cm), veins 12, dark green, chartreuse margin, cordate, rugose. Scape 36 in. (91.5 cm), bare, straight. Flower medium, bell-shaped, lavender, flowers during average period, fertile.
[*H.* 'Beatrice' hybrid].

H. **'Elamae'** Schmid 1985.
Plant erect, 18 in. (46 cm) dia., 18 in. (46 cm) high. Leaf 11 by 1.5 in. (28 by 4 cm), veins 3, yellow (viridescent), not variegated, lanceolate, undulate. Scape 22 in. (56 cm), bare, straight. Flower medium, funnel-shaped, purple striped, flowers during summer period, fertile.
[*H. sieboldii* derivative].

H. **'Elata'.**
H. elata.

H. **'Elata Wavy'** hort. incorrect.
Plant name is an incorrect synonym.
(see *H. elata*).

H. **'Elatior'** Wisley incorrect.
Plant name is an incorrect synonym.
HN: *H. elatior* hort. incorrect.
Wisley No. 821363.
(see *H. nigrescens* f. *elatior*).

H. **'Eleanor J. Reath'** Reath IRA/1986.
AHS-I/3B.
Plant 48 in. (122 cm) dia., 26 in. (66 cm) high. Leaf 18 by 15 in. (46 by 38 cm), veins 16, blue-green, not variegated, cordate, rugose. Scape 30 in. (76 cm), nude, oblique. Flower medium, bell-shaped, white, flowers during average period, fertile.
HN: *H.* 'Eleanor Reath' incorrect.
[*H. sieboldiana* 'Frances Williams' × *H. sieboldiana* 'Elegans'].

H. **'Elephant Ears'** Lewis.
Plant has very large grey-green leaves. Similar to a wide-leaved *H.* 'Elata'.
HN: *H. sieboldiana* 'Sturtevant' Donahue.
Summers No. 1 1967.
Summers No. 92 1963.
[*H.* 'Elata' hybrid].

H. **'Elfin Cup'** Zumbar IRA/1988.
AHS-V/26A.
Plant 9 in. (23 cm) dia., 6 in. (15 cm) high. Leaf 2 by 1.25 in. (5 by 3 cm), veins 6, yellowish green, yellowish white margin, cordate, cupped. Scape 10 in. (25.5 cm), foliated, straight. Flower medium, funnel-shaped, white, flowers during average period, sterile.
[*H.* 'Little Aurora' mutation].

H. **'Elfin Power'** Ruh IRA/1987.
AHS-V/28A.
Plant has pure white margins, streaking into center. Plant erect, 18 in. (46 cm) dia., 10 in. (25.5 cm) high. Leaf 9 by 1.25 in. (23 by 3 cm), veins 3, medium green, white margin, ovate-cupped, flat. Scape 26 in. (66 cm), bare, straight. Flower medium, funnel-shaped, lavender, flowers during summer period, fertile.
[*H. sieboldii* 'Pixie Power' mutation].

H. **'Elf Rim'** Houseworth 1986.

H. **'Elisabeth'** Hensen IRA/1983.
AHS-III/13A.
Plant 38 in. (96.5 cm) dia., 26 in. (66 cm) high. Leaf 9 by 5 in. (23 by 13 cm), veins 9, medium green, not variegated, cordate, wavy-undulate. Scape 38 in. (96.5 cm), foliated, oblique. Flower medium, funnel-shaped, lavender, flowers during average period, fertile.
HN: *H. longissima* var. *brevifolia* Munich BG incorrect.

H. 'Elizabeth Campbell' BHHS IRA/1988.
AHS-III/18B.
Plant is a selected form of *H.* 'Fortunei Albopicta' which retains its variegation longer than the typical form and has wider leaves with broader green margins.
HN: *H.* 'Fortunei Albopicta' sel.
H. 'Panaché Jaune' (= yellow variegated).
(see also *H.* 'Fortunei Albopicta').

H. 'Ellen' Stone/Ruh IRA/1987.
AHS-IV/19A.
Plant 13 in. (33 cm) dia., 6 in. (15 cm) high. Leaf 3 by 2 in. (7.5 by 5 cm), veins 4, medium green, not variegated, cordate, wavy-undulate. Scape 16 in. (40.5 cm), bare, oblique. Flower medium, bell-shaped, whitish, flowers during average period, fertile.
HN: *H.* 'DSM No. 9'.

H. 'Ellen Carder' Carder.
(see *H.* 'Tokudama').

H. 'Ellen F. Weissenberger' Weissenberger IRA/1986.
AHS-II/9B.
Plant 48 in. (122 cm) dia., 24 in. (61 cm) high. Leaf 10 by 7 in. (25.5 by 18 cm), veins 14, blue-green, not variegated, cordate, rugose. Scape 28 in. (71 cm), foliated, oblique. Flower medium, funnel-shaped, lavender, flowers during average period, fertile.
[*H. sieboldiana* 'Elegans' hybrid].

H. 'Ellerbroek' Ellerbroek.
Plant is a form of *H.* 'Fortunei Aureomarginata' received by Ellerbroek from Europe (probably from Hensen).
HN: *H.* 'Ellerbroek L-7'.
H. 'Ellerbrook' incorrect.
H. 'Krossa L-7'.
(see *H.* 'Fortunei Aureomarginata').

H. 'Ellie B'.
Plant is a very small taxon with leaves similar to *H. gracillima*, which see.

H. 'Elsley Runner'.

H. 'Embroidery' Aden.
This unusual cultivar has a deeply crimped, "stitched" margin of a somewhat deeper green than the flat leaf center. The crimping sometimes involves the space between two outer principal veins away from the margin. A mutated form induced by radiation. See Aden (1988, ic. page 109).

H. 'Emerald Carpet'.
[*H.* 'Saishu Jima' hybrid].

H. 'Emerald Crust' Zilis IRA/1988.
AHS-III/14A.
Plant erect, 40 in. (101.5 cm) dia., 20 in. (51 cm) high. Leaf 12 by 8 in. (30 by 20 cm), veins 14, yellow (albescent), green margin, cordate, flat-undulate. Scape 42 in. (106.5 cm), bare, straight. Flower medium, funnel-shaped, lavender, flowers during average period, fertility(?).
[*H.* 'Fortunei Gigantea' mutation].

H. 'Emerald Cushion' Fisher 1968.
Plant is a chartreuse hybrid with leaves similar to *H.* 'Crispula'. Holds color.
HN: *H.* 'Fisher No. 15-68'.

H. 'Emerald Gem' Piedmont Gardens.

H. 'Emerald Isle' Smith.
Similar to *H. sieboldii* 'Louisa' it is white-margined with white flowers and reported to be less vigorous in the United Kingdom.
[*H. sieboldii* derivative].
(see also *H. sieboldii* 'Bunchoko).

H. 'Emerald Ripples' Langdon IRA/1981.
AHS-IV/19A.
Plant is one of the many similar clones of the all-green *H. sieboldii*. Plant erect, 12 in. (31 cm) dia., 8 in. (20 cm) high. Leaf 4 by 1 in. (10 by 2.5 cm), veins 3, medium green, not variegated, lanceolate, wavy-undulate. Scape 12 in. (31 cm), foliated, straight. Flower medium, funnel-shaped, purple striped, flowers during average period, fertile.
HN: *H. sieboldii* f. *spathulata* 'Emerald Ripples'.
[*H. sieboldii* derivative].

H. 'Emerald Skies' Aden/Klehm.
Plant 10 in. (25.5 cm) dia., 4 in. (10 cm) high. Leaf 3 by 2 in. (7.5 by 5 cm), veins 5, medium green, not variegated, ovate, flat. Scape 12 in. (31 cm), nude, straight. Flower medium, funnel-shaped, lavender, flowers during average period, fertile.
[*H.* 'Blue Skies' derivative].

H. 'Emerald Tiara' T & Z/Walters Gardens IRA/1988.
AHS-IV/20A.
Plant 20 in. (51 cm) dia., 14 in. (35.5 cm) high. Leaf 4 by 3 in. (10 by 7.5 cm), veins 6, medium green, not variegated, cordate, flat. Scape 28 in. (71 cm), bare, straight. Flower medium, bell-shaped, purple, flowers during average period, fertility(?).
[*H.* 'Golden Tiara' derivative].

H. 'Emily Dickinson' Lachman IRA/1987.
AHS-III/16A.
Plant 32 in. (81.5 cm) dia., 20 in. (51 cm) high. Leaf 7 by 4 in. (18 by 10 cm), veins 6, medium green, light yellowish white margin, ovate, flat. Scape 28 in. (71 cm), foliated, straight. Flower medium, funnel-shaped, lavender, fragrant, flowers during average period, fertile.
[*H.* 'Neat Splash' hybrid × *H. plantaginea*].

H. 'Emma Foster' Foster IRA/1985.
AHS-III/17A.
Plant is a yellow form of *H. montana*. Reported to be two-thirds the size of the species, but this size has not yet been reached and verified; most plants seen are much smaller than the description. Plant 30 in. (76 cm) dia., 20 in. (51 cm) high. Leaf 7 by 5 in. (18 by 13 cm), veins 16, yellow (lutescent), not variegated, cordate, wavy-undulate. Scape 34 in. (86.5 cm), bare, straight. Flower medium, funnel-shaped, white, flowers during average period, fertile.
HN: *H. montana* 'Emma Foster'.
[*H. montana* 'Aureomarginata' mutation].
(see also *H. montana* 'Ogon').

H. 'Empire State'.
Plant is a very large *H. sieboldiana* form.

H. 'Enchantress' Zumbar IRA/1988.
AHS-V/26A.
Plant 10 in. (25.5 cm) dia., 6 in. (15 cm) high. Leaf 3.5 by 2 in. (9 by 5 cm), veins 6, white (viridescent), green margin, cordate, flat. Scape 8 in. (20 cm), foliated, straight. Flower

medium, white, flowers during average period, sterile.
[*H.* 'Little Aurora' mutation].

H. 'Entreat' Aden 1975.

H. 'Eric Smith' Smith/Archibald IRA/1987.
AHS-IV/21A.
Plant by Eric Smith considered the best progeny in the *H.* Tardiana grex and reported to be TF 2 × 31. Leaf 4 by 4 in. (10 by 10 cm), veins 7, blue-green, round-cordate. Flower lavender.
HN: *H.* Tardiana grex TF 2 × 31.
[*H.* 'Tardiflora' × *H. sieboldiana* 'Elegans'].
(see also *H.* Tardiana grex).

H. 'Erromena'.
Plant name is an incorrect synonym.
HN: *H. erromena.*
(see *H.* 'Undulata Erromena').

H. 'Estelle Aden' Aden IRA/1978.
AHS-II/11A.
Plant 30 in. (76 cm) dia., 24 in. (61 cm) high. Leaf 7 by 6 in. (18 by 15 cm), veins 12, yellow (lutescent), not variegated, round-cordate, cupped-rugose. Scape 28 in. (71 cm), bare, straight. Flower medium, bell-shaped, lavender, flowers during average period, fertile.
HN: Wisley No. 821362.
[*H.* 'Golden Waffles' × *H.* 'Gold Cup'].

H. 'Eunice Choice' Arett No. 39/Ruh IRA/1988.
AHS-IV/23B.
Plant erect, 14 in. (35.5 cm) dia., 14 in. (35.5 cm) high. Leaf 5 by 1.5 in. (13 by 4 cm), veins 5, medium green, not variegated, lanceolate, flat. Scape 37 in. (94 cm), foliated, straight. Flower medium, funnel-shaped, lavender, flowers during summer period, fertile.

H. 'Eunice Fisher' Ruh IRA/1985.
AHS-III/13A.
Plant erect, 24 in. (61 cm) dia., 22 in. (56 cm) high. Leaf 7 by 5 in. (18 by 13 cm), veins 12, medium green, not variegated, cordate, flat. Scape 26 in. (66 cm), foliated, straight. Flower medium, funnel-shaped, lavender, flowers during average period, fertile.
[*H.* 'Crispula' hybrid].

H. 'Evelyn McCafferty' Lehmann IRA/1975.
AHS-II/9B.
Plant 36 in. (91.5 cm) dia., 20 in. (51 cm) high. Leaf 10 by 8 in. (25 by 20 cm), veins 14, blue-green, not variegated, cordate, rugose. Scape 20 in. (51 cm), foliated, straight. Flower medium, bell-shaped, white, flowers during average period, fertile.
[*H.* 'Tokudama' hybrid].

H. 'Evening Magic' Zilis IRA/1988.
AHS-II/8A.
Plant erect, 40 in. (101.5 cm) dia., 20 in. (51 cm) high. Leaf 10 by 8 in. (25.5 by 20 cm), veins 14, yellow (lutescent), white margin, cordate, flat-undulate. Scape 36 in. (91.5 cm), bare, straight. Flower medium, funnel-shaped, white, flowers during average period, fertility(?).
[*H.* 'Piedmont Gold' mutation].

H. 'Everglades' Savory IRA/1988.
AHS-II/8A.
Plant erect, 36 in. (91.5 cm) dia., 26 in. (66 cm) high. Leaf 10 by 9 in. (25.5 by 23 cm), veins 14, chartreuse, green margin, cordate, flat-rugose. Scape 30 in. (76 cm), bare, straight. Flower medium, funnel-shaped, white, flowers during average period, fertility(?).
[*H.* 'Piedmont Gold' mutation].

H. 'Excalibur' Piedmont IRA/1986.
AHS-IV/22A.
HN: *H.* 'Excaliber' incorrect.
(see *H.* 'Ginko Craig').

H. 'Excitation' Aden IRA/1988.
AHS-III/17B.
Plant is the all-yellow stable form of *H.* 'Citation'. Plant 12 in. (31 cm) dia., 8 in. (20 cm) high. Leaf 6 by 3 in. (15 by 7.5 cm), veins 9, chartreuse, not variegated, cordate, flat. Scape 28 in. (71 cm), bare, straight. Flower medium, funnel-shaped, lavender, flowers during average period, sterile.
[*H.* 'Citation' mutation].

H. 'Exotic Frances Williams' Klehm/Wayside Gardens.
(Plate 101).
Plant has a narrow white margin which shows a "drawstring effect" (Pollock, 1988). Plant 24 in. (61 cm) dia., 18 in. (46 cm) high. Leaf 9 by 7 in. (22 by 18 cm), veins 9–13, dark green, very narrow white margin, cordate, cupped. Scape 28 in. (71 cm), bare, straight. Flower medium, funnel-shaped, whitish, flowers during average period, fertile.

F

H. 'Facile' Aden 1974.

H. 'Fairway Green' Minks 1986.
Plant is a small hybrid with dark green spoon-shaped leaves of heavy substance and with a waxy shine.

H. 'Fall Bouquet' Aden IRA/1986.
AHS-III/13B.
Plant is a selected form of the botanical variety *H. longipes* var. *hypoglauca* and by some considered an F$_1$ hybrid of this taxon. This cultivar exemplifies one of the very best forms found among the wild population, with very dark petioles and scapes. Plant 18 in. (46 cm) dia., 12 in. (31 cm) high. Leaf 8 by 3 in. (20 by 7.5 cm), veins 6, medium green, not variegated, lanceolate, flat. Scape 16 in. (40.5 cm), bare, straight. Flower medium, funnel-shaped, lavender, flowers during summer period, sterile.
[*H.* 'Aden No. 322' × *H.* 'Aden No. 324'].
[*H. longipes* var. *hypoglauca* 'Fall Bouquet'].
(see also *H. longipes* var. *hypoglauca*).

H. 'Fall Emerald' IRA/1968.
AHS-II/7B.
Plant is a large early flowering hybrid with leaves that are larger than those of *H. sieboldiana*, deep green, and long lasting during the fall season. Flowers early on tall scapes.
HN: Summers No. 23 Lewis 1963.
[*H. montana* × *H. sieboldiana* ad int].

H. **'Fan Dance'** Benedict IRA/1987.
AHS-III/14A.
Plant has albescent chartreuse center, thin dark green margin. Plant 16 in. (40.5 cm) dia., 12 in. (31 cm) high. Leaf 7 by 4 in. (18 by 10 cm), veins 7, chartreuse (albescent), dark green margin, ovate, flat. Scape 18 in. (46 cm), bare, straight. Flower medium, bell-shaped, lavender, flowers during average period, sterile.
[*H.* 'Dorothy' mutation].

H. **'Fantastic'** Soules IRA/1988.
AHS-II/9B.
Plant has highly contorted-rugose leaf of very heavy substance. Plant 52 in. (132 cm) dia., 30 in. (76 cm) high. Leaf 12 by 10 in. (31 by 25.5 cm), veins 16, blue-grey, not variegated, cordate, contorted-rugose. Scape 30 in. (76 cm), foliated, straight. Flower medium, bell-shaped, white, flowers during average period, fertile.
[*H. sieboldiana* hybrid].

H. **'Fantasy'** Brodeur.

H. **'Fascination'** Aden IRA/1978.
AHS-III/14A.   (Plate 102).
Plant 20 in. (51 cm) dia., 16 in. (40.5 cm) high. Leaf 6 by 4 in. (15 by 10 cm), veins 10, green, streaked chartreuse, yellow, white, cordate, some rugosity. Scape 20 in. (51 cm), foliated, straight. Flower medium, funnel-shaped, lavender, flowers during average period, fertile.
[*H.* 'Flamboyant' × *H.* 'High Fat Cream'].

H. **'Fascinator'** Wilkins-Owens IRA/1989.
AHS-III/14B.
Plant emerges all yellow; later green margin appears. Plant 32 in. (80 cm) dia., 14 in. (35 cm) high. Leaf 7 by 6 in. (18 by 15 cm), veins 10, green, margin on chartreuse to yellow center, cordate, flat. Scape 30 in. (76 cm), foliated, straight. Flower medium, funnel-shaped, lavender, flowers during average period, fertile.
[*H.* 'Golden Fascination' mutation].

H. **'Feather Boa'** O'Harra.
Plant 12 in. (31 cm) dia., 6 in. (15 cm) high. Leaf 4 by 0.75 in. (10 by 2 cm), veins 4, yellow (slightly viridescent), not variegated, lanceolate, wavy. Scape 14 in. (35.5 cm), bare, straight. Flower medium, bell-shaped, purple striped, flowers during average period, fertile.
[*H. sieboldii* derivative].

H. **'Felix'** Houseworth 1986.
Plant 20 in. (51 cm) dia., 12 in. (31 cm) high. Leaf 6 by 4 in. (15 by 10 cm), veins 8, medium green, not variegated, cordate, rugose. Scape 26 in. (66 cm), bare, oblique. Flower medium, bell-shaped, white, flowers during average period, fertile.
[*H.* 'August Moon' hybrid].

H. **'Fernwood'** Moldovan IRA/1983.
AHS-I/1B.
Plant 48 in. (122 cm) dia., 36 in. (91.5 cm) high. Leaf 15 by 12 in. (38 by 31 cm), veins 16, medium green, not variegated, cordate, rugose. Scape 42 in. (106.5 cm), bare, straight. Flower medium, bell-shaped, white, flowers during average period, fertile.
[*H.* 'Big Sam' hybrid].

H. **'Fine Points'** Shaw 1966.
Plant has viridescent narrow leaves. Was *H.* 'Golden Glimmer'; name changed because plant reverted to green.
HN: *H.* 'Golden Glimmer'.
[*H. sieboldii* mutation].

H. **'Finlandia'**.
Plant 20 in. (51 cm) dia., 10 in. (25.5 cm) high. Leaf 6 by 2 in. (15 by 5 cm), veins 7, medium green, not variegated, lanceolate, flat. Scape 24 in. (61 cm), foliated, oblique. Flower medium, funnel-shaped, white, flowers during summer period, fertile.
HN: *H. kikutii* 'Finlandia'.
[*H. kikutii* hybrid].

H. **'Fisher Cream Edge'** Fisher 1960.
Plant is a *H.* 'Fortunei Stenantha' sport with a ("cream") margin on green center. The margin retains its yellowish white color until late into the season and never turns completely white, so this plant is distinct from *H.* 'Fortunei Albomarginata' and other margined forms of *H.* 'Fortunei'. Plant 26 in. (66 cm) dia., 20 in. (51 cm) high. Leaf 8 by 6 in. (20 by 15 cm), veins 8, green, whitish yellow margin (albescent), cordate, flat. Scape 40 in. (101.5 cm), foliated, oblique. Flower medium, funnel-shaped, lavender, flowers during average period, sterile.
HN: *H.* 'Cream Edge'.
        H. 'Fortunei Cream Edge'.
[*H.* 'Fortunei' mutation].

H. **'Flamboyant'** Aden IRA/1978.
AHS-III/16A.   (Plate 103).
Plant has variegation that is unstable and turns into *H.* 'Shade Fanfare'. Plant 22 in. (56 cm) dia., 14 in. (35.5 cm) high. Leaf 6 by 5 in. (15 by 13 cm), veins 10, chartreuse, streaked multicolor, cordate, rugose. Scape 20 in. (51 cm), foliated, straight. Flower medium, funnel-shaped, lavender, flowers during average period, fertile.

H. **'Fleeta Brownell Woodroffe'** O'Harra IRA/1986.
AHS-III/16B.
Plant erect, 28 in. (71 cm) dia., 20 in. (51 cm) high. Leaf 7 by 5 in. (18 by 13 cm), veins 13, blue-green, yellow margin, cordate, cupped-rugose. Scape 22 in. (56 cm), bare, straight. Flower medium, bell-shaped, white, flowers during average period, fertile.
HN: *H.* 'Tokudama Aureonebulosa' group.
[*H.* 'Tokudama' derivation].

H. **'Fleetas Blue'**.

H. **'Floradora'** Aden IRA/1978.
AHS-IV/19A.   (Figure 4-17).
Plant 16 in. (40.5 cm) dia., 6 in. (15 cm) high. Leaf 3 by 2 in. (7.5 by 5 cm), veins 8, medium green, not variegated, cordate, flat. Scape 12 in. (31 cm), bare, straight. Flower medium, bell-shaped, purple, flowers during average period, fertile.
HN: *H.* 'Floral Mass'.
[*H. nakaiana* × *H. longipes* hybrid].

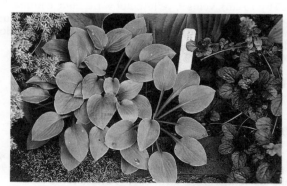

Figure 4-17. *H.* 'Floradora'; general habit (Hosta Hill)

H. 'Floral Mass' Aden.
(see H. 'Floradora').

H. 'Flow Swirls' Aden IRA/1978.
AHS-III/16B.
Plant 18 in (46 cm) dia., 14 in. (35.5 cm) high. Leaf 6 by 4 in. (15 by 10 cm), veins 10, chartreuse, streaky multicolor, cordate, flat. Scape 16 in. (40.5 cm), foliated, straight. Flower medium, funnel-shaped, lavender, flowers during average period, fertile.
[H. 'Flamboyant' × H. 'High Fat Cream'].

H. 'Flower Power' Vaughn IRA/1987.
AHS-II/7A.
Plant is first pruinose then green; slight ruffling. One of the earliest blooming fragrant cultivars. Plant 46 in. (117 cm) dia., 30 in. (76 cm) high. Leaf 12 by 8 in. (31 by 20 cm), veins 8, medium green, not variegated, lanceolate, flat. Scape 50 in. (127 cm), nude, straight. Flower medium, funnel-shaped, lavender, fragrant, flowers during average period, sterile.
[H. nigrescens × H. plantaginea].

H. fluctuans 'Blue Sagae' hort.

H. fluctuans 'Gold Sagae' hort.

H. fluctuans 'Variegated' hort.

H. 'Fond Hope' Fisher IRA/1973.
AHS-II/9B.
Plant 42 in. (106.5 cm) dia., 22 in. (56 cm) high. Leaf 12 by 10 in. (31 by 25.5 cm), veins 16, medium green, not variegated, cordate, rugose. Scape 34 in. (86.5 cm), bare, oblique. Flower medium, funnel-shaped, white, flowers during average period, fertile.
HN: H. 'Fisher No. 60-70'.
[H. sieboldiana Aureomarginata group derivation].

H. 'Formal Attire' Vaughn IRA/1988.
AHS-III/16B.
Plant 36 in. (91.5 cm) dia., 30 in. (76 cm) high. Leaf 11 by 8 in. (28 by 20 cm), veins 12, dark green, wide, even, albescent yellowish margin, cordate, cupped-rugose. Scape 38 in. (96.5 cm), foliated, oblique. Flower medium, funnel-shaped, lavender, flowers during average period, fertility(?).
[H. 'Breeders Choice' × H. sieboldiana 'Frances Williams'].

H. 'Fort Knox' Wilkins IRA/1989.
AHS-III/17A.
Plant 42 in. (106.5 cm) dia., 22 in. (56 cm) high. Leaf 8 by 5 in. (20 by 13 cm), veins 9, yellow, not variegated, cordate, flat. Scape 30 in. (76 cm), foliated, oblique. Flower medium, funnel-shaped, lavender, flowers during average period, fertile.
[H. 'Gold Regal' × H. 'Aspen Gold'].

H. 'Fortunei'.
H. fortunei.

H. 'Fortunei Albomarginata'.
AHS-III/16B.
The cultivar name registered for show purposes (in modified form) as H. fortunei 'Albo-marginata' AHS-NC IRA/1987 for the white-margined form of H. 'Fortunei'.
(see also H. 'Fortunei Albomarginata' group).

H. 'Fortunei Albomarginata' group.
白覆輪レンゲギボウシ(Figures 4-11, 4-18; Plates 104, 158, 178).
A group of white-margined taxa of the H. 'Fortunei' line which includes many cultivars in a broad sense. The margin can vary from narrow to wide and from pure white to pale yellowish white. From this group a clone has been selected, namely H. 'Fortunei Albomarginata', which has been registered with the IRA as H. fortunei 'Albo-marginata'. No description was given with the registration so it is not known to what clone the name applies in a strict sense. The registration is intended to include a number of very similar clones in the trade under the clonal name H. 'Fortunei Albomarginata', all of which are practically identical and well known and recognized by gardeners. A number of other distinct and quite different looking clones exist in this group and have been named; some of these are cataloged following the synonymy and described individually in this chapter. This group does not embrace the several cultivars in the distinctly different H. 'Antioch' line, which see. Hosta 'Antioch' is, unfortunately, quite often incorrectly sold as H. 'Fortunei Albomarginata'; to study the considerable morphological differences compare Plate 88 to Plate 104. This cultivar is extensively used and an outstanding landscape item. Several variegated mutants are known.
Plant conforms to the basic description given under H. 'Fortunei' except that leaf color is dark green with whitish margin.
The following synonyms are used for H. 'Fortunei Albomarginata' in a narrow sense:
SY: H. fortunei marginato alba Bailey 1930 incorrect (H. 'Crispula').
HN: H. albamarginata hort. incorrect.
   H. fortunei albomarginata Everett 1984 incorrect.
   H. fortunei marginata alba Everett 1984 incorrect.
   H. fortunei 'Marginata-alba' hort. UK incorrect.
   H. fortunei 'Marginato-alba' Hensen (pp as applied) incorrect.
   H. fortunei 'Marginato-alba' hort. incorrect.
   H. fortunei 'Obscura Albo-marginata' hort. incorrect.
   H. fortunei 'Silver Crown' hort.
   H. fortunei var. obscura 'Albo-marginata' hort. incorrect.
   H. fortunei 'White Edge' hort.
   H. japonica albomarginata hort. incorrect.
   H. 'Mack No. 4'.
   H. ovata albomarginata hort. pp.
   H. 'Silver Crown' hort.
   H. 'White Band' hort.
   USDA ARS No. 263130 Meyer 1963.
   Wisley No. 821360.
JN: Shirofukurin Renge Giboshi hort.
ON: Grosse Weissrandfunkie (German).
   Riesenweissrandfunkie (German) incorrect.
The following names are used for popular cultivars broadly associated with the H. 'Fortunei Albomarginata' group yet distinct enough to bear their own names. Per the ICNCP use of the group name is optional; for example, H. 'Fortunei Albomarginata' group 'Francee' can be written as H. 'Fortunei Francee' or simply H. 'Francee'. These plants are described under their respective, simplified cultivar names in this chapter:
H. 'Fortunei Carol'.
H. 'Fortunei Francee'.
H. 'Fortunei Gloriosa'.
H. 'Fortunei Klopping Variegated'.
H. 'Fortunei North Hills'.
H. 'Fortunei Zager White Edge'.

H. **'Fortunei Albopicta'.**
H. fortunei var. *albopicta.*

H. **'Fortunei Albopicta'.**
  AHS-III/18B.
  The cultivar name registered for show purposes (in modified form) as *H. fortunei* 'Albo-picta' AHS-NC IRA/1987 for *H. fortunei* var. *albopicta.*
  (see *H. fortunei* var. *albopicta*).

H. **'Fortunei Aoki'.**
  AHS-III/13B.
  The cultivar name registered for show purposes (in modified form) as *H. fortunei* 'Aoki' AHS-NC IRA/1987 for *H. fortunei* (var.) *aoki.*
  (see *H. fortunei* [var.] *aoki*).

H. **'Fortunei Aoki Variegated'** hort.
  A horticultural name of uncertain origin which applies collectively to various variegated sports of *H.* 'Fortunei Aoki'. In addition to the clones listed below, many aureo-nebulosa, aureo-marginata, albo-marginata, mottled, and streaked sports exist, most of which are unstable and revert. Some that are stable have been named and are described under their respective names in this chapter.
  HN: *H.* 'Aoki Variegata' hort. incorrect.
      H. 'Aoki Variegated' hort.
      H. 'Fortunei Aoki Variegated' hort.
  (see also *H.* 'Bensheim').
  (see also *H.* 'Fortunei Variegated').
  (see also *H.* 'Raindance').
  (see also *H.* 'Sundance').

H. **'Fortunei Aurea'.**
  AHS-III/18A.
  The cultivar name registered for show purposes (in modified form) as *H. fortunei* 'Aurea' AHS-NC IRA/1987 for *H. fortunei* var. *albopicta* f. *aurea.*
  (see *H. fortunei* var. *albopicta* f. *aurea*).

H. **'Fortunei Aurea'** group.
  (see *H. fortunei* var. *albopicta* f. *aurea*).

H. **'Fortunei Aureomarginata'.**
  AHS-III/16B.
  The cultivar name registered for show purposes (in modified form) as *H. fortunei* 'Aureo-marginata' AHS-NC IRA/1987 for *H. fortunei* var. *aureomarginata.*
  (see *H. fortunei* var. *aureomarginata*).

H. **'Fortunei Aureomarginata'** group.
  (see *H. fortunei* var. *aureomarginata*).

H. **'Fortunei Gigantea'.**
  H. fortunei var. *gigantea.*

H. **'Fortunei Gloriosa'.**
  AHS-III/16B.
  The cultivar name registered for show purposes (in modified form) as *H. fortunei* 'Gloriosa' AHS-NC IRA/1987 for *H. fortunei* 'Gloriosa'.
  (see *H.* 'Gloriosa').

H. **'Fortunei Hyacinthina'.**
  AHS-III/13B.
  The cultivar name registered for show purposes (in modified form) as *H. fortunei* 'Hyacinthina' AHS-NC IRA/1987 for *H. fortunei* var. *hyacinthina.*
  (see *H. fortunei* var. *hyacinthina*).

H. **'Fortunei Hyacinthina'** group.
  (see *H. fortunei* var. *hyacinthina*).

H. **'Fortunei Mediovariegata'** group.
  (see *H. fortunei* var. *albopicta*).

H. **'Fortunei Obscura'.**
  (see *H. fortunei* var. *obscura*).
  (see also *H. bella*).

H. **'Fortunei Rugosa'.**
  AHS-III/13B.
  The cultivar name registered for show purposes (in modified form) as *H. fortunei* 'Rugosa' AHS-NC IRA/1987 for *H. fortunei* var. *rugosa.*
  (see *H. fortunei* var. *rugosa*).

H. **'Fortunei Stenantha'.**
  AHS-III/13A.
  The cultivar name registered for show purposes (in modified form) as *H. fortunei* 'Stenantha' AHS-NC IRA/1987 for *H. fortunei* var. *stenantha.*
  (see *H. fortunei* var. *stenantha*).

H. **'Fortunei Stenantha Variegated'** hort.
  AHS-III/16B.
  A horticultural name for a number of variegated clones of *H.* 'Fortunei Stenantha'. Some are stable and have been named, but unstable and viridescent forms are frequent. The form most often seen is a viridescent, yellow-margined one that loses much of its margin color by late spring, with only traces remaining. An outstanding, popular form that is stable has been named *H.* 'Viettes Yellow Edge', which see. Some of the variegated forms have lasting, yellowish white margins, and one of these forms has been named *H.* 'Fisher Cream Edge'.
  HN: *H.* 'Cream Edge'.
      H. 'Fisher Cream Edge'.
      H. 'Fortunei Cream Edge'.
      H. fortunei stenantha aureomarginata hort. incorrect.
      H. fortunei 'Stenantha Aureomarginata' hort. incorrect.
      H. 'Fortunei Stenantha Aureomarginata' hort. incorrect.
      H. fortunei var. *stenantha* 'Cream Edge' hort.
      H. fortunei var. *stenantha* 'Variegated' hort.
      H. fortunei var. *stenantha* 'Viettes Yellow Edge'.
      H. fortunei 'Viettes Yellow Edge').
      H. 'Mack No. 23'.
  (see also *H.* 'Viettes Yellow Edge').

H. **'Fortunei Variegated'** hort.
  The *H.* 'Fortunei' hybrid complex in its various forms has a tendency to produce variegated sports that occur in cultivation and are frequently found in tissue culture explants. Aside from the well-known classic white- and yellow-margined or yellow-centered forms described earlier, a multitude of mutants exist in gardens but they often disappear because many are unstable. Over the years stable forms have been found and named; some of the horticulturally important stable taxa are listed below, each also described under its cultivar name in this chapter. Although generally attributed to *H.* 'Fortunei', most are mutants of *H.* 'Fortunei Hyacinthina' or *H.* 'Fortunei Aoki'. Since the names are unique the addition of the specioid epithet is not required; thus it is placed in parenthesis. Many horticulturists retain the epithet to indicate the parentage of these cultivars, but this results in cultivar names longer than three words and thus contrary to ICNCP rules.
  H. '(Fortunei) Crowned Imperial'.
  H. '(Fortunei) Freckles'.

H. '(Fortunei) Green Gold'.
H. '(Fortunei) Jester'.
H. '(Fortunei) Joker'.
H. '(Fortunei)La Vista'.
H. '(Fortunei) Mary Marie Ann'.
H. '(Fortunei) Nancy Lindsay'.
H. '(Fortunei) Raindance'.
H. '(Fortunei) Snowdrift'.
H. '(Fortunei) Sundance'.
H. '(Fortunei) Thea'.
H. '(Fortunei) White Edge'.

H. 'Fortunei Viridis'.
AHS-III/13B. (Figure 4-38).
The cultivar name registered for show purposes (in modified form) as *H. fortunei* 'Viridis' AHS-NC IRA/1987 for *H. fortunei* var. *albopicta* f. *viridis*.
(see *H. fortunei* var. *albopicta* f. *viridis*).

H. 'Fountain' Williams/Hensen IRA/1983.
AHS-II/7B.
Plant was renamed by Hensen because the former name, *H. sieboldiana* 'Longipes', is incorrect. Plant 42 in. (106.5 cm) dia., 30 in. (76 cm) high. Leaf 10 by 8 in. (25.5 by 20 cm), veins 13, medium green, not variegated, cordate, rugose. Scape 50 in. (127 cm), foliated, oblique. Flower medium, funnel-shaped, white, flowers during average period, fertile.
HN: *H. elata* 'Fountain' Hensen 1983.
    H. 'Elata Fountain' hort.
    H. 'FRW No. 490'.
    H. sieboldiana 'Longipes' hort. incorrect.
[*H. montana* × *H. sieboldiana*].

H. 'Fourteen Karat'.
Plant 14 in. (35.5 cm) dia., 8 in. (20 cm) high; veins 8, chartreuse, not variegated, cordate, flat. Scape 16 in. (40.5 cm), bare, straight. Flower medium, bell-shaped, purple, flowers during average period, fertile.

H. 'Fragrant Blue' Aden IRA/1988.
AHS-IV/21A .
Plant 12 in. (31 cm) dia., 8 in. (20 cm) high. Leaf 5 by 3 in. (13 by 7.5 cm), veins 5, blue-green, not variegated, cordate, flat. Scape 20 in. (51 cm), foliated, straight. Flower medium, funnel-shaped, blue opening to white, fragrant, flowers during summer period, fertility(?).
[*H.* '8413' × *H.* '8270'].

H. 'Fragrant Bouquet' Aden IRA/1982.
AHS-III/14A.
The original description calls for "apple green leaves with streaks of yellow and white," but the plants in commerce are margined. Plant 22 in. (56 cm) dia., 18 in. (46 cm) high. Leaf 8 by 6 in. (20 by 15 cm), veins 8, light green, yellowish-white margin, cordate, wavy-undulate. Scape 36 in. (91.5 cm), bare, straight. Flower large, funnel-shaped, white, fragrant, average period, fertile.
[*H.* 'Fascination' × *H.* 'Summer Fragrance'].

H. 'Fragrant Candelabra' Aden IRA/1982.
AHS-III/16B.
Plant's variegation originally described as streaked, but some of the cultivated taxa have irregular yellowish-white margins and no streaking. Plant 26 in. (66 cm) dia., 18 in. (46 cm) high. Leaf 8 by 6 in. (20 by 15 cm), veins 8, medium green, streaked yellow, cordate, wavy-undulate. Scape 30 in. (76 cm), bare, straight. Flower medium, funnel-shaped, white, fragrant, summer period, fertile.
[*H.* 'Fragrant Bouquet' hybrid].

H. 'Fragrant Flame' Zilis IRA/1988.
AHS-III/14A.
Plant 36 in. (91.5 cm) dia., 20 in. (51 cm) high. Leaf 9 by 7 in. (23 by 18 cm), veins 9, streaky multicolor and margined green, cordate, flat. Scape 31 in. (79 cm), foliated, straight. Flower medium, white, fragrant, flowers during average period, fertility(?).
[*H. plantaginea* mutation].

H. 'Fragrant Gold' Aden IRA/1982.
AHS-II/11B. (Plates 97, 159).
Plant's description following is the registered one. The plants offered in commerce have leaves of uniform light green which becomes more yellow with the advancing season and grows larger than the sizes below. There is no streaking. Plant 22 in. (56 cm) dia., 14 in. (35.5 cm) high. Leaf 7 by 5 in. (18 by 13 cm), veins 8, yellow (lutescent) green centerline, streaked green, cordate, wavy-undulate. Scape 34 in. (86.5 cm), bare, straight. Flower medium, funnel-shaped, lavender, fragrant, flowers during summer period, fertile.
[*H.* 'Sum and Substance' hybrid].

H. 'Fragrant Tot' Aden IRA/1982.
AHS-V/26A.
Plant 6 in. (15 cm) dia., 4 in. (10 cm) high. Leaf 1 by 0.75 in. (2.5 by 2 cm), veins 8, yellow (lutescent), streaked green, cordate, flat. Scape 12 in. (31 cm), bare, straight. Flower medium, funnel-shaped, lavender, fragrant, flowers during summer period, sterile.
[*H.* 'Amy Aden' hybrid].

H. 'Fran and Jan' Owens IRA/1986.
AHS-III/14B.
Plant 38 in. (96.5 cm) dia., 14 in. (35.5 cm) high. Leaf 10 by 6 in. (25.5 by 15 cm), veins 9, yellow (viridescent), green margin, cordate, flat. Scape 24 in. (61 cm), bare, straight. Flower medium, funnel-shaped, white, flowers during average period, fertile.

H. 'Francee' Klopping IRA/1986.
AHS-III/16B. (Figure 4-18).
AHS Eunice Fisher Award, 1976, exhibited by Minnie Klopping. Margin narrow and regular. A white-streaked sport exists. One of the best white-margined clones of *H.* 'Fortunei'. Plant 36 in. (91.5 cm) dia., 24 in. (61 cm) high. Leaf 7 by 5 in. (18 by 13 cm), veins 8, dark green, white margin, cordate, flat. Scape 42 in. (106.5 cm), foliated, oblique. Flower medium, funnel-shaped, lavender, flowers during average period, fertile.
HN: *H.* 'Fortunei Albomarginata' group.
    H. 'Fortunei Francee'.
    H. 'Francine' Armstrong incorrect.
    H. sieboldiana 'Francine' Armstrong incorrect.
[*H.* 'Fortunei' derivation].

Figure 4-18. *H.* 'Francee'; mass planting (Honeysong Farm-Falstad)

H. **'Frances Williams'** Williams IRA/1986.
HN: *H.* 'Yellow Edge'.
(see *H. sieboldiana* 'Frances Williams').

H. **'Frances Williams Baby'** Minks IRA/1980.
AHS-III/16B.
Plant 48 in. (122 cm) dia., 22 in. (56 cm) high. Leaf 8 by 6 in. (21 by 15 cm), veins 16, yellow (lutescent), not variegated, cordate, rugose. Scape 26 in. (66 cm), bare, straight. Flower medium, bell-shaped, white, flowers during average period, fertile.
HN: *H. sieboldiana* Aureomarginata group.
     H. sieboldiana (Aureomarginata group) 'Frances Williams Baby'.
     H. sieboldiana 'Frances Williams Baby'.
[*H. sieboldiana* 'Frances Williams' × *H. sieboldiana* 'Frances Williams'].
(see *H. sieboldiana* 'Frances Williams').

H. 'Frances Williams Selection' Soules.

H. 'Frances Williams Gold Sport' hort.
Plant name is given to a yellow sport of the cultivar. It is also an invalid formulation per the ICNCP.
HN: *H. sieboldiana* Aureomarginata group.
(see *H. sieboldiana* 'Frances Williams').

H. 'Frances Williams Sport' hort.
Plant name is given to a number of different mutations of the parent plant. It is a confusing name that should not be used and an illegitimate formulation per the ICNCP.

H. **'Frank Sedgwick'** Davidson.
(see *H.* 'Undulata Albomarginata').

H. **'Freckles'** Viette/Summers No. 53 1966.
Plant's variegation is unstable. Plant 48 in. (122 cm) dia., 26 in. (66 cm) high. Leaf 10 by 8 in. (25.5 by 20 cm), veins 16, medium green, mottled multicolor (viridescent), cordate, rugose. Scape 34 in. (86.5 cm), bare, straight. Flower medium, bell-shaped, white, flowers during average period, fertile.
HN: *H.* 'Fortunei Freckles' pp.
[*H.* 'Fortunei' mutation].

H. **'Freising'** Klose 1982.
Plant is a *H.* 'Fortunei' form with pure white flowers. Named by Klose for the town of Freising, Bavaria, Germany, site of the perennial trial gardens of the University of Munich. Plant 36 in. (91.5 cm) dia., 24 in. (61 cm) high. Leaf 8 by 5 in. (20 by 13 cm), veins 8, medium green, not variegated, cordate, flat. Scape 42 in. (106.5 cm), foliated, oblique. Flower medium, funnel-shaped, white, flowers during average period, fertile.
HN: *H.* 'Fortunei Freising' Klose 1982.
[*H.* 'Fortunei' hybrid].

H. **'Fresh'** Aden.
Plant is small—20 in. (51 cm) dia., 8 in. (20 cm) high—with lanceolate, wavy, yellowish leaves having a yellowish white margin.

H. **'Frilly Puckers'** Fisher 1969 IRA/1986.
AHS-II/7A.
Plant erect, 30 in. (76 cm) dia., 30 in. (76 cm) high. Leaf 10 by 8 in. (25.5 by 20 cm), veins 13, medium green, not variegated, cordate, rugose. Scape 46 in. (117 cm), bare, straight. Flower medium, funnel-shaped, lavender, flowers during average period, fertile.
HN: *H.* 'Fisher No. 41-70'.

H. **'Fringe Benefit'** Aden IRA/1986.
AHS-III/16B.
Plant 36 in. (91.5 cm) dia., 24 in. (61 cm) high. Leaf 9 by 7 in. (23 by 18 cm), veins 9, medium green, yellow margin, cordate, flat, yellow margin. Scape 42 in. (106.5 cm), foliated, oblique. Flower medium, lavender, flowers during average period, fertile.

H. **'Frosted Jade'** Maroushek IRA/1978.
AHS-II/10A.   (Plates 105, 153).
AHS ALAHOSO Bowl 1989, exhibited by Clyde Crockett; AHS 1989 Eunice Fisher Award, Lillian Maroushek, hybridizer. Plant erect, 30 in. (76 cm) dia., 28 in. (71 cm) high. Leaf 12 by 9 in. (31 by 23 cm), veins 10, grey green, white margin, cordate, flat. Scape 42 in. (106.5 cm), foliated, oblique. Flower medium, funnel-shaped, white, flowers during average period, fertile.
[*H. montana* hybrid].

H. **'Frosty'**.

H. **'Frühlingsgold'** Klose.
Plant has yellow-striped, small green leaves with lavender flowers. The name means "Spring Gold.".
[*H. sieboldii* hybrid].

H. **'FRW No. 000'** Williams.
Plants numbered by Frances R. Williams, 1883–1969, a well-known early *Hosta* pioneer and hybridizer who gave identification numbers to species as well as hybrids; for example, *H.* 'FRW No. 152' = *H.* 'Fortunei'. Reference to these numbers is made frequently in this chapter. Because Mrs. Williams numbering ranged into the thousands, only horticulturally important numbers are listed and identified:
H. 'FRW No. 128' = *H.* 'Elata'.
H. 'FRW No. 152' = *H.* 'Fortunei'.
H. 'FRW No. 305' = *H. sieboldiana*.
H. 'FRW No. 383' = *H. sieboldiana* 'Frances Williams'.
H. 'FRW No. 490' = *H.* 'Fountain'.
H. 'FRW No. 502' = *H.* 'Betsy King'.
H. 'FRW No. 511' = *H.* 'Dorothy'.
H. 'FRW No. 537' = *H. sieboldii* 'Alba'.
H. 'FRW No. 541' = *H.* 'Summer Gold'.
H. 'FRW No. 791' = *H.* 'Sprite'.
H. 'FRW No. 851' = *H.* 'Green Ripples'.
H. 'FRW No. 941A' = *H.* 'Glauca Stearn'.
H. 'FRW No. 942A' = *H.* 'Sieboldiana from Engler'.
H. 'FRW No. 1023' = *H.* 'Pancakes'.
H. 'FRW No. 1024' = *H.* 'Purple Profusion'.
H. 'FRW No. 1025' = *H.* 'Lavender Lady'.
H. 'FRW No. 1141' = *H.* 'Golden Circles'.
H. 'FRW No. 1142' = *H.* 'Sunlight'.
H. 'FRW No. 1151' = *H.* 'Sieboldiana from Engler'.
H. 'FRW No. 1154' = *H.* 'Snow Flakes'.
H. 'FRW No. 1155' = *H.* 'Slim Polly'.
H. 'FRW No. 1156' = *H.* 'Tinker Bell'.
H. 'FRW No. 1221' = *H.* 'Kelsey'.
H. 'FRW No. 1246' = *H. sieboldii*.
H. 'FRW No. 1258' = *H.* 'Kathleen'.
H. 'FRW No. 1290' = *H.* 'Green Piecrust'.
H. 'FRW No. 1350' = *H.* 'Sentinels'.
H. 'FRW No. 1373' = *H.* 'White Trumpets'.
H. 'FRW No. 1383' = *H.* 'Sweet Susan'.
H. 'FRW No. 1399A' = *H.* 'Beatrice'.
H. 'FRW No. 1429' = *H.* 'Fortunei Carol'.
H. 'FRW No. 2134' = *H.* 'Sunlight Sister'.

H. **'Fuiri Chishima'** Japan.
斑入チシマギボウシ
(see *H. sieboldii* 'Bunchoko').

H. **'Fuiri Karafuto'**.
斑入カラフトギボウシ
    Fuiri Karafuto Giboshi is a Japanese synonym for *H.* 'Helonioides Albopicta', which see.
(see *H.* 'Helonioides Albopicta').

H. **'Fuiri Unazuki'** Japan.
(see *H. kikutii* var. *caput-avis*).

H. **'Fuji No Akebono'** Japan.
富士のあけぼの
    Fuji No Akebono Giboshi, the "dawn of Fuji hosta," is a *H. montana* mutation with yellow-streaky-center variegated petioles and scapes.
HN: *H. montana* 'Fuji No Akebono'.
JN: *Fuji No Akebono Giboshi* hort.
[*H. montana* mutation].

H. **'Fuji No Yubae'** Japan.
富士の夕映え
    Plant is a *H. montana* mutation that has yellow leaves with narrow green margins.
HN: *H. montana* 'Fuji No Yubae'.
JN: *Fuji No Yubae Giboshi* hort.
[*H. montana* mutation].

H. **'Fukurin Hakuyo'** Japan.
覆輪白洋
    Fukurin Hakuyo Giboshi, the "yellow-margined white-back hosta," is the yellow-margined form of *H.* 'Hakuyo' (*Hakuyo Giboshi*), which see.
JN: *Fukurin Hakuyo Nishiki Giboshi* hort.
[*H. longipes* hybrid].

H. **'Fukurin Tsugaru Komachi'** Japan.
覆輪津軽小町
    Fukurin Tsugaru Komachi Giboshi, the "yellow-margined beautiful maiden hosta from Tsugaru." Found in Tsugaru District, northern Honshu, it is a dwarf, yellow-margined form of *H.* 'Tsugaru Komachi', which see.
JN: *Fukurin Tsugaru Komachi Giboshi* hort.
        Kifukurin Tsugaru Komachi (Koba) Giboshi hort.
[*H. sieboldii* hybrid].

H. **'Fukurin Tsunotori'** Japan.
(see *H.* 'Tsunotori Fukurin').

H. **'Fumiko'** Klose.
    Plant is one of the German Tardiana's (see *H.* Tardiana grex). Medium size, blue, cordate leaves, lavender flowers.
HN: *H.* Tardiana grex.
[*H.* 'Tardiflora' × *H. sieboldiana* 'Elegans'].
(see also *H.* Tardiana grex).

H. **'Fury of Flame'** Zilis IRA/1985.
    AHS-III/16A.
    Plant 40 in. (101.5 cm) dia., 22 in. (56 cm) high. Leaf 10 by 8 in. (25.5 by 20 cm), veins 9, medium green, streaked white, cordate, flat. Scape 40 in. (101.5 cm), bare, oblique. Flower medium, bell-shaped, purple, flowers during average period, fertile.
HN: *H. ventricosa* 'Fury of Flame' Zilis 1985.
[*H. ventricosa* 'Aureomaculata' derivation].

H. **'Fused Veins'** Benedict IRA/1983.
    AHS-IV/19B.   (Figure 4-19).
    Plant obtained by Jack E. Craig from his friend Atsuya Hamada in Japan. It is a natural mutation reportedly from the Hamamatsu area of Aichi Prefecture with contorted leaves and principal veins fused together at various points. Plant erect, 12 in. (31 cm) dia., 12 in. (31 cm) high. Leaf 5 by 1.5 in. (13 by 4 cm), veins 4, medium green, not variegated, lanceolate, flat. Scape 16 in. (40.5 cm), bare, straight. Flower medium, bell-shaped, lavender, flowers during average period, fertile.
HN: *H.* 'Craig No. 42' Craig/Summers No. 189 1969.
        H. 'Hamada Contorted' pp.
[*H. longipes* derivation].

Figure 4-19. *H.* 'Fused Veins'; leaf detail showing fused veins (Hosta Hill)

G

H. **'Ga-Ga'** O'Harra.
    Plant is a yellow cultivar with nonopening flowers. Plant 6 in. (15 cm) dia., 4 in. (10 cm) high. Leaf 3 by 1 in. (7.5 by 2.5 cm), veins 3, yellow (lutescent), not variegated, flat. Flower medium, closed corolla, lavender.

H. **'Gaiety'** Aden IRA/1986.
    AHS-III/14A.   (Plate 106).
    Plant is the white-margined, stable form of *H.* 'Hoopla'. Plant 16 in. (40.5 cm) dia., 10 in. (25.5 cm) high. Leaf 8 by 3 in. (20 by 7.5 cm), veins 6, yellow (lutescent), white margin, in the registration described as lanceolate but mature plants have cordate leaves (see Plate 106), flat. Scape 18 in. (46 cm), foliated, straight. Flower medium, funnel-shaped, white, flowers during average period, fertile.
[*H.* 'Aden No. 421' × *H.* 'Aden No. 425'].

H. **'Gala'** Aden IRA/1978.
    AHS-III/16A.
    Plant erect, 14 in. (35.5 cm) dia., 10 in. (25.5 cm) high. Leaf 8 by 3 in. (20 by 7.5 cm), veins 8, medium green, yellow margin with occasional yellow streaks, lanceolate, flat. Scape 16 in. (40.5 cm), bare, oblique. Flower medium, funnel-shaped, purple, flowers during average period, fertile.
[*H.* 'Tardiflora' derivation].

H. 'Galaxy' Lachman IRA/1987.

AHS-III/16A. (Plate 107).

Plant's variegation is very irregular, streaked yellow on green. No two leaves are alike. Reported to revert to all green. Plant 30 in. (76 cm) dia., 15 in. (38 cm) high. Leaf 12 by 8 in. (31 by 20 cm), veins 9, green, light yellow streaked, cordate, flat. Scape 26 in. (66 cm), foliated, oblique. Flower medium, funnel-shaped, lavender, flowers during average period, fertile.

[*H.* 'Beatrice' hybrid × *H. sieboldiana* 'Frances Williams' hybrid].

H. 'Garden Bouquet' Sellers IRA/1983.

AHS-III/16B.

Plant's variegation reported unstable. Plant erect, 30 in. (76 cm) dia., 24 in. (61 cm) high. Leaf 6 by 4 in. (15 by 10 cm), veins 4, medium green, streaked yellow, lanceolate, flat. Scape 36 in. (91.5 cm), bare, straight. Flower medium, funnel-shaped, lavender, fragrant, flowers during average period, sterile.

HN: *H.* 'Garden Banquet' incorrect.

[*H.* 'Iron Gate Bouquet' mutation].

H. 'Garden Magic' Aden IRA/1980.

AHS-III/16B.

Plant's variegation reported unstable. Plant 36 in. (91.5 cm) dia., 24 in. (61 cm) high. Leaf 6 by 4 in. (15 by 10 cm), veins 9, blue-green, streaky, multicolor, cordate, flat. Scape 34 in. (86.5 cm), foliated, straight. Flower medium, funnel-shaped, lavender, flowers during average period, fertile.

[*H.* 'Intrigue' × *H. sieboldiana*].

H. 'Gay Blade' Lachman IRA/1988.

AHS-IV/22B.

Plant 22 in. (56 cm) dia., 12 in. (31 cm) high. Leaf 5 by 2.5 in. (13 by 6 cm), veins 6, grey-green, white margin, lanceolate, wavy. Scape 22 in. (56 cm), bare, oblique. Flower medium, funnel-shaped, lavender, flowers during average period, fertile.

[(*H.* 'Resonance' × *H.* 'P14') × *H.* 'Halcyon'].

H. 'Gay Feather' Benedict IRA/1983.

AHS-IV/20A. (Plate 108).

Plant reported to be very similar to *H.* 'Celebration' but larger. Both have been reported to "melt out" severely because of lack of chlorophyll, especially during wet springs (Pollock, 1988). Plant erect, 16 in. (40.5 cm) dia., 12 in. (31 cm) high. Leaf 7 by 2 in. (18 by 5 cm), veins 5–6, white (albescent), green margin, lanceolate, flat. Scape 34 in. (86.5 cm), foliated, straight. Flower medium, funnel-shaped, lavender, flowers during summer period, fertile.

HN: *H.* 'Celebration' sim.

(see also *H.* 'Celebration').

(see also *H.* 'Center Stage' pp sim).

H. 'Geisha' Vaughn IRA/1983.

AHS-IV/20B. (Plate 109).

Plant's margin is reported narrower than the *H.* 'Geisha' from Japan (see below). A relationship has not been definitely established. Plant erect, 8 in. (20 cm) dia., 4 in. (10 cm) high. Leaf 4 by 2 in. (10 by 5 cm), veins 5, chartreuse, green margin, ovate, flat. Scape 10 in. (25.5 cm), bare, straight. Flower medium, bell-shaped, lavender, flowers during average period, fertile.

H. 'Geisha' Japan.

(see *H.* 'Ani Machi').

H. 'Gene Summers' Aden IRA/1978.

AHS-III/14A.

Plant's variegation reported unstable. Plant 18 in. (46 cm) dia., 12 in. (31 cm) high. Leaf 6 by 4 in. (15 by 10 cm), veins 8, white (albescent), green margin, cordate, flat. Scape 16 in. (40.5 cm), foliated, straight. Flower medium, funnel-shaped, lavender, flowers during summer period, fertile.

HN: Wisley No. 821373.

[*H.* 'Flamboyant' × *H.* 'Intrigue'].

H. 'Genes Joy' Aden.

Plant 14 in. (35 cm) dia., 10 in. (25 cm) high. Leaf ovate-lanceolate, veins 5–6, greenish-white (albescent), green margin with green streaks to center, flat. Scape 16 in. (40.5 cm), foliated, straight. Flower medium, lavender, flowers during summer period, fertility(?).

H. 'George Smith' George Smith IRA/1983.

AHS-II/8B. (Figure 4-20).

Plant is one of several mediovariegated mutants of *H. sieboldiana* known to exist and by some authors considered the same as *H.* 'Borwick Beauty', but further study is needed. This taxon was formerly called *H.* 'Heslington'. Plant 40 in. (101.5 cm) dia., 24 in. (61 cm) high. Leaf 10 by 8 in. (25.5 by 20 cm), whitish yellow (albescent), blue-green margin, round-cordate, cupped-rugose. Scape 28 in. (71 cm), foliated, straight. Flower medium, bell-shaped, white, flowers during average period, fertile.

HN: *H. sieboldiana* Mediovariegata group.

H. 'Borwick Beauty' sim.

H. 'Heslington'.

[*H. sieboldiana* 'Elegans' mutation].

Figure 4-20. *H.* 'George Smith'; general habit, in the border (private garden, UK/Schmid)

H. 'Gilt Edge' Tompkins.

Plant is similar to other yellow-margined *H. sieboldiana* forms. Plant 42 in. (106.5 cm) dia., 24 in. (61 cm) high. Leaf 13 by 10 in. (33 by 25.5 cm), veins 13, medium green, yellow margin, cordate, rugose. Scape 30 in. (76 cm), foliated, straight. Flower medium, bell-shaped, white, flowers during average period, fertile.

HN: *H. sieboldiana* Aureomarginata group.

[*H. sieboldiana* Aureomarginata group mutation].

H. **'Gin and Tonic'** Vaughn 1990.
Plant has round, rugose, chartreuse leaves with a narrow yellowish white margin.
[*H.* 'William Lachman' hybrid × *H.* 'Aztec Treasure'].

H. **'Gingee'** O'Harra IRA/1986.
AHS-V/29B.
Plant erect, 12 in. (31 cm) dia., 10 in. (25.5 cm) high. Leaf 8 by 1 in. (20 by 2.5 cm), veins 3, yellow (viridescent), not variegated, lanceolate, flat. Scape 18 in. (46 cm), bare, straight. Flower medium, funnel-shaped, purple striped, flowers during summer period, fertile.
[*H. sieboldii* 'Subcrocea' hybrid].

H. **'Ginko Craig'** Craig/Summers IRA/1986.
AHS-IV/22A.   (Figure 2-7)
Plant was purchased by Craig in a Kyoto flower market (Davidson, 1990). Summers named it for Craig's wife Ginko. It has two distinct leaf forms: a small flat juvenile leaf, with uniform margins by which it is known in most gardens, and a mature leaf, which is noticeably larger, with irregular, white undulate margins. Some plants show both leaf forms during a transition stage which occurs 4–6 years after planting. A hosta received from Japan as *H.* 'Bunchoko' (*Bunchoko Giboshi*) has leaves like the juvenile form but its flowers are white. *Hosta* 'Hime' is similar to the mature plant. The juvenile form can be maintained by frequent dividing and is 10 in. (25.5 cm) dia., 4 in. (10 cm) high. Leaf 3 by 1 in. (7.5 by 2.5 cm), veins 3, medium green, white margin, lanceolate, flat. Scape 18 in. (46 cm), bare, straight. Flower medium, funnel-shaped, purple striped, flowers during summer period, fertile.
HN: *H.* 'Excalibur'.
     H. 'Hime Karafuto'.
     H. 'Princess of Karafuto'.
JN: *Hime Karafuto Giboshi* hort.

H. **'Glauca Stearn'** Williams 1951 incorrect.
Plant name is an incorrect formulation of *H. glauca* Stearn (= *H. sieboldiana*).
HN: *H.* 'FRW No. 941A'.
[*H. sieboldiana* form].

H. **'Glockenspiel'** Klose.
Plant is medium size; leaf green; flower lavender. The name means "Carillon" or "Playing Bells."

H. **'Gloriosa'** Krossa IRA/1986.
AHS-III/16B.
Plant's margin is uniform and very narrow. Smaller than most other white-margined forms of *H.* 'Fortunei', but some authors do not believe it is related to the latter. Plant 32 in. (81.5 cm) dia., 18 in. (46 cm) high. Leaf 6 by 4 in. (15 by 10 cm), veins 8, medium green, white margin, ovate, flat. Scape 38 in. (96.5 cm), foliated, oblique. Flower medium, funnel-shaped, lavender, flowers during average period, sterile.
HN: *H.* 'Fortunei Albomarginata' group.
     H. 'Fortunei Gloriosa'.
     H. 'Fortunei Gloriosa Variegated' Savory 1979.
     H. 'Krossa No. A-1'.
     H. rohdeifolia incorrect.
     H. rohdeifolia 'Alba' incorrect.
     H. rohdeifolia 'Albamarginata' incorrect.
     Summers No. 50 1966.
(see also *H.* 'Fortunei Albomarginata' group.
(see *H.* 'Fortunei Gloriosa').

H. **'Glory'** Savory IRA/1985.
AHS-III/17A.
Plant 24 in. (61 cm) dia., 12 in. (31 cm) high. Leaf 5 by 5 in. (13 by 13 cm), veins 8, chartreuse, not variegated, cordate-round, flat. Scape 22 in. (56 cm), bare, straight. Flower medium, funnel-shaped, lavender, flowers during average period, fertile.
[*H.* 'August Moon' hybrid].

H. **'Glowing Heart'** Houseworth 1986.
Plant 12 in. (31 cm) dia., 9 in. (23 cm) high. Leaf 6 by 5 in. (15 by 13 cm), veins 7, medium green, not variegated, cordate, flat. Scape 20 in. (51 cm), bare, straight. Flower medium, bell-shaped, purple, flowers during average period, sterile.
[*H. ventricosa* 'Aureomarginata' hybrid].

H. **'Goddess of Athena'** Kuk's Forest IRA/1987.
AHS-III/16B.
Plant is a chartreuse-margined *H. decorata*. Plant 24 in. (61 cm) dia., 14 in. (35.5 cm) high. Leaf 5 by 3 in. (13 by 7.5 cm), veins 8, dark green, (albescent) chartreuse margin, cordate, flat. Scape 28 in. (71 cm), bare, oblique. Flower medium, bell-shaped, purple, flowers during average period, fertile.
[*H. decorata* hybrid × self].

H. **'Gohonmatsu Fukurin'** Japan.
五本松覆輪
Gohonmatsu Fukurin Giboshi, the "(yellow)-margined hosta from Gohon Matsu," is a *H. montana* form with wide dark yellow margins and with leaves more erect and lanceolate than those of the form.
JN: *Gohonmatsu Fukurin Giboshi* hort.
[*H. montana* mutation].
(see also *H. montana* 'Gohon Matsu Fukurin').

H. **'Gold Bold'** Aden 1976.
Plant is a yellow *H.* 'Tokudama'.
[*H.* 'Tokudama' derivation].

H. **'Gold Cadet'** Aden (No. 381) IRA/1974.
AHS-IV/23B.
Plant 14 in. (35.5 cm) dia., 10 in. (25.5 cm) high. Leaf 5 by 4 in. (13 by 10 cm), veins 8, yellow (lutescent), not variegated, ovate, flat. Scape 14 in. (35.5 cm), foliated, straight. Flower medium, funnel-shaped, purple, flowers during average period, fertile.

H. **'Gold Coast'** Banyai IRA/1986.
AHS-III/17B.
Plant 24 in. (61 cm) dia., 18 in. (46 cm) high. Leaf 9 by 7 in. (23 by 18 cm), veins 12, chartreuse, not variegated, cordate, wavy-undulate. Scape 26 in. (66 cm), foliated, straight. Flower medium, funnel-shaped, white, flowers during average period, fertile.

H. **'Gold Colleen'** Houseworth 1986.
Plant erect, 6 in. (15 cm) dia., 8 in. (20 cm) high. Leaf 5 by 1 in. (13 by 2.5 cm), veins 3, yellow (viridescent), not variegated, lanceolate, flat. Scape 20 in. (51 cm), bare, straight. Flower medium, funnel-shaped, purple striped, flowers during average period, fertile.
[*H. sieboldii* 'Kabitan' hybrid].

H. **'Gold Cover'** Vaughn IRA/1982.
AHS-IV/23B.
AHS Midwest Gold Award, 1980, exhibited by Richard Ward. Plant 10 in. (25.5 cm) dia., 6 in. (15 cm) high. Leaf 5 by 4 in. (13 by 10 cm), veins 8, yellow (lutescent), not variegated,

round-cordate, cupped-rugose. Scape 12 in. (31 cm), bare, straight. Flower medium, funnel-shaped, white, flowers during average period, fertile.

H. 'Gold Crown'.
(see *H.* 'Fortunei Aureomarginata').

H. 'Gold Cup' Aden IRA/1978.
   AHS-III/17A.
   Plant 18 in. (46 cm) dia., 14 in. (35.5 cm) high. Leaf 4 by 3 in. (10 by 7.5 cm), veins 12, yellow (lutescent), not variegated, round-cordate, cupped-rugose. Scape 20 in. (51 cm), bare, straight. Flower medium, bell-shaped, white, flowers during average period, fertile.
   [*H.* 'Tokudama Aureonebulosa' × *H.* 'Golden Prayers'].

H. 'Gold Drop' Anderson IRA/1977.
   AHS-IV/23B.   (Plate 110).
   Plant 10 in. (25.5 cm) dia., 6 in. (15 cm) high. Leaf 3 by 2 in. (7.5 by 5 cm), veins 8, chartreuse, not variegated, cordate, flat. Scape 16 in. (40.5 cm), bare, straight. Flower medium, bell-shaped, white, flowers during average period, fertile.
   [*H. venusta* × *H.* 'August Moon'].

H. 'Gold Edger' Aden IRA/1978.
   AHS-IV/23B.   (Plates 73, 160).
   Plant 12 in. (31 cm) dia., 8 in. (20 cm) high. Leaf 4 by 3 in. (10 by 7.5 cm), veins 8, yellow (viridescent), not variegated, cordate, flat. Scape 14 in. (35.5 cm), bare, straight. Flower medium, bell-shaped, white, flowers during average period, fertile.
   [*H.* 'Blue Cadet' × *H.* 'Blue Cadet'].

H. 'Gold Flush' Bloom IRA/1984.
   AHS-III/16B.
   Plant 30 in. (76 cm) dia., 18 in. (46 cm) high. Leaf 8 by 6 in. (20 by 15 cm), veins 8, medium green, streaky, multicolor, cordate, flat. Scape 32 in. (81.5 cm), bare, straight. Flower medium, bell-shaped, purple, flowers during average period, fertile.
HN: *H. ventricosa* 'Gold Flush' Bloom 1971.
   H. ventricosa 'Aureomaculata Gold Flush'.
   [*H. ventricosa* 'Aureomaculata' mutation].

H. 'Gold Haze' Smith BHHS IRA/1988.
   AHS-III/17A.
   Plant is one of Eric Smith's GL (Gold Leaf) series intended to improve color stability of *H.* 'Fortunei Aurea', but this form also turns green by summer.
HN: *H.* 'Smith GL 5' 1972.
   Wisley No. 821404.
   [*H.* 'Fortunei Aurea' × *H. sieboldiana*].
(see also under *H.* Tardiana grex).

H. 'Gold High Fat Cream' Aden incorrect.
   Plant is the all-yellow form of *H.* 'High Fat Cream', which see. The name is invalid because it does not conform to the ICNCP rules which permit no more than 3 words in a cultivar name.
   [*H.* 'High Fat Cream' mutation].

H. 'Gold Isle' Smith.
(see *H.* 'Golden Isle').

H. 'Gold Leaf' Smith BHHS IRA/1988.
   AHS-III/17A.
   Plant is one of Eric Smith's GL (Gold Leaf) series intended to improve color stability of *H.* 'Fortunei Aurea' but

this form also turns green by summer.
   [*H.* 'Fortunei Aurea' × *H. sieboldiana*].
(see also under *H.* Tardiana grex).

H. 'Gold Mark'.
(see *H.* 'Marble Rim').

H. 'Gold Pan' Aden 1975 IRA/1978.
   AHS-III/17B.
   Plant 28 in. (71 cm) dia., 20 in. (51 cm) high. Leaf 6 by 5 in. (15 by 13 cm), veins 12, yellow (lutescent), not variegated, round-cordate, cupped-rugose. Scape 28 in. (71 cm), bare, straight. Flower medium, bell-shaped, white, flowers during average period, fertile.
   [*H.* 'Golden Waffles' × *H.* 'Gold Cup'].

H. 'Gold Piece' Vaughn IRA/1983.
   AHS-II/12B.
   Plant has a yellow spot near leaf tip that enlarges until the entire leaf is yellow. Veins dark green. Plant erect, 38 in. (96.5 cm) dia., 38 in. (96.5 cm) high. Leaf 13 by 6 in. (33 by 15 cm), veins 8, yellow (lutescent), variegated, ovate, flat. Scape 50 in. (127 cm), bare, straight. Flower medium, bell-shaped, purple, flowers during summer period, fertile.
   [*H. ventricosa*/*H. tibae*/*H. plantaginea*/*H. nigrescens* hybrid].

H. 'Gold Regal' Aden 1970 IRA/1974.
   AHS-II/11B.   (Plate 111).
   Plant not related to *H.* 'Krossa Regal'. Plant erect, 24 in. (61 cm) dia., 20 in. (51 cm) high. Leaf 7 by 5 in. (18 by 13 cm), veins 13, chartreuse, not variegated, ovate, flat. Scape 28 in. (71 cm), bare, straight. Flower medium, bell-shaped, purple, flowers during average period, fertile.
   [*H.* 'Aspen Gold' hybrid al].
   [*H.* 'Tokudama' hybrid].

H. 'Gold Ruffles' Aden.
(see *H.* 'Golden Ruffles').

H. 'Gold Sagae' Japan.
(see *H. fluctuans* 'Gold Sagae').

H. 'Gold Seer' Aden 1972.
   Plant 18 in. (46 cm) dia., 10 in. (25.5 cm) high. Leaf 5 by 4 in. (13 by 10 cm), veins 12, yellow (viridescent), not variegated, round-cordate, cupped-rugose. Scape 16 in. (40.5 cm), bare, straight. Flower medium, bell-shaped, white, flowers during average period, fertile.
   [*H.* 'Tokudama' hybrid].

H. 'Gold Standard' Banyai IRA/1976.
   AHS-III/14B.   (Plate 112, 151, 152).
   AHS multiple award winner: Eunice Fisher Award, 1980; Midwest Gold Award, 1980, exhibited by Pauline Banyai. One of the most popular mediovariegated cultivars. A sport with white streaks in leaf center exists. Plant 36 in. (91.5 cm) dia., 20 in. (51 cm) high. Leaf 7 by 5 in. (18 by 13 cm), veins 8, yellow (lutescent), green margin, cordate, flat. Scape 42 in. (106.5 cm), bare, straight. Flower medium, funnel-shaped, lavender, flowers during average period, fertile.
HN: *H.* 'Fortunei Gold Standard'.
   [*H.* 'Fortunei' mutation].

H. 'Gold Twist' Houseworth 1986.
   Plant erect, 8 in. (20 cm) dia., 8 in. (20 cm) high. Leaf 5 by 1.5 in. (13 by 4 cm), veins 3, yellow (viridescent), not variegated, lanceolate, undulate. Scape 20 in. (51 cm), bare, straight. Flower medium, funnel-shaped, purple striped, flowers during average period, fertile.
   [*H.* 'The Twister' hybrid].

H. **'Gold Vein'** Smith BHHS IRA/1988.
AHS-III/17A.
Plant is one of Eric Smith's GL (Gold Leaf) series.
HN: *H.* 'Smith GL 20'.
(see also under *H.* Tardiana grex).

H. **'Goldbrook'** Goldbrook-Bond/UK IRA/1989.
AHS-III/16A.
Plant is a cultivar similar to *H.* 'Antioch' and *H.* 'Spinners' but the leaves on plants seen are smaller. Plant 36 in. (91.5 cm) dia., 20 in. (51 cm) high. Leaf 7 by 6 in. (18 by 15 cm), veins 7, medium green, white margin, ovate, flat, wavy margin. Scape 28 in. (70 cm), foliated, oblique. Flower medium, funnel-shaped, lavender, flowers during average period, sterile.
HN: *H.* 'Fortunei Goldbrook'.
　　H. 'Fortunei Moerheim' pp sim.
　　H. 'Fortunei Moerheimii' pp sim. incorrect
[*H.* 'Fortunei' mutation].
(see *H.* 'Antioch').

H. **'Goldbrook Genie'** Goldbrook-Bond/UK IRA/1989.
AHS-IV/21B.
Plant similar to parent. Leaf 4 by 3.5 in. (10 by 9 cm), veins 8, medium grey-green, not variegated, cordate, flat. Flower medium, bell-shaped, lavender, flowers during average period, fertile.
[*H. nakaiana* hybrid].

H. **'Goldbrook Glimmer'** Goldbrook-Bond UK.
Plant is reported to be a *H.* Tardiana grex derivation with yellowish white variegation in the leaf center. The margin is grey-green.
[*H.* 'Tardiflora' × *H. sieboldiana* 'Elegans' derivative].

H. **'Goldbrook Gold'** Goldbrook-Bond/UK IRA/1989.
AHS-III/17B.
Plant looks like a large yellow *H.* 'Tokudama'; venation indicates this but it is registered as a *H. sieboldiana* hybrid. Plant 30 in. (76 cm) dia., 23 in. (58 cm) high. Leaf 9 by 7 in. (22 by 18 cm), veins 11, yellow (viridescent), not variegated, cordate, flat. Flower medium, white, flowers during average period, fertile.
HN: *H. sieboldiana* Yellow group.
[*H. sieboldiana* hybrid].

H. **'Goldbrook Grace'** Goldbrook-Bond/UK IRA/1989.
AHS-IV/20B.
Plant is similar to *H.* 'Golden Prayers' but has green margin and is smaller. Plant 10 in. (25 cm) dia., 6 in. (15 cm) high. Leaf 4 by 3 in. (10 by 8 cm), veins 7–8, yellow (lutescent), green margin, ovate, flat. Scape 7 in. (18 cm), foliated, straight. Flower medium, funnel-shaped, purple, flowers during average period, sterile.
[*H.* 'Golden Prayers' mutation].

H. **'Golden Age'** Smith BHHS IRA/1988.
AHS-III/17A.
HN: Wisley No. 821365.
[*H. sieboldii* 'Kabitan' × *H.* 'Tardiflora'].
[*H.* 'Tardiflora' × *H. sieboldiana* 'Elegans' al].

H. **'Golden Anniversary'** Holly IRA/1986.
AHS-II/12B.
Plant is yellow in spring, turns green. Plant 36 in. (91.5 cm) dia., 20 in. (51 cm) high. Leaf 9 by 6 in. (23 by 15 cm), veins 8, yellow (viridescent), not variegated, cordate, flat. Scape 42 in. (106.5 cm), bare, straight. Flower medium, funnel-shaped, lavender, flowers during average period, fertile.
[*H.* 'Fortunei' hybrid ad int].

H. **'Golden Boy'** Aden 1976.

H. **'Golden Bullion'** Bennerup/Ruh IRA/1989.
AHS-III/17B.
Plant in a narrow sense is the yellow sport of *H.* 'Tokudama Flavocircinalis' in commerce. Broadly, this clonal cultivar name has been assigned and is horticulturally used for all yellow-leaved members of the *H.* 'Tokudama Flavocircinalis' group, but this is technically incorrect because several distinct forms of the latter exist. I have established a *H.* 'Tokudama Flavocircinalis Yellow' group per Article 26 of the ICNCP under which all the distinct yellow taxa in this group can be assembled in a broad sense and named. Plant 28 in. (71 cm) dia., 14 in. (35.5 cm) high. Leaf 6 by 4 in. (15 by 10 cm), veins 12, yellow (lutescent), not variegated, cordate, rugose. Scape 20 in. (51 cm), bare, straight. Flower medium, bell-shaped, lavender, flowers during average period, fertile.
HN: *H.* 'Tokudama Flavocircinalis Yellow' group.
[*H.* 'Tokudama Flavocircinalis' mutation].
(see also *H.* 'Tokudama Flavocircinalis Yellow' group).

H. **'Golden Cascade'** Benedict IRA/1984.
AHS-II/11A.
Plant 30 in. (76 cm) dia., 18 in. (46 cm) high. Leaf 9 by 5 in. (23 by 13 cm), veins 10, chartreuse, not variegated, ovate, flat, later rugose. Scape 36 in. (91.5 cm), foliated, straight. Flower medium, funnel-shaped, lavender, flowers during average period, fertile.
[*H.* 'Gold Regal' × *H.* 'Gold Regal' hybrid].

H. **'Golden Chimes'** Grapes IRA/1978.
AHS-III/17A.
Plant 22 in. (56 cm) dia., 12 in. (31 cm) high. Leaf 6 by 5 in. (15 by 13 cm), veins 12, yellow (lutescent), not variegated, cordate, rugose. Scape 18 in. (46 cm), bare, straight. Flower medium, bell-shaped, white, flowers during average period, fertile.
[*H.* 'Tokudama' hybrid].

H. **'Golden Circles'** Williams (No. 1141).
Plant has margins Zilis type C (cfr. Zilis, 1987). Plant 44 in. (112 cm) dia., 24 in. (61 cm) high. Leaf 14 by 10 in. (35.5 by 25.5 cm), veins 16, blue-green, yellow margin, cordate, rugose. Scape 30 in. (76 cm), bare, straight. Flower medium, bell-shaped, white, flowers during average period, fertile.
HN: *H. sieboldiana* Aureomarginata group.

H. **'Golden Crown'** Piedmont Gardens.
(see *H.* 'Fortunei Aureomarginata').

H. **'Golden Fascination'** AHS IRA/1986.
AHS-III/17A.
Plant is a stable yellow form of *H.* 'Fascination'. Plant 20 in. (51 cm) dia., 16 in. (40.5 cm) high. Leaf 6 by 4 in. (15 by 10 cm), veins 10, yellow (viridescent), not variegated, cordate, flat. Scape 20 in. (51 cm), foliated, straight. Flower medium, funnel-shaped, lavender, flowers during average period, fertile.
[*H.* 'Fascination' mutation].

H. **'Golden Francee'** Wallace 1986.
Plant 26 in. (66 cm) dia., 16 in. (40.5 cm) high. Leaf 8 by 5 in. (20 by 13 cm), veins 8, yellow (viridescent), not variegated, cordate, flat. Scape 22 in. (56 cm), foliated, straight. Flower medium, bell-shaped, white, flowers during average period, fertile.
[*H.* 'Fortunei' hybrid ad int].

H. 'Golden Girl' Anderson IRA/1982.
AHS-III/17A.
Plant 24 in. (61 cm) dia., 16 in. (40.5 cm) high. Leaf 8 by 6 in. (20 by 15 cm), veins 10, yellow. Scapes 24 in. (61 cm). [H. 'Tokudama' form].

H. 'Golden Hawk' Benedict IRA/1984.
AHS-IV/23A.
Plant 12 in. (31 cm) dia., 6 in. (15 cm) high. Leaf 3 by 1 in. (7.5 by 2.5 cm), veins 5, yellow (lutescent), not variegated, lanceolate, flat. Scape 14 in. (35.5 cm) foliated, straight.

H. 'Golden Glimmer' Lewis.
HN: Summers No. 100 1963.
(see H. 'Fine Points').

H. 'Golden Globe' Olson.
Plant is a chartreuse H. 'Tokudama' form. Flower medium, funnel-shaped, purple striped, flowers during summer period, fertile.
[H. 'Hadspen Hawk' × H. 'Hadspen Hawk'].

H. 'Golden Haze' Smith UK.
(see H. 'Gold Haze').

H. 'Golden Honey' Anderson.

H. 'Golden Honey' Lewis.
HN: Summers No. 73 1967.

H. 'Golden Honey' Smith.

H. 'Golden Isle' Aden.
Lanceolate leaves with yellow margin.
[H. sieboldii mutation ad int].

H. 'Golden Isle' Smith 1972.
Plant is a hybrid very similar to H. sieboldii 'Kabitan' but has white flowers on very straight scapes.
[H. sieboldii hybrid].

H. 'Golden Lance' Vogel.
HN: H. 'Fortunei Aurea' hort. pp.
H. 'Krossa No. H-6'.
H. 'Lancifolia Aurea' hort. pp.
Summers No. 87 1962.

H. 'Golden Mammoth' Blackthorne.
(see H. 'Golden Sunburst').

H. 'Golden Maple' Minks IRA/1980.
AHS-II/11B.
Plant 36 in. (91.5 cm) dia., 24 in. (61 cm) high. Leaf 10 by 8 in. (25.5 by 20 cm), veins 16, yellow (lutescent), not variegated, cordate, rugose. Scape 30 in. (76 cm), bare, straight. Flower medium, bell-shaped, white, flowers during average period, fertile.
HN: H. sieboldiana 'Golden Maple'.
H. sieboldiana Yellow group.
[H. 'Maple Leaf' mutation].

H. 'Golden Medallion' AHS IRA/1984.
AHS-III/17B.
Plant is a yellow sport of H. 'Tokudama Aureonebulosa'. Several clones exist and form the H. 'Tokudama Aureonebulosa Yellow' group. This clonal cultivar name has been assigned and is horticulturally used for all yellow-leaved members of the H. 'Tokudama Aureonebulosa' group, but this is technically incorrect because several distinct forms of the latter exist. I have established a H. 'Tokudama Aureonebulosa Yellow' group per Article 26 of the ICNCP under which all the distinct yellow taxa in this group can be assembled in a broad sense and named. Plant 24 in. (61 cm) dia., 14 in. (35.5 cm) high. Leaf 6 by 5 in. (15 by 13 cm), veins 12, yellow (lutescent), not variegated, round-cordate, cupped-rugose. Scape 18 in. (46 cm), bare, straight. Flower medium, bell-shaped, white, flowers during average period, fertile.
HN: H. 'Tokudama Aureonebulosa Yellow' group.
[H. 'Tokudama Aureonebulosa' mutation].
(see also H. 'Tokudama Aureonebulosa Yellow' group).

H. 'Golden Nakaiana' hort.
Plant name is incorrect and used for several taxa.

H. 'Golden Nugget' Cooley IRA/1969.
AHS-III/17B.
Plant is smaller than the typical clones in the H. sieboldiana Aureomarginata group. An all-green sport also exists. Plant 26 in. (66 cm) dia., 16 in. (40.5 cm) high. Leaf 6 by 5 in. (15 by 13 cm), veins 16, yellow (lutescent), not variegated, cordate, rugose. Scape 20 in. (51 cm), bare, straight. Flower medium, bell-shaped, white, flowers during average period, fertile.
HN: H. 'Gold Nugget' incorrect.
[H. sieboldiana Aureomarginata group hybrid].

H. 'Golden Oriole' Smith BHHS IRA/1988.
AHS-IV/23A.
Plant small with thin yellow ovate-lanceolate leaves.
[H. 'Hadspen Heron' × H. sieboldii 'Kabitan'].

H. 'Golden Plum' Lewis IRA/1968.
AHS-IV/23B.
Plant is similar to the parent. Leaf 4 by 2.5 in. (10 by 6 cm), yellow (viridescent), turning all green. Slightly pruinose.
HN: H. 'Golden Decorata' incorrect.
H. 'Krossa No. H-4'.
Summers No. 43 1963.
[H. decorata hybrid].

H. 'Golden Prayers' Aden IRA/1976.
AHS-IV/23A. (Plate 113).
Plant 20 in. (51 cm) dia., 12 in. (31 cm) high. Leaf 4 by 3 in. (10 by 7.5 cm), veins 10, yellow (lutescent), not variegated, round-cordate, cupped-rugose. Scape 18 in. (46 cm), bare, straight. Flower medium, bell-shaped, white, flowers during average period, fertile. Often seen labeled H. 'Little Aurora'.
[H. 'Aden No. 381' × H. 'Golden Waffles'].
(see also H. 'Golden Prayers West').

H. 'Golden Prayers Sport' UK.
Plant is identical to H. 'Golden Prayers' but has a light chartreuse margin. According to ICNCP rules this name is illegitimate and cannot be used.
[H. 'Golden Prayers' mutation].

H. 'Golden Prayers West'.
Plant is larger than H. 'Golden Prayers' and reportedly the true form, but is larger than the registration for H. 'Golden Prayers'.

H. 'Golden Rajah' Aden IRA/1976.
AHS-III/17A.
Plant 28 in. (71 cm) dia., 14 in. (35.5 cm) high. Leaf 9 by 6 in. (23 by 15 cm), veins 10, yellow (viridescent), not variegated, cordate, rugose. Scape 20 in. (51 cm), bare, straight.

Flower medium, bell-shaped, white, flowers during average period, fertile.
[*H.* 'Aspen Gold' hybrid × *H.* 'Tokudama Aureonebulosa' hybrid].

H. 'Golden Ruffles' Aden.
Plant is a yellow form of *H.* 'Tokudama'.
[*H.* 'Aden No. 381' × *H.* 'Aden No. 388'].

H. 'Golden Samurai'.
Plant is a yellow form of *H.* 'Samurai'.

H. 'Golden Scepter' Savory IRA/1983.
AHS-IV/23A.   (Plate 156).
Plant is the yellow form of *H.* 'Golden Tiara' which is a derivation of *H. nakaiana* showing vestiges of ridges on the scape. Plant 18 in. (46 cm) dia., 12 in. (31 cm) high. Leaf 4 by 3 in. (10 by 7.5 cm), veins 4, yellow (lutescent), not variegated, cordate, flat. Scape 24 in. (61 cm), bare, straight. Flower medium, bell-shaped, purple striped, flowers during average period, fertile.
HN: Golden Nakaiana incorrect.
    H. nakaiana 'Golden' incorrect.
    H. nakaiana 'Golden Golden Tiara' incorrect.
    H. nakaiana 'Golden Scepter'.
[*H.* 'Golden Tiara' mutation].

H. 'Golden Sculpture' Anderson IRA/1982.
AHS-I/5A.
AHS Alex J. Summers Distinguished Merit Hosta, 1991, selected by Olive B. Langdon. Plant erect, 22 in. (56 cm) dia., 24 in. (61 cm) high. Leaf 12 by 12 in. (31 by 31 cm), veins 16, yellow (lutescent), not variegated, cordate, rugose. Scape 30 in. (76 cm), bare, straight. Flower medium, bell-shaped, white, flowers during average period, fertile.
[*H. sieboldiana* Yellow group].

H. 'Golden Shimmer' Shaw.
HN: Summers No. 395 1970.

H. 'Golden Sieboldiana' incorrect.
(see *H.* 'Golden Sunburst').
(see also *H. sieboldiana* Yellow group).

H. 'Golden Spades' Kuk's Forest IRA/1986.
AHS-V/29B.
Plant erect, 6 in. (15 cm) dia., 4 in. (10 cm) high. Leaf 2.5 by 1.25 in. (6 by 3 cm), veins 4, yellow (viridescent), not variegated, ovate-lanceolate, flat. Scape 12 in. (31 cm), foliated, straight. Flower medium, funnel-shaped, purple striped, flowers during average period, fertile.
[*H. sieboldii* 'Kabitan' hybrid].

H. 'Golden Spider' Harshbarger/Ruh IRA/1987.
AHS-IV/23B.
Plant 18 in. (46 cm) dia., 10 in. (25.5 cm) high. Leaf 4 by 3 in. (10 by 7.5 cm), veins 4, yellow (viridescent), not variegated, ovate, flat. Scape 18 in. (46 cm), oblique. Flower medium, bell-shaped, flowers during average period, fertile.

H. 'Golden Sunburst' AHS IRA/1984.
AHS-II/11B.   (Plates 161, 176).
Plant is a mutation of the yellow-margined *H. sieboldiana* forms and consistent with Zilis type F (cfr. Zilis, 1987). This clonal cultivar name has been assigned and is horticulturally used for all members of the *H. sieboldiana* Yellow group, but this is technically incorrect because, as with the species, many distinct all-yellow forms—some large, some small—exist in

this group and have been named. I have established a *H. sieboldiana* Yellow group per article 26 of the ICNCP under which all the distinct yellow taxa in this group can be assembled in a broad sense and named. The cultivar name *H. sieboldiana* 'Golden Sunburst' represents but one form of the many available in commerce. Plant 44 in. (112 cm) dia., 20 in. (51 cm) high. Leaf 13 by 10 in. (33 by 25.5 cm), veins 16, yellow (lutescent), not variegated, cordate, rugose. Scape 24 in. (61 cm), bare, straight. Flower medium, bell-shaped, white, flowers during average period, fertile.
HN: *H.* 'Golden Mammoth' Blackthorne.
    H. sieboldiana 'Golden Sunburst'.
    H. sieboldiana Yellow group.
    H. sieboldiana (Yellow group) 'Golden Sunburst'.
[*H. sieboldiana* 'Frances Williams' mutation].
(see also *H. sieboldiana* Yellow group).

H. 'Golden Tardiana' Aden 1978.
Plant name is an incorrect synonym.
(see *H.* 'Bright Glow').

H. 'Golden Teacup' Wilkins IRA/1989.
AHS-IV/20A.
Plant 18 in. (45 cm) dia., 12 in. (30 cm) high. Leaf 5 by 5 in. (13 by 13 cm), veins 12, yellow (viridescent), not variegated, cordate, cupped-rugose. Scape 12 in. (30 cm), bare, straight. Flower medium, bell-shaped, white, flowers during average period, fertile.
[*H.* 'Aspen Gold' × *H.* 'Gold Regal'].

H. 'Golden Tiara' Savory IRA/1977.
AHS-IV/22A.   (Plates 13, 154, 156, 166).
AHS Nancy Minks Award, 1980. The yellow-leaved, green-margined form of *H. nakaiana* showing vestiges of ridges on the scape. Plant 22 in. (56 cm) dia., 14 in. (35.5 cm) high. Leaf 4 by 2.5 in. (10 by 6 cm), veins 5, yellow (lutescent), not variegated, cordate, flat. Scape 32 in. (81.5 cm), bare, straight. Flower medium, bell-shaped, purple striped, flowers during average period, fertile.
[*H. nakaiana* derivation].

H. 'Golden Torch' Benedict IRA/1984.
AHS-II/11A.
Plant is chartreuse with a green center. Plant erect, 20 in. (51 cm) dia., 14 in. (35.5 cm) high. Leaf 8 by 5 in. (20 by 13 cm), veins 6, chartreuse, cordate, rugose. Scape 30 in. (76 cm), foliated, straight. Flower medium, bell-shaped, white, flowers during average period, fertile.
[*H.* 'Gold Regal' × *H.* 'Gold Regal'].

H. 'Golden Waffles' Aden IRA/1976.
AHS-III/17B.
Plant 18 in. (46 cm) dia., 10 in. (25.5 cm) high. Leaf 7 by 5 in. (18 by 13 cm), veins 12, yellow (lutescent), not variegated, cordate, rugose. Scape 16 in. (40.5 cm), bare, straight. Flower medium, bell-shaped, white, flowers during average period, fertile.
[*H.* 'Aden No. 381' × *H.* 'Aden No. 388'].

H. 'Golden Wheels' Minks IRA/1976.
AHS-III/17B.
Plant is the all-yellow stable form of *H.* 'Wagon Wheels' (Zilis type F; cfr. Zilis, 1987). Plant 34 in. (86.5 cm) dia., 16 in. (40.5 cm) high. Leaf 12 by 10 in. (31 by 25.5 cm), veins 10, yellow (lutescent), not variegated, cordate, rugose. Scape 18 in. (46 cm), bare, straight. Flower medium, bell-shaped, white, flowers during average period, fertile.
HN: *H. sieboldiana* Yellow group.

[H. 'Wagon Wheels' mutation].
(see H. 'Golden Sunburst').

H. 'Goldilocks' Armstrong IRA/1970.
AHS-III/17A.
Plant 22 in. (56 cm) dia., 12 in. (31 cm) high. Leaf 6 by 5 in. (15 by 13 cm), veins 12, yellow (lutescent), not variegated, round-cordate, cupped-rugose. Scape 14 in. (35.5 cm), bare, straight. Flower medium, bell-shaped, white, flowers during average period, sterile.
HN: H. 'Tokudama Aureonebulosa Yellow' group.
       H. 'Tokudama Goldilocks'.
[H. 'Tokudama' hybrid].

H. 'Goldilocks' UK.
HN: H. Tardiana grex TF 2 × 25?
[H. 'Tardiflora' × H. sieboldiana 'Elegans'].
(see also H. Tardiana grex).

H. 'Goldpfeil' Klose.
Plant is a yellow cultivar related to H. 'Fortunei'; lavender flowers. The name means "Golden Arrow."

H. 'Goldsmith' Smith/Morss BHHS IRA/1988.
AHS-III/17A.
[H. sieboldii 'Kabitan' × H. sieboldiana hybrid].

H. 'Goliath' Harrison 1964 IRA/1986.
AHS-II/7A.   (Figure 4-21).
Plant is a large-leaved plant with a ruffled margin similar to H. 'Ruffles' but with a vein count of 12–13 like H. montana. Leaf 15 by 13 in. (38 by 33 cm), scape tall.
HN: Summers No. 392.
[H. montana × H. sieboldiana].

Figure 4-21. H. 'Goliath'; general habit (Soules garden/Schmid)

H. 'Good as Gold' Aden.
Plant is the all-yellow stable form of both H. 'Gaiety' and H. 'Hoopla'. Plant 24 in. (61 cm) dia., 14 in. (35.5 cm) high. Leaf 6 by 3 in. (15 by 7.5 cm), veins 7, chartreuse, not variegated, cordate, flat. Scape 18 in. (46 cm), foliated, straight. Flower medium, funnel-shaped, lavender, flowers during average period, fertile.
[H. 'Gaiety' mutation].
[H. 'Hoopla' mutation].

H. 'Goody Goody' Benedict IRA/1987.
AHS-V/26A.
Plant has some streaks into white center, narrow margin. Plant spreading, 8 in. (20 cm) dia., 2 in. (5 cm) high. Leaf 2 by 0.5 in. (5 by 1 cm), veins 3, white, green margin, lanceolate, flat.

Scape 10 in. (25.5 cm), bare, straight. Flower medium, funnel-shaped, purple, flowers during average period, fertile.
[H. 'Neat Splash' hybrid × self].

H. 'Gosan August Clouds'.   (Plate 84).
Plant is similar to H. 'August Moon' but has white streaks and "clouding" in the leaves and is a sport of this cultivar. It grows to about the same size.
HN: Mutant WH 13/8703 1987 (Schmid).
[H. 'August moon' mutant].

H. 'Gosan Gold Midget' Schmid IRA/1989.
AHS-VI/35A   (Plate 153).
Plant has yellow leaves with size and shape like those of H. venusta but does not have ridges on scape. Stays small. Plant 5 in. (13 cm) dia., 3 in. (7.5 cm) high. Leaf 1.5 by 0.5–1 in. (10 by 4 cm), veins 4–5, yellow (viridescent), not variegated, ovate-cordate, flat. Scape 6–10 in. (to 25.5 cm), bare, straight, some branching. Flower medium, bell-shaped, lavender, flowers during average period, fertile.
HN: Hybrid WH 13/8307 1983 (Schmid).
[H. venusta × H. Golden Prayers].

H. 'Gosan Gold Sword' Schmid IRA/1989.
AHS-IV/23A   (Figures 2-6, F-2; Plate 114).
Plant has light yellow leaves which are unusually shaped being wider near the tip and continuously decurrent to the petiole as in H. alismifolia. Plant 12–16 in. (30–40 cm) dia., 8 in. (20 cm) high. Leaf 6–8 by 1–2 in. (15–20 by 2–5 cm), veins 4, yellow (lutescent), not variegated, lanceolate, flat. Scape 18 in. (45 cm), foliaceous, straight. Flower medium, funnel-shaped, lavender, flowers during average period, fertile.
HN: Hybrid WH 13/8611 1986 (Schmid).
[H. alismifolia × H. rectifolia 'Ogon'].

H. 'Gosan Hildegarde' Schmid IRA/1989.
AHS-V/29A   (Plate 57).
Plant has yellow leaves like the juvenile leaves of H. 'Ginko Craig'. Good substance and lasting color. Plant 8 in. (20 cm) dia., 3 in. (7.5 cm) high. Leaf 4 in. by 1 in. (10 by 2.5 cm), veins 3, yellow (lutescent), not variegated, lanceolate, flat. Scape 10 in. (25.5 cm), bare, straight. Flower medium, bell-shaped, whitish, flowers during average period, fertile.
HN: Hybrid WH 13/8305 1983 (Schmid).
[H. Golden Prayers × H. 'Ginko Craig'].

H. 'Gosan Lettuce' Schmid.   (Figure 2-5).
Plant is medium size and has erect greenish yellow leaves that are crinkled and deformed like those of certain types of Chinese lettuce whose mound it resembles.
HN: Hybrid WH 13/8613 1986 (Schmid).
[H. rectifolia 'Ogon' × H. alismifolia].

H. 'Gosan Mina' Schmid.
AHS-V/29A   (Plate 115).
Plant has flat yellow-to-chartreuse leaves and makes an excellent edger, about one-fourth the size of H. 'Gold Edger'. Good substance and lasting color. Plant 8 in. (20 cm) dia., 3 in. (7.5 cm) high. Leaf 2.5 in. by 2 in. (6 by 5 cm), veins 7, yellow turning to light chartreuse, not variegated, roundish, cordate, flat. Scape 8 in. (20 cm), bare, straight. Flower medium, bell-shaped, whitish, flowers very early during average period, sterile.
HN: Hybrid WH 13/8304 1983 (Schmid).
[H. Golden Prayers × H. pulchella].

H. **'Gosan Sigi Grey'** Schmid.   (Figure 2-18; Plate 166).
Plant has bluish grey leaves which are similar to those of
H. 'Krossa Regal' but extremely rugose and with heavy substance and elongated tip on a long upright petiole. Plant 16 in.
(40 cm) dia., 16 in. (40 cm) high. Leaf 10 in. by 6 in. (25 by 15
cm), veins 12–14, blue-green, not variegated, elongated-
cordate, flat. Scape 20 in. (50 cm), foliaceous, straight. Flower
medium, bell-shaped, white, flowers during average period,
fertile.
HN: Hybrid WH 13/8619 1986 (Schmid).
[*H. montana* × *H.* 'Tokudama'].

H. **'Gotemba Nishiki'** Japan.
御殿場錦
Gotemba Nishiki Giboshi, the "colorful (brocaded)
Gotemba hosta," is a large white-margined form of *H. longipes*
found near Fuji-san, Gotemba area.
JN: *Gotemba Nishiki Giboshi* hort.
[*H. longipes* derivation].

H. gracillima **'Saizaki'**.

H. gracillima **'Shirofukurin'**.

H. **'Gracillima Variegated'** incorrect.
Plant name is an incorrect synonym.
HN: *H.* 'Gracillima Variegata' incorrect.
(see *H.* 'Vera Verde').
(see also *H. cathayana* 'Shirofukurin').

H. **'Granary Gold'** Smith.
Plant is one of Eric Smith's GL (Gold Leaf) series. It is
larger than *H.* 'Fortunei Aurea', with wider, more cordate
leaves, and retains its yellow color much longer, fading to a
light chartreuse by summer. There are a number of different
plants offered under this name in Britain and no official
description is available. Its exact derivation has been reported
differently and it is by some considered a somatic mutant of *H.*
'Fortunei Aurea'.
HN: Wisley No. 821370.
[*H. sieboldii* 'Kabitan' × *H. sieboldiana* hybrid al].
[*H.* 'Fortunei Aurea' hybrid al].
[*H.* 'Fortunei Aurea' mutation al].

H. **'Grand Master'** Aden IRA/1986.
AHS-III/16B.
Plant erect, 20 in. (51 cm) dia., 20 in. (51 cm) high. Leaf 12
by 9 in. (31 by 23 cm), veins 10, blue-green, white margin, cordate, rugose. Scape 26 in. (66 cm), foliated, straight. Flower
medium, funnel-shaped, lavender, flowers during summer
period, fertile.

H. **'Grandiflora'** hort. incorrect.
Plant name is an incorrect synonym.
(see *H. plantaginea*).

H. **'Gray Cole'** Kuk's Forest IRA/1985.
AHS-I/3B.   (Plate 60).
AHS Eunice Fisher Award, 1985, exhibited by Kuk's
Forest. An outstanding, large, selected clone conforming very
closely to Hylander's classic Western diagnosis and representing the classic "European" *H. sieboldiana*. This plant originated with the firm of Gray & Cole, hence the name. Plant 48
in. (122 cm) dia., 32 in. (81.5 cm) high. Leaf 15 by 13 in. (38 by
33 cm), veins 16, blue-green, not variegated, cordate, rugose.
Scape 34 in. (86.5 cm), foliated, straight. Flower medium, bell-
shaped, white, flowers during average period, fertile.

HN: *H. sieboldiana* 'Gray Cole'.
(see also *H. sieboldiana* 'Elegans').

H. **'Gray Streaked Squiggles'** Ross/Ruh IRA/1978.
AHS-V/28A.
Plant erect, 12 in. (31 cm) dia., 6 in. (15 cm) high. Leaf 5 by
1.5 in. (13 by 4 cm), veins 3, medium green, streaked yellow,
lanceolate, wavy-undulate. Scape 14 in. (35.5 cm), bare,
straight. Flower medium, funnel-shaped, purple striped,
flowers during average period, fertile.

H. **'Great Desire'** Fisher IRA/1973.
AHS-III/13B.
Plant 36 in. (91.5 cm) dia., 22 in. (56 cm) high. Leaf 10 by 8
in. (25.5 by 20 cm), veins 12, medium green, not variegated,
cordate, ribbed. Scape 36 in. (91.5 cm), bare, straight. Flower
medium, funnel-shaped, white, flowers during average
period, fertile.
[*H.* 'Crispula' hybrid].

H. **'Great Expectations'**[PPAF] Bond/Aden IRA/1988.
AHS-III/14A.   (Plate 100, 153).
A mediovariegated mutation of *H. sieboldiana* discovered
in England. In spring the leaf center is a bright golden yellow
but later turns white. There are numerous reports of melting
out during the white phase in late summer. Plant 33 in. (84 cm)
dia., 22 in. (56 cm) high. Leaf 6 by 4 in. (15 by 10 cm), veins 10,
yellow (albescent), dark green irregular margin streaking to
center, cordate, rugose. Scape 33 in. (84 cm), foliated, straight.
Flower medium, bell-shaped, white, flowers during average
period, fertile.
HN: *H. sieboldiana* Mediovariegata group.
[*H. sieboldiana* mutation].

H. **'Great Lakes'** Fisher IRA/1973.
AHS-II/9A.
Plant 46 in. (117 cm) dia., 30 in. (76 cm) high. Leaf 13 by 11
in. (33 by 28 cm), veins 16, blue-green, not variegated, cordate, rugose. Scape 34 in. (86.5 cm), foliated, straight. Flower
medium, bell-shaped, white, flowers during average period,
fertile.
[*H. sieboldiana* Aureomarginata group hybrid].

H. **'Green Acres'** Geissler IRA/1970.
AHS-I/1B   (Figure 4-22).
AHS Eunice Fisher Award, 1973 exhibited by Julia
Geissler. A large *H. montana* form. Many similar forms (listed in
the synonymy) exist and have been named and most conform
in part to the diagnosis of *H. montana* f. *macrophylla*. Plant 52 in.
(132 cm) dia., 42 in. (106.5 cm) high. Leaf 17 by 13 in. (43 by 33
cm), veins 13, medium green, not variegated, cordate, fur-

Figure 4-22. *H.* 'Green Acres'; general habit; *H.* 'Hadspen
Blue' (below) (Coney garden/Schmid)

rowed. Scape 54 in. (137 cm), bare, straight. Flower medium, funnel-shaped, white, flowers during early period, fertile.
HN: H. 'Big Boy' pp sim.
    H. 'King Michael' pp sim.
    H. 'Krossa B-3' (Osaka) Summers No. 78 1967 sim.
    H. 'Mikado' pp sim.
[H. montana f. macrophylla form].

H. 'Green Angel' Aden.
Plant is reportedly a green version of H. 'Blue Angel', which see.

H. 'Green Aspen' Owens IRA/1986.
AHS-III/13B.
Plant 24 in. (61 cm) dia., 12 in. (31 cm) high. Leaf 7 by 6 in. (18 by 15 cm), veins 12, medium green, not variegated, cordate, rugose. Scape 16 in. (40.5 cm), bare, straight. Flower medium, bell-shaped, white, flowers during average period, fertile.
[H. 'Aspen Gold' × H. 'Aspen Gold'].

H. 'Green Beatrice' Williams/Ruh IRA/1987.
AHS-IV/19B.
Plant is the nonvariegated green form of H. sieboldii originating with the unstable H. sieboldii 'Beatrice'. This is a back-mutation to the parental form H. sieboldii f. spathulata. There are many different forms of the latter so exactly which clone this taxon represents is unknown.
HN: H. 'Green Beatrice' hort.
(see H. sieboldii f. spathulata).

H. 'Green Blade' Benedict 1986.
Plant is the stable green form H. 'Yellow Splash'. Plant 24 in. (61 cm) dia., 14 in. (35.5 cm) high. Leaf 6 by 4 in. (15 by 10 cm), veins 7, medium green, not variegated, ovate, flat. Scape 34 in. (86.5 cm), bare, straight. Flower medium, funnel-shaped, lavender, flowers during average period, fertile.
[H. 'Yellow Splash' mutation].

H. 'Green Dome' Minks IRA/1980.
AHS-III/13A.
Plant 24 in. (61 cm) dia., 16 in. (40.5 cm) high. Leaf 7 by 6 in. (18 by 15 cm), medium green, not variegated, ovate, flat. Scape 24 in. (61 cm), bare, straight. Flower medium, funnel-shaped, lavender, flowers during average period, fertile.
[H. 'Crested Reef' × H. 'Candle Wax'].

H. 'Green Eclipse' Summers.
Plant 20 in. (51 cm) dia., 12 in. (31 cm) high. Leaf 5 by 4 in. (13 by 10 cm), veins 10, yellow (lutescent), chartreuse margin, cordate-cupped, rugose. Scape 24 in. (61 cm), foliated, straight. Flower medium, bell-shaped, white, flowers during average period, fertile.
[H. 'Midwest Gold' mutation].

H. 'Green Eyes'.
Plant is a miniature mound of yellow leaves, 2 by 0.75 in. (5 by 2 cm), with a fine green margin. It is smaller than H. sieboldii 'Kabitan'.

H. 'Green Formal' Fisher IRA/1971.
AHS-II/7A.
Plant 38 in. (96.5 cm) dia., 18 in. (46 cm) high. Leaf 10 by 8 in. (25.5 by 20 cm), veins 12, medium green, not variegated, cordate, flat. Scape 36 in. (91.5 cm), bare, straight. Flower medium, bell-shaped, white, flowers during average period, fertile.
[H. sieboldiana Aureomarginata group hybrid].

H. 'Green Fountain' Aden IRA/1979.
AHS-III/13A.
Plant 36 in. (91.5 cm) dia., 26 in. (66 cm) high. Leaf 10 by 3 in. (25.5 by 7.5 cm), veins 7, medium green, not variegated, lanceolate, wavy-undulate. Scape 38 in. (96.5 cm), foliated, straight. Flower medium, funnel-shaped, lavender, flowers during average period, fertile.
[H. 'Green Wedge' × H. longipes al].
[H. kikutii hybrid].

H. 'Green Francee'.
Plant is a green reversion of H. 'Francee'.

H. 'Green Furrows' Schulz IRA/1981.
AHS-III/13B.
Plant 28 in. (71 cm) dia., 20 in. (51 cm) high. Leaf 9 by 7 in. (23 by 18 cm), veins 12, medium green, not variegated, cordate, flat. Scape 28 in. (71 cm), foliated, straight. Flower medium, funnel-shaped, lavender, flowers during average period, fertile.
[H. montana hybrid].

H. 'Green Gold' Mack/Savory IRA/1986.
AHS-III/16B.
Plant 32 in. (81.5 cm) dia., 20 in. (51 cm) high. Leaf 7 by 5 in. (18 by 13 cm), veins 8, dark green, yellow margin, cordate, flat. Scape 34 in. (86.5 cm), foliated, straight. Flower medium, funnel-shaped, lavender, flowers during average period, fertile.
HN: H. 'Fortunei Green Gold'.
    H. 'Mack No. 22' 1965.
[H. 'Fortunei' mutation].

H. 'Green Jeans' Punnett.
[H. 'Nakaimo' hybrid].

H. 'Green Joy' Busse.
Plant is medium green. Fast increaser.

H. 'Green Kabitan' T&Z.
Plant 10 in. (25 cm) dia., 8 in. (20 cm) high. Leaf 5 by 1 in. (13 by 2.5 cm), veins 3–4, medium green, not variegated, lanceolate, wavy. Scape 28 in. (71 cm), bare, straight. Scape 2 in. (33 cm), foliated, straight. Flower medium, funnel-shaped, purple-striped, flowers during summer period, fertile.
[H. sieboldii f. spathulata form].

H. 'Green Lime' Aden IRA/1987.
AHS-IV/23A.
Plant has chartreuse leaves, green midrib. Plant 7 in. (18 cm) dia., 4 in. (10 cm) high. Leaf 6 by 1 in. (15 by 2.5 cm), veins 4, chartreuse, not variegated, lanceolate, flat. Scape 13 in. (33 cm), foliated, straight. Flower medium, bell-shaped, lavender, flowers during average period, fertile.
[H. 'Just So' × H. 'Little Aurora'].

H. 'Green Mantle' Fisher.

H. 'Green Marmalade' Owens IRA/1987.
AHS-III/16B.   (Plate 116).
Plant has glossy green leaves mottled with albescent chartreuse. Plant 24 in. (61 cm) dia., 14 in. (35.5 cm) high. Leaf 8 by 5 in. (20 by 13 cm), veins 8, medium green, mottled multi-colored, ovate, flat. Scape 38 in. (96.5 cm), foliated, oblique. Flower medium, funnel-shaped, white, flowers during average period, fertile.
[H. 'Neat Splash' × H. plantaginea].

H. **'Green Pan'.**

H. **'Green Piecrust'** Williams IRA/1986.
  AHS-I/1B.   (Figure 4-23).
  Plant 44 in. (112 cm) dia., 28 in. (71 cm) high. Leaf 14 by 10 in. (35.5 by 25 cm), veins 12, medium green, not variegated, cordate, piecrust margin. Scape 44 in. (112 cm), foliated, oblique. Flower medium, funnel-shaped, white, flowers during average period, fertile.
  HN: *H.* 'FRW No. 1290' 1951.

Figure 4-23. *H.* 'Green Piecrust'; general habit (Hosta Hill)

H. **'Green Platter'** Fisher IRA/1968.
  AHS-II/7B.
  Plant 26 in. (66 cm) dia., 16 in. (40.5 cm) high. Leaf 9 by 7 in. (23 by 18 cm), veins 8, medium green, not variegated, cordate, flat. Scape 34 in. (86.5 cm), foliated, oblique. Flower medium, funnel-shaped, lavender, flowers during average period, fertile.
  [*H.* 'Fortunei' hybrid].

H. **'Green Rim Nugget'** Summers 1986.
  Plant is an aureonebulosa sport of the parent. Plant 26 in. (66 cm) dia., 16 in. (40.5 cm) high. Leaf 6 by 5 in. (15 by 13 cm), veins 16, yellow (lutescent), green margin, cordate, rugose. Scape 20 in. (51 cm), bare, straight. Flower medium, bell-shaped, white, flowers during average period, fertile.
  [*H.* 'Golden Nugget' mutation].

H. **'Green Ripples'** Williams IRA/1986.
  AHS-II/7A.
  Plant 28 in. (71 cm) dia., 18 in. (46 cm) high. Leaf 10 by 7 in. (25.5 by 18 cm), veins 12, medium green, not variegated, cordate, rippled margin. Scape 28 in. (71 cm), bare, oblique. Flower medium, funnel-shaped, white, flowers during average period, fertile.
  HN: *H.* 'FRW No. 851' 1951.
  [*H.* 'FRW No. 128' hybrid].
  [*H.* 'Elata' hybrid].

H. **'Green Saucers'** Powell IRA/1977.
  AHS-II/7A.
  Plant 42 in. (106.5 cm) dia., 28 in. (71 cm) high. Leaf 11 by 8 in. (28 by 20 cm), veins 16, medium green, not variegated, cordate-cupped, rugose. Scape 28 in. (71 cm), bare, straight. Flower medium, bell-shaped, white, flowers during average period, fertile.

H. **'Green Sheen'** Aden IRA/1978.
  AHS-II/7A.
  Plant 48 in. (122 cm) dia., 32 in. (81.5 cm) high. Leaf 12 by

9 in. (31 by 23 cm), veins 10, medium green, not variegated, cordate, flat. Scape 60 in. (152.5 cm), bare, straight. Flower medium, bell-shaped, white, flowers during summer period, fertile.
[*H.* 'Green Wedge' hybrid].

H. **'Green Smash'** Zilis/Lohman IRA/1988.
  AHS-IV/19A.
  Plant 24 in. (61 cm) dia., 10 in. (25.5 cm) high. Leaf 6 by 3 in. (15 by 7.5 cm), veins 5, medium green, not variegated, ovate-lanceolate, flat. Scape 28 in. (71 cm), bare, straight. Flower medium, funnel-shaped, purple, flowers during summer period, fertile.
  HN: *H.* 'Green Splash' incorrect.
  [*H.* 'Ginko Craig' mutation].

H. **'Green Spot'** Fisher 1968.
  Plant is a green/yellow mosaic sport, viridescent.
  [*H.* 'Starker Aureafolia' mutation].

H. **'Green Valley'** Savory IRA/1988.
  AHS-III/17B.
  Plant 36 in. (91.5 cm) dia., 24 in. (61 cm) high. Leaf 7 by 4 in. (18 by 10 cm), veins 7, yellow, green towards midrib, ovate-lanceolate, flat with wavy margins. Scape 30 in. (76 cm), foliated, straight. Flower medium, funnel-shaped, lavender, flowers during average period, fertility(?).

H. **'Green Velvet'** Zager/Williams.
  (see *H.* 'Fortunei Gloriosa').

H. **'Green Wedge'** Aden IRA/1976.
  AHS-I/1A.   (Figure 3-52).
  Plants in commerce under this name differ. Solberg (1988a) reports two different plants: one introduced by Klehm Nursery, the other originated in Aden's garden. The Aden cultivar was registered without description in 1976, and it was not until 1988 that an official description was published. This plant is a selected clone or an F_1 selfed seedling of *H. nigrescens* 'Elatior' (Figure 3-52).
  (see *H. nigrescens* 'Elatior').
  (see also *H.* 'Green Wedge' Klehm).

H. **'Green Wedge Klehm'** Klehm.   (Figure 4-24).
  Plant's description following characterizes *H.* 'Green Wedge' (Klehm) which is here called *H.* 'Green Wedge Klehm' so as not to conflict with the previous taxon. Klehm has reportedly withdrawn this plant, but there are many examples of this choice cultivar in gardens, which now should be renamed *H.* 'Green Wedge Klehm'. Plant 40 in. (102 cm) dia.,

Figure 4-24. *H.* 'Green Wedge Klehm'; general habit (Coney garden/Schmid)

22 in. (56 cm) high. Leaf 13 by 11 in. (33 by 28 cm), veins 10, very light green, pruinose above, heavier and more white below, not variegated, cordate, flat. Scape 40 in. (102 cm), bare, straight. Flower medium, bell-shaped, white, flowers during summer period, fertile.

H. 'Green Wiggles' Carpenter IRA/1979.
AHS-IV/19B.
Plant erect, 12 in. (31 cm) dia., 8 in. (20 cm) high. Leaf 5 by 1 in. (13 by 2.5 cm), veins 3, medium green, not variegated, lanceolate, flat. Scape 22 in. (56 cm), bare, straight. Flower medium, funnel-shaped, purple striped, flowers during summer period, fertile.
[H. 'Maya' × H. sieboldii 'Kabitan'].

H. 'Greenwood' Fisher.
Plant has leaves of light green similar in form to parent. Leaf 8 by 5 in. (20 by 13 cm).
[H. 'Crispula' hybrid].

H. 'Grey Beauty' Williams/Hensen IRA/1983.
AHS-II/9A.
Plant 36 in. (91.5 cm) dia., 24 in. (61 cm) high. Leaf 10 by 8 in. (25.5 by 20 cm), veins 13, blue-green, not variegated, cordate, rugose. Scape 24 in. (61 cm), foliated, straight. Flower medium, bell-shaped, lavender, flowers during average period, fertile.
HN: H. 'FRW No. 1253'.
H. 'Gray Beauty' incorrect.
H. sieboldiana 'Grey Beauty' Hensen 1983.
[H. sieboldiana hybrid].

H. 'Grey Goose' Smith BHHS IRA/1988.
AHS-III/15B.
Plant 19 in. (48 cm) dia., 10 in. (25.5 cm) high. Leaf 5 by 4 in. (13 by 10 cm), veins 9, blue-green, not variegated, cordate, flat. Scape 11 in. (28 cm), bare, straight. Flower medium, bell-shaped, white, flowers during average period, fertility(?).
HN: H. Tardiana grex TF 2 × 13.
[H. 'Tardiflora' × H. sieboldiana 'Elegans'].
(see also H. Tardiana grex).

H. 'Grey Piecrust' Donahue IRA/1986.
AHS-I/1B.
Plant is like H. 'Green Piecrust', but the leaf color is grey-green. Plant 44 in. (112 cm) dia., 28 in. (71 cm) high. Leaf 14 by 10 in. (35.5 by 25 cm), veins 12, grey-green, not variegated, cordate, piecrust margin. Scape 44 in. (112 cm), foliated, oblique. Flower medium, funnel-shaped, white, flowers during average period, fertile.
[H. 'Green Piecrust' hybrid].

H. 'Grimes Golden'.

H. 'Groo Bloo' Aden.
Plant is a select form of H. sieboldiana.
[H. sieboldiana form].

H. 'Ground Master' Aden IRA/1979.
AHS-IV/22B.
Plant 20 in. (51 cm) dia., 12 in. (31 cm) high. Leaf 5 by 2 in. (13 by 5 cm), veins 5, medium green, white margin, ovate-lanceolate, flat. Scape 20 in. (51 cm), foliated, straight. Flower medium, funnel-shaped, purple, flowers during average period, fertile.
[H. 'Yellow Splash' × H. 'Neat Splash'].

H. 'Ground Sulphur' O'Harra IRA/1986.
AHS-V/29A.
Plant erect, 10 in. (25.5 cm) dia., 8 in. (20 cm) high. Leaf 3 by 1 in. (7.5 by 2.5 cm), veins 12, yellow (viridescent), not variegated, cordate, flat. Scape 28 in. (71 cm), foliated, straight. Flower medium, funnel-shaped, lavender, flowers during average period, fertile.
[H. sieboldii 'Subcrocea' hybrid].

H. 'Grünspecht' Klose.
Plant is one of the German Tardiana's (see H. Tardiana grex). A green H. Tardiana grex hybrid with dark green, round leaves and lavender flowers. The name means "Green Sparrow."
HN: H. Tardiana grex.
[H. 'Tardiflora' × H. sieboldiana 'Elegans'].
(see also H. Tardiana grex).

H. 'Gum Drop' Englerth/Ruh IRA/1987.
AHS-IV/19A.
Plant 13 in. (33 cm) dia., 8 in. (20 cm) high. Leaf 4 by 3 in. (10 by 7.5 cm), veins 7, medium green, not variegated, cordate, flat. Scape 16 in. (40.5 cm), foliated, straight. Flower medium, bell-shaped, lavender, flowers during average period, fertile.

H

H. 'Hadspen Blue' Smith BHHS IRA/1988.
AHS-III/15B. (Figure 4-22; Plate 132).
Plant received RHS Award of Merit. Described as rather small, but clumps undisturbed for a number of years have been measured much larger; the ultimate size may depend on cultivation and microclimate. Plant 14 in. (35.5 cm) dia., 8 in. (20 cm) high. Leaf 5 by 4 in. (13 by 10 cm), veins 11, blue-green, not variegated, ovate, flat. Scape 16 in. (40.5 cm), bare, straight. Flower medium, bell-shaped, white, flowers during average period, fertile.
HN: H. Tardiana grex TF 2 × 7.
Wisley No. 821405, 821417, 821459.
[H. 'Tardiflora' × H. sieboldiana 'Elegans'].
(see also H. Tardiana grex).

H. 'Hadspen Dolphin' Hadspen House.
Plant is a medium-size cultivar belonging to the H. Tardiana grex.
[H. 'Tardiflora' × H. sieboldiana 'Elegans'].

H. 'Hadspen Hawk' Smith BHHS IRA/1988.
AHS-IV/21B. (Plate 117).
Plant 12 in. (31 cm) dia., 8 in. (20 cm) high. Leaf 4 by 2 in. (10 by 5 cm), veins 10, blue-green, not variegated, ovate, flat. Scape 16 in. (40.5 cm), bare, straight. Flower medium, bell-shaped, white, flowers during average period, fertile.
HN: H. Tardiana grex TF 2 × 20.
Wisley No. 821427.
[H. 'Tardiflora' × H. sieboldiana 'Elegans'].
(see also H. Tardiana grex).

H. 'Hadspen Heron' Smith/Aden IRA/1976.
AHS-IV/21B.
Plant 14 in. (35.5 cm) dia., 8 in. (20 cm) high. Leaf 4 by 2 in.

(10 by 5 cm), veins 7, blue-green, not variegated, ovate, flat. Scape 14 in. (35.5 cm), bare, straight. Flower medium, bell-shaped, white, flowers during average period, fertile.
HN: H. 'Blue Heron'.
      H. Tardiana grex TF 2 × 10.
      Wisley No. 821414.
[H. 'Tardiflora' × H. sieboldiana 'Elegans'].
(see also H. Tardiana grex).

H. 'Hadspen Honey' Smith.

Plant 14 in. (35.5 cm) dia., 8 in. (20 cm) high. Leaf 5 by 4 in. (13 by 10 cm), veins 10, yellow (lutescent), not variegated, ovate, flat. Scape 14 in. (35.5 cm), bare, straight. Flower medium, bell-shaped, white, flowers during average period, fertile. In the UK H. sieboldiana 'Golden Sunburst' is sold under this name.
HN: H. sieboldiana 'Hadspen Honey'.
      Wisley No. 821453.

H. 'Hadspen Pink' Smith/Eason BHHS IRA/1988.

AHS-IV/21B.
HN: H. 'Eric Smith' Smith/Archibald.
      H. Tardiana grex TF 2 × 32.
[H. 'Tardiflora' × H. sieboldiana 'Elegans'].
(see also H. Tardiana grex).

H. 'Hadspen Samphire' Smith/Eason 1972.

Plant small with thin yellow viridescent ovate-lanceolate leaves. It is a slow grower. The name is derived from Saint Peter's Herb (Crithmum maritimum), and Rock or Sea Samphire, an aromatic seaside plant with yellowish leaves collected and used in pickles.
[H. sieboldiana 'Elegans' × H. sieboldii 'Kabitan'].

H. 'Hadspen White' Smith 1972.

H. 'Haku Chu Han' Japan 1963 IRA/1986.

AHS-V/26A.   (Plates 30, 68).
Plant is a sport of H. sieboldii and the name means "half (of leaf) white in center." Technically, H. 'Haku Chu Han' is incorrect—due to mistaken transliteration of Japanese kanji characters meaning Shiro Nakafu, "white-centered"—but the cultivar name has been retained because of its extensive use in horticulture and its registration by the AHS. Although the name was registered with hyphens as H. sieboldii 'Haku-chu-han', the proposed 1990 ICNCP (Article 26. e. ii., note) advises that for consistency Japanese transliterations no longer include hyphens. As a consequence I have removed the hyphens to make this name consistent with all other transliterated Japanese cultivar names in this book. A similar taxon received from Japan under the name Shirokabitan Giboshi, the "white Kabitan hosta," is incorrectly named because the Japanese name is botanically linked by several authors (Maekawa 1940, 1969; Ohwi 1942; Hara 1984) with the yellow H. sieboldii 'Subcrocea' (which see), so cannot be used for the white-centered taxon (see nomenclature under H. sieboldii 'Silver Kabitan' in Chapter 3). I have given a new name to the incorrectly named Shirokabitan Giboshi, viz., H. sieboldii 'Silver Kabitan', which represents a different clone of the white-centered H. sieboldii. Hosta 'Haku Chu Han' differs slightly from the latter, and several other similar clones exist. The specimens received from Japan and now named H. sieboldii 'Silver Kabitan' turn more green in summer and are more vigorous (Plate 68). Dwarf forms of this variegated H. sieboldii occur—for example, H. 'Bobbin', which see. The clone H. 'Haku Chu Han' was sent by Craig to Davidson under its present name (Davidson, 1990), but Epstein is also mentioned as a source.
Plant 8 in. (20 cm) dia., 4 in. (10 cm) high. Leaf 3 by 0.75 in.

(7.5 by 2 cm), veins 3, white (viridescent), green margin, lanceolate, flat. Scape 14 in. (35.5 cm), bare, straight. Flower medium, funnel-shaped, purple striped, flowers during summer period, fertile.
HN: H. 'Lancifolia Haku Chu Han' incorrect.
      H. sieboldii 'Haku Chu Han'.
      H. sieboldii 'Silver Kabitan' sim.
      Summers No. 104.
JN: Shiro Kabitan Giboshi incorrect.
(see also H. sieboldii 'Silver Kabitan').

H. 'Hakujima' Craig/Japan.

Plant was introduced from Japan by Davidson (No. 90) who received it from Craig under the name H. nimor in 1967. Davidson (1990) reports that this taxon is a small plant and probably not H. minor. Plants observed under this name are very similar to H. gracillima, but H. 'Saishu Jima' has also been given this label, and these taxa were probably mixed up in cultivation.
HN: H. 'Haku Jima'.
(see H. 'Yakushima').
(see also H. 'Saishu Jima').
(see also H. 'Yakushima Mizu').

H. 'Hakuyo' Japan.

白洋
Hakuyo Giboshi, the "white-backed hosta," is a medium-size hybrid with H. longipes var. hypoglauca ancestry. It has small white-backed oval leaves and purple spots on the petiole.
JN: Hakuyo Giboshi hort.
[H. longipes hybrid].

H. 'Hakuyo Nishiki' Japan.

白洋錦
Hakuyo Nishiki Giboshi, the "colorful (yellow-)variegated white-back hosta," is the yellow-white variegated form of H. 'Hakuyo', which see.
JN: Hakuyo Nishiki Giboshi hort.
[H. longipes hybrid].

H. 'Halcyon' Smith BHHS IRA/1988.

AHS-III/15B.   (Plate 162).
AHS Alex J. Summers Distinguished Merit Hosta, 1987, selected by Diana Grenfell; Award of Merit, Wisley Trials, UK. This cultivar requires time to develop its mature shape. In the United Kingdom many seed-raised plants purported to be this taxon are cultivated (Grenfell, 1988: personal communication). The plants in commerce in North American are true to form. Plant 38 in. (96.5 cm) dia., 20 in. (51 cm) high. Leaf 8 by 5 in. (20 by 12 cm), veins 11, blue-green, not variegated, ovate, flat. Scape 26 in. (66 cm), bare, straight. Flower medium, bell-shaped, white, flowers during average period, fertile.
HN: H. Tardiana grex TF 1 × 7.
      Wisley No. 821408, 822976.
[H. 'Tardiflora' × H. sieboldiana 'Elegans'].
(see also H. Tardiana grex).

H. 'Halo' Aden IRA/1978.

AHS-III/14A.
Plant's name is also used for H. 'Blue Moon'. Plant 16 in. (40.5 cm) dia., 12 in. (31 cm) high. Leaf 5 by 4 in. (13 by 10 cm), veins 12, blue-green, white margin, cordate, flat. Scape 18 in. (46 cm), foliated, straight. Flower medium, funnel-shaped, lavender, flowers during average period, fertile.
[H. 'Flamboyant' × H. 'Estelle Aden'].

H. 'Halo' Smith.

Plant name is an incorrect synonym.
(see H. 'Blue Moon').

H. 'Hanazawa Fukurin' hort. Japan.
ハナザワミズギボウシ

Hanazawa Mizu Giboshi, the "margined swamp hosta," is a white-margined sport of the species found growing in the wild in Shimoyama.

JN: *Hanazawa Mizu Giboshi*.

(see also *H. longissima* 'Hanazawa').

H. 'Hannah Hanson' Brodeur.

H. 'Happiness' Smith BHHS IRA/1988.
AHS-III/15B.

Plant 20 in. (51 cm) dia., 13 in. (33 cm) high. Leaf 5 by 4 in. (13 by 10 cm), veins 12, blue-green, not variegated, cordate, flat. Scape 18 in. (46 cm), foliated, straight. Flower medium, funnel-shaped, lavender, flowers during average period, fertile.

HN: *H.* Tardiana grex TF 1 × 5.

Wisley No. 821409.

[*H.* 'Tardiflora' × *H. sieboldiana* 'Elegans'].

(see also *H.* Tardiana grex).

H. 'Happy Hearts' Fisher IRA/1973.
AHS-III/13A.

Plant 30 in. (76 cm) dia., 16 in. (40.5 cm) high. Leaf 5 by 4 in. (13 by 10 cm), veins 12, blue-green, not variegated, cordate, flat. Scape 28 in. (71 cm), bare, straight. Flower medium, bell-shaped, white, flowers during average period, fertile.

HN: *H.* 'Fisher No. 72'.

[*H. nakaiana* hybrid].

H. 'Harkness' Epstein 1967.

H. 'Harlequin Bells' Craig.
HN: Summers No. 445 1970.

H. 'Harlequin' Aden 1974.

H. 'Harmony' Smith 1961 Aden IRA/1976.
AHS-IV/21B.

Plant 8 in. (20 cm) dia., 8 in. (20 cm) high. Leaf 4 by 3 in. (10 by 7.5 cm), veins 8, blue-green, not variegated, cordate, flat. Scape 12 in. (31 cm), foliated, straight. Flower medium, bell-shaped, white, flowers during average period, fertile.

HN: *H.* Tardiana grex TF 2 × 3.

Wisley No. 821407.

[*H.* 'Tardiflora' × *H. sieboldiana* 'Elegans'].

(see also *H.* Tardiana grex).

H. 'Harrison' Harrison/Ruh IRA/1987.
AHS-I/3B.

Plant 50 in. (127 cm) dia., 28 in. (71 cm) high. Leaf 14 by 11 in. (35.5 by 28 cm), veins 16, blue-green, not variegated, cordate, rugose. Scape 20 in. (51 cm), bare, straight. Flower medium, bell-shaped, white, flowers during average period, fertile.

HN: *H.* 'Harrison Hybrid'.

[*H. sieboldiana* hybrid].

H. 'Harry A. Jacobson' Pierson IRA/1988.
AHS-I/4B.

Plant 36 in. (91.5 cm) dia., 18 in. (46 cm) high. Leaf 11 by 8 in. (28 by 20 cm), veins 12, blue-green, not variegated, cordate, rugose. Scape 20 in. (51 cm), foliated, straight. Flower medium, lavender, flowers during average period, fertility(?).

H. 'Harts Tongue' Kuk's Forest IRA/1987.
AHS-IV/24A.

Plant erect, shaped, 10 in. (25.5 cm) dia., 9 in. (23 cm) high. Leaf 4 by 1 in. (10 by 2.5 cm), veins 8, yellow (viridescent), not variegated, lanceolate, flat. Scape 18 in. (46 cm), bare, straight. Flower medium, funnel-shaped, purple striped, flowers during summer period, fertile.

[*H. sieboldii* 'Kabitan' mutation].

H. 'Haru No Yume' Japan.
春の夢

Haru No Yume Giboshi, "dream of spring hosta," is a sport found in the wild near Fuji-san (Mount Fuji). It has a yellow center with green margin and stripes. It is reported to be viridescent, turning green in summer.

HN: *H. montana* 'Haru No Yume'.

JN: *Haru No Yume Giboshi* hort.

[*H. montana* derivation].

H. 'Harvest Dandy' Summers 1986.

Plant is an intraspecific hybrid of the species collected in the wild and maintained as a cultivar. Plant 20 in. (51 cm) dia., 14 in. (35.5 cm) high. Leaf 7 by 4 in. (18 by 10 cm), veins 7, medium glossy green, not variegated, broadly lanceolate, flat. Scape 22 in. (56 cm), foliated, straight. Flower medium, bell-shaped, white, flowers during late period. Fertile.

HN: *H. longipes* 'Harvest Dandy'.

(see also *H. longipes* 'Harvest Dandy').

H. 'Harvest Dawn' Summers 1986.

Plant 12 in. (31 cm) dia., 6 in. (15 cm) high. Leaf 5 by 1.5 in. (13 by 4 cm), veins 4, medium green, not variegated, lanceolate, flat. Scape 14 in. (35.5 cm), bare, straight. Flower medium, bell-shaped, purple striped, flowers during summer period, fertile.

[*H. sieboldii* derivative].

H. 'Harvest Delight' Summers 1986.

Plant is one of the naturally occurring variants isolated and named. This is a true *H. kikutii*. Plant 24 in. (61 cm) dia., 14 in. (35.5 cm) high. Leaf 8 by 3 in. (20 by 7.5 cm), veins 8, dark green, not variegated, elliptical-ovate/lanceolate, flat. Scape 28 in. (71 cm), foliated, straight. Flower medium, bell-shaped, white, flowers during summer period, fertile.

HN: *H. kikutii* 'Harvest Delight' Summers 1986.

[*H. kikutii* sel].

H. 'Harvest Desire' Summers 1868.

Plant 24 in. (61 cm) dia., 14 in. (35.5 cm) high. Leaf 8 by 3 in. (20 by 7.5 cm), veins 6, medium green, not variegated, lanceolate, flat. Scape 38 in. (96.5 cm), foliated, prostrate. Flower medium, bell-shaped, white, flowers during late period, fertile.

[*H. longipes* × *H. kikutii*].

H. 'Harvest Glow' Walters Gardens IRA/1988.
AHS-III/17B.

Plant 20 in. (51 cm) dia., 16 in. (40.5 cm) high. Leaf 6 by 4 in. (15 by 10 cm), veins 9, chartreuse (lutescent), not variegated, cordate, rugose. Scape 24 in. (61 cm), bare, straight. Flower medium, bell-shaped, white, flowers during average period, fertile.

[*H.* 'Moon Glow' mutation].

H. 'Hatsushimo' Japan.
初霜

Hatsushimo Giboshi, the "first frost hosta," has whitish yellow variegation striped and spotted on a green leaf.

HN: *H. montana* 'Hatsushimo Nishiki' hort.

JN: *Hatsushimo (Nishiki Oba) Giboshi* hort.

[*H. montana* derivation].

H. 'Hatsuyuki Nishiki' Japan.
初雪錦
    Plant is a form with white leaf and green margin.
HN: *H. montana* 'Hatsuyuki Nishiki'.
JN: *Hatsuyuki Nishiki (Oba) Giboshi* hort.
[*H. montana* derivation].

H. 'Hausers Wide Leaf'.

H. 'Hazel' Stone/Ruh IRA/1987.
    AHS-IV/23B.
    Plant starts out lemon-yellow, turns chartreuse. Plant 12 in. (31 cm) dia., 6 in. (15 cm) high. Leaf 4 by 2 in. (10 by 5 cm), veins 8, yellow (viridescent), not variegated, ovate, flat. Scape 24 in. (61 cm), foliated, oblique. Flower medium, funnel-shaped, lavender, flowers during average period, fertile.
HN: *H.* 'DSM No. 1'.

H. 'Headliner' Fisher 1975 IRA/1986.
    AHS-II/9B.
    Plant is a *H. sieboldiana* form with tall scapes.
[*H.* 'Willy Nilly' hybrid].

H. 'Heart Ache' Benedict.
    Plant has viridescent yellow, round-cordate leaves with 6 vein pairs.

H. 'Heart of Chan' Owens IRA/1987.
    AHS-IV/19A.
    Plant 18 in. (46 cm) dia., 8 in. (20 cm) high. Leaf 5 by 3 in. (13 by 7.5 cm), veins 8, medium green, not variegated, cordate, flat. Scape 24 in. (61 cm), bare, straight. Flower medium, funnel-shaped, lavender, flowers during average period, fertile.
[*H.* 'Han Chu Han'(?) hybrid].

H. 'Heart Throb' Anderson IRA/1982.
    AHS-III/15A.
    Plant is medium size with blue-green cordate leaf.

H. 'Heartleaf' Fisher IRA/1971.
    AHS-III/13A.
    Plant 24 in. (61 cm) dia., 12 in. (31 cm) high. Leaf 5 by 4 in. (13 by 10 cm), veins 7, medium green, not variegated, cordate, flat. Scape 24 in. (61 cm), foliated, straight. Flower medium, funnel-shaped, lavender, flowers during average period, fertile.
[*H. nakaiana* hybrid].

H. 'Heartsong' Walters Gardens IRA/1984.
    AHS-IV/22A.
    Plant 28 in. (71 cm) dia., 22 in. (56 cm) high. Leaf 5 by 4 in. (13 by 10 cm), veins 9–11, medium green, white margin, cordate, flat. Scape 28 in. (71 cm), foliated, straight. Flower medium, funnel-shaped, lavender, flowers during average period, fertile.
[*H.* 'Candy Hearts' mutation].

H. 'Heaven Scent'^{PPAF} Walters Gardens IRA/1988.
    AHS-III/16B.   (Plate 118).
    Plant is a sport of *H. plantaginea* that arose in tissue culture. The leaf center is green with some lighter green variegation; the irregular chartreuse margin becomes yellow and streaks towards the center. Plant 32 in. (81.5 cm) dia., 22 in. (56 cm) high. Leaf 9 by 7 in. (23 by 18 cm), veins 10, dark green with yellow (lutescent) margin, cordate, flat. Scape 30 in. (76 cm), foliated, straight. Flower large, funnel-shaped, white, fragrant, flowers during summer period, fertile.
[*H. plantaginea* mutation].

H. 'Helen Doriot' Reath IRA/1982.
    AHS-II/9B.
    Plant 36 in. (91.5 cm) dia., 24 in. (61 cm) high. Leaf 13 by 11 in. (33 by 28 cm), veins 16, blue-green, not variegated, cordate, rugose. Scape 30 in. (76 cm), bare, straight. Flower medium, bell-shaped, white, flowers during average period, fertile.
HN: *H.* 'Blue Max'.
[*H. sieboldiana* 'Frances Williams' × *H. sieboldiana* 'Elegans'].

H. 'Helen Field Fischer' Minks IRA/1970.
    AHS-III/13A.
    Plant is like *H.* 'Fortunei Hyacinthina' but smaller. Plant 18 in. (46 cm) dia., 10 in. (25.5 cm) high. Leaf 6 by 4 in. (15 by 10 cm), veins 8, blue-green, not variegated, cordate, rugose. Scape 22 in. (56 cm), bare, straight. Flower medium, funnel-shaped, lavender, flowers during average period, fertile.
HN: *H.* 'Fortunei Dwarf Grey Leaf'.
       H. 'Fortunei Helen Field Fischer'.
       H. 'Krossa No. C-1'.
       H. 'Olga Thiemans Dwarf Grey Leaf' incorrect.
[*H.* 'Fortunei Hyacinthina' derivation].

H. 'Heliarc' Kuk's Forest IRA/1986.
    AHS-III/16B.
    Plant 36 in. (91.5 cm) dia., 24 in. (61 cm) high. Leaf 6 by 4 in. (15 by 10 cm), veins 8, light chartreuse, dark chartreuse to green margin, cordate, flat. Scape 28 in. (71 cm), foliated, straight. Flower medium, funnel-shaped, lavender, flowers during average period, fertile.
[*H.* 'Fortunei' mutation].

H. 'Helonioides'.
H. helonioides.

H. 'Helonioides Albopicta'.
H. helonioides f. *albopicta*.

H. 'Helonioides Fuiri Karafuto'.
(see *H.* 'Helonioides Albopicta').

H. 'Helonioides Ogata Bunchoko'.
(see *H.* 'Helonioides Albopicta').

H. 'Her Grace' Fisher 1970 IRA/1986.
    AHS-II/7A.

H. 'Herb Benedict' Wilkins.
    AHS Savory Shield Award, 1988, exhibited by James Wilkins. Plant 38 in. (96.5 cm) dia., 24 in. (61 cm) high. Leaf 11 by 8 in. (28 by 20 cm), veins 14–16, blue-green, irregular streaking, cordate, rugose. Scape 30 in. (76 cm). Flower medium, bell-shaped, white, flowers during average period, fertile.
HN: DB-86-1 Hybrid.

H. 'Herifu' Japan/Stone.
ヘリフギボウシ   (Figure 4-14; Plate 119).
    Herifu Giboshi, the "hosta with variegated border around," having size and shape like *H.* 'Lancifolia', has a pure white margin. Plant 12 in. (31 cm) dia., 8 in. (20 cm) high. Leaf 5 by 3 in. (13 by 7.5 cm), veins 4, medium green, white margin, ovate, flat. Scape 20 in. (51 cm), bare, straight. Flower medium, funnel-shaped, purple-striped, flowers during average period, fertile.
HN: Summers No. 145 1967.
JN: *Herifu Giboshi* hort.
[*H. sieboldii* derivative].

H. **'Herifu Tet'.**

H. **'Hertha'** Savory IRA/1988.
   AHS-IV/22B.
   Plant 18 in. (46 cm) dia., 12 in. (31 cm) high. Leaf 5 by 3 in. (13 by 7.5 cm), veins 9, dark green, white margin, cordate, flat. Scape 24 in. (61 cm), foliated, straight. Flower medium, funnel-shaped, lavender, flowers during average period, fertility(?).
   [*H.* 'Neat Splash' × hybrid].

H. **'Heslington'** George Smith/UK.
   A prior synonym for *H.* 'George Smith'.
   HN: *H. sieboldiana* Mediovariegata group.
   [*H. sieboldiana* 'Elegans' mutation].
   (see *H.* 'George Smith').

H. **'Higaki Fukurin'** Higaki.
檜垣覆輪
   Higaki Fukurin Giboshi, the "hosta of Higaki," was named for its discoverer Higaki and is a *H. longipes* form with yellowish white margin.
   JN: *Higaki Fukurin Giboshi* hort.
   [*H. longipes* derivation].

H. **'High Fat Cream'** Aden IRA/1976.
   AHS-III/14A.
   AHS winner of the Nancy Minks Award in 1978, exhibited by Paul Aden. Unstable variegation reported. Plant 14 in. (35.5 cm) dia., 10 in. (25.5 cm) high. Leaf 4 by 3 in. (10 by 7.5 cm), veins 12, medium green, streaky, multicolor, cordate, flat. Scape 14 in. (35.5 cm), foliated, straight. Flower medium, funnel-shaped, lavender, flowers during average period, fertile.
   [*H.* 'Aden No. 270' × *H.* 'Aden No. 275'].

H. **'High Gloss'.**

H. **'High Kicker'** Aden IRA/1987.
   AHS-III/13B.
   Plant erect, shaped, 32 in. (81.5 cm) dia., 28 in. (71 cm) high. Leaf 10 by 5 in. (10 by 13 cm), veins 8, medium green, not variegated, cordate, undulate. Scape 40 in. (101.5 cm), foliated, oblique. Flower medium, bell-shaped, lavender, flowers during summer period, fertile.
   [*H. pycnophylla* fragrant × *H. pycnophylla* yellow].

H. **'High Noon'** Seaver.
   Plant large with yellow round-cordate leaves. Erect habit.

H. **'High Style'** Benedict IRA/1984.
   AHS-II/11A.
   Plant erect, 26 in. (66 cm) dia., 20 in. (51 cm) high. Leaf 10 by 7 in. (25.5 by 18 cm), veins 10, chartreuse, not variegated, cordate, rugose. Scape 30 in. (76 cm), foliated, straight. Flower medium, funnel-shaped, lavender, flowers during average period, fertile.
   [*H.* 'Gold Regal' × *H.* 'Gold Regal'].

H. **'Hilda Wassman'** Savory IRA/1985.
   AHS-III/16B.
   Plant 20 in. (51 cm) dia., 14 in. (35.5 cm) high. Leaf 6 by 4 in. (15 by 10 cm), veins 9, medium green, white margin, cordate, flat. Scape 16 in. (40.5 cm), bare, straight. Flower medium, funnel-shaped, lavender, flowers during average period, fertile.

H. **'Hime Soules'** Hirao/Japan.
ヒメギボウシ
   Hime Giboshi, the "small hosta," is similar to *H. sieboldii* but smaller, and its margin is pure white and lasting. It is similar to the mature form of *H.* 'Ginko Craig' and also to *H.* 'Herifu'. The Japanese name has been applied to several taxa and may be confusing. Plant 18 in. (46 cm) dia., 8 in. (20 cm) high. Leaf 4 by 1 in. (10 by 2.5 cm), veins 3, dark green, white margin, ovate, flat. Scape 24 in. (61 cm), bare, straight. Flower medium, funnel-shaped, purple striped, flowers during summer period, fertile.
   HN: *H.* 'Hime G' incorrect.
   JN: *Hime Giboshi* hort. incorrect.
   (see also *H.* 'Ginko Craig').
   (see also *H.* 'Herifu').

H. **'Hime Arechino Kogarashi'** hort.
姫アレチノコガラシギボウシ
   Hime Arechino Kogarashi Giboshi is an incorrect synonym for *H.* 'Tortifrons', which see.

H. **'Hime Karafuto'** Hirao/Japan.
姫カラフトギボウシ   (Figure 2-7).
   Hime Karafuto Giboshi, the "small hosta from Karafuto," is found in the Karafuto area of Hokkaido and is similar if not identical to *H.* 'Ginko Craig'. Its Japanese name has been incorrectly translated to *H.* 'Princess of Karafuto' (= *Hime No Karafuto*), and so this taxon is also cultivated under the latter name.
   HN: *H.* 'Karafuto G' incorrect.
        H. 'Princess of Karafuto' incorrect.
   JN: *Hime Karafuto Giboshi* hort.
        Hime No Karafuto Giboshi incorrect.
   (see *H.* 'Ginko Craig').

H. **'Hime Koba'** hort.
ヒメコバギボウシ
   Hime Koba Giboshi is a synonym for and applied to several clones of the dwarf group of *H. sieboldii* f. *spathulata*, which see.
   (see *H. sieboldii* f. *spathulata* dwarf form).

H. **'Hime Shirokabitan'** hort.
姫シロカビタン
   Hime Shirokabitan Giboshi is an incorrect synonym for *H. sieboldii* 'Silver Kabitan'.

H. **'Hime Yakushima'** hort.
姫ヤクシマギボウシ
   Hime Yakushima Giboshi is a synonym for and applied to several clones of the dwarf group of *H. sieboldii* f. *spathulata*, which see.
   (see *H. sieboldii* f. *spathulata* dwarf form).

H. **'Hippeastrum'.**
H. hippeastrum.

H. **'Hirao'** Japan.
   Plant 10 in. (25.5 cm) dia., 4 in. (10 cm) high. Leaf 3 by 1 in. (7.5 by 2.5 cm), veins 3, medium green, not variegated, lanceolate, flat. Scape 16 in. (40.5 cm), bare, straight. Flower medium, funnel-shaped, purple striped, flowers during summer period, fertile.
   [*H. sieboldii* hybrid].

H. **'Hirao No. 58'** Japan.
   [*H. sieboldii* form].

H. **'Hirao No. 59'** Japan.
[*H. kikutii* form].

H. **'Hirao Tetra'** Japan.
HN: *H.* 'Hirao Tet' Hirao.
[*H.* 'Tokudama' hybrid tetraploid].

H. **'Hoarfrost'** Fisher IRA/1986.
    AHS-II/9B.
    Plant 38 in. (96.5 cm) dia., 24 in. (61 cm) high. Leaf 12 by 11 in. (31 by 28 cm), veins 16, blue-green, not variegated, cordate, rugose. Scape 30 in. (76 cm), bare, straight. Flower medium, bell-shaped, white, flowers during average period, fertile.
[*H. sieboldiana* Aureomarginata group hybrid].

H. **'Hogyoku'** Japan.
芳玉
    Hogyoku Giboshi, the "excellent treasure hosta," has pruinose leaves with white back and large 3-in. (7.5 cm) purple flowers that are very fragrant and have white-margined lobes.
HN: *H.* 'Kunpu' hort. pp sim.
JN: *Hogyoku Giboshi* hort.
     Ho-Gyoku Giboshi hort.
     Kunpu Giboshi hort. pp sim.

H. **'Hokkaido'** UK.

H. **'Holiday White'** Minks.
    Plant is a white-centered mutation.

H. **'Hollys Dazzler'** Benedict IRA/1987.
    AHS-III/13B.
    Plant 24 in. (61 cm) dia., 15 in. (38 cm) high. Leaf 8 by 4 in. (20 by 10 cm), veins 6, medium green, not variegated, cordate, flat. Scape 24 in. (61 cm), foliated, oblique. Flower medium, bell-shaped, purple, flowers during average period, fertile.
[*H.* 'Hollys Honey' hybrid × self].

H. **'Hollys Green and Gold'** Williams 1968.
[*H. sieboldiana* 'Aureomarginata' hybrid].

H. **'Hollys Honey'** AHS NC IRA/1986.
    AHS-III/13B.
    Plant has shiny leaves that are flat but have a piecrust margin. Plant 28 in. (71 cm) dia., 20 in. (51 cm) high. Leaf 8 by 4 in. (20 by 10 cm), veins 8, shiny dark green, not variegated, cordate, flat with piecrust margin. Scape 38 in. (96.5 cm), bare, straight. Flower medium, bell-shaped, purple, flowers during average period, fertile.
[*H.* 'Hollys Honey' hybrid × self].

H. **'Hollys Hybrid'** Holly 1963.

H. **'Hollys Shine'** Benedict IRA/1987.
    AHS-III/13B.
    Plant has shiny leaves. Plant 28 in. (71 cm) dia., 20 in. (51 cm) high. Leaf 8 by 4 in. (20 by 10 cm), veins 8, medium green, not variegated, cordate, flat. Scape 38 in. (96.5 cm), bare, straight. Flower medium, bell-shaped, purple, flowers during average period, fertile.
[*H.* 'Hollys Honey' hybrid × self].

H. **'Honey'** Savory IRA/1977.
    AHS-III/13A.
    Plant 36 in. (91.5 cm) dia., 14 in. (35.5 cm) high. Leaf 13 by 10 in. (33 by 25.5 cm), veins 12, yellow (lutescent), not variegated, cordate, rugose. Scape 50 in. (127 cm), foliated,

straight. Flower medium, funnel-shaped, lavender, flowers during average period, fertile.
[*H. montana* hybrid].

H. **'Honey Moon'** Anderson IRA/1982.
    AHS-IV/23B.
    Plant 12 in. (31 cm) dia., 8 in. (20 cm) high. Leaf 3 by 2 in. (7.5 by 5 cm), veins 7, chartreuse, not variegated, ovate, flat. Scape 16 in. (40.5 cm), foliated, straight. Flower medium, funnel-shaped, lavender, flowers during average period, fertile.
[*H. venusta* derivative (from *H.* 'Gold Drop')].

H. **'Honeybells'** Cumming 1950 IRA/1986.
    AHS-III/13A.   (Plates 149, 165).
    One of the most vigorous plants with fragrant flowers. An excellent, inexpensive beginner's hosta. Plant 46 in. (117 cm) dia., 26 in. (66 cm) high. Leaf 11 by 8 in. (28 by 20 cm), veins 8, light green, not variegated, cordate, flat. Scape 60 in. (152.5 cm), foliated, straight. Flower medium, bell-shaped, lavender, fragrant, flowers during summer period, fertile.
[*H. plantaginea* × *H. sieboldii*].

H. **'Hoopla'** Aden.
    Plant changes into *H.* 'Gaiety', or *H.* 'Good as Gold', which see. Plant 18 in. (46 cm) dia., 10 in. (25.5 cm) high. Leaf 5 by 3 in. (13 by 7.5 cm), veins 7, chartreuse, streaked white, ovate, flat. Scape 22 in. (56 cm), foliated, straight. Flower medium, funnel-shaped, lavender, flowers during average period, fertile.

H. **'Housatonic'** Payne 1976 IRA/1986.
    AHS-II/9B.   (Plate 93).
    Plant 44 in. (112 cm) dia., 24 in. (61 cm) high. Leaf 13 by 11 in. (33 by 28 cm), veins 16, blue-green, not variegated, cordate, rugose. Scape 32 in. (81.5 cm), foliated, oblique. Flower medium, funnel-shaped, white, flowers during average period, fertile.
[*H. sieboldiana* hybrid].

H. **'Hydon Gleam'** Smith/George.

H. **'Hydon Sunset'** Smith/George BHHS IRA/1988.
    AHS-IV/22B.   (Plate 120).
    Plant is a yellow, probably hybridized form of *H. nakaiana* slightly smaller than the species. The scapes show evidence of the characteristic ridges of section *Lamellatae.* Named for Hydon Nursery, Surrey, England, operated by Arthur George. The cross is frequently given as *H. gracillima* × *H.* 'Wogon', but this appears to be incorrect, because the ridged scapes point to *H. nakaiana* or *H. venusta* as a pod parent. Plants observed in North America retain their yellow variegation, while viridescence has been reported in plants grown in England.
    Plant 8 in. (20 cm) dia., 4 in. (10 cm) high. Leaf 1.5 by 1 in. (4 by 2.5 cm), veins 4, chartreuse, not variegated, cordate, wavy-undulate. Scape 14 in. (35.5 cm), bare, straight. Flower medium, bell-shaped, purple, flowers during average period, fertile.
HN: *H. nakaiana* Yellow group.
[*H. nakaiana* derivation].

H. **hypoleuca** **'Hitotsuba'**.

H. **hypoleuca** **'Ogon'**.

H. hypoleuca 'Urajiro' hort.
    Plant name is an incorrect formulation consisting of the botanical name and the Japanese formal name *Urajiro* (*Giboshi*)

used as a cultivar name. Here considered a superfluous and incorrect name for the species.
(see *H. hypoleuca*).

I

H. 'Iceland' Smith.
Plant is a white-centered cultivar with green margins. Reported to be lost (Grenfell, 1988: personal communication), but may exist in some gardens in the United Kingdom.
[*H.* 'Fortunei Albomarginata' × *H.* 'Fortunei Albopicta'].

H. 'Illusions' Houseworth 1986.

H. 'Immense' Simpers.
Plant, as compared by Herz (cfr. Crockett, 1989), shows this taxon similar to *H. montana* f. *macrophylla* (formerly *H. montana* 'Praeflorens') but slightly larger and with a better leaf form. Plant 50 in. (127 cm) dia., 36 in. (91.5 cm) high. Leaf 16 by 11 in. (40.5 by 28 cm), veins 18, medium green, not variegated, cordate, rugose-furrowed. Scape 42 in. (106.5 cm), bare, straight. Flower medium, bell-shaped, white, flowers during early period, fertile.
[*H. montana* × *H. sieboldiana*].

H. 'Imperial Potentate' Benedict.
Plant is the size of *H.* 'Fortunei' and has a narrow white margin. The interior of the leaf is streaked with chartreuse, yellow, and shades of green.

H. 'Impressive' Goodwin.
Plant has green leaves 8 by 5 in. (20 by 13 cm), veins 13.

H. 'Inaho' Japan.
稲穂   (Plate 66).
Inaho Giboshi, the "golden wave of rice hosta." *Inaho* means "ear of rice," the name picturing the yellow- and green-striped vista of a maturing field of rice. Similar to *H. sieboldii* 'Mediopicta,' but sterile and provisionally linked with *H.* 'Lancifolia'. Plant 10 in. (25.5 cm) dia., 6 in. (15 cm) high. Leaf 3 by 1.5 in. (7.5 by 4 cm), veins 8, yellow (viridescent), streaked green, ovate, wavy. Scape 14 in. (35.5 cm), foliated, straight. Flower medium, funnel-shaped, purple striped, flowers during summer period, practically sterile.
HN: *H.* 'Lancifolia Inaho'.
   H. tardiva 'Aureostriata' hort. incorrect.
(see also *H.* 'Lancifolia Inaho').
(see also *H. sieboldii* f. *mediopicta*).

H. 'Indian Hills' Savory IRA/1989.
   AHS-III/13B.
Plant 20 in. (51 cm) dia., 16 in. (40 cm) high. Leaf 7 by 5 in. (18 by 13 cm), veins 10, dark green, not variegated, cordate, rugose. Scape 17 in. (43 cm), foliaceous, straight. Flower medium, bell-shaped, white, flowers during average period, fertile.
[*H.* 'Black Hills' × hybrid].

H. 'Indian Summer' Summers 1986.
Plant erect, 14 in. (35.5 cm) dia., 10 in. (25.5 cm) high. Leaf 5 by 3 in. (13 by 7.5 cm), veins 5, medium green, not variegated, ovate, flat. Scape 16 in. (40.5 cm).

H. 'Indigo' Savory IRA/1984.
   AHS-IV/21B.
Plant 12 in. (31 cm) dia., 6 in. (15 cm) high. Leaf 4 by 2 in. (10 by 5 cm), veins 8, blue-green, not variegated, cordate, flat. Scape 12 in. (31 cm), bare, straight. Flower medium, funnel-shaped, white, flowers during summer period, fertile.
[*H.* 'Halcyon' hybrid].

H. 'Inniswood' Inniswood Botanical Garden.
(Plate 121).
AHS Savory Shield Award, 1986, exhibited by Inniswood Botanical Garden. A bright yellow *H. montana* form, leaf with a regular, dark green margin. Plant 40 in. (101.5 cm) dia., 20 in. (51 cm) high. Leaf 9 by 6 in. (23 by 15 cm), veins 13, chartreuse, green margin, cordate, rugose. Scape 30 in. (76 cm), bare, straight. Flower medium, funnel-shaped, lavender, flowers during average period, fertile.
[*H.* 'Sun Glow' mutation].

H. 'Innovation' Nesmith 1967.
Plant is a large green *H. montana* form.

H. 'Intrigue' Aden IRA/1978.
   AHS-III/16B.
Plant 16 in. (40.5 cm) dia., 12 in. (31 cm) high. Leaf 5 by 4 in. (13 by 10 cm), veins 8, chartreuse, streaky, multicolor, cordate, flat. Scape 16 in. (40.5 cm), foliated, straight. Flower medium, funnel-shaped, lavender, flowers during average period, fertile.
[*H.* 'Flamboyant' hybrid].

H. 'Invincible' Aden IRA/1986.
   AHS-III/13A.   (Plate 122).
Plant has a very glossy leaf with good substance and large white fragrant flowers. Plant 14 in. (35.5 cm) dia., 10 in. (25.5 cm) high. Leaf 5 by 3 in. (13 by 7.5 cm), veins 6, medium green, not variegated, cordate, wavy-undulate. Scape 20 in. (51 cm), foliated, straight. Flower medium, funnel-shaped, white, fragrant, flowers during summer period, fertile.
[*H.* 'Aden No. 314' × *H.* 'Aden No. 802'].

H. 'Iona' Lavender/Chappell BHHS IRA/1988.
H. 'Fortunei' form with wide, yellowish white margin.
[*H.* 'Fortunei' mutation].

H. 'Irische See' Klose.
Plant is one of the German Tardiana's (see *H.* Tardiana grex). The name means "Irish Sea."
HN: *H.* Tardiana grex.
[*H.* 'Tardiflora' × *H. sieboldiana* 'Elegans'].
(see also *H.* Tardiana grex).

H. 'Irish Spring' Savory IRA/1985.
   AHS-IV/22B.
Plant 20 in. (51 cm) dia., 8 in. (20 cm) high. Leaf 5 by 4 in. (13 by 10 cm), green, mottled yellow, streaked green, cordate, flat. Scape 16 in. (40.5 cm), bare, straight. Flower medium, funnel-shaped, lavender, flowers during average period, fertile.

H. 'Iron Gate Bouquet' Sellers IRA/1983.
   AHS-IV/19A.
Plant 24 in. (61 cm) dia., 14 in. (35.5 cm) high. Leaf 5.5 by 4 in. (14 by 10 cm), veins 8, medium green, not variegated, cordate, flat. Scape 20 in. (51 cm), bare, straight. Flower medium, funnel-shaped, lavender, fragrant, flowers during summer period, fertile.
[*H. plantaginea* hybrid].

H. 'Iron Gate Delight' Sellers IRA/1981.
  AHS-III/16A.
    Plant's variegation reported unstable. Plant 20 in. (51 cm) dia., 14 in. (35.5 cm) high. Leaf 6 by 4 in. (15 by 10 cm), veins 7, medium green, streaked yellow and white, cordate, flat. Scape 24 in. (61 cm), bare, straight. Flower medium, funnel-shaped, lavender, fragrant, flowers during summer period, fertile.
  [*H. plantaginea* × *H.* 'Tokudama Aureonebulosa'].

H. 'Iron Gate Glamor' Sellers IRA/1981.
  AHS-III/16A.   (Figure 4-25).
    Plant 32 in. (81.5 cm) dia., 24 in. (61 cm) high. Leaf 10 by 7 in. (25.5 by 18 cm), veins 7, medium green, white margin, cordate, flat. Scape 36 in. (91.5 cm), bare, straight. Flower medium, funnel-shaped, lavender, fragrant, flowers during summer period, fertile.
  [*H.* 'Iron Gate Supreme' mutation].
  [*H. plantaginea* × *H.* 'Tokudama Aureonebulosa'].

Figure 4-25. *H.* 'Iron Gate Glamor'; general habit (Coney garden/Schmid)

H. 'Iron Gate Supreme' Sellers IRA/1980.
  AHS-III/16A.
    Plant's variegation reported unstable. Plant 22 in. (56 cm) dia., 16 in. (40.5 cm) high. Leaf 6 by 4 in. (15 by 10 cm), veins 7, dark green, streaked multicolor, cordate, flat. Scape 26 in. (66 cm), bare, straight. Flower medium, funnel-shaped, lavender, fragrant, flowers during summer period, fertile.
  [*H. plantaginea* × *H.* 'Tokudama Aureonebulosa'].

H. 'Island Forest' Hatfield.
    Plant 38 in. (96.5 cm) dia., 26 in. (66 cm) high. Leaf 11 by 8 in. (28 by 20 cm), veins 10, medium green, not variegated, cordate, rugose. Scape 38 in. (96.5 cm), foliated, straight. Flower medium, funnel-shaped, lavender, flowers during average period, fertile.

H. 'Island Forest Gem' Carpenter.
    Plant is a large dark green cultivar with *H. montana* form leaves, 13 veins, and white flowers.

H. 'Isshiki Fukurin' hort. Japan.
  イッシキミズギボウシ
    Isshiki Fukurin Mizu Giboshi, the "Isshiki margined swamp hosta," is a yellow-margined sport of the species found growing in the wild in Nukata.
  JN: *Isshiki Fukurin Giboshi* hort.
  (see also *H. longissima* 'Isshiki Fukurin').

H. 'Itasca' Johnson IRA/1974.
  AHS-IV/22A.
    Plant 32 in. (81.5 cm) dia., 22 in. (56 cm) high. Leaf 7 by 5 in. (18 by 13 cm), veins 9, dark green, streaked white, cordate, flat. Scape 38 in. (96.5 cm), foliated, straight. Flower medium,

funnel-shaped, lavender, flowers during average period, fertile.
  [*H.* 'Fortunei Hyacinthina' mutation].

H. 'Ivory Pixie' Seaver IRA/1982.
  AHS-V/26A.
    Plant 8 in. (20 cm) dia., 6 in. (15 cm) high. Leaf 2 by 0.75 in. (5 by 2 cm), veins 5, white (viridescent), green margin, cordate, flat. Scape 10 in. (25.5 cm), bare, straight. Flower small, bell-shaped, lavender, flowers during late period, fertile.
  [*H. nakaiana* 'Allan P. McConnell' mutation].

H. 'Iwa' Horinaka.
    Plant name is an incorrect synonym.
  (see *H.* 'Iwa Soules').

H. 'Iwa Soules' Soules.
  イワギボウシ   (Plate 191).
    Plant is one of the many natural hybrids of *H. longipes* in cultivation, but the use of the formal Japanese name as a cultivar name is technically incorrect because it applies to and is taxonomically linked with the type of *H. longipes* (in P). Since this cultivated taxon originated with a Japanese import by Soules Garden, I have renamed it *H.* 'Iwa Soules'. It flowers later than the species and may be a hybrid with *H. aequinoctiiantha* or one of its variants.
  HN: *H.* 'Iwa G' hort. incorrect.
  JN: *Iwa Giboshi.*
  [*H. longipes* × *H. aequinoctiiantha* ad int].
  (see also *H. aequinoctiiantha*).

H. 'Iwato' Japan.
  岩戸
  JN: *Iwato Giboshi* hort.

J

H. 'Jack Frost' Minks IRA/1983.
  AHS-III/16A.
    Plant 32 in. (81.5 cm) dia., 22 in. (56 cm) high. Leaf 5 by 7 in. (13 by 18 cm), veins 9, medium green, white margin, cordate, flat. Scape 38 in. (96.5 cm), foliated, straight. Flower medium, funnel-shaped, lavender, flowers during average period, fertile.
  [*H.* 'Fortunei Carol' mutation].

H. 'Jack of Diamonds' Savory IRA/1985.
  AHS-III/16B.
    Plant 20 in. (51 cm) dia., 16 in. (40.5 cm) high. Leaf 7 by 6 in. (18 by 15 cm), veins 14, blue-green, yellow margin, cordate, rugose. Scape 18 in. (46 cm), foliated, straight. Flower medium, bell-shaped, white, flowers during average period, fertile.
  [*H. sieboldiana* hybrid].

H. 'Jade Beauty' Zilis IRA/1988.
  AHS-III/13B.
    Plant 40 in. (101.5 cm) dia., 22 in. (56 cm) high. Leaf 9 by 7 in. (23 by 18 cm), veins 10, dark green, not variegated, cordate, flat. Scape 40 in. (101.5 cm), bare, straight. Flower medium, funnel-shaped, lavender, flowers during average period.
  [*H. nakaiana* 'Golden Tiara' mutation].

H. **'Jade Point'** Simpers IRA/1980.
    AHS-II/7B.
        Plant 36 in. (91.5 cm) dia., 22 in. (56 cm) high. Leaf 9 by 6 in. (23 by 15 cm), veins 16, medium green, not variegated, cordate, rugose. Scape 18 in. (46 cm), bare, straight. Flower medium, funnel-shaped, white, flowers during average period, fertile.
[*H.* sieboldiana form].
[*H.* 'Elata Fountain' hybrid].

H. **'Jade Scepter'** Zilis IRA/1988.
    AHS-IV/19A.
        Plant 28 in. (71 cm) dia., 14 in. (35.5 cm) high. Leaf 4 by 3 in. (10 by 7.5 cm), veins 6, medium green, not variegated, cordate, flat. Scape 28 in. (71 cm), bare, straight. Flower medium, bell-shaped, purple striped, flowers during average period.
[*H.* nakaiana 'Golden Tiara' mutation].

H. **'Jadette'** Anderson IRA/1982.
    AHS-IV/22B.
        Plant is a small stoloniferous white-margined hybrid.

H. **'Jambeliah'** Aden IRA/1978.
    AHS-III/16A.
        Plant is medium size. Leaf 5 by 3 in. (12.5 by 7.5 cm), veins 7, medium green, yellow (albescent) margin streaking to center.

H. **'Janet'** Shugart/O'Harra IRA/1981.
    AHS-IV/20A.
        Plant is smaller than *H.* 'Gold Standard' and albescent with leaf center turning white. Plant 24 in. (61 cm) dia., 14 in. (35.5 cm) high. Leaf 6 by 4 in. (15 by 10 cm), veins 8, white (albescent), green margin, cordate, flat. Scape 32 in. (81.5 cm), foliated, straight. Flower medium, funnel-shaped, lavender, flowers during average period, fertile.
[*H.* 'Fortunei' mutation].

H. 'Japonica' nom. confus.
        Plant name is an incorrect and confusing synonym.
H. japonica.

H. 'Japonica Blue' nom. nudum Montreal Botanic Garden.
        Plant name is an incorrect synonym.
(see *H.* 'Montreal').

H. 'Japonica White' nom. nudum Montreal Botanic Garden.
        Plant name is an incorrect synonym.
(see *H.* 'Mount Royal').

H. **'Jelly Bean'** Harstad.
        AHS Savory Shield Award, 1989, grown by Carolyn and Peter Harstad. A small cultivar with ovate-lanceolate leaves that have a yellow-chartreuse center and a medium green wavy margin. Low mound.
[*H.* 'Gold Drop' mutation].

H. **'Jester'**.
HN: *H.* 'Fortunei Jester'.
(see also *H.* 'Fortunei Variegated').

H. **'Jim Cooper'** Aden IRA/1982.
    AHS-II/11B.
        Plant 32 in. (81.5 cm) dia., 24 in. (61 cm) high. Leaf 9 by 7 in. (23 by 18 cm), veins 12, yellow (lutescent), not variegated, round-cordate, cupped-rugose. Scape 36 in. (91.5 cm), bare,

straight. Flower medium, bell-shaped, white, flowers during average period, fertile.
[*H.* 'Sum and Substance' hybrid].

H. **'Jingle Bells'** Grapes IRA/1986.
    AHS-IV/19B.
        Resembles *H.* nakaiana.
[*H.* nakaiana hybrid].

H. 'Jo Anna'.
        Plant name is an incorrect synonym for *H.* 'Johanne', which see.
HN: *H.* 'JoAnna' incorrect.

H. **'Jo Jo'** Stone/Ruh IRA/1987.
    AHS-V/28A.
        Plant has some green on green streaking in leaf. Plant 12 in. (31 cm) dia., 8 in. (20 cm) high. Leaf 3.5 by 1.5 in. (9 by 4 cm), veins 3, medium green, white margin, lanceolate, flat. Scape 15 in. (38 cm), foliated, straight. Flower medium, funnel-shaped, lavender, flowers during average period, fertile.
HN: *H.* 'DSM No. 17'.

H. **'Johanne'** Ellyson/Ruh IRA/1989.
    AHS-III/15B.
        Plant 19 in. (49 cm) dia., 11 in. (28 cm) high. Leaf 7 by 5 in. (18 by 13 cm), veins 12, blue-green, not variegated, cordate, some rugosity. Scape 17 in. (43 cm), bare, foliated. Flower medium, bell-shaped, lavender, flowers during average period, fertile.
HN: *H.* 'JoAnne' incorrect.
        H. 'Jo Anne' incorrect.

H. **'John Wargo'** Weissenberger IRA/1986.
    AHS-II/7A.
        Plant 24 in. (61 cm) dia., 12 in. (31 cm) high. Leaf 8 by 6 in. (20 by 15 cm), veins 9, medium green, not variegated, ovate, flat. Scape 36 in. (91.5 cm), bare, straight. Flower medium, bell-shaped, purple, flowers during average period, fertile.
[*H.* nigrescens hybrid].

H. **'Joker'** Van Vliet/Klijn en Co. Holland.
        Plant is a mutation of *H.* 'Fortunei Hyacinthina' sent to Hosta Hill for evaluation. Grey-green leaf with yellow margins and streaks in spring only and in other respects similar to *H.* 'Fortunei Hyacinthina'.
[*H.* 'Fortunei Hyacinthina' mutation].
(see also *H.* 'Fortunei Variegated').

H. **'Jolly Green Giant'** Armstrong 1970 IRA/1986.
    AHS-I/1A.   (Figure 4-26).
        Plant 44 in. (112 cm) dia., 32 in. (81.5 cm) high. Leaf 10 by 8 in. (25.5 by 20 cm), veins 16, medium green, not variegated,

Figure 4-26. *H.* 'Jolly Green Giant'; general habit (Soules garden/Schmid)

cordate, rugose. Scape 42 in. (106.5 cm), bare, straight. Flower medium, bell-shaped, purple striped, flowers during average period, fertile.
[*H. sieboldiana* × *H.* 'Elata'].

H. 'Josephine' Kuk's Forest IRA/1987.
AHS-IV/22B.
Plant has leaves with narrow whitish yellow margin that is variable in width. Plant erect, 10 in. (25.5 cm) dia., 7 in. (18 cm) high. Leaf 5 by 4 in. (13 by 10 cm), veins 9, medium green, whitish yellow streaks and margin, cordate, flat.
[*H.* 'Neat Splash' hybrid].

H. 'Journeyman' Bond/Savill Gardens UK.
Plant is a cultivar similar to *H.* 'Undulata Erromena' and is growing at Savill Gardens.

H. 'Joybells' Minks IRA/1980.
AHS-III/17B.
Plant 24 in. (61 cm) dia., 20 in. (51 cm) high. Leaf yellow (lutescent), not variegated, cordate, cupped. Scape 24 in. (61 cm), bare, straight. Flower medium, bell-shaped, lavender, flowers during average period, fertile.
[*H.* 'Frances Williams' × *H.* 'Sunlight Sister'].

H. 'Joyce Trott' Vaughn IRA/1980.
AHS-IV/20A.
Plant makes a small clump. Flower medium, purple, flowers during average period.
[*H.* 'Fascination' × *H.* 'Sum and Substance' al].
[*H.* 'Flamboyant' × *H.* 'Sum and Substance'].

H. 'Julia Hardy' Aden IRA/1978.
AHS-II/9B.
Plant 26 in. (66 cm) dia., 18 in. (46 cm) high. Leaf 8 by 6 in. (20 by 15 cm), veins 12, blue-green, not variegated, round-cordate, cupped-rugose. Scape 26 in. (66 cm), bare, straight. Flower medium, bell-shaped, white, flowers during average period, fertile.
[*H.* 'Tokudama' hybrid].

H. 'Julie Morss' Morss IRA/1983.
AHS-III/16B.
Plant was introduced by and is named to honor Julie Morss, an early British hosta pioneer (see Chapter 5). Listed as a sport of a *H. sieboldiana* hybrid, it has 8–10 pairs of veins, so is probably a *H. fortunei* derivative. Considered one of the best English cultivars, it is 18 in. (46 cm) dia., 12 in. (31 cm) high. Leaf 8 by 6 in. (20 by 15 cm), yellow (lutescent), blue-green margin, cordate, rugose. Scape 18 in. (46 cm), bare, straight. Flower medium, bell-shaped, whitish lavender, flowers during average period, fertile.
[(*H. sieboldiana* 'Frances Williams' hybrid) mutation].
[*H. fortunei* derivative al].

H. 'July Gold' Lewis/Summers No. 108 1963.

H. 'Jumbo' Meissner/Summers No. 98 1963.
Plant 48 in. (122 cm) dia., 34 in. (86.5 cm) high. Leaf 13 by 11 in. (33 by 28 cm), veins 16, medium green, not variegated, cordate, rugose. Scape 36 in. (91.5 cm), bare, straight. Flower medium, bell-shaped, white, flowers during average period, fertile.
[*H. sieboldiana* hybrid].

H. 'June Beauty' Zager IRA/1986.
AHS-II/7B. (Figure 4-27).
Plant 38 in. (96.5 cm) dia., 26 in. (66 cm) high. Leaf 10 by 7 in. (25.5 by 18 cm), veins 16, blue-green, not variegated, cordate, rugose. Scape 28 in. (71 cm), foliated, straight. Flower medium, bell-shaped, purple striped, flowers during average period, fertile.
HN: *H. sieboldiana* 'June Beauty'.
[*H. sieboldiana*].

Figure 4-27. *H.* 'June Beauty'; general habit (Honeysong Farm/Schmid)

H. 'Just So' Aden IRA/1986.
AHS-IV/20B.
Plant erect, 14 in. (35.5 cm) dia., 6 in. (15 cm) high. Leaf 5 by 2 in. (13 by 5 cm), veins 8, chartreuse, green margin, cordate, rugose. Scape 12 in. (31 cm), foliated, straight. Flower medium, funnel-shaped, lavender, flowers during average period, fertile.
[*H.* 'Aden No. 421' × *H.* 'Little Aurora'].

K

H. 'Kabitan' AHS NC IRA/1987.
AHS-IV/20B.
The cultivar name registered for show purposes for *H. sieboldii* 'Kabitan'.
(see *H. sieboldii* 'Kabitan').

H. 'Kanagashi' Hydon Nurseries.

H. 'Kara' Horinaka/Soules.
カラギボウシ
Plant is a yellow-margined *H.* 'Tokudama', which is not the same and smaller than *H.* 'Tokudama Flavocircinalis'—the petiole is more winged, the scape shorter, and the leaf is more rounded and not as pointed. Plant 26 in. (66 cm) dia., 14 in. (35.5 cm) high. Leaf 6 by 5 in. (15 by 13 cm), veins 13, blue-green, yellow margin, cordate, rugose. Scape 16 in. (40.5 cm), bare, straight. Flower medium, bell-shaped, white, flowers during average period, fertile.
HN: *H.* 'Kara G' incorrect.
H. 'Tokudama Flavocircinalis' group.
JN: *Kara Giboshi* hort.
(see also *H.* 'Tokudama Flavocircinalis').

H. 'Karafuto' Horinaka.
カラフトギボウシ
Plants under this name are a mix of all-green and variegated forms. The name is used in Japan to indicate small-

ness and has been applied to a number of different taxa. In North America it is utilized for a small white-margined taxon similar to *H.* 'Ginko Craig'.
HN: *H.* 'Karafuto G' incorrect.
(see *H.* 'Ginko Craig').
(see also *H.* 'Hime Karafuto').

H. 'Kasseler Gold' Klose.
Plant is a select hybrid with lasting yellow color. Smaller than the parent.
HN: *H. sieboldiana* 'Kasseler Gold' Klose.
[*H. sieboldiana* 'Semperaurea' hybrid].

H. 'Kathleen' Williams 1958 IRA/1986.
AHS-III/13A.
Plant erect, 6 in. (15 cm) dia., 12 in. (31 cm) high. Leaf 6 by 3 in. (15 by 7.5 cm), veins 6, medium green, not variegated, cordate, flat. Scape 18 in. (46 cm), bare, straight. Flower medium, funnel-shaped, lavender, flowers during average period, fertile.
HN: *H.* 'FRW No. 1258'.
[*H.* 'Fortunei' × *H.* 'Decorata'].

H. 'Kelsey' Williams (No. 1221) 1968.
Plant has lanceolate leaves, lavender flowers.
HN: *H.* 'FRW No. 1221'.

H. 'Kevin Vaughn' Lachman.
AHS President's Exhibitor Trophy, 1986, exhibited by Eleanor and William Lachman.
[*H.* 'Christmas Tree' derivative]'.

H. 'Kifu Hime' Longwood.
Plant 24 in. (61 cm) dia., 20 in. (51 cm) high. Leaf 8 by 3.5 in. (20 by 9 cm), veins 8, medium green, not variegated, lanceolate, flat. Scape 28 in. (71 cm), bare, straight. Flower medium, funnel-shaped, lavender, flowers during summer period, fertile.
[*H. kikutii* form].

H. 'Kifukurin Ko Mame' Japan.
黄覆輪コマメギボウシ
Plant is a yellow-margined form of *H.* 'Yakushima Mizu' found in Kyushu. *Ko* means ""small and *mame* is a pea, so the combination indicates smallness. The name translates to "gold-margined, very small hosta.".
JN: *Kifukurin Ko Mame Giboshi*
Yakushima Mizu Giboshi Kifukurin hort. incorrect.
[*H. gracillima* mutation].

H. 'Kikeika' hort. Japan.
キケイカミズギボウシ
Plant is a form of *H. longissima* with deformed and joined flower lobes and, occasionally, petaloid stamens. It is found in Nukata District and named *Kikeika Mizu Giboshi*.
JN: *Kikeika Mizu Giboshi* hort.
[*H. longissima* mutation].

H. kikutii 'Harvest Delight' Summers.
(see *H.* 'Harvest Delight').

H. kikutii 'Hosoba Urajiro'.

H. kikutii 'Kifukurin'.

H. kikutii 'Soules Pruinose'.

H. kikutii var. polyneuron 'Ogon'.

H. kikutii var. polyneuron 'Shirofukurin'.

H. kikutii var. polyneuron 'Shironakafu'.

H. 'Kilowatt' Armstrong IRA/1970.
AHS-V/25A.
Plant is a selected and named form of the species.
[*H. nakaiana* hybrid].
(see *H. nakaiana*).

H. 'Kinbotan' Japan/Gowen.
Plant has leaves similar to *H. nakaiana* with a wide yellowish white margin and 3–4 pairs of veins.

H. 'King James' Summers.
Plant 42 in. (106.5 cm) dia., 28 in. (71 cm) high. Leaf 9 by 12 in. (23 by 31 cm), veins 12, medium green, not variegated, cordate, furrowed. Scape 34 in. (86.5 cm), bare, straight. Flower medium, funnel-shaped, lavender, flowers during average period, fertile.
[*H. montana* hybrid].

H. 'King Michael' Krossa/Summers.   (Figure 4-28).
Plant resembles *H. montana* f. *macrophylla*, which see. Plant 50 in. (127 cm) dia., 38 in. (96.5 cm) high. Leaf 18 by 12 in. (46 by 31 cm), veins 18, medium green, not variegated, cordate, furrowed. Scape 48 in. (122 cm), bare, straight. Flower medium, funnel-shaped, white, flowers during average period, fertile.
[*H. montana* f. *macrophylla* form].

Figure 4-28. *H.* 'King Michael'; general habit (Honeysong Farm/Schmid)

H. 'King Tut' Harshbarger 1973 IRA/1981.
AHS-III/17A.
Plant 26 in. (66 cm) dia., 12 in. (31 cm) high. Leaf 6 by 5 in. (15 by 13 cm), veins 12, yellow (lutescent), green margin, cordate, flat. Scape 35 in. (89 cm), bare, straight. Flower medium, bell-shaped, white, flowers during average period, fertile.
[*H.* 'Tokudama Aureonebulosa' hybrid].

H. 'Kingfisher' Smith BHHS/IRA 1988.
III/15B.
Plant 22 in. (56 cm) dia., 12 in. (31 cm) high. Leaf 7 by 4 in. (18 by 10 cm), veins 8–10, grey-green, cordate, flat.
HN: *H.* Tardiana grex TF 2 × 17.
[*H.* 'Tardiflora' × *H. sieboldiana* 'Elegans'].
(see also *H.* Tardiana grex).

H. 'Kinkaku' hort. Japan.
Plant is a form of *H. longissima* with double flowers and, occasionally, petaloid stamens. It is found in Tsukude District and named *Kinkaku Giboshi*.
JN: *Kinkaku*.
Kikeika Mizu Giboshi hort.
[*H. longissima* mutation].

H. 'Kinki' Japan.

金輝

Plant is a yellow (lutescent) form of H. 'Tokudama' being larger than H. 'Tokudama Golden Medallion'.

H. 'Kirishima' UK.

Kirishima Giboshi, the "Kirishima hosta," is named for a large volcanic mountain range in south-central Kyushu, primarily Kagoshima and Miyazaki prefectures. An intermediate between H. 'Saishu Jima' and H. 'Yakushima Mizu', which see. The taxon cultivated in Europe may be an interspecific hybrid between H. *gracillima* and a form of the all-green H. *sieboldii* growing in southern Japan. A taxon cultivated in North America under the same name is different—very small, with chartreuse to very light green leaves, 3 pairs of veins. This name is used for several different cultivars and is confusing.

HN: H. 'Karishima' incorrect.
    H. 'Mount Kirishima'.

H. 'Kisuji' Maekawa.

(see H. *sieboldii* 'Mediopicta').

H. 'Kite' Smith BHHS/IRA 1988.

III/15B.

Hosta Tardiana grex TF 2 × 28.

[H. 'Tardiflora' × H. *sieboldiana* 'Elegans'].
(see also H. Tardiana grex).

H. *kiyosumiensis* 'Nakafu'.

H. *kiyosumiensis* 'Shirobana'.

H. 'Klopping 120' Klopping.

(see H. 'Minnie Klopping').

H. 'Klopping Variegated' Klopping/Ruh IRA/1988.

AHS-III/16B.

Plant is similar to H. 'Fortunei Albomarginata'. Plant 28 in. (71 cm) dia., 16 in. (40.5 cm) high. Leaf 8 by 6 in. (20 by 15 cm), veins 10, dark green, white margin, cordate, flat. Scape 24 in. (61 cm), foliated, straight. Flower medium, funnel-shaped, lavender, flowers during average period.

HN: H. 'Fortunei Albomarginata' group.

H. 'Knockout' Aden IRA/1986.

AHS-IV/20A.

Plant 12 in. (31 cm) dia., 8 in. (20 cm) high. Leaf 6 by 3 in. (15 by 7.5 cm), veins 6, yellow (lutescent), green margin, ovate, flat. Scape 12 in. (31 cm), bare, straight. Flower medium, funnel-shaped, lavender, flowers during average period, fertile.

H. 'Ko Iwa' Japan.

小岩

Plant is a small white-backed H. *longipes*.

JN: *Ko Iwa Giboshi* hort.

H. 'Ko Mame' Japan.

コマメギボウシ

Plant is a form of H. 'Yakushima Mizu' found in Kyushu. Both *ko* and *mame* translate to very small or pea-sized and indicate smallness; the name translates to "very small hosta." Similar to H. *gracillima* but smaller. The cultivar H. 'Sugar Plum Fairy' in the United States is similar and so is *Yakushima Mizu Giboshi*, but the latter is slightly larger.

HN: H. 'Sugar Plum Fairy' pp sim.
JN: *Ko Mame Giboshi*.
    Yakushima Mizu Giboshi hort. pp sim.
[H. *gracillima* sel].

H. 'Ko Seto' Japan.

小瀬戸

JN: *Ko Seto Giboshi* hort.

H. 'Kofuki' Japan.

粉吹

Kofuki Giboshi is a name used for a white-backed form of H. *longipes*, viz., H. *longipes* var. *hypoglauca*, which is also known by the formal Japanese name *Kofuki Iwa Giboshi*, which see under H. *longipes* var. *hypoglauca*

JN: *Kofuki Iwa Giboshi*.
(see H. *longipes* var. *hypoglauca*).

H. 'Koki' Japan.

晃輝

Koki Giboshi, the "brilliant hosta," is a hybrid with many different patterns and shades of variegation—yellow-margined, yellow-centered, and striped. Glossy leaves with good substance. The scape is purple-dotted.

JN: *Koki Giboshi* hort.
    Koki Iwa Giboshi hort.
[H. *longipes* hybrid].

H. 'Komachi' Japan.

Plant name is an incorrect synonym.

JN: *Komachi Koba Giboshi*.
(see H. 'Tsugaru Komachi').

H. 'Komyo Nishiki' Japan.

光明錦

Plant is a small hybrid with H. *longipes* parentage. Ovate leaves, truncate base, center clear yellow or whitish yellow, margin narrow, green, and occasional green streaks into center. Variegation stable.

JN: *Komyo Nishiki (Iwa) Giboshi*.
    KoMyo Nishiki (Iwa) Giboshi.
[H. *longipes* var. *latifolia* variegated × H. 'Umezawa Nishiki'].

H. 'Koreana Variegated' hort. incorrect.

This name is invalid per the ICNCP because of its latinate formulation. It is applied to a small cultivar with white-centered leaves and green margin.

H. 'Koriyama' Japan.

コリヤマギボウシ   (Plate 123).

Plant has several clones of slightly different sizes which have been received from Japan; the average is used in the description. Cultural conditions may play a role in ultimate size. Plant erect, 12 in. (30 cm) dia., 8 in. (29 cm) high. Leaf 4 by 2 in. (10 by 5 cm), veins 4, medium green, margin white, ovate, flat. Scape 14 in. (35.5 cm), bare, straight. Flower medium, funnel-shaped, purple striped, flowers during summer period, fertile.

HN: H. 'Kooriyama' incorrect.
    H. 'Koriyama'.
    H. 'Opipara Kooriyama' incorrect.
    H. *sieboldii* 'Koriyama'.
JN: *Koriyama Nishiki Giboshi* hort.
[H. *sieboldii* form mutation].

H. 'Koryu' Japan.
甲竜
　Koryu Giboshi is the "hosta with swollen variegation." The variegation is in relief and looks like Ryu, "dragon on the leaves." Coveted in Japan for its peculiar look. Discovered by Dr. Shuichi Hirao, it is also sometimes called *H.* 'Miyakodori', *Miyakodori Giboshi*. In North America this cultivar name is also used incorrectly for various *H. sieboldii* seedlings.
JN:　*Koryu Iwa Giboshi* hort.
　　　Miyachodori Giboshi hort. incorrect.
　　　Miyakodori Giboshi hort.
(see also *H.* 'Miyakodori').

H. 'Koryu Iwa' Japan.
甲竜イワギボウシ
　Koryu Iwa Giboshi is a synonym for *H.* 'Koryu', which see.
JN:　*Koryu (Iwa) Giboshi.*
(see *H.* 'Koryu').

H. 'Krinkled Joy' Armstrong/Arett IRA/1986.
　AHS-III/15B.
　Plant is much larger than this description in some gardens and classified as a AHS-II/9B. Plant 18 in. (46 cm) dia., 10 in. (25.5 cm) high. Leaf 5 by 4 in. (13 by 10 cm), veins 12, blue-green, not variegated, cordate, rugose. Scape 16 in. (40.5 cm), bare, straight. Flower medium, bell-shaped, white, flowers during average period, fertile.
[*H.* 'Tokudama' hybrid].

H. 'Krossa Asiatic Seedling' Krossa.
　Plant is a seedling received from Japan without name. It is similar to *H. nakaiana* and was used for hybridizing but never renamed.
HN:　*H.* 'Krossa No. E-3'.

H. 'Krossa Cream Edge' Krossa.
　Plant erect, 10 in. (25.5 cm) dia., 10 in. (25.5 cm) high. Leaf 3 by 0.75 in. (7.5 by 2 cm), veins 3, medium green, white margin, lanceolate, flat. Scape 24 in. (61 cm), bare, straight. Flower medium, funnel-shaped, purple striped, flowers during summer period, fertile.
[*H. sieboldii* derivative].

H. 'Krossa No. 00' Krossa.
　Plants numbered by the late Gus Krossa, who imported many hostas from Japan and Europe which he obtained from academic sources and collectors the world over. His connections to Osaka University brought a number of wild taxa into the United States. He numbered many of them, lacking identification, and after their names became known they were renamed. Following are his numbered taxa together with Summers' numbers, for cross-checking, and their current identification, where known. The numbers were compiled from Krossa's lists and his correspondence with Alex Summer, who generously provided originals and/or copies:
H. 'Krossa No. 5'/Summers No. 115 1967
= Small-leaved hybrid.
H. 'Krossa No. 6'/Summers No. 45 1967
= *H.* 'Tall Twister' pp sim.
H. 'Krossa No. A-1'/Summers No. 50 1967
= *H.* 'Fortunei Gloriosa'.
H. 'Krossa No. A-2'/Summers No. 170 1967
= *H.* 'Silver Streak'.

H. 'Krossa No. A-3'/Summers No. 69 1967
= *H.* 'Krossa Regal'.
H. 'Krossa No. B-1'/Summers No. 80 1967
= *H. montana* form.
H. 'Krossa No. B-2'/Summers No. 282 1967
= *H.* 'King Michael'.
H. 'Krossa No. B-3'/Summers Nos. 78 and 484 1967
= *H. montana* f. *macrophylla.*
H. 'Krossa No. B-4'/Summers No. 466 1970
= *H. montana* form.
H. 'Krossa No. B-5'/Summers No. 111 1967
= *H. nigrescens* pp sim.
H. 'Krossa No. B-6'/Summers No. 51 1967
= *H. clausa* var. *normalis.*
H. 'Krossa No. B-7'/Summers No. 46 1967
= *H. clausa.*
H. 'Krossa No. C-1'
= *H.* 'Helen Field Fischer'.
H. 'Krossa No. C-2'
= *H.* 'Chartreuse'.
H. 'Krossa No. C-3'
= A white variegated taxon of unknown parentage.
H. 'Krossa No. C-4'
= *H.* 'Fortunei Aoki'.
H. 'Krossa No. C-5'
= *H.* 'Undulata Univittata'.
H. 'Krossa No. DX-1'/Summers No. 412 1970 PI 274704
= *H.* 'Undulata' form.
H. 'Krossa No. DX-2'/PI 275074
= *H. montana* form.
H. 'Krossa No. DX-3'/Summers No. 280 1968 PI 275393
= *H. sieboldii* form.
H. 'Krossa No. DX-4'/Summers No. 411 1970 PI 274537
= *H. montana* form.
H. 'Krossa No. E-1'
= *H.* 'Elata' form.
H. 'Krossa No. E-2'
= *H.* 'Crispula' form.
H. 'Krossa No. E-3'
= *H.* 'Asiatic Seedling' Krossa hort(?).
H. 'Krossa No. E-4'
= *H. ventricosa.*
H. 'Krossa No. E-5'
= *H. longissima* form.
H. 'Krossa No. E-6'
= *H.* 'Burkes Dwarf' = *H. nakaiana.*
H. 'Krossa No. F-1'
= *H.* 'Tardiflora' form.
H. 'Krossa No. F-2'
= *H.* 'Yellow Splash'.
H. 'Krossa No. F-3'.
H. 'Krossa No. F-4'/Summers No. 27
= *H.* 'Undulata' form.
H. 'Krossa No. F-5'
= *H.* 'Elata' form.
H. 'Krossa No. F-6'
= *H.* 'Elata' form.
H. 'Krossa No. F-7'
= *H.* 'Late Gold' Summers = *H.* 'August Moon'.
H. 'Krossa No. F-8'
= *H.* hybrid form–yellow viridescent.
H. 'Krossa No. F-9'
= *H.* 'Cardwell Yellow'.
H. 'Krossa No. G-1'
= *H.* 'Crispula' hybr.
H. 'Krossa No. G-2'
= A hybrid received from Starker.

H. 'Krossa No. G-3'/Summers No. 125 1967
= *H.* 'Starker Aureafolia'.
H. 'Krossa No. G-4'
= *H.* 'Vilmoriniana'.
H. 'Krossa No. G-5'
= *H.* 'Undulata Albomarginata'.
H. 'Krossa No. H-1'
= *H.* 'Snow Mound'.
H. 'Krossa No. H-2'
= *H. sieboldiana* form.
H. 'Krossa No. H-3'
= *H.* 'Viettes Yellow Edge'.
H. 'Krossa No. H-4'
= *H.* 'Golden Plum'.
H. 'Krossa No. H-5'
= *H.* 'Maya'.
H. 'Krossa No. H-6'
= *H.* 'Golden Lance'.
H. 'Krossa No. H-7'
= *H.* 'Helonioides Albopicta'.
H. 'Krossa No. H-8'/Summers No. 61 1967
= *H.* 'Louisa' Williams IRA/1986 pp.
H. 'Krossa No. J-1'
= An unspecified *H. sieboldii* hybrid received from Fisher.
H. 'Krossa No. J-2'
= Described as an Asiatic dwarf form(?).
H. 'Krossa No. J-3'/Summers No. 86 1967 PI 275394
= A *H. sieboldii* hybrid received from Fisher.
H. 'Krossa No. J-4'/Summers No. 110 1969
= *H.* 'Saishu Jima' pp.
H. 'Krossa No. J-5'
= *H.* 'Crispula'.
H. 'Krossa No. J-6'
= *H.* 'Fortunei' form.
H. 'Krossa No. K-1'/Summers No. 151 1967 PI 318546
= Purportedly *H. minor* but not the true Korean form.
H. 'Krossa No. K-2'/Summers No. 246 1967 PI 318547
= *H. capitata*.
H. 'Krossa No. K-3'/PI 319294
= *H. capitata* form.
H. 'Krossa No. K-4'/PI 319295
= *H. clausa* form.
H. 'Krossa No. K-5'/PI 318545
= *H. sieboldii* form.
H. 'Krossa No. K-6'
= *H.* 'Fortunei Hyacinthina'.
H. 'Krossa No. K-7'
= *H.* 'Crispula Viridis'.
H. 'Krossa No. L-1'
= *H. sieboldii* hybr.
H. 'Krossa No. L-2'
= *H.* 'Fortunei' mutation.
H. 'Krossa No. L-3'.
H. 'Krossa No. L-4'/Summers No. 472
= *H.* 'Samual Blue' Krossa/Ruh IRA/1981.
H. 'Krossa No. L-7'
= *H.* 'Fortunei Aureomarginata'.
H. 'Krossa No. X-1'
= *H. montana* form.
H. 'Krossa No. X-2'
= *H. sieboldiana* form.
H. 'Krossa No. X-3'
= *H. montana* form.
H. 'Krossa No. X-4'/Summers No. 486 1971.
H. 'Krossa No. X-5'
= *H. montana* form.
H. 'Krossa No. Z-4'
= *H.* 'Belles Baby'.

H. **'Krossa Regal'** Osaka University/Krossa/Summers IRA/1980.
AHS-III/15B.   (Figure 2-4; Plates 124, 137, 176).
AHS Eunice Fisher Award, 1974. Plant is a sterile descendant of *H. nigrescens*. Imported from Japan by Krossa in the 1950s and by him cultivated under *H.* 'Krossa No. A-3', it was named and introduced by Alex Summers. It appeared in Summers' listings as No. 69 in 1967. Widely cultivated, it attained a No. 2 position in The American Hosta Society popularity poll in 1988. During tissue culture several mutant forms have appeared and have been named: *H.* 'Porcelain Vase' (Zilis, registered in 1988), which is a mediovariegated, greenish white with dark green margins, and *H.* 'Regal Splendor' (Walters, registered 1987), a whitish yellow margined *H.* 'Krossa Regal'. Plant erect, 30 in. (76 cm) dia., 28 in. (71 cm) high. Leaf 9 by 5 in. (23 by 13 cm), veins 12, blue-green, not variegated, cordate, wavy-undulate. Scape 56 in. (142 cm), bare, straight. Flower medium, funnel-shaped, lavender, flowers during average period, fertile.
HN: *H.* 'Krossa No. A–3'.
    H. nigrescens 'Krossa Regal'.
    Summers No. 69 1967.
[*H. nigrescens* hybrid].

H. 'Krossa Regal Variegated'.
Plant name is a superseded synonym.
[*H.* 'Krossa Regal' mutation].
(see *H.* 'Regal Splendor').

H. 'Krossa White' Krossa.
(see *H.* 'White Christmas').

H. 'Krossa Wide Band' Krossa.
(see *H.* 'Fortunei Aureomarginata').

H. **'Kunpu'** Japan.
薫風
Kunpu Giboshi, the "balmy (fragrant) breeze (hosta)," is much like *H.* 'Hogyoku', *Hogyoku Giboshi*, which see. Flowers fragrant, to 3 in. (7.5 cm), light purple. Leaves whitish pruinose on back.
JN: *Kunpu Giboshi* hort.

H. **'Kyushi'** UK.
A small cultivar of unknown provenance. The Japanese name is a European formulation and not known in Japan.

L

H. **'La Vista'** Walters Gardens IRA/1988.
AHS-IV/20A .
Plant 22 in. (56 cm) dia., 18 in. (46 cm) high. Leaf 6 by 3.5 in. (15 by 9 cm), veins 10, white (albescent), dark green margin, cordate, flat. Scape 28 in. (71 cm), foliated, straight. Flower medium, funnel-shaped, lavender, flowers during average period.
[*H.* 'Fortunei Hyacinthina' mutation].

H. **'Ladies Choice'** Houseworth 1986.
Plant 24 in. (61 cm) dia., 14 in. (35.5 cm) high. Leaf 6 by 4 in. (15 by 10 cm), veins 8, blue-green, not variegated, cordate, rugose. Scape 28 in. (71 cm), foliated, straight. Flower medium, bell-shaped, white, flowers during average period, fertile.
[*H.* 'August Moon' hybrid].

H. 'Lady Helen' Holly 1963 IRA/1968.
 AHS-III/18B.
 Plants are viridescent, yellow in spring, all green later. Some cultivars in commerce under this name are not the true form due to errors in distribution; the incorrect plants look like *H.* 'Nakaimo', which see. Plant 28 in. (71 cm) dia., 16 in. (40.5 cm) high. Leaf 7 by 5 in. (18 by 13 cm), veins 12, yellow (viridescent), not variegated, cordate, flat. Scape 32 in. (81.5 cm), bare, oblique. Flower medium, bell-shaped, purple, flowers during average period, fertile.

H. 'Lady Lou' Meissner.
 Plant is an all-green sport smaller than the parent.
HN: Summers No. 75 1964.
[*H.* 'Fortunei Albopicta' mutation].

H. 'Lady-in-Blue' Arett.
 Plant name is a superseded synonym.
(see *H.* 'Lady-in-Waiting').

H. 'Lady-in-Waiting' Arett IRA/1980.
 AHS-I/3B.
 Plant is a large blue-green *H. sieboldiana* form. Similar to the species.
[*H.* 'Tokudama' × *H. sieboldiana* 'Elegans'].

H. 'Lake Louise' Minks IRA/1975.
 AHS-II/9B.
 Plant 42 in. (106.5 cm) dia., 26 in. (66 cm) high. Leaf 11 by 10 in. (28 by 25.5 cm), veins 16, blue-green, not variegated, cordate, cupped-rugose. Scape 28 in. (71 cm), bare, straight. Flower medium, bell-shaped, white, flowers during average period, fertile.
[*H. sieboldiana* hybrid].

H. 'Lakeport Blue' Tompkins IRA/1984.
 AHS-I/3B.
 Plant is very close in form to the species *H. sieboldiana*. Plant 46 in. (117 cm) dia., 34 in. (86.5 cm) high. Leaf 14 by 11 in. (35.5 by 28 cm), veins 16, blue-green, not variegated, cordate, rugose. Scape 36 in. (91.5 cm), bare, straight. Flower medium, bell-shaped, white, flowers during average period, fertile.
[*H. sieboldiana* hybrid].

H. 'Lakeside Accolade' Chastain IRA/1988.
 AHS-IV/19B.
 Plant 18 in. (46 cm) dia., 12 in. (31 cm) high. Leaf 5.5 by 4 in. (22 by 10 cm), veins 8, blue-green, not variegated, cordate, rugose. Scape 26 in. (66 cm), bare, straight. Flower medium, bell-shaped, white, flowers during average period.
[*H.* 'Little Aurora' hybrid].

H. 'Lakeside Leprechaun' Chastain.
 Plant is small with light green leaves.

H. 'Lakeside Shadow' Chastain.
 Plant has leaves with shape similar to *H.* 'Fortunei'. Leaf 7 by 5 in. (18 by 13 cm), veins 8–10, dark green, developing a mottled yellowish white (lutescent) center, cordate.

H. 'Lakeside Symphony' Chastain IRA/1988.
 AHS-II/8A.
 Plant 24 in. (61 cm) dia., 12 in. (31 cm) high. Leaf 8 by 6 in. (20 by 15 cm), veins 10, yellowish white (lutescent), green margin, cordate, rugose-wavy. Scape 66 in. (1676 cm), bare, straight. Flower medium, bell-shaped, white, flowers during average period.
[*H.* 'Piedmont Gold' mutation].

H. 'Lanceleaf No. 51' incorrect.
H. 'Krossa No. B-6'.

H. 'Lancifolia'.
H. lancifolia.

H. 'Lancifolia Albomarginata' incorrect.
(see *H. sieboldii*).

H. 'Lancifolia Angustifolia' hort. incorrect.
(see *H. sieboldii* f. *angustifolia*).

H. 'Lancifolia Asami Improved' hort. incorrect.
(see *H.* 'Asami').

H. 'Lancifolia Aurea' hort.
 Hosta 'Lancifolia' has in cultivation produced several different, sterile, yellow sports which are either all yellow or yellow spotted. Most are viridescent, but a form which remains yellow has been reported in Germany and is also cultivated in North America. This taxon has 5–6 pairs of veins but is often mistaken for the yellow form of *H. sieboldii* which is fertile, has 3–4 principal veins, and is much smaller. It is also very much like *H. cathayana* 'Ogon' (Plate 167) but is sterile. Plant 20 in. (51 cm) dia., 12 in. (30.5 cm) high. Leaf 4–5 by 2–3 in. (10–13 by 5–7 cm), veins 5–6, yellow (some viridescent, others color stable), not variegated, ovate, flat. Scape 22 in. (56 cm), foliated, oblique. Flower medium, funnel-shaped, purple-striped, flowers during August, fertile.
SY: *H. japonica* var. *aurea* Nobis 1951 pp.
 Hostia japonica f. *lutescens* Voss 1896.
HN: *Hosta lancifolia aurea* hort. incorrect.

H. 'Lancifolia Aurea' hort.
 Plant is yellow leaved and much larger than the taxon described previously. It is sold and cultivated in North America under the incorrect cultivar name *H.* 'Lancifolia Aurea'. It has 10–12 pairs of veins but is not related. Its exact relationship has yet to be determined, but it is certain that it has no connections with *H.* 'Lancifolia'.

H. 'Lancifolia Bunchoko' hort. incorrect.
(see *H. sieboldii* 'Bunchoko').

H. 'Lancifolia Cathy Late' hort.
(see *H.* 'Cathy Late').

H. 'Lancifolia Inaho' hort.
(see *H.* 'Inaho').

H. 'Lancifolia Kabitan' hort. incorrect.
(see *H. sieboldii* 'Kabitan').

H. 'Lancifolia Mediopicta' hort. incorrect.
(see *H. sieboldii* f. *mediopicta*).

H. 'Lancifolia Minor' hort. incorrect.
(see *H. sieboldii* f. *angustifolia* Dwarf group).

H. 'Lancifolia Numor' hort. incorrect
(see *H. sieboldii* f. *spathulata*).
(see also *H. numor*).

H. 'Lancifolia Shirobuchi' hort. Japan incorrect.
(see *H.* 'Shirobuchi').

H. 'Lancifolia Subcrocea' hort. incorrect.
(see *H. sieboldii* 'Subcrocea').

H. **'Lancifolia Tardiflora'** hort. incorrect.
(see *H.* 'Tardiflora').

H. **'Lancifolia Thunbergiana'** incorrect.
(see *H. sieboldii* f. *spathulata*).

H. **'Lancifolia Thunbergii'** incorrect.
(see *H. sieboldii* f. *spathulata*).

H. **'Larry Englerth'** Benedict IRA/1986.
    AHS-III/14B.
HN: *H. sieboldiana* Yellow grex.
[*H.* 'Midwest Gold' mutation].

H. **'Late Gold'** Summers.
HN: *H.* 'Krossa No. F-7'.
(see *H.* 'August Moon').

H. **'Lauman Blue'** Lauman.
    Plant 28 in. (71 cm) dia., 22 in. (56 cm) high. Leaf 8 by 6 in.
(20 by 15 cm), veins 13, blue-green, not variegated, round-
cordate, cupped-rugose. Scape 28 in. (71 cm), bare, straight.
Flower medium, bell-shaped, white, flowers during average
period, fertile.
HN: *H.* 'Lauman Garden Blue'.
        H. 'Lowman Garden Blue' incorrect.
[*H.* 'Tokudama' hybrid].

H. **'Lavender Lady'** Williams 1964 IRA/1986.
    AHS-IV/19A.
    Plant erect, 10 in. (25.5 cm) dia., 10 in. (25.5 cm) high. Leaf
5 by 2 in. (13 by 5 cm), veins 3, medium green, not variegated,
lanceolate, flat. Scape 22 in. (56 cm), bare, straight. Flower
medium, funnel-shaped, purple, flowers during average
period, fertile.
HN: *H.* 'FRW No. 1025'.
[*H. sieboldii* 'Alba' hybrid].

H. **'Lavisière'** Inniswood.
    Plant is similar to *H.* 'Decorata Normalis'. Name means
visor. Seen at Inniswood Botanic Garden, Columbus, Ohio.
(see *H.* 'Decorata Normalis').

H. **'Leather Sheen'** Lohman/Zilis IRA/1988.
    AHS-IV/19B.
    Plant 30 in. (76 cm) dia., 14 in. (35.5 cm) high. Leaf 7 by 3
in. (18 by 7.5 cm), veins 6, glossy dark green, not variegated,
ovate-cordate, flat. Scape 30 in. (76 cm), foliated, straight.
Flower medium, bell-shaped, lavender, flowers during
average period, fertile.
[*H.* 'Sum and Substance' × *H. venusta* hybrid].

H. **'Ledi Lantis'** Aden IRA/1978.
    AHS-III/17A.
    Plant 28 in. (71 cm) dia., 18 in. (46 cm) high. Leaf 9 by 8 in.
(23 by 20 cm), veins 13, chartreuse, not variegated, round-
cordate, cupped-rugose. Scape 24 in. (61 cm), bare, straight.
Flower medium, bell-shaped, white, flowers during average
period, fertile.
[*H.* 'Tokudama' hybrid].

H. **'Lee Armiger'** Reath IRA/1986.
    AHS-III/15B.
    Plant 30 in. (76 cm) dia., 18 in. (46 cm) high. Leaf 5 by 5 in.
(13 by 13 cm), veins 13, blue-green, not variegated, round-
cordate, cupped-rugose. Scape 22 in. (56 cm), bare, straight.
Flower medium, bell-shaped, white, flowers during average
period, fertile.
HN: *H.* 'Lee Arminger' incorrect.
[*H. sieboldiana* 'Elegans' × *H.* 'Tokudama'].

H. **'Lemon Chiffon'** Banyai IRA/1988.
    AHS-II/11A.
    Plant is a vigorous hybridized yellow form of *H. montana*.
28 in. (71 cm) dia., 24 in. (61 cm) high. Leaf 12 by 7 in. (31 by 18
cm), veins 12, yellow, not variegated, cordate, wavy-rugose.
Scape 18 in. (46 cm), bare, straight. Flowers during average
period, fertile.

H. **'Lemon Lime'** Savory IRA/1977.
    AHS-V/29B.   (Figure 4-29).
    Plant 18 in. (46 cm) dia., 12 in. (31 cm) high. Leaf 3 by 1 in.
(7.5 by 2.5 cm), veins 3, chartreuse, not variegated, lanceolate,
flat. Scape 18 in. (46 cm), bare, straight. Flower medium, bell-
shaped, purple-striped, flowers during average period, fertile.
[*H. sieboldii* derivative].

Figure 4-29. *H.* 'Lemon Lime'; general habit; (Walters
Gardens, Inc./Falstad)

H. **'Lemonade'** Anderson IRA/1980.
    AHS-IV/23A.
    AHS Midwest Gold Award, 1982, exhibited by Kenneth
Anderson. Medium size, round leaves are lemon-yellow and
have 6 pairs of veins.

H. **'Leola Fraim'** Lachman IRA/1986.
    AHS-III/16B.   (Plate 125).
    Plant 32 in. (81.5 cm) dia., 18 in. (46 cm) high. Leaf 9 by 7
in. (23 by 18 cm), veins 11, medium green, white margin, cordate, rugose. Scape 28 in. (71 cm), bare, straight. Flower
medium, funnel-shaped, lavender, flowers during average
period, fertile.
HN: Lachman No. L80-4.
[*H.* 'Swoosh' hybrid].

H. **'Leviathan'** Nesmith IRA/1986.
AHS-II/7A.
Plant is a large cultivar similar to *H. montana* or an all-green *H. sieboldiana*.
[*H. montana* or *H. sieboldiana* hybrid].

H. **'Liberty Bell'** Benedict IRA/1985.
AHS-IV/20A.
Plant 16 in. (40.5 cm) dia., 12 in. (31 cm) high. Leaf 5 by 2 in. (13 by 5 cm), veins 4, medium green, streaky white, lanceolate, flat. Scape 40 in. (101.5 cm), foliated, straight. Flower medium, bell-shaped, purple, flowers during summer period, fertile.
[*H.* 'Yellow Splash' × *H.* 'Neat Splash'].

H. **'Lighthouse'** hort. incorrect.
Plants received under this name are *H.* 'Undulata Albomarginata'.

H. **'Lights Up'** Aden IRA/1986.
AHS-V/29A.
Plant erect, 6 in. (15 cm) dia., 4 in. (10 cm) high. Leaf 5 by 0.75 in. (13 by 2 cm), veins 3, yellow (viridescent), not variegated, lanceolate, flat. Scape 8 in. (20 cm), foliated, straight. Flower medium, funnel-shaped, purple striped, flowers during average period, fertile.
[*H.* 'Aden No. 519' × *H.* 'Chartreuse Wiggles'].

H. **'Lilac Giant'** Verboom/Hensen IRA/1983.
AHS-II/7A.
Plant 40 in. (101.5 cm) dia., 30 in. (76 cm) high. Leaf 12 by 9 in. (31 by 23 cm), veins 14, blue-green, not variegated, cordate, rugose. Scape 44 in. (112 cm), foliated, straight. Flower medium, funnel-shaped, lavender, flowers during average period, fertile.
HN: *H. sieboldiana* 'Lilac Giant' Hensen 1983.
[*H. sieboldiana* 'Elegans' hybrid].

H. **'Liliput'** Klose.
Plant has lavender flowers over a flat leaf mound of small green leaves which spread flat on the ground.
[*H. rectifolia* hybrid].

H. **'Lime Krinkles'** Soules IRA/1988.
AHS-III/17B. (Plate 126).
Plant 36 in. (91.5 cm) dia., 20 in. (51 cm) high. Leaf 10 by 8 in. (25.5 by 20 cm), veins 13, chartreuse (viridescent) turning to lime green, not variegated, cordate, rugose-undulate, crinkled. Scape 22 in. (56 cm), foliated, straight. Flower medium, bell-shaped, white, flowers during average period, fertile.
[*H.* 'Tokudama' hybrid].

H. **'Lime Shag'**.
Plant is a dwarf form of *H. sieboldii* f. *spathulata* with light green leaves. Leaf lanceolate, veins 3.

H. **'Lime Twist'** Houseworth 1986.
Plant erect, 8 in. (20 cm) dia., 8 in. (20 cm) high. Leaf 5 by 0.75 in. (13 by 2 cm), veins 3, yellow (viridescent), margin green, lanceolate, flat. Scape 16 in. (40.5 cm), bare, straight. Flower medium, funnel-shaped, purple striped, flowers during summer period, fertile.
[*H.* 'The Twister' hybrid].

H. **'Limelight'** Savory IRA/1988.
AHS-IV/20B.
Plant 12 in. (31 cm) dia., 10 in. (25.5 cm) high. Leaf 4 by 3 in. (10 by 7.5 cm), veins 9, chartreuse (lutescent) turning to yellow green, thin white margin, cordate, flat. Scape 16 in. (40.5 cm), foliated, straight. Flower medium, lavender, flowers during average period.
[*H.* 'Aspen Gold' hybrid × *H.* 'Aspen Gold' hybrid].

H. **'Limon'** Sellers IRA/1983.
AHS-III/17B.
Plant 24 in. (61 cm) dia., 20 in. (51 cm) high. Leaf 5 by 5 in. (13 by 13 cm), veins 13, chartreuse, not variegated, cordate, rugose. Scape 26 in. (66 cm), bare, straight. Flower medium, bell-shaped, lavender, flowers during average period, fertile.
[*H.* 'Tokudama' form].

H. **'Linde'** Ruh/Hofer IRA/1987.
AHS-III/15B.
Plant 20 in. (51 cm) dia., 18 in. (46 cm) high. Leaf 8 by 6 in. (20 by 15 cm), veins 13, blue-green, not variegated, round-cordate, cupped-rugose. Scape 20 in. (51 cm), foliated, straight. Flower medium, bell-shaped, white, flowers during average period, fertile.
[*H.* 'Perrys True Blue' hybrid].

H. **'Little Ann'** Stone/Piedmont Gardens/Ruh IRA/1988.
AHS-V/26A.
Plant is similar to *H.* 'Anne Arett' (Plate 87), erect, 8 in. (20 cm) dia., 8 in. (20 cm) high. Leaf 4 by 1 in. (10 by 2.5 cm), veins 3, yellow (viridescent), white margin, lanceolate, flat. Scape 14 in. (35.5 cm), bare, straight. Flower medium, funnel-shaped, purple striped, flowers during summer period, fertile.
HN: *H. (sieboldii)* 'Anne Arett' sim.
[*H. sieboldii* 'Subcrocea' mutation].

H. **'Little Aurora'** Aden IRA/1978.
AHS-IV/23A. (Figure 6-5; Plates 81, 170).
Plant 12 in. (31 cm) dia., 8 in. (20 cm) high. Leaf 4 by 3 in. (10 by 7.5 cm), veins 8-10, yellow (lutescent), not variegated, cordate, cupped-rugose. Scape 12 in. (31 cm), bare, straight. Flower medium, bell-shaped, white, flowers during average period, fertile.
[*H.* 'Tokudama' hybrid].
(see also *H.* 'Tokudama Ogon Hime').
(see also *H.* 'Golden Prayers').

H. **'Little Blue'** Englerth IRA/1976.
AHS-III/13B. (Figure 4-34).
Plant is similar to the species, but smaller, leaves more elongated. Plant 18 in. (46 cm) dia., 12 in. (31 cm) high. Leaf 6 by 4 in. (15 by 10 cm), veins 8, medium green, not variegated, ovate-cordate, flat. Scape 30 in. (76 cm), bare, straight. Flower medium, bell-shaped, purple, flowers during summer period, fertile.
HN: *H.* 'Lil Blue'.
(see *H. ventricosa* dwarf form).

H. **'Little Early Bird'** Fisher.
[*H. nakaiana* hybrid].

H. **'Little Jim'** Benedict IRA/1986.
AHS-V/28A. (Plate 127).
Plants of similar form have been found in Japan and given the names *H.* 'Tsugaru Komachi' and *H.* 'Tsugaru Nishiki', which see. Another Japanese sport arising from *H. sieboldii* (the parent plant of *H.* 'Saishu Jima') is called *H.* 'Shima Kabitan', which also see. This plant arose independently in the United States and is erect, 8 in. (20 cm) dia., 6 in. (15 cm) high. Leaf 3 by 0.75 in. (7.5 by 2 cm), veins 3, medium green, streaked

yellowish white, lanceolate, flat or wavy. Scape 12 in. (31 cm), bare, straight. Flower medium, funnel-shaped, purple striped, flowers during summer period, fertile.
HN: *H.* 'Saishu Jima Variegated' Aden pp sim.
[*H.* 'Saishu Jima' mutation].
[*H. sieboldii* derivative].

H. 'Little Pearl' Houseworth 1986.
[*H. sieboldii* 'Louisa' hybrid].

H. 'Little Puck' Minks.

H. 'Little Razor' Lohman/Zilis IRA/1988.
　　AHS-V/29B.
　　Plant 16 in. (40.5 cm) dia., 6 in. (15 cm) high. Leaf 3 by 1.25 in. (7.5 by 3 cm), veins 3, light yellow (viridescent), not variegated, ovate-lanceolate, flat. Scape 18 in. (46 cm), bare, straight. Flower medium, lavender, flowers during summer period.
[*H.* 'Sum and Substance' × *H. venusta* hybrid].

H. 'Little Sister' Fisher 1974.
　　Plant is same yellow color as the parent but smaller, leaves more pointed, some rugosity.
[*H.* 'Sunlight Sister' hybrid].

H. 'Little White Edge' Geissler.

H. 'Little White Lines' Zilis IRA/1988.
　　AHS-V/28A.
　　Plant 18 in. (46 cm) dia., 8 in. (20 cm) high. Leaf 4 by 2 in. (10 by 5 cm), veins 5, medium green, white margin, ovate-cordate, flat. Scape 20 in. (51 cm), bare, straight. Flower medium, purple, flowers during summer period.
[*H.* 'Sum and Substance' × *H. venusta* hybrid].

H. 'Little Wonder' Lachman IRA/1989.
　　AHS-V/28B.
　　Plant occasionally develops streaky variegation. Plant 12 in. (30 cm) dia., 6 in. (15 cm) high. Leaf 2.5 by 1.5 in. (4 by 3 cm), veins 4, dark green, wide, yellowish white margin, ovate-cordate, flat or wavy. Scape 12 in. (31 cm), bare, straight. Flower medium, funnel-shaped, purple, flowers during average period, fertility(?).

H. 'Lochness' Lachman IRA/1988.
　　AHS-II/9B.
　　Plant 40 in. (101.5 cm) dia., 24 in. (61 cm) high. Leaf 12 by 11 in. (31 by 28 cm), veins 16, blue-green, not variegated, cordate, cupped-rugose. Scape 36 in. (91.5 cm), bare, straight. Flower medium, bell-shaped, lavender, flowers during average period, fertile.
HN: *H.* 'Loch Ness'.
[*H.* 'Sea Monster' × hybrid].

H. 'Loleta Powell' Aden IRA/1980.
　　AHS-III/14A.
　　Plant 24 in. (61 cm) dia., 18 in. (46 cm) high. Leaf medium, veins 10, medium green, streaky multicolor, lanceolate, flat. Scape 20 in. (51 cm), foliated, straight. Flower medium, funnel-shaped, lavender, flowers during summer period, fertile.
[*H.* 'Fascination' × *H.* 'Intrigue'].

H. longipes f. sparsa 'Kinakafu'.

H. longipes 'Golden Dwarf'.

H. longipes 'Hakuyo'.
(see *H.* 'Hakuyo').

H. longipes 'Harvest Dandy'.
(see *H.* 'Harvest Dandy').

H. longipes 'Koki'.

H. longipes 'Ogon'.

H. longipes 'Ogon Amagi'.

H. longipes 'Okutama Nishiki'.
(see *H.* 'Okutama Nishiki').

H. longipes 'Setsuko'.

H. longipes 'Shirobana'.

H. longipes 'Shirofukurin'.

H. longipes 'Tagi'.

H. longipes 'Urajiro'.

H. longipes 'Usuba'.

H. longipes var. latifolia 'Amagi Nishiki'.

H. longipes var. latifolia 'Izu'.

H. longipes var. latifolia 'Maruba'.

H. longipes 'Viridipes'.
　　Plant in the trade incorrectly under this name is *H.* 'Crispula'.

H. longissima 'Fukurin'.

H. longissima 'Hanazawa'.

H. longissima 'Hosoba'.

H. longissima 'Isshiki Fukurin'.

H. longissima 'Kifukurin'.

H. longissima 'Kikeika'.

H. longissima 'Nikazaki'.

H. longissima 'Shirobana'.

H. longissima 'Sotoyama Fukurin'.

H. longissima var. longifolia 'Kifukurin'.

H. longissima var. longifolia 'Kinakafu'.

H. longissima var. longifolia 'Shirofukurin'.

H. 'Look See' Aden IRA/1980.
　　AHS-III/14A.

H. 'Lorna' Benedict IRA/1983.
　　AHS-V/25B.
　　Plant 6 in. (15 cm) dia., 2 in. (5 cm) high. Leaf 2 by 1.5 in. (5 by 4 cm), veins 4, medium green, not variegated, ovate, flat.

Scape 8 in. (20 cm), bare, straight. Flower medium, bell-shaped, purple, flowers during average period, fertile.
[*H. nakaiana* × *H. venusta*].

_H._ 'Louisa' Williams (No. 537) IRA/1986.
　　AHS-IV/22A.
　　Plant erect, 16 in. (40.5 cm) dia., 12 in. (31 cm) high. Leaf 4 by 1.5 in. (10 by 4 cm), veins 3, medium green, margin white, lanceolate, flat. Scape 24 in. (61 cm), bare, straight. Flower medium, funnel-shaped, white, flowers during summer period, fertile.
[*H. sieboldii* derivative].
(see also *H. sieboldii* 'Bunchoko').

_H._ 'Louise Ryan' Walters Gardens.
　　Plant is a chartreuse-margined mutant found in tissue culture explants. Margins do not burn.
HN: *H.* 'Ryans Big One' mutation.

_H._ 'Love Joy' Aden IRA/1980.
　　AHS-III/14A.
　　Plant 20 in. (51 cm) dia., 16 in. (40.5 cm) high. Leaf medium, veins 10, medium green, streaky yellow, ovate, flat. Scape 20 in. (51 cm), foliated, straight. Flower medium, funnel-shaped, white, flowers during average period, fertile.
[*H.* 'Fascination' hybrid].

_H._ 'Love Pat' Aden IRA/1978.
　　AHS-III/15B.　　　　　　　(Figure 2-16; Plate 128).
　　AHS Midwest Blue Award, 1988, exhibited by Richard Ward. Plant 24 in. (61 cm) dia., 20 in. (51 cm) high. Leaf 6 by 6 in. (15 by 15 cm), veins 13, blue-green, not variegated, cordate, cupped-rugose. Scape 26 in. (66 cm), bare, straight. Flower medium, bell-shaped, white, flowers during average period, fertile.
[*H.* 'Tokudama' form].

_H._ 'Loving Cup' Armstrong IRA/1970.
　　AHS-II/9B.
　　Plant 26 in. (66 cm) dia., 20 in. (51 cm) high. Leaf 8 by 7.5 in. (20 by 19 cm). Veins 13, chartreuse, not variegated, cordate, cupped-rugose. Scape 26 in. (66 cm), bare, straight. Flower medium, bell-shaped, white, flowers during average period, fertile.
[*H.* 'Tokudama' × *H. sieboldiana*].

_H._ 'Lucky Charm' Fisher IRA/1986.
　　AHS-III/13A.

_H._ 'Lucy' Houseworth 1986.
　　Plant 30 in. (76 cm) dia., 20 in. (51 cm) high. Leaf 10 by 8 in. (25 by 20 cm). Veins 9, medium green, not variegated, round-cupped. Scape 32 in. (81.5 cm), bare, oblique. Flower medium, funnel-shaped, lavender, flowers during summer period, fertile.
[*H. hypoleuca* hybrid].

_H._ 'Lucy Vitols' Seaver IRA/1989.
　　AHS-II/8B.
　　Plant medium size. Leaf 10 by 9 in. (25 by 22 cm), veins 10, yellowish green (viridescent), irregular green margin, cordate, rugose. Scape 18 in. (45 cm), foliated, straight. Flower medium, funnel-shaped, lavender, flowers during average period, fertile.

_H._ 'Lucys Little White Seedling' Simpers incorrect.
　　Plant name incorrectly formulated per the ICNCP.

_H._ 'Lunar Eclipse' Zilis IRA/1985.
　　AHS-III/14B.　　　　　　　(Plates 84, 129).
　　Plant is the white-margined sport of *H.* 'August Moon'. Characterized by a spring flush of cupped-rugose leaves which usually stay chartreuse, especially during dry and hot spring seasons. The second summer flush of leaves emerges and stays more yellow and is not quite as rugose and cupped. Some mutants do not have cupped leaves (see Plate 84). Plant 36 in. (91.5 cm) dia., 20 in. (51 cm) high. Leaf 6 by 5 in. (15 by 13 cm), veins 9–10, yellow (viridescent), margin white, cordate, cupped-rugose. Scape 28 in. (71 cm), foliated, straight. Flower medium, bell-shaped, white, flowers during average period, fertile.
[*H.* 'August Moon' mutation].

_H._ 'Lynne' Weissenberger IRA/1986.
　　AHS-IV/21B.
　　Plant 14 in. (35.5 cm) dia., 10 in. (25.5 cm) high. Leaf 2.5 by 1.5 in. (6.5 by 4 cm), veins 6, blue-green, not variegated, cordate, flat, slightly rugose. Scape 18 in. (46 cm), bare, straight. Flower medium, bell-shaped, lavender, flowers during average period, fertile.
[*H.* 'Blue Cadet' hybrid].

M

_H._ 'Macabe Blue' Summers 1968.
　　Plant 18 in. (46 cm) dia., 12 in. (31 cm) high. Leaf 6 by 3.5 in. (15 by 9 cm), veins 12, blue-green, not variegated, cordate, rugose. Scape 20 in. (51 cm), bare, straight. Flower medium, bell-shaped, white, flowers during average period, fertile.

_H._ 'Mackwoods No. 00' Mackwoods Garden.
　　Plants appearing on a numbered list issued by Mackwoods Garden in 1960.
(see Chapter 5).

_H._ 'Maekawa' Aden.
(see *H. hypoleuca*).

_H._ 'Majestic Blue' Aden 1976.
　　Plant 44 in. (112 cm) dia., 26 in. (66 cm) high. Leaf 12 by 10 in. (31 by 25.5 cm), veins 16, blue-green, not variegated, cordate, rugose. Scape 32 in. (81.5 cm), bare, straight. Flower medium, bell-shaped, white, flowers during average period, fertile.
[*H. sieboldiana* hybrid].

_H._ 'Majestic Glow' Anderson IRA/1982.
　　AHS-III/17A.
　　Plant 16 in. (40.5 cm) dia., 12 in. (31 cm) high. Leaf 5 by 3 in. (13 by 7.5 cm), veins 12, chartreuse, not variegated, cordate, cupped-rugose. Scape 20 in. (51 cm). Flower medium, bell-shaped, white, flowers during average period, fertile.

_H._ 'Majestic Gold'.

_H._ 'Maple Leaf' Minks IRA/1972.
　　AHS-II/10B.
　　Plant 44 in. (112 cm) dia., 24 in. (61 cm) high, 30 in. (76 cm), bare, straight; leaf, veins 16, blue-green, margin yellow,

cordate, rugose. Flower medium, bell-shaped, white, flowers during average period, fertile.
HN: *H. sieboldiana* Aureomarginata group.

H. 'Marble Rim' Shaw IRA/1986.
AHS-IV/22B.
Plant belongs broadly to *H. sieboldii* 'Kifukurin' (Plate 65). Plant erect, 12 in. (31 cm) dia., 10 in. (25.5 cm) high. Leaf 4 by 1 in. (10 by 2.5 cm), veins 3, medium green, margin white, lanceolate, flat. Scape 28 in. (71 cm), bare, straight. Flower medium, funnel-shaped, purple striped, flowers during summer period, fertile.
HN: *H.* 'Gold Mark'.
    H. 'Shaw Variegated'.
    H. sieboldii 'Marble Rim'.
    Summers No. 158.
[*H. sieboldii* derivative].
(see also *H. sieboldii* 'Kifukurin').

H. 'Marbled Bouquet' Falstad IRA/1988.
AHS-III/16A.
Plant is a *H. plantaginea* mutant with streaked variegation which develops better in high light levels. Plant 34 in. (86.5 cm) dia., 22 in. (56 cm) high. Leaf 10 by 7 in. (25.5 by 18 cm), veins 11, medium green, streaked in white and yellow, cordate, flat. Scape large medium, funnel-shaped, white, fragrant, 30 in. (76 cm), foliated, straight. Flowers during average period, fertile.
[*H. plantaginea* mutation].

H. 'Marbled Cream' Owens IRA/1985.
AHS-III/16A.
Plant 22 in. (56 cm) dia., 10 in. (25.5 cm) high. Leaf 8 by 4 in. (20 by 10 cm), veins 6, medium green, streaky white and yellowish white, lanceolate, flat. Scape 30 in. (76 cm), foliated, straight. Flower medium, funnel-shaped, lavender, flowers during summer period, fertile.
[*H.* 'Yellow Splash' hybrid].

H. 'Margaret' Stone/Ruh IRA/1987.
AHS-V/25A.
Plant 10 in. (25.5 cm) dia., 6 in. (15 cm) high. Leaf 3 by 1 in. (7.5 by 2.5 cm), veins 3, medium green, not variegated, lanceolate, flat. Scape 10 in. (25.5 cm), foliated, straight. Flower medium, funnel-shaped, lavender, flowers during summer period, fertile.
HN: *H.* 'DSM No. 19'.

H. 'Margie Weissenberger' Weissenberger IRA/1986.
AHS-IV/21B.
Plant 14 in. (35.5 cm) dia., 6 in. (15 cm) high. Leaf 3 by 1 in. (7.5 by 2.5 cm), veins 5, blue-green, not variegated, cordate, flat. Scape 16 in. (40.5 cm), bare, straight. Flower medium, bell-shaped, lavender, flowers during average period, fertile.
[*H.* 'Blue Cadet' hybrid].

H. 'Marilyn' Zilis.
Plant is medium-size with wavy yellow leaves. Flower pale lavender.
[*H.* 'Gold Drop' × *H.* 'Green Piecrust'].

H. 'Marquis' Savory IRA/1982.
AHS-IV/19A.
Plant 16 in. (40.5 cm) dia., 8 in. (20 cm) high. Leaf small, veins 5, medium green, not variegated, cordate, rugose-wavy. Scape 14 in. (35.5 cm), bare, straight. Flower medium, bell-shaped, lavender, flowers during average period, fertile.
[*H. nakaiana* hybrid].

H. 'Maruba Iwa' Japan.
マルバイワギボウシ   (Figure 3-41).
Maruba Iwa Giboshi, the "round-leaved rock hosta," is a variant of *H. longipes* var. *latifolia* found on Izu Hanto (Izu Peninsula). It may represent an intergrading hybrid swarm and is very close in appearance to *H. rupifraga*.
JN: *Maruba Iwa Giboshi* hort.
(see *H. longipes* var. *latifolia* 'Maruba').
(see also *H. longipes*).

H. 'Mary Jo' Stone/Ruh IRA/1987.
AHS-IV/21A.
Plant 17 in. (43 cm) dia., 8 in. (20 cm) high. Leaf 5 by 4 in. (13 by 10 cm), veins 9, medium green, not variegated, lanceolate, flat. Scape 17 in. (43 cm), bare, straight. Flower medium, funnel-shaped, lavender, flowers during average period, fertile.
HN: *H.* 'DSM No. 11'.

H. 'Mary Lou' Banyai IRA/1986.
AHS-II/7A.
Plant 36 in. dia., 18 in. (91.5 by 46 cm) high. Leaf 10 by 8 in. (25.5 by 20 cm), veins 12, blue-green, not variegated, cordate, flat. Scape 36 in. (91.5 cm), foliated, straight. Flower medium, bell-shaped, white, flowers during average period, fertile.
[*H.* 'Fortunei Aoki' hybrid].

H. 'Mary Marie Ann' Englerth IRA/1982.
AHS-IV/20B.   (Plate 130).
Plant 16 in. (40.5 cm) dia., 10 in. (25.5 cm) high. Leaf 7 by 5 in. (18 by 13 cm), veins 7, chartreuse, viridescent center, margin green, cordate, wavy. Scape 16 in. (40.5 cm), bare, straight. Flower medium, funnel-shaped, lavender, flowers during average period, sterile.
[*H.* 'Fortunei Aoki' mutation].

H. 'Mastodon' Vaughn.
Plant very large with very rugose blue-green leaves of heavy substance.
[*H.* 'Polly Bishop' hybrid × *H.* 'Blue Lace' hybrid].

H. 'Maurice Mason' hort.
Plant is a miniature hosta with the name unknown and from the garden of Maurice Mason of England. One of a number of British hostas displayed by Dr. Gilbert S. Daniels during the 1989 AHS convention.

H. 'May T. Watts' Zilis IRA/1985.
AHS-III/14B.
Plant 48 in. (122 cm) dia., 20 in. (51 cm) high. Leaf 9 by 6 in. (23 by 15 cm), veins 16, yellow (lutescent), margin white, cordate, rugose. Scape 30 in. (76 cm), bare, straight. Flower medium, bell-shaped, white, flowers during average period, fertile.
[*H. sieboldiana* 'Golden Sunburst' mutation].

H. 'Maya' Meissner/Summers No. 17 1965.
Plant 18 in. (46 cm) dia., 12 in. (31 cm) high. Leaf 6 by 4 in. (15 by 10 cm), veins 7, medium green, margin white, ovate, flat. Scape 26 in. (66 cm), foliated, straight. Flower medium, funnel-shaped, lavender, flowers during average period, fertile.
HN: *H.* 'Fortunei Maja' incorrect.
    H. 'Fortunei Maya'.
    H. fortunei viridismarginata 'Dwarf' hort. incorrect.
    H. 'Krossa No. H-5'.
    H. 'Maja' incorrect.
[*H.* 'Fortunei Albopicta' mutation].
(see also *H.* 'Fortunei Albopicta').

H. 'Mayan Moon' Mitchell 1986.
III/16B. (Plate 84).
Plant is a dark-green centered, yellow-margined sport of
H. 'August Moon'. Summers (1989a) and others consider this
cultivar equal to H. 'Abiqua Moonbeam' (Plate 84). This has
been confirmed so the latter name, which is registered, is the
correct one. Plant 34 in. (86.5 cm) dia., 22 in. (56 cm) high. Leaf
5 by 5 in. (13 by 13 cm), veins 9, medium green, margin yellow,
cordate, flat. Scape 30 in. (76 cm), bare, straight. Flower
medium, bell-shaped, white, flowers during average period,
fertile.
[H. 'August Moon' mutation].
(see also H. 'Abiqua Moonbeam').

H. 'Mayan Seer' Mitchell.
(see H. hypoleuca).

H. 'Maytime' Simpers.
Plant has leaves slightly larger than the pod parent,
viridescent yellow. Many purple, bell-shaped flowers during
average period on purple-dotted scapes.
[H. nakaiana hybrid].

H. 'Medio Picta' hort. incorrect.
Plant name has been horticulturally applied to several different taxa so is a confusing name.
(see H. 'Undulata').

H. 'Mediovariegata' hort. incorrect.
Plant name has been horticulturally applied to several different taxa so is a confusing name.
(see H. 'Undulata').

H. 'Mentor Gold' Wayside/Ruh IRA/1978.
AHS-IV/22B.
Plant is an unstable sport of H. sieboldii. Some leaves turn
all-whitish yellow, others white margined. Plant erect, 10 in.
(25.5 cm) dia., 8 in. (20 cm) high. Leaf 4 by 1 in. (10 by 2.5 cm),
veins 3, medium green, streaky multicolor, lanceolate, flat.
Scape 22 in. (56 cm), bare, straight. Flower medium, funnel-
shaped, purple striped, flowers during summer period, fertile.
[H. sieboldii derivative].

H. 'Mesa Fringe'.
Plant is a H. montana form with nice piecrust edges. Leaf 9
by 6 in. (23 by 15 cm), veins 11, green, cordate, piecrust
margins. Flower medium, funnel-shaped, white, flowers
during average period, fertile.
[H. montana form].

H. 'Michigan Gold' Benedict IRA/1984.
AHS-III/17A.
Plant 34 in. (86.5 cm) dia., 22 in. (56 cm) high. Leaf 11 by 7
in. (28 by 18 cm), veins 9, yellow (viridescent), cordate,
rugose. Scape 30 in. (76 cm), foliated, straight. Flower
medium, bell-shaped, white, flowers during average period,
fertile.
[H. 'August Moon' × H. 'Aspen Gold'].

H. 'Michinoku Nishiki' Japan.
みちのく錦
(see H. 'Animachi').

H. 'Midas Touch' Aden IRA/1978.
AHS-III/17A. (Plate 131).
Plant has a golden yellow leaf with a metallic sheen
approaching a golden "bronze." Plant erect, 28 in. (71 cm) dia.,
22 in. (56 cm) high. Leaf 9 by 8 in. (23 by 20 cm), veins 12,

yellow (lutescent), not variegated, cordate, cupped, very
rugose. Scape 30 in. (76 cm), bare, straight. Flower medium,
bell-shaped, white, flowers during average period, fertile.
[H. 'Tokudama' hybrid].

H. 'Middle Ridge' Boonstra/Lewis/Ruh IRA/1979.
AHS-III/16A. (Plates 80, 170).
Plant is a select form of H. 'Undulata Univittata' with wide
leaf. Plant 28 in. (71 cm) dia., 16 in. (40.5 cm) high. Leaf 6 by 5
in. (15 by 13 cm), veins 9, medium two-tone green, center
streaky white and white, cordate, wavy. Scape 42 in. (106.5
cm), foliated, oblique. Flower medium, funnel-shaped,
lavender, flowers during average period, sterile.
HN: H. 'Ella Sedgwick' Sedgwick 1936.
H. 'Undulata Middle Ridge'.
[H. 'Undulata Univittata' derivative wide leaf].

H. 'Midwest Gold' Cooley IRA/1969.
AHS-II/11B.
Plant 34 in. (86.5 cm) dia., 18 in. (46 cm) high. Leaf 9 by 9
in. (23 by 23 cm), veins 12, yellow (lutescent), not variegated,
cordate, cupped-rugose. Scape 22 in. (56 cm), bare, straight.
Flower medium, bell-shaped, white, flowers during average
period, fertile.
HN: H. sieboldiana Yellow grex.
[H. sieboldiana 'Aureomarginata' × H. 'Tokudama'].

H. 'Midwest Majesty' Minks IRA/1983.
AHS-II/8B.
Plant 24 in. (61 cm) dia., 16 in. (40.5 cm) high. Leaf 10 by 6
in. (25.5 by 15 cm), veins 8, chartreuse, green variegated,
ovate-cordate, cupped, flat. Scape 42 in. (106.5 cm), bare,
straight. Flower medium, bell-shaped, white, flowers during
average period, fertile.
[H. 'Gold Regal' mutation].

H. 'Mikado' Aden IRA/1982.
AHS-I/1B.
Plant looks very much like H. montana f. macrophylla (Plate
46), which see. Plant 50 in. (127 cm) dia., 38 in. (96.5 cm) high.
Leaf 18 by 10 in. (46 by 25.5 cm), veins 18, medium green, not
variegated, cordate, ribbed. Scape 48 in. (122 cm), bare,
straight. Flower medium, funnel-shaped, white, flowers
during average period, fertile.
[H. montana f. aureomarginata × H. 'Big Sam'].
[H. montana f. macrophylla form].

H. 'Mildred S. Brown'.

H. 'Mildred Seaver' Vaughn IRA/1981.
AHS-III/16B.
Plant registered as a small plant with yellow-mottled
leaves. The plant in the trade is not mottled and may have to be
renamed. Plant 30 in. (76 cm) dia., 14 in. (35.5 cm) high. Leaf 8
by 5 in. (20 by 13 cm), veins 9, medium green, (registered with
yellow mottling) margin yellowish white, cordate, flat, some
leaves rugose. Scape 26 in. (66 cm), foliated, straight. Flower
medium, funnel-shaped, lavender, flowers during average
period, fertile.
[H. 'Vaughn 73-2' × H. sieboldiana 'Frances Williams'].

H. 'Mille Fleure' O'Harra.
Plant has branched scapes and many flowers.

H. 'Ming Dynasty' O'Harra.
Plant has very round, rugose-cupped leaves. Veins 15.
[H. sieboldiana line].

H. **'Ming Jade'** Syre-Herz IRA/1986.
  AHS-II/7A.
    Plant 48 in. (122 cm) dia., 20 in. (51 cm) high. Leaf 10 by 8 in. (25.5 by 20 cm), veins 16, blue-green, not variegated, cordate, rugose. Scape 48 in. (122 cm), foliated, straight. Flower medium, bell-shaped, white, flowers during average period, fertile.
[*H. sieboldiana* hybrid].

H. **'Minnesota Weather'** Kiehne IRA/1980.

H. **'Minnie Bell'** Benedict IRA 1985.
  AHS-V/28B.
    Plant 10 in. (25.5 cm) dia., 6 in. (15 cm) high. Leaf 3 by 1 in. (7.5 by 2.5 cm), veins 3, medium green, margin yellowish white, lanceolate, flat. Scape 14 in. (35.5 cm), foliated, straight. Flower medium, funnel-shaped, lavender, flowers during summer period, fertile.
[*H.* 'Neat Splash' × *H.* 'Neat Splash'].

H. **'Minnie Klopping'** Klopping 1968 Arett IRA/1975.
  AHS-III/13A.   (Figure 4-30).
    Plant 14 in. (35.5 cm) dia., 8 in. (20 cm) high. Leaf 3.0 by 2.5 in. (7.5 by 6 cm), veins 9, medium green, not variegated, cordate, flat. Scape 20 in. (51 cm), foliated, straight. Flower medium, bell-shaped, purple, flowers during average period, fertile.
HN: *H.* 'Klopping No. 120'.
    H. 'Fortunei Minnie Klopping'.
[*H.* 'Fortunei' derivative].

Figure 4-30. *H.* 'Minnie Klopping'; general habit (Soules garden/Schmid)

H. minor 'Alba' hort. incorrect (not *H. minor* f. *alba* Maekawa).
    This name has been used incorrectly and persistently in horticulture for *H. sieboldii* 'Alba', the white-flowered form of *H. sieboldii*. There is also a white-flowered form of *H. minor* which has the correct name *H. minor* f. *alba*, here reduced to cultivar form as *H. minor* 'Alba'. The latter has heart-shaped leaves and ridges on the scape, while the former has lanceolate leaves and no ridges on the scape. The name *H. minor* 'Alba' should be used for the white-margined form of *H. minor* only; its use with *H. sieboldii* is incorrect.
HN: *H.* 'Minor Alba' incorrect.
(see *H. sieboldii* 'Alba').
(see also *H. minor* 'Alba').

H. minor **'Goldbrook'**.

H. **'Minuta'** Soules.
    Plant name is illegitimate per the ICNCP due to its Latin

form. This taxon is a selected form of *H. venusta* and virtually identical to the species clone in commerce (Figure 3-78). There is a much larger plant in commerce, incorrectly called *H.* 'Minuta' because it is not conspecific with *H. venusta*.
(see *H. venusta*).

H. **'Misty Morning'** Kuk's Forest IRA/1986.
  AHS-IV/19A.
    Plant 18 in. (46 cm) dia., 8 in. (20 cm) high. Leaf 4 by 3 in. (10 by 7.5 cm), veins 7, medium green, not variegated, cordate, flat. Scape 16 in. (40.5 cm), bare, straight. Flower medium, funnel-shaped, lavender, flowers during average period, fertile.
[*H. venusta* hybrid].

H. **'Misty Waters'** Fisher 1978 IRA/1986.
  AHS-II/9A.
    Plant is a large blue-green *H. sieboldiana* form. Has a silvery sheen above and below.
[*H. sieboldiana* hybrid].

H. **'Miyakodori'**.
都鳥
(see *H.* 'Koryu').

H. **'Moerheim'**.
HN: *H.* 'Moorheim'.
(see *H.* 'Antioch').

H. 'Moerheimi' incorrect.
(see *H.* 'Antioch').

H. 'Moerheimii' incorrect.
(see *H.* 'Antioch').

H. **'Mogul'** Savory IRA/1988.
  AHS-III/13A.
    Plant 15 in. (38 cm) dia., 12 in. (31 cm) high. Leaf 5 by 4 in. (13 by 10 cm), veins 10, medium green, not variegated, cordate, cupped-rugose. Scape 16 in. (40.5 cm), foliated, straight. Flower medium, bell-shaped, lavender, flowers during average period.
[*H.* 'August Moon' × *H.* 'Tokudama'].

H. montana **'Aureomarginata'**.
H. montana f. *aureomarginata*.

H. montana **'Emerald'** Simpers.
[*H. montana* form].

H. montana **'Gohonmatsu Fukurin'**.

H. montana **'Haru No Yume'**.
(see *H.* 'Haru No Yume').

H. montana **'Hatsushimo'**.
(see *H.* 'Hatsushimo').

H. montana **'Hatsuyuki Nishiki'**.
(see *H.* 'Hatsuyuki Nishiki').

H. montana **'Kurumazaki'**.

H. montana **'Liliiflora'**.
H. montana var. *liliiflora*.

H. montana **'O Fuji Fukurin'**.

H. montana 'Ogon'.

H. montana 'Ogon Fukurin'.

H. montana 'Praeflorens'.
H. montana var. *praeflorens*.

H. montana 'Sagae'.

H. montana 'Shirobana'.

H. montana 'Shirofukurin'.

H. montana 'Taika'.

H. montana 'Transiens'.
H. montana var. *transiens*.

H. montana 'Tsunotori Fukurin'.

H. montana 'Urajiro'.

H. montana 'Yae'.

H. 'Montreal' Montreal Botanic Garden 1936 IRA/1983.
    AHS-IV/19A.
    Plant erect, 12 in. (31 cm) dia., 12 in. (31 cm) high. Leaf 8 by 2 in. (20 by 5 cm), veins 5, medium green, not variegated, lanceolate, flat. Scape 26 in. (66 cm), bare, straight. Flower medium, funnel-shaped, purple striped, flowers during average period, fertile. A yellow form exists.
HN: *H.* 'Japan Boy' UK.
    H. 'Japonica Blue'.
    H. montrealensis nom. nudum 'Montreal' 1936 hort. incorrect.
[*H. rectifolia* × *H. ventricosa* al hybrid incorrect].
[*H. rectifolia* × *H. sieboldii* hybrid].

H. 'Moon Glow' Anderson IRA/1977.
    AHS-III/14B.   (Plate 132).
    Plant is smaller than *H.* 'Moonlight' and the leaves are more cupped. Plant 30 in. (76 cm) dia., 20 in. (51 cm) high. Leaf 7 by 5 in. (18 by 13 cm), veins 10, light yellow (viridescent), margin white, cordate, slightly cupped. Scape 28 in. (71 cm), foliated, straight. Flower medium, funnel-shaped, lavender, flowers during average period, fertile.

H. 'Moon Shadow' Savory IRA/1988.
    AHS-IV/20A.
    Plant 16 in. (41 cm) dia., 12 in. (30.5 cm) high. Leaf 4.5 by 1.5 in. (11.5 by 6 cm), veins 3(or 4), whitish yellow, margin green, lanceolate, flat. Scape 20 in. (51 cm), foliated, straight. Flower medium, funnel-shaped, purple striped, flowers during summer period, fertile.
HN: *H.* 'Moon Shadows'.
[*H.* 'Butter Rim' × hybrid].

H. 'Moonlight' Banyai IRA/1977.
    AHS-III/14A.   (Plate 133).
    Plant 36 in. (91.5 cm) dia., 20 in. (51 cm) high. Leaf 7 by 5 in. (18 by 13 cm), veins 10, yellow (viridescent), margin white, cordate, flat. Scape 28 in. (71 cm), foliated, straight. Flower medium, funnel-shaped, lavender, flowers during average period, fertile.
[*H.* 'Gold Standard' mutation].

H. 'Moonshine' Savory IRA/1988.
    AHS-II/11B.
    Plant 44 in. (112 cm) dia., 26 in. (66 cm) high. Leaf 10 by 9 in. (25.5 by 23 cm), veins 14, chartreuse, not variegated, cordate, flat-rugose. Scape 50 in. (127 cm), bare, straight. Flower medium, funnel-shaped, lavender, flowers during average period.
[*H.* 'Piedmont Gold' mutation].

H. 'Moscow Blue' Arett IRA/1986.
    AHS-III/15B.
    Plant 24 in. (61 cm) dia., 20 in. (51 cm) high. Leaf 6 by 6 in. (15 by 15 cm), veins 13, blue-green, not variegated, cordate, cupped-rugose. Scape 26 in. (66 cm), bare, straight. Flower medium, bell-shaped, white, flowers during average period, fertile.
[*H.* 'Tokudama' hybrid].

H. 'Mount Fuji' Wilkins IRA/1989.
    AHS-II/7A.
    Plant 48 in. (122 cm) dia., 20 in. (51 cm) high. Leaf 10 by 8 in. (25.5 by 20 cm), veins 16, blue-green, not variegated, cordate, rugose. Scape 48 in. (122 cm), foliated, straight. Flower medium, bell-shaped, white, flowers during average period, fertile.
[*H. sieboldiana* hybrid].

H. 'Mount Hood' Minks IRA/1984.
    AHS-III/16A.
    Plant has medium green leaves with an albescent margin that starts green and turns white later.

H. 'Mount Kirishima' UK Hodgkins.
    (see *H.* 'Kirishima').

H. 'Mount Royal' Montreal Botanic Garden 1936 IRA/1983.
    AHS-IV/19A.
    Plant is a selected clone of *H. sieboldii* 'Alba', the white-flowered form of the species. Plant erect, 10 in. (25.5 cm) dia., 8 in. (20 cm) high. Leaf 3 by 1.5 in. (7.5 by 4 cm), veins 3, medium green, not variegated, lanceolate, flat. Scape 22 in. (56 cm), bare, straight. Flower medium, funnel-shaped, white, flowers during average period, fertile.
HN: *H.* 'Japan Girl' UK.
    H. 'Japonica White'.
    H. montrealensis nom. nudum 'Mount Royal' 1936 hort. incorrect.
[*H. rectifolia* × *H. ventricosa* al hybrid incorrect].
[*H. sieboldii* hybrid].

H. 'Mount Tsukuba' hort.
    Plant is a form of *H. montana* collected on the mountain for which it is named.

H. 'Mountain Snow' Zilis IRA/1988.
    AHS-II/10A.
    Plant 60 in. (152.5 cm) dia., 28 in. (71 cm) high. Leaf 14 by 8 in. (35.5 by 20 cm), veins 13, medium green, margin white, cordate, flat-wavy. Scape 40 in. (101.5 cm), bare, straight. Flower medium, funnel-shaped, white, flowers during average period, fertile.
[*H. montana* 'Aureomarginata' mutation].
    (see also *H. montana* 'Shirofukurin').

H. 'Mukayama' hort. UK.
    Plant name is an incorrect synonym.
    (see *H. nakaiana*).

H. **'Muriel Seaver Brown'** Seaver IRA/1984.
AHS-II/9B.
Plant 36 in. (91.5 cm) dia., 20 in. (51 cm) high. Leaf 15 by 8 in. (38 by 20 cm), veins 17, slightly blue-green, not variegated, cordate to ovate-cordate, rugose. Scape 26 in. (66 cm), foliated, straight. Flower medium, bell-shaped, lavender, flowers during average period, fertile.
[*H.* 'Wagon Wheels' hybrid].
[*H. sieboldiana* hybrid]

N

H. **'Nagaeto'** UK/Japan.
Plant is a small, rapidly growing, all-green cultivar of uncertain parentage.
HN: *H.* 'Nageto'.

H. **'Nakafu Tsugaru Komachi'** Japan.
中斑津軽小町
Plant is the aureonebulosa form of *H.* 'Tsugaru Komachi.' Has beautiful yellow variegation. It is also smaller and less vigorous.
JN: *Nakafu Tsugaru Komachi (Koba) Giboshi* hort.
[*H. sieboldii* hybrid].

H. nakaiana **'Ogon'**.
(see also *H. nakaiana* 'Golden').

H. nakaiana **'Shirofukurin'**.

H. **'Nakaimo'** Japan IRA/1986.
AHS-III/13A.   (Figures 2-33, F-4; Plates 157, 181).
Plant is one of the best-blooming hostas with large white capitate translucent buds and bracts. Developed at the Imperial Botanic Garden in Tokyo and imported into the United States before 1939 by Pearce Seed Company, Moorestown, New Jersey. Due to a mix up at the nursery, a hosta with lanceolate leaves and purple flowers is also in commerce under this name, but it is not this taxon which has wide cordate leaves.
Plant 32 in. (81.5 cm) dia., 22 in. (56 cm) high. Leaf 9 by 6 in. (23 by 15 cm), veins 9, dull green, not variegated, cordate, flat. Scape 34 in. (86.5 cm), foliated, oblique. Flower medium, bell-shaped, purple, flowers during average period, fertile.
HN: *H.* 'Nakhima' incorrect.
[*H. capitata* hybrid al.].
[*H. nakaiana* hybrid].

H. **'Nakaimo Minor'** Japan.
Plant name is an incorrect synonym.
(see *H. minor*).

H. **'Nakiomi'**.
Plant name is an incorrect spelling for *H.* 'Nakaimo'.

H. **'Nameoki'** Hensen 1985.
Plant was named as a separate taxon by Hensen (1985). It originated in North America, probably with Krossa, and differs from *H.* 'Nakaimo' by a slightly smaller leaf size. It may be the same plant or a very similar clone with an incorrectly formulated name.

H. **'Nancy Lindsay'** Grenfell/BHHS IRA/1988.
AHS-III/17A.
Plant is named for the late British hosta enthusiast and collector. A mosaic mutant, speckled with dull yellow color on a green background. It turns green in summer and may be unstable as many of the *H.* 'Fortunei Hyacinthina' mutations are. Reportedly similar to *H.* 'Windsor Gold'.
HN: *H.* 'Fortunei Aurea' Longstock form incorrect.
     H. 'Windsor Gold'.
[*H.* 'Fortunei Hyacinthina' mutation].

H. **'Nancy Minks'** Minks No. 747 IRA/1986.
  · AHS-III/14A.
Plant is a medium-size cultivar with rugose leaves that have a yellowish white center and blue-green margins.
HN: *H.* 'Winners Circle'.

H. **'Naomi'** Klose.
Plant is one of the German Tardiana's (see *H.* Tardiana grex) with lavender flowers and large blue-grey leaves. "Naomi" is a female given name.
HN: *H.* Tardiana grex.
[*H.* 'Tardiflora' × *H. sieboldiana* 'Elegans'].
(see also *H.* Tardiana grex).

H. **'Neat and Tidy'** Simpers IRA/1980.
AHS-III/13B.   (Figure 4-31).
Plant 34 in. (86.5 cm) dia., 16 in. (40.5 cm) high. Leaf 9 by 9 in. (23 by 23 cm), veins 12, blue-green, not variegated, cordate, rugose-twisted. Scape 22 in. (56 cm), foliated, straight. Flower medium, bell-shaped, white, flowers during average period, fertile.
[*H. sieboldiana* form].
[*H. (sieboldiana)* 'Golden Circles' hybrid].

Figure 4-31. *H.* 'Neat and Tidy'; general habit (Langdon garden/Schmid)

H. **'Neat Splash'** Aden IRA/1978.
AHS-IV/22B.   (Figure 4-32).
Plant is a highly variegated cultivar which will revert to the stable margined form *H.* 'Neat Splash Rim', which see. Plant 22 in. (56 cm) dia., 14 in. (35.5 cm) high. Leaf 7 by 4 in. (18 by 10 cm), veins 7, medium green, streaky yellow, ovate, flat. Scape 28 in. (71 cm). Flower medium, funnel-shaped, lavender, flowers during average period, fertile.

H. **'Neat Splash Rim'** AHS NC IRA/1986.
AHS-IV/22B.   (Figure 4-32; Plate 93).
Plant 24 in. (61 cm) dia., 14 in. (35.5 cm) high. Leaf 7 by 4 in. (18 by 10 cm), veins 7, medium green, margin yellowish white streaking to center, ovate-lanceolate, flat. Scape 28 in.

(71 cm) Flower medium, funnel-shaped, lavender, flowers during average period, fertile.
[*H.* 'Neat Splash' mutation].

Figure 4-32. *H.* 'Neat Splash'; general habit; some leaves have reverted to the margined form, *H.* 'Neat Splash Rim' (Coney garden/Schmid)

H. 'Needle Point' Jones 1986.
Plant 12 in. (31 cm) dia., 10 in. (25.5 cm) high. Leaf 4 by 2 in. (10 by 5 cm), veins 6, medium green, not variegated, ovate, flat. Scape 24 in. (61 cm), bare, straight. Flower medium, funnel-shaped, white, flowers during average period, fertile.

H. 'Netta Statham' Bloom.
Plant has yellow leaves with a green margin.
[*H. ventricosa* 'Aureomarginata' mutant].

H. 'New Tradition' Zilis IRA/1988.
AHS-IV/20A.
Plant 32 in. (81.5 cm) dia., 14 in. (35.5 cm) high. Leaf 6 by 2 in. (15 by 5 cm), veins 6, white (albescent), green margin, lanceolate, flat-wavy. Scape 24 in. (61 cm), bare, straight. Flower medium, funnel-shaped, lavender, flowers during summer period.
[*H.* 'Lancifolia' mutation].

H. 'New Wave' Lohman/Zilis IRA/1988.
AHS-IV/19A.
Plant 24 in. (61 cm) dia., 12 in. (31 cm) high. Leaf 5 by 3 in. (13 by 7.5 cm), veins 9, medium (lime) green, not variegated, lanceolate, flat-wavy. Scape 26 in. (66 cm), bare, straight. Flower medium, funnel-shaped, lavender, flowers during average period.
[*H.* 'Sum and Substance' × *H. venusta* hybrid].

H. 'Nicola' Eason IRA/1984.
AHS-IV/19A.
Plant is the only green-leaved cultivar of the *H.* Tardiana grex to be named in the United Kingdom. Its flowers are said to be lavender, ranging to pink. Plant 12 in. (31 cm) dia., 12 in. (31 cm) high. Leaf 6 by 3 in. (15 by 7.5 cm), veins 7, medium green, not variegated, ovate, flat. Scape 20 in. (51 cm), foliated, straight. Flower medium, funnel-shaped, lavender, flowers during average period, fertile.
HN: *H.* 'Nicole' incorrect.
H. Tardiana grex TF 2 × 32 (?) ad int.
[*H.* 'Tardiflora' × *H. sieboldiana* 'Elegans'].
(see also *H.* Tardiana grex).

H. 'Nifty Fifty' Benedict IRA/1986.
AHS-II/10B.
Plant 36 in. (91.5 cm) dia., 24 in. (61 cm) high. Leaf 12 by 8 in. (31 by 20 cm), veins 16, blue-green, margin yellow, cor-

date, rugose. Scape 28 in. (71 cm), foliated, straight. Flower medium, bell-shaped, lavender, flowers during average period, fertile.
HN: *H. sieboldiana* Aureomarginata group.
[*H.* 'Dorothy Benedict' mutation].

H. nigrescens 'Elatior'.

H. nigrescens 'Krossa Regal'.
(see *H.* 'Krossa Regal').

H. 'Nioi No Mai' Japan.
匂いの舞
Nioi No Mai (Giboshi), the "dance of fragrance (hosta)," is a large-flowered fragrant hosta with lavender flowers and trumpet-shaped lobes. Vigorous.
JN: *Nioi No Mai Giboshi* hort.

H. 'Noahs Ark' Hatfield.
Plant is similar to the species, but leaves are more elongated. Plant 44 in. (112 cm) dia., 20 in. (51 cm) high. Leaf 12 by 9 in. (31 by 23 cm), veins 16, blue-green, not variegated, cordate, rugose. Scape 34 in. (86.5 cm), foliated, straight. Flower medium, bell-shaped, white, flowers during average period, sterile.
[*H. sieboldiana* form].

H. 'Noel' Benedict IRA/1983.
AHS-IV/20A.
Plant erect, 6 in. (15 cm) dia., 6 in. (15 cm) high. Leaf 4 by 1 in. (10 by 2.5 cm), veins 3, white (albescent), margin green, lanceolate, flat. Scape 16 in. (40.5 cm), bare, straight. Flower medium, funnel-shaped, purple striped, flowers during summer period, fertile.
[*H. sieboldii* 'Beatrice' derivative].

H. 'Nokogiriyama' Klose (?).

H. 'Nokon No Yuki' Japan.
JN: *Nokon No Yuki Giboshi* hort.
(see *H.* 'Zansetsu').

H. 'Nordatlantic' Klose.
Plant is one of the German Tardiana's (see *H.* Tardiana grex). The name means *H.* 'North Atlantic' (Smith/ Archibald?).
HN: *H.* Tardiana grex.
[*H.* 'Tardiflora' × *H. sieboldiana* 'Elegans'].
(see also *H.* Tardiana grex).

H. 'North Atlantic' Smith/Archibald.
(see *H.* 'Nordatlantic' Klose).

H. 'North Hills' Meissner/Summers 1964 IRA/1986.
AHS-III/16B.
Plant 36 in. (91.5 cm) dia., 20 in. (51 cm) high. Leaf 9 by 7 in. (23 by 18 cm), veins 9, medium green, margin white, cordate, flat. Scape 40 in. (101.5 cm), foliated, oblique. Flower medium, funnel-shaped, lavender, flowers during average period, sterile.
HN: *H.* 'Fortunei Albomarginata' group.
H. 'Fortunei North Hills'.
Summers No. 20.

H. 'Northern Halo'™ Walters Gardens IRA/1984.
AHS-II/10B. (Plate 134).
AHS ALAHOSO Bowl, 1988, exhibited by Lloyd Jones.

Plant 34 in. (86.5 cm) dia., 20 in. (51 cm) high. Leaf 12 by 10 in. (31 by 25.5 cm), veins 16, blue-green, margin white, cordate, cupped-rugose. Scape 30 in. (76 cm), foliated, straight. Flower medium, bell-shaped, white, flowers during average period. [*H. sieboldiana* 'Elegans' mutation].

H. 'Northern Lights'™ Walters Gardens IRA/1984.

AHS-III/14A.   (Plate 135).

AHS Nancy Minks Award, 1988. Plant 30 in. (76 cm) dia., 16 in. (40.5 cm) high. Leaf 9 by 6 in. (23 by 15 cm), veins 10, white (albescent), margin green, cordate, rugose. Scape 28 in. (71 cm), foliated, straight. Flower medium, bell-shaped, white, flowers during average period, sterile.
HN: *H. sieboldiana* Mediovariegata group.
[*H. sieboldiana* 'Elegans' mutation].

H. 'Northern Mist'™ Walters Gardens IRA/1988.

AHS-II/10A.

Plant has unique, streaky, white-on-green center and is considered a member of the *H. sieboldiana* Mediovariegata group but difficult to classify. Plant 36 in. (91.5 cm) dia., 30 in. (76 cm) high. Leaf 11 by 10 in. (28 by 25.5 cm), veins 16, green, streaky white and light green on dark grey-green background, a margin sometimes shows, round-cordate, rugose-wavy. Scape 36 in. (91.5 cm), bare, straight. Flower medium, bell-shaped, white, flowers during average period, fertile.
HN: *H. sieboldiana* Mediovariegata group.
[*H. sieboldiana* 'Elegans' mutation].

H. 'Northern Star'™ Walters Gardens.

Plant has leaves with chartreuse center with blue-green margins.
HN: *H. sieboldiana* Mediovariegata group.
[*H. sieboldiana* 'Elegans' mutation].

H. 'Northern Sunray'™ Walters Gardens IRA/1987.

AHS-II/8B.

Plant has leaves with center greenish (viridescent) white, becomes blue-green. Plant 40 in. (101.5 cm) dia., 18 in. (46 cm) high. Leaf 12 by 8 in. (31 by 20 cm), veins 8, white (viridescent), margin green, cordate, rugose. Scape 24 in. (61 cm), foliated, straight. Flower medium, bell-shaped, white, flowers during average period, fertile.
HN: *H. sieboldiana* Mediovariegata group.
[*H. sieboldiana* 'Elegans' mutation].

H. 'Number One' Lighty IRA/1987.

AHS-IV/21A.

Plant 40 in. (101.5 cm) dia., 18 in. (46 cm) high. Leaf 5 by 4 in. (13 by 10 cm), veins 9, blue-green, not variegated, cordate, rugose. Scape 24 in. (61 cm), foliated, straight. Flower medium, bell-shaped, lilac, flowers during average period, fertile.
[*H. venusta* hybrid].

O

H. 'O Fuji Fukurin' Japan.

大富士覆輪

Plant is a yellow-margined and yellow-splashed form of *H. montana* found on lava fields near Gotemba in Shizuoka Prefecture. Multiplies rapidly.
HN: *H. montana* 'O Fuji Fukurin'.
JN: *O Fuji Fukurin Giboshi* hort.

H. 'Oakview' Stone/Ruh IRA/1987.

AHS-IV/19B.

Plant has glossy leaves, flowers bunched at tip. Plant 20 in. (51 cm) dia., 8 in. (20 cm) high. Leaf 4 by 3 in. (10 by 7.5 cm) veins 8, green, not variegated, cordate, flat. Scape 18 in. (46 cm), foliated, straight. Flower medium, bell-shaped, white, flowers during average period, fertile.
HN: *H. 'DSM No. 16'*.

H. 'Obscura' hort. incorrect.

Plant name is an incorrect synonym.
(see *H. bella*).

H. 'Obscura Aureomarginata' hort. incorrect.

Plant name is an incorrect synonym.
HN: *H. 'Fortunei Obscura Aureomarginata'*.
        H. 'Fortunei Obscura Marginata'.
(see *H. 'Fortunei Aureomarginata'*).

H. 'October Skies' Bemis.

H. 'Oga' Japan.

Oga Giboshi, the "hosta from Oga," is purported to be from Oga Hanto (Oga Peninsula) in Akita Prefecture of northwestern Honshu. It is a *H. sieboldii/H. rectifolia* intermediate. Plant 14 in. (35.5 cm) dia., 10 in. (25.5 cm) high. Leaf 4 by 2 in. (10 by 5 cm), veins 5, medium green, slightly pruinose, not variegated, ovate, flat. Scape 24 in. (61 cm), bare, straight. Flower medium, funnel-shaped, lavender, flowers during average period, fertile.
JN: *Oga Giboshi*.

H. 'Ogata Bunchoko'.

大型文鳥香ギボウシ

Ogata Bunchoko Giboshi is a Japanese synonym for *H. 'Helonioides Albopicta'*, which see.
(see *H. 'Helonioides Albopicta'*).

H. 'Ogon' Japan.

(see *H. 'Wogon'*).

H. 'Ogon Kabitan' Japan.

(see *H. 'Ogon Koba'*).

H. 'Ogon Koba' Japan.

(see *H. sieboldii* 'Subcrocea').
(see also *H. 'Ogon Kabitan'*).

H. 'Ogon Sagae' Japan.

Plant is a Japanese cultivar similar to *H. 'Sagae'* (*H. fluctuans* 'Variegated') with yellow, not variegated leaves. It probably is a seedling or sport of the latter.
[*H. 'Sagae'* derivative].

H. 'Ogon Waisei' Japan/Soules.

Ogon Waisei Giboshi, the "dwarf-growing gold hosta," is *H. sieboldii* 'Kabitan' under a fancy Japanese cultivar name.
HN: *H. 'Ougan Waisei'* incorrect.
        H. 'Ougon Waisei'.
        H. 'Wogan Waisei' incorrect.
JN: *Ogon Waisei Giboshi* hort.
(see *H. sieboldii* 'Kabitan').

H. 'Okutama Nishiki' Japan.

オヒガンギボウシ

Okutama Nishiki Giboshi, the "glorious (brocade) hosta from Okutama," was found in Tokyo Prefecture. It is a whitish yellow streaked form of *H. longipes*. Viridescent.

JN: *Okutama Nishiki Giboshi* hort.
[*H. longipes* mutation].

H. 'Olga Thiemann Dwarf Glaucous' incorrect.
(see *H.* 'Helen Field Fischer').

H. 'Olga Thiemann Dwarf Grey Leaf' incorrect.
(see *H.* 'Helen Field Fischer').

H. 'Olgas Shiny Leaf' Thiemann/Fisher.
    Plant 12 in. (31 cm) dia., 6 in. (15 cm) high. Leaf 5 by 1.5 in. (13 by 4 cm), veins 3, medium green, not variegated, lanceolate, flat. Scape 20 in. (51 cm), bare, straight. Flower medium, bell-shaped, purple striped, flowers during average period, fertile.
HN: *H.* 'Shiny Leaf'.
    H. 'Shiny Leaf Hybrid'.
[*H. sieboldii* hybrid].

H. 'Olive Bailey Langdon' O'Harra.
    One of the selected clones of the *H. sieboldiana* Aureomarginata group. Plant is 44 in. (112 cm) dia., 24 in. (61 cm) high. Leaf 14 by 12 in. (35.5 by 31 cm), veins 16, blue-green, margin yellow, cordate, rugose. Scape 30 in. (76 cm), bare, straight. Flower medium, bell-shaped, white, flowers during average period, fertile.
HN: *H.* 'Cover Girl'.
    H. 'Frances Williams' Des Moines Form.
    H. sieboldiana Aureomarginata group.
[*H. sieboldiana* mutation].

H. 'Oliver' O'Harra.
    Plant is small with yellowish white margins.
[*H. sieboldii* form].

H. 'Olympic Gold' Banyai IRA/1986.
    AHS-III/17A.
    Plant 22 in. (56 cm) dia., 14 in. (35.5 cm) high. Leaf 8 by 6 in. (20 by 15 cm), veins 9, yellow (lutescent), not variegated, cordate, flat. Scape 22 in. (56 cm), bare, straight. Flower medium, bell-shaped, white, flowers during average period, fertile.

H. 'Omaha Gold' Geissler.
(see *H.* 'Aksarben').

H. 'On Stage' Aden IRA/1986.
    AHS-III/14B.
    Plant has yellow primary leaf color and a two-tone dark green margin streaking to center. Looks very much like and may be closely related to *H.* 'Choko Nishiki', which see. The latter is in Japan considered a *H. montana* mutation. Plant 24 in. (61 cm) dia., 14 in. (35.5 cm) high. Leaf 8 by 5 in. (20 by 13 cm), veins 8, white or light yellow (albescent), margin two-tone green, cordate, rugose. Scape 24 in. (61 cm), bare, straight. Flower medium, funnel-shaped, lavender, flowers during average period, fertile.
HN: *H.* 'Choko Nishiki' sim.
[*H. montana* derivative ad int].

H. 'Opipara'.
H. opipara.

H. 'Opipara Bill Brincka'.
(see *H.* 'Bill Brincka).

H. 'Opipara Koriyama' Japan.
(see *H.* 'Koriyama).

H. 'Opipara Noble One'.
H. opipara.

H. 'Orange Joy' Carpenter IRA/1979.
    AHS-IV/23B.
HN: *H.* 'Orange Gold'.

H. 'Oriana' Smith/Eason 1966.
    Plant is a light yellowish cultivar similar to *H.* 'Golden Haze'. Reported to be one of Smith's GL series (see Chapter 5).

H. 'Oshkosh' Fisher.
HN: *H.* 'Fisher No. 51-70'.

H. 'Osprey' Smith BHHS IRA/1988.
    AHS-IV/21B.
    Plant has cordate leaves, 10 veins, white flowers on 14 in. (35.5 cm) scape.
HN: *H.* Tardiana grex TF 2 × 14.
[*H.* 'Tardiflora' × *H. sieboldiana* 'Elegans'].
(see also *H.* Tardiana grex).

H. 'Otome No Ka' Japan.
乙女の香
    Otome No Ka Giboshi, the "fragrant maiden hosta," is a day-blooming dwarf with fragrant purple flowers.
JN: *Otome No Ka Giboshi* hort.

H. 'Ovata' hort.
    Plant name has been persistently used for different taxa and is a nomen confusum.

H. 'Oxheart' Minks IRA/1976.
    AHS-III/13A.
    Plant 18 in. (46 cm) dia., 10 in. (25.5 cm) high. Leaf 7 by 5 in. (18 by 13 cm), veins 8, medium green, not variegated, ovate, wavy. Scape 24 in. (61 cm), foliated, straight. Flower medium, bell-shaped, white, flowers during average period, fertile.
[*H.* 'Green Platter' × *H. nakaiana*].

P

H. 'Pagoda' Smith/BHHS IRA/1988.
    AHS-III/18A.
    Plant is one of the Smith GL series and similar to *H.* 'Gold Haze'.
HN: *H.* 'Smith GL(W) 12'.
    Wisley No. 8214401 through 8214403.
[*H.* 'Fortunei Aurea' × *H. sieboldii* 'Kabitan'].
(see also *H.* 'Gold Haze').

H. 'Paintbrush' Minks IRA/1976.
    AHS-III/14B.
    Plant erect, 10 in. (25.5 cm) dia., 8 in. (20 cm) high. Leaf medium, veins 3, medium green, streaky white, lanceolate, flat. Scape 24 in. (61 cm), bare, straight. Flower medium, funnel-shaped, purple striped, flowers during summer period, fertile.
[*H.* 'Undulata' × *H. ventricosa* 'Aureomaculata' al].
[*H. sieboldii* hybrid].

H. 'Painted Lady' Benedict IRA/1984.
    AHS-IV/22A.
    Plant erect, 10 in. dia., 8 in. (25.5 by 20 cm) high. Leaf 4 by

1.5 in. (10 by 4 cm), veins 3, medium green, streaky white, lanceolate, flat. Scape 24 in. (61 cm), bare, straight. Flower medium, funnel-shaped, purple striped, flowers during summer period, fertile.
[*H. sieboldii* mutation].

H. 'Pale Gold' Fisher IRA/1968.
AHS-II/7B.
Plant is pale golden yellow to chartreuse in spring, viridescent. Leaf 7 by 5 in. (18 by 13 cm), pruinose underside.
[*H.* 'Golden Anniversary' hybrid].

H. 'Pancakes' Williams (No. 1023) 1948.
Flat, rounded leaves. Purple flowers.
HN: *H.* 'FRW No. 1023'.
[*H.* 'Decorata' × *H. plantaginea*].

H. 'Park Avenue' Minks.

H. 'Pastures New' Smith.
Plant is similar to *H.* 'Candy Hearts' or *H.* 'Pearl Lake' but smaller. Scapes do not have ridges and the petioles are purple-dotted.
HN: Wisley No. 821458.
[*H. nakaiana* × *H. sieboldiana*].

H. 'Pastures'.
(see *H.* 'Pastures New').

H. 'Paul Aden' Aden.
Plant 22 in. (56 cm) dia., 14 in. (35.5 cm) high. Leaf 7 by 6 in. (18 by 15 cm), veins 8, medium green, streaky white, cordate, flat. Scape 28 in. (71 cm), foliated, straight. Flower large, funnel-shaped, white, fragrant, flowers during average period, fertile.
[*H.* 'Fragrant Candelabra' hybrid].

H. 'Paul Bunyan' Tompkins.   (Figure 4-33).
Plant 42 in. (106.5 cm) dia., 26 in. (66 cm) high. Leaf 11 by 10 in. (28 by 25.5 cm), veins 14, green, not variegated, cordate, ribbed-rugose. Scape 30 in. (76 cm), foliated, straight. Flower medium, bell-shaped, white, flowers during average period, fertile.
[*H. sieboldiana* × *H. montana* hybrid].

Figure 4-33. *H.* 'Paul Bunyan'; general habit; (Kulpa garden/Schmid)

H. 'Paula San Martin' Balletta IRA/1988.
AHS-V/26A.
Plant 8 in. (20 cm) dia., 4 in. (10 cm) high. Leaf 3 by 1.5 in. (7.5 by 4 cm), veins 6, white, (albescent), yellow to chartreuse

margin, ovate, wavy-undulate. Scape 12 in. (31 cm), foliated, straight. Flower medium, lavender, flowers during average period.
[*H.* 'Little Aurora' mutation].

H. 'Pauline' Stone/Ruh IRA/1987.
AHS-IV/19B.
Plant 22 in. (56 cm) dia., 13 in. (33 cm) high. Leaf 6 by 2 in. (15 by 5 cm), veins 5, green, not variegated, lanceolate, flat. Scape 20 in. (51 cm), foliated, oblique. Flower medium, bell-shaped, lavender, flowers during summer period, fertile.
HN: *H.* 'DSM No. 13'.

H. 'Pauline Brac' Weissenberger IRA/1986.
AHS-IV/21B.
Plant 26 in. (66 cm) dia., 10 in. (25.5 cm) high. Leaf 4 by 4 in. (10 by 10 cm), veins 10, blue-green, not variegated, cordate, rugose. Scape 22 in. (56 cm), foliated, straight. Flower medium, funnel-shaped, lavender, flowers during average period, fertile.
[*H.* 'Blue Cadet' hybrid].

H. 'Pauls Glory' Hofer/Ruh IRA/1987.
AHS-III/14A.
Plant has leaves with center yellow, turning whitish. Plant 26 in. (66 cm) dia., 17 in. (43 cm) high. Leaf 6 by 4.5 in. (15 by 11.5 cm), veins 10, yellow (albescent), blue-green margin, cordate, rugose. Scape 24 in. (61 cm), foliated, oblique. Flower medium, bell-shaped, whitish, flowers during average period, fertile.
[*H.* 'Perrys True Blue' mutation].

H. 'Peace' Aden IRA/1987.
AHS-IV/22B.
Plant has leaves with variable white margin, suffused into center. Plant 10 in. (25.5 cm) dia., 5 in. (13 cm) high. Leaf 5 by 1.5 in. (13 by 4 cm), veins 4, blue-green, white margin, cordate, rugose. Scape 12 in. (31 cm), bare, straight. Flower medium, bell-shaped, lavender, flowers during average period, fertile.
[*H.* 'Love Pat'] hybr.

H. 'Pearl Buttons' O'Harra.
Plant is a hybrid selection of *H. venusta*, with spicate flower bud. The leaves are more blue-green and the scape is somewhat shorter than the species. Plant 5 in. (13 cm) dia., 2 in. (5 cm) high. Leaf 2 by 1.5 in. (5 by 4 cm), veins 3 (or 4), medium green with blue cast, not variegated, flat. Scape 8 in. (20 cm), bare, straight. Flower medium, funnel-shaped, flowers during average period, fertile.
[*H. venusta* hybrid].

H. 'Pearl Lake' Piedmont 1974 IRA/1982.
AHS-IV/19A.   (Plate 91).
AHS Alex J. Summers Distinguished Merit Hosta, 1982, selected by Alex J. Summers. The first hosta cultivar to receive this award. Plant 30 in. (76 cm) dia., 14 in. (35.5 cm) high. Leaf 4 by 3.5 in. (10 by 9 cm), veins 9, blue-green, not variegated, cordate, flat. Scape 32 in. (81.5 cm), bare, straight. Flower medium, funnel-shaped, lavender, flowers during average period, fertile.

H. 'Pebble Beach' Woodruff IRA/1972.
AHS-III/14B.
Plant has blue-green leaves which show occasional chartreuse mottling. Leaf 7 by 6 in. (18 by 15 cm), rugose, pruinose underside. Slow grower.

H. **'Peedee Elfin Bells'** Syre-Herz IRA/1987.
　AHS-IV/19B.　　　　　　　　　　(Figure 4-34).
　Plant is a miniature *H. ventricosa*. Reblooms. Much smaller than *H.* 'Little Blue' and with a leaf shape very much like that of *H. ventricosa*. Plant 18 in. (46 cm) dia., 9 in. (23 cm) high. Leaf 4 by 2 in. (10 by 5 cm), veins 4, green, not variegated, cordate, undulate. Scape 24 in. (61 cm), foliated, straight. Flower medium, bell-shaped, purple, flowers during average period, fertile.
[*H. ventricosa* hybrid mutation].

Figure 4-34. *H.* 'Peedee Elfin Bells'; general habit; *H.* 'Little Blue' (right) (Hosta Hill)

H. **'Peedee Gold Flash'** Syre-Herz IRA/1987.
　AHS-IV/23B.
　Plant erect, 18 in. (46 cm) dia., 10 in. (25.5 cm) high. Leaf 4 by 1.5 in. (10 by 4 cm), veins 4, yellow (viridescent), lanceolate, flat. Scape 12 in. (31 cm), foliated, straight. Flower medium, funnel-shaped, purple striped, flowers during average period, fertile.
[*H. sieboldii* 'Kabitan' hybrid].

H. **'Peedee Graymulkin'** Herz IRA/1987.
　AHS-IV/19A.
　Plant has green leaves with grey cast. Reblooms. Plant 18 in. (46 cm) dia., 10 in. (25.5 cm) high. Leaf 4 by 4 in. (10 by 10 cm), veins 8, green, not variegated, cordate, flat. Scape 14 in. (35.5 cm), bare, straight. Flower medium, bell-shaped, lavender, flowers during average period, fertile.
HN: *H.* 'Peedee Gray Mulkin' incorrect.

H. **'Peedee Treasure'** Syre-Herz IRA/1989.
　AHS-IV/23A.
　Plant erect, 15 in. (40 cm) dia., 7 in. (18 cm) high. Leaf 4 by 2 in. (10 by 5 cm), veins 3–4, yellow (viridescent), lanceolate, some rugosity. Scape 18 in. (46 cm), foliated, straight. Flower medium, funnel-shaped, purple striped, flowers during average period, fertile.
[*H.* 'Gold Drop' × *H. ventricosa*].

H. **'Peek-a-Boo'** Aden IRA/1976.
　AHS-III/15B.
　Plant is a selected hybrid with typical *H.* 'Tokudama' form. Leaf blue-green, cupped-rugose.
[*H.* 'Tokudama Aureonebulosa' × *H.* 'Aden No. 355'].

H. **'Peking'**.
　Plant is small and has light green leaves, 4 by 2 in. (10 by 5 cm), with elongated tip.

H. **'Pelham Blue Tump'** Kitchingman IRA/1986.
　AHS-IV/21A.
　Plant 12 in. (31 cm) dia., 6 in. (15 cm) high. Leaf 3 by 2 in.

(7.5 by 5 cm), veins 7, blue-green, not variegated, cordate, rugose. Scape 16 in. (40.5 cm), foliated, straight. Flower medium, funnel-shaped, lavender, flowers during average period, fertile.
[*H.* 'Tokudama' × *H. sieboldiana*].

H. **'Penciled Edge'** Viette.
　(see *H.* 'Viettes Yellow Edge').

H. **'Peoria Knickers'** (incorrect).

H. **'Peppermint Cream'** Hatfield.
　Plant looks like *H.* 'Vanilla Cream', which see, but has a green margin.

H. **'Permanent Wave'** Banyai IRA/1989.
　AHS-IV/19A.
　Plant 32 in. (81.5 cm) dia., 12 in. (30 cm) high. Leaf 7 by 3.5 in. (18 by 9 cm), veins 6, medium green, not variegated, ovate-lanceolate, wavy. Scape 19 in. (48 cm), bare, straight. Flower medium, funnel-shaped, lavender, flowers during average period, fertility(?).

H. **'Perrys True Blue'** Gruelleman/Hofer/Ruh IRA/1981.
　AHS-II/9B.　　　　　　　　　　　(Plate 180).
　Plant is sometimes incorrectly called *H.* 'True Blue', which see. Plant 36 in. (91.5 cm) dia., 22 in. (56 cm) high. Leaf 12 by 9 in. (31 by 23 cm), veins 16, blue-green, not variegated, cordate, rugose. Scape 30 in. (76 cm), bare, straight. Flower medium, bell-shaped, white, flowers during average period, fertile.
HN: *H.* 'True Blue' incorrect.
[*H. sieboldiana* hybrid].

H. **'Peter Pan'** Minks IRA/1980.
　AHS-IV/19A.
　Plant has cupped grey-green leaves.
[*H. nakaiana* × *H.* 'Helen Field Fisher'].

H. **'Petite Gold'** Geissler IRA/1970.
　AHS-IV/23B.
　Plant has leaf color in some areas more chartreuse than yellow. Plant 10 in. (25.5 cm) dia., 6 in. (15 cm) high. Leaf small, veins 8, yellow (lutescent), not variegated, cordate, piecrust margin. Scape 12 in. (31 cm), bare, straight. Flower medium, bell-shaped, white, flowers during average period, fertile.
[*H.* 'Tokudama' form].

H. **'Photo Finish'** Kuk's Forest IRA/1988.
　AHS-III/16B.
　Plant has leaf center that changes from white and green to grey-green. Plant 16 in. (40.5 cm) dia., 10 in. (25.5 cm) high. Leaf 8 by 6 in. (20 by 15 cm), veins 6, green and yellowish white (viridescent) leaf center, green margin, cordate, wavy-undulate. Scape 18 in. (46 cm), foliated, straight. Flower medium, white, flowers during average period, fertile.
[*H.* 'Hoarfrost' hybrid].

H. **'Phyllis Campbell'** Maxted/BHHS IRA/1988.
　AHS-III/16B.
　Plant is a yellow, mediovariegated, viridescent mutant that is reported to be the same as *H.* 'Sharmon'.
HN: *H.* 'Fortunei Phyllis Campbell'.
　Wisley No. 821368.
[*H.* 'Fortunei' mutation].
　(see *H.* 'Sharmon').

H. 'Picta' incorrect.
　　Plant name is an incorrect synonym.
(see *H.* 'Fortunei Albopicta').

H. **'Piecrust Power'** Aden.

H. **'Piedmont Gold'** Piedmont 1974 Stone IRA/1982.
　　AHS-II/11A.   (Plate 136).
　　AHS Eunice Fisher Award, 1978; AHS Midwest Gold
Award, 1988, exhibited by Kenneth Anderson. Plant 40 in.
(101.5 cm) dia., 20 in. (51 cm) high. Leaf 11 by 8 in. (28 by 20
cm), veins 11, yellow (lutescent), not variegated, cordate, flat.
Scape 30 in. (76 cm), bare, straight. Flower medium, funnel-
shaped, white, flowers during average period, fertile.

H. **'Piedmont Stripe'** Goodwin 1989.
　　Plant small. Leaf 3 by 1.5 in. (8 by 4 cm), veins 3(or 4),
green, yellow streaks, lanceolate, flat.

H. **'Pin Stripe'** Vaughn IRA/1983.
　　AHS-III/14A.
　　Plant is a sister seedling of *H.* 'Formal Attire'. Plant 36 in.
(91.5 cm) dia., 26 in. (66 cm) high. Leaf 8 by 6 in. (20 by 15 cm),
veins 12, medium green, streaky white, cordate, rugose. Scape
38 in. (96.5 cm), bare, straight. Flower medium, bell-shaped,
lavender, flowers during average period, fertile.
HN: *H.* 'Pinstripe' incorrect.
[*H.* 'Breeders Choice' × *H.* 'Frances Williams' al].
[*H.* 'William Lachman' × *H.* 'Frances Williams'].

H. **'Pineapple Poll'** Smith BHHS IRA/1988.
　　AHS-IV/19B.
[*H. sieboldiana* × *H.* 'Lancifolia'(?) hybrid].

H. **'Pinwheel'** Savory IRA/1983.
　　AHS-V/28B.
　　Plant 10 in. (25.5 cm) dia., 8 in. (20 cm) high. Leaf 2 by 1 in.
(5 by 2.5 cm), veins 5, viridescent yellowish white, dark green
irregular margin streaking to center, ovate-oblanceolate,
wavy-contorted. Scape 10 in. (25.5 cm), bare, straight. Flower
medium, bell-shaped, lavender, flowers during average
period, fertile.
[*H. venusta* hybrid].

H. **'Pioneer'** Tompkins IRA/1984.
　　AHS-I/1B.
　　Plant 32 in. (81.5 cm) dia., 20 in. (51 cm) high. Leaf 12 by 9
in. (31 by 23 cm), veins 12, medium green, not variegated, cordate, wavy. Scape 34 in. (86.5 cm), foliated, straight. Flowers
medium, funnel-shaped, white, flowers during average
period, fertile.
[*H. montana* hybrid].

H. **'Pipestone'** Johnson.
　　Plant 16 in. (40.5 cm) dia., 10 in. (25.5 cm) high. Leaf 7 by 5
in. (18 by 13 cm), veins 7, medium green, margin white, ovate,
flat. Scape 22 in. (56 cm), foliated, straight. Flower medium,
funnel-shaped, lavender, flowers during average period,
fertile.
[*H.* 'Fortunei Albopicta' mutation].

H. **'Pixie Power'** Aden 1969.
　　Plant 5 in. (13 cm) dia., 3 in. (7.5 cm) high. Leaf 2.5 by 1 in.
(6.5 by 2.5 cm), veins 3, white (albescent) center, wide margin
green, lanceolate, flat. Scape 9 in. (23 cm), bare, straight.
Flower medium, funnel-shaped, purple striped, flowers
during average period, sterile.

H. **'Pizzazz'** Aden IRA/1986.
　　AHS-III/16B.
　　Plant 18 in. (46 cm) dia., 12 in. (31 cm) high. Leaf 7 by 5 in.
(18 by 13 cm), veins 13, medium green, some streaking of
yellow and white, margin white, cordate, rugose. Scape 18 in.
(46 cm), foliated, straight. Flower medium, bell-shaped,
lavender, flowers during average period, fertile.
HN: *H.* 'Pizazz' incorrect.

H. **'Placemat'** Soules 1991.
　　Plant is a large hybrid of *H. sieboldiana* derivation. Leaf 12
by 12 in. (31 by 31 cm), veins 16, blue-green, not variegated,
cordate, rugose. Scape 26 in. (66 cm), bare, straight. Flower
medium, bell-shaped, white, flowers during average period,
fertile.
[*H. sieboldiana* × *H.* 'Tokudama'].

H. plantaginea **'Aphrodite'**.
H. plantaginea f. *aphrodite*.
H. plantaginea var. *plena*.

H. plantaginea **'Flora Plena'**.
(see *H. plantaginea* f. *aphrodite*).

H. plantaginea **'Grandiflora'**.
(see *H. plantaginea*).

H. plantaginea **'Plena'**.
(see *H. plantaginea* f. *aphrodite*).

H. plantaginea **'Stenantha'**.
H. plantaginea f. *stenantha*.

H. **'Platinum Tiara'** Walters Gardens IRA/1987.
　　AHS-IV/20A.
　　AHS Alex J. Summers Distinguished Merit Hosta, 1989,
selected by Eldren Minks. Plant has a variable margin, but
mostly narrow. Plant 14 in. (35.5 cm) dia., 12 in. (31 cm) high.
Leaf 4 by 3 in. (10 by 7.5 cm), veins 5, chartreuse, margin white,
cordate, flat. Scape 26 in. (66 cm), bare, straight. Flower
medium, bell-shaped, purple striped, flowers during average
period, fertile.
[*H.* 'Golden Tiara' mutation].

H. **'Polly Bishop'** Vaughn IRA/1977.
　　AHS-II/9B.
　　Plant has bluish green leaves with tall scapes.
[*H. sieboldiana* 'Frances Williams' × *H. sieboldiana* 'Frances
Williams'].

H. **'Polly Mae'** Savory IRA/1982.
　　AHS-IV/19A.
　　Plant is one of the named selections of *H. sieboldii* 'Alba'.
Plant erect, 22 in. (56 cm) dia., 14 in. (35.5 cm) high. Leaf 5 by
1.5 in. (13 by 4 cm), veins 3, medium green, not variegated,
lanceolate, flat. Scape 28 in. (71 cm), bare, straight. Flower
medium, funnel-shaped, white, flowers during average
period, fertile.
[*H. sieboldii* 'Alba' hybrid].

H. **'Pollyanna'** Banyai IRA/1983.
　　AHS-IV/19A.
　　Plant 12 in. (31 cm) dia., 8 in. (20 cm) high. Leaf 4 by 2 in.
(10 by 5 cm), veins 6, medium green, not variegated, cordate,
flat. Scape 12 in. (31 cm), bare, straight. Flower medium,
funnel-shaped, purple striped, flowers during late period,
fertile.
[*H. sieboldii* f. *spathulata* × *H. longipes*].

H. **'Pooh Bear'** Falstad IRA/1988.
AHS-IV/20B.
Plant 12 in. (31 cm) dia., 8 in. (20 cm) high. Leaf 3 by 2 in. (7.5 by 5 cm), veins 6, yellow, green margin, cordate, flat. Scape 14 in. (35.5 cm), foliated, straight. Flower medium, bell-shaped, lavender, flowers during average period.
[*H.* 'Gold Drop' mutation].

H. **'Popo'** O'Harra 1986.
Plant 10 in. (25.5 cm) dia., 6 in. (15 cm) high. Leaf 2 by 1.5 in. (5 by 4 cm), veins 5, blue-green, not variegated, cordate, cupped. Scape 12 in. (31 cm), foliated, straight. Flower medium, funnel-shaped, white, flowers during average period, fertile.

H. **'Porcelain Vase'** Zilis IRA/1988.
AHS-III/14A.
Plant 42 in. (106.5 cm) dia., 22 in. (56 cm) high. Leaf 9 by 6 in. (23 by 15 cm), veins 12, greenish white (albescent), margin dark green, cordate, flat-wavy. Scape 48 in. (122 cm), bare, straight. Flower medium, funnel-shaped, lavender, flowers during average period.
[*H.* 'Krossa Regal' mutation].

H. **'Powder Blue'** Summers 1986.
Plant is similar to the *H.* Tardiana grex. Plant 22 in. (56 cm) dia., 12 in. (31 cm) high. Leaf 7 by 5 in. (18 by 13 cm), veins 9, blue-green, not variegated, cordate, flat. Scape 18 in. (46 cm), foliated, straight. Flower medium, bell-shaped, white, flowers during average period, fertile.

H. **'President Woodrow Wilson'** Bemis.

H. **'Presidents Choice'** Moldovan IRA/1983.
AHS-I/3B.
Plant 52 in. (13.2 cm) dia., 28 in. (71 cm) high. Leaf 14 by 11 in. (35.5 by 28 cm), veins 14, blue-green, not variegated, cordate, rugose. Scape 34 in. (86.5 cm), foliated, oblique. Flower medium, bell-shaped, white, flowers during average period, fertile.
[*H. sieboldiana* hybrid].

H. **'Princess of Karafuto'** Soules IRA/1984.
AHS-IV/22A.
Plant's name is in dispute. The Japanese name *Hime* used as a adverb means "small, dwarf"; thus *Hime Karafuto (Giboshi)* means "the small hosta from (or in) Karafuto," which is the correct translation. As a noun *Hime* means "princess," as in *Karafuto No Hime Giboshi* or *Karafuto Hime Giboshi* which translates to "Princess of Karafuto." This cultivar is virtually identical to *H.* 'Ginko Craig'.
[*H. sieboldii* mutation].
(see also *H.* 'Hime Karafuto').
(see *H.* 'Ginko Craig').

H. **'Promenade'** Aden 1975.

H. **'Puckered Giant'** Powell IRA/1983.
AHS-II/9B.
Plant 52 in. (132 cm) dia., 34 in. (86.5 cm) high. Leaf 12 by 10 in. (31 by 25.5 cm), veins 14, blue-green, not variegated, cordate, rugose. Scape 22 in. (56 cm), foliated, oblique. Flower medium, bell-shaped, white, flowers during average period, fertile.
[*H. sieboldiana* 'Elegans' hybrid].

H. pulchella **'Kifukurin'**.

H. pulchella **'Sobo'**.

H. pulchella **'Urajiro'**.

H. pulchella **'Variegated'**.
Plant name is an incorrect synonym.
(see *H. pulchella* 'Kifukurin').

H. **'Purbeck Ridge'** Smith BHHS IRA/1988.
AHS-III/15B.
Plant 24 in. (61 cm) dia., 12 in. (31 cm) high. Leaf 8 by 4 in. (20 by 10 cm), veins 11, blue-green, not variegated, cordate, flat. Scape 14 in. (35.5 cm). Flower medium, bell-shaped, white, flowers during average period.
HN: *H.* Tardiana grex TF 2 × 18.
[*H.* 'Tardiflora' × *H. sieboldiana* 'Elegans'].
(see also *H.* Tardiana grex).

H. **'Purple and Gold'** Minks IRA/1976.
AHS-IV/23B.
Plant has purple petioles and flowers contrast the yellow leaves.
[*H.* 'Wogon' × *H.* 'Undulata'].

H. **'Purple Bloomstock'** Summers.
Plant resembles *H.* 'Tardiflora' but may be related to *H. longipes*.

H. **'Purple Bouquet'** Banyai IRA/1986.
AHS-III/13B.
Plant 20 in. (51 cm) dia., 14 in. (35.5 cm) high. Leaf 5.5 by 5 in. (14 by 13 cm), veins 7, blue-green, not variegated, cordate, flat. Scape 22 in. (56 cm), bare, oblique. Flower medium, bell-shaped, purple striped, flowers during average period, fertile.
[*H.* 'Nakaimo' hybrid].

H. **'Purple Dwarf'** Hensen IRA/1983.
AHS-V/25A.
Plant 20 in. (51 cm) dia., 8 in. (20 cm) high. Leaf 2.5 by 2 in. (6.5 by 5 cm), veins 5, medium green, not variegated, cordate, flat. Scape 20 in. (51 cm), foliated, straight. Flower medium, bell-shaped, purple, flowers during average period, barely fertile.
HN: *H. minor* hybrid Hodgkin incorrect.
[*H. nakaiana* hybrid].

H. **'Purple Flame Forever'** Zilis IRA/1988.
AHS-III/17A.
Plant 40 in. (101.5 cm) dia., 20 in. (51 cm) high. Leaf 9 by 6 in. (23 by 15 cm), veins 9, light yellow, not variegated, cordate, flat-wavy. Scape 40 in. (101.5 cm), bare, straight. Flower medium, bell-shaped, purple, flowers during average period.
[*H. ventricosa* 'Aureomaculata' hybrid].

H. **'Purple Lady Finger'** Savory IRA/1982.
AHS-IV/19B.
Plant has many flowers which never open, similar to *H. clausa*. Plant erect, 20 in. (51 cm) dia., 14 in. (35.5 cm) high. Leaf 5 by 1.5 in. (13 by 4 cm), veins 3, medium green, not variegated, lanceolate, flat. Scape 20 in. (51 cm), bare, straight. Flower medium, funnel-shaped, purple striped, flowers during average period, fertile.
[*H. clausa* hybrid al].
[*H. sieboldii* 'Alba' hybrid].

H. **'Purple Profusion'** Williams 1962 IRA/1986.
AHS-IV/19A.
Plant 16 in. (40.5 cm) dia., 8 in. (20 cm) high. Leaf 5 by 2 in.

(13 by 5 cm), veins 5, medium green, not variegated, lanceolate, flat. Scape 28 in. (71 cm), bare, straight. Flower medium, funnel-shaped, purple striped, flowers during average period, fertile.
HN: *H.* 'FRW No. 1024'.
[*H. sieboldii* hybrid].

H. **'Purple Stem'** Fisher.

H. pycnophylla **'Ogon'**.

H. pycnophylla **'Urajiro'**.

Q

H. **'Queen of Hearts'** Savory IRA/1983.
AHS-II/10A.
Plant 40 in. (101.5 cm) dia., 28 in. (71 cm) high. Leaf 10 by 8 in. (25.5 by 20 cm), veins 14, medium green, margin wide, white, cordate, rugose. Scape 34 in. (86.5 cm), bare, straight. Flower medium, bell-shaped, lavender, flowers during average period, fertile.
[*H. sieboldiana* hybrid mutation].

H. **'Quilted Cup'** Minks IRA/1980.
AHS-III/15B.
Plant is a rugose-cupped selection similar to the parent.
[*H.* 'Tokudama' × *H.* 'Crinkle Cup' hybrid].

H. **'Quilted Hearts'** Soules IRA/1989.
AHS-II/9B.
Plant 46 in. (117 cm) dia., 20 in. (50 cm) high. Leaf 11 by 9.5 in. (28 by 24 cm), veins 16, dark green, not variegated, cordate, rugose. Scape 20 in. (50 cm), straight. Flower medium, funnel-shaped, white, flowers during average period, fertile.
[*H. sieboldiana* hybrid].

H. **'Quilted Mound'** O'Harra.

H. **'Quilted Skies'** Soules IRA/1985.
AHS-I/3B.
Plant 48 in. (122 cm) dia., 26 in. (66 cm) high. Leaf 13 by 11 in. (33 by 28 cm), veins 16, blue-green, not variegated, cordate, rugose. Scape 30 in. (76 cm), bare, straight. Flower medium, bell-shaped, lavender, flowers during average period, fertile.
[*H. sieboldiana* × *H. sieboldiana* 'Frances Williams'].

H. **'Quilting Bee'** O'Harra.
Plant is small and has green leaves with grey underside, 3 by 2 in. (8 by 5 cm), and 6 veins.

H. **'Quilting Party'** Simpers IRA/1980.
AHS-I/1A.
Plant has large round green leaves, rugose and many near-white flowers.
[*H.* 'Crispula' × *H. sieboldiana*].

R

H. **'Rabinau'** Rabinau.
(see *H.* 'Tokudama').

H. **'Radiance'** Anderson IRA/1980.
AHS-III/17A.
Plant looks like a yellow *H.* 'Fortunei'. Plant 36 in. (91.5 cm) dia., 20 in. (51 cm) high. Leaf 11 by 9 in. (28 by 23 cm), veins 9, yellow (viridescent), not variegated, cordate, rugose. Scape 34 in. (86.5 cm), bare, straight. Flower medium, funnel-shaped, lavender, flowers during average period, fertile.

H. **'Raindance'** Walters Gardens.
Plant 24 in. (61 cm) dia., 14 in. (35.5 cm) high. Leaf 7 by 5 in. (18 by 13 cm), veins 9, white (albescent), margin green, cordate, flat. Scape 30 in. (76 cm), foliated, straight. Flower medium, funnel-shaped, lavender, flowers during average period, fertile.
HN: *H.* 'Fortunei Raindance'.
[*H.* 'Fortunei Aoki' mutation].

H. **'Ralph'** O'Harra.
Plant is a very rugose, blue-green cultivar which has shown a viridescent, variegated leaf center.

H. **'Razzle Dazzle'** Kuk's Forest IRA/1987.
AHS-III/13A.
Plant has maroon petioles. Plant 12 in. (31 cm) dia., 7 in. (18 cm) high. Leaf 5.5 by 3.5 in. (14 by 9 cm), veins 7, medium green, not variegated, cordate, flat. Scape 14 in. (35.5 cm), bare, straight. Flower medium, bell-shaped, white, flowers during average period, fertile.
[*H. sieboldiana* hybrid].

H. rectifolia **'Albiflora'**.
H. rectifolia var. *chionea* f. *albiflora*.

H. rectifolia **'Chionea'**.
H. rectifolia var. *chionea*.

H. rectifolia **'Kinbuchi'**.

H. rectifolia **'Maruba'**.

H. rectifolia **'Ogon'**.

H. rectifolia 'Oze'.

H. rectifolia 'Rishiri'.

H. **'Regal Rhubarb'** Sellers IRA/1983.
AHS-III/13B.
Plant has purple petioles. Plant erect, 24 in. (61 cm) dia., 30 in. (76 cm) high. Leaf 7 by 4 in. (18 by 10 cm), veins 7, medium green, not variegated, ovate, flat. Scape 60 in. (152.5 cm), bare, straight. Flower medium, funnel-shaped, purple, flowers during average period, fertile.
[*H. longipes* var. *hypoglauca* × *H. nigrescens*(?)].

H. **'Regal Ruffles'** Minks IRA/1980.
AHS-I/3B.
Plant 32 in. (81.5 cm) dia., 18 in. (46 cm) high. Leaf 10 by 8 in. (25.5 by 21 cm), veins 12, medium green, not variegated, round-cupped. Scape 22 in. (56 cm), foliated, oblique. Flower

medium, bell-shaped, white, flowers during average period, fertile.
HN: *H.* 'Krossa Regal Variegated'.
[*H.* 'Ruffles' × *H. sieboldiana* 'Elegans'].

H. 'Regal Splash'.
Plant is a form with pronounced yellowish streaking. The colors are similar to *H.* 'Regal Splendor'.

H. 'Regal Splendor' Walters Gardens IRA/1987.
AHS-II/10B.
Plant is a margined *H.* 'Krossa Regal'. Margin whitish to yellowish, variable in width. Plant erect, 34 in. (86.5 cm) dia., 36 in. (91.5 cm) high. Leaf 12 by 7 in. (31 by 18 cm), veins 9, grey-green, whitish margin, cordate, wavy-undulate. Scape 44 in. (112 cm), bare, straight. Flower medium, bell-shaped, lavender, flowers during average period, fertile.
[*H.* 'Krossa Regal' mutation].

H. 'Reginald Kaye' Kaye/Klose 1982.   (Plate 137).
Plant 32 in. (81.5 cm) dia., 20 in. (51 cm) high. Leaf 9 by 6 in. (23 by 15 cm), veins 12, blue-green, not variegated, cordate, flat. Scape 26 in. (66 cm), foliated, straight. Flower medium, bell-shaped, white, flowers during average period, fertile.
HN: *H.* 'Reginald Kay' incorrect.
 H. 'Reginald Key' incorrect.
[*H. sieboldiana* hybrid].

H. 'Reiho' Japan.
靈峰
Reiho (*Giboshi*), the "Mount Fuji hosta," is a small hybrid with ovate leaves, white (albescent) center, and streaky green margin. Center is yellow in spring. The pattern resembles that seen in *H.* 'Undulata', but leaves are much flatter.
JN: *Reiho Giboshi*

H. 'Reiko' Japan.
麗光
Plant is a large-leaved hybrid resembling *H. montana*. Leaf is pruinose, with powdery white on underside. Primary color is green with irregular streaky whitish yellow variegation. Each leaf has a different pattern. Reported to be stable.

H. 'Rembrandt Blue' Moldovan IRA/1983.
AHS-II/9B.
Plant 48 in. (122 cm) dia., 26 in. (66 cm) high. Leaf 11 by 10 in. (28 by 25.5 cm), veins 16, medium green, not variegated, cordate, rugose. Scape 34 in. (86.5 cm), foliated, straight. Flower medium, bell-shaped, whitish, flowers during average period, fertile.
[*H. sieboldiana* 'Elegans' hybrid].

H. 'Renaissance' Minks IRA/1983.
AHS-III/14A.
Plant registered as streaky variegation but has been observed margined. Plant 22 in. (56 cm) dia., 14 in. (35.5 cm) high. Leaf 5 by 3 in. (13 by 7.5 cm), veins 7–9, dark green with chartreuse to white streaky multicolor center, cordate, flattish. Scape 20 in. (51 cm), foliated, straight. Flower medium, funnel-shaped, lavender, flowers during average period, fertile.
[*H.* 'Flamboyant' mutation].

H. 'Resonance' Aden IRA/1976.
AHS-IV/22A.
Plant 18 in. (46 cm) dia., 8 in. (20 cm) high. Leaf 5 by 2.5 in.

(13 by 6.5 cm), veins 6, medium green, irregular margin wide, white, ovate-lanceolate, wavy. Scape 20 in. (51 cm), bare, straight. Flower medium, funnel-shaped, lavender, flowers during average period, fertile.
[*H.* 'Aden No. 270' × *H.* 'Aden No. 275'].

H. 'Reversed' Aden IRA/1978.
AHS-III/14A.
Plant has white leaf tissue which reportedly melts out (Pollock, 1988). In many gardens this cultivar does not reach its ultimate reported size. Plant 20 in. (51 cm) dia., 10 in. (25.5 cm) high. Leaf medium, veins 9, white (albescent), margin green, cordate, rugose. Scape 20 in. (51 cm), foliated, straight. Flower medium, funnel-shaped, lavender, flowers during average period, fertile.

H. 'Rhapsody' Hatfield No. H82-01.
[*H.* 'Fortunei Stenantha Variegated' mutation].

H. 'Rhodeifolia' incorrect.
Plant name is as originally formulated by Maekawa 1940, but is an orthographic error and has been validly corrected in Chapter 3 and Appendix A. The correct formulation is *H. rohdeifolia* f. *rohdeifolia* which has been reduced to cultivar form as *H.* 'Rohdeifolia'.
(see also *H.* 'Rohdeifolia' in this chapter).

H. 'Rhodeifolia Albomarginata' hort. incorrect.
Plant name is incorrect per the ICBN and the ICNCP. It is used for *H.* 'Fortunei Gloriosa', which in commerce is mistakenly offered as *H.* 'Rohdeifolia'.

H. 'Rhodeifolia Aureomarginata' hort. incorrect.
Plant name is incorrect per the ICBN and the ICNCP. It is used for *H.* 'Fortunei Aureomarginata' which in commerce is mistakenly offered as *H.* 'Rohdeifolia'.

H. 'Ribbon Candy' Minks.

H. 'Richland Gold' Wade IRA/1987.
AHS-III/17A.
Plant is a yellow *H.* 'Fortunei'. Plant 30 in. (76 cm) dia., 16 in. (40.5 cm) high. Leaf 6 by 4 in. (15 by 10 cm), veins 8, yellow (albescent), not variegated, cordate, flat. Scape 18 in. (46 cm), foliated, oblique. Flower medium, funnel-shaped, lavender, flowers during average period, fertile.
[*H.* 'Fortunei Gold Standard' mutation].

H. 'Richland Gold Splash' Wade.
Plant is similar to *H.* 'Sea Lightning' but smaller. Leaf center is yellowish white surrounded by two-tone green margins which streak to center. Plant 30 in. (76 cm) dia., 16 in. (40.5 cm) high. Leaf 6 by 4 in. (15 by 10 cm), veins 8, two-color green, yellowish white, wide center stripe (albescent), cordate, flat. Scape 18 in. (46 cm), foliated, oblique. Flower medium, funnel-shaped, lavender, flowers during average period, fertile.
[*H.* 'Fortunei Gold Standard' hybrid mutation].

H. 'Ridges' Fisher IRA/1970.
AHS-II/9B.
Plant looks like *H. sieboldiana*, but has tall scapes.
[*H. sieboldiana* hybrid].

H. 'Rim Rock' Savory IRA/1982.
AHS-IV/19B.
Plant 18 in. (46 cm) dia., 10 in. (25.5 cm) high. Leaf 5 by 3.5 in. (13 by 9 cm), veins 5, medium green, not variegated, cor-

date, flat. Scape 18 in. (46 cm), bare, straight. Flower medium, funnel-shaped, purple, flowers during average period, fertile. [*H. venusta* hybrid × *H. nakaiana* hybrid].

H. 'Rippling Waves' Nesmith IRA/1986.
AHS-I/1B.
Plant 32 in. (81.5 cm) dia., 22 in. (56 cm) high. Leaf 12 by 10 in. (31 by 25 cm), veins 12, medium green, cordate, wavy, rugose. Scape 34 in. (86.5 cm), foliated, oblique. Flower medium, bell-shaped, white, flowers during average period, fertile.
[*H.* 'Tokudama' × *H. sieboldiana* al].
[*H. montana* hybrid].

H. 'Riptide' Sellers IRA/1987.
AHS-III/13B.
Plant has white on underside of leaf. Plant erect, 30 in. (76 cm) dia., 24 in. (61 cm) high. Leaf 6 by 5 in. (15 by 13 cm), veins 8, blue-green, not variegated, cordate, rugose. Scape 20 in. (51 cm), bare, straight. Flower medium, bell-shaped, white, flowers during late period, fertile.
[*H. sieboldiana* hybrid].

H. 'Rishiri' hort.
利尻ギボウシ
Rishiri Giboshi is an incorrect synonym for *H. rectifolia*, which see.
JN: *Rishiri Giboshi*.
(see *H. rectifolia*).

H. 'Rising Sun' Vaughn IRA/1988.
AHS-III/17A.
Plant 34 in. (86.5 cm) dia., 28 in. (71 cm) high. Leaf 10 by 5 in. (25.5 by 13 cm), veins 9, bright yellow, not variegated, cordate, flat-wavy. Scape 36 in. (91.5 cm), bare, straight. Flower medium, lavender, flowers during average period.
[*H.* 'Summer Fragrance' hybrid × *H.* 'Aztec Treasure' hybrid].

H. 'Rising Tide' Walters Gardens IRA/1984.
AHS-III/16B.
Plant 36 in. (91.5 cm) dia., 20 in. (51 cm) high. Leaf 10 by 6 in. (25.5 by 15 cm), veins 12, blue-green, margin white, cordate, rugose. Scape 26 in. (66 cm), foliated, straight. Flower medium, bell-shaped, white, flowers during average period, fertile.
[*H.* 'Helen Doriot' hybrid mutation].

H. 'River Nile' Moldovan IRA/1983.
AHS-I/3B.
Plant has leaves that emerge blue-green, changing to blue and gold. Plant 42 in. (106.5 cm) dia., 30 in. (76 cm) high. Leaf 12 by 11 in. (31 by 28 cm), veins 16, blue-green, cordate, rugose. Scape 32 in. (81.5 cm), foliated, straight. Flower medium, funnel-shaped, lavender, flowers during average period, fertile.
[*H. sieboldiana* 'Golden Circles' mutation].

H. 'Robert Frost' Lachman IRA/1988.
AHS-II/10B.
Plant 42 in. (106.5 cm) dia., 24 in. (61 cm) high. Leaf 10 by 8 in. (25.5 by 20 cm), veins 12, dark blue-green, margin yellowish white, cordate, flat. Scape 36 in. (91.5 cm), bare, straight. Flower medium, bell-shaped, white, flowers during average period.
[*H.* 'Banana Sundae' × *H. sieboldiana* 'Frances Williams' hybrid].

H. 'Robusta' incorrect.
HN: *H.* 'Fortunei Robusta' Arends 1905.
(see *H. sieboldiana* 'Elegans').

H. 'Rock Baby' Aden.

H. 'Rock Master' Aden IRA/1982.
AHS-V/25A.
Plant is a small frosted green hybrid similar to the parent.
[*H. venusta* hybrid].

H. 'Rock Princess'.
(see *H. gracillima*).

H. 'Rocky Road' Savory IRA/1988.
AHS-III/13B.
Plant 36 in. (91.5 cm) dia., 18 in. (46 cm) high. Leaf 8 by 5 in. (20 by 13 cm), veins 9, dark green, not variegated, cordate, rugose. Scape 26 in. (66 cm), bare, straight. Flower medium, funnel-shaped, lavender, flowers during average period, fertile.
[*H.* 'Fortunei' hybrid].

H. 'Rohdeifolia'.
H. rohdeifolia f. *rohdeifolia*.

H. 'Rohdeifolia Fukurin' hort.
覆輪オモトギボウシ
Fukurin Omoto Giboshi, the "(white-)margined hosta with leaves like Rohdea," looks like *H. sieboldii* but is much larger in all respects. Specialists in Japan consider *H. calliantha* Araki 1942 synonymous to this hosta, but this placement is not corroborated by Araki's holotype. A hosta called *H. rhodeifolia* 'Albo-marginata' is cultivated in the United States; it is not this hosta but *H.* 'Fortunei Gloriosa'. This is a Japanese cultivar selection of minor importance which has not seen horticultural use in Western gardens.
HN: *H. rhodeifolia* 'Albo-marginata' hort. incorrect.
JN: *Fukurin Omoto Giboshi* hort.

H. 'Rohdeifolia Kifukurin' hort.
黄覆輪オモトギボウシ
Kifukurin Omoto Giboshi is a Japanese synonym applied to *H. rohdeifolia*.
JN: *Kifukurin Omoto Giboshi* hort.
(see *H. rohdeifolia*).

H. 'Rohdeifolia Omotoba' hort. incorrect.
オモト葉ギボウシ
Omotoba Giboshi, the "Rohdea-leafed hosta," is an incorrect Japanese synonym applied to *H. rohdeifolia*.
JN: *Omotoba Giboshi* hort.
(see *H. rohdeifolia*).

H. 'Rohdeifolia Rohdeifolia'.
H. rohdeifolia f. *rohdeifolia*.

H. 'Rohdeifolia Viridis' hort.
Plant name is the cultivar name for the naturally occurring, all-green form of *H. rohdeifolia* f. *viridis*.

H. 'Ros Hogh' Curtis/Summers No. 71 1967.

H. 'Rosanne' O'Harra.   (Plate 147).
Plant 20 in. (51 cm) dia., 8 in. (20 cm) high. Leaf 4 by 1 in. (10 by 2.5 cm), veins 3, yellow (viridescent), not variegated, lanceolate, wavy. Scape 28 in. (71 cm), bare, straight. Flower

medium, funnel-shaped, purple striped, flowers during summer period, fertile.
HN: *H.* 'Roseann' incorrect.
[*H. sieboldii* form hybrid].

H. 'Rotunda' Savory IRA/1988.
AHS-III/13A.
Plant 34 in. (86.5 cm) dia., 18 in. (46 cm) high. Leaf 6 by 6 in. (15 by 15 cm), veins 12, medium green, not variegated, round-cordate, rugose. Scape 24 in. (61 cm), bare, straight. Flower medium, lavender, flowers during average period, fertile.
[*H.* 'Pearl Lake' × hybrid].

H. 'Rough Waters' Armstrong IRA/1969.
AHS-II/9A.
Plant 36 in. (91.5 cm) dia., 18 in. (46 cm) high. Leaf 10 by 8 in. (25.5 by 20 cm), veins 13, blue-green, not variegated, cordate, rugose. Scape 26 in. (66 cm), bare, straight. Flower medium, bell-shaped, white, flowers during average period, fertile.
HN: *H.* 'Ruff Waters' incorrect.
[*H.* 'Tokudama' hybrid].

H. 'Roundabout' hort. (?).
Plant described here is sold under the same name Savory registered for another plant, which see. Source unknown. Plant 30 in. (76 cm) dia., 18 in. (46 cm) high. Leaf with 12 veins, yellow (viridescent), not variegated, cordate, rugose. Scape 24 in. (61 cm), bare, straight. Flower medium, bell-shaped, white, flowers during average period, fertile.

H. 'Roundabout' Savory IRA/1988.
AHS-IV/21B.
Plant 24 in. (61 cm) dia., 18 in. (46 cm) high. Leaf small, veins 5, blue-green, not variegated, cordate, rugose. Scape 20 in. (51 cm), bare. Flower medium, lavender, flowers during average period.
[*H.* 'Rough Waters' × hybrid].

H. 'Royal Accolade' Zumbar IRA/1986.
AHS-III/14B.
Plant 30 in. (76 cm) dia., 18 in. (46 cm) high. Leaf medium, veins 8, chartreuse center, streaky with yellow and green, margin green, cordate, moderately rugose. Scape 30 in. (76 cm), foliated, straight. Flower medium, funnel-shaped, white, fragrant, flowers during average period, fertile.
[*H.* 'Royal Standard' mutation].

H. 'Royal Command' Wayside.
(see *H.* 'Royal Standard').

H. 'Royal Flush' Savory IRA/1985.
AHS-IV/22A.
Plant 24 in. (61 cm) dia., 14 in. (35.5 cm) high. Leaf 7 by 4.5 in. (18 by 11.5 cm), veins 9, medium green, margin yellow, wide irregular, cordate, flattish. Scape 30 in. (76 cm), bare, straight. Flower medium, funnel-shaped, purple, flowers during average period, fertile.
[*H.* 'Fortunei' mutation].

H. 'Royal Lady' Holly IRA/1986.
AHS-IV/19B.
Plant is a selected named hybrid form of *H. sieboldii* f. *spathulata*. One of many named all-green *H. sieboldii* hybrids.

H. 'Royal Quilt' Caprice Farm IRA/1988.
AHS-I/3B.
Plant 30 in. (76 cm) dia., 24 in. (61 cm) high. Leaf 13 by 11 in. (33 by 28 cm), veins 12, blue-green, not variegated, round-cordate, cupped-rugose. Scape 36 in. (91.5 cm), foliated, straight. Flower medium, bell-shaped, white, flowers during average period.
[*H.* 'Great Lakes' × *H.* 'Ryans Big One' hybrid].

H. 'Royal Rainbow' Aden IRA/1978.
AHS-III/16B.
Plant is large with variegated leaves.

H. 'Royal Standard' Wayside IRA/1986.
AHS-III/13A. (Figure 4-35).
Plant was awarded Plant Patent Number 2467, registered to Wayside Gardens. In the patent the parentage of this hosta was given as *H. plantaginea* × *H. sieboldiana*, but several reports have disputed this. Plant 38 in. (96.5 cm) dia., 18 in. (46 cm) high. Leaf 8 by 6 in. (20 by 15 cm), veins 8, chartreuse, streaky multicolor, cordate, rugose. Scape 26 in. (66 cm), foliated, straight. Flower medium, funnel-shaped, white, fragrant, flowers during average period, fertile.
HN: *H.* 'Royal Command' obs.
H. 'Wayside Perfection' obs.
H. 'White Knight' pp sim.
U.S. Plant Patent Number 2467.
[*H. plantaginea* × *H.* 'Decorata' al].
[*H. plantaginea* × *H.* 'Fortunei' form al].
[*H. plantaginea* × *H. sieboldiana* form al].

Figure 4-35. *H.* 'Royal Standard'; flower detail (Hosta Hill)

H. 'Royal Standard' yellow form.
Plant is a smaller yellow mutant of the cultivar discovered in tissue culture explants.

H. 'Royal Standard' mediovariegated form.
Plant is a smaller yellow-centered mutant of the cultivar discovered in tissue culture explants. A streaky yellow form also exists.

H. 'Royal Tiara' Walters Gardens IRA/1988.
AHS-V/26A.
Plant 14 in. (35.5 cm) dia., 8 in. (20 cm) high. Leaf 4 by 2.5 in. (10 by 6.5 cm), veins 6, white (albescent), margin green, cordate, wavy. Scape 22 in. (56 cm), bare, straight. Flower medium, bell-shaped, purple, flowers during average period.
[*H. nakaiana* 'Golden Tiara' mutation].

H. 'Royalty' Anderson IRA/1982.
AHS-V/23B. (Figure 4-36).
Plant erect, 14 in. (35.5 cm) dia., 4 in. (10 cm) high. Leaf 3 by 1.5 in. (7.5 by 4 cm), veins 5, chartreuse to yellow, not

208

'Ruffled Queen'

variegated, cordate, flat. Scape 14 in. (35.5 cm), bare, straight. Flower medium, bell-shaped, purple, flowers during average period, fertile.
HN: *H.* 'Anderson Seedling No. 120' obs.
[*H. capitata* hybrid].

Figure 4-36. *H.* 'Royalty'; general habit (Langdon garden/Schmid)

H. 'Ruffled Queen' Shaw.
(see *H.* 'Birchwood Ruffled Queen').

H. 'Ruffled Sieboldiana' Arett.
　　Plant 38 in. (96.5 cm) dia., 20 in. (51 cm) high. Leaf large, veins 16, blue-green, not variegated, cordate, rugose. Scape 26 in. (66 cm), bare, straight. Flower medium, bell-shaped, white, flowers during average period, fertile.
[*H. sieboldiana* form].

H. 'Ruffles' Lehman IRA/1986.
　　AHS-II/7A.　　　　　　　　　(Figure 4-37).
　　Plant 32 in. (81.5 cm) dia., 22 in. (56 cm) high. Leaf 10 by 8 in. (25 by 20 cm), veins 12, medium green, not variegated, round-cupped. Scape 34 in. (86.5 cm), foliated, oblique. Flower medium, bell-shaped, white, flowers during average period, fertile.
[*H. montana* hybrid].

Figure 4-37. *H.* 'Ruffles'; general habit (Hosta Hill)

H. 'Rugosa'.
H. fortunei var. *rugosa*.

H. rupifraga 'Ki Hachijo'.

H. rupifraga 'Kifukurin Ki Hachijo'.

H. rupifraga 'Koriyama'.

H. rupifraga 'Urajiro'.
(see *H. longipes* var. *latifolia* 'Urajiro Hachijo').

H. 'Ryans Big One' Ryan 1963/Englerth IRA/1982.
　　AHS-I/3B.　　　　　　　　　(Plate 138).
　　Plant is a selected large form of *H. sieboldiana* 'Hypophylla'. Plant 52 in. (132 cm) dia., 30 in. (76 cm) high. Leaf 13 by 11 in. (33 by 28 cm), veins 15, blue-green, not variegated, cordate, rugose. Scape 50 in. (127 cm), bare, straight. Flower medium, funnel-shaped, white, flowers during average period, fertile.
[*H. sieboldiana* hybrid].

S

H. 'Sacra'.
H. sacra.

H. 'Sagae' Japan.
寒河江ギボウシ
(see *H. fluctuans* 'Variegated').
(see also *H. montana* 'Sagae').

H. 'Saishu Jima' Korea/Japan/Davidson/Summers.
サイシュウジマギボウシ　　　　(Plate 191).
　　Saishu Jima Giboshi, the "hosta from Saishu Island," is named for an island 80 miles (120 km) off the southern tip of the Korean Peninsula. Once called Quelpart (or Quelpaert) Island, its Korean name is Cheju Do, but the Japanese call it Saishu Jima (Saishu To). Of recent volcanic origin, it has yielded many uncommon species, including *H. venusta*. The clone most frequently available in commerce under this name is a small all-green form of *H. sieboldii*. This name is also used for several other taxa, and the name *H.* 'Saishu Jima', as applied in commerce, is technically not a clonal name. In a broad sense, it and the taxa cultivated under the names listed in the synonymy are considered small or dwarf forms of the all-green *H. sieboldii* and belong to the *H. sieboldii* f. *spathulata* Dwarf group. The anther coloration of some of them suggests infraspecific, hybrid origin. *Hosta gracillima* is also sold under this name. Further study is needed to solve this problem. Variegated and yellow sports exist. The typical plant is 12 in. (31 cm) dia., 8 in. (20 cm) high. Leaf 4 by 1 in. (10 by 2.5 cm), veins 3, medium green, not variegated, lanceolate, flat. Scape 14 in. (35.5 cm), bare, straight. Flower medium, bell-shaped, purple striped, flowers during summer period, fertile.
HN: Cheju Island Hosta.
　　H. 'Craig No. 17'/Summers No. 323 1969.
　　H. 'Crinkled Stars' Blackthorne.
　　H. 'Davidson No. 90'.
　　H. 'Haku Jima' incorrect.
　　H. 'Kirishima' pp sim.
　　H. 'Krossa No. J-4' Hirao/Summers No. 110 1969 pp sim.
　　H. 'Mount Kirishima' pp sim.
　　H. numor incorrect = *H. gracillima* form.
　　H. 'Wee Willy'.
　　Summers No. 298 1968.
JN: *Saishu Jima Giboshi* hort.
　　Yaku Giboshi hort.
[*H. sieboldii* hybrid].
(see *H. sieboldii* f. *spathulata* Dwarf group).

H. **'Saishu Jima Variegated'** Aden.
HN: *H.* 'Little Jim' pp sim.

H. **'Samual Blue'** Krossa/Ruh IRA/1981.
    AHS-II/9B.
    Plant erect, 20 in. (51 cm) dia., 18 in. (46 cm) high. Leaf medium, veins 13, blue-green, not variegated, cordate, rugose. Scape 20 in. (51 cm), foliated, straight. Flower medium, bell-shaped, white, flowers during average period, fertile.
HN: *H.* 'Krossa No. L-4'.
      H. 'Krossa No. LH' incorrect.

H. **'Samurai'** Aden.
    Plant is a selected and named form of the yellow-margined *H. sieboldiana*, reportedly similar to *H.* 'Aurora Borealis', which see. It apparently does not suffer marginal necrosis.
(see *H. sieboldiana* Aureomarginata group).

H. **'Sarah Farmer'** Trafton IRA/1975.
    AHS-III/16B.
    Plant 20 in. (51 cm) dia., 14 in. (35.5 cm) high. Leaf 7 by 5 in. (18 by 13 cm), veins 9, medium green, streaky yellow, cordate, flat. Scape 32 in. (81.5 cm), foliated, straight. Flower medium, funnel-shaped, lavender, flowers during average period, fertile.
[*H.* 'Fortunei Aureomarginata' mutation]

H. **'Sasa No Yuki'** Japan.
笹の雪

H. **'Sassy'** Aden IRA/1987.
    AHS-IV/22A.
    Plant has variable whitish margin. Plant 8 in. (20 cm) dia., 4 in. (10 cm) high. Leaf 4 by 3 in. (10 by 7.5 cm), veins 4, medium green, white margin, cordate, flat. Scape 13 in. (33 cm), bare, straight. Flower medium, bell-shaped, purple, flowers during late period, fertile.
[*H.* 'Art Shane' × *H.* 'Invincible' hybrid].

H. **'Satin Beauty'** Fisher 1976 IRA/1986.
    AHS-II/7A.

H. **'Satin Flare'** Fisher IRA/1971.
    AHS-II/7B.
    Plant 36 in. (91.5 cm) dia., 20 in. (51 cm) high. Leaf 7 by 5 in. (18 by 13 cm), veins 8, medium green, not variegated, cordate, flat. Scape 42 in. (106.5 cm), bare, straight. Flower medium, funnel-shaped, lavender, flowers during average period, fertile.
[*H.* 'Golden Anniversary' hybrid].

H. **'Sawtooth'** Houseworth 1986.
    Plant 12 in. (31 cm) dia., 8 in. (20 cm) high. Leaf 6 by 4 in. (15 by 10 cm), veins 8, medium green, not variegated, cordate, flat. Scape 18 in. (46 cm), bare, oblique. Flower medium, bell-shaped, purple, flowers during average period, fertile.
[*H. ventricosa* 'Aureomarginata' hybrid].

H. **'Schneewittchen'** Klose.
    Plant is similar to *H.* 'Haku Chu Han'. Name is German for 'Snow White'.
HN: *H. sieboldii* 'Silver Kabitan' pp sim.
[*H. sieboldii* hybrid].

H. **'Schwarzer Ritter'** Klose.
    Plant's name is German for 'Black Knight' referring to a very dark green cultivar.

H. **'Sea Aquarius'** Seaver.

H. **'Sea Blue'** Seaver IRA/1978.
    AHS-III/15B.
    Plant is similar to the species *H. sieboldiana*. Plant 32 in. (81.5 cm) dia., 20 in. (51 cm) high. Leaf large, veins 16, blue-green, not variegated, cordate, rugose. Scape 28 in. (71 cm), bare, straight. Flower medium, bell-shaped, white, flowers during average period, fertile.
[*H. sieboldiana* 'Frances Williams' hybrid].

H. **'Sea Blue Leather'** Seaver.

H. **'Sea Blue Monster'** Seaver.

H. **'Sea Bunny'** Seaver IRA/1986.
    AHS-III/17A.
    Plant has glossy light green leaves with some scapes being branched. Plant 18 in. (46 cm) dia., 12 in. (31 cm) high. Leaf 10 by 6 in. (25.5 by 15 cm), veins 9, medium green, not variegated, cordate, flat. Scape 28 in. (71 cm), bare, straight. Flower medium, bell-shaped, white, flowers during average period, fertile.

H. **'Sea Dream'** Seaver IRA/1984.
    AHS-III/14B.
    Plant has lutescent leaves that emerge green and turn yellow with white margin. Plant 30 in. (76 cm) dia., 14 in. (35.5 cm) high. Leaf medium, veins 9, yellow (lutescent), margin white, cordate, flat. Scape 18 in. (46 cm), bare, straight. Flower medium, bell-shaped, lavender, flowers during summer period, fertile.
[*H.* 'Neat Splash' hybrid].

H. **'Sea Drift'** Seaver IRA/1978.
    AHS-I/1B.   (Figure 4-38).
    Plant is much like the parent plant. Plant 30 in. (76 cm) dia., 22 in. (56 cm) high. Leaf 13 by 11 in. (33 by 28 cm), veins 10, medium green, not variegated, cordate, piecrust margin. Scape 28 in. (71 cm), bare, straight. Flowers medium, funnel-shaped, lavender, flowers during average period, fertile.
[*H.* 'Green Piecrust' hybrid].

Figure 4-38. *H.* 'Sea Drift'; general habit, with *H.* 'Fortunei Viridis' (left) (Hosta Hill)

H. **'Sea Foam'** Seaver IRA/1978.
    AHS-II/11A.
    Plant has medium-size lutescent leaves, changing from green to chartreuse. Much like the parent otherwise.
[*H. sieboldiana* 'Frances Williams' hybrid].

H. **'Sea Frolic'** Seaver.
    Plant has dark blue-green leaves with ruffled edges and marginal serration. Smaller than the parent.
[*H.* 'Donahue Piecrust' hybrid].

H. 'Sea Gold' Seaver IRA/1985.
AHS-III/17A.
AHS President's Trophy Award, 1989, exhibited by Mildred Seaver; Midwest Gold Award, 1985, exhibited by Mildred Seaver. Mature leaves have 16 veins. Plant 20 in. (51 cm) dia., 12 in. (31 cm) high. Leaf 9 by 5 in. (23 by 13 cm), veins 12, yellow (lutescent), not variegated, cordate, flat. Scape 16 in. (40.5 cm), foliated, straight. Flower medium, bell-shaped, lavender, flowers during summer period, fertile.
[*H.* 'Ledi Lantis' hybrid].

H. 'Sea Gold Star' Seaver IRA/1984.
AHS-III/17A.
Plant 30 in. (76 cm) dia., 14 in. (35.5 cm) high. Leaf 10 by 8 in. (25.5 by 20 cm), veins 12, yellow (lutescent), not variegated, cordate, slightly rugose. Scape 18 in. (46 cm), bare, straight. Flower medium, bell-shaped, whitish, flowers during average period, fertile.
[*H.* 'Wagon Wheels' hybrid].

H. 'Sea Lightning' Seaver IRA/1981.
AHS-III/16B.
Plant has unstable variegation. Leaves have been observed to mutate to either a wider streaky white center or to all green. Plant erect, 16 in. (40.5 cm) dia., 16 in. (40.5 cm) high. Leaf 8 by 5 in. (20 by 13 cm), veins 7, medium green, narrow whitish streak in white center, ovate, flat. Scape 48 in. (122 cm), bare, straight. Flower medium, funnel-shaped, lavender, flowers during summer period, fertile.
[*H.* 'Neat Splash' hybrid].

H. 'Sea Lotus Leaf' Seaver IRA/1985.
AHS-II/9B.
AHS Midwest Blue Award, 1985, exhibited by Mildred Seaver. Plant erect, 24 in. (61 cm) dia., 20 in. (51 cm) high. Leaf large, veins 12, blue-green, not variegated, cordate, cupped-rugose. Scape 22 in. (56 cm), bare, oblique. Flower medium, bell-shaped, white, flowers during average period, fertile.
[*H.* 'Wagon Wheels' hybrid].

H. 'Sea Master' Seaver.

H. 'Sea Mist' Seaver.
Plant is medium large with cupped-rugose leaves of yellow to chartreuse, light green margin.

H. 'Sea Monster' Seaver IRA/1978.
AHS-I/1B.
AHS Eunice Fisher Award, 1982. Plant 42 in. (106.5 cm) dia., 28 in. (71 cm) high. Leaf 11 by 9 in. (28 by 23 cm), veins 16, blue-green, not variegated, cordate, rugose to cupped-rugose. Scape 30 in. (76 cm), bare, straight. Flower medium, bell-shaped, white, flowers during average period, fertile.
[*H.* 'Brookwood Blue' hybrid].

H. 'Sea Octopus' Seaver IRA/1981.
AHS-IV/19A.
Plant erect, 14 in. (35.5 cm) dia., 8 in. (20 cm) high. Leaf 4 by 1 in. (10 by 2.5 cm), veins 3, medium green, not variegated, lanceolate, wavy. Scape 20 in. (51 cm), bare, straight. Flower medium, funnel-shaped, purple striped, flowers during summer period, fertile.
[*H.* 'Sea Sprite' hybrid].

H. 'Sea Peridot' Seaver.

H. 'Sea Prize' Seaver.
Plant small with green leaves that are streaked with yellow and white. No two leaves are alike. Plant 14 in. (35.5 cm) dia., 12 in. (31 cm) high. Leaf medium, veins 10, medium green, streaky yellow, cordate, flat. Scape 24 in. (61 cm), bare, straight. Flower medium, funnel-shaped, lavender, flowers during average period, fertile.

H. 'Sea Sapphire' Seaver.
Plant has very blue-green leaves. Smooth texture.

H. 'Sea Shells' Arett 1980.
Plant name is a superseded synonym.
(see *H.* 'Shells at Sea').

H. 'Sea Sprite' Seaver IRA/1978.
AHS-IV/20B.
Plant is very similar to *H. sieboldii* 'Kabitan', but this hosta is chartreuse, not yellow, with less undulate leaves. Most plants in commerce are infected with a virus. Plant erect, 14 in. (35.5 cm) dia., 8 in. (20 cm) high. Leaf 5 by 1 in. (13 by 2.5 cm), veins 3, chartreuse (viridescent), margin white, lanceolate, flat. Scape 14 in. (35.5 cm), bare, straight. Flower medium, funnel-shaped, purple striped, flowers during summer period, fertile.
[*H. sieboldii* 'Kabitan' hybrid].
(see also *H. sieboldii* 'Kabitan').

H. 'Sea Sunrise' Seaver IRA/1982.
AHS-IV/20A.
AHS Savory Shield Award, 1982. Plant has variegation which is reportedly unstable and reverts to *H.* 'Sea Yellow Sunrise', which see. Plant 16 in. (40.5 cm) dia., 8 in. (20 cm) high. Leaf 5 by 3.5 in. (13 by 9 cm), veins 7, medium green, very irregularly streaked yellow, white, and chartreuse, ovate, flat. Scape 24 in. (61 cm), bare, straight. Flower medium, funnel-shaped, lavender, flowers during summer period, fertile.
HN: No. 128 Hybrid.
[*H.* 'Neat Splash' hybrid].

H. 'Sea Surf' Moldovan.

H. 'Sea Thunder' Seaver.   (Plate 139)
Plant has white, very wide center streak. Sport of *H.* 'Sea Lightning'. Reversion to all-green leaves reported. Plant erect, 14 in. (35.5 cm) dia., 12 in. (31 cm) high. Leaf 6 by 4 in. (15 by 10 cm), veins 7, medium green, wide, whitish streak in center white, ovate, flat. Flower medium, funnel-shaped, lavender, flowers during summer period, fertile.
[*H.* 'Sea Lightning' mutation].

H. 'Sea Wave' Smith UK.

H. 'Sea Waves' Seaver.

H. 'Sea Wiggles' Seaver IRA/1981.
AHS-IV/23B.
Plant erect, 8 in. (20 cm) dia., 8 in. (20 cm) high. Leaf 5 by 1 in. (13 by 2.5 cm), veins 3, yellow (viridescent), not variegated, lanceolate, wavy-undulate. Scape 10 in. (25.5 cm), bare, straight. Flower medium, funnel-shaped, purple striped, flowers during summer period, fertile.
[*H.* 'Sea Sprite' hybrid].

H. 'Sea Yellow Sunrise' Seaver IRA/1985.
AHS-IV/23A.
Plant is the stable yellow form of *H.* 'Sea Sunrise'. Plant 18 in. (46 cm) dia., 12 in. (31 cm) high. Leaf 5 by 4 in. (13 by 10 cm), veins 7, yellow (viridescent), not variegated, ovate, flat. Scape 20 in. (51 cm), bare, straight. Scape flower medium,

funnel-shaped, lavender, flowers during summer period, fertile.
[H. 'Sea Sunrise' mutation].

H. 'See Saw' Summers IRA/1986.
AHS-IV/22A.   (Figure 4-39).
Plant is one of the selected forms of H. 'Undulata Albomarginata' with a smaller, more cupped leaf. Plant 20 in. (51 cm) dia., 14 in. (35.5 cm) high. Leaf 4 by 3 in. (10 by 7 cm), veins 6, medium green, margin white, ovate, rugose-wavy. Cape 30 in. (76 cm). Flower medium, funnel-shaped, lavender, flowers during average period, sterile.
Summers No. 29 1970.
HN: H. 'Sea Saw' incorrect.
     H. 'Undulata See Saw'.
[H. 'Undulata Erromena' mutation].

Figure 4-39. H. 'See Saw'; general habit (Hosta Hill)

H. 'Seer Master' Aden 1975.
Plant is a very large hybrid with medium green, rugose, heavy textured leaves.

H. 'Seersucker' Savory.

H. 'Semperaurea' Foerster hort.
(see H. sieboldiana 'Semperaurea').

H. 'Sentinels' Williams 1954 IRA/1986.
AHS-IV/19B.
Plant 12 in. (31 cm) dia., 8 in. (20 cm) high. Leaf 6 by 1.5 in. (15 by 4 cm), veins 5, medium green, not variegated, lanceolate, flat. Scape 16 in. (40.5 cm), bare, straight. Flower medium, funnel-shaped, purple striped, flowers during summer period, fertile.
HN: H. 'FRW No. 1350'.
     H. 'Sentinals' incorrect.
[H. sieboldii hybrid].

H. 'September Sun' Solberg IRA/1985.
AHS-III/14B.   (Plates 84, 140).
Plant is a variegated sport of H. 'August Moon' with yellow center and green margin. There is high contrast between margin and center. A plant in the trade with barely distinguishable chartreuse margins and yellowish green center of little contrast is not this taxon. Plant 34 in. (86.5 cm) dia., 22 in. (56 cm) high. Leaf 6 by 5 in. (15 by 13 cm), veins 9, yellow (lutescent), margin green, cordate, flat. Scape 30 in. (76 cm), bare, straight. Flower medium, bell-shaped, white, flowers during average period, fertile.
HN: H. 'September Song' incorrect.
[H. 'August Moon' mutation].

H. 'Serendipity' Aden IRA/1978.
AHS-IV/21B.
Plant 14 in. (35.5 cm) dia., 10 in. (25.5 cm) high. Leaf 5 by 4 in. (13 by 10 cm), veins 12, blue-green, not variegated, cordate, rugose. Scape 16 in. (40.5 cm), bare, straight. Flower medium, bell-shaped, white, flowers during average period, fertile.
HN: H. 'Blue Swarm'.
[H. 'Tokudama' hybrid].

H. 'Serene' Minks IRA/1983.
AHS-III/14B.
Plant 18 in. (46 cm) dia., 10 in. (25.5 cm) high. Leaf 5 by 4 in. (13 by 10 cm), veins 12, chartreuse/yellow (viridescent) center, margin darker green, cordate, cupped-rugose. Scape 16 in. (40.5 cm), bare, straight. Flower medium, bell-shaped, white, flowers during average period, fertile.
[H. 'Tokudama Aureonebulosa' mutation].

H. 'Serenity' Banyai IRA/1986.
AHS-III/13A.
Plant 30 in. (76 cm) dia., 14 in. (35.5 cm) high. Leaf 10 by 6 in. (25.5 by 15 cm), veins 7, medium green, not variegated, cordate, flat. Scape 26 in. (66 cm), foliated, straight. Flower medium, bell-shaped, white, flowers during average period, fertile.
[H. 'Fortunei' mutation or hybrid].

H. 'Seto Hime' Japan.
瀬戸姫
Plant is a small white-backed cultivar.
JN: Seto Hime Giboshi hort.

H. 'Seto No Aki' Japan.
瀬戸の秋
Plant is a white-backed cultivar.
JN: Seto No Aki Giboshi hort.

H. 'Setsuko' Japan.
セツコイワギボウシ
JN: Setsuko Iwa Giboshi hort.
(see H. longipes 'Setsuko').
(see also H. longipes var. hypoglauca).

H. 'Setsurei' Japan.
雪鈴
Plant is a white-backed cultivar.
JN: Setsurei Giboshi hort.

H. 'Shade Beauty' Aden IRA/1982.
AHS-IV/20A.
Plant 10 in. (25.5 cm) dia., 4 in. (10 cm) high. Leaf small, yellow (viridescent), margin white, lanceolate, wavy. Scape 10 in. (25.5 cm), bare, straight. Flower medium, funnel-shaped, lavender, flowers during average period.
[H. Tardiana grex—yellow hybrid].

H. 'Shade Fanfare' Aden IRA/1986.
AHS-III/16A.   (Figure 4-40; Plates 45, 137, 169).
Plant is the stable marginata form derived from H. 'Flamboyant'. A cultivar of high merit having soft colors which are useful in the landscape. Plant 24 in. (61 cm) dia., 16 in. (40.5 cm) high. Leaf 7 by 5.5 in. (18 by 14 cm), veins 9, chartreuse, margin yellowish white (cream), cordate, flat. Scape 22 in. (56 cm), foliated, straight. Flower medium, funnel-shaped, lavender, flowers during average period, fertile.
[H. 'Flamboyant' mutation].

Figure 4-40. *H*. 'Shade Fanfare'; general habit (Hosta Hill)

H. 'Shade Master' Aden IRA/1982.

AHS-III/17A.

Plant 38 in. (96.5 cm) dia., 22 in. (56 cm) high. Leaf 7 by 5 in. (18 by 13 cm), veins 12, yellow (lutescent), not variegated, cordate, flat. Scape 30 in. (76 cm), foliated, straight. Flower medium, funnel-shaped, white, flowers during average period, fertile.

[*H*. 'White Vision' × *H*. 'Gold Regal'].

H. 'Shadow and Substance' Aden 1979.

H. 'Shalimar' Aden IRA/1983.

AHS-III/14A.

Plant 20 in. (51 cm) dia., 14 in. (35.5 cm) high. Leaf 8 by 3 in. (20 by 7.5 cm), veins 5, green center streaked with chartreuse, yellow and white, margin whitish, ovate, flat. Scape 26 in. (66 cm), foliated, straight. Flower medium, funnel-shaped, white, fragrant, flowers during summer period, fertile.

[*H*. 'Fragrant Bouquet' × *H*. 'Fragrant Candelabra'].

H. 'Sharmon' Donahue 1972 IRA/1986.

AHS-III/18B.

Plant is an unstable sport of *H*. 'Fortunei'; reverts to all green. Plant 36 in. (91.5 cm) dia., 24 in. (61 cm) high. Leaf 7 by 5 in. (18 by 13 cm), veins 9, medium green, streaky yellow, cordate, flat. Scape 34 in. (86.5 cm), foliated, oblique. Flower medium, funnel-shaped, lavender, flowers during average period, fertile.

HN: *H*. 'Fortunei Phyllis Campbell' pp sim.

H. 'Phyllis Campbell' pp sim.

[*H*. 'Fortunei' mutation].

H. 'Sharmon D-Improved' Payne 1973.

Plant 36 in. (91.5 cm) dia., 24 in. (61 cm) high. Leaf 7 by 5 in. (18 by 13 cm), veins 9, medium green, streaky yellow, cordate, flat. Scape 34 in. (86.5 cm), foliated, oblique. Flower medium, funnel-shaped, lavender, flowers during average period, fertile.

[*H*. 'Sharmon' × *H*. *sieboldiana* 'Golden Sunburst'].

H. 'Shelleys' Hodgkin/Brickell IRA/1988.

AHS-III/16A.

Plant reportedly collected in Japan by the late British plantsman Elliot Hodgkin and named by Brickell for his garden. Grenfell (1990) spells the name 'Shelleys', but the AHS registration list has it as 'Shellys' and the AHS judges handbook as 'Shelly's'. Plant 28 in. (71 cm) dia., 14 in. (35.5 cm) high. Leaf 9 by 3 in. (23.5 by 7.5 cm), veins close together, lanceolate, green, wavy margin. This may be a *H*. *kikutii* form or hybrid.

HN: *H*. 'Shelly's' incorrect.

H. 'Shellys' incorrect.

H. 'Shells at Sea' Arett IRA/1983.

AHS-IV/19A.

Plant 22 in. (56 cm) dia., 12 in. (31 cm) high. Leaf 4 by 3 in. (10 by 7.5 cm), veins 8, medium green, not variegated, round-cupped. Scape 26 in. (66 cm), foliated, straight. Flower medium, bell-shaped, purple, flowers during average period, fertile.

HN: *H*. 'Sea Shells' incorrect.

H. 'Shenanigans'.

Plant 38 in. (96.5 cm) dia., 26 in. (66 cm) high. Leaf 5 by 2 in. (13 by 5 cm), veins 7, medium green, margin and center streaky white, ovate, flat. Scape 38 in. (96.5 cm), bare, oblique. Flower medium, funnel-shaped, lavender, flowers during average period, fertile.

H. 'Sherborne Profusion' Smith BHHS IRA/1988.

AHS-IV/21B.

Plant 12 in. (31 cm) dia., 8 in. (20 cm) high. Leaf 4 by 3 in. (10 by 7.5 cm), veins 8, grey-green, not variegated, cordate, flat. Scape 10 in. (20.5 cm).

HN: *H*. 'Tardiana Grey'.

H. Tardiana grex TF 2 × 21.

[*H*. 'Tardiflora' × *H*. *sieboldiana* 'Elegans'].

(see also *H*. Tardiana grex).

H. 'Sherborne Songbird' Smith BHHS IRA/1988.

AHS-III/15B.

Plant 32 in. (81.5 cm) dia., 20 in. (51 cm) high. Leaf 12 by 6.5 in. (31 by 16.5 cm), veins 12. Scape 24 in. (61 cm).

HN: *H*. Tardiana grex TF 2 × 19.

[*H*. 'Tardiflora' × *H*. *sieboldiana* 'Elegans'].

(see also *H*. Tardiana grex).

H. 'Sherborne Swallow' Smith BHHS IRA/1988.

AHS-IV/21B.

HN: *H*. Tardiana grex TF 2 × 34.

[*H*. 'Tardiflora' × *H*. *sieboldiana* 'Elegans'].

(see also *H*. Tardiana grex).

H. 'Sherborne Swan' Smith BHHS IRA/1988.

AHS-III/15B.

Plant 25 in. (63.5 cm) dia., 17 in. (43 cm) high. Leaf 9 by 5 in. (23 by 13 cm), veins 10. Scape 24 in. (61 cm).

HN: *H*. Tardiana grex TF 2 × 29.

[*H*. 'Tardiflora' × *H*. *sieboldiana* 'Elegans'].

(see also *H*. Tardiana grex).

H. 'Sherborne Swift' Smith BHHS IRA/1988.

AHS-IV/21B.

Plant 13 in. (33 cm) dia., 8 in. (20 cm) high. Leaf 4 by 3 in. (10 by 7.5 cm), veins 8.

HN: *H*. Tardiana grex TF 2 × 26.

[*H*. 'Tardiflora' × *H*. *sieboldiana* 'Elegans'].

(see also *H*. Tardiana grex).

H. 'Shiho' Japan.

至芳

Shiho Giboshi, the "best treasure hosta," is a fragrant hybrid. Ovate leaves, scape 12 in. (31 cm) with many large flowers.

JN: *Shiho Giboshi* hort.

H. 'Shima Kabitan' Japan.

縞カビタン   (Plate 127).

Shima Kabitan Giboshi, the "striped Kabitan hosta," is smaller than H. sieboldii and very closely related to it. The leaves are green with irregular white stripes; some are white-margined. Variegation highly variable.

JN: Shima Kabitan Giboshi hort.

[H. sieboldii mutation].

(see H. 'Little Jim').

H. 'Shimano' Houseworth 1986.

H. 'Shinano Nishiki' Japan.

信濃錦

Shinano Nishiki Giboshi, the "resplendent (like brocade of gold) hosta from Shinano," was found in Nagano Prefecture, once called Shinano. The golden-yellow striped variegation differs from leaf to leaf. In Japan it is considered to be a mutation of H. kiyosumiensis.

JN: Shinano Nishiki Giboshi hort.

[H. kiyosumiensis mutation].

H. 'Shining Tot' Aden IRA/1982.

AHS-VI/31B   (Figure 4-41).

Plant 6 in. (15 cm) dia., 2 in. (5 cm) high. Leaf 1.25 by 0.75 in. (3 by 2 cm), veins 4, medium shiny green, not variegated, cordate, flat. Scape 6 in. (15 cm), bare, oblique. Flower medium, funnel-shaped, lavender, flowers during average period, fertile.

[H. 'Rock Master' × H. venusta].

[H. pulchella form a1].

Figure 4-41. H. 'Shining Tot' (top right) with H. pulchella (top left) and H. 'Crown Jewel' (bottom center)

H. 'Shipshape'.

Plant 16 in. (40.5 cm) dia., 12 in. (31 cm) high. Leaf medium green, veins 5, margin white, ovate, flat. Scape 34 in. (86.5 cm), foliated, oblique. Flower medium, funnel-shaped, lavender, flowers during average period, fertile.

H. 'Shiro Kabitan'.

シロカビタン

(see H. sieboldii 'Silver Kabitan').

H. 'Shirobana Kika Koba' Japan.

白花奇花コバギボウシ

Shirobana Kika Koba Giboshi, the "white-flowered, strange, small-leaved hosta." An unusual sport with an unstable number of petals (4 to 6) and pure white flowers. Anthers project before flower opens.

JN: Shirobana Kika Koba Giboshi hort.

[H. sieboldii mutation].

H. 'Shirobuchi' Japan.

Shirobuchi Giboshi, the "white-dappled hosta," is named buchi meaning "with patches of a different color," but in a wider sense simply "variegated." A cultivar that is small, veins 3–4, with yellowish white margins.

JN: Shirobuchi Giboshi hort.

[H. sieboldii mutation].

H. 'Shirofukurin Ko Mame' Japan.

Shirofukurin Ko Mame Giboshi, the "white-margined dwarf hosta." Leaf 2 by 0.5 in. (5 by 1 cm), veins 3, medium green, white-margined, lanceolate, flat.

JN: Shirofukurin Ko Mame Giboshi hort.

[H. gracillima mutation].

H. 'Shironami' Horinaka.

シロナミギボウシ

Shironami Giboshi, the "wavy white hosta," is a Japanese cultivar of uncertain parentage.

HN: H. 'Shiranami' incorrect.

JN: Shironami Giboshi hort.

H. 'Shirozasa' (?).

Plant is a Japanese cultivar mentioned by name but not described and not seen.

HN: H. 'Shiro Sasa'.

JN: Shirozasa Giboshi hort.

H. 'Shocking Chartreuse' Vaughn IRA/1982.

AHS-III/17A.

Plant is medium size with cupped-rugose, light chartreuse leaves.

[H. Vaughn SG-3 × H. 'Golden Waffles'].

H. 'Shogun' Aden.

Plant looks very much like H. 'Spinners' and 'Goldbrook' (UK) and H. 'Moerheim' (Netherlands). It also resembles H. 'Antioch', but the latter is larger with wider leaves. The margin in all these plants starts out yellow and turns white. Plant 26 in. (66 cm) dia., 14 in. (35.5 cm) high. Leaf 8 by 4 in. (20 by 10 cm), veins 6, medium green, irregular margin white, ovate, flat. Scape 28 in. (71 cm), bare, oblique. Flower medium, funnel-shaped, lavender, flowers during average period, fertile.

[H. 'Fortunei' mutation].

(see H. 'Antioch').

H. 'Show Piece' Krossa/Fisher 1975.

Plant looks much like the species H. nakaiana, but the leaves start out yellowish and turn green. Plant 12 in. (31 cm) dia., 8 in. (20 cm) high. Leaf 3 by 2 in. (7.5 by 5 cm), veins 5, yellowish (viridescent), turns medium green, not variegated, cordate, flat. Scape 16 in. (40.5 cm), bare, straight. Flower medium, bell-shaped, purple, flowers during average period, fertile.

HN: H. 'Krossa Asiatic Seedling'.

[H. nakaiana hybrid].

H. 'Showtime' Aden IRA/1987.

AHS-III/16B.

Plant has variable white margin. Plant 32 in. (81.5 cm) dia., 22 in. (56 cm) high. Leaf 8 by 6 in. (20 by 15 cm), veins 5, dark green, white margin, cordate, flat. Scape 32 in. (81.5 cm), bare, straight. Flower medium, funnel-shaped, white, fragrant, flowers during summer period, fertile.

[H. 'Fragrant Bouquet' × H. 'Fragrant Candelabra'].

H. 'Shuho Nishiki' Japan.

Shuho Nishiki Giboshi, the "resplendent (like brocade)

excellent peak hosta," has a light yellowish white leaf with a yellow margin. One of the numerous sports with *H. montana* lineage.
JN: *Shuho Nishiki Giboshi* hort.
[*H. montana* mutation].

H. sieboldiana 'Alba'.
(see *H. sieboldiana* 'Elegans Alba').

H. sieboldiana 'Amplissima'.
H. sieboldiana var. *amplissima.*

H. sieboldiana 'Aurea'.
(see *H. sieboldiana* Yellow group).

H. sieboldiana Aureomarginata group.

H. sieboldiana 'Elegans'.
H. sieboldiana var. *elegans.*

H. sieboldiana 'Elegans Alba'.

H. sieboldiana 'Engler' incorrect.
A horticultural name for *H. sieboldiana* (Hooker) Engler.
HN: *H.* 'FRW No. 942A'.
        H. 'FRW No. 1151' 1950.

H. sieboldiana 'Frances Williams'.

H. sieboldiana 'Gigantea' Nesmith incorrect.
This name is used botanically for another taxon.
[*H. sieboldiana* × *H. sieboldiana* 'Elegans'].

H. sieboldiana 'Hypophylla'.
H. sieboldiana var. *hypophylla.*

H. sieboldiana 'Longipes' incorrect.
Plant is of Japanese origin. Seed was received under the name *H. sieboldiana* var. *longipes* by Mrs. F. R. Williams from T. Sataka, Yokohama, Japan (Fisher, 1967). It is not the same plant as *H. sieboldiana* var. *longipes* Matsumura (1905), so the name as applied here is illegitimate under the ICBN and invalid as a cultivar name under the ICNCP because of its Latin form. As a consequence Hensen (1985) renamed it *H.* 'Elata Fountain' writing it *H. elata* 'Fountain'.
(see *H.* 'Fountain').

H. sieboldiana Mediovariegata group.

H. sieboldiana 'Mira'.
H. sieboldiana var. *mira.*

H. sieboldiana 'Mrs Allen' incorrect.
HN: *H. sieboldiana* 'From Mrs Allen' incorrect.
[*H. sieboldiana* hybrid].

H. 'Sieboldiana 942A'.
        H. sieboldiana 'From Engler'.
[*H. sieboldiana* hybrid].

H. sieboldiana 'Semperaurea'.

H. sieboldiana Yellow group.

H. sieboldii 'Alba'.
H. sieboldii f. *alba.*

H. sieboldii 'Bunchoko'.
H. sieboldii f. *bunchoko.*

H. sieboldii 'Fuiri Chishima'.

H. sieboldii 'Hime Kin Cho'.

H. sieboldii 'Kabitan'.
H. sieboldii f. *kabitan.*
(see also *H.* 'Kabitan').

H. sieboldii 'Kifukurin'.
H. sieboldii f. *kifukurin.*

H. sieboldii 'Mediopicta'.
H. sieboldii f. *mediopicta.*

H. sieboldii 'Ogon Hime'.

H. sieboldii 'Ogon Kobano'.

H. sieboldii 'Oze'.

H. sieboldii 'Oze Mizu'.

H. sieboldii 'Shirokabitan'.
(see *H. sieboldii* 'Silver Kabitan').

H. sieboldii 'Silver Kabitan'.

H. sieboldii 'Subcrocea'.
H. sieboldii f. *subchrocea.*
(see also *H.* 'Subcrocea').

H. 'Silberpfeil' Klose.
Plant's name means "Silver Arrow." A *H.* Tardiana grex hybrid with lavender flowers and silver-grey lanceolate leaves.
HN: *H.* Tardiana grex.
[*H.* 'Tardiflora' × *H. sieboldiana* 'Elegans'].
(see also *H.* Tardiana grex).

H. 'Silver Award' Fisher 1977 IRA/1986.
AHS-I/3B.
[*H. sieboldiana* Aureomarginata group hybrid].

H. 'Silver Bowl' Fisher 1977 IRA/1986.
AHS-II/9B.
Plant 24 in. (61 cm) dia., 18 in. (46 cm) high. Leaf 6 by 4.5 in. (15 by 11.5 cm), veins 13, blue-green, not variegated, cordate, piecrust margin. Scape 30 in. (76 cm), bare, oblique. Flower medium, bell-shaped, white, flowers during average period, fertile.
[*H.* 'Tokudama' hybrid].

H. 'Silver Crown'.
(see *H.* 'Fortunei Albomarginata').

H. 'Silver Dust' Fisher 1976.
Plant is small, with silver-bluish pruinose and whitish coated underside. White, bell-shaped flowers.
[*H.* 'Tokudama' hybrid].

H. 'Silver Edge' Hauser.

H. 'Silver Giant' Owens IRA/1987.
AHS-I/3B.
Plant 42 in. (106.5 cm) dia., 28 in. (71 cm) high. Leaf 14 by

13 in. (35.5 by 33 cm), veins 16, blue-green, not variegated, cordate, rugose. Scape 28 in. (71 cm), foliated, oblique. Flower medium, bell-shaped, white, flowers during average period, fertile.
[*H. sieboldiana* 'Mira' hybrid].

H. 'Silver Japanese' Grapes/Summers 1969.
HN: Summers No. 197 1969.

H. 'Silver Kabitan'.
HN: *H. sieboldii* 'Silver Kabitan'.

H. 'Silver Lance' Savory IRA/1982.
AHS-IV/22B.
Plant 12 in. (31 cm) dia., 8 in. (20 cm) high. Leaf 6 by 1.5 in. (15 by 4 cm), veins 4, medium green, margin white, lanceolate, flat. Scape 16 in. (40.5 cm), bare, straight. Flower medium, funnel-shaped, purple striped, flowers during summer period, fertile.
[*H.* 'Sentinels' mutation].

H. 'Silver Parasol' Moldovan.

H. 'Silver Rim' Minks IRA/1980.
AHS-III/15B.
Plant has a thin silvery-white line on the margin of a blue-grey leaf. Much like *H.* 'Helen Field Fischer'.
[*H.* 'Tokudama' × *H.* 'Tokudama'].
[*H.* 'Helen Field Fisher' hybrid al].

H. 'Silver Spoon' Langdon IRA/1985.
AHS-V/26A.
AHS Savory Shield Award, 1984. Plant is a selected and named sport belonging broadly to *H. sieboldii* 'Silver Kabitan' but has white flowers. Plant 6 in. (15 cm) dia., 4 in. (10 cm) high. Leaf 4 by 1 in. (10 by 2.5 cm), veins 3, white (viridescent), margin green, lanceolate, flat. Scape 12 in. (31 cm), bare, straight. Flower medium, funnel-shaped, white, flowers during summer period, fertile.
[*H. sieboldii* 'Butter Rim' mutation].

H. 'Silver Streak' Zager/Krossa IRA/1986.
AHS-IV/20A.   (Figure 4-42).
AHS Nancy Minks Award, 1985. Plant is a unique cultivar with silvery white center and dark green margins. Plant 12 in. (31 cm) dia., 8 in. (20 cm) high. Leaf 4 by 1.5 in. (10 by 4 cm), veins 6, white (albescent), margin dark green, lanceolate, wavy-undulate-contorted. Scape 12 in. (31 cm), bare, straight. Flower medium, funnel-shaped, purple striped, flowers during summer period, sterile.
HN: *H.* 'Krossa No. A-2' Summers No. 170 1968.

Figure 4-42. *H.* 'Silver Streak'; general habit (Chastain garden/Schmid)

H. 'Silver Tiara' Walters Gardens IRA/1988.
AHS-V/26A.
Plant 12 in. (31 cm) dia., 8 in. (20 cm) high. Leaf 3 by 2 in. (7.5 by 5 cm), veins 6, white (albescent), margin yellow turning chartreuse, cordate, flat. Scape 14 in. (35.5 cm), bare, straight. Flower medium, bell-shaped, purple striped, flowers during average period, fertile.
[*H. nakaiana* 'Golden Tiara' mutation].

H. 'Silver Tips' Nesmith 1965.
Summers No. 179.

H. 'Silverado' Kuk's Forest IRA/1987.
AHS-IV/22B.
Plant has chartreuse regular margin that turns white. Plant 9 in. (23 cm) dia., 5 in. (13 cm) high. Leaf 4.5 by 2 in. (11.5 by 5 cm), veins 3, medium green, chartreuse (albescent) margin, lanceolate, undulate-ruffled. Scape 15 in. (38 cm), bare, straight. Flower medium, bell-shaped, purple striped, flowers during late period, fertile.
[*H. sieboldii* mutation].

H. 'Silverdale'.
HN: *H. sieboldiana* 'Silverdale'.
[*H. sieboldiana* hybrid].

H. 'Sir Knight' Moldovan.

H. 'Sitting Pretty' Aden IRA/1987.
AHS-IV/20A.
Plant has light yellow center, two-tone green margin, variable width. Plant 8 in. (20 cm) dia., 4 in. (10 cm) high. Leaf 7 by 1.5 in. (18 by 4 cm), veins 3, yellow, green margin, lanceolate, flat. Scape 12 in. (31 cm), foliated, straight. Flower medium, funnel-shaped, purple striped, flowers during late period, fertile.
[*H.* 'Reiko' × *H.* 'Amy Aden' hybrid].

H. 'Sky Crystal'.

H. 'Sky Kissed' Powell.
Plant 55 in. (140 cm) dia., 19 in. (48 cm) high. Large blue leaves. Flower medium, lavender.

H. 'Skylands' Skylands Nursery.
HN: Summers No. 102 1963.

H. 'Slim Crinkles' Fisher.
Plant is similar to the all-green *H crispula*, but lighter green, with narrower leaves that have crispate margin and are otherwise flat.
[*H.* 'Crispula' hybrid].

H. 'Slim Polly' Williams 1964 IRA/1986.
AHS-IV/19A.
Plant 12 in. (31 cm) dia., 8 in. (20 cm) high. Leaf 4 by 1 in. (10 by 2.5 cm), veins 3, medium green, not variegated, lanceolate, flat. Scape 14 in. (35.5 cm), bare, straight. Flower medium, funnel-shaped, purple striped, flowers during summer period, fertile.
HN: *H.* 'FRW No. 1155'.

H. 'Snow Cap' Aden IRA/1980.
AHS-III/16B.
Plant 36 in. (91.5 cm) dia., 24 in. (61 cm) high. Leaf medium, veins 9, blue-green, margin white, cordate, rugose. Scape 28 in. (71 cm), bare, straight. Flower medium, funnel-shaped, purple striped, flowers during summer period, fertile.
[*H.* 'Wide Brim' × *H.* 'Royal Rainbow'].

H. **'Snow Cream'** Lewis.
  Plant 12 in. (31 cm) dia., 8 in. (20 cm) high. Leaf small, veins 3, medium green, not variegated, lanceolate, flat. Scape 14 in. (35.5 cm), bare, straight. Flower medium, funnel-shaped, white, flowers during summer period, fertile.
HN: Summers No. 159 1963.
[*H. sieboldii* 'Alba' hybrid].

H. **'Snow Crust'** Zilis IRA/1985.
  AHS-II/10A.
  Plant is a sport found in tissue culture explants of what the laboratory calls *H.* 'Fortunei Gigantea'. Plant 54 in. (137 cm) dia., 28 in. (71 cm) high. Leaf 13 by 9 in. (33 by 23 cm), veins 13, medium green, margin white, cordate, flat. Scape 48 in. (122 cm), bare, straight. Flower medium, funnel-shaped, lavender, flowers during summer period, fertile.
[*H.* 'Elata' mutation].

H. **'Snow Flakes'** Williams (No. 1154) 1964 IRA/1986.
  AHS-IV/19A.
  Plant 12 in. (31 cm) dia., 8 in. (20 cm) high. Leaf 4 by 1 in. (10 by 2.5 cm), veins 3, medium green, not variegated, lanceolate, flat. Scape 14 in. (35.5 cm), bare, straight. Flower medium, funnel-shaped, white, flowers during summer period, fertile.
HN: *H.* 'FRW No. 1154'.
[*H. sieboldii* 'Alba' × *H. plantaginea*].

H. **'Snow Flurry'** Vaughn IRA/1973.
  AHS-V/28A.
  Plant has mosaic form variegation which is unstable. Plant 8 in. (20 cm) dia., 4 in. (10 cm) high. Leaf 4 by 1 in. (10 by 2.5 cm), veins 3, medium green, mottled, streaky white, lanceolate, flat. Scape 12 in. (31 cm), bare, straight. Flower medium, funnel-shaped, white, flowers during summer period, fertile.
[*H.* 'Snow Flakes' hybrid].

H. **'Snow Mound'** Lewis IRA/1986.
  AHS-IV/19A.
  Plant 12 in. (31 cm) dia., 8 in. (20 cm) high. Leaf 4 by 1 in. (10 by 2.5 cm), veins 3, medium green, not variegated, lanceolate, flat. Scape 14 in. (35.5 cm), bare, straight. Flower medium, funnel-shaped, white, flowers during summer period, fertile.
HN: *H.* 'Krossa No. H-1'.
    Summers No. 38.
[*H. sieboldii* 'Alba' mutation].

H. **'Snow Mound Variegated'** Summers.
  Plant has several forms of similar, streaky white-variegated sports discovered and numbered by Summers, but reported to be unstable. Plant 12 in. (31 cm) dia., 8 in. (20 cm) high. Leaf 4 by 1 in. (10 by 2.5 cm), veins 3, medium green, streaky white, lanceolate, flat. Scape 14 in. (35.5 cm), bare, straight. Flower medium, funnel-shaped, white, flowers during summer period, fertile.
HN: Summers Nos. 371 to 375 1970.
[*H.* 'Snow Mound' mutation].

H. **'Snow Sport'**.

H. **'Snow White'** Arett No. 240 IRA/1983.
  AHS-IV/20A.
  Plant is a selection of *H.* 'Undulata' with much more white in the leaf. Plant 20 in. (51 cm) dia., 14 in. (35.5 cm) high. Leaf 4 by 2.5 in. (10 by 6.5 cm), veins 7, white (viridescent), margin green, ovate-cordate, wavy-contorted. Scape 34 in. (86.5 cm), foliated, oblique. Flower medium, funnel-shaped, lavender, flowers during average period, sterile.
HN: *H.* 'Undulata Snow White'.
[*H.* 'Undulata' mutation].

H. **'Snowden'** Smith 1972 BHHS IRA/1988.
  AHS-II/9B.   (Plates 141, 163, 192).
  Plant is a stately cultivar showing the general aspects of *H.* 'Fortunei' but attaining the size of *H. sieboldiana*. Plant 52 in. (132 cm) dia., 32 in. (81.5 cm) high. Leaf 14 by 10 in. (35.5 by 25.5 cm), veins 11, blue-green, not variegated, cordate, flat. Scape 38 in. (96.5 cm), bare, straight. Flower medium, funnel-shaped, white, flowers during average period, fertile.
HN: *H.* 'Snowdon' incorrect.
    Wisley No. 854047.
[*H. sieboldiana* × *H.* 'Fortunei Aurea'].

H. **'Snowdrift'** Zilis IRA/1985.
  AHS-IV/20A.
  Plant 36 in. (91.5 cm) dia., 16 in. (40.5 cm) high. Leaf 8 by 5 in. (20 by 13 cm), veins 9, white (albescent), margin green, cordate, flat. Scape 32 in. (81.5 cm), bare, oblique. Flower medium, funnel-shaped, lavender, flowers during average period, fertile.
HN: *H.* 'Snow Drift' incorrect.
[*H.* 'Fortunei Francee' mutation].

H. **'Snowstorm'** Simpers IRA/1986.
  AHS-IV/19A.
  Plant has many white flowers. Plant 12 in. (31 cm) dia., 8 in. (20 cm) high. Leaf 4 by 1 in. (10 by 2.5 cm), veins 3, medium green, not variegated, lanceolate, flat. Scape 14 in. (35.5 cm), bare, straight. Flower medium, funnel-shaped, white, flowers during summer period, fertile.
HN: *H.* 'Snow Storm' incorrect.
    H. sieboldii 'Alba'.
[*H.* 'Fortunei' mutation al incorrect].
[*H. rectifolia* hybrid al].
[*H. sieboldii* mutation].

H. **'So Big'**.
  Plant is a cultivar with very large green leaves.

H. **'So Sweet'** Aden IRA/1986.
  AHS-III/16A.   (Plates 97, 159).
  Plant 12 in. (31 cm) dia., 8 in. (20 cm) high. Leaf 7 by 4.5 in. (18 by 11.5 cm), veins 6, medium green, white margin, lanceolate, flat. Scape 14 in. (35.5 cm), bare, straight. Flower medium, funnel-shaped, purple striped, flowers during summer period, fertile.
[*H.* 'Fragrant Bouquet' × *H.* 'Aden No. 462'].

H. **'Soft Touch'** Savory IRA/1977.
  AHS-IV/19B.
  Plant has heart-shaped, flat leaves. Flowers dark purple.
[*H. nakaiana* hybrid].

H. **'Solar Flare'** Ross IRA/1981 (P.P. 7046).
  AHS-I/5A.
  Plant 52 in. (132 cm) dia., 28 in. (71 cm) high. Leaf giant, veins 16, chartreuse changing to yellow center with green veins, cordate, rugose. Scape 34 in. (86.5 cm), bare, straight. Flower medium, funnel-shaped, lavender, flowers during summer period, fertile.
[*H. montana* hybrid].

H. **'Something Blue'** Simpers.
  Plant medium. Leaf 5 by 4 in. (13 by 10 cm); cordate leaves are pruinose, rugose. Scape short, bare, straight. Flowers white.
[*H.* 'Blue Boy' hybrid].

H. 'Southern Pride' Suggs IRA/1986.
AHS-III/16A.
Plant 12 in. (31 cm) dia., 8 in. (20 cm) high. Leaf 6 by 4 in. (15 by 10 cm), veins 11, light green, irregular chartreuse margin and streaking to the center, ovate, rugose. Scape 15 in. (38 cm), bare, straight. Flower medium, funnel-shaped, lavender, flowers during summer period, fertile.
[*H.* 'Fascination' × *H.* 'Christmas Tree'].

H. 'Sotoyama Fukurin'.
黄覆輪ミズギボウシ
Plant is a yellow-margined *H. longissima* found in Nukata.
JN: *Kifukurin Mizu Giboshi.*
(see *H. longissima* 'Kifukurin').

H. 'Sparkling Burgundy' Savory IRA/1982.
AHS-IV/19A.
Plant 20 in. (51 cm) dia., 12 in. (31 cm) high. Leaf 4 by 3.5 in. (10 by 9 cm), dark green, not variegated, cordate, rugose. Scape 22 in. (56 cm), bare, straight. Flower medium, funnel-shaped, purple, flowers during summer period, fertile.
[*H.* 'Ginko Craig' hybrid].

H. 'Sparky' Aden IRA/1987.
AHS-IV/22A.
Plant has yellow undulate margin that turns white, variable width. Plant 8 in. (20 cm) dia., 4 in. (10 cm) high. Leaf 6 by 1.5 in. (15 by 4 cm), veins 3, medium green, yellow (albescent) margin, lanceolate, flat. Scape 10 in. (25.5 cm), bare, straight. Flower medium, funnel-shaped, purple striped, flowers during late period, fertile.
[*H.* 'Amy Aden' × *H. pulchella*].

H. 'Spartan Gem' Banyai IRA/1989.
AHS-IV/19B.
Plant 24 in. (61 cm) dia., 14 in. (35 cm) high. Leaf 6 by 2.5 in. (15 by 6 cm), veins 6, dark green, not variegated, ovate-lanceolate, wavy margin. Scape purple-dotted, straight. Flower medium, funnel-shaped, lavender, flowers during summer period, fertile.

H. 'Special Gift' Fisher IRA/1973.
AHS-III/13A.
Plant 20 in. (51 cm) dia., 12 in. (31 cm) high. Leaf 4 by 3 in. (10 by 7.5 cm), veins 9, blue-green, not variegated, cordate, flat. Scape 24 in. (61 cm), bare, straight. Flower medium, bell-shaped, purple, flowers during average period, fertile.
[*H. nakaiana* hybrid].

H. 'Special Item' Fisher 1961.
Plant 30 in. (76 cm) dia., 18 in. (46 cm) high. Leaf 10 by 8 in. (25.5 by 20 cm), veins 12, medium green, not variegated, cordate, wavy margin. Scape 26 in. (66 cm), bare, straight. Flower medium, bell-shaped, white, flowers during average period, fertile.
[*H.* 'Elata' hybrid].

H. 'Spilt Milk' Seaver.
AHS Nancy Minks Award, 1989. Plant has leaves that are *H.* 'Tokudama' form with streaky and splashed white and greenish white on darker green background and a more-or-less darker, variable margin; the variegation is quite variable. Plant 24 in. (61 cm) dia., 14 in. (35.5 cm) high. Leaf 9 by 7 in. (23 by 18 cm), veins 13, streaky white and greenish white on green, margin darker green, cordate, cupped-rugose. Scape 18 in. (46 cm), bare, straight. Flower medium, bell-shaped, white, flowers during average period, fertile.
[*H.* 'Tokudama' form].

H. 'Spinners' Smith/Chappell BHHS IRA/1988.
AHS-III/16A. (Plate 192).
Plants sold in the United Kingdom under the names *H.* 'Goldbrook' and *H.* 'Spinners' are similar to *H.* 'Antioch' but may have narrower leaves, although this may equalize as plants mature. Plant 36 in. (91.5 cm) dia., 20 in. (51 cm) high. Leaf 10 by 7 in. (25.5 by 18 cm), veins 7, medium green, white margin, ovate, flat. Scape 32 in. (81.5 cm), foliated, oblique. Flower medium, funnel-shaped, lavender, flowers during average period, sterile.
HN: *H.* 'Albo Aurea' UK incorrect.
H. 'Fortunei Albo Aurea' Smith UK incorrect.
H. 'Goldbrook' Goldbrook pp sim.
H. 'Moerheim' pp sim.
[*H.* 'Fortunei' hybrid].
(see *H.* 'Antioch').

H. 'Spinning Wheel' Seaver 1986.
Plant has variegation that is extremely variable, some leaves more green than yellow. Plant 24 in. (61 cm) dia., 14 in. (35.5 cm) high. Leaf 9 by 7 in. (23 by 18 cm), veins 13, yellow (lutescent), margin green, cordate, cupped-rugose. Scape 18 in. (46 cm), bare, straight. Flower medium, bell-shaped, white, flowers during average period, fertile.
[*H.* 'Tokudama Aureonebulosa' form].

H. 'Spit Shine' Aden IRA/1986.
AHS-III/13A.
Plant 38 in. (96.5 cm) dia., 20 in. (51 cm) high. Leaf 7 by 6 in. (18 by 15 cm), veins 8, shiny medium green, not variegated, cordate, flat. Scape 26 in. (66 cm), bare, straight. Flower large, funnel-shaped, white, flowers during summer period, fertile.
[*H. plantaginea* hybrid].

H. 'Splashes' Minks.
Plant 30 in. (76 cm) dia., 16 in. (40.5 cm) high. Leaf has 14 veins, chartreuse, streaky green, cordate, rugose. Scape 22 in. (56 cm), bare, straight. Flower medium, bell-shaped, white, flowers during average period, fertile.
[*H.* 'Golden Nugget' hybrid].

H. 'Splish-Splash' Aden IRA/1980.
AHS-III/16A.
Plant 22 in. (56 cm) dia., 12 in. (31 cm) high. Leaf 7 by 5 in. (18 by 13 cm), veins 9, medium green, streaky yellow, cordate, flat. Scape 24 in. (61 cm). Flower medium, funnel-shaped, lavender, flowers during average period, fertile.
[*H.* 'Fascination' × *H.* 'Intrigue'].

H. 'Sprengeri' hort.
(see *H.* 'Fortunei Aureomarginata').

H. 'Spring Dream' Japan.
(see *H.* 'Haru No Yume').

H. 'Spring Gold' Klose 1982.

H. 'Spring Gold' Stone.

H. 'Spring Ivory' Lantis IRA/1982.
AHS-IV/24A.
Plant has leaves that start out whitish and turn all green. Plant 12 in. (31 cm) dia., 4 in. (10 cm) high. Leaf 4 by 1 in. (10 by 2.5 cm), veins 4, white (viridescent), not variegated, lanceolate, flat. Scape 14 in. (35.5 cm), bare, straight. Flower medium, bell-shaped, purple, flowers during average period, fertile.
[*H.* 'Wogon' hybrid].

H. **'Sprite'** Williams (No. 791) 1946.
HN: *H.* 'FRW No 791'.

H. **'Spritzer'** Aden IRA/1986.
AHS-III/14A.
Plant erect, 18 in. (46 cm) dia., 18 in. (46 cm) high. Leaf 9 by 5 in. (23 by 13 cm), veins 5, yellowish (viridescent) center, irregular margin light and dark green, ovate-lanceolate, flat. Scape 30 in. (76 cm), foliated, straight. Flower medium, funnel-shaped, purple, flowers during summer period, fertile. [*H.* 'Aden No. 349' × *H.* 'Green Fountain'].

H. **'Spun Sulphur'** O'Harra IRA/1986.
AHS-IV/23A.
Plant 12 in. (31 cm) dia., 8 in. (20 cm) high. Leaf 4 by 3.5 in. (10 by 9 cm), veins 4, yellow (viridescent), not variegated, lanceolate, flat. Scape 14 in. (35.5 cm), bare, straight. Flower medium, funnel-shaped, purple striped, flowers during summer period, fertile.
[*H. sieboldii* 'Subcrocea' hybrid].

H. **'Squash Edge'** Donahue.
Plant is a yellow-margined *H. sieboldiana*.
HN: *H. sieboldiana* Aureomarginata group.
Summers No. 378 1970.
[*H. sieboldiana* mutation].

H. **'Squiggles'** Aden IRA/1978.
AHS-V/26A.
Plant 10 in. (25.5 cm) dia., 6 in. (15 cm) high. Leaf 3 by 1 in. (7.5 by 2.5 cm), veins 4, white (viridescent), margin green streaking to center, lanceolate, wavy. Scape 12 in. (31 cm), bare, straight. Flowers medium, funnel-shaped, purple striped, flowers during summer period, fertile.

H. **'Squire Rich'** Kuk's Forest IRA/1988.
AHS-III/17B.
Plant 24 in. (61 cm) dia., 18 in. (46 cm) high. Leaf 9 by 5 in. (23 by 13 cm), veins 10, light chartreuse (lutescent), not variegated, ovate-cordate, wavy-undulate. Scape 28 in. (71 cm), bare, straight. Flower medium, bell-shaped, lavender, flowers during summer period, fertile.

H. **'Standard Bearer'**.
Plant is a very large *H. sieboldiana* form.

H. **'Standing Ovation'** Vaughn IRA/1987.
AHS-II/10B.
Plant has uniform white margin. Flowers clustered at tip. Plant 34 in. (86.5 cm) dia., 26 in. (66 cm) high. Leaf 12 by 10 in. (31 by 25.5 cm), veins 12, dark green, yellowish white margin, cordate, rugose. Scape 38 in. (96.5 cm), bare, oblique. Flower medium, bell-shaped, lavender, flowers during average period, fertile.
[A variegated seedling × *H.* 'Goliath'].

H. **'Starburst'** Eisel IRA/1973.
AHS-IV/22B.
AHS, Eunice Fisher Award 1972. Variegation unstable. Plant 10 in. (25.5 cm) dia., 6 in. (15 cm) high. Leaf 4 by 1.5 in. (10 by 4 cm), veins 3, medium green, whitish streaks, lanceolate, flat. Scape 12 in. (31 cm), bare, straight. Flower medium, funnel-shaped, purple striped, flowers during summer period, fertile.
[*H. sieboldii* 'Beatrice' hybrid].

H. **'Starburst Stable'** Eisel IRA/1973.
Plant is the stable marginata form *H.* 'Starburst'. Plant 10 in. (25.5 cm) dia., 6 in. (15 cm) high. Leaf 5 by 1.5 in. (13 by 4 cm), veins 3, medium green, margin white, lanceolate, flat. Scape 12 in. (31 cm), bare, straight. Flower medium, funnel-shaped, purple striped, flowers during summer period, fertile.
[*H. sieboldii* 'Starburst' mutation].

H. **'Starker Aureafolia'** Starker.
Plant name is illegitimate per the ICNCP. This taxon has been registered under the name *H.* 'Starker Yellow Leaf', which see.

H. **'Starker Yellow Leaf'** Starker/Ruh IRA/1989.
AHS-II/12B.
Plant 53 in. (132 cm) dia., 27 in. (68 cm) high. Leaf 13 by 10 in. (33 by 25.5 cm), veins 15, yellow (viridescent) turning to dark green, not variegated, cordate, undulate margin. Scape 42 in. (105 cm), bare, oblique. Flower medium, funnel-shaped, lavender, flowers during average period, fertile.
HN: *H.* 'Aurea Folia' Starker incorrect.
H. 'Aurea Folio' Starker incorrect.
H. 'Aureafolia' Starker incorrect.
H. 'Krossa No. G-3'.
H. 'Laella' Tompkins.
H. '1928 No. 11 W E' Tompkins.
H. 'Starker Aureafolia' Starker incorrect.
H. 'Starker No. 1' Starker.
[*H. sieboldii* mutation or hybrid].

H. **'Starlight'** Eisel IRA/1973.
AHS-IV/20A.
Plant 20 in. (51 cm) dia., 12 in. (31 cm) high. Leaf 5 by 3.5 in. (13 by 9 cm), veins 8, white (viridescent), margin green, ovate, flat. Scape 28 in. (71 cm), foliated, straight. Flower medium, funnel-shaped, lavender, flowers during average period, fertile.
[*H.* 'Fortunei' mutation al].
[*H.* 'Undulata' mutation].
(see also *H.* 'White Christmas').

H. **'Stenantha Variegated'** hort. incorrect.
Plant name is an incorrect synonym.
HN: *H.* 'Fortunei Stenantha Variegated'.
[*H.* 'Fortunei Stenantha' mutation].
(see *H.* 'Fortunei Stenantha Variegated').

H. **'Stephen'** Weissenberger IRA/1986.
AHS-V/27B.
Plant 8 in. (20 cm) dia., 4 in. (10 cm) high. Leaf 1.75 by 1 in. (4.5 by 2.5 cm), veins 4, blue-green, not variegated, cordate, flat. Scape 8 in. (20 cm), bare, straight. Flower medium, bell-shaped, purple, flowers during summer period, fertile.
[*H.* 'Blue Cadet' hybrid].

H. **'Stiletto'** Aden IRA/1987.
AHS-IV/22A.
Plant has very narrow white margin. Plant erect, 8 in. (20 cm) dia., 6 in. (15 cm) high. Leaf 7 by 1 in. (18 by 2.5 cm), veins 3, medium green, white margin, lanceolate, undulate. Scape 12 in. (31 cm), foliated, straight. Flower medium, funnel-shaped, purple striped, flowers during summer period, fertile.
[*H.* 'Amy Aden' × *H. pulchella*].

H. **'Stolon'** Klose.
HN: *H. clausa* 'Stolon'.
(see *H. clausa* 'Stolon').

H. **'Stones'** Stone.
Plant is a named selection of the species.
[*H. sieboldiana* form].

H. **'Stones Fantasy'** Stone 1974.
(see *H.* 'Wolcott').

H. **'Stones Golden Sunburst'.**

H. **'Stones Valentine'** Piedmont Gardens/Stone/Ruh IRA/1989.
AHS-IV/23B.
Plant 9 in. (22 cm) dia., 4 in. (10 cm) high. Leaf 3 by 2 in. (7.5 by 5 cm), veins 5, yellowish green, not variegated, cordate, flat. Scape 15 in. (38 cm), bare, straight. Flower medium, bell-shaped, lavender flowers during summer period, fertile.

H. **'Streaked Tiara'** T&Z/Walters.
Plant has variegation that is probably unstable. Plant 18 in. (46 cm) dia., 12 in. (31 cm) high. Leaf 3 by 2 in. (7.5 by 5 cm), veins 5, yellow (lutescent), streaky green, cordate, flat. Scape 28 in. (71 cm), bare, straight. Flower medium, bell-shaped, purple striped, flowers during average period, fertile.
[*H. nakaiana* 'Golden Tiara' mutation].

H. **'Sturtevant'** Donahue.
[*H. sieboldiana* form].

H. **'Subcordata'** hort.
Plant name is an incorrect synonym.
(see *H. plantaginea*).

H. **'Subcordata Grandiflora'** hort.
Plant name is an incorrect synonym.
(see *H. plantaginea*).

H. **'Subcrocea'** AHS NC IRA/1987.
AHS-IV/23B.
The cultivar name registered for show purposes for *H. sieboldii* f. *subcrocea*.
(see *H. sieboldii* 'Subcrocea').

H. **'Sugar and Cream'** Zilis IRA/1984.
AHS-III/16A.   (Figure 4-43).
AHS Savory Shield Award, 1985. Plant is the white-margined form of *H.* 'Honeybells' found in tissue culture explants. Very vigorous and more desirable than the all-green parent. Plant 46 in. (117 cm) dia., 26 in. (66 cm) high. Leaf 10 by 5 in. (20 by 10 cm), veins 8, medium green, margin white, cordate, flat. Scape 54 in. (137 cm), foliated, straight. Flower medium, bell-shaped, lavender, fragrant, flowers during summer period, fertile.
[*H.* 'Honeybells' mutation].

Figure 4-43. *H.* 'Sugar and Cream'; general habit (Wallace garden/Schmid)

H. **'Sugar Plum Fairy'** Briggs IRA/1987.
AHS-V/25B.
Plant is a selected form of *H. gracillima*, usually not growing to the size specified in the registration document (24 in. dia by 12 in. high). Plant 8 in. (20 cm) dia., 4 in. (10 cm) high. Leaf 2 by 0.5 in. (5 by 1 cm), veins 3, shiny green, not variegated, lanceolate, flat, but margin wavy. Scape 10 in. (25 cm), foliated, straight. Flower medium, funnel-shaped, purple striped, flowers during summer period, fertile.
HN: *H.* 'Ko Mame' sim.
[*H. gracillima* sel].

H. **'Sultana'** Zumbar IRA/1988.
AHS-IV/22B.
Plant 11 in. (28 cm) dia., 7 in. (18 cm) high. Leaf 4 by 2.5 in. (10 by 6.5 cm), veins 6, dark green, margin chartreuse, cordate, wavy-undulate. Scape 10 in. (25.5 cm), foliated, straight. Flowers medium, bell-shaped, white, flowers during average period, barely fertile.
[*H.* 'Little Aurora' mutation].

H. **'Sum and Substance'** Aden 1979 IRA/1980.
AHS-I/5B.   (Figures 2-10, 2-11; Plates 147, 151).
AHS multiple award winner: AHS President's Exhibitor Trophy, 1987, exhibited by Richard Ward; Eunice Fisher Award, 1984; and Midwest Gold Award, 1984, exhibited by Olive and Joe Langdon; AHS Alex J. Summers Distinguished Merit Hosta, 1990, selected by Jim Cooper. Plant is a huge cultivar with heavy substance; useful as a specimen plant. White pruinose on back of leaf. Needs some sun to go from chartreuse to yellow, so yellowing depends on location. Plant 60 in. (152.5 cm) dia., 30 in. (76 cm) high. Leaf 20 by 15 in. (51 by 38 cm), veins 14, yellow (lutescent), not variegated, cordate, when young flattish, well-grown older plants become rugose. Scape 38 in. (96.5 cm), bare, oblique. Flower medium, bell-shaped, white, flowers during average period, fertile.

H. **'Sumi'** Moldovan IRA/1983.
AHS-I/3B.
Plant 54 in. (137 cm) dia., 36 in. (91.5 cm) high. Leaf 13 by 11 in. (33 by 28 cm), veins 16, blue-grey green, not variegated, cordate, rugose. Scape 36 in. (91.5 cm), foliated, straight. Flower medium, bell-shaped, white, flowers during summer period, fertile.
[*H. sieboldiana* 'Elegans' hybrid].

H. **'Summer Fragrance'** Vaughn IRA/1983.
AHS-II/10A.   (Figure 2-3).
Plant 40 in. (101.5 cm) dia., 24 in. (61 cm) high. Leaf 8 by 4 in. (20 by 10 cm), veins 8, center medium green with lighter and darker green streaks, margin white, irregular, cordate, flat. Scape 60 in. (152.5 cm), foliated, straight. Flower large, bell-shaped, lavender-purple, fragrant, flowers during summer period, fertile.
HN: *H.* 'Fragrant Summer' incorrect.
[*H. plantaginea* × *H.* 'Vaughn No. 73-2'].

H. **'Summer Gold'** Nesmith/Phillips/Hamblin.
Plant is a viridescent yellow form that is smaller than the species. Turns all green.
HN: *H.* 'FRW No. 541' 1962.
[*H. sieboldiana* hybrid].

H. **'Summer Ripples'.**

H. **'Summer Snow'** Canon IRA/1978.
AHS-II/10B.
Plant 42 in. (106.5 cm) dia., 24 in. (61 cm) high. Leaf 11 by

9 in. (28 by 23 cm), veins 16, blue-green, margin white, cordate, rugose. Scape 30 in. (76 cm), foliated, straight. Flower medium, bell-shaped, white, flowers during average period, fertile.

[*H. sieboldiana* mutation].

H. 'Summers No. 00' Summers.

Plants numbered by the first president and cofounder of The American Hosta Society who exchanged many hostas with other collectors and imported them from Japan and Europe. Keeping careful records he numbered acquisitions, gave the source of the plant, and provided identification where this was required. His 1972 listing is an important historical reference for this present volume. It contains 581 entries, some of those which provided important clues to identification are listed below. Many of Summers' other numbered taxa are of interest to researchers only, so I have not listed them.

Summers No. 1 1963
= *H.* 'Elephant Ears'.
Summers No. 17 1963
= *H.* 'Maya'.
Summers No. 20 1963
= *H.* 'North Hills'.
Summers No. 21 1963
= *H.* 'Viettes Yellow Edge'.
Summers No. 23 1963
= *H.* 'Fall Emerald'.
Summers No. 27 1963
= *H.* 'Undulata' form.
Summers No. 29 1963
= *H.* 'See Saw'.
Summers No. 30 1966
= *H.* 'Krossa F-7'.
Summers No. 30 1966
= *H.* 'August Moon'.
Summers No. 43 1963
= *H.* 'Golden Plum'.
Summers No. 45 1967
= *H.* 'Tall Twister'.
Summers No. 46 1967
= *H. clausa.*
Summers No. 50 1966
= *H.* 'Gloriosa'.
Summers No. 51 1967
= *H. clausa* var. *normalis.*
Summers No. 53 1966
= *H.* 'Freckles'.
Summers No. 61 1967
= *H.* 'Louisa'.
Summers No. 69 1967
= *H.* 'Krossa Regal'.
Summers No. 71 1967
= *H.* 'Ros Hogh'.
Summers No. 73 1967
= *H.* 'Golden Honey'.
Summers No. 75 1964
= *H.* 'Lady Lou'.
Summers No. 78 1967
= *H. montana* 'Praeflorens'.
Summers No. 78 1967
= *H. montana* form.
Summers No. 80 1967
= *H. montana* form.
Summers No. 86 1967
= *H. sieboldii* hybrid (= PI 275394).
Summers No. 87 1962
= *H.* 'Golden Lance'.

Summers No. 92 1963
= *H.* 'Elephant Ears'.
Summers No. 98 1963
= *H.* 'Jumbo'.
Summers No. 100 1963
= *H.* 'Golden Glimmer'.
Summers No. 101 1963
= *H.* 'Black Pod'.
Summers No. 104 1963
= *H.* 'Haku-Chu-Han'.
Summers No. 108 1963
= *H.* 'July Gold'.
Summers No. 110 1969
= *H.* 'Saishu Jima'.
Summers No. 111 1967
= *H. nigrescens* form.
Summers No. 115 1967
= *H. sieboldii* form.
Summers No. 125 1967
= *H.* 'Starker Aureafolia'.
Summers No. 140 1967
= *H.* 'Willimantic'.
Summers No. 143 1968
= *H.* 'Charldon'.
Summers No. 145 1967
= *H.* 'Herifu'.
Summers No. 151 1967
= *H. minor* (= PI 318546).
Summers No. 158 1968
= *H.* 'Marble Rim'.
Summers No. 170 1967
= *H.* 'Silver Streak'.
Summers No. 181 1969
= *H. longipes* hybr.
Summers No. 182 1969
= *H. montana* hybr.
Summers No. 183 1969
= *H.* 'Tortifrons'.
Summers No. 184 1969
= *H. pachyscapa.*
Summers No. 185 1969
= *H. longipes* dwarf form.
Summers No. 189 1969
= *H.* 'Tortifrons' form.
Summers No. 196 1968
= *H.* 'Wogon'.
Summers No. 197 1970
= *H.* 'Silver Japanese'.
Summers No. 246 1967
= *H. capitata* (= PI 318547).
Summers No. 280 1967
= *H. sieboldii* form (= PI 275393).
Summers No. 282 1967
= *H. montana* f. *macrophylla.*
Summers No. 298 1968
= *H.* 'Numor' (= *H.* 'Saishu Jima').
Summers No. 317 1969
= *H.* 'Belle Robinson'.
Summers No. 323 1969
= *H.* 'Saishu Jima'.
Summers No. 324 1969
= *H. sieboldii* f. *spathulata.*
Summers No. 331 1969
= *H. tardiva.*
Summers No. 332 1969
= *H. tardiva.*
Summers No. 334 1969
= *H. longipes* form.

Summers No. 335 1969
= *H.* 'Fortunei Aureomarginata'.
Summers No. 378 1970
= *H.* 'Squash Edge'.
Summers No. 392 1964
= *H.* 'Goliath'.
Summers No. 395 1970
= *H.* 'Golden Shimmer'.
Summers No. 411 1970
= *H. montana* form (= PI 274537).
Summers No. 412 1970
= *H.* 'Undulata' form (= PI 274704).
Summers No. 445 1970
= *H.* 'Harlequin Bells'.
Summers No. 448 1970
= *H. montana* form.
Summers No. 466 1970
= *H. montana* form.
Summers No. 472 1971
= *H.* 'Samual Blue'.
Summers No. 486 1971
= *H. montana* form.

H. **'Sun Glow'** Aden IRA/1974.
　　AHS-III/17B.
　　Plant has yellow leaves retaining their color well. Similar to the parent. Leaf 9 by 6 in. (23 by 15 cm).
[*H.* 'Aspen Gold' hybrid].

H. **'Sun Power'** Aden IRA/1986.
　　AHS-II/11A.
　　AHS Midwest Gold Award, 1986, exhibited by Warren Pollock. Plant erect, 36 in. (91.5 cm) dia., 24 in. (61 cm) high. Leaf 10 by 7.5 in. (25.5 by 19 cm), veins 12, yellow (lutescent), not variegated, ovate-cordate, wavy. Scape 36 in. (91.5 cm), foliated, oblique. Flower medium, funnel-shaped, lavender, flowers during average period, fertile.
HN: *H.* 'Golden Cascade'.
[*H.* 'Aden No. 217' × *H.* 'Aden No. 219'].

H. **'Sun Splash'** Soules.
　　Plant is a reverse mutation of *H.* 'Tokudama Aureonebulosa'.
[*H.* 'Tokudama Aureonebulosa' mutation].

H. **'Sundance'** Walters Gardens IRA/1984.
　　AHS-III/16B.　　　　　　　　　　(Plate 142).
　　Plant 24 in. (61 cm) dia., 18 in. (46 cm) high. Leaf 7 by 3.5 in. (18 by 9 cm), veins 7–9, medium green, margin irregular white, ovate-cordate, flat. Scape 36 in. (91.5 cm), foliated, straight. Flower medium, funnel-shaped, lavender, flowers during average period, fertile.
[*H.* 'Fortunei Aoki' mutation].

H. **'Sunlight'** Williams (No. 1142) 1968.
　　Plant 44 in. (112 cm) dia., 26 in. (66 cm) high. Leaf 10 by 8.5 in. (25.5 by 21.5 cm), veins 12, yellow (lutescent), not variegated, cordate, flat, barely rugose. Scape 32 in. (81.5 cm), foliated, straight. Flower medium, bell-shaped, white, flowers during average period, fertile.
HN: *H.* 'FRW No. 1142'.
[*H.* 'Elata' hybrid].

H. **'Sunlight Sister'** Williams (No. 2134) IRA/1986.
　　AHS-I/5A.
　　Plant is a stable yellow form of *H.* 'Elata'. Plant 42 in. (106.5 cm) dia., 26 in. (66 cm) high. Leaf 12 by 9 in. (31 by 23 cm), veins 12, yellow (lutescent), not variegated, cordate, flat, barely rugose. Scape 32 in. (81.5 cm), foliated, straight. Flower medium, bell-shaped, white, flowers during average period, fertile.
HN: *H.* 'FRW No. 2134'.
[*H.* 'Elata' hybrid yellow].

H. **'Sunny Smiles'** Tompkins.
　　Plant is similar to *H.* 'Shade Fanfare' but has a much darker green center.
[*H.* 'Old Gold Edge' × *H. sieboldiana* 'Frances Williams'].

H. **'Sunnybrook'** Stone/Ruh IRA/1987.
　　AHS-II/10B.
　　Plant has yellow margins varying in width. Looks like a small *H. sieboldiana* 'Frances Williams'. Plant 28 in. (71 cm) dia., 16 in. (40.5 cm) high. Leaf 8 by 6 in. (20 by 15 cm), veins 14, blue-green, yellow margin, cordate, cupped-rugose. Scape 18 in. (46 cm), foliated, oblique. Flower medium, bell-shaped, white, flowers during average period, fertile.
HN: *H.* 'DSM No. 5'.

H. **'Suns Glory'** Vaughn IRA/1982.
(see *H.* 'Sunshine Glory').

H. **'Sunset'** UK.
　　Plant is smaller than *H.* 'Hydon Sunset' but otherwise very similar.
(see also *H.* 'Hydon Sunset').

H. **'Sunshine Glory'** Vaughn IRA/1982.
　　AHS-II/8A.
　　AHS President's Exhibitor Trophy Award, 1988, exhibited by Richard Ward. Plant erect, 28 in. (71 cm) dia., 24 in. (61 cm) high. Leaf 8 by 5 in. (20 by 13 cm), veins 12, yellow margin, irregular, streaking to center in some leaves, ovate-cordate, rugose-wavy. Scape 32 in. (81.5 cm), foliated, oblique. Flower medium, bell-shaped, white, flowers during average period, fertile.
HN: *H.* 'Suns Glory'.
[*H.* 'Breeders Choice' × *H.* 'Golden Waffles'].

H. **'Sunshine Kid'** Aden IRA/1980.
　　AHS-IV/22A.
[*H.* 'Fascination' × *H.* 'High Fat Cream'].

H. **'Super Bowl'** Aden.
　　Plant erect, 22 in. (56 cm) dia., 18 in. (46 cm) high. Leaf 5.5 by 4.5 in. (14 by 11.5 cm), veins 13, yellow (lutescent), not variegated, cordate, deeply cupped, rugose. Scape 26 in. (66 cm), bare, straight. Flower medium, bell-shaped, white, flowers during average period, fertile.
[*H.* 'Tokudama' hybrid].

H. **'Super Seeder'** Houseworth 1986.
[*H.* 'August Moon' hybrid].

H. **'Super Streak'** Vaughn IRA/1982.
　　AHS-III/16A.
　　Plant 14 in. (35.5 cm) dia., 6 in. (15 cm) high. Leaf 4 by 2.5 in. (10 by 6.5 cm), veins 8, medium green, streaky white and yellowish white, ovate-cordate, flat. Scape 17 in. (43 cm), bare, straight. Flower medium, bell-shaped, lavender, flowers during summer period, fertile.

H. **'Superba'** Arends 1933.

Plant is a selected seedling of the species with very dark flowers.

HN: *H. ovata superba* nom. nudum Arends incorrect.

H. ovata 'Superba' hort. incorrect.

H. ventricosa 'Superba' hort.

(see *H. ventricosa*).

H. **'Surprise'** Williams 1961 IRA/1986.

AHS-IV/19A.

Plant 22 in. (56 cm) dia., 14 in. (35.5 cm) high. Leaf 5 by 2.5 in. (13 by 6.5 cm), veins 5, medium green, not variegated, cordate, flat. Scape 22 in. (56 cm), foliated, straight. Flower medium, funnel-shaped, lavender, fragrant, flowers during summer period, fertile.

HN: *H.* 'Sweet Susan' pp sim.

[*H. plantaginea* × *H. sieboldii* 'Alba'].

H. **'Susy'** Harrison 1964 IRA/1986.

AHS-IV/19A.

Plant 12 in. (31 cm) dia., 8 in. (20 cm) high. Leaf 5 by 1 in. (13 by 2.5 cm), veins 3, medium green, not variegated, lanceolate, flat. Scape 14 in. (35.5 cm), bare, straight. Flower medium, funnel-shaped, purple striped, flowers during summer period, fertile.

HN: *H.* 'Harrison No. 964'.

[*H. sieboldii* hybrid].

H. **'Suzuki Thumbnail'** Suzuki/Ruh IRA/1987.

AHS-VI/31A.

Plant bought by Craig in Japan at a market stall and sent to Davidson in 1964 (Davidson, 1990). In 1969 bought by Davidson directly from Suzuki. Cultivated under Davidson nos. 86 and 87. Plant 6 in. (15 cm) dia., 3 in. (7.5 cm) high. Leaf 2 by 1 in. (5 by 2.5 cm), veins 4, medium green, not variegated, cordate, flat. Scape 13 in. (33 cm), foliated, straight. Flower medium, bell-shaped, purple, flowers during average period, fertile.

HN: *H. venusta* 'Thumb Nail' pp.

[*H. venusta* sel].

(see also *H.* 'Thumb Nail').

H. **'Sweet Jill'** Benedict IRA/1986.

AHS-IV/20A.

Plant 15 in. (38 cm) dia., 12 in. (31 cm) high. Leaf 6 by 3.5 in. (15 by 9 cm), veins 6, white (albescent), margin green, streaking to center, ovate, flat. Scape 16 in. (40.5 cm), foliated, straight. Flower medium, funnel-shaped, lavender, fragrant, flowers during summer period, fertile.

[*H. plantaginea* × *H.* 'Tokudama' hybrid mutation].

H. **'Sweet Marjorie'** Benedict IRA/1983.

AHS-III/13A.

Plant 22 in. (56 cm) dia., 12 in. (31 cm) high. Leaf 7 by 4 in. (18 by 10 cm), veins 6, medium green, not variegated, ovate, wavy. Scape 42 in. (106.5 cm), foliated, oblique. Flower medium, funnel-shaped, lavender, fragrant, flowers during summer period, fertile.

[*H. plantaginea* × *H.* 'Ginko Craig'].

H. **'Sweet Standard'** Zilis IRA/1984.

AHS-III/16A.

Plant 24 in. (61 cm) dia., 16 in. (40.5 cm) high. Leaf 8 by 4 in. (20 by 10 cm), veins 8, medium green, streaky white, ovate, flat. Scape 38 in. (96.5 cm), foliated, oblique. Flower medium, funnel-shaped, lavender, fragrant, flowers during summer period, fertile.

[*H.* 'Honeybells' mutation].

H. **'Sweet Susan'** Williams (No. 133) 1958 IRA/1986.

AHS-III/13A.

Plant 30 in. (76 cm) dia., 18 in. (46 cm) high. Leaf 6.5 by 4 in. (16.5 by 10 cm), veins 8, medium green, not variegated, cordate, flat. Scape 32 in. (81.5 cm), foliated, oblique. Flower medium, funnel-shaped, lavender, fragrant, flowers during summer period, fertile.

HN: *H.* 'FRW No. 1383'.

[*H. plantaginea* × *H. sieboldii*].

H. **'Sweet Winifred'** Benedict IRA/1984.

AHS-III/13A.

Plant is similar to *H.* 'Royal Standard' but leaves are longer. Plant 22 in. (56 cm) dia., 12 in. (31 cm) high. Leaf 10 by 7 in. (25.5 by 18 cm), veins 8, medium green, not variegated, cordate, flat. Scape 34 in. (86.5 cm), foliated, oblique. Flower medium, funnel-shaped, white, fragrant, flowers during summer period, fertile.

[*H. plantaginea* hybrid].

H. **'Sweetheart'** Armstrong.

Plant 12 in. (31 cm) dia., 8 in. (20 cm) high. Leaf 3.5 by 2 in. (9 by 5 cm), veins 5, medium green, not variegated, cordate, flat. Scape 18 in. (46 cm), bare, straight. Flower medium, bell-shaped, purple, flowers during average period, fertile.

[*H. nakaiana* hybrid].

H. **'Sweetheart'** Lee.

Plant is a clonal form of *H. nakaiana* or an F₁ hybrid.

(see *H. nakaiana*).

H. **'Sweetheart'** Wallace No. 31 1985.

Plant 22 in. (56 cm) dia., 12 in. (31 cm) high. Leaf 6.5 by 4 in. (16.5 by 10 cm), veins 9, medium green, not variegated, cordate, flat. Scape 22 in. (56 cm), foliated, straight. Flower medium, bell-shaped, purple, flowers during average period, fertile.

[*H. capitata* hybrid].

H. **'Sweetie'** Aden IRA/1988.

AHS-III/16A.

Plant 30 in. (76 cm) dia., 20 in. (51 cm) high. Leaf 8 by 5 in. (20 by 13 cm), veins 11, yellow (viridescent), margin white, cordate, wavy-undulate. Scape 32 in. (81.5 cm), foliated, straight. Flower medium, funnel-shaped, white, flowers during average period, fertile.

[*H.* 'Fragrant Bouquet' × *H.* 'Fragrant Candelabra'].

H. **'Swoosh'** Aden IRA/1978.

AHS-IV/22A.

Plant has variegation reported to be unstable. Reverts to a marginata form. Plant 12 in. (31 cm) dia., 8 in. (20 cm) high. Leaf 4 by 3 in. (10 by 7.5 cm), veins to 8, white-to-yellow-white center, streaky green, ovate, flat. Scape 26 in. (66 cm), bare, oblique. Flower medium, funnel-shaped, lavender, flowers during summer period, fertile.

H. **'Sybl'** Davidson 1969.

Plant 10 in. (25.5 cm) dia., 4 in. (10 cm) high. Leaf 3 by 2 in. (7.5 by 5 cm), veins 5, medium green, not variegated, ovate, flat. Scape 12 in. (31 cm), bare, oblique. Flower medium, bell-shaped, purple, flowers during average period, fertile.

HN: *H. nakaiana* 'Sybl'.

(see also *H. nakaiana*).

T

H. 'Tagi' Japan.
タギイワギボウシ
JN: *Tagi Iwa Giboshi* hort.
(see *H. longipes* 'Tagi').
(see also *H. longipes* var. *hypoglauca*).

H. 'Taika' Japan.
帯化オオバギボウシ
    Taika Oba Giboshi is a form with fasciated scapes and branched racemes at the top.
JN: *Taika Giboshi* hort.
(see also *H. montana* 'Taika').

H. 'Tailored Girl' Aden 1976.

H. 'Tall Boy' J. B. Montreal/Savill/Bond IRA/1983.
    AHS-II/7A.   (Plate 179).
    Award of merit, Wisley, UK. Plant is a large cultivar with very tall, straight scapes. Named in the United Kingdom after being sent there by Gulf Stream Nursery in 1961. Plant erect, 30 in. (76 cm) dia., 24 in. (61 cm) high. Leaf 9 by 6 in. (23 by 15 cm), veins 10, medium green, not variegated, cordate, flat. Scape 38 in. (96.5 cm) to 72 in. (183 cm), foliated, straight. Flower medium, funnel-shaped, lavender, flowers during average period, fertile.
HN: *H.* 'Peerless' Sedgwick 1936 ad int.
      H. 'Tall Blue'.
      H. rectifolia 'Tall Blue'.
      H. rectifolia 'Tall Boy'.
      H. robusta hort. incorrect.
[*H. rectifolia* hybrid].

H. 'Tall Twister' Minks IRA/1973.
    AHS-IV/19B.
    Plant erect, 12 in. (31 cm) dia., 12 in. (31 cm) high. Leaf 6 by 1.5 in. (15 by 4 cm), veins 3, medium green, not variegated, lanceolate, wavy. Scape 12 in. (31 cm), bare, straight. Flower medium, funnel-shaped, purple striped, flowers during summer period, fertile.
HN: *H.* 'Krossa No. 6'.
[*H. sieboldii* hybrid].

H. 'Tama No Yuki' Japan.
多摩の雪
    Plant's name means "Jewel of Yuki hosta." It is a sport of *H. longipes* found in the Okutama area, Tokyo Prefecture. Many pure white bell-shaped flowers. A specimen received from Japan is very small, with glossy leaves, and 3 veins. Similar to *H. pulchella*.
JN: *Tama No Yuki Giboshi* hort.
[*H. longipes* mutation].

H. 'Tamborine' Lachman IRA/1987.
    AHS-III/16A.
    Plant has yellowish white margin which varies in width. Plant 24 in. (61 cm) dia., 14 in. (35.5 cm) high. Leaf 6 by 5 in. (15 by 13 cm), veins 7, medium green, white margin, cordate, flat. Scape 20 in. (51 cm), foliated, straight. Flower medium, bell-shaped, lavender, flowers during average period, fertile.
HN: *H.* 'Tambourine'.
[*H.* 'Resonance' × *H.* 'Halcyon' hybrid].

H. Tardiana grex Smith UK.
    Plants are a complex of cultivars hybridized by Eric Smith, resulting from the unlikely cross *H.* 'Tardiflora' × *H. sieboldiana* 'Elegans'. Smith was able to fertilize the very late blooming *H.* 'Tardiflora' with pollen taken from a reblooming scape *H. sieboldiana*, which normally blooms 4 months earlier. This group of hybrids was initially given the hybrid binomial *H.* × *tardiana*, but this name is illegitimate for several reasons: (1) no Latin description of the plants embraced by this name has ever been published, and (2) it is an illegitimate combination per the latest editions of the ICBN (1988) and the ICNCP (1980, 1990). These governing codes stipulate that a name made up of parts of the names of the parent species is invalid. Furthermore, the proposed 1990 ICNCP rejects grex as well as group names formed in this manner. This means that *H.* × *tardiana* is an invalid name which cannot be legitimized. Because of its widespread and persistent use in horticulture I have not undertaken to change this name; to do so would cause much confusion, and its change, although required by the codes, is not essential at this time. Grounds (1986) reports that the Nomenclature Committee of the BHHS recommends calling this hybrid complex the "Tardiana group." It is, however, correctly a grex inasmuch as all hybrid derivatives of this group come from the same parent species and both parents of the cross are known. Because a grex name better defines this complex, I am retaining the hybrid binomial "Tardiana," calling the complex "*H.* Tardiana grex."
    In 1988 the BHHS Nomenclature Committee registered with the IRA for *Hosta* a number of cultivars belonging to this grex to protect the existing names and to establish new ones for yet unnamed cultivars. Some of them were registered with abbreviated or no descriptions because authentic reference plants have not yet been found. Unfortunately, under the rules of the ICNCP, these registrations are theoretically invalid; the code requires that a full description must be provided. Even the plants with full descriptions have not been authenticated by the BHHS due to much confusion; one example is the mix-up of *H.* 'Blue Wedgwood'. Verification of some of the taxa is difficult because they lack fully mature reference specimens as a result of constant division propagation and very slow growth. Other members of the grex look similar, so it may take some time for the BHHS committee to sort out the muddle. I have listed all known names and provided whatever descriptions are available at this time with the caveat that some of these may have to be changed and/or emended in a future edition of this work.
    Not included in the registrations were the "German Tardianas" which were obtained from Smith by German nurseryman Heinz Klose (1989: personal communication). Klose has named some of these acquisitions, and the names are listed later. There may be many other members of the *H.* Tardiana grex because Smith freely distributed seed and seedlings originating with this cross.
    Smith also bred yellow-leaved cultivars, called the GL (Gold Leaf) series. Some of them are considered Tardianas, but this is incorrect because this yellow-leaved series involves *H. sieboldiana, H.* 'Fortunei Aurea', and *H. sieboldii* 'Kabitan' in the breeding. However, in one of Smith's published records (Smith, 1984), some gold seedlings were recorded in the *H.* Tardiana grex complex.
    Throughout this book and in the following listing, each Tardiana is listed with a number combination preceded by "TF." The "T" means Tardiana and the "F" stands for filial. The first number indicates the generation (filial), and the second number was assigned by Eric Smith to that particular seedling to differentiate it from others in its generation. As an example,

TF 2 × 4 means the fourth seedling among the second-generation Tardianas. It is believed that Smith assigned these numbers in a rather inconsistent manner. According to comparative observations conducted by Pollock in the United Kingdom and the United States (1990: personal communication), some Tardianas grown under the same number or name are different. Most Tardianas were named after Smith numbered them. A few were named by Smith, others in the United States by Aden and Summers. Recently, the BHHS assigned cultivar names to all the known Tardianas on Smith's numbered lists.

HN: *H.* Tardiana.
    H. Tardiana grex.
    H. Tardiana group.
    H. × Tardiana grex incorrect.
    H. × Tardiana group incorrect.
    Tardiana grex.
    Tardiana group.
[*H.* 'Tardiflora' × *H. sieboldiana* 'Elegans'].
(see also individual *H.* Tardiana grex cultivars named in the following list).

Except as noted otherwise, all the cultivars below are by Smith:
H. 'Blaue Venus' Klose TF (?).
H. 'Blaumeise' Klose TF (?).
H. 'Blauspecht' Klose TF (?).
H. 'Blue Belle' TF 2 × 22.
H. 'Blue Blush' TF 3 × 1.
H. 'Blue Danube' TF 2 × 24.
H. 'Blue Diamond' TF 2 × 23.
H. 'Blue Dimples' Smith/Summers TF 2 × 8.
H. 'Blue Moon' Smith/Aden TF 2 × 2.
H. 'Blue Skies' TF 2 × 6.
H. 'Blue Wedgwood' Smith/Summers/BHHS TF 2 × 9.
H. 'Brother Ronald' TF 2 × 30.
H. 'Camelot' TF 2 × 27.
H. 'Curlew' TF 2 × 5.
H. 'Dorset Blue' Smith/Aden TF 2 × 4.
H. 'Dorset Charm' TF 1 × 1.
H. 'Dorset Flair' TF 1 × 4.
H. 'Eric Smith' Smith/Archibald TF 2 × 31.
H. 'Fumiko' Klose TF (?).
H. 'Goldilocks' UK TF 2 × 25 (?).
H. 'Grey Goose' TF 2 × 13.
H. 'Grünspecht' Klose TF (?).
H. 'Hadspen Blue' TF 2 × 7.
H. 'Hadspen Hawk' TF 2 × 20.
H. 'Hadspen Heron' Smith/Aden TF 2 × 10.
H. 'Hadspen Pink' Smith/Eason BHHS TF 2 × 32.
H. 'Halcyon' TF 1 × 7.
H. 'Happiness' TF 1 × 5.
H. 'Harmony' Smith/Aden TF 2 × 3.
H. 'Kingfisher' TF 2 × 17.
H. 'Kite' TF 2 × 28.
H. 'Naomi' Klose TF (?).
H. 'Nicola' Eason TF 2 × 32 (?) ad int.
H. 'Nordatlantic' Klose TF (?).
H. 'Osprey' TF 2 × 14.
H. 'Purbeck Ridge' TF 2 × 18.
H. 'Sherborne Profusion' TF 2 × 21.
H. 'Sherborne Songbird' TF 2 × 19.
H. 'Sherborne Swallow' TF 2 × 34.
H. 'Sherborne Swan' TF 2 × 29.
H. 'Sherborne Swift' TF 2 × 26.
H. 'Silberpfeil' Klose TF (?).
H. 'Tomoko' Klose TF (?).
H. 'Wagtail' TF 2 × 35.

H. 'Tardiflora'.
H. tardiflora.

H. 'Tardiflora Golden' Schaeffer 1967.
Plant name is an incorrect synonym.

H. 'Tardiflora Hybrida' Arends 1911.
Georg Arends (see Chapter 5) made the cross *H.* 'Tardiflora' × *H. ventricosa* to obtain earlier flowering of *H.* 'Tardiflora'. The resulting hybrid was given the cultivar name 'Hybrida' and first sold in 1911.
(see also *H.* 'Tardiflora').

H. 'Tardiflora Kinakafu' hort.
Plant is in Japan called *Kinakafu Aki Giboshi*, the "aureonebulosa Aki hosta," but *Aki Giboshi* is *H. longipes* f. *sparsa* (purple anthers), not *H.* 'Tardiflora' (yellow anthers), so application of the name is questioned here. It is not known if the true form of *Aki Giboshi* (*H. longipes* f. *sparsa*) has mediovariegated mutations, but it probably does. This cultivar is a sport with a yellow center and green margin or a center clouded with yellow. A stable and viridescent forms exist. Aside from the variegation it is identical to *H.* 'Tardiflora'. A hosta offered as *H. tardiva aureostriata* hort. in the United States is not related but belongs to the *H. sieboldii* complex, the main difference is the much heavier substance of the leaves and the much later blooming habit of the variegated *H.* 'Tardiflora'. Most clones of this cultivar are viridescent. It is available and of interest to the collector.
HN: *H. tardiva aureostriata* hort. sim incorrect.
JN: *Kinakafu Aki Giboshi* hort. incorrect

H. 'Tardiflora Minor' hort. incorrect.
Plant name is an incorrect synonym.
[*H. longipes* form].

H. 'Tardiflora Twisted' hort.
Plant is a mutation found in England that has twisted leaves similar to *H.* 'Tortifrons' but wider. Also seen in North America, the sport is frequently not stable.

H. 'Tarnished' Vaughn IRA/1987.
AHS-IV/22B.
Plant has undulate margin, yellow markings on blue-green. Plant 12 in. (31 cm) dia., 6 in. (15 cm) high. Leaf 4 by 3 in. (10 by 7.5 cm), veins 5, medium green, yellow streaking, ovate, flat. Scape 10 in. (25.5 cm), bare, straight. Flower medium, bell-shaped, lavender, flowers during average period, fertile.
[*H.* 'Blue Boy' × *H.* 'Blue Lace'].

H. 'Tatted Lace' Minks.
Plant has chartreuse cupped leaves with ruffled margins.

H. 'Teddy Bear' Falstad.

H. 'Temple Great' Jernigan IRA/1986.
AHS-II/9B.
Plant 54 in. (137 cm) dia., 34 in. (86.5 cm) high. Leaf 14 by 10 in. (35.5 by 25.5 cm), veins 16, medium green, not variegated, cordate, rugose. Scape 44 in. (112 cm), foliated, straight. Flower medium, bell-shaped, lavender, flowers during average period, fertile.
[*H. sieboldiana* hybrid].

H. 'Tenryu' 1985 Japan/Yoshie.
天竜ギボウシ
Tenryu Giboshi, the "Tenryu River Hosta," is cultivated in

the Tenryu River area of Shizuoka Prefecture. A very large hosta with leaves very white, pruinose both sides, leaf mound 36 in. (91.5 cm) high, and scapes to 80 in. (204 cm). Name given by Haruo Yoshie. Reportedly a long-scaped *H. sieboldiana*.
HN: Tenryu River Hosta.
JN: *Tenryu Giboshi* hort.

H. **'Tess Hoop'** Holland.

H. **'Tet-A-Poo'** Aden 1976.

H. **'Thai Brass'** Woodruff IRA/1972.
    AHS-II/11A.
    Plant erect, 20 in. (51 cm) dia., 16 in. (40.5 cm) high. Leaf 5 by 4 in. (13 by 10 cm), veins 12, yellow (lutescent), not variegated, cordate, cupped-rugose. Scape 22 in. (56 cm), bare, straight. Flower medium, bell-shaped, white, flowers during average period, fertile.
[*H.* 'Fortunei' mutation al].
[*H.* 'Tokudama' mutation].

H. **'The Twister'** Savory IRA/1986.
    AHS-IV/19A.
    Plant erect, 12 in. (31 cm) dia., 12 in. (31 cm) high. Leaf 5.5 by 1.25 in. (14 by 3 cm), veins 3, medium green, not variegated, lanceolate, wavy. Scape 12 in. (31 cm), bare, straight. Flowers medium, funnel-shaped, purple striped, flowers during summer period, fertile.
[*H. sieboldii* hybrid].

H. **'Thea'** Statham/Barcock IRA/1985.
    AHS-III/16A.
    Plant is a typical *H.* 'Fortunei Hyacinthina' sport of which many exist and have been named. Unstable variegation. Plant 24 in. (61 cm) dia., 18 in. (476 cm) high. Leaf 7 by 5 in. (18 by 13 cm), veins 9, blue-green, streaky white, cordate, flat. Scape 36 in. (91.5 cm), foliated, straight. Flower medium, funnel-shaped, lavender, flowers during average period, fertile.
HN: *H.* 'Fortunei Thea'.
        H. 'Fortunei Hyacinthina Thea'.
[*H.* 'Fortunei Hyacinthina' mutation].

H. **'Thelma M. Pierson'** Pierson IRA/1988.
    AHS-II/11A.
    Plant 28 in. (71 cm) dia., 21 in. (54 cm) high. Leaf 12 by 6.5 in. (31 by 16.5 cm), veins 9, yellow to light chartreuse (viridescent), not variegated, cordate, wavy-undulate. Scape 24 in. (61 cm), straight. Flower medium, funnel-shaped, white, flowers during average period, fertile.
[*H.* 'Fortunei Hyacinthina' hybrid].

H. 'Thomas Hogg' Hogg 1875.
    Plant name has been applied to several taxa and so is an incorrect and confusing synonym.
HN: *H.* 'Crispula' pp incorrect.
        H. 'Decorata' U.S.A.
        H. 'Undulata Albomarginata' UK.
(see *H.* 'Decorata').
(see *H.* 'Undulata Albomarginata').

H. **'Thor'** Ruh.

H. **'Thumb Nail'** Aden IRA/1982.
    AHS-VI/31A.
    Plant 4 in. (10 cm) dia., 2 in. (5 cm) high. Leaf 1.5 by 1 in. (4 by 2.5 cm), veins 4, medium green, not variegated, cordate, flat. Scape 10 in. (25.5 cm), bare, straight. Flower medium, bell-

shaped, purple, flowers during average period, sterile.
HN: *H.* 'Suzuki Thumbnail' pp sim.
[*H. venusta* hybrid].
(see also *H. venusta*).

H. **'Tiddlywinks'** Banyai IRA/1989.
    AHS-V/28A.
    Plant 14 in. (35 cm) dia., 7 in. (18 cm) high. Leaf 3.5 by 1.5 in. (9 by 4 cm), veins 3, medium green, yellowish white margin, cordate, flat. Scape 25 in. (63 cm), bare, straight. Flower medium, funnel-shaped, purple-striped, flowers during average period, fertile.

H. **'Tijuana Brass'** Vaughn IRA/1988.
    AHS-II/11B.
    Plant 28 in. (71 cm) dia., 20 in. (51 cm) high. Leaf 10 by 8 in. (25.5 by 20 cm), veins 12, yellow (lutescent), not variegated, cordate, flat, cupped-rugose. Scape 30 in. (76 cm), bare, straight. Flower medium, lavender, flowers during average period.
[*H.* 'Golden Waffles' × *H.* 'Polly Bishop'].

H. **'Tinker Bell'** Williams IRA/1986.
    AHS-IV/19A.
    Plant erect, 12 in. (31 cm) dia., 10 in. (25.5 cm) high. Leaf 5 by 1 in. (13 by 2.5 cm), veins 3, medium green, not variegated, lanceolate, flat. Scape 16 in. (40.5 cm), bare, straight. Flower medium, funnel-shaped, purple striped, flowers during summer period, fertile.
HN: *H.* 'FRW No. 1156' 1963.
        H. sieboldii 'Tinker Bell'.
[*H. sieboldii* 'Alba' hybrid].

H. **'Tiny Snowflakes'** Bemis.

H. **'Tiny Tears'** Savory IRA/1977.
    AHS-VI/31A.   (Figure 4-44).
    Plant is a selected small form of the species *H. venusta*. Plant 4 in. (10 cm) dia., 2 in. (5 cm) high. Leaf 1.5 by 1 in. (3 by 1.5 cm), veins 4, medium green, not variegated, cordate, flat. Scape 10 in. (25.5 cm), bare, straight. Flower medium, bell-shaped, purple, flowers during average period, fertile.
HN: *H. venusta* 'Tiny Tears'.
[*H. venusta* sel].

Figure 4-44. *H.* 'Tiny Tears'; general habit, with *Carex morrowii* 'Argenteovariegata' (Langdon garden/ Schmid)

H. **'Tiny Tim'** Summers No. 171.
    Plant erect, 4 in. (10 cm) dia., 2 in. (5 cm) high. Leaf small, veins 3, white (viridescent), margin green, lanceolate, flat. Scape 8 in. (20 cm), bare, straight. Flower medium, funnel-shaped, purple striped, flowers during summer period, fertile.
[*H. sieboldii* mutation].
(see *H. sieboldii* 'Silver Kabitan').

H. 'Tokudama'.
H. tokudama.

H. 'Tokudama Akebono' hort.
アケボノトクダマ

Akebono Tokudama is the Japanese formal synonym for *H.* 'Tokudama Aureonebulosa'.
(see *H.* 'Tokudama Aureonebulosa').

H. 'Tokudama Aofukurin' hort.
青覆輪トクダマ

Aofukurin Tokudama is a name occasionally and incorrectly used as a Japanese synonym for *H.* 'Tokudama Aureonebulosa'.
(see *H.* 'Tokudama Aureonebulosa').

H. 'Tokudama Aureonebulosa'.
H. tokudama f. *aureonebulosa*.

H. 'Tokudama Aureonebulosa' AHS-NC IRA/1987.
AHS-III/14B.

The cultivar name registered (in modified form) as *H. tokudama* 'Aureo-nebulosa' for show purposes for *H. tokudama* f. *aureonebulosa*.
(see *H. tokudama* f. *aureonebulosa*).

H. 'Tokudama Aureonebulosa' group.

Yellow-margined forms similar to *H.* 'Tokudama Aureonebulosa' arise in cultivation and tissue culture and are sufficiently different to be given cultivar names. All of them belong in a broad sense to a group of yellow-margined mutants here called the *H.* 'Tokudama Aureonebulosa' group. This group includes mutants having white, not lavender flowers, and more-cupped and rugose leaves.
(see *H. tokudama* f. *aureonebulosa*).

H. 'Tokudama Aureonebulosa Yellow' group.
黄金トクダマ

Ogon Tokudama, the "golden well-rounded hosta," originated with *H.* 'Tokudama Aureonebulosa', which is unstable in the long term and will occasionally sport to all-yellow forms which occur naturally as well as in tissue culture. Additionally, many different forms and sizes occur when this taxon is hybridized. A number of distinct clones and hybrids have been isolated and named. The horticultural "standard" form which is essentially identical to *H.* 'Tokudama Aureonebulosa', except for the all-yellow leaves, is most often seen cultivated under the name *H. tokudama* 'Golden Medallion', but this name was registered without description. The former group name, *H.* 'Tokudama' Golden group, is too vague because distinct yellow mutants of *H.* 'Tokudama Flavocircinalis' also exist, and it has been replaced by the more specific name. Other distinct clones belonging to this group may exist and may be named in the future.
HN: *H.* 'Golden Medallion' AHS-NC IRA/1984.
　　　 H. tokudama 'Golden' incorrect.
　　　 H. tokudama 'Golden Group' incorrect.
　　　 H. tokudama 'Golden Medallion' AHS-NC IRA/1984.
JN: *Kinki Giboshi* hort. pp sim.
(see *H.* 'Golden Medallion').

H. 'Tokudama Flavocircinalis'.
H. tokudama f. *flavocircinalis*.

H. 'Tokudama Flavocircinalis' AHS-NC IRA/1987.
AHS-III/16B.

The cultivar name registered (in modified form) as *H. tokudama* 'Flavo-circinalis' for show purposes for *H. tokudama* f. *flavocircinalis*.
(see *H. tokudama* f. *flavocircinalis*).

H. 'Tokudama Flavocircinalis' group.

Yellow-margined forms similar to *H.* 'Tokudama Flavocircinalis' arise in cultivation and tissue culture and are sufficiently different to be given cultivar names. All of them belong in a broad sense to a group of yellow-margined mutants here called the *H.* 'Tokudama Flavocircinalis' group. This group includes mutants having lavender, not white flowers, and less-cupped and rugose leaves.
(see *H. tokudama* f. *flavocircinalis*).

H. 'Tokudama Flavocircinalis Yellow' group.
黄金トクダマ

These yellow forms occur as natural mutations of *H.* 'Tokudama Flavocircinalis' and also arise in cultivation and tissue culture. They differ from other yellow *H.* 'Tokudama' mutants by having lavender coloration in the flowers and less-cupped and rugose leaves. Although several clones exist, they are virtually identical and are cultivated under the clonal name *H. tokudama* 'Golden Bullion'. Other distinct clones belonging to this group may exist and may be named in the future.
HN: *H.* 'Golden Bullion'.
　　　 H. tokudama 'Golden' incorrect.
　　　 H. tokudama 'Golden Bullion'.
　　　 H. tokudama 'Golden Group' incorrect.
JN: *Ogon Tokudama* hort. pp sim.
(see *H.* 'Golden Bullion').

H. 'Tokudama Flavoplanata'.
H. tokudama f. *flavoplanata*.

H. 'Tokudama Flavoplanata' AHS-NC IRA/1987.
AHS-III/16B.

The cultivar name registered (in modified form) as *H. tokudama* 'Flavo-planata' for show purposes for *H. tokudama* f. *flavoplanata*.
(see *H. tokudama* f. *flavoplanata*).

H. 'Tokudama Gyakufu' hort.
逆斑ギボウシ

Gyakufu Giboshi is a name occasionally and incorrectly used as a Japanese synonym for *H.* 'Tokudama Aureonebulosa'.
(see *H.* 'Tokudama Aureonebulosa').

H. 'Tokudama Hime' hort.
ヒメトクダマ

Hime Tokudama, the "small Tokudama hosta," is a selected small form of the specioid found in cultivation.
JN: *Hime Tokudama* hort.

H. 'Tokudama Kinakafu' hort.
黄中斑トクダマ

Kinakafu Tokudama is a name occasionally and incorrectly used as a Japanese synonym for *H.* 'Tokudama Aureonebulosa'.
(see *H.* 'Tokudama Aureonebulosa').

H. 'Tokudama Murasaki' hort.
紫トクダマ

Murasaki Tokudama is a name used for a dark-flowered form of *H.* 'Tokudama'.

H. 'Tokudama Ogon Hime' hort.
黄金姫トクダマ

Ogon Hime Tokudama is a dwarf yellow form of H. 'Tokudama' and is made up of several cultivars which form a group. A Western cultivar similar to this form is H. 'Little Aurora'.
(see also H. 'Little Aurora').

H. 'Tokudama Ogon Himechirifu' hort.
黄金姫トクダマ

Ogon Himechirifu Tokudama is small and not so yellow. A specimen observed does not look at all like H. 'Tokudama'. Needs further study.

H. 'Tompkins [Named Hybrids]' Tompkins.

Plants are hybrids made by the Tompkins family over a period of 65 years starting in the early 1920s. Some names are synonyms for contemporary cultivars already validly named, while others have been registered with the IRA, viz., H. 'Cynthia' and H. 'Lakeport Blue'. Detailed accounts of the history of these hybrids can be found in Tompkins (1984, 1985). Following are some of the more important names:
H. 'Aunt Saphrona'.
H. 'Checkerboard'.
H. 'Cynthia'.
H. 'Dandelion Days'.
H. 'Gilt Edge'.
H. 'Lakeport Blue'.
H. 'Lucifer'.
H. 'Old Arrowhead'.
H. 'Old Gold Edge'.
H. 'Pioneer'.
H. 'Sun Showers'.
H. 'Sunny Smiles'.
H. 'Tattletail Gray'.
H. 'The Cemetary One'.
H. 'The Freak'.
H. 'The Graveyard One'.

H. 'Tomoko' Klose.

Plant is a H. Tardiana grex hybrid with lavender flowers and medium heart-shaped leaves of dark blue-grey color. The name honors Tomoko Kamo, the daughter of the eminent Dr. Mototeru Kamo, formerly an associate of Maekawa and master of Kamo Hanashobu-en, a well-known nursery specializing in Hosta and Iris, located near Mount Fuji in Shizuoka Prefecture.
HN: H. Tardiana grex.
[H. 'Tardiflora' × H. sieboldiana 'Elegans'].

H. 'Top Banana' Vaughn IRA/1983.
AHS-III/14A.

Plant 24 in. (61 cm) dia., 20 in. (51 cm) high. Leaf 8 by 8 in. (20 by 20 cm), veins 13, white (albescent) center, streaky green, cordate, flattish. Scape 30 in. (76 cm), bare, straight. Flower medium, funnel-shaped, lavender, flowers during average period, fertile.
[H. sieboldiana 'Frances Williams' × H. sieboldii 'Beatrice'].

H. 'Top Number' Fisher IRA/1971.
AHS-II/7A.

Plant 36 in. (91.5 cm) dia., 26 in. (66 cm) high. Leaf 10 by 8 in. (25.5 by 20 cm), veins 13, medium green, not variegated, cordate, flat. Scape 36 in. (91.5 cm), foliated, straight. Flower medium, funnel-shaped, white, flowers during average period, fertile.
[H. 'Elata' hybrid].

H. 'Tortifrons'.
H. tortifrons.

H. 'Tot Tot' Aden IRA/1978.
AHS-V/25B.

Plant is often connected with the species H. venusta, but it does not have ridges on the flower scape and it looks more like H. pulchella. Plant 8 in. (20 cm) dia., 4 in. (10 cm) high. Leaf 1.5 by 1 in. (4 by 2.5 cm), veins 4, blue-green, not variegated, cordate, flat. Scape 12 in. (31 cm), bare, straight. Flower medium, bell-shaped, purple, flowers during average period, fertile.
HN: H. venusta 'Tot Tot' (?).
[H. pulchella sel] (?).

H. 'Trails End' Ruh IRA/1978.
AHS-I/3B.

Plant 44 in. (112 cm) dia., 26 in. (66 cm) high. Leaf 13 by 11 in. (33 by 28 cm), veins 16, blue-green, not variegated, cordate, rugose. Scape 32 in. (81.5 cm), bare, straight. Flower medium, bell-shaped, white, flowers during average period, fertile.
[H. sieboldiana hybrid].

H. 'Treasure' Harshbarger 1973 IRA/1981.
AHS-III/17A.

Plant 36 in. (91.5 cm) dia., 20 in. (51 cm) high. Leaf 10 by 9 in. (25.5 by 23 cm), veins 16, yellow (lutescent), not variegated, cordate, rugose. Scape 30 in. (76 cm), bare, straight. Flower medium, bell-shaped, white, flowers during average period, fertile.
[H. 'Tokudama Aureonebulosa' × H. sieboldiana hybrid].

H. 'True Blue' Aden 1975 IRA/1978.
AHS-II/9B.   (Figure 4-45).

Plant 38 in. (96.5 cm) dia., 24 in. (61 cm) high. Leaf 12 by 10 in. (31 by 25.5 cm), veins 16, blue-green, not variegated, cordate, rugose. Scape 30 in. (76 cm), bare, straight. Flower medium, bell-shaped, white, flowers during average period, fertile.
[H. sieboldiana hybrid].

Figure 4-45. H. 'True Blue'; general habit (Hosta Hill)

H. 'True Love' Aden IRA/1979.
AHS-II/9B.
[H. 'Blue Vision' × H. 'True Blue'].

H. 'Tsugaru Komachi' Japan.
津軽小町

Tsugaru Komachi Giboshi, the "beautiful (girl) hosta from Tsugaru," is named for a district in northern Honshu (an alternate spelling is Tugaru). A dwarf hosta with lanceolate leaves that have a white center and green margin similar to H. sieboldii

'Silver Kabitan'. Broadly related to *H. sieboldii*, with affinity to *H. rectifolia*.
JN: *Tsugaru Komachi (Koba) Giboshi* hort.
[*H. sieboldii* hybrid].

H. 'Tsugaru Komachi Fukurin' Japan.
覆輪津軽小町
(see *H.* 'Fukurin Tsugaru Komachi').

H. 'Tsugaru Komachi Nakafu' Japan.
中斑津軽小町
(see *H.* 'Nakafu Tsugaru Komachi').

H. 'Tsugaru Nishiki' Japan.
(see *H.* 'Tsugaru Komachi').

H. 'Tsunotori Fukurin' Japan.
角取り覆輪
Plant is an aureomarginata form of *H. montana* found by Koshi Katsuya in the Kanzawa Mountains of Shizuoka Prefecture. The margin is slightly viridescent.
JN: *Tsunotori Fukurin (Oba) Giboshi* hort.
[*H. montana* mutation].
(see also *H. montana* 'Tsunotori Fukurin').

H. *tsushimensis* 'Ogon'.

H. *tsushimensis* 'Sanshoku'.

H. *tsushimensis* 'Shirobana'.

H. 'Tutu' Vaughn.
Plant has large blue-green leaves with white back and ruffled margin. Petiole purple. Flower light purple.

H. 'Tweeny' Heller/Banyai IRA/1989.
AHS-VI/31A.
Plant 4 in. (10 cm) dia., 2.5 in. (6 cm) high. Leaf 1.5 by 0.75 in. (4 by 2 cm), veins 3, medium green, not variegated, lanceolate, flat. Scape 12 in. (31 cm), bare, straight. Flower medium, funnel-shaped, lavender, flowers during summer period, fertile.

H. 'Twinkle Toes' Minks IRA/1973.
AHS-IV/23B.
Plant 8 in. (20 cm) dia., 4 in. (10 cm) high. Leaf 5 by 1 in. (13 by 2.5 cm), veins 3, medium green, not variegated, lanceolate, flat. Scape 12 in. (31 cm), bare, straight. Flower medium, funnel-shaped, purple striped, flowers during summer period, fertile.
[*H. sieboldii* 'Subcrocea' hybrid].

H. 'Twinkles' Van Hoorn.
Plant is often considered a *H.* 'Lancifolia Aurea' form, but this taxon is a yellow (viridescent) hybrid of *H. sieboldii*.

H. 'Twist and Shout' Vaughn IRA/1988.
AHS-II/9A.
Plant erect, 38 in. (96.5 cm) dia., 27 in. (68.5 cm) high. Leaf 12 by 12 in. (31 by 31 cm), veins 14, blue-green, not variegated, round-cordate, cupped-rugose, twisted. Scape 40 in. (102 cm), bare, straight. Flower medium, lavender, flowers during average period.
[*H.* 'Gold Piece' × *H.* 'Aztec Treasure' hybrid].

H. 'Twisted Leaf'.
(see *H. tortifrons* pp sim).

H. 'Two Step' Aden IRA/1987.
AHS-IV/22A.
Plant has yellow margin with streaks into center, variable width. Plant 24 in. (61 cm) dia., 18 in. (46 cm) high. Leaf 9 by 4 in. (23 by 10 cm), veins 4, green, yellow margin, ovate, undulate. Scape 26 in. (66 cm), bare, straight. Flower medium, funnel-shaped, white, flowers during summer period, fertile.
[*H.* 'Embroidery' × *H.* 'Aden No. 341'].

U

H. 'Uguis' Japan.
Uguis Giboshi, the "spring bird hosta." Plant 16 in. (40.5 cm) dia., 10 in. (25.5 cm) high. Leaf 4.5 by 1.5 in. (11.5 by 4 cm), veins 5, medium green, not variegated, lanceolate, flat. Scape 18 in. (46 cm), bare, straight. Flower medium, funnel-shaped, purple striped, flowers during summer period, fertile.
HN: *H.* 'Ugis' hort. incorrect.
H. ventricosa 'Uguis' hort. incorrect.
JN: *Uguis Giboshi* hort.

H. 'Ultraviolet Light' Wilkins IRA/1989.
AHS-III/17B.
Plant erect, 42 in. (105 cm) dia., 18 in. (45 cm) high. Leaf 8 by 5 in. (20 by 13 cm), veins 9, yellow (viridescent), not variegated, round-cordate. Scape 30 in. (75 cm), bare, straight. Flower medium, purple, flowers during average period.
[*H.* 'Gold Regal' × Hybrid].

H. 'Umezawa' Umezawa/Maekawa.
ウメザワギボウシ
Umezawa Giboshi, the "Umezawa hosta," was named by Maekawa for the collector Senkichi Umezawa who found it as a mutation in the wild in Chiba Prefecture. A dwarf white-margined form of *H. longipes*.
JN: *Umezawa Giboshi* hort.
[*H. longipes* mutation].

H. 'Unazuki Soules' Japan.
ウナズキギボウシ   (Figure 2-34).
Plant's name is the Japanese academic name for *H. kikutii* var. *caput-avis*, which see. In North America it is used as a cultivar name for a selected, small clone of *H. kikutii* var. *caput-avis*. This horticultural application of a Japanese academic name is technically incorrect because this name applies to all the natural populations of this taxon, not just a selected clone. For this reason I have added the importer's name to the cultivar name, as *H.* 'Unazuki Soules', to make this clonal cultivar name acceptable under the ICNCP.
JN: *Unazuki Giboshi*.
(see *H. kikutii* var. *caput-avis*).

H. 'Unducosa' Summers IRA/1986.
AHS-III/13A.
Plant 24 in. (61 cm) dia., 14 in. (35.5 cm) high. Leaf 5 by 4 in. (13 by 10 cm), veins 6, medium green, not variegated, cordate, flat. Scape 22 in. (56 cm), bare, straight. Flower medium, funnel-shaped, lavender, flowers during average period, fertile.
HN: *H. × unducosa* hort. incorrect.
Summers No. 428 1970.
[*H.* 'Undulata' × *H. ventricosa*].

V

H. **'Undulata'**.
H. undulata.

H. **'Undulata'** white form.
(see *H.* 'White Trouble').

H. **'Undulata Albomarginata'**.
H. undulata var. *albomarginata*.

H. **'Undulata Albomarginata'** AHS-NC IRA/1987.
　　AHS-III/16A.
　　The cultivar name registered (in modified form) as *H. undulata* 'Albo-marginata' AHS-NC IRA/1987 for show purposes for *H. undulata* var. *albomarginata*.
(see *H. undulata* var. *albomarginata*).

H. **'Undulata Erromena'**.
H. undulata var. *erromena*.

H. **'Undulata Erromena'** AHS-NC IRA/1987.
　　AHS-III/13A.
　　The cultivar name registered (in modified form) as *H. undulata* 'Erromena' AHS-NC IRA/1987 for show purposes for *H. undulata* var. *erromena*.
(see *H. undulata* var. *erromena*).

H. **'Undulata Kifukurin'** Japan.
キフクリンオハツキギボウシ
　　Kifukurin Ohatsuki Giboshi is a yellow-margined form of the specioid reported from Japan.
JN:　*Kifukurin Ohatsuki Giboshi*.

H. **'Undulata Univittata'**.
H. undulata var. *univittata*.

H. **'Undulata Univittata'** AHS-NC IRA/1987.
　　AHS-III/16A.
　　The cultivar name registered (in modified form) as *H. undulata* 'Univittata' AHS-NC IRA/1987 for show purposes for *H. undulata* var. *univittata*.
(see *H. undulata* var. *univittata*).

H. **'Unique'** Fisher.
　　Plant is a sizable cultivar with large leaves, deeply impressed veins, and ruffled margins of a shiny green color. The funnel-shaped flowers are reported to be purple with white centers in the lobes.
HN:　*H.* 'Fisher No. 57-70'.
[*H.* 'Elata' × *H. ventricosa* ad int].

H. **'Uplift'** Aden.

H. **'Urajiro Ko Iwa'** Japan.
裏白小岩
　　Plant is a small white-backed *H. longipes* form.
Urajiro Ko Iwa.

H. **'Uzu No Mai'** Japan.
　　Plant has short petioles, giving the clump a rosette appearance. The name means "Dancing Eddie."

H. **'Valentine Lace'** Armstrong IRA/1970.
　　AHS-III/13B.
　　Plant 22 in. dia., 10 in. (56 by 25.5 cm) high. Leaf 5 by 5 in. (13 by 13 cm), veins 10, blue-green, not variegated, cordate, slightly rugose. Scape 28 in. (71 cm), bare, straight. Flower medium, bell-shaped, purple, flowers during average period, fertile.
[*H. capitata* hybrid].

H. **'Vanilla Cream'** Aden IRA/1986.
　　AHS-IV/23A.
　　Plant 18 in. (46 cm) dia., 10 in. (25.5 cm) high. Leaf 3 by 2.5 in. (7.5 by 6.5 cm), veins 8, yellow (lutescent), cordate, wavy, rugose in part. Scape 12 in. (31 cm), bare, straight. Flower medium, funnel-shaped, lavender, flowers during summer period, fertile.
[*H.* 'Aden No. 456' × *H.* 'Little Aurora'].

H. **'Variegata'**.
　　Plant name has been applied to different taxa and so is an incorrect and confusing name.

H. **'Vaughn 73-2'** Vaughn 1973.
[*H. sieboldii* 'Beatrice' × *H. sieboldii* 'Beatrice'].

H. ventricosa **'Aureomaculata'** Hensen.

H. ventricosa **'Aureomarginata'** Hensen.

H. ventricosa **Dwarf group**.

H. ventricosa 'Uguis' incorrect.
　　Plant's name suggests relationship of *H.* 'Uguis' with the species *H. ventricosa* but this is in doubt.
(see *H.* 'Uguis').

H. ventricosa **Yellow group**.

H. **'Venucosa'** Wister/Summers 1967 IRA/1986.
　　AHS-III/13B.
　　Plant 30 in. (76 cm) dia., 18 in. (46 cm) high. Leaf 7 by 5.5 in. (18 by 14 cm), veins 8, medium green, not variegated, cordate, flat. Scape 22 in. (56 cm), bare, straight. Flower medium, funnel-shaped, lavender, flowers during average period, fertile.
[*H. venusta* × *H. ventricosa*].

H. venusta **'Aureomarginata'** hort.
(see *H. venusta* 'Kifukurin').

H. venusta **'Kifukurin'** hort.

H. venusta **'Ogon'** hort.

H. venusta 'Portor'.
　　Plant is a named clone of the species or an F$_1$ hybrid. The name may be incorrect.

H. venusta 'Rock Princess'.
　　Plant in the trade under this name is a named clone of the species or an F$_1$ hybrid. The true *H.* 'Rock Princess' is, according to Davidson (1990), a form of *H. gracillima*.
(see *H. gracillima*).

H. venusta 'Shikou'.
Plant is a named clone of the species or an F$_1$ hybrid. The name is incorrect.

H. venusta **'Shironakafu'** hort.
(see *H. venusta* 'Variegated').

H. venusta **'Variegated'**.

H. **'Vera Verde'** Klehm 1987.
(Figures 3-68, 4-12; Plate 190).
Plant is the stable margined form of the highly variable *H.* 'Cheesecake' which has white centers and green margins or is half-green and half-white. Plant erect, 12 in. (31 cm) dia., 4 in. (10 cm) high. Leaf 3.5 by 0.75 in. (9 by 2 cm), veins 3, medium green, margin white, lanceolate, flat. Scape 24 in. (61 cm), bare, straight. Flower medium, funnel-shaped, purple striped, flowers during summer period, fertile.
HN: *H. cathayana* 'Shirofukurin' hort. Japan.
  H. 'Gracillima Variegata' incorrect.
  H. 'Gracillima Variegated' incorrect.
  H. gracillima variegata hort. incorrect.
JN: *Shirofukurin Akikaze Giboshi* hort.
(see also *H. cathayana* 'Shirofukurin').

H. **'Verdi Valentine'** Payne/Payne 1979.
Plant is very similar to *H. nakaiana* and may be a selected clone or an F$_1$ selfed seedling.
(see *H. nakaiana*).

H. **'Vicki Aden'** Aden 1975 IRA/1980.
AHS-III/16B.
Plant has variegation that has been observed unstable and reverting to all blue-green. Plant 22 in. (56 cm) dia., 14 in. (35.5 cm) high. Leaf 7 by 5 in. (18 by 13 cm), veins 10, blue-green, streaky yellow, cordate, rugose. Scape 20 in. (51 cm), foliated, straight. Flower medium, funnel-shaped, lavender, flowers during average period, fertile.
[*H.* 'Flamboyant' hybrid].

H. **'Viettes Yellow Edge'** Viette IRA/1986.
AHS-III/16B.
Plant 28 in. (71 cm) dia., 16 in. (40.5 cm) high. Leaf 8 by 6 in. (20 by 15 cm), veins 9, medium green, margin yellow, cordate, flat. Scape 26 in. (66 cm), bare, straight. Flower medium, funnel-shaped, lavender, flowers during average period, fertile.
HN: *H.* 'Krossa Broad Band B' Krossa ob.
  H. 'Fortunei Viettes Yellow Edge'.
  H. 'Krossa No. H-3' Krossa/Summers No. 21 1966.
[*H.* 'Fortunei Stenantha' mutation].

H. **'Vilmoriniana'** Vilmorin et Andrieux 1900.
Plant is a European classic. The French firm of Vilmorin-Andrieux et Cie. cataloged this hosta as early as 1866. Called "Vilmorin's Taxon" on two herbarium specimens in K, its correct name is *H.* 'Vilmoriniana'. My discovery of these specimens in K solves the question regarding the origin of this classic European hybrid. Plant 28 in. (71 cm) dia., 16 in. (40.5 cm) high. Leaf 5 by 3.5 in. (13 by 9 cm), veins 7, medium green, not variegated, cordate, wavy, but flat between the veins. Scape 32 in. (81.5 cm), foliated, straight. Flower medium, bell-shaped, purple striped, flowers during average period, fertile.
HN: *H.* 'Krossa No. G-4'.
  H. 'Vilmorana' incorrect.
  H. 'Vilmoreana' incorrect.
  H. 'Vilmoriana' incorrect.
  H. 'Vilmorineana' incorrect.
  H. 'Vilmorin's Taxon' in schedula, Kew.

W

H. **'Wagners Petite'** Wagner IRA/1985.
AHS-V/25B.
Plant 6 in. (15 cm) dia., 2 in. (5 cm) high. Leaf 1.25 by 0.75 in. (3 by 2 cm), veins 3, medium green, not variegated, lanceolate, flat. Scape 10 in. (25.5 cm), bare, straight. Flower medium, funnel-shaped, purple striped, flowers during summer period, fertile.

H. **'Wagon Wheels'** Minks IRA/1971.
AHS-II/10B.
Plant is a distinct member of the *H. sieboldiana* Aureomarginata group. The leaves are cupped and blunt. Plant 36 in. (91.5 cm) dia., 18 in. (46 cm) high. Leaf 12 by 10 in. (31 by 25.5 cm), veins 16, blue-green, margin yellow, cordate, deeply cupped-rugose. Scape 22 in. (56 cm), bare, straight. Flower medium, bell-shaped, white, flowers during average period, fertile.
[*H. sieboldiana* 'Golden Nugget' mutation].

H. **'Wagtail'** Smith BHHS IRA/1988.
AHS-IV/21B.
Plant 16 in. (40.5 cm) dia., 6 in. (15 cm) high. Leaf 4 by 3 in. (10 by 7.5 cm), veins 8. Scape 10 in. (20.5 cm).
HN: *H.* Tardiana grex TF 2 × 35.
[*H.* 'Tardiflora' × *H. sieboldiana* 'Elegans'].

H. **'Wahoo'** Aden IRA/1976.
AHS-III/16A.
Plant has variegation reported to be unstable. Plant 18 in. (46 cm) dia., 10 in. (25.5 cm) high. Leaf 4.5 by 2.5 in. (11.5 by 6.5 cm), veins 7, medium green, streaky yellow, cordate, flat. Scape 20 in. (51 cm), bare, straight. Flower medium, bell-shaped, white, flowers during average period, fertile.
[*H.* 'Tokudama Aureonebulosa' × 'Tokudama Flavocircinalis'].

H. **'Walden'**.

H. **'Warwick Cup'** Jones.
Plant is a blue-green cultivar with very deeply cupped leaves. Size is between *H. sieboldiana* and *H.* 'Tokudama'.

H. **'Wassman Sport'** Wassman.

H. **'Waterford'** Moldovan IRA/1983.
AHS-II/9B.
Plant 38 in. (96.5 cm) dia., 24 in. (61 cm) high. Leaf 11 by 10 in. (28 by 25.5 cm), veins 16, blue-green, not variegated, cordate, cupped-rugose. Scape 30 in. (76 cm), bare, straight. Flower medium, bell-shaped, white, flowers during average period, fertile.
[*H. sieboldiana* 'Elegans' hybrid].

H. **'Wayside Blue'** Wayside/Ruh IRA/1989.
AHS-III/15B.
Plant 25 in. (63 cm) dia., 15 in. (38 cm) high. Leaf 10 by 7 in. (25 by 18 cm), veins 14, blue-green, not variegated, cordate. Scape 19 in. (48 cm), bare, straight. Flower medium, funnel-shaped, white, flowers during average period, fertile.
[*H.* 'Tokudama' hybrid].

H. **'Wayside Perfection'** Wayside.
(see *H.* 'Royal Standard').

H. **'Wee Willy'** Japan.
JN: *Yaku Giboshi* hort.
(see *H.* 'Saishu Jima').

H. **'Weihenstephan'** Müssel. (Plate 143).
Plant is a hybrid with pure white flowers. The leaves of specimens observed in Europe are wider than those of the parent species and have 5 pairs of veins. This is not *H. sieboldii* 'Alba' which has narrower leaves and 3 pairs of veins. Some authors attribute this taxon a mutant of *H. sieboldii*, but it is probably directly related to the hybrid *H. sieboldii* 'Alba' × *H. ventricosa* made by Arends. Plant 16 in. (40.5 cm) dia., 10 in. (25.5 cm) high. Leaf 5.5 by 2 in. (14 by 5 cm), veins 5, medium green, not variegated, cordate, flat. Scape 18 in. (46 cm), bare, straight. Flower medium, funnel-shaped, white, flowers during summer period, fertile.
HN: *H. albomarginata* 'Weihenstephan' Müssel.
H. minor alba "Improved" hort. Arends.
[*H. sieboldii* 'Alba' × *H. ventricosa*].
(see also 'White Trumpets' pp sim).

H. **'Weisse Glocke'** Klose.
Plant has white flowers that are larger than those of *H. sieboldii* 'Alba'. Name means "White Bell."
[*H. sieboldii* hybrid].

H. **'Wheel of Fortune'** Houseworth 1986.
[*H. sieboldii* 'Louisa' hybrid].

H. **'Whipped Cream'** Zilis IRA/1988.
AHS-IV/20A.
Plant 24 in. (61 cm) dia., 16 in. (40.5 cm) high. Leaf 6 by 3 in. (15 by 7.5 cm), veins 9, white, narrow green margin, ovate, flat. Scape 32 in. (81.5 cm), foliated, oblique. Flower medium, funnel-shaped, lavender, fragrant, flowers during summer period, fertile.
[*H. plantaginea* 'Honeybells' mutation].

H. **'Whirlwind'** Kulpa IRA/1989.
AHS-IV/20A.
Plant 12 in. (30 cm) dia., 5 in. (13 cm) high. Leaf 4.5 by 2 in. (11 by 5 cm), veins 8, yellowish white center (variable), dark green margin, ovate-cordate, flat. Scape 20 in. (51 cm), foliaceous, straight. Flower medium, funnel-shaped, lavender, flowers during average period, fertility(?).
[*H.* 'Fortunei Hyacinthina' mutation ad int].

H. **'White Border'** Japan.
Plant's name is applied to several yellowish white and white-margined taxa, including *H.* 'Helonioides Albopicta' and *H.* 'Rohdeifolia'.
HN: *H.* 'Helonioides Albopicta'.
H. 'Rohdeifolia'.
(see also *H.* 'Helonioides Albopicta').
(see also *H.* 'Rohdeifolia').

H. **'White Cap'** Bemis.

H. **'White Charger'** Aden IRA/1986.
AHS-III/13B.
Plant 36 in. (91.5 cm) dia., 22 in. (56 cm) high. Leaf 10 by 7.5 in. (25.5 by 19 cm), veins 12, medium green, not variegated, cordate, flat. Scape 32 in. (81.5 cm), bare, straight. Flower medium, funnel-shaped, white, flowers during summer period, fertile.
[*H.* 'Aden No. 614' × *H.* 'Aden No. 618'].

H. **'White Christmas'** Krossa 1966 IRA/1971.
AHS-IV/20A.
Plant is a selection of *H.* 'Undulata' with large white areas that stay white longer than the typical form. Plant 20 in. (51 cm) dia., 12 in. (31 cm) high. Leaf 5 by 2.5 in. (13 by 6.5 cm), veins 6, white (viridescent), margin green, ovate, wavy, twisted. Scape 28 in. (71 cm), foliated, straight. Flower medium, funnel-shaped, lavender, flowers during average period, fertile.
HN: *H.* 'Krossa White'.
H. 'Starlight' pp sim].
[*H.* 'Undulata' mutation].

H. **'White Colossus'** Aden IRA/1978.
AHS-II/8A.
Plant has unstable variegation and melting out of leaf center has been reported. Plant 28 in. (71 cm) dia., 16 in. (40.5 cm) high. Leaf 8 by 5 in. (20 by 13 cm), veins 8, white (albescent), margin medium green and chartreuse, streaked into center, cordate, flat. Scape 28 in. (71 cm), foliated, straight. Flower medium, funnel-shaped, lavender, flowers during summer period, fertile.

H. **'White Edge'** Simpers.
Plant 28 in. (71 cm) dia., 16 in. (40.5 cm) high. Leaf 7 by 5 in. (18 by 13 cm), veins 9, medium green, margin white, cordate, flat. Scape 26 in. (66 cm), bare, straight. Flower medium, funnel-shaped, lavender, flowers during average period, fertile.
HN: *H.* 'Fortunei Albomarginata' group 'White Edge'.
H. 'Fortunei White Edge'.
[*H.* 'Fortunei' mutation].

H. **'White Edger'** Aden.
Plant 18 in. (46 cm) dia., 10 in. (25.5 cm) high. Leaf 4 by 2.5 in. (10 by 6.5 cm), veins 9, shiny medium green, not variegated, cordate, flat. Scape 18 in. (46 cm), bare, straight. Flower medium, bell-shaped, white, flowers during average period, fertile.

H. **'White Knight'**.
Plant is very similar to *H.* 'Royal Standard', but slightly pruinose on leaf underside. Flowers are the same (Figure 4-35). Plant 38 in. (96.5 cm) dia., 22 in. (56 cm) high. Leaf 7 by 5 in. (18 by 13 cm), veins 8, dark green, not variegated, cordate, flat. Scape 34 in. (86.5 cm), foliated, straight. Flower medium-large, funnel-shaped, white, fragrant, flowers during summer period, fertile.
HN: *H.* 'Royal Standard' pp sim.

H. **'White Magic'** Aden IRA/1978.
AHS-III/14A.
Plant 20 in. (51 cm) dia., 12 in. (31 cm) high. Leaf 9 by 6 in. (23 by 15 cm), veins 8, white (viridescent), margin green, ovate, flat. Scape 28 in. (71 cm), foliated, straight. Flower medium, funnel-shaped, lavender, flowers during summer period, fertile.

H. **'White Mule'** Summers.
Plant 12 in. (31 cm) dia., 8 in. (20 cm) high. Leaf 4 by 1 in. (10 by 2.5 cm), veins 3, medium green, not variegated, lanceolate, flat. Scape 14 in. (35.5 cm), bare, straight. Flower medium, funnel-shaped, white, flowers during summer period, fertile.
HN: *H. sieboldii* 'White Mule'.
[*H. sieboldii* mutation].

H. 'White Ray' Minks IRA/1974.
AHS-IV/20A.

Plant is a selected form of *H.* 'Undulata Univittata' with the variegation diminished to a narrow white line. One of the transitional stages of *H.* 'Undulata' reverting to all-green. Plant 24 in. (61 cm) dia., 14 in. (35.5 cm) high. Leaf 5 by 2.5 in. (13 by 6.5 cm), veins 8, medium green, white line in center, ovate, wavy. Scape 30 in. (76 cm), foliated, oblique. Flowers medium, funnel-shaped, lavender, flowers during average period, sterile.

HN: *H.* 'Unitalis' hort.

[*H.* 'Undulata Univittata' mutation].

H. 'White Shoulders'ᴾᴾᴬᶠ Walters Gardens IRA/1988.
AHS-III/16A.

Plant is a white-margined mutation of the species *H. plantaginea*. Plant 34 in. (86.5 cm) dia., 22 in. (56 cm) high. Leaf 10 by 6 in. (25.5 by 15 cm), veins 10, medium green, margin white (albescent), ovate-cordate, flat. Scape 32 in. (81.5 cm), foliated, oblique. Flower large, funnel-shaped, white, fragrant, flowers during summer period, fertile.

[*H. plantaginea* mutation].

H. 'White Standard'.
Plant 28 in. (71 cm) dia., 16 in. (40.5 cm) high. Leaf 6.5 by 3.5 in. (16.5 by 9 cm), veins 8, white (albescent), margin green, cordate, flat. Scape 38 in. (96.5 cm), bare, straight. Flower medium, funnel-shaped, lavender, flowers during average period, fertile.

[*H.* 'Fortunei Gold Standard' mutation].

H. 'White Tie Affair' Vaughn.
Plant is related to *H.* 'Formal Attire' but has reverse variegation.

H. 'White Trouble' Schmid.   (Plate 144).
Shiro Ohatsuki Giboshi, the "white leafy-scaped hosta," is a white form that occurs from time to time as a mutation in cultivated *H.* 'Undulata Albomarginata' colonies. It has been reported in Japan and on several occasions in the United States. Its leaves are a uniform near-white with a scarcely noticeable greenish-yellow tint, the overall impression being white. A difficult subject in cultivation—hence the name—because of its lack of chlorophyll. The Japanese cultivate it in pots so it can be moved around. It makes a fine showing in spring when it requires shade, but later it must be grown in sun so that the white-streaked, green summer leaves can build up enough food for survival. Its other morphological features are like *H.* 'Undulata' except that the leaves are flat and, being a difficult subject, it is definitely for experienced collectors only.

JN: *Shiro Ohatsuki Giboshi* Schmid.

H. 'White Trumpets' Williams/Hensen IRA/1983.
AHS-IV/19A.

Plant 16 in. (40.5 cm) dia., 10 in. (25.5 cm) high. Leaf 5.5 by 2 in. (14 by 5 cm), veins 5, medium green, not variegated, cordate, flat. Scape 18 in. (46 cm), bare, straight. Flower medium, funnel-shaped, white, flowers during summer period, fertile.

HN: *H. albomarginata* 'White Trumpets' Hensen 1985.
     H. 'FRW No. 1373'.

[*H. sieboldii* hybrid].

(see also *H.* 'Weihenstephan' pp sim).

H. 'White Vision' Aden IRA/1978.
AHS-III/17A.

Plant has light yellow leaves, cupped, medium size.

H. 'Whoopee' Aden IRA/1980.
AHS-III/16A.

Plant has very variable variegation, with some leaves observed more green than yellow. Plant 20 in. (51 cm) dia., 14 in. (35.5 cm) high. Leaf medium, veins 10, medium green, streaky yellow, cordate, flat. Scape 20 in. (51 cm), foliated, straight. Flower medium, funnel-shaped, lavender, flowers during average period, fertile.

[*H.* 'Flamboyant' × *H.* 'Fascination'].

H. 'Wide Brim' Aden IRA/1979.
AHS-III/16B.   (Plate 73).

Plant 36 in. (91.5) dia., 22 in. (56 cm) high. Leaf 7 by 5 in. (18 by 13 cm), veins 10, medium green, margin yellow turning to white, cordate, rugose. Scape 32 in. (81.5 cm), bare, straight. Flower medium, funnel-shaped, white, flowers during summer period, fertile.

[*H.* 'Bold One' × *H.* 'Bold Ribbons'].

H. 'William Lachman' Vaughn IRA/1981.
AHS-III/16B.

Plant has unstable variegation which has been reported to revert to green. The typical form has rather small leaves which enlarge during reversion process. Plant 14 in. (35.5 cm) dia., 8 in. (20 cm) high. Leaf 6 by 5 in. (15 by 13 cm), veins 7, blue-green, streaky white and yellow, cordate, flat, barely rugose. Scape 18 in. (46 cm), foliated, oblique. Flower medium, funnel-shaped, lavender, flowers during average period, fertile.

[*H.* 'Breeders Choice' × *H. sieboldiana* 'Frances Williams'].

H. 'Willimantic' Lauman.
Summers No. 140 1967.

[*H. sieboldiana* hybrid].

H. 'Willy Nilly' Holly 1963 IRA/1968.
AHS-II/9A.

Plant 40 in. (101.5 cm) dia., 22 in. (56 cm) high. Leaf 13 by 10 in. (33 by 25.5 cm), veins 16, blue-green, not variegated, cordate, rugose. Scape 30 in. (76 cm), foliated, oblique. Flower medium, funnel-shaped, white, flowers during average period, fertile.

[*H. sieboldiana* hybrid].

H. 'Windsor Gold'.
(see *H.* 'Nancy Lindsay').

H. 'Winning Edge' Zilis IRA/1988.
AHS-III/16B.

Plant 36 in. (91.5 cm) dia., 16 in. (40.5 cm) high. Leaf 7 by 6 in. (18 by 15 cm), veins 15, blue-green, margin yellow, cordate. Scape 30 in. (76 cm), bare, straight. Flower medium, lavender, flowers during average period.

[*H.* 'Tokudama Aureonebulosa' × 'Tokudama Aureonebulosa'].

H. 'Witches Brew' Ross IRA/1981.
AHS-II/9B.

Plant 48 in. (122 cm) dia., 24 in. (61 cm) high. Leaf 13 by 11 in. (33 by 28 cm), veins 16, medium green, not variegated, cordate, rugose. Scape 32 in. (81.5 cm), foliated, oblique. Flower medium, funnel-shaped, white, flowers during average period, fertile.

[*H. sieboldiana* hybrid].

H. 'Woad Courts'.

H. **'Wogon'** Japan/Epstein IRA/1986.
AHS-IV/23B.
黄金ギボウシ

Plant name is an old spelling of *ogon* which means "gold." The correct Japanese name is *Ogon Giboshi*, and the Western cultivar name should correctly be *H.* 'Ogon'. *Hosta* 'Wogon' has been registered with the IRA and is here reluctantly accepted as a valid cultivar name. All other synonyms listed below are incorrect and should not be used. This cultivar is one of the many named yellow forms of *H. sieboldii* and is very similar to *H. sieboldii* 'Subcrocea'. Plant 12 in. (31 cm) dia., 6 in. (15 cm) high. Leaf 4 by 1.5 in. (10 by 4 cm), veins 4, yellow (viridescent), not variegated, ovate, flat. Scape 14 in. (35.5 cm), bare, straight. Flower medium, bell-shaped, purple, flowers during average period, fertile.
HN: *H.* 'Ogon' (alternate, but correct spelling).
      H. 'Wogon Giboshi' UK ex Rokujo.
      H. 'Wogon (Gold)' hort. incorrect.
      H. 'Wogan Gold' incorrect.
      Summers No. 196.
JN: *Ogon Giboshi* hort.
      Wogon Giboshi hort.
[*H. sieboldii* mutation or hybrid].

H. **'Wolcott'** Piedmont Gardens IRA/1982.
AHS-II/12B.

Plant has been originally described as yellow variegated, but most plants in existence have reverted to all-green. Plant 48 in. (122 cm) dia., 24 in. (61 cm) high. Leaf 13 by 11 in. (33 by 28 cm), veins 16, blue-green, not variegated, cordate, rugose. Scape 32 in. (81.5 cm), foliated, oblique. Flower medium, funnel-shaped, white, flowers during average period, fertile.
HN: *H.* 'Stones Fantasy' Stone.
[*H.* 'Fortunei Sharmon' × *H. sieboldiana* 'Golden Sunburst'].
[*H. sieboldiana* hybrid].

H. **'Woodland Blue'** Simpers.

Plant is medium size, with dark bluish green rugose leaf. It is similar to *H.* 'Tokudama'.
[*H. sieboldiana* hybrid].

H. **'Woodland Green'** Simpers.

Plant has large dark green cordate leaves with elongated, contorted tip.
HN: *H. sieboldiana* form.
[*H.* 'Elata Fountain' hybrid].

H. **'Wrinkles and Crinkles'** Englerth IRA/1985.
AHS-II/7A.

Plant 38 in. (96.5 cm) dia., 16 in. (40.5 cm) high. Leaf 9.5 by 6 in. (24 by 15 cm), veins 16, blue-green, not variegated, cordate, very rugose. Scape 32 in. (81.5 cm), foliated, oblique. Flower medium, funnel-shaped, white, flowers during average period, fertile.
HN: *H.* 'Wrinkly Crinkly'.

H. **'Wunderbar'** Harrison.
HN: *H.* 'Wonderbar' incorrect.

Y

H. **'Yakushima'** Japan.
ヤクシマギボウシ

Plant name is a derivation of the botanical name *H. yakusimensis* (Masamune) Maekawa 1950 which is based on *H. sieboldiana* var. *yakusimensis* Masamune (1932). As such it was considered a synonym of *H. sieboldiana* by Fujita (1976a). Unfortunately, in Japan the name is applied to a number of different, small taxa, usually belonging to *H. sieboldii, H. gracillima,* or *H. kikutii.* Yaku Island is noted for the occurrence of scarce dwarf forms of a number of different genera, so Japanese nursery operators use "Yaku" or "Yakushima" in the descriptors for small plants to imply scarcity. The plants I have observed under this name are forms of *H. gracillima.* Because this name has been used persistently for a number of different taxa it is a nom. confusum in its botanical forms and when used as a cultivar name as well.
HN: *H.* 'Hakujima' hort.
      H. 'Yakushimana' incorrect.
      H. 'Yakusimana' incorrect.
JN: *Yakushima Mizu Giboshi* hort.
[*H. gracillima* sel].
(see *H. gracillima*).
(see also *H.* 'Yakushima Mizu').
(see also *H. yakusimensis*).

H. **'Yakushima Mizu'** Japan.
ヤクシマミズギボウシ

Plant from Yaku Island which is notable for the occurrence of scarce dwarf forms of a number of different genera. Japanese nursery operators use "Yaku" or "Yakushima" in the descriptors for small plants to imply scarcity. The plants most commonly grown under this name are forms of *H. gracillima* (Figure 3-14). Most Japanese authorities consider this an incorrect name.
HN: *H.* 'Hakujima'.
JN: *Yakushima Mizu Giboshi* hort.
[*H. gracillima* sel].
(see *H. gracillima*).

H. **'Yellow Blade'** Benedict 1986.

Plant is the stable yellow form of *H.* 'Yellow Splash'. Plant 20 in. (51 cm) dia., 14 in. (35.5 cm) high. Leaf 6 by 2.5 in. (15 by 6.5 cm), veins 5, yellow (lutescent), not variegated, ovate-lanceolate, flat. Scape 28 in. (71 cm), bare, straight. Flower medium, funnel-shaped, lavender, flowers during average period, fertile.
[*H.* 'Yellow splash' mutation].

H. **'Yellow Boa'** O'Harra.

Plant 12 in. (31 cm) dia., 6 in. (15 cm) high. Leaf 4 by 0.75 in. (10 by 2 cm), veins 4, yellow (viridescent), not variegated, ovate, flat. Scape 14 in. (35.5 cm), bare, straight. Flower medium, bell-shaped, purple striped, flowers during average period, fertile.
[*H. sieboldii* 'Suberocea' hybrid].

H. **'Yellow Boy'**.

Plant name is a superseded synonym.
HN: *H.* 'Fortunei Yellow Boy'.
(see *H.* 'Antioch').

H. **'Yellow Edge'** Williams.

Plant name is a superseded synonym.
(see *H. sieboldiana* 'Frances Williams').

H. **'Yellow Emperor'** Savory IRA/1987.
AHS-II/11A.
Plant has yellow ruffled leaves with green veins. Plant 30 in. (76 cm) dia., 20 in. (51 cm) high. Leaf 12 by 8 in. (31 by 20 cm), veins 12, yellow (lutescent), not variegated, cordate, undulate. Scape 32 in. (81.5 cm), bare, straight. Flower medium, funnel-shaped, lavender, flowers during average period, fertile.
[*H. montana* 'Honey' hybrid].

H. **'Yellow River'** Aden.
AHS Benedict Award, 1989, exhibited by Van Wade. Ruh (1985) reports seeing this unregistered cultivar in Julie Morss' garden (UK). Burto (1989) relates it was sent by Aden to Benedict around 1980. Plant 48 in. (122 cm) dia., 24 in. (60 cm) high. Leaf 13 by 10 in. (33 by 25 cm), veins 12–15, grey-green, margin whitish yellow, cordate, ribbed, wavy margin. Scape 48 in. (122 cm), straight. Flower medium, white, flowers during average period, fertile.
[*H. montana* mutation].

H. **'Yellow Splash'** Aden 1973 IRA/1976.
AHS-IV/22B.
Plant has unstable variegation, reverting to the all-yellow or margined form. Plant 20 in. (51 cm) dia., 14 in. (35.5 cm) high. Leaf 6 by 2.5 in. (15 by 6.5 cm), veins 5, medium green, streaky white, ovate, flat. Scape 28 in. (71 cm), bare, straight. Flower medium, funnel-shaped, lavender, flowers during average period, fertile.
[*H.* 'Aden No. 270' × *H.* 'Aden No. 275'].

H. **'Yellow Splash Rim'** AHS IRA/1986.
AHS-IV/22B.   (Figure 4-46; Plate 154).
Plant is the stable margined form of *H.* 'Yellow Splash'. Plant 32 in. (81.5 cm) dia., 16 in. (40.5 cm) high. Leaf 6 by 2.5 in. (15 by 6.5 cm), veins 5, medium green, margin white, ovate, flat. Scape 32 in. (81.5 cm), bare, straight. Flower medium, funnel-shaped, lavender, flowers during average period, fertile.
[*H.* 'Yellow Splash' mutation].

Figure 4-46. *H.* 'Yellow Splash Rim'; general habit (Hosta Hill)

H. **'Yellow Splashed Edged'** Ruh.
Plant has lanceolate green leaves, sometimes mottled with yellow and yellow margin.

H. **'Yellow Surprise'** Fisher/Hensen IRA/1983.
AHS-III/18B.
Plant 20 in. (51 cm) dia., 14 in. (35.5 cm) high. Leaf 5.5 by 3 in. (14 by 7.5 cm), veins 6, yellow (viridescent), not variegated,

ovate, flat. Scape 20 in. (51 cm), foliated, straight. Flower medium, funnel-shaped, lavender, flowers during average period, fertile.
HN: *H.* 'Fisher Clone No. 4'.
     H. 'Fisher No. 12.
     H. rectifolia 'Yellow Surprise' Hensen 1983.
[*H. rectifolia* hybrid].

H. **'Yellow Waves'** Aden 1974 IRA/1978.
AHS-IV/23B.

Z

H. **'Zager Blue'** Zager/Ruh IRA/1987.
AHS-III/15A.
Plant 34 in. (86.5 cm) dia., 24 in. (61 cm) high. Leaf 9 by 6 in. (23 by 15 cm), veins 12, blue-green, not variegated, cordate, flat. Scape 48 in. (122 cm), foliated, straight. Flower medium, bell-shaped, white, flowers during average period, fertile.
HN: *H.* 'Zager Blue Leaf' Zager.
[*H.* 'Fortunei' sel al].
[*H. sieboldiana* × *H. montana*].

H. **'Zager Giant Puckered'** Zager/Ruh IRA/1989.
AHS-III/15B.
Plant 26 in. (66 cm) dia., 17 in. (43 cm) high. Leaf 9 by 7 in. (23 by 18 cm), veins 14, light blue-green, cordate, rugose. Scape 28 in. (71 cm), foliated, oblique. Flower medium, funnel-shaped, white, flowers during average period, fertile.
[*H. sieboldiana* hybrid ad int].

H. **'Zager Green'** Zager/Ruh IRA/1987.
AHS-III/13A.
Plant 32 in. (81.5 cm) dia., 22 in. (56 cm) high. Leaf 9 by 6 in. (23 by 15 cm), veins 12, blue-green, not variegated, cordate, flat. Scape 35 in. (89 cm), foliated, straight. Flower medium, bell-shaped, white, flowers during average period, fertile.
HN: *H.* 'Zager Green Leaf' Zager.
[*H. sieboldiana* × *H. montana*].

H. **'Zager Green Rim'** Zager/Ruh IRA/1987.
AHS-III/18B.
Plant has viridescent light green margin that turns all green. Plant 26 in. (66 cm) dia., 20 in. (51 cm) high. Leaf 7 by 4 in. (18 by 10 cm), veins 8, green, light green margin (viridescent), cordate, flat. Scape 34 in. (86.5 cm), foliated, oblique. Flower medium, funnel-shaped, white, flowers during average period, fertile.

H. **'Zagers Pride'** Zager/Ruh IRA/1987.
AHS-II/10B.
Plant is similar to *H. sieboldiana* 'Frances Williams'. Chartreuse margin. Plant 34 in. (86.5 cm) dia., 16 in. (40.5 cm) high. Leaf 10 by 7 in. (25.5 by 18 cm), veins 14, blue-green, chartreuse margin, cordate, rugose. Scape 24 in. (61 cm), foliated, straight. Flower medium, bell-shaped, white, flowers during average period, fertile.
HN: *H.* 'Zager Frances Williams' Zager.
     H. sieboldiana Aureomarginata group.
[*H. sieboldiana* mutation].

H. **'Zager Puckered Giant'** Zager.
(see *H.* 'Zager Giant Puckered').

H. **'Zager White Edge'** Simpers IRA/1980.
    AHS-III/16A.
    Plant is similar to *H.* 'Fortunei Albomarginata', but has a more elongated leaf shape and one of the whitest margins in this group, so is very distinct.
HN: *H.* 'Fortunei Albomarginata' group.
    H. 'Zager White Border'.
[*H.* 'Fortunei' mutation].

H. **'Zansetsu'** Japan.
残雪
    Nokon No Yuki Giboshi, the "lingering snow hosta," is a mosaic mutant form with snow-flurry form variegation.
HN: *H.* 'Nokon No Yuki' hort.
JN: *Nokon No Yuki Giboshi* hort.
    Zansetsu Giboshi hort.
(see also *H.* 'Nokon No Yuki').

H. **'Zircon'**.

H. **'Zitronenfalter'** Klose.
    Plant has violet-striped flowers over yellowish green leaves. The name means "Lemon Butterfly".
[*H. sieboldii* hybrid].

H. **'Zounds'** Aden 1975 IRA/1978.
    AHS-II/11A.   (Plates 145, 160).
    AHS Midwest Gold Award, 1989, exhibited by Richard Ward. Plant 30 in. (76 cm) dia., 16 in. (40.5 cm) high. Leaf 11 by 8.5 in. (28 by 21.5 cm), veins 12, yellow (lutescent), not variegated, cordate, rugose-twisted. Scape 24 in. (61 cm), foliated, straight. Flower medium, funnel-shaped, white, flowers during average period, fertile.
[*H. sieboldiana* 'Elegans' hybrid].

CHAPTER 5

Historical Account of the Genus *Hosta* With Emphasis on Nomenclature

THE BEGINNING—EARLY JAPAN

Early representatives of the genus *Hosta* evolved in the land areas bordering the East China Sea and the Sea of Japan. They have been found growing in the wild in eastern China (northeast, east-central, and some southeastern areas, and southern Manchuria), Korea, throughout the Japanese archipelago (including the South Kurile islands and Sakhalin to the north and Yaku and Oshima islands to the south, but excluding the Ryukyu Islands), and the southern Sikhote-Alin mountains of the far eastern USSR.

The Japanese formal (academic) and horticultural name for the genus is *Giboshi* (the exact transliteration from the Japanese katakana is *Gi-bo-u-shi*). The Japanese generic name is transliterated as *Giboshi Zoku*. According to *Brinkley's Japanese-English Dictionary*,[1] the word has its roots in the word *gibo* or its synonym *giboshi*, an old Japanese floristic name for *H. cærulea*.[2] Spelled *giboshu* it has another meaning: a leaf-shaped decoration on temples and bridges, which looks much like hosta leaves.

The ancient beginnings of hosta history are shrouded with mystery, but records show that Japanese landscape gardening (Zoen), based on Chinese models, predates the Nara period of the 8th century and was, at first, greatly influenced by religion. Around the 11th century court nobility started to build pleasure gardens designed for walking and boating. Two examples survive today: the Motsuji Temple garden in Iwate Prefecture and the Joruri-ji at Kyoto. Old Japanese records mentioning hostas have survived from this period. For example, *Giboshi* is mentioned in a story entitled "Hanada no Hyogo" by Tsutsumi Chunagon Monogatari, who wrote during the second half of the Heian period (10th–12th centuries):

> *Eldest Princess*: The Gentian as a companion plant in the garden is excellent. It is comparable to the highest rank of the Imperial families.
> *Second Princess*: Giboshi must be compared to the rank of Empress.

This brief dialogue makes it clear that hostas were held in high esteem as garden plants in Japan as early as the Heian period (8th–12th centuries).

The Edo period, also called the Tokugawa period, is of considerable importance in the history of the cultivation of the genus *Hosta*. The period was named for Shogun Tokugawa Ieyasu, who centralized governmental control in Edo, now Tokyo, and lasted from 1603 until 1867.[3]

During this period hosta plants and a likeness of hosta leaves began to appear in Japanese art. In 1682 Moronobu Hishikawa published a picture book under the title *Miyagino*.[4] A beautiful print depicts a courtesan resting on a tatami[5] and gazing into a garden in which the only plant visible is a hosta (Figure 5-1). The floristic work *Ehon Noyamagusa*, written and published by Yasukuni Tachibana in 1755, described and included an excellent illustration of *Giboshi* (Figure 5-2). Shortly thereafter, in 1788, a picture book of satirical poems,

Mushi Erami, by Utamaro Kitagawa shows a rendering of *Giboshi* with an insect perched upon a leaf (Figure 5-3). A number of other works dated before 1800 also include illustrations of hostas. Just what species were figured is difficult to determine.

Figure 5-1. Courtesan. Moronobu Hishikawa in *Miyagino*, 1682

At the beginning of the Edo period Japan opened its previously closed borders to Western trade and culture. Proselytizing by Western missionaries—principally Portuguese—created problems almost immediately, with the result that in only 30 years the Tokugawa shogun again closed the country to all Westerners except the Dutch. More interested in developing trade than religion, the Dutch were the only Western colonial power to enjoy access to Japan until around 1850. Their port of call was Nagasaki on the west coast of Kyushu.

In addition to the Dutch, Chinese and Korean traders were permitted in Japanese ports. This fact is significant in hosta history, because the Chinese and Korean species found their way into Japanese cultivation by virtue of trade and plant exchanges between these countries.

While Japanese horticulture and garden design flourished during the Edo period, the science of systematic botany, as we know it today, was unknown to the Japanese.

Figure 5-2. *Giboshi*. Yasukuni Tachibana in *Ehon Noyamagusa*, 1755

Their plant classification system was based primarily on traditional herbalistic methods. It was not until the beginning of the Meiji restoration[6] that systematic studies were initiated by Western-educated Japanese botanists who had been exposed to Western science some time before this. These studies, which began on an individual basis in 1774, were called "rangaku"—literally "Dutch learning," for it was primarily through the

Dutch that the Japanese were introduced to Western medicine, botany, chemistry, physics, geography, and the military sciences. Botany went hand in hand with medicine, because it was important to the understanding and practice of herbalistic methods of healing. European physicians and naturalists working for the Dutch East India Company were the primary teachers.

Three of these teachers are immortalized by stone monuments located in Nagasaki Park (Nagasaki Koen), near Uma-Machi (a borough). These monuments survived the ravages of the nuclear explosion at the end of the Second World War and the names cut into them can still be clearly read: Kaempfer, Thunberg, and von Siebold. It is not by coincidence that these three names are inseparably linked with the history of the genus *Hosta*.

ENGELBERT KAEMPFER (1651–1716)

Although no hosta has been named for Kaempfer, his name is nevertheless closely linked to the genus. He was the first to mention the genus in Western scientific literature. Kaempfer was born in Lemgo, Germany, in 1651. He studied languages, history, physics, and medicine. After completing his education he was invited to join the embassy sent by King Charles XI of Sweden to the shah of Persia. While in Isfahan, the capital of Persia, he joined the Dutch East India Company as ship physician, arriving on the island of Java (Indonesia) in 1686. In recognition of his abilities he was asked to accompany Dutch officials on their annual journey to Edo (also Yedo, now Tokyo), which was the seat of the Tokugawa shogunate. He arrived in Nagasaki in 1690. During his stay he studied Japanese history, customs, geography, and its flora. In 1693 he returned to Java. After a brief sojourn, he sailed back to Holland, arriving there late that year after an arduous journey of six months.

In 1712 Kaempfer published *Amoenitates Exoticae*, which contains a catalog of Japanese plants. Among them are two hostas: *Joksan, vulgo Giboosi* and *Giboosi altera*.[7] His drawings of

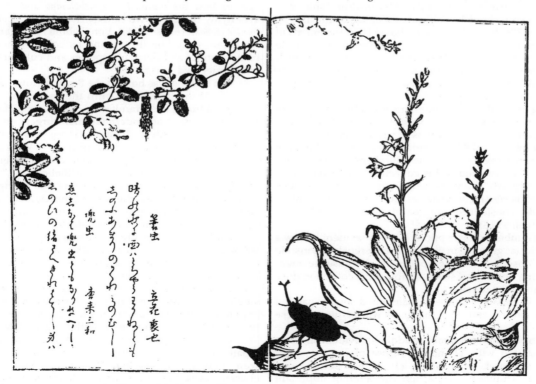

Figure 5-3. Poems. Utamaro Kitagawa in *Mushi Erami*, 1788

these species are now in the Sloan Collection of the British Museum. *Joksan, vulgo Giboosi* is by all indications conspecific with *H.* 'Tokudama' in a broad sense (Stearn, 1931b; Maekawa, 1940), while most scientific references regard *Giboosi altera* as *H.* 'Lancifolia'. Aside from the drawings mentioned, Kaempfer brought neither herbarium specimens nor plants nor seed from Japan.

CARL PEHR THUNBERG (1743–1828)

The name "Thunberg" was first used for a hosta by Stearn,[8] who refers to *H.* 'Lancifolia' as *H. lancifolia* var. *Thunbergii*. Maekawa[9] used the name for the same plant in a corrupt Latin form, viz., "Thunbergiana," but described quite another species—namely the all-green form of *H. sieboldii*, viz. *H. sieboldii* f. *spathulata*.

Thunberg was born at Jönköping, Sweden, in 1743. The young Thunberg aspired to be a physician and enrolled at the University of Uppsala in 1761. He had the good fortune to have Carolus Linnaeus,[10] the founder of systematic botany, as his teacher. Thunberg soon became an intimate disciple of Linnaeus. He studied medicine, which in his day also required the study of botany and natural history. Accepted as a candidate for a doctorate in medicine he successfully defended his thesis and was awarded his doctorate in 1772. His diploma was signed by Linnaeus.

Upon completion of his schooling he was appointed surgeon extraordinary and medical officer with the Dutch East India Company. The company selected their physicians with great care because maintaining good relations with the Japanese depended largely on these very few chosen individuals. Before going to Japan, Thunberg was sent to the Cape Colony (now South Africa), where he became fluent in Dutch. He remained there for three years, studying, among other subjects, the flora of the Cape. His collections and descriptions earned him the title "Father of Cape Botany."

Thunberg eventually arrived in Japan in 1775. There he found a treasure trove of botanical and horticultural splendor. He worked feverishly, collecting and cataloging. By the time he left Japan in 1776, he had collected almost 1000 specimens of plant species. His collection is now preserved at the Institute for Systematic Botany at the University of Uppsala, Sweden. It was the basis for Thunberg's classic work *Flora Japonica*. Published in 1784, this work is considered one of the cornerstones of botany in Japan.

Among his collections Thunberg brought a number of herbarium specimens. Included were *H.* 'Lancifolia', which he described in different publications at various times as *Aletris japonica* Thunberg (1780), *Hemerocallis japonica* Thunberg (1784), and *Hemerocallis lancifolia* Thunberg (1794). Interestingly, also represented in his collection is a specimen of *Hemerocallis undulata* Thunberg, with variegated and undulate leaves, which is *Hosta* 'Undulata', as far as this determination can be made, considering the condition of the herbarium specimen (Juel, 1918).

From Thunberg's descriptions it is now evident he saw a number of hostas growing in the wild in different locations. He must have observed fruiting specimens, because he mentioned fruiting bodies and seeds, although his collection does not contain such material.

While in Japan, Thunberg maintained and expanded Kaempfer's garden and won the good will of his Japanese hosts.

Some of the nomenclature muddle so evident in *Hosta* taxonomy started with Thunberg, whose placements were difficult to interpret, as Hylander (1954) has pointed out. Nevertheless, Thunberg's collection was another important step towards the introduction of the genus into Europe. For the first time botanists were able to examine and work with herbarium specimens.

THE FIRST HOSTAS IN EUROPE

A number of European settlements and colonies existed along the Chinese coast long before Japanese cities became ports of call for European merchant ships. The Chinese species *H. plantaginea* and *H. ventricosa* became known to European botanists and naturalists travelling in China, so the first hostas grown in Europe originated not in Japan but in China.

The first hosta introduced to the continent of Europe was *H. plantaginea*. It was grown from seed which arrived in France before 1784, sent from Macao[11] by the French consul Charles de Guignes. Planted at the Jardin des Plantes in Paris they quickly grew to maturity, and in 1789 Lamarck[12] first described this hosta on the basis of specimens growing there. Lamarck used the species name *Hemerocallis plantaginea*.

Not long after the introduction of *Hosta plantaginea* into France as seed, the first live specimens of the genus were imported into England. In 1790 George Hibbert, a wealthy Englishman and amateur naturalist, imported both *H. plantaginea* and *H. ventricosa*. These hostas, considered rare specimens, were at first grown under glass. Soon their suitability to the English climate became apparent and they became popular garden plants. In 1797 Andrews[13] first described *H. ventricosa* Stearn as *Hemerocallis cærulea*.

For almost half a century these two species remained the only cultivated representatives of the genus in European gardens, until 1829 when an importation of a large number of hostas changed this. The von Siebold era had begun.

PHILIPP FRANZ BALTHASAR VON SIEBOLD (1796–1866)

The one name most associated with hostas is Siebold's. Two species bear his name: *Hosta sieboldiana* and *H. sieboldii*. In synonymy there are two others: *Hemerocallis sieboldtiana* and *Funkia sieboldi* (not *sieboldii*). Von Siebold had a gardener's eye for plants, including hostas, and he collected and imported many distinct and desirable species and cultivars, a number with variegated foliage.

Von Siebold was born in the Bavarian town of Würzburg in 1796. At the time of his birth the name von Siebold was already famous. His grandfather, Karl von Siebold, is considered the father of modern German surgery and obstetrics. Von Siebold's father, Johann Georg von Siebold, was professor of physiology at the University of Würzburg. It is no wonder that young Philipp became the fifth member of the family to enroll in the "Academia Sieboldiana," a name by which the medical faculty at Würzburg was jokingly referred. Philipp studied botany, chemistry, physics, anatomy, geology, and various medical subjects. He completed his studies in 1820, receiving his diploma as a doctor of medicine.

Von Siebold's one great love was natural history. He also wanted to travel. Not satisfied with settling down to what he considered a boring medical practice, he requested a commission in the military forces of the East Indies in Holland. To prepare himself for this undertaking he undertook further studies in botany and natural history. In 1822 he was appointed surgeon major to the East India Army and late in that year sailed for the Dutch settlement in Batavia, Java.

The Dutch, intent on maintaining their trade monopoly in Japan, were eager to impress and please the Japanese. They were looking for another "Thunberg." Von Siebold was chosen. His skill as an eye surgeon, his broad scientific knowledge, and his linguistic aptitude were precisely what the Dutch in Batavia were looking for. Thus von Siebold's greatest dream was realized: He received a commission to go to Japan. He sailed into Nagasaki harbor in August 1823. With him he brought unbounded enthusiasm, and more significantly, all Kaempfer's and Thunberg's writings on Japan which he had very painstakingly studied and analyzed. He was well prepared.

The Dutch settlement in Japan was on Dejima, an artificial island in Nagasaki harbor. Its 130 acres (32 hectares) were the only place Westerners, principally Hollanders, were allowed to live. No one was permitted to leave the island, except for the obligatory ceremonial visits to the shogun in Edo. Women were barred from the island. To many who served there, Dejima was like a prison, and by all accounts it was a miserable place.

Undaunted, von Siebold set up a medical school to train the Japanese in Western medicine. Then, as now, the Japanese suffered hereditary eye problems. Von Siebold performed the first Western-style cataract surgery in Japan and cured many with his special skills as an ophthalmic surgeon. He earned the gratitude of his patients not least because he steadfastly refused to accept payment for his medical services. He was the first physician to systematically teach Western surgery and medicine and has been described as the father of modern obstetrics in Japan. His students were not required to pay tuition (Bowers, 1970). To show their appreciation and realizing the doctor's interest in botany and natural history, they frequently brought von Siebold botanical specimens, art objects, and other ethnographic material.

Von Siebold's ability with the Japanese language very quickly won him other generous friends. Soon he amassed a large collection covering every aspect of Japanese life and culture.

Refurbishing the garden Kaempfer had started was one of von Siebold's first priorities. The little garden on Dejima had deteriorated after Thunberg (with whom he corresponded) had returned to Sweden. Von Siebold redesigned and enlarged the plot, carefully laying out row upon row of saplings, bushes, herbs, and flowering plants. Among the plants he cultivated were several species of hostas that abounded in the mountains around Nagasaki. Much later one of these was named for the city, namely, *Nagasaki Giboshi*, scientifically known as *Hosta tibae*, although it was not validly published as a species until 1984 when Maekawa described it on the basis of a plant found and collected in 1940 by Tsunesaburo Chiba on Mount Inasa-dake. In 1827 von Siebold collected this hosta on that same mountain which can be seen from the site of his house in Katafuchi-machi across Nagasaki harbor. Two of his specimens of *H. tibae* exist in the Leiden Herbarium, both marked syntypes of *Funkia ovata* Sprengel var. *ramosa* Miquel.[14]

Von Siebold's garden soon became a botanical garden of sorts. Every plant was labeled and categorized. Expanding constantly to make room for new specimens brought to him, von Siebold quickly ran out of space, and his school, by adding more and more students, also became too small. One of his grateful students bought him a house and a large piece of property on a mountainside in the Narutaki section (Katafuchi-machi) of Nagasaki. There he established his Narutakijuku, a medical school which bestowed the degree of "Doktor" on many Japanese aspiring to be physicians. He became the only foreigner permitted to leave Dejima Island on a regular basis to continue his teaching. On these short trips he used every opportunity to gather more plant specimens. Eventually he was permitted to move into the house and soon started a garden on his new property. Now free to move through the Nagasaki area and its environs he was able to collect additional plant specimens, including hostas. One of

these was the white-margined *H.* 'Crispula'. This taxon is a mutation which does not come true from seed so is now considered a specioid. Reported by others as originating in temple gardens, this taxon was in fact found by von Siebold in the wild as a mutation as evidenced by annotations on two herbarium specimens in L, nos. 86 and 87: "in valle montis (in mountain valleys)" and "in locis uvis umbrens prope rupiculum Umesima ins (in moist, shady areas near rock on the island of Umeshima)." Clearly, this establishes that von Siebold was able to travel to and collect on nearby islands.

In 1826 von Siebold accompanied Dutch officials on the *hofreis*, (a Dutch word meaning "travel to the royal court"), the obligatory ceremonial visit to the shogun in Edo. The journey took several weeks and spanned a distance of 650 miles (1046 kilometers) both overland and by sea. Von Siebold and his companions had ample opportunities to gather botanical material because the route traversed areas rich in flora: across Kyushu to the Shimonoseki Strait, barely 1 km (1100 yards) wide; crossing over to the western tip of Honshu, thence along the Inland Sea to Himeji, past Shirasagi-jo, the 13th-century Castle of the White Heron, and by land and sea on to Edo, with stops at Osaka and Kyoto.

The Western clinical demonstrations and scientific instruments von Siebold had brought as gifts to Edo made him the center of attention of the learned men at the shogun's court. He befriended many of them, and they, in return, gave him Japanese artifacts of scientific and historic interest. Von Siebold left with a wealth of new materials for his collections, returning to Dejima in July 1927 after an absence of five months.

Von Siebold worked 18 hours a day, seven days a week. Only by driving himself in this way was he able to accomplish the assemblage of his enormous Japanese ethnographic collection.

With the end of his term nearing, von Siebold made plans to return to Holland in the fall of 1928. He carefully packed hundreds of crates and sent them in stages to Holland. Ready to sail on the East Indiaman *Cornelius Houtteman*, he put on board the final shipment of 80 crates containing a secret "forbidden" map of the Japanese coast line which had been given to him in Edo by the court astronomer Takahashi Sakuzaemon (Kageyasu) whose Dutch sobriquet was Globius. In September 1828 a typhoon grounded the ship at Inasa, across the bay from Nagasaki. When the map was discovered in the wreckage, enemies of Takahashi accused von Siebold of being a spy in Russian service, an accusation which was aggravated because he was German by birth yet posing as a Dutchman. Many of his Japanese friends were arrested and von Siebold himself was put under house arrest. Globius later died in prison and his body was formally "executed." Notwithstanding, von Siebold continued to smuggle botanical specimens to Batavia.

In October 1829 von Siebold was pardoned, but banished from his beloved Japan for life. He left Nagasaki in January 1830. His first stop was the Dutch settlement of Batavia, on the island of Java (Indonesia). There he went to work in the gardens of Buitenzorg to identify and classify the plants he had sent the year before and to ready them for the trip to Holland.

When von Siebold sailed from Batavia he carried with him over 5000 botanical specimens—many of them live plants that had been dug up in his gardens at Nagasaki and Buitenzorg—and a like number of zoological specimens (Bowers, 1970). He was the first European to cultivate the Japanese *Hosta* species, which he must have treasured, for on the deck of the ship, among his other botanical treasures, were hostas. Secure in their pots, he lovingly cared for them during the long, arduous journey. Included among those hostas sent by von Siebold from Japan are the following:

1829 *Funkia cucullata* Siebold = *H. sieboldiana*
'Hypophylla'.
1829 *Funkia lanceolata* Siebold = *H. longissima*.
1829 *Funkia lancifolia* Sprengel = *H.* 'Lancifolia'.
1829 *Funkia marginata* Siebold = *H.* 'Crispula'.
1829 *Funkia sieboldiana* Loddiges = *H. sieboldiana*,
Hooker type.[15]
1829 *Funkia undulata* Siebold *foliis variegatis* = *H.*
'Undulata'.
1830 *Funkia maculata* Siebold = *H. sieboldiana*.
1830 *Funkia spathulata* Siebold *foliis albomarginatis* =
H. sieboldii.

Those hostas listed as introduced in 1829 were sent while von
Siebold was under house arrest and arrived in 1929 in Leiden,
Netherlands, where he was to establish residence. The hostas
introduced in 1830 were most likely those that accompanied
him on the return trip from Japan. Further study is required to
determine the full extent of von Siebold's collections because
we know today that some of his accessions were subsequently
lost—for example, the unrecognized species *H. tibae*.

Von Siebold also grew other hosta species and varieties in
his garden at Leiden, which he did not bring back from Japan,
but obtained from European sources. Some of these were
planted soon after his return but did not appear in catalog
listings until later. Those are mentioned in his 1844 and 1856
catalogs are:

1844 *Funkia ovata* Sprengel = *Hosta ventricosa*.
1844 *Funkia subcordata* Sprengel = *Hosta plantaginea*.
1856 *Funkia ovata* Sprengel *aureomaculata* hort =
Hosta ventricosa 'Aureomaculata'.
1856 *Funkia grandiflora* = *Hosta plantaginea*.
1856 *Funkia subcordata* Sprengel *grandiflora* = *Hosta*
plantaginea var. *japonica*.

In 1841, at von Siebold's request, J. Pierot of the Rijksherbarium, Leiden, travelled to Indonesia (and also to Japan) and
sent back some of the tropical and Japanese plants von Siebold
had cultivated there. (He also sent back a number of von
Siebold's herbarium specimens.) Among the plants were
hostas, including *Funkia grandiflora*. In 1844 von Siebold listed
this hosta as *Funkia subcordata grandiflora*, but it was
undoubtedly the var. *japonica* because the species—that is, the
typical form of *Hosta plantaginea*—was not grown in Japan at
that time.[16] The latter hosta had already been grown in
England for some time and had been described by Sprengel[17]
as *Funkia subcordata* in 1825. In 1863 Ascherson[18] transferred
this taxon to *Hosta* as *H. plantaginea*. Even today some of these
old names for *H. plantaginea* are incorrectly used in nursery
catalogs and horticultural references.

Also grown by von Siebold at Leiden was *H. ventricosa*
Stearn. It was listed as *Funkia ovata* in von Siebold's first catalog
published in 1844. The species name *Funkia ovata* was first
used by Sprengel in 1825. It was probably grown by von
Siebold at Leiden soon after he arrived in 1830. Now we know
the epithet *ovata* was also used for several other hostas, among
them *Hosta tibae* and *H.* 'Undulata Erromena'.

Interestingly, he also listed a variegated form of *H. ventricosa*, namely, *H. ventricosa aureomaculata*, with gold variegated
centers in spring.

Von Siebold brought *H. sieboldii* with him from Japan
listing it as *Funkia spathulata foliis albomarginatis*. This hosta has
a narrow white margin on a green leaf. When grown from seed
it occasionally sports to lutescent or mediovariegated forms.[19]
The latter is now called *Hosta sieboldii* 'Silver Kabitan' and is
similar to *H.* 'Haku Chu Han'. All indications are that this was
the plant described by von Siebold under the species name

Funkia undulata angustifolia. This plant looks like a small, very
narrow leaf *Hosta* 'Undulata', hence the name given by von
Siebold.

The only link to his beloved Japan remaining for von
Siebold were the trees and plants he had brought from his
gardens. One of his main objectives was to introduce them into
the gardens and landscape of Europe, so to realize this aim he
bought land in the village of Leiderdorp near Leiden. There he
built a garden patterned after the Japanese gardens he had
seen and put many of his plants on display. In the meantime he
also sent live plants and seed to many botanical gardens of
Europe. These activities eventually led to the establishment of
the nursery Von Siebold & Coy which published a series of
catalogs starting in 1844 and continuing until 1882. By 1879 a
total of 38 species and cultivars of *Hosta* had been listed. In
addition to these von Siebold introduced more than 1000 trees
and plants, including *Ginkgo biloba*, *Prunus serrulata*, *Viburnum
sieboldii*, hydrangeas, magnolias, maples, ornamental cherries,
bamboo, lilies, irises, chrysanthemums, and a host of other
plants. Today many of his important introductions carry the
epithet "Sieboldii" or "Sieboldiana."

Desperately wanting to return to Japan, in the early 1850s
von Siebold negotiated with the U.S. State and Navy depart-
ments to serve on one of the up-coming expeditions to Japan.
He provided U.S. officials with detailed information on Japan
and furnished a copy of the map that led to his exile 20 years
earlier. This material was later used by Commodore Perry's
expedition. Von Siebold realized the "opening of Japan" was
about to take place and he wanted to be part of it, so redoubled
his efforts to gain permission from the Japanese authorities to
return. He pleaded with kings, dukes, and heads of state all
over Europe to intercede on his behalf. In 1855 the Dutch
consul in Nagasaki was successful in having von Siebold's life
banishment revoked. Still it was not until 1858 that he received
his call to travel. In 1859 the Nederlandsche Handels-
Maatschapij (successor to the Dutch East India Company)
appointed von Siebold advisor for Japanese affairs and he
came to realize his dream to see Japan again. He left Bonn,
Germany, for the first stage of his trip in April 1859. With him
went the best wishes of many, including a farewell letter from
Alexander von Humboldt.[20] He sailed into Nagasaki Bay in
August of that year, almost 36 years to the day after he arrived
on his first trip.

Soon after his arrival von Siebold returned to his former
hillside home in Nagasaki. The garden von Siebold had built
over 30 years earlier was still there having been lovingly cared
for by his former Japanese students, now established physicians, and friends who had not forgotten him. The garden contained thousands of pharmaceutical plants and a multitude of
perennials. Among these were a number of hostas he had
planted.

Many of his old Japanese friends came to see him and
occasionally even visitors from abroad arrived there. Robert
Fortune was one who paid him a visit late in the summer of
1860. He left with several plants given to him by von Siebold,
among them a hosta which was later named *H. sieboldiana* var.
fortunei (= *H.* 'Tokudama'). Von Siebold himself also brought
this plant back from Japan under the name *Funkia glauca*.

The Japan von Siebold knew in the 1830s had changed.
Many Japanese felt threatened by increasing Western aggres-
siveness. To many of the samurai,[21] the foreigners were "barbarians" bent on destroying Japanese customs and traditions.
This created bitter antagonism which resulted in many
kidnappings and assassinations. No "Western barbarian" was
safe and many hired bodyguards or carried guns. Von Siebold,
convinced by his former students and friends to practice and
teach medicine again, had no such problems. At age 64 he was
a handsome six-foot-two giant among his hosts. He always

wore traditional Japanese clothes and was still fluent in Japanese. To the Japanese around him he was a friend and teacher whom they called *Shiboruto sensei*.[22] He could be seen visiting patients after dark, his long, snow-white beard illuminated by the soft glow of lanterns carried by Japanese servants. On the rice paper shielding the lamps were printed the Japanese characters for his name. Even the most radical and vengeful *ronin*[23] left him in peace.

Von Siebold wished to become advisor to the shogun and a negotiator for the Western embassies. He was a highly skilled surgeon and a consummate naturalist, but a diplomat he was not. He only got in the way of both Japanese and Western politicians so von Siebold had to go. The Dutch consulate arranged for his transfer as an advisor to the governor of Batavia with the promise that he could return to Japan after the political situation cooled down.

Late in 1861 von Siebold embarked for Batavia, Java. Again he went to work in the gardens of Buitenzorg while awaiting the call to go back to Japan—a call that never came. Von Siebold realized his diplomatic efforts had failed, so disillusioned he returned to Holland in 1862. His second trip to Japan certainly dashed all his ambassadorial hopes and ambitions, but for botany and horticulture it was a triumph. During his stay he made many new contacts for his nursery and exported a considerable number of new plants, including hostas, to Holland. The following table lists the hostas introduced during his second stay in Japan, all of which (except *Funkia striata*) were sent to Holland before his return and some of which were sent shortly after his arrival in Japan:

1859 *Funkia striata* Siebold = *Hosta* 'Undulata'.
1859 *Funkia glauca variegata* = *Hosta sieboldiana* or *H.* 'Tokudama' variegated form.
1859 *Funkia undulata* f. *angustifolia* = *H.* 'Haku Chu Han' = *Hosta sieboldii* 'Silver Kabitan'.
1859 *Funkia argenteostriata* = *Hosta* 'Undulata'.
1860 *Funkia spathulata* Siebold = *Hosta sieboldii* f. *spathulata*.
1862 *Funkia glauca* Siebold = *Hosta tokudama* or *H. sieboldiana* form.

Funkia striata and *Funkia argenteostriata*, both aberrant forms of *Hosta* 'Undulata', which is known to take on a white-on-green striate variegation during summer, are listed only once in the catalog. Von Siebold apparently realized the temporary nature of this variegation so dropped listings of these hostas from subsequent catalogs.
Funkia glauca and its variegated form have been considered *H.* 'Tokudama' or forms of *Hosta sieboldiana* since the publication of the name by both Witte (1868) and Miquel (1869). Witte (1868) includes an illustration, which attests to this placement. This is the same plant von Siebold gave to Fortune. Both brought it back to Europe in 1862. The variegated form is still grown in Germany under the original species name as *H. glauca variegata* and looks very much like *H. (tokudama)* 'Blue Shadows'.
Funkia spathulata is none other than the green-leaved form of *Hosta sieboldii*. Hostas were rare plants so seeds were carefully harvested and grown. It is well known that *H. sieboldii* seedlings are mostly green plants and these seedlings no doubt came from the white-margined form listed as *Funkia spathulata* Siebold *foliis albomarginatis* (= *Hosta sieboldii*) which was introduced in 1830 and first listed in 1844.

Upon returning to Holland von Siebold brought additional hostas with him and continued to import plants from Japan. The following is a compilation of hostas introduced by his nursery during the years following his return in 1862:

1863 *Funkia undulata argenteovittata* Siebold hort = *Hosta* 'Undulata', a selected clone.
1863 *Funkia univittata* van Houtte = *Hosta* 'Undulata Univittata'.
1863 *Funkia viridimarginata* hort = *Hosta* 'Fortunei Albopicta'.
1863 *Funkia mediovariegata* hort = *Hosta* 'Undulata'.
1867 *Funkia cærulea variegata* = *Hosta ventricosa* variegated form.
1867 *Funkia japonica* hort = *Hosta sieboldii* f. *spathulata*.
1867 *Funkia viridis* hort = *Hosta* 'Undulata Erromena'.
1868 *Funkia japonica flore albo* hort = *Hosta sieboldii* 'Alba'.
1871 *Funkia fortunei* = *Hosta* 'Tokudama'.
1871 *Funkia fortunei* var. *variegata* = *Hosta* 'Tokudama', variegated form.
1872 *Funkia sinensis* var. *marmorata* = *Hosta* 'Fortunei', variegated form.
1874 *Funkia aurea* = *Hosta fortunei aurea* (Wehrhahn) = *H.* 'Fortunei Aurea'.
1874 *Funkia aureamaculata* = *H.* 'Fortunei' form with mottled or streaky variegation.
1875 *Funkia liliiflora* = *Hosta plantaginea*.
1876 *Funkia (albo-)marginata* var. *lutescens* = *Hosta* 'Crispula Lutescens'; a mutant sporting to yellow.
1876 *Funkia spathulata albomarginata* var. *lutescens* = *Hosta sieboldii* lutescent form.
1877 *Funkia glaucescens* = *Hosta* 'Fortunei Hyacinthina'.
1879 *Funkia japonica gigantea* = *Hosta* 'Elata' or *H.* 'Fortunei Gigantea'.
1879 *Funkia aokii* = *Hosta* 'Fortunei Aoki'.

Many of these names are still used in the trade in Europe, especially in Holland and Germany. *Funkia japonica flore albo* is widely sold under the incorrect species name *Hosta minor alba*, which correctly is *H. sieboldii* 'Alba'. The hosta still grown in Europe under the species name *H. fortunei variegata* looks like a variegated form of *H.* 'Tokudama', but is slightly larger and has less of its characteristic puckering. It appears more like *H.* 'Blue Shadows' and may, in fact, be none other than the variegated form of *H. glauca* mentioned above. *Funkia cærulea* hort. *variegata* was a variegated form of *Hosta ventricosa*, possibly the marginata form *H. ventricosa* 'Aureomarginata'. The *maculata* form *H. ventricosa* 'Aureomaculata' had previously been listed by von Siebold under the name *Funkia ovata foliis aureomaculatis*. The epithet *ovata* was used in 1856, followed by *cærulea* in 1863, both pertaining to *Hosta ventricosa*. A century later a *H. cærulea aureovariegata* was listed in the 1960 Mackwoods Gardens[24] catalog (no. 29; synonyms given were *H. ventricosa aureovariegata* and Variegated Blue Plantain Lily). Another possible interpretation is that of Nakai,[25] who determined that Thunberg's specimen no. 2, namely, *H.* 'Undulata', was *H. cærulea* var. *variegata* (Lowe).

The list of hostas introduced since 1870 includes a number which, without question, did not originate in Japan but were the result of hybridizing or mutation in von Siebold's gardens in Holland. In the following list the respective placements are based on historical botanical research and current horticultural knowledge:

Funkia mediovariegata hort. is a selected clone of *Hosta* 'Undulata'.
Funkia liliiflora is mentioned in an early Dutch horticultural journal (Anonymous, 1891b, 20:531–533, 535) as *Funkia*

liiiflora alba and described as a plant with numerous stems and white flowers. The description fits *Hosta sieboldii* 'Weihenstephan' pictured in a recent *The American Hosta Society Bulletin* (1985, no. 16, opposite page 42). This cultivar originated with Arends[26] and is sold in Europe under the incorrect name *H. minor alba* 'Improved'. It was further developed by Weihenstephan.[27] Its correct name is *H. sieboldii* 'Alba'. In 1903 and again in 1915 Bailey lists this hosta in the synonymy of *H. plantaginea*.[28] In Germany the latter was called *H. liliiflora* as recently as 1953 by Foerster. Maekawa (1940) lists a *H. montana* var. *liliiflora*, which is not the same taxon as Siebold's *Funkia liliiflora*.

Funkia japonica gigantea was most likely *Hosta fortunei* var. *gigantea* Bailey, a large green-leaved, tall-scaped form of *H. sieboldiana*.

Funkia spathulata foliis albomarginatis lutescens. The possible placement of this hosta is quite interesting, in that it was a seedling similar to the unstable *Hosta sieboldii* 'Beatrice', which may account for the disappearance of the taxon. It is known that this cultivar was a mutation of *H. sieboldii* with streaky lutescent variegation. In addition to *H. sieboldii* 'Beatrice' other cultivars fit this description, namely, *H. sieboldii* f. *kabitan* and *H. sieboldii* f. *mediopicta* (= *Suji Giboshi*). Occurrence of lutescent variegation in *H. sieboldii* seedlings is well documented (Yasui, 1929) and also occurs in the wild. Von Siebold's variety *lutescens* was most likely a yellow sport or mutated seedling of *H. sieboldii*. Exactly which one cannot be determined from the brief description available.

Funkia glaucescens. Early references link this hosta with *Hosta sieboldiana*, but this is *H. bella* (Wehrhahn) or *H. fortunei* var. *hyacinthina* Hylander. The question arises as to where Hylander's variety *hyacinthina* came from. The epithet *glaucescens* originated in 1877 and the plant given this name was certainly of cultivated origin. The name's meaning ("somewhat glaucous") points to *H.* 'Bella' or *H.* 'Fortunei Hyacinthina'. The appearance of *H. aokii* in 1879 further strengthens this placement as the latter is now considered *Hosta* 'Fortunei (Hyacinthina) Aoki'.

Funkia aokii is in the nursery trade as *Hosta* 'Fortunei Aoki'. The name of this hosta has been the subject of considerable speculation. In my opinion, it was named by von Siebold before his death in honor of Aoki Kon'yo, who in 1740 was ordered by the shogun Yoshimune to study the Dutch language after which he produced the first Japanese-Dutch dictionary and a study of the Dutch monetary system. Aoki's work was of great value and unquestionably vital to von Siebold when he studied the Japanese language. *Hosta* 'Fortunei Aoki' is listed as early as 1903 in U.S. horticultural literature. *Hosta* 'Fortunei Aoki' is a selection of *H.* 'Fortunei Hyacinthina' released in 1879.

Friedrik Miquel's[29] 1869 monograph on the hostas grown by von Siebold, which is reviewed in Appendix B, is largely ignored by botanists and horticulturalists. Instead of referring to Miquel, later authors continued to use von Siebold's listings and catalogs and the names appearing there. This has given rise to considerable confusion in the nomenclature of many of the species and varieties. Von Siebold did not provide botanical descriptions of his hostas so his names were considered botanically nomina nuda. Due to the lack of descriptions, some of his names were applied incorrectly after his death.

Von Siebold was a prolific writer. Soon after he arrived in Japan in 1823 he started sending accounts to Germany and Holland, reporting principally on the state of botany and natural history, his favorite subjects (Siebold, 1824, 1825, 1828, 1830). After he returned from Japan he turned down a professorship, explaining in a letter to his mother that he had enough writing to do to last him 10 years (Körner, 1967). His principal aim was to catalog all his acquisitions and write about Japan, but in the summer of 1834 he was invited on a tour of European capitals, where he was given audiences, honored, and decorated at the royal courts in Petersburg, Berlin, Vienna, and Munich, in his native Bavaria. Finally settling down to his writing task in Leiden, he assembled a team of assistants to bolster his efforts: from Munich came botanist Joseph G. Zuccarini; from Würzburg came the linguist J. J. Hoffman; from Saxony came H. Schlegel to assist with fauna; and C. J. Temminck, curator of the Rijksmuseum, came to support his ethnographic studies. Von Siebold's 5-volume *Fauna Japonica* (Siebold et al., 1833) was the first of his trilogy of major works and the first comprehensive description of Japanese fauna to be published in the West. The second work, covering floristic subjects, was written in collaboration with Zuccarini and published as *Flora Japonica* (Siebold and Zuccarini, 1835–1841). It contained several excellent illustrations of *Hosta*. Von Siebold was the sole author of the third work, *Nippon* (Siebold, 1850), an enormous 7-volume documentation of his 1824–1830 Japanese diaries. Beginning in 1844 he began publishing plant lists and catalogs through his nursery, the first of which was *Kruidkundige Naamlijst* (Siebold, 1844).

Von Siebold died in 1866 in Munich. His nursery business was continued by his master gardener, J. Mater, and his catalogs continued to be published by the establishment Feu von Siebold & Coy until 1882. They were most likely compiled by Heinrich Witte, von Siebold's friend and curator of the botanical garden at Leiden. It was he and Mater who carried on the business in the name of von Siebold's widow.

Philipp Franz Balthasar von Siebold is buried in the famous old Südfriedhof in Munich, where the well-known chemist Justus Liebig, Pettenkoffer, father of German hygiene, and many of the elite of German science and medicine have found a final resting place. Among the many classical tombstones, von Siebold's is easy to find for it is of Japanese design, a spire of concentric, tapering circles, like one might find on top of Japanese shrines. Engraved on one side of the large monument are four Japanese kanji characters which mean: "How strong a bridge." Bowers (1970) writes: "No man in history has been such a remarkable bridge of knowledge that spanned the thousands of miles separating Europe and Japan." It is that bridge which gave us most of the classical hostas.

Von Siebold's greatest recognition came from the Japanese. There he is fondly remembered as *sensei*, the great teacher, for von Siebold's horticultural accomplishments described here were only coincidental to his other achievements. As a medical doctor he was responsible for inaugurating Western medical teaching in Japan which later led to the adoption of German medical science by the Japanese. The site of his house in the Narutaki section of Nagasaki is maintained as a shrine by the Japanese and a plaque proclaims: "Siebold is the one who deserves the glory of the great achievement to have introduced knowledge to the Japan of today." The Museum Hall of the Nagasaki Prefecture Library exhibits his medical and surgical instruments and his military uniform. Every school child knows the name *Shiboruto* (Siebold) belongs to Japan's great foreign *sensei* (teacher).

ROBERT FORTUNE (1812–1880)

The name "Fortune" is used for two distinctly different hostas: *H. fortunei* (Baker) Bailey, the species name for a group of hybrids described by Hylander; and *H. sieboldiana* β *fortunei* Regel. Hylander's *H. fortunei* complex is a multifaceted assemblage of cultivars and has been popular for years. Regel's taxon is *H.* 'Tokudama'.

Robert Fortune was born in Kelloe, Berwickshire, England, in 1812. Interested in plants since boyhood he studied to be a botanist and horticulturist at the Royal Botanical Garden at Edinburgh. He quickly rose through the ranks and became superintendent of the Hothouse Department at the Royal Horticultural Society's Garden at Chiswick. In 1843 he was called to go on a collecting trip to China. This become Fortune's main area of activity; in all he made three celebrated journeys to China. The 1858 trip to China and India was made on behalf of the U.S. government to find tea suitable for cultivation in the southern states and to collect, as well, but rebellions and mutinies chased him from one place to another. His tea eventually reached the United States only to be neglected due to the outbreak of the Civil War (Coats, 1969). It was probably because of all these problems that he decided to go to Japan, so he boarded a Chinese vessel bound for Yokohama. He arrived in Nagasaki, a port of call along the way, on 12 October 1860.

Being well aware of von Siebold's importations and horticultural renown and realizing that the naturalist was in Japan at that time, Fortune took time to visit von Siebold at his home in Nagasaki, a meeting he describes in one of his books (Fortune, 1863). Von Siebold had arrived in Nagasaki only 14 months prior to Fortune's visit, but according to Fortune's description "his house was already surrounded by small nurseries for the reception and propagation of new plants, and for preparing them for their trip to Europe." Fortune also tells of underbrush being cleared from the hillside to make room for more propagating areas. Among the many plants in the garden, Fortune saw von Siebold's hostas, and he went away with one of them, which later was called *Funkia fortunei*.

Fortune went on to Yokohama to collect plants in the local nurseries, including one operated by the American George R. Hall, where he purchased a male *Aucuba japonica*. Later he gathered plant material in and around Tokyo, having arrived there on 12 November 1860. He met Veitch and both, rushed by the onset of winter, deposited their collections on the steamer *England* which went via Nagasaki to Shanghai where it docked on 2 January 1861. Fortune wanted to see the spring flowers so returned to Japan in May. Again he went via Nagasaki but did not visit von Siebold and stayed there only two days. After his arrival in Yokohama he decided to go to Tokyo as soon as possible so as not to miss the blooming. In the absence of the British consul he received an invitation from the U.S. consul Townsend Harris, who, by the way, was replaced by Thomas Hogg the following year. Fortune never met Hogg. He did some collecting in the wild—for example, gathering *Lilium auratum* in the fields around Kamakura—but most of the wild plants were available in nurseries. After one collection trip into the surrounding hillsides he brought home some "rare" primulas only to find them offered by the basket load by enterprising Japanese. Late in July he packed all his collections and sailed for China to pick up the plants he had previously brought there and which had been planted in a friend's garden. Von Siebold's hosta was among them. He arrived back in England on 2 January 1862 bringing a wealth of plants. The single specimen hosta and the other plants in his collection were not destined for the Royal Horticultural Society, but were consigned to the firm of Standish & Noble, Bagshot, an expedition sponsor. A year later this hosta was the only representative of the genus shown at the Royal Horticultural Society's summer show of 1863 (Anonymous, 1863). Described as a "Japanese *Funkia* with glaucous leaves and French white flowers," it undoubtedly is the one that came from von Siebold's garden in Nagasaki.

Von Siebold, who also returned in early 1862, brought this same hosta with him and simply planted it in his garden. Apparently, it was forgotten until after his death in 1866. A short time later, Miquel (1867) made a note of it under the name *Funkia sieboldiana* var. *condensata*. It was introduced by Witte in 1870 who states that it had been grown in the Netherlands for some time and also mentions that it is a slow grower (which explains the delay in introduction). It should be pointed out that this hosta, although shown in England in 1863, was also not introduced in that country to the public until some time later and then probably from Holland. This taxon was not validly published until 1876, when Regel published his diagnosis under the name *Funkia sieboldiana* β *fortunei*. The honorific epithet suggests that Regel got his plant via England or that after von Siebold's death Witte accepted the English name in lieu of *Funkia glauca* given by von Siebold. If the latter is the case, Regel's taxon could have come from Holland as well. Regel also provides an excellent illustration which aids in the identification and placement of this hosta with H. 'Tokudama'. Maekawa (1940) lists this name as a synonym under *H. tokudama*. Today this hosta is still occasionally grown and sold under the name *H. fortunei* in both Germany and in Holland, and was offered under this name in the United States as late as 1960. This name is slowly being replaced by *H. tokudama*, the name Maekawa assigned in 1940, when he elevated it from a variety of *H. sieboldiana* to the rank of species.

Also in 1876, just prior to Regel's publication, Baker[30] described quite another hosta as *H. fortunei*. Regel's description and illustration opposite Baker's herbarium specimen at Kew Herbarium show these two hostas are not conspecific. It is possible that Baker's plant was a hybridized seedling of the plant brought by Fortune in 1862, hence retaining the epithet *fortunei*. The hosta Baker describes gave its name to a large group of cultivars, some of which originated before 1876 with von Siebold and had been given different names. This group is referred to as the *fortunei* complex. Some of its representatives were elevated by Hylander[31] in 1954 to the rank of varieties of the "species" *H. 'Fortunei'*. To date no satisfactory explanation has been offered as to why some of these hostas cultivated in the Netherlands since the 1850s came to be associated with Baker's plant of 1876. In fact, there seems to be no species *H. 'Fortunei'* (in the strict sense) in cultivation today. Nonetheless, there are today a considerable number of "varieties" in the horticultural trade, and some of the variegated cultivars of this complex are very popular with the gardening public. Thus, the complex bearing Fortune's name has, in fact, little to do with the original *H. fortunei* exhibited by Fortune in 1863 which is now called *H. 'Tokudama'*.[32] While there seems to be no acceptable "true" form of *H. 'Fortunei'*, the epithet *fortunei* as applied to *H. 'Tokudama'* when considered a botanical variety of *H. sieboldiana*, viz., *H. sieboldiana* var. *fortunei*, is beyond question.

After his return in 1862 (concurrently with von Siebold) from what was to be his last collecting trip abroad, Fortune settled down to a quiet and tranquil retirement in Kensington. He wrote several pieces, among them *Yedo and Peking* published in 1863. This book is a recollection of his travels in Japan and China, in which he recalls his visit to von Siebold. He frequented horticultural affairs at which he received much deserved praise as one of the leading introducers of fine Oriental plants. Fortune died in London in 1880.

THE FIRST HOSTAS IN THE UNITED STATES

Nothing can be found about hostas in U.S. botanical and horticultural literature of the 18th century. A diligent search under all the names given to the genus *Hosta*—namely, *Aletris*, *Hemerocallis*, *Niobe*, *Bryocles*, *Hostia*, *Funckia*, and *Funkia*—located no specific references.

In the early 19th century, however, hosta names appear in

the horticultural literature. Surprisingly, in 1839, only nine years after von Siebold's return to Holland, an entry on *Funkia* shows up in *The American Flower Garden Directory* edited by the U.S. florist Robert Buist. He mentions "three species, all beautiful": One was *Hosta ventricosa* (as *Funkia cærulea*) "with blue flowers"; another was *Hosta plantaginea* (as *Funkia japonica*), "pure white"; and the other, *Hosta* 'Undulata' (as *Funkia variegata*), with Buist's annotation, "The latter is yet rare, and but recently introduced (into Europe) from Japan." Also mentioned is the fact that "this genus has been separated from *Hemerocallis*." In 1854 Buist added one new species to that year's edition of his directory: *Funkia laurifolia*, "early blue." Its identity is not known definitely, but I daresay it was probably *H.* 'Lancifolia'.

Edward Sprague Rand's *Garden Flowers* appeared in 1866 and shows that the selection available in the United States had increased as compared to Buist's listings. Rand includes:

> *Hosta ventricosa* as *Funkia ovata*.
> *Hosta plantaginea* as *Funkia subcordata*.
> *Hosta sieboldiana* as *Funkia sieboldiana*.
> *Hosta* 'Undulata' as *Funkia undulata*.
> *Hosta* 'Lancifolia' as *Funkia lancifolia*.
> *Hosta sieboldii* as *Funkia albomarginata*.

These accounts indicate that hostas were imported into the United States from Europe in the early 1800s, though *Hosta plantaginea* and *H. ventricosa* may actually have come earlier, possibly in the late 1790s.

In the 1850s U.S. horticulturists and plant collectors gained access to Japan. Among them was Hall,[33] who came to Japan in 1855. By 1860 he had a large collector's garden in Yokohama, and, according to Keough et al. (1982), the first plants sent directly from Japan to the United States arrived in 1861 and probably came from Hall. Many new plants were represented in this garden and it was there that Fortune found his celebrated male *Aucuba japonica*. It is not known if Hall cultivated hostas.

In addition to the hostas imported by Thomas Hogg directly from Japan in the 1870s, additional hostas originating with von Siebold were also imported into the United States from Holland or by way of England. This we can postulate with some certainty, because many hostas were labeled with and retained the names given by von Siebold.

By the 1890s several other hostas made an appearance in North America, and the unstable *H.* 'Undulata' certainly had sported to the variety *H.* 'Undulata Erromena', which was sold under a number of different names. Plant exchanges between U.S. botanists and their European counterparts increased thanks to improved technology for maintaining plants in good health and improved transportation in the late Victorian era. No doubt, additional hostas were brought into the country by early travellers visiting Europe. By 1900 the hosta selection in North America reflected the European selection very closely, right down to the names used.

One notable example is that of *Funkia lanceolata*, offered by the nursery of Jakob W. Manning, Reading, Massachusetts. I examined a specimen which the Bailey Herbarium obtained in 1897 and found it labeled "*Funkia lancifolia* Sprengel; trade name *Funkia lanceolata*. From the nursery of Jakob W. Manning, Reading, Mass. cat. 1897; Sep. 26–27, 1898." Von Siebold imported this hosta in 1829 and listed it in his first catalog of 1844 also as *Funkia lanceolata*. Today it is considered conspecific with *Hosta longissima*. In this case the European source is proven, because the epithet *lanceolata* was originated by von Siebold. Thus, with exception of Hogg's importations, all the hostas in the United States around 1900 originated from European stock.

As pointed out earlier, hosta names had been included in North American garden directories since at least 1839. Hosta advertising by way of catalog listings probably began with Hogg, although a date cannot be established. But even before his time some plants and seeds were certainly imported or brought in by travellers returning from Europe and Japan.

A few hostas found their way to the United States not by way of Europe but through direct importation from Japan. One of the leading plant collectors was Thomas Hogg.

THOMAS HOGG, JR. (1819–1892)

The "opening of Japan" began in earnest in 1862, the year both von Siebold and Fortune returned to Europe. The days of the "great collectors" of Japanese flora were ending. The Russian Maximowicz[34] prepared to leave Japan in 1864. The Englishmen Oldham[35] and Veitch[36] had sent back their collections, and the American Hall, who conducted a nursery business in Yokohama, also left for home in 1862. Collecting plant speciments in the Japanese countryside had become a dangerous task. The "invasion of the barbarians", which began in 1855, generated a lot of ill will and the feudal princes, seeing their political power and status slip away, had a fanatical hatred for the foreigners. Many naturalists felt it was time to go.

Thomas Hogg, Jr., was the oldest son of the celebrated English florist and horticulturist Thomas Hogg of Paddington, who at one time was head gardener to William Kent. Shortly after his birth in 1819 his family emigrated to the United States where in 1820 they established a nursery and florist business on Manhattan Island, not far from where 23rd Street and Broadway intersect today. There was considerable demand for nursery stock and the business soon flourished and had to move to larger grounds at 79th Street and the East River. The elder Hogg made important connections with plant collectors who supplied him with new plant material; among them was Douglas,[37] of Douglas fir fame, who collected in North America from 1823 to 1834. The elder Hogg died in 1855 and left his nursery to Thomas, Jr., and his younger son James, who was born shortly after the Hogg family arrived in the United States.

In 1855 Commodore Perry made his first expedition to Japan and regular trade between the United States and Japan soon developed. When the U.S. consul and U.S. Marshal Townsend resigned in 1862, President Lincoln sent Thomas Hogg, Jr., to Japan to take over the post of U.S. Marshal for Japan. By then Fortune and von Siebold were safely back in Europe. Hogg remained in Japan until 1870 but returned in 1873 for another stay in a private capacity, remaining until 1875, during which time he reportedly served as an agent for the Japanese Customs Service. Hogg sent many fine plant discoveries back to the United States, where his brother James built the Hogg nursery into one of the best sources for Asiatic and Japanese plants. Among his introductions were a number of lilies, of which he made a special study. He also brought into horticultural use the Kousa dogwood (*Cornus kousa chinensis*), umbrella pine (*Sciadopitys verticillata*), several wisterias and clematis, and many other plants, including hostas. As with Fortune, Hogg found it easier and safer to purchase his plants in the nurseries of Tokyo and Yokohama, so did very little collecting in the wild.

By the 1860s the Japanese began to realize the great commercial value of their plants, so began to collect them and gave them fancy names for the sole purpose of selling them to Western collectors. These names were virtually entirely descriptive in nature. The trade in Japanese plants became so important that most plants exported after 1862 were bought from dealers rather than collected in the wild. Oldham reported a flourishing plant business in the streets of

Yokohama taking place as early as 1863, but even before collecting became risky business, many collectors, including Hogg, preferred to purchase their plants.

The Japanese plant vendors also realized that variegated plants commanded higher prices, and Hogg, who was looking for variegated plants to expand his already extensive Asiatic plant offerings, bought a number of his variegated hosta introductions from these street merchants. It is not known exactly when Hogg brought what was to become his famous introduction—what the Japanese called *Fukurin Fu Giboshi*, "green-leaf-with-variegated-edge hosta"[38]—to the United States. In Japan just about everything variegated is considered *fu*, and there are numerous translations of this concept word. Horticulturally, it refers to mottling, spots, streakings, margins, or any mark on a different-colored background, usually on leaves. Undoubtedly, Hogg brought at least two hostas under this name from Japan: one is now identified as *H.* 'Decorata', another is *H.* 'Undulata Albomarginata'. Both have green leaves with white margins and may have been, by indifferent Japanese sellers, called by the same name *Fukurin Fu Giboshi*. Since Western gardeners had difficulty with the Japanese name it was quickly changed to *Funkia* 'Thomas Hogg', and it should be noted that to casual observers young plants of these two "species"[39] are virtually identical—which may explain why both were sold as *Funkia* "Thomas Hogg" by the nursery. The plants, being rare, were probably never allowed to grow to maturity due to constant propagation. Cultivars under this name in England are considered to be *Hosta* 'Undulata Albomarginata', while in North America the name is applied to *H.* 'Decorata'.

The time of Hogg's importations is most commonly quoted as in the horticultural literature as "around the turn of the century", but this is incorrect. He unquestionably brought hostas with him when he returned from his second trip in 1875 (Hansen et al., 1964, 1974; Schmid, 1986b), or shipped them back shortly before or after his departure. Reports indicate a *Funkia* 'Thomas Hogg' was growing at the Lexington Botanic Garden in the early 1880s, described as a "deep green Funkia with the edge white." The Hogg nursery experienced its peak of prosperity as one of the leading suppliers of Asian plant material in the 1870s. Hogg travelled to Europe several times after 1875, and he undoubtedly brought his *Funkia* 'Thomas Hogg' and other plants with him. He died in 1892 at the age of 73. The nursery carried on for some time after his death before it ceased to operate.

The Hogg nursery exported hostas to Europe; *H.* 'Undulata Albomarginata' went to England as "Thomas Hogg's Funkia" and is still called by that name on occasion. Probably because they look so much alike as small plants, both *H.* 'Decorata' and *H.* 'Undulata Albomarginata' went to Holland, also under the name "Thomas Hogg's Funkia." The presence of *H.* 'Decorata' is confirmed by the account of the German geneticist A. Ernst, who published a paper in 1918 (pp. 446–447) describing genetic experiments "mit einer von Tubergen in Harlem, Holland, bezogenen 'Thoss. Högg Funkia' " (i.e., a hosta named 'Thoss. Högg Funkia' which he obtained from the Tubergen nursery in Holland) which turns out to be *H.* 'Decorata'. Ernst's research on pollination of hostas took years to complete, so he would have acquired his hostas around 1910. It can be safely assumed that "Funkia Thomas Hogg" (= *H.* 'Decorata') was in Holland before 1900. This date fits agreeably with de Noter's 1905 date for his *Funkia alba* "Thomas Hogg" hort., described as a white-flowered cultivar. Hylander (1954), in his synonymy for *Hosta* 'Decorata', stated this taxon was not conspecific with the hostas labeled today *H.* 'Thomas Hogg'. Although de Noter's descriptions are quite difficult to interpret, I believe that the "French Thomas Hogg" was in fact *H. plantaginea*, so the name attached by de Noter

suggests this hosta also came from Hogg. In this way *H. plantaginea* came full circle: from Europe to the United States, where it was mentioned as early as 1839 (Buist, 1839, 1854; Rand 1866), only to be exported back to Europe around the 1880s as 'Funkia Thomas Hogg' or 'Funkia Alba Thomas Hogg'. The white-margined taxa bearing the Hogg name were mixed up, due to their likeness, and traded under the same name for a long time.

Recorded use of this name for at least three, and probably more, unrelated taxa gave rise to considerable confusion. For this reason the name has been eliminated as a cultivar name, but this should in no way diminish the great contribution Hogg made to the introduction of hostas into commerce.

HOSTAS IN EARLY HORTICULTURE AND GARDENING

By the last decade of the 19th century hostas had become an accepted and desirable garden plant. More importantly, professional horticulturists and landscape architects were using them in landscapes. The horticultural literature of Europe and North America contains many references to hostas, albeit under many of the earlier names—funkia, plantain lily, daylily—or in Germany as Funkie, Herzlilie, or Herzblatt Lilie, while in Sweden Thunberg's old genus name *Hemerocallis* still persists for hostas, there commonly called daglilie (daylily).

Victorian parks, cemeteries, and private gardens were soon displaying collections of hostas and hosta plantings which were especially useful in such shady settings. The plants' rugged constitution and low-maintenance requirements made them ideal for public plantings. In Europe they were planted in city parks, along avenues, and in beds fronting public buildings, some of which survive today. They fit well in the naturalistic gardens of the "Robinsonian" period when they were used in groups and mass plantings. With their lush, tropical appearance they were welcomed in private gardens and provided a steadying element for the multicolored perennial borders then in vogue.

The leading gardeners and landscape architects of that time began to illustrate and describe the use of hostas. In England William Robinson mentioned *Funkia sieboldiana* in 1883, and Gertrude Jekyll[40] included hostas in several of her books (1899, 1901, 1908). In the United States Beatrix Farrand[41] specified *Hosta sieboldiana* in her borders. Many other noted landscape gardeners included representatives of the genus in their projects.

Von Siebold & Coy was the first firm to publish a catalog of sorts (actually a listing), offering a selection of hostas in 1844. As demand developed, other nurseries in Europe and the United States offered hostas, providing a limited choice of species and varieties and, no doubt, a number of seedlings. Most of these originated from stock imported by von Siebold and Hogg. Very little fresh hosta material seems to have come from Japan after the initial importations of these two plant hunters.

From 1830 until the late 1890s the original stock of hostas expanded through propagation—planned hybridizing as well as open pollination. Additionally, some mutations occurred in the original pool of plants. Von Siebold, Miquel, and contemporaries listed a number of forms, mostly variegated, under the designation *lusus*, which means "mutation" or "sport." These did not see wide distribution, because they were regarded as oddities. The landscape gardeners of that period looked for uniformity and stability in plants, a requirement which was satisfied by the cool grey of *H. sieboldiana* and the uniform emerald-green of *H. ventricosa*, in addition to the large, pure white flowers of *H. plantaginea*, which had the added attraction of being fragrant. This may explain why many of von Siebold's variegated forms never reached the public, in spite of having been grown in botanical gardens across Europe. For example, *H. sieboldiana β fortunei aureovariegata*, a variegated form of *H.* 'Tokudama', has been grown in the Munich Botanic Garden for years, and is still there under the name given it in 1870 by the von Siebold firm. This is probably the same hosta which was named *Funkia glauca mediovariegata* in 1859. This taxon is difficult to find outside botanical gardens in Germany, because its uneven variegation did not fit the landscape requirements of yesteryear. Today, variegated hostas are in vogue, so this taxon is now finding its way into private gardens.

THE EARLY HOSTA HYBRIDIZERS

The beginnings of Japanese hosta hybridizing are obscure. Certainly, some hosta breeding was carried out by Japanese gardeners during the reign of Shogun Tokugawa and possibly before this time. During that period gardening flourished and was extensively pursued by the ruling class. Although we know little about early hybridizing, some facts are known: Thunberg's visit to Japan brought a specimen of *H.* 'Undulata', which is now preserved at the Institute of Systematic Botany, the University of Uppsala, Sweden.[42] This hosta is today one of the most popular and has been widely grown in Western gardens for over 150 years. Although raised to species rank by Otto & Dietrich in 1833, it is a pod-sterile hybrid. It may have been one of the early successes of Japanese hosta breeding when Thunberg obtained it in 1797. If so, it is an example of Japanese hybridizing in the 18th century or earlier.

The first European to hybridize the genus was von Siebold. He assembled enough of a genetic hosta base at his gardens in Nagasaki, Batavia, and later in Leiden, to make significant crosses. His catalogs listed a number of garden varieties marked with the suffix "hort." Many of these may have been the result of planned crosses. As more and more hosta collections were assembled at botanical institutions, nurseries, and private gardens, open pollination also began to play a rather unpredictable role. Initially hostas were relatively rare plants, so all seeds were carefully harvested and planted. Many of the seedlings from these planned and accidental crosses were allowed to develop to maturity, some of which are probably still growing in old gardens. A few were named, propagated, and sold in commerce.

Many of the classic and horticulturally important hostas in Japan listed in the early floristic works of the second half of the 19th century were in fact hybrids. One of them, *Tokudama Giboshi* (Iinuma 1856, 1874), is today considered of cultivated (hybrid) origin, although it was validly published as the species *H. tokudama* by Maekawa in 1940. A number of similar examples can be found in Japanese horticulture.

In Europe, scientific pollination experiments were carried out as early as the 1870s. First alluded to by Brown in 1810 (cfr. Jones in Aden, 1988), Strasburger (1878) determined the apomictic (see Schmid, 1985e) nature of *H. ventricosa*, and published his findings in 1878 under the name *H. ovata*.

Following the cessation of catalogs by von Siebold and his successors in the 1880s there seems to have been a hiatus of sorts in hybridizing with horticultural goals; little has been reported in the literature of such efforts. Vegetative propagation aimed at producing uniform nursery stock by division of rootstock curtailed pollination because quite often the flower scapes were removed to channel the plants' vigor into producing more leaves and divisions, not seed. The vegetative method was rapidly accepted because seeds do not come

reliably true. Von Siebold brought with him the Japanese way of forcing side shoots from the crown—which requires severing the entire leaf crown after it emerges in the spring and cutting of the flower scape—which, of course, prevents seed formation (see Appendix G).

German nurseries began offering von Siebold's hostas at almost the same time they were marketed in the Netherlands. Soon after his return from Japan in 1830 he sent many hostas to scientific contacts and friends in his native Germany for morphologic and taxonomic evaluation, and so most found their way into university trial gardens, for then, as now, horticultural testing of plants was largely done by universities. The botanic gardens developed what in Germany is called a "Sortiment"—a selection of recommended cultivars, which had been successful in extensive garden and field trials after which they were propagated by nurseries and offered for sale. Nurserymen in turn usually refined the selection by further hybridizing and clonal selection.

One of these nurserymen was Georg Arends of Wupperthal-Ronsdorf, located in the German Ruhr valley. Arends' work with the genus *Astilbe* is world famous today. In his autobiography he recounts his work with *Hosta* (Arends, 1951). He offered his first cross in 1905, a plant called *H. fortunei robusta* which resulted from a cross between *H. sieboldiana* and *H. fortunei* (= *H.* 'Tokudama'). In 1954 Hylander gave it "varietal" rank, naming it *H. sieboldiana* var. *elegans*, but it is now recognized as Arends' hybrid.

Arends also worked on improving the flower size of *H. sieboldii* var. *alba*, which he and many other nurseries referred to under the incorrect name *H. minor* 'Alba'. This cross was in the trade soon after 1905 as *H. minor* 'Alba' (Improved form); it was further improved and is now in the trade as *H. sieboldii* 'Weihenstephan'. Arends next concentrated on *H.* 'Tardiflora' because the flowers of this popular, late-flowering specioid are spoiled year after year by early freezes. He was able to advance its flowering period sufficiently to prevent this by crossing it with *H. ventricosa* (then called *H. ovata*) as the pollen parent. He named the new cultivar *H. tardiflora* 'Hybrida' in its first catalog listing in 1911. Arends also worked on darkening the color of *H. ventricosa* flowers, offering the plants as *H. ovata* 'Superba'. His hybrids are still grown in Germany and are beginning to find their way into U.S. specialty hosta collections.

Another early hybridizer was Karl Foerster of Potzdam-Bornim, Germany, who is well known for his many German language books on gardening. His writing career spanned from 1911 until the late 1950s. Hostas played an important part in his landscaping philosophy in which he juxtaposed large leafy plants with grasses and ferns, making for a very pleasing, balanced arrangement. He called this "Dreiklang," which is the German word for the sounding of three musical notes in perfect harmony. Relating this to gardening, Foerster meant it to be the combination of three plant elements into a harmonious triad: bold hosta leaves, tall grasses, and delicate fern fronds. Unfortunately, Foerster recounted little in his books about his hosta breeding efforts, but his firm handled a number of hybrids.

English and Dutch nurseries were also active in early hosta breeding, although records of these efforts are extremely scanty. It was not until the International Registration Authority for *Hosta* was established in 1969 that hostas could be registered by name, so for this reason only the names of those early cultivars enjoying wide distribution have survived. Many other hybrids, both named and unnamed, were either lost or exist unnoticed in obscure corners of old gardens. Some of these survivors include the Arends' hybrids already mentioned.

The French firm of Vilmorin-Andrieux et Cie. cataloged hostas as early as 1866, one of which was *H.* 'Elata'.[43] Later, other hostas were also cataloged, including one named cultivar "Vilmorin's Taxon," now called *H.* 'Vilmoriniana'. Two herbarium specimens of this hosta exist in K,[44] the discovery of which solves the questions surrounding the origin of this hosta.

THE BEGINNING—LANDSCAPE USE IN THE UNITED STATES

As detailed earlier, a considerable number of hostas were distributed in the United States in the years before 1900, apparently most of them in the northern tier of states. Just how widely they were distributed can be assessed in a paper published by Tompkins (1984:8), who recalled that members of his family collected hostas in such out-of-the-way places as St. Joseph, Missouri, and Valley City, North Dakota. In both locations the hostas were planted in cemeteries.

After 1918 the great parks and garden cemeteries designed by Downing[45] and his followers during the 19th century and those of the garden cemetery movement[46] were "opened up." Magnificent old shade trees were cut down to "let in the sun." Their cool shade gave way to rolling, manicured lawns. Hostas, along with a host of other shade-tolerant shrubs and perennials, were no longer required. They all but disappeared from many of the redesigned and replanted parks and cemeteries. In some locations hosta plantings remained; though mowed down year after year, they returned to their old magnificence after mowing stopped.

This new fashion in park and cemetery gardening curtailed the landscapers' demand for hostas. As a consequence hostas became more difficult to obtain through regular commercial sources although a few varieties remained on some nurseries lists. The hostas purchased during that time were usually relegated to dark, shady corners of public parks, typically away from the public eye. Many found their way into private gardens, where they flourished in secluded grandeur to be seen only by the owner and a few friends. Nonetheless, hostas did find satisfactory presentation in some botanical gardens and in the perennial borders of several of the great estate gardens which were created or refurbished during the 1920s. Garden plans which have survived reveal the utilization of hostas in these gardens. The landscape gardener Beatrix Farrand, for example, included *H. sieboldiana* in the north border of the outside garden of the John D. Rockefeller Estate at Seal Harbor, Maine (Farrand, 1985:46–47). Many other estate gardens incorporated this seemingly obligatory hosta in their borders which were patterned after the archetypal English perennial borders that also included some of the classic hostas.

The relative scarcity of hostas did not deter determined gardeners from obtaining them. Some were imported from Europe or brought back when returning from trips abroad. A few resourceful and determined gardeners who were unable to buy hostas through nurseries got their start from small divisions taken in remote graveyards (Tompkins, 1984).

To satisfy a modest but insistent demand for hostas by landscapers, a few North American nurseries continued to bring in hostas from Europe, principally from the Netherlands, England, and Germany. These, together with stock already in place, were propagated and offered by nurseries without finding their way into nursery catalogs. Thus, few records exist.

In the 1930s public interest in hostas increased. With this attention specialty nurseries were started to satisfy a rebuilding demand and established nurseries added hostas to their catalog selections.

THE FOUNDATION—THE U.S. NURSERY TRADE

Aside from Hogg's nursery, many others existed to satisfy the demand for plant material. Very few, though, offered hostas or specialized in hostas. William Borsch & Sons of Multnomah, Oregon, listed four hostas in 1930: Borsch no. 1, no. 2, no. 3, and no. 4. Some clues were given by Krossa who described them in a 1967 list as follows: "Borsch No. 1, 2 and 4: Heavy green leaves 10 by 7 inches, plant 25 inches high, July bloom." These were *H. montana* or *H. sieboldiana* seedlings. Borsch No. 3: "Similar to *H. cærulea* (= *H. ventricosa*)." The old Borsch plants are still offered in nursery catalogs. The fact that no names were given by Borsch indicates the identification struggle which was always present. Apparently, by 1944 some of the hostas had been identified and Borsch listed the following:

> *Hosta fortunei* = (?).
> *H. fortunei robusta* (Arends) = *H. sieboldiana* 'Elegans'.
> *H. lancifolia*.
> *H. minor alba* = *H. sieboldii* 'Alba'.
> *H. plantaginea*.
> *H. sieboldiana* form hybrids.
> *H. undulata variegata* = *H.* 'Undulata'.

Another of the early nurseries for which there are records is Ruh's Sunnybrook Farms Nursery in Chesterland, Ohio, whose catalog, published 1937–38, had a fairly comprehensive collection which included a *H. aureo variegata*. Ruh (1987: personal communication) informed me that this taxon has disappeared so is no longer grown and that he also carried *H.* 'Decorata' and *H.* 'Thomas Hogg' (= *H.* 'Undulata Albomarginata') which were originally purchased in Holland. This is confirmation that both of these "Thomas Hogg" hostas were exported from the United States to Holland only to be reimported after propagation.

By the mid-1930s a number of nurseries were offering hostas: Morningside Nurseries of Sioux City, Iowa; Sass Brothers Garden in Omaha, Nebraska; Napierville Nurseries of Napierville, Illinois; Wayside Gardens of Mentor, Ohio; and Skyland Nursery of Ringwood, New Jersey. Undoubtedly there were more, but unfortunately, very little printed material has survived. Most hosta cultivars existed in small numbers only and were still relatively scarce, but propagation of these cultivars by a few individuals and nurseries increased, as confirmed by Tompkins (1985), who reported deliveries of cultivar 1928-7W.E. (now *H.* 'Antioch') made by his mother in the 1930s to Wayside Nurseries. According to his account, 100 plants were delivered in 1936, 500 in 1937, and a total of 1100 in 1938, which indicates a considerable increase in demand for hostas at that time.

The well-publicized story (Williams, 1938) of the discovery of *H. sieboldiana* 'Frances Williams' at Bristol Nurseries in Bristol, Connecticut, in 1936 confirms this nursery also had hostas for sale in the 1930s. Among them was *H. sieboldiana*, from which *H. sieboldiana* 'Frances Williams' sported. A search among Mrs. Williams' papers[47] for listings of the hostas available at this nursery has yielded nothing, but she did leave a number of catalogs from other nurseries dating from the 1940s which give us a comprehensive account of the hosta selections available then.

One of the important hosta specialist nurseries during the 1930s and 1940s was H. A. Zager of Des Moines, Iowa. Like Mrs. Williams, Zager also contributed reference material for Hylander's 1954 study. Through this connection he obtained many of the European hostas. He was one of the first to offer them and became an important source for other nurseries. Gray & Cole, for example, offered *H. glauca* (Zager) and *H. glauca variegata* (also from Zager) in their 1965 *Hosta* List.

Krossa and Summers obtained many of their hostas from Zager and documented this source in their respective lists (Krossa, 1966–1970; Summers, 1972). Zager's own hosta records are extremely interesting because they show how the horticultural nomenclature evolved during that period. Furthermore, his descriptions were very comprehensive and his later catalogs provided photographs for a number of the hostas listed. Some of the descriptions he used were written by Mrs. Williams.

The hosta names cataloged by Zager in the 1940s had been in use since von Siebold's days which again confirms that the primary source of most hosta material in the United States at that time were from Europe, although a number of names were incorrectly spelled or formulated by Zager. In 1941 he listed the following:

> *Hosta cærulea* = *H. ventricosa.*
> *H. fortunei albo marginata* = *H.* 'Fortunei Albomarginata'.
> *H. fortunei gigantea.*
> *H. robusta.*
> *H. glauca.* [48]
> *H. lancifolia.*
> *H. lancifolia aurea margista* = *H.* 'Fortunei Albopicta'.
> *H. minor alba* = *H. sieboldii* f. *alba.*
> *H. sieboldiana* (as "seiboldiana").
> *H. subcordata grandiflora* = *H. plantaginea.*
> *H.* 'Thomas Hogg' = *H.* 'Decorata'.
> *H. undulata* = *H.* 'Undulata Erromena'.
> *H. undulata variegata* = *H.* 'Undulata'.

In the 1945–1946 edition Zager added *H.* 'Fortunei Aoki'. He also corrected the description of *H. glauca* from shiny green to glaucous blue. Today most hosta specialists consider this as one of the *H. sieboldiana* form plants, possibly a cross between *H. sieboldiana* and *H.* 'Tokudama'. Zager described it "with good size glaucous leaves . . . foliage not quite as large and more pointed than *H. sieboldiana.*" In the 1966 listing of Gray & Cole (see below), Zager was given as the source of *H. glauca* which is described as the "extremely rare 'true' glauca, very blue leaves and slow growing." But Summers (1987: personal communication), who grew practically all of Zager's plants, informed me that Zager's *H. glauca* was in fact *H.* 'Fortunei Hyacinthina', and plants that sold as *H. fortunei gigantea* and *H. robusta* were *H. montana* seedlings. Clearly, many of the hosta specialists conducting business during that time were offering seedlings labeled with various legitimate as well as invalid horticultural names.[49]

In 1958 Zager cataloged several new varieties in addition to some name changes. This perhaps indicates that most reputable nurserymen were willing to follow changes made by botanists in hosta nomenclature. For example, Zager brought his catalog of 1958 into line with Hylander's 1954 monograph:

> *Hosta alba marginata* = *H.* 'Undulata Albo-marginata'.
> *H. fortunei viridis-marginata* = *H.* 'Fortunei Albopicta'.
> *H.* 'Honey Bells' (Zager: "from Bristol Nurseries").
> *H. lancifolia* 'Aurea' = *H.* 'Fortunei Aurea'.
> *H.* 'Nakaimo'.
> *H. undulata univittata* = *H.* 'Undulata Univittata'.

The appearance of *H.* 'Nakaimo' is significant. Listed by Zager as a species from Japan, it was one of the first hostas to appear in U.S. listings with a Japanese name. It is known that it did not come from Krossa, who began importing hostas from Japan in 1950, because he documented (Krossa, 1966) that his source for this taxon was none other than Zager. In analyzing pertinent segments of Mrs. Williams' papers, which were provided by the IRA registrar, Mervin C. Eisel, I discovered that this hosta came from Pearce Seed Company, Moorestown, NJ. Mrs.

Williams, on an order for this hosta (dated 5 May 1954), inquired about its origin to which Pearce replied that they had received it from the Imperial Botanic Garden, Tokyo, before World War II.

The firm of Gray & Cole of Ward Hill, Massachusetts, was another early source of hostas as part of their perennial selection. Their 1942 catalog bears some interesting contrasts to Zager's in the choice of some of the hosta names, all of which were of European origin. The list (below) is also important because it gives English common names to the various taxa. Interestingly, *H.* 'Decorata' is included with the name given to it by Bailey in 1930, while other nurseries were still using *H.* 'Thomas Hogg', Zager being one of them.

> *Hosta cærulea* = *H. ventricosa* = Blue Plantain Lily.
> *H. decorata* = Blunt Plantain Lily.
> *H. fortunei albomarginata* = *H.* 'Fortunei Albomarginata' = Tallcluster Plantain Lily.
> *H. fortunei viridis-marginata* = *H.* 'Fortunei Albopicta'.
> *H. lancifolia* = *H.* 'Lancifolia', also listed as *H. japonica* = Lanceleaf Plantain Lily.
> *H. lancifolia albomarginata* = *H. sieboldii.*
> *H. lancifolia tardiflora* = *H.* 'Cathy Late', not the *H.* 'Tardiflora'.
> *H. minor alba* = *H. sieboldii* 'Alba'.
> *H. plantaginea* = White Plantain Lily.
> *H. sieboldiana* = Cushion Plantain Lily (also listed as *H. subcordata*).
> *H. undulata* = Wavyleaf Plantain Lily.
> *H. undulata univittata* = *H.* 'Undulata Univittata'.

A list issued by Gray & Cole in 1966 no longer included English common names but offered essentially the same selection as in 1942. *Hosta glauca* was listed as "Extremely rare true glauca, very blue leaves, slow growing," which was the European equivalent of *H.* 'Tokudama', but represents a different and larger variant which has more-pointed leaves.[50] Obviously, this was not the *H. glauca* sent to Summers by Zager, but one of European origin. *Hosta glauca variegata* was listed as "Also extremely rare. Blue with darker blue edge(?)," which was perhaps what is today called *H.* 'Blue Shadows', which in turn is the European variegated *H.* 'Tokudama'. The plant called *H. sieboldiana aureomarginata* also came from Zager who obtained it from Mrs. Williams. Zager gave it this species name in a slightly different, incorrect form, namely, *H. sieboldiana aureus marginata*. Interestingly, in 1962 Gray & Cole still listed this taxon as *H. sieboldiana* 'Yellow Edge', which perhaps indicates that Zager assigned the new name in the period between 1962 and 1964. The yellow form of *H. sieboldiana*, now registered as *H. sieboldiana* 'Golden Sunrise', was listed as *H. sieboldiana aurea* and noted as a sport of *H. sieboldiana aureomarginata*.

Napierville Nurseries, already mentioned, had a limited selection in 1941 which included *H. aurea variegata* (= *H.* 'Fortunei Aureomarginata') and *H. fortunei* (= Fortune Plantain Lily). What Napierville sold as *H. fortunei* is not known.

The nursery of Carl Starker, Jennings Lodge, Oregon, advertised the basic selection in 1949.

Rockmont Nursery of Boulder, Colorado, carried a hosta selection in their 1944 catalog, indicating hostas were available even during the war years. Again, with the exception of *H.* 'Decorata', all were from the original von Siebold listings, and the inclusion of *H. subcordata*, which had been an invalid name from its very start in 1825, indicated how persistent such obsolete, old names were in the North American nursery trade. Rockmont's *H. fortunei gigantea* was described as "a very scarce Plantain Lily with exceptionally large blue-green or glaucus foliage . . . flowers white tinged with blue." Although this name is today considered a synonym for *H. elata*, judging by the description provided, this hosta was probably not *H.* 'Elata', but a *H. sieboldiana* seedling.

Wayside Gardens, formerly of Mentor, Ohio, listed only one hosta in their 1959 catalog, namely, *H.* 'Undulata', as *H. undulata media picta*. This nursery, now operated by the George W. Park Seed Company, Inc., is still in business and carries a large selection of hostas, including some of the latest tissue-cultured cultivars. Several varieties were sold by Wayside as *H. albo marginata. Hosta fortunei aurea marmorata* was *H.* 'Antioch' (see Tompkins, 1985), but other cultivars were also sold under this name. In 1973 I purchased a hosta from this nursery under this name which proved to be *H.* 'Fortunei Creamedge' (= *H.* 'Fisher Creamedge'). Not all plants sent out under the label were *H. sieboldiana,* and occasionally *H.* 'Fortunei Hyacinthina' was substituted; this was confirmed by another of my orders. *Hosta japonica* 'Blue' and *H. japonica* 'White' date back to the Montreal Botanical Garden and were also listed. Today they are registered as *H.* 'Montreal' and *H.* 'Mount Royal', respectively (Ruh, 1983).

The sampling of hosta listings for 1930–1960 would not be complete without reference to Mackwoods Gardens operated by Carl Mack and located at Lotus Woods, Spring Grove, Illinois. This nursery published lists exclusively devoted to hostas. Its 1960 list is important because it includes synonyms for the various hostas, giving some indication of the different names used for the same taxon in horticulture. Today, however, some of these synonyms are incorrect. The hostas are here listed in the order in which they were printed in the 1960 catalog:

1. *Hosta sieboldiana,* Siebold Plantain Lily; syn. *Hosta glauca.*
2. *Hosta glauca,* Shortcluster Plantain Lily; syn. *Hosta sieboldiana* var. *elegans;* syn. *Hosta fortunei robusta.*
3. *Hosta erromena,* Midsummer Plantain Lily; syn. *Hosta undulata* var. *erromena.*
4. *Hosta fortunei* var. *albomarginata,* Whiterim Fortune Plantain Lily; syn. *Hosta crispula;* syn. *Hosta fortunei* var. *marginato-alba.*
5. *Hosta undulata* var. *albomarginata,* Wavyleaf Whiterim Plantain Lily.
6. *Hosta undulata* var. *univittata,* Wavyleaf Plantain Lily.
7. *Hosta cærulea,* Blue Plantain Lily; syn. *Hosta ventricosa;* syn. *Hosta cærulea;* syn. *Funkia ovata.*
8. *Hosta fortunei* var. *stenantha;* syn. *Hosta aokii.*
9. *Hosta fortunei* var. *viridis-marginata,* Greenrim Plantain Lily.
10. *Hosta fortunei* var. *gigantea,* Giant Fortune Plantain Lily; syn. *Hosta elata.*
11. *Hosta fortunei,* Tallcluster Plantain Lily or Fortune Plantain Lily.
12. *Hosta decorata,* Blunt Plantain Lily or Whiterim Blunt Plantain Lily; syn. *Hosta decorata* f. *marginata;* syn. *Funkia* 'Thomas Hogg'.
13. *Hosta decorata* f. *normalis,* Greenleaf Blunt Plantain Lily; syn. *Hosta decorata.*
14. *Hosta plantaginea,* Fragrant Plantain Lily; syn. *Funkia subcordata;* syn. *Funkia grandiflora.*
15. *Hosta minor alba,* Dwarf White Plantain Lily; syn. *Hosta albomarginata* var. *alba;* syn. *Hosta minor;* syn. *Hosta albiflora.*
16. *Hosta lancifolia* var. *fortis,* Lanceleaf Plantain Lily or Narrowleaf Plantain Lily; syn. *lancifolia;* syn. *Hosta japonica* var. *fortis.*
17. *Hosta lancifolia* var. *tardiflora,* Autumn Plantain Lily; syn. *Hosta tardiflora;* syn. *Hosta japonica* var. *tardiflora.*
18. *Hosta* species not positively identified ("resembles *H. kikutii* var. *yakusimensis*").
19. *Hosta sieboldiana* var. *marginata,* Yellowedge Siebold Plantain Lily; syn. *Hosta glauca* var. *aureovariegata* = *H. sieboldiana* 'Frances Williams'.
20. *Hosta fortunei* var. *albopicta* f. *viridis,* Fortune Greenleaf Plantain Lily.
21. *Hosta albomarginata,* White-flowered Whiterim White Plantain Lily = *H. sieboldii* 'Louisa'.
22. *Hosta* white-margined form (name not established) = *H.* 'Fortunei Green Gold'.
23. *Hosta fortunei* var. *stenantha,* variegated form—Green Rim = *H.* 'Fortunei Stenantha Aureomaculata'.
24. *Hosta lancifolia* var. *alba,* name probably incorrect.
25. *Hosta* hybrid 'Honey Bells', Honey Bells Plantain Lily.
26. *Hosta decorata* form.
27. *Hosta* white-margined form of no. 8.
28. *Hosta fortunei* variety (name not established).
29. *Hosta cærulea aureovariegata,* Variegated Blue Plantain Lily = *H. ventricosa* 'Aureomaculata'; syn. *Hosta ventricosa aureovariegata.*
30. *Hosta* species not positively identified ("it resembles *H. fluctuans*").
31. *Hosta fortunei* variety (name not established).
32. *Hosta lancifolia albomarginata,* Whiterim Plantain Lily or Whiterim Purple Plantain Lily = *H. sieboldii.*
33. *Hosta fortunei* var. *albopicta* f. *aurea,* Fortune Yellowleaf Plantain Lily.
34. *Hosta lancifolia albomarginata,* green-leaved form, Green-leaved Violet Plantain Lily = *H. sieboldii* f. *spathulata;* syn. *Hosta albomarginata,* green-leaved form.
35. *Hosta glauca,* variegated dwarf form.
36. *Hosta undulata,* Wavyleaf Plantain Lily or Variegated Plantain Lily; syn. *Hosta undulata variegata.*

I have included the list because, when it was published in 1960, it was one of the most extensive available. It indicates the considerable selection available to those who were determined to seek out the hosta specialist. The catalog also evidences that, with exception of a few Japanese imports, the basic selection in 1960 still consisted chiefly of the European von Siebold varieties.

Fairmount Gardens is also of considerable interest, because it was through the owner of this nursery, Mrs. Thomas Nesmith, that Mrs. Frances Williams marketed her hosta hybrids and discoveries. Many of them were listed in the 1964 catalog, including *H. sieboldiana* 'Yellow Edge' (= *H. sieboldiana* 'Frances Williams').

Comparing these later catalogs with those published in the 1930s clearly demonstrates how the selection of hostas had improved by 1960. Hybridizing was in full swing, and hybridizers and hosta specialists began to supply the market with an ever-increasing selection.

Pricing of hostas provides interesting information (all in U.S. $): In the 1930s and 1940s hosta divisions could be obtained for as little as $0.25 per division and were usually generous in size. Ruh's Sunnybrook Farms Nursery sold its hostas in the late 1930s for $0.25–$0.50. By the time the Mackwoods Gardens list appeared in 1960, prices had risen to $1 to $3. *Hosta sieboldiana* 'Frances Williams' was quite expensive at $8 per division. Also expensive at $4 was the green form of *H.* 'Fortunei Albopicta', apparently sported from the variegated form, and considered rare then. In the 1964 Fairmount Gardens catalog, prices had increased again. Most of the new introductions, marked by FRW numbers (for Frances R. Williams), were $8. The remainder were priced from $1 for the older classic varieties to $6–$8 for named hosta cultivars. In 1965 Gray & Cole sold four of their selections for $15 each: *H. glauca*, *H. glauca variegata*, *H. sieboldiana aurea* (a "Golden Sieboldiana"), and *H. sieboldiana aureomarginata*. In spite of the seemingly high cost, they were sold out most of the time.

TRAILBLAZERS—THE HOSTA SPECIALISTS

One of the prime reasons for the availability of a significantly expanded selection of hostas was the emergence of hosta specialists in the late 1960s and early 1970s. These individuals were trailblazers who were not content with the few bits of information available at the time or to simply obtain what was available in the local nursery trade. They actively engaged in searching out all available sources for hostas. They went to Japan and other countries where hostas are cultivated and acquired them from friends and colleagues who also grew hostas, and from universities, botanical gardens, and arboreta worldwide. In addition, some of them researched, identified, hybridized, and distributed the new plant material.

These hosta specialists come from all over the world and all walks of life. Their work continues today. Some are botanists, professional horticulturists, and landscape architects, while others are nursery owners and operaters and hybridizers, with a large number of keen amateur gardeners among their ranks. Judging by the correspondence between many of them,[51] they had one thing in common: a passionate interest in the genus *Hosta*. Their names are known to many hosta gardeners today: Aden, Allen, Arett, Armiger, Armstrong, Banyai, Barquist, Benedict, Bloom (UK), Brickell (UK), Cannon, Carder, Cooper, Craig, Davidson, Donahue, Eisel, Ellerbroek, Englerth, Epstein, Fischer (Germany), Fisher, Flintoff, Fraim, Geissler, Grapes, Grenfell (UK), Harrison, Harshbarger, Hatfield, Hensen (Netherlands), Jernigan, Kiehne, Kitchingman (UK), Klehm, Klopping, Klose (Germany), Krossa, Lantis, Lewis, Maroushek, McConnell, Minks, Morss (UK), Müssel (Germany), Nesmith, O'Harra, the Paynes, Plater-Zyberk, Pollock, Reath, Ross, Ruh, Savory, Schaeffer, Schutt, Seaver, Sellers, Shaw, Simpers, Smith (UK), Stark, Stone, Summers, Tiemann, Tompkins, Van Hoorn, Vaughn, Viette, Vogel, Wherry, Williams, Wister, Woodroffe, and Zager. In Japan, aside from botanists researching the genus, the nurseries of Kamo, Suzuki, and others, as well as a number of enthusiasts like Hirose and many unnamed others, laid the foundation of today's high interest in the genus. In the mid-1970s many more, too numerous to mention, joined this prominent group.

What set these enthusiasts apart from the average hosta gardener was their ardent pursuit of anything connected with hostas. This included seeking out other enthusiasts, sources for new plants, and whatever limited information they could find in print. Many of them not only shared plants but, more importantly, wrote about them. Some, including Craig and Davidson, were fortunate enough to reside in Japan for some time where they actively searched for hostas in the wild and in commerce and were responsible for the importation of many species and varieties. Other hosta specialists hybridized them, no doubt recognizing the great potential for new varieties existing in the genus. And finally, a handful of these enthusiasts, among them Summers, investigated and observed the plants arriving from Asiatic sources and matched them to the available botanical diagnoses, thereby identifying many of these nameless or misidentified imports.

Foremost among these specialists was Frances R. Williams. A professional landscape architect, she was trained, among other things, in botany and horticulture. Apparently, in the 1930s she transferred all her gardening energies to the genus. She grew many varieties, hybridized them, sought out sports, and wrote about them. She numbered and named her seedlings and selections. Williams collaborated with the scientific community, providing valuable information to botanists, among them Hylander, who used material provided by her in his 1954 monograph on the Swedish hostas. A number of articles have been written about her.[52] She was honored in 1969 by The American Hosta Society with a plaque in recognition for her "devotion to the genus, for hybridizing, naming and introducing many new varieties, and for inspiring others with a love for hostas." In 1986 she was posthumously awarded the AHS Alex Summers Distinguished Service Award. Mrs. Williams and a handful of hosta gardeners provided the nucleus of what was to become a growing number of hosta gardeners and specialists.

Another specialist, who was and still is one of the leading proponents of hostas in horticulture, is Alex J. Summers. He has been collecting hostas since about 1938 and was cofounder and the first president of The American Hosta Society. As editor of *The American Hosta Society Bulletin* he wrote many useful articles on the genus and was instrumental in having major botanical works translated and made available to hosta gardeners. On his large estate in Delaware, USA, he and his wife Gene maintain a very large and possibly the most comprehensive hosta planting anywhere. Summers kept an accurate acquisition list over the years, which is important historically because it records many of the sources and dates of European and Japanese imports (Summers, 1972). He also numbered his acquisitions which I have used extensively in my horticultural historical comments[53] on the various taxa. The Alex Summers Distinguished Service Award of The American Hosta Society was established in his honor, and he was the first recipient of this award.

In 1967 Eunice V. (Mrs. Glen) Fisher, co-founder (with Summers) and the first secretary-treasurer of The American Hosta Society, published a small booklet entitled *Hosta—The Aristocratic Plant for Shady Gardens*. That pioneering work and her service to the Society earned her an honorary life membership in this body. The book contained all the listed species and botanical varieties included in Maekawa (1940) and Araki (1942), as well as many of the "European" hostas described by Hylander (1954). Also described were most of the named cultivars then in commerce. It was revised in 1973 and a final issue released in 1979. Fisher hybridized, named, introduced, and registered a number of cultivars starting in 1970.

Peter Ruh, who served as vice president of The American Hosta Society for eight years, maintains a large hosta collection to which he constantly adds. Ruh was and still is a prolific correspondent with wide-ranging connections to other hosta specialists the world over. His services to the AHS have garnered him the 1986 Distinguished Service Award of The American Hosta Society.

Several other individuals were also awarded the Alex J. Summers Distinguished Service Award:

In 1985 to Dr. Warren I. Pollock, editor of *The American Hosta Society Bulletin* (later *The Hosta Journal*) from 1982 until 1987. He and coeditor Russell O'Harra turned this publication into a professionally produced and edited journal, featuring color photographs and informative articles, and utilizing good typography and layout. Pollock also served on the AHS Awards and Honors Committee, the Finance Committee, and as chairperson of the Nomenclature Committee which he organized into a productive group with international participation. He has written extensively on the subject (see Bibliography).

In 1987 to Mrs. Diana Grenfell of England, who was honored as co-founder of the British Hosta and Hemerocallis Society, for her service as chairman of this society for five years, and for her many contributions to the genus *Hosta*. She is one of the best-known and prolific writers on the genus.

In 1988 to Mrs. Charles (Mildred) Seaver, who is well known for her many hosta hybrids and the donation of rare hosta material to The American Hosta Society auction fund. She continues to enthusiastically support the cause for *Hosta*.

In 1989 to Eldren Minks, who served as president and has been an active supporter and hybridizer in the Midwest.

In 1900 to Luther J. (Jim) Cooper, who served as president, board member, and newsletter editor.

In 1991 to Olive Bailey Langdon, who served as secretary, president, and board member.

Three hosta collectors—Jack E. Craig, Leroy B. Davidson, and Gus F. Krossa—hold special positions because of their role in importing many species and varieties from Japan. A detailed account of their contributions follows.

IMPORTS FROM JAPAN 1950–1970

In the 1958 Zager catalog a hosta bearing a Japanese cultivar name first appeared before the U.S. gardening public: *H.* 'Nakaimo'. Zager described it as "a species from Japan." Almost immediately this taxon acquired several synonyms—such as "Nakaima," "Nakina", and "Nakhima"[54]—due to the unfamiliarity of most North Americans with Japanese kana.

By 1960 *H.* 'Nakaimo' had found its way to Hensen at Wageningen, Netherlands, indicating how quickly newly imported hostas from Japan found their way to Europe.

With the importation of a number of unknown Japanese hostas, a considerable problem arose in U.S. horticulture: the identification of plants either sent from Japan or collected there by U.S. hosta enthusiasts. Unfortunately, most plants arriving from Japan were not properly named or were graced with common, descriptive Japanese names given by Japanese collectors and nurseries. Examples of such cultivar names are 'Herifu' and 'Haku Chu Han'.[55] These descriptive Japanese names were not correlated to the Japanese botanical literature. It is true that some hostas came in under their Japanese academic names, but a botanical association could not be made at that time because Maekawa's 1940 work and other botanical papers had not been translated so were little known to non-professionals in the United States when the first plants arrived in the 1950s. Most of the recipients of new hostas were, in fact, laypersons who knew neither botanical Latin nor Japanese kana. This led to incorrect spellings such as "Kibuti" for *H. kikutii* and "Kikutchiana Huga" for Kikuchi's *Hyuga Giboshi*

(= *H. kikutii*). The imports were usually given an identifying code or number until positive identification could be made, as was the case with most of Krossa's Japanese imports. A few of the imported hostas were given English cultivar names which are still used in spite of the fact that the correct botanical identity and names are known today.

As pointed out earlier, the first hostas to arrive in the United States directly from Japan were sent by Hogg around 1875. After Hogg's imports very little new material seems to have come from Japan or Korea, save for a few species collected in the wild before 1940. Being mostly all-green and possessing no outstanding features, they were often relegated to obscure corners and forgotten.

Following the cessation of hostilities in 1945, access to the Japanese archipelago was again possible. By 1950 conditions in Japan were beginning to return to a more-or-less normal state, so scientific interchange recommenced. About this time several Japanese universities began to assemble collections of native *Hosta* species and varieties, and hosta exportations resumed from Japan. One of the importers was the late Gus F. Krossa, then living at Livonia, Michigan. In his letters to Summers, Krossa (1966) made it clear he considered himself a plant collector possessed of much enthusiasm but little botanical knowledge. He was principally interested in true species and botanical varieties and to that end corresponded with Japanese universities, including the University of Osaka. He also knew a number of private Japanese hosta collectors, and received *Hosta* material from several Japanese sources starting in 1950.

Enough of Krossa's correspondence has survived[56] to permit reconstruction of an acceptable time frame. In a letter to Summers dated 19 September 1966, he wrote: "From Osaka University and with the aid of Creech[57] I was able to obtain 11 species that were never in this country [United States] before." In the same letter he included a list of these: *H. akebono, H. gracillima, H. wogon, H. kikutii, H. sacra, H. tosana, H. clavata, H. venusta, H. tokudama, H. tokudama variegata,* and *H. sparsa.* These apparently came labeled with their respective names but some were misidentified due to switched labels and others were not validly published species. In fact, Krossa closed this letter with the remark: "I doubt that the names of any of these are correct." As it turned out, Krossa's postscript was right: Many of the named hostas he received were subsequently found to be labeled incorrectly.

On 26 February, 1967, Krossa added: "All the Japanese hostas I have did not come from Osaka University. I got 5 from an industrialist in Tokyo." On 28 July, 1968, he further noted: "My B-1[58] is the hugest hosta I have in height and came in a shipment from Japan (Osaka) about 1950."

Direct importation from Japan was not the only way Krossa acquired hostas from Oriental sources. He obtained some from E. G. Corbett, J. L. Creech, and R. W. Lighty at the U.S. Department of Agriculture, Agricultural Research Station, and additional plants came from S. (Skip) March, plant explorer and propagator at the National Arboretum as well as F. G. Meyer. Some of these originated in Korea. Quite a few were sent to him by Summers after they arrived from Japan at Summers' garden.

Krossa also contacted and received plants from other collectors including Cardwell, Ellerbroek, Epstein, Grapes, Holly, Schaeffer, Shaw, Williams, and Zager. Other hosta gardeners and specialists who were known to have imported hostas were included in Krossa's extensive correspondence, so he obtained plants from every possible source. Some of these had originally come from Europe, while others were of Japanese origin. In 1967 Krossa received a shipment of hostas from Hensen in the Netherlands which, in turn, he sent to his correspondents and plant contributors, including Summers.

Several of the lists compiled by Krossa between 1966 and 1970 show his sources by name and place of origin. These records indicate a number of other individuals who also imported hostas directly from Japan after 1960.

The key individual in this undertaking was Summers. He assembled many of the Japanese species and varieties and made a number of identifications which are documented in his 1972 acquisition list. This list includes 581[59] hostas which Summers obtained between 1962 and 1972 from a variety of sources, including Krossa. The most important contributions to the Summers collection came from two Japanese botanists, Dr. Hirao and Dr. Kaneko, and from two private collectors, Jack E. Craig and Leroy B. Davidson.

Kaneko (1966, 1968a, 1968b, 1969, 1970) is well known for his study of *Hosta* chromosome numbers. Hirao (1981) contributed to the understanding of inducing polyploidy in the genus.

Both Craig and Davidson resided in Japan for some time. Their activities are partially documented in early issues of *The American Hosta Society Bulletin* (1970, 1971, 1972, 1976). They sent many specimens, some quite rare, to Summers, and their articles gave fascinating glimpses of hostas growing in the wild. They were assisted in their explorations by Japanese botanists, among them Drs. Moria and Miyazawa, and several private collectors, including Hirano and Hamada. Aside from collecting hosta material in the wild, Davidson reported purchases of plants at the Yokohama nursery of Suzuki. Craig (1970, 1971, 1972) and Davidson (1970) worked independently, but together they made important contributions to the understanding of several species by Western specialists. Especially significant was Davidson's importation of representatives of the *H. longipes* complex, and Craig's collection of specimens belonging to *H. rupifraga*, *H. hypoleuca*, *H. gracillima*, and the popular *H. sieboldii* 'Haku Chu Han'.

Recently, Davidson detailed his activities in a personal communication (1990) and cleared up several issues. His trips to Japan and collecting activities took place in 1969–70. After his return in 1970 he received many plants from Jack Craig. His primary outlet for the species and cultivars which he had collected or which he had received from Craig was George Schenk's Wild Garden Nursery. For some time Siskiyou Rare Plant Nursery, Medford, OR, also listed some of the plants in its catalog. Robert Putnam's Plant Farm, Seattle, WA, did the propagating, and after the owner's death about 1985 the stock went to Grand Ridge Nursery, Seattle, WA, where some of the stock is still grown. Some of the plants attributed by some authors to Davidson actually originated (labeled with Japanese names) with Craig, who sent pieces of most of his collections and purchases to Davidson, among them *Kanzashi Giboshi* (*H. nakaiana*) 1962, *Hime Iwa Giboshi* (*H. gracillima*) 1964, and *H.* 'Suzuki Thumbnail' (*H. venusta*) 1969.

In the late 1960s several U.S. botanists went on collecting expeditions to the Orient. Corbett and Lighty visited Korea and Japan, and Creech traveled to Japan. These excursions brought a number of Korean and Japanese plants collected in the wild to the United States. As noted earlier these U.S. scientists contributed to both the Krossa and Summers collections. The very recent explorations of Yinger (in 1985) and Chung (in 1985, 1987, 1988) to remote Korean islands have led to the naming of several new species.

This brief review would not be complete without mentioning the Japanese and Korean imports by institutions and individuals in Europe.

Foerster in Germany reportedly secured Japanese hostas in the 1930s, including *H. sieboldiana* 'Semperaurea' (Fischer, 1983; Schmid 1985b, 1985c). Hensen (1963a, 1985) reports that most of the listed Japanese species and varieties cultivated at Wageningen came to the Netherlands via the United States. One exception appears to have been *H. rectifolia* 'Chionea' which was sent (from Japan) by E. Hodgkin in 1964, and other plants were imported by Hodgkin as well. Also well known are the importations of botanical institutions, which are reflected in living and herbaria collections. One of these is the Royal Botanic Garden, Kew, which through courtesy of others made a number of specimens available to me.

According to Stearn (1966) and Brickell (1968), *H. venusta* was introduced into cultivation in Britain—sent to Roy C. Elliott from Dr. Rokujo of Tokyo before 1956—which confirms some importations to the United Kingdom took place in recent times. Unfortunately, an inordinate amount of seed was grown in gardens in that country before it was generally known that it cannot be expected to come true. Growing from seed is a method accepted by botanists the world over as an appropriate and inexpensive way to bring wild species into cultivation.[60] But the species and botanical varieties of the genus do not reliably come true from seed, so some of the British specimens may be intra- or interspecific natural hybrids or hybridized cultivated material.[61] As an example, some of the cultivated specimens of *H. venusta*, which I examined in England, lack the ridges on the flowering scape, so cannot be this taxon. I have found morphological problems in most plants grown from collected seed imported to Europe and North America.

Although postwar importations from Japan began around 1950, such acquisitions were still rather uncommon until recently. Today many connections exist between scientists, nursery owners and operators, and private individuals in the United States and their Japanese counterparts. Travel to Japan by plant enthusiasts has become commonplace. New plant material and additional specimens of known species and cultivars arrive rather frequently now. This influx has created a significant identification problem, because now, as before with earlier imports, many of the plants are incorrectly labeled or furnished with common Japanese cultivar names which are difficult to place.

In recent years the Japanese also have taken renewed interest in their *Giboshi*, especially those growing in the wild. As a result many new discoveries are being made. Sources in Japan have provided profuse evidence of these finds by sending color photographs and slides revealing the many exiting variegated sports found in the wild. Many of these are being observed, named, and propagated and will eventually find their way into hosta gardens the world over.

THE GROUNDWORK AND BEYOND—ENGLAND

In 1988 I visited southern England, a veritable paradise of gardens, both large and small. My hosts, Diana Grenfell and Roger Grounds, knew all the best places, and they introduced me to many fine gardens and their creators. Introduced in one such garden as historian of The American Hosta Society, I was asked about the beginnings of what we now call the "new hosta renaissance." Surrounded by aged clumps of hostas, the answer came easy: It all started in England.

The early involvement of English botanists in the taxonomy of the genus is well known, and I have covered this subject in Appendix B. Among them, important contributions came from Baker (1868, 1870, 1876), Banks (1791), Hooker (1838, 1839), Ker-Gawler (1812), Lindley (1839), Paxton (1838), Salisbury (1807, 1812), Sims (1812), and Sweet (1827). Around the turn of the century Farrar (1919), Irving (1903), and Wright (1916) also wrote on the subject.

Private gardening, having reached the highest state of the art in England, had for many years fostered use of the genus. The work of William Robinson and Gertrude Jekyll mentioned earlier led to the inclusion of several of the classic hostas, foremost *H. sieboldiana*, into the standard assortment of foliage plants for the border. The books written by these innovators of garden style were widely read and studied the world over and set in motion new trends in gardening. Together, with the ideas advanced, an increased, yet restrained use of hostas in the landscape occurred. By 1900 the inclusion of at least a few members of the genus in the shade garden or the border became almost obligatory. While this cannot be called the beginnings of a hosta renaissance, it was certainly part of the necessary groundwork which had radiated from England to the continent of Europe, particularly Germany, and to North America where hostas had also became important shade garden and border plants and were planted in large drifts in parks and cemeteries.

No planned hybridizing programs seem to have been carried out in England up to the end of the Victorian era, at least no records of such activities have been found. Undoubtedly, some English nurseries and private gardeners made hybrids, and some of these may still be around undetected. There was, in any case, very little planned hybridizing anywhere, except for some hybrids made by Arends starting in 1905 and by Foerster somewhat later in Germany, but they were not widely distributed and none appear to have reached England during that period, although some did much later.

The available selection of hostas was limited to a few classic species and specioids, like *H. sieboldiana*, *H. plantaginea*, *H. ventricosa*, *H.* 'Undulata', and a few of the garden varieties originating with von Siebold who supplied nurseries in England and Germany. *Hosta* 'Decorata' had not yet been given a binomial and was called *H.* 'Thomas Hogg' in North America, and the *H.* 'Fortunei' group later classified by Hylander (1954) was an unrecognized conglomeration of garden varieties, each having multiple and confusing names.

Clearly needed were stability in the plant material as well as order in the nomenclature. Most English gardeners are very keen on the scientific aspects of gardening, so it is no surprise that English botanists had considerable influence on the horticultural development of the genus.

Beginning in the late 1920s, botanists started to take a serious look at individual species and at classification and nomenclature as a whole. About that time Liberty Hyde Bailey, a well-known U.S. botanist, began studying the genus (as detailed in Appendix B). On the other side of the Atlantic a young English botanist, William T. Stearn, published his research, and soon the two scientists were collaborating very closely. Bailey produced a new classification system in 1930 and a follow-up paper in 1932 (see Bibliography and Appendix B), after which no further work dealing exclusively with the genus was published by him. Stearn, on the other hand, who first published on the genus in 1931 with his own revision of *Hosta*, continued to produce valuable contributions on the subject for several decades (1931a, 1931b, 1932b, 1947, 1948, 1951, 1953, 1966, 1971). His work is also reviewed in Appendix B. Combined with Bailey's work, Stearn's studies led to an increased awareness of the genus among English gardeners and, more importantly, a system of nomenclature, albeit one that was only partially correct.

Another key event in publicizing the genus was the appearance of a very detailed listing of hostas in C. H. Grey's *Hardy Bulbs* in 1938. Collaborating with Bailey and Stearn, Grey integrated all their work with that of Maekawa (1937, 1938) and provided gardeners their first true glimpse into the extent of the plant species involved. Grey's work was the first English translation to appear in the West to use Maekawa's Latin text. Regard for the genus grew after 1954 when Stearn, collaborating closely with Hylander in Sweden, revised the listings in the authoritative *Dictionary of Gardening* produced by the Royal Horticultural Society (1956, 1969). Within a short period of time horticulturist were applying this new and not-so-new scientific information to gardening. This kindled renewed interest in the genus among gardeners and soon led to increased commercial production. In 1950, for example, Eldon Nurseries of Wimborne, Dorset, listed 21 hosta varieties. Small articles—for example, F. P. Lee's 1957 *Plantainlilies*—were soon followed by more extensive works by Graham Stuart Thomas, who wrote detailed accounts on the genus in 1960 and 1961 (see Bibliography).

Unfortunately, very few of the new hostas were actually available; some, indeed, had not been seen alive. A young English botanist realizing this shortcoming undertook to change this deficiency. Today he is well known as one of the world's leading gardener-botanists: Christopher D. Brickell.

Brickell's idea was to put together a scientific exhibit of all known cultivated hostas at the Chelsea Flower Show, where a maximum number of gardeners could see them. He began working with Sir George Taylor (then director of Kew Garden), Sir Eric Savill (then director of Savill Garden, Windsor Great Park), Hylander, Hensen in the Netherlands (see Appendix B), Stearn, A. F. George, G. S. Thomas, and R. C. Elliott—all of whom offered advice and donated plants for the exhibit which was placed in the 1968 Chelsea Flower Show. The exhibit featured many hostas planted around a water feature in a natural setting, as well as a small building which contained display boards giving detailed botanical and horticultural information on the plants. The exhibit was a huge success and created considerable interest among gardeners which, unfortunately, was short-lived because many of these glorious plants were simply not readily available. Existing nursery stocks were quickly exhausted and all many frustrated gardeners could do was look at the beautiful color illustrations which accompanied Brickell's article about the show in the September 1968 issue of the *Journal of the Royal Horticultural Society*. This is, perhaps, the reason hosta cultivation shifted to North America where larger nurseries—supported by Dutch imports—and a great many small family enterprises were able to fill an ever-increasing demand. The result was the building of what must be considered the first gardens to use hostas as the principal element.

Thus, the beginning year of the new hosta renaissance must be 1968, which was not only the year of Brickell's Chelsea exhibit, but, coincidentally, also the year when, across the Atlantic, The American Hosta Society was formed and an international registrar for the Genus *Hosta* was appointed at the University of Minnesota, USA.

Although the development of hosta cultivation moved at a much faster pace in North America, it was by no means neglected in England, carried on there by a few quiet individuals whose names are well known in hosta circles today: Jim Archibald, Sandra Bond, Ann and Roger Bowden, Diana Grenfell, Roger Grounds, Julie Morss, and last, but not least, Eric Smith. Also contributing to the growing interest in hosta cultivation were some of the best garden writers in the world, who are still active today: Alan Bloom, Beth Chatto, Penelope Hobhouse, Christopher Lloyd, and Graham Stuart Thomas.

Recognizing widespread local interest, hosta enthusiasts formed a group called the British Hosta and Hemerocallis Society (BHHS) in 1981. In the autumn of 1982 the society published its first *BHHS Newsletter*. C. D. Brickell is listed as the first president, with Eric Smith and Graham Stuart Thomas serving as vice-presidents.

Eric Smith of Southampton, England, is internationally the best known of the early English hosta pioneers and breeders. He died in 1986 and was a shy and unassuming person who never married and preferred plants above anything else. Trained as an architect, he did not stay with this profession long but returned to his plants, becoming propagator at Hilliers of Winchester, where he worked in the walled garden for four years. There he made many famous crosses in the genus *Helleborus* and selected his first famous *Hosta* cultivar, *H.* 'Buckshaw Blue', a *H.* 'Tokudama' derivative, which remained unnamed while he was at Hilliers. Much later this cultivar won him the Award of Merit after trial at Wisley.

Smith's dream was to have a nursery of his own, so after resigning from Hilliers and spending yet another year working for an architectural firm, he went into partnership with Jim Archibald in 1965. Together they formed the Plantsmen Nursery at Buckshaw Gardens, near Sherborne, Dorset. In this partnership Eric Smith seems to have been the raiser of plants while Archibald was the promoter/businessman. Soon, their enterprise became world famous because they were able to supply all kinds of rare plants. Eric did extensive breeding work in several plant genera, including *Bergenia*, *Brunnera*, *Camassia*, *Crocosmia*, *Kniphofia*, *Rheum*, and others. In 1970 their nursery list included 21 hostas, probably the most extensive selection in England.

Eric's hosta breeding efforts concentrated on two lines: (1) his *H.* × *tardiana* (nom. illegitimum) cross, and (2) his GL (Gold Leaf) series. The former was a cross he made earlier, when employed at Hilliers, while work on the latter cross took place at Plantsmen Nursery. The GL series arose out of a desire to permanently fix the fine, but fleeting golden-yellow variegation of *H.* 'Fortunei Aurea' and to impart more substance to *H. sieboldii* 'Kabitan'. He crossed *H. sieboldiana* with the latter—an unlikely and difficult cross that is itself an achievement because these taxa bloom several months apart. Smith was able to make the cross only because his *H. sieboldiana* rebloomed in late summer (Smith, [1971] 1982). From this he obtained *H.* 'Goldsmith' and *H.* 'Hadspen Samphire', both named much later. The *H.* 'Fortunei Aurea' cross with *H. sieboldiana* resulted in *H.* 'Gold Haze' and *H.* 'Granary Gold'. This early work has now been replaced by breeding efforts in North America with the yellow lines of *H. sieboldiana* and *H.* 'Tokudama'.

As noted earlier, while still at Hilliers, Eric was able to cross the late-flowering *H.* 'Tardiflora' with a large, robust form of *H. sieboldiana*, most often alluded to as *H. sieboldiana* 'Elegans'. This accomplishment won him lasting fame as a British hosta hybridizer of note. The resulting hybrids in the F_1 and F_2 generations have become classics, and many have been named and registered. A complete listing and details can be found in Chapter 4. For many years these hybrids have been known under the collective name *H.* × *tardiana* (nom. illegitimum). As reported by Grounds (1986), the nomenclature committee of the BHHS suggested calling it the *H.* Tardiana group following recommendation 18A of the ICNCP. Unfortunately, the formulation of this hybrid binomial violates both the ICBN and the ICNCP rules, so is a nomen illegitimum and cannot be legitimized under the present rules nor can it be used for a grex or group name. In this book I have, nevertheless, retained the name due to its persistent and historical use, leaving to someone else the task of renaming it. In spite of the committee's recommendation and overlooking the name's illegitimacy, a group name is not indicated here, because all derivatives of this cross are from the same two parents, both known, so *H.* Tardiana grex better indicates this relationship. Smith gave away many small plants and seed, some of which, now mature, have been misidentified because all seem to have similar characteristics. Recently the BHHS has identified and registered many of Smith's hybrids and has begun building a reference collection of authentic plants to help in identifying these taxa. Smith corresponded with Alex Summers and together they named many of the more popular hybrids, giving them the "Dorset" and "Hadspen" prefixes.

In my opinion, one of Smith's best hybrids is *H.* 'Snowden', raised at Buckshaw Gardens, a cross between *H. sieboldiana* and a *H.* 'Fortunei' form. It takes time to mature, but will eventually become a magnificent specimen, as the one growing at Hadspen House attests (see Plate 141).

In 1975 the Plantsmen Nursery went out of business and Smith went to Hadspen House, where he became head gardener and propagator for Penelope Hobhouse, a position he held until his retirement five years later. He named many of his earlier successes at Hadspen House, and plant collectors from all over the world visited him there to buy and exchange plants. In 1982 he was made honorary life member of the AHS, and shortly thereafter, in 1983, he was elected vice-president of the newly founded BHHS.

One of the prime movers in the founding of this society was Diana Grenfell, who is also well known for her many written contributions starting with her thorough opus on cultivated hostas in *The Plantsman* in 1981 followed by other articles which are detailed in the Bibliography. Diana has held chairmanship in the BHHS from its founding until 1987 and is now a vice-president. She has unflinchingly supported the cause for *Hosta*, which is just one of the reasons why, in 1987, she was honored with the Alex J. Summers Distinguished Service Award, given by The American Hosta Society. More specifically, she was given this award for her work as co-founder of the British Hosta and Hemerocallis Society, for her service as chairperson of this society for five years, for her many contributions to the popularizing of hostas, and for being one of the best-known and prolific writers on the genus.

I visited her in the summer of 1988 on the occasion of being asked to give a lecture on *Hosta* species to the BHHS membership in the Lecture Theater of the RHS Old Hall, Vincent Square, London. I became acquainted with Apple Court, a garden she is building with Roger Grounds at Lymington, Hampshire, which now houses the National Reference Collection of small *Hosta* species and cultivars. During my stay she asked me to review the species chapter of a book on hostas she was writing at the time, because some parts of that chapter are based on my translations of Japanese texts previously unavailable in the West. Diana's latest contribution, entitled *Hosta: The Flowering Foliage Plant*, is reviewed in Appendix B.

Also during my 1988 visit I met Sandra Bond and Ann and Roger Bowden. Sandra Bond of Goldbrook Plants, Hoxne, Eye, in Suffolk, has for many years exhibited collections of *Hosta* at the RHS Vincent Square shows and Chelsea Flower shows and has received many gold medals for her efforts, one of which I was privileged to see. These exhibits are an excellent means to educate the public and to show the new cultivars as well as rare botanical forms. On that occasion Sandra also received the Eric Smith Award for 1988, the highest honor the BHHS can bestow. Today she is recognized as one of the leading promoters of the genus in England and her Goldbrook Plants nursery, currently featuring over 100 varieties, has become a mecca for enthusiasts seeking out new cultivars.

Ann and Roger Bowden live at Cleave House in the village of Sticklepath, near Okehampton, Devon. Their gardens are actually several sites spread about the village, but all of them are close to the house. Roger is general secretary of the BHHS, and both he and Ann are registrars for a committee overseeing the registration of British hostas with the IRA. The Bowdens offer many of the latest cultivars and have a fine exhibition area where fully mature clumps can be seen. Their promotion of the genus and their hard work in making many fine cultivars available to British gardeners has put them in the position of one of the leading suppliers of hostas in England.

Several other gardens should be mentioned and given credit for having contributed to the new hosta renaissance.

Floreat Garden, Poole, Dorset, the nursery of Julie and David Morss, started to offer hostas in the early 1970s but, unfortunately, no longer operates. In 1983 *H.* 'Julie Morss', a *H. sieboldiana* 'Frances Williams' derivative, was named in Julie's honor and registered with the IRA. A few other gardens with historical significance which are still in business and continue to contribute as well are Bloom's Bressingham Gardens in Diss, Norfolk; Hadspen House, Castle Cary, Somerset, where I met Nori and Sandra Pope, nursery managers and head gardeners; Beth Chatto's horticultural paradise in Colchester, Essex; and Spinners, Boldre, Hampshire, a fine garden created by Peter Chappell. A number of other important nurseries are listed at the end of Chapter 6. Photographs taken at Bressingham, Hadspen House, and Spinners are featured in this book.

Finally, credit must be given to the English writers who so diligently sought out much information on the genus and published on it: Graham Stuart Thomas, who has been writing about hostas for three decades and included one of the most comprehensive, horticultural lists published to date in his *Florilegium* (Thomas, [1982] 1985); Alan Bloom, who first built island beds at Bressingham in 1952, an idea that is now almost universally copied in hosta gardens, particularly in North America (Bloom, 1981), and which has been incorporated in Chapter 6; Christopher Lloyd, whose garden has been seen all over North America on the television series "Victory Garden" and whose ideas about the inclusion of foliage plants in gardens have been widely emulated (Lloyd, 1973); and Beth Chatto, whose book *The Damp Garden* (1983) is another important contribution in addition to the many hostas she offers at her nursery. Her garden has also been seen on "Victory Garden".

Gardening tends to be somewhat more organized in Britain than in the rest of the world; the establishment of the National Hosta Reference collections is an example. In North America the only similar collection is at the Landscape Arboretum of the University of Minnesota, USA—although there is a now a move to establish several national display gardens, but rules and sites have not yet been determined. Forging ahead, Britain has established national reference collections for many plant genera. These are operated under the auspices of the National Council for the Conservation of Plants and Gardens (NCCPG) which was formed in 1980. Several sites have been selected, and all are now in the process of assembling comprehensive collections of the particular species and cultivar groups they have been elected to grow. The collection holders cooperate in the acquisition of plant material and the exchange of information on the effects of abiotic and biotic factors on cultivation. Another important task is the identification of the taxa in the collections and the production of standard herbarium specimens for each, to be held at the RHS Herbarium at Wisley. These reference collections occupy different sites in Britain and so provide dissimilar growing conditions. All are in addition to the hosta collections already growing at the various botanic gardens in Britain.

A comprehensive collection will be grown in the Wild Garden of the RHS Garden at Wisley, Woking, Surrey. The collection was established under the direction of Christopher Brickell. Whenever available I have given the old Wisley numbers in Chapters 3 and 4. The larger species and cultivars have been assigned to the collection at Golden Acre Park, a facility owned and operated by the Council of the City of Leeds in West Yorkshire. The 137-acre (55-hectare) park is located near Bramhope, northwest of Leeds, and already houses reference collections of other genera. The collection will be managed by the city's horticultural officer, Terry Exley, an early proponent of the NCCPG. Small species and cultivars will be placed within the protective walls and under the highly qualified eyes of the owners of Apple Court—Diana Grenfell

and Roger Grounds—near Lymington, Hampshire. The Scottish national reference collection will be housed at old Kittoch Mill, a few miles south of Glasgow. It is the home of Colonel and Mrs. Howard Jordan who have been growing hostas for a relatively short time but now have over 150 species and cultivars.

The cultivation of hostas in Britain has come a long way since the 1968 scientific exhibit at Chelsea, and the use of hostas in gardens may take a somewhat different path than that in North America where hostas have become key elements in many gardens. The British love all their plants and, usually, many kinds, so they will certainly find new and exiting ways to use them in combination with hostas.

THE HOSTA RENAISSANCE—HOSTA PIONEERS IN NORTH AMERICA

In North America, as in England, the assiduous work of the relatively few hosta pioneers laboring from 1950 to 1970 finally came to fruition in the late 1960s. In 1968 two milestones extremely important to a more generalized acceptance of the genus *Hosta* were reached in the United States. Together with Brickell's scientific exhibit at Chelsea, these achievements must be considered the beginning of the hosta renaissance.

The first event was the founding of The American Hosta Society (AHS) by Mrs. Eunice V. Fisher and Alex J. Summers. This society has international membership and has aggressively pursued its goals of fostering and promoting interest in the genus, introducing new and improved varieties into cultivation, and using correct nomenclature. The society's publication *The American Hosta Society Bulletin*, renamed *The Hosta Journal* in 1986, has presented a cross section of horticultural as well as scientific information on the genus. The inclusion of color photographs started by the new editors O'Harra and Pollock in 1982 has added an important visual dimension to the articles.

Among the founding charter members of the AHS were Dr. R. C. Allen, Harold Epstein, Mrs. Eunice V. Fisher, David Stone, Alex J. Summers, and Dr. and Mrs. John C. Wister. The founding president was Mr. Summers, who held this post as well as that of editor of *The American Hosta Society Bulletin* from 1968 until 1978. Under his leadership the society grew into a smoothly functioning organization and is today the world's leading association promoting the genus.

Secondly, primarily because of the work done by U.S. hosta enthusiasts, the International Society for Horticultural Science, The Hague, Netherlands, appointed the University of Minnesota as the International Registration Authority (IRA) for the genus *Hosta*. Mr. Mervin C. Eisel was named international registrar and is still performing this function today.

With the IRA for *Hosta* firmly in place and promotional efforts for the genus on the rise, interest in hostas advanced considerably during the late 1960s and the 1970s. One of the most important contributions to the new popularity of hostas was the work of a new generation of hosta hybridizers. Registration of new *Hosta* cultivars reflects this trend. In 1969 three new hostas were registered, while in 1978, Alex Summer's final year as president, 52 hostas were registered. Many of these hosta cultivars have become classics and their names are known internationally.

One of these hybridizer's was Mrs. Williams. Her hosta discoveries and cultivars predate the establishment of the IRA for Hosta. Most were not registered by her initially, but they are nevertheless in the trade (Wister, 1970a). Recently many of her named varieties were registered by the Nomenclature Committee of the AHS together with some other classic cultivars. One of Mrs. Williams' discoveries, *H. sieboldiana*

'Frances Williams', which has been at the top of the AHS popularity polls for many years, was named in her honor by Mr. George W. Robinson of England's Oxford University Botanic Garden (Pollock and Schmid, 1986).

Other hybridizers either discovered or created the hosta classics of today: Eunice Fisher's H. 'Candy Hearts' of 1971; Ann Arett's H. 'Anne Arett' in 1975; Pauline Banyai's H. 'Gold Standard' in 1976; Bob Savory's H. 'Golden Tiara' in 1977; Mildred Seaver's H. 'Sea Drift' in 1978; and Van Seller's H. 'Iron Gate Supreme' in 1980. There were others who introduced and registered new cultivars: Anderson, Armstrong, Benedict, Bloom, Carpenter, Cooley, Cummings, Eisel, Englerth, Fisher, Geissler, Holly, Klose (Germany), Krossa, Minks, Moldovan, O'Harra, Ruh, Sellers, Simpers, Soules, Stone, Tompkins, Vaughn, and Woodruff.

One U.S. hybridizer merits special mention: Paul Aden of Baldwin, New York. He has registered more hostas than any other breeder and is well known as editor of *The Hosta Book*. Using the genetic precepts subsequently published by Vaughn (Vaughn et al., 1978; Vaughn and Wilson, 1980a, 1980b, 1980c; Vaughn, 1981, 1982), Paul began naming and registering hostas in 1974. That year he introduced four cultivars, including *H.* 'Blue Cadet'. In 1978 he registered 40 out of a total of 52 cultivars for the year; in 1980, 15; and in 1982, another 15. He developed a number of hybrids with a highly streaked and splashed form of white and yellow variegation, although most have been found unstable and thus have reverted to stable periclinal chimeras, usually of the *marginata* type. Those with gold or yellow variegated leaves have become exemplary. He also bred for heavy substance and long-lasting pruinosity coupled with pronounced rugosity—characteristics which found their best expression in his blue and grey cultivars, which are now widely distributed. Aden, realizing better than anyone else the commercial possibilities of hybridizing the genus, was instrumental in getting his many cultivars into mass production by way of tissue culture. In this he gained the collaboration of Roy Klehm of Charles Klehm and Son Nursery, South Barrington, Illinois. The Klehm organization, recognizing the genus' horticultural merit, initiated mass production by way of tissue culture and followed up with a plant development program which resulted in the publication of the first full-color hosta guide catalog, featuring many of Aden's hybrids and making recommendations for their use in the landscape. Published in 1982, it was the first color publication solely devoted to hostas and was eminently successful in

attracting many gardeners to the genus. Aden keeps adding to the list of available cultivars and Klehm, offering many of Aden's cultivars as well as other classics, is continuing to actively popularize the genus.

At present there is no organized hosta activity on the European continent. But gardeners of many countries, including Germany, the Netherlands, and Sweden, have joined the AHS and the BHHS. Several have contributed to the publications of these societies, notably K. J. W. Hensen of the Netherlands (see Appendix B) and Ullrich Fischer of Germany.

Although there is intense interest in the genus in Japan, no Japanese *Hosta* specialty societies are known to exist. Many Japanese enthusiasts have therefore joined Western societies. Nevertheless many articles on the subject have been published in Japanese journals[62] and many of the nursery catalogs feature hostas. Discoveries of new variegated forms of hostas continue to be made in the wild and also among those under cultivation. They are carefully nurtured, propagated, and named. Some of these are already in the United States—for example, *Sagae Giboshi*, *H.* 'Sagae', one of Japan's finest cultivars. This cultivar is also known in Japan as *H.* 'Sagae', but unfortunately, in the West is known under a different synonym, viz., *H. fluctuans* 'Variegated', which is technically incorrect but retained because of widespread use. Many more exciting Japanese discoveries are currently finding their way into North American and European gardens.

As the hosta following increased in the United States, regional societies were formed all over the country. The popular press has taken up the subject worldwide and even the prestigious *Wall Street Journal* (Hagan, 1986) featured an article on the genus *Hosta*. The professional horticulturist as well as the general gardening public has found sturdy, virtually maintenance-free perennials in the genus. At a time when help in the garden is too expensive or impossible to find and gardeners must rely on their own means, the genus *Hosta* has caught the public's fancy. Much of this is due to the perseverance and hard work of the hosta pioneers. A contingent of hosta enthusiasts and specialists—building on the foundation laid by these hosta pioneers—will undoubtedly perpetuate the hosta renaissance. The highly developed skills of the leading tissue culture propagators and proficient nurserypersons are doing much to aid this renaissance and to get modern hostas into the gardens of both the hosta enthusiast and the average gardener.

CHAPTER 6

Hostas in the Landscape

THE PERFECT PERENNIAL

Over the years, visiting many gardens, both large and small, I discovered long before making my first garden that the elaborate schemes, grand herbaceous borders, and crowded collections of multicolored perennials and annuals demonstrate one important fact: The handling of color combinations and placement of plants by size, blooming season, and habit requires a very delicate and professional touch to look like a poem of color.

Obviously, most gardeners develop their own idea of what a garden should look like, but for the majority of modern gardeners this vision includes, to an ever-increasing degree, a longing for peace, restfulness, and quiet repose. The garden has become a place of refuge from an increasingly synthetic world, providing a private place to relax.

Grandiose borders and tapestries of color, even when designed with consummate skill, somehow do not fit this tranquil goal. Neither do the many strongly colored individual elements of these borders, perennials, and some annuals. Yet, many years ago, I found my perfect perennial in one of these borders. Unaffected by its kaleidoscopic neighbors it presented a picture of serenity and dignity. The name on the label hidden under the leaf mound was barely legible: Siebold's Funkia. The stately mound, almost three feet high, was just overtopped by sturdy stalks with white flowers. Large heart-shaped leaves held high by strong petioles were dusted with a comforting, deep blue-grey frosting. Up close their indescribable texture added visual excitement to the otherwise serene habit. Traversed by many parallel veins following the curvature of the margins, the leaf surface was dimpled, wrinkled, and pleated—a veritable dance of light and shadow of almost infinite contrast. Soon after, I found this magnificent plant was correctly called a *Hosta*. I learned there were others—green ones with white margins, yellow-variegated ones, and a host of others. In one garden I followed a delicious scent to find a hosta with bright green leaves and large, waxy, white flowers emanating that fragrance.

Now, 40 years later, I know my own personal search for the perfect perennial ended with the discovery of Siebold's Funkia. Making my third garden, called Hosta Hill, and growing hostas for almost 30 years it has become quite obvious that these plants are simple to use, require little maintenance other than clean-up—no staking, tending, lifting, dividing, babying—and fit anywhere. Reportedly, insects do not bother them, but larger slugs and snails may eat holes through the arising shoots resulting in perforated leaves. Most U.S. gardeners meet this challenge by applying poisons, while the more pragmatic Japanese gardeners most often leave things as they are and consider holes in hosta leaves as being nature's way.

Few perennials offer a 6- to 8-month display (depending on latitude) in the garden. Granted, the plants pass through different stages, looking their best in late spring, but they remain attractive from the time they emerge until the first frost turns their leaves into a warm buff or golden yellow to brighten up the usually dreary, grey, late autumn garden (Plate 43).

I daresay no other perennial plant offers the tremendous diversity seen in the modern hosta assortment: plant sizes from tiny crowns fitting into the palm of a hand to huge mounds of shrub-size proportions; plant habits from tall, erect vase shapes to starry pinwheels lying flat on the ground; leaf shapes from grasslike strap leaves to nearly perfectly round circles; leaf features from flat to dimpled, wrinkled, cupped, or twisted; leaf substances from thin and papery to thick as leather; surface effects from polished and shiny to matte, pruinose, even powdery white; leaf colors from blue-green through the entire green range to chartreuse, yellow, and almost silvery white; variegation patterns from narrow and wide margins to bright centers on dark surrounds and multicolored streakings and splashings; scapes from tall and erect, some overtopping a tall man, to oblique, with some scapes lying flat on the ground. Some hostas start blooming in early June, but by carefully combining early, average-, and late-flowering hostas, a succession of bloom lasting into October can be established providing a cool, white or lavender show during the hot summer months and beyond. Flowers are diverse and come as large, waxy, white trumpets emanating a delicious fragrance or as purple, wide-open bells, with almost every combination in between. Even the seed capsules show great variety. The combinations are almost infinite.

Aside from all other considerations mentioned, hostas give a high return on investment of initial costs and labor. They are long-lived, frequently outliving the gardener. Compared to other perennials, the more common hostas cost about the same, although some of the newer cultivars can be very expensive. Once planted and given reasonable care, hostas multiply faithfully and, in most cases, rapidly, so offsetting the initial cost by quickly providing root divisions which can be sold, exchanged, or planted elsewhere in the garden.

In the final analysis, hostas are makers of gardeners because what makes enthusiastic gardeners out of reluctant ones is the sweet smell of success. Hostas practically guarantee success, and with success comes a willingness to work harder to achieve more.

SELECTION—A DAUNTING TASK

A quick glance at the many names in Chapters 3 and 4 quickly shows that the most daunting task facing gardeners is sorting out the available diversity and choosing from the ever-increasing selection of hostas. In this chapter I give basic directions for placing hostas in the landscape and help for selecting appropriate species and cultivars by referring to selected groups using abbreviations enclosed in parenthesis, thus (VMG) = variegated margin group. Whenever these group abbreviations appear in the following text, any one of the hostas listed under the group names given in the "List of Recommended Species and Cultivars" at the end of this chapter can be used, provided the instructions pertaining to size are followed as well. For this reason some major groups listed are subdivided into several size categories. Other minor groups are listed alphabetically, and size can be determined from the descriptions in Chapters 3 and 4. The group abbreviations follow (for color definitions see Chapter 2 and Appendix D).

Color Groups

As pointed out in Chapter 2 and Appendix D, some colors in these groups are neither true colors nor are they permanent. For example, the "blue" appearance of the leaves in the blue group may turn to green or dark green with the advancing seasons. As a consequence, groupings of hostas selected from this group will look bluish in May but green in August. Likewise, yellow can turn to chartreuse or green, and chartreuse can change to whitish. Variegation can change to plain green as it does in members of the irregularly variegated group which are color-unstable. Some taxa are viridescent and emerge with variegated leaves that normally turn green later. The impact of these changes on color balance and harmony should be considered when making selections from these groups.

GG = Green Group: Light, medium, or dark green leaves.

BG = Blue Group: Bluish grey-green or blue-green leaves.

YG = Yellow Group: Any shade of yellow or chartreuse leaves. (Although technically considered a yellowish green, most gardeners consider chartreuse a yellow color, so it is included here.)

VMG = Variegated Margin Group: Dark principal leaf color with light (whitish or yellow) whitish margin.

VCG = Variegated Center Group: Light (whitish, chartreuse, or yellow) principal central leaf color with darker-(usually green-) margin.

VIG = Irregularly Variegated Group: Light (whitish, chartreuse, or yellow) streakings, stripes, blotches, or other irregular variegation on a darker (usually green) colored leaf. It has been reported that many of these variegation types are unstable and will eventually revert to solid color or margined forms.

Size Groups

Special consideration has been given to the very small group and to some of the giant-leaved hostas to allow rapid selection of these two extreme sizes for special plantings.

TG = Tiny Group: Selected very small hostas classified as dwarf.

MG = Mammoth Group: Selected very large hostas classified as giant.

Special Purpose Groups

Hostas suitable for edging or accents, and those known to be fragrant or having a distinct, erect habit, have been singled out and grouped because of their special use in gardens.

EG = Edger Group: Hostas suitable for edgings. Most selections are inexpensive to allow purchase of large numbers usually required for landscaping. Many are small and lance-leaved, but other types are included, so please refer to individual descriptions for details.

RG = Erect Group: A selection from the many erect-leaved hostas available which have pronounced vertical habit, such as H. 'Krossa Regal'.

AG = Accent Group: Any of the giant hostas make good accent plants, particularly the yellow or variegated ones and large erect hostas, so only outstanding selections are repeated. Those listed are exceptional hostas, some expensive, which deserve planting in special accent positions.

FG = Fragrant Group: Hostas which have fragrant blooms.

Rules of Selection

The basic rules I have followed for selecting species and cultivars are as follows:

1. *Availability*: The selected hostas are available either in North America, Europe, or Japan usually in specialty nurseries or by mail order. Those widely available are marked with an asterisk, thus *. Some Japanese cultivars are becoming available in North America, but most of them may have to be ordered from Japanese nurseries, and conversely, varieties generally available in North America may have to be imported by Japanese buyers. In Europe the list of available varieties is growing steadily, but some of the newer U.S. and Japanese varieties may also require direct overseas purchase. In areas where no specialty nurseries exist, direct mail-order buying is the only way to obtain the newer varieties. Some of those described in this book have entered propagation stage or tissue culture while this book was in preparation and are projected to be available, but their commercial availability is uncertain. Occasionally, some of the more exceptional types may be withdrawn for increase, so may be hard to get. A worldwide list of hosta nurseries is printed at the end of this chapter. Some of these sell only locally, but most of them will accept mail orders and ship internationally. I recommend gardeners contact them for catalogs and ordering instructions.

2. *Cost*: In North America, where availability is best, advertised prices of individual plants (usually 1–3 eye divisions or potted, tissue-cultured plants) range from U.S. $3 to $200 with the average price being around U.S. $10. In Europe and Japan costs are about the same in the respective local currencies, but because of their relative scarcity some of the newer U.S. cultivars may demand much higher prices there. Most of the plants I have selected are available for U.S. $5 to $10, but some outstanding cultivars and species costing between U.S. $15 and $50 also have been selected. The price of a particular cultivar can vary considerably depending on available stock at a given nursery, and it pays to obtain catalogs and compare before buying. When ordering from foreign countries, special import permits may have to be obtained and shipping costs may be high, adding to the cost of the plants.

3. *Adaptability*: In the wild, hosta species grow from latitude 30° (Yaku Island) to 55° (Sakhalin) north. In cultivation I have observed them as far north as 60° latitude (Uppsala, Sweden), and some cultivated species are reported from south-central China near 25° north. In the Southern Hemisphere cultivation is recorded in New Zealand and Australia from 35° to about 45° south latitude. All selections are based on adaptability to these climatic zones with the stipulation that in the colder areas some hostas may not flower or, if they do, their flowers may be spoiled by early frosts. Conversely, in the warmer latitudes hosta shoots may arise early, only to be cut down by late freezes. Very generally, optimum growing conditions exist in the following zones: In North America from a line between the south-central parts of the southeastern states of Georgia and Alabama to and along the southern Canadian border, across the Midwest and Plain states, and from central California to Vancouver Island; in Europe from south-central France, southern Germany, and the Balkan countries north of Greece to a line between Edinburgh, Scotland, and north of Stockholm, Sweden (Uppsala); in Japan from Yakushima to northern Hokkaido; in all Korea; in southern Australia and New Zealand north of latitude 45° south; in the temperate western areas of the USSR and along the Japan Sea coast; and in central and north-central China, although cultivation extends into parts of

southeastern China. Obviously, there are many other areas in the temperate climatic zone in which hostas can be cultivated successfully.

A PROPER FIT

Use of hostas as garden perennials is nothing new. Some have been included in gardens for a century and a half. What is new and exciting is the exclusive use of hostas in isolated areas of gardens and the making of gardens in which hostas are the key perennial, used almost exclusively, aside from inclusion of a few companion plants. One example is the consummate garden of Mr. Toshihiko Satake in Higashi-Hiroshima city (Plate 146). The sudden spurt of interest in hostas during the last 20 years is primarily due to a change in basic gardening practice. With competent and inexpensive help no longer easily available, contemporary gardeners are forced to reduce their garden maintenance by turning to labor-saving machinery, methods, and plants. The rediscovery of hostas as premier maintenance-free plants coincides with this change. More importantly, hybridizers began to work with the genus and in a few, short years have created hundreds of cultivars which fit properly into the modern garden.

Proper fit means appropriateness, suitability, and adaptability. Fortunately, most hostas have built-in proper fit, provided some of the basic rules of garden design are applied, but hostas are so adaptable that occasionally even a few rules can be ignored. As to garden design, hundreds of books have been written dealing with this subject in glowing terms and using a special language replete with technical terminology: asymmetry, balance, composition, density, focal point, harmony, proportion, scale, structure, unity, variety, and many others. The profession and practice of landscape architecture and landscape gardening grew up around the making of gardens. Rich novice gardeners about to design and plant a large garden should not hesitate to seek the help of these design professionals. But today's average gardeners plan on a much smaller scale. Most are already maintaining a modest garden or are in the process of making their own small garden. For them the plethora of garden design can be reduced to three simple rules which will almost always give proper fit:

1. **Right place**
2. **Right number**
3. **Right color**

In addition to these three rights, there is a fourth, implicit one: *Right for the gardener*. Never mind all the books and rules. Gardens must be right for their owners and makers, reflecting their individual personalities and tastes. Most gardens are planted for private viewing and should therefore show the owners' and makers' individuality. The very best private gardens are not only designed well, but they also have that certain mien which only the makers' individuality can impart on the overall scheme. This can be seen in many of the photographs included with this chapter.

Right Place
Common Sense. For an existing garden border or a small flower bed, tucking in a hosta here and there will whet the appetite. The simple and inexpensive ones are the best choices for a start. Because they are inexpensive it is possible to buy a dozen or more and plant what can be considered the most effective way to show hostas in a garden: groups of the same variety. Good choices are the shiny green *H.* 'Lancifolia' (EG) (Figure 3-37), the blue-green *H.* 'Fortunei Hyacinthina' (Figure 3-12; Plate 24), or the white-margined *H.* 'Decorata' (VMG) (Plate 13). If there is no border, but a few trees or shrubs hold their

place in the garden, congregating a few hosta plants around and at the base of these will quickly result in improvement. This is not expensive if *H. ventricosa* is selected as it comes true from seed so can be seed-raised by patient gardeners and planted round the base of a tree (Figure 6-1). This is certainly the easiest approach to hosta gardening, because it does not require careful balancing of many different elements. In most situations it works very well because hostas fit in almost anywhere. For novice gardeners this is one of the best ways to start, because it results in the little successes so necessary to gain confidence. A majority of gardeners need to experiment and make occasional mistakes and in so doing add to their skills. With this they usually have a lot of fun by learning, maturing, and realizing the many rewards of gardening, which include a sense of achievement, pride, and satisfaction.

Figure 6-1. *H. ventricosa*; landscape use (Cochran garden/Schmid)

Carrying the common-sense approach a little further, it should be obvious to all that a huge clump of a *H. sieboldiana* cultivar (MG) (Plates 60, 138) in the middle of a small rock garden is totally out of place. Likewise, putting the tiny *H. venusta* (TG) (Figure 3-78) or equally minute hostas (Figure 4-44) among dense ground cover or under large hosta clumps will hide them from view, and they will be lost in the landscape.

Unfortunately, quite a few gardeners do not have the ability to visualize a garden scene before it is actually planted nor can they visualize what it might look like when the plants reach maturity. To them I suggest keeping hostas, even large ones, in plastic pots of adequate size which they can place in holes in the garden, pot and all, backfilling as required. This technique allows observation of a particular design for a season or two, and modification, if necessary, will be easy. If a hosta looks out of place it can simply be lifted out of the ground, again pot and all, and moved to a more appropriate location. The potted hostas are not hurt by this move, and after final positions are found, the plastic containers can be removed and the hostas planted permanently. Using this method the right place can be found by trial and error. Some will call this a shotgun approach, but it works. It is down-to-earth and suits many gardeners because it allows them to visualize different arrangements by actual trial.

Some highly skilled gardeners use a similar method, without digging the holes, but for a different reason. They place the pots on top of the ground, mound up topsoil around them, and dress the mounds or berms with pine bark chips or another decorative mulch. Simple and effective, this method is used principally to eliminate competition from the roots of maples, willows, tulip trees, and other trees with greedy root systems near the surface. It is important to water the potted

Chapter 6

hostas inside the mounds regularly because the potted soil concentrates the roots and dries faster than the surrounding soil. Trickle irrigation to each pot is an ideal solution to this problem. Having the same portability as pots sunk into the ground, these berms can be taken down and rebuilt elsewhere on the property during a weekend. Warren and Ali Pollock, whose fine hosta garden near Wilmington, DE, U.S.A., won the coveted AHS Harshbarger landscape award in 1987, employ such a method, and to show that very large clumps can be maintained this way I have provided a color illustration with the owners among their hostas (Plate 147).

More technically inclined gardeners will try to educate themselves before they dig the first hole. Buying a few good books on garden layout and design and applying the principles learned to hosta placement will go a long way to realizing an exceptional garden without making too many mistakes in the process.

Perspective. There are a few tricks that can be used to enhance the chance of giving hostas the right place. One is a visual phenomenon called perspective. To the human eye objects look smaller as they become more distant. Gardeners can take advantage of this by planting larger plants up front and progressively smaller ones toward the rear. This accentuates normal perspective and makes the garden plot look larger than it really is. The same effect can be obtained by planting bright-colored hostas in front and darker ones, especially the blue-green and grey shades, to the rear.

Lining a walk with hostas on both sides directs the view and accentuates perspective (Plate 148), thus setting the stage for surprises just around the corner (Plate 149).

Surprises. Experienced gardeners use surprises, which are perhaps just another trick. Laying out garden walks with curves and corners will increase their visual length (Figure 6-2; Plate 150) and afford the opportunity to plan surprises. Large or colorful variegated hostas planted at or just around the bend will be a visual surprise and lead the visitor on to the next, maybe even bigger surprise. The surprise can also be a garden sculpture (Figure 6-3), a water feature, or garden seating. Some say this surprise technique works only the first time a person goes through a garden. This is not true because garden surprises, though no longer true surprises, retain a powerful visual impact at every visit.

Figure 6-3. *H. sieboldiana*; landscape use at focal point (Villa de Bella Fiore, Dorough design/Schmid)

Accents. Hostas make outstanding accents. The bold shapes of large hosta clumps belonging to the *H. sieboldiana* group and its many named hybrids (in BG) make perfect accent plants and so do the larger varieties of *H. montana* parentage. Selected large-leaved yellow cultivars, such as *H.* 'Sum and Substance' (Plate 151) or *H.* 'Sun Power', are suitable for prominent accents particularly in the darker areas of the garden. Special places in gardens often require special selections, and *H. montana* 'Aureomarginata' (Plate 45), *H.* 'Color Glory', *H. fortunei* 'Gold Standard' (Plate 152), and *H.* 'Great Expectations' (Plate 153), all in AG, are good choices. Even very inexpensive plain green hostas can be accents if used correctly. An example is *H.* 'Undulata Erromena' planted at the entrance to a moss garden (Plate 150). Accents should be used sparingly because too many cancel each other out and thus defeat the purpose for which they were planted.

Focal Points. Surprises are among the eye-catchers of a garden and often become focal points—places in a landscape where lines of sight come to rest. When a focal point is close, garden accents can be planted at that spot; some examples are a very large (MG) (Plate 154) or colorful hosta (VMG or VCG) or a garden sculpture (Figure 6-3). The focal point can also be an archway that opens to another part of the garden (Figure 6-4) or perhaps a closed gate leading nowhere (usually a neighbor's garden is on the other side). A narrow walk lined, for example, with *H.* 'Lancifolia' (EG), and leading up to a gate in the focal point makes observers think there is more on the other side, tricking them into visualizing a property much larger than it actually is. By borrowing the neighbors' trees and shrubs gardeners can visually expand their own domain beyond its actual boundaries.

Figure 6-2. *H.* 'Undulata Albomarginata' planted alongside the hosta walk of Hosta Hill (Hosta Hill)

Figure 6-4. *H.* 'Undulata Albomarginata' (left) and annuals as edgings leading to an archway (Villa de Bella Fiore, Dorough design/Schmid)

Definition of Space. Hostas make great edging plants. Lining walks laid out with sinuous curves, hostas will define them, stretch their visual length, and guide the visitor to the next view or a place of rest. Many of the small lance-leaved hostas are ideally suited for this. *Hosta* 'Lancifolia', all the members of the *H. sieboldii* group, such as *H. sieboldii* 'Kabitan' and 'Subcrocea', and *H.* 'Gold Edger' or *H.* 'Ginko Craig' (all in EG), serve this purpose well (Plates 67, 159). Larger edgings can be obtained by using the inexpensive *H.* 'Undulata' and *H.* 'Undulata Univittata' (Plate 155), *H.* 'Undulata Albomarginata' (Figures 6-2, 6-4), or a small group of *H. rectifolia* (Plate 55) to define a walk. Even very large cultivars mixed with other hostas can define garden pathways (Plate 92). Except for the very large varieties almost any hosta can be used for edgings, but those just mentioned have the advantage of being inexpensive, a plus because many plants are usually required for edgings. Gardeners using medium-size hostas like *H.* 'Undulata Albomarginata' need to consider that eventually the edging will expand to a width of up to three feet or more and cover part of the walk if planted right at the walk's boundary line. To define a small collector's bed of dwarf hostas, edgings of *H. nakaiana* or the even smaller *H. venusta* are excellent.

Whether defining small areas with edgings of hostas or using boundaries on a larger scale, such as trees, hedges, walls, fences, and shrubs, the effect is to demarcate outdoor garden rooms in which collections of perennials, including hostas, can be grown. These defined garden spaces may be formal, square or rectangular designs, or they may be free-flowing, irregular spaces. They may be small, isolated spaces alongside a walk, providing small, colorful vignettes shading off into a green background (Plate 156). Regardless of their layout, all of them afford privacy and thus increase the intimacy of space. They cause gardeners to linger, and they invite closer inspection of hosta collections and other plants presented there (Plate 157). These outdoor spaces can be very large, and placing garden seating in them makes them true places of repose into which hostas fit superbly (Plate 158). On the other hand, these defined spaces adapt well to today's cramped conditions and can be realized in very small areas (Plate 159). Larger gardens benefit from being divided into a number of smaller areas that are separated from each other, each featuring its own marvels.

Balance and Harmony. Depending on tastes and intentions, balance and harmony are complicated subjects. Some gardeners like symmetry and formality, while others prefer a more natural, informal look. Balance and harmony can exist in either of these settings. Aside from color, a subject covered later, the achievement of balance and harmony involves careful selection and placement of the individual plants and garden elements, so many gardeners resort to experimentation. Attainment of this goal is probably the most important requisite to transforming gardens into works of art, but it should be remembered gardeners frequently have their own vision of paradise. Mine includes hostas. While they can contribute to a formalized layout (Plate 160), they are superb additions in a natural garden, and I recommend the latter style as one which best fits modern layout (Plate 157).

Hostas can be placed in just a few spots in a garden where they make excellent accents (Plate 161) or they can be companion plants to a majority of other types of herbaceous plants and shrubs. They usually fit splendidly into established borders (Plate 162). If the elements forming a landscape already have balance and harmony, the addition of hostas will frequently improve the composition when the blue-green hostas (BG) of the *H.* Tardiana grex or other blue-green or grey-green (BG) hostas, like *H.* 'Fortunei Hyacinthina' (Plate 24) or *H.* 'Snowden' (Plate 163), are selected. Using hostas in larger borders as balancing elements requires larger ones such as *H. sieboldiana*, *H.* 'Blue Angel', *H.* 'True Blue', or any of the larger blue hostas (BG) (Plates 92, 164). Sizable green hostas (GG) can also be used, particularly if they provide visual texture such as the rugose, deeply furrowed leaves of *H. montana* f. *macrophylla* (Plate 46) or the piecrust margins of *H.* 'Birchwood Ruffled Queen' or *H.* 'Ruffles'. The smaller, inconspicuous, green types may get lost in the other greenery. The lesson is that balance and harmony require some contrast.

Planting a few hostas here and there reveals their many positive features and soon compels most gardeners to add more. Currently in North America many gardens are being made where hostas are the dominant element, so harmony and balance must be found in the selection and placement of the hostas.

Essential to balance and harmony are the bones of the garden—the trees, shrubs, and hedges, and perhaps also a few man-made constructions. Perish the thought, but if a garden plot must be started from a bare piece of ground, these bones should always be planted first. They will eventually determine the essence of a garden and therefore should be located with great care and forethought. I highly recommend gardeners copy from nature and use natural groupings, remembering that 3 and 5 are better than 2 and 4, a principle that applies to planting hostas as well (Plate 160). If trees and shrubs are already present, they should be retained, if at all possible, and permitted to dictate the layout. The only thing gardeners might want to do is cut some paths and plant hostas in groups alongside and in between trees and shrubs. This natural approach befits hostas and results in balance and harmony much more frequently than the approach which imposes a formalized layout on nature. Square and rectangular beds can be used around the house (Plate 165) and terrace but are difficult to fit in the garden. Yet I have seen some where this rule was violated, and the formal beds looked good because the hostas had happily obliterated the geometric patterns with their overhanging leaves by growing beyond the straight boundaries, thus softening them and again showing their great adaptability.

Companion Plants. Where hostas are the predominant element in a garden and other perennials become companion plants, the most successful companions are those perennials that contrast the large bold masses of hosta leaves. But it is equally important to select plants which emerge in spring coincidentally with the hostas and which retain their habit in good condition until late fall, just like the hostas. In the following I have left out some excellent plants simply because they disappear leaving empty spots in the planting.

Premier companions for hostas are the many ferns whose delicate fronds are in perfect contrast to bold hosta leaves (Plates 52, 110, 119). Grasses and sedges offer vertical accents, as do any of the plants with lance-shaped leaves: iris (Plate 166), daylily (*Hemerocallis*), lily of the valley (*Convallaria*), *Crocosmia* (Plate 149), *Liriope* (Plate 160), *Carex* (Figure 4-44), *Ophiopogon*, cast iron plant (*Aspidistra elatior*) (Plate 157), *Rohdea japonica*, and yucca. The gracefully arching stems of *Polygonatum* and toad lily (*Tricyrtis*) provide exciting highlights and are easy to grow. The near-evergreen *Epimedium* (Figure 6-5) and all members of the genus *Helleborus* fit in well (Plate 167). Small-leaved ground covers such as purple and bronze *Ajuga* provide an excellent foil for yellow, chartreuse, and light green, indeed, all hostas (Plates 149, 156), and the silvery lamium (*Lamium roseum*) or variegated strawberry geranium (*Saxifraga sarmentosa* or *stolonifera*) go well with blue-green or dark green varieties (Plates 54, 128, 156, 168, 169). Excellent companions can be found in plants with incised and divided leaves, first and foremost *Astilbe* (Figure 6-5; Plate 170) and *Rodgersia* (Plates 90, 163, 171), *Acanthus*, goat's beard

(*Aruncus*), bugbane (*Cimicifuga*), false dragonhead (*Physostegia*), and *Kirengeshoma palmata* (Plate 86). *Asarum*, *Bergenia*, and *Brunnera* make fine additions and so do lungwort (*Pulmonaria*), *Ligularia* (Plate 164), and the evergreen beetleweed (*Galax urceolata*) of southeastern North America. Even the very large-leaved foliage plants, like *Rheum palmatum* 'Atrosanguineum' (Plate 179), make good companions, although they must be used in the background and with some judgment. The horsetails (*Equisetum arvense*, *praealtum*, and *laevigatum*) and some smaller bamboos provide excellent contrast but are invasive and need to be planted in heavy plastic or stone pots sunk into the ground to keep them from taking over the garden. Except for some evergreen plants among these, all those listed come up with the hostas and go dormant about the same time the hostas do.

Figure 6-5. *H.* 'Antioch' with *Epimedium* (top left); *H.* 'Little Aurora' next to Japanese Painted Fern (*Athyrium niponicum* var. *pictum*) hiding under *Astilbe* (bottom right); *H.* 'Undulata Albomarginata' (bottom left); followed by *H. longipes* (center), and *H.* 'Fortunei Viridis' (Hosta Hill)

I do not recommend underplanting hostas with spring bulbs, like tulips or hyacinths, because unsightly ripening foliage in and among the hosta clumps spoils the picture during the best hosta display period. The true lilies, however, make excellent companions and so do all the bulbous plants that retain their leaves all season, provided they are color compatible. I am using some rather exotic bulbs for this purpose. An example is *Amorphophallus rivieri* (Araceae) (Plate 157), which is also called *Hydrosme rivieri* or snake palm, and which I retain in the ground where it multiplies by offsets. In colder areas the bulbs can be kept in pots and plunged outdoors in late spring after danger of frost has passed. Snake palm has a rather unpleasant smell, but its lacy and very unusual divided leaf form goes well with hostas. Other exotics make fine companions, as for example, the calla lilies (*Zantedeschia aethiopica*) (Plate 172). Where ground conditions are suitable, primulas are excellent companions (Plates 24, 173).

Inclusion of these companions will not automatically assure balance and harmony, but it will provide contrast. Contrast in the right places and in the right proportions will go a long way toward establishing balance and proper fit. In the end, it is up to gardeners to seek the balance and harmony which most appropriately fit their own individual proclivity. Above all, gardeners should experiment, for experimentation will lead to invention, and invention to uniqueness. Playing it safe can only lead to boredom.

A Place in the Shade. Most gardeners consider hostas shade plants. A few even think that hostas must be grown in the shade. However, the right place for hostas may not be in the shade but rather in the sun (literally), and this placement has nothing to do with art and garden design, but is very important nevertheless. Shade can mean many different levels of light. Some gardeners consider as shady those deep, dark corners of a garden where almost nothing will grow. Others see only light overhead shade with lots of sunshine coming through. Actually shade exists in both these situations and comes in many intensities, from very light to very dark.

In their natural habitat hostas usually do not grow in very dense shade. They frequently colonize at the margins of deciduous forests, around and in forest canopy openings, on rock outcrops usually along sunny banks and waterfalls in open river valleys, and even out in open, sunny, usually swampy or moist grasslands where in spring they emerge early and get a lot of full sun until the leaf crowns are shaded out in early summer by tall grasses, weeds, and sub-shrubs.

Using natural habitat as a guide, it becomes obvious that hostas are not the true shade plants most horticultural authorities make them out to be. This idea may have started because they do grow quite well in shady places, better than many other plants. The blue-green varieties actually succeed in shady cool places, keeping their blue-grey pruinosity much longer in shade than they would in sunshine. Hostas with green, chartreuse, and yellow leaf colors can stand quite a lot of direct sun as long as their root systems have plenty of moisture available at all times. Too much sun, especially in more southern regions, will bleach the lighter green and yellow colors. In cases of high exposure, burning can occur, and thin leaves are more prone to burning than leaves of heavy substance.

Conversely, too much shade can also adversely affect hosta growth rates and prevent flowering altogether. Hostas will not thrive in dark corners where nothing else will grow. They may exist and persist, but flourish they will not. Some cultural failures with hostas are probably due to the plants not getting enough sun or strong, indirect light to photosynthesize (Schmid, 1990). Gardeners should be circumspect when planting hostas in very dense shade.

Relative exposure, length of day, average cloud cover, and light intensity all have something to do with correct and optimum hosta placement. The right place for hosta varieties is usually one that closely approximates the natural conditions under which their parents dwell in the wild. The species and associated varieties coming from southern China, southern Korea, and southern and central Japan usually require a good amount of sunshine and longer seasons for flowering. Those from northern Japan—Hokkaido and farther north—have shorter seasons, prefer cooler climates, and can usually take more shade.

Aside from geographic considerations, parental native habitat influences the endurance of species and varieties in the garden. This means grassland hostas and their offspring can take considerable amounts of sun in spring but require some cover during the hot summer months. Forest-dwelling hostas prefer a more shady environment, but this does not mean dense shade. They do best in filtered shade, with occasional direct sun, preferably morning sun, on their leaves.

Some gardeners may want to determine the right place by experimenting with different locations. It is difficult to make specific recommendations on planting location because the number of potential microclimates is incalculable. When placing hostas in the garden, it is very important to remember they will thrive in some shade but will also need a fair amount of sun or high light levels for maximum increase and flowering. That is why many commercial growers raise their hostas in sun-drenched field rows.

Detailed information on the habitat of species is given in Chapter 3, while Chapter 4 gives the specific breeding lines (parentage) for cultivars, when known. Study of this information will provide a guide to the preferable sun exposure for a given species or variety.

Visit and Learn. One of the best ways to find out about the concept of right place and what balance and harmony are all about is to visit gardens. Next best is the study of recently published, illustrated books on gardens, most of which feature excellent color photography and thus permit gardeners to develop visual concepts of harmonious design before they dig their first planting hole. Emulating good design may be considered copying by some, but it will educate gardeners, and the learning experience will eventually contribute to the development of original concepts.

The American Horticultural Society and many of the national horticultural or specialty societies feature annual garden tours. More specifically, national and regional hosta societies exist in North America and the United Kingdom, and publish membership lists. These societies can be contacted for membership and annual regional and national garden tours, and they will frequently help with visits. The AHS has regional coordinators who can arrange local garden visits. The gardens are too numerous to be listed but the addresses of the AHS and BHHS are given at the end of this chapter.

In North America fine hosta collections can be found at the Minnesota Landscape Arboretum, Chanhassen. In England several National *Hosta* Reference Collections exist and large hosta displays can be seen at the gardens of the Royal Horticultural Society at Wisley (Plate 174), at Savill Gardens in Windsor Great Park (Plate 164), and at Hadspen House (Plate 175). In Germany botanical-horticultural schools at several universities (Fachhochschulen) maintain Stauden-Sichtungs-gärten (literally "perennial-viewing grounds"), which feature hosta selections, as do many of the German botanic gardens (Figure 3-63). Many other temperate-zone botanical and public gardens and parks in Japan, North America, and Europe feature large hosta plantings as well, and gardeners should plan visits if they are near them. A telephone inquiry can usually confirm the existence of such plantings. Finally, most hosta specialty nurseries listed at the end of this chapter have large display gardens, maintain collections of mature *Hosta* cultivars, and encourage visits and viewing.

Right Number

Good gardening is, among other things, a numbers game, so it is important to get the right number. The rules are simple: For accents there should never be more than one in a given, defined area, and the total number of accents in a garden should be limited because too many become commonplace and cease to be accents. When using hostas as accents, one may be enough. Any of the large (MG) or dominant (AG) hostas can serve this purpose, or a single, large yellow one, depending on the foil (Plate 161). A small group of identical varieties, no more than 3 or 5, planted closely together can also serve as an accent group (Plate 176). When planting small groups of less than 20 hostas, always plant in odd numbers—3s, 5s, 7s, or more. Odd numbers force odd geometry and assure a more natural look.

When planting for mass effect (Figures 3-13, 3-37, 4-18; Plates 47, 63, 143, 177, 178), the odd or even numbers no longer matter because the human eye can no longer quickly perceive a count of individual plants but discerns only masses. For mass plantings which stretch over large areas of a border and require large numbers of hostas, inexpensive hostas like *H.* 'Undulata Albomarginata' can be used (Plate 165), although the somewhat more expensive *H.* 'Tall Boy' is spectacular in mass plantings (Plate 179). In these plantings, the adjacent plants usually grow together into a continuous group, although fine displays can be seen where they are carefully

spaced (Plate 178). Mass plantings using large numbers of hostas can be magnificent if correctly designed, but even on a much smaller scale they make fine displays (Plate 169). Gardeners with very limited space can have mass plantings, of sorts, by filling a planter box or a small patio bed with small or tiny hostas (TG) of the same kind (Figure 3-78; Plate 63).

Numbers are all-important when selecting color and visual contrast. A glut of all kinds of variegated hostas may be too garish, or too many yellow ones in one area may be distracting, while too much plain green (GG) or blue-green (BG) may be boring. Accent (AG) hostas add excitement and color to the hosta garden but should be carefully selected and placed (Plate 146). Often the expensive and newer varieties are chosen for this purpose, ostensibly to give them prominent display (Plate 153). But less-expensive, multicolor variegated (VIG), all-yellow (YG), or variegated (VMG and VCG) serve equally as well as accents (Plate 180). Additional information about this is given later under "Right Color." Accent hostas can also be 1, 3, or 5 tall erect types, like *H.* 'Krossa Regal', either as a solitary group (Plate 124) or in a field of lower-growing, small green (GG) hostas, such as *H. nakaiana*, or underplanted by a mass of small yellow (YG) ones.

Numbers are all-important to what is called plant mix. Plant mix comprises all the different types of plants combined in a garden. If a garden has a lot of color already by way of flowering shrubs and a multitude of perennials, blue (BG) and green (GG) hostas better realize correct mix and balance. As with all basic rules, there is an exception to this one, too. Some gardeners may want to build an all-yellow garden in which all flowers and accent leaf colors are yellow. In this case large numbers of yellow-variegated hostas will contribute, not detract. Good displays of such schemes are difficult to accomplish, and they are often too garish and intense. Much easier to place in the overall scheme of hosta gardens or gardens in general are monochromatic island beds, berms, or borders in which hostas of a single leaf color are displayed. These arrangements almost always work because they can be juxtaposed against other, major garden elements. When using bright colors, such as yellow (YG), I caution against making group arrangements too large (i.e., using too large a number of individual plants) because they may upset a garden's total balance. Binding such beds with green edger hostas (EG) or *Liriope* cultivars will contain the color and give better definition to the bed.

Obviously, the number of hostas selected for any given spot in the garden will depend not only on the three rights discussed here, but also on other factors, such as available garden space and ultimately on the individual gardener's pocket book. Some years ago financial considerations forced me to adopt a number tactic which I recommend to all: When buying expensive hostas always buy two. As contradictory as this may sound as a strategy to save money, it will do so in the long run. The larger and better one of the two can be planted in that favorite spot and left undisturbed to grow into an exemplary specimen clump. The other can be relegated to the propagating area and divided as many times as practical year after year to build up stock. With this strategy twice the money is spent initially, but after a few seasons gardeners wind up with tenfold their investment (hostas are an investment!) and are able to exchange the extra hostas for other plant material. This tactic requires one other ingredient which no amount of money can buy, namely, patience, but I assume gardeners sooner or later learn to be patient.

The tactic just outlined can be used when gardeners with adequate space want to install massed hostas which they propagate themselves. Propagating is an easy process: Lift a clump and with a sharp knife cut it into wedge-shaped sections, each with an eye (shoot) and some attached roots. The best time to do this is late summer or early fall (see Appendix G). Each will grow into a plant, even very small pieces, as I found out when dividing a very expensive hosta: The knife slipped, producing a very thin sliver of the rhizome with a couple of tiny roots, but planted this small root piece quickly produced a small plant.

Right Color

In the triad of the "three rights," color selection is easily the most perplexing one. Technical definitions of hosta color are given in Chapter 2 and Appendix D, where color is considered more for classification and as a morphological tool. In this chapter color is dealt with as an artistic attribute, albeit a very vague one, because the nature of color in the art of gardening is imprecise and differently perceived and understood.

Color Perception. Scientifically, color is reflected light of different wavelengths. Pigments in plants absorb some of the natural light that illuminates them, and the reflected light is modified in this way to be combinations of red, yellow, and blue which result in an infinity of color variations. What makes the subject so vast and difficult is the distinction between the physical basis of this reflected light (wavelength in angstroms) and the different sensations produced by these light waves in humans.

Most individuals will feel colors more than they see them, so color combinations are either pleasant sensations or they evoke disdain. These color feelings have a lot to do with personal likes and dislikes; some individuals are more drawn towards yellow or red, while others prefer cool colors like blue or even white (yes, white is a color). Even when they see colors, people see them differently because the impulses transmitting light waves from the optical nerve of the eye register in slightly dissimilar fashion on the human brain. Some individuals are even color blind and have a distorted color image.

Quite frequently observers may even be mentally influenced as to what color they want to see: Blue hostas are not really blue, and the terms "gold" and "silver" as they relate to colors in hosta leaves are strictly in the eyes of the beholder. I have discussed this phenomenon in Chapter 2.

Because colors are reflected light, the quality of the natural light which is reflected also influences color. Brilliant direct sunshine or light filtered through a cloudy overcast affects the resulting color. Moreover, colors are almost never viewed in isolation, but in combination with others and so are visually (and mentally) modified. It is easy to see that the important judgment and selection of color is a difficult task.

Complicating things further is the temporal nature of plant colors which undergo changes from spring until after the first frost. Hosta societies are well aware of this and time their annual conventions and garden visits to dates when they expect leaf colors to be near perfection. The seasonal change of hosta leaf color from pruinose blue-green to just plain green, from golden yellow to chartreuse, or from bright yellow to off-white, is well known and documented. The early spring leaves of some yellow hostas have a different color than the leaves arising later. An example is *H.* 'Lunar Eclipse' which has greenish vernal leaves and bright yellow summer leaves. The combination can look strange indeed (Plate 129). Technical terms used for classification in Chapter 2, such as viridescent (becoming green), lutescent (turning yellow), and albescent (changing to white), point to the importance of considering the impermanent nature of natural color when making selections.

Those who have dealt with the subject of color on a more scientific and technical level have a pretty good idea just how vast and complicated a subject it is. For the many gardeners who have been feeling their way through the world of color, perhaps discerning only good or bad and likes or dislikes, I recommend a review of one of the many books devoted to color or any of the basic garden books which include chapters on colors in flowers and plants and their selection.

Color of Flowers. Although hostas are considered foliage plants, many have attractive flowers. These play a minor role in gardening, individually lasting only one day (with some exceptions), and being either white or colored in the red-blue range. The colors purple, violet, mauve, lavender, lilac, and even gentian and delphinium have been used to characterize hosta flowers. Hybridizers are working to improve hosta flowers, and improved forms may be available in coming years. For the time being some gardeners, not wanting to deal with hosta flowers at all, simply cut the flower scapes before they expand. This may be justified to avoid the clash of deep lavender flowers on chartreuse or greenish yellow hosta clumps, but for most, hosta flowers should not be ignored. *Hosta plantaginea* with its large, waxy, white, fragrant flowers (Figure 3-56) and *H. ventricosa* with its purple bells (Figure 2-37) are examples of good-looking flowers found on hostas. Less well known are the dark violet, dense flower heads on *H. capitata* and the heavy, porcelainlike buds of its hybrid *H.* 'Nakaimo' which are followed by a spectacular, long-lasting display of almost transparent, mauve flowers (Plate 181). The spidery, deep lavender shapes of the flowers of *H. yingeri* and *H. laevigata* (Figure 2-38; Plate 182) are very attractive. Some clones of *Ezo Giboshi, H. rectifolia* var. *sachalinensis,* have what I consider beautiful flowers. In any case, most hosta flowers are good-looking while in bloom. It is the obnoxious habit of the spent petals hanging on the swelling seed pod which makes the whole picture quite unattractive (Figure 3-43), and frequently parts of the disintegrated corolla hang on until the pods ripen. Hosta blooms open in succession from bottom to top, so the first blooms to open are replaced by developing seed pods, when flowers further up the raceme are still closed.

Flowers of Leaves. Although their flowers are by many gardeners considered rather ordinary, when it comes to leaves hostas are the premier foliage plants. Their leaves offer excellent color variations from white, to all shades of yellow, to green and blue. Many come in shades of green, from dark green to chartreuse, with medium and light green being the most prevalent. Many varieties are variegated, and their leaf mounds or foliaceous bracts have been compared by some hosta enthusiasts to large flowers of leaves (Plate 183).

As foliage plants, hostas are ideal companion plants in a border of multicolored perennials. Proper color fit is relatively easy to accomplish because particularly the large blue (BG), but also the green (GG) varieties combine easily in the standard flower border and add to the color balance. The highly variegated hosta mounds blend in as flowers of leaves, particularly when a yellow-green-white primary color mix is desired. In established borders where other flowering perennials are usually in the majority, adding hostas is easy. Finding the right color combinations is not difficult because their mostly benign coloration gives them innate proper fit (Plate 162).

Color in the Hosta Garden. Making gardens where hostas are by design the dominant flowering plant requires a more-calculated approach. The easiest solution is to opt for a monochromatic or two-color garden. Aside from the temporal flower colors, the most obvious contrast colors for the green hosta garden are blue (BG), yellow (YG), and white (in VMG, VIG, and VCG). Blue has been included because it is important during the prime display season of May–June, but keep in mind that blue is but a fleeting stage, which is most pronounced in spring but later turns to plain green. The larger blue-green (BG) hostas, whether in their blue or green stage, make superb background plants, however, and can add dignity and stateliness to a flamboyant border (Plate 162). Yellow hostas on a deep green-and-grey foil can result in an exciting yellow garden.

Aside from the companion plants already mentioned, annuals can be one of the many yellow-flowering border plants available for spring, summer, and autumn bloom (Plate 184). In this garden it may be justified to cut the flower scapes of deep lavender flowering hostas, using only the leaf color. White flowers on yellow cultivars fit in well and add an extra touch of brightness and contrast to the yellow garden, but apposing hostas with white in the leaves (in VCG and VMG) with pure yellow (YG) ones must be done very carefully. They should be kept separate, for white is akin to cool, while yellow is most conspicuous and a hot color. They can be isolated by surrounding them with smaller green (GG) hostas. Many hostas variegated with yellow in spring will slowly change that color to white, so as the outside temperature climbs, this whitening of the variegation makes it look cooler, a definite plus. For this reason white-flowering plants for summer bloom, particularly *H. plantaginea*, can be introduced as companions to these hostas. The combination makes a garden a warm yellow in spring, but changes to a cool, white dominant coloration by summer. For balance it is important that all the plants in such a garden—including the flowering trees, shrubs, and hedges—are selected to blend into the monochromatic or two-color scheme and provide a strong green foil to balance the yellow. Obviously, too much yellow or white can be ruinous.

The Green Garden. Green is nature's predominant color. It is used as a foil so is often called the canvas upon which gardeners paint. Nevertheless, all-green gardens should not be ruled out because hostas display a tremendous range of greens—more so than most other perennials—from a yellow that is almost chartreuse to a green that is nearly blue. This diversity of green hues and shades coupled with a boundless variety of shapes, forms, and habits can establish interesting all-green beds or borders, indeed entire gardens, with a soothing and relaxing background color, while individual plant habits, shapes, and textures bring excitement and contrast. In such a garden, hosta flowers and those of companion plants become more important, and the selection of plants should include consideration for year-round bloom. The descriptions in Chapters 3 and 4 contain information on flowering periods and so are useful for this selection process.

Color Combinations. Gardeners concerned about using incorrect color combinations in gardens which mix hostas and other flowering perennials or annuals can relax because most colors fit happily together. One rule should be observed: Orange flowers (pink and red with yellow mixed in) clash with those having bright blue in their composition. They can be used, of course, but should be kept well apart, perhaps separated by green (GG) or blue (BG) hostas with white flowers or, if flowering occurs at different times, the mix still works. While hosta flowers fit almost everywhere, flowering companion plants require careful color selection. A classic English book on this subject, *Colour Schemes for the Flower Garden*, was written by Gertrude Jekyll and originally published in 1908. It is available as a reprint. Another outstanding modern treatise is *Color in Your Garden* by Penelope Hobhouse (1984). An excellent work with a North American point of view is L. B. Wilder's *Color in My Garden* (1990).

The Collector's Garden. Many hosta aficionados are collectors first and gardeners second, so their gardens, which frequently resemble a collector's album, usually start out as assemblies of hostas placed in beds or segregated areas of the garden. Some scientifically inclined collectors prefer to arrange their plants systematically, while horticulturists arrange by type or color for comparison—yellow with yellow, green with green, white-margined with white-margined—each with its own kind. Some public collections—whose primary purpose is to teach—for example, the reference collection in the Minnesota Landscape Arboretum—are planted in this manner with the express purpose of educating the public. Even these technically arranged gardens are on the average very attractive because hosta colors are rather benign and adapt well to the landscape. Many collectors compartmentalize their gardens into outdoor rooms, assigning each hosta collection to a different area. These can then be tied together by walks. My advice is to avoid arrangements of rectangular beds and use the much more appealing free-form island beds on the model of those at Bressingham Gardens (Plate 158). In small gardens borders can be utilized for this purpose, letting trees and shrubs act as a background. With the addition of architectural elements and companion plants, these arrangements cease to be collections and become hosta gardens (Plate 185). In this manner, even very large gardens of hosta collections can be pleasing to the eye, although considerable skill is required to get the desired color balance. To novice gardeners I recommend designs which copy nature because hosta collections fit well into natural gardens and so balance almost without forethought in such settings.

Gardening as Art. Gardening has been compared to painting living pictures using plants as the medium. Some gardens are considered works of art, but it is rather more complicated. Standard works of art are hung on the wall or put on a pedestal, while artfully designed gardens are forever changing in color, texture, overall balance, and appearance. Some of them become living art. Some gifted makers of gardens have enough creative genius plus the ability to travel through time and visualize their creations 20 years hence so that their gardens are the ones making it into the many illustrated compendiums of gardens which are published today. These gardens serve as guide and inspiration to many gardeners still struggling with the basic rules of garden design.

These rules tell gardeners, for example, to be mindful when combining yellow and white, or to avoid using yellow with lavender or purple. Hostas, of course, have a mind of their own and frequently combine yellow with white on the same plant or raise dark lavender flowers over a yellow leaf mound. Gardeners going by the book remove dark lavender flowers from yellow hostas, but most of them put up with the idiosyncracies of the genus, letting nature take its course and ignoring a temporary clash of colors. Yet, even uncompromising observance of these rules does not guarantee that a garden will become a work of art and make the pages of a book on gardening. In my opinion, even the most commonplace garden becomes art if it honestly manifests the maker's individualism, and never mind critics who may disagree because, after all, most gardens are made for the gardener's own benefit and satisfaction. I believe the creation of a personal landscape transcends some of the rules usually applied to garden design and that gardeners should develop their own sources of inspiration. I highly recommend reading *Personal Landscapes* by Malitz (1989), which deals not only with practical aspects but also with the philosophy of this concept.

One rule should be observed concerning highly variegated hostas, which are streaked with shades of green, chartreuse, yellow, and white (VCG), and whose color patterns often differ from leaf to leaf and are frequently mixed with all-yellow, all-chartreuse, or all-green leaves on a single plant. Some hosta gardeners and collectors are willing to pay high prices for these mutations which they congregate in flashy patches of color. This may work in the larger hosta gardens where large areas of green and blue-green can be used to balance such flamboyant aggregations. However, in the small gardens of today, flashy variegations should be used judiciously, perhaps only as solitary contrasts or accents. When assembling collections of these highly variegated hostas in one place gardeners should treat them like any other grouping of very prominent, brightly colored flowers and, following the advice of Gertrude Jekyll, surround these dazzling cultivars with a progression of milder-colored neighbors or back them up with a foil of tranquil green (GG) or blue (BG). As an example, a small accent group of 3 of the flamboyant cultivar *H.* 'Flamboyant' (Plate 103) in front of a bed could be partially encircled by its attractive, color-stable cousin *H.* 'Shade Fanfare' (Figure 4-40) and backed up by a large group of dark green or blue-green (BG) hostas, such as *H.* 'Fortunei Hyacinthina', *H.* 'Royal Standard', or *H.* 'Hadspen Blue'.

Strong Hosta Colors. Strong or bright flower colors do not exist in the genus except perhaps for the temporal whites, but hosta leaves are a different matter. Leaf mounds of yellow or yellow-white variegated provide strong and bright colors. Gardeners seeking to brighten dark garden corners with yellow hostas must keep in mind that colors have a considerable influence on how observers perceive their surroundings. Yellow (YG) hostas will literally jump at the viewer and, if planted in the rear of a border or bed, will bring the background forward. They will also brighten a dark corner (Plate 152). Others, like blue, blue-green, and grey (BG), produce an illusion of greater depth thus making the garden look larger than it really is. Gardeners with small gardens can take advantage of this. On the other hand, yellow and yellow-variegated hostas and those with a lot of white (VCG, VMG, and YG) develop and show their colors better in strong light or even some direct sunlight. Perhaps they should be congregated in island beds or berms, out in the open shade, surrounded by an edging of dark green *Liriope* in a pool of cool green grass and leaning against dark green dwarf evergreens planted in the center.

Seasons and Color. Most flowering plants undergo drastic seasonal changes affecting color composition, but fortunately, most hostas remain relatively unchanged in their leaf colors from spring to fall, an advantage altogether evident in gardens using hostas as the principal perennial. A few varieties, however, are yellow variegated in spring turning green by summer, or they are blue-green changing to plain dark green, or they have yellow margins becoming white. Gardeners need to consider these seasonal changes in their overall scheme. Luckily, most variegated hostas and a majority of the chartreuse and yellow ones retain their colors as long as the weather allows. At Hosta Hill, this period lasts from the first of May until the middle of November, six and a half months, but in more northern latitudes the duration is shorter.

A definite plus is the fall coloration of hosta leaves which develops after the first few frosts or light freezes have stopped photosynthesis (Plate 43). At a time when practically all flowers have faded away and most other plants have dried and gone to seed, hostas begin to turn a glowing yellow, some even light orange, which brightens dark autumn days until a hard freeze cuts down the petioles. With this the hostas start their dormancy which lasts until next spring's warming. This will leave most or all the planting beds bare, not just for the hostas, but for most perennials with annual leaves or top growth. A

late-fall or early winter cleaning should remove dead hosta leaves and scapes in time for winter snow cover, or in more southern regions, in time for a mulch of pine needles or thin leaves which descend from nearby trees and shrubs and may remain on the bed until spring. Thicker leaves from oaks should probably be removed because they do not easily disintegrate but pack down over the hosta causing crown rot in some cases.

Winter is the only season without color in the hosta garden but trees and shrubs with colored bark and attractive shapes and textures as well as winter-flowering herbaceous perennials—the members of the genus *Helleborus*, for example—can add color and interest for those who insist on appealing winter landscapes. These plants carry on until spring and mix happily with the hostas after they reemerge. But many gardeners turn inward during this time, making plans for new garden projects and plantings for the coming spring season, and letting winter take over the bare garden for the duration without unduly worrying about attractiveness and color.

HOSTA GARDENS

Following the dictates of the three rights detailed earlier, specific recommendations for using hostas in the landscape can be made. It is very difficult to adequately describe such use in words alone, so I have resorted to illustrations to convey the various concepts of using hostas. Group abbreviations refer to the listings at the end of this chapter which give alternate selections for hostas described and illustrated.

Small Beginnings
In hosta gardening, as in other endeavors, keeping it small always contributes to a good start because it fosters simplicity, costs less money, and results in attractive displays with satisfying rapidity. A small garden can be built with one or two hostas. It is not the quantity that counts, but the design (Plates 186, 187). Gardeners need to experience a measure of success to spur them on to bigger and better things, and it is easier to succeed from small beginnings which are also less likely to become a burden.

The Potted Garden
Not every gardener is lucky enough to own a piece of land, so the smallest gardens in the world are in pots. Population densities in North America, and to a lesser degree in Europe, still permit personal ornamental gardening on a relatively large scale. In Japan and other populous countries, private gardens in or near cities are yielding to the necessity of housing and industrialization. Notwithstanding, all over the world many gardeners who lack a piece of land give evidence—with a multitude of pots, containers, and window gardens—that gardening is possible even without owning a plot.

Pot culture may be the most frequently practiced form of gardening in the world today, and it is easily the most controllable and least expensive. For planting hostas, any pot or container will do as long as it is at least as deep as it is wide, has drainage holes, and is correctly sized for the chosen hostas. There are exceptions: In Japan single hosta clumps are sometimes grown bonsai style in shallow dishes with most of the external roots exposed, but this requires constant care and watering. Many gardeners opt for attractive, colorful china or stoneware containers, but it is best to use unobtrusive colors so as not to detract from the planting.

Very small, even tiny species and varieties (TG) allow the making of very small gardens. If a window sill is all that is available for gardening, it is possible to create interesting and attractive dish gardens or shelf gardens. Because these small hostas have small root systems, shallower dishes can be used, provided regular watering can be accomplished. Stone troughs and planters make fine containers for miniature landscapes combining hostas, hardy ferns, moss, and decorative stones. The design possibilities are endless. Hostas can be the tranquil element, using mostly miniature and dwarf green- (GG) or grey-leaved (BG) varieties, or they can be showy accents. Placing variegated or yellow miniatures (YG) in pastures of green moss or natural, dark gravel is very showy, and in this case the small, highly variegated hosta clumps take on the role of low-growing, long-lasting flowers.

In these small gardens different leaf shapes can be combined to add to the visual interest, but it is usually best not to overplant and to use identical hostas either singly or several together, remembering the odd-number principle discussed earlier.

Pot gardens are undemanding, but frequent watering is required because hosta leaves have high transpiration rates and pots dry out faster than the ground. Fertilizing can take the form of light foliar feeding, or osmotic pellets which release nutrients very slowly by osmosis can be added once a year (see Appendix F).

One problem always arises with small container gardens: Most hostas are rapid growers, and after 3–4 growing seasons their root systems will outgrow the container. They must be lifted and divided. This is almost never required in open ground, but in pots it is unavoidable. I do not recommend root pruning for hostas because it will affect leaf top-growth patterns and may upset the balance. For dish gardens it may be best to start with fresh plant material. Container-grown hostas can be moved to larger containers.

Being portable and attractive, potted hostas are often moved to what is called the front porch in southeastern United States, and the arrangement can be very inviting and attractive (Plate 188). Some gardeners even bring them indoors. This is possible in humid parts of Japan where houses are kept open during the warm seasons. These potted hostas become focal points on the *engawa*, a narrow deck without railing which is considered an essential part of a Japanese house and forms the transition between house and garden. An occasional airing in light rain ameliorates temporary indoor placement, but hostas are not house plants. They need winter chilling, so the containers in which these miniature gardens or single specimens are planted should be weather- and freezeproof. Gardeners using valuable containers that could be subject to damage by freezing should equip them with removable plastic or wooden liners so that plants can be removed with their root ball intact to overwinter outdoors while the valued pots are safe inside. Hosta root structures easily withstand being frozen solid for extended periods, but frequent thawing and refreezing can be damaging, so winter chilling should take place in shaded or north-facing locations where brief sunny warm spells do not cause thawing.

Western houses have patios, terraces, verandas, or balconies, vaguely comparable to the Japanese *engawa*, except they are customarily defined by railings, fences, or hedges. Pots and containers with single hosta specimens of almost any type can be used here, but it is best to stay away from the highly variegated (VCG) ones and to select from the medium-to-giant green (GG) and blue (BG) groups or, if more color is desired, any one of the margined (VMG) hostas will do. Yellow (YG) hostas may clash with red brick backgrounds and are more difficult to incorporate. It is worth while to try them, though, since they are portable and can be moved around. Pots and containers of neutral earth-tone color combine happily with the background colors of bricks, stone, wood, or concrete (Plate 189). Some gardeners prefer to use stronger colors, which brings the requirement for careful consideration of color harmony. Some variegated hostas (in VMG and VCG) that change color with the advancing seasons—for example, H. 'Fortunei Albopicta', H. 'Janet', or even H. 'Gold Standard'—should not be used in heavy, practically immovable containers as their color change can disturb planned color harmony, but in smaller pots they present no problem because they can be relocated elsewhere.

Species with white pruinose coatings on the leaf underside, such as *H. hypoleuca*, *H. pycnophylla*, and the several white-backed varieties of *H. longipes* and *H. kikutii*, present a special display problem because the attractive white is not visible from above. Planting these species in pots and elevating them on columns or stands will provide a good look at this unusual and fascinating feature.

Occasionally in the Northern Hemisphere hostas are grown beyond their perceived southern limit of culture. In Europe they are found in northern Italy and along the French Mediterranean coast; in North America they are grown in Florida, along the Gulf Coast, in southern California, and in northwestern Mexico. In these locations they are almost always seen in pots or containers, so they do get some winter chilling because in the pots they are exposed to relatively cold winter air. In the ground they would probably not succeed because the occasional cold in these areas never penetrates to the root ball.

When planting hostas in such southern regions, selection also becomes an important factor. Gardeners should select species or the offspring of species which are native in the southern parts of Japan or China; for example, *H. plantaginea*, *H. kikutii*, *H. pulchella*, or the southeastern Korean species *H. venusta*, *H. yingeri*, and *H. laevigata* are all suitable selections which will often withstand considerable amounts of sun, a definite plus in warmer climates. In North America the Mediterranean theme is occasionally copied, and invariably the ever-present *H.* 'Undulata Albomarginata' is used, also in pots (Plate 189).

Small Gardens

Where space allows, the progression from potted plants to small gardens, including small beds and borders, is a natural one. Many hosta gardeners remember with fondness their first hostas, usually planted around trees (Figure 6-1). These surrounds are gardens of sorts, albeit quite simple ones. They almost always work because in these situations practically any hosta will fit.

Aside from container planting, small or miniature hosta gardens can be made in very small outdoor gardens or garden beds, either isolated or adjacent to other garden areas (Plate 190), or in planting squares left open in terraces. Small beds alongside patios can be converted into hosta gardens (Plates 159, 170, 180). If no natural shade is available on a patio or terrace, a portable or permanent overhead trellis or containerized small trees can solve this problem. Some gardeners specialize in dwarf (TG) hostas. Their entire collection can be planted in less than 2 square yards (1.5 square meters) with room left for rocks, mosses, and a few other tiny companion plants, such as small ferns.

Because of space restrictions Japanese gardeners have become masters in the art of designing and building very small gardens. By utilizing small symbolic plants and rocks, usually combined with a water feature, they create marvels of simplicity and expression and bring the majestic Japanese landscape into their private quarters. In these small and even tiny gardens each element is chosen and planted with utmost care. To the purist a single tiny hosta planted on a rocky ledge covered with moss often advocates the use of the genus better than many crowded collections (Figure 6-6). It is gardening in its most basic terms. The lesson is simple: In small gardens the

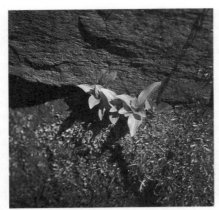

Figure 6-6. *H. sieboldii* dwarf form; growing on mossy rock ledge, making a garden in its most basic terms (Hosta Hill)

number and variety of elements should be in keeping with the available space.

In Europe and North America private gardens are also becoming smaller. With this trend comes the temptation to crowd as many trees, shrubs, and decorative plants, including hostas, into small areas, resulting in overcrowded jungles. Fewer is better, but it never hurts to let plants cover up the ground between them (Plate 190) because that cuts down on weeding. A small garden corner can be created with yellow hostas next to ferns and companions of different shades of green (Plate 167). Those inclined towards the naturalistic style can take their inspiration from nature, planting hostas on rocks, and adding a few ferns and a water feature (Plate 191).

Hostas and Water
Hostas go great with water (Plates 146, 187). The Japanese have taught us that water features do not have to be large. They use small water basins, usually made from stone, which are used for a ceremonial washing of the hands and the symbolic ritual cleansing of the spirit before partaking in the tea ceremony. These water basins come in two types: A low one, *tsukubai*, translated to "having to crouch" (Figure 6-7), and a taller one, *chozubachi*, literally "a hand-water place." Adapted for decorative use in Western gardens they represent a refined and minimum addition of water to a small garden, although some purists have shunned such use.

Figure 6-7. *H. ventricosa* with *Tsukubai* (Japanese Garden, Minnesota Landscape Arboretum/Schmid)

Another Japanese water feature is the *sozu kakehi* (or *shishi odoshi*) made from two lengths of bamboo, one acting as a flume, the other balanced on a cradle with one end closed. The flume slowly fills the balanced tube causing it to tip and empty at the open end after which the closed end tips back striking a

stone with an audible sound. This water feature can be built in a small corner surrounded by ferns and small green (GG) or blue (BG) hostas, rocks, and a tiny pool into which the bamboo empties. The combination of artistic design, seemingly perpetual motion, and the sounds of splashing and clanking makes a captivating display.

For Western-style gardens small streams (Plate 191) or small ponds in natural settings are good minimum additions. Semiformal arrangements, such as a classic fountain (Plate 149), will also provide engaging settings for hostas. Obviously, where space permits, small streams, waterfalls, or ponds and lakes make magnificent additions to a garden and are superb for displaying hostas (Plates 163, 187). In the wild many hosta species congregate around water, so emulating this habitat in our gardens is one of the best ways to show them (Plates 187, 191). *Hosta longipes* and its many forms and *H. kiyosumiensis* are good choices for these situations, although almost any hosta looks good planted near water.

A HAPPY MIX

More has been written about British-style gardens than any other because they epitomize a happy mix of plant material in beds and borders. This style fits equally well in grand parks and small suburban or cottage gardens (Plates 162, 164).

Herbaceous Borders
The evolution of the English herbaceous border is an outgrowth of the tremendous increase in available kinds of plants towards the end of the 19th century when a gardener's greatest problem became that of choice. Under the leadership of Robinson (1883) and Jekyll (1899, 1901, 1908) a reformation started which led gardeners away from massed plantings and formalism and appealed for a return to simpler ideas. Robinson drew his inspiration from nature itself, while Jekyll, with the eye of an artist and painter, took as a model the happy, but often haphazard mixture of plants in the cottage gardens of Surrey. During the last 100 years a combination of these two philosophies has resulted in the preferred layout of our modern Western gardens. It has also led to further innovation, of which an example is the island beds advocated by Bloom (1981) (Plate 158). It is not by coincidence that beds, borders, and island beds lend themselves supremely for planting a happy mix of hostas and companions.

In North America the average plot varies from 0.25 to 1 acre (1000 to 4000 square meters). Plots in Europe may be somewhat smaller, and in crowded Japan gardens are often reduced to tiny interior courtyards (*tsubo*), though some purists do not consider the latter true gardens. Regardless of physical size, gardens require a good deal of work to keep them attractive, and experienced gardeners know that gardens are forever growing and changing. Those lucky enough to own a piece of the earth know very well that with that ownership comes an obligation for maintenance, which can very easily become a burden. For this reason I advocate the inclusion of low-maintenance plants, especially hostas, which, as discussed earlier, require less upkeep than the traditional multi-perennial garden based on the English model.

A century ago Robinson and Jekyll pointed the way for gardeners, and I believe we are again at the threshold of better things to come. A new school of low-maintenance gardening is rapidly developing. It is strongest in the United States and may be that nation's contribution to garden fashion. It is not by coincidence that hostas and similar labor-saving plants are being used increasingly in the borders and beds formerly reserved for Jekyll's happy, but back-breaking mix of perennials. Modern gardeners have no gardening help, so are turning to simpler models, such as the Japanese gardens, and most importantly, to nature itself. The trend is towards native plants and wild flowers mixed with easy-care, long-lasting foliage plants, among which hostas are supreme because they contribute not only diversity in shape and texture but also provide long-lasting color.

In England, the beautiful, traditional, labor-intensive, multiperennial borders can still be seen everywhere. An example is in the Ivy Cottage garden of Ann Stevens in Dorset (Plate 162), but even there hostas and other low-maintenance plants are increasingly planted. This can be observed also at Spinners, Peter Chappell's garden at Boldre (Plate 192), and at Diana Grenfell's Apple Walk at Hordle, both near Southampton, England. Spinners comes very close to representing a preferred U.S. style. Easily one of the finest borders using hostas and low-maintenance plants almost exclusively is at Hadspen House, Castle Cary, Somerset (Plate 175). Gardeners around the world have adopted hostas to an ever-increasing degree in the border, and fine examples can be seen at Gordon Collier's Titoki Point garden, Taihape, New Zealand, where the happy mix includes exotic plants like tree ferns (Plate 173).

Greenscape Solutions

Visitors to North America often comment on the sameness of most of the suburban landscape. These look-alike gardens have the bare essentials: a lawn, some evergreens around the home (foundation planting), and perhaps a tree in the middle of the front lawn. Except for the occasional flowering shrub, the seasonal color of the garden is more or less green. Many homeowners are satisfied with the status quo and struggle to maintain these greenscapes, diligently trimming the evergreens, mowing the lawn, raking the leaves (and throwing them away), aerating the ground, fertilizing, watering, and spending the better part of each weekend competing with their neighbors for the greenest lawn on the block. The development of lawn services in North America is an outgrowth of gardeners getting tired of this maintenance aggravation, and nowadays in North America perpetual lawn care is only a phone call away. Costs for these services are on the rise, so the more frugal gardeners opt for alternative ways to solve their greenscape problems.

Greenscapes present another problem in areas where increasing water shortages have brought about restrictions on watering. These water-hungry lawns are being replaced by xeriscapes, natural settings that require less water and retain moisture through the use of mulches and leafy perennials which shade the ground. Here again hostas are easily the best choice. In these gardens trickle irrigation replaces wasteful sprinkler systems.

In many existing greenscape gardens the areas under trees, where grass will not thrive have been planted with ivy or other ground covers which frequently get out of bounds and make periodic trimming necessary. In this situation the addition of hostas results in immediate improvement. Correctly selected leaf colors will improve the greenscape with long-lasting color: Large yellow cultivars (YG) provide shining accents, inexpensive blue-green and grey-green varieties (BG) or green forms (GG) soften the transition between reduced lawns and shrubbery borders, and walks can be defined by edging them with the smaller lance-leaved species or cultivars (EG). Alongside houses the traditional foundation planting can be replaced by hostas (Plate 165), and the base of shade trees can be ringed with all-green (GG) or white-margined hostas of a single variety (VMG) (Figure 6-1). Moreover, the selection of several hostas flowering at different times provides a long flowering season from May until October. The flowers are not spectacular, but they provide bright spots all year, and by choosing fragrant varieties, a pleasant aroma can be added to permeate the garden during the summer months.

Island Beds

One of the best ways to reduce lawn area is to install one or more island beds on the model of Bloom (1981) (Plate 158). These can be large or small, and their shape can be adjusted to best fit the available space. They can be placed in the open lawn or anchored to trees. In this way labor-intensive front lawns can be reduced in area by creating island beds filled with the more-sunproof yellow-leaved cultivars (YG). If the sun is too strong, plant fast-growing, small lawn trees—like dogwoods (*Cornus florida* or *Cornus kousa chinensis*), redbuds (*Cercis canadensis*), hawthorns (*Crataegus oxycantha*), or any of the smaller flowering cherry, plum, and peach trees—so they cast some shade on the hostas during the hottest time of day. During the first two or three years while the young trees are growing, the hostas may get burned and bleached a little. Nevertheless, they will photosynthesize intensely in the strong light, thus developing a strong root system and growing quickly into fine specimens.

Island beds require more planning than borders because they are seen from all sides. Taller plantings should be in the center, unlike borders which are viewed from the front only so require background plantings. Gardeners who shy away from such design tasks can resort to leaving everything in pots and experiment as described earlier. Sooner or later they will find an arrangement that is pleasing enough to be made permanent. On sloping ground, island beds can be terraced using retaining walls of brick or stone on the low side, so becoming an architectural feature as well.

In older, established greenscapes, where the once-small trees have grown to maturity, lawns usually suffer from lack of sunshine and become unsightly. Hostas are a supreme revitalization tool for these gardens. Gardeners who are tired of being slaves to lawn culture and have become aware of the low-maintenance requirements of hostas have converted large parts of their landscape to growing hostas predominately. Removing most of their lawns and converting the areas to natural gardens with walks, they plant native shrubs, hostas, wild flowers, shade-tolerant companion plants, and ferns along the walks, to outline shrubbery and trees, and in beds in clearings of filtered shade, thus creating a natural woodland garden that is attractive and has low upkeep and maintenance requirements.

Woodland Gardens

Hostas are happiest in woodland gardens, because the microclimate closely approximates natural habitat with open as well as shady areas, and in border areas surrounding canopy openings and clearings where high light levels exist at least during part of a day. A woodland setting can be very small, ranging from 0.25 acre (1000 square meters) to areas encompassing thousands of acres. Most of these gardens are patterned on the model of English woodland gardens. One of the finest examples exists in Windsor Great Park, near London, in an area known as Savill Garden, named for Sir Eric Savill, its creator. Starting in the 1970s John Bond, keeper of the garden, has added considerably to the hosta plantings which, in keeping with the garden's large size, are planted in great drifts or as ground cover of one variety backed by other flowering perennials (Plate 164), flowering shrubs, or large ferns. Also near London is Wisley Garden, the garden of the Royal Horticultural Society, where large plantings of hostas exist in the herbaceous borders of Battleston Hill (Figures 3-12, 3-13; Plate 174), in the rock garden (Figure 3-3), and in the wild garden (Plates 55, 179) where a large woodland setting houses one of the British National Reference Collections under the auspices of the (British) National Council for Conservation of Plants and Gardens (Plate 177). In the United States the hosta collections at the Minnesota Landscape

Arboretum, University of Minnesota, Chaska, are also in a woodland garden.

Woodland settings can be made on a much smaller scale. Even very small gardens qualify as woodland gardens, such as the plantings at Hosta Hill which grow under a canopy of pines with a dogwood understory. In large woodland settings the walks and paths are spaced well apart and follow nature's dictates, but in small gardens the layout of meandering walks becomes an essential design feature because it, together with the strategic planting of shrubs and hedges, creates the nooks and crannies which visually separate the various plantings and so make the garden appear much larger than it really is.

Garden Walks

The circulatory systems of gardens are walks and paths. Some are grassy and wide, leading the visitor's glance toward flowering shrubs and trees planted there, or flanked by large herbaceous borders, while others are narrow with all manner of plants crowding both sides and vying for attention. Paths are a most important design element in gardens because, as Johnson (1979) so aptly put it, "Their business is to conduct you to all the best places, and it is just as well if they let you know when you have arrived by bringing you to a landmark; a seat or summer house or a view."

Some walks are dictated by necessity since most gardens are also places where people live, and so there must be utilitarian walks to the front door, the refuse storage, and to other daily stops. Frequently these walks are beelines, giving the shortest possible route. But there is no reason why they cannot be made pleasant by incorporating them into a decorative scheme, perhaps even bending them a little for it is the curved walk that best fits gardens nowadays.

Curving paths and walks look more natural, and winding through a small garden they visually expand it and provide opportunities for placing hostas and other plants alongside (Figure 6-2). Hosta Hill, my garden, has a rear garden measuring about 100 by 80 feet (30 by 25 meters), a relatively small area, but it includes a walk which is 1000-feet (300-meters) long. This walk provides 2000 feet (600 meters) of linear planting, counting both sides of the walk. Visitors are baffled when they come for a quick visit only to spend over an hour walking through the garden, lingering here and there

and never seeing the same view twice. Although a semiformal area with some straight walks exists near the rear garden entrance, principally to demonstrate the use of hostas in formal and semiformal settings (Figure 6-8), the remainder of Hosta Hill is a woodland garden criss-crossed by a meandering hosta walk. Because of the limited size, the path at Hosta Hill is one-way obliging visitors to see every part of the garden and so serving its purpose well to conduct to all the best places. Lucky gardeners with more land can make their walks wider and bidirectional, as well as spaced further apart. For a very small garden, the walk will be short, leading to a vantage point from which all can be observed. Often this walk leads to a central lawn or paved area open to the house and surrounded on three sides by plantings. Many tiny city gardens in Europe and North America are designed on this principle. Smaller still are the minimal Japanese interior gardens (*tsubo*), traversed by stone paths which are often just symbolic.

The design of walks and paths, being absolutely crucial to the way visitors see the garden, requires a lot of advance planning. Before finalizing a layout I recommend gardeners study a few good books on garden design and visit established gardens for inspiration and guidance.

A New Gardening Philosophy

In February 1989 Christopher Lloyd, visiting Atlanta, Georgia, stated that Yankee gardeners are too wrapped up in low-maintenance gardens and that gardeners never get more out of a garden than what they put in it (Foster, 1989). I quite agree, if one attempts to build a garden on the English model, with labor-intensive herbaceous borders and such. These gardens, attractive as they may be while being well maintained, will show neglect almost immediately. Many gardeners the world over do not have the time nor the inclination to spend much of their free time maintaining a garden. They have opted for a new philosophy in gardening, one which optimizes what little time can be spent on gardening while still permitting the upkeep of a delightful garden which can even be neglected a week or two without showing ill effect. Using hostas and other low-maintenance perennials in a natural woodland setting will contribute greatly to the realization of such a garden.

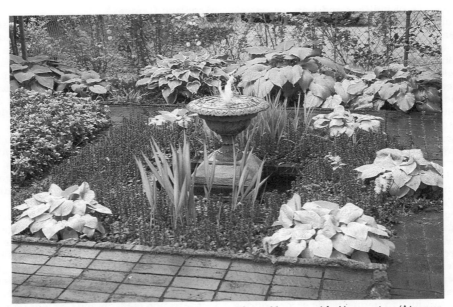

Figure 6-8. *H.* 'August Moon'; clumps in a semiformal layout, with *Ajuga reptans* 'Atropurpurea' ground cover. (Hosta Hill)

LIST OF RECOMMENDED SPECIES AND CULTIVARS

Nota bene

In the following listing, color specifications have been streamlined considerably to simplify selection. The color green (GG) includes all shades of green from light to dark, but blue-green and grey-green taxa are listed in a separate category (BG). For variegated types all greens, including blue-green and grey-green, have been combined under green. Yellow embraces all shades of yellow, including yellowish green (chartreuse) which is technically green but considered yellow by many gardeners. White can be anything from greenish white to yellowish white. Some of the taxa listed may start with yellow coloration later turning to green (viridescent); others have yellow centers turning to white (albescent); and a few have chartreuse or very light green variegation changing to yellow (lutescent). The descriptions and photographs in Chapters 3 and 4 give further details for each listed taxon regarding their changing color characteristics, and it is advisable to refer to these chapters before making final selections. Definitions and explanations of color and color terms are given in Chapter 2 and Appendix D.

Taxa followed by an asterisk thus, *, are widely available in North America.

Species and cultivar names are arranged in alphabetic order.

The Blue-Green and Grey-Green Group (BG)

Giant Sizes

H. 'Abiqua Parasol'
H. 'Big Mama'*
H. 'Blue Angel'*
H. 'Blue Mammoth'*
H. 'Blue Umbrellas'*
H. 'Bressingham Blue'
H. 'Buckanon'
H. 'Duke'
H. 'Empire State'
H. 'Gray Cole'*
H. 'Great Lakes'
H. 'Grey Piecrust'
H. 'Harrison'
H. 'Harry A. Jacobson'
H. 'King Tut'
H. 'Lakeport Blue'
H. 'Presidents Choice'
H. 'Quilted Skies'
H. 'River Nile'
H. 'Royal Quilt'
H. 'Ryans Big One'*
H. 'Sea Monster'*
H. 'Sea Sapphire'
H. sieboldiana*
H. sieboldiana 'Amplissima'
H. sieboldiana 'Elegans'*
H. sieboldiana 'Hypophylla'
H. sieboldiana 'Mira'*
H. 'Silver Giant'
H. 'Sky Crystal'
H. 'Trails End'*

Large Sizes

H. 'Alabama Bowl'*
H. 'Aqua Velva'
H. 'Big Daddy'*

H. 'Blue Bayou'
H. 'Blue Beauty'
H. 'Blue Betty Lou'
H. 'Blue Blazes'
H. 'Blue Lace'
H. 'Blue Piecrust'*
H. 'Blue Rock'
H. 'Blue Saucers'
H. 'Blue Skirt'
H. 'Blue Vision'
H. 'Buckeye Blue'
H. 'Edina Heritage'
H. 'Ellen F. Weissenberger'
H. 'Evelyn McCafferty'
H. 'Grey Beauty'*
H. 'Hoarfrost'
H. 'Housatonic'*
H. 'Julia Hardy'
H. 'June Beauty'
H. 'Lake Louise'
H. 'Lilac Giant'
H. 'Lochness'
H. 'Mary Lou'
H. 'Ming Jade'
H. 'Muriel Seaver Brown'
H. nigrescens*
H. 'Noahs Ark'
H. 'Perrys True Blue'*
H. 'Puckered Giant'
H. 'Rembrandt Blue'
H. 'Rough Waters'
H. 'Samual Blue'
H. 'Sea Lotus Leaf'
H. sieboldiana var. glabra
H. 'Silver Bowl'
H. 'Snowden'*
H. 'True Blue'*
H. 'Twist and Shout'
H. 'Waterford'
H. 'Willy Nilly'*
H. 'Wrinkles and Crinkles'

Medium Sizes

H. 'Abiqua Blue Jay'
H. 'Birchwood Blue'*
H. 'Birchwood Parkys Blue'*
H. 'Blue Arrow'
H. 'Blue Boy'*
H. 'Blue Diamond'
H. 'Blue Dimples'*
H. 'Blue Dome'
H. 'Blue Fan Dancer'
H. 'Blue Heaven'*
H. 'Blue Horizon'
H. 'Blue Jay'
H. 'Blue June'
H. 'Blue Lagoon'
H. 'Blue Tiers'
H. 'Blue Troll'
H. 'Blue Velvet'
H. 'Blue Wedgwood'*
H. 'Blue Whirls'
H. 'Bluebird'
H. 'Bonnie'
H. 'Bressingham Blue'
H. 'Brooke'
H. 'Brother Ronald'
H. 'Buckshaw Blue'*

H. 'Buffy'
H. 'Camelot'
H. 'Candy Hearts'*
H. 'Crinkled Joy'
H. 'Curlew'
H. 'Devon Blue'
H. 'Edge of Night'
H. 'Edward Wargo'
H. 'Grey Goose'
H. 'Hadspen Blue'*
H. 'Halcyon'*
H. 'Happiness'
H. 'Happy Hearts'
H. 'Kingfisher'
H. 'Krinkled Joy'
H. 'Krossa Regal'*
H. 'Lauman Blue'
H. 'Lee Armiger'
H. 'Linde'
H. 'Love Pat'*
H. 'Moscow Blue'
H. 'Neat and Tidy'*
H. 'Purbeck Ridge'
H. 'Purple Bouquet'
H. 'Reginald Kaye'*
H. 'Riptide'
H. 'Sacra'
H. 'Sea Blue'
H. 'Special Gift'
H. 'Tokudama'*
H. 'Valentine Lace'
H. 'Zager Blue'

Small Sizes
H. 'Abiqua Blue Edger'
H. 'Abiqua Trumpet'
H. 'Baby Bunting'
H. 'Barbara'
H. 'Blue Belle'
H. 'Blue Blush'
H. 'Blue Cadet'*
H. 'Blue Danube'
H. 'Blue Moon'*
H. 'Blue Skies'*
H. 'Daniel'
H. 'Dear Heart'
H. 'Dorset Blue'
H. 'Fragrant Blue'
H. 'Hadspen Hawk'*
H. 'Hadspen Heron'*
H. 'Harmony'*
H. 'Indigo'
H. 'Lakeside Accolade'
H. 'Lynne'
H. 'Margie Weissenberger'
H. 'Number One'
H. 'Pauline Brac'
H. 'Pearl Lake'*
H. 'Pelham Blue Tump'
H. 'Roundabout'
H. 'Serendipity'*
H. 'Yakushima Mizu'*

Miniature Sizes
H. 'Blue Line'
H. 'Popo'
H. 'Stephen'

Dwarf Sizes
H. 'Blue Ice'

The Green Group (GG)

Giant Sizes
H. 'Behemoth'
H. 'Bethel Big Leaf'
H. 'Big Boy'
H. 'Big John'
H. 'Big Sam'
H. 'Birchwood Elegance'*
H. 'Birchwood Ruffled Queen'*
H. 'Black Hills'
H. 'Century One'
H. 'Champion'
H. 'Colossal'
H. 'Corduroy'
H. 'Duke'
H. 'Elata'*
H. 'Fernwood'
H. 'Green Acres'*
H. 'Green Piecrust'*
H. hypoleuca*
H. 'Immense'
H. 'Jolly Green Giant'
H. 'King James'
H. 'King Michael'
H. 'Leviathan'
H. 'Mikado'
H. montana f. macrophylla*
H. nigrescens 'Elatior'*
H. 'Pioneer'
H. 'Regal Ruffles'
H. 'Sea Drift'*
H. 'Sumi'

Large Sizes
H. 'Abiqua Blue Madonna'
H. 'Abiqua Blue Shield'
H. 'Aqua Velva'
H. 'Black Beauty'
H. 'Challenger'
H. 'Circus Clown'
H. 'Classic Delight'
H. 'Crested Reef'*
H. 'Fall Emerald'*
H. 'Flower Power'
H. fluctuans
H. 'Fond Hope'
H. 'Fortunei Gigantea'*
H. 'Fountain'
H. 'Frilly Puckers'
H. 'Green Formal'*
H. 'Green Platter'*
H. 'Green Ripples'
H. 'Green Saucers'
H. 'Green Sheen'
H. 'Jade Point'
H. 'Jumbo'
H. montana*
H. montana 'Liliiflora'
H. 'Paul Bunyan'
H. 'Rembrandt Blue'
H. 'Ruffles'*
H. 'Satin Flare'
H. 'Tall Boy'*
H. 'Temple Great'
H. 'Top Number'
H. 'Witches Brew'

Medium Sizes
H. 'Abiqua Ambrosia'
H. alismifolia
H. 'Bette Davis Eyes'
H. 'Betty'
H. 'Big Hearted'
H. 'Black Hills'
H. 'Bon Voyage'
H. 'Buckwheat Honey'
H. 'Candle Wax'
H. capitata*
H. 'Crispula Viridis'
H. 'County Park'
H. 'Daily Joy'
H. densa
H. 'Elisabeth'
H. 'Eunice Fisher'
H. 'Fortunei Aoki'*
H. 'Fortunei Hyacinthina'*
H. 'Fortunei Obscura'*
H. 'Fortunei Rugosa'*
H. 'Fortunei Stenantha'*
H. 'Fortunei Viridis'*
H. 'Great Desire'
H. 'Green Aspen'
H. 'Green Dome'
H. 'Green Fountain'*
H. 'Green Furrows'
H. 'Hippeastrum'
H. 'Jade Beauty'
H. 'John Wargo'
H. jonesii
H. 'Kathleen'
H. kikutii*
H. kikutii f. leuconota*
H. 'Lime Krinkles'
H. 'Little Blue'
H. 'Maruba Iwa'*
H. 'Minnie Klopping'
H. 'Mogul'
H. 'Nakaimo'*
H. 'Oxheart'*
H. pachyscapa
H. plantaginea*
H. plantaginea 'Aphrodite'
H. plantaginea 'Stenantha'
H. plantaginea var. japonica*
H. pycnophylla
H. 'Razzle Dazzle'
H. 'Regal Rhubarb'
H. 'Rocky Road'
H. 'Rotunda'
H. rupifraga*
H. 'Sea Bunny'
H. 'Serenity'
H. shikokiana
H. 'Spit Shine'
H. 'Sweet Marjorie'
H. 'Sweet Susan'
H. 'Sweet Winifred'
H. takahashii
H. tibae*
H. tsushimensis
H. 'Unducosa'*
H. 'Undulata Erromena'*
H. ventricosa*
H. 'Venucosa'*
H. 'Vilmoriniana'*

H. 'White Charger'

Small Sizes

H. aequinoctiiantha
H. 'Alpine Dream'
H. 'Amanuma'*
H. 'Apple Green'
H. atropurpurea
H. 'Ballerina'
H. 'Betsy King'*
H. 'Booka'
H. 'Bountiful'
H. calliantha
H. cathayana*
H. clausa*
H. clausa var. ensata
H. clausa var. normalis*
H. clavata
H. 'Curley Top'
H. 'Dark Victory'
H. 'Decorata Normalis'*
H. 'Dixie Queen'
H. 'Drummer Boy'
H. 'Egret'
H. 'Ellen'
H. 'Emerald Ripples'
H. 'Emerald Tiara'
H. 'Eunice Choice'
H. 'Fairway Green'
H. 'Floradora'*
H. 'Freising'
H. 'Green Splash'
H. 'Green Wiggles'
H. 'Gum Drop'
H. 'Helonioides'
H. 'Iwa Soules'*
H. 'Jade Scepter'
H. 'Kelsey'
H. kikutii var. caput-avis
H. kikutii var. polyneuron
H. kikutii var. tosana
H. kikutii var. yakusimensis
H. kiyosumiensis
H. laevigata
H. 'Lancifolia'*
H. 'Lavender Lady'*
H. 'Leather Sheen'
H. longipes*
H. longipes f. hypoglauca*
H. longipes f. sparsa
H. longipes f. viridipes
H. longipes var. caduca
H. longipes var. latifolia
H. longipes var. vulgata
H. 'Marquis'
H. 'Mary Jo'
H. minor
H. 'Misty Morning'
H. 'Montreal'*
H. 'Mount Royal'*
H. 'New Wave'
H. 'Nicola'
H. 'Oakview'
H. okamotoi
H. 'Pauline'
H. 'Peedee Elfin Bells'
H. 'Peedee Gray Mulkin'
H. 'Polly Mae'

H. 'Pollyanna'
H. 'Purple Lady Finger'
H. 'Purple Profusion'
H. rectifolia*
H. rectifolia f. pruinosa
H. rectifolia var. sachalinensis
H. 'Rim Rock'
H. 'Rohdeifolia Virdis'
H. 'Sea Octopus'
H. 'Sentinels'
H. 'Shells at Sea'
H. sieboldii*
H. sieboldii 'Alba'*
H. sieboldii f. angustifolia*
H. sieboldii f. campanulata
H. sieboldii f. okamii
H. sieboldii f. spathulata*
H. 'Slim Polly'
H. 'Snow Mound'
H. 'Snowstorm'
H. 'Sparkling Burgundy'
H. 'Surprise'
H. 'Susy'
H. takiensis
H. 'Tall Twister'*
H. tardiva
H. 'The Twister'*
H. 'Tinker Bell'
H. 'Twinkle Toes'
H. 'White Trumpets'
H. 'Snow Flakes'*
H. 'Uguis'*
H. 'Unazuki Soules'*
H. yingeri

Miniature Sizes

H. 'Abiqua Ground Cover'
H. 'Bitsy Green'
H. 'Cathy Late'
H. gracillima*
H. longissima*
H. longissima var. longifolia
H. 'Lorna'
H. 'Margaret'
H. minor 'Alba'
H. nakaiana*
H. pulchella
H. 'Purple Dwarf'
H. 'Saishu Jima'*
H. 'Sugar Plum Fairy'
H. 'Tortifrons'
H. 'Tot Tot'
H. 'Wagners Petite'

Dwarf Sizes

H. 'Abiqua Miniature'
H. pulchella
H. 'Shining Tot'*
H. 'Suzuki Thumbnail'
H. 'Thumb Nail'*
H. 'Tiny Tears'*
H. venusta*

The Yellow Group (YG)

Giant Sizes

H. sieboldiana 'Semperaurea'
H. 'Sum and Substance'*

Large Sizes

H. 'Alabama Gold'*
H. 'Bold and Brassy'
H. 'City Lights'
H. 'Golden Maple'
H. 'Golden Sculpture'*
H. 'Golden Sunburst'*
H. hypoleuca 'Ogon'
H. 'Jim Cooper'
H. 'Midwest Gold'
H. 'Piedmont Gold'*
H. 'Sun Power'*
H. 'Sunlight Sister'*
H. 'Thai Brass'
H. 'Tijuana Brass'
H. 'Yellow Emperor'
H. 'Zounds'*

Medium Sizes

H. 'Alpine Aire'
H. 'August Moon'*
H. 'Birchwood Gold'*
H. 'Birchwood Parkys Gold'*
H. 'Blondie'
H. 'Bright Glow'*
H. 'Cardwell Yellow'
H. 'Emma Foster'
H. 'Estelle Aden'
H. 'Fortunei Aurea'*
H. 'Frances Williams Baby'
H. 'Gold Cup'
H. 'Gold Pan'
H. 'Golden Chimes'
H. 'Golden Medallion'*
H. 'Golden Nugget'
H. 'Golden Waffles'
H. 'Golden Wheels'
H. 'Goldilocks'
H. 'Honey'
H. longipes 'Ogon Amagi'
H. 'Midas Touch'*
H. montana 'Ogon'
H. 'Olympic Gold'
H. 'Sea Gold'
H. 'Sea Gold Star'
H. 'Shade Master'
H. 'Sun Glow'
H. 'Treasure'

Small Sizes

H. 'Bengee'*
H. capitata 'Ogon'
H. 'Gold Cadet'
H. 'Gold Cover'
H. 'Gold Edger'*
H. 'Golden Bullion'*
H. 'Golden Prayers'*
H. 'Golden Scepter'*
H. 'Golden Tiara'*
H. 'Good as Gold'*
H. 'Lancifolia Aurea'
H. 'Little Aurora'*

H. 'Petite Gold'
H. *rectifolia* 'Ogon'
H. 'Super Bowl'
H. *tsushimensis* 'Ogon'

Miniature Sizes
H. 'Bitsy Gold'
H. 'Gosan Hildegarde'
H. 'Gosan Mina'
H. *nakaiana* 'Ogon'
H. *sieboldii* 'Subcrocea'*
H. 'Wogon'*

Dwarf Sizes
H. 'Gosan Gold Midget'

The Variegated Margin Group (VMG)

White Margin with Green Center
H. 'Allan P. McConnell'*
H. 'Antioch'*
H. 'Asahi Comet'
H. 'Beaulah'
H. 'Bold Edger'*
H. 'Bold Ribbons'*
H. 'Bridgeville'
H. 'Brim Cup'
H. 'Butter White Rim'
H. 'Carol'*
H. 'Carrie Ann'*
H. *cathayana* 'Shirofukurin'
H. 'Chameleon'
H. 'Change of Tradition'
H. 'Chantilly Lace'
H. 'Christmas Tree'*
H. 'Citation'
H. 'Coquette'
H. 'Cream Edge'
H. 'Crepe Suzette'
H. 'Crescent Moon'
H. 'Crested Surf'
H. 'Crispula'*
H. 'Crowned Imperial'*
H. 'Decorata'*
H. 'Dew Drop'
H. 'Diamond Tiara'
H. 'Dustin'
H. 'Elfin Power'
H. 'Fortunei Albomarginata'*
H. 'Francee'*
H. 'Frosted Jade'*
H. 'Gay Blade'
H. 'Ginko Craig'*
H. 'Gloriosa'*
H. 'Gotemba Nishiki'
H. 'Grand Master'
H. 'Ground Master'*
H. 'Heartsong'
H. 'Helonioides Albopicta'*
H. 'Herifu'*
H. 'Hertha'
H. 'Hilda Wassman'
H. 'Hime'*
H. 'Iron Gate Glamor'*
H. 'Jack Frost'

H. 'Jo Jo'
H. 'Karafuto'
H. 'Kifukurin Ko Mame'
H. 'Klopping Variegated'
H. 'Krossa Cream Edge'*
H. 'Leola Fraim'
H. *longipes* 'Shirofukurin'
H. *longissima* 'Asahi Comet'
H. *nakaiana* 'Allan P. McConnell'*
H. 'Peace'
H. 'Regal Splendor'
H. 'Sassy'
H. 'Showtime'
H. *sieboldii*'*
H. *sieboldii* 'Bunchoko'
H. 'Silverado'
H. 'So Sweet'
H. 'Spinners'
H. 'Standing Ovation'
H. 'Stiletto'
H. 'Tambourine'
H. 'Undulata Albomarginata'*
H. 'Vera Verde'*

White Margin with Yellow Center
H. 'Amy Aden Rim'
H. 'Anne Arett'*
H. 'Bizarre'
H. 'Blessings'
H. 'Crown Jewel'*
H. 'Elfin Cup'
H. 'Emerald Crust'
H. 'Evening Magic'
H. 'Gaiety'
H. 'Little Ann'*
H. 'Platinum Tiara'
H. 'Umezawa'

Yellow Margin with Green Center
H. 'Amagi Nishiki'
H. 'Amber Maiden'
H. 'Asahi Sunray'
H. 'Aurora Borealis'*
H. 'Bill Brincka'
H. 'Bunchoko'*
H. 'Carnival'
H. 'Cartwheels'
H. 'Chariot Wheels'
H. 'Columbus Circle'
H. 'Connie'
H. 'Double Edge'
H. 'Duchess'
H. 'El Capitan'
H. 'Ellerbroek'*
H. 'Emily Dickinson'
H. 'Fleeta Brownell Woodroffe'
H. *fluctuans* 'Variegated'*
H. 'Formal Attire'
H. 'Fortunei Aureomarginata'*
H. 'Frances Williams'*
H. 'Fringe Benefit'*
H. 'Gilt Edge'
H. 'Goddess of Athena'
H. 'Golden Circles'
H. 'Green Gold'*
H. 'Heaven Scent'™'
H. 'Jack of Diamonds'
H. 'Kara'*

H. *longissima* 'Asahi Sunray'
H. *montana* 'Aureomarginata'*
H. 'Opipara'
H. *rectifolia* 'Chionea'
H. *rectifolia* 'Chionea Albiflora'
H. *rectifolia* 'Kifukurin'
H. 'Rohdeifolia'
H. 'Sparky'
H. 'Sunnybrook'
H. 'Tokudama Flavocircinalis'*
H. 'Tsunotori Fukurin'
H. 'Two Step'
H. *ventricosa* 'Aureomarginata'*
H. 'Zagers Pride'*

The Variegated Center Group (VCG)

Green Margin on White Center
H. 'Bobbin'
H. 'Borwick Beauty'
H. 'Calypso'
H. 'Celebration'*
H. 'Center Stage'
H. 'Cheesecake'
H. 'Cupids Arrow'
H. 'Enchantress'
H. 'Gay Feather'
H. 'Gene Summers'
H. 'Goody Goody'
H. 'Haku Chu Han'*
H. 'Hatsu Yuki Nishiki'
H. 'Ivory Pixie'
H. 'Janet'*
H. 'La Vista'
H. 'New Tradition'
H. 'Photo Finish'
H. 'Pixie Power'
H. 'Raindance'
H. *sieboldii* 'Silver Kabitan'*
H. 'Undulata'*
H. *venusta* 'Variegated'*
H. 'Whipped Cream'
H. 'White Christmas'

Green Margin with Yellow Center
H. 'Abiqua Moonbeam'*
H. 'Ani Machi'
H. *cathayana* 'Chinese Sunrise'*
H. 'Chinese Sunrise'*
H. 'Choko Nishiki'
H. 'Color Glory'
H. 'Everglades'
H. 'Fan Dance'
H. 'Fortunei Albopicta'*
H. 'Fran and Jan'
H. 'Fuji No Yubae'
H. 'Geisha'*
H. 'George Smith'
H. 'Gohon Matsu Fukurin'
H. 'Gold Standard'*
H. 'Great Expectations'
H. 'Green Eclipse'
H. 'Green Rim Nugget'
H. 'Inniswood'

H. 'Joyce Trott'
H. 'Julie Morss'
H. 'Just So'
H. 'Kara'*
H. 'King Tut'
H. kiyosumiensis 'Nakafu'
H. 'Knockout'
H. 'Lakeside Symphony'
H. 'Pauls Glory'
H. 'Poo Bear'
H. 'September Sun'
H. sieboldii 'Kabitan'*
H. 'Sitting Pretty'
H. 'Tokudama Aureonebulosa'*
H. 'Tokudama Flavoplanata'*
H. ventricosa 'Aureomaculata'*

The Irregularly Variegated Group (VIG)

Large Sizes
H. 'Cynthia'
H. 'Dorothy Benedict'
H. 'Northern Mist™'

Medium Sizes
H. 'Amanogawa'
H. 'Blue Shadows'*
H. 'Boots and Saddles'
H. 'Breeders Choice'
H. 'Dianne'
H. 'Fascination'
H. 'Flamboyant'
H. 'Fragrant Flame'
H. 'Fuji No Akebono'
H. 'Fury of Flame'
H. 'Galaxy'
H. 'Garden Bouquet'
H. 'Haru No Yume'
H. 'Hatsu Shimo Nishiki'
H. 'Heaven Scent™'
H. 'Iron Gate Delight'*
H. 'Iron Gate Supreme'*
H. 'Marbled Bouquet'
H. 'Marbled Cream'
H. 'Middle Ridge'*
H. 'Pin Stripe'
H. 'Reiho'
H. 'Reiko'
H. 'Sea Prize'
H. 'Sharmon'
H. 'Spilt Milk'
H. 'Spritzer'*
H. 'Sweet Standard'
H. 'Thea'
H. 'William Lachman'

Small Sizes
H. 'Bensheim'
H. 'Inaho'*
H. 'Irish Spring'
H. 'Coquette'
H. 'Goody Goody'
H. 'Komyo Nishiki'
H. 'Mentor Gold'*

H. 'Neat Splash'*
H. 'O Fuji Fukurin'
H. 'Okutama Nishiki'
H. 'Painted Lady'
H. 'Piedmont Stripe'
H. 'Richland Gold Splash'
H. 'Shima Kabitan'
H. sieboldii 'Mediopicta'
H. 'Starburst'
H. 'Streaked Tiara'
H. 'Sweet Jill'
H. 'Swoosh'
H. tardiva 'Aureostriata'
H. 'Undulata'*
H. 'Undulata Univittata'*
H. 'Yellow Splash'*
H. 'Zansetsu'

Miniature Sizes
H. 'Artists Palette'
H. 'Little Jim'

The Tiny Group (TG)

Dwarf Sizes
H. 'Abiqua Miniature'
H. 'Blue Ice'
H. 'Gosan Gold Midget'
H. 'Ivory Pixie'
H. 'Shining Tot'*
H. 'Thumb Nail'*
H. 'Tiny Tears'*
H. 'Tot Tot'

The Mammoth Group (MG)

Green Color
H. 'Behemoth'
H. 'Bethel Big Leaf'
H. 'Big Boy'
H. 'Big Sam'
H. 'Birchwood Elegance'*
H. 'Century One'
H. 'Colossal'
H. 'Corduroy'
H. 'Elata'*
H. 'Fernwood'
H. 'Goliath'
H. 'Green Acres'*
H. 'Green Piecrust'*
H. 'Green Wedge'*
H. 'Grey Piecrust'
H. hypoleuca*
H. 'Jolly Green Giant'
H. 'Mikado'
H. montana f. macrophylla*
H. nigrescens 'Elatior'*
H. 'Pioneer'
H. 'Quilting Party'
H. 'Sea Drift'*
H. 'Sea Monster'

Blue-Green or Grey-Green Color
H. 'Abiqua Parasol'

H. 'Aksarben'
H. 'Aretts Wonder'
H. 'Big John'
H. 'Big Mama'
H. 'Blue Angel'*
H. 'Blue Frost'
H. 'Blue Umbrellas'*
H. 'Bold Ruffles'
H. 'Buckanon'
H. 'Champion'
H. 'Eleanor J. Reath'
H. 'Gray Cole'*
H. 'Harrison'
H. 'Lakeport Blue'*
H. 'Presidents Choice'
H. 'Quilted Skies'
H. 'Regal Ruffles'
H. 'River Nile'
H. 'Royal Quilt'
H. 'Ryans Big One'*
H. sieboldiana*
H. sieboldiana 'Amplissima'
H. sieboldiana 'Elegans'*
H. sieboldiana 'Hypophylla'
H. sieboldiana 'Mira'
H. 'Silver Award'
H. 'Silver Giant'
H. 'Sumi'
H. 'Trails End'*

Variegated White or Yellow
H. 'Harry A. Jacobson'
H. 'Snow Crust'

Yellow Color
H. 'Chartreuse Wedge'
H. 'Golden Sculpture'*
H. sieboldiana 'Semperaurea'
H. 'Solar Flare'
H. 'Sum and Substance'*
H. 'Sunlight Sister'*

The Edger Group (EG)

Medium to Miniature Sizes
H. 'Abiqua Blue Edger'
H. 'Allan P. McConnell'*
H. 'Amanuma'*
H. 'Anne Arett'*
H. 'Betsy King'*
H. 'Birchwood Parkys Gold'*
H. 'Bold Edger'*
H. 'Bunchoko'*
H. 'Carrie Ann'*
H. cathayana*
H. 'Emerald Ripples'
H. 'Floradora'*
H. 'Ginko Craig'*
H. 'Gloriosa'*
H. 'Golden Scepter'*
H. 'Golden Tiara'*
H. gracillima*
H. 'Hadspen Heron'*
H. 'Haku Chu Han'*
H. 'Helonioides Albopicta'*
H. 'Herifu'*

H. 'Hime'*
H. kikutii*
H. 'Lancifolia'*
H. 'Little Ann'*
H. 'Little Aurora'*
H. longipes*
H. 'Montreal'*
H. 'Mount Royal'*
H. nakaiana*
H. rectifolia*
H. 'Saishu Jima'*
H. sieboldii*
H. sieboldii 'Alba'*
H. sieboldii f. angustifolia*
H. sieboldii f. spathulata*
H. sieboldii 'Kabitan'*
H. sieboldii 'Silver Kabitan'*
H. 'Tall Twister'*
H. tibae*
H. 'Undulata'*
H. 'Undulata Albomarginata'*
H. 'Undulata Erromena'*
H. venusta*
H. 'Vera Verde'*
H. 'Weihenstephan'
H. 'Wogon'*
H. 'Yakushima Mizu'*

The Erect Group (RG)

Large Sizes
H. 'Big Daddy'*
H. 'Gold Piece'
H. 'Gold Regal'*
H. 'Golden Sculpture'*
H. 'Golden Torch'
H. 'High Style'
H. montana f. macrophylla*

H. nigrescens 'Elatior'*
H. 'Regal Splendor'
H. 'Samual Blue'
H. 'Sea Lotus Leaf'

Medium Sizes
H. 'Abiqua Ambrosia'
H. 'Ada Reed'
H. 'Aspen Gold'*
H. 'Blue Arrow'
H. 'Blue Velvet'
H. 'Bold Edger'
H. 'Comeuppance'
H. 'Debutante'
H. 'Gala'*
H. 'Garden Bouquet'
H. 'Grand Master'
H. 'High Kicker'
H. 'Kathleen'
H. 'Krossa Regal'*
H. 'Midas Touch'*
H. 'Regal Rhubarb'
H. 'Riptide'
H. 'Sea Lightning'

Small Sizes
H. 'Anne Arett'*
H. 'Artists Palette'
H. 'Bizarre'
H. 'Calypso'
H. 'Cathy Late'
H. 'Celebration'*
H. 'China Doll'
H. clausa*
H. 'Coquette'
H. 'Crown Prince'
H. 'Eunice Choice'
H. 'Fused Veins'
H. 'Gay Feather'

H. 'Geisha'*
H. 'Green Wiggles'
H. 'Harts Tongue'
H. 'Josephine'
H. 'Just So'
H. 'Krossa Cream Edge'*
H. 'Lavender Lady'*
H. 'Louisa'*
H. 'Marble Rim'*
H. 'Mentor Gold'*
H. 'Montreal'*
H. 'Mount Royal'*
H. 'Noel'
H. 'Painted Lady'
H. 'Polly Mae'
H. 'Purple Lady Finger'
H. rectifolia*
H. 'Sea Octopus'

Miniature Sizes
H. 'Asahi Comet'
H. 'Asahi Sunray'
H. 'Chartreuse Wiggles'
H. 'Elfin Power'
H. 'Gingee'
H. 'Golden Spades'
H. 'Gray Streaked Squiggles'
H. 'Ground Sulphur'
H. 'Koriyama'
H. 'Lights Up'
H. 'Little Ann'
H. 'Little Jim'
H. longissima*
H. 'Peedee Gold Flash'
H. 'Royalty'

Dwarf Sizes
H. 'Bobbin'

The Fragrant Group (FG)

Large Sizes
H. 'Flower Power'
H. 'Summer Fragrance'*

Medium Sizes
H. 'Abiqua Ambrosia'
H. 'Bette Davis Eyes'
H. 'Emily Dickinson'
H. 'Fragrant Bouquet'
H. 'Fragrant Candelabra'
H. 'Fragrant Flame'
H. 'Fragrant Gold'
H. 'Garden Bouquet'
H. 'Heaven Scent'™
H. 'Hogyoku'
H. 'Honeybells'*
H. 'Invincible'*
H. 'Iron Gate Delight'*
H. 'Iron Gate Glamor'*
H. 'Iron Gate Supreme'*
H. 'Marbled Bouquet'
H. 'Niohi No Mai'

H. plantaginea*
H. plantaginea 'Aphrodite'
H. plantaginea 'Stenantha'
H. plantaginea var. japonica
H. 'Royal Accolade'
H. 'Royal Standard'
H. 'Shiho'
H. 'Showtime'
H. 'So Sweet'*
H. 'Sugar and Cream'*
H. 'Sweet Marjorie'
H. 'Sweet Standard'
H. 'Sweet Susan'*
H. 'Sweet Winifred'
H. 'Sweetie'
H. 'White Knight'*
H. 'White Shoulders'

Small Sizes
H. 'Fragrant Blue'
H. 'Iron Gate Bouquet'*
H. 'Sweet Jill'
H. 'Whipped Cream'

Miniature Sizes
H. 'Fragrant Tot'

Dwarf Sizes
H. 'Asuka'
H. 'Kunpu'
H. 'Otome No Ka'

The Accent Group (AG)

Any of the hostas in MG as well as any of the giant hostas in the BG, GG, YG, and other groups can serve as accent plants. Because of their prominent variegation and habit, the following hostas make outstanding accents:

All Sizes

    H. 'Aurora Borealis'*
    H. 'Color Glory'
    H. fluctuans 'Variegated'*
    H. 'Frances Williams'*
    H. 'Gold Standard'*
    H. 'Golden Sculpture'*
    H. montana 'Aureomarginata'*
    H. nigrescens*
    H. nigrescens 'Elatior'*
    H. opipara
    H. 'Regal Splendor'
    H. 'Sum and Substance'*
    H. 'Sun Power'*

A FAVORITE COLLECTION

The following group of hostas was selected as the favorite group by gardeners visiting Hosta Hill on several occasions. All are available. Some are inexpensive; others expensive, but prices will drop with increased availability.

All Sizes

    H. 'Antioch'
    H. 'August Moon'
    H. 'Big Daddy'
    H. 'Blue Angel'
    H. 'Blue Cadet'
    H. capitata
    H. 'Crispula'
    H. 'Decorata'
    H. fluctuans 'Variegated'
    H. 'Francee'
    H. 'Geisha'
    H. 'Gold Standard'
    H. 'Golden Tiara'
    H. 'Great Expectations'
    H. 'Hadspen Blue'
    H. 'Honeybells'
    H. hypoleuca
    H. kikutii
    H. 'Krossa Regal'
    H. longipes (all forms)
    H. 'Little Aurora'
    H. 'Midas Touch'
    H. montana (all forms)
    H. montana 'Aureomarginata'
    H. montana f. macrophylla
    H. 'Moonlight'
    H. nigrescens
    H. 'Northern Halo'
    H. plantaginea
    H. 'Regal Splendor'
    H. 'Royal Standard'
    H. 'September Sun'
    H. 'Shade Fanfare'
    H. sieboldii 'Kabitan'
    H. sieboldii 'Mediopicta'
    H. 'So Sweet'
    H. 'Sugar and Cream'
    H. 'Sum and Substance'
    H. 'Sun Power'
    H. 'Tardiflora'
    H. tokudama 'Aureonebulosa'
    H. tokudama 'Flavocircinalis'
    H. 'Undulata Albomarginata'
    H. ventricosa
    H. ventricosa 'Aureomarginata'
    H. venusta

INTERNATIONAL HOSTA SOCIETIES

There are 2 large hosta societies with international membership. One was founded in the United States and the other in the United Kingdom. The latter, called the British Hosta and Hemerocallis Society, counts among its members Hosta and Hemerocallis enthusiasts, while The American Hosta Society deals exclusively with the genus Hosta. Both societies publish newsletters and journals, and membership in one or both of these societies is highly recommended as the best way to keep up with the latest horticultural developments concerning the genus.

In addition to these international groups, regional groups have been organized in the United States. Many of these groups sponsor annual garden tours, conduct cut-leaf shows, and present interesting and educational programs at their meetings.

Readers can obtain details regarding membership by writing to the membership secretaries listed in the following:

The American Hosta Society
Dennis Paul Savory, Membership Secretary
5300 Whiting Avenue
Edina, MN 55435
USA

British Hosta and Hemerocallis Society
The Hon. Secretary, Rodger Bowden
Cleave House, Sticklepath
Okehampton, Devon EX20 2NN
UK

U.S. REGIONAL HOSTA SOCIETIES

The Alabama Hosta Society
Francis Watkins
93 Lucerne Boulevard
Birmingham, AL 35209

Carolina Hosta Society
Bob Solberg
5715 Hideaway Drive
Chapel Hill, NC 27516

Central Illinois Hosta Society
Janis Lee
R.R. No. 1, Box 160
Tremont, IL 61568

Chattanooga Area Hosta Society
Mary Chastain
8119 Roy Lane
Ooltewah, TN 37363

The Cincinnati Daylily and Hosta Society
Don Hawke
205 Summit Street
Lebanon, OH 45036

Delaware Valley Hosta Society
Melissa Levy
43 Harlech Drive
Delaware, DE 19807

The Georgia Hosta Society
Claudia Walker
10525 Timberstone Road
Alpharetta, GA 30201

Harshbarger Hosta Society
Marilyn A. Gaffey
R.R. No. 6, Box 14B
Iowa City, IA 52240

The Indianapolis Hosta Society
Carolyn Harstad
5952 Lieber Road
Indianapolis, IN 46208

The Maine Hosta Society
Ron Burnham
RFD 1, Box 82
Monmouth, ME 04259

The Michigan Hosta Society
Jim Wilkins
2585 Spring Arbor Road
Jackson, MI 49203

Midwest Regional Hosta Society
Frank Riehl
630 East Washington Avenue
Iowa City, IA 52240

The New England Hosta Society
Barbara Jones
46 Bartlett Street
Chelmsford, ME 01824

Northwest Hosta Society
Warren Starnes
11002 South Mount Hope Road
Molalla, OR 97038

The Potomac Hosta Club
Tony Weisbacher
1740 Brookside Lane
Vienna, VA 22180

Willamette Valley Hosta Group
Chet Tompkins
185 NE Territorial Road
Canby, OR 97013

HOSTA NURSERIES (WHOLESALE AND RETAIL)

Nota bene
In the following list many of the nurseries are small specialty nurseries with limited facilities. Before placing orders, contact the nursery by mail or phone to obtain catalogs or lists of available plant material and to establish if the nursery ships by mail or overseas. Overseas shipments usually require inspection and import permits. Investigate cost of shipping, which can be considerable if air mail is utilized.

USA
A majority of North American hosta growers are members of the American Hosta Growers Group, which can be contacted by writing to Bruce Banyai, Secretary, 11 Gates Circle, Hockessin, DE 19707. The following listing is in alphabetic order by state:

Arizona
> Bob Hambuchen
> 2740 Prince Street
> Conway, AR 72032

California
> Marca Dickie
> PO Box 1270
> Boyes Hot Springs, CA 95416

Connecticut
> Sharon Carvalho
> PO Box 1986
> Madison, CT 06443

Delaware
> Alex Summers
> PO Box 430
> Bridgeville, DE 19933
>
> Bruce Banyai Nursery
> 11 Gates Circle
> Hockessin, DE 19707

Georgia
> Sam and Carleen Jones
> Piccadilly Farms
> 1971 Whippoorwill Road
> Bishop, GA 30621

Illinois
> Bob Keller
> 6145 Oak Point Court
> Peoria, IL 61614
>
> Jan Lee
> Rt. 1, Box 160
> Tremont, IL 61568
>
> Jim Van Hoorn
> PO Box 776
> Wauconda, IL 60084
>
> Klehm Nursery
> Rt. 5, Box 197
> South Barrington, IL 60010
>
> Mary Pratt
> 151 West Detweiler Drive
> Peoria, IL 61615

Nancy Crawford
202 Wolf Road
Peoria, IL 61614

Rich Hornbaker
R.R. 4
Princeton, IL 61356

T & Z Nursery
28 West 571 Roosevelt Road
Winfield, IL 44601

Indiana
Leo Sharp, Sr.
600 East Ninth Street
Michigan City, IN 46360

Olga Petryszyn
1514 Teale Drive
Chesterton, IN 46304

Randy Goodwin
7401 Shadow Wood Drive
Indianapolis, IN 46254

Soules Garden
5809 Rahke Road
Indianapolis, IN 46217

Iowa
Frank Riehl
630 East Washington
Iowa City, IA 52240

Stark Gardens
631 G24 Highway
Norwalk, IA 50211

Massachusetts
Ian Donovan
Laboratory Botanica
22 Charles Street
Newton, MA 02166

Maryland
Carroll Gardens, Inc.
PO Box 310
Westminster, MD 21157

Richard Watson
12017 Glen Arm Road
Glen Arm, MD 21057

Michigan
David Reath
100 Central Boulevard
Vulcan, MI 49892

Englerth Gardens
2461 22nd Street
Hopkins, MI 49328

Fraleigh Nursery
2351 East Delhi
Ann Arbor, MI 48103

Hosta Gate Gardens (wholesale only)
8030 Sugarloaf Trail
Clarkston, MI 48016

Leo Sharp, Sr.
303 Fir Street
Michigan City, MI 46360

Nick Balash
26595 H Drive North
Albion, MI 49224

Pauline Banyai Nursery
626 West Lincoln Avenue
Madison Heights, MI 48071

Pete DeGroot
PO Box 575
Coloma, MI 49038

Sam Defazio, Praxis
PO Box 134
Allegan, MI 49101

Walters Gardens, Inc.
PO Box 137
Zeeland, MI 49464

Minnesota
Busse Gardens
Rt. 2, Box 238
Cokato, MN 55321

Fairway Enterprises
114 The Fairway
Albert Lea, MN 56007

Jan Cox
12909 Otchipwe Avenue, North
Stillwater, MN 55082

Kelley and Kelley
2325 South Watertown
Long Lake, MN 55356

Ken Anderson Nursery
Rt. 1, Box 108
Farwell, MN 56327

Mike Heger
8015 Krey Avenue
Waconia, MN 55387

Savory Gardens, Inc.
5300 Whiting Avenue
Edina, MN 55435

New York
Bill Bilodeau
390 Jervis Avenue
Copiague, NY 11726

Irene Schaefer
691 Deer Park Avenue
Dix Hills, NY 11746

Phil Hees
PO Box 1649
Mattituck, NY 11952

Ransom Lydell
10749 Bennett Road
Dunkirk, NY 14048

North Carolina
Bob Solberg
5715 Hideaway Drive
Chapel Hill, NC 27516

Jernigan Gardens
Rt. 6, Box 593
Dunn, NC 28334

Jim Cooper
5206 Hawkesbury Lane
Raleigh, NC 27606

Powell's Garden
Rt. 3, Box 21
Princeton, NC 27569

Van Sellers Gardens
Rt. 3, Box 250
Kings Mountain, NC 28086

Ohio
Bauer's Nursery
9859 St., Rt. 42
Cincinnati, OH 45241

Bill Zumbar
855 Parkway Boulevard
Alliance, OH 44601

Dorothy Parker
3 West Page Avenue
Trenton, OH 45067

Handy Hatfield
22799 Ringgold Southern Road
Stoutsville, OH 43154

Kuk's Forest Nursery
10174 Barr Road
Brecksville, OH 44141

Peter Ruh, Homestead Division
9448 Mayfield Road
Chesterland, OH 44026

Rocknoll Nursery
9210 US 50
Hillsboro, OH 45133

Van Wade
RD No. 3
Bellville, OH 44813

Oregon
Al Rogers
15425 South West Pleasant Hill Road
Sherwood, OR 97140

Hyslop and Purtymun
5744 Crooked Finger Road
Scotts Mills, OR 97395

Pennsylvania
Bette Comfry, Silvermist
RD 2, Box 2146A
Stonesboro, PA 16153

Clifton Russell
725 New Road
Churchville, PA 18966

Vickie Mayer
540 Phillips Street
Baden, PA 15005

South Carolina
Coastal Gardens and Nursery
4611 Socastee Boulevard
Myrtle Beach, SC 29575

Wayside Gardens
Hodges, SC 29695

Tennessee
Roy Chastain, Lakeside Acres
8119 Roy Lane
Ooltewah, TN 37363

Virginia
Andre Viette Nursery
Rt. 1, Box 6
Fisherville, VA 22939

Vermont
Rock Crest Gardens
Rt. 1, Box 1690
Hinesburg, VT 05461

Washington
Robyn Duback
7802 NE 63rd Street
Vancouver, WA 98662

Canada
Jim Stirling
R.R. 1
Morpeth, Ontario N0P 1X0

Ken Knechtel
R.R. 1, Site 2, Box 22
Anmore, BC V3H 3C8

United Kingdom
A large number of plant nurseries in the UK are beginning to offer collections of hostas but it was not possible to include all of them in the following list, which includes nurseries offering 30 varieties or more. I recommend readers consult the *Plant Finder* for additional sources of hostas in the UK. This book was devised and compiled by Chris Philip, edited by Tony Lord, and published by Headmain Ltd. for the Hardy Plant Society. An excellent reference publication, it is updated periodically and available in most book stores handling books on gardening. It can also be ordered in North America. The following listing is in alphabetic order by nursery name:

Apple Court
(National Reference Collection for Small-leaved Hostas)
Hordle Lane
Lymington, Hampshire SO41 0HU

Ann and Rodger Bowden
Cleave House, Sticklepath
Okehampton, Devon EX20 2NN

Bressingham Gardens
Diss, Norfolk IP22 2AB

Beth Chatto Gardens
Elmstead Market
Colchester
Essex CO7 7DB

Goldbrook Plants
Sandra Bond
Hoxne
Eye, Suffolk IP21 5AN

Great Dixter Nurseries
Northiam
Rye, East Sussex TN31 PH6

Hadspen House
Castle Cary, Somerset BA7 7NG

Kittoch Plants
(Scottish National Reference Collection)
Kittoch Mill
Carmunnock, Glasgow C76 9BJ

Lyford Garden Plants
West Lyford
Somerton, Somerset TA11 7BU

Mallorn Gardens
Lanner Hill
Redruth, Cornwall TR16 6DA

Mickfield Market Garden
Mickfield, Suffolk IP14 5LH

Park Green Nurseries
Wetheringset
Stowmarket, Suffolk IP14 5QH

Rushfields of Ledbury
Ross Road
Ledbury, Hereford HR8 2LP

Sinden Nursery
John Sinden
10 Derwentwater Road
Merley Ways
Wimbourne, Dorset BH21 1QS

Spinners
Boldre
Lymington, Hampshire SO41 5QE

Unusual Plants
White Bam House, Elmstead Market
Colchester, Essex CO7 7DB

Germany

Gärtnerischer Pflanzenbau
Dr. Hans und Helga Simon
Georg Mayr Strasse 70
8772 Marktheidenfeld, Germany

Friesland Staudengarten
Husumer Weg 16
2942 Jever 3, Rahrdum, Germany

Heinz Klose
3503 Lohfelden/Kassel
Rosenstrasse 10, Germany

Staudengärtnerei Gräfin von Zeppelin
7811 Sulzburg 2/Laufen
Baden, Germany

Netherlands

Arie van Fliet
C. Klyn and Co.
Zuidkade 97
2771DS Boskoop, Netherlands

Belgium

Ignace van Doorslaer
De Ten Ryen
Kapellendries 52
B9231 Melle Gontrode, Belgium

Japan

Hiroo Ishiguro
Kami-Maracuchi
Sofue Cho, Nakajima
Aichi Prefecture, Japan

Kamo Nurseries
Harasato, Kagewawa
Shizuoka Prefecture, 436-01, Japan

Kogoro Suzuki Nursery
2222 Tomioka-machi
Yokohama
Kanagawa Prefecture, Japan

APPENDIX A—PART 1

The Taxonomy of the Genus *Hosta*

HISTORY OF GENUS NAME

Representatives of the genus have been known to botanists since 1712 when Engelbert Kaempfer published *Amoenitates Exoticae*, which contains a catalog of Japanese plants. Among them are two hostas: *Joksan, vulgo Giboosi* and *Giboosi altera*.[1] These taxa remained without scientific names until Thunberg (1780) assigned the binomial *Aletris japonica* to the latter and validly published it. Thus, *Aletris* was the first generic name used for *Hosta*, but soon this arrangement was found rather unnatural and Thunberg (1784) transferred the genus to *Hemerocallis* (Daylily), as *Hemerocallis japonica*, and with this a long-standing association between these genera began.

Salisbury (1807) suggested the generic name *Saussurea*, but this name was not validly published and so is a nomen nudum. Salisbury's *Saussurea* is no longer important to *Hosta* taxonomy, because A. P. de Candolle's later homonym *Saussurea* (A. P. de Candolle, 1810, cfr. Hylander, 1954) was conserved against it for Compositae. Kuntze (1891) attempted to reestablish Salisbury's name but this proposal was equally invalid and so rejected, as was *Saussuria* (Moench, 1802) spelled slightly differently.

In 1812 the Austrian botanist Leopold Trattinnick (1764–1849) suggested the genus be classified under the generic name *Hosta* honoring his contemporary Nicolaus Thomas Host (1761–1834). But Trattinnick's *Hosta* was illegitimate because earlier validly published homonyms existed against it: *Hosta* Jaquin[2] 1797 (= *Cornutia* L., 1753, Verbenaceae) and *Hosta* Vellozo ex Pfeiffer (1874) (= *Horta*, Vellozo; = *Clavija*, Ruiz-Lopez et Pavón, Myrsinaceae). The slightly different *Hostia* by Voss and Siebert (1896) is taxonomically unimportant because it is an incorrect horticultural spelling of *Hosta* and the homonym *Hostia* by Moench (1802) (= *Crepis* L., Compositae) exists against it. The even earlier name *Hostea* by Willdenow[3] (1797) (= *Matalea* Aublet, Asclepiadaceae) is also considered homonymous, although different slightly in the ending. In spite of the existence of these homonyms, *Hosta* Trattinnick was conserved in 1905 by the International Botanical Congress (IC) of Vienna in accordance with Articles 20 (cfr. IR, 1935) and 24 (ICBN 1952).

In 1817 German botanist Kurt Polycarp Sprengel published the generic name *Funkia* to honor Heinrich Funk (1771–1839), a Bavarian collector of alpine ferns. This name is still occasionally used in horticulture and is a popular name for the genus in several European countries ("Funkia" in the Netherlands and Scandinavia and "Funkie" in Germany). The name also saw considerable horticultural use in North America, because most of the early cultivated species and cultivars were received from Europe. *Funkia* was preceded by several homonyms: *Funkia* Bentham and Hooker (1880/1883) (= *Funckia* Willdenow 1808 = *Astelia*, Banks et Solander, Asteliaceae); *Funkia* Endlicher (1841) (in syn. = *Funckia* Dennstaedt 1818 = *Lumnitzera* Willdenow, Combretaceae); and *Funckia* Dennstaedt (1818) (= *Lumnitzera* Willdenow, Combretaceae). In relation to *Hosta*, this generic name has been set aside.

Dumortier[4] (1822) applied still another name to the genus, namely, *Libertia*, which is unimportant to *Hosta* as it was rejected in favor of the conserved *Libertia* Sprengel (Iridaceae).

Nash (1911) proposed the hitherto subgeneric or sectional name *Niobe* as a name for the genus, but did so in conflict with the earlier conservation of *Hosta* by the IC, so was also ignored.

TYPIFICATION OF THE GENUS

Under the *International Rules of Botanical Nomenclature* (IR, 1935) and the *International Code of Botanical Nomenclature* (ICBN, 1952) the genus *Hosta* is typified by *H. plantaginea*. This species was the first in the genus to reach Europe in the early 1780s and was one of the first of the taxa in the genus to receive formal taxonomic treatment. Its position as generic type is based on the illustration in the original reference by Trattinnick (1812). This taxonomic position has generally been unchallenged, but some recommendations for change have come forward.

Hylander (1954) made a very thorough analysis of the taxa involved in Trattinnick's proposal and gave convincing reasons for changing the typification of the genus from *H. plantaginea* to *H. sieboldiana*. His proposal is based on the circumstance of misidentification of the taxa referred to by Trattinnick (1812). Hylander supposed that the citation of the type species should have been given as "*Hosta japonica* [Thunberg] Trattinnick; quoad basionym illeg. = *Hemerocallis japonica* Thunberg 1794 [non *Hemerocallis japonica* (Thunberg) Thunberg 1784]—non quoad plant. descriptam (quae = *Hemerocallis japonica* 'Thunberg' in sensu Redouté et Ker-Gawler = *Hosta plantaginea*)." Because Thunberg's 1794 basionym was derived from Banks' *Icones Selectae* (1791), tab. 2, the above citation means that the plant cited is not *H. plantaginea* but *Hemerocallis tokudama* (Stearn, 1931b; Maekawa, 1940). As a consequence Hylander proposed that Trattinnick's type was actually *Hosta* 'Tokudama' and that the generic type should be changed to a form of *H. sieboldiana* in a broad sense. This proposal has not been followed by subsequent authors, including Fujita (1976a), and little is to be gained from making this change, because (1) *H. plantaginea*, the most atypical, primitive species in the genus would be replaced by *H.* 'Tokudama', now known to be a cultigen; (2) even the election of *H. sieboldiana* in place of *H.* 'Tokudama' as the type species is not entirely satisfactory due to the former's atypical macromorphology when compared with the standard Japanese population; and (3) Trattinnick undoubtedly illustrates *H. plantaginea* but, unfortunately, none of the three species "transferred" by him can be legitimately associated with this taxon. Here, rather than upsetting long-established nomenclatural positions supported by a preponderance of key authors and the ICBN, I take the pragmatic view that two of the taxa involved in this mixup are now considered specioids (*H.* 'Lancifolia' and *H.* 'Tokudama'—see also discussion of Trattinnick under "The Early Period" in Appendix B) and have been reduced to cultivar form. As such they are no longer important to the taxonomy of the natural populations, and under my classification *H. plantaginea* remains the type species for the genus and the monotypic subgenus *Hosta* (formerly *Niobe*) as well. Nonetheless, for the record, Hylander (1954) is correct, at least in part, in his analysis considering the state of *Hosta* taxonomy at that time. Some might argue that *H. plantaginea* as a nomenclatural type is not typical of most of the taxa in the genus, but per Article 7.2 of the ICBN that circumstance does not prevent its use.

PHYLOGENETIC PLACEMENTS

Classic texts—for example, Baker (1870)—place *Hosta* in the Liliaceae usually in association with genus *Hemerocallis*, and Baker proposed inclusion of both genera in a tribe he calls Hemerocallideae. For over a century placement with the Liliaceae has been the most accepted taxonomic position on the familial level (Gray, 1950; Hylander, 1954; Hutchinson, 1964). Very recently, Cronquist (1981: 1121–1122) redefined this classic position by including the genus in Hemerocallideae, a tribe *Hosta* forms with *Hemerocallis* (daylily), *Hesperocallis* A. Gray (mountain queen, quixote plant) and *Leucocrinum* Nutt. ex A. Gray (star lily), still within the Liliaceae.[5]

No serious objections were raised against the earlier placements until the 1930s when cytologists found *Hosta* to be karyotypically similar to *Yucca*, *Agave*, *Camassia*, and other genera. Thus it was proposed principally on cytological grounds[6] to include *Hosta* with the Agavaceae. Evidence for this and similar placements was provided by a number of researchers who investigated this subject: cytological data were provided by McKelvey and Sax (1933), Whitaker (1934), Akemine (1935), Sato (1935, 1942), Suto (1936), and Granick (1944); embryological information was added by Cave (1948) and Wunderlich (1950); and serological findings were supplied by Chupov and Kutiavina (1981). These arrangements found support among cytologists, but because karyotypical similarities appear to be common among plants formerly placed in the Liliaceae, placements based on cytological evidence alone are no longer considered conclusive. In fact, Yasui (1935) argued against the earlier evidence and supported separation of *Hosta* from Hemerocallideae, but she proposed no other placement.

Traub (1953) nevertheless elevated the genus *Hosta* to tribal status, still within the Agavaceae, but did not give a valid diagnosis for his tribe Hosteae, so this proposal is invalid under the rules of the ICBN. As a consequence, Hylander (1954) was correct in validating the tribal status of Hosteae with a Latin diagnosis, but his validation related to Hosteae as a tribe under Liliaceae not Agavaceae.

Accordingly, on various grounds, close affinity with *Agave*, *Camassia*, *Hemerocallis*, *Hesperocallis*, *Leucocrinum*, *Manfreda*, and *Yucca* has been suggested, which has created rather numerous phylogenetic placements, each one with its proponents.

It became obvious that simplification was highly desirable, so in one of the latest proposals for classification of the monocotyledons, Dahlgren et al. (1985) have taxonomically separated the daylilies and hostas by placing *Hemerocallis* in the monotypic Hemerocallidaceae and the genus *Hosta* along with *Hesperocallis* A. Gray and *Leucocrinum* Nutt. ex A. Gray in the Funkiaceae in the order Asparagales. It is important to note Dahlgren emphasized that the inclusion of *Hesperocallis* and *Leucocrinum*—both endemic to western North America—in the Funkiaceae, which also contain the eastern Asia genus *Hosta*, does not represent a truly satisfactory phylogenetic relationship. According to Mathew (1987) *Leucocrinum* has recently been placed in the Anthericaceae and the taxonomically difficult and monotypic *Hesperocallis* has been connected with Hyacinthaceae; a new arrangement of the petaloid monocotyledon families at Kew Herbarium reflects the removal of the latter from Funkiaceae

and leaves only *Hosta* in the Funkiaceae.

Mathew (1988) further clarified Dahlgren's fragmentation of the old family of Liliaceae into smaller homogeneous families as it relates to *Hosta*. Because of its distinct taxonomic and morphological isolation he proposed placing the genus *Hosta* in a monotypic family. Mathew pointed out that Funkiaceae P. Horaninow (cfr. Mathew, 1988) was based on the earlier name *Funkia* Sprengel (1817) which is a later homonym of *Funckia* Willdenow (1808). As such, according to the rules, it cannot pass its name on to the family. Mathew suggested that the name *Hosta* (a nomen conservandum) would indeed be eminently suitable as a family name for the genus *Hosta* as Hostaceae, and he provided a Latin diagnosis to validate this name. Thus, the latest proposed systematic position of the genus *Hosta* is in a monotypic family, called Hostaceae, which supersedes Hylander's tribal name Hosteae.

Breaking new ground, M. G. Chung and S. B. Jones (1989) have studied the pollen morphology of *Hosta* and provided palynological evidence which is important to understanding phylogenetic relationships and also has implications on evolutionary theories. The arrangement of the genus into three subgenera—first suggested by Bailey (1930) and accepted by me in this book—has attained important micromorphological support by way of the typification of pollen grains presented in Chung and Jones (1989). Additionally, it has contributed key data for delimiting and circumscribing *Hosta* species.

DIVISIONS OF THE GENUS

Before dealing with nomenclatural problems and describing the relative taxonomic positions of *Hosta* species, a short review of the historic divisions of the genus is helpful. The initial division of the genus was carried out by Salisbury (1812) who published the generic names *Niobe* for *H. plantaginea* (founded on *Hemerocallis japonica*) and *Bryocles* for *H. ventricosa* (founded on *Bryocles ventricosa* = *Hemerocallis cærulea*). Both of these names were without valid descriptions and so invalid as nomina nuda. This early division (see Table 1) was based on distinct and obvious morphological differences between *Hosta plantaginea* and *H. ventricosa*; for example, the former is night-flowering with a small bracteole at the base of the pedicel and the latter flowers during the day.

Trattinnick (1812), who created the new genus, divided it into three species: *H. japonica*, *H. lancifolia*, and *H. cærulea*. This division came very close to the present key species concept explained later. Regrettably, none of these names were formally transferred to *Hosta* and only *H. lancifolia* is still used in nomenclature. Nonetheless, Trattinnick's three species represent the current major divisions, namely, *H. japonica* for *Hosta*, *H. cærulea* for *Bryocles*, and *H. lancifolia* for *Giboshi*. Although only a division on the species level, it shows that early botanists had developed a concept of delimitation which is still valid today.

Notwithstanding their status as invalid names, Baker (1870) published *Niobe* and *Bryocles* as sectional names under *Funkia* and subsequently Engler (Engler and Prantl, 1888) did so with respect to *Hosta*, thereby giving them taxonomic significance. This arrangement was strengthened by Bailey (1930) who adopted these sectional names also with respect to *Hosta*. Maekawa (1940) raised both to subgeneric rank with subgenus *Niobe* containing only *H. plantaginea* and subgenus *Bryocles* embracing all the other species. Such an arrangement has been accepted by several authorities, including Fujita (1976a), M. G. Chung (1989), and S. B. Jones (Aden, 1988; Jones, 1989), but Fujita changed the subgeneric name *Niobe* to *Hosta* in accordance with the ICBN which requires that any subgenus incorporating the type species of the genus must

Table 1
THE GENUS HOSTA
DIVISION OF 1812
(Morphological Division)

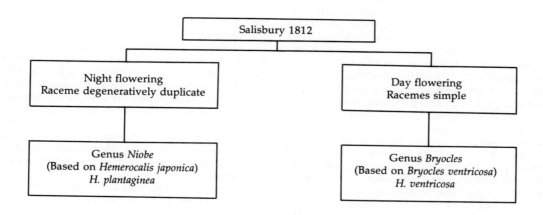

Table 2
THE GENUS HOSTA
DIVISIONS OF 1870–1940 (1976)
(Two Sections or Subgenera)

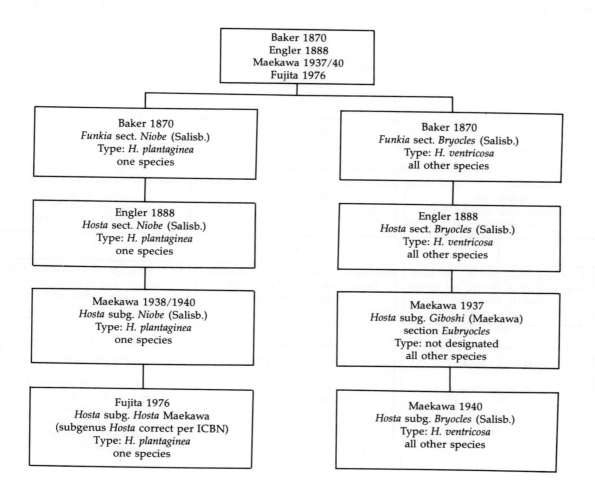

bear the same name as the genus (see also under Fujita, Appendix B). *Niobe* (Salisbury in the sense of Baker) Maekawa (1937, 1938b, 1940) has, of course, priority in this rank and has been used by most authors publishing on the genus. Hensen (1985) was the only other author to follow ICBN in this placement. The historic bisectional and bigeneric subdivisions of the genus result in a very unnatural arrangement because they require, on grounds of priority, that the type species for subgenus *Bryocles*—embracing all Japanese species—must be *H. ventricosa*, an ecologically, as well as macro- and micromorphologically, isolated Chinese species (Table 2).

The first botanist to deal with this problem was Bailey (1930) and he did so from a very narrow base of species available to him for study. He suggested the genus be divided into three sections with *Niobe* representing *H. plantaginea*, *Bryocles* incorporating *H. ventricosa*, and the new section *Alcyone* embracing a number of other species, most endemic in Japan (Table 3). Maekawa (1938a, 1938b) apparently also realized the artificiality of prior placements and proceeded to correct the problem by proposing a new subgenus *Giboshi* for the species native to the Japanese archipelago proper and by raising *Niobe* to the rank of subgenus for *H. plantaginea*. In line with his even earlier 1937 proposal in 1937, *H. ventricosa* was placed into a separate section in subgenus *Giboshi*, which he called *Eubryocles* (= the "real" *Bryocles*) (see Table 2, right hand group). Palynological evidence by M. G. Chung and S. B. Jones (1989) supports Maekawa in that *H. ventricosa* pollen represents a distinct type so far not seen in Japanese species.

In 1972 Maekawa came full circle and divided the Japanese populations of the genus, now subgenus *Giboshi*, into three lines: *Hosta lancifolia* (actually *H. sieboldii*), *H. sieboldiana*, and *H. longipes*. (I have maintained this division as Groups I, II,

and III in Tables 6 and 7.) This division by Maekawa is significant, because it gathers the three key-specific groups of Japanese taxa in subgenus *Giboshi*, while implying that all other taxa are relegated to two other subgenera: the monotypic *Niobe* (= *Hosta*) containing *H. plantaginea*; and *Bryocles* embracing the Chinese *H. ventricosa* and—with the exception of *H. jonesii*—all the Korean taxa. Thus, Maekawa (1972) did, in fact, adopt a tri-subgeneric system of division (see Table 4).

According to ICBN rules, as long as *Bryocles* is part of any new subdivision it must have *H. ventricosa* as the type species. Maekawa stopped short of separating *Bryocles* (*H. ventricosa*) from the new subgenus *Giboshi* and so disabled his efforts for a more natural arrangement. In 1940 he superseded his 1937–1938 scheme by raising *Bryocles* to the rank of subgenus and retaining *H. ventricosa* as a subgeneric type species but at the same time leaving *H. ventricosa* in section *Eubryocles*. This arrangement looks like his 1938 proposals except that the subgenera *Giboshi* and *Bryocles* have reversed roles (Table 2, right hand group).

Later Maekawa became keenly aware that his 1940 placements were flawed and he resurrected his earlier 1937–1938 proposal by assigning new species to subgenus *Giboshi* (Maekawa, 1976, 1984).

Hylander (1954) also pointed out the artificiality of the original placements under *Bryocles* on macromorphological grounds, and he used Maekawa's already validly published subgenus *Giboshi* for the hostas studied by him in Sweden, so reinforcing current classification. Since Maekawa (1938a) had mentioned no type species for his new subgenus, Hylander suggested *H. sieboldiana* as the lectotype for this group.

Bailey (1930) proposed the separation of *Bryocles* as a sec-

Table 3

THE GENUS HOSTA
DIVISIONS OF 1930 AND 1990
(Three Subgenera)

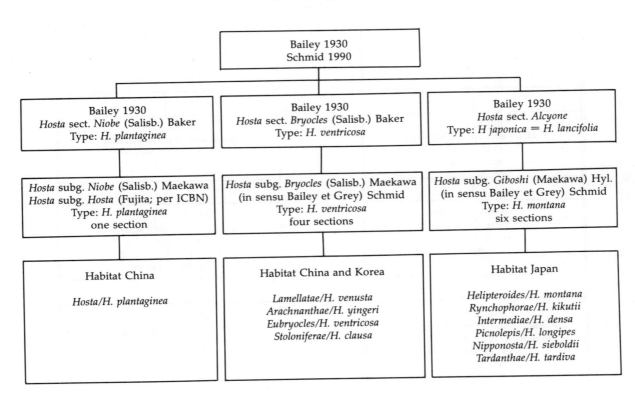

tion (or division) from the indigenous Japanese taxa. This clearly offers a most natural arrangement not only from a macro- and micromorphological point of view, but from an ecological one as well—because it divides the taxa growing in Japan from those native to China and Korea. It also allows the election of a morphologically more representative, and thus systematically correct type species for subgenus *Giboshi* representing the native Japanese taxa. The ecological separation of *H. ventricosa* from the hostas native to Japan is also supported by Fujita (1976a) who does not include this taxon in his systematic keys because it evolved in China.

Aside from the support for this separation founded in morphology and ecology, the recent micromorphological work of M. G. Chung and S. B. Jones (1989) provides positive evidence based on palynology. Their study of pollen morphology provides fresh data for delimiting the genus. The 22 taxa of *Hosta* which they investigated were found to be represented by 5 distinct pollen grain types.[7] One of the distinct types is seen only in *H. ventricosa*, so supports its separation and placement in the monotypic section *Eubryocles* (Maekawa, 1940). Likewise, the monotypic separation of *H. plantaginea* in subgenus *Hosta* is confirmed by its unique pollen size and type. The Korean taxa have a general pollen type similar to that found in indigenous Japanese species but are of a different subtype, so the separation of these groups initially undertaken by Bailey (1930) also has micromorphological support. Following Bailey (1930) and Maekawa (1972), and weighing data by M. G. Chung and S. B. Jones (1989) and Chung (1990), I have divided the genus into three subgenera (see Table 4), all of which have been validly published before but not arranged in this manner. Maekawa (1940) does not suggest a type for subgenus *Giboshi* in this arrangement so Hylander's (1954) choice of *H. sieboldiana* is an acceptable one, but *H. sieboldiana* as circumscribed by Hylander is a secondary

choice for representing the native Japanese taxa. Several morphologically distinct key species typify the native Japanese hostas so I have adopted Hylander (1954) and Fujita (1976a) to accomplish this selection and followed this arrangement which forms the basis for the graphic generic key in Part 2 of this Appendix.

BREEDING SYSTEM AND ORIGIN

Breeding systems have been linked directly with genetic variation so it is important to determine the several mechanisms active in the genus. The spatial separation of mature anthers and stigmas varies considerably with the species. Chung (1990) has shown that there is considerable distance between the sexual organs in the Korean taxa, and this separation is also seen in most Japanese populations but not all of them. Impeding self-pollination, this separation fosters entomophily (insect pollination) and promotes outcrossing (outbreeding) with the resulting fusion of distantly related gametes. Preliminary tests show little fruit set in the screened greenhouse with a lack of congruous pollinators. According to my own studies the distance between anthers and stigma in some lines of interspecific and horticultural hybrids seems to diminish with succeeding generations, so favoring self-pollination and eventual backcrossing to a parental species. Inbreeding reduces genetic variability and increases the number of lethal and semilethal recessive genes produced in successive crosses. Eventually, the vigor of a particular natural group undergoing intensive inbreeding is sufficiently weakened so as to result in declining membership, which may be an evolutionary mechanism to eliminate natural hybrid populations. The breeding system in most natural populations of confirmed *Hosta* species appears to support outcrossing but, undoubtedly, other mating mechanisms are at

Table 4

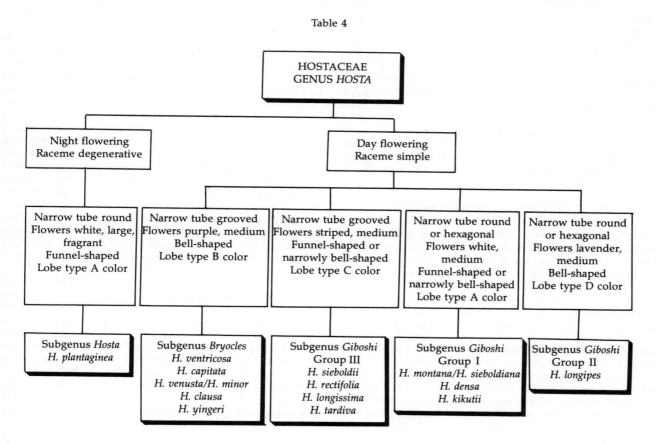

work. If it can be shown that over a protracted period of time heterozygosity affects the distance between anthers and the stigma, this feature may eventually become a diagnostic tool for the detection of hybrids, but further studies are needed. In some Japanese natural populations the spatial anther/stigma separation is relatively small and these taxa are intensely self-fertile, but due to persistent and early entomophily most of these populations still outcross to a high degree. Many of the cultivated specioids have very little anther/stigma separation (H. 'Crispula') and inbreed profusely, occasionally even self-fertilizing within the unopened flower. Hybridizers have taken note and remove the anthers and all perianth lobes, leaving only the ovary with pistil and stigma attached to be fertilized when ready. True outcrossing appears to be active only in populations where reproductive isolation is sustained by geographical, seasonal, and ecological factors. Japan has many populations of mixed specific origin with attendant favorable pollination systems and, as a consequence, interspecific hybridization is rapid but mixed mating systems also occur in these groups. Hosta capitata has bicolor anthers and according to Chung (1990) shows patterns of fixed heterozygosity along with little spatial anther/stigma separation. As a consequence self-pollination occurred under screened greenhouse conditions pointing to possible tendencies for inbreeding. Field studies show that the Korean natural populations of H. capitata are very small and few pollinators exist in the habitat, so the disposition for self-pollination may be an evolutionary adaptation which, incidentally, is also coupled with a proclivity for clonal reproduction also observed by Chung under screened greenhouse conditions. The inbreeding may explain why some of the natural populations of H. capitata are in a recessive state caused by a loss of vigor and consequent failure to adapt to new environments. Some horticultural hybrids—for example, H. 'Honeybells'—have extreme anther/stigma separation. The significance of this is not fully understood, but in this case the hybrid is sterile, which may be partially due to morphological barriers.

The diploid number for Hosta was determined by Kaneko (1968a) and Chung and Chung (1982) to be 2n = 60. Rare triploid (2n = 90; H. clausa var. clausa, H. clausa var. stolonifera nom. nudum, and H. alismifolia) and tetraploid (2n = 120; H. ventricosa) forms have also been found. The diploid number of 2n = 60 has been confirmed for the Korean taxa, including the recently named H. jonesii and H. yingeri, by M. G. Chung (1990) using the colchicine-aceto-orcein squash method of Smith described in Jones and Luchsinger (1968). Chung also determined that gene duplications exist, and this knowledge, together with the confirmed and relatively high diploid number, points to a polyploid origin for Hosta.

HISTORIC NOMENCLATURE PROBLEMS

The identification of many problems existing within the total published base of Hosta classification is tantamount to a new system of classification. For this reason Appendix B presents analytical reviews of all previous classifications.

None of the authors of the recent past attempted to evaluate and merge previously published research of botanists and hosta specialists. Many of the studies on record are of limited scope and omit the subject of general classification altogether. Hylander, for example, accepted Maekawa's subgenus Giboshi but refrained from classifying the hostas in Swedish gardens according to Maekawa's proposals. It would have been difficult for him to integrate the "European" species with Japanese and Korean material not seen by him. Likewise, Maekawa (1938a, 1938b, 1940, 1969) and Fujita (1976a) did not consider or incorporate Hylander's European hostas.[8]

Maekawa, by his own pronouncement (1971), used some rather secondary criteria for delimiting the species. In 1972 he divided the genus into three key-specific lines—Hosta lancifolia (actually H. sieboldii), H. sieboldiana, and H. longipes—using macromorphological characteristics as a basis—position of bracts, absence or presence of the translucent line in the perianth lobes, the size of plants, and scape structure. Maekawa (1976) pointed out several errors in his 1940 treatise. According to his statement, the main defect in his delimitation was the almost exclusive use of taxa furnished by Professor A. Kikuchi and cultivated at the botanical gardens of the Imperial University of Tokyo. The use of this limited, cultivated material and the lack of field studies may have restricted Maekawa's understanding of the total variability of natural populations. The use of cultivated material led to the inclusion of a number of taxa which were not true species and so today are considered cultivars. Notwithstanding, Maekawa's system based strictly on macromorphology is the most methodical available, and most authors who have published on the genus Hosta after 1940 have embraced it. More importantly, Maekawa used a very detailed macromorphological analysis which apparently mirrors to some degree the genetic make-up of the taxa examined and this, in turn, led to a taxonomic system which has been, in part at least, confirmed by palynology (M. G. Chung and Jones, 1989) and in a broad sense by biosystematic studies (M. G. Chung, 1990). Unfortunately, Chung's biosystematic work concentrated mostly on the Korean taxa so cannot be directly applied to Japanese populations.

Fujita (1976a) made significant changes to Maekawa's taxonomy but nevertheless used Maekawa's taxonomic framework and macromorphological methods. Fujita's principal contribution to Hosta taxonomy is the very important elimination of cultivated taxa not found as natural populations though some had been validly published. His de facto elimination of horticultural forms is very convenient as it separates numerous problems from the consideration of classification. Yet, Fujita, by completely eliminating all specioids, has created new problems because many of these taxa of cultivated origin have survived for over 150 years and their taxonomic consideration within the genus has been far-reaching and comprehensive, particularly in Europe. Research concerning such taxa can comfortably exist next to that relating to natural populations, but it is best to separate the two, which I have done in this book. Regrettably, Fujita's delimitation is based on very broad ecological judgments, and so he also eliminates or submerges in synonymy a number of taxa representing natural populations that were collected in the wild, assigned a type, and validly published. Most of these are still recognized as species by more detail-oriented authorities, and some have become acknowledged horticultural items. Consequently, after careful examination of the holotypes and other herbarium specimens and after comparative analysis of macromorphological features, most of these natural taxa have been retained in this book as species or infraspecific taxa, but I hasten to add that some of them may represent only very specialized and limited natural populations.

In addition to considering macromorphology, Fujita's valuable work analyzed ecological factors and the geographic distribution of specific populations. Thus he comes much closer than Maekawa to representing a natural system of delimitation. As the electrophoretic studies conducted by M. G. Chung (1990) on the Korean taxa indicate (see "The Korean Species" below), a high level of isoenzyme variation exists among the latter, and it can be assumed that this may to some degree also be the case within and among the Japanese populations. As biosystematic information becomes available, phylogenetic analysis can be applied and will eventually clarify the evolutionary relationships among the Japanese taxa.

Currently, no biosystematic or other modern systematic techniques have been applied to the indigenous Japanese populations so the historic macromorphological/ecological methodology coupled with some limited palynological data (M. G. Chung and Jones, 1989) are the only tools available for delimitation.

The validly published morphological diagnosis and, when available, type specimens, have traditionally been essential to identification. In some cases, however, the several botanical diagnoses published for a given taxon under the same species name are in conflict. The *H.* 'Elata'/*H. montana* problem (discussed under Maekawa in Appendix B) is one of these cases.

It is obvious that nomenclature must accommodate botanic and historic precedent and conform to the rules of the ICBN. The history of *Hosta* nomenclature reveals a number of cases where some of these principles are seemingly neglected due to differing nomenclatural perspectives or judgments, misinterpretation, misidentification, or misunderstanding, but regardless of why they are made, such placements have had considerable disturbing effect on nomenclature.

Examples of such placements are (1) Fujita (1976a) who gave the large, native *Oba Giboshi* complex (*Hosta montana*) the botanical name *H. sieboldiana* var. *sieboldiana*, considering *H. sieboldiana* synonymous with *H. montana* and realizing the nomenclatural priority of *H. sieboldiana*; (2) Maekawa (1940) who maintained *H. lancifolia* as the type for an unrelated taxon, namely, *H. sieboldii*; and (3) Hylander (1954) who decided that *H. montana* is actually *H.* 'Elata' based on Swedish cultivated material. These cases are fully discussed in Appendix B. In horticulture the effects of these placements have been felt for many years and are still evident today.

Labeling cultigens with Latin names has always been problematic when the recipients of these names are horticultural hybrids and sports or nonperpetuating mutants originating among wild populations. Among a number of Japanese sports received in the United States recently are taxa called *H. kikutii* var. *polyneuron* 'Albomarginata' and *H. kikutii* 'Aureomarginata', for example. These cultivar names are invalid per the ICNCP, Articles 27–32, which specifically invalidates horticultural names published in Latin form after 1 January 1959. These taxa have perfectly valid Japanese cultivar names—*H. kikutii* var. *polyneuron* 'Shirofukurin' and *H. kikutii* 'Kifukurin'—and these should be used.

The status of cultivated taxa for which Latin binomials have been published in conformity with the ICBN (regardless of date of publication) is dealt with in Article 27B of the ICNCP. Many such hostas have since been determined to be cultigens, either hybrids or mutants originating in gardens. Hylander's elevation of such taxa to specific and varietal rank are examples of such names. *Hosta fortunei* and its varieties, as well as *H. sieboldiana* var. *elegans*, were validly published as botanical varieties of species, albeit with Hylander's assertion that these placements may have to changed in the future. In these cases, the ICNCP (Article 10: Note 4) permits cultivars to be treated as taxa coextensive with the botanical species, variety, or form. An example of such a taxon is *H. fortunei* var. *aureomarginata*, but to give it a varietal botanical name does not serve taxonomy well, because it is clearly a cultigen and, moreover, a clonal cultivar originating with a single clone. To rank this taxon on the same level as a botanical variety growing in the wild is inaccurate and confusing. I have therefore considered such taxa as specioids (see Introduction), writing the name in the main headings of Chapter 3 enclosed in double quotation marks to signify this—as in "*H. fortunei* var. *aureomarginata*"—and then reducing these taxa to cultivar form—for example, *H.* 'Fortunei Aureomarginata'. Yet, even in seemingly well-defined situations such as this one, problems

still exist. Some authors, including Brickell (1968, 1983), have argued that some of Hylander's varieties are not represented by a single clone, but by several different ones and therefore should not be given the same clonal cultivar name, because doing so would certainly be contrary to the definition of a clonal cultivar. Upon close examination, however, Hylander (1954) characterized most of his varieties as very uniform and "probably belonging to the same clone." These include *H.* 'Fortunei Albopicta', *H.* 'Fortunei Aurea', *H.* 'Fortunei Viridis', *H.* 'Fortunei Aureomarginata', and *H.* 'Fortunei Rugosa', so my reduction of these names to cultivar form presents no problem. The AHS has, in fact, registered them as cultivars in a slightly modified form—for example, *H. fortunei* 'Albo-picta'.

In a few cases, however, Brickell's dissension must be carefully considered: *H. fortunei* var. *hyacinthina* and *H. fortunei* var. *stenantha* are clearly groups of similar plants by Hylander's definition. Hylander mentioned as many as seven different clones making up the former variety and stated that several clones, slightly different in leaf form, make up the latter. Proposing the use of a clonal cultivar name, such as *H.* 'Fortunei Hyacinthina', raises the immediate question as to which one of these clones the name applies. Theoretically, this problem could present a serious impediment to the reduction of these names to cultivar form, as long as one considers these taxa as originally described by Hylander. In horticulture, however, these two varieties are for practical purposes no longer cultivated, as implied by Hylander's definition (i.e., representing groups of plants), but are propagated and in the trade as homogeneous, clonal cultivar populations. I have inspected numerous plantings of these taxa in Europe and North America and found the cultivated material to be extremely uniform, so much so I daresay they are all from the same respective clone, or perhaps several virtually identical clones, selected years ago in Holland and propagated vegetatively ever since. The AHS Nomenclature Committee has also recognized that the plants in commerce are of uniform stock and has registered these taxa as cultivar forms under the names *H. fortunei* 'Hyacinthina' and *H. fortunei* 'Stenantha'. In these cases I believe the first edition of the ICNCP (1953: Article C3, Note) better serves the situation because it recommends that the term *varietas* be confined to plants which occur in the wild, although later editions of the ICNCP (1980: Article 10, Note 5; 1990: Article 11, Note 1) permit a cultivar that is exactly coextensive with a botanical taxon to be treated either as a botanical taxon bearing a Latin name *or* as a cultivar. As pointed out earlier, I prefer to treat such taxa as cultivars to indicate their origin as cultigens. The ICNCP serves to standardize and simplify horticultural nomenclature, for it is confusing to many gardeners who are used to clonal material to encounter botanical names—which imply a variation of phenotypes—when in fact virtually all the material in commerce is vegetatively propagated clonal material, even the true species.

I have reduced the entire *H.* 'Fortunei' complex to cultivar form because (1) none of the taxa within this group are found in the wild but all are cultigens; (2) these taxa, being primarily of interest to horticulture, are now propagated and sold from uniform, clonal stock readily recognized by gardeners under Hylander's original names, so the reduction has already been accomplished de facto in gardens and the nomenclature needs simplification; and (3) the AHS has registered all Hylander's varietal names as cultivar names with the International Registration Authority for *Hosta* and the registrar has accepted these names.

Some might argue, under the ICNCP, that the above assemblies of similar clones should be considered groups under Article 26 (ICNCP, 1980) from which individual cultivars can be selected and named. One of these groups, for example, could have been called *H.* 'Fortunei Hyacinthina' group. This is also a workable and an admissible solution to the problem of what to do with Hylander's cultigens. I did not elect this solution because the garden material grown under the names is of clonal origin and uniform in nature. Splitting up homogeneous garden populations into theoretical groups would only confuse gardeners. Although I have not elected to use the group concept just described, I have nevertheless included a group name in the synonymy whenever such a name has been suggested by other authors.

Other problems are rather easy to solve, as Hylander's *H. sieboldiana* var. *elegans,* which is actually a hybrid made by Arends (1905) and a clone which could be called *H. sieboldiana* 'Elegans'. Unfortunately, there is now more than one clone in cultivation under this name and no one knows which is the true Arend's 'Elegans'. Theoretically, employing the clonal name for this assembly of seedlings is not appropriate but plant nurseries and gardeners apply it routinely to the typical European forms of *H. sieboldiana.*[9]

Other difficulties are found in the placement of identical taxa in different ranks, as, for example, *H. tokudama* Maekawa (*Tokudama Giboshi*). This hosta was known to von Siebold and has been, and still is, considered by some Western botanists to be a variety of *H. sieboldiana.* Its name in this rank is *H. sieboldiana* var. *fortunei* (Regel) Ascherson and Gräbner. Maekawa raised this variety to specific rank and called it *H. tokudama.* There is no reason why, from a botanical standpoint, these two names cannot coexist; in fact, they do, and without too much argument, but this coexistence confuses gardeners. In this case, the horticultural community has settled on using the much more appealing name *H. tokudama.* Recent research (Fujita, 1976a; Schmid, 1988b) indicates that *H.* 'Tokudama' is a cultigen[10] (probably selfed *H. sieboldiana* progeny). Accordingly, I have reduced this taxon to cultivar form as *H.* 'Tokudama', representing the form described by Maekawa (1940). The various other clones in this collection can be isolated and considered cultivars coextensive with the specioid. They can be given cultivar names, as has already been done with *H.* 'Blue Dome', *H.* 'Love Pat', and *H.* 'Rabinau'.[11] The name *H. sieboldiana* var. *fortunei,* a synonym of *H.* 'Tokudama', is also reduced to cultivar form so is effectively eliminated from consideration in the classification of wild taxa.

Use of obsolete botanical names has always been a problem in horticulture. One example is the use of the epithet *japonica,* which originated with Trattinnick, who applied it to *H. plantaginea.* Hylander (1954) devoted an entire chapter to the vagaries connected with this name. Even after the acceptance of the Cambridge rule on absolute homonymy,[12] *japonica* continued to be used in botanical and horticultural works. Foerster in Germany used the name as late as 1957 applied to *H. sieboldiana.* It was also used for *H. lancifolia,* and in a broad sense applied to *H. undulata.* Even now, it occasionally appears in horticultural articles and nursery catalogs in Europe in the names of a number of different hostas. Under present botanic rules the name has been set aside, though it may take some time for it to be purged from horticultural use.

Another classic case is use of the epithet *glauca. Funkia glauca* was introduced by von Siebold in 1862, the year he returned from his second trip to Japan. This is the same hosta Fortune had obtained from von Siebold during his stay in Japan and introduced in England also in 1862. Today this taxon is considered to be *Hosta sieboldiana* var. *fortunei* or *H.* 'Tokudama'. Stearn (1931b), on the other hand, proposed use of *H. glauca* for *H. sieboldiana* on the basis that Hooker's *Funckia Sieboldiana* (Hooker, 1838, 1839) must have been another species than that nowadays called by this name in gardens. But what is today called *Hosta sieboldiana* is an idealized, selected, hybridized form of the species and is by no means typical of

the natural populations of this taxon which are extremely polymorphic. If one takes the stand that today's form represents the type in a very narrow sense, then Stearn is correct: Hooker's *Funckia Sieboldiana* is certainly not representative of this form. But neither are Lindley's *Funkia Sieboldi* (1839) (Figure A-1), which is similar to *Hosta montana* and illustrated as having 12 pairs of veins and widely opening flowers, nor Loddiges' *Hemerocallis Sieboldtiana* (Figure A-2), also a *Hosta montana* form, which is even more aberrant when compared to today's typical *H. sieboldiana.* The latter was more or less "created" by Hylander, so Stearn was correct in suggesting that many of the old taxa were not *H. sieboldiana* as we know it today.

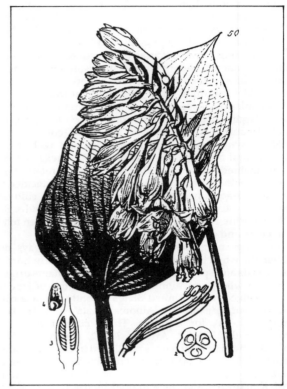

Figure A-1. *Funkia Sieboldi;* from J. Lindley in Edward's *Botanical Register* 25, Plate 50 (1839)

Unfortunately, in the 1930s and later, all the European taxonomists who were dealing with the delimitation of *H. glauca* and *H. sieboldiana* did so from a very narrow basis and used material which had been cultivated and hybridized for 100 years, while Hooker, Loddiges, and Lindley were working with material that had just arrived from Japan. More important, none of the European botanists saw natural populations of the taxa they were dealing with. Fujita (1976a) made an ecological study of these populations and decided to combine all of them under *H. sieboldiana* var. *sieboldiana* and so recognized for the first time the polymorphism of the natural populations. With this recognition came the opportunity to simplify the taxonomy but, regrettably, Fujita's consolidation went too far. He not only included under var. *sieboldiana* all the infraspecific varieties of *H. sieboldiana* that Maekawa and others had described, but also macromorphologically distinct taxa such as the *H. montana* group. My position is somewhere in between: I have given *H. sieboldiana* a much wider interpretation by including *H. glauca* and *H. sieboldiana* forms under the species name and reducing Maekawa's botanical varieties to cultivar form. This much wider interpretation makes the *H.*

Figure A-2. *Hemerocallis Sieboldtiana* Loddiges, 1832: Plate 1869

glauca/H. sieboldiana argument unnecessary. In any case, the name *H. glauca*, originally connected with *Funkia* and still used in Germany by Foerster (1965a, 1965b), was applied to many taxa other than its type and should be discarded as a nomen confusum due to these many different nomenclatural associations.

It is quite obvious that a few nomenclatural problems still need to be solved, but most of the required adjustments in *Hosta* nomenclature have been made in this appendix and in Chapter 3. Benson (1962) points out: "Scientific names are not to be thrown lightly aside." Nothing is gained by inventing new names to replace many of the perfectly legitimate botanical names given to cultigens, such as *H. undulata, H. decorata, H. tokudama, H. lancifolia*, all the *H. fortunei* varieties, *H. elata* and many others. Notwithstanding the valid urge to retain such names, the fact that they are cultivated taxa with no representation in the wild requires some indication. For this reason I have retained these names but reduced them to cultivar form, realizing that technically some are not true clones but collections or groups of very similar plants. However, most of the taxa in commerce under these clonal/cultivar names are readily recognizable and any taxa not fitting a particular macromorphological pattern can be assigned different cultivar names.

Generally, all the Latin binomials validly published under the ICBN rules have been retained in this book, but those not represented in the wild have been reduced to cultivar form. Following the valid transfers of Fujita (1976a), Hara (1984), and others, some names have been declared synonymous to other taxa while others have been placed in different ranks. All the historical names have been considered and appropriately placed. In some cases, especially those involving variegated hostas, a group name has been established under which many of the various clones of a certain specific type can be assembled.

DELIMITATION OF THE SPECIES

Before species can be delimited, the concept of species must first be defined. Unfortunately, the question of what constitutes a species has been answered by botanists in quite diverse ways. Some theoretical botanists have argued that plant species lack reality and simple evolutionary and ecological roles. I am looking at this subject from a more practical standpoint. It is the species concept which facilitates the naming and identification of taxa, and in the ICBN well-defined, established rules exist to govern this naming process. Thus, disregarding the arguments posed by theoretical botanists, in botany, all a species might be is a natural, evolved or even hybridized, population that maintains itself in the wild and conforms to a given systematic type within the morphological limits of a valid diagnosis given for this type. Botanists simply recognize distinct assemblages—in this case members of the genus *Hosta*—define them within specific morphological limits, and conveniently confer specific rank upon each of these assemblages. In the past, with relatively little field work to go on, such placements often became judgment calls, and as a consequence, true species, as well as a number of heterozygous members of the many hybrid swarms existing in the wild, have been declared species. Furthermore, in this genus it is quite common to find hybrids and other cultivated taxa originating not in the wild in Japan, but in Europe, upon which specific rank has been conferred. On the other hand, there exist some natural, self-perpetuating specific populations which have not yet been discovered and named in accordance with the rules, and so are not recognized species in a taxonomic sense. Regardless of the theoretical definition of a species, assuming natural, wild origin, in taxonomy any taxon with a type of a name and a diagnosis valid in accordance with the rules of the ICBN qualifies as a species or subspecific taxon no matter where it originated. Under present ICBN rules, it is obligatory to accept these qualifications, but many botanists caution against further naming of "species" unless the essential field studies have been carried out. Although the ICBN obligates the acceptance of a validly published species, it unfortunately does not provide a method or category which could serve to categorize and separate natural, botanical taxa perpetuating in the wild from validly published cultigens. The only procedure permitted is the reduction of botanical taxa to cultivar form, and this is the method I have used in this book to separate botanical taxa from specioids.

Although field investigation is indispensable, under normal circumstances collecting botanists have access to only a small part of the total natural population of a species. Thus their systematic conclusions may not adequately incorporate the total natural variability of a given taxon's population or its total natural distribution. As a result, the complete characterization of an entire natural population is difficult to achieve. This is especially true when natural populations overlap and interbreed, as is frequently the case with *Hosta*. Referred to as intergradation of phenotypes, this interbreeding results in the formation of hybrid swarms which are frequently quite fertile and maintain themselves in the wild. These hybrids also interbreed freely with each other and often backcross to a parental type. Called introgression, this process greatly increases the complexity of classification because the genes from one species are gradually absorbed into another species and many intermediate types may exist among a natural, intergrading population. Thus, one of the classic definitions—"a species is a population of similar individuals, alike in structural and functional characteristics, *which in nature breed only with each other, and which have a common heritage"*—is of only limited utility when applied to the genus *Hosta* because species, as currently delimited, do interbreed. This may yet be erroneous, because what we define in *Hosta* as "species" and "overlapping specific populations" may in fact not be different species at all but local races of the same species differentiated by local circumstances and habitat or, on the other hand, they may be intergrading hybrid swarms. Fujita (1976a), an ecologist, recognized this and pointed out the very narrow definition of *Hosta* species proposed by earlier botanists. He sought to solve this difficulty by submerging many of these narrowly defined taxonomic units within the synonymy of more broadly demarcated species. From a purely analytical standpoint, he may not have gone far enough because even some of his very broadly defined species hybridize. At some future date it may be shown that only the reproductively isolated species within the genus—such as *H. plantaginea, H. ventricosa*, and unspecified Japanese and Korean species—do not interbreed in nature. Even in some of these cases reproductive isolation may not be an absolute morphological factor, but one that is probably sustained by geographical, seasonal, ecological, and other nongenetic factors. Assuming the italicized part of the above definition of a species is taken at face value (which it should not be), these few taxa would then be the only true species. Adoption of such a rudimentary system of delimitation would obviously have a devastating effect on existing *Hosta* nomenclature.

The subject of what constitutes a *Hosta* species, already complicated by apparently unrestrained interbreeding (especially in Japan), is further compounded by the assumption that the resulting hybrid swarms originated from two fully evolved species. This may not be true in a number of cases where an incompletely evolved species is involved in cross-pollination, resulting in intermediate types which are partially intergrading, retrograding, and evolving, all at the same time. This problem can be investigated only through extensive field studies, but because of the required effort, very little has been done.

Over the years I have seen many fundamental definitions of a species, some formulated by eminent authorities, including Bentham and Cronquist. Most of these definitions require that species are 1) natural, self-perpetuating units (populations) with distinct morphological boundaries and 2) reproductively isolated from other species within the genus, requiring that hybrids made between species be sterile. Unfortunately, as discussed earlier, most of the species in the genus *as currently delimited* fail to conform to one or both of these requirements. Fujita (1976a) attempted to solve this problem, partially at least, by taxonomic consolidation, but an absolute solution would require almost total abrogation of the current system of delimitation and nomenclature. In the final analysis I found it necessary to adopt a "legal" species definition rather than a theoretical one. The legal definition (see introduction to Chapter 3) is based on the rules promulgated by the ICBN. Under this legal definition a species becomes an accepted, fundamental unit (population) of study in taxonomy which is recognized under the rules and conforms to all requirements of a genetic definition of a species except that a reproductive barrier (absolute reproductive isolation) does not exist between most species in the genus. Within the framework of this book this definition has utility for both the scientific and horticultural communities because it permits retention of established nomenclature. Thus, under this definition, the principle of delimitation followed by prior authors is continued, except that the taxa not represented by natural populations have been reduced to cultivar form.

Most previous authors have used macromorphological limits to circumscribe the species. This system of classification aids in the rapid identification of the taxa because of obvious, and occasionally weighted external characters. Its principal goal is identification, but frequently it also conveys natural relationships. Occasionally, certain characters are given added importance (i.e., they are weighted more than others), so that a particular trait stands out among all others. For this reason the classification is sometimes unjustly called "one character taxonomy." As an example, the lamellar, parallel ridges found along the scapes of *H. capitata, H. minor, H. nakaiana*, and *H. venusta* represent such a character which, in this case, is used to differentiate Maekawa's section *Lamellatae*. Admittedly, his sectional classification is based on this single, very prominent character, but in conjunction with it he also uses many other qualitative and quantitative characters in his very detailed and comprehensive macromorphological analysis, most of which have been applied in this book. Chung (1990) also published a comprehensive list of 51 morphological characters (29 quantitative and 22 qualitative characters with 59 variables) which he used for phenetic analysis. For delimiting the taxa in this book I have used 60 morphological characters (33 quantitative and 27 qualitative with 75 variables); they are detailed in the following listing. A reduced set of these characters has been used for horticultural classification (see Chapter 2 and Appendix D).

Rhizome (RH).
RHS = structure.
    RHS1 = short, erect.
    RHS2 = creeping.
    RHS3 = stoloniferous, wide ranging.

Petiole (PT).
PTL = length.
PTW = width.
PTC = coloration.
    PTC1 = green.
    PTC2 = purple-dotted, entirely or in part.

Leaf blade (LF).
LFL = length.
LFW = width.
LFB = length from tip to broadest part of leaf blade.
LFN = number of principal nerves.
LFU = surface of principal nerves below.
    LFU1 = glabrous, smooth.
    LFU2 = papillose, rough.
LFS = surface condition.
    LFS1 = shiny, polished.
    LFS2 = dull, opaque.

Scape (SC).
SCB = diameter at base.
SCR = diameter at raceme (at first fertile bract).
SCL = length.
SCC = coloration.
    SCC1 = green.
    SCC2 = purple-dotted full length.
    SCC3 = purple-dotted lower half.
    SCC4 = purple-dotted upper half.
SCP = direction, posture.
    SCP1 = straight, erect.
    SCP2 = arching, inclined.
    SCP3 = prostate, supine.
SCS = surface.
    SCS1 = terete, smooth.
    SCS2 = ridges, parallel costal elevation.

SCG = branching.
    SCG1 = absent, no consistent branching.
    SCG2 = consistent branching.

Raceme (RA).
RAL = length (from first fertile bract).
RAN = number of flowers.

Bracts, sterile (ground bracts) (BG).
BGN = number.
BGL = length (first ground bract).
BGW = width (first ground bract).
BGC = coloration (ground bracts).
    BGC1 = green.
    BGC2 = whitish green.
    BGC3 = whitish purple.
BGI = insertion (ground bracts).
    BGI1 = amplexicaul, stem-clasping.
    BGI2 = projected from scape, leafy.
BGN = shape (ground bracts).
    BGN1 = linear-lanceolate.
    BGN2 = boat-shaped, keeled.
    BGN3 = leafy, straight.
    BGN4 = leafy, undulate.

Bracts, fertile (first flowering bract) (BF).
BFL = length (first flowering bract).
BFW = width (first flowering bract).
BFC = coloration (first flowering bract).
    BFC1 = green.
    BFC2 = whitish green.
    BFC3 = whitish purple.
    BFC4 = green with purple markings.
BFN = shape (first flowering bract).
    BFN1 = linear-lanceolate, flat.
    BFN2 = boat-shaped, keeled.
    BFN3 = broadly ovate, flat.
    BFN4 = lanceolate, tip rolled under, revolute.
BFW = withering condition after anthesis (first flowering bract).
    BFW1 = withering, within 2–3 days after anthesis.
    BFW2 = withering within 2–3 weeks after anthesis.
    BFW3 = not withering, remaining fresh until dormancy.
BFB = large, leafy initial bud bract.
    BFB1 = absent.
    BFB2 = present.

Pedicel (PD).
PDL = length.
PDD = diameter.
PDC = coloration.
    PDC1 = green.
    PDC2 = purple-dotted, purple.

Bud (BD).
BDS = shape (before opening).
    BDS1 = ovoid, pointed or sharply pointed.
    BDS2 = ovoid, club-shaped.
    BDS3 = ball-shaped, capitate, blunt.
BDC = coloration (before opening).
    BDC1 = green, remaining green at opening.
    BDC2 = green, turning white or purplish white at opening.
    BDC3 = green, remaining green but with purple markings.

Flower (F).
FTL = length (from pedicel to lobe tip).
FLN = length of narrow tube.
FDN = diameter of narrow tube.
FLI = length of inflated tube.
FDI = diameter of inflated tube.
FLL = length of inner lobe.
FWL = width of inner lobe.
FLX = length of outer lobe.
FWX = width of outer lobe.
FLR = ratio of inner lobe to outer lobe length.
FWR = ratio of inner lobe to outer lobe width.
FLA = length of transparent lines.
FCS = cross section of narrow tube.
    FCS1 = grooved.
    FCS2 = round or hexagonal, not grooved.
FLC = coloration of inner perianth lobe (per Appendix D).
    FLC1 = Type A, colorless, white.
    FLC2 = Type B, homogeneous color.
    FLC3 = Type C, striped.
    FLC4 = Type D, colored center field.
FPS = shape of perianth.
    FPS1 = bell-shaped.
    FPS2 = funnel-shaped.
    FPS3 = spider-flowered.
FST = length of stamens.
    FST1 = equal to or shorter than lobe tips.
    FST2 = projected beyond lobe tips.
FSP = stamens length pairing.
    FSP1 = equal length.
    FSP2 = 3 long and 3 short.
FAC = anther coloration.
    FAC1 = yellow, whitish yellow.
    FAC2 = uniformly purple-dotted, from light to dark.
    FAC3 = bicolor anthers, one locule yellow, one purple; or nonuniform, graduated pattern or purple markings.
FDP = period of flowering.
    FDP1 = early.
    FDP2 = average.
    FDP3 = late.
    FDP4 = very late.

Capsule (CP).
CPL = length.
CPW = width.
CPR = length:width ratio.
CPC = coloration.
    CPC1 = green.
    CPC2 = green with purple markings.
    CPC3 = pruinose, light green to grey-green.
CPP = posture on scape.
    CPP1 = hanging down, pendant.
    CPP2 = held horizontally.

Virtually all the comprehensive, authoritative systems of delimitation currently in use are based on macromorphology. Fujita (1976a) added ecological information but otherwise accepted Maekawa's basic arrangement. Recently, the results of limited phenetic analysis and biosystematic data have become available (Chung, 1990), and these new data indicate biological relationships that are not currently reflected in classification systems. Revisions in current classifications may be required, but as pointed out earlier, it is premature to make such adjustments now. As long as these data affect supraspecific placements only, their effect on nomenclature is minimal, because the latter is concerned primarily with species names. Any consolidation of several species into one—as proposed by Fujita (1976a), for example—becomes a serious matter for the horticulturist and gardener who look at species from a very detailed, macromorphological viewpoint. Obviously, the delimitation of species cannot follow the dictates of horticulture; quite to the contrary, it must observe scientific rules and methodology. The valuable work of Fujita (1976a), which includes wholesale "lumping" of validly published species into a single taxon with a very broadly based taxonomic structure, has been ignored by horticulturists and gardeners simply because it did not fit their need for a more detailed and perhaps more practical system dealing with specific horticultural problems.

The question as to whether the taxonomist should pay attention to basic horticultural requirements is a philosophical one. Bailey (1930), Stearn (1931b), Hylander (1954), and Hensen (1963a, 1985) dealt principally with horticultural material of garden origin so their work had almost immediate impact on horticultural nomenclature. On the other hand, the basic and important research conducted by many of the Japanese authors like Hara (1984) found its way into *Index Kewensis* but was otherwise ignored by the horticultural community although it had great significance for horticultural nomenclature. Language difficulties are partially to blame for this dilemma and I have corrected this by considering all the applicable works (see Bibliography) and their effect on horticultural nomenclature. *Hosta clausa* is a good example of how scientific delimitation can plague the horticulturist and gardener. Lee (1973) and Y. H. Chung and Y. C. Chung (1982) determined that *H. clausa* var. *clausa* (closed flowers) and *H. clausa* var. *normalis* (open flowers) are the same taxon and that varietal rank not be recognized. Maekawa (1969) also concluded that *H. clausa* var. *clausa* is very rare in the wild, but on the other hand, very common in cultivation. Likewise, the sword-leaved *H. clausa* var. *ensata* (sword-shaped, smaller leaves) also occurs among natural populations and appears to be an environmentally precipitated adaptation of the normal-flowered *H. clausa* var. *normalis*. Another variant observed at Hosta Hill experimental garden never develops flower stalks but propagates aggressively by a wide-ranging stoloniferous root system. No botanical name has been assigned to this form but I am provisionally calling it *H. clausa* var. *stolonifera* (nom. nudum). This shows there are four distinct forms occurring in the wild which, according to Chung (1990), are biologically one and the same species but are macromorphologically quite distinct having adapted to different environments. All these forms have been cultivated for many years in Western gardens where they have proven to be absolutely stable forms, and so each form requires its own name.

A similar case occurs with *H. minor*, *H. venusta*, *H. nakaiana*, and *H. capitata*—all belonging to section *Lamellatae* (Maekawa, 1940). Maekawa (1969) and others have determined that *H. nakaiana* and *H. capitata* are the same species, some distinct macromorphological differences in the cultivated as well as wild forms notwithstanding. In gardens they are definitely distinct entities and labeled accordingly (per Maekawa, 1940), but most taxonomists no longer recognize *H. nakaiana*. They consider it synonymous to *H. capitata* because in this case the equation *H. nakaiana* = *H. capitata* makes eminent sense to taxonomists, who look for fundamental, biological relationships, while horticulturists and gardeners, for obvious reasons, require and advocate a more detailed nomenclature. It is left to the judgment of the individual researcher to determine how much consideration can be given to horticulture within the boundaries of a given science project, although it should be obvious that such regard is difficult in most cases.

In any case, scientific work is a slow task and many years will be required to arrive at a reasonably complete compilation of data from which systematic conclusions can be drawn. In the meantime, subgeneric and sectional specifications

developed by Maekawa are quite comprehensive and have been accepted by virtually all authorities. The taxa not originally considered by him (Araki, 1942, 1943; Fujita, 1976a; S. B. Jones, 1989; M. G. Chung, 1989; Schmid, in the present volume) have been, as much as possible, placed within his taxonomic structure. Such placements are reflected in the keys given in Part 2 of this Appendix. While future taxonomic investigation may suggest further revisions in the relationships and placements of some of the taxa, I do not believe that *H. ventricosa* will ever be called by any other name. It also seems very unlikely that existing divisions will be supplanted by declaring the genus monotypic, which it clearly is not.

Accepting macromorphology as an important key to identification, herbarium specimens and valid diagnoses should customarily settle the question of identification of previously described taxa. Unfortunately, this is not always possible for the following reasons:

First, herbarium specimens of *Hosta*, especially the historical specimens, are often very poor quality. The considerable bulk of roots and, in the larger varieties, also the leaf structure, do not lend themselves to pressing. The anthocyanin pigments giving hosta flowers their lavender-to-purple coloration are water-soluble and unstable, and consequently not permanent. Thus, the herbarium specimens I inspected did not always provide conclusive morphological evidence for identification. There were notable exceptions: The herbarium specimens I used to determine that *H. tibae* was identical to *Funkia ovata* Miquel var. *ramosa* Siebold (*mihi*), collected by von Siebold around Nagasaki, were in excellent condition after 130 years in storage.

Second, there are descriptions which do not seem to agree fundamentally with the respective type material in herbaria or with authentic specimens either collected or obtained in Japan. The latter problem is illustrated by the difference between authentic, cultivated specimens and the herbarium holotype specimen illustrated in Fujita (1976a) for *H. pulchella*; the pictured specimen is quite different from cultivated plants obtained in the wild. Frequently, two individual plants within the same population of a species are very different looking. Gardeners comparing them may believe they belong to different species. To settle the discrepancy with *H. pulchella*, additional herbarium specimens were examined. An isotype[13] cited by Fujita but not illustrated was collected by Fujita and Takahashi on Mount Sobo-san, 18 July 1970. It depicts a much larger hosta and is more representative of the cultivated population (see Fig. 3-58 and Plate 53). For botanists these differences cause absolutely no problems because they expect variation of phenotypes within a species. To gardeners, on the other hand, it is confusing to have two different-looking hostas represent one and the same species because they deal mostly with asexually propagated, horticultural material, even in species, and so expect unvarying morphological uniformity not phenotypical variation. The term *phenotype* is taken to mean the manifest characteristics of a species collectively (i.e., those traits which result from heredity and environmental exposure and which characterize all the members of a species). Analysis of a botanical diagnosis for a particular species shows the wide range often stipulated for these phenotypical characteristics, as in the above example by Fujita for *H. pulchella*. Botanists seeking to characterize all the traits of a species quite often resort to mass collections of specimens within its entire natural range, if known. Unfortunately, aside from isotypical representation by several duplicate specimens in herbaria, mass collections have not been reported in the botanical literature and *Hosta* phenotypes are frequently based on a single type specimen. The accompanying diagnosis, however, almost always encompasses a much broader range of traits than the holotype which is, after all, only a sample. Consequently, the description is more useful.

Third, another seemingly unsurmountable problem arises from differences in taxonomic interpretation. A botanist studying a particular species may disagree with the findings of prior researchers and conclude that corrections are required. The case of *H. calliantha* illustrates this: The taxon was validly described by Araki (1942) and the holotype is in KYO. In 1963 Maekawa examined this specimen and affixed his *determinavit* (= I have determined) in which he declared this species to be *H. rohdeifolia* f. *viridis*. In 1976 Fujita again looked at this specimen and validly placed it in synonymy with *H. sieboldii*. Each of these opinions is valid because it was made in accordance with taxonomic rules, but they are judgments, and to solve such disagreements is very difficult. In this case, in the opinion of two eminent researchers—Fujita (1976a) and Maekawa (1963)—there is no *H. calliantha*, and furthermore, according to Fujita, there is also no *H. rohdeifolia* because he declared it together with *H. calliantha* and 10 other species to be synonymous with *H. sieboldii* (*Koba Giboshi*). Analysis shows that Fujita is correct if one considers his placements on a sectional level (i.e., from a very broad viewpoint, which places all the taxa in his 1976 synonymy under *H. sieboldii*, all of them belonging conclusively to section *Nipponosta*). Reassessing this placement from a more detailed macro- and micromorphological standpoint, the *H. sieboldii* group in section *Nipponosta* has yellow anthers, while the other interrelated *H. rectifolia* complex has purple anthers. This and other differences create two distinct groups in this section which are clearly not synonymous. Additional palynological support for this comes from M. G. Chung and S. B. Jones (1989) who discovered two distinct pollen types within section *Nipponosta*. Judging this case on the species level, *H. calliantha* has yellow anthers and although closely related to *H. sieboldii*, as Fujita determined, it is in other respects morphologically akin to *H. rectifolia*, although the latter has purple anthers and belongs to a different group. Eventually, it may be determined that *H. calliantha* is a member of one of the many intergrading hybrid swarms that exist within the confines of the *H. sieboldii* range. Until this can be confirmed, I have maintained these taxa under the names originally published because many botanists and most horticulturists and gardeners look upon classification as a means to recognize, identify, and differentiate botanical and cultivated taxa using the detailed descriptions available. The very broad-based approaches to delimitation, such as Fujita's, are not very useful for this purpose. In my opinion it is not simple botanical name changing which confounds gardeners, but these differences in opinion and interpretation which are difficult to resolve.

A review of the applicable material on *Hosta* taxonomy referenced in the Bibliography produced little agreement on how to delimit the rank of species. Maekawa (1940) circumscribed the individual taxa in a very narrow sense and arrived at 39 species, further reducing this number to 25 in 1969 although he excluded some important taxa in the more recent work. Fujita (1976a) recognized 15 native Japanese species in his very broad delimitation, but his work excluded the Korean and Chinese species. Hylander (1954) listed 10 species grown in Sweden of which 2 are "European" species (*H. fortunei* and *H. elata*). He included another 3 species (*H. tardiflora*, *H. rectifolia*, and *H. longissima*) which he did not observe personally. From the considerable differences in

taxonomic interpretation it is quite obvious that simply combining and repeating what other authors have proposed will not suffice for delimiting the genus on the specific level.

Clearly, new facts are needed, such as those provided by Fujita (1976a), who introduced ecological data; by M. G. Chung and S. B. Jones (1989), who added palynological evidence; and by M. G. Chung (1990), who provided extensive biosystematic and morphometric data. Eliminating taxa which are obviously not natural species but horticultural or natural hybrids of long standing must also be considered; Fujita (1976a) eschewed such hybrids and thus pointed to a more realistic approach. A new delimitation of the genus should also consider data of ongoing biosystematic research, involving flavonoid chemosystematics (Currie, 1988: personal communication) and starch gel electrophoresis (Chung, 1990), as well as new field studies of Korean taxa and those on Tsushima Island of Japan (M. G. Chung, 1989: personal communication; 1990)—all of which are available.

Delimitation of the species in the past has progressively reduced their number by eliminating some taxa altogether or at least submerging them in synonymy. This does not always provide a supportable solution; the very broad submergence of macromorphologically distinct taxa under *H. sieboldiana* var. *sieboldiana* as proposed by Fujita (1976a) is an example. The historic work of Japanese and European taxonomists as well as evolutionary, ecological, cytological, palynological, and biosystematic considerations supports a concept of delimitation which considers key species as unique, natural groups of individuals which are identical or correlated in form and structure and which are reproductively associated (not isolated). I define key species as taxa which satisfy the requirements of being the type for a subgenus or a section and have elected Fujita's *Oba Giboshi* as the type for subgenus *Giboshi*, using the botanical equivalent *H. montana* as the type species.

The taxonomic arrangement for the graphic, morphological keys given in Part 2 of this Appendix is based on a tri-subgeneric system which was first proposed by Bailey (1930) and supported by Grey (1938) and Maekawa (1937, 1938a). It has been updated and revised to reflect Maekawa (1944, 1950, 1960, 1969, 1971, 1972, 1976, 1984), Araki (1942, 1943), Hylander (1954), Fujita (1976a), Hara (1984), Schmid (1988b), S. B. Jones (1989), and M. G. Chung (1989, 1990). Most of these investigations are based on traditional macromorphological evidence, except for Fujita, S. B. Jones, and M. G. Chung, who also considered ecology. Furthermore, pivotal micromorphological data based on palynology are contributed by M. G. Chung and S. B. Jones (1989), while Currie (1988: personal communication) added some preliminary chemosystematic evidence by providing collected flavonoid data. Finally the results of M. G. Chung's (1990) extensive biosystematic and morphometric studies on the Korean species and *H. tsushimensis* are also considered.

1. There are three key specific groups in Japan:
   1a. *Hosta montana*/*H. sieboldiana*, *H. densa*, *H. kikutii*.
   1b. *H. longipes*.
   1c. *H. sieboldii*.
2. There are three key specific groups in Korea:
   2a. *H. venusta*/*H. minor*/*H. capitata*.
   2b. *H. yingeri*/*H. laevigata*.
   2c. *H. clausa*.
3. There may be several other key species in China, in addition to *H. ventricosa* and *H. plantaginea*.

THE JAPANESE KEY SPECIES

Fujita (1976a) combined many of Maekawa's taxa in synonymy under broad, key-specific groups without actually suggesting changes in rank. Slightly modified, Fujita's groupings fit agreeably into this arrangement and provide the names needed to typify the subgenus *Giboshi*. Nonetheless, palynological evidence by M. G. Chung and S. B. Jones (1989) indicates some modifications are required to Fujita's placements: *H. sieboldiana* representing section *Helipteroides* and *H. kiyosumiensis* representing section *Intermediae* have rugulate-granulate (RG) pollen, but the latter has a distinct subtype RG(VIII), while the former has type RG(III), supporting the separation of these taxa in sections *Helipteroides* and *Intermediae* as originally proposed (Maekawa, 1940). This separation is supported also by Currie (1988) based on preliminary flavonoid data. Chung and Jones (1989) support segregation of *H. longissima* which has subtype RG(VII), unlike subtype RG(II) found in *H. sieboldii*, so these taxa have been maintained as species within section *Nipponosta* which contains many diverse species. Likewise, contrary to Fujita, *H. rectifolia* with a distinct pollen type RG(IV) is maintained separately from *H. sieboldii* on palynological grounds as well as macromorphology (anther coloration). I have not followed Maekawa's further division of *Nipponosta* into two subsections (viz., *Nipponosta-vera* and *Brachypodae*), because (1) pollen morphology as well as morphometric data indicate the existence of three, not two distinct specific groups (key species) within *Nipponosta*—namely, the *H. sieboldii*, *H. rectifolia*, and *H. longissima* complexes; and (2) these specific groups are not sufficiently differentiated to further divide them into subsections.

Following are the Japanese key species, each grouping having distinct macromorphological and palynological, subgeneric features:

1. *Hosta sieboldiana/H. montana/H. kiyosumiensis*[14] complex (= sections *Helipteroides* and *Intermediae*).
2. *H. kikutii* complex = section *Rhynchophorae*.
3. *H. longipes* complex = section *Picnolepis*.
4. *H. sieboldii/H. rectifolia/H. longissima* complex = section *Nipponosta* and allied groups, including *Tardanthae*.

Two troublesome problems remain: (1) the European species and (2) Japanese cultivars originally and validly described as species, but now considered of cultivated origin or hybrids (i.e., specioids). The first group includes *H. lancifolia*, *H. decorata*, *H. undulata*, *H. elata*, and *H. fortunei* and its many variants. The latter group consists of *H. tokudama*, *H. opipara*, *H. hippeastrum*, *H. tortifrons*, and others. Fujita (1976a) dealt with these problems in two ways: He either submerged them in the form of synonyms under his major groupings, or he ignored them entirely. His tenet was simple: Any hosta not found as a perpetuating (Japanese) population was excluded from his treatment.

Fujita's treatment of species not occurring in the wild was rooted in his very broad delimitation of species. Most taxonomists and botanists studying the genus have no problems accepting this approach, but horticulturists may well dissent. Many of the species names assigned to these cultigens, aside from being perfectly legitimate and valid names botanically, are accepted horticultural names used in gardening publications and instantly recognized by gardeners. To retain them, Brickell (1968, 1983) suggested a "species of convenience" concept which would consider these cultivated species to be assemblages of similar clones under a specific name.[15] Hensen (1985), elaborating upon this scheme, suggested that taxa known only in cultivation be viewed as "specioids" having the same rank as species. Others have called them "species of cultivated origin." I have made occasional use of Hensen's term specioid, although I realize this terminology is currently not sanctioned under ICBN rules (see Introduction).

Many of the taxa initially described in Europe are in fact cultigens so Fujita eliminated them. There are a number of Japanese taxa, principally described by Maekawa, which are also cultigens. *Hosta tortifrons* is an example, which, being a somatic mutation, must be propagated vegetatively to retain its twisted leaf formation.[16] Likewise, *H. opipara*, another of Maekawa's cultigens and also a somatic mutation, has selfed offspring which are always all-green, whereas retention of its beautiful yellow-golden margin requires asexual propagation. Both taxa are ignored by Fujita and I have reduced them to cultivar form as *H.* 'Tortifrons' and *H.* 'Opipara'.

Some of the taxa which have been reduced to cultivar form exhibit long-term variability; an example is *H. undulata*, an unstable, female-sterile hybrid which is now called *H.* 'Undulata'. A few clonal variants of this hosta have already been named. In its typical form it is called *H.* 'Undulata', but after a few years the same plant—as it progressively loses its white coloration—becomes *H. undulata* 'Univittata', now *H.* 'Undulata Univittata', and still later—when it has turned completely green—it is *H. undulata* 'Erromena', now *H.* 'Undulata Erromena'. There are a multitude of intermediate forms in cultivation—for example, narrow-leaved, wide-leaved, and in-between types of *H.* 'Undulata Univittata'—some of which have been isolated and given cultivar names, but these are also unstable in the long term and may eventually mutate to a stable form.

While cultivated specioids and other cultigens are primarily of interest to horticulturists, a portentous problem remains for the taxonomist: Inter- and intraspecific hybridization occurs where specific populations overlap and where cultivated populations introduced by humans exist in close proximity to natural populations. Many F_1 and F_2 hybrid swarms arising in such proximal populations behave like species in the short term and do, in fact, propagate themselves in the wild. *Hosta densa* and *H. kikutii* var. *densa* are examples of this transitional type population. Showing characteristics of both section *Helipteroides* and *Rhynchophorae*, *H. densa* Maekawa was made the type species for section *Intermediae*, implying its intermediate position. Fujita included *H. densa* with section *Helipteroides* by making section *Intermediae* synonymous to section *Helipteroides*, a transfer not supported by pollen morphology. But he also pointed out that in certain areas of its habitat *H. densa* takes on the appearance of *H. kikutii* and so he considered these differentiated colonies part of the *H. kikutii* complex. In fact, Maekawa (1969) described these taxa as *H. kikutii* var. *densa*. It is apparent that the latter is an interspecific hybrid between members of sections *Helipteroides* and *Rhynchophorae*. These borderline cases are more difficult to solve because distinct natural populations do exist. Here it becomes rather evident that many *Hosta* species may not be true species after all because they will produce intra- and interspecific hybrids where no other reproductive barriers exist.[17] A great deal of field and laboratory work will be needed to segregate these hybrids from truly natural (evolved) populations. Maekawa (1940, 1969), Araki (1942, 1943), and Fujita (1976a) have treated some of these putative natural hybrids as species because they represent natural populations. This stand, for the time being, is perhaps the best approach, so I have retained validly published, intergrading, transitional types as species.

THE KOREAN SPECIES

Korea has yielded a rich harvest of very distinct *Hosta* species. It is the evolutionary fount of section *Lamellatae*, unique with its ridged scapes. This section is typified by *H. venusta/H. minor*.

Two new species discovered and named recently are *H. yingeri* and *H. laevigata* with very distinct leaf morphology and a spider-flowered perianth with very narrow purple lobes. The wild population of the spider-flowered taxa varies greatly, with *H. yingeri* being the type for this group. *Hosta laevigata* differs with its long, narrow leaves, which have very undulate margins, and a normal arrangement of anthers. Both species belong in section *Arachnanthae*, having spider-flowered perianths—unlike those of any other *Hosta*—and this very obvious character prompted the naming of this section. Breeding tests (author's data, 1989) have shown this group of hostas does not readily hybridize with other species, including those belonging in section *Lamellatae*, so its populations can therefore be considered quite "pure" and reproductively isolated. Preliminary findings also indicate the species in this group come true from seed. Field studies by M. G. Chung (1989: personal communication) verify the ecological, geographical, seasonal, and probably also evolutionary isolation of these taxa.[18]

Other Korean species also evolved in geographic isolation. Chung (1990) suggests that morphological divergence coupled with a uniformly low-similarity index (Jaccard) and a high number of unique alloenzyme bands in *H. capitata*, *H. clausa*, *H. minor*, and *H. yingeri* indicate these species have been isolated for a long time. This evolutionary isolation points to a probable geographic mode of speciation.

Hosta jonesii is another new Korean species found only on the southern islands. It is related to the other late-flowering taxa which grow on land surrounding the Korea Straight: *H. tsushimensis* on Tsushima Island and *H. tibae* in the coastal regions of northeastern Nagasaki Prefecture, Japan.

Another sectional *Hosta* type which evolved in Korea is section *Stoloniferae*, typified by *H. clausa* var. *clausa*, a sterile natural triploid which propagates by means of an extensive subterranean stoloniferous root system. The unique systematic position of this taxon is confirmed by M. G. Chung and S. B. Jones (1989) who found that it has a distinct rugulate-baculate (RB) pollen type. Additional morphometric and biosystematic support for this position was published by M. G. Chung (1990).

Originally, information on the Korean taxa was researched and published by Japanese and Western botanists (see Appendix B), including Baker (1870), Komarov (1901, 1935), Palibin (1901), Léveillé (1911), Nakai (1911, 1914, 1915, 1918, 1930), Mori (1922), Maekawa (1935, 1937, 1938a, 1938b, 1940), and Kitagawa (1939). It was Maekawa who developed the sectional specifications for the Korean taxa based on weighted macromorphological analysis.

In 1937 Korean botanists began publishing on the genus. Chung, Lee, and Lee (1937) followed the basic arrangement published by Nakai (1918). After 1945, Korean botanists started to focus on the genus and considerable work has been accomplished (see Appendix B), culminating in the recent phenetic, micromorphological, and biosystematic investigations conducted by M. G. Chung (1989, 1990) at the University of Georgia under the direction of S. B. Jones. Because of this valuable research we have more scientific data on six Korean species than we have on all the Japanese populations combined. The palynological studies by M. G. Chung and S. B. Jones (1989) have been examined earlier. In 1990 M. G. Chung completed several papers and generously provided me prepublication copies. Two of the titles are very important contributions: *Morphometric and Isoenzyme Analysis of the Genus*

Hosta Tratt. (with S. B. Jones and J. L. Hamrick) and *Isoenzyme Variation Within and Among Populations of Hosta in Korea* (with J. L. Hamrick, S. B. Jones, and G. S. Derda). Chung's work is examined in Appendix B. His survey recognizes six Korean species—*H. jonesii*, *H. yingeri*, *H. clausa*, *H. minor*, *H. venusta*, and *H. capitata*. Several of these species are discussed below. *Hosta laevigata* was not yet published.

Hosta minor: Morphometric multivariate analysis (M. G. Chung, 1990) shows a very close relationship between *H. minor* and *H. venusta*. Chung postulates that based on macromorphology and distribution patterns *H. venusta* (Cheju Island) is a relatively recent derivative of *H. minor* (southeastern and southern peninsular Korea). He suggests that the propagules of *H. venusta* were moved from southeastern Korea to Cheju Island after the last glacial epoch. The geological age of Cheju Island is estimated to be 13,000 years, so *H. venusta* found only on this island must have speciated after the volcanic island became habitable. During the process of adapting to a new, hostile, basaltic island habitat of recent origin, *H. venusta* underwent subsequent genetic changes. Chung was able to determine that 49 enzyme bands of *H. venusta* are a subset of 72 bands found in *H. minor*, thus establishing a very close relationship.

Hosta capitata is a difficult taxon to resolve taxonomically. Although M. G. Chung (1990) included this taxon in his study, he removed it together with *H. yingeri* from analysis because they "can be easily differentiated from the other (Korean) taxa based on gross morphology." Chung's cluster analysis shows distinct isolation for *H. capitata*, and he determined that electrophoretic patterns of fixed heterozygosity are present at three enzyme systems. The data currently available on *H. capitata* are very comprehensive, but a problem remains: the 18 population samples studied originated in southwestern Korea, although the type of the name, *H. capitata* (in TI), was collected in Japan near Iya-mura (Higashiiyayama-mura) in the old province of Awa, eastern Tokushima Prefecture, Shikoku Island. Maekawa (1940) gave it the Japanese formal name *Iya Giboshi*. The obvious question here is what connection, if any, do the type populations on Shikoku have with the samples taken in south-central peninsular Korea, 700 km (430 miles) away and separated by the waters of the Korea Straight and the Inland Sea. Fujita considers and includes this taxon as a Japanese species stating: "*H. capitata* is scattered in western Japan" and giving as habitat "Chugoku, Shikoku, Kyushu; mainly outcrops of limestone." No mention of Korea is made. Chung, on the other hand, considers *H. capitata* a Korean species, one that evolved and speciated in southwestern Korea, although he mentions it also occurs in western Japan (Chung, 1990:88). He determined that a low interspecific similarity index, a high number of species-specific unique enzyme bands, and considerable morphological differences point to long periods of prior isolation and a (probable) geographic mode of speciation (in Korea). In my opinion, the problem lies not with Chung's research, but with the prior declarations of synonymy between *H. capitata* and *H. nakaiana* (Maekawa, 1969; Fujita, 1976a) which Chung accepted. Analysis of the types and collections on record shows that all the historic specimens of *H. capitata* were collected in Japan (see Maekawa, 1940), including the type of the name, while all the *H. nakaiana* specimens, except one, came from peninsular Korea, including the holotype, with the area of collection of *H. nakaiana* being exactly the same as for the collected populations listed by Chung (1990). The sole Japanese specimen listed by Maekawa (1940) was collected a very long distance from Korea near Osaka, Honshu, Japan. Examination of the types and living material of *H. capitata* and *H. nakaiana* obtained in Japan and Korea indicates considerable morphological, genetic diversity—a fact not corroborated by Chung who examined only Korean material and determined that the populations of *H. capitata* in Korea are very small and show very little genetic diversity and polymorphism. From Fujita's statement and Maekawa's listed collections it appears that the taxa examined by Chung are the phase of the species called *H. nakaiana*. In fact, Chung's research clearly shows that the Korean populations he calls *H. capitata* have been isolated for a long time and speciated in Korea in geographic isolation. This finding is simply not congruent with the synonymy of *H. nakainana* and *H. capitata*, which requires the inclusion of phenotypically differentiated Japanese populations far removed from the Korean taxa. The type of the name *H. capitata* has papillose veins and bicolor anthers not found in the Korean populations, so the possibility of interspecific hybridization for the Japanese populations of section *Lamellatae* exists. The acceptance of synonymy of *H. capitata* with *H. nakaiana*, in my opinion, must wait until the Japanese populations can be subjected to the same precise biosystematic analysis carried out by M. G. Chung for the Korean populations of this group and the results compared. This may also settle the question whether *H. capitata* is a Korean species (Chung, 1990) or a Japanese endemic (Fujita, 1976a).

Hosta jonesii, H. tsushimensis, and *H. tibae* form a very closely related group, but, unfortunately, Chung (1990) did not include the latter in his studies. Ohba et al. (1987) suggest that *H. tsushimensis* migrated from Korea to Tsushima Island and Kyushu, Japan, during the Pleistocene and speciated on the island together with other glacial remnants. In my opinion, it is also possible that the reverse took place and that *H. jonesii* and *H. tsushimensis* originated with the ancestral populations of *H. tibae* in northwestern Kyushu. Although Chung (1990) argues that *H. jonesii* and *H. tsushimensis* may have developed from elements of *H. minor* separated by the last glacial event, it seems more likely—based on macromorphological similarities and distribution patterns—that the propagule was a Japanese species. *Hosta jonesii* and *H. tsushimensis* are morphologically much closer to the Japanese populations than the highly differentiated endemic Korean species: *H. yingeri, H. laevigata, H. clausa, H. minor, H. venusta,* and *H. capitata*. Although scape branching has been observed in many species, it is not a consistent character. The natural populations of *H. jonesii, H. tsushimensis,* and *H. tibae* include many clones exhibiting consistent branching of the scapes; this may be an evolutionary response to a lack of compatible pollinators in a windswept insular and coastal environment. Specimens (in L) collected by von Siebold in 1827 also show this branching (in *H. tibae*). These species are closely related and form a group, which has its largest representation on Kyushu.

Hosta clausa extends from Chungchongnam-do and Chungchongbuk-do in central Korea to north of the Yalu River in Liaoning and Jilin provinces of northeastern China. This multivariate species has undergone substantial changes while responding to environmental conditions. It grows along river banks where it is exposed to periodic flooding, brought about by typhoons, during the time of flowering and seed maturation; this severely disturbs normal sexual propagation and brought about evolutionary changes from the impaired mode of sexual propagation to a more efficient vegetative method by way of extensively creeping rhizomes (in horticulture, referred to as stoloniferous roots). All forms of *H. clausa* occur among the natural populations (Chung, 1990). They are merely differentiated by environmental factors. The sword-leaved variant *H. clausa* var. *ensata* is a form which migrated from the river banks to rock outcrops and was modified by different growing conditions. *Hosta clausa* var. *normalis* grows in open areas on sandy soil, while *H. clausa* var. *stolonifera* occurs under the dense cover of native willows (*Salix*). It never develops flower stalks, which would be useless in the dense cover, but competes aggressively with the willow roots. According to Chung (1990) all these forms are biologically one and the same species. Because they have been cultivated extensively in Western gardens for many years and have proven stable, I have retained their individual botanical names but drawn attention to their taxonomic positions as proposed by Chung.

The unique features found in the taxa of sections *Lamellatae, Arachnanthae,* and *Stoloniferae* indicate the species evolved in relative isolation from the Japanese forms. Some of their traits, but only some, are also evident in Japanese hostas, but they may have been imported during the last 1000 years.[19] *Hosta ventricosa* also occurs but probably migrated from China. *Hosta longipes* and a number of cultivars are also found in Korea.

THE CHINESE SPECIES

Being the first hostas to be brought to Europe and thus fetching the attention of European botanists early on, *H. ventricosa* and *H. plantaginea* are taxonomic key species. Like the Korean species, these two Chinese species are morphologically quite distinct from the native Japanese taxa. A majority of the natural populations of *H. ventricosa* (perhaps all) appear to be natural, apomictic tetraploids (Kaneko, 1968a, 1968b), and they also have a characteristic rugulate (RU) pollen type (M. G. Chung and S. B. Jones, 1989). *Hosta plantaginea* is a night-blooming, fragrant taxon with very large flowers, unlike any in Japan. Its inflorescence is degeneratively duplicate with one-flowered, sessile branches. It appears racemose, though it is not, which points to an ancient lily-scaped and lily-flowering ancestor. It has a unique reticulate (R) pollen type (M. G. Chung and S. B. Jones, 1989). None of these traits occur in Japanese or Korean hostas and this isolation supports its placement in the monotypic subgenus *Hosta* (formerly *Niobe*).

Unfortunately, little is known about other Chinese species. In checking many of the available *Hosta* herbarium specimens I came upon a number of exsiccata collected in central and northeastern China that are not identified and may, in time, be declared species (Figures A-3, A-4). Some of the

Figure A-3. Undetermined *Hosta* species collected in China.

Figure A-4. Undetermined *Hosta* species collected in China.

specimens from eastern China look very much like *H. clausa* and may, in fact, be that taxon. Unfortunately, such determinations cannot be made from dried material alone. As with the new discoveries in Korea, China may also yield botanical surprises.

EVOLUTIONARY CONSIDERATIONS

Analysis of the divergent morphologies of the original populations in Japan, Korea, and China reveals a fascinating picture of how the genus evolved. Many consider Japan the evolutionary birthplace of the genus, but the native Japanese species yield no morphological eye-openers because the entire Japanese population is morphologically quite uniform when regarded in a broad sense. M. G. Chung and S. B. Jones (1989)

advanced the theory based on palynological evidence that the progenitor of *Hosta* may have been lily-type ancestors from which *H. plantaginea* evolved. An evolutionary trend can be seen in the developing pollen types, from reticulate through rugulate or rugulate-baculate to rugulate-granulate type. I believe this trend is also seen in the variability of macro-morphological characters when correlated to geographic location and environment.

Predecessors of the genus probably migrated from the east-central Chinese mainland, where the most "primitive" hosta still exists (*H. plantaginea*), through southern Manchuria into the Korean peninsula and via this southern route to southern Japan. The northern route extended along the coast of southeastern USSR, following the Ussuri/Amur river valleys north of the Sikhote-Alin mountain range and migrating to Sakhalin and from there south into Hokkaido and Honshu. The main Japanese islands provided a climatologically and ecologically very diverse habitat that gave rise to increased speciation. I believe that the taxa growing in northern Kyushu (*H. tibae*), on Tsushima Island (*H. tsushimensis*), and on the southernmost islands of Korea (*H. jonesii*) may have originated with the northern branch of evolution, while all other highly differentiated Korean taxa originated with the southern evolutionary branch after becoming geographically isolated in insular Korea. It was only through geographic isolation that these species remained distinct. On the main Japanese islands natural proximal populations probably have been hybridizing and intergrading for centuries. Hybridization is usually assumed to take place between completely divergent species, but this may not be totally correct because it assumes that the two hybridizing stocks are composed of individuals which have gone through past complete divergence (i.e., they evolved over centuries with the attendant production of a reproductive barrier). While the Chinese night-blooming *H. plantaginea* and the day-blooming Japanese and Korean taxa are reproductively isolated from each other morphologically, this barrier can be easily overcome by human intervention. There seems to be no absolute reproductive isolation among most of the Japanese and Korean taxa; they readily hybridize unless geographic, ecological, or seasonal barriers prevent cross-pollination. Their diversified morphologies are probably due to ecological and environmental factors helped along by the fact that many of the segregated populations may be in a stage of incomplete divergence in evolution.

A Revised Systematic Listing and Graphic Keys

The removal of species not occurring in the wild ("specioids," "species of convenience," or "species of cultivated origin") from the keys developed for natural populations, first advocated (de facto) by Fujita (1976a), has been carried out in this book by reducing them to cultivar form. So as not to play havoc with horticultural nomenclature, this has been done in conformance with the rules of the ICBN and the ICNCP so that long-established names familiar to gardeners, horticulturists, and botanists have been maintained as valid names.

The relationships established in the following listing are reflected in the graphic keys given for the three subgenera and the sections associated with them, but the systematic keys do not include the taxa found only in cultivation.

Nota Bene
The following listing is printed in systematic order exactly as arranged in Part 5 of this Appendix. Species found as natural populations in the wild are printed in bold type, species which do not occur in the wild or are occasional, nonperpetuating mutations found in the wild which survive only through human maintenance and vegetative propagation (i.e., cultivars) are printed in regular type and listed by their respective cultivar names. Type species for each subgenus and section are listed at the beginning of each section and marked by "(type)." For systematic relationships refer to the graphic keys following the listing and peruse Part 3 of this Appendix (see Tables 5, 6, 7).

When required, the taxa in each section have been arranged into groups of species and specioids which have general morphological affinity. Adjacent groups within a section may be differentiated by one or more micro- or macromorphological attributes; for example, the *H. venusta* group with spike-shaped flower buds and the *H. capitata* group with ball-shaped bud. I have refrained from formalizing these groups because it would unnecessarily complicate the taxonomy; they should be considered informal groupings provided for convenience only.

HOSTACEAE.
GENUS *HOSTA*.

H. plantaginea (type).

Subgenus *Hosta* (formerly subgenus *Niobe*).

H. plantaginea (type).
H. plantaginea var. *japonica*.[20]
H. plantaginea 'Aphrodite'.
H. plantaginea 'Stenantha'.

Subgenus *Bryocles*.
Section *Eubryocles*.

H. ventricosa (type).
H. ventricosa 'Aureomaculata'.
H. ventricosa 'Aureomarginata'.

Section *Lamellatae*.

H. venusta (type).

H. minor.
H. minor 'Alba'.

H. capitata.
H. nakaiana.

Section *Arachnanthae*.

H. yingeri (type).
H. laevigata.

Section *Stoloniferae*.

H. clausa var. *clausa* (type).
H. clausa var. *normalis*.
H. clausa var. *ensata*.
H. clausa var. *stolonifera* in obs.

Subgenus *Giboshi*.
Section *Helipteroides*.

H. montana (type).
H. montana f. *macrophylla*.
H. montana f. *ovatolancifolia*.
H. montana 'Aureomarginata'.[21]
H. montana 'Liliiflora'.
H. montana 'Praeflorens'.
H. montana 'Transiens'.

H. sieboldiana var. *sieboldiana*.
H. sieboldiana var. *glabra*.
H. sieboldiana 'Amplissima'.
H. sieboldiana 'Elegans'.
H. sieboldiana 'Hypophylla'.
H. sieboldiana 'Mira'.
H. sieboldiana 'Semperaurea'.
H. 'Tokudama'.
H. 'Tokudama Aureonebulosa'.
H. 'Tokudama Flavocircinalis'.
H. 'Tokudama Flavoplanata'.
H. 'Elata'.

H. nigrescens.
H. nigrescens 'Elatior'.
H. fluctuans.
H. crassifolia.

H. 'Bella'.[22]
H. 'Crispula'.[23]
H. 'Fortunei'.
H. 'Fortunei Albomarginata'.
H. 'Fortunei Albopicta'.
H. 'Fortunei Aoki'.
H. 'Fortunei Aurea'.
H. 'Fortunei Aureomarginata'.[24]
H. 'Fortunei Hyacinthina'.
H. 'Fortunei Rugosa'.
H. 'Fortunei Stenantha'.
H. 'Fortunei Viridis'.

Section *Intermediae*.

H. densa (type).
H. kiyosumiensis.
H. pachyscapa.

H. 'Hippeastrum'.
H. 'Sacra'.

Section *Rynchophorae*.

H. kikutii var. *kikutii* (type).
H. kikutii var. *kikutii* f. *leuconota*.
H. kikutii var. *caput-avis*.
H. kikutii var. *polyneuron*.
H. kikutii var. *tosana*.
H. kikutii var. *yakusimensis*.
H. shikokiana.

Section *Picnolepis*.

H. longipes var. *longipes* (type).
H. longipes f. *hypoglauca*.
H. longipes f. *sparsa*.
H. longipes f. *viridipes*.
H. longipes var. *caduca*.
H. longipes var. *latifolia*.
H. longipes var. *vulgata*.
H. aequinoctiiantha.
H. hypoleuca.
H. okamotoi.
H. pulchella.
H. pycnophylla.

H. rupifraga.
H. takiensis.

H. 'Tardiflora'.
H. 'Tortifrons'.

Section *Tardanthae*.

H. tardiva (type).
H. cathayana.
H. gracillima.
H. jonesii.
H. takahashii.
H. tibae.
H. tsushimensis.

H. 'Lancifolia'.

Section *Nipponosta*.

H. sieboldii (type).[25]
H. sieboldii f. *angustifolia*.
H. sieboldii f. *campanulata*.
H. sieboldii f. *okamii*.
H. sieboldii f. *spathulata*.
H. sieboldii 'Alba'.
H. sieboldii 'Bunchoko'.
H. sieboldii 'Kabitan'.
H. sieboldii 'Kifukurin'.
H. sieboldii 'Mediopicta'.
H. sieboldii 'Subcrocea'.
H. atropurpurea.
H. calliantha.

H. clavata.
H. ibukiensis.
H. rohdeifolia 'Rohdeifolia'.
H. rohdeifolia f. *viridis*.[26]

H. longissima var. *longissima*.
H. longissima var. *longifolia*.

H. rectifolia var. *rectifolia*.
H. rectifolia var. *rectifolia* f. *pruinosa*.
H. rectifolia var. *australis*.
H. rectifolia var. *sachalinensis*.
H. rectifolia 'Albiflora'.
H. rectifolia 'Chionea'.

H. alismifolia.

H. 'Decorata'.
H. 'Decorata Normalis'.
H. 'Opipara'.

H. 'Helonioides'.
H. 'Helonioides Albopicta'.

[Section *Foliosae*].[27]

H. 'Undulata'.
H. 'Undulata Albomarginata'.
H. 'Undulata Erromena'.
H. 'Undulata Univittata'.

Table 5

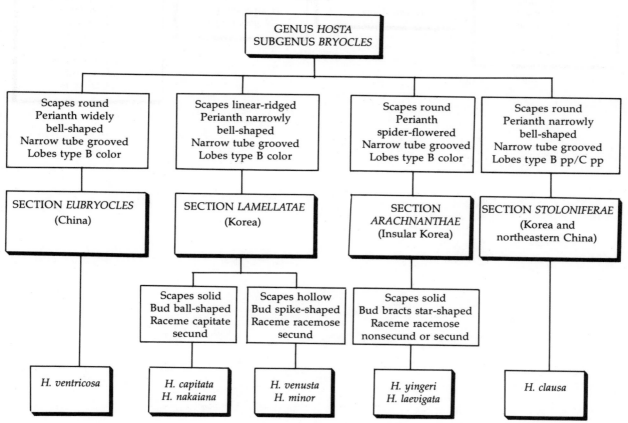

Table 6

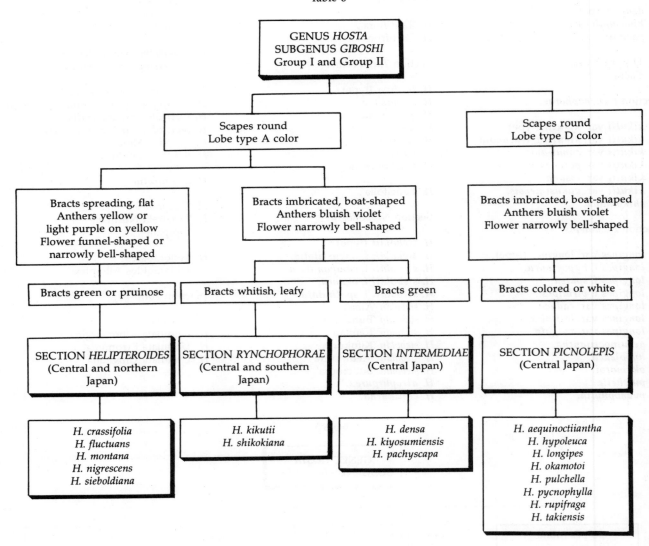

Table 7

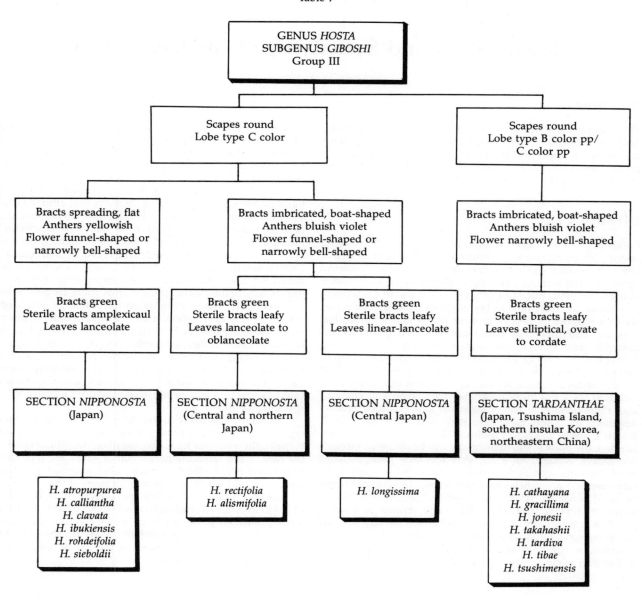

Classification and Synonymy of the Genus *Hosta*

Nota bene

The classification which follows is arranged in systematic order by subgenus and section, with the generic, subgeneric, and sectional type species listed at the beginning of each group. Taxa within each systematic grouping follow the type and are arranged in alphabetic order.

INTRODUCTION

Following is the classification and synonymy for all *Hosta* species, including specioids reduced to cultivar form as well as some important cultivar forms with legitimate, historical synonyms but without valid names per the ICNCP. Inclusion of the latter, while not absolutely necessary, was undertaken to provide an account of all valid synonyms involved in the transfer of a number of taxa to cultivar forms and for historical reasons. The following pages are intended primarily for botanists and other professionals as well as very keen gardeners. In some cases, botanical annotations are given in Latin. Chapter 3 includes complete and expanded English text for all species for those readers who are not able to read the technical texts. For those unfamiliar with taxonomic citations and abbreviations, a list of standard abbreviations follows Appendix H. Keen gardeners may wish to acquire W. T. Stearn's *Botanical Latin*. Published by David and Charles, London, the book is still in print and can be obtained through bookstores. Aside from a few very technical parts, Stearn's work includes comprehensive sections on measurement, Latin use and pronunciation, color terms, standard abbreviations, descriptive terminology with illustrations, and a dictionary-type vocabulary useful to any serious gardener.

The morphology of all taxa reduced to cultivar form has not been considered in the systematic keys. The latter are described in the horticultural as well as the botanical literature and so references may include key horticultural writings.

It should be pointed out that names published in Latin form in the horticultural literature before 1 January 1959 are considered valid under the rules of the ICNCP and have therefore been listed, when appropriate, to provide particular references.

The Eighth International Botanical Congress meeting in Paris in 1954 adopted the requirement that after 1 January 1958 the name of a new taxon is valid only if a nomenclatural type is indicated. This type of a name of a species or infraspecific taxon is a single specimen mounted on a herbarium sheet and scrupulously conserved (ICBN, Article 9). Unfortunately, before 1958 numerous taxa were validly published by description and/or illustration only. This is true particularly of the classic species. Thus, there are a number of taxa published before 1958 which have no type indicated or which, by way of transfers, refer to a type of older synonyms which also have no type indicated. In these cases the type may be a description or figure, or both. Some of the recent Japanese taxa, including Maekawa's, fall into this category. Whenever a type was not found or indicated in the literature for taxa described before 1 January 1958, the name stands on the indicated description and/or illustration and no herbarium type specimen is given.

Furthermore, many of the older European and Japanese type specimens are without identifying numbers and, occasionally, the numbers have become illegible. Whenever this is the case I have listed the herbarium in which the type can be found and given other pertinent label information which I have seen and which will permit location of the type.

Abbreviations for herbaria are taken from the 6th edition of *Index Herbariorum* (Holmgren and Keuken, 1974), with additions published periodically in *Taxon*. Readers not having access to this publication, can find the abbreviations and full information on all the herbaria in the list of abbreviations which follows Appendix H.

APPENDIX A—PART 4

Phyletic Placement, Morphology, and Subgenera

PHYLETIC PLACEMENT

Division: SPERMATOPHYTA

Class 2: ANGIOSPERMAE

Subclass 1: MONOCOTYLEDONEAE

Family HOSTACEAE, Mathew.

Kew Bulletin, 43, 2:302. 1988.
Synonyms:
FUNKIACEAE Dahlgren et al., The Families of Monocotyledons. 1985 (nom. illegitimum).
LILIACEAE Cronquist, An Integrated System of Classification of Flowering Plants. Columbia University Press, New York. pp. 1121–1122.
HOSTEAE Traub ex Hylander, Acta Horti Bergiani, 16, 11:339. 1954 (with respect only to the nom. tribus in Liliaceae).

Genus HOSTA, Trattinnick.

Archiv der Gewächskunde, 1, 2:55, tab. 89. 1812 (nom. conservandum).
Type: *H. plantaginea* (Lamarck) Ascherson (as *H. japonica*).
Synonyms:
Saussurea Salisbury, Transactions of the Linnean Society, London, 8:11. 1807.
Funkia Sprengel, Anleitung zur Kenntniss der Gewächse, 2. Ausgabe, 2, 1:246. 1817; Miquel, Verslag Mededelingen Akademie Wetenschappen Amsterdam, 2,3:295–305. 1869; Baker, J. of the Linnean Society of London, 11:366–368. 1870; Regel, Gartenflora, 25:161–163. 1876.
Funckea Kuntze, Revisio Generum Plantarum, 2:711. 1891.
Bryocles Salisbury, Transactions of the Horticultural Society, London, 1:335. 1812 (with respect only to *H. ventricosa*).
Niobe Salisbury, Transactions of the Horticultural Society, London, 1:335. 1812 (with respect only to *H. plantaginea*); Nash, Torreya, 2, 1:1–9. 1911 s.l.
Libertia Dumortier, Comment. Bot., 9. 1822.

MORPHOLOGY AND PALYNOLOGY

PERENNIAL. ROOTS rhizomes short, nonfusiform, long fibrous thick roots covered with hairs, white, some stoloniferous; some with fibrous remains of leaf sheath; multicrowned. PETIOLE canaliculate, broadly expanded top, margins smooth, very short to very long. LEAVES radical, spirally arranged, petiolate, unsheathed, linear-lanceolate to cordate to orbicular; flat to wavy, or rugose; some cupped; with parallel campylodrome venation; margins smooth never serrate (with rare atypical exceptions); dark green or dark bluish green to light yellow-green, some variegated, some pruinose; annual. SCAPE straight erect or obliquely arching; racemes simple, terminal, occasionally branched, overtopping the leaves, some much shorter, bracteate; some with bracteate leaves. FLOWERS horizontal or pendulous, bracteate, pedicellate, campanulate, perianth formed by 6 tepals in 2 series combining calyx and corolla, gamopetalate, in the lower part tubular, expanding lobes, fleshy, imbricate in bud, white to deep bluish purple. STAMENS free (with rare atypical exceptions), 6 in two series; filaments filiform, white, smooth, elongated, thickened at the tip, superior, curving ascending to tip. ANTHERS small, versatile, oblong, 2-locular, parallel, introversely dehiscent, yellow or purple, several distinct color hues and patterns. POLLEN globose, ovoid, principally oblate-spheroidal, oblate, and suboblate, yellow. PISTIL superior, overtopped by stamens, stile smooth, filiform, elongated. STIGMA capitate, 3-lobed. OVARY superior, 3-locular. CAPSULES round or triangular, subhorizontally inclined or pendulous, loculicidal, 3-valved. SEEDS many, broad wings, testa shiny black, embryo linear to ovoid-oblong.

KARYOTYPE—CHROMOSOMES: Normal 60—12 large, 48 small, diploid (2n); rarely triploid (2n = 90) or tetraploid (2n = 120).

PALYNOLOGICAL CHARACTERISTICS (as typified by Chung and Jones, 1989; pollen shape after Erdtman, 1966): At least 5 distinct pollen grain types with sizes given in μm ±2–10% polar axis (P) × equatorial axis (E).

Type R (reticulate) as found in *H. plantaginea*; shape oblate-spheroidal; size P 100–120 × E 90–110 (Figures A-5, A-6).

Figure A-5. *H. plantaginea*; pollen Type R (reticulate), proximal polar view of whole grain; SEM × 650 (M. G. Chung)

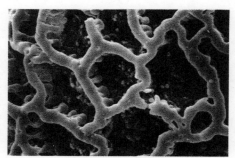

Figure A-6. *H. plantaginea*; pollen Type R (reticulate), grain surface detail; SEM × 2000 (M. G. Chung)

Type RL (reticulate-like) as found in cultivars with *H. plantaginea* parentage (*H.* 'Honeybells', *H.* 'Royal Standard'); shape suboblate; size P 70–72 × E 54–56.

Type RU (rugulate) as found in *H. ventricosa*; shape oblate-spheroidal; size P 79–90 × E 72–83 (Figures A-7, A-8).

Type RB (rugulate-baculate) as found in *H. clausa*; shape suboblate; size P 79 × E 68 (Figure A-9).

Type RG (rugulate-granulate) as found in species belonging to subgenus *Bryocles* or *Giboshi*; several subtypes with shape oblate-spheroidal (OS) and suboblate (SO) as follows:

1. Subtype RG(I): *H. minor*; SO; size P 73 × E 63.
2. Subtype RG(II-A): *H. capitata*; OS; size P 88 × E 81; *H. tardiva*; OS; size P 75 × E 67; *H. tsushimensis*; OS; size P 69 × E 65 (Figure A-10); *H. pulchella*; OS; size P 78 × E 68.
3. Subtype RG(II-B): *H. sieboldii*; SO; size P 77 × E 65; *H.* 'Crispula'; OS; size P 73 × E 67.
4. Subtype RG(II-C): *H.* 'Decorata'; OS; size P 72 × E 64.
5. Subtype RG(III): *H. sieboldiana*; SO and OS; size P 74–96 × E 63–90; *H.* 'Elata'; SO; size P 74 × E 64.
6. Subtype RG(IV): *H. rectifolia*; OS; size P 80 × E 76.
7. Subtype RG(V): *H. longipes*; OS; size P 86–91 × E 83–86; *H.* 'Tardiflora'; OS; size P 83 × E 80.
8. Subtype RG(VI): *H.* 'Undulata'; SO; size P 56 × E 46 (Figure A-11).
9. Subtype RG(VII): *H. longissima*; OS; size P 74–96 × E 66–86.
10. Subtype RG(VIII): *H. kiyosumiensis*; OS; size P 71–74 × E 65–67.

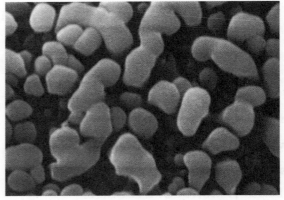

Figure A-9. *H. clausa*; pollen Type RB (rugulate-baculate), grain surface detail; SEM × 4000 (M. G. Chung)

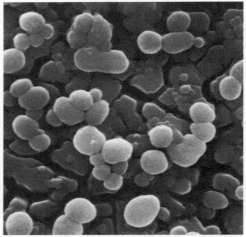

Figure A-10. *H. tsushimensis*; pollen Subtype RG(II-IA) (rugulate-granulate), grain surface detail; SEM × 4000 (M. G. Chung)

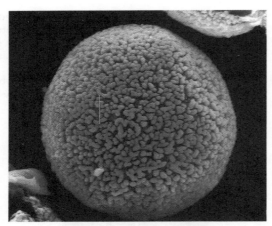

Figure A-7. *H. ventricosa*; pollen Type RU (rugulate), proximal polar view of whole grain; SEM × 650 (M. G. Chung)

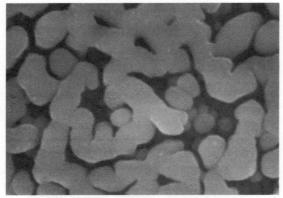

Figure A-8. *H. ventricosa*; pollen Type RU (rugulate), grain surface detail; SEM × 4000 (M. G. Chung)

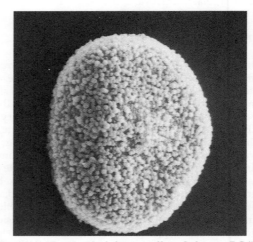

Figure A-11. *H.* 'Undulata'; pollen Subtype RG(VI) (rugulate-granulate), proximal polar view of whole grain; SEM × 650 (M. G. Chung)

DISTRIBUTION MAPS

Endemic in eastern Asia, including Japan, Korea, central and southern China, and far eastern USSR; in cultivation worldwide; 3 subgenera, 43 species; ±2000 named cultivars of hybrid or somatic mutant origin, of which ±850 have been registered with the International Registration Authority for *Hosta* (1989); many unreported and unrecorded garden hybrids, both named and numbered. See Figures A-12 through A-18 for general distribution maps.

SUBGENERA

Subgenus *Hosta* (formerly Subgenus *Niobe*).

Hosta—Subgenus *Hosta*.

(In accordance with the Article 22 of the ICBN, the subgenus name containing the generic type species becomes an autonym and must adopt the generic name, i.e., *Hosta*. In this listing the long-used historical name *Niobe* is also cited to draw attention to this ruling.)

Type: *H. plantaginea.*
Synonyms:
Niobe Salisbury, Transactions of the Horticultural Society, London, 1:335. 1812.
Funkia section *Niobe* Baker, J. of the Linnean Society of London, 11:367. 1870.
Hosta section *Niobe* Engler et Prantl, Die Natürlichen Pflanzenfamilien, 2, 3:39. 1888; Bailey, Gentes Herbarum, 2, 3:125. 1930.
Hosta subgenus *Niobe* (Salisbury) Maekawa, Botanical Magazine, Tokyo, 52:40–44. 1938.
Hosta subgenus *Hosta* Fujita, Acta Phytotaxonomica et Geobotanica, 27, 3/4:74. 1976; Hensen, The Plantsman, 7:7. 1985.

Subgenus *Bryocles.*

Hosta—Subgenus *Bryocles* (Salisbury) Maekawa emend. and in the sense of Bailey et Grey.
J. of the Faculty of Science, Imperial University, Tokyo, Section 3 Botany, 5:349. 1940.

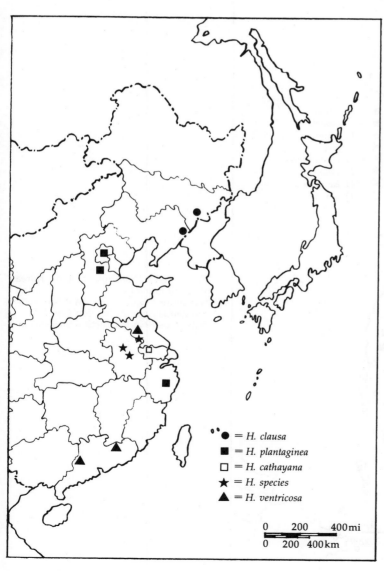

Figure A-12. Distribution Map—China.
Primary habitat of
Subgenus *Hosta*
Subgenus *Bryocles*, Section *Eubryocles*
Note: Populations of *H. clausa, H. cathayana,* and *H. ventricosa* also occur in Korea and Japan; *H. species* are undetermined taxa (see Figures A-3, A-4)

● = *H. clausa*
■ = *H. plantaginea*
□ = *H. cathayana*
★ = *H. species*
▲ = *H. ventricosa*

0   200   400 mi
0   200   400 km

Type: *H. ventricosa*.
Synonyms:
Bryocles Salisbury, Transactions of the Horticultural Society, London, 1:335. 1812.
Funkia section *Bryocles* Baker, J. of the Linnean Society of London, 11:367. 1870.
Funkia B. *bracteae solitariae* Regel, Gartenflora, 25:161. 1876 (under *Funkia subcordata*).
Hosta section *Bryocles* Engler et Prantl, Die Natürlichen Pflanzenfamilien, 2, 3:40. 1888; Ascherson et Gräbner, Synopsis der Mitteleuropäischen Flora, 3:54. 1905; Bailey, Gentes Herbarum, 2, 3:126. 1930.
Hosta section *Bryocles* subsection *Eubryocles* Maekawa, J. of Japanese Botany, 13:892. 1937.
Hosta subgenus *Giboshi* section *Bryocles* subsection *Eubryocles* Maekawa, Botanical Magazine, Tokyo, 52:41, 43. 1938.
Hosta subgenus *Bryocles* sections *Eubryocles*, *Lamellatae*, and *Stoloniferae* (excl. sections *Helipteroides*, *Intermediae*, *Picnolepis*, *Rhynchophorae*, and *Tardanthae*) Maekawa, J. of the

Faculty of Science, Imperial University Tokyo, Section 3 Botany, 5:349–351. 1940.

Subgenus *Giboshi*.

Hosta—**Subgenus *Giboshi*** Maekawa in the sense of Bailey et Grey (emend. W. G. Schmid).
Botanical Magazine, Tokyo, 52:40–43. 1938 (in annotation).
Type: *H. montana*.
Synonyms:
Hosta section *Alcyone* Bailey, Gentes Herbarum, 2, 3:117–142. 1930; Grey, Hardy Bulbs, pp. 92–293. 1938.
Hosta subgenus *Bryocles* sections *Helipteroides*, *Intermediae*, *Picnolepis*, *Rhynchophorae*, and *Tardanthae* (excl. sections *Eubryocles*, *Stoloniferae*, and *Lamellatae*) Maekawa, J. of the Faculty of Science, Imperial University Tokyo, Section 3 Botany, 5:349–351. 1940.
Hosta subgenus *Giboshi* Hylander, Acta Horti Bergiani, 16, 11:339–340. 1954 (in annotation).

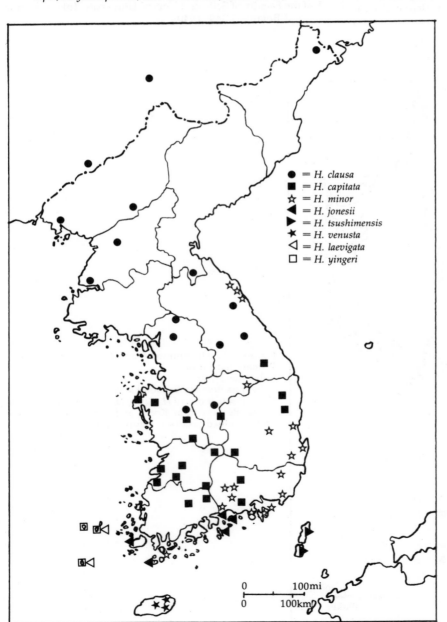

Figure A-13. Distribution Map—Korea. Primary habitat of
Subgenus *Bryocles*, Section *Arachnanthae*
Subgenus *Bryocles*, Section *Lamellatae*
Subgenus *Bryocles*, Section *Stoloniferae*

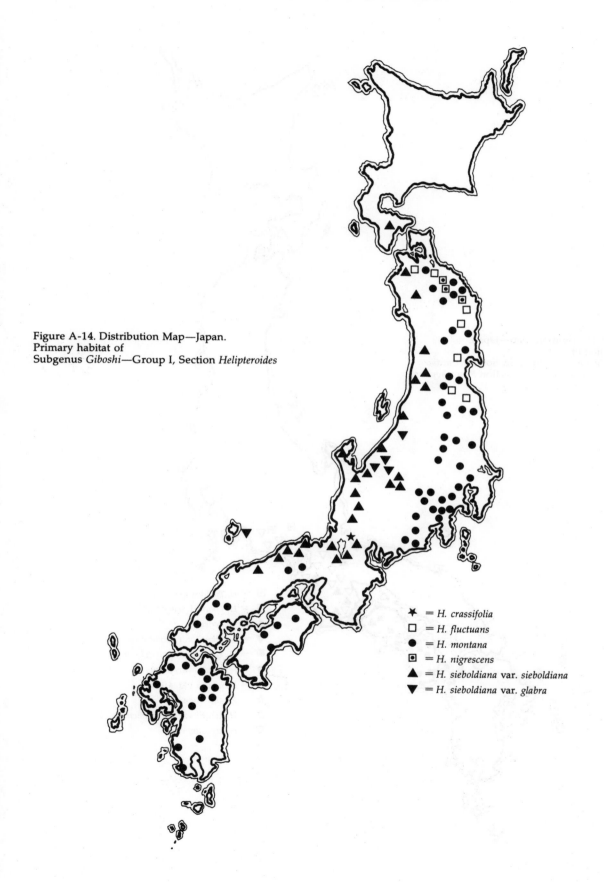

Figure A-14. Distribution Map—Japan.
Primary habitat of
Subgenus *Giboshi*—Group I, Section *Helipteroides*

✱ = H. crassifolia
□ = H. fluctuans
● = H. montana
⊡ = H. nigrescens
▲ = H. sieboldiana var. sieboldiana
▼ = H. sieboldiana var. glabra

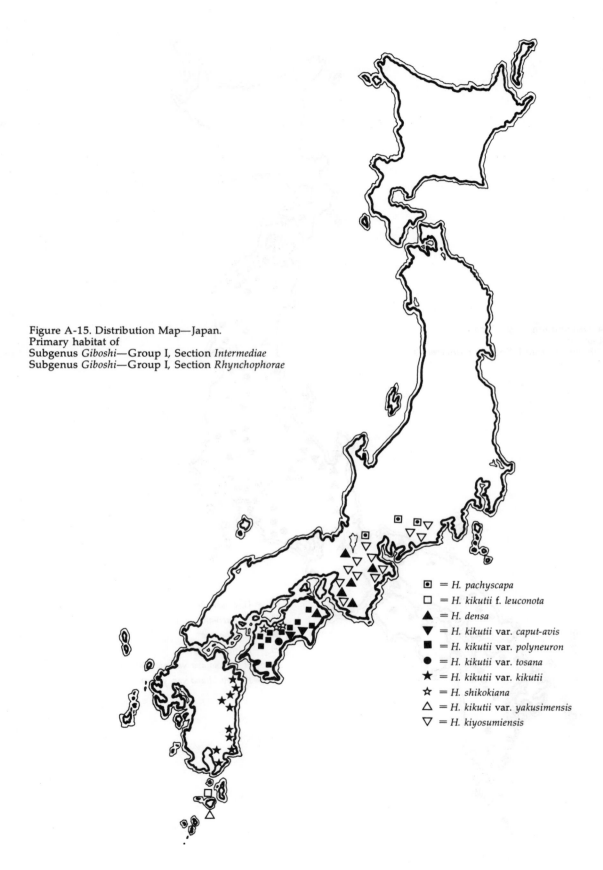

Figure A-15. Distribution Map—Japan.
Primary habitat of
Subgenus *Giboshi*—Group I, Section *Intermediae*
Subgenus *Giboshi*—Group I, Section *Rhynchophorae*

⊡ = *H. pachyscapa*
□ = *H. kikutii* f. *leuconota*
▲ = *H. densa*
▼ = *H. kikutii* var. *caput-avis*
■ = *H. kikutii* var. *polyneuron*
● = *H. kikutii* var. *tosana*
★ = *H. kikutii* var. *kikutii*
☆ = *H. shikokiana*
△ = *H. kikutii* var. *yakusimensis*
▽ = *H. kiyosumiensis*

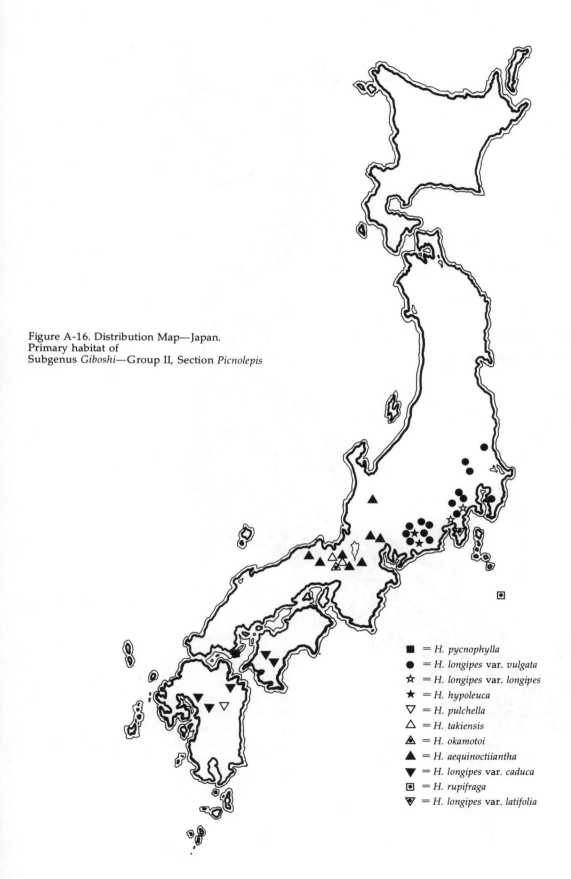

Figure A-16. Distribution Map—Japan.
Primary habitat of
Subgenus *Giboshi*—Group II, Section *Picnolepis*

■ = *H. pycnophylla*

● = *H. longipes* var. *vulgata*

☆ = *H. longipes* var. *longipes*

★ = *H. hypoleuca*

▽ = *H. pulchella*

△ = *H. takiensis*

⊿ = *H. okamotoi*

▲ = *H. aequinoctiiantha*

▼ = *H. longipes* var. *caduca*

▣ = *H. rupifraga*

▼ = *H. longipes* var. *latifolia*

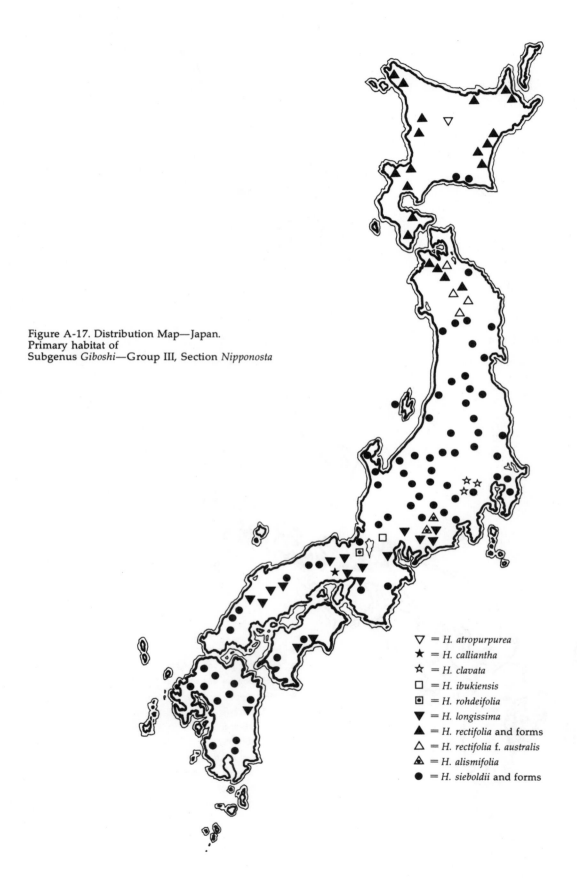

Figure A-17. Distribution Map—Japan.
Primary habitat of
Subgenus *Giboshi*—Group III, Section *Nipponosta*

▽ = *H. atropurpurea*

★ = *H. calliantha*

☆ = *H. clavata*

□ = *H. ibukiensis*

⊡ = *H. rohdeifolia*

▼ = *H. longissima*

▲ = *H. rectifolia* and forms

△ = *H. rectifolia* f. *australis*

⧊ = *H. alismifolia*

● = *H. sieboldii* and forms

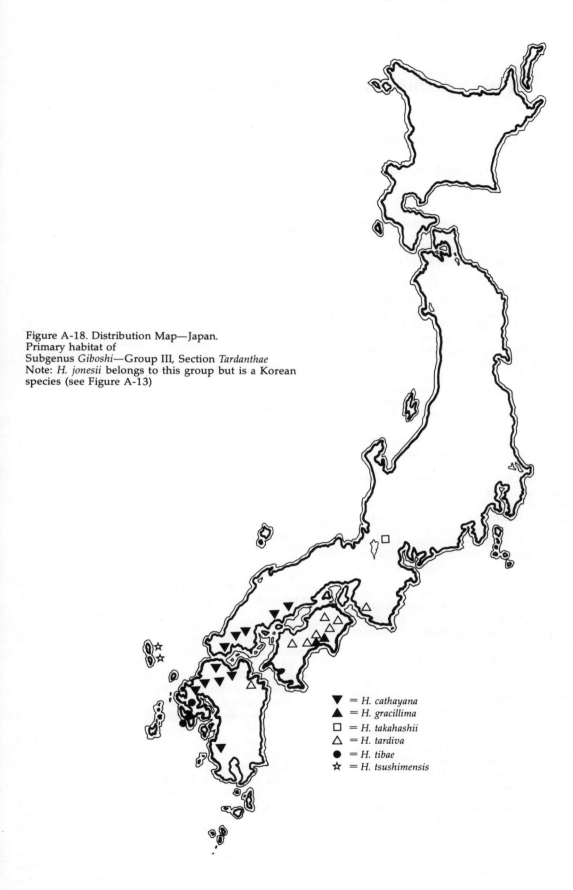

Figure A-18. Distribution Map—Japan.
Primary habitat of
Subgenus *Giboshi*—Group III, Section *Tardanthae*
Note: *H. jonesii* belongs to this group but is a Korean
species (see Figure A-13)

▼ = *H. cathayana*
▲ = *H. gracillima*
□ = *H. takahashii*
△ = *H. tardiva*
● = *H. tibae*
☆ = *H. tsushimensis*

APPENDIX A—PART 5

The Species of the Genus *Hosta*

Subgenus *Hosta* (ICBN).
Archiv der Gewächskunde, 1,2:55, tab 89. 1812 (nomen conservandum).

H. plantaginea (Lamarck) Ascherson (type) var. **plantaginea**.
Botanische Zeitung, 21:53, ic. pl. 24. 1863.
Synonyms:
Hemerocallis plantaginea Lamarck, Encyclopédie méthodique Botanique, 3:103. 1789.
Hemerocallis alba Andrews, Botanist. Repos. 3, tab. 194. 1801.
Hemerocallis cordata Cavanilles, Descripcion de las plantas que Cavanilles, p. 124. 1801.
Hemerocallis japonica in the sense of Redouté, Les Liliacées, 1, tab. 3. 1802 (with respect to the description and illustration); in the sense of Ker-Gawler apud Sims, Curtis's Botanical Magazine, 35, tab. 1433. 1812 (with respect to the description and illustration; not *Hemerocallis japonica* as originally described by Thunberg 1784 and 1794).
Hemerocallis cordifolia hort. Salisbury, Transactions of the Linnean Society, London, 8:11. 1807 (nom. nudum).
Hosta Iaponica (Thunberg; as incorrectly interpreted by Redouté et Ker-Gawler) Trattinnick, Archiv der Gewächskunde, 1, 2:55, tab. 89. 1812 (excluding all the synonyms).
Niobe cordifolia Salisbury, Transactions of the Horticultural Society, London, 1:335. 1812 (nom. nudum and illegitimum).
Funkia subcordata Sprengel, Caroli Linnaei Systema Vegetabilium, ed. 16, 2:40. 1825 (nom. illegitimum and superfluum); and incl. *Funkia* var. *grandiflora* Siebold ex Miquel, Verslag Mededelingen Akademie Wetenschappen Amsterdam, 2, 3:304. 1869 (excluding the synonyms by Banks et Houttuyn); Baker, J. of the Linnean Society of London, 11:367. 1870; Regel, Gartenflora, 25:162. 1876; de Noter, Revue Horticole, Paris, N.S. 5, 77:390. ic. 163. 1905.
Funkia alba (Andrews) Sweet, Hort. Brit., p. 409. 1827.
Funkia sieboldiana bracteata Miquel, Annales Musei Botanici Lugdano-Batavi, p. 152. 1867 (p.p. nom. confusum).
Saussurea plantaginea (Lamarck) Kuntze, Revisio Generum Plantarum 2:714. 1891 (nom. nudum).
Funkia japonica (Thunberg; as incorrectly interpreted by Redouté et Ker-Gawler) Mottet, Revue Horticole, 69:115, ic. 37. 1897; and incl. *Funkia* var. *β subcordata* (Sprengel) Lilja, Fl. Sveriges odl. växter, p. 49. 1839; Druce, Second Supplement to Bot. Soc. and Exchange Club Report for 1916, p. 623. 1917.
Hosta plantaginea f. *grandiflora* (Siebold et Zuccarini) Ascherson et Gräbner, Synopsis der Mitteleuropäischen Flora, 3:53–55. 1905 (not as pictured in Lemaire 1846); Stearn, Gardener's Chronicle, 3 ser., 90:48. 1931.
Niobe plantaginea (Lamarck) Nash, Torreya, 11:3. 1911.

H. plantaginea var. ***japonica*** Kikuchi ex Maekawa.
J. of the Faculty of Science, Imperial University Tokyo, Section 3 Botany, 5:343, 344, 348, ic. 6, 12. 1940.
Synonyms:
Funkia grandiflora Siebold et Zuccarini ex Lemaire, Flore de Serres, 2:10, tab. 158–159. 1846.
Hosta plantaginea Ascherson et Gräbner in the sense of

Matsumura, Index plantarum japonicarum, 2:200. 1905; Makino in Iinuma, Somoku Dzusetsu, ed. 3, 2:468, pl. 6/255. 1910; Shirai et Oonuma in Iwasaki, Honzo-Dzufu, ed. 2, 20:fol. 13, 14. 1921; Makino et Nemoto, Nippon-shokubutsu-soran, ed. 1:1262. 1925.
H. plantaginea var. *grandiflora* in the sense of Hylander, Acta Horti Bergiani, 16, 11:414. 1954; Hylander, RHS Dictionary of Gardening, ed. 2, p. 349. 1969; Grenfell, The Plantsman, 3:37. 1981; Hensen, The Plantsman, 7:7. 1985.

H. plantaginea 'Aphrodite' (a cultivar form).
J. of the Faculty of Science, Imperial University Tokyo, Section 3 Botany, 5:343, 344, 347, 348, ic. 11. 1940.
Synonyms:
H. plantaginea f. ***aphrodite*** Maekawa, J. of the Faculty of Science, Imperial University Tokyo, Section 3 Botany, 5:347. 1940 (here reduced to cultivar form).
H. plantaginea var. *plena* Fei, Huahui Ji Guanshang. Shouce Press, Taipei. 1983.

H. plantaginea 'Stenantha' (a cultivar form).
J. of the Faculty of Science, Imperial University Tokyo, Section 3 Botany, 5:343, 344, 347, ic. 7, 9. 1940.
Synonyms:
H. plantaginea f. ***stenantha*** Maekawa, J. of the Faculty of Science, Imperial University Tokyo, Section 3 Botany, 5:347. 1940 (here reduced to cultivar form).

Subgenus *Bryocles* (Salisbury) Maekawa.
Section *Eubryocles* Maekawa. 1940.
J. of the Faculty of Science, Imperial University Tokyo, Section 3 Botany, 5:414. 1940.
Synonyms:
Hosta section *Bryocles* subsection *Eubryocles* Maekawa, J. of Japanese Botany, 13:892. 1937.
Hosta subgenus *Giboshi* section *Bryocles* subsection *Eubryocles* Maekawa, Botanical Magazine, Tokyo, 52:41, 44. 1938.

H. ventricosa Stearn (type).
Gardener's Chronicle, 3 Ser., 90:27, ic. Pl. 22, 23. 1931. (in annotation).
Synonyms:
Hemerocallis cærulea Andrews, Botanist. Repos. 1, tab. 6 1797; Redouté, Les Liliacées, 1, tab. 106. 1805.
Hemerocallis cærulea β flore violaceo Ker-Gawler apud Sims, Curtis's Botanical Magazine, 35, in annotation under tab. 1433. 1812.
Bryocles ventricosa Salisbury, Transactions of the Horticultural Society, London 1:335. 1812 (nom. illegitimum and not validly published.).
Hosta cærulea (Andrews) Trattinnick, Archiv der Gewächskunde, 2:144, tab. 189. 1814 (not Jaquin 1797); Ascherson et Gräbner, Synopsis der Mitteleuropäischen Flora, 3:54. 1905; Bailey, Standard Encyclopedia of Horticulture, p. 1605–1605, ic. 1909–1910. 1915; and Gentes Herbarum, 2, 3:127–129, ic. 71. 1930.
Funkia ovata Sprengel, Caroli Linnaei Systema Vegetabilium, ed. 16, 2:40. 1825 (nom. illegitimum); Baker, J. of the Linnean Society of London, 11:367. 1870; and incl. var. *α*

typica Regel, Gartenflora, 25:162. 1876.

Funkia cærulea (Andrews) Sweet, Hort. Brit., p. 409. 1827.

Hosta japonica var. *cærulea* Ascherson, Botanische Zeitung, 21:53. 1863.

Funkia ovata var. *cærulea* Miquel, Verslag Mededelingen Akademie Wetenschappen Amsterdam, 2, 3:299. 1869.

Funkia latifolia Miquel, Verslag Mededelingen Akademie Wetenschappen Amsterdam, 2, 3:299–302. 1869.

Saussurea cærulea (Andrews) Kuntze, Revisio Generum Plantarum 2:714. 1891; Salisbury apud Jackson, Index Kewensis, 4:811. 1895.

Hosta latifolia (Miquel) Matsumura, Index plantarum japonicarum, 2:200. 1905 (not in the sense of Wehrhahn 1936).

H. japonica var. *cærulea* Iinuma apud Makino, Somoku Dzusetsu, ed. 3, 2:462, pl. 349. 1910 (with respect only to the name).

Niobe cærulea (Andrews) Nash, Torreya, 11:7. 1911.

Hosta miquelii Moldenke, in Fedde, Repertorium Specierum Novarum Regni Vegetabilis, 40:196–199. 1936 (with respect to a new name for *H. latifolia* (Miquel) Matsumura.

H. ventricosa f. *ventricosa* Hensen, Mededelingen van de Directeur van de Tuinbouw, 26:725–735. 1963.

H. ventricosa 'Aureomaculata' Hensen (a cultivar form).
Mededelingen van de Landbouwhogeschool te Wageningen, 63, 6:19. 1963; The Plantsman, 7:19–21. 1985.

Synonyms:

Funkia ovata foliis *aureomaculatis* Siebold (nom. nudum), Catalogue raisonné et prix-courant, p. 12. 1856; and Nederland Tuinbouwblad Sempervirens, 20:533. 1891.

Funkia latifolia lusus γ *aureomaculata* Miquel, Verslag Mededelingen Akademie Wetenschappen Amsterdam, 2, 3:302. 1869 (basionym).

(?)*Funkia ovata* f. *aureo-variegata* Regel, Gartenflora, 25:162. 1876.

(?)*Hostia cærulea* f. *aureo-variegata* Voss, Voss et Siebert, Vilmorin's Blumengärtnerei, ed. 3, 1:1076. 1896.

Hosta cærulea (gold-variegated form) Bailey, Standard Encyclopedia of Horticulture, p. 1605. 1915 (with respect to the description).

H. cærulea var. *viridimarginata* hort. Hensen, Mededelingen van de Directeur van de Tuinbouw, 26:725–735. 1963.

H. ventricosa 'Aureomarginata' Hensen (a cultivar form).
The Plantsman, 7:19–21. 1985.

Synonyms:

(?)*Funkia cærulea* variegata (hort.) Siebold (nom. nudum), Catalogue et prix-courant, p. 50–51. 1867.

Funkia ovata f. *late-(aureo) marginata* Regel, Gartenflora, 25:162. 1876.

(?)*Hostia cærulea* f. *late-marginata* Voss in Voss et Siebert, Vilmorin's Blumengärtnerei, ed. 3, 1:1076. 1896.

Subgenus *Bryocles* (Salisbury) Maekawa.
Section *Lamellatae* Maekawa 1940.
J. of the Faculty of Science, Imperial University Tokyo, Section 3 Botany, 5:416, 417. 1940.

Synonyms:

Hosta section *Bryocles* subsection *Lamellatae* Maekawa, J. of Japanese Botany, 13:897. 1937.

Hosta subgenus *Giboshi* section *Lamellatae* (*Spicatae* and *Capitatae*) Maekawa, Botanical Magazine, Tokyo, 52:41, 44. 1938.

H. venusta Maekawa (type).
J. of Japanese Botany, Tokyo, 11:245, ic. 2–3. 1935.
Type: Original description based on cultivated material (by T.

Terasaki, July 1934) and collections at Sensyogahara Nikko from displaced, cultivated material. In E (ex Plantae Coreaneae): Taquet 4067, 4 August 1910, Mount Halla, 1700 m.s.m.; recent accession by M. G. Chung, on Cheju-do, Cheju City, near Ch'onwangsa, 600 m.s.m., 6 August 1988. In K (ex Plantae Coreaneae): Faurie 2076, July 1907; Taquet 380, September 1907 (topotypes to indicate earlier accessions). Hab. in mountainous forests, in shade, on the island of Cheju-do (Quelpaert Island).

Synonyms:

Funkia subcordata var. *taquetii* Léveillé in Fedde, Repertorium Specierum Novarum Regni Vegetabilis, 9:322. 1911.

Hosta venusta var. *decurrens* Maekawa, J. of Japanese Botany, 13:897. 1937; Maekawa, J. of the Faculty of Science, Imperial University Tokyo, Section 3 Botany, 5:417 ic. 100, 101. 1940.

H. minor Nakai.
J. of the College of Science, Imperial University Tokyo, 31:251. 1911 (excluding the synonym *H. longipes*).
Type: In L, A147/55; recent accessions by M. G. Chung, 18 July 1988, Kyongsangnam-do and Chollanam-do, Wan-do and Kojae-do (Koje) Islands. Hab. in Korea, provinces Kyongsangnam-do and Chollanam-do along the southern and southeastern coast and coastal islands.

Synonyms:

Funkia ovata var. *minor* Baker, J. of the Linnean Society of London, 11:368. 1871 p.p.

Hosta minor Maekawa, J. of the Faculty of Science, Imperial University Tokyo, Section 3 Botany, 5:419–420, ic. 102. 1940.

H. minor 'Alba' (a cultivar form).
J. of the Faculty of Science, Imperial University Tokyo, Section 3 Botany, 5:418. 1940.
Hab. occasionally found as nonperpetuating mutations among natural populations of *H. minor*.

Synonyms:

H. minor f. *alba* (Nakai) Maekawa, J. of the Faculty of Science, Imperial University Tokyo, Section 3 Botany, 5:418. 1940 (here reduced to cultivar form).

H. longipes f. *alba* Nakai, Report on the Vegetation of Diamond Mountains, p. 167, pl. 5. 1918.

H. capitata (Koidzumi) Nakai.
Botanical Magazine, Tokyo, 44:514. 1930.
Type: In TI; coll. Koidzumi, Mount Higashiiyayama, Tokushima Prefecture from Japanese populations; recent accessions of native Korean material by M. G. Chung in Korea, Chollanam-do, Mount Chiri National Park, near Nogodan, 1300 m.s.m., 29 July 1988 (the *H. nakaiana* phase). Hab. in Korea, provinces Chollanam-do, Chollabuk-do, Kyongsangnam-do, and Kyongsangbuk-do; migrated populations (?) in Nagasaki Prefecture, Kyushu, Japan.

Synonyms:

H. cærulea var. *capitata* Koidzumi, Botanical Magazine, Tokyo, 30:326. 1916 (basionym).

H. nakaiana Fujita, Acta Phytotaxonomica et Geobotanica, 27, 3/4:93. 1976 p.p. in syn.

H. nakaiana Maekawa.
J. of Japanese Botany, 11:687, ic. f. 13, 14. 1935 and 13:897. 1937.
Type: In TI; coll. Nakai, August 1934. Hab. in southern Korea, provinces Chollanam-do, Chollabuk-do, Kyongsang-nam-do, and Kyongsangbuk-do; migrated populations

in southwest Japan, Saga and Nagasaki Prefectures, Kyushu.
Synonyms:
H. nakaiana (Nakai) Maekawa, J. of the Faculty of Science, Imperial University Tokyo, Section 3 Botany, 5:419–420 ic. 103, 104. 1940.
H. capitata Fujita, Acta Phytaxonomica et Geobotanica, 27, 3/4:93. 1976 s.l.

Subgenus *Bryocles* (Salisbury) Maekawa.
Section *Arachnanthae* W. G. Schmid sect. nov.
Corolla tubus dilatatus late arachnanthoides, lobis perangustoribus.
Type: *H. yingeri* S. B. Jones.

H. yingeri S. B. Jones 1989.
Annals of the Missouri Botanical Garden, Vol 76, 2:602–604. 1989.
Type: In NA, 3616, 23 September 1985; coll. B. R. Yinger, T. R. Dudley, J. C. Raulston, A. P. Wharton, and Y. J. Chang; east side of Yeri village, Taehuksan Island (Taehuksando), Chollanam-do, Shin An Gun, Huksan Myeon; among rocks on northwest-facing talus slopes, shade, on cut-over hill side (holotype); Sohuksan Island (Sokuksan-do), Yinger et al., in NA, 3164 (paratype). Hab. island along the southwestern coast of Korea.

H. laevigata W. G. Schmid sp. nov.
Type: In NCU; based on the cultivated plant ex hort. Hosta Hill, grown from natural material collected near the coast on rocky slopes in the shade on Taehuksan Island (Taehuksan-do), Chollanam-do, Shin An Gun, Huksan Myeon; coll. September 1985, B. R. Yinger, T. R. Dudley, J. C. Raulston, A. P. Wharton, and Y. J. Chang. Hab. island along the southwestern coast of Korea, province Chollanam-do, southern Huksan-chedo (Figure 4-35).
H. yingeri et *H. laevigata* similis sed lamina folii suberecta, laevigata, anguste lanceolata, 9–12 cm longa 2–3 cm lata, basi ad petiolum decurrentia, ad marginem undulato-crispata, utrinque 3 nervata, nervis infra laevibus, apex longe acuminatus, paullo contortus; petioli 2 cm longi; scapus erectus, foliis longe exsertus, 35–90 cm longus; bracteae inferiores 3–5, ascendentes, lanceolatae; pedicelli breves 4–6 mm; flores secundi, perianthum sexpartitum; corollae tubus angustus 18–20 mm longus, tubus dilatatus 30–35 mm longus, late infundibiliforme, arachnanthoides, lobi perangustoribus; stamina 6, libera, non exserta, declinata, filamenta aequilonga; antheris 2–3 mm longis, purpurascentibus; stylus corollam exsertus, apice incurvata (also see Chapter 3).

Subgenus *Bryocles* (Salibury) Maekawa.
Section *Stoloniferae* (Maekawa) Maekawa 1938.
Botanical Magazine, Tokyo, 52:42, 44. 1938.
Synonyms:
Hosta subgenus *Bryocles* section *Stoloniferae* Maekawa, J. of the Faculty of Science, Imperial University Tokyo, Section 3 Botany, 5:390, 391. 1940.

H. clausa var. *clausa* Nakai (type).
Botanical Magazine, Tokyo, 44:27. 1930; Maekawa, J. of Japanese Botany, 13:899, ic. f. 5. 1938.
Type: In TI; coll. T. Nakai, in Kyonggi (Keiki) Province. Hab. in provinces Kyonggi-do, Kangwon-do (1988 accessions by M. G. Chung), Hwanghae-do, Pyongannam-do, Hamgyongnam-do and Pyonganbuk-do, central and northern Korea; and provinces Liaoning and Jilin in northeastern China.

H. clausa var. *normalis* Maekawa.
J. of Japanese Botany, 13:898. 1938.
Type: In TI, 3255; coll. T. Nakai, Mount Kongosan, Kangwon-do (Kogen) Province. Hab. in provinces Kyonggi-do, Kangwon-do (1988 accessions by M. G. Chung), Hwanghae-do, Pyongannam-do, Hamgyongnam-do, and Pyonganbuk-do, central and northern Korea; and provinces Liaoning and Jilin in northeastern China.
Synonyms:
Funkia lancifolia (Sprengel) Czerniakovska in Komarov, Flora USSR, 4:55, tab. 5/2. 1935 p.p. in syn.
Hosta cærulea (Trattinnick) Nakai, J. of the Faculty of Science, 31:251. 1911.
H. japonica var. *lancifolia* Nakai, Report on the Vegetation of Diamond Mountains, p. 167. 1918 p.p. in syn.

H. clausa var. *ensata* (Maekawa) W. G. Schmid stat. nov.
Type: In TI, 3253; coll. T. Nakai, Mount Kongosan, Kangwon-do (Kogen) Province; in TI, 366; coll. V. Kamarov, Yalu River, Manchuria (topotype to show distribution). Hab. in provinces Kyonggi-do, Kangwon-do, Hwanghae-do, Pyongannam-do, Pyonganbuk-do, Hamgyong-namdo, and Hamgyong-bukdo, central and northern Korea; and provinces Liaoning and Jilin in northeastern China (Yalu Basin); and far eastern USSR.
Synonyms:
Funkia lancifolia (Sprengel) Komarov, Flora Manchuriae, 1:441. 1901 p.p. in syn.
Hosta ensata Maekawa, J. of Japanese Botany, 13:900. 1938 (basionym); and J. of the Faculty of Science, Imperial University of Tokyo, Section 3 Botany, 5:393, 394 ic. 70. 1940.
H. clausa var. *ensata* Maekawa (in schedula), Annotation on herbarium sheet in TI. 1937 (nomen nudum).
H. japonica var. *lancifolia* Nakai apud Mori, An Enumeration of Plants Hitherto Known From Korea, p. 89. 1922 p.p.
H. lancifolia (Engler) Nakai, J. of the Faculty of Science, 31:250. 1911.

H. clausa var. *stolonifera* W. G. Schmid in obs.
Hab. in provinces Kyonggi-do, Kangwon-do, Hwanghae-do, Pyongannam-do, Pyonganbuk-do, Hamgyongnam-do, and Hamgyongbuk-do, central and northern Korea; observed growing with *Salix* as an evolved, non-flowering phase of *H. clausa* var. *normalis*. Reported in M. G. Chung (1990). Binomial assigned as nom. nudum pending further investigation. Cult. in Korea and North America.

Subgenus *Giboshi*.
Section *Helipteroides* (Maekawa) Maekawa 1938.
Botanical Magazine, Tokyo, 52:42. 1938.
Synonyms:
Hosta section *Helipteroides* Maekawa, J. of Japanese Botany, 13:901. 1937.
Hosta subgenus *Bryocles* section *Helipteroides* Maekawa, J. of the Faculty of Science, Imperial University Tokyo, Section 3 Botany, 5:351. 1940.

H. montana Maekawa excl. var. et syn (emend. W. G. Schmid).
J. of the Faculty of Science, Imperial University of Tokyo, Section 3 Botany, 5:356–357, 361 ic. 21, 23. 1940 (emend. excluding *H. montana* var. *transiens* and the synonym *H. bella* Wehrhahn 1936 and *H. elata* Hylander 1954 which are not conspecific and have been reduced to cultivar forms).
Type: In TI; coll. F. Maekawa, near Lake Yamanaka, Yamanashi

Prefecture and at roadsides Kanagawa Prefecture. In SAP; coll. K. Miyabe, 4 August 1881, Shiribeshi (topotype to show northern distribution). Hab. at forest margins in mountain valleys, Tsukude and Aichi Prefecture; common in Omote-Nihon, Tohoku, Kanto, Chubu and Kansai regions, eastern Honshu; and in southern Hokkaido, Shiribeshi Province, above rocks at seaside at the Niseko-Shakotan-Otaru coast and Mount Shakotan, Japan.

Synonyms:

Funkia sieboldi Lindley Botanical Register 25, tab. 50. 1839 (not *Hemerocallis sieboldii* Paxton 1838) (with respect only to the illustration) (Figure A-1).

Hemerocallis sieboldtiana Loddiges, Botanical Cabinet, 19, tab. 1869. 1832 (p.p. nom. nudum, with respect to the flowers and leaf illustrated) (Figure A-2).

Hosta sieboldiana (Engler) Makino in Iinuma, Somoku Dzusetsu, ed. 3, 2:469, ic. pl. 6/20. 1910.

H. cucullata Koidzumi, Acta Phytotaxonomica et Geobotanica, 5:39. 1936 (p.p.: excluding the basionym and synonyms).

H. fortunei (Bailey) Maekawa, Botanical Magazine, Tokyo, 52:43. 1938.

Funkia sieboldiana bracteata Miquel, Annales Musei Botanici Lugdano-Batavi, p. 152. 1867 (p.p. nom. confusum).

H. sieboldiana var. *sieboldiana* Fujita, Acta Phytotaxonomica et Geobotanica, 27, 3/4:75. 1976 s.l.

H. montana f. *macrophylla* W. G. Schmid f. nov.

Forma macrophylla et *H. montana* similis sed formae lamina folii suberecta, macrophylla, cordata, 40–45 cm longa 25–30 cm lata, utrinque 16–20 nervata; petioli 45–60 cm longi; scapus erectus, foliis breve exsertus, 100–120 cm longus; bracteae superiores revolutae (also see Chapter 3).

Type: In NCU; based on the cultivated plant ex hort. Hosta Hill, Krossa No. B-3 ex coll. OSA, 1951, Nara; Hab. Nara and Kyoto prefectures, west-central Honshu, Japan.

H. montana f. *ovatolancifolia* (Araki) W. G. Schmid comb. nov.

Acta Phytotaxonomica et Geobotanica, 11:328. 1942.

Type: In KYO, 15682; coll Y. Araki, Kitakuwada-gun, Kuroda-mura, Kyoto Prefecture. 11235; coll. Y. Araki, Amada-gun, Kamimutobe-mura; 11233 and 11234; coll. Y. Araki, northern Kyoto, Kasa-gun, Mount Iwatoyama (topotypes in KYO to show distribution). Hab. in Kyoto, Hyogo and Shiga Prefectures, west-central Honshu, Japan.

Synonyms:

H. liliiflora var. *ovatolancifolia* Araki (nom. nudum), Acta Phytotaxonomica et Geobotanica, 11:328. 1942.

H. montana 'Aureomarginata' (a cultivar form).

J. of the Faculty of Science, Imperial University of Tokyo, Section 3 Botany, 5:360, 362 ic. 27. 1940.

Synonyms:

H. montana f. *aureomarginata* (Makino) Maekawa, J. of the Faculty of Science, Imperial University of Tokyo, Section 3 Botany, 5:360, 362 ic. 27. 1940 (here reduced to cultivar form).

H. sieboldiana Engler var. *aureomarginata* (Makino) Maekawa, J. of Japanese Botany, 5:22. 1928.

Ogon Fukurin Oba Giboshi hort. Watanabe (nom. Jap.), The Observation and Cultivation of Hosta, p. 44. 1985.

H. montana Aureomarginata group hort.

H. montana 'Aureomarginata' hort. (AHS).

H. montana 'Liliiflora' (a cultivar form).

J. of the Faculty of Science, Imperial University of Tokyo, Section 3 Botany, 5:360, 361, ic. 24. 1940.

Synonyms:

H. montana var. *liliiflora* Maekawa, J. of the Faculty of Science, Imperial University of Tokyo, Section 3 Botany, 5:360, 361, ic. 24. 1940 (here reduced to cultivar form).

H. liliiflora Maekawa (nom. nudum, with Japanese description), Botanical Magazine, Tokyo, 52:43. 1938.

H. liliiflora Maekawa ex Araki, Acta Phytotaxonomica et Geobotanica, 11:328. 1942.

H. montana 'Praeflorens' (a cultivar form).

J. of the Faculty of Science, Imperial University of Tokyo, Section 3 Botany, 5:363. 1940.

Synonyms:

H. montana var. *praeflorens* Maekawa, J. of the Faculty of Science, Imperial University of Tokyo, Section 3 Botany, 5:363. 1940 (here reduced to cultivar form).

H. montana 'Transiens' (a cultivar form).

J. of the Faculty of Science, Imperial University of Tokyo, Section 3 Botany, 5:363, 362 ic. 25. 1940.

Synonyms:

H. montana var. *transiens* Maekawa (excluding synonym *H. bella* Wehrhahn 1936), J. of the Faculty of Science, Imperial University of Tokyo, Section 3 Botany, 5:363, 362 ic. 25. 1940 (here reduced to cultivar form).

H. sieboldiana var. *sieboldiana* (Hooker) Engler.

In Engler et Prantl, Die Natürlichen Pflanzenfamilien, 2, 3:39–40. 1888.

Hab. among seashore rocks and at forest margins in coastal and lowland areas bordering the Japan sea side in southeastern Hokkaido and in the Ura-Nihon, Tohoku, Kanto, Chubu, and Kansai regions of Honshu, with non-pruinose types extending into Chugoku, Japan.

Synonyms:

Hemerocallis sieboldtiana Loddiges, Botanical Cabinet, 19, tab. 1869. 1832 (p.p.; nom. nudum; with respect only to the name only, not the illustration).

Funckia sieboldiana Hooker, Curtis's Botanical Magazine, 65, tab. 3663. 1839.

Funkia cucullata Siebold (nom. nudum), Jaarb. Kon. Ned. Mij Aanomoed. Tuinbouw, p. 29. 1844; Witte, Flora., 221–224, pl. 56. 1868.

Funkia cordata Siebold ex Steudel, Nom., ed. 2, p. 651. 1840.

Funkia sieboldiana bracteata Miquel, Annales Musei Botanici Lugdano-Batavi, p. 152. 1867 (p.p. nom. confusum).

Funkia umbellata hort., Gardener's Chronicle, p. 1040. 1886.

Funkia glauca Siebold ex Miquel, Verslag Mededelingen Akademie Wetenschappen Amsterdam, 2, 3:303. 1869 (p.p.; with respect to var. β *cucullata*).

Funkia sieboldiana (Hooker) Baker, J. of the Linnean Society of London, 11:367. 1870.

Funkia sieboldiana var. α *typica* (Hooker) Regel, Gartenflora, 25:162 ic. 7; pl. 1, 2. 1876 (considered the typical form by Hylander in a strict sense).

Saussurea sieboldiana (Hooker) Kuntze, Revisio Generum Plantarum 2:714. 1890.

Hostia sieboldiana Voss in Voss et Siebert, Vilmorin's Blumengärtnerei, ed. 3, 2, ic. 228. 1896.

Hosta sieboldiana var. *glauca* Makino, Botanical Magazine, Tokyo, 16:103. 1902.

Niobe sieboldiana (Hooker) Nash, Torreya, 11:6. 1911.

Hosta glauca (Siebold) Stearn, Gardener's Chronicle, 3 ser., 90:80. 1931; Grey, Hardy Bulbs, p. 295. 1938; Bailey, Manual of Cultivated Plants, p. 207. 1951.

H. sieboldiana var. *sieboldiana* Hensen, Mededelingen van de Directeur van de Tuinbouw, 26:725–735. 1963; and Fujita, Acta Phytotaxonomica et Geobotanica, 27, 3/4:75. 1976 s.l.

H. sieboldiana var. glabra Fujita.
Acta Phytotaxonomica et Geobotanica, 27, 3/4:76–78. 1976.
Type: In KYO, 729-18, 20 July 1975; coll. M. Ibuka, leg. H. Nozu, Oki Islands, Fuse-mura, Suki-gun, Shimane Prefecture. Hab. in Toyama, Nagano, Niigata and Shimane Prefectures, Ura-Nihon, Chubu, and Chugoku regions, west-central Honshu, Japan.
Synonyms:
H. sieboldiana var. *longipes* (annotation on herbarium sheet), in KYO. N. Kinashi (in schedula), August 1903; coll. N. Kinashi, Nagano city, Nagano Prefecture, Ura-Nihon, west-central Honshu.
H. nigrescens Fujita, Acta Phytotaxonomica et Geobotanica, 27, 3/4:78. 1976 s.l. p.p.
H. fluctuans, Fujita, Acta Phytotaxonomica et Geobotanica, 27, 3/4:78. 1976 s.l. p.p.

H. sieboldiana 'Amplissima' (a cultivar form).
J. of the Faculty of Science, Imperial University of Tokyo, Section 3 Botany, 5:370, 372, ic. 37. 1940.
Synonyms:
H. sieboldiana var. **amplissima** Maekawa, J. of the Faculty of Science, Imperial University of Tokyo, Section 3 Botany, 5:370, 372, ic. 37. 1940 (here reduced to cultivar form).

H. sieboldiana 'Elegans' (a cultivar form).
Acta Horti Bergiani, 16, 11:386 ic. pl. 3, 4. 1954.
Synonyms:
H. sieboldiana var. **elegans** Hylander, Acta Horti Bergiani, 16, 11:381. 1954 (here reduced to cultivar form).
Funkia fortunei var. *robusta* Arends ex Silva-Tarouca, Unsere Freilandstauden, p. 103. 1910 (nom. subnudum).
Hosta fortunei robusta Bailey, Standard Encyclopedia of Horticulture, p. 1604. 1915.
H. fortunei robusta hort. Arends, Georg Arends Nursery Catalog. 1905; and Grundlagen, 91:138. 1951.
H. sieboldiana fortunei robusta Foerster (nom. nudum), Der Steingarten der Sieben Jahreszeiten, p. 346. 1955.
H. sieboldiana 'Robusta' Hensen, The Plantsman, 7:15. 1985.

H. sieboldiana 'Hypophylla' (a cultivar form).
J. of the Faculty of Science, Imperial University of Tokyo, Section 3 Botany, 5:371, 373, ic. 38–39. 1940.
Synonyms:
H. sieboldiana var. **hypophylla** Maekawa, J. of the Faculty of Science, Imperial University of Tokyo, Section 3 Botany, 5:371, 373, ic. 38–39. 1940 (here reduced to cultivar form).
Funkia cucullata Siebold (p.p.; nom. nudum), Jaarb. Kon. Ned. Mij Aanomoed. Tuinbouw, p. 29. 1844 p.p.; Witte, Flora, 221–224, pl. 56. 1868.
Funkia glauca β *cucullata* Siebold ex Miquel, Verslag Mededelingen Akademie Wetenschappen Amsterdam, 2, 3:303. 1869.
Funkia cucullata hort. Bailey, Standard Encyclopedia of Horticulture, p. 1605. 1915

H. sieboldiana 'Mira' (a cultivar form).
J. of the Faculty of Science, Imperial University of Tokyo, Section 3 Botany, 5:372, 373 ic. 40. 1940.
Synonyms:
H. sieboldiana var. **mira** Maekawa, J. of the Faculty of Science, Imperial University of Tokyo, Section 3 Botany, 5:372, 373 ic. 40. 1940 (here reduced to cultivar form).
H. mira Maekawa (nom. nudum, with Japanese description), Botanical Magazine, Tokyo, 52:43. 1938.

H. sieboldiana 'Semperaurea' (a cultivar form).
Neuer Glanz des Gartenjahres, p. 124, 173. 1952.
Synonyms:
H. sieboldiana var. *semperaurea* Foerster (nom. nudum), Neuer Glanz des Gartenjahres, p. 124, 173. 1952.
H. grandifolia semperaurea Foerster (nom. nudum), Neuer Glanz des Gartenjahres, p. 124, 173. 1952.
H. japonica semperaurea Foerster (nom. nudum), Der Steingarten der Sieben Jahreszeiten, p. 346. 1956; and Einzug der Grässer und Farne in die Gärten, p. 191, 195, 218. 1957.
H. semperaurea Foerster (nom. nudum), Pflanze und Garten, 11:294–297. 1965.

H. 'Tokudama' (a cultivar form).
J. of the Faculty of Science, Imperial University of Tokyo, Section 3 Botány, 5:366, 367, ic. 31–33. 1940.
Synonyms:
H. tokudama Maekawa, J. of the Faculty of Science, Imperial University of Tokyo, Section 3 Botany, 5:366. 1940 (here reduced to cultivar form).
Hemerocallis japonica Thunberg apud Banks (not Thunberg 1784), Icones selectae Kaempfer, tab. 2. 1791.
Funkia sieboldiana var. *condensata* Miquel, Annales Musei Botanici Lugdano-Batavi, p. 153. 1867.
Funkia fortunei Anonymous in Siebold (nom. nudum), Catalogue et Prix-courant 1871, p. 43. 1870–71; and Anonymous, Nederland Tuinbouwblad Sempervirens, 20:535. 1891a; Jäger, Die Schönsten Pflanzen des Blumen- und Landschaftsgartens, 378–380. 1873 (not H. fortunei Baker 1876).
Funkia sieboldiana f. β *fortunei* Regel, Gartenflora, 25:162. 1876.
Funkia sieboldiana var. *fortunei* Witte, Sieboldia, 3:14. 1877.
Hostia sieboldiana f. *fortunei* Voss in Voss et Siebert, Vilmorin's Blumengärtnerei, ed. 3, 1:1075. 1896.
Hosta sieboldiana var. *glauca* Makino, Botanical Magazine, Tokyo, 16:173. 1902; and Matsumura, Index plantarum japonicarum, 2:201. 1905; and Makino, Somoku Dzusetsu, ed. 3, 2:468. 1910 (not Funkia var. glauca Witte 1868).
H. sieboldiana fortunei minor Foerster (nom. nudum), Der Steingarten der Sieben Jahreszeiten, p. 346. 1956; and Einzug der Grässer und Farne in die Gärten, p. 190, 195. 1957.
H. sieboldiana var. *fortunei* Regel Ascherson et Gräbner, Synopsis der Mitteleuropäischen Flora, 3:55. 1905 (with respect to the name in synonymy only, not the description = H. 'Fortunei').
H. sieboldiana var. *fortunei* Maekawa, J. of the Faculty of Science, Imperial University Tokyo, Section 3 Botany, 5:371. 1940 (p.p.; with respect to the description = H. sieboldiana; and excluding the synonyms = H. 'Fortunei').
H. glauca minor Foerster (nom. nudum), Einzug der Grässer und Farne in die Gärten, p. 189, 190, 195. 1957.

H. 'Tokudama Flavocircinalis' (a cultivar form).
J. of the Faculty of Science, Imperial University Tokyo, Section 3 Botany, 5:368. 1940.
Synonyms:
H. tokudama f. **flavocircinalis** Maekawa, J. of the Faculty of Science, Imperial University Tokyo, Section 3 Botany, 5:368. 1940 (here reduced to cultivar form).

H. 'Tokudama Aureonebulosa' (a cultivar form).
J. of the Faculty of Science, Imperial University Tokyo, Section 3 Botany, 5:368. 1940.
Synonyms:
H. tokudama f. *aureonebulosa* Maekawa, J. of the Faculty of Science, Imperial University Tokyo, Section 3 Botany, 5:368. 1940 (here reduced to cultivar form).
H. glauca var. *variegata* Siebold (nom. nudum), Catalogue prodrome 1861, p. 6. 1861.
Funkia fortunei variegata Anonymous in Siebold (nom. nudum), Catalogue et Prix-courant 1871, p. 43. 1870–71; and Anonymous, Nederland Tuinbouwblad Sempervirens, 20:532. 1891a.
Hosta tokudama 'Variegata' Hensen, Mededelingen van de Directeur van de Tuinbouw, 26:725–735. 1963; and Hansen-Müssel, Jahresbericht, Staatliche Lehr- und Forschungsanstalt für Gartenbau, p. 4–5. 1964; and Hansen-Sieber-Müssel, Jahresbericht, Institut für Stauden, p. 10. 1974.
H. tokudama f. *mediopicta* Kaneko, J. of Japanese Botany 43, 7:10. 1968.
H. sieboldiana 'Aureonebulosa' Hensen, The Plantsman, 7:16. 1985.
H. tokudama Mediovariegata group hort.

H. 'Tokudama Flavoplanata' (a cultivar form).
J. of the Faculty of Science, Imperial University Tokyo, Section 3 Botany, 5:368. 1940.
Synonyms:
H. tokudama f. *flavoplanata* Maekawa, J. of the Faculty of Science, Imperial University Tokyo, Section 3 Botany, 5:368. 1940 (here reduced to cultivar form).
H. tokudama Mediovariegata group hort.

H. 'Elata' (a cultivar form).
Acta Horti Bergiani, 16, 11:394 ic. pl. 10, 11, 12, 2c. 1954.
Synonyms:
H. elata Hylander, Acta Horti Bergiani, 16, 11:381. 1954 (excluding the synonym *H. montana* and here reduced to cultivar form).
Funkia sinensis Siebold (nom. nudum), Catalogue raisonné et Prix-courant 1856, p. 12. 1856; Witte, Flora, 223. 1868.
Funkia latifolia β *sinensis* Miquel, Verslag Mededelingen Akademie Wetenschappen Amsterdam, 2, 3:303. 1869.
Funkia ovata f. β *latifolia* Regel, Gartenflora, 25:162. 1876.
Hostia cærulea f. *latifolia* Voss in Voss et Siebert, Vilmorin's Blumengärtnerei, ed. 3, 1:1075. 1896.
Hosta fortunei (Baker) Bailey var. *gigantea* Bailey, Standard Encyclopedia of Horticulture, p. 1604. 1915; and Gentes Herbarum, 2, 3:137, 130 ic. 72, 134 ic. 76. 1933 (p.p.; excluding the synonym *Funkia gigantea* de Noter 1905); Grey, Hardy Bulbs, p. 295. 1938 (p.p.; excluding the synonym *Funkia gigantea* de Noter 1905); Bailey, Manual of Cultivated Plants, p. 207. 1951 (p.p.; excluding the synonym *H. montana* Maekawa); (all p.p., because some taxa under these names are *H. sieboldiana* green-leaved forms).
H. gigantea Koidzumi, Acta Phytotaxonomica et Geobotanica, 5:39. 1936 pp.
H. sieboldi gigantea Foerster (nom. nudum), Neuer Glanz des Gartenjahres, p. 1, 172–173. 1952.
H. sieboldiana gigantea Foerster (nom. nudum), Der Steingarten der Sieben Jahreszeiten, p. 346. 1956 and Einzug der Grässer und Farne in die Gärten, p. 191, 196, 218. 1957.
H. sieboldiana var. *sieboldiana* Fujita, Acta Phytotaxonomica et Geobotanica, 27, 3/4:75. 1976 s.l.
H. sinensis hort. p.p.

H. nigrescens (Makino) Maekawa.
Botanical Magazine, Tokyo, 13:901, ic. 8. 1938; and J. of the Faculty of Science, Imperial University Tokyo, Section 3 Botany, 5:368 ic. 13–15. 1940.
Hab. in mountain valleys, Iwate Prefecture (Rikuchu), northern Honshu, Japan.
Synonyms:
H. sieboldiana var. *nigrescens* Makino, Botanical Magazine, Tokyo, 13:173. 1902; and Makino in Iinuma, Somoku Dzusetsu, ed. 3, 2:469, pl. 6/27. 1910; and Makino et Nemoto, Nippon-shokubutsu-soran, ed. 1:1262. 1925.
H. sieboldiana var. *glabra* Fujita, Acta Phytotaxonomica et Geobotanica, 27, 3/4:75. 1976 s.l. (with respect only to the name in annotation).

H. nigrescens 'Elatior' (a cultivar form).
J. of the Faculty of Science, Imperial University of Tokyo, Section 3 Botany, 5:355, ic. 2, p. 323. 1940.
Synonyms:
H. nigrescens f. *elatior* Maekawa, J. of the Faculty of Science, Imperial University of Tokyo, Section 3 Botany, 5:355. 1940 (here reduced to cultivar form and with respect to the taxon without pruinosity as illustrated).

H. fluctuans Maekawa.
J. of the Faculty of Science, Imperial University of Tokyo, Section 3 Botany, 5:355–358, ic. 17, 18, 19, 20. 1940.
Type: In TI; s.n. coll. Sin Narumi, Hirosaki, Aomori Prefecture. Hab. in mountain valleys, Yamagata Prefecture, and near Hirosaki, Aomori Prefecture, Ura-Nihon, northwestern and northern Honshu, Japan.
Synonyms:
H. sieboldiana var. *glabra* Fujita, Acta Phytotaxonomica et Geobotanica, 27, 3/4:75. 1976 s.l. (with respect only to the name in annotation).
H. sieboldiana var. *fluctuans* (hort.) (Japan).
H. fluctuans f. *parvifolia* Maekawa, J. of the Faculty of Science, Imperial University Tokyo, Section 3 Botany, 5:356. 1940.

H. crassifolia Araki.
Acta Phytotaxonomica et Geobotanica, 12, 118. 1943.
Type: In KYO, 15798; coll. Araki, Mount Ibukiyama, Shiga Prefecture. Hab. in central Honshu, Japan.
Synonyms:
H. sieboldiana var. *sieboldiana* Fujita, Acta Phytotaxonomica et Geobotanica, 27, 3/4:75. 1976 s.l.

H. 'Bella' (a cultivar form).
Gartenflora, p. 247–249, ic. p. 248 and 249. 1936.
Synonyms:
H. bella Wehrhahn, Gartenflora, p. 248–249. 1936 (here reduced to cultivar form).
H. fortunei var. *nova* Hylander (nom. nudum), Lustgården, p. 33–34. 1952–53.
H. fortunei var. *obscura* Hylander, Acta Horti Bergiani, 16, 11:392. 1954.
H. 'Fortunei Obscura' hort.

H. 'Crispula' (a cultivar form).
Botanical Magazine, Tokyo, 52:42. 1938 (nom. nudum, with a Japanese description); and J. of the Faculty of Science, Imperial University of Tokyo, Section 3 Botany, 5:364, 365 ic. 28–30. 1940.
Synonyms:
H. crispula Maekawa, J. of the Faculty of Science, Imperial University of Tokyo, Section 3 Botany, 5:364, 365 ic. 28–30. 1940 (here reduced to cultivar form).

Funkia marginata Siebold (nom. nudum), Jaarb. Kon. Ned. Mij Aanomoed. Tuinbouw, p. 29. 1844; and Catalogue et Prix-courant 1869, p. 43. 1869.

Funkia sieboldiana α *marginata* Miquel, Annales Musei Botanici Lugdano-Batavi, p. 153. 1867.

Funkia sieboldiana lusus β *marginata* Miquel, Verslag Mededelingen Akademie Wetenschappen Amsterdam, 2, 3:302 1869.

Funkia albomarginata Anonymous in Siebold (nom. nudum), Prix-courant 1882, p. 25. 1882; and Anonymous, Nederland Tuinbouwblad Sempervirens, 20:532. 1891a (nom. nudum; not Hooker 1838).

Funkia ovata var. β *intermedia* f. *marginata* Baker, J. of the Linnean Society of London, 11:367. 1870.

Funkia ovata δ *albomarginata* Regel, Gartenflora, 25:162. 1876.

Funkia ovata marginata Regel, Gartenflora, 30:23. 1881.

Hostia cærulea f. *albomarginata* Voss in Voss et Siebert, Vilmorin's Blumengärtnerei, ed. 3, 1:1076. 1896.

Hosta latifolia var. *albimarginata* Wehrhahn, Gartenflora, 85:7. 1936.

H. fortunei (Baker) Bailey var. *marginato-alba* Bailey, Gentes Herbarum, 2, 3:137. 1930 p.p.; Stearn, Gardener's Chronicle, 3 ser., 90:88. 1931; Bailey, Manual of Cultivated Plants, p. 207. 1951.

H. 'Fortunei' (a cultivar form).
Standard Encyclopedia of Horticulture, p. 1604. 1915 (with respect to the basionym and for a taxon no longer in cultivation in a strict sense).
Type: In K.
Synonyms:
H. fortunei (Baker) Bailey, Standard Encyclopedia of Horticulture, p. 1604. 1915 (here reduced to cultivar form).

Funkia fortunei Baker, Gardener's Chronicle, n.s. 6, p. 36. 1876.

H. sieboldiana var. *fortunei* (Baker) Ascherson et Gräbner, Synopsis der Mitteleuropäischen Flora, 3:53–55. 1905 (with respect to the name in synonymy and not *Funkia sieboldiana* β *fortunei* Regel = *H.* 'Tokudama').

Niobe fortunei (Baker) Nash, Torreya, 11:7. 1911.

Hosta fortunei (Bailey) Stearn, Gardener's Chronicle, 3 ser., 90:88. 1931; Foerster (nom. nudum), Der Steingarten der Sieben Jahreszeiten, p. 346. 1956; and Einzug der Grässer und Farne in die Gärten, p. 191, 196, 189 ic. 1. 1957.

H. sieboldiana var. *fortunei* Maekawa, J. of the Faculty of Science, Imperial University Tokyo, Section 3 Botany, 5:371. 1940 (p.p.; with respect to the synonyms only, not description = *H. sieboldiana*).

H. 'Fortunei Albomarginata' (a cultivar form).
Zager, Price List of Hemerocallis and Hosta, H. A. Zager, Des Moines, Iowa, USA, p. 17. 1941; and Gray & Cole, Hardy Plants for New England Gardens, p. 7. 1942. (nom. nuda).
Synonyms:
H. fortunei marginato-alba Bailey, Gentes Herbarum, 2, 3:137. 1930 (p.p., incorrectly applied to this taxon = *H.* 'Crispula').

H. fortunei 'Marginato-alba' Hensen, Mededelingen van de Directeur van de Tuinbouw, 26:725–735. 1963; Hansen-Müssel, Jahresbericht, Staatliche Lehr- und Forschungsanstalt für Gartenbau, p. 4–6. 1964; Hansen-Sieber-Müssel, Jahresbericht, Institut für Stauden, p. 10. 1974; Grenfell, The Plantsman, 3:29. 1981; Hensen, The Plantsman, 7:29. 1985; Jellito-Schacht-Fessler (Müssel) p.p., Die Freiland-Schmuckstauden, p. 300. 1986 (p.p. incorrectly applied).

H. fortunei 'Obscura Albo-marginata' (hort.).

H. fortunei Albomarginata group

H. 'Fortunei Albopicta' (a cultivar form).
Acta Horti Bergiani, 16, 11:389. ic. pl. 6, 8, 11. 1954.
Synonyms:
H. fortunei var. *albopicta* (Miquel) Hylander, Acta Horti Bergiani, 16, 11:389. 1954 (here reduced to cultivar form).

Funkia viridimarginata (hort.) Siebold (nom. nudum), Catalogue et Prix-courant, p. 45. 1863.

Funkia ovata (var.) *albopicta* Miquel, Verslag Mededelingen Akademie Wetenschappen Amsterdam, 2, 3:299. 1869.

Funkia aurea maculata Siebold (nom. nudum), Prijslijst, p. 8. 1874; and Anonymous, Nederland Tuinbouwblad Sempervirens, 20:532. 1891a.

Hosta viridis-marginata (hort.) Bailey, Standard Encyclopedia of Horticulture, p. 1605. 1915.

H. lancifolia var. *aureo-maculata* Wehrhahn, Gartenschönheit, 15:204. 1934.

H. aureo-marmorata Foerster (nom. nudum), Neuer Glanz des Gartenjahres, p. 124, 173. 1952; and Pflanze und Garten. 1965.

H. japonica aureo-marmorata Foerster (nom. nudum), Der Steingarten der Sieben Jahreszeiten, p. 346. 1956; and Einzug der Grässer und Farne in die Gärten, p. 191, 195 ic. 191. 1957.

H. fortunei 'Aureo-maculata' Hensen, Mededelingen van de Directeur van de Tuinbouw, 26:725–735. 1963; Hansen-Müssel, Jahresbericht, Staatliche Lehr- und Forschungsanstalt für Gartenbau, p. 4–6. 1964; Foerster (nom. nudum), Pflanze und Garten, 11:297. 1965; Hansen-Sieber-Müssel, Jahresbericht, Institut für Stauden, p. 10. 1974.

H. fortunei Mediovariegata group.

H. 'Fortunei Aoki' (a cultivar form).
Standard Encyclopedia of Horticulture, p. 1604. 1915.
Synonyms:
Funkia aokii Siebold (nom. nudum), Prix-courant 1879, p. 22–23. 1879 (basionym).

Hosta aoki Bailey, Standard Encyclopedia of Horticulture, p. 1604. 1915.

H. 'Fortunei Aurea' (a cultivar form).
Acta Horti Bergiani, 16, 11:391. 1954.
Synonyms:
H. fortunei var. *albopicta* f. *aurea* Hylander, Acta Horti Bergiani, 16, 11:391. 1954 (here reduced to cultivar form).

Funkia aurea Siebold (nom. nudum), Prijslijst 1874, p. 8. 1874; and Anonymous, Nederland Tuinbouwblad Sempervirens, 20:532. 1891.

Hosta lancifolia var. *aurea* Wehrhahn (nom. nudum; with a German description), Gartenschönheit, 15:204. 1934 p.p. only, also used p.p. with respect to *H.* 'Lancifolia Aurea'.

H. aurea (hort.) Bailey, Standard Encyclopedia of Horticulture, p. 1605. 1915.

H. japonica aurea Nobis, Die Freiland-Schmuckstauden, 4:113. 1951; Der Steingarten der Sieben Jahreszeiten, p. 346, ic. p. 71. 1956; and Einzug der Grässer und Farne in die Gärten, p. 191, 195, ic. p. 188–189. 1957 (nom. nuda, with respect to the description and illustrations only.).

H. japonica f. *lutescens* Voss (with respect only to f. *aureomaculata*) in Voss et Siebert, Vilmorin's Blumengärtnerei, ed. 3, 1:1074–1076. 1896.

H. fortunei var. *albopicta* f. *lutescens* Hylander (nom. nudum). Lustgården, 33/34:27. 1952–53.

H. aurea praecox Foerster (nom. nudum), Pflanze und Garten, 11:294. 1965.

H. fortunei var. *aurea* hort.

H. fortunei 'Aurea' hort. (AHS).

H. fortunei Aurea group.

H. 'Fortunei Aureomarginata' (a cultivar form).

Die Gartenstauden, p. 68. 1931 (nom. nudum); RHS Dictionary of Gardening, Supp., ed. 2, p. 349. 1969.

Synonyms:

H. fortunei var. **aureomarginata** (Wehrhahn) Hylander, Die Gartenstauden, p. 68. 1931; RHS Dictionary of Gardening, Supp,, ed. 2, p. 349. 1969 (here reduced to cultivar form).

H. lancifolia f. *aureimarginata* Wehrhahn, Gartenschönheit, p. 68. 1931 (basionym).

H. japonica var. *aurea-marginata* Nobis, Die Freiland-Schmuckstauden, 4:113. 1951.

H. fortunei var. *obscura* f. *marginata* Hylander (nom. superfluum), Acta Horti Bergiani, 16, 11:393. 1954.

H. japonica aureomarginata Foerster (nom. nudum), Der Steingarten der Sieben Jahreszeiten, p. 346. 1956; and Einzug der Grässer und Farne in die Gärten, p. 191, 195. 1957.

H. fortunei 'Aureo-marginata'.

H. fortunei Aureomarginata group.

H. 'Fortunei Hyacinthina' (a cultivar form).

Acta Hort. Bergiani, 16, 11:393, ic. pl. 5, 9, 10. 1954.

Synonyms:

H. fortunei var. **hyacinthina** Hylander, Acta Hort. Bergiani, 16, 11:393. 1954 (here reduced to cultivar form).

Funkia glaucescens Siebold (nom. nudum), Prix-courant, p. 13–14. 1877.

Hosta sieboldiana glaucescens Foerster (nom. nudum), Der Steingarten der Sieben Jahreszeiten, p. 346. 1956; and Einzug der Grässer und Farne in die Gärten, p. 191, 195. 1957.

H. glauca (hort.) Hensen, Mededelingen van de Directeur van de Tuinbouw, 26:725–735. 1963 p.p. (not Stearn); and Hensen, The Plantsman, 7:18. 1985 (as cultivated in Holland only).

H. fortunei 'Hyacinthina' hort.

H. fortunei Hyacinthina group.

H. 'Fortunei Rugosa' (a cultivar form).

Acta Horti Bergiani, 16, 11:391, ic. pl. 5. 1954.

Synonyms:

H. fortunei var. **rugosa** Hylander, Acta Horti Bergiani, 16, 11:391. 1954 (here reduced to cultivar form).

H. fortunei var. *hyacinthina* 'Rugosa' hort.

H. fortunei 'Rugosa' hort.

H. 'Fortunei Stenantha' (a cultivar form).

Acta Horti Bergiani, 16, 11:388, ic. Pl. 7, 8. 1954.

Synonyms:

H. fortunei var. **stenantha** Hylander, Acta Horti Bergiani, 16, 11:388. 1954 (here reduced to cultivar form).

H. fortunei 'Stenantha' hort.

H. fortunei Stenantha group.

H. 'Fortunei Viridis' (a cultivar form).

Acta Horti Bergiani, 16, 11:391. 1954.

Synonyms:

H. fortunei var. **albopicta** f. **viridis** Hylander, Acta Horti Bergiani, 16, 11:391. 1954 (here reduced to cultivar form).

Funkia viridis (hort.) Siebold (nom. nudum), Catalogue et Prix-courant, p. 50–51. 1867. p.p.

Hosta viridis Foerster (nom. nudum), Neuer Glanz des Gartenjahres, p. 125, 173. 1952.

H. japonica cærulea viridis Foerster (nom. nudum), Der Steingarten der Sieben Jahreszeiten, p. 346. 1956.

H. cærulea viridis Foerster (nom. nudum), Einzug der Grässer und Farne in die Gärten, p. 191, 196. 1957.

H. fortunei var. *albopicta* 'Viridis' hort.

H. fortunei 'Viridis' hort.

Subgenus *Giboshi* Maekawa.

Section *Intermediae* (Maekawa) W. G. Schmid comb. nov.

Synonyms:

Hosta section *Intermediae* Maekawa, J. of Japanese Botany, 14:46. 1938; and Botanical Magazine, Tokyo, 52:42. 1938.

Hosta subgenus *Bryocles* section *Intermedia* Maekawa, J. of the Faculty of Science, Imperial University Tokyo, Section 3 Botany, 5:376. 1940.

H. densa Maekawa (type).

Botanical Magazine, Tokyo, 52:42. 1938 (nom. nudum, with a Japanese description); J. of Japanese Botany, 14:46. 1938; and J. of the Faculty of Science, Imperial University Tokyo, Section 3 Botany, 5:377–378, ic. 47–48. 1940 (excluding the plants in Mie Prefecture = *H. kikutii* var. *densa* Maekawa [1969] and conspecific with *H. kikutii*).

Type: In TI; coll. F. Maekawa, Mount Odaigahara, Nara Prefecture. Hab. in Kansai, west-central Honshu, Japan.

H. kiyosumiensis Maekawa.

J. of Japanese Botany 11:689 ic. f. 15. 1935; and J. of the Faculty of Science, Imperial University Tokyo, Section 3 Botany, 5:380, 382, ic. 53–55. 1940.

Type: In TI; coll. T. Nakai, Mount Kiyosumi, Chiba Prefecture; in TI, 249 (topotype to indicate distribution), 5 August 1962; coll. M. Hotta and N. Fukuoka, Sekkyu-no-syuku, between Ichinotao and Mount Mi-zen, ca. 1600 m.s.m., Tekawa-mura, Yoshino-gun, Kii Peninsula, Nara Prefecture, west-central Honshu. Hab. banks of Oto River, Nukata-cho, Aichi Prefecture; Mount Zyubusan, Kyoto Prefecture and Mount Saniyo, Nara Prefecture; in south Kanto, Chubu, Kansai (incl. Kii Peninsula), central Honshu, Japan.

Synonyms:

H. praecox Maekawa, Botanical Magazine, Tokyo, 52:42. 1938.

H. petrophila Maekawa, Botanical Magazine, Tokyo, 52:42. 1938.

H. kiyosumiensis var. *petrophila* Maekawa, J. of the Faculty of Science, Imperial University Tokyo, Section 3 Botany, 5:380, 382, ic. 55. 1940.

H. pachyscapa Maekawa.

J. of the Faculty of Science, Imperial University Tokyo, Section 3 Botany, 5:383 ic. 58–59. 1940.

Type: Based on the cultivated plant; coll. M. Toyama, Inae, Shiga Prefecture; in hort. TI. Hab. in Shiga and Shizuoka prefectures, southern Chubu and Kansai, central Honshu, Japan.

H. 'Hippeastrum' (a cultivar form).

J. of the Faculty of Science, Imperial University of Tokyo, Section 3 Botany, 5:383 ic. 56–57. 1940.

Synonyms:
H. hippeastrum Maekawa, J. of the Faculty of Science, Imperial
    University of Tokyo, Section 3 Botany, 5:383, 384, ic. 56–
    57. 1940 (here reduced to cultivar form).

H. 'Sacra' (a cultivar form).
J. of Japanese Botany, 14:47. 1938; and Botanical Magazine,
    Tokyo, 52:42. 1938 (nom. nudum, with a Japanese
    description); and J. of the Faculty of Science, Imperial
    University of Tokyo, Section 3 Botany, 5:379, 380, 381, ic.
    50–52. 1940.
Synonyms:
H. sacra Maekawa, J. of Japanese Botany, 14:47. 1938 (here
    reduced to cultivar form).

Subgenus *Giboshi* Maekawa.
Section *Rhynchophorae* (Maekawa) W. G. Schmid comb. nov.
Synonyms:
Hosta section *Rhynchophorae* Maekawa, J. of Japanese Botany,
    14:46. 1938; and Botanical Magazine, Tokyo, 52:44.
    1938.
Hosta subgenus *Bryocles* section *Rhynchophorae* Maekawa, J. of
    the Faculty of Science, Imperial University Tokyo,
    Section 3 Botany, 5:375. 1940.

H. kikutii var. *kikutii* Maekawa (type).
J. of Japanese Botany, 13:48, ic. f. 9. 1937; and J. of the Faculty of
    Science, Imperial University of Tokyo, Section 3 Botany,
    5:375, ic. 3, 4 p. 324. 1940.
Type: Based on the cultivated plant. Coll. B. Miyazawa, Mount
    Boroishizan, Hyuga Prefecture. Hab. in Oita and
    Miyazaki prefectures, southeastern Kyushu, Japan.
Synonyms:
H. kikutii var. *kikutii* Maekawa in Ishii, Engei-daijiten, 2:633.
    1950 p.p.; Kitamura et al., Col. Ill. Herb. Plant. Jap., p.
    138. 1964 p.p.; Fujita, Acta Phytotaxonomica et
    Geobotanica, 27, 3/4:78. 1976.
H. kikutii var. *densa* Maekawa in Ishii, Engei-daijiten, p. 1105–
    1106. 1969.

H. kikutii var. *kikutii* f. *leuconota* W. G. Schmid f. nov.
Differt ab *H. kikutii* var. *yakusimensis*: Lamina folii supra
    manifeste pruinosa, subtus intense pruinosa, albo-
    glaucissima (also see Chapter 3).
Type: In NCU; based on the cultivated plant ex hort. Hosta
    Hill, coll. 1970, Kagoshima (Summers 406). Hab. among
    standard populations in Kagoshima Prefecture, south-
    ern Kyushu, Japan.
Synonyms:
Urajiro Hyuga Giboshi and *Hosoba Urajiro Hyuga Giboshi* hort. in
    Watanabe (with respect only to the Japanese names),
    The Observation and Cultivation of *Hosta*. p. 30, 88.

H. kikutii var. *caput-avis* Maekawa.
In Ishii, Engei-daijiten, 2:633. 1950.
Type: Based on the cultivated plant; coll. K. Yasui, Yanase,
    Kochi Prefecture. Hab. in southern Shikoku, Japan.
Synonyms:
H. tosana var. *caput-avis* Maekawa, J. of Japanese Botany, 22:64.
    1948.
H. caput-avis Maekawa in Nakai, Iconographia Plantarum
    Asiae-Orientalis 5:495. 1952; Ohwi, The Flora of Japan,
    11:291. 1965; Grenfell, The Plantsman, 3:32. 1981.

H. kikutii var. *polyneuron* (Maekawa) Fujita.
Acta Phytotaxonomica et Geobotanica, 27, 3/4:78. 1976.
Type: Based on the cultivated plant; coll. Fujita, Ikegawa-cho,
    Kochi Prefecture. Hab. in Shikoku, Japan.

Synonyms:
H. polyneuron Maekawa in Nakai, Iconographia Plantarum
    Asiae-Orientalis 5:496–497. 1952 (excluding the
    synonyms).

H. kikutii var. *tosana* (Maekawa) Maekawa.
In Ishii, Engei-daijiten, 2:633. 1950; and Kitamura et al.; Col. Ill.
    Herb. Plant. Jap., p. 138. 1964.
Type: Based on the cultivated plant; coll. T. Yoshinaga, Mount
    Kajigamine, Kochi Prefecture. Hab. in southern and
    western Shikoku, Japan.
Synonyms:
H. kikutii var. *caput-avis* Fujita, Acta Phytotaxonomica et
    Geobotanica, 27, 3/4:78. 1976 s.l.
H. tosana Maekawa, J. of the Faculty of Science, Imperial
    University of Tokyo, Section 3 Botany, 5:376, 377, ic. 45,
    46. 1940; and Ohwi, The Flora of Japan, 11:291. 1965 p.p.

H. kikutii var. *yakusimensis* (Masamune) Maekawa.
J. of the Faculty of Science, Imperial University of Tokyo,
    Section 3 Botany, 5:374, 375, 376, ic. 42. 43, 44. 1940.
Type: Based on the cultivated plant; coll. Suzuki, ins. Yaku,
    Kagoshima Prefecture. Hab. in Kagoshima Prefecture,
    incl. ins. Yakushima and Tanegashima, southern
    Kyushu, Japan (excluding the plants on Shikoku).
Synonyms:
H. sieboldiana var. *yakusimensis* Masamune, J. Society of
    Tropical Agriculture, 4:301. 1932 (basionym); and
    Florist. Geobotanical Studies of Yakushima, p. 553.
    1934; Ohwi, The Flora of Japan, 11:291. 1965.
H. yakusimensis Maekawa, in Ishii, Engei-daijiten, 2:633. 1950
    (p.p., excluding Masamune's early blooming form from
    Kosugidani, Yakushima).
H. kikutii var. *polyneuron* Fujita, Acta Phytotaxonomica et
    Geobotanica, 27, 3/4:78. 1976 (p.p.; with respect only to
    the name in synonymy).
H. polyneuron Ohwi, The Flora of Japan, 11:291. 1965 p.p.

H. shikokiana Fujita.
Acta Phytotaxonomica et Geobotanica, 27, 3/4:93, ic. 10. 1976.
Type: In KYO, 22475, 7 August 1957; coll. T. Yamanaka. Hab. in
    open mountain valleys, on rocks at 1300–1800 m.s.m. on
    Mount Higashiakaishi, Ehime Prefecture (G. Murata,
    14981, in KYO) and Mount Akaishi (G. Koidzumi in
    KYO), Mount Nishiakaishi (T. Tsuyama in TI), Mount
    Kanpu (S. Yamawaki in TI), Mount Ishizuchi (N. Fujita
    and H. Takahashi 226 and S. Takafuji in KYO) in Ehime
    Prefecture, and Mount Shiragayama (N. Fujita and H.
    Takahashi in KYO) in Kochi Prefecture, western
    Shikoku, Japan (all topotypes to show distribution).

Subgenus *Giboshi* Maekawa.
Section *Picnolepis* (Maekawa) Maekawa 1938.
Botanical Magazine, Tokyo, 52:42, 44. 1938.
Synonyms:
Hosta section *Picnolepis* Maekawa, J. of Japanese Botany,
    13:901. 1937.
Hosta subgenus *Bryocles* section *Picnolepis* Maekawa, J. of the
    Faculty of Science, Imperial University Tokyo, Section 3
    Botany, 5:385. 1940.

H. longipes var. *longipes* (Franchet and Savatier)
    Matsumura (type).
Plant List, 21. 1894 (nom. seminudum); and Okuiyama, J. of
    Japanese Botany, 13:34. 1937 (with respect only to the
    populations conforming to the type in P and excluding
    major phases of *H. longipes* Maekawa, 1940, type in TI.
    The latter has been reclassified under the name *H.*

longipes var. *vulgata*, which see, and represents a macro-morphologically different phase of *H. longipes*).

Differt a var. *vulgata* Maekawa lamina folii late cordata acuminata 10–13 cm longa 5–7 cm lata, chartacea utrinque 5–6 nervata, nervis glabris, costa basi utrinque purpureo-punctata. Petioli toto purpureo-punctati rigidi 10–30 cm longi. Scapi toto purpureo-punctati teretes 15–20 cm longa flores 8–12 sparsi.

Type: In P, Savatier, 1297; coll. in the area of Hakone-machi, near Mount Hakone, Kanagawa Prefecture. Hab. near Mount Hakone, Kanagawa Prefecture, and in Kanagawa, Saitama, Tochigi, and Tokyo prefectures; Kanto Plain and Izu-Hanto, south-central Honshu, Japan.

Synonyms:
Funkia longipes Franchet et Savatier, Enumeratio Plantarum Japonicarum, 2–1:82, 529. 1876 (basionym).
Hosta sieboldiana var. *longipes* Matsumura, Cat., p. 203. 1886 and Index Plantarum Japonicarum, p. 201. 1905 p.p.
H. longipes f. *hypoglauca* Maekawa, J. of the Faculty of Science, Imperial University Tokyo, Section 3 Botany, 5:388. 1940 (p.p.; with respect only to the plants in the area of original collection in Mount Hakone region which are identical to the type in P).
H. longipes var. *longipes* Fujita, Acta Phytotaxonomica et Geobotanica, 27, 3/4:81. 1976 p.p. (published with respect to Maekawa's type in TI, incl. in syn., not the holotype in P).
H. longipes Bailey, Gentes Herbarum, 2, 3:142, ic. 78, p. 138. 1930.

H. longipes f. *hypoglauca* Maekawa.
J. of the Faculty of Science, Imperial University of Tokyo, Section 3 Botany, 5:388. 1940 (with respect to the plants occurring and collected in Shimotsuke which are differentiated from the type in P).
Type: Coll. Nakai and Maekawa, Tochigi Prefecture (Shimotsuke Province), Fubasami; and in Shizuoka and Aichi prefectures; also in Kanagawa, Saitama, Tokyo, Yamanashi and Tochigi prefectures, Kanto and Fuji-Hakone districts, south-central Honshu, Japan.

H. longipes f. *sparsa* (Nakai) W. G. Schmid stat. nov.
Botanical Magazine, Tokyo, 44:514. 1930 (with respect only to the populations in southern Chubu).
Type: In TI. Hab. on wet rocks at the banks of Tenryu River. Hab. Shizuoka and Aichi Prefectures, southern Chubu Region, south-central Honshu, Japan.
Synonyms:
H. longipes var. *lancea* Honda, Botanical Magazine, Tokyo, 49:696. 1935 (p.p.; with respect only to the sparse-flowered populations observed in the Tenryu District).

H. longipes f. *viridipes* Maekawa.
J. of the Faculty of Science, Imperial University of Tokyo, Section 3 Botany, 5:388. 1940.
Type: Coll. T. Nakai and F. Maekawa, Tochigi Prefecture (Shimotsuke Province), Fubasami, Tochigi Prefecture. Hab. in Yamanashi and Tochigi prefectures, Kanto and Fuji-Hakone districts, south-central Honshu, Japan.

H. longipes var. *caduca* Fujita.
Acta Phytotaxonomica et Geobotanica, 27, 3/4:83, ic. 6. 1976.
Type: In KYO, 6531; coll. M. Hotta, 16 August 1961, between Omaekoharu and Omae, Shiiba-mura, Higashiuzuki-gun in Miyazaki Prefecture. Hab. in Miyazaki, Fukuoka, Kagoshima, and Kochi prefectures, eastern Kyushu and western Shikoku, Japan.
Synonyms:
H. leptophylla Maekawa, in Ishii, Engei-daijiten, 2:636. 1950.

H. longipes var. *latifolia* Maekawa.
J. of the Faculty of Science, Imperial University of Tokyo, Section 3 Botany, 5:388. 1940.
Type: In TI; based on the cultivated plant; coll. F. Maekawa, Yoshina, Mount Amagi, Shizuoka Prefecture, southern Chubu Region, south-central Honshu, Japan.

H. longipes var. *vulgata* (Maekawa) W. G. Schmid et G. S. Daniels var. nov.
J. of the Faculty of Science, Imperial University of Tokyo, Section 3 Botany, 5:388, ic. 60–64. 1940 (excluding the synonyms *Funkia longipes* Franchet et Savatier and *Hosta longipes* [Franchet et Savatier] Bailey. This taxon is a phase which is morphologically different from the type in P and represents major common populations in Kanagawa, Shizuoka, and Aichi prefectures and southern Chubu and is here emend.; see Chapter 3.).
H. longipes var. *vulgata* (typus in TI) differt ab *H. longipes* var. *longipes* (typus in P). Petioli toto purpureo-punctati rigidi 14–15 cm longi 4–5 mm lati leviter sed late canaliculati. Lamina folii chartacea basi patentia, dilatata ovato-cordata vel elliptico-ovata subito cuspidata basi subcordata opaca planata 12–14 cm longa 8–9.5 cm lata, ad marginem 4–5 undulata utrinque 7–8 nervata, nervis glabris, costa basi utrinque purpureo-punctata. Scapi patentes toto purpureo-punctata teretes 20–30 cm longi. Alabastra ovoidea cum lobis interioribus obtuse costato-elevatis et interioribus valde planato-convexis. Flores pallidissimo caeruleo-purpurei, secundi, perianthum sexpartitum. Inflorescentia 10–15 cm longa 20–40-flora. Pedicelli erecto-patentes 10–20 mm longi. Bracteae membranaceae albo-purpurascentes. Corollae tubus angustus 15–17 mm longus 2.5 mm latus teres dilutissime caeruleo-purpurascentibus perfectis numquam impressis tubus dilatatus 20 mm longus 25 mm latus, lobi rectim recurvato-patentes. Stamina libera exserta declinata 4–5 cm longa filamenta aequilonga. Antheris 2–3 mm longis, purpurascentibus (also see Chapter 3).
Type: In TI; coll. Maekawa, Tokura, Kanagawa Prefecture. Hab. in open mountain valleys at rocky river banks and waterfalls along Tenryu and Keta rivers, Mount Tamayama and Osuzu, Shizuoka, and Aichi prefectures, and in southern Chubu region, south-central Honshu, Japan.
Synonyms:
H. longipes var. *longipes* Fujita, Acta Phytotaxonomica et Geobotanica, 27, 3/4:81. 1976; and Kitamura et al., Col. Ill. Herb. Plant. Jap., p. 136. 1964 (p.p.; when applied with respect to Maekawa's type, a nom. illegitimum).

H. aequinoctiiantha Koidzumi ex Araki.
Acta Phytotaxonomica et Geobotanica, 11, 321. 1942.
Type: In KYO, 329; coll. S. Kitamura, 19 September 1941, Yoromura, Gifu Prefecture. Hab. in rocky areas, shady mountain valleys, Gifu Shiga, Nara, Kyoto, Hyogo prefectures, west-central Chubu and Kansai regions, central and west-central Honshu, Japan.
Synonyms:
H. longipes var. *aequinoctiiantha* Kitamura et al. (nom. nudum), Col. Ill. Herb. Plant. Jap., p. 136. 1964; and Kitamura, Acta Phytotaxonomica Geobotanica, 22:68. 1966; and Fujita, Acta Phytotaxonomica et Geobotanica, 27, 3/4:81. 1976 s.l. n.a.

H. hypoleuca Murata.
Acta Phytotaxonomica et Geobotanica, 19:67. 1962.
Type: In KYO, 6645; coll. Murata, 21 September 1953,

Kamebuchi-dani, Miwa-mura, Aichi Prefecture. Hab. in open mountain valleys near streams clinging to ledges on near-vertical rock faces, Mount Chiiwa, with limited, allopatric populations in Aichi Prefecture and near Tenryu River, Shizuoka Prefecture, southern Chubu region, central Honshu, Japan.

H. okamotoi Koidzumi ex Araki.
Acta Phytotaxonomica et Geobotanica, 11, 321. 1942.
Type: In KYO, 15699, 12 September 1947; coll. S. Okamoto, Kitakuwada-gun, Chii-mura, Kyoto and Hyogo prefectures. Hab. in wooded mountain valleys lithophytically on wet rocks and epiphytically on tree trunks. Hab. in Kyoto and Hyogo prefectures, western Kansai, west-central Honshu, Japan.

H. pulchella Fujita.
Acta Phytotaxonomica et Geobotanica, 27, 3/4:89, ic. 8. 1976.
Type: In KYO, 1001, 18 July 1970; coll. N. Fujita and H. Takahashi, Ogata-cho between Tengu and Eboshi, Mount Sobo-san, Oita Prefecture (isotype). Hab. in open mountain valleys on and between rocks at 1600 m.s.m. and in Oita and Miyazaki prefectures, western Kyushu, Japan.

H. pycnophylla Maekawa.
J. of Japanese Botany, 51, 3:80. 1976.
Type: In TI, 35673; coll. K. Oka, Mount Genmei, ins. Oshima, near Yanai, Yamaguchi Prefecture. Hab. in Chugoku region, western Honshu, Japan.
Synonyms:
H. pycnophylla Maekawa (nom. nudum), Garden Life, 8:31–33. 1972.

H. rupifraga Nakai.
Botanical Magazine, Tokyo, 44:27, ic. f. 3. 1930; and Maekawa, Botanical Magazine, Tokyo, 52:42, ic. f. 2. 1938.
Type: In TI; coll. T. Nakai, ins. Hachijojima, Mount Nishi (Hachijo-fuji), a limited allopatric population in grassy and open volcanic rock and cinders, at the northwest-facing rim, 845 m.s.m., Hachijojima, Izu-Shichito, Tokyo Prefecture (administratively), 350 km (220 miles) off southern Honshu, Japan.
Synonyms:
H. longipes var. latifolia Fujita, Acta Phytotaxonomica et Geobotanica, 27, 3/4:81. 1976 s.l.

H. takiensis Araki.
Acta Phytotaxonomica et Geobotanica, 11, 322. 1942.
Type: In KYO, 15099, 11 September 1941; coll. Y. Araki, Taki-gun, Murakumo-mura, Kyoto and Hyogo prefectures. Hab. in moist woodland, shade, in Kyoto and Hyogo prefectures, western Kansai, west-central Honshu, Japan.

H. 'Tardiflora' (a cultivar form).
Hardy Bulbs, p. 303, pl. 20. 1938.
Synonyms:
H. tardiflora (Irving) Stearn apud Grey, Hardy Bulbs, p. 303, pl. 20. 1938 (here reduced to cultivar form).
Funkia lancifolia var. tardiflora (nom. nudum), ex Kew Handlist of Herbaceous Plants, ed. 2:489. 1902; and Wright, Curtis's Botanical Magazine, 142, tab. 8645. 1916.
Funkia tardiflora Leichtlin ex Irving, The Garden, 64:297. 1903.
Niobe japonica var. tardiflora Nash, Torreya, 11:5. 1911.
Hosta lancifolia var. tardiflora Bailey, Standard Encyclopedia of Horticulture, p. 1605. 1915; Stearn, Gardener's Chronicle, 3 ser., 90:89. 1931; Wehrhahn, Gartenschön-

heit, 15:204. 1934 (with a German description); Bergmann, Vaste Planten and Rotsheesters, ed. 2:412. 1939; Nobis, Die Freiland-Schmuckstauden, ed. 4:113. 1951 (with a German description).
H. japonica var. tardiflora (Leichtlin ex Irving) Bailey, Gentes Herbarum, 1:137. 1923; Gentes Herbarum, 2, 3:132–133.

H. 'Tortifrons' (a cultivar form).
Botanical Magazine, Tokyo, 52:42. 1938 (nom. nudum, Japanese description); and J. of the Faculty of Science, Imperial University of Tokyo, Section 3 Botany, 5:389, 390 ic. 1, p. 323. 1940.
Synonyms:
H. tortifrons Maekawa, J. of the Faculty of Science, Imperial University of Tokyo, Section 3 Botany, 5:389. 1940 (here reduced to cultivar form).

Subgenus Giboshi Maekawa.
Section Tardanthae (Maekawa) Maekawa 1938.
Botanical Magazine, Tokyo, 52:42, 44. 1938.
Synonyms:
Hosta section Bryocles subsection Tardanthae Maekawa, J. of Japanese Botany, 13:898. 1937.
Hosta subgenus Bryocles section Tardanthae Maekawa, J. of the Faculty of Science, Imperial University Tokyo, Section 3 Botany, 5:394. 1940.

H. tardiva Nakai (type).
Botanical Magazine, Tokyo, 44:513. 1930; and J. of the Faculty of Science, Imperial University of Tokyo, Section 3 Botany, 5:394, 395 ic. 71, 72, 73. 1940.
Type: In TI; coll. Z. Nikai, Chiba Prefecture. Hab. in Chiba and Mie prefectures, south Kanto and Kansai regions, eastern and western central Honshu, Japan.

H. cathayana Nakai ex Maekawa.
Botanical Magazine, Tokyo, 52:42. 1938 (nom. nudum, Japanese description); and J. of the Faculty of Science, Imperial University of Tokyo, Section 3 Botany, 5:394, 397, ic. 74. 1940.
Type: Based on the cultivated plant; coll. H. Yamamoto, Mukomachi, Kyoto Prefecture. Hab. in Liaoning, Hebei, Anhui, Jiangsu, and Zhejiang provinces, China; Nagasaki, Hiroshima, and Kyoto prefectures, south-central Honshu, Japan (probably migrated populations).

H. gracillima Maekawa in Nakai.
Iconographia Plantarum Asiae-Orientalis, 1:72. 1936 (with respect only to the late-blooming populations described by Maekawa on Shikoku and excluding early blooming variants included by Fujita).
Type: In TI; coll. M. Okamoto, Tosa Prefecture, Shikoku, Japan.
Synonyms:
H. longipes var. gracillima Fujita, Acta Phytotaxonomica et Geobotanica, 27, 3/4:82. 1976 s.l.

H. jonesii M. G. Chung 1989.
Annals of the Missouri Botanical Garden, 76, 3:920–922. 1989.
Type: In GA, 1613, 28 August 1988; coll. M. G. Chung and M. S. Chung; on Mount Kumsan, ascent from River Yangha, Kyongsangnam-do, Namhae-gun, Sanju-Myon, Namhae Island (Namhae-do); common; Hb. GA, 957, Chollanam-do, Yoch'on Gun, Dolsan Island (Tolsan-do) (paratype). Hab. among rocky and humus soil on south-facing slopes at 250 s.m.s., shady pine-oak forests near the ocean. Hab. island along the southern coast of Korea.

H. takahashii Araki.

Acta Phytotaxonomica et Geobotanica, 11, 327. 1942.

Type: In KYO, 14833, 9 September 1938; coll. S. Takahashi, Mount Ibukiyama, Shiga Prefecture, central Honshu, Japan.

H. tibae Maekawa (as *H. tibai*, l.c. corr. ICBN).

J. of Japanese Botany, 59, 5:154–157, ic. fig. 1, p. 155. 1984.

Type: In TI, September 1943; coll. Hara, Mount Insayama, Nagasaki Prefecture; in L, 8147/36 and 8147/37; coll. Siebold, 1827(?) (topotypes to show original collections). Hab. in open mountain valleys and clearings, Nagasaki, Nagasaki Prefecture, Kyushu, Japan.

Synonyms:

Funkia ovata var. *ramosa* Miquel, (in schedula), annotation on herbarium sheets in L, 8147/36 and 8147/37. 1867.

H. tibai Maekawa ex Toyama (nom. nudum), Flora Nagasaki, p. 5. 1940; and Flora Nagasaki, rev. ed., pp. 46 and 264. 1980; Maekawa (nom. nudum, with Japanese diagnosis), in Ishii, Engei-daijiten, 2:633–638; Okuyama (nom. nudum), Col. Ill. Wild Plant. Japan. 7:118, tab. 587, 4. 1963.

H. chibai Kaneko (nom. nudum), Botanical Magazine, Tokyo, 79:133. 1966; and J. of Japanese Botany, 43, 7:10. 1968.

H. tibae, Index Kewensis. suppl. 18. 1987.

H. tsushimensis Fujita.

Acta Phytotaxonomica et Geobotanica, 27, 3/4:91, ic. 9. 1976.

Type: In KYO, 3037; coll. H. Koyama, Mount Ariake, Nagasaki Prefecture, Kyushu, Japan.

Synonyms:

H. minor Maekawa (not in the sense of Nakai), J. of the Faculty of Science, Imperial University, Imperial University Tokyo, Section 3 Botany, 5:418. 1940.

H. 'Lancifolia' (a cultivar form).

Die Natürlichen Pflanzenfamilien, 2 3:40, ic. 2, 3, 4, 6; pls. 17, 18. 1888.

Synonyms:

H. lancifolia Engler in Engler et Prantl, Die Natürlichen Pflanzenfamilien, 2, 35:40, ic. 2, 3, 4, 6; pls. 17, 18. 1888 (here reduced to cultivar form).

Aletris japonica Thunberg, Nova Acta, 3:208 1780 (p.p.: with respect to the description and excluding the plant called *Joksan vulgo giboosi* Kaempfer); Thunberg ex Houttuyn, Natuurlyke Historie, 2/12:413, tab. 34:2 1781.

Hemerocallis japonica Thunberg, Flora Iaponica, p. 142 1784 (with respect to the description of the lectotype Thunberg 1780 in UPS).

Hemerocallis lancifolia Thunberg, Transactions of the Linnean Society of London, 2:335 1794 (to provide a new name for *Hosta japonica* Thunberg 1784 which is a nom. illegitimum).

Funkia lancifolia (Thunberg) Sprengel, Caroli Linnaei Systema Vegetabilium, ed. 16, 2:41. 1825 (nom. illegitimum); Siebold (nom. nudum), Jaarb. Kon. Ned. Mij Aanomoed. Tuinbouw, p. 29. 1844.

Funkia ovata var. *lancifolia* Siebold ex Miquel, Verslag Mededelingen Akademie Wetenschappen Amsterdam, 2, 3:300. 1869.

Funkia japonica α *typica* Regel, Gartenflora, 25:163. 1876.

Saussurea japonica (Thunberg) Kuntze, Revisio Generum Plantarum, 2:714. 1891.

Hostia japonica f. *typica* Voss in Voss et Siebert, Vilmorin's Blumengärtnerei, ed. 3, 1:1076. 1896.

Hosta cærulea f. *lancifolia* Matsumura, Index plantarum japonicarum, 2:199. 1905.

Funkia japonica (Thunberg) Druce, Second Supp. to Bot. Soc.

and Exch. Club Rep. for 1916, p. 623. 1917 (with respect to the type).

Niobe japonica (Thunberg) Nash, Torreya, 11:5. 1911 (p.p.: with respect to var. *tardiflora* in a broad sense, but not *Hosta tardiflora* Stearn).

H. japonica Koidzumi, Botanical Magazine, Tokyo, 39:307. 1925; Bailey, Gentes Herbarum, 2, 3:137. 1930.

H. japonica var. *fortis* Bailey, Gentes Herbarum, 2, 7:434–437. 1932 (with respect to ic. 186 and 187 not showing the 1930 plant which is *H. undulata* var. *erromena*).

H. viridis Foerster (nom. nudum), Neuer Glanz des Gartenjahres, p. 127. 1952.

H. cærulea viridis Foerster (nom. nudum), Der Steingarten der Sieben Jahreszeiten, p. 346. 1956; Einzug der Grässer und Farne in die Gärten, p. 191, 196, 218. 1957.

H. angustifolia Foerster (nom. nudum), Pflanze und Garten, p. 44–45. 1965.

H. sieboldii var. *sieboldii* f. *lancifolia* (Miquel) Hara, J. of Japanese Botany, 59, 6:179. 1984.

Subgenus *Giboshi* Maekawa.

Section *Nipponosta* (Maekawa) W. G. Schmid comb. nov.

Synonyms:

Hosta section *Bryocles* subsection *Nipponosta* Maekawa, J. of Japanese Botany, 13:894. 1937.

Hosta subgenus *Giboshi* section *Bryocles* subsection *Nipponosta* Maekawa, Botanical Magazine, Tokyo, 52:41, 44. 1938 (basionym).

Hosta subgenus *Bryocles* section *Nipponosta* subsection *Nipponosta-vera* Maekawa, J. of the Faculty of Science, Imperial University Tokyo, Section 3 Botany, 5:398. 1940.

Hosta subgenus *Bryocles* section *Nipponosta* subsection *Brachypodae* Maekawa, J. of the Faculty of Science, Imperial University Tokyo, Section 3 Botany, 5:407. 1940.

H. sieboldii (Paxton) Ingram (type).

Baileya, 15, 1:29. 1967; and Hara, J. of Japanese Botany, 59, 6:179. 1984 (excl. all the synonyms for the lectotype of *Aletris japonica* in UPS = *H. 'Lancifolia'*).

Synonyms:

Hemerocallis sieboldii Paxton, Paxton's Magazine of Botany, 5:25, 139, 211. March 1838 (basionym).

Funckia albo-marginata Hooker, Curtis's Botanical Magazine, 65, tab. 3567. May 1838 (ic. S. Curtis, Glazenwood, Essex, May 1838, W. Fitch, del., Swan Sc.).

Funkia spatulata Siebold *foliis albomarginatis* Siebold (nom. nudum), Jaarb. Kon. Ned. Mij Aanomoed. Tuinbouw, p. 29. 1844.

Funkia ovata var. *albomarginata* Miquel, Annales Musei Botanici Lugdano-Batavi, 3:153. 1867; and var. β *albomarginata* Miquel, Verslag Mededelingen Akademie Wetenschappen Amsterdam, 2, 3:299. 1869 (with respect only to the basionym by Hooker and excluding the plant described).

Funkia ovata f. *spathulata* lusus α Miquel, Verslag Mededelingen Akademie Wetenschappen Amsterdam, 2, 3:300. 1869.

Funkia lancifolia f. *albomarginata* Baker, J. of the Linnean Society of London, 11:368. 1870.

Funkia lancifolia f. *albomarginata* Regel, Gartenflora, 25:163. 1876.

Hostia japonica f. *albomarginata* Voss in Voss et Siebert, Vilmorin's Blumengärtnerei, ed. 3, 1:1076. 1896.

Hosta cærulea f. *albomarginata* Matsumura, Index Plantarum Japonicarum, 2:199. 1905.

Niobe japonica var. *albomarginata* Nash, Torreya, 11:5. 1911.

Hosta japonica var. *albimarginata* Ascherson et Gräbner,

Synopsis der Mitteleuropäischen Flora, 3:55. 1905; var.
albomarginata Bailey, Gentes Herbarum, 2, 3:131. 1930;
Foerster (nom. nudum), Einzug der Grässer und Farne
in die Gärten, p. 196. 1957.

H. lancifolia var. *albomarginata* Bailey, Standard Encyclopedia of
Horticulture, p. 1605. 1915; Grey, Hardy Bulbs, p. 296.
1938; Bailey, Manual of Cultivated Plants, p. 206. 1951.

H. lancifolia var. *thunbergiana* f. *albomarginata* Maekawa, J. of the
Faculty of Science, Imperial University Tokyo, Section 3
Botany, 5:402, 403, ic. 82. 1940; and New Encyclopedia
of Horticulture, p. 1106. 1969.

H. lancifolia var. *thunbergiana* f. *sieboldii* Maekawa, in Ishii,
Engei-daijiten, 2:638. 1950.

H. albomarginata Ohwi, Acta Phytotaxonomica et Geobotanica,
11:265. 1942; Hylander, Acta Horti Bergiani, 16, 11:401.
1954; Kitamura et al., Col. Ill. Herb. Plant. Jap., p. 135.
1964; Ohwi, The Flora of Japan, 11:290. 1965; Fujita,
Acta Phytotaxonomica et Geobotanica, 27, 3/4:89. 1976
(excluding all the synonyms); Grenfell, The Plantsman,
3:40. 1981 (for the name *H. sieboldii* in synonymy only).

H. albomarginata f. *albomarginata* Hensen, Mededelingen van de
Directeur van de Tuinbouw, 26:730. 1963 ('Albo-
marginata'); Hansen-Müssel, Jahresbericht, Staatliche
Lehr- und Forschungsanstalt Gartenbau, p. 8. 1964
('Albomarginata'); Hansen-Sieber-Müssel, Jahres-
bericht für Stauden, p. 10. 1974 ('Albomarginata');
Hensen, The Plantsman, 7:25. 1985.

H. sieboldii Hara, J. of Japanese Botany, 59, 6:179. 1984 (excl. all
the synonyms for the lectotype of *Aletris japonica* in UPS
= *H.* 'Lancifolia').

H. sieboldii var. *sieboldii* f. *sieboldii* Hara, J. of Japanese Botany,
59, 6:179. 1984.

H. albomarginata albomarginata (hort.) Watanabe, The Observation and Cultivation of Hosta, p. 31. 1985.

H. sieboldii f. **angustifolia** (Regel) W. G. Schmid f. nov.
Differt ab *H. sieboldii* forma typica formae foliis pure viridis et
anguste elongatis. Scapus erectus 65–80 cm altus (cfr. *H.
longissima*: Scapus similis sed 35–45 cm altus). Antheris
lutescentibus (cfr. *H. longissima*: Antheris purpurascentibus).
Type: In MAK, 643/137725, 10 September 1916. Hab.
common in Kanto, Chubu, Kansai, and Chugoku
regions, Honshu; Shikoku; Kyushu, Japan.
Synonyms:
Funkia lancifolia ε *angustifolia* Regel, Gartenflora, 25:163. 1876
p.p. (basionym); Gaerdt, Wredow's Gartenfreund, ed.
17:448. 1886 p.p.
Hosta japonica var. *angustifolia* Ascherson et Gräbner, Synopsis
der Mitteleuropäischen Flora, 3:55. 1905 p.p.
H. coerulea f. *lancifolia* Matsumura, (in schedula), annotation on
type in MAK, 643/137725.

H. sieboldii f. **campanulata** (Araki) W. G. Schmid comb.
nov.
Type: In KYO, 14562–b, 14 August 1937; coll. Y. Araki,
Kumobe-mura; and in KYO, 14562–a, 5 September
1937; coll. Y. Araki, Kumobe-mura (holotype for var.
parviflora to show distribution). Hab. in Kyoto and
Hyogo Prefectures, central Honshu, Japan.
Synonyms:
H. campanulata Araki, Acta Phytotaxonomica et Geobotanica,
11, 325. 1942 (basionym).
H. campanulata var. *parviflora* Araki, Acta Phytotaxonomica et
Geobotanica, 11, 326. 1942.
H. albomarginata Fujita, Acta Phytotaxonomica et Geobotanica,
27, 3/4:84–85. 1976 s.l.

H. sieboldii f. **okamii** (Maekawa) Hara.
J. of Japanese Botany, 59, 6:179. 1984.
Type: In TI; coll. Y. Okami, 21 September 1936; cult. in Tokyo,
F. Maekawa. Hab. in Mie, Kyoto, and Hyogo prefec-
tures, Kansai region, west central Honshu, Kochi Prefec-
ture, Shikoku.
Synonyms:
H. lancifolia var. *thunbergiana* f. *okamii* (Maekawa) Maekawa, in
Ishii, Engei-daijiten, 2:639. 1950.
H. lancifolia var. *thunbergiana* f. *murasame* Maekawa, New
Encyclopedia of Horticulture, p. 1106. 1969.
H. okamii Maekawa (nom. nudum, with Japanese description),
Botanical Magazine, Tokyo, 52:41. 1938; J. of the Faculty
of Science, Imperial University Tokyo, Section 3 Botany,
5:398, 399. 1940 (basionym); and Ohwi, The Flora of
Japan, 11:289. 1965.

H. sieboldii f. **spathulata** (Miquel) W. G. Schmid comb.
nov.
Differt ab *H. sieboldii* forma typica: Lamina folii pure viridis.
Type: In BH, BH63-318/9327 (lectotype). Hab. widespread in
Hokkaido, Tohoku, Kanto, Chubu, Kansai, Chugoku,
Shikoku, and Kyushu; common in many areas of Japan.
Synonyms:
Funkia spatulata Siebold (nom. nudum), Catalogue et Prix
Courant, p. 12. 1860.
Funkia japonica foliis *viridimarginatis* Rodigas, Bulletin Congr.
Internat. Hort., p. 140–141. 1864.
Funkia ovata (var.) f. *spathulata* Miquel, Verslag Mededelingen
Akademie Wetenschappen Amsterdam, 2, 3:299–300.
1869 (basionym).
H. lancifolia f. *carpellata* Maekawa, J. of Japanese Botany, 20:27,
ic. 3, 4, 5, 6. 1944.
Hosta lancifolia var. *thunbergiana* Maekawa, J. of the Faculty of
Science, Imperial University Tokyo, Section 3 Botany,
5:402. 1940; and Maekawa, New Encyclopedia of Horti-
culture, p. 1006. 1969 (with respect to the description
only and excluding all the synonyms applicable to the
cultigen *H.* 'Lancifolia').
H. lancifolia var. *thunbergiana* f. *monstr. polycarpellata* Maekawa, J.
of Japanese Botany, 20:28–29, ic. 3, 4, 5, 6. 1944.
H. lancifolia var. *thunbergiana* f. *polycarpellata* Maekawa, J. of
Japanese Botany, 20:28–29, ic. 3, 4, 5, 6. 1944.
H. albomarginata f. *viridis* Hylander, Acta Horti Bergiani, 16,
11:407. 1954.
H. albomarginata f. *spathulata* Hensen, Mededelingen van de
Landbouwhogeschool te Wageningen, 63, 6:17. 1963.
H. albomarginata f. *spathulata* Hansen-Müssel, Jahresbericht,
Staatliche Lehr- und Forschungsanstalt für Gartenbau,
p. 8. 1964.
H. albomarginata f. *spathulata* (and 'Spathulata') Hansen-Sieber-
Müssel, Jahresbericht, Institut für Stauden, p. 10. 1974
('Spathulata'); Hensen, The Plantsman, 7:25. 1985
(forma *spathulata*).
H. sieboldii f. *polycarpellata* (Maekawa) Hara, J. of Japanese
Botany, 59, 6:180. 1984.

H. sieboldii 'Alba' (a cultivar form).
J. of Japanese Botany, 59, 6:180. 1984.
Type: In TNS, 27652; coll. Y. Ikegami, Shirasaka, Fukushima,
Honshu. Hab. occasionally found as a nonperpetuating
mutation among natural populations of *H. sieboldii* and
H. sieboldii f. *spathulata*.
Synonyms:
H. sieboldii var. *sieboldii* f. *alba* (Irving) Hara, J. of Japanese
Botany, 59, 6:180. 1984 (here reduced to cultivar form).

Funkia japonica (hort.) *flore albo* Siebold (nom. nudum), Catalogue et Prix-courant, p. 43. 1868–1869.

Funkia ovata f. *spathulata* lusus β Miquel, Verslag Mededelingen Akademie Wetenschappen Amsterdam, 2, 3:300. 1869.

Funkia lancifolia var. *alba* Robinson, The English Flower Garden, ed. 3, p. 423. 1893 (basionym).

Funkia lancifolia (var.) *alba* Irving, The Garden, 64:297. 1903.

Hosta cærulea var. *minor albiflora* Nobis, Die Freiland-Schmuckstauden, 4:112. 1951.

H. albomarginata var. *alba* (Irving) Hylander, Acta Horti Bergiani, 16, 11:401. 1954.

Hosta minor alba grandiflora Foerster (nom. nudum), Der Steingarten der Sieben Jahreszeiten, p. 346. 1956; and Einzug der Grässer und Farne in die Gärten, p. 191, 196, 219. 1957.

H. lancifolia var. *thunbergiana* f. *albiflora* Maekawa, in Ishii, Engei-daijiten, 2:639. 1950.

H. albomarginata f. *alba* (Robinson) Hylander apud Hensen, Mededelingen van de Directeur van de Tuinbouw, 26:730. 1963; Hensen, The Plantsman, 7:28. 1985.

H. lancifolia var. *thunbergiana* f. *albiflora* Ikegami, J. of Japanese Botany, 32:128. 1967.

H. albomarginata alba Grenfell, The Plantsman, 3:25. 1981.

H. minor alba or *H. minor* 'Alba' hort. (not *H. minor* f. *alba* [Nakai] Maekawa).

H. sieboldii 'Alba' hort.

H. sieboldii 'Bunchoko' (a cultivar form).

New Encyclopedia of Horticulture, p. 1106. 1969.

Synonyms:

H. lancifolia var. **thunbergiana** f. **bunchoko** Maekawa, New Encyclopedia of Horticulture, p. 1106. 1969 (here transferred to *H. sieboldii* and reduced to cultivar form).

H. sieboldii 'Bunchoko' hort.

H. sieboldii 'Kabitan' (a cultivar form).

J. of Japanese Botany, 59, 6:179. 1984.

Type: In TI; F. Maekawa, 26 August 1936; cult. in Hort. Bot. KYO, 15 (lectotype). Hab. occasionally found as a non-perpetuating mutation among natural populations of *H. sieboldii* and *H. sieboldii* f. *spathulata*.

Synonyms:

H. sieboldii var. **sieboldii** f. **kabitan** (Maekawa) Hara, J. of Japanese Botany, 59, 6:180. 1984 (here reduced to cultivar form).

H. lancifolia var. *thunbergiana* f. *kabitan* Maekawa, J. of the Faculty of Science, Imperial University Tokyo, Section 3 Botany, 5:402, ic. 78, 79. 1940.

H. albomarginata f. *kabitan* Ohwi, Acta Phytotaxonomica et Geobotanica, 11:265. 1942.

Funkia spathulata albomarginata var. *lutescens* Siebold (nom. nudum), Prix-courant, p. 13–14. 1877 (with respect only to the description).

Hosta japonica var. *angustifolia* (Ascherson et Gräbner) f. *variegata* Oonuma in Iwasaki, Honzo-Dzufu, ed. 20, fol. 18, ic. 4. 1916–1918 (with respect only to the description).

H. lancifolia f. *kabitan* Grenfell, The Plantsman, 3:33–34. 1981; Jellito-Schacht-Fessler (Müssel), Die Freiland-Schmuckstauden, p. 300. 1986.

H. sieboldii 'Kabitan' hort. (AHS).

H. sieboldii 'Kifukurin' (a cultivar form).

New Encyclopedia of Horticulture, p. 1106. 1969.

Synonyms:

H. lancifolia var. **thunbergiana** f. **kifukurin** Maekawa, New Encyclopedia of Horticulture, p. 1106. 1969 (here transferred to *H. sieboldii* and reduced to cultivar form).

H. sieboldii 'Kifukurin' hort.

H. sieboldii 'Mediopicta' (a cultivar form).

J. of Japanese Botany, 59, 6:179. 1984.

Type: In TI; F. Maekawa, 5 September 1936; cult. in Amanuma, Tokyo (lectotype). Hab. occasionally found as a non-perpetuating mutation among natural populations of *H. sieboldii* and *H. sieboldii* f. *spathulata*.

Synonyms:

H. sieboldii var. **sieboldii** f. **mediopicta** (Maekawa) Hara, J. of Japanese Botany, 59, 6:180. 1984 (here reduced to cultivar form).

H. lancifolia var. *thunbergiana* f. *mediopicta* Maekawa, J. of the Faculty of Science, Imperial University Tokyo, Section 3 Botany, 5:402, ic. 80, 81. 1940.

H. albomarginata f. *mediopicta* Ohwi, Acta Phytotaxonomica et Geobotanica, 11:265. 1942.

H. sieboldii 'Mediopicta' hort.

H. sieboldii 'Subcrocea' (a cultivar form).

J. of Japanese Botany, 59, 6:180. 1984.

Synonyms:

H. sieboldii var. **sieboldii** f. **subchrocea** (Maekawa) Hara, J. of Japanese Botany, 59, 6:180. 1984 (here reduced to cultivar form with the cultivar name changed to 'Subcrocea' to correct an orthographic error).

H. lancifolia var. *thunbergiana* f. *subchrocea* Maekawa, J. of the Faculty of Science, Imperial University Tokyo, Section 3 Botany, 5:402. 1940.

H. albomarginata f. *subchrocea* Ohwi, Acta Phytotaxonomica et Geobotanica, 11:265. 1942.

H. albomarginata (forma *variegata*) Ohwi, The Flora of Japan, 11:290. 1965 (in annotation).

H. sieboldii 'Subcrocea' hort. (AHS).

H. atropurpurea Nakai.

Botanical Magazine, Tokyo, 44:26, 58. 1930.

Type: In TI; coll. T. Nakai, Mount Daisetzu, Ishikari, Sorachi, Kamikawa provinces. Hab. in central and southern Hokkaido (Ezo), Japan.

Synonyms:

H. rectifolia f. *atropurpurea* (Nakai) Nakai ex Maekawa, in Ishii, Engei-daijiten, 2:639. 1950.

H. rectifolia subsp. *atropurpurea* (Nakai) Inagaki et Toyokuni, in Report Taisetsu Inst. Sci. 2:17. 1963.

H. rectifolia var. *atropurpurea* (Nakai) Tatewaki et S. Kawano [in Tatewaki et Samejima, Alp. Pl. Cent. Mt. Dist. Hokkaido, 21. 1956.] ex Ito, J. Geobot. Hokuriko, 17:92. 1969.

H. albomarginata Fujita, Acta Phytotaxonomica et Geobotanica, 27, 3/4:84–85. 1976 s.l.

H. sieboldii var. *rectifolia* f. *atropurpurea* (Nakai) Hara, J. of Japanese Botany, 59, 6:181. 1984.

H. calliantha Araki.

Acta Phytotaxonomica et Geobotanica, 11, 324. 1942.

Type: In KYO, 15062, 19 August 1939; coll. Y. Araki, Higashibetsuin-mura. Hab. in Kyoto and Hyogo prefectures, central Honshu, Japan.

Synonyms:

H. albomarginata Fujita, Acta Phytotaxonomica et Geobotanica, 27, 3/4:84–85. 1976 s.l. n.a.

H. clavata Maekawa.

Botanical Magazine, Tokyo, 52:41. 1938 (nom. nudum, with Japanese description); J. of Japanese Botany, 14:45. 1938; J. of the Faculty of Science, Imperial University Tokyo, Section 3 Botany, 5:407, 408, ic. 87. 1940.

Type: In TI; coll. Y. Satake; Urawa, Saitama Prefecture (Musashi Province). Neotype for syn. *H. japonica* var. *intermedia* Makino in TI; coll. F. Maekawa, August 1935,

Mount Tsukuba, cult. in Tokyo. Hab. in Kanto region, central Honshu, Japan.
Synonyms:
H. japonica var. *intermedia* Makino in Iinuma, Somoku Dzusetsu, 2:464, 465. 1910.
H. intermedia (Makino) Maekawa (nom. nudum, with Japanese description), Botanical Magazine, Tokyo, 52:41, ic. f. 1. 1938.
H. albomarginata Fujita, Acta Phytotaxonomica et Geobotanica, 27, 3/4:84–85. 1976 s.l. n.a.
H. sieboldii var. *intermedia* (Makino) Hara, J. of Japanese Botany, 59, 6:180. 1984.

H. ibukiensis Araki.
Acta Phytotaxonomica et Geobotanica, 11, 325. 1942.
Type: In KYO, 14823, 26 July 1938; coll. Y. Araki, Mount Ibukiyama, Shiga Prefecture. Hab. in central Honshu, Japan.
Synonyms:
H. albomarginata Fujita, Acta Phytotaxonomica et Geobotanica, 27, 3/4:84–85. 1976 s.l. n.a.

H. rohdeifolia f. *viridis* Maekawa.
J. of the Faculty of Science, Imperial University Tokyo, Section 3 Botany, 5:407. 1940.
Type: In KYO, 643/39519; coll. M. Tagawa, Tagawa No. 652, 18 August 1931, Koosodani, in Mount Hiei, Kyoto Prefecture (lectotype). Hab. in west-central Honshu, Japan.
Synonyms:
H. albomarginata Fujita, Acta Phytotaxonomica et Geobotanica, 27, 3/4:84–85. 1976 s.l. n.a.

H. rohdeifolia 'Rohdeifolia' (a cultivar form).
J. of Japanese Botany, 13:897 ic. f. 3. 1937 (with respect only to the yellow-margined form. The species epithet cited by Maekawa as *rhodeifolia* is an orthographic error and is here corrected to *rohdeifolia* to reflect the author's original meaning based on the name of Michael Rohde for whom *Rohdea japonica* was named and on which the formal Japanese name *Omoto Giboshi* is founded).
Synonyms:
H. rohdeifolia f. *rohdeifolia* Maekawa (here reduced to cultivar form) published as *H. rhodeifolia* Maekawa, J. of the Faculty of Science, Imperial University Tokyo, Section 3 Botany, 5:406, 407, ic. 85, 86. 1940.
H. albomarginata Fujita, Acta Phytotaxonomica et Geobotanica, 27, 3/4:84–85. 1976 s.l. n.a.

H. longissima Honda var. *longissima* mut. char. p.p. excl. syn. (emend. W. G. Schmid).
J. of Japanese Botany, 13:894. 1937; and J. of the Faculty of Science, Imperial University Tokyo, Section 3 Botany, 5:404. 1940 (emend.; with respect only to the description; excluding the synonyms *H. japonica* var. *longifolia* Honda and *H. lancifolia* var. *longifolia* Honda = *H. longissima* var. *longifolia*; and excluding the synonyms *Funkia lancifolia* ε *angustifolia* Regel and *Hosta japonica* var. *angustifolia* Ascherson et Gräbner = *H. sieboldii* f. *angustifolia*).
Type: In TI; coll. S. Akiyama, Mount Noroyama, Hiroshima Prefecture. Hab. in marshes and wet meadows, open in spring, shaded in summer by weeds and grasses; common; Chubu, Kansai, and Chugoku regions, central and western Honshu, Japan.
Synonyms:
Funkia lanceolata Siebold (nom. nudum), Jaarb. Kon. Ned. Mij Aanomoed. Tuinbouw, p. 29. 1844 (nom. nudum and including the synonym *Hemerocallis lanceolata*).

Funkia ovata var. *lancifolia* Miquel, Verslag Mededelingen Akademie Wetenschappen Amsterdam, 2, 3:300. 1869 (with respect only to the plant described and excluding the various synonyms).
Funkia (with respect to the Japanese formal names *Mizu Giboshi* and *Sazi Giboshi*) Iinuma, Somoku Dzusetsu, ed. 2, 1:6. 1874.
Hosta japonica var. *angustifolia* Ascherson et Gräbner (p.p.; with respect only to taxa with purple anthers), Synopsis der Mitteleuropäischen Flora, 3:55. 1905 p.p.; Makino in Iinuma, Somoku Dzusetsu, ed. 3, tab. 353, 2:466. 1910 p.p.
H. longissima var. *brevifolia* Maekawa, J. of Japanese Botany, 13:894. 1937; Ohwi, The Flora of Japan, 11:289. 1965; Fujita, Acta Phytotaxonomica et Geobotanica, 27, 3/4:89. 1976; Grenfell, The Plantsman, 3:34. 1981; Jellito-Schacht-Fessler (Müssel), Die Freiland-Schmuckstauden, p. 300. 1986.

H. longissima var. *longifolia* (Honda) W. G. Schmid var. nov.
Differt ab *H. longissima* forma typica laminis foliorum pro ratione perangustoribus, linearibus (cum ratio = 1:12–1:20), apicibus obtusis (cfr. *H. longissima* cum ratio = 1:8–1:10).
Type: In TI. Hab. in Okazaki and Nukata, Aichi Prefecture, Chubu, Kansai, and Chugoku regions, west-central and central Honshu, Japan.
Synonyms:
H. japonica var. *longifolia* Honda, Botanical Magazine, Tokyo, 44:410. 1930 (basionym).
H. lancifolia var. *longifolia* Honda, Botanical Magazine, Tokyo, 49:696. 1935.
H. lancifolia var. *angustifolia* Koidzumi, Acta Phytotaxonomica et Geobotanica, 5:38. 1936 (p.p., with respect only to the strap-leaf form described and excluding the synonyms).

H. rectifolia Nakai var. *rectifolia*.
Botanical Magazine, Tokyo, 44:26 and 58, pl. 21. 1930; and J. of the Faculty of Science, Imperial University Tokyo, Section 3 Botany, 5:410, 411, ic. 90–93. 1940.
Type: In TI; coll. T. Nakai, Mount Apoi, Ishikari Province. Hab. in northern Honshu; southern Hokkaido (Ezo): Oshima, Hiyama, Shiribeshi, Ishikari, Iburi, Hidaka, Tokachi, Kushiro and Nemuro provinces; southern Kurile Islands; Habomai Islands; all in northern Japan.
Synonyms:
Funkia longipes Franchet et Savatier sec. Irving, The Garden, 64:297. 1903 (with respect only to the misidentified specimen at Kew of *Hosta rectifolia* called incorrectly *H. longipes*).
Funkia ovata Czerniakowska, Flora USSR, 4:54. 1932 (emend. as *Hosta rectifolia* in Czerepanov, Corrections to Flora USSR, 332. 1979.
H. apoiensis Nakai ex Miyabe et Kudo, J. Fac. Agr. Hokkaido Univ., 26:315. 1932 (with respect only to the name in synonymy).
H. harunaensis Honda, J. of Japanese Botany, 11:572. 1930 (with respect to the populations observed in Gumma Prefecture only and conforming to the type in TI; coll. T. Sakai, near Shiwukawa, Mount Haruna).
H. albomarginata Fujita, Acta Phytotaxonomica et Geobotanica, 27, 3/4:84–85. 1976 s.l. n.a.
H. sieboldii var. *rectifolia* Hara, J. of Japanese Botany, 59, 6:180. 1984.

H. rectifolia var. *rectifolia* f. *pruinosa* Maekawa.
J. of the Faculty of Science, Imperial University Tokyo, Section 3 Botany, 5:413. 1940.
Type: In TI; coll. F. Maekawa, cult. 8, 2 August 1937, Mount Chishima, Higashi-kushiro, Kushiro Province (lectotype). Hab. in southwestern central Hokkaido (Ezo).
Synonyms:
H. sieboldii var. *rectifolia* f. *pruinosa* (Maekawa) Hara, J. of Japanese Botany, 59, 6:181. 1984.
H. rectifolia f. *pruinosa* Ito, J. Geobot. Hokuriko, 17:92. 1969.

H. rectifolia var. *australis* Maekawa ex W. G. Schmid var. nov.
In schedula, annotation on herbarium sheet in TI, 643 225/6560; Maekawa (basionym).
Differt ab *H. rectifolia* forma typica laminis foliorum late ovatis, apicibus obtusis.
Type: In TI, 643 225/6560; coll. M. Mizushima, 29 August 1954, Tone-gun, Mount Ozegahara (applies to the populations with widely ovate leaves observed in Gumma Prefecture, Oku Nikko).

H. rectifolia var. *sachalinensis* (Koidzumi) Maekawa.
J. of the Faculty of Science, Imperial University Tokyo, Section 3 Botany, 5:413. 1940.
Type: In KYO; coll. G. Koidzumi, 13 August 1930, Sakaehama, Sakhalin (lectotype). Hab. in Sakhalin.
Synonyms:
H. sachalinensis Koidzumi, Acta Phytotaxonomica et Geobotanica, 5:40. 1936.
H. rectifolia var. *sachalinensis* (Koidzumi).
H. albomarginata Fujita, Acta Phytotaxonomica et Geobotanica, 27, 3/4:84–85. 1976 s.l. n.a.

H. rectifolia 'Albiflora' (a cultivar form).
J. of the Faculty of Science, Imperial University Tokyo, Section 3 Botany, 5:412, 413, ic. 95. 1940
Synonyms:
H. rectifolia var. *chionea* f. *albiflora* (Tatewaki) Maekawa, J. of the Faculty of Science, Imperial University Tokyo, Section 3 Botany, 5:410–413, ic. 95. 1940 (here reduced to cultivar form).
H. atropurpurea f. *albiflora* Tatewaki, Transactions of the Sapporo Natural History Society, 13:111. 1934.
H. rectifolia var. *chionea* f. *albiflora* Tatewaki, Transactions of the Sapporo Natural History Society, 13:111. 1934 (basionym).
H. sieboldii f. *albiflora* (Tatewaki) Hara, J. of Japanese Botany, 59, 6:180. 1984.
H. sieboldii f. *leucantha* (Ito) Hara, J. of Japanese Botany, 59, 6:180. 1984.
H. rectifolia 'Albiflora' hort.

H. rectifolia 'Chionea' (a cultivar form).
J. of Japanese Botany, 14:45. 1938.
Type: In TI; cult. in hort. bot. KYO, F. Maekawa, 20 August 1936 (neotype).
Synonyms:
H. rectifolia var. *chionea* Maekawa, J. of Japanese Botany, 14:45. 1938 (here reduced to cultivar form); and J. of the Faculty of Science, Imperial University Tokyo, Section 3 Botany, 5:412, 413, ic. 94. 1940.
H. sieboldii f. *chionea* (Maekawa) Hara, J. of Japanese Botany, 59, 6:181. 1984.
H. rectifolia 'Chionea' hort.

H. alismifolia Maekawa.
J. of Japanese Botany, 59, 5:156–157, ic. fig. 2. 1984.
Type: In TI, 21 July 1937; coll. K. Inami, Mikuni-san, Tsurusato-mura, Gifu Prefecture. Hab. in sunny peat bogs and wet grasslands; open in spring, shaded by weeds and grasses in summer; Aichi and Gifu prefectures.
Synonyms:
H. alismifolia Maekawa apud Fujita, Acta Phytotaxonomica et Geobotanica, 27, 3/4:88. 1976; Maekawa in Inami (as *Baran Giboshi*) in Aichi-shokubutsu, 40, ic. 11. 1971 (with respect to the nom. Jap. only).

H. 'Decorata' (a cultivar form).
Gentes Herbarum, 2, 3:141, ic. 69d, 70e, 77. 1930.
Synonyms:
H. decorata f. *decorata* Bailey, Gentes Herbarum, 2, 3:141, ic. 69d, 70e, 77. 1930 (here reduced to cultivar form); and Maekawa, J. of the Faculty of Science, Imperial University Tokyo, Section 3 Botany, 5:408, 409, ic. 89. 1940.
Funkia 'Thomas Hogg' hort. (1875).
Funkia hybr. 'Thomas Hogg' hort.
Hosta 'Thomas Hogg' hort.
H. decorata f. (or var.) *marginata* Stearn, Gardener's Chronicle, 3 ser., 90:89. 1931.
H. decorata minor hort.
H. lancifolia var. *albomarginata* hort. (Hensen 1963; in Holland only).

H. 'Decorata Normalis' (a cultivar form).
Gardener's Chronicle, 3 ser., 90:89. 1931; and Maekawa, J. of the Faculty of Science, Imperial University Tokyo, Section 3 Botany, 5:408, 409, ic. 88. 1940.
Synonyms:
H. decorata f. *normalis* Stearn, Gardener's Chronicle, 3 ser., 90:110. 1931 (here reduced to cultivar form).
H. decorata 'Normalis' hort.

H. 'Opipara' (a cultivar form).
J. of Japanese Botany, 13:895. 1937.
Synonyms:
H. opipara Maekawa, J. of Japanese Botany, 13:895. 1937 (here reduced to cultivar form); and Maekawa, J. of the Faculty of Science, Imperial University Tokyo, Section 3 Botany, 5:412–414, ic. 96, 97. 1940.

H. 'Helonioides' (a cultivar form).
J. of Japanese Botany, 13:895, i.c. 3. 1937.
Synonyms:
H. helonioides Maekawa, J. of Japanese Botany, 13:896 i.c. 3. 1937 (here reduced to cultivar form); and Maekawa, J. of the Faculty of Science, Imperial University Tokyo, Section 3 Botany, 5:402, 405, ic. 83. 1940.

H. 'Helonioides Albopicta' (a cultivar form).
J. of Japanese Botany, 13:896, i.c. 2. 1937.
Synonyms:
H. helonioides f. *albopicta* Maekawa, J. of Japanese Botany, 13:896, i.c. 2. 1937 (here reduced to cultivar form); and Maekawa, J. of the Faculty of Science, Imperial University Tokyo, Section 3 Botany, 5:402, 405, ic. 84. 1940.

Subgenus *Giboshi* Maekawa.
[Section *Foliosae* Maekawa 1940].
Botanical Magazine, Tokyo, 52:42, 44. 1938.
All taxa in this section have been reduced to cultivar form.
Synonyms:
Hosta section *Foliosae* Maekawa, J. of Japanese Botany, 13:901. 1937.

Hosta subgenus *Bryocles* section *Foliosae* Maekawa, J. of the Faculty of Science, Imperial University Tokyo, Section 3 Botany, 5:420–424, ic. 105–110. 1940.

H. 'Undulata' (a cultivar form).
Gentes Herbarum, 1, 3:133, pl. 15. 1923.
Synonyms:
H. **undulata** var. **undulata** (Otto et Dietrich) Bailey, Gentes Herbarum, 1, 3:133, pl. 15. 1923; and 2:139 ic. f. 77 (here reduced to cultivar form).
Hemerocallis undulata Thunberg (nom. nudum), Mus. Bot. Upsal., App. 5:107 1797; and Siebold apud Miquel, Verslag Mededelingen Akademie Wetenschappen Amsterdam, 2, 3:300. 1869.
Funkia undulata Otto et Dietrich, Allgemeine Gartenzeitung, 1:119. 1833; (Otto et Dietrich) Kunth, Enumeratio Plantarum pl. 4, 552. 1843.
Funkia undulata foliis *variegatis* Siebold (nom. nudum), Jaarb. Kon. Ned. Mij Aanomoed. Tuinbouw, p. 29. 1844; and Extrait du catalogue raisonne et du prix-courant, p. 44.
Funkia argenteo-striata Siebold (nom. nudum), Catalogue prodrome, p. 6. 1861.
Funkia undulata argenteo-vittata Siebold (nom. nudum), Catalogue et Prix-courant, p. 45. 1863; Anonymous (nom. nudum), Nederland Tuinbouwblad Sempervirens, 20:388–389, 391. 1891b.
Funkia undulata medio-variegata Siebold (nom. nudum), Catalogue et Prix-courant, p. 50–51. 1867.
Funkia ovata var. *undulata* (Otto et Dietrich) Miquel, Annales Musei Botanici Lugdano-Batavi, 3:152. 1867.
Funkia sieboldiana variegata Lowe et Howard, Beautiful Leaved Plants, p. 69, ic. 34. 1868.
Funkia lancifolia δ *undulata* (Otto et Dietrich) Regel, Gartenflora, 25:163. 1876.
Hostia japonica f. *undulata* (Otto et Dietrich) Voss in Voss et Siebert, Vilmorin's Blumengärtnerei, ed. 3, 1:1076. 1896; Foerster (nom. nudum), Der Steingarten der Sieben Jahreszeiten, p. 346. 1956.
Hosta cœrulea f. *undulata* (Otto et Dietrich) Matsumura, Index Plantarum Japonicarum, 2:199. 1905.
H. lancifolia var. *undulata* Bailey, Encyclopedia of American Horticulture, p. 619. 1900; and Standard Encyclopedia of Horticulture, p. 1605. 1915.
Niobe undulata (Otto et Dietrich) Nash var. *variegata* hort. in Nash, Torreya, 11:5. 1911.
Hosta japonica var. *angustifolia* f. *undulata* Ascherson et Gräbner, Synopsis der Mitteleuropäischen Flora, 3:55. 1905 p.p.
H. japonica var. *undulata* f. *albo-variegata* Makino, Nippon shokubutsu-dzukan, p. 398. 1935.
H. japonica albo-undulata Foerster (nom. nudum), Einzug der Grässer und Farne in die Gärten, p. 196. 1957; and Pflanze und Garten, p. 45. 1965.

H. 'Undulata Albomarginata' (a cultivar form).
J. of Japanese Botany, 12:506, ic. f. 5–9. 1936.
Synonyms:
H. **undulata** var. **albomarginata** Maekawa, J. of Japanese Botany, 12:506. 1936 (here reduced to cultivar form).
Funkia 'Thomas Hogg' hort. (p.p.; vix *Funkia alba* 'Thomas Hogg' ex de Noter and p.p. *Hosta* 'Decorata').
H. undulata var. *decolorans* Maekawa, J. of Japanese Botany, 12:507. 1936.
H. undulata 'Albo-marginata' hort.

H. 'Undulata Erromena' (a cultivar form).
J. of Japanese Botany, 12:506 ic. f. 3, 4. 1936.
Synonyms:
H. **undulata** var. **erromena** (Stearn) Maekawa, J. of Japanese Botany, 12:506 ic. f. 3, 4. 1936 (here reduced to cultivar form).
Funkia viridis Siebold (nom. nudum), Catalogue et Prix-courant, p. 50–51. 1867.
Funkia sieboldiana Siebold ex Miquel, Verslag Mededelingen Akademie Wetenschappen Amsterdam, 2, 3:301. 1869 (nom. nudum; not in the original sense ascribed by Hooker and éxcluding var. lusus α et lusus β).
Niobe undulata (Otto et Dietrich) Nash, Torreya, 11:5. 1911 (excluding var. *variegata* but not *Funkia undulata* [Otto et Dietrich] in the original sense).
Hosta japonica var. *fortis* Bailey, Gentes Herbarum, 2, 3:132. 1930.
H. lancifolia var. *fortis* (Bailey) Stearn, Gardener's Chronicle, 3 ser., 90:48. 1931 (with respect to the description).
H. erromena Stearn apud Bailey, Gentes Herbarum, 2, 7:438, ic. 188, 189. 1932.
H. viridis (Siebold) Koidzumi, Acta Phytotaxonomica et Geobotanica, 5:39. 1936.
H. undulata 'Erromena' hort.

H. 'Undulata Univittata' (a cultivar form).
Acta Horti Bergiani, 16, 11:399. 1954.
Synonyms:
H. **undulata** var. **univittata** (Miquel) Hylander, Acta Horti Bergiani, 16, 11:399. (here reduced to cultivar form).
Funkia univittata van Houtte ex Siebold (nom. nudum), Catalogue et Prix-courant, p. 45. 1863.
Funkia sieboldiana lusus α *univittata* Miquel, Verslag Mededelingen Akademie Wetenschappen Amsterdam, 2, 3:227, 302. 1869 (basionym).
Funkia lancifolia var. *univittata* Bailey, Standard Encyclopedia of Horticulture, p. 1605. 1915.
Hosta univittata (Siebold) Grey, Hardy Bulbs, 3:303. 1938 (excluding the annotation, this is not *H. erromena*).
H. japonica univittata Foerster (nom. nudum), Der Steingarten der Sieben Jahreszeiten, p. 346. 1956; and Einzug der Grässer und Farne in die Gärten, p. 196. 1957.
H. undulata 'Univittata' hort.

APPENDIX B

Critical Analysis of Prior Accounts

THE EARLY PERIOD—1712–1900

E. Kaempfer and C. P. Thunberg

Starting with Kaempfer (1712) and Thunberg (1780), members of the genus *Hosta* were included in Western scientific commentary, most of which deals with single species and varieties. A considerable number of these limited individual papers were published between 1712 and 1850 and are listed in the Bibliography. Except for a few true species, such as *H. plantaginea* and *H. ventricosa*, these early studies analyzed and described cultigens and hybridized taxa of Japanese or European origin. Most of these taxa have been reduced to cultivar form; as a consequence they are of little or no importance to the taxonomy of Japanese species. Nevertheless, they were given considerable attention by early botanists simply because they were the only representatives of the genus available for study in Europe. Hylander (1954) has given a very thorough analysis of the early taxonomic and nomenclatural history of these species and cultivated forms and his monograph has been reprinted in *The American Hosta Society Bulletin*, 6, 7, and 8. Hensen (1963b) has also researched and published considerable historical information on this subject.

L. Trattinnick

In 1780 the first scientific name was applied to a member of the genus, namely, *Aletris japonica* (Thunberg, 1780). Only four years later Thunberg (1784) made the transfer to another Linnean genus, viz., *Hemerocallis*. The first independent generic name *Hosta* was proposed by Trattinnick in 1812 with a Latin diagnosis and the separation of three species from *Hemerocallis* to *Hosta*, viz., *Hemerocallis japonica*, *Hemerocallis lancifolia*, and *Hemerocallis cærulea*. The transfer of these names was made without synonyms or descriptions, so was illegitimate. Similarly, Trattinnick's new name *Hosta japonica* was illegitimate for the same reason: It is without synonyms or a description and stands as a heading only of the paragraph with which the new genus *Hosta* was proposed. Aside from being illegitimate, *Hemerocallis japonica* and *Hosta japonica* have been persistently used for different taxa, namely, *H. plantaginea*, *H.* 'Tokudama' and *H.* 'Lancifolia'. In any case, the validation of the name *Hosta japonica* (based on *Hemerocallis japonica* Thunberg 1784 or *Aletris japonica* Thunberg 1780) under *Hosta* did not take place until Voss (1896). Even then it was under an illegitimate orthographic formulation, viz., the combination *Hostia japonica*.

Trattinnick's second name *Hosta cærulea* is also problematic. *Cærulea* was certainly the first validly published epithet to be applied to *H. ventricosa* as *Hemerocallis cærulea* Andrews (1797), but the combination *Hosta cærulea* is illegitimate because an earlier homonym exists against it under *Hosta cærulea* Jaquin (1797 = *Cornutia cærulea* [Jaquin] Moldenke). Thus, under the 1930 homonymy rules, Trattinnick's name is invalid.

Under *Hosta* the names *H. japonica* and *H. cærulea* should be placed on a list of rejected names (nomina rejicienda) per Article 69 of the ICBN or, at least, considered ambiguous names (nomina ambigua). Only *H. lancifolia* still figures in *Hosta* nomenclature, but it represents a sterile, nonperpetuat-

ing hybrid of long standing and so has joined the ranks of cultivar names.

The generic name *Hosta* is a later homonym, so by today's taxonomic rules a nomen illegitimum, but it has nevertheless been conserved (see Appendix A).

C. S. Kunth

With the arrival of many new hostas imported as live plants by von Siebold and the discovery of new garden varieties, botanists were beginning to attempt taxonomic classification of the genus and its species. The German botanist Kunth[1] (1843) published the first work which dealt with the genus as a whole. Using macromorphology as the principal taxonomic tool, Kunth's division of the genus came remarkably close to the concept of key species that I have presented in this work. He placed the genus in the Asphodelaceae, under the generic name *Funkia*, dividing it into five species:

> *Funkia subcordata* = *Hosta plantaginea*.
> *Funkia ovata* = *Hosta ventricosa*.
> *Funkia undulata* = *Hosta* 'Undulata'.
> *Funkia sieboldiana* = *Hosta sieboldiana*.
> *Funkia albomarginata* = *Hosta sieboldii*.

Kunth's study was published a year before von Siebold (1844) produced his first catalog listing, so it is limited to the few taxa cultivated in Europe at that time. *Hosta* 'Lancifolia', known since Kaempfer (1712) and Thunberg (1794), was not included by Kunth. This is puzzling because it was well known in Germany then, having been sent there by von Siebold. The astute Kunth probably excluded it because its sterility gives indication it is not a true species, but the also-sterile *H.* 'Undulata' was, on the other hand, included by him. He gave *H. sieboldii* (as *Funkia albomarginata*) a very prominent position which was unfortunately ignored by later authors, starting with Miquel (1867).

F. A. W. Miquel

Over a quarter of a century passed before the next study of the genus was produced by Dutch botanist Friedrik Miquel (1867, 1869), a contemporary of von Siebold, professor of botany at Utrecht University and director of the Leiden Herbarium, who had access to all von Siebold's dried material, as well as all von Siebold's hostas planted at Ghent and Leiden (see Chapter 5). This association is important because all von Siebold's names, lacking descriptions, are nomina nuda (names without valid descriptions), and so it is only through Miquel that the botanical validity of some of the names has been established. Two years after issuing preliminary findings in 1867, Miquel published *Bijtragen* (1869) which contains a treatment of the genus *Hosta* including five species and twenty varieties. I have added the important *Funkia ovata* var. *ramosa*, which is now known as *Hosta tibae*, on contemporary herbarium sheets (my discovery is discussed in detail under von Siebold in Chapter 5).[2] Miquel apparently was unable to place this taxon. This notable case illustrates that true species brought to Europe and recognized by early botanists as distinct taxa were subsequently lost and forgotten only to be rediscovered and named in Japan years later.[3] Miquel recognized and pointed out the differences between *H. plantaginea* and *H. plantaginea* var. *japonica*, so separated them as distinct variations (the latter as *Funkia subcordata β grandiflora*).

Miquel's review was based primarily on living material collected and obtained by von Siebold,during his two sojourns in Japan. Most of his 1869 taxonomical conclusions and placements are now considered erroneous—for example, *Hosta latifolia* was identified by Bailey (1930) as *H. ventricosa* and *H. cærulea* is now *H.* 'Lancifolia'; *Funkia sieboldiana* was actually *Hosta* 'Undulata Erromena'. For these reasons it is perhaps fortunate that Miquel's work was largely ignored. Miquel, who started his study soon after von Siebold's death in 1866, went public with the results only two years before he also died in 1871, and so his work went into obscurity with him. It was not until recently that a comprehensive analysis of it by Hylander (1954) and additional information by Hensen (1963b) shed new light on Miquel's contributions. Determination and placement of his taxa based on present knowledge are possible because Miquel provided very accurate morphological descriptions:

1. *Funkia subcordata* = *Hosta plantaginea*.
   1a. *Funkia subcordata* Siebold = *Hosta plantaginea*.
   1b. *Funkia subcordata β grandiflora* = *Hosta plantaginea* var. *japonica* (*Funkia grandiflora* Siebold and Zuccarini ex Lemaire).
2. *Funkia glauca* = *Hosta sieboldiana*.
   2a. *Funkia glauca β cucullata* = *Funkia cucullata* Siebold = *Hosta sieboldiana* ('Hypophylla'?).[4]
3. *Funkia sieboldiana* = *Hosta* 'Undulata Erromena'.
   3a. *Funkia sieboldiana α univittata* = *Hosta* 'Undulata Univittata'.
   3b. *Funkia sieboldiana β marginata* = *Funkia marginata* Siebold = *Hosta* 'Crispula'.
   3c. *Funkia sieboldiana bracteata* = *Hosta sieboldiana*.
4. *Funkia ovata*.
   4a. *Funkia ovata* = *Hosta* 'Lancifolia' pp and *H. sieboldii* pp.
   4b. *Funkia ovata cærulea* = *Hosta* 'Lancifolia'.
   4c. *Funkia ovata albomarginata* = *Hosta* 'Fortunei Albomarginata'? pp sim.
   4d. *Funkia ovata albopicta* = *Funkia viridimarginata* Siebold = *Hosta* 'Fortunei Albopicta'.
   4e. *Funkia ovata maculata* = *Hosta* 'Lancifolia' (variegated).
   4f. *Funkia ovata undulata* = *Hosta* 'Undulata'.
   4g. *Funkia ovata spathulata* = *Hosta sieboldii* f. *spathulata*.
   4h. *Funkia ovata spathulata α albomarginatis* = *Funkia spathulata albomarginatis* Siebold = *Hosta sieboldii*.
   4i. *Funkia ovata spathulata β floribus subalbidis* = *Funkia japonica flore albo* Siebold = *Hosta sieboldii* 'Alba'.
   4j. *Funkia ovata lancifolia* = *Hosta longissima* pp and = *H. sieboldii* f. *angustifolia* pp.
   4k. *Funkia ovata* var. *ramosa* (Hb. annotation) = *Hosta tibae*.
5. *Funkia latifolia* = *Hosta ventricosa*.
   5a. *Funkia latifolia α maculata* = *Funkia maculata* Siebold.
   5b. *Funkia latifolia β sinensis* = *Funkia sinensis* Siebold = *Hosta* 'Elata' (?) pp sim.
   5c. *Funkia latifolia γ aureomaculata* = *Funkia ovata aureomaculata* Siebold = *Hosta ventricosa* 'Aureomaculata'.

This list shows the considerable alteration of names by Miquel and marks the beginning of the unfortunate submergence of the taxonomically important *H. sieboldii* under *H.* 'Lancifolia', a sterile cultigen, which has had long-term taxonomic implications. Today it seems incredible that in light of the considerable morphological differences *H. sieboldii* could be considered a variety of the sterile *H.* 'Lancifolia', yet this arrangement was repeated by many botanists until finally corrected by Ohwi (1942). Some of Miquel's misapplied names saw horticultural use and so contributed to the ensuing nomenclatural muddle. The epithet *latifolia* employed by Miquel for *H. ventricosa* was used as late as 1905 by Matsumura[5]. In 1862 von Siebold and Fortune imported *H.* 'Tokudama', which was listed by Miquel (1867) as *Funkia sieboldiana* var. *condensata* but reappeared in 1869 as *Funkia glauca*. A hosta called "True Glauca" was sold for many years in both Europe and North America and is very close to *Hosta* 'Tokudama'. This taxon eventually sported to a yellow-variegated form which von Siebold called *Funkia glauca variegata*.

J. G. Baker

Baker (1870) published a brief schematic survey of the genus as part of a revision of the Liliaceae. He listed only four species, which follow Kunth's arrangement, but substituted the hybrid *Hosta* 'Lancifolia' for the green-leaved *H. sieboldii*. Of interest is the number of principal veins he ascribed to *H. sieboldiana* (i.e., 12–13, which is correct for *H.* 'Tokudama' or *H. montana*, but should be 14–20 for *H. sieboldiana*):

Order: Liliaceae.
Suborder: Liliaceae verae.
Tribe: Hemerocallideae.
Genus: *Funkia*.

1. *Funkia subcordata* = *Hosta plantaginea*.
2. *Funkia sieboldiana* = *Hosta sieboldiana*.
3. *Funkia lancifolia* = *Hosta* 'Lancifolia'.
4. *Funkia ovata* = *Hosta ventricosa*.

Japanese Floristic Works

By the middle 1800s Japanese floristic works covering members of the genus (as *gibo, gibooshi, giboushi*, or *giboshi*) began to appear: Ono (1847) produced *Zyusyu Honzo Somoku Keimo*; Iinuma[6] (1856) published the first edition of *Somoku Dzusetsu*, which was followed by a second edition in 1874 and subsequently revised by Makino[7] (1910); Iwasaki (1874) released *Honzo-Dzufu*, which was revised by Shirai and Oonuma in 1916–1918. There were others, mostly horticultural in nature because taxonomy, as practiced by Western botanists, was just beginning to be accepted in place of the traditional, herbalistic, botanical system used up to this time in Japan. These works were used by Maekawa (1940) and others as sources for many of the formal (academic) Japanese names in use today.

E. A. von Regel

Nine years after Miquel's initial review, Regel (1876) published a short paper, which, in spite of its brevity, had considerable subsequent influence on *Hosta* nomenclature. Regel followed Baker's basic delimitation into four species, but he broadened the subject by including several varieties of these species. He also placed *H. sieboldii* as a variety under *H.* 'Lancifolia' (as *Funkia lancifolia α typica*). All the varieties are variegated taxa, but while adding these, Regel eliminated many of von Siebold's garden varieties, which included most of the hostas which Hylander (1954) assembled as the *fortunei* complex.

1. *Funkia subcordata* = *Hosta plantaginea*.
2. *Funkia sieboldiana*.
   2a. *Funkia sieboldiana* α *typica* = *Hosta sieboldiana*.
   2b. *Funkia sieboldiana* β *fortunei* = *Hosta* 'Tokudama'.
3. *Funkia lancifolia*.
   3a. *Funkia lancifolia* α *typica* = *Hosta* 'Lancifolia'.
   3b. *Funkia lancifolia* β *latifolia* = *Hosta* 'Undulata Erromena'.
   3c. *Funkia lancifolia* γ *albomarginata* = *Hosta sieboldii*.
   3d. *Funkia lancifolia* δ *undulata* = *Hosta* 'Undulata'.
   3e. *Funkia lancifolia* ε *angustifolia* = *Funkia lancifolia* var. *angustissima* = *Hosta sieboldii* f. *angustifolia* pp and *H. longissima* pp.
4. *Funkia ovata*.
   4a. *Funkia ovata* α *typica* = *Hosta ventricosa*.
   4b. *Funkia ovata* β *latifolia* = *Hosta* 'Elata' (?).
   4c. *Funkia ovata* γ *aureovariegata* = *Hosta ventricosa* 'Aureomaculata'.
   4d. *Funkia ovata* δ *albomarginata* = *Hosta* 'Crispula'.
   4e. *Funkia ovata* ε *latemarginata* = *Hosta ventricosa* 'Aureomarginata'.

Anonymous

An unknown author writing in *Nederland Tuinbouwblad Semper-virens* (Anonymous, 1891a, 1891b) must have been familiar with von Siebold's importations. Ignoring Miquel (1867, 1869) completely, this writer resurrected von Siebold's names and included several cultigens which later were associated with the *H.* 'Fortunei' group. This list establishes that by 1891 many of the variegated garden varieties placed by Hylander (1954) under *H.* 'Fortunei' had emerged in cultivation.

Funkia albomarginata = *Hosta* 'Crispula'.
Funkia albomarginata lutescens = *Hosta* 'Crispula Lutescens'.
Funkia aurea = *Hosta* 'Fortunei Aurea'.
Funkia aurea maculata = *Hosta* 'Fortunei Albopicta'.
Funkia glauca = *Hosta sieboldiana* or *H.* 'Tokudama'.
Funkia glaucescens = *Hosta* 'Fortunei Hyacinthina'.
Funkia cucullata = *Hosta sieboldiana* 'Hypophylla'.
Funkia fortunei = *H.* 'Tokudama'.
Funkia fortunei variegata = *Hosta* 'Tokudama', variegated form.[8]
Funkia liliiflora = *Hosta plantaginea*.
Funkia ovata foliis aureomaculatis = *Hosta ventricosa* 'Aureomaculata'.
Funkia sinensis = *Hosta montana* pp.
Funkia sinensis marmorata.
Funkia spathulata albomarginata = *Hosta sieboldii*.
Funkia undulata argenteovittata = *Hosta* 'Undulata Univittata'.

This list also shows how deep-rooted von Siebold's names were in horticulture. *Hosta glauca* and *H. fortunei* were still listed in nursery catalogs as late as the 1960s. Foerster (1965b) wrote *H. glauca* for *H. sieboldiana* and *H. glauca minor* for *H.* 'Tokudama'. In Europe *H.* 'Tokudama' is also still occasionally sold under the name *H. fortunei*, and the name *H. liliiflora* (spelled "lilieflora") for *H. plantaginea* was still used in Germany by Foerster (1965).

A. Voss

Voss and Siebert (1896) published a treatise on cultivated plants, which included hostas, following Regel (1876). They changed the generic name to *Hostia*—a later homonym of *Hostia* Moench (1802) = *Crepis* L., Compositae—and dropped the specific epithets *ovata* and *lancifolia*, replacing them with *cærulea* and *japonica*, respectively. Interestingly, in North America *H.* 'Undulata' was still being sold under Voss' name *H.*

japonica undulata as late as the middle 1940s (Rockmont Nursery, 1944). The incorrect placement of *H. sieboldii* (under the name *Hostia japonica* f. *albomarginata*) as a variety under *H.* 'Lancifolia' is obvious.

1. *Hostia subcordata* = *Hosta plantaginea*.
2. *Hostia sieboldiana*.
   2a. *Hostia sieboldiana* f. *typica* = *Hosta sieboldiana*.
   2b. *Hostia sieboldiana* f. *fortunei* = *Hosta* 'Tokudama'.
3. *Hostia japonica*.
   3a. *Hostia japonica* f. *typica* = *Hosta* 'Lancifolia'.
   3b. *Hostia japonica* f. *albomarginata* = *Hosta sieboldii*.
   3c. *Hostia japonica* f. *lutescens* = *Hosta sieboldii* 'Subcrocea' (?).
   3d. *Hostia japonica* f. *undulata* = *Hosta* 'Undulata'.
4. *Hostia cærulea*.
   4a. *Hostia cærulea* f. *typica* = *Hosta ventricosa*.
   4b. *Hostia cærulea* f. *latemarginata* = *Hosta ventricosa* 'Aureomarginata' or *H.* 'Fortunei Aureomarginata'.
   4c. *Hostia cærulea* f. *latifolia* = *Hosta* 'Elata'.
   4d. *Hostia cærulea* f. *aureovariegata* = *Hosta ventricosa* 'Aureomaculata'.
   4e. *Hostia cærulea* f. *albomarginata* = *Hosta* 'Crispula'.

S. Mottet

Mottet (1897) published a review of *Funkia* which contains taxa that are difficult to identify. For this reason his work has been ignored and is no longer considered important to the classification of the natural population.

These early listings of the genus show the reason for the confused nomenclature. They also point to the cause for later misinterpretations—for example, the placement of *Hosta sieboldii* with *H.* 'Lancifolia'. The persistent horticultural and botanical use of the generic name *Funkia* is conspicuous.

GENERIC REVIEWS—1900–1930s: EARLY JAPANESE, EUROPEAN, AND KOREAN STUDIES

Major Early Japanese Authors

Most significant for *Hosta* nomenclature and taxonomy was the appearance of Japanese authors around 1900. Although pre-dated by a number of floristic works, including Iinuma (1856, 1874, rev. 1910), no botanical study of the genus came out of Japan before that time. Between 1840 and 1880 Japanese botanists were developing the science of botany according to the Western system. By 1900 they had trained a formidable nucleus of their own qualified scientists and teachers and were beginning to publish botanical works on the flora of Japan. Among these works were *Nippon shokubutsu mei-i* [Japanese seed plants] (Matsumura, 1884); *Index plantarum japonicarum* [Catalog of Japanese plants] (Matsumura, 1905); *Somoku Dzusetsu* [An Iconography of Japanese plants] (Makino 1910, revised from Iinuma); *Nippon shokubutsu soran* [Flora of Japan] (Makino and Nemoto,[9] 1925); *Nippon shokubutsu dzukan* [Illustrated Flora of Japan] (Makino, 1935); *Flora of Hokkaido and Saghalien* (Miyabe and Kudo[10] 1930–1934); *Flora Nagasaki* (Toyama 1940, rev. 1980); and an unfinished work, *Nova Flora Japonica* (Nakai with Honda,[11] 1935–1951). All these major works are known for their comprehensive coverage of the flora in the entire Japanese archipelago and include basic or partial treatments of the genus. Short articles covering individual species were published by Honda (1930, 1935a, 1935b), Ibuyama (1937), Kikuchi (1934), Koizumi[12] (1916, 1936, 1942), Mori (1922), Makino (1902, 1928, 1938), Masamune[13] (1932, 1934), Nakai (1911, 1914, 1918, 1930), Ohwi (1942), Okamoto (1934), and Tatewaki[14] (1934). Maekawa (whose work will be discussed later) released his first paper in 1928.

J. Matsumura

Matsumura (1905) clearly manifests European influence in his work. Well acquainted with European botany because he studied at the University of Heidelberg, Germany, Matsumura was able to refer to a number of European authors, making his study one of the first Japanese studies to include European synonyms. One of the names Matsumura resurrected was Miquel's specific name *H. latifolia* for *H. ventricosa*:

> *Hosta plantaginea* f. *grandiflora* = *H. plantaginea*.
> *H. sieboldiana* = *H. sieboldiana*.
> *H. sieboldiana* var. *glauca* = *H.* 'Tokudama'.
> *H. sieboldiana* var. *longipes* = *H. longipes* pp.
> *H. cærulea* f. *lancifolia* = *H.* 'Lancifolia'.
> *H. cærulea* f. *albomarginata* = *H. sieboldii*.
> *H. cærulea* var. *minor* f. *undulata* = *H.* 'Undulata'.
> *H. latifolia* = *H. ventricosa*.

P. F. A. Ascherson and K. O. R. P. P. Gräbner

In Europe botanists continued their classification efforts, and Ascherson and Gräbner[15] (1905) jointly published a classic reference work on the European flora in which the genus *Hosta* was included. Of note are the incorrect application of *H. sieboldiana* var. *fortunei* to *H. fortunei* Baker (in the sense of Bailey) and the revival of the name *H. japonica*:

> *Hosta plantaginea* f. *grandiflora* = *H. plantaginea*.
> *H. sieboldiana* = *H. sieboldiana*.
> *H. sieboldiana* var. *fortunei* = *H. fortunei* (Baker) Bailey, not *H.* 'Tokudama'.
> *H. japonica* = *H.* 'Lancifolia'.
> *H. japonica* var. *angustifolia* = *H. longissima* pp and *H. sieboldii* f. *angustifolia* pp.
> *H. japonica* var. *angustifolia* f. *undulata* = *H.* 'Undulata'.
> *H. japonica* var. *albomarginata* = *H. sieboldii*.
> *H. cærulea* = *H. ventricosa*.

R. de Noter and E. Graf von Silva-Tarouca

A treatment by de Noter (1905) is particularly difficult to interpret, as is Graf von Silva-Tarouca's (1910) effort, and so subsequent authors disregarded them.

T. Makino

Makino (1902) listed *H.* 'Tokudama' as *H. sieboldiana* var. *glauca*. The name *H. nigrescens* also appeared as *H. sieboldiana* var. *nigrescens*.

A revision of Iinuma's *Iconography* by Makino (1910) introduced several new hostas, including *H. nigrescens*, with descriptions that figure prominently in the synonymy of subsequent authors, including Maekawa. The displacement of names started by European botanists continues unabated; for example, Makino's *H. sieboldiana* was later placed in the synonymy of *H. montana* by Maekawa (1940). *Hosta sieboldii* is still incorrectly associated with *H. japonica* = *H.* 'Lancifolia'.

> *Hosta plantaginea*.
> *H. sieboldiana* = *H. montana*.
> *H. sieboldiana* var. *nigrescens* = *H. nigrescens*.
> *H. sieboldiana* var. *glauca* = *H.* 'Tokudama'.
> *H. japonica* = *H.* 'Lancifolia'.
> *H. japonica* var. *angustifolia* = *H. longissima* pp and *H. sieboldii* f. *angustifolia* pp.
> *H. japonica* var. *intermedia* = *H. clavata*.
> *H. japonica* var. *albomarginata* = *H. sieboldii*.
> *H. cærulea* = *H. ventricosa*.

It is notable that neither Ascherson and Gräbner nor Makino perceived the difference between *H. longissima* and *H. sieboldii*

f. *angustifolia*; all taxa were ascribed to the former when, in fact, some had yellow anthers and were actually the latter.

The basionym for *H. montana* 'Aureomarginata' was published by Makino (1928) as *H. sieboldiana* var. *aureomarginata*.

G. V. Nash

The first monograph by a North American author was by Nash[16] (1911) who decided to go against the conservation of the name *Hosta*. He resurrected the subgeneric name *Niobe*, which was coined by Salisbury (1812), and changed it to generic rank, applying it to the genus as a whole. His classification scheme was ignored because it was confusing and contrary to the international rules, but it should be noted that Nash was at that time working under the rules of the American Code of Nomenclature. Under this code two identical generic names cannot exist even though, as in this case, the older may be invalid or unused. As a consequence Trattinnick's *Hosta* becomes unacceptable and one of the other, still earlier names can be selected—either *Niobe* or *Bryocles*. Nash chose the former because it appears in print ahead of the latter in Salisbury (1812).

> *Niobe plantaginea* = *H. plantaginea*.
> *Niobe undulata* = *H.* 'Undulata Erromena'.
> *Niobe undulata* var. *variegata* = *H.* 'Undulata'.
> *Niobe japonica* = *H.* 'Lancifolia'.
> *Niobe japonica* var. *albomarginata* = *H. sieboldii*.
> *Niobe caerulea* = *H. ventricosa*.

Nash's placement of *Niobe undulata* is particularly interesting; he apparently believed the all-green *H.* 'Undulata Erromena' must be the species, with *H.* 'Undulata' a variety under it. Nash must have been well aware of the mutability of the highly variegated *H.* 'Undulata' to the all-green *H.* 'Undulata Erromena', the only reasonably stable form of this cultigen taxon.

T. Nakai

In Nakai (1911) the name *H. minor* surfaced, and three years later Nakai (1914) repeated this mention in a study of the flora of Quelpaert Island (Cheju Do).

Nakai (1930) described *H. rectifolia*, *H. rupifraga*, *H. clausa*, and *H. atropurpurea*.

His extensive contributions to our knowledge of the Korean taxa are detailed below.

G. Koidzumi

Koidzumi (1916) originated the varietal epithet *capitata* which he applied under *H. cærulea* as *H. cærulea* var. *capitata*. The latter was raised to specific rank by Nakai (1930) as *H. capitata*.

Major Authors on the Korean Taxa

Until recently only Japanese and Western botanists studied the Korean taxa. The first author of record is Baker (1870), who published *Funkia ovata* var. *minor*, based on a specimen collected by Oldham in 1863; the type is in K. Although dried specimens of taxa with coastal elevation usually show traces of these lamellar ridges on the scape, Baker's type does not. Some years later two Russians contributed significantly: Komarov[17] included Korean taxa in *Flora Manchuriae* (1901), and many years later dealt with *Funkia lancifolia* Sprengel (= *Hosta clausa*) in *Flora USSR* (1935). Palibin,[18] the other Russian contributor, listed a *Funkia ovata* var. *ovata* and *Funkia ovata* var. *minor* in *Conspectus Florae Coreae* (1901). The latter may have been what is today considered *Hosta tsushimensis*. The French missionary Taquet collected on Cheju Island between 1907 and 1910 and several specimens exist from these accessions: the holotype in

E, no. 153/86 43, Taquet no. 4067, August 1910; also in C, Taquet no. 380, September 1907 and Taquet no. 1896, July 1908. Based on these collections Léveillé[19] published *Funkia subcordata* var. *taquetii*. These taxa belong without doubt to *Hosta venusta*, and the former name is now considered a synonym.

The Japanese botanist Takenoshin Nakai (mentioned earlier) did much research on Korean species, which includes his 1911 "Flora Koreana," "his 1914 *Report of Collection on Cheju and Wan Islands*, his 1915 *Flora of Chiisan*, and his 1918 *Report on the Vegetation of Diamond Mountains* in which he listed *H. japonica*, *H. japonica* var. *lancifolia*, *H. longipes*, *H. longipes* var. *alba*[?], *H. minor*, and *H. minor* var. *alba*. Mori (1922) also dealt with the Korean taxa. In 1930 Nakai recognized the macromorphological differentiation of the Korean taxa hitherto called *H. lancifolia* and published the new species *H. clausa*.

Maekawa (1935) named *H. venusta* on the basis of a cultivated specimen and *H. nakaiana* from a specimen collected by Nakai on Mount Paekun and by Smith on Mount Chiri, in province Chollanam-do, southern Korea. Maekawa (1937) named another species, *H. ensata* also from collected material (Nakai No. 5253 in TI). Maekawa (1937, 1938a, 1938b, 1940) dealt with the sectional classification of the Korean taxa. He named sections *Lamellatae* to encompass *H. capitata*, *H. nakaiana*, *H. minor*, and *H. venusta*; and *Stoloniferae* to include *H. clausa*, *H. clausa* var. *normalis*, and *H. ensata*. Finally, in 1939 Kitagawa discussed the economic applications and distribution of *H. clausa* var. *normalis* and *H. ensata* in "Lineamenta Florae Manshuricae."

It was not until 1937 that Korean botanists began publishing on the genus. Chung, To, Lee, and Lee (1937) wrote *Nomina Plantarum Coreanum*. The list of taxa recognized as Korean species follows very closely that published by Nakai (1918).

After 1945 Korean botanists began to focus on the genus and considerable work has been accomplished, culminating in the recent micromorphological and biosystematic work conducted by M. G. Chung (1989, 1990). Due to its considerable effect on taxonomy, this recent work is covered in Appendix A—Part 1.

THE 1930S: BAILEY, STEARN, AND WEHRHAHN

Beginning in 1930, considerable research into the genus commenced. Botanical accounts published since then form the foundation for today's system of *Hosta* classification and nomenclature. All these papers are of limited scope (i.e., none of them includes all the hostas known then). Most of the reviews take into account the major works and expand on this historical knowledge.

Much of this work was done in the West by three well-known botanists: L. H. Bailey[20] in the United States, W. T. Stearn in England, and H. R. Wehrhahn[21] in Germany. Quite independently, though, Japanese botanists also dealt with specific facets of the genus, but unfortunately, with very few exceptions, the language barrier kept the Japanese studies from being considered in the West.

Japanese authors published many short papers dealing with one or several new species. These include Honda, Kudo, Koidzumi, Maekawa, Makino, Masamune, Miyabe, Nakai, and Tatewaki (bibliographic references for these were given earlier under "Generic Reviews").

Japanese botanists were also active in *Hosta* genetics and several important contributions were published: Teresawa (1923), Yasui (1929, 1935), Sato (1935, 1942), and Suto (1936).

L. H. Bailey

Bailey (1903) released an exhaustive horticultural encyclopedia; the 1915 edition included an extensive reference listing of hostas. It is of particular interest to horticulturists and *Hosta* specialists because it includes variegated cultivars usually neglected by botanists and solves some nomenclatural puzzles by Bailey's application of certain synonyms which appear in the following list:

Hosta plantaginea.
  H. plantaginea var. *grandiflora* = *H. plantaginea*.
  Syn. *H. macrantha* hort.
H. sieboldiana.
  Syn. *Funkia glauca*, *F. glaucescens*, *F. cucullata*, *F. sinensis* hort., and *F. cordata* hort. Siebold.
H. fortunei = *H.* 'Tokudama'.
  Syn. *Funkia fortunei* Baker (incorrect).
  H. fortunei gigantea = *H.* 'Elata'.
  H. fortunei var. *robusta* = *H. sieboldiana* 'Elegans'.
  H. fortunei var. *argenteovariegata* = *H.* 'Fortunei Albomarginata'(?) or *H.* 'Decorata'(?).
H. lancifolia = *H.* 'Lancifolia'.
  H. lancifolia var. *albomarginata* = *H. sieboldii*.
  H. lancifolia var. *tardiflora* = *H.* 'Tardiflora'.
  H. lancifolia var. *undulata* = *H.* 'Undulata'.
  H. lancifolia var. *univittata* = *H.* 'Undulata Univittata'.
H. longipes = *H. rectifolia*.
H. Aoki = *H.* 'Fortunei Aoki'.
H. elata hort. = *H.* 'Crispula Viridis' pp sim.
H. gigantea hort. = *H. sieboldiana* or *H. montana* type.

Bailey (1915) stated that a considerable number of variegated hostas existed during that time; for lack of accurate descriptions they can no longer be positively placed, although knowledge of the stock available at that time allows supposition. For example, under *H. sieboldiana* Bailey mentioned "there is a form with the body of the leaf yellowish white and the edge green"; this form has disappeared but could have been a mediovariegated sport of the species. It was not the modern *H.* 'Fortunei Albopicta' because the latter was already known as *Hosta viridis-marginata* hort. *Hosta fortunei* var. *argenteovariegata* is probably a member of the *H.* 'Fortunei' Albomarginata group. Also listed are *H. aurea* hort., which Bailey described as "(gold) variegated forms of various species," and *H. variegata* hort., characterized as "variegated forms of various species"— usually of *H. cærulea* (= *H. ventricosa*) or *H. lancifolia*— indicating variegated forms of *H. ventricosa* were known at this time. The variegated forms of *H. lancifolia* may have included von Siebold's *Funkia spathulata foliis albomarginatis lutescens* (= *H. sieboldii* 'Subcrocea') and yellow forms of other species and cultigens. The encyclopedia was revised and reissued in 1927 with about the same listing of names. Highly significant is Bailey's adoption of names long known in European horticulture. This gives testimony to the European origin of many hostas cultivated in North America at that time.

Bailey (1930) produced a limited revision of the genus *Hosta* in *Gentes Herbarum*, in which he divided the genus into three divisions (subsections):

Niobe.
  H. plantaginea.
Bryocles.
  H. ventricosa.
Alcyone.
  H. japonica group.
  H. sieboldiana group.
  H. undulata group.

Although limited in scope because of the narrow range of living material available for study, Bailey's contribution is nevertheless of major importance to the delimitation of the genus as detailed in Appendix A. He used the group concept of classification which was changed to generic rank in the endorsements of Grey (1938) and Hylander (1954). His section *Alcyone* is equivalent to subgenus *Giboshi* Maekawa:

Section (division) *Alcyone*.

Sieboldiana group.
  H. sieboldiana.
  H. sieboldiana var. *fortunei* (Baker) Bailey = *H.* 'Fortunei' (not *H.* 'Tokudama').
  H. sieboldiana var. *marginato-alba* = *H.* 'Crispula'.
  H. sieboldiana var. *nigrescens* = *H. nigrescens*.
Japonica group.
  H. japonica = *H.* 'Lancifolia'.
  H. japonica var. *albomarginata* = *H. sieboldii*.
  H. japonica var. *fortis* = *H.* 'Undulata Erromena'.
  H. japonica var. *tardiflora* = *H.* 'Tardiflora'.
Undulata group.
  H. undulata = *H.* 'Undulata'.
  H. decorata = *H.* 'Decorata'.

Other hostas mentioned include:

Hosta latifolia.[22]
H. legendrei = *H. plantaginea*.
H. longipes = *H. rectifolia*.
H. minor.
H. argyi = This is not a hosta, but the tuberose (*Polyanthes tuberosa*).

Bailey discussed *H. latifolia* and came to the conclusion it must have been *H. cœrulea* = *H. ventricosa*, based primarily on the diagnosis of the flowers which points to a dark bluish bell-shaped perianth. He mentioned three variegated forms of this hosta were known to Miquel, who first used this name. *Hosta legendrei* was first mentioned by Lévillé (1911) and is interesting because it may represent a lost hybrid. The description seemed to combine characteristics of *H. plantaginea* and *H. ventricosa*.

W. T. Stearn

Stearn (1931b) produced a limited critical review of the genus *Hosta* which was largely based on Bailey (1930) and which considered new regulations adopted by the International Botanical Congress of 1930. The new rules rejected homonymy; a homonym is a name spelled exactly like a name previously and validly published for a taxon of the same rank but based on a different type (ICBN, 1988: Article 64). Stearn pointed out the epithet *japonica* must fall before *lancifolia* because *H. japonica* Trattinnick was not an originally published species with a valid diagnosis but was accepted in name only as a new combination. Only the year before, Bailey (1930) still used *H. japonica*. Equally, *H. caerulea* Trattinnick must yield to *H. ventricosa* Stearn. The epithet *ventricosa* was first used by Salisbury in *Bryocles ventricosa*. Incredible as it may be, *Hosta ventricosa*, in Europe since the 1790s, did not have a valid name under *Hosta* until Stearn (1931b) assigned one. He also rejected the name *H. sieboldiana* in favor of *H. glauca*, a placement not followed by later authors. Since von Siebold's importations, this taxon has been known by two different names, namely, *H. sieboldiana* and *H. glauca*.

Stearn was instrumental in identifying a plant long grown at Kew Botanic Garden under the erroneous name *H. longipes* as being *H. rectifolia*.

Later, Stearn produced a number of individual papers, including detailed accounts of *H. rectifolia*, *H.* 'Tardiflora', and *H. venusta*, in the new series of *Curtis's Botanical Magazine* (Stearn 1951, 1953, 1966). Stearn did not mention the very prominent ridges on the scapes of his *H. venusta* and his illustration shows other atypical features: leaves too lanceolate, scapes too short, and indication of at least two sterile bracts. My observations in England and Germany indicate that some of the European cultivated material purported to be *H. venusta* may be hybridized or another species because it does not fundamentally match the morphology of this species as confirmed by recent accessions on Mount Halla, Cheju Do (M. G. Chung). One of the taxa grown in Europe and labeled *H. venusta* turned out to be *H. gracillima*, another was a dwarf *H. sieboldii* f. *spathulata* form, neither having ridges on the scape.

H. R. Wehrhahn

Wehrhahn (1931) produced a general survey of perennial garden plants, including hostas, which was followed in 1934 by an article covering hostas (as "Funkien"), both were horticultural in nature and without new data significant to the classification of the genus. On the other hand, Wehrhahn's (1936) "Zwei übersehene *Hosta*-Arten" produced a valid diagnosis for a new species which he called *H. bella* (now considered a cultigen). Wehrhahn states he received specimens of this taxon from England and Holland under the names *H. glauca* and *H. japonica*, and records show this taxon was considered *H. glauca* by Miquel (1869) and illustrated as *H. glauca* in Jensen et al. (1949). As far as can be determined from dried material, the type specimen of *H. fortunei* (Baker) Bailey in K very closely matches Wehrhahn's line drawing (Figure 3-4) and photographs. Hylander (1954) included this taxon under *H. fortunei* var. *obscura*, and Maekawa (1940) held it to be synonymous with his *H. montana* var. *transiens*. Both botanists reached their conclusions without actually having seen the plant and so started the exceedingly difficult *H.* 'Elata'/*H. montana* problem discussed later under "Maekawa."

1938—GREY'S REVIEW

In 1938 Charles Harvey Grey published a three-volume work, *Hardy Bulbs*, which in Part 3, Liliaceae, contains detailed descriptions of most of the species of the genus known to exist at that time. It is the first of the Western reviews to reflect Japanese botanical research then available, using as main references Maekawa (1937, 1938b). Grey includes descriptions for *H. capitata* and *H. atropurpurea*, which were somehow left out of Maekawa's 1940 monograph, and incorporates most of the European specioids.

Grey supports the system of classification proposed by Bailey (1930), but ranks them as subgenera—contrary to Bailey who placed his subdivisions of the genus on a sectional (or divisional) level. I have cited Grey as one of the proponents of a tri-subgeneric system of division.

Grey describes the flower stem of *H. capitata* as "terete"[23] and bright green, overlooking the most differentiating feature of this species—namely, its parallel ridges along the scape—so his description is not based on actual observation, and it is doubtful this taxon was in England in 1938.

Hosta cordata is incorrectly quoted as a synonym for *H. sieboldiana* with von Siebold as the author, but Hensen (1963b) does not list this name and *cordata* may be based on *Hemerocallis cordata* Thunberg (1784) (not *Hemerocallis cordata* Cavanilles, 1801 = *Hosta plantaginea*).

Hosta cucullata is given as a synonym for *H. glauca*, and *cucullata* (hoodlike) apparently refers to hoodlike leaves covering the flower stems, as in *H. sieboldiana* 'Hypophylla' and *H. glauca* (Siebold) Hensen.

Hosta legendrei collected by Maire in China is described as close to *H. ventricosa* with larger flowers and broad greenish yellow bracteolate leaves, but according to Grey is no longer in cultivation.

Maekawa (1940) specifically excluded from the synonymy of *H. minor* a taxon referred to as *H. longipes*, which Nakai had included previously. *Hosta minor*, per Maekawa, has ridges along the scapes, the distinct sectional characteristic of *Lamellatae* native to Korea. Grey correctly disputed Nakai's synonymy, suspecting there may be two taxa bearing this name, one of which has been incorrectly used in horticulture (as *H. minor alba*) for a long time.

The name *H. violacea* Glück[24] (1919), occasionally seen in modern works, is listed, but is by Hylander (1954) called a *"lapsus calami"* ("slip of the pen") for *H. cærulea* = *H. ventricosa*.

Grey's review is important because it describes many of the new Japanese hostas for the first time in English in a European work and so made an important contribution to the understanding of the Japanese native taxa. Unfortunately, he did not have access to most of them and merely repeated the diagnoses, some incorrectly, from Japanese sources.

This review also shows how the old hosta names, most of them originating with von Siebold, persisted in the horticultural and botanical literature of Europe for a considerable period of time after they had been declared invalid.

1940—MAEKAWA'S MONOGRAPH

Published under the title "The Genus *Hosta*" by Fumio Maekawa on 10 August 1940 in the *Journal of the Faculty of Science*, Imperial University, Tokyo, this monograph was the most extensive and detailed work published to date, culminating many years of study which began in 1928. Maekawa's taxonomic studies, initially carried out under the able direction of his father-in-law and mentor, Professor Nakai, resulted in his first paper in 1928, while still a young student. Following Maekawa's 1984 posthumous work, Yosio Kobayashi mentions in his eulogy that Maekawa was called up for military service before he was able to gain his Ph.D., although he finished his 1940 monograph, which was published. After his return, Kobayashi assisted Maekawa in finishing his studies and in obtaining his Ph.D. Many additional publications on the genus were originated by Maekawa and are itemized in the Bibliography. Detailed information of his contributions after his return from military service before 1944 are given in Chapter 3 under the individual taxa he described.

Maekawa (1937, 1938a, 1938b) made preliminary proposals for a new system of classification, followed by a definitive plan in 1940, which created two distinct subgenera for the genus, first (1938a) as *Niobe* and *Giboshi*, and later (1940) as *Niobe* and *Bryocles*, dividing the latter into ten sections and several subsections. Just why Maekawa did not follow Bailey (1930), who separated subgenus *Bryocles* from subgenus *Giboshi* (using the name *Alcyone*), is not known. Without this separation *H. ventricosa* had to remain the type species for the subgenus, perpetuating the previous unnatural arrangement which was based totally on European cultivated taxa. Hylander (1954) pointed out that Maekawa's (1938b) proposal for a new subgenus *Giboshi* for the main group of indigenous Japanese taxa would permit a more natural arrangement; later Maekawa realized this and restored his 1938(a) proposal, reinstating subgenus *Giboshi* for the Japanese hostas and applying it to his new species, although he never validly separated the taxa in *Giboshi* from those in *Bryocles*.

A list of the hostas described in Maekawa's monograph is not included here because the graphic keys and synonyms given in Appendix A follow Maekawa's basic delimitation of

1940 and 1969, with later revisions incorporated. As Fujita (1976a) has pointed out, Maekawa raised a number of cultivated taxa to specific rank; I have reduced many of them to cultivar form, following Fujita (1976a). Except for Hara (1984), who revised Maekawa's *H. sieboldii* complex, no comprehensive correction of Maekawa (1940) has been published to date, so the required corrections are made in Appendix A. Following is a brief analysis of Maekawa's monograph.

The Japanese *H. plantaginea*

There is universal agreement that subgenus *Hosta*, represented by *H. plantaginea*, is a natural grouping from both an ecological and macromorphological standpoint. Micromorphological evidence (M. G. Chung and S. B. Jones, 1989) has corroborated this delimitation recently. The Japanese have assigned a unique formal name, viz., *Maruba Tama No Kanzashi*, and are not using the genus name *Giboshi* in this combination of names. According to Maekawa *H. plantaginea* f. *typica* (*Maruba Tama No Kanzashi*) is synonymous to *Funkia grandiflora* Siebold and Zuccarini (ex Lemaire), but this is incorrect because the excellent illustration in Lemaire (1846), clearly shows the leaves elongated, not round, and the anthers not pure yellow, but discolored with purple, so the plant is *H. plantaginea* var. *japonica* (see jacket back). Maekawa mentions that it was undoubtedly introduced from China at one time, but I believe it is an interspecific hybrid with a Japanese species produced long ago because it was described and named by Ono (1847) and may have been known earlier.

Maekawa erroneously lists under the Chinese species *H. plantaginea* a number of European synonyms which clearly belong to his *H. plantaginea* var. *japonica*, so the validity of Maekawa's name *japonica* has been questioned since Hylander (1954) published the name var. *grandiflora* for the same taxon citing the correct synonyms. Both Maekawa (1940) and Hylander (1954), however, cite the same correct synonym by which the valid transfer was made, namely, *H. plantaginea* f. *grandiflora* (Siebold) Matsumura (1905), so Maekawa's name is valid on grounds of priority. His synonymy of the typical Chinese form of *H. plantaginea* (not the variety) has been corrected in Appendix A.

The round-leaved, typical *H. plantaginea*, *Maruba Tama No Kanzashi* (*maruba* means "round leaf") came into Europe directly from China, via Macao, while the Japanese form, *H. plantaginea* var. *japonica* (*Tama No Kanzashi*), was imported from Japan, via Java (Buitenzorg), by von Siebold in 1841.[25]

The *H. 'Elata'/H. montana* Problem

Hosta montana[26] and its many forms are common in extensive areas of Japan; the name is in botanical as well as horticultural use the world over. Notwithstanding, the name *H. montana* has become a point of nomenclatural contention because Maekawa equated the European cultivated taxon *H. bella* Wehrhahn (1936) to his *H. montana* var. *transiens* by listing it in the synonymy of the latter. In the scientific and horticultural literature this is referred to as the *H. 'Elata'/H. montana* problem. According to Hylander (1954), Maekawa's synonymy makes the name *H. montana* illegitimate because *H. bella* Wehrhahn (1936) has priority. Hylander considered, in a broad sense, the two names to apply to different phases of a single taxon, so under the ICBN only the earliest name under this classification is the correct name. Hylander's citation suggests this: "*H. montana* Maekawa . . . (quoad syn. Bail., et pl. in p. 361, fig. 22 depictam et quoad descr. ad hanc pertinentem)—n. illeg. (ob. *Hosta bellam* Wehrh. prius descriptam a Maekawa inclusam)." Undoubtedly, under Hylander's classification *H. montana* is superfluous but not illegitimate, and becomes a metanym, or antedated name (ICBN: Art. 62–72). Incredibly, both Maekawa and Hylander arrived at their theoretical placements without either of them (according to their own admissions) first having studied living material or herbarium specimens of these plants. These botanical proceedings become even more incredible when Hylander, contrary to his own taxonomic arguments, did not adopt the earlier correct name *H. bella* as a name for *H. montana*, but decided to give it the new name *H.* 'Elata', which is obviously also a metanym, so superfluous under his classification as well. *Hosta bella*, on the other hand, was transferred by Hylander as a synonym to *H. fortunei* var. *obscura*, and his taxonomic equation *H.* 'Bella' = *H. montana* = *H.* 'Fortunei' simply makes no sense morphologically.

Today *H.* 'Bella' exists in name only and *H. montana* 'Transiens' cannot be located anywhere in Japan; it was ignored by Ohwi (1965), Maekawa (1969), and Fujita (1976a) as a cultigen not represented in the wild. *Hosta montana*, on the other hand, has major populations of allopatric as well as sympatric character in large areas of Japan. For this reason I am not accepting Hylander's classification and have reclassified the taxa involved. According to the ICBN the metanym *H. montana* may be used in a modified classification and become a correct name for a segregated taxon, viz., *H. montana*. Aside from reasons based in the ICBN, the following arguments were considered:

1. Synonymy requires that the taxa involved have converging morphologies and this is clearly not the case. Maekawa describes *H. montana* var. *transiens* as having 14–15 veins and states it looks like *H.* 'Tokudama', while *H.* 'Elata' has 8–10 veins, according to Hylander. More importantly, *H. montana* has purple anthers and those of *H.* 'Bella' and *H.* 'Elata' are yellow, which confirms they are not the same taxon.

2. Technically, Hylander only made a partial transfer. For the transfer to be applicable in a broad sense to all taxa belonging to the species *H. montana*, it should have been made in the rank of species, but this is not reflected in Hylander's citation—"p.p. (pro parte[!]), quoad syn. Bail. et pl. in p. 361, fig. 22 depictam et quoad descr. hanc[!] pertinentem . . ."—which indicates only a partial application was intended by Hylander based on illustration no. 22 in Maekawa (1940) and parts of the description. *Index Kewensis*, in fact, clearly corroborates that partial application only was intended by citing "p.p." with the name *H. elata*.

3. The name *H. elata* itself may be invalid because it was not published with a Latin diagnosis per the ICBN, and what some might consider (validly published) homonyms (Vilmorin, 1866; Bailey, 1903, 1915) exist against it. Obviously, Hylander cited *H. montana* as the type for his nomen novum *H. elata*, which ordinarily negates the requirement for a Latin diagnosis under the rules. He did, however, not cite the basionym correctly, and it can be argued that his new name requires a Latin diagnosis. *Hosta bella* Wehrhahn, which according to Hylander is the correct name for *H. montana*, was not directly mentioned as a synonym but transferred by him to a segregated taxon, viz., *H. fortunei*.

4. Hylander's assertion that the name *H. montana* is illegitimate is incorrect per the ICBN. It must be considered a metanym when judged on the basis of Hylander's classification, and as such is superfluous (nomen superfluum), but per the ICBN it is not permanently so. More importantly, it is not illegitimate (nomen illegitimum) and may be used under a different classification for segregated taxa under the rules of the ICBN. I have undertaken this reclassification and maintained *H. montana* as the name for the segregated taxon described by Maekawa (1940).

All the authors investigating this problem have followed Hylander without further examination of the taxa involved so were not able to offer a valid solution. Hensen (1983, 1985) suggested rejection of the name *H. montana* based on Fujita's classification, which he in turn did not follow himself. Fujita (1976a) proposes to incorporate *H. montana* in the *H. sieboldiana* complex under *H. sieboldiana* var. *sieboldiana* giving the latter the widest possible taxonomic meaning; this makes him the only taxonomist who sought to replace Maekawa's name. Significantly, he retained *Oba Giboshi* for his *H. sieboldiana* var. *sieboldiana*, which happens to be the Japanese formal name for *H. montana*. Araki (1943), Maekawa (1950, 1969, 1971), Ohwi (1965), and Grenfell (1981) continued the use of the name *H. montana* even if such use was technically inappropriate based on Hylander's classification. Later, Grenfell (1988: private communication) realized this and suggested that the epithet in *H. montana* be enclosed in double quotation marks, thus *H.* "montana", indicating its provisional status until it can be reclassified. Similarly, Hensen (1985) referred to it as "*H. montana*", enclosing the entire name in double quotation marks.

For reasons detailed earlier, the cultigens *H.* 'Bella' and *H.* 'Elata' have been segregated from the natural populations representing the *H. montana* complex, and I have reclassified the latter in Appendix A to permit use of this species name as originally intended by Maekawa (1940).

Additional information about *H.* 'Elata' is given later in this chapter under "Hylander."

The *H.* 'Tardiflora'/*H. sparsa* Relationship
Hosta tardiflora (Irving) Stearn was included by Maekawa in the synonymy of *H. sparsa* as *Funkia japonica* var. *tardiflora*. *Hosta* 'Tardiflora' was not otherwise listed by Maekawa, and this problem is discussed further in my review of Hylander (1954) later in this appendix. Maekawa (1969) dropped the name *H. sparsa* in favor of *H. tardiflora*, realizing the latter's priority, while maintaining the Japanese formal name *Aki Giboshi* used for *H. sparsa*. It appears that European data available to Maekawa after the war years indicated to him the priority of the name *H. tardiflora* in the rank of species, when one considers *H. sparsa* synonymous to *H.* 'Tardiflora'. This is, however, not the case, and I have identified *H. sparsa* as a taxon belonging to *H. longipes* and reclassified it in Appendix A as *H. longipes* f. *sparsa*. *Hosta* 'Tardiflora', only broadly related, has been reduced to cultivar form.

The *H.* 'Lancifolia'/*H. sieboldii*/*H. cathayana* Confusion
Since Miquel (1869), *H. sieboldii* has been classified as a variety under *H.* 'Lancifolia', and all major authors dealing with this problem have followed this classification which is still used by many commercial sources who list *H. sieboldii* as *H. lancifolia* var. (or f.) *albomarginata*. Maekawa also followed this basic arrangement but muddled the placement further by adopting Stearn's *H. lancifolia thunbergii* (Stearn, 1931b), quoting it incorrectly as *H. lancifolia* var. *thunbergiana* and, while citing many of the synonyms for *H.* 'Lancifolia', describing some of the morphological features of *Koba Giboshi*, the green-leaved form of *H. sieboldii*, viz., *H. sieboldii* f. *spathulata*. Maekawa followed previous authors and incorrectly used the hybrid *H.* 'Lancifolia' as the type for the *H. sieboldii* complex including a number of variegated mutant forms of the latter (Yasui, 1929; Pollock, 1984b; Schmid, 1988c).

This classification was finally recognized as erroneous and corrected by Ohwi (1942) who identified *H. sieboldii* (as *H. albomarginata*) as belonging to a species distinct from the sterile *H.* 'Lancifolia'. Only two years later Maekawa (1944) recognized the priority of the name *H. sieboldii* and published the species name *H. lancifolia* var. *thunbergiana* f. *sieboldii* but did not sever its connection to *H*. 'Lancifolia'. Stearn corrected his earlier position in 1953 (in adnot.), followed by Hylander (1954). Ingram (1967) proposed a transfer from *H. albomarginata* to *H. sieboldii* on grounds of priority. Ohwi (1965), while recognizing *H. sieboldii* (as *H. albomarginata*) as a distinct taxon, nevertheless still listed *H*. 'Lancifolia' as a synonym under it; this may account for the fact that *H*. 'Lancifolia' and *H. sieboldii* (as *H. albomarginata*) are still considered the same in Japan. In this case Japanese horticulture has not yet caught up with the valid transfer of *H. albomarginata* and its associated varietal and forma names to *H. sieboldii* made in Japan by Hara in 1984. Unfortunately, Hara also continued to connect *H*. 'Lancifolia' with *H. sieboldii* by listing many of the former's synonyms under the latter (see Hara below).

I consider the European *H*. 'Lancifolia' a taxon of hybrid origin and not consequential to the taxonomy of natural Japanese populations. I have therefore reduced it to cultivar form.

As to what taxon the Japanese formal (academic) name *Koba Giboshi* (*koba* meaning "small leaf") should be applied remains problematic. Maekawa (1940, 1969) used it under the erroneous *H. lancifolia* var. *thunbergiana*, following the wider application most European botanists gave to the name *H*. 'Lancifolia' until recently. In Japan *Koba Giboshi* applies taxonomically (and horticulturally) to a wide range of small-leaved, all-green or variegated hostas reflecting the very broadly based application in Fujita (1976a). Maekawa gave the new formal name *Fukurin Giboshi* to the familiar white-margined *H. sieboldii*, although an earlier formal Japanese name already existed, namely, *Heritori Giboshi* (Makino and Tanaka, 1928). Due to the elimination of *H*. 'Lancifolia' from the keys of naturally occurring taxa in Japan, I am following Japanese nomenclatural practice by adopting Maekawa's *Fukurin Giboshi* for the species *H. sieboldii*, which in Japan is still called *H. albomarginata*, and *Koba Giboshi* in a broad sense for all the botanical forms of *H. sieboldii* growing in the wild. The variegated forms listed by Maekawa (1940, 1969) do not belong to *H*. 'Lancifolia' but to *H. sieboldii*, and Hara (1984) has made all the required formal transfers. In the horticultural literature some of these taxa have been informally reduced to cultivar forms under *H. sieboldii* (Summers, 1984; S. B. Jones in Aden, 1988; Schmid, 1988c). I have undertaken formal reduction to cultivar form in Chapter 3 and Appendix A.

Maekawa (1940) described *H. cathayana* under section *Tardanthae*, giving it the Japanese name *Akikaze Giboshi*. The true taxonomic position of this species has not been realized in earlier reviews, and it is often confused with *H*. 'Lancifolia'. Hylander (1954) included *H. japonica* var. *fortis* (which is *H*. 'Lancifolia' in Bailey, 1931, but *H*. 'Undulata Erromena' in Bailey, 1930) as a synonym under its name, and a number of other botanists and hosta specialists have since come to the same conclusion (Fujita, 1976a; Summers, 1984). This incorrect placement was repeated until just recently by Hensen (1985) who listed *H. cathayana* and *H. tardiva* in the synonymy of *H*. 'Lancifolia'. I consider the fully fertile *H. cathayana* a segregated taxon and not conspecific with the sterile hybrid *H*. 'Lancifolia'; this placement is reflected in Chapter 3 and Appendix A.

There is a yellow variegated form of *H. cathayana* that evolved in Europe and has not been mentioned by Maekawa; it has also been associated with *H*. 'Lancifolia'. Its leaves are clear yellow with a narrow green margin in spring. The yellow fades to a lighter green and is barely visible by late summer. This hosta is a fully fertile mutation of the species now known as *H. cathayana* 'Chinese Sunrise' (*H. cathayana* 'Kinakafu'). Additional variegated forms of *H. cathayana* have been found in the wild, one a fertile, all-yellow form which retains its leaf color.

The Identities of *H. longissima*

One of the many different forms of Maekawa's polymorphic *H. longissima* has been known in Europe since the time of von Siebold, who imported it in 1829 and named it *Funkia lanceolata*. A herbarium specimen in L (no. 908. 106:1023), is named *Sasi Kiboosi*, in von Siebold's own handwriting.

Maekawa lists the Japanese formal names *Mizu Giboshi* and *Sazi Giboshi*, which date back to Iinuma (1856, 1874), under *H. longissima* var. *brevifolia*. Apparently, Maekawa considered this variety to be identical to Iinuma's taxon and consequently to von Siebold's plant named *Sazi Giboshi*. This raises the question why Maekawa chose to separate a variety *brevifolia* from the species *H. longissima* when his diagnoses for either taxon are virtually identical, as Hylander (1954) pointed out. Neither Hylander nor Hensen (1985) listed the variety *brevifolia*, except as a synonym under the specific form *H. longissima*, and Fujita (1976a) also considered them synonymous, so I have maintained these recent placements. Notwithstanding, Maekawa was aware of the wide morphological range this species exhibits in the wild; this must have been his reason for naming two taxa each with its own description. I believe his diagnosis for what he calls *Nagaba Mizu Giboshi* is incorrect as it does not describe the narrow, long-leaved form found among the natural population, which was reported earlier by Honda (1935a) under the varietal epithet *longifolia*. I have emended Maekawa's diagnosis in Appendix A under the new combination *H. longissima* var. *longifolia*, using Honda's name as the basionym. Recent Japanese horticultural publications speak of an "ordinary" type, a "long-leaf" type, several variegated forms, and some with white flowers, deformed flowers, and flowers with petaloid stamens (Sugita, 20 May 1984: personal communcation).

There is also a form of the all-green *H. sieboldii* which has very long, narrow leaves. It is often mistaken for *H. longissima* because superficially it fits Maekawa's diagnosis for var. *brevifolia*; however, it differs in two key respects: It has yellow anthers and its scape is longer with 15 to 20 flowers. This taxon is not a *H. longissima* but is the narrow-leaved form of *H. sieboldii*, previously, and at least in part, known under the names *H. lancifolia* var. *angustifolia* Regel, *H. lancifolia* var. *angustifolia* f. *angustissima* Regel, or *H. japonica* var. *angustifolia*. To place this taxon I have formed the new combination *H. sieboldii* f. *angustifolia* (Regel) Schmid using Regel's (1876) basionym. I believe this form was also known to von Siebold and represents Iinuma's (1856, 1874) *Sazi Giboshi* in part.

The Name *H. rohdeifolia*

Within section *Nipponosta* Maekawa described a hosta under the name "*H. rhodeifolia*." This name was first used by him in 1937. According to Schmid (1988b), its original spelling must be considered an orthographic error and has been corrected in Appendix A. *Omoto Giboshi* is the Japanese formal name for this taxon, with *Omoto* being the Japanese name for *Rohdea japonica*, a broadly related petaloid monocotyledon taxon indigenous to Japan that was formerly placed in the Liliaceae but has recently been reclassified in the Convolariaceae (Mathew, 1987). It was named for Michael Rohde, a physician and naturalist of Bremen, Germany. Maekawa's spelling, viz., *rhodeifolia*, was incorrectly derived from the Greek *rhodon* (rose) and *rhodeifolia* (with leaves like a rose) is obviously orthographically incorrect.

In Japan the margined *H*. 'Rohdeifolia' is considered a mutant cultivar and called *H. rohdeifolia* 'Rohdeifolia'. Only the all-green form described by Maekawa under *H. rohdeifolia* var. *viridis*, *Aoba Omoto Giboshi*, occurs in the wild in Kyoto Prefecture, so is maintained as a botanical form.

A New Species: *H. tibae*

Maekawa (1940) did not include *H. tibae* in section *Tardanthae*, but he published this species name in *Flora Nagasaki* (Toyama, 1940) as a nomen nudum (with a Japanese diagnosis). He included it in his (1969) listing, yet the name was not validated until his 1984 publication. My discovery of two herbarium specimens in L confirms von Siebold collected this species in the mountains surrounding Nagasaki and is detailed in Chapters 3 and 5. Maekawa's spelling *tibai* has been corrected to *tibae* to conform to the ICBN.

The Japanese *H. fortunei*

In Japan *Renge Giboshi* is equivalent to *H. fortunei* (Baker) Bailey, and Maekawa includes this taxon under the name *H. sieboldiana* var. *fortunei* in his classification with all the correct synonyms and excluding *Funkia sieboldiana β fortunei* Regel (= *H.* 'Tokudama'). Maekawa's species name *H. sieboldiana* var. *fortunei*, when applied to *H. fortunei* (Baker) Bailey, must be considered a nomen illegitimum because it is a later homonym of *H. sieboldiana* var. *fortunei* (Regel) Ascherson and Gräbner (1905), which is a synonym for *H.* 'Tokudama' when considered as a variety of *H. sieboldiana*, and thus a different taxon. A serious problem also exists with Maekawa's description: "Round leaves . . . 15–17 pairs of principal veins . . . scape surpassing leaves only a little . . . flowers shiny, white" This obviously does not describe *H.* 'Fortunei' and exactly what taxon Maekawa had in mind is not known, but it appears to be a *H. sieboldiana* form. Complicating matters even more, in Japan the name *Renge Giboshi* has been accepted in horticulture and is applied to *H.* 'Fortunei' and its variegated forms—for example, *H.* 'Fortunei Albomarginata' (from America) is known as *Shirofukurin Renge Giboshi*. Fortunately, the solution to this problem is not crucial to the classification of the genus because, as Maekawa pointed out, his *H. sieboldiana* var. *fortunei* is a cultivar form and as a consequence has been eliminated from the morphological keys.

Maekawa's Cultigens

Hosta montana—Maekawa (1940) mentions four infraspecific forms of this abundant species. *Hosta montana* var. *transiens*, reportedly found in the wild in the mountains of Kyoto and Mie prefectures, apparently represents an intergrading population and was no longer listed by Maekawa in 1969. *Hosta montana* var. *praeflorens* is modified from the very polymorphic, typical form only by its earlier blooming period and was also eliminated by Maekawa in 1969. It should be noted that this taxon is not the hosta cultivated in North America under the name *H. montana* 'Praeflorens' (see Chapter 3). *Hosta montana* var. *liliiflora* is modified only by its more flared, trumpet-shaped perianth, and *H. montana* f. *aureomarginata* is a nonperpetuating, yellow-margined mutant form. All four have been reduced to cultivar forms.

Hosta sieboldiana and *H.* 'Tokudama'—Maekawa (1940) described *H. sieboldiana* var. *hypophylla*, *H. sieboldiana* var. *fortunei*, *H. sieboldiana* var. *amplissima*, and *H. sieboldiana* var. *mira* and also listed all of them in his 1969 treatise. In my opinion these "varieties" represent clones selected from the natural populations of *H. sieboldiana*, which is an extremely polymorphic species. Fujita (1976a) held them to be synonymous to his *H. sieboldiana* var. *sieboldiana*, thereby eliminating them. *Hosta* 'Tokudama' and its variegated forms are clearly garden varieties that are maintained in cultivation only. All Maekawa's varieties belonging to this group are in cultivation in Japan and in Western gardens and have been reduced to cultivar forms.

Hosta nigrescens and *H. fluctuans*—The specific forms described by Maekawa are found in the wild. *Hosta nigrescens* 'Elatior' is a cultivar originating in Yamanaka's Kyoto garden. *Sagae Giboshi*, known in Western gardens as *H. fluctuans* 'Variegated' is a cultivar form and treated as such.

Hosta 'Crispula'—This cultivated form, discussed earlier, is by some considered a mutant cultigen (Summers, 1984). It was found by von Siebold and Pierot as a mutation among the purportedly all-green population in shady mountain valleys of Nagasaki Prefecture (see Chapter 5). It does not come true from seed and I have classified it as a cultivar form.

Hosta 'Hippeastrum' and *H.* 'Sacra'—These taxa classified by Maekawa (1940) in section *Intermediae* are no longer included by Maekawa (1969) and excluded by Fujita (1976a). In Japan they are considered cultivars and as a consequence they are reduced to cultivar forms.

Hosta 'Tortifrons'—This is a mutant form originating with *H. longipes*. It must be vegetatively propagated to maintain its twisted leaf form, so is reduced to cultivar form.

Hosta sieboldii—All variegated forms of *H. sieboldii* are treated as cultivar forms. This obviously includes the white-margined species, which is a nonperpetuating form in the wild. Technically, it is a specioid, but it has been continuously used in taxonomy as the type for the *H. sieboldii* complex, so changing this taxon would cause great difficulties and probably require reclassification of the entire group of species. All previous authors have accepted the historic placement and I also consider it best to continue the present delimitation.

Hosta rohdeifolia and *H.* 'Helonioides'—With the exception of the green-leaved form of *H. rohdeifolia*, which is documented as a wild species on several herbarium sheets (in KYO), all other taxa under these names were eliminated as botanical taxa by Maekawa (1969) and Fujita (1976a). I have reduced them to cultivar forms.

Hosta rectifolia—The white-margined and white-flowered forms of this species are mutant forms that must be asexually propagated to remain true, so are maintained as cultivar forms.

Hosta 'Decorata'—The typical white-margined form of *H.* 'Decorata', *Otafuku Giboshi*, as well as the green-leaved *H.* 'Decorata Normalis', *Midori Otafuku Giboshi*, although treated as a species by most earlier authors, are considered cultivar forms following Maekawa's note on their habitat: "Hab.: Honshu, in hortis colitur [cultivated in gardens]." Fujita (1976a) mentions this taxon and states he could not confirm the existence of natural populations so eliminated it from the keys.

Hosta 'Opipara'—This species name was first listed as a nomen nudum in Maekawa (1937) and published by him (1940). It has several practically identical clones in existence, pointing to a variable cultivar population. It does not come true from seed, is a cultigen, and so is considered a cultivar form.

Section *Foliosae*

Maekawa (1940) states:

> No wild plant has ever been found. The report that it grows on Mount Kurokami, Hizen Province (near Arita, Saga Prefecture), is very doubtful. It may be that a form of it, resembling in shape *H. pachycarpa* [!] (incorrect = *H. pachyscapa*), of section *Intermediae*, exists unknown somewhere in Honshu or Kyushu.

All the taxa belonging to section *Foliosae* are sterile hybrids so have been eliminated from the taxonomic keys. I have reduced them to cultivar forms and as a consequence section *Foliosae* has technically been eliminated from consideration in the classification of the genus.

Brief Comments on Maekawa

Hosta capitata is listed by Maekawa without diagnosis. *Hosta pachycarpa* is mentioned in the introductory text, but this name is an incorrect name for *H. pachyscapa*. *Hosta tardiva* var. *lucida* is included in the introductory text but Maekawa's classification does not reflect this name. *Hosta atropurpurea* is listed by Maekawa without diagnosis. *Hosta rectifolia* var. *sachalinensis* has no description. *Funkia ovata* (var.) *minor* in section *Lamellatae*, collected by Oldham in Korea and described by Baker (1870), is included by Maekawa as a synonym for *H. minor*, but an examination of the type specimen (in K) shows no traces of lamellar ridges on the scape and Baker's diagnosis also does not mention them. Maekawa (1940) included two Japanese formal names under *H. minor*, namely, *Keirin Giboshi* and *Ko Giboshi* (Nakai, 1914). *Ko Giboshi* (Makino, 1910) is also applied to *H. clavata*, which is widely distributed in the mountains of Honshu. Consequently, *H. minor*, *Keirin Giboshi*, is the Korean species described by Maekawa that belongs in section *Lamellatae*, while Baker's (var.) *H. minor* is now impossible to place, but could be related to *Ko Giboshi* = *H. clavata*.

1942—ARAKI "THE NEW HOSTAS OF JAPAN"

Yeiichi Araki (1942, 1943) published diagnoses of several new species. In his 1942 introduction he remarks: "[T]he genus *Hosta* seems to be in a period of mutation, thus many new species will be found," which may allude to his recognition of the state of incomplete divergence and interspecific hybridization in the genus. Araki's field work and accessions centered on the Kinki District of central Honshu, with the new species being indigenous to the prefectures of Gifu, Hyogo, Kyoto, and Shiga.

Araki adopted Maekawa's (1940) sectional classification and intricate morphological flower analysis as a basis for naming new species which may be true species or representatives of intergrading hybrid swarms. Many of the taxa have indicated holotypes (in KYO) and represent wild populations so have been retained as species. As Fujita (1976a) pointed out, some are morphologically very close to other taxa, so he combined them in synonymy.

Araki's epithet *liliiflora* in the rank of species is invalid because the basionym published by Maekawa in 1938 was a nomen nudum and Araki does not provide a valid description. Although Araki provides a diagnosis for var. *ovatolancifolia*, the combination is obviously also invalid. Maekawa (1940) used the name *liliiflora* in varietal rank under *H. montana*, as *H. montana* var. *liliiflora*, with a valid description, but this placement has no priority outside its rank. The latter has been retained as a cultivar form and Araki's invalid types, which are similar to it, are listed in its synonymy. Variety *ovatolancifolia* has been transferred to *H. montana*.

Hosta crassifolia is placed in synonymy under *Oba Giboshi* by Fujita (1976a) who considers it related to *H. montana*. As the epithet (*crassifolia* meaning "thick-leaved") implies, it has leaves of considerable substance, an attribute more normally associated with *H. sieboldiana*. It may be an interspecific hybrid between the latter and *H. montana* because it occurs in Shiga Prefecture of central Honshu where proximal populations of these species exist.

Araki states that *H. aequinoctiiantha* (*Ohigan Giboshi*) is a new species comparable to *H. longipes*, but that it differs from it by being an "exceedingly tiny plant, with thin smaller leaves and by the fewer lateral ribs." Summers (1970) describes this hosta as "an exceedingly tiny plant, with leaves thumbnail size," but in 1985 Summers states the plants were ten times thumbnail size. More recently he wonders if plants collected in the wild may have been under stress which resulted in dwarfing (Summers, 29 July 1985: personal communication).

Fujita (1976a) treated this taxon as a variety of *H. longipes*, and my examination of authentic, living material and the holotype (in KYO) confirms it is a variant of the latter with smaller leaves, 2.5–4 in. (6.5–10 cm), 4–5 pairs of veins, and later blooming period. Because of these distinct differences I have maintained Araki's specific placement, which is confirmed by Maekawa (1969).

Hosta okamotoi (*Okuyama Giboshi*) and *H. takiensis* (*Taki Giboshi*) are regarded by Fujita (1976a) as synonyms of *H. longipes* var. *aequinoctiiantha*, but Maekawa (1969) did not include them, nor did Ohwi (1965). Both undoubtedly belong in section *Picnolepis*, growing lithophytically on rocks and as epiphytes on tree trunks, so Araki's comparison of *H. takiensis* to *H. cathayana* is not accepted. I have examined the holotypes[27] and living plants of both taxa and find enough differences to maintain them as species related to *H. longipes*.

Hosta campanulata (*Tsurigane Giboshi*) and *H. campanulata* var. *parviflora* (*Kobana Tsurigane Giboshi*) were placed by Araki in section *Nipponosta* and declared to be similar to *H. rectifolia*. As the Latinized scientific and Japanese epithets (*campanulata* "bell-shaped"; *tsurigane* "temple bell") indicate, the configuration of the flowers is broadly expanded, ovate, shaped like a Japanese temple bell. Fujita is correct to associate these taxa with *H. sieboldii*, and after examining Araki's type specimens[28] and living material, I have followed Murata (herbarium annotation) and Fujita (1976a) and placed this taxon as a forma under *H. sieboldii*. Variety *parviflora* is identical to the type except for moderately smaller flowers; this slight difference is not adequate to justify taxonomic separation, and the variety has also been included in the synonymy of *H. sieboldii* f. *campanulata*.

Araki assigns *H. calliantha* (*Omoto Giboshi*) to section *Nipponosta* and incorrectly relates it to the sterile *H.* 'Lancifolia' (probably meaning the all-green *H. sieboldii*), but the holotype (in KYO) shows broadly winged petioles like *H. rectifolia* and widely bell-shaped flowers. *Hosta calliantha* is placed with *H. rohdeifolia* by Japanese horticultural authors because the type specimen bears a label linking it with this taxon.[29] I have maintained it as a species because it is morphologically distinct and represents wild populations.

Hosta ibukiensis (*Ibuki Giboshi*) is described by Araki as closely related to *H. sieboldii* and having yellow anthers, so Fujita (1976a) lists this name in the synonymy of *H. sieboldii*. It is similar to the all-green form *H. sieboldii* f. *spathulata*, but there are sufficient differences in the morphology of the bracts and leaves to maintain it as a separate taxon.

Hosta takahashii (*Shihizo Giboshi*) is close to *H. tardiva*, to which Fujita considered it synonymous, but the latter has much narrower leaves with an approximate length-to-width ratio of 3–4:1. *Hosta takahashii* has a 1.5:1 ratio and cordate leaves. I have cultivated authentic, living material and examined the holotype;[30] I consider this to be a macromorphologically distinct taxon which is here retained as a species.

1954—HYLANDER: "THE GENUS *HOSTA* IN SWEDISH GARDENS"

Hylander's research into the genus began in 1945 and culminated with his 1954 study entitled "The Genus *Hosta* in Swedish Gardens—With Contributions to the Taxonomy, Nomenclature, and Botanical History of the Genus." A preliminary review in Swedish preceded this monograph in 1953. Hylander stresses his findings are limited to hostas growing in Swedish gardens, but he contributes substantially to the classification of a number of "European" hostas in cultivation for over a century. More importantly, he covers in great detail all aspects of the early botanical history of the genus in Europe and investigates a number of the taxonomical and nomenclatural conflicts that had developed during that time. His treatise is the most comprehensive in Western botanical literature.

Although his study has been taken as doctrine by some authors, Hylander himself cautioned the scientific community in his introduction: "I am fully aware that my results must still be considered preliminary, even in regard to the limited task I have tried to fulfill," and "the problem whether certain cultivars are true species or interspecific hybrids could only be dealt [with] in a preliminary theoretical manner." Additionally, he was aware that some of the new nomenclature he postulated might subsequently have to be changed, stating "some entities of lower rank, which I have described as new—e.g. within the H. 'Fortunei' complex—may in future be identified with taxa described earlier, and perhaps assigned other names than those I have used." One of these—for example, H. 'Fortunei Obscura Marginata'—is conspecific with H. lancifolia f. aureimarginata Wehrhahn (1934), which has priority in the rank of varietas, and consequently Hylander (1969) changed his 1954 name to H. fortunei var. aureomarginata, which is now considered a cultivar form as H. 'Fortunei Aureomarginata'.

Hylander also explicitly limits his study to cultivated species and hybrids growing in Sweden and states:

> I am not sufficiently acquainted with the genus as a whole to form detailed opinion of the correctness of Maekawa's groupings ... [and] have therefore refrained from classifying the hostas in Swedish gardens according to Maekawa's proposals.

Thus, he clearly distanced himself from dealing with the Japanese natural populations. His findings, nevertheless, directly challenge certain placements in Maekawa's 1940 classifications (these problems were discussed and solved earlier under "Maekawa").

Hylander supports Maekawa (1938a) in regard to a generic classification system, proposing the use of subgenus Giboshi for all the indigenous Japanese hostas and recommending it as the most natural placement in this rank. He suggests H. sieboldiana as the type for this subgenus.

The Sieboldiana Complex

Hylander recognizes the polymorphism of H. sieboldiana in Europe as partly due to the extensive use of seed for propagation and that many of the hostas bearing the name H. sieboldiana are, in fact, not the species in a strict sense or clones of it, but hybrids.[31]

One of these examples is H. sieboldiana 'Elegans', which was raised by Hylander to varietal rank as H. sieboldiana var. elegans. At the time he wrote his study, Hylander was not able to settle the question whether this taxon was in fact the cultivar H. fortunei robusta (Arends, 1905), a hybrid of H. sieboldiana × H. sieboldiana var. fortunei (= H. 'Tokudama'). Later research shows Hylander's var. elegans is in fact Arends' cultivar 'Robusta', so this taxon is treated as a cultivar form and has been eliminated from the systematic keys. Notwithstanding, the cultivar name H. sieboldiana 'Elegans' has been horticulturally transferred to the species H. sieboldiana, giving it a very narrow definition, and quite often the species is cultivated in Europe and North America under the incorrect name 'Elegans'. While the species should not be labeled H. sieboldiana 'Elegans', this cultivar name is perfectly legitimate for the hybrid Arends made, and it has been registered by the AHS. In gardens the popular species itself has taken on an "idealized" morphology that comes very close to what H.

sieboldiana 'Elegans' actually looks like, so many gardeners use the names interchangeably. In fact, few gardeners know what the total morphological character of the species really is and frequently ascribe their own perception of this character. On the other hand, hybridizers have not hesitated to give cultivar names to over 100 selected seedlings and clones of this species which basically look exactly like the idealized image of the species. It should be noted that botanists, including Maekawa and Fujita, give this taxon a much broader interpretation, which more accurately reflects the natural populations and includes nonglaucous, tall-scaped, and green forms (see Maekawa, 1940: Photo 35; also see Figures 3-64, 3-65).

The H. 'Fortunei' Complex

Hylander devoted considerable space to the investigation of a group of hostas now known as the H. 'Fortunei' complex. Some representatives of this group were known to von Siebold and originated in his gardens, where they were identified by different names, viz., Funkia aokii, Funkia aurea, Funkia viridimarginata, and Funkia viridis. Hylander raised these and other obviously hybridized cultivars to varietal rank under the specific name H. fortunei. They do not come true from seed nor are they found in the wild, so they are not true botanical varieties. I have reduced them to cultivar forms. To simplify cut leaf show classification, the AHS has registered a number of names belonging to this complex with the International Registration Authority.

Although there is a specimen in K for H. 'Fortunei', this taxon seems to have disappeared from cultivation, and Hylander notes his search for living material at Kew was futile. In spite of extensive correspondence with botanical institutions and visits to Sweden, England, and Germany, I have been unable to unearth a specimen with direct lineage to H. fortunei (Baker) Bailey. Most of the cultivars obtained and cultivated as H. 'Fortunei' in North America are either H. 'Tokudama' or an all-green form of one of the many variegated H. 'Fortunei' garden varieties. The only taxon which comes, by description and illustration, close to being Hylander's H. 'Fortunei' is H. bella Wehrhahn, and the latter name was included in the synonymy of H. fortunei var. obscura Hylander. I believe that little is gained by changing names long established in horticulture and recognized by gardeners the world over, but for historical reasons I have included H. 'Bella' as a cultivar form— on account of its valid Latin diagnosis and priority. I have used it in a narrow sense as the correct name for H. 'Fortunei Obscura'. The names of individual taxa in Hylander's H. 'Fortunei' complex have been maintained but are written as cultivar forms.

The H. 'Elata' Problem

This problem has been dealt with earlier in this chapter (under "Maekawa"). Hylander states he created his new species from hybrid taxa represented in Sweden "by several clones which differ mainly in the leaf form." He gives as his sources several nurseries in Sweden, obtaining these clones as H. sieboldiana from Alnarp, as H. glauca sieboldii from Sävedalen, and as H. fortunei glauca robusta from Skogsholm. It is evident that Hylander's H. 'Elata' is based on hybridized, cultivated material, and my examination of a number of herbarium specimens (in L, K, UPS, and HB) also shows this quite clearly.

I examined 17 groups of H. 'Elata' in botanic gardens in Sweden, England, and Germany and found considerable macromorphological differences. Hansen and Müssel (1964) identify two different "types," and Summers (1984) reports that H. 'Elata' stock received from Hensen, who worked closely with Hylander, and formerly grown at the Case Estates of the Arnold Arboretum under numbers, varied considerably from one to another. He concludes: "H. 'Elata' is a group or assembly of closely related seedlings arising from cultivation in Europe."

It is no longer possible to trace the ancestry of all the hybrids now lumped under the name *H.* 'Elata'. All have yellow anthers, so *H. sieboldiana*, and probably also *H. fortunei* (Baker) Bailey, are considered part of the gene pool for the group. The close relationship of *H.* 'Elata' and *H. sieboldiana* is also supported with palynological evidence by M. G. Chung and S. B. Jones (1989), who determined identical pollen type RG(III) for both taxa (based on specimens in GA and HB). On the other hand, *H. montana* has purple anthers and it is unlikely that it had anything to do with the creation of this group. I must emphasize that the broad macromorphological relationship of *H.* 'Elata' within section *Helipteroides* is not at all in doubt, but it is very clear that *H.* 'Elata' as described by Hylander is not *H. montana* as diagnosed by Maekawa (1940). Rather it is a collection of hybrids with *H. sieboldiana* lineage. I have refrained from creating a *H.* 'Elata' grex because very little of the material now cultivated under this name has anything to do with the *H.* 'Elata' diagnosed by Hylander.

The name *H. elata* was not new when Hylander applied it as a specific name, albeit superfluously as a metanym. It appears in Vilmorin (1866) and in Bailey (1915) with a very brief description: "*Hosta elata* Hort., bears tall scapes and pale blue flowers." Some researchers may consider this a valid publication in spite of its typification as a cultivated form (i.e., hort., with no author given[32]) because a number of other taxa in the same reference—for example, *H. fortunei* var. *gigantea*—have already been accepted as validly published. Hylander further complicates the placement by including *H. fortunei* var. *gigantea* (Bailey, 1915, 1930) in the synonymy of his *H. elata* (Hylander) because the latter, while broadly related to the *H.* 'Elata' group of hybrids, is nevertheless judged a different taxon by virtue of published descriptions. It can be argued that the earlier *H. elata* (Bailey) has priority and *H. elata* (Hylander), published under an English diagnosis after 1935, might therefore be, per the ICBN, an invalid name (nomen illegitimum). In any case, its use as a metanym makes it superfluous. There is, however, absolutely no impediment to consider the name *H. elata* (Hylander), reduced to cultivar form as *H.* 'Elata', as the name for the cultigen narrowly described by Hylander and to apply it only to the cultivated, hybridized population originating with Hylander in Sweden. All other taxa now cultivated under the name *H.* 'Elata' but not conforming to Hylander's diagnosis—most of them do not—should be given other names.

The *H.* 'Undulata' Complex

Hosta 'Undulata' and its varieties, except *H.* 'Undulata Albomarginata', are confirmed by Hylander and called a "polymorphic, probably hybridogeneous group of sterile clones." He validly publishes *H. undulata* var. *univittata* for the first time, transferring Miquel's 1869 name to *Hosta*. It is rather surprising that it took over 120 years to have the entire complex adequately described in the literature. *Hosta* 'Undulata' was first described by Otto and Dietrich in 1833 under *Funkia*, but their diagnosis was not transferred to Hosta until 90 years later, when Bailey (1923) published on it.

Hosta 'Undulata' is an unstable, sterile hybrid developed in Japan before 1800, as substantiated in Juel (1918) who listed a Thunberg herbarium specimen (in UPS, no. 107, 1797, *Hemerocallis undulata*) dating from the 1790s.

As hybrids the members of this complex no longer figure in the taxonomy of the natural populations and are treated as cultivar forms.

The *H.* 'Lancifolia'/*H. sieboldii* Relationship

Hylander is sometimes credited as having been first to transfer Hooker's *Funckia albomarginata* to *Hosta* by publishing the name in a rather obscure seed list *Delectus Seminum* (Hylander, 1945). There exists, however, an earlier transfer in Ohwi (1942) as *H. albomarginata* (Hooker) Ohwi, and this is the correct citation for the effective transfer of *Funkia albomarginata* to *Hosta albomarginata* and the simultaneous, indirect correction of the erroneous placement *H. lancifolia* var. *albomarginata*.

Hylander uses correct delimitation and describes *H.* 'Lancifolia' as well as *H. sieboldii* (as *H. albomarginata*) with all the correct synonyms, including Stearn's *H. lancifolia* var. *thunbergii* which was used by Maekawa as a basionym for his *H. lancifolia* var. *thunbergiana*. Stearn (1931b) first pointed out the priority status of Paxton's *Hemerocallis sieboldii* over Hooker's *Funkia albomarginata*; Hylander also draws attention to Paxton's priority by citing the earlier publication date (March 1838 vs. May 1838) of the document but declines acceptance of *H. sieboldii* on grounds it would cause endless confusion. He retains Hooker's name as *H. albomarginata* (Hooker) Hylander (1954), but the author's citation should be corrected to "(Hooker) Ohwi" (1942). Following the research of Stearn and Hylander, most European taxonomists considered the separation of the cultigen *H.* 'Lancifolia' from the *H. sieboldii* (usually as *H. albomarginata*) as an accomplished fact, but 40 years later in Japan these distinct taxa were still considered varieties of the same taxon (see Hara, 1984). Even today, in Japanese horticulture *H.* 'Lancifolia' and all-green forms of *H. sieboldii* are called by the same Japanese name, namely, *Koba Giboshi*.

On the other hand, and conflicting with Maekawa (1940, 1969), Hylander still erroneously includes *H. cathayana* in the synonymy of *H.* 'Lancifolia'.

The *H.* 'Tardiflora'/*H. sparsa* Confusion

Hylander repeats Maekawa's error of including *H. sparsa* in the synonymy of *H.* 'Tardiflora'. Hylander's placement of *H. sparsa* with *H.* 'Tardiflora' is not accepted in my classification because Nakai gave his hosta the name *H. sparsa* (from *sparsus* meaning far between, sparse) alluding to its sparse flowering habit, which is depicted by Maekawa as "6 to 13 flowered, sparse." In contradiction, Hylander references Stearn (1953), who reported 12–50 flowers, and described the flowers as "rather numerous and crowded." Stearn described the scape as obliquely ascending at about 45 degrees from the surface. Nakai depicted the scape as erect. These differences were by some considered clonal only, but there is a decisive difference in the color of the anthers, which is deep purple in *H. sparsa* and yellow in *H.* 'Tardiflora'. I have therefore not followed Hylander and Stearn (1953) and reclassified these taxa in Appendix A, the former being placed as a forma under *H. longipes*, the latter being reduced to cultivar form.

The Japanese *H. plantaginea*

Hylander's conclusion that *H. plantaginea* var. *grandiflora* is a distinct variety is correct. This taxon is the Japanese form with elongated leaves which distinguishes it from the round-leaved Chinese form. The name *H. plantaginea* var. *grandiflora* is correctly applied as a synonym for *H. plantaginea* var. *japonica* and a superfluous name as explained earlier under "Maekawa." An excellent illustration labeled *Funkia grandiflora* (Siebold and Zuccarini)[33] ex Lemaire[34] (1846) (see jacket back) confirms that *grandiflora* applies to the Japanese form; it shows characteristic elongated leaves, and was first listed as *Funkia grandiflora* in von Siebold's 1844 catalog. It was brought to Holland by J. Pierot in 1841 as described in Chapter 5. Maekawa (1940) disclosed that the Chinese form—*Maruba Tama No Kanzashi* (*maruba* means round-leaved)—was not in Japan until the 1930s:

344   Appendix B

This plant [the typical *H. plantaginea*] was introduced into Japan recently [1930s] through Europe. It is strange that such a remarkable garden plant, so very widely cultivated in China, was overlooked by its neighbor Japan.

There is a longstanding horticultural problem, however, because the plants which are cultivated in Europe and North America as *H. plantaginea* var. *grandiflora* are none other than the round-leaved Chinese form so are incorrectly named. This incorrect naming goes back to its association with Sprengel's (1825) illegitimate *subcordata* as *Funkia subcordata grandiflora*, a name dating to Miquel (1869) which is even now incorrectly used in horticulture for the Chinese species as *Hosta subcordata grandiflora* hort. (Figure B-1).

1963—HENSEN: THE HOSTAS CULTIVATED IN THE NETHERLANDS

Beginning in the 1950s Karel J. W. Hensen investigated the taxonomy of the *Hosta* assortment cultivated in the Netherlands. Formerly taxonomist at the Agricultural University at Wageningen, Netherlands, one of his first efforts (Hensen, 1960) is a brief listing of hostas followed by "De in Nederland gekweekte Hosta's" (1963a). Additional important contributions were produced later (Hensen 1963b, 1963c, 1970, 1983, 1985).

Hensen's (1963b) study "Identification of the Hostas ("Funkias") Introduced and Cultivated by von Siebold" is the key document concerning the hostas introduced into cultivation by the German doctor and naturalist. Most of Hensen's research has been included in the history dealing with von Siebold in Chapter 5, and I have made frequent reference to this valuable work.

Hensen (1963a) covers a limited subject but is nevertheless important to classification because it provides one key based on vegetative and floral characteristics and another based on vegetative attributes only. The latter is important to horticultural applications, where the minute floral differences the botanist must consider are of less importance. The list is important because of its horticultural synonyms which provide considerable support for the placement of some long-known horticultural varieties; these synonyms are incorporated into the individual descriptions in Chapters 3 and 4.

Hensen continues the use of the name *H. albomarginata*, a position he still adhered to in his 1985 paper. The many variants of *H.* 'Fortunei' listed by him are well known in North America. Some of his nomenclature is now considered incorrect. For example, his cultivar name *H. fortunei* 'Marginato-alba' used for *H.* 'Fortunei Albomarginata' is not supported by the Nomenclature Committee of The American Hosta Society, which prefers *H.* 'Fortunei Albomarginata' because *H.* 'Fortunei Marginato-alba' was used by Bailey (1930), Maekawa (1940), and Hylander (1954) as a synonym for *H.* 'Crispula'.

Hensen's use of the epithet 'Variegata' as applied to variegated cultivars is rather imprecise. *Variegata* provides no information about the specific type of variegation in a leaf when several variegated forms occur within a given species (i.e., *marginata* or *mediovariegata*). Additionally, the epithet *variegata* orginated in most cases as a nomen nudum in horticulture and there is no valid reason for continuing it.

Hensen's 1963 contributions provided important evidence for the further investigation of the history, taxonomy, and classification of the genus *Hosta*. I feel his 1985 study is important enough to be covered separately later in this chapter.

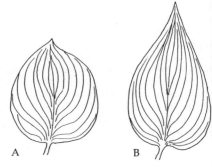

Figure B-1. *H. plantaginea* var. *japonica*; Herbarium specimen in L (1828?) labeled "Hemerocallis Gibbosi v. Sieb." Hylander det. (1953): *H. plantaginea* var. *grandiflora* (top). (A) Average leaf shape of *H. plantaginea*, (B) Elongated leaf shape of *H. plantaginea* var. *japonica* (drawing by author)

1964—HANSEN AND MÜSSEL: A SURVEY OF HOSTAS IN EUROPEAN COMMERCE

The Fachhochschule Weihenstephan at Freising near Munich, Germany, has long been active in researching the genus for horticultural applications. The results of these studies were published in the annual reports for 1963/64 and 1974 (Hansen and Müssel, 1964, 1974). The 1974 study presents a supplement to the 1964 work. Both Hylander (1954) and Hensen (1963a) are referenced.

Weihenstephan houses a collection of hostas in its Staudensichtungsgarten, literally "perennial viewing and trial garden," where the school assembled all the historically important Arends hostas, as well as many of the "classic" hostas of Germany and Europe, which have been growing in this garden for many years. It collaborates with the Munich Botanic Garden, which also houses a notable hosta collection that is very important from the historical perspective.

Both Weihenstephan studies contribute to the rectification of the nomenclature used in German horticulture which was greatly influenced by von Siebold's invalid names (nomina nuda). For example, five different hostas were sold under the name *H. japonica albomarginata*: *H. sieboldii*, *H.* 'Crispula', *H.* 'Decorata', *H.* 'Fortunei Albomarginata', and *H.* 'Undulata Albomarginata'. These studies permit determination of the types sent by von Siebold to his native Germany and their identification and distribution.

Also meaningful are the synonyms which are given in this commentary as they present an overview of the entire synonymy from a somewhat different perspective and add valuable comment. German common names in the synonymy allow identification by German-speaking gardeners:

Hosta sieboldiana (*H. glauca* Stearn), Blaublattfunkie—Polymorphic, imported in several variants, includes seedlings.

Hosta sieboldiana 'Elegans' (*H. fortunei robusta* hort.), Grosse Blaublattfunkie—Five distinct variants, some of which may be seedlings and not necessarily clones, Weihenstephan states.

Hosta tokudama Maekawa (*H. fortunei* hort., *H. glauca* hort., *H. sieboldiana fortunei* Ascherson and Gräbner), Blaue Löffelblattfunkie—"Diese Art könnte... als Zwergform von der *H. sieboldiana* 'Elegans' angesehen werden [this variety could be considered a dwarf form of *H. sieboldiana* 'Elegans']." Further comment on the variegated form indicates that two distinct variants of *H.* 'Tokudama Variegata' exist at Weihenstephan. I examined one of these at the Munich Botanic Garden and it does not look like the form grown in North America as *H.* 'Tokudama Aureonebulosa' but more like *H.* 'Blue Shadows' with somewhat less yellow and more-mottled variegation in the leaf center.

Hosta sieboldiana 'Semperaurea', Dauergoldfunkie—Included in the 1974 report. It is a very large gold-yellow-leaved variety reportedly imported by Foerster from Japan in the 1930s (Fischer, 1983). Not listed is Foerster's Blaue Gelbrandfunkie, *H. sieboldiana fortunei aureomarginata*, a name that appeared in the German literature before 1940. This was a yellow-margined *H. sieboldiana* similar to *H. sieboldiana* 'Frances Williams' which was reported to have grown in the Munich Botanic Garden in the 1930s.[35] It could also have been a margined sport of an intermediate between *H. sieboldiana* and *H.* 'Tokudama'.

Hosta elata Hylander (*H. fortunei gigantea* Bailey), Grüne Riesenfunkie—Special emphasis is placed on the wavy leaf margin and *H. montana* is not mentioned. Also cited is the existence of two "clones"—a wide-leaf and a narrow-leaf form—and it is significant that *H.* 'Elata' is considered a *H.* 'Fortunei'.

Hosta fortunei Bailey (not *H. fortunei* hort.)—No German name or description was given for the type, and there is no plant called *H.* 'Fortunei' (Baker) Bailey in German collections. The *H.* 'Fortunei' hort. sold by German commercial sources is *H.* 'Tokudama'.

Hosta fortunei 'Obscura', Dunkelgrüne Schattenfunkie—The description for this hosta carries the very interesting remark: "Kann als Prototyp für *H. fortunei* gemäss der Beschreibung von Bailey angesehen werden [this hosta can be considered the prototype according to Bailey's diagnosis]." Under the name 'Obscura' the report mentioned *H. fortunei* 'Aureomarginata', Grüne Goldrandfunkie, and *H. fortunei* 'Albomarginata', Grosse Weiss-randfunkie. The latter is described as larger than 'Obscura', with a broad white margin.

Hosta fortunei 'Albopicta', listed by Weihenstephan as *H. fortunei* 'Aureomaculata', Gelbe Grünrandfunkie—According to this study, the core plant for a group of variable cultivars. Bud sporting to golden forms is reported in this group (*H. fortunei* 'Aurea', Frühlingsgoldfunkie) and an unnamed yellow-spotted form with green margin has also been found, as well as the all-green *H. fortunei* 'Viridis' (Frühgrüne Schmalblattfunkie). All these forms apparently come from two original sources, as each of them exists as a wide-leaf and a narrow-leaf form.

Hosta fortunei 'Stenantha' and *H. fortunei* 'Rugosa' (both called Runzelblattfunkie)—Reported to be similar, with wide leaves and more-or-less rugose leaves. This is inaccurate because leaves of cultivar 'Stenantha' are a lighter green, scapes shorter, and the leaflike bracts on the scapes disappear soon after anthesis.

Hosta fortunei 'Hyacinthina', Hyazinthenfunkie—Considered the best form of the *H.* 'Fortunei'.

Hosta crispula (*H. japonica albomarginata* hort., *H. ovata albomarginata* Wehrhahn), Riesen-Weissrandfunkie—All the plants in North America and Europe of this hosta are characterized as being clones of the plant von Siebold imported from Japan.

Hosta undulata Bailey (*H. japonica undulata* Voss), Wellblattfunkie—The several forms listed correspond to the variants in North America exactly: 'Undulata' (Zierrliche Schneefederfunkie, but in the 1964 report incorrectly called Weissgrüne Wellblattfunkie) is the typical plant; 'Univittata', (Schneefederfunkie) with narrow variegation; 'Albomarginata, (Weissgrüne Wellblattfunkie), the typical white-margined form; and 'Erromena' (Grüne Wellblattfunkie), the all-green form.

Hosta decorata Bailey, Ziehrliche Weissrandfunkie—The document states this hosta had been in cultivation in Japan for a long time and was imported into the United States in 1875. This date confirms my own research and coincides with Hogg's return from Japan but unfortunately no source is given for this date. The all-green form is reported to be growing wild in Japan and has been grown at Weihenstephan and at the Munich Botanic Garden, Nymphenburg, for some time.

Hosta albomarginata Hylander 'Albomarginata' (*H. lancifolia* var. *albomarginata* Stearn), Schmale Weissrandfunkie—The white-margined form and the all-green form 'Spathulata' both occur in the wild in Japan according to the study. The white-flowered variety 'Alba' is said to have originated with von Siebold and cultivated in Holland since 1860.

Hosta lancifolia Engler (*H. japonica* Voss), Lanzenfunkie—It is significant that this taxon has been recognized as separate from the *H. sieboldii* complex.

Hosta rectifolia Nakai—Reported as being rare in cultivation, but available from botanic gardens in 1964.

Hosta longissima Honda (*H. japonica* var. *angustifolia* Ascherson and Gräbner), Schmalblattfunkie, also Langblattfunkie—Not much in cultivation. Judging by herbarium specimens of this taxon in UPS, *H. japonica* var. *angustifolia* is not *H. longissima* but a narrow-leaved green form of *H. sieboldii*.

Hosta tardiflora Stearn (*H. lancifolia* var. *tardiflora* hort.), Zwerg-Herbstfunkie—Not much in cultivation in Germany in 1963. The 1974 report lists it as a cultivated variety.

Hosta ventricosa Stearn (*H. cærulea* Trattinnick), Glockenfunkie—The apomictic nature of this taxon was recognized in this work. It was stated that the form

'Aureomaculata' is not found in Germany. Several forms of a smaller *H. ventricosa* appear to be in cultivation in Europe as well as North America. *Hosta ventricosa* 'Minor' listed in the 1974 tabulation probably belongs to this variant.

Hosta plantaginea (*Funkia subcordata* Sprengel), Lilienfunkie— The variety 'Grandiflora' was listed as a garden form with elongated leaves, and this is *Hosta plantaginea* var. *japonica* Maekawa.

Hosta venusta, Zwergfunkie—Mentioned in the 1974 report.

1965—OHWI: *GIBOSHI* ZOKU (*HOSTA* TRATTINNICK)

Jisaburo Ohwi first published on the genus in 1942 when he corrected Maekawa's *H. lancifolia* var. *thunbergiana* f. *albomarginata* to *H. albomarginata*, at the same time changing Maekawa's forms to *H. albomarginata* f. *kabitan*, *H. albomarginata* f. *lancifolia*, *H. albomarginata* f. *mediopicta*, and *H. albomarginata* f. *subchrocea*. This is the first valid correction of Maekawa's *H. lancifolia* var. *thunbergiana* to *H. sieboldii*, albeit under the synonym *H. albomarginata*.

Ohwi (1965) published a translation of *Flora of Japan* and *Flora of Japan—Pteridophyta* (both originally published in Japanese in 1953 and 1957, respectively) under the sponsorship of the Smithsonian Institution, Washington, DC. It includes under Class 2, Angiospermae, Subclass 1, Monocotyledonae, Family 52, Liliaceae, the genus *Hosta* Trattinnick (*Giboshi Zoku*). Ohwi includes the title byline "Treatment based mainly on the monograph by Dr. F. Maekawa," but makes some important changes.

Ohwi does not divide the genus into subgenera and sections along Maekawa's lines but simply catalogs the taxa and provides a morphological key. Ohwi omits many of the cultivated taxa formerly included by Maekawa and does not include taxa originating outside Japan, namely, *H. ventricosa* and the entire section *Stoloniferae*, encompassing *H. clausa*, *H. clausa* var. *normalis*, and *H. clausa* var. *ensata*—all native to Korea and China.[36]

Ohwi considered *H. sparsa* to be identical to *H.* 'Tardiflora' and replaces *H. sparsa* with *H.* 'Tardiflora', probably on grounds of priority, but I do not support this synonymy for the reasons discussed under Maekawa and Hylander. He adds *H. caput-avis* which belongs to section *Rynchophorae* and was not included by Maekawa (1940). Both Maekawa (1969) and Fujita (1976a) retained this taxon, but included it as *H. kikutii* var. *caput-avis*, the rank I have maintained.

Ohwi recognizes the taxonomic problems created by Maekawa's use of the name *H. lancifolia* for the taxon *H. sieboldii*. He eliminates Maekawa's name, viz., *H. lancifolia* var. *thunbergiana*, and substitutes *H. albomarginata* (Hooker) Ohwi—a substitution originally made much earlier (Ohwi, 1942:265), but overlooked by most European botanists. However, Ohwi repeats the error of including most classic synonyms pertaining to *H. lancifolia* Engler, including Thunberg's *Aletris japonica*. *Hosta lancifolia* Engler is not included as a separate entry, reflecting its cultivar status, but importantly, *H. cathayana*, *Akikaze Giboshi*, is listed as a separate species.

The study provides a diagnosis for *H. capitata* which was left out of Maekawa's monograph. The inclusion of this taxon indicates Ohwi agrees with Maekawa that it is an indigenous Japanese plant, contrary to Chung (1990) who considers it Korean. Under section *Foliosae* Ohwi incorporates *H.* 'Undulata Erromena' but excludes *H.* 'Undulata Albomarginata'. Ohwi alludes to the hybridogeneous nature of *H.* 'Undulata Erromena' with the statement: "Known only in cultivation."

1976—FUJITA: "THE GENUS *HOSTA* (*LILIACEAE*) IN JAPAN"

Noboru Fujita (1976a) published a major revision of the genus under the title "The Genus *Hosta* (*Liliaceae*) in Japan." Additional important investigations concerning ecological facts produced by him and considered in this book are listed in the Bibliography under Fujita (1976b, 1978a, 1978b). To fully correlate Fujita's treatment of the genus to other proposals is difficult because of his ecological approach to delimitation. He eliminates or combines many of Maekawa's species. He brings a new viewpoint to the arrangement of the various groups and points out that in this mutable genus, genetic variations based on ecology and geography must be expected within the species; I have elaborated on this in Appendix A. In spite of this expanded methodology, Fujita's system has not been accepted by most Western botanical and horticultural authors, although it has found some acceptance in Japanese horticultural circles.

As an ecologist, Fujita weighs ecological and systematic considerations to the exclusion of possible negative consequences on horticultural nomenclature. He gives the native species the broadest possible interpretation so helps in the very necessary elimination of many cultivated taxa (specioids) from the systematic keys, but his classification is tantamount to the deletion and renaming of quite a number of macromorphologically distinct and horticulturally widely recognized taxa. Further discussion of this subject is in Appendix A.

The trepidations of horticulturists and gardeners viewing Fujita's proposal are easy to understand, because systematics and ecology mean little to them if they are considered without the inclusion of obvious morphological differences as illustrated by the following: To consider *H. montana* synonymous with *H. sieboldiana* var. *sieboldiana* would mean that the very popular *H. sieboldiana* 'Frances Williams' technically becomes synonymous to *H. montana* 'Aureomarginata'. Such an arrangement is obviously unacceptable from a horticultural standpoint and not easily justified on morphological grounds. Likewise *H. nigrescens* and *H. fluctuans* would now be called *H. sieboldiana* var. *glabra*. To other botanists and most horticulturists this "lumping" went too far, because these admittedly broadly related taxa are plainly very distinct and easily recognizable even to untrained eyes and acceptance of Fujita's proposal would cause utter chaos in horticultural nomenclature.

Fujita deals only with native Japanese hostas so omits some of the Chinese species, as well as the Korean species.[37] He ignores all the hostas validly published in Europe as well. Fujita adopted the basic taxonomic framework of Maekawa but makes some fundamental changes within this framework by combining many of the taxa, thus reducing the total number of species to 15, including 3 new species named by him and validly published with diagnosis. Fujita eliminates 27 out of 39 species accounted for by Maekawa.

A New Subgenus Name

Under *Hosta* Trattinnick Fujita designates a new subgeneric name, namely, subgenus *Hosta*, referencing Maekawa's *Niobe* (1940:341). Fujita, following the latest rules of the ICBN, used the subgeneric name *Hosta* for what all other authors call subgenus *Niobe*. According to Article 22 of the ICBN, any subgenus that includes the type of the name of the genus must repeat that generic name as its epithet. Such names are termed autonyms by the ICBN. To bring *Hosta* nomenclature in line with this ruling, I have adopted *Hosta* as a subgeneric name. However, on grounds of its persistent historic use, I am citing the former subgeneric name along with it to draw attention to the required name change. The only other author who adopted the name *Hosta* under the new rules of the ICBN for the subgenus containing *H. plantaginea* is Hensen (1985).

A Combination of Sections

Fujita's proposal to consolidate sections *Helipteroides*, *Rynchophorae*, and *Intermediae* is ecologically well based but macromorphologically and micromorphologically controversial. This recommendation places *H. kikutii* (Hyuga Giboshi), *H. kiyosumiensis* (Kiyosumi Giboshi), and *H. pachyscapa* (Benkei Giboshi) in section *Helipteroides*. I have grown populations of these taxa originating in the wild for a number of years and observed them as wild species; they are distinct, so I have maintained them as separate taxa. I am supported in this by palynological evidence (M. G. Chung and S. B. Jones, 1989; see Appendix A) which shows different pollen subtypes for the various taxa involved. Macromorphological differences include the flower structure and coloration, anther color, shape of bud, sterile bracts, fertile bracts, scapes, racemes, and a number of other obvious differences.

Hosta pycnophylla and *H. hypoleuca* are included by Fujita in section *Helipteroides*. I have placed both in section *Picnolepis*, a placement supported by Maekawa (1984) who initially classified *H. pycnophylla* under this section. *Hosta hypoleuca* is difficult to place but has also been included in this section on macromorphological grounds.

Section *Picnolepis*

Hosta longipes var. *caduca* (Saikoku Iwa Giboshi) is included as a new variety under section *Picnolepis*. This hosta has been previously published as *H. leptophylla* (Usuba Iwa Giboshi) by Maekawa (1950), but this binomial is a nomen nudum. Fujita states he used this name for forms of var. *H. longipes* var. *gracillima* growing in Shikoku, but the diagnosis describes a much larger hosta, which may nevertheless be related. In Japanese horticulture *Usuba Iwa Giboshi*, growing in Aichi Prefecture, Honshu, is still considered separate from Fujita's *H. longipes* var. *caduca* (Watanabe, 1985).

Section *Nipponosta*

Within *H. sieboldii* (as *H. albomarginata*) Fujita assembled a great many hostas, most of which are correctly placed with this complex in a broad sense. Some of the inclusions made are clearly incorrect, however; for example, *H.* 'Lancifolia', a sterile cultivar form not related to *H. sieboldii* has been discussed earlier under Maekawa and Hylander. According to M. G. Chung and S. B. Jones (1989), *H. rectifolia* pollen is Type RG(IV) and *H. sieboldii* Type RG(II-B), so separation for these taxa is supported on palynological grounds as well as anther coloration, which is yellow in the latter and purple in the former.

Section *Tardanthae*

Hosta pulchella, a new species found in a single, remote location in Oita Prefecture on Mount Sobosan at altitude 1600 m (5250 ft.), is included in this section by Fujita. It flowers early in June/July so this placement is questioned.

Hosta cathayana and *H. takahashii* are included in the synonymy of *H. tardiva*. Although there is a morphological resemblance, *H. cathayana* is a much smaller plant than *H. tardiva*. Fujita considers the latter a taxon that may have originated in cultivation and from there escaped into roadsides and fields near human habitations in Shikoku, where it can be found. He further states: "Elsewhere it is definitely a cultivated plant." It must be propagated by human intervention because it is a sterile triploid (Kaneko, 1968a). On the other hand, *H. cathayana* and *H. takahashii* are quite fertile diploids and for this reason I have maintained them as segregated taxa.

Hosta tsushimensis is another new species included in this section. The only synonym given is *H. minor*, but not in the

sense of Nakai. Initially, the taxa on Tsushima Island were called *H. minor*, but they do not have ridged scapes so are not conspecific with *H. minor* growing in southwestern Korea and belonging to section *Lamellatae*. Fujita reported that his species *H. tsushimensis* has flowers that vary in color; near white as well as lavender-colored flowers have been observed. The natural populations are quite polymorphic. A "tri-color" cultivar *H. tsushimensis* 'Sanshoku' is being cultivated in North America (see Chapter 3). Chung (1990) reports that convincing biosystematic evidence links *H. tsushimensis* with *H. jonesii* occurring on the southern Korean island. Macromorphological evidence points to *H. tibae*, growing in northern Kyushu, as also belonging to this group.

Fujita contributes key information to the understanding of the indigenous Japanese hostas. His research is very important to those who seek to simplify the delimitation of the genus by eliminating validly described horticultural hybrids and cultivar forms (specioids). His ecological viewpoint gives a better understanding of the mechanism of interspecific and intraspecific natural hybridization patterns. The addition of several species and clarification of the taxonomy of existing taxa in his valuable work provides much-needed, new information on the genus.

1981—GRENFELL: "A SURVEY OF THE GENUS *HOSTA*"

Diana Grenfell (1981) produced a treatise entitled "A Survey of the Genus *Hosta* and Its Availability in Commerce," which is a detailed horticultural survey. It is based on the classification of Maekawa and mirrors it very accurately in regard to botanical species and varieties. The survey also presents descriptions of a number of cultivars and provides a thorough inventory of the *H.* 'Fortunei' complex. Following is a short analysis concerning debatable comments.

In the sectional treatment, Grenfell recounts the unverified reports of members of section *Foliosae*, viz., *H.* 'Undulata' growing on Mount "Kurami." The correct name is Mount Kurokami, in the old province of Hizen, Saga Prefecture. Maekawa (1940:338) and other authors have repudiated this report.

Grenfell still lists *H. sieboldii* as *H. albomarginata*, but points out that *H. sieboldii* is the correct name. Her comment relating *H. sieboldii* to the sterile *H.* 'Lancifolia' is incorrect as pointed out in my examination of Maekawa.

The survey lists *H. caput-avis* in the rank of species. Both Maekawa (1950) and Fujita (1976a) reduced this taxon to a botanical variety, a placement accepted by me.

Hosta 'Elata' and *H. montana* are listed as separate species, but the inclusion of *H. fortunei* var. *gigantea* as a synonym of *H. montana* is questionable.

In her discourse of *H. hypoleuca* she cites Suzuki as the author of the name. The correct citation is Murata (1962). The type specimen—no. 6645 in KYO—was also collected by Murata in Miwa-mura, Province Mikawa. *Hosta* 'Tardiflora' and *H. sparsa* are incorrectly listed as synonyms (see Maekawa).

The name *H. venusta yakusimana* mentioned by Grenfell is not botanically valid, but is the invention of the Japanese nursery trade. It is well known that the epithets *yakusimana* and *yakusimensis* are used frequently in Japanese horticulture to signify smallness. In 1988 I inspected specimens labeled *H. venusta* in England, but they turned out to be *Yakushima Mizu Giboshi*, a Japanese cultivar similar to *H. gracillima* but lacking the ridges on the scape and therefore not *H. venusta*.

Grenfell's survey is a highly useful document to horticulturists and gardeners. Its descriptions are concise and easily understood and address the requirements of gardeners. Especially helpful is the inclusion of a number of English cultivars.

1984—HARA: THE *H. SIEBOLDII* COMPLEX

The priority of *H. sieboldii* over *H. albomarginata* has been pointed out by several authors, starting with Stearn (1931b), followed by Hylander (1954), and, finally, Ingram (1967), who formally proposed the name change. This proposed transfer of names has been debated by botanists and horticulturists ever since. Nevertheless, even before Ingram's proposal, Maekawa (1950) recognized the name *H. sieboldii* and cited *H. sieboldii* as *H. lancifolia* var. *thunbergiana* f. *sieboldii*. The rules of priority under Article 11 of the ICBN were followed eventually and the name *H. sieboldii* is now considered correct. Unfortunately, nomenclature is slow to change and in North America and Europe, as well as in Japan, the species is still called *H. albomarginata* in disregard of the valid transfers made by Hara in 1984, writing in the *Journal of Japanese Botany*, vol. 59, no. 6. Regrettably, the basic system of delimitation on which these transfers were based was that of Fujita (1976a), so they reflect the very broad-based synonymy advocated by the latter. The following varietal and forma names were transferred to the species *H. sieboldii* with Hara's synonyms and/or basionyms given in parenthesis and, where required, I have included the correct synonym with respect to the classification which I have followed:

Hosta sieboldii (*Hemerocallis sieboldii*, Paxton).

H. sieboldii var. *sieboldii*.
    H. sieboldii var. *sieboldii* f. *sieboldii* (*Hemerocallis sieboldii*) = *Hosta sieboldii*.
    H. sieboldii var. *sieboldii* f. *alba* (*Funkia lancifolia* [var.] *alba*) = *Hosta sieboldii* 'Alba'.
    H. sieboldii var. *sieboldii* f. *kabitan* (*H. lancifolia* f. *kabitan*) = *H. sieboldii* 'Kabitan'.
    H. sieboldii var. *sieboldii* f. *lancifolia* (*Funkia ovata* var. g. *lancifolia*) = *Hosta* 'Lancifolia'.
    H. sieboldii var. *sieboldii* f. *mediopicta* (*H. lancifolia* f. *mediopicta*) = *H. sieboldii* 'Mediopicta'.
    H. sieboldii var. *sieboldii* f. *okamii* (*H. okamii*) = *H sieboldii* f. *okamii*.
    H. sieboldii var. *sieboldii* f. *polycarpellata* (*H. lancifolia* f. *polycarpellata*) = *H. sieboldii* f. *spathulata*.
    H. sieboldii var. *sieboldii* f. *subchrocea* (*H. lancifolia* f. *subchrocea*) = *H. sieboldii* 'Subcrocea'.
H. sieboldii var. *intermedia* (*H. japonica* var. *intermedia*) = *H. clavata*.
H. sieboldii var. *rectifolia* (*H. rectifolia*) = *H. rectifolia*.
    H. sieboldii var. *rectifolia* f. *albiflora* (*H. rectifolia* var. *albiflora*) = *H. rectifolia* 'Albiflora'.
    H. sieboldii var. *rectifolia* f. *atropurpurea* (*H. atropurpurea*) = *H. atropurpurea*.
    H. sieboldii var. *rectifolia* f. *chionea* (*H. rectifolia* var. *chionea*) = *H. rectifolia* 'Chionea'.
    H. sieboldii var. *rectifolia* f. *leucantha* (*H. rectifolia* var. *leucantha*) = *H. rectifolia* 'Albiflora'.
    H. sieboldii var. *rectifolia* f. *pruinosa* (*H. rectifolia* var. *pruinosa*) = *H. rectifolia* var. *pruinosa*.

Some of Hara's synonyms are problematic: *Funkia ovata* var. g. *lancifolia* Miquel (1869) is listed as a synonym under *Hosta sieboldii* var. *sieboldii* f. *lancifolia* (Miquel) Hara. Hylander (1954), working with von Siebold's and Miquel's dried material from the Rijksherbarium, Leiden, determined the former to be synonymous with *H. longissima*. My examination of the same herbarium material corroborates Hylander's determination. Although Miquel lists most of the synonyms found under *H. lancifolia* Engler, according to his description and herbarium material, the taxon is plainly *H. longissima*. I

would like to add, however, that it could also be *H. sieboldii* f. *angustifolia*, which, with exception of its yellow anthers (the former's are purple), has a similar morphology, but an exact determination cannot be made from dried material. Hara's use of Miquel's synonym casts doubt on the actual identity of this taxon. If it does represent *H.* 'Lancifolia', then the correct basionym for this taxon is *H. lancifolia* Engler.

Hara made all the correct transfers, but his inclusion of *H. lancifolia* as a forma under *H. sieboldii* marks the first time in over 125 years that *H. sieboldii* has been elected the species under which *H. lancifolia* now becomes a forma, reversing the traditional role in which the former was included as a taxon of lower rank under *H.* 'Lancifolia', as, for example, in *H. lancifolia* f. *albomarginata*. But Hara failed to recognize that *H.* 'Lancifolia' is a sterile hybrid taxon that does not belong to *H. sieboldii*, so his application in synonymy is incorrect and, in any case, no longer important because *H.* 'Lancifolia' has been reduced to cultivar form. The separation of synonyms applying to *H.* 'Lancifolia' and *H. sieboldii* respectively, undertaken by Hylander (1954), has been augmented by me with respect to Hara's synonyms.

Hosta japonica var. *intermedia* is used a synonym for *H. sieboldii* var. *intermedia*, and Maekawa (1938a) also employs the epithet *intermedia* in the rank of species as *H. intermedia* (Makino) Maekawa. A short time later, he named a new taxon, namely, *H. clavata* Maekawa (1940), and transferred *H. japonica* var. *intermedia* to it, apparently realizing that the name *H. japonica* has been widely and persistently used for other taxa not including its type; its application here is incorrect. I have maintained Maekawa's name *H. clavata*.

I am not accepting Hara's placement of taxa belonging to the *H. rectifolia* complex as belonging to *H. sieboldii* in a strict sense as implied by some of Hara's transfers which follow the basic system used by Fujita (1976a). Macromorphological and micromorphological evidence suggests the existence of three major groups within section *Nipponosta*: (1) *H. sieboldii*, (2) *H. longissima*, and (3) *H. rectifolia*. According to M. G. Chung and S. B. Jones (1989), *H. rectifolia* pollen is Type RG(IV) and *H. sieboldii*, Type RG(II-B), so separation of these taxa is supported by palynology as well as anther coloration which is yellow in the latter and purple in the former. Preliminary flavonoid chemosystematic evidence (Currie, 1988: personal communication) also supports separation. Consequently, under my classification all taxa previously classified (by Maekawa) under *H. rectifolia* remain with this species and their transfer to *H. sieboldii* proposed by Fujita (1976a) and undertaken by Hara is not accepted here.

Hosta atropurpurea occupies an intermediate position macromorphologically, having yellow anthers but otherwise typical *H. rectifolia* morphology, so has been maintained as a species. It may yet turn out to be an interspecific hybrid but further field studies are needed.

All the variegated and white-flowered taxa listed by Hara have been reduced to cultivar forms because they are non-perpetuating in the wild and must be vegetatively propagated to retain their characteristics. Although no longer important to taxonomy, these taxa are very important in horticulture so a brief inventory and comparison of Maekawa's and Hara's variegated forms are helpful: Both botanists include *H. sieboldii* 'Alba', *H. sieboldii* 'Kabitan', *H. sieboldii* 'Mediopicta', and *H. sieboldii* 'Subcrocea'. The latter cultivar name appears in a slightly modified form identical to that registered with the IRA because the epithet *subchrocea* turns out to be an orthographic error (Pollock, 1984e) so has been changed. Maekawa (1969) added two new forms under Japanese formal names: *Bunchoko Giboshi* and *Kifukurin Giboshi*. The former, not dealt with by Hara, has been transferred by me to *H. sieboldii* and reduced to cultivar form. The latter's identity is in doubt; it may be *H.*

'Rohdeifolia'. There are, however, a number of cultivars with yellowish margins closely related to *H. sieboldii* and these are described in Chapter 3 under the cultivar name *H. sieboldii* 'Kifukurin'. One confounding problem remains: *H. sieboldii* f. *subchrocea* is *Shirokabitan Giboshi* and is described as a yellow taxon by Maekawa (1940) when, in fact, plants received from Japan under the latter Japanese name have white leaf centers with green margins, similar to the plant grown in North America under the cultivar name *H.* 'Haku Chu Han'. The Japanese formal name *shirokabitan* which means "White Kabitan", is a fitting descriptive name because the leaves of the latter are just like *H. sieboldii* 'Kabitan' except with white leaf centers instead of yellow ones. The name *H.* 'White Kabitan', however, is merely a translation of *shirokabitan*, so is not a useful name for a segregated taxon under the rules of the ICNCP. As a consequence I have assigned a new cultivar name, viz., *H. sieboldii* 'Silver Kabitan' (which see in Chapters 3 and 4). None of my Japanese contacts have been able to provide a solution to this problem. Interpreting data by Watanabe (1985) shows that in Japanese horticulture Maekawa's yellow *H. sieboldii* f. *subchrocea* is not *Shirokabitan Giboshi* but *Ogon Koba Giboshi*. The Japanese names have, of course, no standing in botany, and all the taxa involved have been reduced to cultivar forms, so I have made a correction under the ICNCP. *Hosta sieboldii* f. *subchrocea* is taxonomically linked to Maekawa's very brief diagnosis ("folia aureovariegata margine valde undulata"), which describes a yellow-leaved taxon, so in Chapter 3 I have retained the botanical name (in cultivar form) as applying to the yellow form *Ogon Koba Giboshi*. *Shirokabitan Giboshi*, on the other hand, as used by Japanese horticulturists, has taken on a completely different meaning; such usage is technically incorrect so, to avoid confusion, I recommend use of the new cultivar name *H. sieboldii* 'Silver Kabitan', at least in Western gardens.

Hara's contribution is very important because it comprehensively corrected the nomenclature of the *H. sieboldii* complex in regard to the specific name; his transfers helped end a nomenclatural muddle that has persisted for over a century.

1984—KITCHINGMAN: "*HOSTA*—A NOMENCLATURE STUDY"

Kitchingman (1984) published a brief survey on nomenclature. He pulled together key information from scientific sources and the experience and opinions of many of today's hosta authorities.

Commentary on this survey was provided by Schmid and Pollock (1985),[38] giving additional information to Kitchingman's survey and correcting a number of errors. Both papers are available from the British Hosta and Hemerocallis Society.[39]

1985—HENSEN: "A STUDY OF THE TAXONOMY OF CULTIVATED HOSTAS"

After a hiatus of 22 years, Hensen published again on the genus; his 1985 work includes only the hostas cultivated in the collections at the Agricultural University at Wageningen, Netherlands, which were available to him for study, and some recently named cultivars.

Hensen bases his survey on the classification of Maekawa, in combination with Hylander's contributions, and comments on his reasons for declining acceptance of Fujita's new classification.

A tabulation of key morphological criteria required for identification and classification are included by Hensen. Most important is his brief mention of the significance of the coloration of the anthers. I have briefly discussed this matter in the introduction to Chapter 3 and used this morphological attribute in cases where taxonomic disagreements required additional data for conclusions. Hensen concludes that (all?) putative hybrids have purple anthers, but my own investigation has shown this is not always the case. Hensen also incorporates sprouting as one of the key considerations. He did not, however, include sprout pigmentation as one of the salient features for identification although it may be another of the useful features for classification; more study is needed.

Hensen is the only recent author to adopt Fujita's correction of the subgeneric name *Hosta* for the subgenus containing the generic type species *H. plantaginea*, as required by the ICBN. Further comment on this matter was given earlier under Fujita.

Hensen presents *H. sieboldiana* 'Elegans' and *H. sieboldiana* 'Robusta' as separate varieties, but they are the same. The cultivar 'Robusta', originated by Arends (1905), was renamed 'Elegans' by Hylander who listed the earlier cultivar name 'Robusta' in its synonymy. I compared type I and type II of Hylander's *H. sieboldiana* 'Elegans' growing at Uppsala, Sweden, with *H.* 'Fortunei Robusta' received directly from Arends and growing at the Staudensichtungsgarten, Weihenstephan, near Freising, Bavaria, Germany, and their morphological match was evident.

In section *Picnolepis*, Hensen considers *H. rupifraga* as synonymous to *H. longipes* var. *latifolia*. This synonymy, originating with Fujita (1976a), has not been confirmed. Correspondingly, the synonymy of *H.* 'Tardiflora' with *H. sparsa* is incorrect, as explained under Maekawa.

Hensen corrects a nomenclature problem that has long existed with the placement of *H.* 'Lancifolia' in section *Nipponosta*; he suggests changing it to section *Tardanthae*, which is taxonomically correct; I have followed this arrangement but eliminated the taxon from the systematic keys. Hensen put *H. cathayana* in synonymy with *H.* 'Lancifolia', which is incorrect for reasons explained earlier under Maekawa.

Hensen also suggests an epithet (i.e., *spathulata*) for the common green-leaved form of *H. sieboldii* which has had many different names, all incorrect, among them *H. lancifolia* var. *thunbergiana* and *H. lancifolia* f. *viridis*. Von Siebold named it *Funkia spathulata*, which was published as a nomen nudum in 1860. Miquel included it as *Funkia ovata* f. *spathulata* in 1869. Valid specimens of these could not be found by Hensen at Leiden Herbarium, so Hensen provides several neotypes now in WAG. Unfortunately he characterizes this taxon as having 5–7 pairs of veins, which is incorrect for *H. sieboldii*, which has 3–4 pairs, so his determination as well as his lectotypification are here considered incorrect and based on misinterpretation. As a consequence, a new lectotype has been assigned in accordance with Article 8 of the ICBN, selected from North American material originating in Japan and supplied by Mrs. Fisher to Hensen, who, in fact, referred to it but did not use it. Several specimens of this taxon are in BH, from which a lectotype has been selected. The specimen is now labelled *H. longissima*, but this determination is incorrect macromorphologically. Hensen has not favored the name *H. sieboldii*, and he published his new name for the all-green form of the latter under *H. albomarginata* f. *spathulata* (Miquel) Hensen (1963b). Following Hensen I have transferred his name to *H. sieboldii* in Appendix A.

Hensen's work on the genus *Hosta* is most important to *Hosta* nomenclature, and he has been instrumental in the resolution of difficult taxonomical problems.

1985—WATANABE: *THE OBSERVATION AND CULTIVATION OF* HOSTA

Kenji Watanabe is a well-known hybridizer and master gardener of the Gotemba Nouen, a Japanese *Hosta* exhibition nursery (Pratt, 1986). Gotemba is a small town on the east flank of Fuji-san (Mount Fujiyama). Watanabe's book, although not a scientific treatise, is nevertheless a very important Japanese language contribution to the understanding of the indigenous Japanese wild and cultivated hostas. With few exceptions, Japanese botanists mentioned little about variegated forms found in the wild or cultivars of obvious hybrid origin. Watanabe, who has made many observation trips, has extensively studied the genus in the wild, and his detailed report is extremely valuable to students of the genus. Aided by his sons, he discovered many variegated, wild forms which are undoubtedly bud mutations of described species and intra- or interspecific hybrid swarms. A number of them have been given Japanese cultivar names and are detailed in Chapters 3 and 4.

Watanabe includes information on history, morphology, nomenclature, and cultivation. He accounts for most of the names previously published by Japanese authors and adds a number of names of horticultural standing. All are briefly diagnosed. His analysis of the Japanese nomenclature as compared to Western hosta nomenclature clears up some misunderstandings. It should be remembered that many of the Japanese imports arriving in the United States in the 1950s and 1960s were without names or carried names given by Japanese nurserypersons and, regrettably, as a consequence, some of these hostas carry different names in the West.

As in the West, nomenclature is also a problem in Japan. Watanabe's inclusion of corrections for duplicate and erroneous Japanese metaphorical names resolves a number of questions and materially aids in the identification of specimens arriving from Japan under some of these epithets, so they have been included in Chapters 3 and 4 as synonyms. Most of the morphological information was presented by arranging the taxa into groups by size, without regard to botanical classification.

Watanabe has also contributed a number of articles to the Japanese horticultural press, including the *Journal of the Japan Horticultural Society* (1984).

1988—ADEN: *THE HOSTA BOOK*

The first English language book devoted entirely to the genus *Hosta* (but including some companion plants) was published in 1988 by Timber Press under the title *The* Hosta *Book*. It was edited and compiled by Paul Aden, a well-known hybridizer, who wrote six chapters, with the remaining eight chapters contributed by Dr. Lillian Eichelberger Cannon, John Elsley, Harold Epstein, Nora Fields, Mabel Maria Herweg, Yoshimichi Hirose, Dr. Samuel B. Jones, Jr., Graham Stuart Thomas, and Andre Viette.

With 133 pages lavishly illustrated on fine paper, the book deals with basic information concerning the genus, covering nomenclature, landscape uses, and hybridizing, as well as other elementary subjects. It serves its purpose well and is recommended to all *Hosta* enthusiasts.

1989/1990—M. G. CHUNG: *HOSTA* PALYNOLOGY AND BIOSYSTEMATICS

Field studies and accessions of *Hosta* populations on the Korean peninsula and the offshore islands of this region in 1985–1988 by Dr. Myong Gi Chung led to the naming of a new species, *H. jonesii*, and to several important papers on the palynology (pollen morphology) and enzyme systems analysis using starch gel electrophoresis. These studies were carried out at the Department of Botany, University of Georgia, USA, under the direction of Dr. S. B. Jones, who coauthored some of the work.

In 1989 Chung, in collaboration with Jones, published a study entitled "Pollen Morphology of *Hosta* Tratt. (Funkiaceae) and Related Genera." This work represents a limited but very pivotal look at the importance of pollen morphology to the classification of the genus; the results of this study have been incorporated in this book and are detailed in Appendix A—Part 1. Also in 1989, Chung named a new Korean species, *H. jonesii*, which is included in Chapter 3 and Appendix A.

The most recent investigations by Chung (1990) deal with the biosystematics of the Korean taxa and will be published during 1991 in several journals. A prepublication copy received from M. G. Chung through the courtesy of Dr. S. B. Jones is entitled "A Biosystematic Study on the genus *Hosta* (Liliaceae/Funkiaceae) in Korea." The study contains three parts: (1) *H. jonesii*, (2) Morphometric and Isozyme Analysis of the Genus *Hosta*, Trattinnick, and (3) Isozyme Variation Within and Among Populations of *Hosta* in Korea.

As pointed out in Appendix A, the genus has never been comprehensively reviewed from a taxonomic viewpoint and all the scientific efforts to date hinge on macromorphological concepts. Chung's valuable contributions are the first applications of biosystematics (starch gel electrophoresis) to the classification of the genus. His palynological work is preceded only by general Korean studies, and so can be considered the first detailed pollen study. Although only a limited number of taxa were subjected to pollen analysis and the enzyme system variations were investigated for only the species native to Korea and Tsushima Island, these efforts are nevertheless extremely important to *Hosta* taxonomy and classification and have a decisive impact on the evolutionary understanding of the genus. It is hoped Chung's work will encourage other researchers to apply modern analytical methods to further examine the genus, particularly as far as the Japanese populations are concerned.

The results of Chung's 1989 and 1990 investigations have been considered throughout this work.

1990—GRENFELL: *HOSTA: THE FLOWERING FOLIAGE PLANT*

Diana Grenfell's initial, pioneering contributions and her 1981 horticultural survey are covered earlier in this Appendix and in Chapter 5.

Grenfell's valuable horticultural treatment of the genus was released by Batsford Books, London, in 1990, under the title *Hosta: The Flowering Foliage Plant*. In North America the book is copublished by Timber Press. It begins with a detailed chapter on the historical development of hostas, including the early collectors who brought the native Japanese and Chinese plants into Western cultivation. This is followed by an extensive treatise on the problems encountered with early attempts by botanists and taxonomists to classify the genus and the resulting confusion in nomenclature. The work of specialists who have contributed to the introduction and use of hostas in gardens is also covered in great detail.

Another large part of the volume offers basic descriptions for over 140 cultivars which the author considers good garden plants, including a few which have historic and botanical interest or are of particular interest to collectors. This is followed by a chapter devoted to the uses of hostas, covering the use of hosta leaves in flower arranging and dealing with landscape use by describing several gardens in Britain and North America in which hostas are grown extensively and well. I have visited several of the English gardens discussed, including Apple Court, the author's garden; Spinners; Hadspen House; and Savill Garden, all good choices in my opinion and worth seeing. These and several others mentioned exemplify the use of hostas in the landscape, as does the one private garden included from North America, which I have mentioned in Chapter 6 of the present volume, namely the garden of Dr. Warren I. and Ali Pollock. The Hosta Reference Collection at the Landscape Arboretum of the University of Minnesota, Chanhassen, MN, USA, is also represented, as are the comparable British National Reference Collections, which I have covered in Chapter 5. Following are separate chapters on cultivation and propagation and how to fight pests and diseases which occasionally plague hosta plantings. A list of hosta suppliers follows, together with an unfortunately very abbreviated bibliography which does not include all sources referred to in the text.

By far the largest part of the book is dedicated to an extensive treatment of the *Hosta* species, marking the first time that all species have been included in a horticultural treatise and consigned to the various subgenera and sections. Grenfell

supports the arrangement of the genus into three subgenera first proposed by me in 1988 (Schmid, 1988b). She also endorses the placement of *H. montana* as the type for subgenus *Giboshi*, representing the native Japanese taxa. In general, Grenfell's subgeneric and sectional classification follows Maekawa (1937, 1938a, 1938b, 1940, 1969), Fujita (1976a; in part), and Schmid (1988b).

A few of the author's placements are not in accord with current taxonomic positions. As an example, Grenfell includes *H. jonesii* in section *Arachnanthae* (Schmid) but this section only encompasses *H. yingeri* and *H. laevigata*. M. G. Chung has placed *H. jonesii* in section *Tardanthae*, a position maintained in this book, so Grenfell's synonymy of *H. laevigata* with *H. jonesii* deviates from the original placements.

Diana Grenfell's contributions to the knowledge of the genus have been extensive (see Chapter 5). Quoting from the introduction, her book is "for those whose interest in the genus has already been awakened, who need to know about hostas now and who may not want to wait a decade or more until the taxonomists have completed their researches" (Grenfell, 1990:19). Her book will assist gardeners and horticulturists for many years to come and undoubtedly will be a key reference in the horticultural hosta literature.

APPENDIX C

AHS Awards, Cut-Leaf Show Schedule, and Leaf Sizes

AMERICAN HOSTA SOCIETY EXHIBITIONS

The AHS holds annual shows at the site of the national convention. These exhibitions are usually divided into three divisions: Division I, Horticulture, is the horticultural event featuring the cut-leaf show competition; Division II, Artistic Design, embraces the art of flower arranging with hosta leaves incorporated into the designs; and Division III which consists of Section 1, Educational Exhibits, and Section 2, Container Grown Hostas.

Awards are given in all these divisions and also for outstanding hostas in tour gardens as well as for landscape design. There are three basic groups of major AHS awards: (1) Tour Garden Awards, marked *"TGA"* in the following listing; (2) Cut-Leaf Show Awards, including artistic design awards, identified with *"CSA"*; and (3) Special and Service Awards, indicated by *"SPA."*

AMERICAN HOSTA SOCIETY AWARDS

Eunice Fisher Award (EFA) *(TGA)*.

Established in 1972, the EFA honors the first secretary-treasurer of the AHS, the late Mrs. Glen (Eunice) Fisher of Oshkosh, WI. It is awarded for the best *large*-leaved, registered cultivar growing in an AHS national convention tour garden and selected by vote of the convention attendees. The walnut plaque is awarded to the hybridizer or introducer of the winning cultivar for permanent retention.

Nancy Minks Award (NMA) *(TGA)*.

Established in 1976, the NMA honors the second secretary-treasurer of the AHS, Mrs. E. W. (Nancy) Minks of Albert Lea, MN. It is awarded for the best *small-to-medium*-leaved registered cultivar growing in an AHS national convention tour garden and selected by vote of the convention attendees. The walnut plaque is awarded to the hybridizer or introducer of the winning cultivar for permanent retention.

Savory Shield Award (SSA) *(TGA)*.

Established in 1980, the SSA honors Robert W. Savory, AHS board member and well-known hybridizer, Edina, MN. It is awarded for the best *seedling or sport* growing in an AHS national convention tour garden and selected by vote of the convention attendees. The walnut plaque is awarded to the hybridizer or introducer of the winning seedling or sport whose name is engraved each year on the plaque.

Harshbarger Landscape Design Award (HDA) *(TGA)*.

Established in 1980, the HDA honors Gretchen Harshbarger of Iowa City, IA. It is awarded for the best *landscape use* of hostas in an AHS national convention tour garden and selected by vote of the convention attendees. A certificate is awarded to the garden owner.

Alabama Hosta Society Award (AlaHoSoA) *(TGA)*.

Established in 1985 and sponsored by the Alabama Hosta Society, the AlaHoSoA is awarded for the best *variegated*-leaved (with 3 or more divisions) cultivar growing in an AHS national convention tour garden and selected by vote of the convention attendees. A silver bowl and certificate are given to the garden owner for permanent retention.

Lucille Simpers Award (LSA) *(TGA)*.

Established in 1989 and sponsored by the Indianapolis Hosta Society, the LSA honors Mrs. Lucille Simpers of Salem, IN, a charter member of the AHS. It is awarded for the best registered *giant or large blue*-leaved cultivar growing in an AHS national convention tour garden and selected by vote of the convention attendees. A sundial and certificate are given to the hybridizer for permanent retention.

President's Exhibitor Trophy (PET) *(CSA)*.

Established in 1978, the PET is awarded to the overall champion in the cut-leaf exhibit at the AHS national convention. This individual is selected by the panel of show judges and a plaque is given to the exhibitor for permanent retention.

Midwest Blue Award (MBA) *(CSA)*.

Established in 1980, the MBA is sponsored by the Midwest Regional Hosta Society. It is awarded for the best *blue*-leaved exhibit in the cut-leaf exhibit at the AHS national convention and selected by vote of the convention attendees. The walnut plaque is awarded to the exhibitor for permanent retention.

Midwest Gold Award (MGA) *(CSA)*.

Established in 1980, the MGA is sponsored by the Midwest Regional Hosta Society. It is awarded for the best *gold*-leaved exhibit in the cut-leaf exhibit at the AHS national convention and selected by vote of the convention attendees. The walnut plaque is awarded to the exhibitor for permanent retention.

Schutt Silver Cup Award (SSC) *(CSA)*.

Established in 1980, the SSC honors Theresa A. Schutt of Woolstock, IA. It is awarded for the best *artistic design arrangement* in the artistic exhibit at the AHS national convention and selected by one or more artistic show judges. The winning exhibitor's name is engraved on the silver cup.

Benedict Award (BA) *(CSA)*.

Established in 1986, the BA honors Dr. Ralph H. Benedict, a well-known hybridizer, and is sponsored by Drs. Lloyd C. Jones and James W. Wilkins. It is awarded for the best *variegated*-leaved exhibit in the cut-leaf exhibit at the AHS national convention and selected by vote of the convention attendees. A certificate and gift are awarded to the exhibitor for permanent retention.

Alex J. Summers Distinguished Merit Award (AJSA) *(SPA)*.

Established in 1982, the AJSA honors Alex J. Summers, of Bridgeville, MD, cofounder and first president of the AHS. It is awarded to a member of the AHS in recognition of *outstanding service* to the development of the genus *Hosta*, the AHS, or both. The recipient is selected by a special awards committee and receives a certificate. The award is sponsored by the Delaware Valley Regional Hosta Society.

Alex J. Summers Distinguished Merit Hosta (AJSH) (*SPA*).

Established in 1982, the AJSH is *a hosta with excellence*. It is chosen by the recipient of the Alex J. Summers Distinguished Merit Award who details the merits of the chosen hosta in the acceptance address and receives a certificate. The award is sponsored by the Delaware Valley Regional Hosta Society.

'Big Bucks' Award (BBA) (*SPA*).

Established in 1986, the BBA recognizes the *largest contributor to the auction* at the AHS national convention based on dollar value obtained for plant material given by the contributor. A plaque is awarded for permanent retention.

INTRODUCTION TO DIVISION I SHOW RULES

The American Hosta Society classifies species and cultivars for the purpose of cut-leaf shows. During the past five years the AHS has published several documents concerning show classification: *Handbook for Classification Clerks and Listing of Species and Cultivars* (Schmid, 1987a) was written for the 1987 AHS national convention, and "The American Hosta Society—National Standard Show Schedule" (Minks, 1989) was written in 1989 for the AHS national cut-leaf show in Indianapolis, IN. The latest classification resulted in *Exhibition Judges Handbook* (Minks, 1990c), which is now the official document used by The American Hosta Society for cut-leaf shows, and is the basis for the AHS classification numbers given in the present volume.

The AHS classification does not follow established morphological standards in regard to color identification nor does it specifically mention and categorize difficult colors—for example, chartreuse and grey-green. The former has been considered a greenish yellow or a yellowish green, the latter has been included with the blues, as bluish grey, or with greens, as greyish green. As an example, some taxa that are described as blue-green in the registration document are classified in class 1 rather than class 3. Analogous to this problem is the requirement of listing "light," "medium," and "dark" shades and hues for the various colors. This classification is relatively simple for distinct color shadings such as in the green color group. In the yellow group, however, it presents a difficulty because abiotic factors determine the color development in leaves and so identical taxa growing in one particular area may be "darker" than those from another microclimate and, further, in extreme cases some taxa have light and dark leaves on the same clump (Plate 129). Resolution of these difficulties is left to the discretion of the classification clerks.

To aid classification clerks the AHS publishes a classification list as part of the *Judges Handbook* which specifies the classification numbers of registered varieties and "recognized" species, but this list currently does not include classification numbers for unregistered seedlings, "non-recognized species," and mutations (sports).

The term "non-recognized species" is not defined by the 1990 Classification Committee of the AHS nor is it defined under the latest show rules. As a consequence several species long known to science are missing from the "recognized" list, so ostensibly are nonrecognized and this results in an incomplete list of species. Since the delimitation and recognition of species is regulated by the ICBN, the AHS technically has no authority in this matter. Thus I have provided the AHS classification numbers for those taxa not included in the AHS species list. It is hoped the Classification Committee of the AHS will remove the regrettable terminology and "recognize" and include all species validly described under the rules of the ICBN.

A further problem with the AHS species list concerns the classification of some of the taxa included, which does not conform to validly published diagnoses. To name a few examples, *H. alismifolia* is characterized as IV/1A when in fact translation of Maekawa's (1984) Latin diagnosis results in II/1A. *Hosta capitata* is described with leaves 3–5 in. (8–13 cm) long (Grey, 1938) and they are about one-half as wide, so they belong in Section IV not III. Most species are described with an extremely wide morphological range of leaf characteristics and sizes so classification under the leaf show rules of the AHS is very difficult.

Another problematic group is one composed of cultivars which undergo a complete or partial color change as the season progresses. One example is *H.* 'Fortunei Albopicta' which has its best variegation very early in the season but turns completely green by late spring or early summer. These cultivars are difficult to classify due to their change in leaf color. Although it is not specifically mentioned in the cultivar list, the class titled "Any other" in each section appears to be the category used for these changeable cultivars.

DIVISION I—HORTICULTURE

The show classification numbers shown for individual taxa in Chapters 3 and 4 are composed of the section number followed by the class number and letter, thus II/1B. The required number of leaves is indicated in parenthesis in the section headings (i.e., "(2 leaves)" means that 2 leaves must be shown in the section).

Division I is subdivided by size into 12 sections as follows:

Section I: Giant-Leaved Registered Varieties and Recognized Species (1 leaf).

Class 1: Green—All shades of green from the lightest to the darkest.
　　　A = Light and Medium; B = Dark.
Class 2: Variegations—All shades of yellow to all shades of light green with creams and whites (including blendings, borders, patterns, stipplings, washings).
　　　A = Light and Medium; B = Dark.
Class 3: Blue—All shades of blue from the lightest to the darkest.
　　　A = Light and Medium; B = Dark.
Class 4: Variegations—All shades of medium green to all shades of dark green with creams and whites (including blendings, borders, patterns, stipplings, washings).
　　　A = Medium; B = Dark.
Class 5: Yellow—All shades of yellow from the lightest creams to the darkest golds.
　　　A = Light and Medium; B = Dark.
Class 6: Any Others
　　　A = Light and Medium; B = Dark.

Section II: Large-Leaved Registered Varieties and Recognized Species (1 leaf).

Class 7: Green—All shades of green from the lightest to the darkest.
　　　A = Light and Medium; B = Dark.
Class 8: Variegations—All shades of yellow to all shades of light green with creams and whites (including blend-

ings, borders, patterns, stipplings, washings).
A = Light and Medium; B = Dark.

Class 9: Blue—All shades of blue from the lightest to the darkest.
A = Light and Medium; B = Dark.

Class 10: Variegations—All shades of medium green to all shades of dark green with creams and whites (including blendings, borders, patterns, stipplings, washings).
A = Medium; B = Dark.

Class 11: Yellow—All shades of yellow from the lightest creams to the darkest golds.
A = Light and Medium; B = Dark.

Class 12: Any Others
A = Light and Medium; B = Dark.

Section III: Medium-Leaved Registered Varieties and Recognized Species (2 leaves).

Class 13: Green—All shades of green from the lightest to the darkest.
A = Light and Medium; B = Dark.

Class 14: Variegations—All shades of yellow to all shades of light green with creams and whites (including blendings, borders, patterns, stipplings, washings).
A = Light and Medium; B = Dark.

Class 15: Blue—All shades of blue from the lightest to the darkest.
A = Light and Medium; B = Dark.

Class 16: Variegations—All shades of medium green to all shades of dark green with creams and whites (including blendings, borders, patterns, stipplings, washings).
A = Medium; B = Dark.

Class 17: Yellow—All shades of yellow from the lightest creams to the darkest golds.
A = Light and Medium; B = Dark.

Class 18: Any Others
A = Light and Medium; B = Dark.

Section IV: Small-Leaved Registered Varieties and Recognized Species (3 leaves).

Class 19: Green—All shades of green from the lightest to the darkest.
A = Light and Medium; B = Dark.

Class 20: Variegations—All shades of yellow to all shades of light green with creams and whites (including blendings, borders, patterns, stipplings, washings).
A = Light and Medium; B = Dark.

Class 21: Blue—All shades of blue from the lightest to the darkest.
A = Light and Medium; B = Dark.

Class 22: Variegations—All shades of medium green to all shades of dark green with creams and whites (including blendings, borders, patterns, stipplings, washings).
A = Medium; B = Dark.

Class 23: Yellow—All shades of yellow from the lightest creams to the darkest golds.
A = Light and Medium; B = Dark.

Class 24: Any Others
A = Light and Medium; B = Dark.

Section V: Miniature-Leaved Registered Varieties and Recognized Species (3 leaves).

Class 25: Green—All shades of green from the lightest to the darkest.
A = Light and Medium; B = Dark.

Class 26: Variegations—All shades of yellow to all shades of

light green with creams and whites (including blendings, borders, patterns, stipplings, washings).
A = Light and Medium; B = Dark.

Class 27: Blue—All shades of blue from the lightest to the darkest.
A = Light and Medium; B = Dark.

Class 28: Variegations—All shades of medium green to all shades of dark green with creams and whites (including blendings, borders, patterns, stipplings, washings).
A = Medium; B = Dark.

Class 29: Yellow—All shades of yellow from the lightest creams to the darkest golds.
A = Light and Medium; B = Dark.

Class 30: Any Others
A = Light and Medium; B = Dark.

Section VI: Dwarf-Leaved Registered Varieties and Recognized Species (3 leaves).

Class 31: Green—All shades of green from the lightest to the darkest.
A = Light and Medium; B = Dark.

Class 32: Variegations—All shades of yellow to all shades of light green with creams and whites (including blendings, borders, patterns, stipplings, washings).
A = Light and Medium; B = Dark.

Class 33: Blue—All shades of blue from the lightest to the darkest.
A = Light and Medium; B = Dark.

Class 34: Variegations—All shades of medium green to all shades of dark green with creams and whites (including blendings, borders, patterns, stipplings, washings).
A = Medium; B = Dark.

Class 35: Yellow—All shades of yellow from the lightest creams to the darkest golds.
A = Light and Medium; B = Dark.

Class 36: Any Others
A = Light and Medium; B = Dark.

Section VII: Giant-Leaved Unregistered Seedlings, Nonrecognized Species, and Mutations (Sports) (1 leaf).

Class 37: Green—All shades of green from the lightest to the darkest.
A = Light and Medium; B = Dark.

Class 38: Variegations—All shades of yellow to all shades of light green with creams and whites (including blendings, borders, patterns, stipplings, washings).
A = Light and Medium; B = Dark.

Class 39: Blue—All shades of blue from the lightest to the darkest.
A = Light and Medium; B = Dark.

Class 40: Variegations—All shades of medium green to all shades of dark green with creams and whites (including blendings, borders, patterns, stipplings, washings).
A = Medium; B = Dark.

Class 41: Yellow—All shades of yellow from the lightest creams to the darkest golds.
A = Light and Medium; B = Dark.

Class 42: Any Others
A = Light and Medium; B = Dark.

Section VIII: Large-Leaved Unregistered Seedlings, Nonrecognized Species, and Mutations (Sports) (1 leaf).

Class 43: Green—All shades of green from the lightest to the darkest.
A = Light and Medium; B = Dark.

Class 44: Variegations—All shades of yellow to all shades of light green with creams and whites (including blendings, borders, patterns, stipplings, washings).
A = Light and Medium; B = Dark.

Class 45: Blue—All shades of blue from the lightest to the darkest.
A = Light and Medium; B = Dark.

Class 46: Variegations—All shades of medium green to all shades of dark green with creams and whites (including blendings, borders, patterns, stipplings, washings).
A = Medium; B = Dark.

Class 47: Yellow—All shades of yellow from the lightest creams to the darkest golds.
A = Light and Medium; B = Dark.

Class 48: Any Others
A = Light and Medium; B = Dark.

Section IX: Medium-Leaved Unregistered Seedlings, Nonrecognized Species, and Mutations (Sports) (2 leaves).

Class 49: Green—All shades of green from the lightest to the darkest.
A = Light and Medium; B = Dark.

Class 50: Variegations—All shades of yellow to all shades of light green with creams and whites (including blendings, borders, patterns, stipplings, washings).
A = Light and Medium; B = Dark.

Class 51: Blue—All shades of blue from the lightest to the darkest.
A = Light and Medium; B = Dark.

Class 52: Variegations—All shades of medium green to all shades of dark green with creams and whites (including blendings, borders, patterns, stipplings, washings).
A = Medium; B = Dark.

Class 53: Yellow—All shades of yellow from the lightest creams to the darkest golds.
A = Light and Medium; B = Dark.

Class 54: Any Others
A = Light and Medium; B = Dark.

Section X: Small-Leaved Unregistered Seedlings, Nonrecognized Species, and Mutations (Sports) (3 leaves).

Class 55: Green—All shades of green from the lightest to the darkest.
A = Light and Medium; B = Dark.

Class 56: Variegations—All shades of yellow to all shades of light green with creams and whites (including blendings, borders, patterns, stipplings, washings).
A = Light and Medium; B = Dark.

Class 57: Blue—All shades of blue from the lightest to the darkest.
A = Light and Medium; B = Dark.

Class 58: Variegations—All shades of medium green to all shades of dark green with creams and whites (including blendings, borders, patterns, stipplings, washings).
A = Light and Medium; B = Dark.

Class 59: Yellow—All shades of yellow from the lightest creams to the darkest golds.
A = Light and Medium; B = Dark.

Class 60: Any Others
A = Light and Medium; B = Dark.

Section XI: Miniature-Leaved Unregistered Seedlings, Nonrecognized Species, and Mutations (Sports) (3 leaves).

Class 61: Green—All shades of green from the lightest to the darkest.
A = Light and Medium; B = Dark.

Class 62: Variegations—All shades of yellow to all shades of light green with creams and whites (including blendings, borders, patterns, stipplings, washings).
A = Light and Medium; B = Dark.

Class 63: Blue—All shades of blue from the lightest to the darkest.
A = Light and Medium; B = Dark.

Class 64: Variegations—All shades of medium green to all shades of dark green with creams and whites (including blendings, borders, patterns, stipplings, washings).
A = Medium; B = Dark.

Class 65: Yellow—All shades of yellow from the lightest creams to the darkest golds.
A = Light and Medium; B = Dark.

Class 66: Any Others
A = Light and Medium; B = Dark.

Section XII: Dwarf-Leaved Unregistered Seedlings, Nonrecognized Species, and Mutations (Sports) (3 leaves).

Class 67: Green—All shades of green from the lightest to the darkest.
A = Light and Medium; B = Dark.

Class 68: Variegations—All shades of yellow to all shades of light green with creams and whites (including blendings, borders, patterns, stipplings, washings).
A = Light and Medium; B = Dark.

Class 69: Blue—All shades of blue from the lightest to the darkest.
A = Light and Medium; B = Dark.

Class 70: Variegations—All shades of medium green to all shades of dark green with creams and whites (including blendings, borders, patterns, stipplings, washings).
A = Medium; B = Dark.

Class 71: Yellow—All shades of yellow from the lightest creams to the darkest golds.
A = Light and Medium; B = Dark.

Class 72: Any Others
A = Light and Medium; B = Dark.

Table 8. Determination of Leaf Sizes.

For AHS show purposes the terms GIANT, LARGE, MEDIUM, SMALL, MINIATURE, and DWARF are determined by the size of an average leaf on an adult plant. Each leaf has an aspect ratio (length:breadth). Total leaf size is determined by multiplying length times breadth; the result determines the section number to which the leaf belongs. The total area in square inches or centimeters is an averaged value.

LEAF SIZES (IN INCHES)

SECTION	DIMENSIONS (length by breadth)					IN.^{2}($\pm$)
I & VII—GIANT, larger than	12×12	13×11	14×10	16×8.5	18×8	144
II & VIII—LARGE, between	12×12	13×11	14×10	16×8.5	18×8	144
	9×9	10×8	11×7.5	12×6.5	14×6	81
III & IX—MEDIUM, between	9×9	10×8	11×7.5	12×6.5	14×6	81
	5×5	6×4	7×3.5	8×3	10×2.5	25
IV & X—SMALL, between	5×5	6×4	7×3.5	8×3	10×2.5	25
	2.5×2.5	3×2	4×1.5	5×1.25	6×1	6
V & XI—MINIATURE, between	2.5×2.5	3×2	4×1.5	5×1.25	6×1	6
	1.5×1.5	2×1	3×0.6	4×0.5	5×0.4	2
VI & XII—DWARF, smaller than	1.5×1.5	2×1	3×0.6	4×0.5	5×0.4	2

LEAF SIZES (IN CENTIMETERS)

SECTION	DIMENSIONS (length by breadth)					CM^2($\pm$)
I & VII—GIANT, larger than	30×30	33×28	35×25	40×36	46×20	900
II & VIII—LARGE, between	30×30	33×28	35×25	40×36	46×20	900
	23×23	25×51	28×19	30×16	35×15	530
III & IX—MEDIUM, between	23×23	25×51	28×19	30×16	35×15	530
	13×13	15×10	18×9	20×8	25×6	160
IV & X—SMALL, between	13×13	15×10	18×9	20×8	25×6	160
	6×6	8×5	10×4	13×3	15×2.5	36
V & XI—MINIATURE, between	6×6	8×5	10×4	13×3	15×2.5	36
	3.6×3.6	5×2.5	8×1.5	10×1.3	13×1	13
VI & XII—DWARF, smaller than	3.6×3.6	5×2.5	8×1.5	10×1.3	13×1	13

APPENDIX D

Macromorphological Concepts

The purpose of Appendix D is to elaborate on the fundamental macromorphological standards used in Chapters 2, 3, and 4. It has been included for professional horticulturists and very keen gardeners who desire further definition of color groupings and variegation, as well as flower and leaf morphology.

COLOR GROUPS

Color Standards. Over the years a number of botanical and horticultural color standards and guides have been developed. One very comprehensive color wheel is published by and available from the Royal Horticultural Society in association with the Flower Council of Holland.[1] There are others. Unfortunately, none of them has a sufficiently wide distribution among gardeners to be used as a universal guide. I have therefore employed the classic color descriptions used by botanists.

Such standardized color groupings used in botany and horticulture are found in Lindley[2] (1832) with identification numbers quoted from Stearn (1986). The basic color terms were considerably expanded by Jackson's review of Latin terms used in botany to denote color (Jackson, 1899); occasional reference is made to these expanded terms but not all of them have been included here because the limited range of colors appearing in the genus does not require this.

Golden Yellow. Easily the two most debatable colors in the spectrum of *Hosta* leaf colors are gold and blue. This is because these colors are not true gold or blue but only perceived as such; a discussion of color sagacity was published by Deane (1987). Notwithstanding the absence of a true gold in the genus, the latinate qualifier *aureo-*, meaning golden, is found in many cultivar names. Equally abundant are the descriptors gold or golden. Lindley's only reference to gold is in the yellow-orange group under number 37, and described as: "Golden yellow (*aureus, auratus;* in Greek derivation = *chryso-*); pure yellow, but duller than lemon-yellow, and bright." (Lemon-yellow is described as "the purest yellow, without any brightness.")

The Yellow Group. To simplify color classification, only the term *yellow* is used in the listings. Yellow, according to Lindley, includes:

36. Lemon-yellow (*citreus, citrinus*).
37. Golden yellow (*aureus, auratus*).
38. Plain yellow (*luteus*).
39. Pale yellow (*flavus, lutescens, flavescens*).
40. Sulphur yellow (*sulphureus*).
41. Straw-colored (*stramineus*).
42. Leather-yellow (*alutaceus*).
43. Ochre-colored (*ochraceus*).
45. Waxy yellow (*cerineus*).
46. Yolk of egg (*vitellinus*).
47. Apricot-colored (*armeniacus*).
48. Orange-colored (*aurantiacus, aurantius*).
49. Saffron-colored (*croceus*).
50. Greyish yellow (*helvolus*).
52. Brownish yellow (*testaceus*).
53. Tawny yellow (*fulvus*).
55. Livid, a yellow clouded with greyish and bluish (*lividus*).

Of these colors, only those approaching orange occur rarely in *Hosta* cultivars. Although I have not observed such leaf coloration, nos. 47–49 have been included above because occasional reference is made to orange leaf colors.

One color sometimes incorrectly included in this group by horticulturists and gardeners is ivory or cream, apparently because many yellows fade or bleach to much lighter colors. Ivory or cream is, however, considered a white with a tinge of yellow and is included in the white group. Another color often considered a yellow color is chartreuse which correctly belongs in the green group and is discussed there.

The Blue-Violet-Purple Group. Undoubtedly equally as arguable as the term *gold* in leaves is the descriptor *blue*. Just as there is no true gold color, there is no true blue color in hosta leaves. Lindley's blue-violet-purple group includes:

63. Prussian-blue (*cyaneus*).
64. Indigo (*indigoticus*).
65. Plain blue (*caeruleus*).
66. Sky-blue (*azureus*).
67. Lavender (*caesius*).
68. Violet (*violaceus, ianthinus*).
69. Lilac (*lilacinus*).

While many of these true blue colors are quite common in *Hosta* flowers (see "Flower Color" below), they do not occur in leaves.

Surface Coatings. The color in "blue" leaves is a bluish or greyish green, which is enhanced by an epidermal, opaque, waxy coating. Technically, this color is a sea-green (*glaucus, thalassicus, glaucescens*), defined as a dull green passing into greyish blue in Lindley's green group. It is commonly accompanied by surface features falling into one of the following botanical categories. It is these surface coatings which contribute to the manifestation of what many gardeners refer to as a "blue" color:

289. Farinose, mealy (*farinosus*), covered with a whitish, scurvy coating.
305. Pruinose, frosted (*pruinosus*), a frosted, dewy appearance, as with *H.* 'Frosted Jade'.
306. Powdery (*pulverentus*), covered with a fine bloom.
307. Glaucous (*glaucus*), a fine bloom the color of cabbage, as with *H. sieboldiana*.
308. Caesious (*caesius*), like glaucous but greener, as with *H. nigrescens*.
309. Whitened (*dealbatus*), powdered with very opaque white, as with *H. hypoleuca*.

The Green Group. Sea-green is mostly associated with nos. 305–309 to produce the "blue" appearance.

Many cultivars are characterized as plain green by the casual observer. Upon close examination, the range of greens shown is extremely diverse. In fact, all Lindley's green colors listed above can be found in the genus.

Adding to the complexity of classifying the green colors are many surface effects characterized by terms such as frosted, shiny, glossy, dull, opaque, and metallic. Some of these surface effects change with the seasons and affect the hue and shading of the green coloration.

Frequently a green color is composed of two or three shades of different greens which are obvious at close range but may blend into a monochrome appearance at a distance. These effects must be assessed during the prime growing season. Lindley's green group includes:

56. Grass-green (*smaragdinus, prasinus*).
57. Clear green (*viridis, viridescens*).
58. Verdigris-green (*aeruginosus*), deep green with a mixture of blue.
59. Sea-green (*glaucus, thalassicus, glaucescens*), a dull green passing into greyish blue.
60. Deep green (*atrovirens*), a green verging on black.
61. Yellowish green (*flavovirens*).
62. Olive-green (*olivaceus*).

Chartreuse-Yellow Green. The term *chartreuse* is not a valid botanical color descriptor. It is a yellowish green and is customarily referred to as *flavovirens*. The terms *chlorascens, chlorinus*, and *chloroticus* are also used for yellow-green and I have used these botanical terms as appropriate in Chapter 3; but in Chapter 4 I have maintained the use of the term chartreuse, because it is in common use in horticulture and describes a yellowish green. Many of the cultivars characterized as having golden or yellow leaves have, in fact, chartreuse leaves.

The White Group. A white color does occur in several hues and shades both in flowers and leaves. The general expression for white is *albus*, a dead white. Lindley further defines in the white group:

1. Snow-white (*niveus*).
2. Pure white (*candidus*).
3. Ivory-white (*eburneus, eborinus*), white with yellow.
4. Milk-white (*lacteus*), white with blue.
5. Chalk-white (*cretaceus, calcareus, gypseus*).
6. Silvery (*argenteus*), white changing to bluish grey with luster.
7. Whitish (*albidus*).
8. Turning white (*albescens*), from another color.
9. Whitened (*dealbatus*), covered with white.

Silvery White. The term *silver* has been used in cultivar descriptions. There is, of course, no true silver color, but some of the whites in leaves verge on being silvery white. There are also a few cultivars with white in the leaves approaching a pure white but a true pure white is not found. Nonetheless, most whites in leaves are ivory, the result of yellow colors bleaching to white, or whitish green, the result of greening-up of white leaf areas. Lindley listed no greenish white, so it is considered a whitish green under the green group, although both are used in horticulture.

White Surface Effects. The leaf underside of some species, including *H. hypoleuca* and *H. pycnophylla*, has a near white color which is actually a coating of very opaque, white powder. Some hybrids have inherited this trait—for instance, *H.* 'Sum and Substance'. This effect is included by botanists under leaf surface polish or texture (see no. 309 under "Surface Coatings" above), described as whitened (*dealbatus*). For the purpose of simplification, it is considered a color and included in the descriptions as such.

VARIEGATION

The biological mechanism of variegation in *Hosta* was researched by Yasui (1929), Vaughn (1979, 1981, 1982), Vaughn and Wilson (1980a, 1980b, 1980c), and a popular treatise of this subject is included in Aden's *The Hosta Book* (1988).

Technically, variegation in leaves is caused by periclinal chimeras in which the tissues of one genetic type are completely surrounded by those of another. These chimeras originate from plastid mutations preventing chlorophyll synthesis (i.e., greening of leaf tissue). The mutation usually occurs in the tip of a new shoot, either in the second layer of the tip, called *tunica* (L2), or in the body of the shoot-tip, called *corpus* (L3). Differences in color appear because the margins are derived from the L2 while the body is composed of both the L2 and L3. For example, if the mutation occurs in the L2, the margin is white and the center is green. Well-understood natural processes cause these changes, but for the purpose of this book it is not necessary to dwell upon the biological mechanism of plastid mutations which produce these color changes; I recommend perusal of the above references to those desiring more information. Because transfer of variegation does not follow standard Mendelian rules of inheritance, hybridizers are urged to acquaint themselves with the occurrence of maternally inherited plastid mutation which has far-reaching implications to *Hosta* breeding. Simply put, variegation is almost always acquired from the maternal (pod) parent of a cross (see Appendix G).

Variegation Types. Mutation to variegated leaf color occurs in the wild and in cultivation. Variegated sports have also been found in tissue culture and as mutated seedlings after having been exposed to chemical or radiation treatment. Chodat (1919) and Yasui (1929) have used terminology which qualifies five distinct types of variegation occurring in the genus:

1. *Marginata* (Chodat) or margined, in which the primary color green occurs in the center and the variegation is limited to the leaf margins as either white (*albomarginata*) or yellow (*aureomarginata*).
2. *Mediovariegata* (Chodat) or center-variegated (*picta*), in which the primary leaf color occurs in the center of the leaf as white (*medioalbinata*) or either yellow or chartreuse (*mediochlorinata*).
3. *Variegata* (Yasui) or streaky-variegated, in which the leaves have a green primary color but are irregularly streaked with white (*albovariegata*), yellow (*chlorovariegata*), or white and yellow (*albochlorovariegata*) stripes.
4. *Striata* (Yasui), in which distinct white (*albostriata*) or yellow (*chlorostriata*) stripes occur on a green primary color.
5. *Maculata* (Yasui), in which leaves have a green margin and a variegated center of a lighter color, becoming spotted or mottled with white (*Albomaculata*) or yellow (*aureomaculata*).

The above categories are an outgrowth of research into plastid systems and are not useful in horticultural classification and identification. For this reason a revised set of the classification used by Vaughn (1979) has been adopted in Chapter 2 with the exclusion of snow flurry and mosaic mutants which are unstable and horticulturally not significant. For horticultural identification three basic types remain: solid colors, margined and picta (reverse) types, and streaky variegation, of which the latter is also unstable to a considerable degree although many of its forms have nevertheless been introduced into commerce. How these unstable types of variegation behave in cultivation is explained by the Benedict Cross.

The Bendict Cross. The phenomenon of changes in unstable, streaky (splashed) variegated cultivars has been studied and systematized by Benedict (1986) and has been labeled the "Benedict Cross" (Table 9) by Pollock (in Benedict, 1986). At the center of this cross are the mottled, splashed, streaked, multicolored cultivars. A number of reports characterize these cultivars as consistently unstable, meaning they display the splashed and streaky variegation only temporarily and then revert to a more stable variegation pattern or to a solid green or yellow. These monochromatic, stable cultivars form the end points of one of the bars of the Benedict Cross.

The two other possible stable variegation patterns are the margined (*marginata*) type and the reversed (*picta*) type. The margined type is usually a light-colored yellow, chartreuse or white margin on a darker green or yellow primary color background. The reversed type is a light colored yellow, chartreuse, or white primary color center with a white, darker yellow, or green margin. Both of these types are stable and form the end points of the other bar of the Benedict Cross.

Types With Margins. The most frequently observed variegation in cultivars is the margined (or *marginata*) type in which the margins are either dark on a light primary color or light on a dark primary color. All conceivable color combinations have appeared and with very few exceptions all of them are color stable. A few—for instance, *H. sieboldii*—have a margin that is viridescent, so it greens up as the season advances and almost disappears.

Other cultivars undergo the same margin color degradation but change from one color to another—for example, from yellow to white, as in *H. ventricosa* 'Aureomarginata'. During the prime observation time in May/June this change has not yet occurred and is not considered a factor in classification.

While more-or-less color stable in the short term (1–6 years), many cultivars with variegated margins show considerable modification of the area covered by the margins in the longer term (more than 6 years). The margins become progressively wider, reducing the primary color and eventually turning into a solid color, nonvariegated leaf. A study of this phenomenon was published by Zilis (1987) who classified the intermediate steps of this color transformation in *H. sieboldiana* 'Frances Williams' as type A through type F: type A has a very narrow margin; type D has a much wider squash-edge margin; Type E has irregular margins, with some leaves having yellow on one side of the central vein and green on the other; the transformation is complete in type F, which is all-yellow. Zilis points out these changes may take several years and may occur only if the clump remains undisturbed. Most gardeners divide their plants for increase so may not see such changes. This serves to illustrate that variability exists even in cultivars heretofore thought to be permanently stable.

The descriptions in Chapter 4 do not distinguish between absolutely stable, never-changing, variegated cultivars (if there is such a thing) and long-term stable, variegated cultivars. They simply indicate the type of margined variegation. On the other hand, cultivars reported in the literature as being noticeably unstable are listed as unstable.

Table 9

THE BENEDICT CROSS
The 4 Stable Forms
Arising From Unstable Type UN/SP

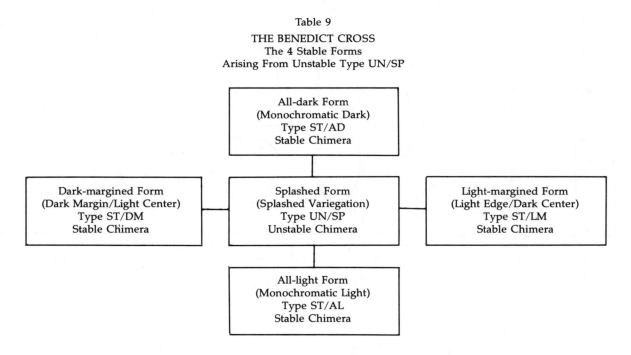

Explanation of Codes:
UN/SP = Unstable splashed
ST/AD = Stable all dark
ST/AL = Stable all light
ST/DM = Stable dark margin   ST/LM = Stable light margin

LEAF SHAPE

Three main components make up the outline shape of a leaf: the basic shape, the shape of the leaf tip, and the shape of the leaf base. It is the combination of these three attributes that makes up the actual leaf shape. The combined leaf characteristics used in the descriptions are given in Chapter 2. Following are details for these attributes:

Leaf Shape. Leaf shapes have been systematized by the Systematics Association, Committee for Descriptive Biology (1962: chart 1a). Mathematical ratios of length to breadth used as guidelines in these descriptions are standardized ratios as published by W. B. Turrill (1925; cfr. Stearn, 1986) and illustrated in Chapter 2. I have correlated Turrill's mathematical organization of leaf shapes with the numbers quoted by the Systematics Association (Figure D-1). Definitions for basic leaf shapes are important cultivar and species recognition and classification so they have been given in Chapter 2 and are also included in the Glossary.

Leaf Apex. The manner in which the leaf tip (apex) is formed is of considerable importance in the identification of leaves. Several very distinct tip shapes are recognized:

140. Mucronate (*mucronatus*), abruptly terminated by a sharp point (Figure D-2A).
141. Cuspidate (*cuspidatus*), tapering gradually to a sharp point (Figure D-2B).
149. Acute (*acutus*), coming straight to a point (Figure D-2C).
153. Obtuse, blunt-pointed (*obtusus*), terminated by a rounded end (Figure D-2D).

Leaf Base. The shape of the leaf base is the third important element making up the shape of a leaf. Only a few specific types are found:

166. Cordate, heart-shaped (*cordatus*), having two equal, rounded lobes (Figure D-3A).
171. Truncate (*truncatus*), as if cut straight across (Figure D-3B).
175. Cuneate, wedge-shaped (*cuneatus*), with straight sides converging (Figure D-3C).
176. Attenuate (*angusatus*), with curved sides converging (Figure D-3D).

Combinations of these basic leaf shapes, leaf tips, and leaf bases form the leaf shapes most frequently seen in cultivar leaves. A few exceptions exist, and they are pointed out in the individual descriptions in Chapter 4.

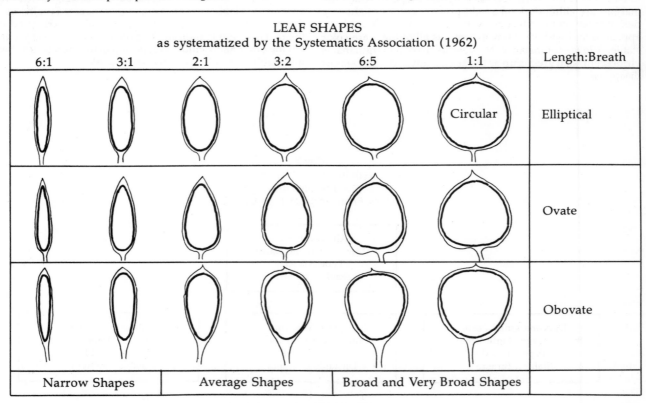

Figure D-1. Leaf shapes

Figure D-2. Leaf apices

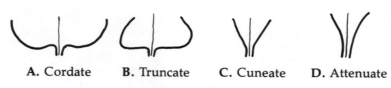

A. Cordate　　**B.** Truncate　　**C.** Cuneate　　**D.** Attenuate

Figure D-3. Leaf bases

Margin Features. Leaves are classified by botanists as being no. 179, entire (*integer*) or no. 180, quite entire (*integerrimus*). This means the margins are free or perfectly free of marginal divisions, such as those found in serrated, toothed, or sawed margins. Although microscopic divisions of the margins have been reported in *H. kiyosumiensis*, these are unimportant for horticultural classification (see Figure 3-34).

While lacking teeth or incisions, hosta leaves have many different margin configurations. Aside from being virtually flat and even, the margins can have slight waves, many undulations, piecrust edges, even what might be called shirred borders. Margins can be flat with the leaf or turned up or down.

LEAF SURFACE (TOPOGRAPHY)

General. The leaf itself can take on several distinct surface forms: flat and even, cupped, wavy, twisted, contorted, or distinctly ribbed. The surface shape of the leaf in combination with margin characteristics make for compound shapes which are, again, extremely difficult to describe so illustrations are provided in Chapter 2 to adequately portray the leaf surface and margin features. Fortunately, a majority of leaf surface and margin features belong to well-recognized types. However, there are a few unusual ones, such as *H. tortifrons*, which are provided with additional comment in their descriptions.

The leaf surface features are determined by a combination of several factors: (1) markings or evenness, (2) superficial processes, and (3) polish or texture.

Markings or Evenness. Markings or evenness are most difficult to qualify and quantify. Usually not all the leaves of a given plant show the same amount and density of markings or evenness. When combined with general leaf and margin forms—such as cupping, waviness, undulations, curling, and uneven twisting and contorting—characterization of the leaf becomes very complicated.

Botanists have specific terms which can be applied, such as rugose (*rugosus*) and furrowed (*sulcatus*). Horticulturists and gardeners use terms such as dimpled, puckered, pursed, ruffled, pleated, embossed, wrinkled, crinkled, and, of course, smooth. All these characterizations are attempts to describe surfaces which are very difficult to describe in words alone. To simplify matters, many of these terms have been combined into the most frequently seen types, and illustrations in Chapter 2 are provided to typify the major leaf types. Following are the principal features used to portray leaf surfaces.

245. Rugose, wrinkled (*rugosus*) (Figure 2-18). Any leaf surface with uneven surface features is classified as rugose. This includes dimpled, puckered, pursed, embossed, ruffled, pleated, wrinkled, and crinkled leaf surfaces. Examples include *H. sieboldiana* and its hybrids. Many cultivars are rugose.
256. Furrowed (*sulcatus*) (Figure 2-23). Most cultivars have principal veins impressed on the leaf surface. Nonetheless, the leaf is quite flat and can be considered smooth in broad terms. In some, the principal veins are very

deeply impressed with the intervening leaf surface arching highly and forming rather deep V-shaped channels or furrows. The depth of these furrows can reach ⅛ in. (4 mm) or more. In these cases the leaf surface is called furrowed, as in *H. montana* f. *macrophylla*.
259. Even, smooth (*aequatus*) (Figure 2-17). Although having slightly impressed principal veins, most hosta leaves have a relatively even, smooth surface. For this reason any cultivar not definitely falling into categories 245 or 256 has been classified as having a "flat," smooth, even surface with no rugosity but not "flat as a board."

Hair Coverings and Superficial Processes. Hair coverings are not found in leaves of *Hosta* cultivars. Superficial processes include mealy (*farinosus*) coatings (as no. 289). But since mealy is also treated as polish or texture, it has been combined with this category and included above under "Surface Coatings."

Polish and Texture. Disappearing or permanent polish and texture features, such as powdery white or grey coatings (*dealbatus*, *pulverentus*), glaucous blooms (*glaucus*, *glaucescens*, *caesius*), and others are treated as color phenomena falling into the blue/grey category; they are included above under "Surface Coatings" because the "blue" in leaves is a combination of color and surface textures. The leaf polish of most cultivars is smooth (*laevis*, *glaber*), with some leaves having either a shiny (*nitidus*) or dull (*opacus*, *impolitus*) surface. In rare cases a very smooth, polished (*laevigatus*, *politus*) surface exists. The following descriptions are applied to leaf polish and texture:

294. Shining (*nitidus*), having a smooth, even, very shiny surface, as in *H. tardiflora* and *H. longipes*.
295. Smooth, glabrous (*glaber*), free of unevenness, as in *H.* 'Lancifolia'.
296. Polished (*politus*, *laevigatus*), having the appearance of a polished substance, as in *H. laevigata* or *H. yingeri*.
299. Opaque (*opacus*, *impolitus*), dull, the reverse of shining.
304. Dusty (*lentiginosus*), covered with minute dots, as if dusted.
305–309. See "Surface Coatings" above.

The polish of the leaf surface changes with the season in most taxa of the genus so it is difficult to characterize it. In late spring, after the disappearance of surface effects such as pruinosity, most leaves have a shiny surface. Some have a polished surface lasting all season—as for example, *H. yingeri* and *H. laevigata*—and when this is the case it is mentioned in the descriptions. In most taxa, however, no mention is made of leaf polish; in these cases it is considered changeable during the prime season of observation and more-or-less shiny during summer and fall.

Texture and Substance. Identification is quite often visual only, relying on color, size, and visible surfaces. In this case, texture means visible texture, as in "Polish and Texture" above. Botanists recognize a tactile texture which is more akin to substance and can be determined only by touch. Claims are made that thick leaves (of heavy substance) can actually be seen, but this has no basis in fact. Since heavy texture or substance is approximately equal to thickness, it can be measured for scientific applications with a micrometer, but this is beyond the needs of the average gardener. Aside from thickness, other factors, such as stiffness and succulence, enter into the determination of texture and substance, another matter too complicated to be defined in great detail.

The following characterizations deal with texture and substance in leaf morphology and are used primarily in Chapter 3:

310. Membranaceous (*membranaceus*), thin, translucent.
311. Papery (*papyraceus, chartaceus*), having the substance of writing paper in combination with being opaque.
312. Coriaceous, leathery (*coriaceus*), having the consistency of leather, as with *H. rupifraga*.
323. Carnose, carnous, fleshy (*carnosus*), firm, juicy.
324. Ceraceous, waxy (*ceraceus, cereus*), having the texture of new wax.
326. Thick (*crassus*), thicker than usual, as with *H. crassifolia*.
327. Succulent (*succulentus*), very thickly cellular and juicy.
334. Herbaceous (*herbaceus*), thin, green, and cellular, as the tissue of membranous leaves.

OTHER MACROMORPHOLOGICAL FEATURES

Various other morphological characters important to identification and classification are listed in Appendix A—Part 1 and are utilized in Chapters 3 and 4. Definitions are given in Chapter 2 and the Glossary. Aside from other key characteristics, they concern direction, insertion, mode of attachment or adhesion, and arrangement of sterile and fertile bracts.

FLOWER SHAPE AND COLOR

Flower Shape. The flower is composed of a narrow tubular section (*tubus angustus*) followed by an expanding section (*tubus dilatatus*) formed by six lobes. The three exterior lobes (the calyx) are technically sepals and the three interior lobes (the corolla) are petals, but there is little difference between them so they are called tepals. All are either white or colored and together form the perianth. Because there is no distinction between calyx and corolla the entire structure has been referred to as a corolla by Maekawa (Figure 2-35), while other authors correctly call it a perianth (Fujita, 1976a).

The center section of the perianth—beginning at the point of expansion to the onset of the lobes—is either funnel-shaped (*corolla infundibuliformis*) or bell-shaped (*corolla campanulata*) with many in-between shapes. Most cultivars have a more-or-less bell-shaped flower (Figure 2-37), while a few have a truly funnel-shaped inflorescence (Figures 2-36, D-4). Figure D-4 also shows the relative size difference between the largest, flowering species—*H. plantaginea*—and the average-sized flowers. The spider-flowered species of section *Arachnanthae* are basically funnel-shaped in outline, but the lobes are separated giving a spider-flowered appearance.

One exception to these two major types of flower shapes is the closed perianth (*corolla clausa*) type. Flowers develop to the point where they would normally open their lobes, but, in these cases, they remain closed until they dry and separate from the pedicel, as in *H. clausa*. This characteristic is not limited to one taxon, but has also been observed in rare hybrids in which the perianth expands but the lobes remain closed and attached to the raceme for two to three weeks until the closed flower drops from the pedicel.

The three classifiers used in the cultivar descriptions are covered in Chapter 2.

Figure D-4. *H. montana* 'Liliiflora' (left) and *H. plantagina* (center) flowers are funnel-shaped; *H. tibae* (right) shows slightly ventricose perianth (left measure = 1 cm; right = 1 in.) (Hosta Hill)

Flower Color. Identification of cultivars by the average gardener depends mostly on shape and color of leaves only; this is possible because of distinct leaf shapes and variegations. Flowers, observable for only a short period during each season, are usually not considered. However, close inspection of flower color is in many species an absolute necessity for correct identification because leaf morphology in species can vary considerably.

Flower colors have been commonly characterized as lilac, rose-purple, purple, blue, lavender, mauve, white, and even pink. Obviously, some of these colors are personal interpretations of the color spectrum, and just as "gold" and "silver" are in the eye of the beholder, so is "pink." Exact description of flower color is as difficult as describing leaf colors, but botanical guidelines are available and given later.

Factors Controlling Color. There are several other factors which affect the development and recognition of color. A very important one is the relative exposure of a given cultivar to sunlight. Exposure to strong light levels usually deepens the shades of flower coloration, while deep shade lightens colors, except perhaps for the blues. Strong light levels are not the same as continuous direct sunlight but may involve periodic exposures to direct sunlight and are also beneficial to leaf color development, flowering, and fruiting.

Other factors that control color are:

1. Geographic Latitude. During a data-gathering visit to England in July 1988, I noticed flower colors in southern England are very intense. This may indicate that the latitude at which plants are grown affects the colors. Lobe color is much darker in gardens south of London at 51° north latitude than in those in Atlanta, Georgia, at 34° north latitude or anywhere else in North America below 45° north latitude. Not only are the colors deeper near London, but in some cases buds take on a transparent, bone-china look. My hosts described this as a normal occurrence. The flowers of *H. kikutii* which are near white in their native habitat on Kyushu and Shikoku (between 30° and 34° north latitude) and near Atlanta, Georgia (34° north latitude), are deep lavender suffused

near London. Occasionally in my garden, some taxa rebloom in the fall; these flowers are usually darker, indicating perhaps that night-time temperatures may also be involved. More study is needed to determine the reasons, and readers should make adjustments depending on their geographical location on the globe. I invite reports on this subject from readers to be used in a future edition.

2. Timing. The exterior of a flower bud is initially more intensely colored than the interior, becoming paler as the flower expands so that after opening the interior of the perianth is more strongly colored than the exterior. In the morning the colors are stronger and fade as the day progresses.

3. Location and Pattern. Maekawa (1940) was the first to classify the location and pattern of color fields on the interior of the lobe: (1) very dark colored veins on a lighter colored background, (2) dark-colored veins on pale or white, and (3) white or near-white lobes.

Maekawa's system requires the colors to be assessed on the inside of the perianth, because that is where the most intense coloring occurs in the opened flower. This method requires more care and better timing than the casual observance of the exterior flower color. It is, nevertheless, the only precise way to utilize flower pigmentation patterns for identification purposes, and gardeners intent on using this method must regard this principle. Maekawa's method also includes consideration of transparency or nontransparency of the veins in the perianth, as well as the placement of colored field alongside them, but these are difficult to detect in the flower so I have disregarded them.

Flower pigmentation can be of some use in cultivar identification, but it must be used with knowledge and caution. Hybridization causes the characteristic color patterns of species to be muddled, and so their interpretation becomes inexact. Early generation hybrids originating from parents that belong to the same taxonomic section and removed one or two generations from these parents (F_1 and F_2) can carry over some distinct color patterns, but succeeding hybrids no longer show the standard configurations consistently and reliably. For species identification, however, pigmentation of the perianth is important. It is indispensable for the determination of pure specific material versus inter- and intraspecific natural hybrids occurring in the wild.

Some species are very easily identified. Most gardeners recognize a *H. montana* type or *H. sieboldii*, for example, without resorting to the examination of flower coloration. The general appearance of the plants and their leaves allow positive identification in most cases.

A large group of taxa in the genus have white flowers with little coloration. Although there are distinct differences in veining, they are too minute and difficult for most gardeners to detect. Fortunately, most white-flowered species are well known and possess other, very distinct features useful for identification.

Flower pigmentation patterns are most effective in identifying the lesser known groups of wild hostas, such as the *H. kikutii* group (section *Rhynchophorae*) and the *H. longipes* group (section *Picnolepis*).

It is obvious that flower colors must be judged from a common basis. I have expanded Maekawa's system to include my own research and established the following rules of observance:

Timing of Observation. For the purpose of arriving at a standard, color should be observed at the time the flower opens, which is just before or just after sunrise in day-blooming cultivars and during the evening hours in night bloomers.

Typification of Coloration. The coloration on flowers is not simple or uniform but occurs as complex patterns, more visible on the inside of the flower perianth than on the outside. The color appears as stripes or colored fields, usually in purple, on white, lavender, or purple background. This system recognizes four types which are reflected in the systematic keys and used for the classification of cultivars in Chapter 2:

Type A. White or near-white (Plates 193–196): *H. plantaginea*; sections *Helipteroides* and *Rhynchophorae*; section *Intermediae* pp.

Type B. More-or-less uniform medium-to-dark background color, stripes visible but not obvious and blending into background. Margins partially or entirely white (Plates 197–200): sections *Eubryocles*, *Lamellatae*, and *Arachnanthae*; sections *Tardanthae* and *Stoloniferae* pp.

Type C. Obvious dark colored stripes on colored background of different intensities (Plates 201–204): section *Nipponosta*; sections *Tardanthae*, *Stoloniferae*, and *Intermediae* pp.

Type D. Colored field in center of lobe with no obvious stripes, surrounded by mostly white or very lightly tinted background color (Plates 205–208): section *Picnolepis*.

There are obvious, overlapping characteristics which may be due to the extensive intra- and interspecific hybridization in the natural habitat. In some of the key groups—for example, sections *Picnolepis* and *Nipponosta*—the coloration of the lobes is quite distinct and can be used for positive identification.

Detecting Flower Color Patterns. To permit easy observation and side-by-side comparison of color patterns, I have developed a procedure for analysis which can be performed by the average gardener, although it might require some patience and dexterity:

1. Collect a single flower, cutting it flush with the stem. Remove the bract. Cut off the pedicel with the base section of the ovary to permit easy removal of the stamens and style.

2. With a sharp blade, cut the flower lengthwise between two lobes all the way to the narrow tube end. Unroll the perianth to create a fan consisting of the six lobes. Flatten out the fan on a dark surface and place a small pane of glass over it. The inside of the perianth (the tepals), now on top facing the observer, will look like the perianths in plates 193–208.

3. The color pattern can now be analyzed and studied in detail.

Obviously, the practiced observer can look into the open flower without severing it from the stem. When side-by-side comparisons of several flowers are necessary, however, the above method is helpful.

Typical pigmentation patterns for several species are shown on Plates 193–208. Without providing further detailed analysis, which is beyond the scope of this book, these photographs provide a key to the recognition of some of the more difficult species as well as some of the more common groups.

Most *Hosta* flowers are colored in shades of purple. Since "one observer's purple may be another's blue," an examination of the color purple follows.

Red-Blue Perception. Blue as is relates to leaves is discussed below (under "Blue-Violet-Purple Group") and in Chapter 2.

Characterizing colors belonging to the red-blue same group is very difficult and varies with different observers.

For example, botanists have had difficulty with the placement of purple and some confusion exists. A quote from Jackson (1899) explains:

> Purple is variously understood. Practically, it is any mixture of blue and red. Saccardo (1891) treats it as synonymous with crimson, but the majority regard it as having more blue in its composition. *Purpureus, porphyreus*, therefore, are general in their application, followed by *purpurascens, purpurellus, purpurinus* and *porphyreo-leucus. Atropurpureus* is familiar to most in the old cultivated 'Sweet Scabious', *Scabiosa atropurpurea; lilacinus, lilaceus, syringus* recall the tint of *Syringa vulgaris* (Common Lilac). Colder in hue we have *violaceus, violeus, ianthinus, ionides* to recall the violet in all its shades, deeper tones denoted by *amathysteus, amathystinus, hyacinthinius,* and *atro-violaceus*.

Clearly, some botanists analyzing color consider purple more red than blue and liken it to crimson. But a majority of botanists consider it more blue than red, and this is the posture I have adopted. Names denoting the bluer hues of purple are well presented in the genus as in *Funkia cærulea* (blue-flowered), *Hosta atropurpurea*, and *H. fortunei* var. *hyacinthina*.

The Blue-Violet-Purple Group. In the listing of colors for this group given earlier, I did not include colors with a predominance of red, such as rose (*roseus, rosaceus, rhodellus*) or pink (*salmonaceus, salmoneus*), because there is no scientific foundation to indicate these colors actually occur in the genus. Among the colors in Lindley's blue-violet-purple group that are used to describe flower colors are purple (*purpureus*), here regarded more blue than red, also mauve (*malvinus*), violet (*violaceus, ianthinus, hyacinthus, amethystinus*), and lilac (*lilacinus, syringus*).

REPRODUCTIVE ORGANS

All flowers in the genus are bisexual, meaning they contain both male and female reproductive organs. The female organ is a compound-type pistil fused together from three carpels and comprising the ovary at the base of the flower, a long, tubular style, and the three-lobed stigma which receives the pollen. Frequently, the lobes are not fully developed and appear to be one structure. The ovary has three cavities (locules) in which the ovules are arranged in two rows attached to the central axis of the ovary. The ovary develops into a seed capsule which, when it becomes dry, splits open, starting at the tip; each of the three parts progressively curves away from the initial point until it finally is attached to the pedicel only.

The stamens are the male reproductive organs of the flower and consist of six filaments (long, slender stalks) and six anthers. In most species the filaments are attached below the ovary, but in *H. plantaginea* they are attached to the lower inside of the tepals above the ovary. The anthers are pollen sacks; each is bilocular, meaning that it is composed of two sacks. In the cavity (*loculus*) of each sack mother cells undergo meiosis which eventually results in the production of pollen grains. In the genus the anther surface cells have characteristic coloration and patterns which are useful in classifying the taxa.

Fertilization is accomplished through pollination, the process of depositing pollen on the stigma—usually carried out by insects (entomophily), wind (anemophily), gravity, or human intervention. Once deposited a pollen tube grows from the stigma towards the eggs. This tube is an outgrowth of the inner pollen grain wall (intine) which pushes through the outer pollen wall (exine) and carries the male gametes with it as it grows through a canal in the style (stylar canal). This growth is fast, in some taxa reaching 3 mm/hr. Once the eggs are reached the pollen tube discharges its contents resulting in fertilization, which is the fusion of haploid male and female gametes to form a diploid zygote from which seed develops.

APPENDIX E

Japanese, German, and Korean Names and Their Meanings

JAPANESE

When I began my bibliographic search to write this book, examination of the available titles made it very clear that anyone writing a comprehensive treatise on the genus *Hosta* would have to be able to translate many of the Japanese references never before available and considered in the West. After a few courses in Japanese it became apparent they were trying to teach me to *speak* the language; this was not my goal so I found myself back with the books and dictionaries: I wanted to be able to read and that was all.

I found out that Japanese is the world's most complex writing system, but even more complex is the spoken language because most kanji ideograms, derived from Chinese characters, have a Japanese and a Chinese reading and may have several dialectic readings. The way Japanese pupils learn these readings (pronunciations) in school is by rote. Even then, the Japanese often refer to written characters during the course of a conversation so as to indicate the true meaning. Television news is occasionally accompanied by subtitles clarifying the spoken text.

Fortunately, it is not necessary to speak Japanese in order to translate it. Moreover, many technical terms cannot be expressed in kanji so are expressed in one or both Japanese phonetic syllabaries. *Hosta* names utilize one or a combination of the three Japanese writing systems:

1. *Kanji* is the original Japanese writing system which was first employed in the fourth century using Chinese characters. These are the familiar ideograms, or word symbols. In Chinese each expresses one syllable, so the Japanese use two or more of these complicated-looking characters to write relatively simple words, and the resulting compound words are called *jukugo*. For example, the word *kifukurin* (yellow-margined) requires three kanji ideograms resulting in two jukugo.
2. *Hiragana* is a phonetic syllabary which was developed by the twelfth century. It is capable of expressing all the sounds of the Japanese language. The characters do not stand for letters but for sounds (syllables), of which there are over 100. Many common plant names are written in hiragana or a combination of kanji and hiragana.
3. *Katakana* is also capable of expressing all the sounds required for a Japanese phonetic syllabary and it evolved last. The characters have a simplified style and there are over 100. Katakana is utilized almost exclusively for foreign language translations and for academic (formal) Japanese *Hosta* names. All Western cultivar names are written by "sounding them out" in katakana script; for example, *H.* 'Neat Splash' is phonetically spelled with the following phonetic katakana characters: 'ni-to su-pu-ra-tsu-sho'. It is pronounced "Nito Sprasho" with the letter *r* being phonetically somewhere between the English *r* and *l*, and the ending *o* barely audible. The Japanese practice of not actually translating Western modern names into Japanese but merely writing or sounding them out

phonetically has led to the adoption of an enormous number of loanwords taken from English, German, Portuguese, and French.

Japanese botanical and horticultural texts are written with a combination of kanji, jukugo, hiragana, and katakana. Classic, and occasionally even modern, horticultural texts are written in vertical columns from right to left. All scientific texts I have seen were written horizontally, top to bottom, on the Western model.

The Japanese phonetic language can be transcribed into the Latin alphabet without difficulty. The standard method for doing this was developed by a committee of scholars in 1885 and is known as the *Hebonshiki romaji*, after the U.S. philologist Hepburn, and I have adopted this method in this book.

The Hepburn romanization requires the consonants to be pronounced as in English and the vowels as in Italian; for instance, *f* and *w* are pronounced like in English, and *e* is pronounced as in "letter." Vowels are short, unless they are marked to indicate length, and double consonants are pronounced double. *I* or *u* between consonants or at word endings is usually inaudible; so is an initial *y*; *s* is unvoiced, as in "so"; the sound for *r* is between the English *r* and the *l*; and the combination *ng* is always pronounced separately as in "ungainly."

Most of Japanese metaphorical names are translated and transliterated in the individual descriptions given in Chapters 3 and 4, so I am not repeating these names here. There are, however, a number of frequently used descriptive (literal) names which are translated below with the caution that several of them may also have other meanings; for example, *hime* as a noun can mean "princess." The translations I have given are the prevalent horticultural meanings:

Aki = late, fall.
Ama = rain.
Aoba = green leaf, suggests blue-green.
Aocha = yellowish green.
Aofukurin = green margined.
Aojiku (aoziku) = green petiole.
Atsuba = thick leaf.
Buchi = with patches of variegation, dappled, variegation (any kind).
Chirifu = with dispersed variegation, also dusty.
Fu = variegation, any kind.
Fuiri = variegated, spotted.
Fukurin = variegated margin.
Giboshi, also *giboushi* or *gibooshi* = *Hosta*.
Gin = silver, silvery-white.
Ginbuchi = silvery white variegated edge.
Goshiki = many colors.
Haya = early.
Herifu = variegated border.
Hime = miniature, small.

Hiroha, hiroba = wide leaf.
Hosoba = strap leaf, very narrow.
Iwa = rock, crag.
Kara = ancient China, Chinese.
Ki = yellow.
Kifukurin = yellow margined.
Kin = golden yellow, gold.
Kinakafu = yellow in center.
Kisuji = yellow striped.
Ko = small.
Koba = small leaf.
Kobana = small flower.
Kofuki = small pruinose.
Koki = small or dwarf yellow.
Komame = very small, dwarf.
Kuro = black, dark color.
Kurobana = dark flower.
Mame = pea; tiny as a pea.
Maruba = rounded leaf.
Midori = green, greenish.
Mizu = water, damp place.
Murasaki = dark violet, purple.
Nagaba = long leaf.
Naka = in the center, middle.
Nakafu = variegated center.
Nami = wavy.
Nikazaki = double-flowered.
Nishiki = brocade, excellently colorful.
No = of.
O = pretty, nice.
Ohba, ooba, oba = large leaf.
Ogon = golden.
Oo, Oh, Ou = large, big.
Sakuhana = open flower.
Saji (sazi) = small, little, trifling.
Shima = striped.
Shiro = white.
Shirobana = white flower.
Shirofukurin = white margined.
Shironakafu = white in center.
Suji = striped.
Tachi = erect, stately.
Tama = jewel, gem.
To = old, of old.
Tsubomi = closed bud flower.
Tsurigane = temple bell.
Urajiro = white back.
Waisei = dwarf in stature.
Wogon = golden (wogon is obsolute, but in use—ogon is correct).
Yae = double (as in double flowers).

GERMAN

Relatively few German metaphorical names exist, and those extant have been translated in Chapter 4. A number of German descriptive names are translated in the following. Note that the typographic character for the German "sharp *s*" has been replaced by an *ss*.

Blau = blue.
Dauergold = permanently gold.
Dunkel = dark.
Früh = early.
Frühlingsgold = spring gold.
Funkie = *Hosta*.
Gelb = yellow.
Gelbrand = yellow margined.
Glocke = bell.
Gold = gold, golden.
Goldrand = gold margined.
Grau = grey.
Graublau = blue-grey.
Grosse = large.
Grün = green.
Hell = light.
Herbst = fall.
Herzblattlilie = heartleaf lily = *Hosta*.
Herzlilie = heartlily = *Hosta*.
Lang = long.
Langblatt = long leaf.
Lanzenblatt = lance leaf.
Löffelblatt = spoonleaf.
Panaschiert = variegated.
Riese = giant.
Runzelblatt = rugose leaf.
Schatten = shadow.
Schmal = small.
Schmalblatt = small leaf.
Wegerichblättrige Funkie = plantainleaf lily = *Hosta*.
Weiss = white.
Weissrand = white margined.
Wellblatt = undulate leaf.
Ziehrlich = dainty, nice.
Zwerg = dwarf.

KOREAN

The Korean common names are included for Korean taxa.

Banwool-bibich'u = ball-shaped hosta.
Bibich'u = *Hosta*.
Ch'am-bibich'u = lanceolate hosta.
Hanra-bibich'u = Mount Halla hosta.
Huksando-bibich'u = Huksan Island hosta.
Ilwol-bibich'u = ball-shaped hosta.
Jookug-bibich'u = lanceolate hosta.
Tadohae-bibich'u = several islands hosta.

APPENDIX F

Abiotic and Biotic Factors in Cultivation

The cultivation of the genus *Hosta* requires specific ecosystems, and the interrelationship between abiotic and biotic factors in a given environment provides the ecological basis for these systems. Fortunately, the species and hybrids of the genus are relatively unaffected by external factors due to their very high degree of adaptability and their relatively low susceptibility to plant pathogens. Many hybrids have persisted in old gardens and graveyards without any care, and there are unconfirmed reports that some species and fertile varieties have escaped into the wild where they appear to have naturalized.

In most gardens where collections of hostas coexist next to many other living things, attention to biotic and abiotic considerations affecting the cultivation of this plant mixture is highly advisable. While it is beyond the scope of this book to deal with these environmental components in great detail, a brief survey is presented here to alert gardeners as to what they are, how they affect the taxa, and what gardeners can do to minimize harmful effects caused by some while at the same time optimizing abiotic, environmental elements to create the best possible microclimate for the cultivation of hostas. While the following treatment is general, abiotic and biotic factors of high interest to gardeners have been covered in more detail.

Abiotic factors are nonliving components which make up the environment of a given site. Aside from natural habitat or geographic location of cultivated populations already discussed in detail, three abiotic elements merit consideration:

1. Climatic considerations, including summer and winter maximum and average temperatures, average annual rainfall, light (and shade) levels, exposure to direct sunlight, seasonal humidity levels, and air movement, including highest expected wind velocities, occurrence of storms, and hail events.
2. Edaphic constituents, which are the biological, chemical, and physical properties of the soil, including texture, pH level, water content, entrained air, organic content, mineral content, and percolation.
3. Physiographic factors, the "lay of the land," including topographic characteristics such as flat or sloping ground, prevailing surface drainage conditions, erosion, and altitude.

Biotic factors are all the living components of the environment which can influence hosta cultivation. These include microbiota—such as bacteria, fungi, viruses, and other unseen pests usually giving only symptomatic clues to their existence—as well as all other living beings which can damage hostas, including night-feeding insects and insect larvae, leaf-cutting bees, weevils, mollusks (slugs and snails), and larger animals that feed on hostas, such as rabbit and deer, even dogs chasing cats through hosta beds.

ABIOTIC FACTORS

Climate
Climatic factors are obviously related to geographic location as well as to physiographic conditions, principally altitude, which has an effect on climate. The totality of abiotic condi-

tions results in the microclimates which are purely local conditions and can vary even within a small garden from one planting bed to another. Good gardeners are aware of these localized growing conditions and modify them after analysis to provide optimum growing condition regardless of original microclimate.

Climatic zone. Optimum growing conditions for the genus exist in the temperate zone ranging into some subtropical areas (refer to brief discussions under "Rules of Selection" in chapter 6 and references to habitat given under each species in chapter 3).

Optimum temperature ranges. Summer: 75–100° F (24–38° C); winter: −40° F (−40° C). The genus is reliably winter hardy to very low temperatures, which have been reported below −40° F (−40° C) in some areas of cultivation. Winter chilling to around 32° F (0° C) or below for several weeks is required for all taxa in the genus, more so for specific types originating in northern Honshu and Hokkaido. For small taxa repeated soil freezing/thawing cycles can be injurious to root structures. The underground parts of all taxa are fully and reliably winter hardy and can remain frozen solid for extended periods so I have not included maps of hardiness zones.

Average annual precipitation (rain and snow). In cultivation hostas rarely receive as much rain as the species in Japan where the average annual rainfall is a high 61.2 in. (1555 mm)—excluding Ryu-kyu and Okinawa, which have high precipitation but no native populations of *Hosta*. Four distinct regions of precipitation can be isolated: Hokkaido = September high 5.6 in. (142 mm); May low 2.4 in. (61 mm); annual average 40 in. (1016 mm). Ura-Nihon (Japan Sea side) = December high 10.4 in. (264 mm); May low 3.8 in. (97 mm); annual average 73 in. (1854 mm). Omote-Nihon (Pacific Ocean side) = October high 8.7 in. (221 mm); January low 1.9 in. (48 mm); annual average 56 in. (1422 mm). Kyushu region = June high 11.4 in. (290 mm); January low 2.7 in. (69 mm); annual average 76 in. (1930 mm). At least 12 typhoons impact the Japanese islands every year and can add as much as 10–20 in. (254–1016 mm) of rain per event to some areas, principally in the southern regions. The Chinese natural populations receive less rain; in central China 40–60 in. (1016–1524 mm), in northeastern China 20–40 in. (508–1016 mm). Korean species receive 20–40 in. (508–1016 mm), except in the northern parts where dry conditions exist.

For comparison, following are averages of precipitation in other geographic regions where hostas are cultivated: North America = Southeast 40–50 in. (1016–1270 mm); Northeast and Midwest 20–40 in. (508–1016 mm); Northern Plains 10–20 in. (254–508 mm); Northwest Coast 60–80 in. (1524–2032 mm). Central Europe and England 20–40 in. (508–1016 mm); Scotland 50–60 in. (1270–1524 mm); Southeastern Australia 20–40 in. (508–1016 mm); New Zealand 80 in. (2032 mm) east coast to 40 in. (1016 mm) west coast.

Study of the natural habitat given for species in Chapter 3 and references to breeding lines in Chapter 4 permits some conclusions as to the water economy of particular species and their breeding lines, but even without this analysis it is quite obvious that most cultivated populations either do not receive enough precipitation or they receive it during the wrong season so artificial irrigation is required in many areas. Overhead sprinkler systems have been reported to adversely affect the attractive pruinosity or blueness of hostas and should be avoided. The best way to water is by trickle irrigation, which gives a constant supply of moisture to balance the high transpiration rate of hostas.

Lack of moisture results in water stress which first shows as drooping of petioles and leaves followed by the shutdown of the circulatory system and cessation of photosynthesis, causing the yellowing of leaves and onset of premature dormancy, which is called heat dormancy and should not be confused with yellowing caused by biotic factors, which see. Restoration of water supply can produce another set of leaves during the same season but they will be much smaller. The plants, having employed this survival tactic, will almost always come through a drought but are usually set back for a time.

There seems to be a direct relationship between available moisture and growth rates during periods of active growth as reported by Fujita (1976b), so while hostas are highly drought tolerant, the addition of artificial irrigation to cultivated environments will result in larger and better looking plants. Quantitatively, enough artificial watering should be provided to supplement natural precipitation to an equivalent minimum total of 1 in. (25 mm) per week. In case natural rainfall is equal to or exceeds this amount, supplementary watering can be stopped. The addition of clean, nonpacking, loose mulches (ground bark, salt hay, pine needles, ground corn cobs) to reduce surface evaporation is beneficial. Rotting, organic mulches belong on the compost pile until they become humus and should not be applied to hosta beds.

Flooding tolerance. Investigations by Fujita (1976b, 1978b) on water economy and flooding tolerance indicate most taxa in the genus have a high tolerance to temporary flooding. Long-duration submergence is detrimental particularly during periods of dormancy and with the presence of biotic pathogens can cause crown rot. It is best to cultivate hostas in areas where flooding is rare.

Light (and shade) levels. See discussion under "A Place in the Shade" in Chapter 6. For maximum flowering an increased exposure to direct sunlight should be adjusted to the maximum tolerated by a given cultivar with morning sun providing optimum exposure conditions.

Humidity levels. High humidity levels are tolerated better than very low ones, but the entire range of relative-humidity conditions occurring within temperate and subtropical areas of cultivation falls within acceptable limits for the genus. In Japan low-elevation humidity levels in the north (N) are lower than in the south (S), as expected: April, 68% N and 74% S; July, around 80% N and S; October, around 74% N and S; and January, 75% N and 70% S. Some of the thin-leaved taxa originating in areas of wet soil show marginal deterioration during drought periods coincident with low humidity but this damage is cosmetic only and does not affect plant viability and vitality.

Air movement. Low velocity air movement of up to 15 mph (24 kmh) is beneficial to the overall microclimate. In areas having frequent high-velocity wind gusts or sustained winds exceeding 35 mph (56 kmh), the installation of fences or shelterbelt shrubs and trees is required to avoid physical damage, such as breaking of petioles or leaf shredding, particularly in the larger varieties.

Inclement weather. Early fall ice and snowstorms can occur before full dormancy and are not harmful but will hasten the onset of dormancy. If they happen in spring after the tender leaves have unfurled, they are very damaging to the aboveground portions of plants but not fatal, although the plants are set back for a time and leaves are deformed and unattractive for the rest of the season. The underground parts of the plants are not affected because these weather events are usually of short duration.

Hail storms occur frequently in some areas and perforate or shred leaves causing severe cosmetic and physical damage (Plate 16). Even if total defoliation results, the affected plants usually recover in due time. Given advance notice some plants can be covered with inverted pots or other suitable coverings, but this is impractical for large gardens. Location of plantings under sheltering trees may help and some commercial establishments build trellises or canopies not only for partial shading but also for protection from inclement weather.

Catastrophic weather events, such as violent tropical cyclones—hurricanes in the Atlantic Ocean and typhoons in the Pacific Ocean—or other windstorms occasionally affect cultivated populations. Realistically, nothing can protect against these devastating incidents. Most taxa in the genus will survive destruction of top growth and eventually recover.

Frosts and freezes. The stipulations listed earlier under "Inclement Weather" apply. Most hostas, particularly those with heavy leaf substance, can withstand several degrees below freezing (32° F/0° C) for short periods of time, but slight damage can occur. When exposed to temperatures below 28° F (−2° C) for 3–4 hours or more, damage can be widespread, particularly when the freezing episode occurs in late spring while the leaves are still tender. Late fall and early winter frosts and freezes are normal events and are in no way detrimental to the cultivation but will hasten winter dormancy when they happen early in the season. Obviously, they will also spoil the flowers of late-blooming varieties.

The Soil

Crucial to the continuing vitality of cultivated populations is the maintenance of correct edaphic conditions. In their native habitat species adapt to a number of very different soil conditions; some in fact grow epiphytically on trees or lithophytically on sheer rock cliffs virtually without benefit of soil. Gardeners can take advantage of this adaptability by providing soils which are better than those supporting natural populations, growing cultivated taxa that are more vigorous and usually larger than those making up wild populations.

There is a vast number of different soils found in gardens the world over. This subject so important to agriculture and horticulture has been extensively covered in great detail in many books and periodicals, so I am dealing with the aspects affecting the cultivation of hostas only and my comment principally concerns top soils, the surface layer of soil in which cultivation occurs. In gardens this layer is usually modified by soil amendments, tillage, and addition of fertilizers. Natural topsoils are built by the accumulation of decomposing organic matter mixed with natural mineral components.

Physical properties of basic mineral soils. Particles making up mineral soil mixtures are classified by their physical size: Gravel (fine) 2–1 mm; sand (coarse to fine), 1 mm–0.05 mm particle size; silt 0.05–0.005 mm; and clay 0.005 mm and smaller.

Natural soil mixtures. Depending on the ratio of coarse-to-fine particles, key groups of soil types can be isolated: sandy soils, loamy soils, and clayey soils. Loams are mixtures of mineral particles with an optimum combination of coarse and fine particles. There are many intermediate types such as gravelly sands, fine sands, sandy loams, silt loams, sandy clays, heavy clays, and so forth. I recommend reading the section on soil in any of the better garden encyclopedias which cover this involved subject in great detail.

Garden soils. Although I have successfully grown hostas in heavy clay, most natural soils encountered in gardens need improvement to attain good physical structure and openness, a condition sometimes referred to as good tilth. Etymologically, tilth also means cultivation, so it is difficult to define. In most sites good garden soil can be made only by developing and improving natural soils. Preeminent is the addition of organic matter to clay or sandy soils, indeed to any type of natural soil composed chiefly of mineral particles. Organic matter can be ready-to-use, which, for practical reasons, usually takes the form of packaged products, such as a fine-graded ground bark, coarse sphagnum peat, or natural waste products like sawdust, but the latter also requires the addition of slow-release, high-nitrogen fertilizers to feed the decomposition process. Gardeners can collect pine needles, leaves, or other natural waste and compost them to make fine soil amendments. When raw organic materials are digested by soil organisms they become humus, an amorphous, colloidal, black or brown substance that has the ability to retain water; it is an excellent amendment to garden soils—particularly rapid draining, sandy soils—making them water retentive. It also helps the formation of soil crumbs in clayey soils, improving aeration and drainage. Humus is classified as mor humus, formed in acid conditions, and mull humus, formed in circumneutral or alkaline environments. The addition of humus is one of the best ways to improve garden soil because its chemical constituents are directly available to plants. Gardeners often regard the brown, decayed matter on their compost piles as pure humus, but it is in actuality a mixture of raw and decomposed organic matter, some of it colloidal humus, some moder, an intermediate form of humus, and the balance is reduced, raw organic matter in different stages of decomposition. Raw vegetable garbage, grass clippings, and plant waste materials have no place in the garden but should be composted first.

pH level. Soils can be acid, alkaline, or neutral. In their native habitat hostas often grow near pine and oak forests which impart acidity to the surrounding soil, but they also grow on limestone rock where the soil is more alkaline. The genus has great adaptability to soil pH levels, seemingly preferring slightly acid soils, a condition found in most garden soils, so adjustment of pH is normally not required. A condition called *chlorosis* is occasionally encountered in hosta plantings in which the leaves turn slowly yellow but the veins stay dark green. This condition can also be caused by overfertilizing, poorly drained soils, or biotic factors, so spraying the leaves with iron sulphate (1 oz. per 2 gallons or 4 g per liter) can quickly fix the cause. If the leaves temporarily turn green after this treatment, chlorosis is the cause and the pH balance of the soil requires adjustment usually towards the acid side to make the iron in the soil more available; sometimes the addition of chelated iron is required. Aside from this problem, a wide variety of pH levels are tolerated by hostas.

Water content. Hostas have high transpiration rates so require considerable, available amounts of water in the soil to support the required water economy. Watering has been discussed earlier under "Average Annual Precipitation." With

rare, atypical exceptions, wild populations grow in relatively wet soils or near water and this condition is fortified by high humidity and rainfall. For this reason the waterholding capacity of garden soils should be held at an optimum level by the addition of organic matter and thoroughly composted material containing humus. During the spring growing season soil moisture must be maintained at field capacity. The latter is the amount of water which can be held by capillary action in the soil after excess gravitational water has percolated to the water table. As moisture is withdrawn from the soil by absorption through roots or evaporation, the moisture amount becomes less than field capacity and the difference between the actual amount of moisture in the soil and its field capacity is referred to as soil moisture deficit. This deficit can be held to a minimum by supplemental irrigation and the addition of clean mulches to reduce surface evaporation as discussed earlier.

Entrained air and percolation. Soils must be able to breathe, and good garden soils have a high percentage of pore space, which is the empty space in soils usually occupied by air and water. Optimum soils have around 50% solid matter and 50% pore space. At field capacity, the pore space is filled half with water and half with air. Obviously, these are average values which can vary greatly given the many possible combinations. In very fine, natural clay soils the volumetric dimensions of the individual pore spaces become very small, but surface tension increases so the soil can hold larger amounts of water. Heavy clay soils have poor percolation, which is the rate at which water can move through the soil. These soils are called sticky and wet and retain large quantities of water but are difficult to bring back up to field capacity because of poor percolation. Percolation in these soils can be improved by addition of liberal amounts of coarse organic matter as explained earlier. I do not recommend the addition of sands alone to pure clay soils, because they can form concretelike masses through chemical interaction.

Mineral and organic content. Natural, solid top soil matter is composed of 90% mineral and 10% organic matter, but in garden soil the organic constituent can be as much as 50% by volume of the solid soil matter. It depends on how much organic matter gardeners add to the naturally occurring soil. A high percentage of mineral content should be maintained for balance.

Fertilizers and trace elements. Cultivated hostas are heavy feeders and the eventual addition of fertilizers to the soil is inevitable if continued maximum performance is required from the plants. Nutrients can be added in many ways and volumes have been written about different techniques of fertilizing. Because nutrients are absorbed at a fairly high rate by fast-growing hostas, the danger of overfertilizing is always present. For this reason I resort to only one type fertilizer, which not only contains nitrogen, phosphorus, and potassium, but many required trace elements, such as magnesium, iron, and calcium. This fertilizer comes in the form of osmotic pellets and feeds through osmosis for extended periods. Available as Osmocote® it comes in two formulas: 14–14–14 with 2–4 months time release, and 18–6–12 with 8–9 months time release. I use the latter which is available in 20- and 50-pound bags for U.S. $35 and $50, respectively. A 50-pound bag will feed my entire cultivated hosta population in 10,000 square feet (930 square meters) of beds, applied sparingly at the base of each plant. Other fertilizers will do but many are water soluble so are depleted by heavy spring rains that wash most of the nutrients away. If Osmocote® is not available, other, slow-release, nonwater soluble, urea-based fertilizers like Nitroform® can be used. I do not recommend the use of raw chemical fertilizers, such as ammonium nitrate or superphosphate, due to the danger of burning nor do I employ foliar feeding because it deposits a residue marring the attractive pruinosity of blue hostas. In most areas application should be made in early spring, but in more southern latitudes where the ground rarely freezes and some root growth continues through winter, fertilizer can be applied in late winter.

Physiographic factors

Topography. The lay of the land requires some consideration in the cultivation of hostas. Some rules are obvious, such as avoiding areas where temporary flooding occurs (see "Flooding Tolerance" above), or where frequent landslides or heavy erosion can have a detrimental effect on plantings. On the other hand, hosta plantings, once established, can help considerably in the stabilization of moving soils so actually prevent erosion.

Another consideration is the existence of frost pockets in certain areas, where year after year frosts spoil the awakening plantings. Acutely sloping ground may excessively speed the drainage of rain water and prevent maximum absorption of moisture, particularly if the soil is heavy and requires soaking, so terracing is frequently required to remedy this situation. Soil in low areas, having no way of draining surface water, can become waterlogged; some adjustment in topography must be made to improve surface or subsurface drainage. Conversely, unsheltered, high places in the landscape can expose plantings to high winds, cause continuous, rapid drying conditions, and present difficulties in maintaining soil moisture field capacity. Gardeners should consider topography when establishing hosta plantings but not unduly so because hostas in the wild grow in some of the most unbelievably difficult places and appear to thrive under such conditions.

Physiogenic factors. One or more of the various environmental conditions described above can act in concert and become detrimental to hosta cultivation: There may be too much sun, not enough nutrients in the soil, a too dry or perhaps waterlogged soil, a lack of trace elements, or too much fertilizer, so the plants are put under stress. Unfortunately that environment is frequently created by overzealous or uninformed gardeners, who can literally kill with kindness.

BIOTIC FACTORS

Coming to grips with the abiotic environment of a garden is relatively easy when compared to the many creatures, both large and small, which invade cultivated hosta populations. Many are beneficial—for example, pollinators, insect-eating birds, some soil bacteria, earthworms, and mycorrhiza (symbiotic soil fungi, although they have not been shown to be a factor in the cultivation of hostas). Unfortunately, there is also a high percentage of living, environmental components which can adversely affect hosta cultivation. These include microbiota, such as bacteria, fungi and viruses, as well as all the visible living beings which can damage hostas plantings. Following is a brief survey of biotic considerations, starting with the smallest components.

Viruses. The existence of viruses in *Hosta* tissue has been suspected for some time but has not been verified (Vaughn, 1989a). Later reports (Vaughn, 1989b; Pollock, 1989) discuss the presence of viruses in the genus in a manner which allows the presumption that viruses are indeed present. Unconfirmed reports connect tobacco virus (TMV) with the genus.

Viruses consist of ultramicroscopic, pathogenic nucleoprotein molecules which, once inside a living plant, start behaving like living organisms. As long as a virus is outside a host plant (actually the cells of plants), it can be characterized as deoxyribonucleic acid (DNA) or ribonucleic acid (RNA) surrounded by a protein shell, called a capsid, which protects the DNA and RNA of the virus. The nature of the capsid determines what host plants the virus will attack, and is also important in the identification of a virus based on the serological reaction to the capsid proteins.

The symptoms induced by viral pathogens are chlorosis (yellowing of the leaves), mottling or mosaicism (presence of white or yellowish spots), blotching (whitened areas larger than spots), wilting and collapse of plant tissue, streaking of flower petals, and a general reduction in vigor and stunting caused by partial shutdown of the vascular system and consequently also photosynthesis. Not all viruses are pernicious; some types are actually welcome because they produce attractive markings on flower petals and so are tolerated. In most cases, though, viruses are harmful or sometimes even lethal so must be eliminated because they can spread and infect healthy plant populations.

No conclusive data are available as to how viral infections are spread in *Hosta* from one plant to another. Informal experiments by Vaughn (1989b) point to a requirement for cell sap exchange. Leaves from infected plants were ground and the extract spread on seedlings which were subsequently infected by the virus. It can be assumed that the virus is spread by any action which transfers cell sap from one plant to another—for example, by cutting or sucking insects or by gardeners who use the same garden tools first on infected and then on healthy plants. The virus can also spread through asexual propagation methods and often through seed. Because there is no known control or cure of viral diseases and due to their infectious behavior, I recommend that plants showing the above symptoms be destroyed as soon as symptoms are definitely identified as viral in nature. Mosaicism is almost always a viral infection, but leaf yellowing can have a number of other causes—for example, the normal yellowing occurring due to vascular shutdown at the onset of dormancy. Occasionally many leaves turn yellow during very hot and dry weather; this is normal, signaling a high degree of soil moisture deficit and the onset of heat stress due to lack of water, and it usually results in heat dormancy until watering is resumed. In this case the leaves will remain firm for quite some time and dry up slowly, just like they do at the onset of winter.

The leaf yellowing often attributed to virus can also be caused by fungi, usually starting with the outer leaves and progressing to the inner leaves. When leaves turn yellow in a sporadic fashion, perhaps just one or two on a crown, and they collapse fairly rapidly but are hard to separate from the crown, a viral problem may exist. Caution should always be exercised and perhaps professional help in identifying the problem may be needed in cases of severe infestations. Although the exact mechanism of how viruses spread is not known, viral infections are usually localized and may initially affect only one or, at the most, a few plants. At present no effective treatment against viral infections is known and the only certain cure is to ruthlessly destroy all infected plants before the virus can spread throughout a garden. It may be a good idea to buy inexpensive garden tools for use in this procedure which afterwards can be thrown away.

Parasitic biota. Bacteria and fungi are the most prevalent of the microscopic pathogens found affecting the genus. They usually enter plant tissue at cut, torn, or abraded sites and once inside the plant tissue multiply rapidly. They can cause decay, contribute to secondary infections, and may in the end result in the demise of the plant.

Crown rot, a frequently observed problem, belongs in this category (Schmid, 1987c). Infections can start anytime, but most often pathogens invade the rhizome in fall and early winter. The old leaves having been killed by a freeze are invaded by ever-present bacteria and fungi starting decomposition which normally stops at the healthy tissue of the crown. At this point injury to the crown, perhaps stepping on it, cutting it for increase, or damaging it while digging it can open wounds through which bacteria can enter healthy tissue with the result of bacterial rot accompanied by fungal action. In this type of infection, the top of the rhizome is first affected. Other adverse conditions, such as frequent freeze and thaw cycles or waterlogged soil, may also provide the right conditions for healthy tissue to be affected. Most of the time this happens below ground and cannot be detected. During the winter season while the ground is frozen or very cold the bacterial action is slowed or halted. When the soil warms up in spring with plenty of moisture in the ground, small, localized infections spread rapidly and soon the entire crown including the large feeder roots are involved. Detection is difficult because it only affects the underground portions of the plant so no symptoms show. In severe cases the entire rhizome turns to mush and no leaves appear in spring so treatment is usually too late; the remains should be dug up and burned or disposed of outside the garden in approved disposal sites. Infected plant tissue has no place on the compost pile. The cause for this is frequently *Botrytis cinera* (Schmid, 1987c), the grey mold fungus, but other microorganisms are usually involved, acting in concert.

Another fungal malady strikes hostas after they have leafed out, and its symptoms are easy to recognize. During hot, wet and humid weather outwardly healthy-looking leaves suddenly collapse. Inspection of the petiole usually shows softening and disintegration of the petiole base tissue where it joins the rhizome. White fungus threads and orange-brown or light brown sclerotia, a certain growth stage of fungi, are visible. Other leaves when pulled will separate from the crown with little effort, and leaf color is normally not affected, although in some cases mild yellowing before collapse has been reported. This condition is usually caused by *Sclerotium rolfsii* (syn. *Corticium rolfsii*), in Japan called *Shira Kanu*, in North America called southern blight, white silk fungus, or white mold fungus (Schmid, 1987c; Solberg, 1988b; Sugita, 1988). This problem almost always happens in crowns which stay submerged for extended periods, are covered with heavy, suffocating layers of rotting, organic mulch, or are planted in low spots in heavy, poorly draining, acid clay soils subject to waterlogging.

In these cases yellowing is attributed to *Fusarium oxysporum* and *Verticillium alboatrum* which are prevalent during hot weather and should be treated by repeated applications of a systemic fungicide like Benlate® (DuPont Chemical Company) or Benomyl®, following the manufacturer's directions to the letter. These remedies will not cure the parts already yellow because photosynthesis has been terminally interrupted in these leaves by blockage of the vascular system, so only unaffected leaves can be saved.

Early detection is absolutely essential. Once a crown is affected the decay process is irreversible and affected parts cannot be cured because there is no magic bullet for curing hosta crown or petiole rot. Only surgery together with a sanitizing treatment to prevent reinfection can save the unspoiled part of a crown.

I have saved hostas using the following procedure but must admit I would go through all this trouble only for very expensive or rare plants. The procedure begins by digging up the plant and washing off all soil in a place away from other plants to prevent infection of other garden areas. Inspection of the rhizome may reveal the existence of healthy, white, firm tissue and roots which are the parts to be saved. All soft tissue is diseased and must be ruthlessly removed with a sharp knife; this should include removal of all suspicious tissue realizing that some affected tissue may still be firm but has discolored and must be cut away.

During this procedure it will quickly become evident if the crown is worth saving and as long as a small piece of the crown with some healthy roots attached can be isolated and treated it will usually live. Obviously, this procedure is a radical measure and it will set the plant back for a long time. After being separated the healthy piece or pieces should be air-dried on paper towels or clean newspapers in a sunny spot, turning several times to let the ultraviolet rays sanitize all surfaces; the pieces must be completely dry before submerging them in a solution containing a fungicide and an antibiotic. Both of the chemicals recommended here are systemic. That means they are absorbed by the plant and permeate the plant tissue. They can, therefore, treat systemic diseases. Some reports have suggested dipping in weak bleach, but this will only eliminate surface microbes and contaminants so I do not recommend it. During this treatment a final check should be made to make certain no diseased or soft spots have been missed previously.

The broad spectrum treatment recommended here requires two chemicals. Both are biodegradable and will not pollute the environment. They are: (1) an antibiotic Agrimycin 17® (Pfizer Company) or Agristrep® (Merck and Company) containing 17% streptomycin as streptomycin sesquisulfate with a recommended dilution of one ounce per 6 gallons of water (1.25 grams per liter), and (2) a fungicide Benlate® (DuPont Chemical Company) or Benomyl®, using 3 tablespoons per 6 gallons of water (about 1/3 teaspoon per liter). Both chemicals can be added to the same 6 gallons (23 liters) of water or, if less solution is needed, a smaller amount can be prepared proportionately adjusting the ingredients. A clean plastic container is ideal for the treatment, immersing the healthy part for 6 to 8 hours, making certain all the roots are completely covered. Several crowns can be treated in the same container. After this soaking period they can be planted, without drying, in sterile soil in new plastic containers of adequate size, adding a mild, liquid fertilizer or osmotic pellets. The top of the crown should be planted slightly above the soil surface to allow periodic inspection and these pots should be kept in an isolated area. If winter is approaching the pots can be sunk into well-drained ground for overwintering. After this severe treatment the plant may not leaf out until the next growing season, and frequent checks should be made for appearance of any softness by pushing down with a finger on the crown which should feel firm and hard. The solution used for immersion can be utilized to drench the holes from which the affected hostas were removed. The systemic fungicide treatment has also been reported effective by Solberg (1988b). Additionally, some reports suggest sanitizing the area around the infection site with PCNB (Terrachlor®; Brassicol®; pentachloronitrobenzene) or hydroxyisoxasol (3-Hydroxy-5-Methylisoxasole) applied as recommended by the manufacturers (Sugita, 1988; Solberg, 1988b). Treatment continues by watering the pots sparingly with freshly prepared solution every three to four days for a three-week period after which watering with plain water can be resumed as needed. Patience is required for the results are not definitively known until the following growing season or until the rescued piece decides to leaf out. Before using PCNB or similar chemicals gardeners should carefully consider environmental consequences.

While crown rot appears to be the most prevalent form of systemic hosta diseases, occasionally leaf spot and anthracnose blight can be seen, which are similar to leaf spot on roses and caused by *Fungi imperfecti* (deuteromycotina). They can be treated by spraying the plant every day for four days with the same solution described above, then repeating the treatment once a week for four weeks. Spraying with a systemic insecticide, such as Ortho's Orthene®, in accordance with directions, will keep insects from attacking the weakened plant. In this case the plant need not be dug up but should be checked for soft spots or fungal action around the top of the rhizome at soil level.

Prevention is unquestionably the best way to avoid all these problem. Good cultural practices go a long way toward reducing diseases: Avoid low spots that get flooded every spring; improve soil if it is mostly clay; stay away from heavy, rotting, organic mulches in the fall, instead apply light, clean mulches, like pine needles, or better, none at all, because hostas are very hardy. Plant pathogens, particularly bacteria and fungi, are everywhere, and sterilizing the planting hole with PCNB or a similar chemical and backfilling with clean planting soil goes a long way in eliminating microbiota as well as insect larvae and other subterranean pests. Another important factor in preventing these diseases is the reduction of physical damage to the plants caused by slugs and insects which can result in secondary infections. If widespread damage has occurred only a regular spray program using an insecticide/fungicide combined with a slug poison can eradicate the problem, but some gardeners are hesitant to employ continuous spray programs for fear of poisoning the environment.

A compromise which I have instituted at Hosta Hill has worked well and uses a minimum of chemicals: During a windfree, sunny morning in very early spring, when the first hosta shoots appear, the entire property is sprayed by way of an overhead irrigation system with a systemic fungicide/insecticide combination (Benlate®/Orthene®) employing a timed, automatic mixing/suction device to apply correct amounts of chemicals. Precautions are taken, such as covering bird baths and feeders, and I stay indoors while application takes place. This process is repeated one more time 3–4 weeks later, and my experience shows a majority of the problems are eliminated. Any problems showing up after June are treated locally if action is warranted.

Above all, gardeners should regularly visit the hosta sites, checking the progress and health of all plants, particularly in early spring. Use of all the gardener's senses are decisive: look, touch, and smell. When dealing with fungal diseases and bacterial rot, early detection is absolutely necessary or it may be too late to rescue affected hostas.

Nematodes: Phylum Aschelmintes, the round worm or thread worm, encompasses class Nematoda also called eelworms or nematodes, thus are microbiota in the length range of 0.02–0.2 in. (0.5–5 mm) although some grow much larger and are visible. Eelworms colonize virtually every habitat from the equator to the poles. Nematodes specializing on agricultural crops are serious pests causing an estimated U.S. $1 billion in damage yearly to U.S. agriculture. Common horticultural afflictions are the cyst-forming nematodes belonging to genera *Heterodera*, and in warmer regions *Meliodogyne*—rootknot eelworms or root gall nematodes, which invade the root structures and lay eggs in cysts formed from root tissue. These cysts or galls are visible when the roots are exposed. The damage is done by the release of poisons or enzymes which alter cell content leading to stunted growth or loss of vigor. The cysts, full of eggs formed by some species, detach themselves awaiting another cycle and staying viable for many years. Other species form permanent galls which remain part of the roots, and the nematodes do not leave the host plant

until it dies or the roots are severed. No truly effective control exists for living plants, but the ground can be fumigated before planting, a process best left to professionals. Some granular nematicides are available and should be tried. Good cultural practices, watering, and fertilizing can overcome some of the damage.

Insects and other macrobiotic pests: There are no records that any particular insect species specializes on hostas. More often than not the hostas happen to be in a site where, for example, weevils have infested azaleas, and their proximity also leads to weevil damage on hosta leaves (Figure F-1). It is impossible to list all the insect pests which could possibly affect cultivated populations in the northern and southern temperate zones. The larvae of butterflies and moths in the order Lepidoptera include some of the most damaging of the insect pests, and there are over 100,000 species. Some of the 50,000 species of true weevils that exist around the world feed on hosta roots and superstructures. Gastropods in phylum Mollusca, encompass the destructive land snails, a group counting over 10,000 species, and it is easy to see that comprehensive, worldwide treatment of these problematic biota would take considerably more space than can be allocated, so I am limiting myself to those pests which have been identified in the literature as pandemic in the genus: mollusks (Summers, 1970b; Waters, 1982; Pollock, 1984c; Schmid 1986c; Wilkins, 1986); weevils (Stevens, 1984; Pollock, 1985d; Webster and Rutherford, 1986); caterpillars (private correspondence; numerous reports). According to my own observations during my travels as well as those of correspondents in Europe and Japan, many of the harmful species in North America are also troublesome in Europe and in Japan, so the commentary applies to all areas where hostas are cultivated except that different, but related species may be involved in causing damage.

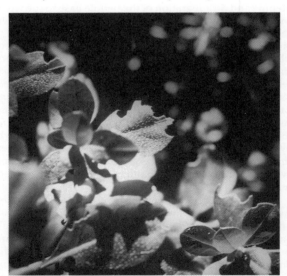

Figure F-1. *Azalea* 'Pink Pearl'; Black Vine Weevil damage (Hosta Hill)

Mollusks: While some snails are harvested to make an epicurean meal for daring gourmets as escargot (*Helix pomotia*), gardeners consider a number of mollusk species as serious pests. The latter belong to the large phylum Mollusca, class Gastropoda, which has 40,000 species, many of which are marine and freshwater varieties. Of interest to gardeners are principally the soft-bodied, invertebrate, gastropod, hermaphrodite land snails and slugs in Stylommatophora, of which there are over 10,000 species.

Slugs belonging to the Arionidae, chiefly of European origin, are now well known all over the world having been accidentally introduced in many other areas. Identified as garden plagues have been *Arion hortensis*, the common garden slug, the red slug (*A. rufus*), the black slug (*A. ater*) growing to 6 in. (15 cm), and the dusky slug (*A. subfusus*). The Limacid slugs in the Limacidae, known as keeled slugs, cause extensive damage in gardens and include the great garden slug (*Limax maximus*) and the ash-black slug (*L. cineroniger*). A species known as *Deroceras reticulatum*, the field slug, is widespread, causes considerable horticultural and agricultural damage, and will invade gardens.

Snails are morphologically similar to slugs but are characterized by having a shell of various, occasionally very attractive designs, and include the garden snail, *Helix aspersa*, which is quite common, and the banded snails belonging to *Cepaea* (*C. normalis* and *C. hortensis*).

As soft as the mollusk's body may be, it has horny, rasplike teeth (radula) with which it can eat through even the most substantive hosta leaf or sprout. The larger mollusks get to be several inches long, and they can devour the entire top of an emerging hosta during the course of one night. Against these large mollusks even the very heavy substance of *H.* 'Tokudama' is no defense (Figure 3-75). The medium-size and smaller mollusks (1–3 in./2.5–7.5 cm in length) are also voracious eaters, so to minimize the damage all kinds of countermeasures have been suggested.

Slugs and snails are hermaphrodites, meaning they can produce offspring without benefit of a sexual union, but they do also mate. The egg clusters are produced in batches from a few to many laid in moist places under vegetation, abandoned flower pots, wood piles, and other hiding places including soil fissures and hollows. Depending on the species involved, during a life cycle hundreds to thousands of eggs are produced with a high survival rate, so the fight against mollusks is a constant one. Successful gardeners are able to reduce the adult population to a minimum and put up with minor damage caused by newly hatched generations climbing onto the leaves (Figure F-2) but adults cause extensive damage, occasionally eating an entire shoot at the ground line in spring, and so must be controlled. The plant will still emerge, but the leaves will be extensively damaged.

Figure F-2. *H.* 'Gosan Gold Sword'; damage caused by small slugs (Hosta Hill)

Usually, application of broad-spectrum insecticides in early spring, as discussed earlier, will kill some baby snails, so reducing this problem also. Because many of the mollusks become sexually mature very early on, the generation gap is very brief and attention must be paid to this problem consistently. A study of the mollusk population in a given site should precede any countermeasures at which time the area can also

be inspected for possible hiding places which must be eliminated. A good cleanup goes a long way. Some reports find the maximum damage during summer (Grenfell, personal communication; Pollock, personal communication), but this may be due to a lapse in vigilance during the late season. In spring, when cultivated hostas are at prime condition, gardeners are more alert so spend more time and effort on detecting and eliminating pests. During the lazy summer days mollusks and other pests get the upper hand; resigned gardeners often put up with them because the first freeze is not too far away so considerable damage is frequently tolerated. Unfortunately, during this time many eggs are laid which hatch with the new broods generally hibernating during winter and literally overrunning the garden in spring. Often this requires drastic methods to eliminate at least some of the burgeoning gastropod population. Following is a very successful method I have used for some time, with other methods mentioned as well.

At Hosta Hill control consists of preventative measures described earlier and a molluskicide which will not hurt the lovely song birds and other wildlife in the garden and which has minimum environmental impact. Keeping these restrictions in mind my program involves (1) patience, (2) timing, (3) cleanup, (4) persistence, and (5) Ortho Deadline®. It is impossible to control snail and slug populations overnight so patience is required, and gardeners must realize total eradication is probably an elusive goal because they can infiltrate from neighboring areas and constantly regenerate from egg clusters. Correct timing is absolutely crucial to success. The spring warmup produces the biggest crop of new slugs and snails, and at this time the application of poison is most effective; in most areas of cultivation this time period occurs shortly before early hosta sprouts appear. Outside air temperature may still be cold, but in protected areas warmed by the sun hibernation ends and the slugs commence their search for food. Some vigilance is required in the warmer sections of the temperate regions to detect very early infestations. A thorough cleanup is an absolute must, so leaves, sticks, pine cones, and other debris must be removed from beds, paths, and planting areas, and this sanitation should take place as early as possible in spring or started in late fall, at least to some extent. Anything that is lying on the ground can be a hiding place for mollusks during the daytime when ultraviolet rays endanger their existence and force them to seek cover. During cloudy, rainy days they can be seen climbing to the top of leaves. Feeding takes place during night.

While eliminating the hiding places, leaves and other debris should be inspected on the underside for hiding mollusks which can be scraped into a container with denatured alcohol eliminating them cleanly. As described earlier under "Bacteria and Fungi," I apply Orthene® (Ortho-Chevron) in combination with a fungicide twice each spring because of the relatively warm climate of the site which has virtually no winter-kill of insects and so requires strong measures. The insecticide usually also kills small mollusks, but is not an essential part of this program. I have found Bug-Geta-Deadline® (Ortho-Chevron) to be the ultimate slug killer. Formerly made by Pace National Corporation and now marketed by Ortho Chemical, a division of Chevron, it comes in a plastic squeeze bottle with a spout in the familiar yellow-red Ortho label and reportedly is now also being marketed in Europe. The 16-ounce bottle is most economical and lasts a long time. The product is a bluish-grey, thickened water system containing 4% metaldehyde, a synergist, and a selective, mollusk-specific attractant which has proven to be highly effective. This is squeezed out of the bottle in a thin bead or in small drops; small amounts only are required. Drawn out of their hiding places by the attractant, the mollusks consume some of the product which together with the synergist results in fast dehydration and death. Unlike poisoned bran products, this grey slug-killer does not attract birds and other wildlife. I have most of my more-expensive hostas in brick-bordered beds, with others bordering walks or fences. I simply squeeze a bead of Deadline® around each bed and along the walks, near the hostas. The product will last two weeks or more before it dries up and becomes ineffective, but light rain will revitalize it and it again becomes effective. Heavy rains will obviously wash it into soil as a nontoxic residue. I use it sparingly all summer and into the fall, using up to four 16-ounce bottles during this time. Initially more may have to be applied to get the gastropod infestation under control. Finally, persistence is the key to success. After the initial application a few boards with a few leaves of fresh lettuce underneath as bait will indicate if slugs are still present. Checking frequently for some light damage (Figure F-2) I apply more Deadline®. With this method I have been able to get the mollusk populations under control or at least limited to new broods which, due to their size, cause minimal damage.

Similar products and control methods are in use in England and other European countries, where Impregnated Tapes, Ltd. markets a paper tape which is permeated with metaldehyde and a selective attractant. The product works similar to Deadline® and is nontoxic to wild life and biodegradable. Reportedly, there are other products employing the metaldehyde/attractant combination including the bran/metaldehyde combination mentioned earlier. Slugit® also uses metaldehyde as the active ingredient. Manufactured by Murphy Chemical, Ltd., England, it is a liquid product which contains 22.8% metaldehyde in solution together with 9.37% surface active agent, thickener, inert base, and bacteriostat; 10% ethylene glycol, and the balance water (Pollock, 1987b). The product is distributed by MAC-PAK, a division of McHutchison & Co., Ridgefield, NJ. Reduced to a 2–5% solution of metaldehyde with water, frequent applications are required starting in early spring before the hosta shoots emerge.

Nonpoisonous methods include spreading diatomaceous earth, wood ashes, soot, sharp cinders, and other, similar material around the plants. I have tried some but unsuccessfully. Finely ground pine bark seems to have some effect when loose and dry because it coats the gastropods' foot with bark fines which apparently cannot be overcome by increased secretion of slime, so repels them, but this is only marginally useful because the bark fines must be loose and dry, a difficult state to achieve during rainy spring. Some reports call for adding short, broken cedar shingle fibers (shingle tow).

Biological controls include birds, skunks, shrews, and turtles. At Hosta Hill a family of chipmunks—a species of ground squirrels, the striped squirrel (*Tamias striatus*)—consumes a considerable number of snails judging by piles of broken snail shells at the entrance to their burrows, and they probably eat slugs, too, without leaving a trace. Unfortunately, they dig extensive tunnels and can be a real nuisance. Finally, some gardeners sink containers into the ground, the tops level with the surface adding a small amount of beer in which the attracted mollusks drown. Other lures include inverted grapefruit skins, lettuce, and other preferred foods around which slugs congregate during the night for feeding; they can be gathered in the early morning before sunrise and disposed of.

Leaf cutters: The nonsocial, solitary bees are little known but include agriculturally important groups like those in the Andrenidae, known as effective pollinators in apple orchards. The Megachilidae, containing about 1000 species, includes the leaf-cutter bees (*Megachile* ssp). To line their nests, these bees

cut sometimes perfectly round or oval sections measuring 0.2–0.5 in. (5–12 mm) out of leaf margins (Figure F-3). Damage is very characteristic but usually isolated to a few plants so can be tolerated. I have found that these bees prefer certain soft-leaved taxa—for instance, the redbud (*Cercis canadensis*) in eastern North America—so leave nearby hostas alone (as shown in Figure F-3). I have never seen leaf cutter damage on hosta leaves with thick substance; they seem to prefer soft-textured leaves as in *H.* 'Honeybells' or *H. plantaginea*. Control is difficult, although systemic insecticides reportedly have some effect.

Figure F-3. *H. montana* leaf; untouched but damage by leaf-cutter bee evident on nearby Redbud (*Cercis canadensis*) leaf (Hosta Hill)

Weevils: Belonging in Coleoptera, the snout beetles, are a large group of insects containing 50,000 species, some of which present a serious agricultural problem in many areas—for example, the cotton boll weevil (*Anthonomus grandis*) in southeastern North America where its devastating effects on the cultivation of cotton are well known. Many of the species in the Curculionidae, the true weevils, tend to specialize on specific plants or plant groups so have become a significant pest for some ornamentals, as for example in azaleas and rhododendrons (Figure F-1). One of the species identified as causing damage is the black vine weevil (*Otiorhynchus sulcatus*), but other species of true weevils are occasionally involved (the strawberry root weevils, *Otiorhynchus ovatus* and *O. rugosostriatus*). Visual damage caused by the adult beetles feeding at night and consists of irregular notches eaten out of leaf margins (Figure F-4). Even more destructive are the beetle larvae, cream colored with orange heads, feeding on the roots. Control is difficult, but the adults can be killed with repeated applications of a systemic insecticide. The larvae are more difficult to eradicate but drenching the area with PCNB (terrachlor; brassicol; pentachloronitrobenzene) has been reported to be effective as has granular diazinon. A novel biological approach to control has been described by Simon

Figure F-4. *H.* 'Nakaimo'; Black Vine Weevil damage (Hosta Hill)

Frazer University in British Columbia (Webster and Rutherford, 1986), where researchers have discovered that the nematode *Heterohabditis heliothidis* causes death in weevils by being eaten and releasing deadly blood-poisoning bacteria and also by penetrating the skin of the insect and feeding on its blood cells. The selective, specialized nematode is harmless to other plants and humans and should be the control of choice.

Larvae of butterflies and moths: The order Lepidoptera encompasses 112,000 species of butterflies and moths having worldwide distribution and with a large number of species endemic to the temperate zones. The adults are mostly very attractive and admired as beautiful insects. Nevertheless, during their larval stage, representing the second stage of metamorphosis, many of the species of this large group cause great damage to food crops and ornamentals. Some are migratory in the adult stage so can infest certain areas overnight. Even the larvae of some species are migratory—for example, the army worms or striped caterpillars which occasionally move in huge numbers. Fortunately, many of the butterfly and moth larvae have specialized feeding habits so usually bypass hostas in favor of other food plants. The well-known migratory monarch, *Danaus plexippus,* for example, feeds only on milkweed, genus *Asclepias.* However, the larvae of some night-feeding owlet or noctuid moths belonging to the Noctuidae have a voracious appetite for anything green, and their damage can be devastating in cultivated hosta populations (Figures F-5, F-6; Plate 29).

Figure F-5. *H. ventricosa;* night-feeding caterpillar (moth larvae) damage (Hosta Hill)

Figure F-6. *H. montana;* multiple damage from moth larvae of night-feeding caterpillar (center), weevils (top), and holes made by needles of several species of pine (Hosta Hill)

Both chemical and biological controls are available. Unfortunately, only chemical methods will work fast enough to control overnight infestation so at present it is the only choice in difficult, but usually localized situations. One of the prime considerations in using pesticides is their toxicity or potential ill effects on the environment. If food crops are grown among or nearby hostas, systemic insecticides should be ruled out, but contact poisons can be used if the foods are carefully cleaned before consumption. In any case the instructions on the manufacturer's label should be followed absolutely, and one very important caution implores the users not to apply the poison during windy days to avoid drift. The choice is a broad-spectrum systemic type which kills a broad range of insects, is absorbed by the plant through its roots and leaves, and remains effective for up to two weeks. I found two products conform to this specification: Orthene® and Isotox®, made by Chevron/Ortho Division and available in many places and also under different names from other manufacturers the world over. Orthene® and Isotox-Formula II® contain 9.4% by weight of active, systemic ingredient (acephate = O,S-Dimethyl acetylphosphoramidothioate), while Isotox® has 8% by weight of the same ingredient, plus an additional 3% of Kelthane® miticide. As described earlier, at Hosta Hill application is made during the first really warm weekend after young hosta shoots have appeared. In the warmer areas of hosta cultivation this may be in February, but it is usually safe to wait until March. In northern regions it is advisable to wait until the snow has melted and the soil has started warming up. The best timing device for application may be the hostas themselves, signaling correct time when the very first hostas emerge.

Biological controls include predatory wasps and insect-eating birds and mammals. Repeated applications of *Bacillus thuringiensis,* which is eaten by the caterpillars and kills them, have proved effective. Gardeners not wanting to use chemical poisons should find out about these methods and utilize them. Timing is of the essence with this biological control and slight, beginning damage (not as extensive as shown in Figure F-5) signals immediate application is required.

Mammals: Several species of mammals reportedly feed on hostas—principally in spring when the growth is young and tender—and these include members of the deer family, Cervidae, and rabbits belonging to the hare family, Leporidae. Damage consists of partially eaten sprouts or the destructive removal of entire, emerging leaf bundles. Rabbits can be easily fenced out. Deer are another matter, because many species easily can and will jump over standard-height (4 ft./1.2 m) chain-link fencing to get to a food supply. To reliably keep out deer, animal control experts recommend fences with a minimum height of 8 ft. (2.4 m), topped with barbed and electric wire. Many gardeners have neither the funds nor the inclination to convert their property into a cage so other methods have been tried. One apparently successful method (Descloux, 1989) uses a foul-smelling concoction consisting of two eggs, one clove of garlic, a cup of green onion, and two cups of water. These ingredients are liquefied in a blender with two tablespoons of chili pepper, then poured into a 1-quart (1-liter) container, after which a bar of deodorant soap is added and the mixture topped off with water. This preparation is stored unrefrigerated for some time and then sprinkled on the hostas, leaves, buds, and scapes. During the main growing season the applications are repeated weekly if it rains or biweekly during dry periods. Since deer are no problem at Hosta Hill, I have no personal experience dealing with them and have not tried this method. Yinger (1990), who fences out deer on his property, states:

My experiences with deer leave me very pessimistic about most forms of control. Most anything will work if the population is small, but as the competition for food increases, deer become more bold. They soon become disdainful of most controls.

Other experienced gardeners have written about this subject, and I recommend reading McGourty (1989), who has devoted an entire chapter of his book to his own problems with deer, all the while keeping enough of a sense of humor to deal with it in a funny, but thoroughly educational way.

Severe physical damage can be inflicted on plantings, primarily by the larger breeds of domesticated dogs (*Canis*) and cats (*Felis domesticus*) when running or chasing through gardens. Some cats have the odious habit of using hosta clumps as a cooling bed on hot summer days, flattening them and breaking many, if not every petiole in the clump (Figure F-7).

Figure F-7. *H.* 'Blue Cadet'; used by a cat as a cooling summer bed (this is the same plant shown during its prime in Figure 2-1) (Hosta Hill)

In North America and Europe several species of voles invade hosta plantings: the field mouse (*Microtus agrestis*), the meadow vole (*M. pennsylvanicus*), the European red or bank vole (*Evotomys glareolus* or *Clethrionomys glareoulus*) and its North American counterpart (*C. gapperi*). The southeastern North American pine vole (*Microtus pinetorum*) and the central European water vole (*Arvicola terrestris*) may also play a role. The rodent species native to particular areas have been reported as serious pests (Blanchette, 1989; Solberg, 1989) and terrestrial squirrels, such as the striped ground squirrel or chipmunk (*Tamias striatus*), also damage cultivated populations by digging tunnels in planting beds and in some cases feeding on the rhizomes and roots. Burrowing rodents, principally gophers belonging to the genera *Geomys* and *Thomomys*, also ravage hosta plantings by their extensive tunneling.

Digging rodents, such as various species of squirrels belonging to the genus *Sciurus*, damage individual clumps by digging holes to bury seeds and acorns in the fall and retrieving them in spring. I have observed smaller clumps being completely dug up and thrown aside during this search for buried food.

Control of these pests is difficult and involves passive methods, such as fencing or chaining, but more often active controls, principally trapping and poisoning, are employed on wild animals. Before using any of these methods, the existence of local restrictive laws should be investigated. Biological controls are obvious—for example, cats against voles or trained dogs against rabbits—but this control can backfire when the animals engage in fast pursuit through hosta plantings.

Physical and cosmetic damage by falling natural products: Cultivated hosta populations are frequently planted under trees so are exposed to a continuous rain of micro- and macro-particles, bits of bark, sap, seed, leaves, pollen, living and dead insects, animal droppings, and numerous other natural products. Although most of these do no physical damage, they accumulate in the pockets of rugose leaves (Figure 2-18) and in the cup-shaped leaves of some varieties, as for example *H. tokudama* and its hybrids and forms (Figure 2-19). Neither rain nor wind will dislodge them and they eventually become attached and so adversely affect the appearance of a leaf or an entire plant.

Gardeners should also avoid planting hostas under trees which produce large seed pods or fruit, including most of the fruit and nut trees, but also many of the pine trees, magnolias, and other, large-fruited trees. Falling pine cones can cause considerable leaf damage (Figure F-8) and even pine needles driven by wind or height can pierce leaves (Figure F-6).

Another problem is caused by tree droppings, such as the resinous droplets descending from many of the pine trees or the sticky nectar exuded by some flowering trees, for example, the tulip tree (*Liriodendron tulipifera*) of North America, a magnificent forest tree. These secretions are impossible to remove and usually turn black in short order by way of fungal action and so discolor the hosta leaves (Figure F-9).

Figure F-8. *H.* 'Elata'; leaf damaged by falling pine cones (Hosta Hill)

Figure F-9. *H.* 'Bright Glow'; leaf damaged by fungi growing on tree sap droppings; holes (lower right) are snail damage (Hosta Hill)

Impact damage by falling dead branches is a rather obvious hazard under trees, principally those with brittle wood. Not so obvious are falling, spent flower petals (or bracts in some cases) which attach themselves to moist leaves and because of the sugars in their chemical composition become literally glued to the leaves. In North America the dogwood

(*Cornus florida*) is one such flowering tree. If left on the leaves, fungal action will eventually decay part of the leaf tissue covered (Figure F-10).

Careful siting and selection of suitable shade tree species under which hostas will be planted can reduce or eliminate these problems. They can also be diminished somewhat by planting shielding, leafy, understory trees (redbud, *Cercis canadensis*; flowering dogwood, *Cornus florida*; or other, similar trees in other parts of the world). But as described earlier, while the flowering dogwood will shield hostas, partially at least, from falling objects, it may itself present a hazard.

Figure F-10. *H.* 'Crispula'; damage caused by falling petals (bracts) of Dogwood (*Cornus florida*); bract (left) peeled away to reveal damage underneath (Hosta Hill)

CONCLUSION

Compared to other perennials, the cultivation of members of the genus *Hosta* is easy, and their vigorous response to improved soils, watering, fertilization, and general care makes the effort worthwhile. But unlike many other perennials, hostas will adapt to neglect and an environment turning hostile for various reasons; they will persist under extraordinarily poor conditions and outlive most other cul-

tivated monocotyledons. They will, in fact, give a measure of success even to gardeners who neglect to exercise most of the very basic rules of good plant cultivation. Hostas are survivors as witnessed by many very old plantings which have outlived their creators and still carry on unattended.

Some of the more common diseases and pests on record have been discussed above, but this does not mean they will occur inevitably in hosta plantings. In more than 20 years of cultivating hostas at Hosta Hill I have had only one incident of bacterial crown rot, and it was probably my own fault. I kept a group of expensive hostas in pots over winter; the tops thawed out in spring while the soil in the bottoms remained frozen solid, preventing drainage and creating an artificial swamp. The submerged rhizomes already injured by freezing/thawing cycles began to rot. I discovered the problem in time to save a few pieces by the method described earlier, and these pieces are now big clumps. I have never had bacterial crown rot in populations planted in the ground, because most are in elevated beds with relatively good drainage. My garden is located in the insect-rich, humid, moist climate of the southeastern United States so my struggle with mollusks, cut worms, and army worms continues. Until recently I have been willing to use some of the biodegradable chemicals to combat these pests. Lately, however, I am increasingly leaning towards accepting the philosophy of Japanese fellow gardeners who not only gracefully accept some damage to their precious hostas as being nature's way but even feature such damaged hostas on the title page of one of their books (Watanabe, 1985).

The universal presence of plant pathogens in gardens is indeed nature's way, and the very best means by which gardeners can contribute to a balanced environment is to provide optimum growing conditions in which to raise healthy, disease-resistant plants. Larvae that eat holes in leaves and cut off petioles can appear seemingly overnight, but the damage starts almost imperceptibly and as the caterpillars grow, it becomes more severe; frequent, close checks can start control when the infestation is in its early stages and less chemicals are required or gardeners can use slower-acting biological controls. Ideally, gardeners should learn to accept some slight damage, taking comfort in the thought that by so doing a little less poison is released into our environment. As for mammalian pests the use of passive methods is preferable; deer can be fenced out, dogs kept on a leash, and squirrels and rabbits trapped and released in the woods. Good gardeners are becoming increasingly aware that their responsibility includes not only the welfare of plants and animals inhabiting their own plots, but extends far beyond to the protection of the environment we live in—planet Earth.

APPENDIX G

Propagation and Hybridization

SEXUAL BREEDING SYSTEM

The abundance of seed produced by species and fertile hybrids, as well as a high germination rate generally exhibited by this seed, is tempting to uninformed gardeners who frequently seek to propagate hostas by way of seed. Most of these seedling trials appear to be successful in that a large number of seedlings can be raised in short order, but practically all of them are *not* true to the variety the gardener is trying to increase and for this there are several well-based reasons:

1. Reproductive barriers do not exist between most species, so they will make hybrids with other varieties within the same specific populations (intraspecific hybrids) or with other species (interspecific hybrids) in the genus. In the wild many species come true because they are ecologically and geographically isolated, so breed only with members of an isolated specific population. Where natural species overlap and flower together, as is frequently the case, many hybrid, intergrading populations are created. There is some evidence (Chung, 1989: personal communication) that some of the isolated and consequently more specialized Korean and Japanese taxa are not only geographically but reproductively isolated as well, but in cultivation they will occasionally make rare hybrids with other species when carefully and persistently hand-pollinated. Additionally, a number of taxa that have been declared species (*H.* 'Undulata', *H.* 'Lancifolia', *H.* 'Crispula') are either infertile (female sterile) mutations or intra- and interspecific hybrids, so do not conform to the botanical definition of a species. Only one species in the genus has been recorded as coming absolutely true from seed, namely, the tetraploid, apomictic *H. ventricosa* (Schmid, 1985e; Jones, in Aden, 1988). Detailed discussions on apomixis, hybridization in the natural habitat, and intergradation of natural populations can be found in Appendix A.
2. In cultivation species and fertile hybrids are grown in close proximity so there is a great chance for cross-pollination or self-pollination by insects, which is referred to as random or "open" pollination. Additionally, most species are self-fertile, meaning the stigma in a flower can be pollinated by the pollen produced in the adjacent anthers of the same flower. With the exception of the night-blooming *H. plantaginea*, the fertile taxa in the genus are receptive to pollination very early in the morning, usually before daylight, so insects pollinate the flowers before controlled pollination can be performed by human intervention. Gardeners must do their pollinating before the insects become active, which is almost impossible in areas where night-feeding insects are present. The only way to make uncontaminated, controlled (planned) crosses is to emasculate the flower by removing the anthers and subsequently employ mechanical barriers, such as hoods (plastic bags, paper bags) to prevent pollen carried by insects from reaching the flower. Some hybridizers recommend careful removal of the entire perianth (six tepals) and the anthers with the filaments from an unopened flower the evening before the cross, leaving only the pistil which can be protected overnight by a hood; pollination can be accomplished the next morning when the stigma becomes receptive.
3. Seedlings of white- or yellow-margined cultivars will invariably be all green because variegated taxa in the genus do not follow standard Mendelian rules for inheritance of variegation. Yasui (1929), Vaughn (1979, 1981), and Vaughn and Wilson (1980a) have demonstrated that variegation is a nonnuclear trait carried by genes in the plastids and that this character can only be transferred maternally (i.e., by the pod parent) (see Appendix D for discussion). Carefully selfed all-yellow cultivars will produce around 40% yellow offspring in the first generation (F_1), but color may be the only transferred character; other morphological features frequently differ to a high degree from those of both parents, so it is clear that neither variegation nor morphology is reliably transferred through sexual propagation.

To gardeners this means that seedlings will not reliably come true so, with the exception of *H. ventricosa*, the normal, natural breeding process cannot be employed to dependably propagate the taxa. On the other hand, the strong inclination of the mostly fertile taxa to form hybrids is a boon to hybridizers and has resulted in the creation of many unique and attractive hybrids.

Raising hostas from seed is a simple procedure and can be accomplished by first collecting seed pods when they start turning yellow, drying them, extracting and separating the seeds, and planting them in open ground in fall or early spring, or anytime in seed trays under lights in sterilized soil, covering them very lightly with fine seed-starter soil. Liquid fertilizer and a small amount of systemic fungicide (Benlate® or Benomyl®) in the irrigation water will reduce damping off and keep the seedlings growing at a fast rate. When planted indoors, the continuous application of light has been reported to increase growth rates dramatically (Wilkins, 1987). It is not necessary to break dormancy by storing the seed in the refrigerator before germination nor is heating, soaking, or stratifying required because the seeds are ready to germinate when harvested. During wet fall periods I have observed the sprouting of seeds in the slightly opened seed capsules; these can be carefully removed and planted as they will usually grow. While raising hostas from random pollinated seed is fascinating and a worthwhile activity, it must be stated that most of the seedlings will not be outstanding hostas and are not worth naming, although they may be useful in mass plantings or ground covers.

ASEXUAL PROPAGATION

Frequently referred to as vegetative propagation, asexual reproduction involves either division of the rhizome or tissue culture. The latter, also called micropropagation or meristem culture, involves the microcutting of meristem tissue, sterile conditions and growing media, controlled temperature and other highly developed techniques, as well as special chemicals and materials which are not normally available to average gardeners, so are best left to commercial tissue culture laboratories (Hammer, 1976; Zilis et al., 1979; Zilis, 1981; M. Meyer, 1982; DeFiglio, 1983; Falstad, 1988).

On the other hand, division of the rhizome is a process easily undertaken by the average gardener and is widely practiced and successful. It is the procedure employed by a majority of small specialty nurseries to generate additional stock for sale, and it obviously provides divisions which are absolutely true to the mother plant. For large clumps, divisions can be accomplished in the ground—after first determining the extent of the root structure—by removing a small amount of soil covering the rhizome and then either splitting the root into two or four pieces with a sharp spade or a heavy-duty knife. I have observed old mature clumps being lifted out of the ground with mechanical equipment because their size (200 lbs./100 kg) precluded manual lifting. For these very large clumps dividing in the ground may be the only practical way, and once division has been accomplished, the more-manageable smaller pieces can then be dug up individually. Smaller clumps can be dug up and cut into wedge-shape pieces, taking care that each division has an "eye" (dormant shoot or bud) and some roots attached. If the leaf bundles are still on the crown, cutting should be done between these bundles or between the visible, emerging shoots in spring. It is not necessary to remove the soil from the divisions which should be replanted as soon as possible.

The best time for dividing is in very early spring when the dormant shoots are clearly visible and before active growth has started, or division can be performed in late fall before the ground freezes. Although I do not recommend it, if absolutely required, hostas can be divided at any time during the year; I have divided hostas even when in full bloom without ill effect, taking a lot of original soil with the divided clump and replanting immediately. Dusting the cut surfaces with a systemic fungicide and an insecticide is said to be helpful in areas where diseases have been a problem (see Appendix F).

The divisions heal unusually fast and additional dormant buds are forced into growth so the divisions may have somewhat smaller, substandard leaves for a season or two, but with abundant watering and fertilizing they will quickly grow into normal-size plants.

To force more dormant buds into growth, two techniques are available. The oldest one on record has been practiced in Japan for centuries and was brought to Europe by von Siebold. It consists of cutting off at ground level the entire leaf crown about the time the flower scapes are emerging and elongating. This drastic measure forces numerous new growing buds and allows the production of more divisions the following season. These will, of course, be small but more numerous than those produced by normal growth. Another procedure is described as the "Ross Method" (Ross, 1982) and involves cutting the rhizome in place. The latter method is probably a better one because it does not require the removal of chlorophyll-producing leaf tissue so it barely sets the plant back, but it does require a somewhat more-delicate touch, particularly with the smaller rhizomes, and it may not force as many buds as the Japanese method.

Some species and their hybrids have stoloniferous root systems with elongated rhizomes that are difficult to locate so it is recommended that they be dug up completely and divided in late summer. Division is simple and consists of severing the stolons so that each division has a leaf bundle and some attached stoloniferous roots. The division should be replanted as quickly as possible and well watered with liquid fertilizer and a small amount of systemic fungicide (Benlate® or Benomyl®) added to the irrigation water.

Many novice gardeners shudder at the thought of taking a knife to the roots of their precious hostas and seeing them literally cut to pieces, but they should relax because root division is a simple and relatively foolproof method which is universally utilized for vegetatively propagating *Hosta*. It is a tried and well-proven way to increase many other herbaceous plants. One word of caution is in order: Vegetative propagation (i.e., division of rhizomes) should not be overdone. Many gardeners, in their continuing quest for maximum increase, will divide clumps as soon as they show three or more divisions. In so doing they prevent the plants from reaching maturity and from showing their full potential. I advise setting aside at least one plant of each variety and permitting it to grow unmolested. There are possible exceptions: Some unstable, mediovariegated hostas need to have reverted shoots cut off to maintain their unique variegation without being overpowered by the more vigorous reversions; this technique has been reported from Japan and North America.

HYBRIDIZATION

Many of the best hybridizers working with the genus (see Chapter 5) agree that it is becoming increasingly more difficult to produce truly distinct hybrids worthy of naming and registration with the registration authority for *Hosta*. A few of the master hybridizers have a self-imposed code of standards which regulates the criteria for selection and naming. Unfortunately, many other hybridizers use less judgment in their selection process, so there are now, in some of the breeding lines, numerous hybrids named and registered which are very similar if not completely alike in appearance. As Eisel and Pollock (1984) have pointed out, the responsibility for selecting hybrids which are distinct from those already named and registered rests with the hybridizer, but with the number of registrations increasing at a fast rate most hybridizers do not have access to all the plants so cannot compare; as a consequence quite a few of the named and registered taxa are very similar and can hardly be told apart. This is particularly true in the *H. montana*, *H. sieboldiana*, and *H. sieboldii* breeding lines, and Chapter 4 indicates how serious the problem is. As more information on the various named cultivars becomes available both hybridizers and buyers will be in a better position to judge the merit of a particular plant, and in the end buyers will decide on the success or failure by voting with their purchases. As a general rule, the more distinct a hybrid is, the better its acceptance with gardeners.

The process of hybridizing is very simple and involves putting some pollen on the female organ of the flower, called the stigma, supported on a central style (see "Other Macromorphological Features" and "Reproductive Organs" in Appendix D). If the plant's own pollen is used the procedure is called "selfing"; this is the way specific populations propagate in the wild, the pollinating being taken care of by insects. Although some incorrectly consider selfing to be hybridizing, it is not because it does not result in a hybrid between two different species but rather in the creation of more of the same taxon. Thus, selfing is sexual propagation. Technically, true hybridizing results from the cross-fertilization of two taxa; the plant supplying the pollen is called the "pollen parent" or male parent, and the seed-producing plant is the "pod parent" or female parent. Pollination by insects, already referred to earlier, is considered "open" pollination which in isolated, natural populations results in selfing. In gardens, where many varieties of hostas are present, open pollination creates hybrids in an uncontrolled fashion so is referred to as "random" pollination. The pollination undertaken by hybridizers involves careful selection of breeding lines and partners and controlled cross-fertilization between taxa, so is called "controlled" pollination.

Success or failure of hybridization depends on the hybridizer's knowledge of the basic Mendelian laws of inheritance, the transfer process of cytoplasm and plastids, and the maternal inheritance of variegation, among other factors. Although this sounds very complicated it is in actuality simple and can be reduced to the following rules:

1. In principle, the transfer of standard morphological features, excluding variegation, follows Mendelian rules, and both parents contribute according to their genetic basis.
2. Variegation is determined by nonnuclear factors involving plastids, and its transfer is controlled by the pod parent.
3. Stable variegation patterns (i.e., margined patterns) are not transferred by either the pollen or pod parent, and parents with margined variegation will produce only monochromatic hybrids.
4. Unstable mediovariegated variegation patterns are transferred by the pod parent only (i.e., the center-variegated parent must be the pod parent). The resulting hybrids will inherit the instability of the mediovariegated pattern and eventually change to a stable margined or monochromatic (all-yellow or all-green) type (see "The Benedict Cross," Appendix D).

Although these rules are simple, the inheritance mechanism at work in hosta hybridizing is very complicated and entails both nuclear and nonnuclear factors. Novice hybridizers often misunderstand the process. In Appendix A, I deal with intergradation and introgression of specific populations, and the basic principles discussed there also pertain to hybridizing of cultivars. Sexual propagation and hybridization in the natural habitat are, in fact, simple when compared with the hybridization of cultivars because the breeding stocks existing in most gardens have already been extensively hybridized in the past so contain many "hidden" genes (i.e., dormant morphological characteristics). These hidden traits can show up at any time resulting in hybrids which have nothing in common with either parent, and this is puzzling to the novice.

Experienced hybridizers give due consideration to the performance of a given breeding line, and this knowledge can be gained only through working with many different lines for a number of years. There is always beginner's luck, and occasionally gardeners come up with a rare, distinct hybrid either by random or controlled pollination, but as a rule the consistent production of hybrids that are distinct and worthy of naming and registration requires many years of experience. Nevertheless, Paul Aden, the most productive hybridizer of hostas, states that "the genus is still open to committed hybridizers" (Aden, 1988), so gardeners wanting to join the ranks of hybridizers should realize that commitment and a great deal of patience are required. Once the decision is made to make planned crosses, at least 2–3 years are required before the first promising seedlings can be recognized; it takes another 5 years to grow seedlings to a stage of maturity that allows judgment to be made on the distinctiveness and general merit of the plant, and during this time the hybrid plant should remain undivided; another 4–5 or more years pass before the plant is in full production. Obviously, careful record keeping is essential to hybridizing because it eliminates duplicate crosses and optimizes the breeding effort.

Last but not least, many successful hybridizers have rather unique plant material available for the task and so are able to make hybrids which are impossible to repeat elsewhere.

Much reference material has been written about hybridizing but it is scattered throughout many publications, so Aden's comprehensive and exemplary treatment is recommended as a source for further information (Aden, 1988).

Not willing to wait for the long-lasting hybridization process, gardeners occasionally resort to exposing seeds or seedlings to strong chemicals, microwaves, radiation treatment, and other dangerous methods designed to produce mutations. I advise against this, although in rare cases these methods may be successful under carefully controlled laboratory conditions. The resulting plants are mutants (sports), and obviously hybridization has nothing to do with their creation.

Recently, genetic engineering and gene splicing have been addressed increasingly in the literature as well as in public information media. A new branch of biological science called biotechnology is rapidly finding new, practical applications in agricultural and horticulture (Jones, in Aden, 1988). Tissue culture is one of these and specifically relates to macro-biotechnology. On the micro-biotechnological, nuclear level, a specialized branch called plant molecular biology is attempting to produce intergeneric crosses—for example, between *Hemerocallis* (daylily) and *Hosta*—by transferring chromosomes between the genera. What a cross between these genera would look like is unknown, but I must admit at this point that a taxon sporting large, red daylily flowers over-topping a *H. ventricosa* 'Aureomarginata' leaf mound will most likely never grace my garden. Hopefully, instead of fooling around with nature, these new methods will be used to improve insect resistance, solve sterility problems, provide immunity against diseases, give more texture to leaves, and sunproof some of the taxa.

To keep up with the latest developments concerning hybridizing and propagation, membership in one or both of the international hosta societies and a local regional society is highly recommended. The addresses of The American Hosta Society and the British Hosta and Hemerocallis Society are given at the end of Chapter 6. Both organizations publish journals which contain material concerning all aspects of *Hosta* taxonomy, nomenclature, hybridizing, propagation, and cultivation.

APPENDIX H

Economic and Miscellaneous Uses

DECORATIVE USE IN RELIGION AND ART

In Japan some of the large-leaved varieties of *Hosta* belonging to *H. sieboldiana* and *H. montana* have been used to clothe or wrap religious statuary during festivals or to construct raftlike platforms on which religious objects are carried (Y. Hirose, in Aden, 1988), and similar uses are reported by a number of authors. More conventional is the use of hostas as a landscape object on temple grounds; the stately, larger varieties with glaucous, blue coloration fit well into this environment. There are reports of certain varieties being raised specifically to support these uses.

A likeness of hosta leaves can be seen on carved balusters for bridge railings, and leaf-shaped decorations on temples and bridges, looking much like hosta leaves, are called *giboshu*.

Hostas have figured in Japanese art since at least the 11th century and probably before. This use has been covered in detail in Chapter 5.

AGRICULTURAL USE

A large part of the Japanese land area is mountainous and covered by forests, so is marginal for agricultural purposes. In Aomori Prefecture of northern Honshu the inhabitants of mountain villages supplement their diet by growing hostas and other wild herbs as vegetable crops, using varieties belonging to the *H. sieboldiana* group (Maekawa, 1940), and farmers in the mountains of Hokkaido grow hostas as a cash crop (Y. Hirose, in Aden, 1988). The leaf stems (petioles) are sold in vegetable shops under the name *urui*. The petioles can be eaten raw or cooked, but they are bitter when taken from mature plants and, not unlike many staple green vegetables, such as asparagus, are best cut when young and tender. The leaves require boiling until tender and are best harvested at the point of maximum moisture content which occurs in the morning hours (Pratt, 1990).

As food hostas can be used in several ways, and it is usually the larger varieties which are grown for this purpose. The young petioles are skinned and parboiled; the instructions admonish the cook not to let the green color fade during boiling because it indicates overcooking. The petioles are cut into sections and dressed with butter made from peanuts or other nuts or sesame (*Sesamum indicum*), seasoned with vinegar, salt, and sugar, and served hot as part of dinner (*ban-gohan*). The pieces are also sometimes used in *shabu-shabu*, similar to a fondue, in which thinly sliced beef, mushrooms, hosta or other vegetables, and bean curd (*tofu*, coagulated soy bean protein colloid) are boiled in stock and dipped in vinegar before eating. The boiled pieces are also served cold as a salad, dressed with sesame paste, soy sauce, and a little sugar to taste. Y. Matsumura (1958) reports that in some parts of the Nikko area hostas are considered the best wild vegetable for pickling and the petioles can also be dried and stored as preserved (dehydrated) food. He also gives one of his own recipes for a type of *sushi*: Soak the previously skinned, dried hosta petioles overnight, then boil them well and marinade them in soy sauce with salt and sugar added to taste. In this form they are used instead of dried gourd shavings as center filling for rolled rice covered with sea weed (*nori*). The dish is called *nori-maki-sushi*.

The smaller hostas of the *H. sieboldii* group are used whole, utilizing both the leaf tissue and the petioles in bean paste soup (*misoshiru*), which is served with rice, raw egg, pickles (*tsukemono*), dried seaweed, and soy sauce as part of the traditional Japanese breakfast (*asa-gohan*). The shoots of larger plants like *H. montana* are fried with *abura age*, itself a fried bean curd (*tofu*) (Y. Matsumura, 1958). Another delicious dish consists of young hosta leaves dipped in *tempura* batter, made of wheat flour and egg, and lightly fried in vegetable oil. The freshly made tempura is dipped in soy sauce. Several recipes exist for *sushi* made with hosta leaves which are first boiled to make them tender (15–20 minutes). The leaves are used for casing Japanese rice made with *shiso*, the dried, crushed, reddish purple leaf of the Japanese beefsteak plant (almost like red basil), and the food is called *shiso (giboshi) sushi* (Pratt, 1990).

Westerners can also cook with hostas, of course, but need to avoid plants that have been treated with systemic insecticides. Gardeners who want to eat their hostas should grow them in the organic vegetable plot.

EROSION CONTROL

The very dense and intertwining roots of some taxa in the genus are ideal for erosion control on steep hillsides and banks. Planted closely together they are frequently mowed several times during the year to force new leaf initials into growth. After 2–3 seasons a solid mat of hosta plants becomes an extremely hardy and lasting erosion control measure.

FLOWER ARRANGING

Flower arranging is an integral part of Eastern religions. It started with the veneration of religious objects through the use of flower decoration and in this form arrived in Japan with Buddhism from China via Korea around A.D. 600. At first decoration with flowers was a religious practice, but it soon was taken up by the ruling class and became an independent art form. By the 8th century (Heian period, from *Heiankyo* meaning Kyoto) competitions in flower arranging (*hana-wasa*) were held at court. Later, during the Muromachi period (14th–16th centuries), ordinary people took up the art of flower arranging (*ikebana*) which reached its peak during the Edo period (17th–19th centuries). In the early days flowers only were used, but vases and bowls were soon added and this culminated in the evolution of ornamental niches (*tokonama*) into which the arrangements were placed. In Japan *ikebana* is more than just a hobby. It is an idealized expression of the trinity of heaven, humankind, and earth, so it still shows religious roots. Today flower arranging is deeply rooted in Japanese cultural life and has long been an essential part of the education of Japanese girls. Several schools and styles have developed over 13 centuries and include Ikenobo, Nisho, Enshu, Ohara, Sogetsu, and a number of other variations. Many of these schools advocate the use of foliage in designs, and it is no surprise that the leaves of hostas have been used for this purpose for a long time, perhaps since the very beginning of the art in Japan. Historical records show hostas were grown in court gardens since the 11th century and by all indications were cultivated before this time (see Chapter 5).

In Europe the great still life paintings of flowers produced by some of the Dutch and Flemish masters show that arranging flowers was a practiced art at that time. But, as in Japan, the art of decorating with flowers initially had a religious application: Christians adorned their altars and religious statuary with the simple, but beautiful wild flowers available locally. The tremendous increase in the kinds of beautiful and exotic plants available for use in flower arranging near the end of the 18th century and lasting well into the 19th century included not only new flowers but increasingly also foliage plants which were joined by hostas after 1830. It is difficult to determine when hostas were first used for flower arranging in Europe, but the importation of live plants from abroad was accompanied also by new ideas and concepts. Leaves had always been an important element of the Japanese styles, so their influence was slowly felt in European arrangements, and hosta leaves were undoubtedly utilized starting about the middle of the 19th century. In this way the principally naturalistic artistry of Japanese ikebana became known in European countries.

Due to the temporal nature of flower arrangements, only paintings and sketches of the early efforts have survived. Much has been written, though, and in 1907 Gertrude Jekyll published *Flower Decoration in the House* which gives a good idea of the state of the art at that time. Although the art always had a following of dedicated enthusiasts, it was not until the 1950s that a literal explosion of clubs and societies dedicated to flower arranging took place. During this period in England, the Royal Horticultural Society (RHS) sponsored its first exhibit on flower arranging, and in Europe and North America flower arranging became an integral activity of many garden clubs and societies where teachers not only taught the Chinese school and Japanese styles of ikebana but also revived and further developed the Western styles, like gardenesque and Victorian, and the North American styles of art nouveau and modern. Also during this time the universal availability of color photography allowed exact records to be made. They show that in many of these arrangements hosta leaves were part of the composition. This trend has continued and even increased as variegated hosta leaves became available to the general public, and in Europe some flower growers have developed stock just to serve this purpose.

Quite obviously, an exhaustive treatment of flower arranging would fill volumes and is beyond the scope of this book, but a good selection of European and North American books is available covering the Oriental as well as the Western styles of flower arrangement. Unfortunately, due to the language barrier, a wealth of Japanese information on ikebana is inaccessible to Western enthusiasts. For those principally interested in the use of hosta leaves as elements of flower arranging I recommend Mabel-Maria Herweg's large chapter "Flower Arranging with Hostas" in Aden's (1988) *The Hosta Book*.

HORTICULTURAL EXHIBITS

In many parts of the world late-winter flower shows give a foretaste of coming spring bloom, and in some countries flower exhibits are held on different dates the year round with most of them falling between April and July to take advantage of spring blooming periods. The late-winter shows require most exhibition plants to be forced from dormancy; this necessitates rather complicated techniques of freezing potted plants and carefully "awakening" them at precisely the correct time, so careful scheduling is a must (Pollock, 1984d;

Haskell 1984). Because the various forced plants have different time requirements to grow from dormancy to full bloom, or in the case of hostas, to full leaf development, the entire process requires great skill and experience. In most of these shows hostas have been used for a number of years to provide foliage background for flowering plants. Increasingly, the exhibits feature hostas, and in some cases parts of the displays are devoted solely to hostas.

Probably the best known of these shows is the RHS Chelsea Flower Show, an outdoor show conducted each spring in London, England, but Germany has its Floriade and hosts other international horticultural shows, the United States has its New England Flower Show, almost 120 years in the running, and there are many others, too numerous to mention. Indicative of the popularity of the genus and its decorative and landscape potential are the many gold medals garnered by exhibitors who display principally hostas. I had the pleasure of seeing the excellent Goldbrook Nursery (Mrs. S. Bond) hosta display at the RHS Summer Show in London in July 1988, which was awarded a gold medal; this nursery had previously won gold medals for similar exhibits. In the United States A. C. Haskell won the Massachusetts Horticultural Society's top honor, the President's Award, at the 1983 New England Flower Show (March 12–20), by exhibiting the largest collection of hostas ever assembled indoors (Hotton, 1983). He considers hostas perfect flower show plants but warns a lot of hard work and planning are involved in this process (Haskell, 1984). These displays are instrumental in educating the public about the genus and the many forms now available for gardening, flower arranging, and exhibitions. Readers interested in learning more about exhibiting hostas at flower shows should peruse the above references available from The American Hosta Society (AHS), and contact their local garden clubs, horticultural societies, and international hosta societies (some addresses in Chapter 6).

A different type of exhibit is the cut-leaf show. The AHS and its many regional groups, as well as the British Hosta and Hemerocallis Society (BHHS) conduct these shows. Appendix C gives a complete cut-leaf show schedule, and details on dates and locations can be obtained from the societies mentioned. A series of articles relating to this subject was published in volume 16 of *The American Hosta Society Bulletin* pp. 37–42), and this publication is available from the AHS. These exhibitions are usually open to the public and similar to cut-flower shows exhibiting blossoms, but display cut leaves only, in matching containers with the petioles in water. Sponsored and endorsed by the AHS and BHHS, the shows are also competitions sanctioned by these societies, and many awards are given in the various categories listed in Appendix C.

MEDICAL USE

Hostas are not medicinal plants. They contain no substances which might be extracted for medical use. There are unconfirmed reports indicating that in remote areas of Japan, large fresh hosta leaves are occasionally used for temporarily dressing wounds when more suitable materials are not available on the spot.

One published report speaks, somewhat funnily, yet quite seriously, of the therapeutic value of one patient's obsession with hostas during a 12-week confinement in a cast (Grovatt, 1978). By studying all available written materials on the subject, this patient was helped mightily by making time spent flat on his back go seemingly faster, so avoiding "cabin fever" and forgetting pain and suffering. The therapy worked for healing broken bones, but the patient, in his own words, came down with a different, incurable disease: hosta fever.

Abbreviations and Acronyms

ad int; *ad interim*: For the present; meanwhile; on a provisional basis. In cases where some research has been conducted but not enough information is available to make exact determinations and decisions, provisional placement was made on the basis of preliminary results. This placement may change at a later date.

AHS: The American Hosta Society.

BH: The herbarium at Ithaca; L. H. Bailey Hortorium, Mann Library Building, Cornell University, Ithaca, New York 14853, USA.

BHHS: British Hosta and Hemerocallis Society.

BM: The herbarium at London; British Museum, Natural History, Cromwell Road, London SW7 5BD, Great Britain.

cfr.; *confer*: Compare or refer to; usually used in regard to information given in another reference or bibliographic source.

comb. nov.; *combinatio nova*: A new combination of botanical names. Occasionally new research supports the placement of botanical taxa in different ranks, species, or affiliations. A new name combination is assigned to indicate the new placement.

E: The herbarium at Edinburgh; Royal Botanic Garden, Edinburgh EH3 5LR, Scotland, Great Britain.

emend.; *emendatus*: Emended, revised, corrected.

f.; *forma*: Used in botanical name combinations to indicate a botanical rank below species and varietas (variety). It is the lowest rank used within the genus for botanical forms. Example: *H. sieboldii* var. *rectifolia* f. *albiflora*.

f. nov.; *forma nova*: A new or redefined taxon in the rank of forma.

F_1 and F_2: The first and second generation of offspring, called filial. Here the F_1 offspring is considered a cross between two homozygous taxa (pure specific lines). In this case the F_1 generation will be heterozygous and the resulting phenotypes are usually very similar. When the F_1 hybrids are selfed or allowed to breed in isolation among themselves, the resulting F_2 generation manifests segregation of characteristics. For those traits covered by Mendelian genes, the typical Mendelian ratios of inheritance, such as 3:1 or 9:3:3:1, become notable.

GA: The herbarium at Athens; Department of Botany, Herbarium of the University of Georgia, Athens, Georgia 30602, USA.

H.: *Hosta*; used for the generic name, as in *H. montana*.

hab.; *habitat*: It inhabits, place of growth or occurrence.

hort.; *hortorum*; *hortulanorum*: Of gardens or gardeners; used to designate names which have horticultural origin and are not valid botanically, even though they may be quoted in botanical publications. When this is the case, they are usually designated as *nomina nuda*, which see.

i.e.; *id est*: That is.

ic.; *icon*: Illustration; usually given with a reference number.

IC: International Botanical Congress of Vienna.

ICBN: *International Code of Botanical Nomenclature*.

ICNCP: *International Code of Nomenclature for Cultivated Plants*.

IR: *International Rules of Botanical Nomenclature*.

IRA: International Registration Authority for *Hosta*.

K: The herbarium at Kew; The Herbarium and Royal Library, Royal Botanic Garden, Kew, Richmond, Surrey TW9 3AE, Great Britain.

KYO: The herbarium at Kyoto; Department of Botany, Faculty of Science, Kyoto University, Kyoto 606, Japan.

L: The herbarium at Leiden; Rijksherbarium, Schelpenkade 6, Leiden, Netherlands.

LM: Light microscopy.

m.s.m.; *metra supra mare*: Meters above sea level.

M: The herbarium at München; Botanische Staatssammlung, Menzingerstrasse 67, D-8 München 19, Germany.

MAK: Makino Herbarium, Faculty of Science, Tokyo Metropolitan University, Fukazawa, Setagaya, Tokyo 158, Japan.

NA: National Herbarium, United States National Arboretum, Washington, DC 20002, USA.

na, n.a.; *not accepted*: Used to designate taxonomic placements and/or name combinations of other authors which have not or cannot be accepted under the particular classification of the genus presented in this work. These nonaccepted names have been included as synonyms. This abbreviation is also used in combination as *sl na*, which see.

NC: Nomenclature Committee (of The American Hosta Society).

NCU: The herbarium at Chapel Hill, University of North Carolina, Department of Botany, Chapel Hill, North Carolina 27415, USA.

nom. ambig.; *nomen ambiguum*: An ambiguous name, usually one that has been applied to several different taxa.

nom. confus.; *nomen confusum*: A confusing name.

nom. illeg.; *nomen illegitimum*: An illegitimate name; one that is published in violation of one or more of the rules of the ICBN.

nom. nudum; *nomen nudum* (pl. *nomina nuda*): A botanical name published invalidly without description or a designated nomenclatural type; literally a "naked" name.

nom. superfl.; *nomen superfluum*: A superfluous name, usually a validly published name that has an earlier name with priority existing against it. The rules of the ICBN permit only one binomial for each taxon.

nom. typ.; *nomen typus*: The name of the nomenclatural type.

P: The herbarium at Paris; Muséum National d'Histoire Naturelle, Laboratoire de Phanérogamie, 16 Rue Buffon, 75005 Paris, France.

PE: The herbarium at Peking; Institute of Botany, Academia Sinica, Peking, China.

pp, p.p.; *pro parte*: In part, partially.

pp sim; p.p. sim.; *pro parte similis*: Partially similar, similar in part. Used to indicate partial morphological similarity of two taxa which may or may not be related. See also *pp* and *sim*.

SAP: The herbarium at Sapporo; Laboratory of Plant Taxonomy, Botanical Institute, Faculty of Agriculture, Hokkaido University, Hokkaido, Japan.

sel.; *selectus*: Selected clone or form; occasionally outstanding clones are selected from a wild or cultivated population and named. ·

SEM: Scanning electron microscopy.

SHIN: Biological Institute and Herbarium, Faculty of Liberal Arts, Shinshu University, 3-1-1 Asahi, Matsumoto, Japan (formerly at Ueda).

sim; *similis*: Similar. Used when a taxon resembles another morphologically.

sl, s.l.; *in sensu lato*: In a broad sense. Used when a placement is a wide or general interpretation of the facts. For instance, *H.* 'Elata' is broadly related to *H. montana*, but it is not the same taxon.

sl na, s.l. n.a.: Not accepted even in a broad sense (see also *sl* and *na*). Placements made with a broad interpretation of the facts, but not accepted by the author.

SNU: The Herbarium, Seoul National University, Seoul, Korea.

sp. nov.; *species novum*: New species; indicates a species new to science.

sphalm.; *sphalmate*: By mistake, mistakenly.

ss, s.str.; *in sensu stricto*: In a narrow sense.

ssp.; subspecies, subspecific: A group of closely related plants comprising a subdivision of species; not a varietas or forma. Variously defined but usually considered groups of plants within a specific population that are ecologically or morphologically different in some character but genetically the same. Taxonomists rank a population as a subspecies when more than 90% of the individuals of an infraspecific group are recognizably distinct.

stat. nov.; *status novus*: New rank.

STEM: Scanning transmission electron microscopy.

syn.; *synonymon, synonymia*: Synonym, in synonymy; a name having the same or nearly the same meaning and application as another name; in botany, different names applied to the same taxon.

tab.; *tabula*: Plate.

TEM: Transmission electron microscopy.

TF: Tardiana grex numbers. A cross made in 1961 by the late Eric Smith of England, with *H. tardiflora* as pod parent and *H. sieboldiana* as pollen parent. Smith assigned "TF" numbers to selected seedlings of this cross. *T* stands for Tardiana and *F* signifies filial (see F_1). TF 1×7 means the 7th seedling given a number in the 1st generation of the Tardianas, which was later named *H.* 'Halcyon'.

TI: The herbarium at Tokyo; Department of Botany, Faculty of Science, University of Tokyo, Hongo, Tokyo, Japan.

TNS: The herbarium at Tokyo; National Science Museum, Department of Botany, Hyakunin-cho 3-23-I, Shinjuku-ku, Tokyo, Japan.

trans. nov.; *translatio nova*: New transfer; used of names transferred without change in rank of the taxon.

TUS: The herbarium at Sendai; Biological Institute, Faculty of Science, Tonhoku University, Sendai, Miyagi-Ken, Japan.

U: The herbarium at Utrecht; Institute for Systematic Botany, Tweede Transitorium, Heidelberglaan, 2, de Uithof, Utrecht, Netherlands.

UPS: The herbarium at Uppsala; The Herbarium, Institute of Systematic Botany, University of Uppsala, PO Box 51, S-751 0 21 Uppsala I, Sweden.

var.; *varietas*: Variety; indicates a botanical rank lower than species. Example: *H. longipes* var. *hypoglauca*.

viz.; *videlicet*: Namely; that is; that is to say. Used to introduce a more precise explanation of a previous name or phrase.

WAG: The herbarium at Wageningen; Laboratory for Plant Taxonomy and Geography, 37, Generaal Foulkes Weg, Wageningen, Netherlands.

Endnotes

CHAPTER 2

1. From 1969 until 1985 the main publication of the AHS was known as *The American Hosta Society Bulletin* and afterwards as *The Hosta Journal*.

2. This is obviously a rough approximation. The January isotherms do not directly follow the lines of latitude, but are influenced by geographic features and other factors. In eastern North America they run from southwest to northeast; in Great Britain they run almost south to north, influenced by the Gulf Stream.

CHAPTER 5

1. The first edition of this dictionary was published by Sanseido, Tokyo, in 1896. Captain Frank Brinkley, 1841–1912, was professor of mathematics at Tokyo Imperial Engineering College from 1867 until 1876. The Japanese botanist Jinzo Matsumura (1856–1928) collaborated with Brinkley and provided the definitions and translations of botanical terms.

2. In the botanical literature *cærulea* is frequently spelled *coerulea* or *caerulea*. These words have been used in the names of a number of different species. It is not known which particular species Matsumura had in mind. In the present book the classic ligature *æ* is used.

3. Shogun is an abbreviation of Seiitaishogun, which translates as "barbarian-killing general." The barbarians in this case were Westerners. The title shogun was first used in 1192 and given by the emperor to key leaders. It was abolished in 1867.

4. Only two copies of this book still exist, one at Kamakura in Japan and the other at the Boston Museum, United States.

5. "Tatami" literally means "folding." It refers to a floor mat woven from rushes, *Juncus effusus*, which covers the wooden floors of Japanese dwellings. Rooms are usually measured by how many tatamis can be spread on the floor.

6. In 1867 the crown prince Mutsuhito was enthroned as emperor (called Meiji posthumously). The following year the office of shogun was abolished, and Emperor Meiji became the sole ruler. As part of the Meiji restoration, a central government was established in Tokyo which began to pattern governmental and educational policies along Western lines.

7. According to Maekawa (1940) "Joksan" is an incorrect reading of "Gyokusan" from the Chinese *Yu-san*.

8. William Thomas Stearn, b. 1911–, botanist, United Kingdom.

9. Fumio Maekawa, 1908–1984, botanist, Japan.

10. Carolus Linnaeus, 1707–1778, botanist and physician, Sweden; the name is frequently shortened to Carl (von) Linnè.

11. Macao is a Portuguese colony established on the coast of southern China in 1557.

12. Jean Baptiste Pierre Antoine de Monet de Lamarck, 1744–1829, botanist, France.

13. Henry C. Andrews, 1769–1828, botanist, United Kingdom.

14. The epithet *ramosa* given by Miquel means "branched." The specimens—nos. 908.106 1041 and 908.106 1043— are numbered in L 8147/37 and 8147/36, respectively. Von Siebold identified the former as *Hemerocallis japonica* and *Hemerocallis japonica* var. *β mihi* (*mihi* = mine, indicating it was collected by him), and the latter he identified as *Giboosi varietas*. In 1957 Hylander believed these specimens were varieties of *Hosta* 'Lancifolia' and affixed his incorrect determination to the specimens over his signature. The species name *Hosta tibai*, published by Maekawa in 1950 (in obs.) as a nomen nudum (with a Japanese diagnosis), was validly published by him in 1984. His illustration of the holotype exactly matches that of von Siebold's specimen. Both were collected on Mount Inasa on the west side of Nagasaki harbor. Both clearly show the scape with multiple branches so characteristic of this species. Although known to von Siebold and recognized by Miguel as a botanical variety, this hosta was forgotten and did not make an appearance in Western gardens until it was sent to the United States by Kaneko in the late 1960s under a new species name, *H. chibai* Kaneko, a nomen nudum. How such a characteristic hosta escaped the attention of European botanists studying the genus is not clear.

15. This was the specific form which was sent to England in 1830 and described under the basionym *Sieboldtiana* by Loddiges (1832).

16. Maekawa (1940) stated that this species was a relatively recent importation into Japan. I have in my collection an original 1846 van Houtte drawing of this taxon, which shows the typical elongated leaves of *H. plantaginea* var. *japonica*.

17. Kurt Polykarp Joachim Sprengel, 1766–1833, botanist and naturalist, Germany.

18. Paul Friedrich August Ascherson, 1834–1913, botanist, Germany.

19. K. Yasui (1929) was the first to report this in the scientific literature.

20. Baron Friedrich Heinrich Alexander von Humboldt, 1769–1859, naturalist and explorer, Germany.

21. *Samurai* means literally "loyal servant." It refers to a group of individuals granted the unique right to carry a sword. They were the "knights" of feudal Japan but were totally dependent upon their *daimyo*, "lord and master," who granted the "right to the sword."

22. *Shiboruto* (sometimes *Shiiboruto*) is the transliterated equivalent of the Japanese phonetic spelling for Siebold. *Shiboruto sensei* means "the teacher Siebold."

23. *Ronin* means literally "floating person." During the Meiji restoration many samurai lost their jobs. No longer supported by their former masters, they became very bitter. Many a ronin vented his anger on the Western barbarians, frequently with tragic results.

24. Mackwoods Gardens of Lotus Woods, Spring Grove, Illinois, published a number of specialized hosta catalogs in the 1960s.

25. Takenoshin Nakai, 1882–1952, botanist, Japan.

26. Georg Arends, 1863–1951, horticulturist and plant breeder, Germany.

27. Staudensichtungsgarten Weihenstephan, the perennial trial grounds of Institut für Stauden, Gehölze und

Angewandte Pflanzensoziologie, Fachhochschule Weihen-stephan, associated with the Department of Botany, University of Munich, Germany.

28. One of the German names for this hosta is "Lilienfunkie."

29. Friedrik Anton Willem Miquel, 1811–1871, botanist, Netherlands.

30. John Gilbert Baker, 1834–1920, botanist, United Kingdom.

31. Nils Hylander, 1904–1982, botanist, Sweden.

32. The possibility exists that H. 'Tokudama' was one of the progenitors of this undoubtedly hybrid complex.

33. George R. Hall, 1820–1899, physician and plant collector, United States.

34. Carl Johann Maximowicz, 1827–1891, botanist, USSR.

35. Richard Oldham, 1838–1864, botanist, United Kingdom.

36. John Gould Veitch, 1839–1870, botanist and nurseryman, United Kingdom.

37. David Douglas, 1798–1834, botanist, Scotland.

38. Several Japanese "descriptive" words were used: "herifu" (variegated margin), "shirofukurin", and "kifukurin" (white- and gold-margined), or simply "fukurin."

39. Although validly published botanically, both are now considered species of cultivated origin.

40. Gertrude Jekyll, 1843–1932, master gardener and landscape architect, United Kingdom.

41. Beatrix Jones Farrand, 1872–1959, landscape gardener, United States.

42. Sheet no. 2, consisting of one flowering stem, one flower, and one loose leaf. The specimen is identified as *Hemerocallis undulata*—Japon. Th.

43. *Hosta* 'Elata' was incorrectly named *Hemerocallis lancifolia* Thunberg by Vilmorin-Andrieux et Cie. (1866: Figure 470).

44. The specimens in K—nos. H. 1428/86/7 and H. 1428/86/42—are both ex Herbarium W. T. Stearn. No. 7 is annotated as *Hosta* sp. ex *Hort.* Vilmorin, 6/8/1932. Stearn: "This was raised by Messrs. Vilmorin-Andrieux et Cie. from seeds collected by Taquet on Quaelpert Island (Cheju Do) . . . I gathered these specimens at Vilmorin's trial ground at Verrieres-le-Buisson near Paris." Diagnosis in English follows. Taquet was in Korea and Cheju Do in August 1910 collecting specimens of *H. venusta* and apparently also seed of *H.* 'Vilmoriniana'. It appears to be an interspecific hybrid between *H. minor* and *H. tsushimensis*.

45. Andrew Jackson Downing, 1815–1852, landscape architect, United States. His book (1841) was widely influential and popularized gardens for public use.

46. The garden cemetery movement originated in the United States with the Massachusetts Horticultural Society at Mount Auburn Cemetery, Cambridge, MA; Spring Green, Cincinnati, OH; and Cave Hill, Louisville, KY.

47. The papers of Mrs. Frances R. Williams were bequeathed to the library of the University of Minnesota.

48. Zager described this hosta as having shiny green leaves. It could not have been the true pruinose *H. glauca* (= *H.* 'Tokudama').

49. In 1972 I ordered *H. sieboldiana* from an Ohio nursery of good integrity and received *H.* 'Fortunei Hyacinthina'.

50. There is still a question whether this was the "true" Japanese *H.* 'Tokudama' Maekawa or a European form, which conforms closely to it but has more-pointed leaves. Both are in the trade in the United States.

51. I have been able to build an extensive collection of private correspondence extending from the early 1960s to the present.

52. Wister, 1969, 1970a, 1970b; E. V. Fisher, 1983; McGourty and McGourty, 1985.

53. The information contained in his lists was supplemented by an extensive correspondence with Summers during the writing of this book.

54. Hensen (1985) listed these incorrect names as synonyms.

55. Translated, *herifu* means "border-variegated" and *haku chu han* comes out as "white-half (of leaf) in center."

56. I have drawn these conclusions from an analysis of copies of Krossa's letters to Summers and other hosta specialists.

57. In the early 1960s Dr. Creech participated in a plant exploration to Japan for the U.S. National Arboretum. Krossa received divisions of most of the plants brought back by this expedition.

58. Krossa B-1 may have been the same as or very similar to B-3. To facilitate record keeping Krossa numbered many of the hostas he received if they came without names or could not be identified. According to one of his letters most—but not all—of these came from Osaka University.

59. Quite a number were duplicate hostas under different names.

60. This is not possible with several sterile taxa declared species by Maekawa (1940) and Fujita (1976a).

61. The hybridization of the wild hosta population has been accelerated by the many years the genus has been cultivated in Japan. Cultivation brought about dislocations of unique local populations and the consequent interbreeding of wild stock. The resulting polymorphism of many of the "wild" species has been documented. This is not to say that there are no "pure" species still in existence in the wild.

62. A series of articles on hostas featuring many color illustrations was published in *The Journal of the Japan Horticultural Society* 88(1984):4–15.

APPENDIX A

1. The meaning of *joksan* has not been determined. It may refer to *H. plantaginea* which is cultivated in China under the name *Yu-san* (玉簪). The Japanese translation of *Yu-San* is *Tamanokanzashi* which means jewel of the hairpiece (Maekawa 1940). *Vulgo Giboosi* means "the common hosta," while *Giboosi altera* is "other hosta."

2. Baron Nicolaus Joseph von Jaquin, 1727–1817, botanist, Austria.

3. Karl Ludwig Willdenow, 1765–1812, botanist, Germany.

4. Count Barthèlemy Charles Joseph Dumortier, 1797–1887, botanist, Belgium.

5. Although new evidence based on pollen studies (Chung and Jones, 1989) indicates that *Hosta, Hesperocallis,* and *Leucocrinum* may have originated from a common group of ancestors, it is obvious that the genus is morphologically and ecologically quite isolated based on its current evolutionary development.

6. It was determined that *Yucca* and *Agave* have similar karyotypes with 10 large and 50 small chromosomes (2n); *Hosta* also has a total of 60 chromosomes, with 12 large and 48 small, while *Hesperocallis undulata* has 12 large and 36 small. This led to proposals which would include *Hosta* in the Agavaceae. The genus *Camassia*, because of its karyotype—12 large and 24 small—has also been connected with these groups and so is considered related.

7. Palynology is the study of pollen grains utilizing light microscopes (LM), scanning electron microscopes (SEM), and transmission electron microscopes (TEM). Pollen can be typi-

fied and these data are useful in systematics giving additional, and occasionally decisive, evidence for delimiting the taxa. On the basis of distinct surface features of the outer wall of the pollen grain (exine ornamentation) and outer grain wall architecture (wall ultrastructure), distinct types of pollen can be defined. These types are so distinct that individual genera and even species can be recognized. Accordingly, *Hosta* has at least five distinct pollen grain types: reticulate, reticulatelike, rugulate, rugulate-baculate and rugulate-granulate. Unfortunately for gardeners, this type of investigation requires electron microscopy so relegates it to the laboratories of scientific institutions. On the other hand, it is fortunate that the University of Georgia, School of Botany, under the leadership of Professor S. B. Jones, has devoted considerable time and resources to the biosystematic study of the genus and so continues to contribute pivotal evidence which has been considered in writing this book.

8. Maekawa refers to the *fortunei* group but he includes only the type, viz., *H. fortunei* (Baker) Bailey, the *Renge Giboshi*. His description does not match that of the type in K so is a segregated taxon. None of the taxa described by Hylander are listed by Maekawa.

9. *Typical* here means the form described by Hylander, not Maekawa. In Western gardens Hylander's description is considered the typical species. This is, of course, not the case, because the natural population is extremely polymorphic and may represent several intergrading hybrid swarms. This example is only one of many where botanists have applied different morphological limits to the description of a species: Hylander (1954) in a very narrow sense, Maekawa (1940) with broader definitions, and Fujita (1976a), in the broadest sense possible, equates *H. sieboldiana* to *H. montana* and combines both under the Japanese formal name *Oba Giboshi*. The original botanical concept of what this species looks like was much closer to Fujita's proposal which recognizes the polymorphism of this hosta. I examined many herbarium specimens of *H. sieboldiana* dating back to von Siebold and found a number of taxa under this name. Today, in Europe and in North America, *H. sieboldiana* is considered, in a very narrow sense, a short-scaped, very blue-grey, very large, rugose taxon. This presumption started in the late 1800s when master gardeners like Gertrude Jekyll included this clonal type in their garden books and designs. It was no doubt helped along by many gardeners who liked the idea of a species being an easily recognizable clone-type with a very narrow morphological definition. Nothing, of course, could be further from the botanical truth.

10. Originally, the description of such species was frequently based on a single cultivated clone. Over the years, seedlings with identical or similar characteristics were selected and added to the original material resulting in a mixed population of similar clones of different origins.

11. *Hosta tokudama* 'Rabinau' (also spelled 'Rabineau', as in Summers, 1972) is by some considered the true *H.* 'Tokudama'. This assumption is inaccurate. Although the latter is now considered of cultivated origin and has been reduced to cultivar form, Maekawa's original diagnosis still stands. In it this hosta is described with somewhat wider morphological limits. The 'Rabinau' form is a selected, named clone with deeply cupped leaves. I recommend to those who maintain that the real *H.* 'Tokudama' must have deeply cupped, round leaves that they refer to Maekawa's photo 31 (Maekawa, 1940: 367; reprinted in *The American Hosta Society Bulletin*, 1972, 4:59). Maekawa describes the leaf as often somewhat concave but the photograph conclusively shows that the leaves can be somewhat flat as well.

12. Homonyms are valid botanical names given at different times to different taxa, such as genera or species. In *Hosta* nomenclature each of the potential generic names—*Hosta* and *Funkia*—had been used for other taxa prior to their intended and proposed use for *Hosta*. This makes them later homonyms of the names applied earlier. The Cambridge rule rejects homonyms and allows old, rejected names to be revived on the basis of priority. Although *Hosta* (Trattinnick, 1812) was a later homonym of earlier valid names, it was nevertheless conserved by a vote of the members of the International Botanical Congress in 1905. Thus it is a nomen conservandum (conserved name). At the same time the IC rejected *Funkia* Sprengel (1817) and with this rejection all names used under *Funkia* also became invalid.

13. This isotype, no. 1001 (in KYO, no. 32413) looked more like the imported authentic specimens than the holotype. It may be that the cultivated specimens grown in the United States are a distinct selection of the natural population. Compare illustrations of the specimen (Fig. 3-58 and Plate 53) to Fujita's holotype reprinted in *The American Hosta Society Bulletin*, 1978, 10:39.

14. *Hosta kiyosumiensis* is included here because it is very closely associated with the other two named species. Maekawa (1969) included it with *H. crispula*.

15. Brickell coined the phrase "Species of convenience" at a lily group discussion at the RHS hall in 1970. It was republished in Brickell (1983:13).

16. *Hosta* 'Tortifrons' is a fertile somatic mutation. Controlled selfed crosses which I made over a period of years have never yielded offspring with contorted leaves. All seedlings turned out to be small versions of *H.* 'Tardiflora' (or similar). Fujita ignored this taxon.

17. A reproductive barrier (absolute reproductive isolation) has been cited as one of the requirements to qualify as a species. In *Hosta*, as currently delimited, this requisite is mostly ignored. Most taxa in the genus that are classified as species readily hybridize in their natural habitat.

18. These populations are reproductively isolated by virtue of their remote habitat. Once removed from this habitat they will interbreed with at least some of the other taxa in the genus and produce interspecific and intraspecific hybrids.

19. *Hosta minor* or *H. nakaiana* may be among these imports which introduced the ridged scape trait into Japan by interbreeding with a native Japanese species.

20. *Hosta plantaginea* var. *japonica* may be an interspecific hybrid.

21. *Hosta montana* 'Aureomarginata' may have been found as a mutation in the wild. The type is of cultivated origin.

22. *Hosta* 'Bella' is *H. fortunei* var. *obscura*. Wehrhahn's *H. bella* is the same and has priority.

23. *Hosta* 'Crispula' was originally found in the wild by von Siebold as a mutation near Nagasaki (see Chapter 5).

24. *Hosta* 'Fortunei Aureomarginata' is *H. fortunei* var. *obscura* f. *marginata*. Wehrhahn's var. *aureomarginata* has priority.

25. The white-margined and green forms of *H. sieboldii* are found as natural, wild populations. The variegated forms of *H. sieboldii* are found in the wild, but only as isolated mutants that revert and do not perpetuate themselves.

26. Herbarium specimens for the all-green form of *H. rohdeifolia* f. *viridis* which were collected in the wild were examined. The margined, specific form is a mutation which does not perpetuate in the wild.

27. All taxa in section *Foliosae* have been reduced to cultivar form. They are hybrids which I have retained for historic reasons only.

APPENDIX B

1. Carl Sigismund Kunth, 1788–1850, German botanist and vice-director of the Berlin Botanic Garden (now called the Berlin-Dahlem Botanical Museum). His monumental seven volume *Nova genera et species plantarum* contains 700 plates. The entire garden and his herbarium containing 45,000 specimens were destroyed during the Second World War.

2. Several herbarium specimens exist with the name *Funkia ovata* var. *ramosa* (= branched), which Miquel used to indicate their branching scapes (in L, nos. 8147/36 and 8147/37, both marked syntypes). Miquel's specimens collected by von Siebold in 1827 as well as Maekawa's holotype of 1984 show this branching. The specimens of both were collected from the populations growing on Mount Inasa-dake across Nagasaki harbor. In Japan this hosta was named *Nagasaki Giboshi* (Maekawa ex Toyama, 1940) and described under the species name *H. tibai* (Maekawa, 1984). Maekawa did not use Miquel's name because it has no priority outside its rank. (Per the ICBN the correct name is *H. tibae*.)

3. This case also shows the communication and language difficulties existing between European and Japanese botanists. Hylander examined Miquel's syntypes in 1952–53 and incorrectly identified these taxa as *H.* 'Lancifolia'. In light of the considerable differences between *H.* 'Lancifolia' and *H. tibae* (= Miquel's var. *ramosa*) and because Miquel judged this taxon a distinct variety and gave it a varietal name, Hylander's determination was obviously made without first comparing Japanese records (Maekawa ex Toyama, 1940; Maekawa 1950) concerning this taxon, which unfortunately are in Japanese.

4. It should be remembered than some forms of *H. sieboldiana* are in Japan considered to be *Oba Giboshi*, which technically is *H. montana*. Fujita (1976a) made an opposite placement and the exact borderline is muddled. Maekawa (1940) stated that *H. sieboldiana* was "glaucina vel viridis (glaucous OR green)."

5. Jinzo Matsumura, 1856–1928, botanist, Japan.

6. Jokusai Iinuma, 1782–1865, botanist, Japan.

7. Tomitaro Makino, 1862–1957, botanist, Japan.

8. This taxon is still growing at the Munich Botanic Garden where I saw it in 1939 and again examined it in 1984 (Schmid, 1985b).

9. Kwanji Nemoto, 1860–1936, botanist, Japan.

10. Kingo Miyabe, 1860–1951, botanist, Japan; Yushun Kudo, 1887–1932, botanist, Japan.

11. Masaji Honda, 1897–(?), botanist, Japan.

12. Gen'ichi Koidzumi, 1883–1953, botanist, Japan.

13. Genkei Masamune, 1899–(?), botanist, Japan.

14. Misao Tatewaki, 1899–(?), botanist, Japan.

15. Karl Otto Robert Peter Paul Gräbner, 1871–1933, botanist, Germany.

16. George Valentine Nash, 1864–1921, botanist and head gardener at the New York Botanic Garden, United States.

17. Vladimir Leontievtch Komarov, 1869–1946, botanist, USSR.

18. Ivan Vladimirovitch Palibin, 1872–1949, botanist, USSR.

19. Augustin Abel Hector Léveillé, 1810–1880, botanist, France.

20. Liberty Hyde Bailey, 1858–1955, botanist, United States.

21. Heinrich Rudolf Wehrhahn, 1882–1940, botanist, Germany.

22. There is a *H. longipes* var. *latifolia* (also *H. latifolia*) in Japan, where it is known under the name *Amagi Iwa Giboshi* and a similar hosta known as *Maruba Iwa Giboshi* hort. These taxa are not conspecific with the "European" *H. latifolia* but belong to section *Picnolepis*.

23. The *Oxford University Dictionary* defines "terete" as "smooth and round, having a cylindrical form, circular in cross-section and a surface free from furrows or ridges."

24. Christian Maximilian Hugo Glück, 1868–1940, botanist, Germany.

25. According to Hensen (1963b), J. Pierot, a member of the Rijksherbarium at Leiden stayed in Indonesia and sent back several hostas which were cultivated at the garden of Buitenzorg, Java, in 1840. This garden was used by von Siebold ten years earlier as an acclimatization garden and staging point for sending plants on to Holland. *Hosta plantaginea* var. *japonica* was one of these plants, and I believe it was originally sent to Java from Japan by von Siebold and subsequently retrieved by Pierot.

26. In Japan *Oba Giboshi* grows on the Pacific Ocean side of the main islands. This hosta has various scientific synonyms, which include *H. sieboldiana* var. *gigantea*, *H. montana*, and *H. fortunei* var. *gigantea*. These synonyms are taken from Fujita (1976a). Maekawa's holotype of *H. montana* was collected near Lake Yamanaka, Yamanashi Prefecture, and cultivated as no. 31 in his garden. The lake is due northeast of Mount Fujiyama (Fuji-san) and occupies 2.5 square miles (6.5 sq. km) at an altitude of 3222 ft (982 m). Recently, a number of variegated *H. montana* mutants have been found in this lake district. All the more than two dozen specimens of *H. montana* cited by Maekawa (1940) were collected in the central part of Honshu (the areas bounding the Pacific Ocean coastal regions of eastern Kansai, Chubu, Kanto, and southern Tohoku), an area not accessible to von Siebold and therefore outside his collecting area. He could, of course, have received *H. montana* types cultivated in Kyushu, but as Hensen (1963b) pointed out, the taxa most often thought to have been *H. montana* in von Siebold's gardens were, in fact, nonglaucous, tall-scaped forms of a "green" *H. sieboldiana*. Maekawa (1940) included this type in his broad diagnosis of the taxon, and this would account for the yellow anthers in *H.* 'Elata'. I believe *H. sinensis* was *H.* 'Fortunei Gigantea', a relationship also mentioned by Hensen (1963b).

27. The holotype for *Hosta okamotoi* is in KYO, Araki no. 15699, dated 12 September 1947, and was collected in Kyoto Prefecture, Chii-mura. The holotype for *Hosta takiensis*, also in KYO, Araki no. 15099, dated 16 September 1941, was collected in Kyoto Prefecture, Murakumo-mura.

28. The holotype for *Hosta campanulata* is in KYO, Araki no. 14562b, dated 14 August 1937, and was collected in Kyoto Prefecture, Takigun, Kumobe-mura. The specimen has a determinavit by Murata, dated March 1967 and cosigned by Fujita, which judges this taxon to be *H. sieboldii* (as *H. albomarginata* [Hooker] Ohwi). This specimen shows two scapes—one with two branches—and three leaves. The holotype for *Hosta campanulata* var. *parviflora* is also in KYO, Araki no. 14562a, dated 5 November 1937, and was collected in Kyoto Prefecture, Kumobe-mura.

29. The holotype for *Hosta* calliantha is in KYO, Araki no. 15062, dated 19 August 1939, and was collected in Kyoto Prefecture, Higashibetsuin-mura. It is also labeled *H. rohdeifolia* var. *viridis*.

30. The holotype for *Hosta takahashii* is in KYO, Araki no. 14833, dated 6 September 1938, and was collected in Shiga Prefecture on Mount Ibukiyama.

31. Even when carefully selfed, *H. sieboldiana* does not come true but produces seedlings—some green, others pruinose—which vary considerably in size and other morphological traits.

32. Bailey apparently also did not know when the name *H. elata* was first used, indicating he was not the author and that the name had been used previously. His use is considered the first botanically valid one.

33. Joseph Gerhard Zuccarini, 1797–1848, botanist, University of Munich, Germany. He collaborated with von Siebold on *Flora Japonica* (1835–1841), a major illustrated work on the Japanese flora.

34. Charles Antoine Lemaire, 1801–1871, botanist, Belgium.

35. Wister reports (1969:26): "Here are further notes on the yellow-edged hosta sent to Robinson: Looking over some old notes I find a statement by Charles Stockman of Newburyport that he had seen the yellow edged hosta in Germany. On 23 September 1935, Mr. Stockman had seen these in Munich Botanic Garden."

36. According to Kaneko (1968a) *H. clausa* has a chromosome number of 90 (2n). The normal chromosome count for the genus is 60 (2n).

37. Fujita apparently considered inclusion of some of the Korean species under section *Tardanthae*. He mentioned *H. venusta* and *H. minor*. On the latter he made the statement: "There remains a question whether it should be included in this section (*Tardanthae*) or not." Such an arrangement would, in my opinion, be rather unnatural because these taxa bloom very early, and macromorphologically they clearly belong to section *Lamellatae*. The new Korean species *H. jonesii* M. G. Chung (1989) does, however, belong to section *Tardanthae*, together with *H. tibae* and *H. tsushimensis*.

38. Alex J. Summers, Bridgeville, DE, also contributed information to this article.

39. Write to: The Hon. Secretary, Roger Bowden, Cleave House, Sticklepath, Okehampton, Devon, EX20 2NN, England.

APPENDIX D

1. This chart comprises four color fans, each with 50 sheets in four different shades—a total of 200 sheets with four color shades on each. The cost is £25 (in 1990) postage paid. Order from the Royal Horticultural Society Enterprises, Ltd., RHS Garden, Wisley, Woking, Surrey, England.

2. John Lindley, 1799–1865, botanist, United Kingdom. Lindley adopted the works of Link (1789; cfr. Stearn, 1986), Illiger (1800; cfr. Stearn, 1986), and de Candolle ([1813] 1844; cfr. Stearn, 1986). He published major contributions in 1832 (with subsequent editions in 1835, 1839, and 1848) as *An Introduction to Botany* and in 1847 as *The Elements of Botany*—both published in London. His work was subsequently embraced by Bentham and Gray and forms the foundation of English botanical terminology. Lindley's terms have been extracted from Bischoff (1833) and the characteristic numbers are quoted from Stearn (1986).

Glossary

The following subject vocabulary defines botanical terminology used in this book and gives the English-Latin and in some cases the Latin-English equivalents. The application of descriptive terms is in many cases specific to the taxa in the genus *Hosta* so may have other meanings. A number of terms and specific micro- and macromorphological characters directly affecting classification have been defined and explained in other chapters and appendices. Readers are encouraged to first study these chapters to familiarize themselves with the botanical/morphological terminology and concepts explained.

Standard technical nomenclature in general use can be looked up in any popular dictionary so is also excluded. Occasionally, scientific words originating with Latin have two or more correct orthographic forms; for example, "membranaceous" and "membranous." To determine the application and correctness of multiple spellings, several editions of *The Oxford Universal Dictionary* have been consulted and used as authority.

Where ratios are given in conjunction with technical terms applying to leaf shapes, as "ratio = 6:1," the first number indicates leaf length and the second, width (or breadth) of leaf.

Abiotic: The nonliving components of the environment which comprise the microclimate and so affect plant life.

Acute (*acutus*): Coming straight to a point.

Agamospermy: See apomixis.

Albescent: Turning white (with age).

Allele: A form in which a gene occurs on a chromosome occupying always the same site. A diploid having two identical alleles is homozygous while one with two different alleles is heterozygous (see heterozygous).

Allopatric: See population.

Amplexicaul, stem-clasping (*amplexicaulis*): Wrapped around the stem, as in the sterile bracts of *H. sieboldii*.

Anemophily: The process of pollination by wind action.

Anthers: The pollen sacks, six in *Hosta*, which are bilocular, meaning each anther is composed of two sacks. In the cavity (*loculus*) of each sack mother cells undergo meiosis which eventually results in the production of pollen grains. The anther surface cells have characteristic coloration and patterns which are useful in classifying the taxa.

Anthesis: The specific period in time when a flower is fully open until fruit set. Broadly applied to an entire raceme when it is "in full bloom."

Apex, apices (pl): The leaf tip(s).

Apomixis, apomictic: In *Hosta* used in narrow sense, as agamospermy, meaning the production of seed without actual fertilization. Apomixis is frequently found in combination with polyploidy, which see. The only apomict on record in the genus is the tetraploid *H. ventricosa*, and it is an obligate apomict, which can reproduce only by apomixis, so is incapable of producing hybrids as a pod parent although it has excellent, fertile pollen and has produced a number of hybrids as a pollen parent. Because apomixis is asexual, all the resulting plants are identical as in vegetative reproduction.

apud: By; in the writings of. This word is used in connection with the author's citation of a botanical name. "Author A

apud author B" means a name proposed by A and published by (in the writings of) B.

Arcuate: Curved like a bow, shaped like a arc.

Ascendent, ascending (*ascendens*): Having a direction upwards, with an oblique base.

Asexual reproduction: The propagation of plant material without fusion of the gametes (the male and female reproductive cells). Also considered vegetative reproduction. Root division and tissue culture are types of asexual reproduction and so is apomixis, which see.

Attenuate (*angusatus*): With curved sides converging.

Baculate: Stick-shaped.

Band-shaped (*fasciarius*): Ratio = 12 (or more):1.

Binomial: The scientific name of an organism; also the standard method of naming species in botanical nomenclature. The first part (usually abbreviated) is the genus name and the second part is the species epithet, as in *H. sieboldiana*.

Biosystematics: The study of relationship and variation in natural populations. Instead of studying individual plants, entire groups (populations) are analyzed using comparative morphological, cytological, chemosystematic, palynological, ecological, and various other techniques.

Biotic: The living elements of a given environment which by their activities affect plant life.

Bract: A leaf subtending a flower and for this reason often called a fertile bract where the pedicel supporting the flower emanates in the axil of the bract and scape. Many taxa in the genus have 1–5 amplexicaul or foliaceous sterile bracts below the raceme, so called because they do not subtend a flower although occasionally remnants of aborted flowers can be seen in the axil. Sterile bracts are also called ground bracts.

Bracteate: Having a bract.

Bracteole: A leaf subtending a flower in an inflorescence that is itself subtended by a bract.

Broadly ovate (*late ovatus*): Ratio = 6:5.

Caesious (*caesius*): Like glaucous, but greener, as with *H. nigrescens*.

Calyx: See corolla.

Caespitous (*caespitosus*): A population of plants forming dense patches or colonies, as in *H. venusta*.

Carnose, carnous, fleshy (*carnosus*): Firm, juicy.

Ceraceous, waxy (*ceraceus, cereus*): Having the texture of new wax.

Cernuous, drooping (*cernuus*): Inclined from the perpendicular and directed more to the horizon.

Chemosystematics, chemotaxonomy: The application of results obtained principally by chemical analysis to classification. The routine utilization of chromatography, electrophoresis, and other modern methods of chemical analysis allow biosystematic conclusions to be drawn which are applied to delimit taxa.

Chimera, or chimaera: Plant parts which contain two or more genetically different cells. Periclinal chimeras play an important role in variegation (see Appendix D).

Chlorophyll: Pigments which absorb red and violet-blue light and reflect green, giving plants their green color. Usually located in leafy areas, they are essential to photosynthesis.

Clone: Generally this term is applied to a line of genetically identical plants breeding true by mitotic (cell) division when sexually propagating, so clones are often referred to as pure lines or pure strains. In *Hosta* this is normally not the case so the terms pure line or pure strain are not applicable and should not be used. The word "clone" is used, however, with its meaning modified: Because most taxa in the genus are heterozygous (genetically not identical), so do not breed true, clonal lines can be maintained only by asexual propagation, such as root division or tissue culture and this is the case with all hybrids in the genus.

Connation: Joined together, as in the abnormal fusion of petals or reproductive organs. In *Hosta*, fusion of the carpels has been observed (Maekawa, 1944) resulting in monstrosities.

Conspecific: Of the same species, the state of belonging to the same specific group.

Convolute (*convolutus*): Rolled up, as leaves before unfurling.

Cordate, heart-shaped (*cordatus*): Having two equal, rounded lobes.

Coriaceous, leathery (*coriaceus*): Having the consistency of leather, as with *H. rupifraga*.

Corolla: By definition the corolla is formed by the petals (i.e., the inner lobes of the perianth). In the genus three exterior lobes (the calyx) are technically sepals and three interior lobes (the corolla) are petals, but both are either white or colored and there is little difference between them so they are called tepals. Together they form the perianth which combines calyx and corolla parts into a narrow tubular section (*tubus angustus*) followed by an expanding tubular section (*tubus dilatatus*) formed by six tepals (lobes). Because there is no distinction between calyx and corolla, the entire structure has been referred to as a corolla (Maekawa, 1940), while other authors correctly call it a perianth (Fujita, 1976). The center section of the perianth beginning at the point of expansion to where separation of the exterior lobes begins is either funnel-shaped (*corolla infundibuliformis*) or bell-shaped (*corolla campanulata*) with many in-between shapes. This central shape gives the flower either a funnel-shaped or bell-shaped character. Most cultivars have a more-or-less bell-shaped flower, while a few have truly funnel-shaped inflorescence.

Cultigen: A plant that originated in cultivation and is unknown as a perpetuating wild plant.

Decumbent (*decumbens*): Reclining upon the earth, then rising again from it at the apex.

Decurrent (*decurrens*): Prolonged below the point of insertion, as if running downwards. The smooth, continuous merging of leaf margin into petiole margin, without any noticeable break or change of direction as in *H. alismifolia*, *H.* 'Opipara', and *H.* 'Decorata'.

Dehisce, dehiscence: The splitting open of plant organs to release their content; as anthers releasing pollen or seed capsules releasing seeds.

Delimit, delimitation: Setting the morphological and other limits which define a taxon; as defining and circumscribing the distinctive bounds of a species.

Dependent, hanging down (*dependens*): Having a downward direction, caused by weight.

Descending (*descendens*): Directed gradually downwards.

Differentiate: The act of determining differences between plants. Also applied as the state of being different or found different after careful morphological analysis.

Diffuse (*diffusus*): Spreading widely.

Diploid: See polyploidy.

Dusty (*lentiginosus*): Covered with minute dots, as if dusted.

Entire (*integer*): Margins are free of divisions, such as serrated, toothed, or sawed margins (see also quite entire).

Entomophily: The process of pollination by insects.

Epidermal: Related to the outer layer of skin; specifically the top layer of cells in a leaf, as in epidermal wax.

Epiphyte, epiphytic: One plant growing upon another plant, as species occasionally growing on tree trunks and in tree crotches. In a broad sense this is also (and incorrectly) applied to hostas growing on rocks with only sparse soil available, but the latter are technically lithophytes.

Epithet: The part of a taxonomic name identifying a subordinate unit within a genus (see also binomial).

Even, smooth (*aequatus*): Although having slightly impressed principal veins, most hosta leaves have a relatively even, smooth surface. For this reason cultivars not definitely falling into distinctly rugose or furrowed types have been classified as "flat," smooth, having an even surface with no rugosity but not "flat as a board" (see also smooth, as applied to principal veins).

ex: Used in connection with the author's citation of a botanical name. When a name is proposed but not validly published by one author and subsequently it is validly published by another, who supplied a valid description, the name of the later author is appended to the citation with the connecting word *ex*. "Author A ex author B" means that A formulated an invalid name (usually a nomen nudum), and subsequently B validly published the taxon.

Farinose, mealy (*farinosus*): Mealy, covered with a whitish scurvy coating.

Fasciate, fasciated (*fasciatus*): Several contiguous parts growing unnaturally together into one part, such as fasciated scapes.

Fasciculate (*fasciculatus*): Bundled, as in the petioles of many species.

Fastigiate, tapered (*fastigiatus*): Arranged like a narrow pyramid, as in some cultivars which have sterile, leafy bracts growing from the scape and progressively smaller towards the top.

Filiform: Having a threadlike form.

Flavonoid: Several compounds found in plants all of which contain a 2-phenyl-benzo-pyran nucleus. Anthocyanins, for example, are flavonoids giving the flowers of the genus their lavender or purple coloration.

Floristic: Primarily used to characterize publications and books which deal with the flora of certain regions. Some of the historic works may not be considered scientific, botanical works but are nevertheless extremely useful to classification.

Form, type: Used in Chapters 3 and 4 when a plant conforms to a specific typical look well known to gardeners but cannot be positively identified as the true species.

Furrowed: Most cultivars have principal veins impressed on the leaf surface. Nonetheless, the leaf is quite flat and can be considered smooth in broad terms. In some, the principal veins are very deeply impressed with the intervening leaf surface arching highly and forming rather deep V-shaped channels or furrows. The depth of these furrows can reach 1/8 in. (4 mm) or more. In these cases the leaf surface is called furrowed, as in *H. montana* f. *macrophylla*.

Gamopetalate: Having petals that are fused together at the base forming a corolla tube.

Genotype: The genetic makeup of a living organism, in this context the taxa belonging to the genus *Hosta*. A given genotype can develop several phenotypes (which see) by the interaction of genes and their relative dominance as well as environmental factors.

Genus, genera (pl): A group of closely related plants comprising the subdivision of a plant family. The genus embraces all taxa, including the species, subspecies, hybrids, and mutants.

Glabrous, smooth (*glaber*): Being free of unevenness. In the genus applied to smooth nerves on underside of leaf, as opposed to papillose, which see.

Glaucous (*glaucus*): A fine bloom the color of cabbage, as with *H. sieboldiana*.

Granulate: Composed of granules, covered with uniform, knoblike prominences.

Herbaceous (*herbaceus*): Thin, green, and cellular, as the tissue of membranous leaves.

Herbalistic: In reference to early botany, when it was chiefly a science dealing with the knowledge of herbs and their medical use in healing. Until the establishment of systematic botany, herbalism was the main practical reason for studying herbs and plants. Herbalistic writings are now considered botanical texts which predate systematic botany.

Herbarium, herbaria (pl) (*hortus siccus*): A place where collections of dried, pressed type specimens and other specimens are kept, usually arranged according to a taxonomic system, and scrupulously preserved. The specimen sheets carry labels giving the name of the plant collector, the place of collection, notes on habitat, uses, and other pertinent data. In the text, standard abbreviations as listed in *Index Herbariorum* (Holmgren and Keuken, 1974) have been used.

Heterozygous: Most taxa in the genus appear to be heterozygous; this can be inferred from the frequency of failure to breed true. Normally, diploid plants have identical alleles (a form in which a gene can occur) on a chromosome, so breed true; they are called homozygous. Those plants having different alleles are called heterozygous; they usually do not breed true because one allele is dominant while the other is recessive, resulting in different phenotypes or exhibiting incomplete dominance, where the morphological character of a plant is somewhere between that of the parents. It should be pointed out that the total genetic makeup of a plant determines its morphology and only certain characteristics may be affected by heterozygosity.

Holotype: See type.

Homonym, homonymous: A homonym is a name identical in spelling to another which has been previously and validly published for a taxon of the same rank based on a different type. Even if the homonym is illegitimate, or is generally treated as a synonym on taxonomic grounds, the later homonym must be rejected, unless it has been conserved (ICBN, Article 64). The ICBN rules allow old, rejected names to be revived on the basis of priority. Names with slightly different spellings (cfr. *Funkia* vs. *Funckia*) are under the ICBN treated as homonyms when they are based on a different type. The case of *Hosta* (Trattinnick, 1812) is an exception because a vote by the members of the International Botanical Congress in 1905 made this name a nomen conservandum (conserved name) and rejected *Funkia* (Sprengel, 1817). With this all the epithets used with *Funkia* also became invalid (see Appendixes A and B).

Horizontal (*horizontalis*): Aligned with the horizon.

Hybrid swarm: Interspecific or intraspecific hybrid populations produced in the wild between two original, parental species or forms. These populations are usually in a continuous process of intergrading so are constantly variable until they (1) eventually disappear; (2) backcross to one of the parental forms; (3) evolve and adapt (speciate) to new or changed habitat following the forces of genetic recombination so developing into new species or forms; or (4) undergo mutation resulting in transitional taxa which are usually unable to perpetuate.

Hybrid (definition): The offspring resulting from crossing two genetically different parental forms.

Hybrid (notation): A hybrid of the taxon listed; for example: "(*H. montana* hybrid)" signifies that the listed plant is undoubtedly a hybrid of *H. montana* (by virtue of its macromorphology), but its exact parental combination is unknown. Where the parents are known, both names are listed and connected by a multiplication sign: *H. sieboldiana* × *H. kikutii* signifies a hybrid between *H. sieboldiana* as a pod parent (listed first) and *H. kikutii* as a pollen parent (listed second).

Hybridizer: One who sexually crosses two different hostas to make a new offspring.

Imbricate, imbricated (*imbricatus*): overlapped; tiled, like the bracts of unopened flower buds and racemes, with tightly packed, overlapping bracts and flowers.

Inclined (*inclinatus*, *declinatus*): Falling back from the perpendicular.

Indigenous: Native. Used to indicate a taxon is native to a certain area.

Interspecific (hybrid): Between species. A hosta hybrid resulting from the cross-fertilization of two different species.

Intraspecific, infraspecific (hybrid): Within a species. A hybrid resulting from the cross-fertilization of taxa belonging to the same species.

Introgression, intergradation, intergrading: The process of incorporating genes from one species or subspecies into another related species or subspecies. In natural populations this is an important step in evolution and adaptation to different environments. Many of the taxa in the genus are broadly related so introgressive hybridization takes place frequently as does subsequent backcrossing with one of the parental types. The transitional populations of hybrids are considered intergrading types.

Involute (*involutus*): Rolled inward, as some leaf margins.

Isotype: See type.

Juvenile: An immature development, such as immature leaves that do not have typical shapes.

Karyotype, karyotypical: During a particular stage of mitosis the chromosomes of a cell take on a highly characteristic configuration—determined by number, size, and shape—which can be seen in a light microscope and recorded by a photograph or drawing, called an idiogram (or karyogram) of a karyotype. The latter is used as evidence in plant classification and delimitation.

Lacunose (*lacunosus*): Having numerous large, deep depressions or excavations.

Lanceolate, lance-shaped (*anguste ellipticus*): Ratio = 6:1 to 3:1.

Lectotype: See type.

Lined (*lineatus*): Marked by longitudinal lines.

Lithophyte, lithophytic: Growing on rocks.

Locule, loculicidal: A cavity in a plant organ, as in anthers, where pollen develops (see anther). The seed capsules of the genus contain three locules and dehisce in a loculicidal manner, meaning along the dorsal slits (sutures) in the capsule wall of each locule (here seed cavity).

Lusus: Literally, a game for amusement or sport. Here its derived meaning is mutation. This term is now rarely used and has been replaced by "mutation" or "sport." It is listed here because earlier botanists made frequent use of the term—for example, Miquel (1867, 1869)—and so the term is used in historical names.

Lutescent: Turning yellow (with age).

Macromorphology: The branch of morphology that deals with features visible to the naked eye, such as flowers and leaves.

Meiosis, meiotic: The process in which a diploid cell undergoes reduction division to form haploid cells, each containing a single set of chromosomes.

Membranaceous, membranous (*membranaceus*): Thin, translucent. Also having a papery texture, parchmentlike. Mostly of leaves. In contrast to thick leaves, with heavy substance.

Meristem: A part of the plant which contains potentially actively dividing cells, such as dormant shot tips. These areas can be cut out and used in tissue culture (meristem culture), which see. In the genus the rhizome contains meristematic tissue.

Metanym: An antedated name which may be superfluous under a given classification but not necessarily permanently so; it may be used if the ruling classification is not accepted or revised. Per the ICBN metanyms are not illegitimate (nom. illegitima) and can be used for reclassified or segregated taxa.

Micromorphology: The branch of morphology that investigates "invisible" characters, such as pollen and cellular systems, which require the application of light (optical) microscopy, as well as scanning electron (SEM), transmission electron microscopy (TEM), or scanning transmission electron microscopy (STEM).

Mitosis, mitotic: The mechanism of cell division having several distinct phases by which a cell divides forming two identical daughter cells each having the same number of chromosomes with matching genetic composition.

Monocotyledonae, monocotyledons: A subclass of the Angiospermae (flowering plants) having one cotyledon (seed leaf) and to which the genus *Hosta* belongs. All are segments of division Spermatophyta (seed plants).

Monograph: A book or treatise written about a single topic, as the detailed aspects of a specific subject, usually a class of plants, animals, or minerals; or devoted to a single genus or species.

Monotypic: Any taxon that has only one subordinate taxon is monotypic. For example, the genus *Hosta* is the only genus in the monotypic family known as Hostaceae, and the monotypic subgenus *Hosta* (formerly *Niobe*) has just one species, viz., *H. plantaginea*.

Monstrous, monstrosity: Abnormal and unusual growth patterns often due to connation, which see, of plant tissue.

Morphology, morphological: A branch of botany that deals with the study of form and external structure of taxa. Two distinct branches exist: macromorphology and micromorphology, which see.

Mucronate (*mucronatus*): Abruptly terminated by a sharp point.

Mutability: Prone to change or sport.

Mutant: A sport or mutant. Usually variegated forms or monstrosities which arise spontaneously but do not have the ability to perpetuate. All variegated hostas are mutants (see Appendix D).

Narrowly obovate (*anguste obovatus*): Ratio = 6:1 to 3:1.

Narrowly ovate (*anguste ovatus*): Ratio = 6:1 to 3:1.

Natural (sometimes called spontaneous in the literature): Populations of species and botanical varieties which arose and exist as a result of natural processes, without modification by human intervention or cultivation. Cultivated populations existing near natural colonies in Japan may give rise to hybrids between natural populations and cultivated ones. The resulting wild plants may or may not be considered natural. Purists argue that interspecific or intraspecific hybrids resulting from cross-fertilization of cultivated populations with natural ones are considered modified by human intervention so the hybrids are not truly natural plants.

Navicular: Boat-shaped. The bracts in many species are boat-shaped and distinctly keeled.

Necrosis: The death of a certain part of a plant or the whole plant. In *Hosta* most often applied to the browning and drying up ("burning") of leaf margins, as occurs in *H. sieboldiana* 'Frances Williams'.

Neotype: See type.

Nomenclature: An established system of names and the rules applied thereto.

Nutant, nodding (*nutans*): Inclining markedly from the perpendicular and directed downwards.

Oblique: Slanting away from the vertical. Used primarily for flower scapes.

Obovate, sides curved with greatest breadth above the middle (*obovatus*): Ratio = 2:1 to 3:2.

Obtuse, blunt-pointed (*obtusus*): Terminated by a rounded end. Blunt ended, as leaf tips. *Hosta decorata* has blunt ends, *H. sieboldii* has pointed ends.

Opaque (*opacus, impolitus*): Dull, the reverse of shining.

Orbicular, round or almost round (*circularis*): Ratio = 1:1.

Oval, sides curved with greatest breadth at the middle, elliptic (*ellipticus*): Ratio = 2:1 to 3:2.

Ovate, sides curved with greatest breadth below the middle, egg-shaped (*ovatus*): Ratio = 2:1 to 3:2.

Palynology, palynological: The study of pollen grains. Pollen can be typified and these data are useful in systematics giving additional, and occasionally decisive, evidence for delimiting the taxa.

Papery (*papyraceus, chartaceus*): Having the substance of writing paper in combination with being opaque.

Papillose: Having short, nipple-shaped protuberances, such as on the surface of the veins on the backside of leaves of several species, including *H. montana*. When sliding the fingertip along the vein, these are felt as a slight roughness (in contrast to many other species, which have very smooth vein surface). These features are used in classification.

Paratype: See type.

Patent, spreading (*patens*): Gradually spreading outward, as most leaf crowns; opening wide, as flower petals; diverging widely.

Pedicel: The individual flower stem. A short stem carrying the flower originating on the scape and extending to the flower base, usually subtended by a bract, which see.

Pedicellate: Having a pedicel.

Pendulous (*pendulus*): Hanging down.

Perennation: The process by which herbaceous perennials survive the winter season. In the genus the mechanism involves annual top growth, which disappears during winter, and the organ of perennation, which is the below-ground rhizome that produces new, annual leaf bundles and flowers scapes every spring. In most taxa of the genus the flower scapes are woody and remain upright on the plant throughout winter.

Perianth: The exterior structure of the flower composed of the calyx and the corolla which are not differentiated in the genus and form a tubular flower consisting of three exterior lobes (calyx) and three interior lobes, also called the corolla, which see.

Periclinal: Parallel to the surface. Periclinal chimeras play an important role in variegation (see Appendix D).

Perpendicular (*perpendicularis, verticalis*): Being at right angles with a surface. Used for scapes that are very straight and vertical

Petiole: The leaf stem of a plant extending from the crown to the base of the leaf. Some taxa in the genus have no discernable petiole and the expanding leaf tissue originates directly from the rhizome, while others represent intermediate forms having blade tissue continuing into a barely differentiated petiole which is called a pseudopetiole.

Phenotype: The manifest characteristics of a species collectively, namely, all the traits which result from gene interaction and dominance (inheritance), as well as environmental exposure in a given genotype and which morphologically characterize all the members of a species. Wide-ranging species usually undergo considerable gene modification and are influenced by vastly different habitats so show considerable differentiation of phenotypes (infraspecific variation), while species which have adapted to highly specialized environments commonly have very homogeneous phenotypical representation.

Phylogenetic, phyletic: The application of comparative morphology (shared characteristics) to the classification of taxa above the rank of genus and pointing to common ancestry on the familial and higher levels.

Pistil: The female organ of the flower comprising the ovary at the base of the flower, a long, tubular style, and the three-lobed stigma, which receives the pollen.

Polished (*politus, laevigatus*): Having the appearance of a polished substance, as in *H. laevigata* or *H. yingerii*.

Pollination: The act of depositing pollen on the stigma of a flower resulting in fertilization. This can be accomplished by insects or pollen carried by the wind, which is referred to "open" pollination, or it can be performed by human hands. The former is uncontrolled fertilization, because insects and wind forces are not selective as to the source of the pollen deposited. Ordinarily, human intervention is planned pollination (hybridization), using either the plant's own pollen (selfing) or pollen from another species (hybridizing).

Polymorphism, polymorphic: The existence of a number of different forms (phenotypes) within the same species, usually caused by genetic or environmental factors.

Polyploidy: A state in which plants have three or more complete sets of chromosomes in its cell nuclei. In the genus the normal condition is diploid, where two sets of chromosomes exist for a total of $2n = 60$. The genus has several triploid representatives ($2n = 90$) and one tetraploid species ($2n = 120$), namely, *H. ventricosa*, which also is apomictic.

Population: A local, perpetuating community of interbreeding plants usually of the same species. Populations may be allopatric—specialized and limited to small, isolated areas of habitat so usually separated geographically—or they may be sympatric, meaning they cover contiguous habitats encompassing large land areas and overlapping with other populations of plants either of the same genus or other genera or both. (see also specific population).

Powdery (*pulverentus*): Covered with a fine bloom.

Procumbent (*procumbens, humifusus*): Spread over the surface of the ground, as in leaf crowns.

Pruinose, frosted (*pruinosus*): A frosted, dewy appearance, as with *H.* 'Frosted Jade'. Covered with a white, powdery looking substance. For a more detailed, technical explanation see Chapter 2.

Pseudogamy, pseudogamous: In the genus meaning a type of apomixis in which seed tissue is developed without actual fertilization, but stimulus from the male gamete is required to initiate the process, so pollination is necessary. Pseudogamous apomixis is found in *H. ventricosa*.

Quite entire (*integerrimus*): Margins perfectly free of marginal divisions, such as serrated, toothed, or sawed margins.

Raceme: The flowering part of the scape on which the flowers are formed (inflorescence) and carried on individual, usually short, pedicels (flower stems). In the genus the inflorescence is a raceme forming a spike which is branched occasionally.

Recurving: Turned upon itself. In some species, like *H. sieboldii*, the tips of the lobes (flower petals) will curve outward and back upon themselves.

Reproductive isolation: The inability of sexual propagation between groups in a population or between proximal populations resulting in the prevention of gene flow between these non-interbreeding groups. This is due to the development of sterility barriers, which are obvious in geographically isolated, allopatric populations, but the mechanism is more complicated in sympatric, proximal populations and may have several causes: Different flowering times, different pollinators, or different niches in a common habitat; also hybridization may in fact occur but the hybrids are either sterile or inviable so are unable to perpetuate. Reproductive isolation is commonly considered one of the conditions required for qualifying a species but this is clearly not the case in the genus (see Appendix A) where interbreeding and introgressive hybridization is common.

Reticulate: Forming a network, shaped like a network.

Revolute (*revolutus*): Rolled backwards from the direction ordinarily assumed, as in leaf margins.

Rhizome: The thickened, underground part of the stem, also sometimes called rootstock, serving as organ of perennation. In most hostas the rhizome grows horizontally into a tuberlike mass but some hostas have a near-vertical rhizome, while others spread out to form underground, stoloniferous roots. The buds, from which aboveground leaf bundles and flower scapes emanate, as well as the underground roots grow from the rhizome

Roundish (*late ellipticus*): Ratio = 6:5.

Rugose, wrinkled (*rugosus*): Any leaf surface with uneven surface features. This includes dimpled, puckered, pursed, embossed, ruffled, pleated, wrinkled, and crinkled leaf surfaces. Examples include *H. sieboldiana* and its hybrids. Many cultivars are rugose.

Rugulate: Wrinkled; a slightly rugose surface.

Scape: The stem of the inflorescence bearing a number of flowers in the upper part, called a raceme, which see. Usually a leafless stem but in the genus frequently furnished with amplexicaul or foliaceous bracts.

Scrobiculate, pitted (*scrobiculatus*): Having numerous small, shallow depressions or excavations.

Secund, one-sided (*secundus*): Having all stalks (or pedicels) twisted one way, as with many racemes, flowers pointing to one side.

Selfing: Natural or hand-pollination of a flower with its own pollen.

Semiamplexicaul, half-stemclasping (*semiamplexicaulis*): Wrapped halfway around the stem, as with the sterile leafy bracts of *H. pachyscapa*.

Serotaxonomy, serology: The study of blood serum and its application to classification by analyzing the reaction of living animals to injections of plant protein extracts and comparing the similarities between antiserum and antigen produced by proteins obtained from different species.

Sessile, stalkless (*sessilis*): Without any sensible stalk, stalkless branches, as in *H. plantaginea*.

Shining (*nitidus*): Having a smooth, even, very shiny surface, as in *H. tardiflora* and *H. longipes*.

Speciation, speciate: The development of new species either by natural adaptation and selection or by polyploidy with attendant development of absolute reproductive isolation.

Species: A group of closely related plants comprising a subdivision of a genus.

Specific populations: A number of like plants growing together in the wild; a specific population may occur in a very limited area, such as *H. rupifraga* (Hachijo Island), or may be native to large land areas and consist of many individual plants and colonies, as *H. sieboldii*.

Spiral (*spiralis*): Twisted, spiral as the placement of leaves emerging from the rhizome.

Sport: See lusus.

Stamen: The male reproductive organ of the flower consisting of the filaments, long, slender stalks, 6 in the genus *Hosta*, and the anthers.

Stellate, star-shaped (*stellatus*, *stelliformis*): Arranged in a star shape around a common axis, as in the buds of *H. sieboldiana*.

Sterile, sterility: A taxon not producing viable seed but viable pollen is pod-sterile. If it produces neither it is absolutely sterile.

Sterility barrier: See reproductive isolation.

Stoloniferous: Characterizing a root stock which sends out horizontal stems, often far reaching, from which new and independent plants arise, as *H. clausa*.

Striate, striated (*striatus*): Marked with stria—fine linear markings, streaks, or grooves.

Succulent (*succulentus*): Very thickly cellular and juicy, fleshy.

Sympatric: See population.

Sympodial: In the genus an underground stem (stolon) with nodes at which leaf bundles arise. The stolon grows from node to node in a series of axillary branches so giving the effect of a simple stem (stolon), when in fact each section is technically a branch.

Syntype: See type.

Taxon, taxa (pl): A taxonomic plant category, such as genus or species. The hierarchy of taxa applicable to the genus are (in descending order): genus, species, subspecies, variety (varietas), and form (forma).

Taxonomist, taxonomy: The scientist and science of classifying (animals and) plants into natural, related groups (taxa) based on common features.

Terete: Smooth round, cylindrical, or tapering. Applied to scapes being smooth and round.

Tetraploid: See polyploidy.

Thick (*crassus*): Thicker than usual, thick, as with *H. crassifolia*.

Tissue culture: A highly successful method of plant propagation, also called micropropagation or meristem culture, which involves micro-cutting of meristem tissue and growing it on sterile growing medium with the aid of special chemicals and materials. Many popular cultivars are propagated by tissue culture which is an asexual process so produces a high rate of true offspring in most cases.

Triploid: See polyploidy.

Truncate (*truncatus*): As if cut straight across.

Type, type specimens: The type of a name of a species or infraspecific taxon, called a *holo*type, is the herbarium type specimen designated by the author as the nomenclatural type at the time of publication of the name. An *iso*type is a duplicate herbarium specimen of the holotype which was collected by the original author at the same time and place as the original specimen. *Syn*types are two or more specimens designated together and cited by the author as the type, usually when no holotype was specified. A *para*type is a specimen cited together with the original description. When a holotype was not designated or is missing a *lecto*type may be substituted and this type is usually chosen from the original specimens or one studied by the author. If no type material can be found or all original type material was lost a *neo*type may be selected to serve as a nomenclatural type. The term *topo*type is used in this text applied to specimens which are applied to illustrate distribution or limits of habitat.

Typica (*typos*): Type; occasionally used in botanical names: Forma or f. *typica*, meaning the typical form of a species, the type.

Ultrastructure: The structure of cells walls and other cellular details below the limits of resolution of light microscopy so only visible with electron microscopes.

Undulate: Wavy, either the leaf margin or the entire leaf is wavy.

Venation: The several major pairs of veins in leaves having a campylodrome arrangement (see Chapter 2). The number of vein pairs is useful for classification.

Vernal: Occurring in spring; shoots or leaves appearing in spring.

Versatile: Describing the attachment of an anther to the filament about halfway along its length, so being able to pivot and move relatively freely.

Verticillate, whorled (*verticilatus*): Arranged around the stem, as occasionally occurs in cultivars where groups of flowers are whorled around the stem and separated by portions of a bare raceme.

Very broadly ovate (*perlate ovatus*): Ratio = 1:1.

Very straight (*strictus*): Absolutely not deviating from a straight direction.

Viridescent: Turning green.

Whitened (*dealbatus*): Powdered with very opaque white, as with *H. hypoleuca*.

Bibliography

REFERENCES

To write this book I depended upon literally thousands of references, including everything from botanical works to scraps of paper handed to me by hybridizers at conventions. The references used were written in many languages, but principally English, botanical Latin, Japanese, German, Dutch, French, and Swedish, in that order by frequency. Rather than rely on translations made by others, I have in most cases obtained copies of the originals from which I made my own translations. I did so because, unfortunately, existing translations are not always correct and some contain serious errors.

The reference material includes significant letters from correspondents whose names are listed in the Acknowledgments. Also scrutinized were several important *Hosta* reference collections, including the Frances Williams collection at the Landscape Arboretum of the University of Minnesota and the Alex J. Summers collections of correspondence with Gus Krossa, Eunice Fisher, and Frances Williams, of which the former generously provided copies. I have also examined hundreds of nursery catalogs and articles in magazines and newspapers.

Following are the key botanical and horticultural reference works and a listing of catalogs. The references marked "in schedula" are taken from herbarium sheets. References marked "(cat.)" in the text are taken from the catalog listing which follows the reference works.

Aden, P. 1983. Hostas. *American Horticulturist* (August): pp. 31–33.

Aden, P., ed. 1988. *The* Hosta *Book*. Portland, OR: Timber Press.

Ahlburg, M. 1984. More about *H. sieboldiana* 'Semperaurea'. *British Hosta and Hemerocallis Society Bulletin*, 1, 2:41–42.

Airy-Shaw, H. K. 1931. The botanical name of the Japanese "Old-Women" lily. *Kew Bulletin* 3:159–160.

Akemine, T. 1935. Chromosome studies in *Hosta*. *J. Faculty of Science, Hokkaido Univ.*, ser. 5, 5,1:25–32.

Akemine, T., and H. Kanazawa. 1975. High frequency of chromosome breakage in *H. undulata*. *Kromosomo* 100:3108–3117.

Anderson, E. 1948. Hybridization of the habitat. *Evolution* 2:1–9.

Anderson, E. 1951. Concordant versus discordant variation in relation to introgression. *Evolution* 5:133–141.

Anderson, E. 1957. An experimental investigation of judgements concerning genera and species. *Evolution* 11:260–262.

Andrews, H. C., 1797. Rare and new plants. *Botanist. Repos.* 1, tab. 6.

Andrews, H. C. 1801. *Hemerocallis alba*. *Botanist. Repos.* 3, tab. 194.

Anonymous. 1863. Royal Horticultural Society. The Third Great Show. *Gardener's Chronicle*. pp. 626, 628.

Anonymous. 1891a. Een prachtsierplant, De *Funkia*. *Nederland Tuinbouwblad Sempervirens*. 20:531–533, 535.

Anonymous. 1891b. *Funkia undulata argenteo-vittata*. *Nederland Tuinbouwblad Sempervirens*. 20:388–389, 391.

Araki, Y. 1942. The new hostas of Japan. *Acta Phytotaxonomica et Geobotanica* 11:322–328. Reprinted in *The American Hosta Society Bulletin* 2(1970).

Araki, Y. 1943. *Hosta crassifolia*. *Acta Phytotaxonomica et Geobotanica*. 12:118. Reprinted in *The American Hosta Society Bulletin* 2(1970).

Arends, G. 1905. *Georg Arends Nursery Catalog* (cat.).

Arends, G. 1951. Mein Leben als Gärtner und Züchter. *Grundlagen und Fortschritte im Garten- und Weinbau* (Ludwigsburg) 91:138.

Asano S., and K. Odaki. 1973. Notes on the distribution of *Hosta longipes* Matsumura in Chiba Prefecture, Japan. *Col. and Breed.* (Tokyo) 35, 3:52–53.

Ascherson, P. F. A. 1863. *Hosta plantaginea*. Botanische Zeitung 21:53, pl. 24.

Ascherson, P. F. A., and K. O. R. P. P. Gräbner. 1905. *Synopsis der Mitteleuropäischen Flora* (Leipzig) 3:53–55.

Bailey, L. H. 1903. *Cyclopedia of American Horticulture*. New York: McMillan. Ed. 2. 618–619.

Bailey, L. H. 1915. *Standard Encyclopedia of Horticulture*. New York: McMillan. 1605–1606, figs. 1909–1910.

Bailey, L. H. 1923. Various cultigens, and transfers in nomenclature. *Gentes Herbarum* 1, 3:113–136.

Bailey, L. H. 1930. *Hosta*, the plantain lilies. *Gentes Herbarum* 2, 3:117–142.

Bailey, L. H. 1932. *Hosta*, and the case of the new homonym regulations. *Gentes Herbarum* 2, 7:434–435.

Bailey, L. H. 1951. *Manual of Cultivated Plants, Liliaceae*. New York: McMillan. 13:206–207.

Bailey, L. H. and E. Z. Bailey. 1941. *Hortus Second: A Concise Dictionary of Plants Cultivated in the United States and Canada*. New York: McMillan.

Bailey, L. H. and E. Z. Bailey. 1976. *Hortus Third: A Concise Dictionary of Plants Cultivated in the United States and Canada*. Rev. New York: McMillan.

Baker, J. G. 1868. The genus *Funkia*. *Gardener's Chronicle* (London). 1015.

Baker, J. G. 1870. *Funkia* in: A revision of the genera and species of herbaceous capsular gamophyllous Liliaceae. *J. of the Linnean Society of London*, Bot. 11:54–55, 366–368.

Baker, J. G. 1876. *Funkia Fortunei*. *Gardener's Chronicle* (London). N.S. 6:36.

Banks, J. 1791. *Icones selectae Plantarum quas in Japonien collegit et delineavit Engelbertus Kaempfer es archetypis in Museo Britannico Asservatis*. London.

Barr, P. 1967. *The Coming of the Barbarians*. New York: Dutton and Company.

Benedict, R. H. 1986. Taming the wild ones. *The Hosta Journal* 17, 2:28–29.

Benson, L. 1962. *Plant Taxonomy. Methods and Principles*. New York: The Ronald Press Company. 250.

Bentham, G. and W. J. Hooker. 1880/1883. *Genera Plantarum*. 3:774, 781.

Bergmann, J. [1924] 1939. *Vaste Planten and Rotsheesters*. Haarlem. Netherlands.

Bischoff, G. W. 1833. *Handbuch der Botanischen Terminologie*. Nuremberg, Germany.

Blanchette, L. 1989. Combating the vole. *The Hosta Journal* 20, 1:58.

Bloom, A. 1981. *Hardy Perennials*. Chicago: Floraprint.

Blume, K. L. 1849–1856. *Museum Botanicum Lugdano-Batavum* 1–2.

Bond, J. 1983. *Hosta 'Tall Boy'. The American Hosta Society Bulletin* 14:45.

Boom, B. K. 1970. *Flora der Gekweekte Kruidachtige Gewassen*. Ed. 2. Wageningen, Netherlands: Veenman and Zonen.

Bowers, J. Z. 1970. *Western Medical Pioneers in Feudal Japan*. Baltimore and London: The Johns Hopkins Press.

Brandies, M. 1988. A restful garden of hostas. *Flower and Garden*. 32, 4:34–38.

Breck, J. 1859. *The Flower Garden; or, Breck's Book of Flowers*. New York: A. O. Moore, Agricultural Book Publishers.

Brickell, C. D. 1968. Scientific exhibit at the Chelsea flower show. A survey of the genus *Hosta* in cultivation. *J. of the Royal Horticultural Society* 93:365–372.

Brickell, C. D. 1983. Some thoughts on *Hosta* nomenclature. *British Hosta and Hemerocallis Society Bulletin* 1, 1:5–19.

Brickell, C. D. 1984. Note on *H. decorata* nomenclature. *The American Hosta Society Bulletin* 15:101.

Brinkley, F. [1896] 1963. *Brinkley's Japanese-English Dictionary*. Tokyo: Sanseido. Reprint. Brooklyn: Saphrograph.

Buist, R. 1839. *The American Flower Garden Directory*. Philadelphia: E. L. Carey & A. Hart. 40.

Buist, R. 1854. *The American Flower Garden Directory*. Philadelphia: A. Hart, Late Carey & Hart. 44.

Burto, W. C. 1989. Some personal choices in Indianapolis. *The Hosta Journal* 20, 2:52–53.

Burto, W. C. 1990. Index to (names and illustrations in) *The American Hosta Society Bulletin* and *The Hosta Journal*.

Candolle, A. P. de. 1810. *Saussurea. Ann. Mus. Hist. Natl*. 15:156, 196.

Candolle, A. P. de. [1813] 1844. *Théorie élémentaire de la Botanique*. Ed. 3. Paris.

Cavanilles, A. J. 1801. *Descripcion de las plantas que D. Antonio Josef Cavanilles demostró en las leciones públicas del año 1801*. Madrid. p. 124.

Cave, M. S. 1948. Sporogenesis and embryo sac development of *Hesperocallis* and *Leucocrinum* in relation to their systematic position. *American J. of Botany* 35, 6:343–349.

Chatto, B. 1983. *The Damp Garden*. London: J. M. Dent & Sons.

Cho, I., and K. Kazuo. 1961. Kemperu no shokubutsu kenkyu (Kaempfer's research on Japanese Botany). *Rangaku Shiryo Kenkyu Kai* (Society for Research on Dutch Studies). Report No. 98.

Chodat, R. 1919. La panachure et les chimères dans le genere *Funkia. Compt. Rend. Sèenees Soc. Phys. Hist. Nat. Gèneve* 36, 3:81–84.

Chung, M. G. 1989. *Hosta jonesii* (Liliaceae/Funkiaceae): A new species from Korea. *Annals of the Missouri Botanical Garden*. 76, 3:920–922.

Chung, M. G. 1990. *A Biosystematic Study on the Genus* Hosta *(Liliaceae/Funkiaceae) in Korea and Tsushima Island of Japan*. Ph.D. Dissertation, University of Georgia, Athens. Includes: "Morphometric and isoenzyme analysis of the genus *Hosta* Tratt." with S. B. Jones and J. L. Hamrick and "Isoenzyme variation within and among populations of *Hosta* in Korea" with J. L. Hamrick, S. B. Jones, and G. S. Derda.

Chung, M. G., and S. B. Jones. 1989. Pollen morphology of *Hosta* Tratt. (Funkiaceae) and related genera. *Bulletin of the Torrey Botanical Club* 116, 1:31–44.

Chung, T. H. 1956. *Korean Flora, 2*. Sinjisa, Seoul, Korea. pp. 965–967.

Chung, T. H. 1965. *Illustrated Encyclopedia of Fauna and Flora of Korea, 5, Trachephyta*. Seoul, Korea: Ministry of Education. 1510–1512.

Chung, T. H., B. S. To, D. B. Lee, and H. J. Lee. 1937. *Nomina Plantarum Coreanum*. Seoul, Korea: Chosen Natural History Institute. 31–32.

Chung, Y. C. 1985. *A Taxonomic Study of the Genus* Hosta *in Korea*. Ph.D. Dissertation, Seoul National University, Korea.

Chung, Y. C. 1988. Interspecific relationships of some species of the genus *Hosta* on artificial hybridization experiments. *Korean J. of Plant Taxonomy* 18:153–160.

Chung, Y. H., and Y. C. Chung. 1982. A taxonomic study of the genus *Hosta* in Korea. In *Proc. Coll. Nat. Sciences*. Seoul, Korea: Seoul National University. 7:87–122.

Chupov, V. S., and N. G. Kutiavina. 1981. Serological studies in the order Liliales. Botanicheskii Institut Komarov, Leningrad, USSR. *Botanicheskii Zhurnal* 66:75–81.

Coats, A. M. 1969. *The Plant Hunters: Being a History of the Horticultural Pioneers, Their Quests and Discoveries*. New York: McGraw-Hill.

Cooke, J. F. 1968. *The Chromatography and Cytology of Some Cultivated Taxa of the Genus* Hosta *Tratt*. Ph.D. Dissertation. Ohio State University, Columbus, Ohio.

Coombes, A. J. 1985. *Dictionary of Plant Names*. Portland, OR: Timber Press.

Craig, J. E. 1970. In search of *H. hypoleuca. The American Hosta Society Bulletin* 2:36–37.

Craig, J. E. 1971. *Hosta rupifraga*—The Hachijo Giboshi. *The American Hosta Society Bulletin* 3:36–37.

Craig, J. E. 1972. Patio plant supreme (*H. hypoleuca). The American Hosta Society Bulletin* 4:11.

Craig, J. E. 1990. Letter to Dr. R. C. Olson (cfr. *H. hypoleuca). Hosta Leaves* 26.

Crockett, C. 1989. The hostas of Lucille Simpers. *The Hosta Journal* 20, 1:49–51.

Cronquist, A. 1981. *An Integrated System of Classification of Flowering Plants*. New York: Columbia University Press. 1121–1122.

Cronquist, A. 1988. *The Evolution and Classification of Flowering Plants*. Ed. 2. New York: The New York Botanical Garden.

Currie, H. E. 1988. *Biosystematics of the Eastern Asian Species of* Hosta. Preliminary title for a dissertation. University of Georgia, Athens. (Personal communication).

Dahlgren, R. M. T., H. T. Clifford, and P. F. Yoe. 1985. *The Families of Monocotyledons. Structure, Evolution and Taxonomy*. Berlin: Springer Verlag. 187–188.

Dandy, J. E. 1958. *The Sloan Herbarium: An Annotated List of the Horti Sicci Composing It*. New ed. London: Balding and Mansell.

Davidson, R. 1970. Japan Report. *The American Hosta Society Bulletin* 2:38–40.

Davidson, R. 1990. Letter to Dr. R. C. Olson (January).

Deane, R. H. 1987. Singing the Blues in New England. *The Hosta Journal* 18, 1:10–12.

DeFiglio, P. [1983] 1985. Tissue Culturing Hostas at T&Z Nursery. *The American Hosta Society Bulletin* 15:71–75.

Descloux, J. 1989. Repelling Deer. *The Hosta Journal*. 20, 2:20–21.

Dick, L. W. 1978. An investigation of the plant *H. fortunei* 'Aureo Maculata' to find rapid methods of propagation. West Scottland Agricultural College, Auchincruive, Ayre. *Comb. Proceed. of the IPPS* 27:43–44.

Downing, A. J. 1841. *A Treatise on the Theory and Practice of Landscape Gardening Applied to North America*. New York.

Druce, C. G. 1917. Nomenclatorial notes (*Funkia japonica). Second Supplement to Bot. Soc. and Exchange Club Report for 1916*. 623.

Dumortier, D. C. J. 1822. *Libertia, Comment. Bot.*, 9.

Dutta R., and G. N. Bhattacharya. [1970] 1981. Cytological studies on *Funkia* and *Hemerocallis. Acta Botanica Indica* 9, 2:314–317.

Eddy, A. M. 1990. *General Hosta List.* Unpublished.

Eisel, M. C. 1977. *H. plantaginea,* fragrant plantain lily. *American Horticulture* 56, 4:4.

Eisel, M. C., and W. I. Pollock. 1984. IRA for Hosta. *The American Hosta Society Bulletin* 15:98–100.

Ellerbroek, P. 1970. Source List for *Hosta* Plants. Des Moines.

Endlicher, S. F. L. 1841. *Gen.* 1182.

Engler, H. G. A. 1888. Liliaceae, *Hosta.* In *Die Natürlichen Pflanzenfamilien.* Eds. Engler and K. A. E. Prantl. Leipzig. 2/3:39–40.

Engler H. G. A. 1900. *Das Pflanzenreich.* Leipzig: Wilhelm Engelmann.

Erdtman, G. 1966. *Pollen Morphology and Plant Taxonomy. Angiosperms.* New York: Hafner Publishing Company.

Ernst, A. 1918. *Bastardierung als Ursache der Apogamie im Pflanzenreich.* Jena, Germany. 435/458, pp. 446–447.

Everett, T. H. 1984. *The New York Botanical Garden Illustrated Encyclopedia of Horticulture, Hosta.* New York: Garland Publishing. 1703–1707.

Fagerlind, F. 1946. Hormonale Substanzen als Ursache der Frucht-und Embryobildung bei pseudogamen Hosta-Biotypen. *Svensk Bot. Tidskr.* (Uppsala) 40,3:230–234.

Falstad, C. 1988. Propagation by tissue culture. *The Hosta Journal* 19, 29–31.

Farrand, B. 1985. *Beatrix Farrand's American Landscapes.* New York: Sagapress.

Farrar, R. 1919. *Hosta tardiflora. The English Rock Garden.* London. 356.

Faust, J. L. 1985. Hostas. *The New York Times* (7 July).

Fei, Y. L., et al. 1983. *Huahui Ji Guangshang.* Taipei: Shouce Press.

Figdor, W. 1914. Über die panaschierten und dimorphen Laubblätter einer Kulturform der *Funkia lancifolia* Sprengel. *Sitz. Ber. Akademie der Wissenschaften,* Vienna, Mathematik-Naturwissenschaft, Kl., 123, Abt. 1.

Fischer, U. 1983. *Hosta sieboldiana* 'Semperaurea'. *British Hosta and Hemerocallis Society Bulletin* 1, 1:59–62.

Fischer, U. 1984. *Hosta sieboldiana* 'Elegans' and other Arends' Hybrids. *The American Hosta Society Bulletin* 15:28–29.

Fisher, E. V. 1966–1976, Letters to Mr. A. J. Alex Summers.

Fisher, E. V. [1969, 1973] 1979. *Hosta,* The Aristocratic Plant for Shady Gardens. Self-published.

Fisher, E. V. 1983. A Note on *H.* 'Frances Williams'. *The American Hosta Society Bulletin* 14:12–14.

Foerster, K. 1950. *Blauer Schatz der Gärten.* Radebeul and Berlin: Neumann.

Foerster, K. 1952. *Neuer Glanz des Gartenjahres.* Radebeul and Berlin: Neumann. 127.

Foerster, K. 1955, 1956. *Der Steingarten der sieben Jahreszeiten. Eine Provinz aller Baulichen und Naturhaften Gartenkunst.* Radebeul and Berlin: Neumann. 346.

Foerster, K. 1957. *Einzug der Gräser und Farne in die Gärten.* Sowie einiger bedeutungsvoller Blattschmuckstauden. Radebeul: Neumann. 19, 196, 218.

Foerster, K. 1965a. Die vierzehn Ideal-Funkien. *Pflanze und Garten* 2:44–45.

Foerster, K. 1965b. Endlich eine neue Ordnung im Durcheinander der Funkien. *Pflanze und Garten* 11:294–297.

Fortune, R. 1863. *Yedo and Peking: A Narrative of a Journey to the Capitals of Japan and China.* London.

Foster, M. F. 1989. Americans are gaining ground on the British. *The Atlanta Journal/Constitution.* 26 February. P-1, P–8.

Franchet, A., and P. A. Savatier. L. 1876. *Enumeratio Plantarum in Japonia Sponte Crescentium Hucusque Rite Cognitarum.* Paris. 82, 529.

Fujita, N. 1976a. The genus *Hosta* (*Liliaceae*) in Japan. *Acta*

Phytotaxonomica et Geobotanica 27, 3/4:66–96. Reprinted in *The American Hosta Society Bulletin* 10:14–43.

Fujita, N. 1976b. Habitat and water economy of Japanese *Hosta. Japanese J. of Ecology* 26:71–81.

Fujita, N. 1978a. Reproductive capacity and leaf development of Japanese *Hosta* as viewed from ecology and evolution. *Memoirs of the Faculty of Science, Kyoto University, Series Biology* 7:59–68.

Fujita, N. 1978b. Flooding tolerance of Japanese *Hosta* in relation to habitat preference. *Memoirs of the Faculty of Science.* Kyoto University, Series Biology 7:45–57.

Gaerdt, H. 1886. *Wredow's Gartenfreund.* 17:448 (with text same as Regel, 1876).

Glück, H. 1919. *Blatt- und blütenmorphologische Studien: Hosta violacea.* Jena, Germany. 561, 593.

Gottlieb, L. D. 1977. Electrophoretic evidence and plant systematics. *Annals of the Missouri Botanical Garden* 64:161–180.

Graf, A. B. 1978. *Exotica Third.* Ed. 7. E. Rutherford, NJ: Roehrs. 1092–1093.

Granick, E. B. 1944. A karyosystematic study of the genus *Agave* (*Hosta*). *American J. Bot.* 31:283–297.

Grant, V. 1971. *Plant Speciation.* New York: Columbia University Press.

Gray, A. 1950. *Manual of Botany.* Ed. 8. New York and London: American Book Company.

Gray, B. 1953. Sloane and the Kaempfer collections. *British Museum Quarterly* (London) 18:2–23.

Gréen, S. 1937. *Perenna växter.* Stockholm. *Hosta.* 140–142.

Grenfell, D. 1981. A survey of the genus *Hosta* and its availability in commerce. *The Plantsman* 7:1–35.

Grenfell, D. 1982. The hostas of England's Eric Smith. *The American Hosta Society Bulletin* 13:15–17.

Grenfell, D. 1983. Hostas—The golden age. *The American Hosta Society Bulletin* 14:8–11.

Grenfell, D. 1984. *Hosta* 'George Smith' and *H.* 'Thea', two new hostas. *The American Hosta Society Bulletin* 15:25.

Grenfell, D. 1987. Eric B. Smith. 1917–1986. *The Hosta Journal* 18, 1:13–15.

Grenfell, D. 1989. *Hosta.* In *Encyclopedia of Plants.* Ed. C. Brickell. New York: Macmillan Publishing Company.

Grenfell, D. 1990. *Hosta: The Flowering Foliage Plant.* London: Batsford Books; Portland, OR: Timber Press.

Grey, C. H. 1938. *Hardy Bulbs,* 3, Liliaceae. London: William and Norgate. 292–305. Section on *Hosta* reprinted in *The American Hosta Society Bulletin* 3:44–53.

Grounds, R. 1986. Hostas of the Tardiana group. *British Hosta and Hemerocallis Society Bulletin* 1, 4:25–27.

Grovatt, E. F. 1978. Hosta therapy. *The American Hosta Society Bulletin* 10:44–45.

Gustafson, Å. 1946–1947. Apomixis in Higher Plants. Parts 1–3. *Lunds Univ. Årsskr.,* N. F., Avd. 2, 42/43, *Hosta coerulea.* 38, 74, 155, 315.

Hadfield, M. 1955. *Pioneers in Gardening.* London: R. and K. Paul.

Hagan, P. 1986. The shadow grows: Planting in the dark. *The Wall Street Journal* (22 October).

Hamblin, S. F. 1936. Re. Funkia 'Thomas Hogg'. *Lexington Leaflets* (Lexington Botanic Garden, MA). 211–224.

Hammer, P. A. 1976. Tissue culture propagation of *H. decorata* Bailey. *HortScience* 11:309. (Abstract).

Hansen, R. 1972. *Namen der Stauden.* Stuttgart: Ulmer.

Hansen, R., and H. Müssel. 1964. Eine Übersicht über die in Europa eingeführten und im Handel verbreiteten Arten und Sorten der Gattung *Hosta, Jahresbericht, Staatliche Lehr- und Forschungsanstalt für Gartenbau.* Freising, Germany: Weihenstephan. 4–7.

Hansen, R., J. Sieber, and H. Müssel. 1974. Der Gehölzrand

und seine Stauden, *Jahresbericht, Institut für Stauden, Gehölze und Angewandte Pflanzensoziologie.* Freising, Germany: Fachhochschule Weihenstephan. 10.

Hara, H. 1938. *Hosta rectifolia. Botanical Magazine* (Tokyo) 52:510.

Hara, H. 1984. *Hosta sieboldii. J. of Japanese Botany* 59:176–181.

Harshbarger, G. 1981. Hostas: Multi-purpose perennials for the shade. *Flower and Garden* 25, 3:6–10.

Haskell, A. C. 1984. Hosta: The perfect flower show plant. *The American Hosta Society Bulletin* 15:50.

Henderson, P. 1881. *Handbook of Plants.* New York: Henderson.

Hensen, K. J. W. 1960. Hosta-sortiment. *Tuinbouwgids.* 473–475.

Hensen, K. J. W. 1963a. De in Nederland gekweekte Hosta's. *Mededelingen van de Directeur van de Tuinbouw* 26:725–735.

Hensen, K. J. W. 1963b. Identification of the hostas ("Funkias") introduced and cultivated by von Siebold. *Mededelingen van de Landbouwhogeschool te Wageningen* 63, 6:1–22.

Hensen, K. J. W. 1963c. Preliminary Registration List of Cultivar Names in *Hosta* Tratt. Wageningen: Veenman and Zonen.

Hensen, K. J. W. 1965. De in Nederland gekweekte Hosta's. *Belmontia* 3, 7, 43.

Hensen, K. J. W. 1970. Letter to the editor. *The American Hosta Society Bulletin* 2:42.

Hensen, K. J. W. 1983. Some nomenclature problems in *Hosta. The American Hosta Society Bulletin* 14:41–44.

Hensen, K. J. W. 1985. A study of the taxonomy of cultivated hostas. *The Plantsman* 7:1–36.

Hirao, S. 1981. Inducing tetraploids. *The American Hosta Society Bulletin* 12:36.

Hobhouse, P. 1984. *Color in Your Garden.* Toronto: Little, Brown & Company.

Hobhouse, P. 1988. *Garden Style.* Toronto: Little, Brown & Company.

Holmgren, P. K., and W. Keuken. 1974. *Index Herbariorum.* Ed. 6. Ed. F. Stafleu. Ultrecht: Oosthoek, Scheltema and Holkema, for the International Bureau of Plant Taxonomy and Nomenclature.

Honda, M. 1930. *Hosta japonica* var. *longifolia. Botanical Magazine* (Tokyo) 44:410.

Honda, M. 1935a. *Hosta longissima* and *H. longipes* var. *lancea. Botanical Magazine* (Tokyo) 49:696.

Honda, M. 1935b. *Hosta harunaensis. J. of Japanese Botany* 11:572.

Hooker, W. J. 1838. *Funckia albo-marginata. Curtis's Botanical Magazine* 65, tab. 3567.

Hooker, W. J. 1839. *Funckia sieboldiana. Curtis's Botanical Magazine* 65, tab. 3663.

Hornemann, J. W. 1813. *Hortus regius hafniensis,* 1, Hauniæ, *Hemerocallis alba.* 343.

Hotton, P. C. 1983. A host of hostas at the flower show. *Boston Sunday Globe* (13 March).

Houttuyn, M., 1781. *Natuurlyke Historie van den Heer Linnaeus.* Amsterdam. *Aletris japonica* 2, 12:413–414, tab. 34:2.

Hu, S. I., and C. Chu. 1979. The fusion of male and female nuclei in fertilization of higher plants (*H. caerulea*). Beijing: *Acta Botanica Sinica* 21, 1:1–10.

Hutchinson, T. 1964. *The Families of Flowering Plants.* Vol. 2, *Monocotyledons.* Oxford: Clarendon Press. 601.

Hylander, N. 1945. *Delectus seminum Hortus Botanicus Gotoburgensis.* Göteborg, Sweden. 3, pls. 4, 1,7 18.

Hylander, N. 1948. *Våra prydnadsväxters namn på svenska och latin.* Stockholm. 49, 149–154.

Hylander, N. 1953. *Hosta.* En översikt över de svenska trägårdarnas funkior eller blålijor. *Lustgården* 33/34:27.

Hylander, N. 1954. The genus *Hosta* in Swedish gardens. *Acta Horti Bergiani* 16, 11:331–420. Reprinted in *The American Hosta Society Bulletin* 6(1974):19–65; 7(1975):14–48; 8(1976):13–46.

Hylander, N. 1960. The genus *Hosta. J. of the Royal Horticultural Society* 85:356–365.

Hylander, N. 1969. *Dictionary of Gardening.* Ed. 2. Supplement. London: The Royal Horticultural Society. 347–350.

Hylander, N., and W. T. Stearn. 1956. *Dictionary of Gardening.* Supplement. London: The Royal Horticultural Society. 233.

Ibuyama, 1937. *Iwa Giboshi. J. of Japanese Botany* 13:34.

Iinuma, Y. 1856. Somoku Dzusetsu. *An Illustrated Flora of Japan.* Ed. 1. Tokyo.

Iinuma, Y. 1874. Somoku Dzusetsu. *An Illustrated Flora of Japan.* Ed. 2. Tokyo.

Iinuma, Y. 1910. Somoku Dzusetsu, *An Iconography of Plants, Indigenous to, Cultivated in or Introduced into Nippon.* Rev. by T. Makino. *Herbaceous Plants* 6. Tokyo. 462–470, pl. 19–27.

Ikegami, Y. 1967. *Hosta rectifolia* var. *atropurpurea.* In *Rep. Taisetsu Inst. Science* 2:17.

Illiger, J. K. W. 1800. *Versuch einer systematischen vollständigen Terminologie für das Thierreich und Pflanzenreich.* Helmstedt, Germany.

Inagaki and Toyokuni. 1963. *Hosta lancifolia* var. *thunbergiana* f. *albiflora. J. of Japanese Botany* 32:128.

Inami, K. 1971. *Baran Giboshi.* In *Aichi-shokubutsu* 40, ic. 11.

Index Kewensis Plantarum Phanerogamarum. Linnaeus to 1885; 1895–1987. Main vols. 1 and 2; supplements 1–18. Oxford University Press; Koenigstein, Germany: Koeltz Scientific Books.

Ingram, 1967. Notes on the cultivated Liliaceae. *Hosta sieboldii* and *H. sieboldiana. Baileya* 15, 1:27–32.

International Code of Botanical Nomenclature. 1983. Ed. F. Stafleu Forestburgh, NY: Lubrecht and Cramer.

International Code of Botanical Nomenclature. 1988. Adopted by the 14th International Botanical Congress, Berlin, July–August 1987. Regnum Vegetabile, ser. 118, vol. 14. Ed. W. Greuter. Königstein, Germany: Koeltz Scientific Books. Also referenced: ICBN 1969, adopted by the 11th International Botanical Congress; ICBN 1956, adopted by the 8th International Botanical Congress; and ICBN 1950, adopted by the 7th International Botanical Congress.

International Code of Nomenclature for Cultivated Plants. 1980. Adopted by the International Commission for the Nomenclature of Cultivated Plants of the International Union of Biological Science, IUBS Division of Botany. Utrecht, Netherlands: Bohn, Scheltema and Holkema. Also referenced: ICNCP 1956; ICNCP 1953.

International Code of Nomenclature for Cultivated Plants. 1990. Preliminary Proposal to Revise the 1980 ICNCP, dated 1990, by the Horticultural Taxonomy Group, ISHS Commission for Nomenclature and Registration. (Preliminary copy furnished by the commission, unpublished).

International Rules of Botanical Nomenclature. 1935. Ed. 3. Jena, Germany.

Irving, W. 1903. The *Funkias. The Garden* 64:297.

Itazawa, T. 1960. *Shiboruto.* Tokyo: Yoshikawa kobunkan.

Ito, K. 1969. *Hosta rectifolia* var. *atropurpurea* f. *leucantha. J. Geobot. Hokuriku* 17:91–92.

Iwasaki. 1874. *Honzo-Dzufu:* (cfr. Maekawa, F. 1940.)

Iwasaki. [1874] 1916–1918. *Honzo-Dzufu.* Ed. 20. Rev. by M. Shirai and T. Oonuma. Fol. 12–18.

Jackson, B. D. 1895. *Index Kewensis.* London. 4:811.

Jackson, B. D. 1899. Color. *J. Botany* 37:97–106.

Jaquin, N. J. von. 1797. *Pl. Hort. Schoenbr.* 1:60, 114.

Jekyll, G. 1907. *Flower Decoration in the House.* Country Life.

Jekyll, G. [1908] 1983a. *Colour Schemes for the Flower Garden.* Reprint. Salem: The Ayer Company.

Jekyll, G. [1901] 1983b. *Wall and Water Gardens.* Reprint. Salem: The Ayer Company.

Jekyll, G. [1899] 1983c. *Wood and Garden*. Reprint. Salem: The Ayer Company.

Jellito, L., and W. Schacht. 1963. *Die Freiland-Schmuckstauden*. Stuttgart: Ulmer.

Jellito, L., and W. Schacht. 1986. *Die Freiland-Schmuckstauden*. Ed. 2. Rev. by W. Schacht and A. Fessler. Stuttgart: Ulmer. 299–303. Eng. trans. by M. Epp. 1990. *Hardy Herbaceous Perennials*. 2 vols. Portland, OR: Timber Press. 300–306.

Jensen, S., et al. 1949. *Frilandsblomster*. 223.

Jentsch, A. 1989. *Hosta*—Eine Schattenpflanze rückt ins Licht (Dr. U. Fischer's garden). *Deutscher Gartenbau*. Vol. 43. Stuttgart: Ulmer.

Johnson, H. 1979. *The Principles of Gardening*. New York: Simon and Schuster.

Jones, D. L. 1987. *Encyclopedia of Ferns*. Portland, OR: Timber Press.

Jones, S. B., and A. E. Luchsinger. 1979. *Plant Systematics*. New York: McGraw-Hill Book Company.

Jones, S. B., and A. E. Luchsinger. 1986. *Plant Systematics*. 2nd ed. New York: McGraw-Hill Book Company.

Jones, S. B., et al. 1981. Basic systematic research. In *Trends, Priorities and Needs in Systematics Biology*. Eds. Stuessy and Thomson. Lawrence, KS: Amer. Assoc. Syst. Coll. 3–8.

Jones, S. B. 1989. *Hosta yingeri* (Liliaceae-Funkiaceae): A new species from Korea. *Annals of the Missouri Botanical Garden* 76, 2:602–604.

Juel, H. O. 1918. *Plantae Thunbergianae*, 5. Uppsala: Ekmans Universitetsfond. 21:124–125.

Kaempfer, E., 1692. *Yoksan, vulgo Gibboosi*, original drawing no. 52; *Gibboosi altera*, original drawing no. 166. Sloane Collection, British Museum (Bloomsbury), London.

Kaempfer, E. 1712. *Amoenitatum exoticarum politico-physico-medicarum fasciculi 5, quibus continentur varieae relationes, observationes et descriptiones Rerum Persicarum et Ulterioris Asiae*. Meyer-Lemgo. 5:863.

Kamo, M. 1985. Article on *Hosta*. *Garden Magazine* 18:22–26.

Kaneko, K. 1966. Cytology *Hosta*. *Botanical Magazine* (Tokyo) 79:131–137.

Kaneko, K. 1968a. Chromosome numbers of 26 species of *Hosta*. *J. of Japanese Botany* 43:202–203.

Kaneko, K. 1968b. Chromosome study *Giboshi*. *Botanical Magazine* (Tokyo) 81:267–277, 396–403.

Kaneko, K. 1968c. *Hosta chibai* with F. Maekawa. *J. of Japanese Botany* 43:202.

Kaneko, K. 1969. Cytological studies on some species of *Hosta*. *Botanical Magazine* (Tokyo) 82:32–39, 253–262.

Kaneko, K. 1970. Cytological studies on some species of *Hosta*. *Botanical Magazine* (Tokyo) 83:27–35.

Keough, J. S., J. Powell, and B. W. Ellis. 1982. *North American Horticulture*. Compiled by The American Horticultural Society. New York: C. Scribner's Sons.

Ker-Gawler, J. 1812. *Hemerocallis japonica*. Sweet-scented daylily of Japan. *Curtis's Botanical Magazine* 35, tab. 1433.

Kew. 1902. *Handlist of Herbaceous Plants*. Ed. 2. London. 489.

Kikuchi, M. 1934. *Giboshi. Zissai Engei* [Practical Gardening] 17, 4:263–272, (*H. gracillima*, p. 272 as *Hime Iwa Giboshi*).

Kintya, P. K., N. E. Mashchenko, and G. V. Lazurevskii. 1977. Steroidal glycocides in *Funkia ovata* leaves (several studies). Kishinev, Moldavian SSR: Institut Khimii. *Khimiya Prirodnykh Soedinenii* 1:60–72, 123–124.

Kitagawa, M. 1939. Lineamenta Florae Manshuricae. *Rep. Inst. Scient. Res. Manch*. 3:137.

Kitamura. 1966. *Hosta sieboldiana* var. *gigantea, H. longipes* var. *aequinoctiiantha. Acta Phytoxonomica et Geobotanica* 22:68.

Kitamura, et al. 1964. *Hosta longipes. Col. Ill. Herb. Plant. Jap.* (Monocotyledons). 135–138.

Kitchingman, R. M. 1984. *Hosta*—A nomenclature study. *British Hosta and Hemerocallis Society Bulletin* 1, 2:4–29.

Klose, H. de re. 1979. Neue Herzlilien aus Kassel. *Mein Schöner Garten* 8, 10:56–61.

Klose, H. 1980, 1983: Perennial Catalog. Kassel, Germany: Lohfelden.

Kodansha Encyclopedia of Japan. 1983. Tokyo: Kodansha.

Koidzumi, G. 1916. *Hosta cærulea* var. *capitata. Botanical Magazine* (Tokyo) 30:326.

Koidzumi, G. 1925. *Giboshi. Botanical Magazine* (Tokyo) 39:307.

Koidzumi, G. 1936. *Hosta lancifolia* var. *angustifolia (Sazi Giboshi), H. rectifolia* var. *sachalinensis (Ezo Giboshi), H. viridis. Acta Phytotaxonomica et Geobotanica* 5:38–40.

Koidzumi, G. 1942. *Acta Phytotaxonomica et Geobotanica* 11:321.

Komarov, V. L. 1901. *Flora Manchuriae*. Leningrad. 327–330, 441.

Komarov, V. L. 1935. *Funkia lancifolia* Sprengel. *Flora USSR* (Leningrad) 4:55, tab. 5/2.

Kooiman, H. N., and H. J. Venema. 1938. De catalogi van von Siebold en de introductie van planten uit Japan (Enkele aanvullingen). *Gedenkboek J. Vackenier Suringar Ned. Dendr. Ver.* 264–265; and *Jaarboek Ned. Dendr. Ver.* 12:124–126.

Korea Annual 1987. 1987. Seoul, Korea: Yonhap News Agency.

Körner, H. 1967. Siebold: Beitrage zur Familiengeschichte. Die Würzburger Siebold. *Archiv der Deutschen Familien*. Neustadt an der Aisch: Degener und Co.

Krossa, G. 1966–1970. Coded and Numbered Acquisition Lists (unpublished; derived from Krossa's private correspondence with Summers).

Krossa, G. 1966–1972. Letters to A. J. Alex Summers.

Kunth, C. S. 1843. *Enumeratio Plantarum Omnium Hucusque Cognitarum*. Stuttgart. 4:590–592.

Kuntze, C. E. O. 1891. *Funkea. Revisio Generum Plantarum* (Leipzig) 2:711–714.

Kure, S. 1926. *Shiboruto sensei sono shogai oyobi kogyo*. Tokyo: Tohodo shoten.

Küster, E. 1919. Über weissrandige Blätter und andere Formen der Buntblättrigkeit. *Biologisches Zentralblatt*., 39, *Hostia japonica*. 232–233.

Lacy, A. 1986. Hosta revival. *Horticulture* 64, 1:28–34.

Lamarck, J. B. P. A. de Monet de. 1789. *Encyclopédie méthodique Botanique* (Paris) 3:103.

Lee, C. Y., and H. S. An. 1963. *Nomina Plantarum Coreanum*. Seoul, Korea: Bumhaksa. 307–308.

Lee, F. P. 1957. Plantainlilies. *National Hort. Magazine* (Washington) 36, 4:313–333.

Lee, T. B. 1980. *Illustrated Flora of Korea*. Seoul, Korea: Hyangmunsa. 199–200.

Lee, Y. N. 1973. A taxonomic study on two taxa: *H. clausa* Nakai and *H. clausa* Nakai var. *normalis* Maekawa. *J. K.R.I.B.L.* 10:37–41.

Lee, Y. N. 1980. *Illustrated Fauna and Flora of Korea, 18, Flowering Plants*. Seoul, Korea: Ministry of Education. 458–459.

Leighton, A. 1987. *American Gardens of the Nineteenth Century*. Amherst: University of Massachusetts Press. Appendix, 332, 335.

Lemaire, C. A. 1846. *Funkia grandiflora* Sieb. et Zucc. (del. van Houtte). *Flore de Serres* 2:10, tab. 158–159.

Léveillé, A. A. H. 1911. *Funkia subcordata* var. *taquetii*. In Fedde, *Repertorium Specierum Novarum Regni Vegetabilis* 9:322.

Licht, J. L. 1989. Rediscovering an old *H. plantaginea*—Double the pleasure, twice the fun. *The Hosta Journal* 20, 2:11–12.

Lilja. 1839. *Funkia. Fl. Sveriges odl. växter*. Stockholm, 49.

Lindley, J. 1832. *An Introduction to Botany*. London.

Lindley, J. 1839. *Funkia sieboldi. Edwards Botanical Reg.* 25, pl. 50.

Lindley, J. 1847. *The Elements of Botany*. London.

Link, H. F., 1798. *Philosophiae botanicae novae seu Institutionum phytographicarum Prodromus*. Göttingen, Germany.

Lloyd, C. 1973. *Foliage Plants*. London: Collins Sons & Co.

Lloyd, C. 1984. *The Well-Chosen Garden*. London.

Loddiges, C. 1832. *Hemerocallis sieboldtiana. Botanical Cabinet* 19, tab. 1869.

Long, E. A. 1891. *Ornamental Gardening for Americans.* New York: Orange Judd Company. 127–128.

Maekawa, F. 1928. *Giboshi. J. of Japanese Botany* 5:22.

Maekawa, F. 1935. Studia Monocotyledonearum Japonicarum (1 and 5) *H. kiyosumiensis, H. venusta, H. nakaiana. J. Japanese Botany* 11:244–248, 687–689.

Maekawa, F. 1936a. *Hosta undulata. J. Japanese Botany* 12:5–7.

Maekawa, F. 1936b. *Hosta gracillima.* See Nakai, 1936.

Maekawa, F. 1937. Divisiones et Plantae Novae Generis *Hostae* (1). *J. of Japanese Botany* 13: 892–905.

Maekawa, F. 1938a. A new classification of *Hosta* (preliminary note). *Botanical Magazine* (Tokyo) 52:40–44.

Maekawa, F. 1938b. Divisiones et Plantae Novae Generis *Hostae* (2). *J. of Japanese Botany* 14:45–49.

Maekawa, F. 1940. The genus *Hosta. J. of the Faculty of Science,* Imperial University Tokyo, Section 3 Botany, 5:317–425. Reprinted in *The American Hosta Society Bulletin* 4(1972):12–64; 5(1973):12–59.

Maekawa, F. 1944. Carpel-studies of the monocotyledonous genus *Hosta* (*H. lancifolia* var. *thunbergiana* f. monstr. *poly-carpellata*). *J. of Japanese Botany* 20:26–29, ic. 3, 4, 5, 6.

Maekawa, F. 1948. *Hosta tosana* var. *caput-avis. J. of Japanese Botany* 22:64.

Maekawa, F. 1950. *Giboshi* in Ishii, *Engei-daijiten* [Big Dictionary of Garden Craft] (Tokyo) 2:633–638.

Maekawa, F. 1952. *H. caput-avis.* In Nakai. 1952a.

Maekawa, F. 1954. In schedula (TI).

Maekawa, F. 1960. Evolutional aspects to the inter-generic or inter-specific hybrids. In *Darwin Shinkaron Hyakunen-Kinen.* 115–119.

Maekawa, F. 1963. In schedula (TI).

Maekawa, F. 1968. *Hosta chibai* (with K. Kaneko). *J. of Japanese Botany* 43:202.

Maekawa, F. 1969. *Hosta* Trattinnick. In *New Encyclopedia of Horticulture.* Tokyo: Seibundoshinkosha. 3:1105–1109.

Maekawa, F. 1971. The genus *Hosta* in Japan. *New Flowering Plants* (Tokyo) 70:3–7.

Maekawa, F. 1972. The distribution map of *Hosta* in Japan. In *Garden Life* Tokyo: Seibundoshinkosha. 8:31–33.

Maekawa, F. 1976. Note on a new species of *Hosta. J. of Japanese Botany* 51:79–81.

Maekawa, F. 1984. Two new species of *Hosta* from Japan. *J. of Japanese Botany* 59:154–157.

Maekawa, F. and K. Kaneko. 1968. Evolution of karyotype in *Hosta. J. of Japanese Botany* 43:132–140.

Makino, T. 1902. Observations on the flora of Japan. *Botanical Magazine* (Tokyo) 13:173.

Makino, T. 1910. Somoku Dzusetsu, *An Iconography of Plants, Indigenous to, Cultivated in or Introduced into Nippon.* Revised from Iinuma 1856, 1874. Tokyo. 2:462–468.

Makino, T. 1928. *Hosta sieboldiana* var. *aureomarginata. J. of Japanese Botany* 5:22.

Makino, T. 1935. *Nippon shokubutsu-dzukan* [Illustrated Flora of Japan]. Tokyo. 398.

Makino, T. 1938. *Hosta intermedia* (*Ko Giboshi*). *Botanical Magazine* (Tokyo) 52:41.

Makino, T., and K. Nemoto. 1925. *Nippon shokubutsu-soran* [Flora of Japan]. Ed. 1. Tokyo. 1262.

Makino, T., and Y. Tanaka. 1928. *Heritori Giboshi;* cfr. Hara 1984.

Malitz, J. I. 1989. *Personal Landscapes.* Portland, OR: Timber Press.

Masamune, G. 1932. *Hosta sieboldiana* var. *yakusimensis. J. of Society of Tropical Agriculture* 4:301.

Masamune, G. 1934. *Hosta sieboldiana* var. *yakusimensis. Florist. Geobotanical Studies of Yakushima* 553.

Mathew, B. 1987. Rearrangement of petaloid monocotyledon families at Kew. *British Hosta and Hemerocallis Society Bulletin* 2, 1:24–34.

Mathew, B. 1988. Hostaceae, a new name for the invalid Funkiaceae. *Kew Bulletin* 43, 2:302.

Matsumura, J. 1884. *Nippon shokubutsu-mei-i* [Japanese seed plants]. Tokyo.

Matsumura, J. 1886. *Cat.,* Nikko Bot. Gard. 203.

Matsumura, J. 1894. *Hosta longipes. Plant List.* Nikko Bot. Gard. 21.

Matsumura, J. 1905. *Index Plantarum Japonicarum* (Tokyo) 2:199–200.

Matsumura, Y. 1958. Letter to Mrs. F. R. Williams. 12 March. See Rogier, et al. 1980.

McGourty, F., and M. A. McGourty. 1985. The McGourty's on *H.* 'Frances Williams'. *The American Hosta Society Bulletin* 16:17.

McGourty, F. 1989. *The Perennial Gardener.* New York: Houghton Mifflin Company.

McKelvey, S. D., and K. Sax. 1933. Taxonomic and cytological relationships of *Yucca* and *Agave. J. Arnold Arb.* 14:76–81.

Meikle, R. D. 1963. *Garden Flowers.* (The Kew Series). Eyre & Spottiswoode, (*Hosta,* Trattinnick). 417–421.

Merrill, E. D. 1938. A critical consideration of Houttuyn's new genera and new species of plants. *J. Arnold Arb.* 19, 4:324.

Meyer, F. G. 1963. Ornamental Plant Explorations. USDA. Numbered List of *Hosta*s.

Meyer, M. M., Jr. 1976. Propagation of *Hosta* by *in vitro* techniques. *HortScience* 11:309. (Abstract).

Meyer, M. M., Jr. 1982. Basic terms and techniques of tissue culture propagation. *The American Hosta Society Bulletin* 13:38–42.

Minks, N. M. 1989. The American Hosta Society national standard show schedule. In *National Convention Handbook.* AHS Exhibition Committee, AHS National Convention, Indianapolis.

Minks, N. M. 1990a. The American Hosta Society national standard show schedule. AHS Exhibition Committee. Personal communication.

Minks, N. M. 1990b. The American Hosta Society national standard show schedule. *The Hosta Journal* 21 (1):96–101. AHS Exhibition Committee.

Minks, N. M. 1990c. The American Hosta Society national standard show schedule. In *Exhibition Judge's Handbook.* AHS Exhibition Committee.

Miquel, F. A. W. 1867. Prolusio Florae Iaponicae, 5. *Annales Musei Botanici Lugdano-Batavi.* 152.

Miquel, F. A. W. 1869. Bijdragen tot de Flora van Japan, 1. *Funkia* Sprengel. *Verslag Mededelingen Akademie Wetenschappen, Amsterdam,* Natuurkunde Series 2, 3:299–302.

Mitchell, H. 1983. The giant August lily. *The American Hosta Society Bulletin* 14:26–27.

Miyabe, K., and Y. Kudo. 1930–1934. Flora of Hokkaido and Saghalien. *J. Fac. Agr. Hokkaido Univ.* (Sapporo) 3:315.

Moench, C. 1802. *Methodus, Suppl.* 221.

Moldenke, H. N. 1936. A monograph of the Genus *Cornutia. Repertorium Specierum Novarum Regni Vegetabilis* (Berlin-Dahlem) 40:196–199.

Mori, T. 1922. *Hosta minor. An Enumeration of Plants Hitherto Known from Korea.* Seoul, Korea: Government of Chosen. 89.

Morren, E., and A. de Vos. 1887. *Index bibliographique de l'Hortus Belgicus.* Catalogue méthodique des plantes ornamentales qui ont été décrites, figurées ou introduites en Belgique de 1830 à 1880, *Funkia.* 95.

Mottet, S. 1897. Les *Funkia. Revue Hortic.* (Paris) 69:114–116.

Murata, G. 1962. *Hosta hypoleuca. Acta Phytotaxonomica et Geobotanica* 19:67.

Murray, J. A., 1784. *Hemerocallis. Caroli a Linné Systema*

Vegetabilium. Ed. 14. Gottingæ. 339.

Müssel, H. 1976. Funkien—Beachtungswerte Stauden für Schattige Plätze. *Garten Praxis* 8:372–375.

Müssel, H. See R. Hansen; also Jellito-Schacht-Fessler.

Nakai, T. 1911. Flora Koreana, Pars Secunda (*H. minor*). *J. of the College of Science,* Imperial University Tokyo 31:250–251.

Nakai, T. 1914. Report of Collection on Cheju and Wan Islands. Seoul, Korea: Government of Chosen. 30–31.

Nakai, T. 1915. *Flora of Chiisan.* Seoul, Korea: Government of Chosen.

Nakai, T. 1918. *Hosta minor.* In: *Report on the Vegetation of Diamond Mountains, Corea.* Seoul, Korea: Government of Chosen. 167.

Nakai, T. 1930. Notulae ad Plantas Japoniae et Koreae (38/39) (*H. rectifolia; H. rupifraga*). *Botanical Magazine* (Tokyo) 44:7–40, 507–537 (26, 58, 513).

Nakai, T. 1936. *H. gracillima* by Maekawa. In *Iconographia Plantarum Asiae-Orientalis* (Tokyo) 1, 4:tab. 33 (1:72).

Nakai, T. 1952a. *H. caput-avis* by Maekawa. In *Iconographia Plantarum Asiae-Orientalis* (Tokyo) 5:495.

Nakai, T. 1952b. A synoptical sketch of Korean flora. *Bul. Nat. Sci. Mus. Tokyo* (Tokyo) 31:1–152.

Nash, G. V. 1911. The funkias or day-lilies. *Torreya* 11, 1:1–9.

Nelson, A. N. 1983. *The Modern Reader's Japanese-English Character Dictionary.* 2nd rev. ed. Ruttland and Tokyo: Tuttle.

Nobis, F. 1951. *Die Freiland-Schmuckstauden, Grundlagen und Fortschritte im Garten- und Weinbau* (Ludwigsburg) 85–86, 4:112–114.

Noter, R. de. 1905. *Hemerocallis en Funkia.* Vertaald en van opmerkingen voorzien door H. Witte. *Nederland Tuinbouwblad Sempervirens* 3:445; *Revue Horticol.* (Paris). N.S. 5, 77:390, ic. 163.

Ohba, H., N. Ishii, and S. Saito. 1987. Biogeography of Tsushima Island. In *Report on the Natural Resource Investigation of Tsushima Island; Nature of Tsushima Island.* 259–271.

Ohba, H., and K. Midorikawa. 1987. Some remarks on the flora of Tsushima Island, NW Kyushu, Japan. In: *Report on the Natural Resource Investigation of Tsushima Island; Nature of Tsushima Island.* 63–78.

Ohwi, J. 1942. *H. albomarginata. Acta Phytotaxonomica et Geobotanica* 11:265.

Ohwi, J. 1965. *The Flora of Japan.* Eds. F. G. Meyer and E. H. Walker. Washington, DC: Smithsonian Institution. Fam. 52, 11:287–291.

Okamoto, S. See Kikuchi, 1934.

Okuyama, S. 1937. *H. longipes. J. of Japanese Botany* 13:34.

Okuyama, S. 1963. *H. tibai. Col. Ill. Wild Plant. Japan.* (Tokyo) 7:118, tab. 587, 4.

O'Neill, H. B. 1987. *Companion to Chinese History.* New York, U.S.A., and Oxford, England: Facts On File Publications.

Ono, R. 1847. *Zyusyu Honzo Somoku Keimo.* Vol. 12. In facsimile Ed. 2(1929):337; cfr. Maekawa, 1940. 349.

Otto, C. F., and A. Dietrich. 1833. Kultur und Beschreibung the *Funkia undulata.* *Allgemeine Gartenzeitung* 1:119.

Palibin, J. 1901. Conspectus Florae Coreae, Pars Tertia. *Acta Hort. Petrop.* 19, 3:112.

Papachatzi, M., P. A. Hammer, and P. M. Hasegawa. 1980. *In vitro* propagation of *H. plantaginea. HortScience* 15:506–507.

Park, M. K. 1949. *An Enumeration of Korean Plants.* Seoul, Korea: Ministry of Education. 320–321.

Paxton, J. 1838. *Hemerocallis sieboldii. Magazine of Botany* 5:25–26.

Payne, F. H., and P. R. Payne. 1985. The *Hosta* legacy of the late David Stone. *The American Hosta Society Bulletin* 16:32–34.

Pearson, R., and E. Napier. 1981. *The Wisley Book of Gardening.* London: Norton and Company.

Philip, C., and T. Lord. 1989. *The Plant Finder.* Whitbourne: Headmain, for the Hardy Plant Society.

Pollock, W. I. 1982. Hostas: The new colored-foliage perennials. *The Green Scene* 11, 1:21–24.

Pollock, W. I. 1983. *Hosta* 'Thomas Hogg'. *The American Hosta Society Bulletin* 14:35–38.

Pollock, W. I. 1984a. Letter from America, *Hosta* nomenclature. *British Hosta and Hemerocallis Society Bulletin* 1, 2:34–37.

Pollock, W. I. 1984b. Much ado about *H. sieboldii. The American Hosta Society Bulletin* 15:108–111.

Pollock, W. I. 1984c. Start your slug abatement program—Early. *The American Hosta Society Bulletin* 15:87.

Pollock, W. I. 1984d. Forcing hostas—An interview with Allen C. Haskell. *The American Hosta Society Bulletin* 15:51–53.

Pollock, W. I. 1984e. What's in a *Hosta* name. (Part 1). *The American Hosta Society Bulletin* 15:41.

Pollock, W. I. 1985a. *H. ventricosa* 'Aureo-marginata'. *The American Hosta Society Bulletin* 16:8–11.

Pollock, W. I. 1985b. *Hosta* nomenclature—Where are we today? *The American Hosta Society Bulletin* 16:87–92.

Pollock, W. I. 1985c. On *H. fortunei* 'Aureo-marginata' and 'Albo-marginata'. *The American Hosta Society Bulletin* 16:75.

Pollock, W. I. 1985d. More on black vine weevil. *The American Hosta Society Bulletin* 16:95.

Pollock, W. I. 1986. Nomenclature of stable and unstable *Hosta. The Hosta Journal* 17, 1:66–71.

Pollock, W. I. 1988. High on hostas . . . drawstring effect, melting out, scorching and reverting. *The Hosta Journal* 19, 1:58–63.

Pollock, W. I. 1989. Virus in *Hosta. The Hosta Journal* 20, 2:81.

Pollock, W. I. 1990. Hostas in Britain. Part 2. *The Hosta Journal* 21, 1:61–68.

Pollock, W. I., and W. G. Schmid. 1986. A note on *H.* 'Frances Williams'. *The Hosta Journal* 17, 1:11.

Pollock, W. I., et al. 1986a. *H.* 'Golden Sunburst' and *H.* 'Golden Medallion'. *The Hosta Journal* 17, 1:48–65.

Pollock, W. I., et al. 1987b. Slugs . . . bugs . . . countermeasures. *The Hosta Journal* 18, 2:33–35.

Pratt, M. E. 1986. Kenji Watanabe: Guardian of Mt. Fuji's hostas. *The Hosta Journal* 17, 2:12–14.

Pratt, M. E. 1990. Cooking with hosta. *The Hosta Journal* 21, 1:58–60.

Rand, E. S., Jr. 1866. *Garden Flowers. How to Cultivate Them.* Boston: J. E. Tilton and Company. 170.

Redouté, P. J. 1802. *Les Liliacées.* 1. Paris: Jardin de Malmaison. Tab. 3.

Redouté, P. J. 1805. *Les Liliacées.* 1. Paris: Jardin de Malmaison. Tab. 106.

Regel, E. A. von. 1876. Die *Funkia*-Arten der Gärten und deren Formen. *Gartenflora* 25:161–163.

Regel, E. A. von. 1881. Funkia. *Gartenflora* 30:23.

Robinson, W. [1883] 1933. *The English Flower Garden.* Ed. 15. London: John Murray.

Robyns, W., and A. Louis, 1942. Beschouwingen over de poly-embryonie en polyspermie by den bedektzadigen. *Verh. Vlaam. Academie Wet.* 4, 3:63.

Rodigas, 1864. *Funkia albomarginata. Bulletin Congr. Internat. Hort.* 140–141.

Rogier, J., and J. Brown. 1980. *The Frances R. Williams Hosta Letters.* Chaska, MN: Andersen Horticultural Library, Minnesota Landscape Arboretum.

Ross, H. A. 1982. A foolproof method of rapidly propagating hostas. *The American Hosta Society Bulletin* 13:51–53.

Ross, N. L. 1989. A haven for hostas. *The Washington Post* (3 August).

Ruh, P., et al. 1980. Preliminary Checklist of Genus *Hosta.* Cleveland. 1–58.

Ruh, P. 1982. Hostas from the original Wayside gardens. *The American Hosta Society Bulletin* 13:23–24.

Ruh, P. 1983. Return to the origins of 'Japonica Blue' and

'Japonica White'. *The American Hosta Society Bulletin* 14:28–29.

Ruh, P. 1984. Update on *H.* × *tardiana*. *The American Hosta Society Bulletin* 15:26–27.

Ruh, P. 1985. Sojourns in English gardens. *The American Hosta Society Bulletin* 16:27–29.

Ruh, P., and W. I. Pollock. 1985. On *H. tardiflora* and "*H. lancifolia tardiflora*". *The American Hosta Society Bulletin* 16:52–53.

Ruh, P., and M. R. Zilis. 1989. Whoops! Mistaken identity! *The Hosta Journal* 20, 1:32–33.

Saccardo, P. A., 1912. *Chromotaxia* [1891]. Ed. 3. Padua.

Salisbury, R. A. 1807. Observations on the perigynous insertion of the stamina of plants (*Saussurea*). *Transactions of the Linnean Society of London* 8:1–16.

Salisbury, R. A. 1812. On the cultivation of rare plants, especially such as have been introduced since the death of Mr. Philip Miller. *Transactions of the Horticultural Society, London*, 1:262–366.

Sato, D. 1935. Analysis of the karyotypes in *Yucca, Agave* and the related genera with special reference to the phylogenetic significance. *J. of Japanese Genetics* 11, 5:272–278.

Sato, D. 1942. Karyotype alternation and phylogeny in Liliaceae and allied families. *Jap. J. of Botany* 12:57–132.

Savory, R. R. 1985. *H.* 'Golden Tiara' and 'Golden Scepter'. *The American Hosta Society Bulletin* 16:35.

Schmid, G. 1942. Über Ph. Fr. v. Siebold's Reise Nach Japan. *Botanisches Archiv* 43:487–530.

Schmid, W. G. 1985a. A commentary on Japanese *Hosta* names. *The American Hosta Society Bulletin* 16:83–85.

Schmid, W. G. 1985b. Hostas in Germany. *The American Hosta Society Bulletin* 16:22–26.

Schmid, W. G. 1985c. More on *H. sieboldiana* 'Semperaurea'. *The American Hosta Society Bulletin* 16:56.

Schmid, W. G. 1985d. On *H. ventricosa* 'Aureo-maculata' and 'Aureo-marginata'. *The American Hosta Society Bulletin* 16:57–59.

Schmid, W. G. 1985e. Apomixis in *H. ventricosa*. *The American Hosta Society Bulletin* 16:68.

Schmid, W. G. 1986a. Survey of the *H. kikutii* complex. *British Hosta and Hemerocallis Society Bulletin* 1, 4:7–12.

Schmid, W. G. 1986b. Don't forget the species. *The Georgia Hosta Society Newsletter* 2, 2; 3, 1, 3; 4, 1, 3.

Schmid, W. G. 1986c. Deadline for slugs. *The Hosta Journal* 17, 2:47–49.

Schmid, W. G. 1987a. *Handbook for Classification Clerks and Listing of Species and Cultivars*. The American Hosta Society.

Schmid, W. G. 1987b. It's *H. rohdeifolia* not *H. rhodeifolia*. *The Hosta Journal* 18, 2:24–25.

Schmid, W. G. 1987c. Hosta diseases and their prevention. *The Hosta Journal* 18, 1:30–31.

Schmid, W. G. 1987d. Caveat hostae emptor. *The Hosta Journal* 18, 1:48–52.

Schmid, W. G. 1988a. *Handbook for Classification Clerks and Listing of Species and Cultivars*. The American Hosta Society.

Schmid, W. G. 1988b. Hosta taxonomy—A revised overview. *British Hosta and Hemerocallis Society Bulletin* 2, 2:25–35.

Schmid, W. G. 1988c. One more time: *H. sieboldii* vs. *H. albomarginata*. *The Hosta Journal* 19, 2:64–67.

Schmid, W. G. 1990. A place in the shade? *The Hosta Journal* 21, 1:78–80.

Schmid, W. G., and W. I. Pollock. 1985. Commentary to a nomenclature study. *British Hosta and Hemerocallis Society Bulletin* 1, 3:34–50.

Schulze, E. 1965. Unverwüstliche Funkie. *Pflanze und Garten*. 94–95.

Shiboruto Sensei Toray Hyakunen Kinenkai. 1924. *Shiboruto*

Sensei Toray Hiakunen Kinen Rombunshu (100-year memorial to von Siebold). Nagasaki.

Shirai, M., and T. Oonuma, revisers. 1921. *Honzo-Dzufu*, by Iwasaki. Ed. 20. Fol. 12–18. Tokyo.

Siebold, P. F. von. 1824. De historiæ naturalis in Japonia statu. Oken, *Isis*, Batavia.

Siebold, P. F. von. 1825. Einige Wörter über den Zustand der Botanik auf Japan. *Acad. Cæs. Leopold Nova Acta*. 14:670–696.

Siebold, P. F. von. 1827. In schedula (L).

Siebold, P. F. von. 1828. Nachrichten aus Japan. *Flora* 11:753–762.

Siebold, P. F. von. 1830. Synopsis plantarum oeconomicarum universi regni Japonici. *Batavia Genootsch. Verhand.* 16:1–73.

Siebold, P. F. von. 1844. Kruidkundige Naamlijst von oud en nieuw ingevoerde Japansche planten van het jaar 1824 tot 1844. *Jaarb. Kon. Ned. Mij Aanmoed. Tuinbouw*. 29.

Siebold, P. F. von. 1848. Extrait du catalogue raisonne et du prix-courant des plantes et graines du Japon et des Indes-Orientales et Occidentales Néerlanddaises cultivées dans l'établissement de von Siebold & Comp. à Leide. *Jaarb. Kon. Ned. Mij Aanmoed. Tuinbouw, Funkia*. 44.

Siebold, P. F. von. 1850. *Nippon: Archiv zur Beschreibung von Japan und dessen Neben- und Schutzländern Jezo mit den südlichen Kurilen, Sachalin, Korea und den Liukiu-Inseln*. 7 vols. Leiden, Netherlands.

Siebold, P. F. von. 1856. *Catalogue raisonne et prix-courant des plantes et graines du Japon cultivées dans l'établissement de von Siebold & Comp. à Leide*. Leiden, Netherlands.

Siebold, P. F. von. 1860. *Catalogue et prix courant des plantes du Japon, cultivées dans l'établissement de von Siebold & Company à Leide (Hollande)*. Leiden, Netherlands.

Siebold, P. F. von. 1861. *Catalogue prodrome des plantes du Japon, introduites en Hollande dans les annees 1859, 1860 et 1861 et cultivées dans l'établissement de von Siebold et Comp. à Leide (Hollande)*. Leiden, Netherlands.

Siebold, P. F. von. 1862. *Catalogue supplémentaire et prix courant des plantes nouvelles, introduites du Japon en 1862 et cultivées dans l'établissement de von Siebold & Company à Leide (Hollande)*. Leiden, Netherlands.

Siebold, P. F. von. 1863. *Catalogue raisonne et prix-courant des plantes et graines du Japon et de la Chine, cultivées dans l'établissement de von Siebold & Comp. à Leide*. Leiden, Netherlands.

Siebold, P. F. von. 1867. *Catalogue et prix-courant des plantes, cultivées dans le Jardin d'Acclimatation de Feu Mons. Ph. F. von Siebold à Leide, (Hollande)*. Leiden, Netherlands.

Siebold, P. F. von. 1868. *Catalogue et prix-courant des plantes, cultivées dans le Jardin d'Acclimatation de Feu Mons. Ph. F. von Siebold à Leide (Hollande)*. Leiden, Netherlands.

Siebold, P. F. von. 1871. *Catalogue et prix-courant des plantes, cultivées dans le Jardin d'Acclimatation de Feu Mons. Ph. F.von Siebold à Leide (Hollande)*. Leiden, Netherlands.

Siebold, P. F. von. 1872. *Plantes nouvelles récemment introduites, et qui ont livrées au commerce au 1er Mars 1872. Feu Mons. von Siebold & Company à Leide (Hollande)*. Leiden, Netherlands.

Siebold, P. F. von. 1874. *Prijslijst van bol- & knolgewassen, vaste planten & Liliums. Fa. von Siebold & Comp. à Leide*. Leiden, Netherlands.

Siebold, P. F. von. 1875. *Prix-courant de plantes bulbeuses, Amaryllis-Liliums, plantes vivaces-Iris kaempferii, etc. Feu Ph. F. von Siebold & Comp. à Leide*. Leiden, Netherlands.

Siebold, P. F. von. 1876. *Prix-courant de plantes bulbeuses, Amaryllis-Liliums, plantes vivaces-Iris kaempferii, etc. (Nouveatés de 1876) Feu Ph. F. von Siebold & Comp. à Leide*. Leiden, Netherlands.

Siebold, P. F. von. 1877. *Prix-courant de plantes bulbeuses, Amaryllis-Liliums, plantes vivaces-Iris kaempferii, etc. (Nouveatés de 1877) Feu Ph. F. von Siebold & Comp. à Leide*. Leiden, Netherlands.

Siebold, P. F. von. 1879. *Prix-courant de plantes bulbeuses, Amaryllis-Liliums, Iris kaempferii-plantes vivaces, Orchidées de pleine terre, Fougéres de pleine terre. (Nouveatés de 1879). Feu Ph. F. von Siebold & Comp. à Leide.* Leiden, Netherlands.

Siebold, P. F. von. 1882. *Prix-courant de plantes bulbeuses, Amaryllis-Liliums, Iris kaempferii-plantes vivaces, Orchidées de pleine terre, Fougéres de pleine terre. (Nouveatés de 1882). Feu Ph. F. von Siebold & Comp. à Leide.* Leiden, Netherlands.

Siebold, P. F. von, Letters to his daughter Ine. Nagasaki Prefectural Library, Nagasaki.

Siebold, P. F. von, C. J. Temminck, H. Schlegel, and W. deHaan, 1833. *Fauna Japonica.* 5 vol. Leiden, Netherlands.

Siebold, P. F. von, and J. G. Zuccarini. 1835–1841. *Flora Japonica.* Leiden, Netherlands.

Siebold, P. F. von, and J. G. Zuccarini. 1836. Flora Japonica, sive plantæ in imperio Japonico collectæ. *Ann. Sci. Nat. 6 (Bot.).*

Siebold, P. F. von, and J. G. Zuccarini. 1837/1843. Plantarum in Japonica collectarum genera nova, notis characteristicis illustrata. (Munich), *Abhandlungen,* 3:717–750.

Siebold, P. F. von, and J. G. Zuccarini. 1843. Plantarum, quas in Japonia Collegit Dr. Ph. Fr. de Siebold, *Genera Nova,* Notis Characteristicis Delineationibusque Illustrata Proponunt (General). Leiden, Netherlands.

Siebold, P. F. von, and J. G. Zuccarini. 1844/1846. Floræ japonicæ familiæ naturales, adjectis generum et specierum exemplis selectis. *Abhandlungen* (Munich) 4.

Siebold, W. 1943. *Ein Deutscher Gewinnt Japan's Herz.* Leipzig, Germany: Hase und Köhler.

Silva-Tarouca, E. Graf von. 1910. *Unsere Freiland-Stauden.* Ed. 1. Vienna: F. Tempsky. 103.

Sims, J. 1812. *Hemerocallis japonica. Curtis's Botanical Magazine* 35, tab. 1433.

Smith, A. W. 1963. *A Gardener's Book of Plant Names.* New York: Harper & Row.

Smith, E. B. 1971. Hosta × tardiana. *The American Hosta Society Bulletin* 3:57–58. Reprinted in *The American Hosta Society Bulletin* 13(1982):18–21.

Smith, E. B. 1985. Eric Smith on his *H. Tardianas. The American Hosta Society Bulletin* 16:48–49.

Smith, E. B. 1982. *H. × tardiana. The American Hosta Society Bulletin* 13:18–21.

Smith, R. (notes by E. B. Smith). 1984. Eric Smith's hostas. *British Hosta and Hemerocallis Society Bulletin* 1, 2:30–32.

Sneath, P. H. A., and R. P. Sokal. 1973. *Numerical Taxonomy: The Principles and Precise Numerical Classification.* San Francisco: Freeman Company.

Solberg, R. M. 1988a. A conversation with the registrar. *The Hosta Journal* 19, 2:43.

Solberg, R. M. 1988b. Southern blight (*Sclerotium rolfsii*) and southern hostas. *The Hosta Journal* 19, 1:36–37.

Solberg, R. M. 1989. More vole control. *The Hosta Journal* 20, 1:58.

Soules, M. C. 1984. Some recent *Hosta* cultivars from Japan. *The American Hosta Society Bulletin* 15:36–38.

Sprengel, K. P. J. 1817. *Anleitung zur Kenntniss der Gewächse.* Ed. 2. Halle, Germany. 2, 1:246.

Sprengel, K. P. J. 1825. *Caroli Linnaei Systema Vegetabilium.* Ed 16. Gottingen, Germany. 2:40–41.

Stace, C. A. 1973. *Plant Taxonomy and Biosystematics.* London: E. Arnold, Division of Hodder and Stoughton.

Stearn, W. T. 1931a. The *Lilium cordatum* and *Hosta japonica.* Two Thunbergian species. *Gardener's Chronicle,* 3 ser., 89:111.

Stearn, W. T. 1931b. The hostas or funkias, a revision of the plantain lilies. *Gardener's Chronicle,* 3 ser., 90:27, 47–49, 88–89, 127.

Stearn, W. T. 1932a. Schedæ ad Sertum Cantabrigiense Exsiccatum a W. T. Stearn editum; Decades 1–2; in Notes from the University Herbarium, Cambridge, 3. (*H. lancifolia* var. *Thunbergii*). *J. of Botany* 70 (Suppl.):14–15.

Stearn, W. T. 1932b. *Hosta (Funkia) rectifolia.* A newly identified plantain-lily. *Gardener's Chronicle,* 3 ser., 91:23.

Stearn, W. T. 1947. The name *Lilium japonicum. RHS Lily Year Book* 11:101–108.

Stearn, W. T. 1948. Kaempfer and the lilies of Japan. *RHS Lily Year Book,* 12:65–70.

Stearn, W. T. 1951. *Hosta rectifolia. Curtis's Botanical Magazine,* N.S. vol. 168, tab. 138.

Stearn, W. T. 1953. *Hosta tardiflora. Curtis's Botanical Magazine,* N.S. vol. 169, tab. 204.

Stearn, W. T. 1966. *Hosta venusta. Curtis's Botanical Magazine,* N.S. vol. 176, tab. 499.

Stearn, W. T. 1971. Philipp Franz von Siebold and the lilies of Japan. *RHS Lily Year Book* 34:11–20.

Stearn, W. T. 1986. *Botanical Latin, History, Grammar, Syntax, Terminology and Vocabulary.* London: David & Charles.

Stevens, D. 1984. Black vine weevils—My experience. *British Hosta and Hemerocallis Society Newsletter* 5.

Stevens, D. 1987. *Hosta* 'Gold Standard'. *British Hosta and Hemerocallis Society Bulletin* 2, 1:37.

Stewart, R. N., and H. Dermen. 1979. Ontogeny in monocotyledons as revealed by studies in the developmental anatomy of periclinal chloroplast chimeras. USDA Agricultural Research. *American J. of Botany* 66, 1:47–58.

Stork, A. L. 1978. Plantes striees, tachetees, panachees—causes diverses. *Revue Horticole Suisse* 51, 3:76–82.

Strasburger, E. 1877. *Befruchtung und Zellteilung.* Jena, Germany.

Strasburger, E. 1878. Über die Polyembryonie. *Jenaische Zeit. Naturwissenschaft* 12:648–650.

Sugita, H. 1987. List of Japanese species and cultivars (private correspondence).

Sugita, H. 1988. Prevention of the white silk fungus (*Corticium rolfsii*) on *Hosta. The Hosta Journal* 19, 1:36.

Summers, A. J. [1969] 1982. Hosta and the shady garden. gardening in the shade. In *Plants and Gardens (Brooklyn Botanic Garden Record).* Brooklyn Botanic Garden. 7th printing, vol. 25, 3:42–46.

Summers, A. J. 1970a. *Hosta venusta* Maekawa. *AGS Bulletin* no. 160, 38, 2:174–177.

Summers, A. J. 1970b. Slugs and meadow mice. *The American Hosta Society Bulletin* 2:52–53.

Summers, A. J. 1972. Numbered Acquisition List, Hortus. 1964 through 1972. (Unpublished).

Summers, A. J. 1982. Notes on the tardianas. *The American Hosta Society Bulletin* 13:21.

Summers, A. J. 1984. On *Hosta* nomenclature. *The American Hosta Society Bulletin* 15:102–107.

Summers, A. J. 1985. *H. tokudama. The American Hosta Society Bulletin* 16:47.

Summers, A. J. 1989a. Companion plants. *The Hosta Journal* 20, 1:39–41.

Summers, A. J. 1989b. The Frances Williams complex. *The Hosta Journal* 20, 1:28–29.

Summers, A. J. 1990. History of *H.* 'August Moon'. *The Hosta Journal* 21, 1:41.

Suto, T. 1936. List of chromosome number and idiogram types in Liliaceae and Amaryllidaceae. *Jap. J. Genetics* 12, 2:107.

Sweet, R. 1827. *Funkia alba. Hort. Brit.* 409.

Systematics Association. 1962. Descriptive terminology. *Taxon* 11:145–156, 245–247.

Takehara. 1924. *Standard Japanese-English Dictionary.*

Tatewaki, M. 1934. *Transactions of the Sapporo Natural History Society.* 13:111.

Tatewaki, M., and Samejima. 1956. *H. atropurpurea. Alp. Pl. Cent.*

Mt. Dist. Hokkaido. 21.

Taylor, N. 1961. *Taylor's Encyclopedia of Gardening.* Ed. 4. Boston: Houghton Mifflin Company.

Teresawa, Y. 1923. On the inheritance of *Giboshi (Hosta). Jap. J. Genetics* 2:13–21.

Thomas, G. S. 1960. Notes on the genus *Hosta. Hardy Plant Society Bulletin* 2, 5:92–101.

Thomas, G. S. 1961. Notes on the Genus *Hosta. Gardener's Chronicle* 2 (5):92–101.

Thomas, G. S. 1977. *Plants for Ground Cover.* Rev. ed. London: J. M. Dent & Sons.

Thomas, G. S. [1982] 1985. *Perennial Garden Plants or The Modern Florilegium.* Ed. 2. London: J. M. Dent & Sons. 8 (ic. 4-5/6, 7-3), 181–189.

Thompson, P. 1980. Hostas from seed. *J. of the Royal Horticultural Society* 105:371–372.

Thunberg, C. P. 1780. Kaempferus illustratus. *Nova Acta Regiae Societatis Scientiarum Upsaliensis* (Uppsala) 3:208.

Thunberg, C. P. 1784. *Flora Iaponica* Lipsiæ, Germany. 142.

Thunberg, C. P. 1794. *Icones Plantarum Japonicarum: Quas in Insulis Japonicis Annus 1775 et 1776 Collegit et Descripsit.* Uppsala: J. F. Edman.

Thunberg, C. P. 1797. *Hemerocallis undulata.* Mus. Bot. Upsal., App. 5:107.

Thunberg, C. P. 1826. Horti Upsaliensis plantæ cultæ ab initio sæculi. *Hemerocallis japonica. Diss. Upsaliæ.* 25.

Tilney-Bassett, R. 1975. Genetics of variegated plants. In *Genetics and Biogenesis of Mitochondria and Chloroplasts.* Eds. C. Birky, P. Perlman, and T. Byers. Columbus, OH: Ohio State University. 268–309.

Tompkins, C. 1984. Through the years with hostas. *The American Hosta Society Bulletin* 15:8–13.

Tompkins, C. 1985. The odyssey of Cynthia's no. 1928–7W.E. *The American Hosta Society Bulletin* 16:20–21.

Toyama, H. 1940. *Flora Nagasaki.* Nagasaki. 5.

Toyama, H. 1980. *Flora Nagasaki.* Rev. ed. Nagasaki. 46, 264

Trattinnick, L. 1812. *Archiv der Gewächskunde* (Vienna) 1, 2:14, tab. 89.

Trattinnick, L. 1814. *Archiv der Gewächskunde* (Vienna) 2:144, tab. 189.

Traub, H. P. 1953. The tribes and genera of the Agavaceae (Hoseae). *Plant Life* (Arcadia, CA) 9:134–135.

Trehane, P. 1989. *Index Hortensis.* Vol. 1, *Perennials.* Dorset: Wimborne; Portland, OR: Timber Press.

Trigg, L. B. 1988. Splendid, colorful hostas. *Southern Living* 23, 8:38–40.

Trigg, L. B. 1989. Splendid, colorful hostas. *Southern Living-Garden Guide.* (Spring-Summer).

Turill, W. B. 1925. Standardization on a mathematical basis of the commonly used terms for the shapes of leaves and petals. (Unpublished manuscript widely known and adopted in part by the Systematics Association.)

Ullrich's International Periodicals Directory. 1984. Ed. 23. Bowker.

Vaughn, K. C. 1979. Chloroplast mutants in *Hosta. The American Hosta Society Bulletin* 11:36–49.

Vaughn, K. C. 1981. Using genetics to improve *Hosta. The American Hosta Society Bulletin* 12:21–28.

Vaughn, K. C. 1982. The genetics of *Hosta. The American Hosta Society Bulletin* 13:44–49.

Vaughn, K. C. 1989a. Viruses in *Hosta. The Hosta Journal* 20, 1:24–25.

Vaughn, K. C. 1989b. More on virus. *The Hosta Journal* 20, 2:80.

Vaughn, K. C. 1990. Twenty-three years of frustration hybridizing *Hosta.* Summarized by L. Jones in *Michigan Hosta Happenings* 5, 1:4–8.

Vaughn, K. C., and K. G. Wilson. 1980a. Genetics and ultrastructure of a dotted leaf pattern in *Hosta. J. Hered.* 71:121–123.

Vaughn, K. C., and K. G. Wilson. 1980b. An ultrastructural survey of plastome mutants of *Hosta. Cytobios* 28:71–83.

Vaughn, K. C., and K. G. Wilson. 1980c. A dominant plastome mutation in *Hosta. J. Hered.* 71:203–206.

Vaughn, K. C., K. G. Wilson, and K. D. Stewart. 1978. Light-harvesting pigment-protein complex deficiency in *Hosta. Planta* 143:275–278.

Vellozo, J. M. da C. 1874. *Nomencl.* Rio de Janeiro. 1674.

Vilmorin-Andrieux et Cie. 1866. *Les fleurs de pleine terre* (with Atlas). Ed. 2. Paris. 404–406, 468–470.

Voss, A., and A. Siebert. 1896. *Vilmorin's Blumengärtnerei,* Berlin. Ed. 3, 1:1074–1076.

Wade, V. R., and S. Wade. 1990. *American Hostas.* Bellville, OH: Wade and Gatton Nurseries. 1–174.

Walker, J. W., and J. A. Doyle. 1975. The bases of angiosperm phylogeny: Palynology. *Annals of the Missouri Botanical Garden* 62:664–723.

Watanabe, J., and K. Watanabe. 1985. Articles on *Hosta. Garden Magazine* 18:15–21.

Watanabe, K. 1984. Articles on *Hosta. J. of the Japan Horticultural Society* 88.

Watanabe, K. 1985. *The Observation and Cultivation of Hosta.* Gotemba, Tokyo: New Science Company.

Waters, G. 1982. A beginner's guide to slugs and snails. *The American Hosta Society Bulletin* 13:57–60.

Webster, J., and T. A. Rutherford. 1986. Bad news for black vine weevils. *The Hosta Journal* 17, 1:46.

Wehrhahn, H. R. 1931. *Die. Gartenstauden.* Berlin and Altenburg: Parey. 66–68.

Wehrhahn, H. R. 1934. Die Funkien unserer Gärten. *Gartenschönheit* (Berlin) 15:180–181, 203–204.

Wehrhahn, H. R. 1936. Zwei übersehene *Hosta*-Arten. *Gartenflora* (Berlin) 85:246–249.

Weist, J. 1989. Nursery grows plants in laboratory (Walters Gardens, Inc.). *The Detroit News* (22 May). 3D–4D.

Wherry, E. T. 1946. A key to the cultivated hostas. *National Hort. Magazine* (Washington) 25, 3:253–256.

Whitaker, T. W. 1934. Chromosomal constitution in certain monocotyledons. *J. Arnold Arbor* 15:135, 143.

Wilder, L. B. 1990. *Color in My Garden; An American Gardener's Palette.* New York: Atlantic Monthly Press.

Wilkins, J. W., Jr. 1987. Accelerated growth of *Hosta. The Hosta Journal* 18, 1:55–56.

Wilkins, J. W., Jr. 1987. Do-it yourself slug bait. *The Hosta Journal* 17 (1):54–55.

Wilkins, J. W., Jr., and L. C., Jones. 3. 1989. *Convention Handbook.* The American Hosta Society.

Willdenow, K. L. 1797. *Hosta. Spec. Plant.* Berlin. 1274.

Willdenow, K. L. 1808. *Funckia* in *Ges. Naturf. Fr. Berl. Mag.* 2:19.

Williams, C. 1983. *Hosta* 'Frances Williams'. *The American Hosta Society Bulletin* 14:12–14.

Williams, F. R. 1947. The plantain lilies. Good plants for shady gardens. *Brooklyn Bot. Gard. Rec.,* N.S. 3, 3:186–189.

Williams, F. R. 1949. They will thrive on neglect but they do better if babied. *Horticulture* 27, 10:368, 382.

Williams, F. R. 1966–1968, Private correspondence with Mr. A. J. Alex Summers.

Williams, F. R. 1983. *H.* 'Frances Williams'. *The American Hosta Society Bulletin* 14:12–15. Reprint.

Winge, Ö. 1919. On the non-Mendelian inheritance in variegated plants. *Compt. Rend. Trav. Carlsb. Lab.* 14, 3:1–20.

Wilson, K. 1986. Hot hostas. *Rodale's Organic Gardening* 33, 8:65–69.

Wister, G. S. 1969. *Hosta* 'Louisa'. *The American Hosta Society Bulletin* 1:25–27.

Wister, G. S. 1970a. Frances R. Williams and her hostas. *The American Hosta Society Bulletin* 2:13–22.

Wister, G. S. 1970b. Frances Williams and her garden adventures. *Arnoldia* 30, 4:148–154.

Witte, H. 1868. *Flora. Afbeeldingen and beschrijvingen van boomen, éénjarige planten enz. voorkomende in de Nederlandsche Tuinen.* Leiden. 221–224, pl. 56.

Witte, W. 1873. *Funkia sieboldiana* en andere soorten. *Nederland Tuinbouwblad Sempervirens.* 2:279–282.

Witte, W. 1877. Nieuwe planten. *Sieboldia* 3:14.

Witte, W. 1892. Vaste planten, 3. *Nederland Tuinbouwblad Sempervirens* 21:49–52.

Woodcock, H. D., and W. T. Stearn, 1950. *Lilies of the World.* London.

Woods, M., and H. Dubuy, 1946. Seasonal changes in biological equilibria involving two chromosomal systems in variegated *Hosta. Phytopathology* 36:472–478.

Wright, C. H. 1916. *Funkia lancifolia* var. *tardiflora. Curtis's Botanical Magazine* 142, tab. 8645.

Wunderlich, R. 1950. Die *Agavaceae* Hutchinson's im Licht der Embryologie, ihres Gynözeum-, Staublatt- und Blattbaues. *Öster. Botanische Zeit.* 97, 3/5:495.

Wyatt, R. 1989. Grow hostas in a shady garden spot. *The Atlanta Journal/Constitution* (14 May) P-4.

Yasui, K. 1929. Studies on the maternal inheritance of plastid characters in *Hosta japonica* Aschers. et Graeb. f. *albomarginata* Mak. and its derivatives. *Cytologia* 1:192–215.

Yasui, K. 1935. Cytological studies in diploid and triploid *Hosta. Cytologia* 6:484–491.

Yinger, B. R. 1990. Letter to the Editor. *The Hosta Journal* 21, 1:13–14.

Yuasa. 1987. List of Japanese species and cultivars. Private Correspondence.

Zilis, M. R. 1981. Tissue propagation of *Hosta. The American Hosta Society Bulletin* 12:19–20.

Zilis, M. R. 1987. Classifying the variability of *H. sieboldiana* 'Frances Williams'. *The Hosta Journal* 18, 1:39–41.

Zilis, M. R. 1989. *Listing of Species and Cultivars.* The American Hosta Society, Classification and Nomenclature Committee.

Zilis, M. R., D. Zwagerman, D. Lamerts, and L. Kurtz. 1979. Commercial production of herbaceous perennials by tissue culture. *Proceedings of the Intern. Plant Propagation Soc.* 29:404–414.

Zoku-Tsushin zenran, Ranjiin Shiboruto choko ikken. n.d. Medical Library, Tokyo University, Kure Collection (a collection of von Siebold's personal articles).

Zollinger, H. 1854–1855. *Systematisches Verzeichnis der im Indischen Archipel in den Jahren 1842–1848 gesammelten, sowie der aus Japan empfangenen Pflanzen* (BO; formerly Hb. Buitenzorg, Bogor, Java). Zurich.

Zuccarini, J. G. 1844. Weitere Notizen über die Flora von Japan etc. *Gelehrte Anzeigen* 18.

CATALOG LISTING

The many catalogs offering *Hosta* information used in the preparation of this book were:

Aden, Paul. 1975–1981. *Hosta* Price Lists. Baldwin, NY, U.S.A.

Ambergate Gardens. 1990. Perennial Catalog. Waconia, MN, U.S.A.

Banyai's Hostas. 1985–1989. *Hosta* Catalog. Madison Heights, MI, U.S.A.

Benkhuysen (H. G.) & Sons. 1987. *Hosta* Price List. Boskoop, Holland.

Blue Mount Nurseries. 1985, 1986. Monkton, MD, U.S.A.

Bluebird Nursery. 1986. Wholesale Price List. Clarkson, NE, U.S.A.

Bluemel. 1987. Wholesale Price List. Baldwin, MD, U.S.A.

Borsch, W., & Sons. 1930. *Hosta* List. Multnomah, OR, U.S.A.

Bowden, A., and R. Bowden. 1987. *Hosta* List. Cleave House, Okehampton, Devon, UK.

Breeze Hill Laboratories. 1987. *Hosta* Price List. Centreville, DE, U.S.A.

Bressingham Gardens. 1986–1989. Perennial Catalog. Bressingham, Diss, Norfolk, UK.

Briggs Nursery, Inc. 1986, 1987. Lining Out Stock. Olympia, WA, U.S.A.

Busse Gardens. 1978–1989. Wholesale and Retail *Hosta* Catalogs. Cocato, MN, U.S.A.

Caprice Farm Nursery. 1985–1989. *Hosta* Catalogs and Lists. Sherwood, OR, U.S.A.

Carroll Gardens. 1987, 1988, 1989. Perennial Catalog. Westminster, MD, U.S.A.

Coastal Gardens and Nursery. 1983–1989. *Hosta* Price Lists and Catalogs. Myrtle Beach, NC, U.S.A.

Country Lane Nursery. (Ken Anderson). 1978–1989. *Hosta* Catalog. Farwell, MN, U.S.A.

Englerth Gardens. 1974–1989. *Hosta* Catalogs. Hopkins, MI, U.S.A.

Fairmount Gardens. 1964. *Hosta* Price Lists. Lowell, MA, U.S.A.

Fairway Gardens. 1975–1985. *Hosta* Catalogs. Albert Lea, MN, U.S.A.

Fisher, Mrs. Glen. 1975–1978. *Hosta* Lists. Oshkosh, WI, U.S.A.

Fleur de Lis Gardens. 1987, 1988. *Hosta* Price List. Canby, OR, U.S.A.

GM Nurseries, Inc.. 1986, 1987. *Hosta* Price List. Holland, MI, U.S.A.

Gotemba Nursery. 1978, 1988. Price List. Gotemba-shi, Shizuoka, Japan.

Gray & Cole. 1941, 1942. Hardy Plants for New England Gardens. Ward Hill, MA, U.S.A.

Gray & Cole. 1963, 1966. *Hosta* Price Lists. Ward Hill, MA, U.S.A.

Grootendorst, A. M., Inc. 1985, 1986. *Hosta* Price List. Benton Harbor, MI, U.S.A.

Hadspen House Gardens and Nursery. 1987. Price List. Castle Cary, Somerset, UK.

Hatfield Gardens. 1976–1989. *Hosta* Catalogs. Stoutsville, OH, U.S.A.

Holbrook Farm and Nursery. 1984–1989. Perennial Catalogs. Fletcher, NC.

Homestead Division, Sunnybrook Farms. 1982–1989. *Hosta* Catalogs. Chesterland, OH, U.S.A.

Iron Gate Gardens. 1980–1989. Kings Mountain, NC, U.S.A.

Jernigan Gardens. 1984, 1985. *Hosta* List. Dunn, NC, U.S.A.

Kamo Nurseries. 1987. *Hosta* Catalog. Kakegawa, Japan.

Kelways. 1984. Perennial Catalog. Kelways Nurseries, Langport, Somerset, UK.

Klehm, Charles, & Son Nursery. 1982–1989. *Hosta* Price Lists and Catalogs. East Barrington, IL, U.S.A.

Klose, Staudengärtner. 1980, 1983. Perennial Catalog. Lohfelden bei Kassel, Germany.

Klyne, C. & Co.. 1986, 1987. *Hosta* Price List. Boskoop, Holland.

Lamb Nurseries. 1987. *Hosta* Price List. Spokane, WA, U.S.A.

Lee Gardens. 1988,1989. *Hosta* Catalog. Tremont, IL, U.S.A.

Mack. 1960. Mackwoods Gardens *Hosta* Listing. Spring Grove, IL, U.S.A.

Malorn Gardens. 1984. *Hosta* List. Carn View, Redruth, Cornwall, UK.

Maroushek Gardens. 1983–1986. *Hosta* Catalog. Hastings, MN, U.S.A.

Midwest Groundcovers. 1987. *Hosta* Price List. St. Charles, IL, U.S.A.

Milaeger's Gardens. 1987. Perennial Catalog. OH, U.S.A.

Millcreek Gardens. 1985. *Hosta* Price List. Ostrander, OH, U.S.A.

Napierville Nurseries. 1941. *Hosta* Price Lists. Napierville, OH, U.S.A.

Nieuwesteeg Nurseries. 1957. *Hosta* Price Lists. Boskoop, Holland.

Oosterwijk, Jr. 1987. *Hosta* Price List. Holland.

Piccadilly Farm. 1984–1989. *Hosta* Price Lists. Bishop, GA, U.S.A.

Piedmont Gardens. 1980–1987. *Hosta* Price Lists. Waterbury, CT, U.S.A.

Powell's Gardens. 1976–1989. Perennial Catalogs. Princeton, NC, U.S.A.

Redman Nurseries. 1985. *Hosta* List. Oxford Road, Abington, Oxon, UK.

Rijnbeek & Zoon. 1986, 1987. Perennial Price List. Boskoop, Holland.

Rockmont Nursery. 1944. Price List of *Hosta*. Boulder, CO, U.S.A.

Rocknoll Nursery. 1985–1989. Perennial Catalogs. Hillsboro, OH, U.S.A.

Savory's Greenhouses and Gardens. 1970–1989. *Hosta* Catalog. Edina, MN, U.S.A.

Shady Oaks Nursery. 1985, 1986. Perennial Catalogs. Waseca, MN, U.S.A.

Simpers, L. 1978. *Hosta* List. Salem, IN, U.S.A.

Soules Gardens. 1983–1989. *Hosta* Price Lists and Catalogs. Indianapolis, IN, U.S.A.

Spinners. 1985. Price List. Boldre, Lymington, Hampshire, UK.

Springbrook Gardens, Inc. 1986, 1987. *Hosta* Price List. Mentor, OH.

Stark Gardens. 1983–1989. *Hosta* Price Lists. Norwalk, Iowa, U.S.A.

Starker, Carl. 1949/1950, 1959. Price List of *Hosta*. Jennings Lodge, OR, U.S.A.

Sunny Border. 1987. *Hosta* Price List. U.S.A.

T & Z Nursery, Inc. 1985, 1987. Wholesale Liner and *Hosta* Price List. Winfield, IL, U.S.A.

Van Burgondien, K., & Sons, Inc. 1987. *Hosta* Price List. Babylon, NY, U.S.A.

Van Hoorn, J., & Co. 1975–1987. *Hosta* Price Lists. Lake Zurich, IL, U.S.A.

Vandenberg Bulb Company. 1987. *Hosta* Price List. Chester, NY, U.S.A.

Viette Farm and Nursery. 1980–1989. Perennial Catalogs. Fishersville, VA, U.S.A.

Wade and Gatton Nurseries. 1990. Pricelist. Bellville, OH, U.S.A.

Walters Gardens, Inc. 1987–1989. Wholesale Pricelist. Zeeland, MI, U.S.A.

Watanabe, Kenji. 1985. *Hosta* List. Gotemba, Shizuoka, Japan.

Watanabe, Kenzi. 1983, 1985. *Hosta* Price Lists. Fukutami Kuroishi, Aomori, Japan.

Wayside Gardens. 1948–1989. Price List of *Hosta*. Mentor, OH and Hodges, SC, U.S.A.

Weir Meadow Nursery. 1986. Wholesale Catalog. Wayland, MA, U.S.A.

Weston Nurseries. 1987. *Hosta* Price List. U.S.A.

Zager, H. A. 1941, 1945, 1958. Price List of *Hemerocallis* and *Hosta*. Des Moines, IA, U.S.A.

Zeppelin, Staudengärtnerei Gräfin von. 1986–1989. Perennial Catalog. Sulzburg-Laufen, Germany.

General Index

Index of Names Associated with the Genus *Hosta*

Nota Bene

Bold numbers indicate pages of primary name entries, major discussions, or critical explanations; italic numbers refer to figures (including distribution maps) and color plates; however, figures included with a main entry are *not* indexed.

Many of the names long known to gardeners are in abbreviated, horticultural form. To name two examples: the full botanical name for *H. sieboldiana*, according to ICBN rules, must be *H. sieboldiana* var. *sieboldiana*; likewise, the taxon known to many as *H. decorata* is correctly *H. decorata* f. *decorata*, and now reduced to cultivar form as *H. 'Decorata'*. Whenever the simplified, horticultural naming convention is used in this

book, it is intended to apply to the basic form of a species (*forma typica*), whose name repeats the species epithet as a *varietas* or *forma* name; thus, *H. sieboldiana* = *H. sieboldiana* var. *sieboldiana*, and *H. decorata* = *H. decorata* f. *decorata* = *H. 'Decorata'*. When a particular taxon has been reduced to cultivar form, as, for example, *H. 'Elata'*, most of the historic name entries will be a scientific binomial (i.e., *H. elata*) so *H. 'Elata'* = *H. elata*. As a consequence readers should check references under both of these name formulations. Appropriate cross references have been provided in such cases.

Names occurring in the Introduction, Botanical Summary, and Endnotes have not been indexed.

Index of Foreign Names

East Asia